MASS
TORT LITIGATION

CASES AND MATERIALS

By

Linda S. Mullenix

Bernard J. Ward Centennial Professor of Law
University of Texas

AMERICAN CASEBOOK SERIES®

WEST PUBLISHING CO.

ST. PAUL, MINN., 1996

COPYRIGHT © 1996 By WEST PUBLISHING CO.
            610 Opperman Drive
            P.O. Box 64526
            St. Paul, MN 55164–0526
            1–800–328–9352

Library of Congress Cataloging-in-Publication Data

Mullenix, Linda S., 1950–
     Cases and materials on mass tort litigation / by Linda S.
Mullenix.
          p.   cm. — (American casebook series)
     Includes index.
     ISBN 0–314–06635–7 (hardcover)
     1. Torts—United States—Cases.   2. Class actions (Civil
procedure)—United States—Cases.   3. Complex litigation—United
States—Cases.   I. Title.   II. Series.
KF1249.M85   1996
346.7303—dc20
[347.3063]   95–38919
                                                                      CIP

ISBN 0–314–06635–7

This book is dedicated to my sons,
Rob, Jack, and Will,
and in memory of Mickey

*

Preface

This book collects cases and materials that deal with a set of problems related to mass tort litigation. As a new casebook organizing a body of legal materials, there is some need to justify this endeavor: why a new casebook that further subdivides and balkanizes legal study? What makes mass tort litigation different from civil procedure, complex litigation, federal courts, conflicts, environmental law, administrative law, products liability or remedies? Are the problems of mass tort litigation a temporary phenomenon of the late twentieth century, unlikely to require continuing attention?

The answers to these questions suggest that mass tort litigation has evolved as a separate and compelling set of legal and social problems that are worthy of discrete study. Although complicated substantive litigation and mass disaster cases such as airplane crashes have existed for some time, mass tort litigation, with its distinctive characteristics, began to emerge only in the 1980s. And through the 1980s it became clear, as the courts attempted to grapple with hundreds and thousands of repetitive, individual tortious injury claims, that the American adjudicatory system was and is not capable of handling these claims in a just, efficient, and inexpensive fashion. The history of mass tort litigation, when it is eventually written, will be a story of repeated procedural frustration—of systemic false starts and failures. Similarly, the substantive law issues raised in mass tort cases have questioned and challenged the boundaries of existing rules and principles, across a wide spectrum of legal doctrine.

What is equally clear, now, is that mass tort litigation is not likely to go away: in our unending quest to improve life, we have demonstrated our unending ability to poison our environment, spoil our food supply, and manufacture toxic and defective products that cause injury on unprecedented and unimaginable scale. Therefore, the mass tort litigation crisis that has occurred at the end of this century is worthy of separate study precisely because this legal phenomenon presents challenging, difficult problems that require creative legal and non-legal solutions. Most obviously, mass tort litigation first presents a set of difficult procedural issues common to any complex, multiparty, multiforum litigation: joinder of parties and claims, jurisdiction, transfer, consolidation, joint trial, and jury functions. In addition, repeated litigation of the same or similar claims implicates the scope of preclusion doctrine. But beyond procedural issues, mass tort litigation has engendered interesting problems across a range of other legal fields: constitutional law and federalism, conflicts of law, tort law and products liability, environmental law, remedies, professional responsibility, bankruptcy, and alternative dispute resolution. Mass tort litigation, in all its dimensions, has pushed the boundaries of existing procedural and substantive law and forced re-examination of existing statutes, rules, and doctrine.

This casebook is a collection of cases, readings, and materials on the mass tort litigation crisis that began in the 1980s. The fundamental concept of this casebook is that late twentieth-century mass tort litigation has generated a series of stimulating legal and social problems that have, in turn, engendered concentrated efforts at legal reform. Thus, in the broadest sense, these cases and materials collectively explore the fabric of legal process: how legal problems are defined and how these problems generate a cycle of debate, reaction, and reform. It is a casebook about cases, rules, and doctrine in the traditional sense, but also about dispute resolution and social justice. It is a casebook about public policy and the allocation of societal resources to solve problems involving private, rather than public or institutional harm. It is a collection of cases and readings that raise questions of justice, fairness, efficiency, and professional ethics.

Students most commonly understand legal change that results from judicial rulings overturning precedent, or through the gradual erosion of doctrine, evidenced, for example, in the development of strict products liability law. What law students more often fail to comprehend is the way in which legal change is accomplished through the interplay of legal problems, judicial process, and extra-judicial process: public-policy debate, institutional law reform efforts, legislative initiative, and interest-group lobbying. The collection of cases and readings in this casebook, then, is intended to illuminate the process of how legal problems are defined, and how various judicial and non-judicial bodies propose, refine, and attempt to solve these problems.

This casebook is divided into five parts. Part One introduces the subject of mass tort litigation by first examining the human dimensions of this problem. In the effort to articulate legal problems and to debate reform proposals, it is often easy to lose sight of the fact that real people with real injuries underlie the mass tort litigation crisis. This section of the casebook is intended to focus attention on people—individually, collectively, or corporately—who present competing claims upon societal resources for redress of injuries. Included are selections from best-selling books published in the mid-1980s dealing with the Dalkon Shield litigation, the asbestos cases, and Agent Orange. This section also introduces analytical frameworks for thinking about aggregative procedure, the jurisprudential debate surrounding aggregative procedure, and some special problems of professional responsibility especially pertinent to mass tort cases.

Part Two deals with the series of problems relating to procedural difficulties implicated in mass tort litigation. The chapters in this part examine a set of procedural "failures": failure of the class action rule, consolidation rules, and the multidistrict litigation statute, as well as preclusion doctrine, to supply a procedural solution that avoids repetitive litigation of mass tort cases. This section next examines procedural problems in a federal dimension: how the two-court system, through various rules, doctrine, and constitutional law, constrains the ability to accomplish a unified, intersystem solution to mass tort litigation. The materials here examine issues of supplemental jurisdiction, the Anti-Injunction Act, and problems and possibilities relating to intersystem transfer. This section concludes with an examination of some procedural problems relating to the trial of mass tort cases—problems in post-aggregative procedure relating to trial structure, presentation of evidence, jury competence, jury instructions, verdicts, and findings. Mass tort litigation has revitalized the debate surrounding the jury function, with proponents urging the use of special or scientific juries in toxic tort litigation. Obviously, these problems raise questions concerning the meaning of the Seventh Amendment guarantee to a right to trial by jury. In addition, many mass tort cases have experienced troubling episodes relating to entrepreneurial litigation and attorneys' fees, and these issues are explored in the readings.

Part Three focuses on problems relating to substantive tort and products liability law. The mass tort cases that have progressed through pretrial proceedings or even to trial have produced challenging questions of substantive tort law: problems relating to indeterminate plaintiffs and defendants; old and new theories of joint liability; latent injury; general and specific causation; scientific proof; and available defenses, including the "state of the art" defense, the government contract defense, and limitations defenses. In addition, mass tort litigation has brought into sharp focus issues relating to aggregate damages, proof of aggregate damages, punitive damages, and ultimately, applicable law. This section examines how courts and commentators have attempted to address this array of substantive law problems, and how the law of substantive liability has been shaped in the mass tort context.

Part Four focuses on choice-of-law problems related to mass tort litigation. The complexity of applicable law questions is first illustrated through choice-of-law analysis that frequently occurs in litigated airplane crash disasters. The transposition of choice-of-law problems into mass tort cases is then explored in the ensuing materials. In the absence of complete federalization of substantive tort or products liability law, mass tort cases have raised incredibly complex issues of applicable law. This is a function of the fact that most mass tort cases, unless litigated in a single forum or federal district, inevitably involve multiple parties from multiple forums. When the cases are in federal court by virtue of federal diversity jurisdiction, the applicable law must be determined according to *Erie* doctrine, *Klaxon, Van Dusen*, and *Ferens* rules. These materials not only include cases grappling with applicable law problems, but also include proposed solutions for the choice-of-law problem in mass tort cases.

Part Five addresses the burgeoning movement to resolve mass tort litigation through auspices other than the litigation system. This section examines various attempts to use special masters, alternative dispute resolution, claims facilities, and trust mechanisms for resolving mass tort litigation. This section also explores the use of bankruptcy as a means for settling claims in mass tort, and reviews possible administrative solutions to mass tort litigation. Each of these alternative dispute resolution techniques, as applied to mass tort, has received a good deal of criticism, and these objections are presented for study and debate. Taken together, these readings raise questions about the extent and limits of Article III power, as well as the appropriate role of court-appointed adjuncts in achieving a just and fair resolution of claims outside the adversarial, adjudicative process.

Clearly, complex large scale litigation is not a new phenomenon and the judicial system has long had both substantive and procedural means of adjudicating collective claims, most notably through the class action rule. But what history has taught is that legal problems appear that were unanticipated by the rulemakers, so that rules and statutes become ineffective or incapable of resolving new legal problems. The last major complex litigation crisis, in the 1950s, related to large-scale prosecution of manufacturers of electrical equipment for price-fixing in violation of the antitrust laws. The inability of the existing judicial system to handle these cases resulted in a round of reform, ultimately yielding the multidistrict litigation statute. In the same way that crisis induced procedural reform, the mass tort litigation crisis of the 1980s has encouraged another round of efforts at procedural law reform, as procedural rules prove ineffective as a means for litigating these cases.

This casebook, therefore, has been assembled in the belief that mass tort litigation is a rich and exciting frontier of the legal landscape that merits both study and meaningful reform. The materials collected in this book set forth the major problems, debates, and core innovative proposals. The materials have been selected to illustrate the interaction between emerging legal problems, the identification of systemic inadequacies, and the efforts of law reform bodies to assist in changing the law. The primary purpose of these materials is to generate discussion on the issues of mass tort litigation, as well as on the merits of proposed solutions. A secondary purpose is to encourage debate on how legal reform is accomplished or frustrated. In this regard, the materials are intended to show the interplay between judicial process, legal theory, empirical study, legislative initiative, and *real politik*.

NOTE ON THE INSTITUTIONAL LAW REFORM EFFORTS

Since the mid-1980s, a number of significant developments relating to mass tort litigation reform have been going forward under the auspices of various law reform organizations and the federal judiciary. The American Law Institute undertook a *Complex Litigation Project;* the American Bar Association created a Commission on Mass Torts; Congress through both branches has proposed and considered multiparty, multiforum legislation; the Commission on Uniform State Laws promulgated a Transfer of Litigation statute; and Chief Justice Rehnquist appointed a judicial committee, the "Reaveley Committee," to formulate proposals for dealing with the federal courts' asbestos litigation crisis. In addition, the specially appointed Federal Courts Study Committee issued a Report in 1990 with recommendations for complex litigation, and in that same year Congress enacted the Judicial Improvements Act which in Title I (the Civil Justice Reform Act), outlines procedural reforms for complex cases. The following summarizes these various efforts relating to the mass tort litigation crisis, and excerpts from these institutional law reform proposals are included throughout this casebook.

(1) COMPLEX LITIGATION: STATUTORY RECOMMENDATIONS AND ANALYSIS (THE AMERICAN LAW INSTITUTE 1994): The ALI COMPLEX LITIGATION: STATUTORY RECOMMENDATIONS AND ANALYSIS began as an Institute project in 1986–87 and progressed through multiple drafts, culminating in a final draft in May 1993 which has now been published in a final bound volume (American Law Institute 1994). The Reporters for the PROJECT were Professor Arthur R. Miller (Harvard) and Professor Mary Kay Kane (Dean, Hastings). The COMPLEX LITIGATION project surveys defining the problem of complex litigation; federal intrasystem consolidation; federal intersystem consolidation; proposed complex litigation statutes; and choice-of-law. Among reforms contemplated, proposed, or recommended are the creation of a Complex Litigation Panel, modified jurisdictional, consolidation, and transfer rules, expanded injunctive powers, and mandatory intervention rules. The Reporters also proposed a federalized choice-of-law scheme. The COMPLEX LITIGATION project recommendations are discussed in a symposium in 54 La. L. Rev. 833 (1994).

(2) ENTERPRISE RESPONSIBILITY FOR PERSONAL INJURY (*Reporters' Study,* The American Law Institute, 1991): This project was conceived and endorsed by the American Law Institute in 1986 in response to "a major crisis in [the] tort litigation/liability insurance system." During the five years of drafting, however, the study's focus changed to analyze and appraise the present state of the personal injury tort system. This study identifies three tiers of tort litigation: ordinary vehicular accidents; medical and products liability cases; and mass torts. The project focuses on these latter two "high-stakes" and "very high-stakes" litigation; and the study's second volume deals especially with environmental and other mass torts. The Reporters' Study was presented to the American Law Institute membership at the May 1991 meeting.

(3) REVISED REPORT OF THE ABA COMMISSION ON MASS TORTS: After the February 1987 meeting of the ABA House of Delegates, that body created a Commission on Mass Torts to study and make recommendations concerning the handling of mass tort litigation arising out of single event disasters or negligent product design. The Commission issued its first REPORT for the August 1989 meeting, but withdrew the REPORT for revisions before the House of Delegates acted. A revised REPORT was issued before the February 1990 midyear meeting, but it was not considered at that meeting when the REPORT encountered substantial criticism.

The revised REPORT contained a detailed set of recommendations on the processing of mass torts with broad ramifications for mandatory consolidation of state and federal actions, expanded removal jurisdiction, choice of law, punitive damages, burden of proof, issue preclusion, expanded expert witness use, broadened use of ADR mechanisms (including settlement), and increased regulation of attorneys fees. At the February 1990 meeting, the delegates instead considered a proposal from the Standing Committee on Federal Judicial Improvements similar to proposals in the Federal Courts Study Committee Report and the Multiparty, Multiforum bill in Congress, recommending modification of 28 U.S.C. § 1407 to permit consolidated trial of multiparty, multiclaim cases after transfer and consolidation. Although supported by the Sections on Litigation and Tort and Insurance Practice, the proposal was defeated. *See* 58 U.S.L.W. 2747, 2477 (1990). The Reporter for the ABA Commission on Mass Tort was Professor Frank E. Flegal (Georgetown).

(4) THE MULTIPARTY, MULTIFORUM JURISDICTION ACT: The Multiparty, Multiforum Jurisdiction Act of 1993 (H.R. 1100, 103d Cong., 1st Sess.) is the most recent in a series of similarly-named legislation that has been successively introduced in the House and Senate since 1988. Earlier versions include the Multiparty, Multiforum Jurisdiction Act of 1991 (H.R. 2450, 102nd Cong., 2d Sess.); the Multiparty, Multiforum Jurisdiction Act of 1990 (H.R. 3406, 101st Cong., 2d Sess.), and Title IV of the Court Reform and Access to Justice Act (H.R. 3152) that was not passed with the final bill (the 1988 Judicial Improvements and Access to Justice Act). There are extensive legislative histories to H.R. 2450 (1991) and H.R. 3406 (1989-90). In addition, a two-volume legislative history to H.R. 3152 (1988) that includes testimony on the multiparty, multiforum title. Although the first Multiparty, Multiforum Jurisdiction Act was passed by the House on June 1, 1990, it died in committee after referral to the Senate. In 1991, the bill was reintroduced in the House of Representatives, but it again failed in the Senate during spring 1992. A new version was introduced in the House in 1993, but as of June 1995, no new version has yet been introduced during the 104th Congress.

The legislation, in its various incarnations, was intended to amend Title 28 to add a new section on multiparty, multiforum jurisdiction. This section would confer original diversity jurisdiction over civil actions arising from a single accident where at least 25 persons have either died or incurred injury "at a discrete location" and the injury results in damages that exceed $50,000 per person. The jurisdictional proposal relaxes the complete diversity rule. The legislation includes conforming venue and removal provisions, and would amend 28 U.S.C. § 1407 to permit trial of transferred actions. Finally, the legislation proposes a federalized choice-of-law scheme to determine applicable law.

(5) REPORT OF THE FEDERAL COURTS STUDY COMMITTEE (APRIL 2, 1990): As part of the 1988 Judicial Improvements Act, Congress authorized the creation of a committee to study the federal courts and issue recommendations to relieve congestion, delay, and expense in adjudicating actions. After fifteen months of study, deliberation, and public hearings, the Committee's REPORT was issued and it contained three recommendations relating to complex litigation. First, the REPORT recommended amending the multidistrict litigation statute to permit consolidated trials in addition to consolidated pretrial proceedings and to provide special minimal diversity for such multiparty, multiforum litigations. Second, the REPORT recommended that the MANUAL FOR COMPLEX LITIGATION include guidelines for consolidation and severance. And third, the REPORT recommended that the Federal Judicial Center analyze and disseminate information about special procedures tailored for complex mass tort cases. The Reporters also suggested that Congress be alert to the need for statutory change to facilitate resolution of such mega-cases.

(6) TRANSFER OF LITIGATION ACT (National Conference of Commissioners on Uniform State Laws): At its August 1991 meeting, the National Conference of Commissioners on Uniform State Laws considered and approved a Transfer of Litigation Act that would establish a framework for transferring and consolidating cases in state courts. The Uniform Act must now be considered and adopted by individual states. The Act would supplant *forum non conveniens* principles and require joint consent of the transferring and receiving courts. The statute would permit transfer of a case from a court with jurisdiction to one that could not independently establish jurisdiction, with a joint determination of fairness. The criteria for transfer look to the interest of each plaintiff in selecting a forum and the judicial system's interest in securing a single disposition of related matters. The transfer order can designate specific terms for the transfer, but the receiving court can depart from these orders for good cause. An order granting transfer would be reviewable only by extraordinary writ or permissive interlocutory appeal in the transferring state.

(7) AD HOC COMMITTEE ON ASBESTOS LITIGATION (The Reaveley Committee Report, March 1991): This committee was appointed by Chief Justice Rehnquist in September 1990 to consider problems confronting the federal courts arising from asbestos litigation. The committee recommended that Congress consider a national legislative scheme for resolution of asbestos personal injury claims, or new legislation that would expressly authorize consolidation and collective trials of asbestos cases. The Committee also recommended that the Standing Committee on Rules of Practice and Procedure direct the Advisory Committee on Civil Rules to study whether Federal Rule of Civil Procedure 23 should be amended to better accommodate the requirements of mass tort litigation. Finally, the committee recommended that the Administrative Office of the United States Courts be given broader supervisory authority to enable that office to function as a clearing house.

(8) ADVISORY COMMITTEE ON CIVIL RULES OF THE JUDICIAL CONFERENCE OF THE UNITED STATES COURTS: In early 1993 the Committee on Rules of Practice and Procedure of the Judicial Conference of the

United States issued a request for comments on a preliminary Draft of Proposed Amendments to Federal Rule of Civil Procedure 23. As of early 1995, the Advisory Committee was still soliciting comments from the bench and bar relating to proposed revisions of the class action rule.

LINDA S. MULLENIX

August, 1995

Acknowledgements

My students at the University of Texas School of Law and the Harvard Law School studied versions of this manuscript. I am grateful for their interest and comments on the materials.

I am indebted to Ms. Cynthia Bright, Georgetown Law Center '94, for preparing the manuscript for West Publishing Company. Without her patient assistance and care, it would not have been completed.

I am indebted to the copyright holders identified below for permission to reprint excerpts from the following copyrighted materials (listed in the order they appear in the book). Except for granting me permission to reprint in this book, the following copyright holders have retained all rights:

Mintz, At Any Cost: Corporate Greed, Women, and the Dalkon Shield (1985), copyright © 1985, by Morton Mintz. Reprinted by permission of Pantheon Books, a division of Random House, Inc.

Brodeur, Outrageous Misconduct: The Asbestos Industry on Trial (1985), copyright © 1985, by Paul Brodeur. Reprinted by permission of Pantheon Books, a division of Random House, Inc.

Schuck, Agent Orange on Trial: Mass Toxic Disasters in the Courts (1986), copyright © 1986, 1987 by Mary Schuck Trust. Reprinted by permission of the publishers, Cambridge, Mass.: Harvard University Press.

Peterson and Selvin, Resolution of Mass Torts: Toward a Framework for Evaluation of Aggregative Procedures (1988), copyright © RAND, N–2805–ICJ, 1988. Reprinted by permission of RAND and the Institute for Civil Justice.

McGovern, Resolving Mature Mass Tort Litigation, 69 B.U.L.Rev. 659 (1989), copyright © 1989, Boston University Law Review.

The American Law Institute, Enterprise Responsibility for Personal Injury, Reporter's Study (1991), copyright © 1991 by the American Law Institute. Reprinted with the permission of the American Law Institute.

Transgrud, Mass Trials in Mass Tort Cases: A Dissent, 1989 U.Ill.L. Rev. 69 (1989), copyright © 1989, by Roger H. Transgrud and the Board of Trustees of the University of Illinois.

Hensler, Resolving Mass Toxic Torts: Myths and Realities, 1989 U.Ill.L. Rev. 89 (1989), copyright © 1989, by Deborah Hensler and the Board of Trustees of the University of Illinois.

Rosenberg, Class Actions for Mass Torts: Doing Individual Justice by Collective Means, 62 Ind. L.J. 561 (1987), copyright © 1987, by the Trustees of Indiana University. Reprinted by permission.

Roth, Confronting Solicitation of Mass Disaster Victims, 2 Geo.J. Legal Ethics 967 (1989), copyright © 1989, The Georgetown Journal of Legal Ethics. Reprinted with the permission of the publisher, The Georgetown Journal of Legal Ethics © 1989, and Georgetown University.

Jackson, A Controversial Settlement Approach: The Alpert Letter, 49 J. Air L. & Com. 213 (1983), copyright © 1983, The Journal of Air Law & Commerce. Reprinted with permission of the Journal of Air Law and Commerce, published by the SMU Law Review Association, Southern Methodist University, Dallas, Texas.

Sanders, The Bendectin Litigation: A Case Study in the Life Cycle of Mass Torts, 43 Hastings L.J. 301 (1992), copyright © 1992, by University of California, Hastings College of the Law. Reprinted by permission.

Silver, Comparing Class Actions and Consolidations, published originally in 10 The Review of Litigation 495 (1991). Copyright © 1991 by the University of Texas at Austin Publications, Inc. Reprinted by permission.

Schuck, The Role of Judges in Settling Complex Cases: The Agent Orange Example, 53 U. Chi.L.Rev. 337 (1986), copyright © 1986, The University of Chicago Law Review.

Henderson and Brett, A Trial Lawyer's Commentary on One Jurist's Musing of the Legal Occult: A Response to Judge Weinstein, 88 Nw. U.L.Rev. 592 (1994), copyright © 1994, Northwestern University Law Review.

The American Law Institute, Complex Litigation: Statutory Recommendations and Analysis, copyright © 1994 by the American Law Institute. Reprinted with the permission of the American Law Institute.

Rowe and Sibley, Beyond Diversity: Federal Multiparty, Multiforum Jurisdiction, 135 U. Pa.L.Rev. 7 (1986), copyright © 1986, University of Pennsylvania Law Review.

Sedler and Twerski, The Case Against All Encompassing Federal Mass Tort Legislation: Sacrifice Without Gain, 73 Marq.L.Rev. 76 (1989), copyright © 1989, Marquette University Law Review.

Kelner, Note, "Adrift on an Uncharted Sea:" A Survey of Section 1404(a) Transfer in the Federal System, 67 N.Y.U.L.Rev. 612, 615–617 (1992), copyright © New York University Law Review.

Weinstein, Ethical Dilemmas in Mass Tort Litigation, 88 Nw.U.L.Rev. 469 (1994), copyright © 1994, by Hon. Jack B. Weinstein.

Schwarzer, Judicial Federalism in Action: Coordination of Litigation in State and Federal Courts, 78 Va.L.Rev. 1689 (1992), copyright © 1992, Virginia Law Review Association.

Ratliff, Special Master's Report in Cimino v. Raymark Industries, Inc., published originally in 10 The Review of Litigation 521, copyright © 1991 by the University of Texas at Austin School of Law Publications, Inc. Reprinted by permission.

Saks and Blanck, Justice Improved: The Unrecognized Benefits of Aggregation and Sampling in the Trial of Mass Torts, 44 Stan.L.Rev. 815 (1992), copyright © 1992 by the Board of Trustees of the Leland Stanford Junior University.

Bone, Statistical Adjudication: Rights, Justice, and Utility in a World of Process Scarcity, 46 Vand.L.Rev. 561 (1993), copyright © 1993, Vanderbilt Law Review.

Drazan, The Case for Special Juries in Toxic Tort Litigation, 72 Judicature 292 (February/March 1989), copyright © 1989, The American Judicature Society.

Bordens and Horowitz, Mass Tort Civil Litigation: The Impact of Procedural Changes on Jury Decisions, 73 Judicature 22 (June/July 1989), copyright © 1989, The American Judicature Society.

Selvin and Pincus, The Debate over Jury Performance—Observations from a Recent Case (1987), copyright © 1987, The Institute for Civil Justice, RAND.

Sobol, Bending the Law: The Story of the Dalkon Shield Bankruptcy (1991), copyright © 1991, University of Chicago Press.

Robinson, Multiple Causation in Tort Law: Reflections in the DES Cases, 67 Va. L. Rev. 713 (1982), copyright © 1982, Fred B. Rothman & Co.

Delgado, Beyond Sindell: Relaxation of Cause-in-Fact Rules for Indeterminate Plaintiffs, 70 Calif.L.Rev. 881 (1982), copyright © 1982 by California Law Review, Inc.

Brennan, Helping Courts with Toxic Torts: Some Proposals Regarding Alternative Methods for Presenting and Assessing Scientific Evidence in Common Law Courts, 51 U.Pitts.L.Rev. 1 (1989), copyright © 1989, Troyen A. Brennan.

Abraham and Robinson, Aggregative Valuation of Mass Tort Claims, 53 Law & Contemp.Probs. 137 (Autumn 1990), copyright © 1990, Law & Contemporary Problems.

Ayres, Optimal Pooling in Claims Resolution Facilities, 53 Law & Contemp.Probs. 159 (Autumn 1990), copyright © 1990, Law & Contemporary Problems.

Lowenfeld, Mass Torts and the Conflict of Laws: The Airline Disaster, 1989 U.Ill.L.Rev. 157 (1989), copyright © 1989 by the Board of Trustees of the University of Illinois.

Juenger, Mass Disasters and the Conflict of Laws, 1989 U.Ill.L.Rev. 105 (1989), copyright © 1989 by the Board of Trustees of the University of Illinois.

Vairo, Multi-Tort Cases: Cause for More Darkness on the Subject, or a New Role for Federal Common Law?, 54 Fordham L.Rev. 167 (1985), copyright © 1985, Fordham Law Review.

Mullenix, Federalizing Choice of Law in Mass Tort Litigation, 70 Texas L.Rev. 1623 (1992), copyright © 1992, Texas Law Review.

McGovern, Toward a Functional Approach for Managing Complex Litigation, 53 U.Chi.L.Rev. 440 (1986), copyright © 1986, University of Chicago Law Review.

Brazil, Special Masters in Complex Cases: Extending the Judiciary or Reshaping Adjudication, 53 U.Chi.L.Rev. 394 (1986), copyright © 1986, University of Chicago Law Review.

Fitzpatrick, The Center for Claims Resolution, 53 Law & Contemp. Probs. 13 (1990), copyright © 1990, Law & Contemporary Problems.

Mullenix, Beyond Consolidation: Post-Aggregative Procedure in Asbestos Mass Tort Litigation, 32 Wm. & Mary L.Rev. 475 (1991), copyright © 1991, William & Mary Law Review.

Berman, The Agent Orange Veteran Payment Program, 53 Law & Contemp.Probs. 49 (1990), copyright © 1990, Law & Contemporary Problems.

Note, The Manville Bankruptcy: Treating Mass Tort Claims in Chapter 11 Proceedings, 96 Harv.L.Rev. 1121 (1983), copyright © Harvard Law Review Association.

Smith, Resolving Asbestos Claims: The Manville Personal Injury Trust, 53 Law & Contemp.Probs. 27 (1990), copyright © 1990, Law & Contemporary Problems.

McKay, Asbestos Property Damage Settlement in a Bankruptcy Setting, 53 Law & Contemp.Probs. 37 (Autumn 1990), copyright © 1990, Law & Contemporary Problems.

Vairo, The Dalkon Shield Claimants Trust: Paradigm Lost (or Found), 61 Fordham L.Rev. 617 (1992), copyright © 1992, Fordham Law Review.

Cooper, Interstate Consolidation: A Comparison of the ALI Project with the Uniform Transfer of Litigation Act, 54 La.L.Rev. 897 (1994), copyright © 1994, Louisiana Law Review.

Weber, Complex Litigation and the State Courts: Constitutional and Practical Advantages of the State Forum over the Federal Forum in Mass Tort Cases, 21 Hastings Const.L.Q. 215 (1994), copyright © 1994, by University of California, Hastings College of the Law.

*

Summary of Contents

*

Table of Contents

PART THREE. SUBSTANTIVE LAW ISSUES IN MASS TORT LITIGATION

*

Table of Cases

The principal cases are in bold type. Cases cited or discussed in the text are roman type. References are to pages. Cases cited in principal cases and within other quoted materials are not included.

*

Table of Authorities

H

Y

Z

MASS
TORT LITIGATION
CASES AND MATERIALS

*

Part One

INTRODUCTION

Chapter I

INTRODUCTION TO THE PROBLEM OF MASS TORT LITIGATION

On August 10, 1990, ten federal district court judges from around the country handling large asbestos personal injury dockets issued an unprecedented order creating a nationwide, mandatory class action.[1] The very fact that a group of judges had convened to take action to do something about mass tort litigation was a unique event in judicial history. Within a week of the judges' order, the Sixth Circuit struck down the novel class action plan stating that it was "unable to find any Congressional authority for an 'ad hoc coordinating committee' to issue orders as an Article III court." The appellate court went further to opine that the federal judges had exceeded their Article III constitutional powers in their efforts to coordinate asbestos litigation on a nationwide basis.[2]

What had impelled the federal judges to take this unusual step that caused such a swift rebuke from the Sixth Circuit? The federal judges were reacting to the very concrete crisis on federal civil dockets relating to asbestos litigation. Although asbestos litigation, as a discrete mass tort phenomenon, first was noticeable on federal dockets in the late 1970s, the asbestos crisis is still very much upon the federal courts at the end of this century. The incidence of newly filed personal injury and product liability cases continues apace, without a correlative capacity of the judicial system to efficiently or fairly adjudicate these cases. As of January 1, 1990 there were approximately 30,000 asbestos cases pending in all districts of the federal court system. While a significant number of cases have been terminated through various means, statistics reflect a steady flow of new cases into the system with a total net increase in pending cases. Moreover, whereas in the 1970s these cases were centered primarily in six judicial districts, the trend of the 1980s and 1990s is that asbestos personal injury claims are now dispersed throughout the

---

1. This introduction is adapted from Linda S. Mullenix, *Problems in Complex Litigation,* 10 Rev. Litig. 213 (1991).

2. *In re* Allied–Signal, Inc., 915 F.2d 190, 191 (6th Cir.1990).

entire federal system. In this sense, then, asbestos litigation has become the Sisphyean task of the federal court system: no matter how efficiently the courts have been able to process asbestos lawsuits, more cases keep coming into the system without any signs of respite.

While the judges' meeting and subsequent class action order seemed to have appeared from the blue, causing some asbestos attorneys to label the judges' behavior as "truly bizarre" and "getting stranger and stranger," to any close observer of the mass tort phenomenon the judges' action seemed a logical, if perhaps desperate, outgrowth of nearly a decade of frustrated attempts at legal reform. What was going on here was judicial action to remedy a litigation crisis in the face of legislative lassitude. If institutional law reform groups were ineffective to induce change and Congress was unable to enact meaningful legislative measures, then the judges would take matters into their own hands and begin to solve the complex mass tort litigation crisis. The response of the Sixth Circuit to the district judges, predictably, was "Thou shalt not legislate."

How had it come to pass that federal judges hoped to usurp the prerogatives of legislators? The answer lies, in part, in surveying the last decade's complex mass tort litigation problems as well as the failed reform efforts to relieve this phenomenon. To be sure, the concept of complex litigation is not new. Complex cases involving multiple parties, with claims dispersed over time and place, have existed as long as litigation has existed. The Federal Rules of Civil Procedure, as enacted in 1938, recognized the need for a procedural vehicle for collective action in the class action rule. In addition, the rules encouraged increasingly complex litigation through various liberal joinder provisions relating to claims and parties.

Notwithstanding these procedural vehicles for adjudicating large scale litigation, the complex litigation phenomenon did not fully evolve until mid-century. In the 1950s the federal courts experienced the massive electronics antitrust litigation, and in the 1960s, with amendment of the class action rule, the judicial system experienced vigorous prosecution of civil rights and institutional reform litigation. This first experience with system-wide complex litigation revealed problems with the judicial system's ability to fairly and efficiently adjudicate complex cases under rules and procedures then governing the system. This recognition, in turn, fostered the first reform efforts directed specifically at complex cases, resulting in the enactment of the multidistrict litigation statute.

Complex civil rights, antitrust, securities, and institutional reform cases remained fixtures of the litigation landscape through the 1980s. But the 1980s witnessed the advent of a new kind of complex case, with new characteristics and new challenges for the judicial system: the multiparty, multiforum mass tort litigation. The roll call of such mass tort cases is now well known to the general public and well documented in the academic literature: litigation involving Agent Orange, Bendectin, the Dalkon Shield, swine flu vaccine, and asbestos. Added to this parade of horribles have been mass disaster cases, most notably spectacular hotel calamities such as the collapse of the skywalk at the Kansas City Hyatt–Regency hotel, and the MGM Grand and Dupont Plaza hotel fires—events that killed or injured thousands of people. Rounding out this gloomy scenario are environmental pollution disasters such as Bhopal, Love Canal, and Three Mile Island.

These large scale mass tort litigations have refocused attention on the various inabilities of the judicial system to resolve these cases in a fair, expeditious, and equitable fashion. The academic literature of the 1980s is replete with discussion and analysis of the failure of the judicial system to adequately deal with this newer phenomenon of complex litigation. In turn, these new problems of complex mass tort litigation have fostered reform efforts by various academics and institutional law reform groups, such as the American Bar Association, the American Law Institute, the Federal Judicial Center, and the Rand Institute for Civil Justice.

The following readings are intended to introduce the problem of mass tort litigation. This chapter begins with a selection of stories about the people who, through their personal injuries, unwittingly became involved in dispute resolution on a grand scale. These are the stories of the people behind the mass tort cases. The readings then shift to a wider-lens, academic view of the mass tort phenomenon, setting forth analytical frameworks for thinking about mass torts. After these analytical frameworks are set out, the chapter presents the overarching jurisprudential problem raised by modern mass tort litigation: the fundamental question tension between the litigant autonomy and aggregate procedure. Finally, the chapter examines some special problems of professional responsibility engendered by mass tort cases.

A. CASE STUDIES IN MASS TORT LITIGATION

MORTON MINTZ, AT ANY COST: CORPORATE GREED, WOMEN, AND THE DALKON SHIELD *

New York: Pantheon Books (1985) at 3–8.

In January 1971, the A.H. Robins Company began to sell the Dalkon Shield, promoting it as the "modern, superior," "second generation," and—most importantly—"safe" intrauterine device for birth control. Robins, a major pharmaceutical manufacturer in Richmond, Virginia, distributed 4.5 million of the IUDs in eighty countries before halting sales in the mid–1970s. There followed a catastrophe without precedent in the annals of medicine and law.

The seriously injured victims number in the tens of thousands. Nearly all suffered life-threatening forms of infections known as pelvic inflammatory disease (PID). In the United States alone, PID killed at least eighteen women who had been wearing Shields. Most of the infections impaired or destroyed the women's ability to bear children.

Not only was the Shield unsafe, it was surprisingly ineffective. The number of wearers who became pregnant with the devices in place was on the order of 110,000, or 5 percent—a rate nearly five times the one falsely claimed in advertising and promotion to physicians and women, and a rate sharply higher than that for many other IUDs. More than ordinary commercial puffery, the exaggerated and bogus claims led women to reject more effective birth control in favor of the Shield; and this led directly to consequences far worse than unwanted pregnancies. Statistically, half of all women who became pregnant with an IUD miscarry. But in fact, of the estimated 110,000 women who conceived while wearing the Dalkon Shield, 66,000—or 60 percent—miscarried. Most suffered the previously rare miscarriages called *spontaneous abortions* in either the first or second trimester. Others, in the fourth to sixth months of pregnancy, experienced the still rarer infected miscarriages, or *septic spontaneous abortions*. By the count of the Food and Drug Administration, 248 women just in this country endured this dangerous, Shield-related complication; for 15 of them, these septic abortions were fatal.

Moreover, hundreds of women throughout the world who conceived while wearing the Shield gave birth prematurely, in the final trimester, to children with grave congenital defects including blindness, cerebral palsy, and mental retardation, or that were stillborn. No one can pinpoint the exact number of such women, partly because no one knows how many times women or their doctors failed to make a proper connection between the Shield and the premature birth of a defective baby.

Robins distributed about 2.86 million Shields in the United States, and doctors implanted them, by the company's estimate, in 2.2 million women. Abroad, Robins distributed about 1.7 million Shields, and in June 1974 it estimated that 800,000 to one million were implanted. The Agency for International Development (AID) brought more than 697,000 Shields for use in the Third World, slightly more than half of them for the International Planned Parenthood Federation and most of the rest for the Pathfinder Fund, the Population Council, and the Family Planning International Assistance. AID said in a report in 1985 that nearly half of the Shields it had bought were returned unused to Robins and that a review of cables to the agency left the impression "that very few Dalkon Shield insertions were made." But whatever the precise numbers of Shield insertions in African, Asian, Middle Eastern, Caribbean, Latin American, and South American countries, poor medical conditions made lethal complications more likely. My guess is that Shield-related PID killed hundreds—possibly thousands—of women outside of the United States. Dr. Richard P. Dickey, a former member of the Food and

Drug Administration's obstetrical and gynecological devices advisory panel, has seen at first hand the conditions faced by a woman who suffers PID. An infected Shield wearer, "where there are no doctors, no antibiotics, she's going to die," he told me.

In 1974, increasing numbers of Shield-related spontaneous septic abortions became known to the FDA, and the agency asked Robins to suspend Shield sales in the United States. It did so on June 28, 1974. After the sales suspension, the company retrieved unsold Shields from supply channels in this country. Plaintiffs' lawyer Dale I. Larson asked company chairman E. Claiborne Robins why this had been done. Because "it was the proper thing to do," the chairman swore. Larson, trying to find out if the retrieved devices may have been exported, asked if the Shields had been destroyed, and how and when—and why "the proper thing" had not also been done for less-developed countries— where product liability lawsuits and adverse publicity about a defective product are rarities. To all such questions the chairman's answer was that he did not know.

In fact, after halting domestic sales, the company continued to distribute Shields abroad for as long as nine months—"at the request of * * * specific governments," Robins swore at a deposition in January 1984. Asked who had told him that, he replied, "I don't know that. It seems to me I saw a memo somewhere, but I don't remember when or where."

In El Salvador in 1975—a year after the suspension of Shield sales here—Martine Langley was a volunteer in a family-planning clinic. Now a lawyer in Austin, Texas, she recalls that the only IUD the clinics's doctors were inserting was the Shield, and that some clinics in El Salvador continued to implant Shields until 1980. "Sometimes the doctor would say to the patient, 'This is from the United States and it's very good,'" Langley told David Phelps, a Washington correspondent for the *Minneapolis Star and Tribune*. Then, she said, the doctor would motion toward her and tell the woman, "She is from the United States and people [there] use it."

Today, more than a decade after Shield sales officially ended, legacies of death, disease, injury, and pain persist. Even women who have had the Shield removed are not out of danger. Because PID is not an affliction that is simply treated and is then over and done with, large numbers of former Dalkon Shield wearers suffer chronic pain and illness, sometimes requiring repeated hospitalizations and surgery; many have waged desperate battles to bear children despite severe damage to their reproductive systems. More cheerless news came in April 1985 from two studies funded by the National Institutes of Health. They showed that childless IUD wearers who have had PID run a far higher risk of infertility if their devices were Shields than if they were other makes. Not even women who currently wear the Shield with no apparent problem are safe: they run the risk of suddenly being stricken by PID. In the words of Judge Lord, they are wearing "a deadly depth charge in their wombs, ready to explode at any time."

The exact number of women still wearing the Shield is unknown. By early 1983, some Food and Drug Administration officials and OB–GYNs were confident that few American women, probably only hundreds, still used it. Other qualified observers, however, were estimating the figure to be much higher, anywhere from 80,000 to more than half a million. Certainly the response to Robin's own call-back campaign of October 1984 suggests that the higher figures are closer to the mark. By February 1985, a $4–million advertising drive, which urged women still wearing the Shields to have them removed at Robins's expense, had drawn more than 16,000 phone calls on toll-free hotlines; by the end of March 4,437 women had filed claims for Shield removals. The claims were flowing in at the dramatic rate of more than one hundred a week.

And what of women in the seventy-nine other countries where the Shield was distributed? The company told the FDA that it had notified first the countries' ambassadors in Washington and then their senior health officials at home of its Shield-removal campaign in the United States, and had "sought direction on whether a similar program would be appropriate in those countries." By early April 1985, Australia, Canada, and the United Kingdom had requested, and the company had put into effect, one or another kind of removal program. New Zealand, too, was considering a program. Sixteen other countries had simply acknowledged receipt of Robins's letter. Eight others—Denmark, Mexico, Norway, Pakistan, the Philippines, South Africa, Tanzania, and Zambia—had declined any removal program. From the rest of the countries, of which there were fifty-one, Robins had received no response almost a half-year after inviting one. If this record suggests indifference to the health and safety of women, at least a partial explanation may be found in the company's adamant refusal to admit to the special dangers inherent in its device. "Robins believes that serious scientific questions exist about whether the Dalkon Shield poses a significantly different risk of infection than other IUDs," it said in an interim report to the FDA.

Another measure of the extent of the damage is provided by the lawsuits and unlitigated claims filed by Shield wearers in the United States. Nearly all of these women had suffered PID followed by damage to or loss of their ability to bear children. The large majority had not been pregnant when stricken. Through June 30, 1985, by the company's own count, the total number of cases was 14,330, and new ones were being filed at a rate of fifteen a day. The company continues to experience a dramatic upsurge in the number of new Shield claims, president E. Claiborne Robins, Jr., told the annual stockholders' meeting on May 30, 1985. "I want to emphasize that the company anticipates that a substantial number of new claims will be filed in the future," he said. Through June 30, 1985, Robins and its former Shield insurer, Aetna Life & Casualty Company, had paid out $378.3 million to dispose of cases, plus $107.3 million in legal expenses. Juries have awarded $24.8 million in punitive or exemplary damages, which are intended to punish wanton or reckless behavior and to deter it repetition or emulation.

Still, no summary of suits and claims can come close to accounting for the total number of Shield injuries. By Robins's own conservative estimate in April 1985, 4 percent of the wearers were injured—that is, nearly 90,000 women in the United States alone. Of course, only a fraction of these will file suit. It is conventional wisdom among medical scientists that adverse reactions to drugs are always grossly underreported, and this is surely true of Shield injuries, too. Also, some Shield victims who stood to win substantial damages chose not to sue, either because they wanted to put a horrifying experience behind them, or because they placed a higher value on avoiding public disclosure of a matter as private and sensitive as the impairment or destruction of their ability to bear children. Other victims did not know or had forgotten the makes of their IUDs, as confirmed by Robins in its report to the FDA. By January 17, 1985, it said, 3,939 calls had come in on its special phone lines "from women presently wearing an IUD but of unknown type."

Furthermore, some of the women who might have sought compensation were certainly intimidated by Robins's brutal invasions of privacy and courtroom techniques. Judge Lord charged:

> When the time came for these women to make their claims against your company, you attacked their characters. You inquired into their sexual practices and into the identity of their sex partners. You exposed these women—and ruined families and reputations and careers—in order to intimidate those who would raise their voices against you. You introduced issues that had no relationship whatsoever to the fact that you planted in the bodies of these women instruments of death, of mutilation, of disease.

Again, if the claims against Robins in the United States represent only a fraction of the incidence of injury, they represent an even smaller fraction worldwide, since figures are simply unavailable from most of the countries where the Shield was used.

* * *

PAUL BRODEUR, OUTRAGEOUS MISCONDUCT: THE ASBESTOS INDUSTRY ON TRIAL *

New York: Pantheon Books (1985) at 3–6.

When the Manville Corporation, the world's largest asbestos company, with twenty-five thousand employees and more than fifty factories and mines in the United States and Canada, filed a debtor's petition for reorganization and protection under Chapter 11 of the federal Bankruptcy Code, on August 26, 1982, it did so in order to force a halt to thousands of lawsuits that had been brought against it by workers who claimed that they had developed lung cancer and other diseases as a result of their exposure to asbestos in Manville's insulation products, and who were alleging that the company had failed to warn them of the dangers involved. The story made the front page of virtually every major newspaper in the country, because Manville (formerly the Johns–Manville Corporation) was not only the largest American industrial company ever to file under Chapter 11—at the time, it ranked 181st on *Fortune's* list of the nation's 500 leading industrial corporations—but, with assets of more than $2 billion, was also one of the most financially healthy companies ever to take such action. In a full-page statement that appeared on August 27 in the New York *Times*, the Washington *Post,* the *Wall Street Journal*, and other leading papers, John A. McKinney, Manville's chairman and chief executive officer, announced that the company was "overwhelmed by 16,500 lawsuits related to the health effects of asbestos." McKinney said that lawsuits were being brought against Manville at a rate of 500 a month, and that the company could expect to be named as a defendant in at least 52,000 asbestos-disease lawsuits before the litigation ran its course. He estimated that at present settlement cost of about $40,000 per case the lawsuits would create a potential liability of $2 billion, requiring Manville to set aside a reserve fund that would wipe out most of its net worth and cripple its operation. For these reasons, he declared, the company's board of directors had decided to file for relief in the hope of establishing an effective system for handling the asbestos claims under Chapter 11.

In his statement, McKinney took pains to point out those people whom he considered responsible for Manville's predicament. He began by blaming the federal government for refusing to admit responsibility for asbestos disease that had developed among Second World War shipyard workers, who made up half the plaintiffs in the lawsuits brought against Manville. He criticized Congress for failing to enact a statutory compensation program for the victims of asbestos disease "so that the thousands of citizens and voters caught up in this problem will be spared the expensive, inefficient, and haphazard litigation system we have been saddled with." In addition, he castigated the insurance companies with which Manville had been doing business over the years for refusing to pay claims against product-liability policies totaling hundreds of millions of dollars. As for any responsibility that Manville might have incurred for the plight of the insulation workers, McKinney implied that the company was not at fault because "not until 1964 was it known that excessive exposure to asbestos fiber released from asbestos-containing insulation products can sometimes cause certain lung diseases." Since the mid–1970s, he said, Manville had disposed of some thirty-five hundred lawsuits by settlement or trial, and in a significant number of the cases that had gone to trial, he said, "juries have found that we are not at fault and acted responsibly in light of then existing medical knowledge."

In many ways, McKinney's statement was more revealing for its omissions than for what it contained. By neglecting to mention that Manville and its insurance carriers had settled out of court approximately thirty-four hundred of the thirty-five hundred lawsuits it had disposed of, and that it had paid out some $50 million in doing so, he ignored the extent to which his company had already acknowledged responsibility for the incidence of asbestos disease in insulation workers. In claiming that insulation materials containing asbestos were not known to be dangerous until 1964—an assertion that had constituted Manville's chief legal defense for many years—he ignored the fact that this defense had been rejected by juries across the country, and had recently been struck down by the New Jersey Supreme Court. Far and away the most self-serving of the omissions in McKinney's statement, however, was his failure to go beyond a bare mention of the fact that punitive damages had been awarded against Manville. Not only had juries found Manville liable for punitive damages in ten of some sixty-five asbestos lawsuits involving the company that had been tried in the United States during 1981 and the first half of 1982, but the average amount of punitive damages in the first six months of 1982 was about $600,000 a case. It is usually not possible to insure against punitive damages, which are assessed for outrageous and reckless misconduct, and McKinney could not have been unaware of their potential effect upon his company, for the simple reason that the likelihood of their being awarded in subsequent trials had been listed as a chief reason for Manville's financially uncertain future in a sworn affidavit that Manville's treasurer had submitted to the United States Bankruptcy Court of the Southern District of New York on the previous day. Moreover, in testimony given before the Senate Committee on Labor and Human Resources two years earlier, McKinney himself had underscored the devastating implications of punitive damages when, in order to substantiate his denial of the charge that employers had knowingly exposed workers to the hazards of excessive asbestos dust, he had pointed out that in all the litigation to date there had not been a single instance in which a jury or a trial judge had awarded punitive damages against any asbestos company. "I can think of no greater demonstration that the cover-up charge is a complete fabrication," he declared.

By and large, the newspaper stories that appeared on August 27 tended to describe Manville as a beleaguered giant reeling under the burden of mass litigation, and to portray McKinney as an embattled business manager fighting for his company's survival. Few of them reported the fact that juries had assessed punitive damages against Manville after hearing evidence that the company had engaged in a cover-up of the asbestos hazard for nearly five decades. The *Times*, for example, not only neglected to tell its readers initially that punitive damages had been assessed but also ran an editorial that compared the suffering of asbestos workers with the fiscal woes afflicting the asbestos companies. "Asbestos is a tragedy, most of all for the victims and their families but also for the companies, which are being made to pay the price for decisions made long ago," the editorial read. The editorial warned Congress to address the asbestos problem "before more victims die uncompensated and other companies follow Manville into the bankruptcy courts."

During the remainder of August and in the first part of September, the economic, legal, and political ramifications of Manville's Chapter 11 petition received daily attention in the press, which speculated at length on the dilemma it presented to Manville's stockholders and creditors, on the problems it posed for bankruptcy court, and on the pressure it placed on Congress to enact legislation that would help Manville overcome its financial difficulties. Considerably less attention was given to a grim prediction made by Dr. Irving J. Selikopff, who was director of the Environmental Sciences Laboratory at the Mount Sinai School of Medicine, in New York, and was widely acknowledged as the world's leading expert on asbestos disease. Selikopff estimated that among the twenty-one million living American men and women who had been occupationally exposed to asbestos between 1940 and 1980 there would be between eight and ten thousand deaths from asbestos-related cancer each year for the next twenty years. As for the culpability of Manville and other leading asbestos companies in helping to create this immense human tragedy, it either went unreported or was mentioned only in passing. By the last week of September, when the story of Manville's Chapter 11 petition had dropped from the headlines, few people were aware that the bankruptcy filing was simply the latest episode in a fifty-year history of corporate malfeasance and inhumanity to man that is unparalleled in the annals of the private enterprise system.

* * *

PETER H. SCHUCK, AGENT ORANGE ON TRIAL: MASS TOXIC DISASTERS IN THE COURTS *

The Belknap Press of Harvard University Press (1986).
3–6; 10–12, 13–15.

This * * * is about two urgent social problems and about the extraordinary lawsuit they have spawned.

The first problem arose from the smoldering ashes of Vietnam. For many of the millions of American soldiers who returned home from that charnel house, the future was filled with bitterness, dread, controversy, and debilitating illness. In 1978 the veterans sued a number of chemical manufacturers, blaming them for various diseases and traumas that they and their families had allegedly suffered because of exposure to Agent Orange, a herbicide the United States Army had used to defoliate Vietnam's luxuriant jungle cover. The law, the veterans hoped, would assuage their pain and vindicate their sacrifices. Today, almost a decade later, they are still waiting. For many of them, the law has become a mockery of justice, an object of derision.

The second problem arose from a very different set of social facts. We live in the midst of a burgeoning technological revolution. For several decades a torrent of new synthetic chemicals has cascaded out of our laboratories. Complex industrial processes have been developed, and intricate patterns of distribution, consumption, and disposal have evolved. These innovations have benefited American society enormously, but they have also created new kinds of risks. Agent Orange, originally hailed by some environmentalists and even by one of the veterans' lawyers as a model herbicide, was later found to harbour insidious dangers as well; in this respect it was a characteristic product of the great scientific advance.

It might seem surprising that these two disparate social problems—the one produced by unspeakable human suffering, the other by unparalleled human ingenuity—came together in a courtroom. On the surface, each of these problems seems quite unsuited to resolution at the instance of private parties wrangling before a judge. War, after all, leaves many bitter legacies; distributing its burdens is ordinarily the stuff of national politics, not of private litigation. By the same token, environmental risk management is an immensely complex technical task; controlling such risks is usually the responsibility of legislatures and regulatory agencies, not of courts.

Students of the contemporary legal system, however, know better. Times have changed. Traditionally, tort (personal injury) cases were generally regarded as essentially isolated disputes in which the law's role was simply to allocate losses between putative injurers and victims according to a moral conception that Aristotle called corrective justice; the law required that a wrongdoer return to a victim, typically in the form of money damages, what the former had "taken" from the latter. Such disputes were readily managed by the parties and the court system. Typically, the parties would adduce a relatively simple, comprehensible body of evidence before a detached arbiter, usually a jury. Applying general and familiar norms of conduct to the facts of the case, the jury would reach a decision, one that bound the parties but, because it was so fact-specific and was not explained by the jury, had little precedential effects on other cases.

Today, the law books abound with tort cases, especially in the product liability area, that involve not a few individuals but large aggregations of people and vast economic and social interests. These cases are not preoccupied with corrective justice between individuals concerned solely with past events. Instead, they concern the public control of large-scale activities and the distribution of social power and values for the future. The court and the jury in these cases do not simply prescribe and apply familiar norms to discrete actions; they function as policy-oriented risk regulators, as self-conscious allocators of hard-to-measure benefits and risks, and as social problem solvers.

The Agent Orange case carries this trend to its logical (or, as we shall see, perhaps illogical) extreme. Apart from its locus in a courtroom, its bears little resemblance to traditional tort adjudication. Its magnitude and complexity beggar imagination, as a few crude numerical indicators will suggest. The case is actually a consolidation into one class action of more than 600 separate actions originally filed by more than 15,000 named individuals throughout the United States, and almost 400 individual cases not included in the class action ("opt out" cases). The parties in these consolidated actions consist of some 2.4 million Vietnam veterans, their wives, children born and unborn, and soldiers from Australia and New Zealand; a small number of civilian plaintiffs; seven (originally twenty-four) corporate defendants; and the United States government.

In a typical case litigated in the federal district court in which the Agent Orange case was heard, the docket sheet is one or two pages long and contains perhaps sixty individual entries, each representing a filed document. The Agent Orange docket sheet in the district court alone is approximately 425 single-spaced pages long. It contains over 7,300 individual entries, many representing documents that are hundreds of pages long. The files of briefs, hearing transcripts, court orders, affidavits, and other court documents in the case were so voluminous that the already cramped clerk's office had to take the unprecedented step of devoting an entire room, staffed by two special clerks, to house them.

The financial and personnel demands of the case are even more staggering. The plaintiffs are represented by a network of law firms that numbered almost 1,500 by May 1984, located in every region of the country; the documented cost of their activities to date certainly exceeds $10 million and increases daily. It has been estimated that defendants spent roughly $100 million merely to prepare for the trial, utilizing hundreds of lawyers and corporate staff in their Herculean effort.

The court has also borne an enormous administrative burden. The current district court judge—the second to preside over the Agent Orange case—had to create a considerable bureaucracy within its chambers simply to enable him to run it, employing additional law clerks and paralegals. And although it is highly unusual for a judge to appoint even one special master to handle particular aspects of a litigation for him, this judge used no fewer than six special masters (four or five of them simultaneously) plus a federal magistrate, and they in turn sometimes hired consultants to assist them.

Finally, the case resulted in the largest tort settlement in history. That settlement, reached in May 1984 after almost six years of litigation, created a fund of $180 million; with accrued interest, it now totals more than $200 million, increasing at the rate of more than $40,000 each day. The case is now on appeal; since the settlement has been challenged, the court will not be in a position to begin distributing that fund for years, even if the plan is ultimately upheld. Nevertheless, simply to maintain the fund, the court has already been obliged to disburse more than two million dollars. For example, it had to create an Agent Orange computer center to process the almost 250,000 claims that class members have filed against the fund.

But the significance of the Agent Orange case is not confined to the features that have been mentioned—its symbolic reenactment of the war, its heralding of a new role for courts and juries, or its gigantic dimensions. Even more important is what the case reveals about a new and far-reaching legal and social phenomenon—the "mass toxic tort"—and society's response to it. The Agent Orange case is not the first mass toxic tort litigation (the diethylstilbestrol, or DES, and asbestos litigations began earlier), but it is probably the most revealing and perplexing example of the legal genre. In the Agent Orange case, we confront an unprecedented challenge to our legal system: a future in which the law must grapple with the chemical revolution and help us live comfortably with it.

The mass toxic tort has only become possible in recent years, as a vibrant chemical technology converged with mass distribution techniques and mass markets. We have not yet grasped its full meaning and implications. To begin to understand what is truly distinctive about it, we must isolate the three constitutive elements—mass, toxic, and tort.

* * *

The Agent Orange case dramatically illustrates each of these distinctive characteristics of mass toxic tort litigation. Its *mass* aspect, as we have already seen, is especially striking, creating the prospect of ruinous liability for defendants, stupefying organizational complexity for plaintiffs, and unprecedented problems of procedural, evidentiary, and substantive law for the court.

Even more than the mass character of the claims, however, the *toxic* nature of the injury in Agent Orange defines the case as extraordinary. This is especially evident when Agent Orange is compared with the two most important and difficult toxic tort litigations that had been brought previously, those involving asbestos and DES. Although each of these litigations presented its own unique array of complications, the issue that would prove most perplexing in Agent Orange—the question of whether the chemical caused plaintiffs' injuries—was far more straightforward in the asbestos and DES cases. First, the objective symptoms of asbestosis and mesothelioma, the two most common asbestos-related diseases, and the vaginal adenocarcinoma caused by DES, are relatively exposure-and-disease-specific, distinctive, and easily observed. Second, the long latency periods for those diseases (often twenty years or more) had already run their courses by the time many of the cases reached trial. Third, the exposure levels of asbestos workers and of women who had ingested DES during pregnancy were relatively high and sustained.

None of these conditions obtained in the case of Agent Orange: the cancers and birth defects that it allegedly caused were not distinctive; the exposures had occurred less than fifteen years earlier and thus may not yet have fully revealed their toxic effects; and the levels of dioxin (the highly toxic contaminant of Agent Orange) to which the veterans were exposed were generally quite low. For these and other reasons, the obstacles to establishing general causation and damage, easily overcome in the earlier toxic tort cases, would prove decisive in shaping the Agent Orange litigation and settlement and the public reaction to them.

By the same token, the task of establishing the liability of particular defendants was far more daunting in the Agent Orange case. The DES cases presented the indeterminate defendant problem; the pills, although manufactured by many different drug companies, were fungible and had been consumed long ago. Some asbestos cases presented the problem of indeterminate plaintiffs; certain injuries, especially cancer, were not asbestos-specific.

The Agent Orange case, however, presented both the indeterminate defendant and indeterminate plaintiff problems and in extreme forms. The Agent Orange was produced by different companies, but their formulations were mixed together in nonidentifiable steel drums before being sent to Vietnam. The most serious injuries of which the veterans complained apparently are not dioxin-specific. And although in the asbestos cases the issue of which particular firms were liable was sometimes complicated by a number of variables (type of asbestos, condition of packaging and handling, use of respirators) that were not usually relevant to Agent Orange, the issues of which individuals were exposed and at what levels were even more difficult in Agent Orange.

But this case also reveals in an unusually clear and arresting form the distinctive moral dilemma that characterizes tort disputes. From the perspective of the veterans who sued, the case's significance lay less in large questions of public policy, such as the conduct of the Vietnam War and the social control of toxic substances, than in their claim to what tort law has traditionally promised—corrective justice. The veterans viewed the case as their opportunity to settle accounts, to recover from the government and the chemical manufacturers some portion of what the Vietnam War had taken from them in the name of duty: their youth, their vigor, and their future. The case came to symbolize their most human commitments and passions: their insistence upon respect and recognition, their hope for redemption and renewal, and their hunger for vindication and vengeance. For them, it was a searing morality play projected onto a national stage. These deeply personal aspirations pervaded the case, influencing the strategies of plaintiffs' counsel, shaping certain issues, and casting a shadow over the negotiated settlement that would obscure its legal status for years to come.

Agent Orange, however, is more than a paradigm of a particularly difficult kind of mass toxic tort case. It also exemplifies a long historical development in the structure and underlying assumptions of tort law generally. This development consists of three interwoven themes. * * * First, tort law has moved from an individualistic grounding toward a more collective one. In defining the parties' legal rights and duties, tort law has come to be concerned with them less as discrete, idiosyncratic actors than as relatively interchangeable units of large, impersonal aggregations—broadly defined classes, epidemiological populations, or stochastic events. Second, the criteria for evaluating the parties' behavior have moved from moral categories to more functional ones. Evaluations of conduct based on fault, specific causation, and corrective justice norms have increasingly given way to considerations of compensation, deterrence, and administrative efficiency. Third, tort law has come to legitimate a judicial role that is less arbitral and more managerial in nature. Today's judge does not simply decide between the competing proofs and legal theories offered by the parties; he or she is also widely expected to administer large-scale litigation with an eye to achieving broad social purposes. The judge is supposed to allocate scarce resources wisely, develop legal rules that advance sound public policy, ensure that lawyers adequately represent their clients, and consider the social and political implications of settlements.

* * *

But for all its unique features, it would be profoundly mistaken to regard the case as only an interesting oddity, a sort of legal sideshow of interest to veterans, to be sure, but without larger significance for American society generally. * * * In reality, the Agent Orange litigation prefigures a grim dimension of our future; it is a harbinger of mass toxic tort cases yet to come. Future disputes will surely possess their own idiosyncratic elements; for example, they may involve pharmaceuticals, food additives, industrial compounds, pollutants, toxic wastes deposited in landfills, radiation, or some other effusion of modern technology. The causal linkages between toxic agents, exposure levels, and pathological symptoms may be more or less elusive than was true of Agent Orange. The injurers' identity and responsibility may be more or less determinate than in this case. The judges who adjudicate future cases may have very different conceptions of the court's role and of the nature of mass toxic tort litigation than did Judges Pratt and Weinstein. Other differences will surely exist. The contours of the new cases are no more predictable today than the Agent Orange case was twenty-five years ago.

* * *

But emphasizing the case's significance as a lodestar for future litigants and judges is to miss what in the end may be an even more profound lesson. The Agent Orange case is not simply a response to the veterans' anguish and to the social risks from toxic chemicals. It is, most pointedly, an attempt to solve these problems in a particular way. Tort litigation is an exceedingly valuable mechanism of social integration and control, a mechanism of which Americans appear to be unusually fond. But it is by no means our only, or necessarily our most promising, remedy for mass toxic harms. It is only one in a repertoire of policy instruments, including regulation, administrative compensation schemes, collective bargaining, and insurance, by which society can attempt to control risks and compensate harms.

* * *

It may seem odd to close this introduction by emphasizing the particularized, idiosyncratic, human dimension of the Agent Orange case. After all, [it has been] stressed that its causes, character, and consequences are firmly rooted in technological developments, fundamental legal structures, and large historical and political forces. These are social phenomena in which the role of individuals might seem insignificant or at most merely epiphenomenal. Yet the truth is that almost every aspect of the Agent Orange litigation has been influenced by contingent human choices. Dedicated but deeply divided veterans; flamboyant trial lawyers; class-action financial entrepreneurs; skillful, Machiavellian special masters; a Naderesque litigation organizer; a brilliant, crafty judge—these forceful personalities continually collided in a kind of Brownian motion of strategic choice, high idealism, seat-of-the-pants innovation, and human folly. Seldom has the contradiction between the popular, intuitive aspiration for law and its technical, formal reality been more vividly revealed. The Agent Orange case reminds us that the great historic developments not only play upon, but may also be the playthings of, ordinary men and women who are sometimes capable of doing extraordinary things.

* * *

Notes and Questions

1. The Dalkon Shield litigation, the asbestos cases, and the Agent Orange litigation represent three complex mass torts that have merited in-depth case studies of the social and legal problems surrounding resolution of these cases. These three mass torts will provide a continuing source for many of the case excerpts presented in this text. For other book-length treatments of mass tort litigation, *see* Ronald J. Bacigal, THE LIMITS OF LITIGATION: THE DALKON SHIELD CONTROVERSY (1990); Henry S. Cohn and David Bollier, THE GREAT HARTFORD CIRCUS FIRE: CREATIVE SETTLEMENT OF MASS DISASTERS (New Haven: Yale University Press, 1991); Sheldon D. Engelmayer and Robert Wagman, LORD'S JUSTICE: ONE JUDGE'S BATTLE TO EXPOSE THE DEADLY DALKON SHIELD I.U.D. (1985); Michael Green, BENDECTIN AND BIRTH DEFECTS: THE CHALLENGE OF MASS TOXIC SUBSTANCES LITIGATION (1995); Karen M. Hicks, SURVIVING THE DALKON SHIELD IUD: WOMEN v. THE PHARMACEUTICAL INDUSTRY (1994); Susan Perry & James Dawson, NIGHTMARE: WOMEN AND THE DALKON SHIELD (1985); and Richard B. Sobol, BENDING THE LAW: THE STORY OF THE DALKON SHIELD BANKRUPTCY (Chicago: The University of Chicago Press, 1991); Jack B. Weinstein, INDIVIDUAL JUSTICE IN MASS TORT LITIGATION (1995). *See also* VIETNAM VETERANS, THEIR FAMILIES, THEIR LEGACY (1994).

In addition, there is a growing academic literature of case studies of mass tort litigation aimed at "[expanding] the analytical literature describing new case management techniques" so that "[w]ith a sufficient database of case histories, it may be possible by reasoning inductively to develop a functional approach for the judicial management of complex cases." *See* Cheryl Frank, *Mass Tort: Salmonella Cases; A Model?*, A.B.A.J., Aug. 1985, at 5; Francis E. McGovern, *Resolving Mature Mass Tort Litigation*, 69 B.U.L.Rev. 659 (1989). Professor McGovern has been a leading expositor of mass tort case studies. *See* McGovern, *An Analysis of Mass Torts for Judges*, 73 Texas L.Rev. 1821 (1995); (descriptive analysis of mass tort litigation); McGovern, *The Alabama DDT Settlement Fund*, 53 Law & Contemp. Probs. 61 (1990); *Resolving Mature Mass Tort Litigation, id.* (case studies of *Jenkins v. Raymark Industries, Inc.* and *In re A.H. Robins Co.*); McGovern, *Toward a Functional Approach for Managing Complex Litigation*, 53 U.Chi.L.Rev. 440 (1986)(case studies of Michigan fishing rights litigation, Alabama utility ratemaking, and Ohio asbestos litigation); *see also*, Linda S. Mullenix, *Beyond Consolidation: Postaggregative Procedure in Asbestos Mass Tort Litigation*, 32 Wm & Mary L.Rev. 475 (1991)(case studies of the *In re School Asbestos Litigation* and *Cimino v. Raymark Industries* cases); Joseph Sanders, *The Bendectin Litigation: A Case Study in the Life Cycle of Mass Torts*, 43 Hastings L.J. 301 (1992); Peter H. Schuck, *The Role of Judges in Settling Complex Cases: The Agent Orange Example*, 53 U.Chi.L.Rev. 337 (1986)(case study of the Agent Orange litigation with a focus on settlement techniques).

2. The excerpts from Mintz, Brodeur, and Schuck books concerning the Dalkon Shield, asbestos, and Agent Orange litigations suggest similarities and differences in these mass tort cases. What commonalities exist across these cases? What differences? To what extent do these cases suggest a paradigmatic mass tort case? The Dalkon Shield litigation, in addition to its intrinsic mass tort characteristics, raises interesting questions concerning the legal and ethical obligations of corporations in their activities in the international arena. What is a corporation's legal liability for marketing and distributing a defective product abroad? How is this determined? Does it make a difference if distribution is in a so-called "third world" country, or, as Mintz describes, that a foreign country's government requests that a product continue to be distributed? What are a corporation's ethical responsibilities once the product has been recalled or suspended in the American market? *See e.g.,* Renee B. Allen, *International Regulation of Defective Medical Devices: Protecting the Foreign Consumer Through Recall*, 7 B.U. Int'l L.J. 85 (1989); Bruce F. Meyers, *Soldier of Orange, The Administrative, Diplomatic, Legislative and Litigatory Impact of Herbicide Agent Orange in South Vietnam*, 8 B.C. Envtl. Aff. L. Rev. 159 (1979); Laurel E. Miller, Comment, *Forum Non Conveniens and State Control of Foreign Plaintiff Access to U.S. Courts in International Tort Actions*, 58 U. Chi. L. Rev. 1369 (1991); Russell J. Weintraub, *A Proposed Choice-of-Law Standard for International Products Liability Disputes*, 16 Brook. J. Int'l L. 225 (1990).

3. Paul Brodeur's book raises the issue of the appropriateness of bankruptcy as a vehicle for resolving mass tort claims. The literature of mass tort litigation tends to focus on the harm to individual victims, with less attention paid to the effects of mass tort litigation on corporate solvency. The Brodeur excerpt also raises the issue of the impact of possible repetitive punitive damages on corporate malfeasors. The issues relating to mass torts and bankruptcy will be considered in Chapter XIII, and punitive damages in Chapter VII.

4. The excerpt from Professor Schuck's book suggests that Professor Schuck views the Agent Orange litigation as the paradigmatic mass tort litigation. Professor Richard Marcus has disagreed, stating: "The message he chose to emphasize, however, seems to be the wrong one. Treated as a parable for the failure of the tort system, the Agent Orange story is a poor fit because it is such a special case. Even as a harbinger of mass exposure litigation, it is of doubtful value; the recent books on asbestos and Dalkon Shield litigation suggest that the tort system serves a purpose in such cases." Richard L. Marcus, *Apocalypse Now?*, 85 Mich.L.Rev. 1267 (1987)(reviewing Schuck, AGENT ORANGE ON TRIAL). Professor Marcus believes that the real value to be derived from the Agent Orange litigation is in its lessons for active judicial promotion of settlement. *See also* Robert L. Rabin, *Tort System on Trial: The Burden of Mass Toxic Tort Litigation*, 98 Yale L.J. 813 (1989)(reviewing Schuck's AGENT ORANGE ON TRIAL); Frank A. Lalle, Comment, *Agent Orange As A Problem of Law and Policy*, 77 Nw. U.L. Rev. 48 (1982). The Dalkon Shield settlement is discussed in Chapter II, and the Dalkon Shield bankruptcy trust fund is explored in Chapter XIII. One of the recurring themes of this casebook is the extent to which both the procedural and substantive law "systems" have failed in the context of mass tort litigation.

5. It is perhaps useful, at the outset, to distinguish between "mass-accident" cases and "mass tort" litigation, as a number of commentators and courts do. Most so-called mass-accident or mass-disaster cases involve situations in which a number of persons are simultaneously harmed by a single act of the defendant. Usually these cases do not involve complex questions concerning the time between the defendant's wrongful conduct and the plaintiff's injury, remoteness of damage, contributory negligence, or assumption of risk. Typical examples are airplane crashes, explosions, catastrophic fires, and oil spills. *See In re Beverly Hills Fire Litigation*, 639 F.Supp. 915 (E.D.Ky.1986)(nightclub fire killing or injuring over 300 persons); *In re Federal Skywalk Cases*, 93 F.R.D. 415 (W.D. Mo.1982), *vacated* 680 F.2d 1175 (8th Cir.1982), *cert. denied sub nom.* Rau v. Stover, 459 U.S. 988, 103 S.Ct. 342, 74 L.Ed.2d 383 (1982)(Hyatt–Regency hotel skywalk collapse killing more than 100 people and injuring over 220); *In re Air Crash Disaster at Florida Everglades on December 29, 1972*, 549 F.2d 1006 (5th Cir.1977). The so-called "modern" mass tort is characterized by multiple occurrences of various related harms over time, with geographical dispersion of claims and claimants. For a discussion of this distinction, *see* Linda S. Mullenix, *Class Resolution of the Mass–Tort Case: A Proposed Federal Procedure Act*, 64 Tex.L.Rev. 1039, 1044 n.19 (1986); *see also* Sherrill P. Hondorf, *A Mandate for the Procedural Management of Mass Exposure Litigation*, 16 N.Ky.L.Rev. 541, 546–48 (1989)(distinguishing mass accident cases from mass exposure cases); Georgene M. Vairo, *Multi-Tort Cases: Cause For More Darkness on the Subject, or a New Role for Federal Common Law?*, 54 Fordham L.Rev. 167 n.1 (1985)(distinguishing mass accident cases from toxic tort cases); Spencer Williams, *Mass Tort Class Actions: Going, Going, Gone?*, 98 F.R.D. 323, 324 n.1 (1983)(distinguishing mass-accident cases from mass products-liability cases); Deborah Deitsch–Perez, Note, *Mechanical and Constitutional Problems in the Certification of Mandatory Multistate Mass Tort Actions Under Rule 23*, 49 Brook.L.Rev. 517, 517 n.6

(1983)(distinguishing mass-accident cases from products liability cases); Note, *Mass Accident Class Actions,* 60 Cal.L.Rev. 1615, 1616–17 (1972).

6. The Advisory Committee's note to Federal Rule of Civil Procedure 23 indicates that the class action rule is generally not a suitable procedural mechanism for litigating mass-accident cases. Through the 1970s and 1980s this Advisory Committee note was frequently cited to justify denying class certification in mass-tort cases. *See e.g.,* In re Northern Dist. of Cal., Dalkon Shield IUD Prods. Liab. Litig., 693 F.2d 847, 852 (9th Cir.1982)(decertifying classes in Dalkon Shield litigation), *cert. denied* 459 U.S. 1171, 103 S.Ct. 817, 74 L.Ed.2d 1015 (1983); Ikonen v. Hartz Mountain Corp., 122 F.R.D. 258, 263 (S.D.Cal.1988)(denying class certification in flea and tick spray products liability litigation). For a further discussion of this problem, *see* Chapter II, A, *infra,* discussing the class action rule and mass torts.

7. For capsule descriptions of a number of recent mass accident and mass tort cases, *see* William W. Schwarzer, Nancy E. Weiss, and Alan Hirsch, *Judicial Federalism in Action: Coordination of Litigation in State and Federal Courts,* 78 Va.L.Rev. 1689 (1992). Of what possible importance, as a matter of substantive and procedural law, is the distinction between mass accident and mass tort cases? For recent discussions of current issues in mass tort, *see* Jack B. Weinstein, *An Introduction to Who's Who in Mass Toxic Torts,* 80 Cornell L. Rev. ___ (1995); Jack B. Weinstein, *Procedural and Substantive Problems in Complex Litigation Arising From Disasters,* 5 Tuoro L. Rev. 1 (1988); Symposium, *Mass Torts After Agent Orange,* 52 Brook. L. Rev. 329 (1986).

B. ANALYTICAL FRAMEWORKS

THE AMERICAN LAW INSTITUTE, COMPLEX LITIGATION: STATUTORY RECOMMEN-DATIONS AND ANALYSIS

(1994) at 7—18.

THE PROBLEM OF COMPLEX LITIGATION

a. Introduction. "Complex litigation" has no uniform definition, and the term sometimes is used to refer to litigation that concerns complex issues even if the dispute takes place only between two parties in a single forum. As used in this Project, however, "complex litigation" refers exclusively to multiparty, multiforum litigation; it is characterized by related claims dispersed in several forums and often over long periods of time and presents one of the greatest problems our courts currently confront. Repeated litigation of the common issues in a complex case unduly expends the resources of attorney and client, clogs already over-crowded dockets, delays recompense for those in need, and brings our legal system into general disrepute. Creative lawyers and judges have shown that both justice and efficiency can be achieved by those willing to stretch the bounds of the existing procedural scheme, but as Congress, the profession, and newspaper journalists have noted, we are in urgent need of procedural reform to meet the exigencies of the complex litigation problem.

Complex cases may arise under state or federal law and in the courts of either system. They are generated by a variety of circumstances—from a single mass disaster such as the collapse of a Hyatt Hotel skywalk, from myriad individual contacts with a hazardous product such as asbestos, or from allegations of antitrust violations committed by one of the world's largest corporations or a number of small ones. The claims in a complex case may accrue all at once as in an air crash, or they may be latent for generations and mature at different times, as in the case of DES. *See, e.g.,* Payton v. Abbott Labs, 386 Mass. 540, 437 N.E.2d 171 (1982). But complex cases share two defining characteristics: they all involve duplicative relitigation of identical or nearly identical issues, and consequently, they all involve the enormous expenditure of resources.

* * *

b. A description of the history of complex litigation. The history of complex litigation is a litany of gargantuan and often well-known cases that have posed unprecedented challenges for the courts. An outline of some of the most important developments in that history follows and illustrates the current problem posed by this form of litigation.

In the early 1960's, as the House Judiciary Committee has noted, "[f]ollowing the successful Government prosecution of the electrical equipment manufacturers for antitrust law violations, more than 1,800 separate damage actions were filed in 33 federal district courts. This wave of litigation threatened to engulf the courts." House Judiciary Committee Report No. 1130 (1968). As a result, a Coordinating Committee for Multiple Litigation was established, without whose efforts, in the late Chief Justice Earl Warren's view, "district court calendars throughout the country could well have broken down." *Manual for Complex Litigation* vii (4th rev.ed.1977). Congress eventually responded to the electrical equipment cases by creating the Judicial Panel on Multidistrict Litigation, *see* 28 U.S.C. § 1407, one of the most important tools for processing complex litigation that the federal system has developed to date. As of December 31, 1987, after two decades of operation, the Multidistrict Litigation Panel had consolidated 16,173 separate civil actions for pretrial proceedings. Report of the Proceedings of the Judicial Conference of the U.S., March 15, 1988, at 5. Despite the Multidistrict Litigation Panel's past success and undoubted future potential, however, the much-criticized provisions that limit its authority to consolidation for pretrial purposes have prevented it from serving as anything like a comprehensive solution for the complex litigation problem.

* * *

After a 1963 grand jury indictment charged the Wm. Merrell Company with falsifying data submitted to the Food and Drug Administration, fifteen hundred plaintiffs brought suit claiming injuries due to MER/29. MER/29 cases "were begun in almost every state and in many different courts, both state and federal, within most states." Rheingold, *The MER/29 Story—An Instance of Successful Mass Disaster Litigation,* 56 Cal.L.Rev. 116, 121 (1968). MER/29 was one of the great success stories of voluntary cooperation among litigants—a lawyers' committee was able to consolidate pretrial discovery effectively, and because there was only a single defendant, the few cases that went to trial served as test cases that facilitated settlement. The lawyers even established a MER/29 "school" to train plaintiffs' attorneys in the facts of the case. Nevertheless, MER/29 was the type of exception that proves a rule—altogether extraordinary effort, trust, and good faith were necessary to prevent the disintegration of the litigation into a fight to the last ditch that could have generated immense legal fees at the expense of the tort victims and the defendant.

The giant of complex litigation has been and continues to be asbestos. Asbestos litigation on a large scale began in the mid–1970s and has continued to grow. As a result, so many asbestos-related personal injury claims now have been brought that, in 1986, "[a]pproximately 20,000 damage actions by asbestos disease victims, mostly workers, [were] pending in state and federal courts across the country, and the number [was] increasing by several hundred new claims each month." Rosenberg, *Book Review,* 99 Harv.L.Rev. 1693, 1693–94 (1986). An even larger estimate was suggested in a 1987 study for the Federal Judicial Center: "Exact counts of pending asbestos cases are impossible to find. Recent estimates * * * range from about 33,000 to 50,000. New cases continue to be filed, and Johns–Manville estimates that it will have to pay between 83,000 and 100,000 personal injury claims." T. Willging, *Trends in Asbestos Litigation* 12 (1987). Asbestos also has spawned a great number of ancillary suits seeking to determine responsibility for removing the substance from buildings or to apportion blame among defendants. It should not be surprising, therefore, that "[t]he estimated legal bill for all facets of the asbestos litigation easily exceeds a billion dollars." Rosenberg, *supra,* at 1694.

Many complex cases over the past three decades have arisen from single mass catastrophes. United States Circuit Judge Alvin Rubin provides a simple but moving catalog:

> We all know of the Bhopal disaster in which, as a result of the release of noxious chemicals from a Union Carbide plant in Bhopal, India, more than 1700 persons were killed and 200,000 were injured. When a Pan American Boeing 727 crashed into a residential area near the New Orleans airport on July 9, 1982, 179 people died. The collapse of a skywalk at the Hyatt Regency Hotel in Kansas City in 1981 resulted in 114 deaths and hundreds of injuries. In 1985, 500 people died in an airline crash in Japan, 174 in a Delta Airlines crash at the Dallas airport, and 57 persons in a crash of a Midwestern Airlines plane.

Rubin, *Mass Torts and Litigation Disasters,* 20 Ga.L.Rev. 429, 432 (1986). Because catastrophes like these invariably raise complex issues of fact, they can have a much greater impact on the courts than the small number of the cases suggests. It is not uncommon that cases may be dispersed in both the state and federal judicial systems. For example, after the Hyatt Hotel skywalk collapse, hundreds of virtually identical lawsuits were filed in state court as well as before United States District Court Judge Scott Wright. *See* Williams, *Mass Tort Class Actions, Going, Going, Gone?*, 98 F.R.D. 323, 331 (1983).

In the early 1980's, "Agent Orange" was perhaps the most highly visible complex case in the federal system. After more than 600 individual suits were filed, first Judge Pratt and then Chief Judge Jack Weinstein of the United States District Court for the Eastern District of New York certified a plaintiff class containing an estimated 2.4 million members. Efficient handling of the case was made more difficult by the decision of 2,440 individuals to opt out of the plaintiff class, although 600 of them later asked to be reinstated. The controversy over Judge Weinstein's aggressive management of this case, his tactics in achieving settlement, and the adequacy of the settlement he obtained, may not abate for years to come. Nevertheless, a seemingly hopeless litigation morass was resolved. The case is a perfect example of the inadequacy of our traditional procedural system to cope with mass disasters or the demands of modern substantive law. *See* P. Schuck, *Agent Orange on Trial: Mass Toxic Disasters in the Courts* (1986).

The sometimes devastating impact of complex litigation is suffered by large defendants, as well as individual plaintiffs. This fact was underscored recently when two mass tort defendants, asbestos producer Johns–Manville and Dalkon Shield manufacturer A.H. Robins, resorted to bankruptcy in order to resolve the outstanding tort claims against them. *See* In re Johns–Manville Corp., Nos. 82 B 11,656 to 82 B 11,676 (S.D.N.Y., filed Aug. 26, 1982). Although the invocation of bankruptcy procedures may be one method of achieving the consolidated adjudication of a complex case, it is by no means obvious that it is the optimal means for handling mass tort claims. Indeed, the very propriety of using bankruptcy in this setting has proved extremely controversial. *See, e.g.*, Note, *The Manville Bankruptcy: Treating Mass Tort Claims in Chapter 11 Proceedings*, 96 Harv.L.Rev. 1121 (1983). Serious questions also can be raised as to whether bankruptcy courts can cope with the massive litigation ancillary to a complex case, or can achieve equity between early-and-late filing claimants.

At times the complexity of some cases goes beyond what appears on the surface of the litigation. For example, in massive environmental clean-up litigation what already is a highly complex basic dispute is compounded by the complexity of deciding the applicability of insurance coverage as well as assigning the liability among multiple insurers.

Even this brief summary suffices to show that huge multiparty, multiforum disputes have become a recurring feature of modern litigation. In many cases systemic resources have been saved and costs reduced by good sense, procedural creativity, and judge or lawyer initiative. Nevertheless, the time has come to replace ad hoc innovation with procedures developed specifically for complex cases. This is especially true because the essential features of complex litigation are predictable, and the number of cases is bound to increase.

* * *

c. Cost of duplicative litigation. Rule 1 of the Federal Rules of Civil Procedure specifies a tripartite goal for the federal procedural system: "the just, speedy, and inexpensive determination of every action." Unfortunately, complex litigation can yield determinations that are slow, enormously expensive, and potentially unjust.

Complex litigation as defined in this proposal is not limited to cases involving complex substantive issues. Rather, it is characterized by the wasteful multiplication of proceedings, needless costs, and the likelihood of injustice resulting from inconsistent adjudications. Judicial overload also leads to delay and costs throughout the entire judicial system. *See* D. Hensler, *Trends in Tort Litigation: The Story Behind the Statistics* 33 (1987). It is worth stressing, however, that the effect of long court delays does not fall equally on all members of society—although a large corporation may be able to wait many years to obtain a tort or contract recovery, or may be content to defer liability for that length of time, someone who is poor and seriously injured may find that justice delayed is indeed, as the saying goes, justice denied.

Duplicative litigation of the issues in a complex case also can lead to injustice in more direct ways. "[B]eyond the sheer economy of not having to litigate the same matters twice," authors Rowe and Sibley point out, "consolidation of related proceedings can reduce such problems as inconsistent outcomes, whipsawing (from the ability of defendants in separate litigation to point to a nonparty as the one truly liable), and uncoordinated scrambles for the assets of a limited fund." Rowe & Sibley, *Beyond Diversity: Federal Multiparty, Multiforum Jurisdiction,* 135 U.Pa.L.Rev. 7, 15 (1986). The ultimate result of an "uncoordinated scramble," of course, can be a defendant's bankruptcy before all potential plaintiffs have been paid, and this risk particularly is plausible in cases allowing plaintiffs to obtain large and often widely differing punitive damage awards. In addition, consolidation of related claims can ensure that people with modest means or those with relatively small claims can gain access to justice; forcing individual litigation of propositions that are true but expensive to demonstrate can be tantamount to barring the courthouse doors.

Finally, the most striking problem caused by complex litigation is its enormous cost. That cost cannot be measured precisely, but every indication is that it is staggering.

> Even saving one week of judicial time per case would, as most trial judges know, be substantial * * *. [I]n the Dalkon Shield litigation, the record disclosed that, if the usual percentage (90) of the 100 members [in a] statewide class settled their cases, the savings of

judicial resources in the trial of the remaining 100 would amount to 400 weeks, or, roughly eight years of trial time. In addition, there would be an estimated savings of $26 million in litigation expense to the parties and $7 million of court expenses.

Williams, *supra* at 328. If a 90% settlement rate in a single thousand-member portion of a nationwide complex case can achieve savings of $33 million plus eight years of judicial time, it seems clear that the savings from a carefully planned consolidation procedure for all types of complex litigation might prove to be billions of dollars. This conclusion is reinforced by the fact * * * that the legal bill for asbestos cases alone already has been estimated at over $1 billion. *See* Rosenberg, *supra*, at 1694.

The economic expense of complex litigation also can be estimated by tabulating the cost of its component parts. As of 1982, an hour of judicial time cost approximately $600. *See* Levin & Colliers, *Containing the Cost of Litigation*, 37 Rutgers L.Rev. 219, 27 (1985). In addition, studies have shown that each dollar of plaintiff recovery typically costs two dollars in attorney's fees. Thus, assume that the crash of a small plane injured ten plaintiffs and that the litigation brought by each cost the defendant $100,000 in legal fees and compensation after an individual ten-hour trial. Based on that, and even without adjusting the estimated system costs to take into account of cost-of-living increases in judicial salaries, it can be estimated that the plaintiffs will take $333,-000, the lawyers $666,000, and the court system $60,000. In other words, it will have cost $726,000 to generate only $333,000 in plaintiff recovery.

This example of a ten-person air crash, a case almost certainly too small to be considered complex and consolidated by current procedures, demonstrates that a two-thirds reduction in court and lawyer time would save almost $500,000, or half of the total costs of compensation. Equally, a reduction in litigation time of only fifty percent would save $363,000, or 36% of the costs of compensation. Moreover, because this estimate is based on only three assumptions—that legal services take two-thirds of compensation costs, that court time costs $600 per hour, and the claims will require on average one hour per $10,000 to litigate—it should be subject to generalization. That is, so long as a case requires about one hour of court time per $10,000 of compensation, any consolidation that cuts legal time in half will save an average of 37% of the total costs of compensation, and this is true even if the parties' own expenditure of time and effort is left out of the equation. Thus, to the extent that empirical data are available, they provide a dramatic confirmation of Professor Chafee's statement that "[i]n matters of justice * * *, the benefactor is he who makes one lawsuit grow where two grew before." Chafee, *Bills of Peace with Multiple Parties*, 45 Harv.L.Rev. 1297 (1932).

* * *

AMERICAN LAW INSTITUTE, ENTERPRISE RESPONSIBILITY FOR PERSONAL IN-JURY (REPORTERS' STUDY 1991)

389–93.

* * * From the process perspective, the salient defining characteristics of a mass tort include:

(1) numerous victims who have filed or might file damage claims against the same defendant(s);

(2) claims arising from a single event or transaction, or from a series of similar events or transactions spread over time;

(3) questions of law and fact that are complex and expensive to litigate and adjudicate—frequently questions that are scientific and technological in nature;

(4) important issues of law and fact which are identical or common to all or substantial subgroups of the claims;

(5) injuries that are widely dispersed over time, territory, and jurisdiction;

(6) causal indeterminacy—especially in cases involving toxic substance exposure—that precludes use of conventional procedures to determine and standards to measure any causal connection between the plaintiff's injury and the defendant's tortious conduct;

(7) disease and other injuries from long delayed latent risks, especially in cases involving toxic substance exposure.

The standard lawsuit embodies the ideal of individual justice through its strong procedural preference for adjudicating tort claims de novo, one by one, and for customizing judgments according to the particular facts and circumstances of each case. Yet, as Holmes put it, this ideal may be more consistent with, if not largely the creation of, "[o]ur law of torts . . . from the old days." In contrast to the bygone era "of isolated, ungeneralized wrongs, assaults, slanders, and the like," modern tort law is primarily concerned with the "incidents of certain well known businesses . . . injuries to person or property by railroads, factories, and the like." Since Holmes's observations nearly a century ago, substantive tort rules have undergone major reforms that take account of the systemic and statistically predictable risks created by business activity.

Tort process, however, remains largely unchanged. In mass tort cases the wholesale infliction of injury is still redressed at retail. Adjudicating mass torts on an individual basis entails great costs that may preclude or disable the effective preparation and prosecution of a large number of claims. This means that many claims are redressed at a steep—and, in fact, standardized—discount, while a substantial number are not redressed at all. Consequently, standard tort process not only sacrifices potential gains in compensation, prevention, and administrative efficiency, but also undermines its patron norm of individual justice.

* * *

MARK A. PETERSON AND MOLLY SELVIN, RESOLUTION OF MASS TORTS: TOWARD A FRAMEWORK FOR EVALUATION OF AGGREGATIVE PROCEDURES

Rand, The Institute for Civil Justice (1988) at vii, 31–37.

Mass tort litigation presents unique problems for courts and litigants:

- The large number of litigants, plaintiffs as well as defendants, makes mass litigation burdensome. These large numbers significantly complicate the processing and resolution of litigation with procedures that evolved primarily for "simple" lawsuits—i.e., those involving one or two parties on each side.

- Mass tort litigation can involve enormous personal, financial, and political stakes for parties on all sides. It also imposes large burdens on the court system in terms of both public costs and concentration of cases within particular jurisdictions.

- Timing is critical for plaintiffs with significant disabilities and expenses. Yet as the number of claims increases, the need of plaintiffs for prompt compensation becomes harder to satisfy. The complex issues and larger numbers of parties can result in long delays in processing and resolving cases.

- Litigation involving toxic torts presents particular difficulties centering on issues, both technical and legal, about the causation and documentation of injuries and diseases. The frequently long latency period between exposure to a toxic substance and injury, together with the need to identify the products to which exposure occurred, further complicates legal and technical issues.

- Finally, mass litigation presents special threats to the fairness of our justice system, raising the possibilities that outcomes will be inconsistent; that defendants faced with a great number of claims may be forced to make significant settlements even when liability is unlikely; that defendants can avoid responsibility by aggressively pursuing litigation; that compensation is not related to the seriousness of injuries; and that the burdens on defendants might not accurately reflect their relative culpability.

* * *

Conceptual Overview of Mass Tort Litigation

The impact aggregative procedures is both complex and significant, primarily because of the complexity of mass tort litigation. Each instance of mass personal injury litigation involves a multitude of parties and a maze of issues, procedures, and strategies, and each can lead to outcomes that can have varying effects on hundreds or thousands of participants * * *. The overview also provides a common way of looking across various instances of mass tort litigation so that inferences can be drawn about similarities and differences in the effects of aggregative procedures.

The overview is primarily intended as a means for organizing elements of mass tort litigation by grouping those elements in the following manner (Fig. 2, next page):

Characteristics

> What is the litigation about?

> Who are the participants?

> What are the objectives and strategies of the participants, and what are the relationships among them?

Approach

> What is the formal organization of the litigation?

> What aggregative procedures are used?

> What are the features of those aggregative procedures?

Course of the litigation

> What procedural actions have been taken?

> How have those actions been carried out?

> What informal actions have been taken, such as negotiations and contacts among parties?

Outcomes

> Has the litigation been resolved?

> Was the resolution comprehensive—i.e., did it include all issues and all parties?

> How was compensation distributed among plaintiffs?

> What were defendants' relative contributions?

> How satisfied are the parties with the outcome?

> How much did the litigation cost? What were the transaction costs?

> How long did the litigation take?

Figure 3 provides a working list of * * * elements. Some of the characteristics listed are obvious determinants of the course and outcomes of litigation, while others have been deemed important in previous discussions of mass litigation. * * *

FIGURE 2—GENERAL OVERVIEW OF MASS TORT LITIGATION

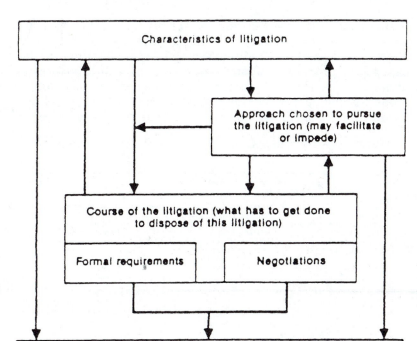

This overview lists characteristics that are particularly critical to mass litigation—i.e., traits that seem to have a direct effect on the course and outcomes of mass litigation or that interact with aggregative procedures to have such effects.* Figure 3 lists these characteristics, grouping them as "issues," "participants," and "organization of litigation." We used these groupings to stress relationships among various characteristics rather than to draw sharp definitional lines for each group.

In addition to listing elements important to mass litigation, the overview serves as a kind of flow chart; the arrows on the overview suggest relationships among the elements in mass litigation. For example, the course of litigation, subsuming both informal and formal (procedural) activities, contributes to the determination of outcomes. In turn, the activities of litigation are affected by the characteristics of that litigation, such as the nature and strength of liability claims or the relative resources of the parties. The course of litigation is also affected by the approach toward handling the litigation—i.e., whether it is

---

* The overview lists characteristics that may be systematically related to the use of aggregative procedures in mass litigation. Other characteristics might be important in particular litigation but may not have such a systematic relationship. For example, the quality of defense attorneys might play a critical role in a particular case, but there may be less case-by-case variance in the organization, strategies, and experience of defense lawyers than among plaintiffs' lawyers. And differences among cases do not have as much significance for the course and outcome of litigation as do differences in plaintiffs' lawyers, who usually finance and control litigation for plaintiffs.

handled through traditional means or through specific types of aggregation.

While some of the relationships shown on the overview are obvious, others are more complex. For example, the choice of approach to handling mass litigation—traditional case-by-case litigation or the type of aggregative procedure, if any,—is driven by characteristics of the litigation, particularly the complexity of issues and number of parties. Decisions bearing on whether to aggregate and on the type of aggregative procedure to apply will also be affected by the progress of the

FIGURE 3—DETAILED OVERVIEW OF MASS TORT LITIGATION

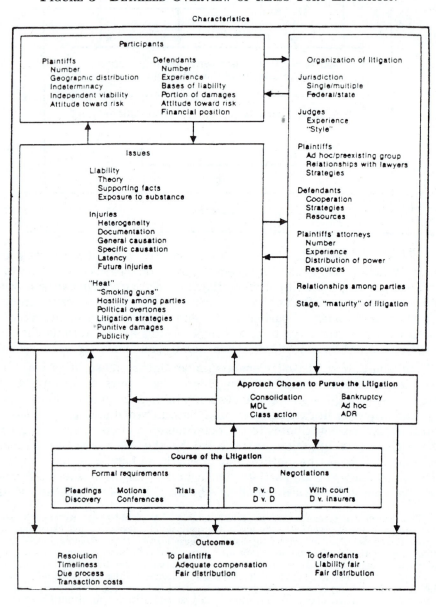

litigation. Different types of aggregative procedures have been used at different stages of the same mass litigation.

Issues and participants can combine in several ways to change the nature of litigation. For example, mass toxic litigation in which there are questions about exposure to a toxic agent—or about injury causation or latency—may pose the problem of "indeterminate plaintiffs." Plaintiff indeterminacy makes it difficult to fashion aggregative procedures that will produce comprehensive and final resolution.

The characteristics of litigation will affect the impact of aggregative procedures. Differences among claims may diminish the effectiveness of aggregative procedures. Issues of liability and injuries usually vary among plaintiffs so that there is a distribution in the strength of claims. This distribution affects matters of cooperation and power among plaintiffs' attorneys as well as their likely response to aggregative procedures. * * * The distribution of injuries—i.e., the relative number of plaintiffs with weak as opposed to strong claims—may markedly affect the success of aggregative procedures. Aggregative procedures can be frustrated if the strength of claims is varied and plaintiffs with strong claims choose not to cooperate in the aggregative procedure, as in the Hyatt Skywalk case.

The overview illustrates the complex relationships among the characteristics of mass litigation. Issues and litigants' characteristics not only shape but can also be affected by the organization of litigation. In Fig. 3, for example, we have described a set of issues as "heat": emotional matters that can inflame jurors, producing extreme verdicts, and that can upset litigants, making settlement difficult. Emotional issues might arise with (or even before) the filing of claims (as occurred following the 1984 Union Carbide gas leak at Bhopal, India) or they may grow out of the process of litigation (as in the discovery of incriminating documents or attempts to frustrate litigation). Heat might also be generated, however, by the manner in which litigation is organized or carried out. Much of the fervor among plaintiffs and plaintiffs' lawyers in the Dalkon Shield litigation grew out of an aggressive litigation strategy by the defendant that included thorough investigation and trial of claimants' sexual histories.

The general overview also identifies several other hypotheses that will be explored. * * * We expect to find that the approach adopted to handle mass litigation—the type of aggregative procedure—affects many of the litigation outcomes. Aggregative procedures are employed to change litigation activities and are intended to change some outcomes, such as faster resolution of claims or comprehensive resolution of all claims, but the procedures may also change substantive results. For example, a given aggregative procedure might affect the comprehensiveness of resolution. Bankruptcy and class actions are both methods that might be used to resolve all claims. In contrast, MDL [multidistrict litigation procedure] has no formal legal provisions for comprehensive resolution of claims.

Another hypothesis of our * * * studies is that aggregative procedures and characteristics interact to determine the course and outcome of mass litigation; the characteristics of litigation will influence how those aggregative procedures affect the course and outcome.

A third hypothesis is that aggregative procedures can change other important characteristics of litigation—e.g., redefining and adding issues, adding or subtracting parties, changing jurisdictions or judges, or altering the organization of litigants and their lawyers.

Observations and hypotheses suggested by the arrows indicate the complex relationships between aggregative procedures and characteristics that complicate our research. Since each aggregative procedure is used in distinctive litigation, we must understand the central characteristics of that litigation, how those characteristics shape the litigation in their own right, how they affect the consequences of the aggregative procedure, and how aggregative procedures in turn reshape the characteristics. * * *

* * *

Notes and Questions

1. There can be little doubt that complex mass tort cases, however described or defined, present a litigation model distinct from the traditional model of adjudication described by Professor Chayes in his famous article on public law litigation. *See* Abram Chayes, *The Role of The Judge in Public Law Litigation*, 89 Harv.L.Rev. 1281 (1976). In that article, Professor Chayes discussed five characteristics of the traditional civil case: (1) the lawsuit is bipolar, (2) the litigation is retrospective, (3) the right and remedy are interdependent, (4) the lawsuit is a self-contained episode, and (5) the process is party-initiated and party-controlled. Professor Chayes then described a new "public law" model of adjudication as one "sprawling and amorphous," "subject to change over the course of the litigation," "suffused and intermixed with negotiating and mediating processes at every point," with the judge as a dominant figure in organizing and guiding the case, as well as continuing involvement in administration and implementation of relief. The paradigmatic public law litigations have involved school desegregation, employment discrimination, and prisoners' or inmates' rights cases.

The question is whether complex mass tort cases, based as they are in the adjudication of private harms, are emerging as yet another model of civil dispute resolution anchored in the "public law" concept of the 1960s. A consistent proponent of engrafting a "public law" litigation model onto the mass tort context has been Professor David Rosenberg. *See e.g.,* David Rosenberg, *The Causal Connection in Mass Tort Exposure Cases: A "Public Law" Vision of the Tort System*, 97 Harv.L.Rev. 849 (1984); Rosenberg, *Class Actions For Mass Torts: Doing Individual Justice By Collective Means*, 62 Ind. L.J. 561 (1987); Rosenberg, *Toxic Tort Litigation: Crisis or Chrysalis? A Comment on Feinberg's Conceptual Problems and Proposed Solutions*,

24 Hous.L.Rev. 183 (1987). For a competing view questioning the wisdom of the trend towards a new model of aggregative procedure, exemplified in mass tort litigation, *see* Judith Resnik, *From "Cases" to "Litigation,"* 54 Law & Contemp. Probs. 5 (1991); *cf.* Ralph K. Winter, Comment: *Aggregating Litigation,* 54 Law & Contemp. Probs. 69 (summer 1991)(responding to Resnik). In addition, this view has been endorsed by Judge Weinstein; *see* Jack B. Weinstein, INDIVIDUAL JUSTICE IN MASS TORT LITIGATION (1995); Jack B. Weinstein, *Ethical Dilemmas in Mass Tort Litigation,* 88 Nw. U.L.Rev. 469 (1994). *See also* section C, note 6, *infra* (on the aggregation debate).

2. Professor Francis McGovern, who has served as special master in several mass tort and complex litigations (*see supra* n.1 at p. 17), has developed a concept of the "mature" mass tort litigation. Writes Professor McGovern:

> The traditional view of the civil litigation system as an individualized, rights-based adjudicatory system dedicated to victim compensation has faced mounting pressures in recent years. In particular, the litigation process has been challenged by notions that emphasize the collective interests of society by centralizing rulemaking and by fostering inquisitorial fact-finding. The paradigm cases for these alternative views are "mature mass torts" or mass tort litigation, where there has been full and complete discovery, multiple jury verdicts, and a persistent vitality in the plaintiffs' contentions. Typically at the mature stage, little or no new evidence will be developed, significant appellate review of any novel legal issues has been concluded, and at least one full cycle of trial strategies has been exhausted. The East Texas asbestos class action in *Jenkins v. Raymark* and the Dalkon Shield bankruptcy in *In re A.H. Robins Company* are examples of mature mass tort litigation.

Francis E. McGovern, *Resolving Mature Mass Tort Litigation,* 69 B.U.L.Rev. 659 (1989); *see also* Francis F.E. McGovern, *An Analysis of Mass Torts for Judges,* 73 Tex.L.Rev. 1821 (1995). Professor Rosenberg has challenged the usefulness of this concept of "mature" mass torts, noting: "On its face, the maturity standard is simply too vague to provide courts with useful guidance in determining when to use class actions and other collective procedures. McGovern's criteria * * * are not only slippery tests, [but] they also require courts to engage in a highly complex analysis. More seriously, the 'maturity' prerequisite ironically fails to fulfill its objective of providing a reliable and fair predicate for collective settlement and disposition precisely because it effectively *forbids* collective processing." *See* Rosenberg, *Of End Games and Openings in Mass Tort Cases: Lessons From a Special Master,* 69 B.U.L.Rev. 695, 707–08 (1989).

3. The American Law Institute's COMPLEX LITIGATION: STATUTORY RECOMMENDATIONS AND ANALYSIS is interesting not only for the scope of that enterprise, but for what it deliberately leaves out. As the excerpt suggests, the Reporters decided at the outset to exclude from consideration any alternative dispute resolution techniques for resolving mass torts, or other compensation systems. As it turns out, administrative models, claims facilities, alternative dispute resolution, bankruptcy, and trust funds have been, to

date, the chief vehicles for resolving mass tort claims. *See* Chapters XI–IV *infra* for a discussion of these methods for dealing with mass tort litigation.

4. The ALI COMPLEX LITIGATION project focused exclusively on procedural problems relating to mass tort, dealing primarily with issues relating to jurisdiction, intra-system and intersystem consolidation, and applicable law. Not only has the project eschewed discussion of alternative dispute resolution techniques, but it also has excluded consideration of substantive tort issues. This gap is somewhat filled by the ALI *Reporter's Study* in ENTERPRISE RESPONSIBILITY FOR PERSONAL INJURY (1991), in which the Reporters divide contemporary tort litigation into three tiers: (1) ordinary accident litigation, (2) products defects and medical malpractice, and (3) mass toxic tort cases. Discussing this "third-tier" tort litigation, the Reporters note, at 10:

> Even graver concerns arose about the capacity of our centuries-old tort regime to grapple with a new third tier of litigation. This category involves the "mass" tort of toxic exposure of a large number of people to a product or environmental hazard that may cause cancers or other serious illnesses a decade later. Although such mass tort episodes have been relatively few in number and their legal treatment is still in a state of flux, the third tier involves the highest stakes of all. A single product from a single firm, such as the Dalkon Shield, can produce tens of thousands of disabling injuries and tort claims, and, like the asbestos cases, can threaten to swamp the legal system with several hundred thousand lawsuits around the country. At the same time, because of the long latency period between initial exposure and eventual manifestation of diseases such as cancer without a single standard cause, knotty questions were presented to the tort system about precisely which product or firm was responsible for a particular victim's present condition or fatality. And liability insurers, themselves not much better able than their policyholders to predict the scope and limits of mass tort liability, displayed greater and greater reluctance to provide any future coverage against it.

5. How does one calculate the costs of complex mass tort litigation? The Rand Institute for Civil Justice has conducted a series of empirical studies of the costs of litigation. *See* Kakalik, James S., et al., *Costs and Compensation Paid in Aviation Accident Litigation* (1988); Kakalik, James S. and Nicholas M. Pace, *Costs and Compensation Paid in Tort Litigation* (1986); Kakalik, James S., et al., *Variation in Asbestos Litigation Compensation and Expenses* (1984); Kakalik, James S., et al., *Costs of Asbestos Litigation* (1983); Kakalik, James S., *et al.*, *Costs of Civil Justice System: Court Expenditures for Various Types of Civil Cases* (1983); and Kakalik, James S., et al., *Costs of the Civil Justice System: Court Expenditures for Processing Tort Cases.* *See also* Mark A. Peterson, *Giving Away Money: Comparative Comments on Claims Resolution Facilities,* 53 Law & Contemp. Probs. 113 (1991). A highly contentious area of mass tort litigation has centered on the question of attorneys' fees, which will be discussed at D.3, *infra,* and Chapter IV.G, *infra.*

C. THE JURISPRUDENTIAL DEBATE: LITIGANT AUTONOMY VERSUS AGGREGATIVE JUSTICE

MERTENS v. ABBOTT LABORATORIES

United States District Court, District of New Hampshire, 1983.
99 F.R.D. 38.

FRANCIS J. BOYLE, CHIEF JUDGE, Sitting by Designation.

This action was brought by twelve Plaintiffs. Eight of them are women who allege that by reason of exposure to diethystilbestrol (hereinafter referred to as DES) *in utero*, they suffered various injuries, including cancerous or pre-cancerous conditions, repeated pregnancy losses, infertility, incomplete, defective or abnormal development of their reproductive tracts and other adverse effects. They seek damages and a variety of other forms of relief, including the establishment of a fund, treatment facilities for themselves and persons who in the future might suffer similar injury. The eight female Plaintiffs contend that they have sustained a variety of injuries by reason of their in utero exposure to DES. One of these eight Plaintiffs seeks damages for multiple surgeries to eradicate adenocarcinoma and sterility. The other seven seek damages for the following, respectively: genital tract abnormalities requiring frequent medical procedures; spontaneous abortions, tubal pregnancy and uterine and cervical adenosis; chronic cervicitis dysplasia with foci of carcinoma in situ requiring frequent medical procedures; irregular cervix necessitating surgery and the development of tissue abnormalities; adenosis in the genital tract and deformed cervix; irregular cervix; and hyperkeratosis and glycogenital squamous epithelium of the genital tract.

Defendants are eleven firms that allegedly manufactured DES. They assert that the companies which manufactured DES numbered in the hundreds. Some of the Plaintiffs can produce evidence to identify a specific Defendant as manufacturer of the product that allegedly harmed them. In other claims, the manufacturer is probably either one of two Defendants, and in still other actions the manufacturer of the DES is not and cannot be identified.

Plaintiffs seek a determination that this action can be maintained as a class action. * * *

* * *

Rule 23(b)(3) requires a finding "that the questions of law or fact common to the members of the class predominate over any questions affecting only individual members, and that a class action is superior to other available methods for the fair and efficient adjudication of the controversy. The matters pertinent to the findings include: "(A) the interest of members of the class in individually controlling the prosecution or defense of separate actions; (B) the extent and nature of any litigation concerning the controversy already commenced by or against members of the class; (C) the desirability or undesirability of concentrating the litigation of the claims in the particular forum; (D) the difficulties likely to be encountered in the management of a class action."

* * *

While there are enough common issues of law and fact in this action to satisfy the 23(a) analysis, 23(b)(3) requires that these common questions predominate over individual issues. In Ryan v. Eli Lilly & Co., 84 F.R.D. 230 (D.S.C.1979), the court observed:

> Apparently it is not sufficient that common questions merely exist, rather the common issues must outweigh the individual ones in terms of quantity or quality. In deciding the issue of predominance this Court must predict the evidence likely to be introduced at trial.

In a sense, Plaintiffs would have the question of global liability be the predominant one in this litigation. They seek a blanket determination that DES causes injury to a female *in utero*, and believe that this common issue predominates over any questions affecting only individual class members. The telling inquiry is what would such a determination do to advance the cause of the class members as a group?

It is this Court's view that a mere finding that DES causes injury in utero would do substantially nothing to advance the common cause of class members. In light of the varied degrees of use, exposure and harm in each Plaintiff's case, a determination in principle would serve no useful purpose in resolving the individual claims made in this action. As in *Ryan,*

> The mothers of the proposed plaintiffs * * * each used a synthetic estrogen; however, the length of exposure, the reason for the drug's use, the specific chemical formulation of the drug, the state of the art at the time of consumption or the manufacturer's knowledge of synthetic estrogen's carcinogenic effect and possible medical result in the absence of the estrogens are all specific points going toward proximate causation which will require proof for each individual class member.

Although common questions need not be dispositive of the entire class action, their resolution should at least provide a definite signal of the beginning of the end. This is not the type of litigation, however, that lends itself to establishing a global result that a product causes harm with details merely to be tidied up thereafter. The importance of the "details" in each individual claim would clearly outweigh the single determination that DES causes injury.

If the damages question were the only one to be determined on an individual basis for each class member, bifurcating the trial as to liability and damages would be a practical consideration. It is clear, however, that a per se rule that DES causes injury could not possibly result in a per se rule of liability. The liability issue would require separate and individual proof for each claimant and therefore could not be the predominant issue in the proposed class action. In Yandle v. PPG Industries, Inc., 65 F.R.D. 566 (E.D.Tex.1974), former employees and survivors of former employees of the defendant's asbestos plant, sought class certification. Like that case, the litigation presently before this Court,

> is very different from the single mass accident case that have in the past allowed a class action to proceed on the liability issues. Those cases have normally involved a single tragic happening which caused physical harm or property damage to a group of people, and affirmative defenses are absent. Usually, one set of operative facts will establish liability. * * * The Court is in agreement with the defendant that there is not a single act of negligence or proximate cause which would apply to each potential class member and each defendant.

* * *

The difficulties with a class determination of the liability issue weight heavily in a consideration of the prerequisite of predominance from the Defendant's perspective as well. Although there may be some advantage to litigation which establishes what the industry manufacturing DES knew at specified intervals of time concerning the deleterious effects of the drug, there is nothing to show that knowledge at a given point in time essentially settles anything with respect to liability to a particular claimant. Moreover, the manufacturers are so disparately situated in terms of market participation that little, if anything, would be accomplished except as to those specifically identified. * * *

What has already been said about the individual nature of proof in the context of predominance applies with equal force to the issue of superiority. In addition, the Court notes that this is not a situation involving a large number of small claims which would otherwise not be brought since it is unlikely that any claim for DES inflicted injury would have an ad damnum of less than $10,000. Nor is this a situation where the "floodgate" argument is appropriate. If thousands of claims are brought, they will be dealt with in the same fashion as any other litigation. Indeed, judicial resources applied to each claim on an individual basis would doubtless be effective than a general pronouncement applied to all cases without any real effect. These factors militate against a finding that the proposed class action in these circumstances is superior to other available methods of adjudication.

The advantage of certifying a class in this action is at best obscure, and the gain difficult to perceive. Other than the possibility of seeking to commit the law of New Hampshire in a particular direction, it is unlikely that anything of real value could be determined that would aid in the resolution of the claims of any individual Plaintiff. * * *

* * *

CIMINO v. RAYMARK INDUSTRIES, INC.

United States District Court, Eastern District of Texas.
Order, December 29, 1989.

ROBERT M. PARKER, UNITED STATES DISTRICT JUDGE.

On October 26, 1989, this Court consolidated 3031 [asbestos] cases for resolution of the state of the art and punitive damages issues. The Court also certified, under Fed.R.Civ.P. 23(b)(3), a class of plaintiffs in personal injury asbestos cases pending in the Beaumont Division of the Eastern District of Texas as of February 1, 1989, for a determination of the exposure and actual damage issues. The Defendants informed the Court of their desire to respond to the certification Order. Subsequently, the Defendants filed numerous objections and requests for modification of the Order as well as numerous requests for certification of issues pursuant to 28 U.S.C. 1292(b). For reasons given below, the Defendants' objections are overruled; the requests for modification of the Court's Order are denied and the requests for certification of issues pursuant to 28 U.S.C. 1292(b) are denied.

This memorandum will discuss, in more detail, the procedure set out in the Court's October 26, 1989, Order for the trial of this action and, then, will discuss the Defendants' objections to the Court's Order.

[The Order then set forth a three-phase trial procedure, with phases one and two to be tried before a jury, and phase three to be tried without a jury. In phase one the jury was to try the issue of gross negligence and to formulate a multiplier for each defendant for which the jury returned an affirmative finding. In phase two, the court was to try the cases of the class representatives. In addition, the plaintiffs and the defendants would be allowed to introduce evidence as to fifteen claimants, chosen by that side. The jury was to make classwide findings on the issues of exposure and actual damages, and would be able to award lump sum punitive damages in place of the multiplier in phase one. In phase three, the court was to distribute the jury's award of actual and punitive damages. The defendants objected to this trial plan on a number of grounds, including applicable law under *Erie* doctrine; use of statistical evidence; class action and mass tort case law precedents; court-supervised distribution; statute of limitations; amount in controversy; punitive damages; and violation of the Rules Enabling Act. The following portion of the order deals solely with the defendants' objections based on Seventh Amendment grounds.—*ed.*]

* * *

DEFENDANTS' RIGHTS TO A JURY TRIAL

The Defendants' position is that the Court's plan for the disposition of these cases violates the Defendants' right to a jury trial. Contrary to the Defendants' belief, the Court's procedure more than adequately protects the Defendants' right to a Jury trial. First, by trial date, the defendants will have performed 45–minute depositions of all 3031 Plaintiffs in this consolidated action and class action. With respect to the eleven class representatives and the thirty illustrative Plaintiffs, the defendants will have conducted full, extensive depositions. The Defendants will have also completed medical examinations on all 3031 Plaintiffs. Due to the need to bring these cases to trial once and for all, the discovery in this action will have some restrictions * * *. Nevertheless, as explained in the Discovery Plan and Schedule, the defendants will have had a reasonable opportunity to conduct discovery in this action.

By deposing and testing every member of this consolidated action and class action, the defendants will be able to gather all the necessary information for their defense of this action. Specifically, this information will form the basis of the Defendants' expert testimony at trial. By having looked at and investigated each and every one of the Plaintiffs in this action, the Defendants will be able to expose the Jury to the full range of defenses contained in the class.

The Defendants will have the chance to contest each one of the cases of the eleven class representatives in this action. The Defendants will have the opportunity to expose the Jury to the weaknesses of the representatives' cases.

The Jury will hear the testimony of thirty illustrative Plaintiffs (fifteen chosen by each side) in addition to the testimony of the class representatives. In selecting fifteen Plaintiffs, the Defendants will once again have the opportunity to ensure that a variety of defenses are exposed to the Jury. In addition, by cross-examining the Plaintiffs' fifteen witnesses, the Defendants will once again have the chance of showing the weaknesses in the Plaintiffs' claims.

Given these procedural safeguards, the Court finds that its certification Order does not violate the Defendants' right to a Jury trial. Nevertheless, the defendants urge that they have the right to contest each one of these 3031 cases on an individual basis. Trial of these cases individually or by a procedure of mini-trials would only serve to violate the Plaintiffs' right to a jury trial. The Court does not have the resources to utilize such an alternative procedure. Many plaintiffs would simply wait in vain for their day in court.

These cases have been pending for over three years. The Defendants would have this Court delay these cases for another day. Yet many of the class members are ill; some of them have died since the filing of this action. Any procedure other than a single adjudication of these cases can by no means protect the Plaintiffs' right to a jury trial. This Court can see no justice in denying the Plaintiffs their day in court in the interest of providing Defendants with a procedure for the repetitive assertion of their defenses.

The Defendants' opposition to the Court's plan lies in their hope that these cases will eventually just "go away." The "[D]efendants enjoy all the advantages, and the [P]laintiffs incur the disadvantages, of [this] class action—with one exception: the cases are to be brought to trial." *Accord Jenkins v. Raymark*, 782 F.2d at 473. The defense costs attributable to trying these cases individually or in groupings would be astronomical. Attorneys' fees for the Defendants, as well as for the individual Plaintiffs, will be greatly reduced under this plan as the Court will control the fees collected from all class members. *See Jenkins v. Raymark*, 782 F.2d at 473. The Court's Order protects the Defendants' right to a trial by jury while ensuring that the Plaintiffs receive their day in court.

IN RE FIBREBOARD CORPORATION

United States Court of Appeals, Fifth Circuit, 1990.
893 F.2d 706.

Before Higginbotham, Davis, and Duhe, Circuit Judges. Patrick Higginbotham, Circuit Judge:

Defendants Fibreboard Corporation and Pittsburgh Corning Corporation, joined by other defendants, petition for a writ of mandamus, asking that we vacate pretrial orders consolidating 3,031 asbestos cases for trial entered by Judge Robert Parker, Eastern District of Texas.

In 1986 there were at least 5,000 asbestos-related cases pending in this circuit. We then observed that "because asbestos-related diseases will continue to manifest themselves for the next fifteen years, filings will continue at a steady rate until the year 2000." That observation is proving to be accurate. In *Jenkins v. Raymark,* we affirmed Judge Parker's certification of a class of some 900 asbestos claimants, persuaded that the requirements of Rule 23(b)(3) were met for the trial of certain common questions including the "state of the art" defense. After that order and certain settlements, approximately 3,031 asbestos personal injury cases accumulated in the Eastern District of Texas.

The petitions for mandamus attack the district court's effort to try these cases in a common trial. * * *

* * *

Defendants find numerous flaws in the procedures set for Phase II of the trial. They argue with considerable force that such a trial would effectively deny defendants' rights to a jury trial under the seventh amendment, would work an impermissible change in the controlling substantive law of Texas, would deny procedural due process under the fifth amendment of the United States Constitution, and would effectively amend the rules of civil procedure contrary to the strictures of the enabling acts. * * *

* * *

The contentions that due process would be denied, the purposes of *Erie* would be frustrated, and the seventh amendment circumvented are variations of a common concern of defendants. Defendants insist that one-to-one adversarial engagement or its proximate, the traditional trial, is secured by the seventh amendment and certainly contemplated by

Article III of the Constitution itself. Defendants point out, and the plaintiffs quickly concede, that under Phase II there will inevitably be individual class members whose recovery will be greater or lesser than it would have been if tried alone. Indeed, with the focus in Phase II upon the "total picture", with arrays of data that will attend the statistical presentation, persons who would have had their claims rejected may recover. Plaintiffs say that "such discontinuities" would be reflected in the overall omnibus figure. Stated another way, plaintiffs say that so long as their mode of proof enables the jury to decide the total liability of defendants with reasonable accuracy, the loss of one-to-one engagement infringes no right of defendants. Such unevenness, plaintiffs say, will be visited upon them, not the defendants.

With the procedures described at such a level of abstraction, it is difficult to describe concretely any deprivation of defendants' rights. Of course, there will be a jury, and each plaintiff will be present in a theoretical, if not practical, sense. Having said this, however, we are left with a profound disquiet. First, the *assumption* is that its proof of omnibus damages is in fact achievable; that statistical measures of representativeness and commonality will be sufficient for the jury to make informed decisions concerning damages. We are pointed to our experience in the trial of Title VII cases and securities cases involving use of fraud on the market concepts and mathematical constructs for examples of workable trials of large numbers of claims. We find little comfort in such cases. It is true that there is considerable judicial experience with such techniques, but it is also true we have remained cautious in their use.

* * *

We are also uncomfortable with the suggestion that a move from one-on-one "traditional" modes is little more than a move towards modernity. Such traditional ways of proceeding reflect far more than habit. They reflect the very culture of the jury trial and the case and controversy requirement of Article III. It is suggested that the litigating unit is the class and, hence, we have the adversarial engagement or that all are present in a "consolidated" proceeding. But, this begs the very question of whether these 3,031 claimants are sufficiently situated for class treatment; it equally begs the question whether they are actually before the court under Fed.R.Civ.P. Rules 23 and 42(b) in any more than a fictional sense. Ultimately, these concerns find expression in defendants' right to due process.

* * *

We are told that Phase II is the only realistic way of trying these cases; that the difficulties faced by the courts as well as the rights of the class members to have their cases tried cry powerfully for innovation and judicial creativity. The arguments are compelling, but they are better addressed to the representative branches—Congress and the State Legislature. The Judicial Branch can offer the trial of lawsuits. It has no power or competence to do more. We are persuaded on reflection that the procedures here called for comprise something other than a trial within our authority. It is called a trial, but it is not.

* * *

We admire the work of our colleague, Judge Robert Parker, and are sympathetic with the difficulties he faces. This grant of the petition for writ of mandamus should not be taken as a rebuke of an able judge, but rather as another chapter in an ongoing struggle with the problems presented by the phenomenon of mass torts. The petitions for writ of mandamus are granted. The order for Phase II trial is vacated and the cases are remanded to the district court for further proceedings.

ROGER H. TRANGSRUD, MASS TRIALS IN MASS TORT CASES: A DISSENT

1989 U.Ill.L.Rev. 69, 74–76 (1985).

In the last decade, mass trials have come to be seen in much of the academic literature as the proper and efficient answer to mass torts in our mass society. Burdened by lengthening dockets, federal judges have begun to experiment with mass trials to try many claims at once. In this way, we appear ready to reject a centuries old tradition of individual claim autonomy in tort litigation involving substantial personal injuries or wrongful death. Insufficient attention has been paid, however, to the impact of mass trials on the fairness of such proceedings to individual plaintiffs, on the relationship of counsel to client, on the role of the judge in coercing settlement, and on the temptation to distort substantive law to skirt important procedural obstacles to mass trial. As explained below, all of these concerns argue against using mass trials to adjudicate mass tort cases. The better course is to coordinate and consolidate pretrial discovery and motions practice but then individually try the tort cases in an appropriate venue. After a number of cases have been tried substantial incentives will operate to encourage the private settlement of many of the remaining claims.

* * *

The Traditional Justifications for Individual Claim Autonomy Remain Important in Mass Tort Cases

The English and American judicial systems have long favored individual control and disposition of substantial personal injury and wrongful death claims for several reasons. Such claims usually involve incidents of tremendous importance to the individual plaintiff or the plaintiff's family. A mother who perishes in a hotel fire or airplane crash, a father who works in a trade for many years and now has terminal lung cancer, or a child born with foreshortened limbs are catastrophic human tragedies of the first order. Until recently, our system treated such incidents and the tort claims they created with uncompromised due process. This we should continue to do.

The purpose of our civil justice system is and should be to offer corrective justice in disputes arising between private parties. While today we burden our courts with many claims arising out of government regulatory and entitlement programs and even ask our judges to manage prisons, mental health institutions, and schools, we should not let these cases obscure the original and first purpose of our civil courts—to adjudicate justly disputes between individuals. Among such private disputes, cases involving substantial personal injury or wrongful death claims are as important, or more important, than any other. Regardless of the burden of such claims put on the judicial resources of our courts, we ought not to compromise in the quality of process we afford these tort plaintiffs.

Underlying our tradition of individual claim autonomy in substantial tort cases is the natural law notion that this is an important personal right of the individual. While much less celebrated than other natural rights, such as the right to practice one's own religion or to think and speak freely, the right to control personally the suit whereby a badly injured persons seeks redress from the alleged tortfeasor has long been valued both here and in England. The responsibility for asserting such a claim rested with the injured individual or his family, and the exercise of this right was protected. It was not the duty of the government or some third party to initiate such a suit, nor could the government or some third party interfere in the prosecution of the action.

This jealous protection of the individual's absolute right to control his own tort claim was respected for practical as well as philosophical reasons. For example, English and American courts have held for many years that a tort action for personal injury is not assignable before judgment. Limiting ownership and control of such claims to the injured party was believed to be important for several reasons that remain important today. Unless control of such tort claims was left with the injured party, a "litigious person could harass and annoy others if allowed to purchase claims for pain and suffering and pursue the claims in court as assignees." There was also the risk of overreaching, deception, and other misconduct by the party seeking to acquire the right to bring a tort claim on another's behalf. These remain major concerns today, as evidenced by the methods used by attorneys to solicit clients in mass tort cases and to obtain control over the cases of nonclients by bringing class actions or becoming lead counsel in huge consolidated tort cases. The attorney's fees at stake in mass tort cases are so high as to strain the norms that ought to govern professional conduct. The questionable activities of many of the counsel in the Agent Orange litigation, for example, has been well documented in Professor Schuck's history of that case.

Our traditional justifications for individual claim autonomy remain important today in mass tort cases. From a purely economic point of view, our system operates mainly on the assumption that economic decisions are best made by the true owner of property rather than by any other person. Control and disposition of a valuable piece of property, such as a substantial tort claim, ought to rest with its owner, the injured party or his family, and not with some stranger such as a class representative or lead counsel in a mass tort case consolidated in a common venue. In addition, parties often wish to settle or litigate claims based upon a variety of personal economic considerations and intangible personal beliefs or concerns which are unique to them. If the plaintiffs enjoy autonomy over the settlement or trial of their particular claim, they can obtain the outcome best suited to their personal views on the proper disposition of this property. If others assume control over their claim, then this is less likely to happen because these strangers will often not be aware of the special circumstances attending this claim or will have a divided loyalty because the stranger will often be responsible for many other substantial tort claims as well.

Traditionally, our civil justice system avoided mass trials of mass tort claims for another reason grounded in efficiency. The more parties and claims lumped together in a single proceeding, the greater the procedural and substantive complexity of the litigation. While the repetitious trial of common fact issues is regularly deplored today, less concern is voiced about the enormous additional costs created by consolidation and mass trials. Large numbers of plaintiffs and defendants often create a matrix of cross-claims, a web of choice-of-law issues, and a host of peripheral and satellite litigation that would never exist if the claims had been tried separately.

These and other concerns * * * argue strongly against the use of mass trials in mass tort cases and help explain the nearly unbroken tradition of individual claim autonomy in substantial tort cases that characterized Anglo–American litigation until the last decade.

* * *

DEBORAH R. HENSLER, RESOLVING MASS TOXIC TORTS: MYTHS AND REALITIES

1989 U.Ill.L.Rev. 89, 91–97 (1989).

* * *

II. The Traditional Tort Version of Reality

Beliefs about the traditional tort approach relate to both process and outcomes. As [Professor] Schuck indicates, the version of legal reality implicit in the traditional tort approach assumes that "private [litigant] control of litigation" and "intimate contact and consultation" between litigants and lawyers "force lawyers to educate their clients, respond to their wishes, and litigate faithfully and vigorously." The quite widely noted lawyer opposition to class actions for tort claims partly derives from concern that aggregating cases will "corrode [ ] the individual attorney-client relationship," which, it is assumed, would otherwise exist. According to Schuck, Judge Weinstein told one of the leading Agent Orange litigators that in class actions "the nominal representative plaintiffs are only names and the case is turned over to the lawyers." Implicit in this admonition is the notion that such a state of affairs would not exist, absent a class action.

Although the "sanctity and indissolubility of the conventional attorney-client relationship" is one of the primary underpinnings of the tort process, there are other important elements. Trial by jury and general adjudication hold out the promise that parties will be fairly treated, carefully, and with dignity.

Just as traditional tort process values are highly individualistic in nature, so are criteria for judging the outcomes of the system.

> Each individual possesses an absolute right to the integrity of his or her personhood. If injured, he or she possesses the right to recover damages that compensate not simply for out-of-pocket expenses and other economic losses wrongfully caused by the defendants but for invasion of dignitary and other subjective interests, particularly pain and suffering.

Another argument against class actions for tort claims is motivated by concern about "the inequities of subjecting all individuals to uniform class treatment * * * [leading to settlement funds which] when distributed on a wholesale basis [are] almost certain to result in a lower recovery than some individuals (especially the most seriously injured) would receive by litigating on their own."

According to the traditional tort approach, fair outcomes not only require adequate compensation and similar levels of compensation for similarly situated plaintiffs but also proper attention to defendants' varying degrees of fault. More generally, the deterrence objective of the tort system can only be satisfied, according to modern economic theory, if the full losses of plaintiffs are imposed upon negligent defendants.

III.   PROCEDURAL REALITIES

Systematic empirical research on litigation suggests that the tort process in practice diverges substantially from the picture painted above. Although most of the research concerns routine litigation, some involves mass torts. The version of legal reality drawn from this research posits a litigation process in which (1) lawyer-client relations are more often perfunctory and superficial than intimate; (2) the locus of control is shifted towards lawyers rather than clients; (3) lawyers educate their clients to a view of the legal process that serves the lawyer's interests as much, if not more than clients' interests; (4) litigants are frequently only names to both lawyers and court personnel; and (5) trial is rarely desired, except perhaps by litigants, or delivered.

A.   *Lawyer–Client Relations and Litigant Control*

One of the first researchers to document the character of lawyer-client relations was Douglas Rosenthal, who surveyed a small number of litigants in routine tort cases. Within his sample, he found that most lawyers spent little time with their clients and that most clients had little control over the progress or outcomes of their cases.

In a more recent and larger survey of litigants in personal injury cases involving amounts up to $50,000, respondents were asked how many times they met in person with their lawyer and how many times they talked to their lawyer on the telephone. Table 1 summarizes the results. Twenty-five percent either never met with their lawyers or met with them only once, and thirty-two percent talked by telephone fewer than three times. Because this survey deliberately overrepresented litigants whose cases were resolved after some sort of court intervention (e.g., arbitration, judicial settlement conference, or trial) these numbers may overestimate the average time spent by lawyers with clients whose cases are more typically resolved through bilateral bargaining. Some support for this caveat is provided in Table 2, which shows the pattern of interaction for only those litigants whose cases were bargained to resolution. Although both tables show significant fractions of litigants do interact multiple times with their attorneys, a sizeable number would seem to have little opportunity to establish the "intimate" relationship envisioned by the traditional tort version of reality. Data from several other studies documenting the modest number of hours attorneys typically spend on civil cases bolster this interpretation. For example, the Civil Litigation Research Project (CLRP) estimated that lawyers spend an average of about forty-five to fifty hours on a typical case. Not surprisingly, the range of hours spent on cases was large, with very high stakes cases receiving more effort. A study of 222 New Jersey lawyers who handle routine automobile personal injury cases found the median number of billable hours spent on such cases was twenty.

Table 1

TORT LITIGANTS' INTERACTION WITH LAWYERS

Number	In-Person Meetings	Telephone Calls
	%	%
Zero	11	11
One	14	9
Two	15	12
Three	15	9
Four	12	7
Five or more	33	52
Total Number of Cases	363	359

Table 2

INTERACTION WITH LAWYERS: BI–LATERAL
BARGAINING CASES ONLY

Calls Number	In-Person Meetings %	Telephone %
Zero	24	16
One	12	8
Two	14	16
Three	18	9
Four	10	5
Five or more	22	46
Total Number of Cases	118	110

The New Jersey survey of tort litigants' experiences also inquired into their perceptions of their control over the litigation process. Researchers asked a number of questions about the litigants' role in key decisions in the litigation process. Table 3 shows how litigants described the decision to file the lawsuit rather than settle out of court. About half of the litigants saw filing the lawsuit as mainly the lawyer's decision. Litigants' views of their role varied across different decisions (e.g., to settle or appeal), but for most decisions, only a minority of litigants viewed themselves as the dominant decision maker.

Tables 4 and 5 show how litigants summarized their role in the litigation process. Table 4 illustrates that a majority of litigants felt they had little or no control over how their cases were handled. Table 5 shows that about half of those who felt relatively lacking in control attributed this to their lawyers; only a few litigants said they exercised little control by choice.

Table 3

TORT LITIGANTS' PERCEPTIONS OF WHO
DECIDED TO FILE THE LAWSUIT

Responsible Person	%
Litigant on Own	27
Mainly Litigant	11
Shared Equally	9
Mainly Lawyer	22
Lawyer on Own	30
Total Number of Cases	331

Table 4

TORT LITIGANTS' PERCEPTION OF CONTROL
OVER THEIR CASE

How Much Control Was Exercised	%
A Lot	18
Some	26
A Little	18
Not Much	38
Total Number of Cases	372

Table 5

TORT LITIGANTS' PERCEPTIONS OF WHY THEY LACKED CONTROL

Reason For Lack of Control	%
Court	21
Lawyer	46
Self	8
Lawyer & Court	10
Insurance Company or Other	15
Total Number of Cases	299

The New Jersey study did not inquire into the content of litigant-attorney interactions, but recent research by Sarat and Felstiner suggests that educating the client to the attorney's version of legal reality is an important dimension of the litigation process, at least in family law cases. Felstiner and Sarat's analysis of transcripts of lawyer-client conversations depicts a process where lawyers gradually wean clients from their views of what the justice system ought to provide in the way of equitable dispute resolution to a more realistic—or even, cynical—view of the systems's goals and operations, a view that serves both the lawyer's and the legal order's interests. This type of education does not appear to accord well with the idealized education process envisaged in the traditional tort version of reality.

None of the research described above deals with mass toxic tort cases, and no one has yet surveyed litigants in these cases. However, descriptions of the mass tort litigation process give little reason to believe that the traditional tort approach to such cases provides more interaction between lawyers and clients, more intimate relations between lawyers and clients, or more opportunity for clients rather than lawyers to control the litigation process. In fact, the reverse is likely to be true: when lawyers handle cases individually, the already tenuous client relationship described above is attenuated further by the press of the sheer number of claims. More frequently, cases are aggregated *informally*, despite strictures against such groupings.

The RAND Corporation's Institute for Civil Justice first studied asbestos litigation practices during a period when no formal aggregative procedures were in place and found plaintiff attorneys with inventories of several hundred to several thousand claimants per firm. In the Dalkon Shield litigation, two plaintiff attorneys represented nine hundred clients over a relatively brief time. In asbestos litigation, initial lawyer contacts with claimants often involved mass meetings or bureaucratic intake procedures rather than intimate conversations between lawyer and client. Pleadings and discovery were highly standardized, and rulings made in a single case were often applied by judicial order to hundreds of other cases. By the time of the RAND study, many law firms were so overburdened with asbestos suits—or their staffs were so "burned out"—that junior attorneys were assigned to important pretrial activities and opportunities for settling cases expeditiously were lost.

Some courts with large mass tort caseloads encouraged or ordered plaintiff and defense attorneys to group cases for pretrial preparation and settlement discussions. Where courts were able to provide a credible threat of trial, attorneys with large caseloads were forced to settle on different grounds from those possible with a real option of trial. Litigants were rarely, if ever, included in the settlement discussions directed by the court.

In his description of another mass litigation, DDT cases in Alabama, Brazil notes that several hundred named DDT claimants could not be located by the court for discovery purposes "suggest[ing] that attorney-client communication left something to be desired." In these and other examples of mass litigation conducted under apparently traditional formal procedures, the pressures to aggregate cases informally are so great that it is difficult to discern a qualitative difference between litigant-attorney relations in such situations and the relationships that typically exist under formal class actions. In the latter, however, by reviewing settlements and fees, the court is assigned the role of protecting clients' interests. In the former, the court performs no such review.

* * *

Notes and Questions

1. The *Mertens* DES district court opinion, as excerpted here, presents at least three recurring themes. The first theme concerns the use of the class action procedure to aggregate and adjudicate mass tort claims. In *Mertens*, the attempt to certify a Rule 23(b)(3) class action failed on commonality, superiority, and predominance grounds. *See generally* Federal Rule of Civil Procedure 23(a) and (b)(3). Is the court's reasoning convincing? The *Mertens* decision exemplifies an early trend to deny class certification to mass tort cases. *See e.g.,* Ryan v. Eli Lilly & Co., 84 F.R.D. 230 (D.S.C.1979)(action by woman who took synthetic estrogen during pregnancy, on behalf of others similarly exposed, not suitable for class certification); Yandle v. PPG Indus., Inc., 65 F.R.D. 566 (E.D.Tex.1974)(action by employees and survivors of employees of asbestos exposure in the workplace not proper for class certification); Rosenfeld v. A.H. Robins Co., 63 A.D.2d 11, 407 N.Y.S.2d 196 (1978) (denying class certification to plaintiff purporting to represent New York women suffering pelvic inflammatory disease), *appeal dismissed* 46 N.Y.2d 731, 413 N.Y.S.2d 374, 385 N.E.2d 1301 (1978)(denying class certification both to residents of chemical waste disposal site and to their unborn children). For a discussion of the aggregation problem in relation to the class action rule, *see generally* Chapter II. A, *infra*. To what extent is the court's refusal to certify class actions in these mass tort cases grounded in a preference for individual, as opposed to aggregate, procedure?

The second concern expressed in *Mertens* relates to the substantive tort law requirement of proof of specific causation for each individual plaintiff, as opposed to proof of general causation as to the class. In *Mertens*, Chief Judge Boyle construes the causation problem to defeat the commonality requirement for class certification. As a legal matter, are the defendants entitled to proof of specific causation for each individual plaintiff? Can tort cases ever be aggregated, under this principle? As a jurisprudential or philosophical matter, should defendants be entitled to specific proof? Why? Do we require specific causation in all class actions? Should the nature of the underlying claims make a difference? We will examine the causation and proof problems in Chapter V.E., *infra*.

The third concern flagged by the court in *Mertens* runs to the need for individualized proof of liability as a prerequisite for determination of damages. Why can't the court, as it suggests is a possibility, make a global determination of liability with an individualized assessment of damages, using a bifurcated proceeding? Isn't this procedural model a sensible compromise between aggregative and individualized procedure? Is the court here correct in declaring that the advantages of certifying a class action are obscure, and the gains difficult to perceive? The problem of aggregative as opposed to individualized damages continues to bedevil the courts confronted with mass tort litigation. *See generally* Chapter IV.D., *infra*.

2. The district court in *Mertens* refers to *Yandle v. PPG Industries, Inc.* to draw a distinction between single mass accident cases and true mass tort litigations. The distinction resonates in the similar statement in the Advisory Committee's Note to Federal Rule of Civil Procedure 23, which specifically indicates that mass-accident cases are not suitable for adjudication under Rule 23:

> A "mass accident" resulting in injuries to numerous persons is ordinarily not appropriate for a class action because of the likelihood that significant questions, not only of damages but of liability and defenses to liability, would be present, affecting the individuals in different ways. In these circumstances an action conducted nominally as a class action would degenerate in practice into multiple lawsuits separately tried.

See Fed.R.Civ.P. 23 Advisory Committee Note, 39 F.R.D. 98, 103 (1966). The 1966 Advisory Committee Note, which has yet to be amended or superseded, has remained an obstacle to class certification of true mass tort cases, as opposed to single-accidents. Does the Advisory Committee Note make sense? Should it be accorded continuing vitality in the face of post–1980s mass tort litigation?

3. The defendants in *Cimino v. Raymark* couched their legal claim to individualized procedure in terms of a right to a trial by jury. To what extent did Judge Parker's proposed pre-trial procedures and trial plan meet this concern? Do either plaintiffs or defendants have a constitutional right to an *individualized* trial by jury? The Fifth Circuit in *In Re Fibreboard Corp.* struck down Judge Parker's trial plan on a request for mandamus from the defendants. Other than a "profound disquiet" for Judge Parker's contemplated trial procedures, has the Fifth Circuit stated a good case why Judge Parker's plan violates due process or the Seventh Amendment right to trial by jury?

4. Professor Transgrud grounds the sanctity of "individual claim autonomy" in "the natural law notion that this is an important personal right of the individual." Is there a "natural right" ("less celebrated than other natural rights") to prosecute a tort claim individually as opposed to collectively? What is the source of this natural right? Is there a similar natural right say, of a Title VII employment discrimination plaintiff to litigate his or

her own claim individually? For a critique of Professor Trangsrud's position, *see* David Rosenberg, *Class Actions for Mass Torts: Doing Individual Justice by Collective Means,* 62 Ind. L.J. 561, 581–82:

> Significant rights-based objections to mass tort class actions arise in connection with claims that would gain access to the system without the cost savings afforded by aggregate and averaging processes. Achieving process efficiency at the expense of these claimants' substantive rights would seem offensive to notions of individual justice. However, opposition to aggregative treatment of otherwise marketable claims is often mistakenly predicated on a definition of the baseline of an individual's substantive rights that uncritically equates individual justice with separate actions. It is simply assumed that any benefits claimants may derive from proceeding separately from one another are necessarily entailed by the substantive rights they are asserting. Thus, arguments that class treatment deprives claimants of power to control the destiny of their cases frequently confuse the substantive right of action with advantages gained by strategic exploitation of the process.

* * *

> * * * But such opportunistic manipulation of judicial processes to secure a systematically biased or myopic forum hardly comports with notions of even-handed fairness implicit in corrective justice. Corrective justice similarly would appear to offer little support for the proposition that individuals are entitled to have the public subsidize their personal preference for separate lawsuits to relitigate common questions. The fact that tort litigation confers public benefits—including deterrence of socially inappropriate risks, delivery of compensation to victims, fair and peaceful resolution of disputes, and the elaboration of legal norms,— certainly does not require committing public resources beyond the point of negligible return.

5. In the conclusion to her study, Deborah Hensler notes a trend for judges dealing with mass tort cases to use informal aggregative procedures to process hundreds, if not thousands, of claims. She views this as a somewhat unfortunate trend: "And informal aggregation, while often the only feasible alternative to dispose of cases, may be embarked upon in such an *ad hoc* fashion that its implications are not carefully considered nor its consequences subjected to careful scrutiny. Faced with the realities of current mass tort litigation, courts—and legal scholars—should be open to the possibility that expanding the use of formal aggregative procedures may provide more litigant control over the litigation process, more opportunity for litigant participation in the process, and a better match between victims' losses and compensation for those losses." *See* Hensler, *Resolving Mass Toxic Torts,* 1989 U.Ill.L.Rev. at 104. *See also* Deborah R. Hensler, *A Glass Half Full, A Glass Half Empty: The Use of Alternative Dispute Resolution in Mass Personal Injury Litigation,* 73 Texas L.Rev. 1587 (1995); Judith Resnik, *Procedural Innovations (Sloshing Over): A Comment on Deborah Hensler,* 73 Texas L.Rev. 1627 (1995). The use of informal or alternative dispute resolution techniques to resolve mass tort litigation will be explored in Chapters XI–XIII, *infra.* For a discussion of the general problems of

client control of class actions, *see* Lawrence M. Grosberg, *Class Actions and Client–Centered Decisionmaking*, 40 Syracuse L.Rev. 709 (1989).

6. A number of commentators have analyzed the tensions between individual and aggregate justice in mass tort litigation. *See generally* Kenneth S. Abraham, *Individual and Collective Responsibility: The Dilemma of Mass Tort Reform,* 73 Va. L. Rev. 845 (1987); Kenneth S. Abraham & Lance Liebman, *Private Insurance, Social Insurance, and Tort Reform: Toward a New Vision of Compensation for Illness and Injury,* 93 Colum. L. Rev. 75 (1993); Robert A. B. Bush, *Between Two Worlds: The Shift From Individual to Group Responsibility,* 33 U.C.L.A. L. Rev. 1473 (1986); Kenneth R. Feinberg, *The Toxic Tort Litigation Crisis: Conceptual Problems and Proposed Solutions,* 24 Hous. L. Rev. 155 (1987); Mark A. Peterson & Molly Selvin, *Mass Justice: The Limited and Unlimited Power of the Courts,* 54 Law & Contemp. Probs. 227 (Summer 1991); Edward F. Sherman, *Aggregate Disposition of Related Cases: The Policy Issues,* 10 Rev. Litig. 231 (1991); Edward F. Sherman, *Introduction, Symposium on Problems in Disposition of Mass Related Cases and Proposals for Change,* 10 Rev. Litig. 209 (1991); Jay Tidmarsh, *Unattainable Justice: The Form of Complex Litigation and the Limits of Judicial Power,* 60 Geo. Wash. L. Rev. 1683 (1992); Stephen C. Yeazell, *Collective Litigation as Collective Action,* 1989 U. Ill. L. Rev. 43 (1989). *See also* Lea Brilmayer, *Comment on Peterson and Selvin,* 54 Law & Contemp. Probs. 249 (Summer 1991).

7. With the evolution of the settlement class as a primary means for resolving mass tort litigation, some critics have become concerned with the "crisis mentality" surrounding mass tort cases and the resulting reform efforts. *See generally* Richard L. Marcus, *They Can't Do That, Can They? Tort Reform Via Rule 23,* 80 Cornell L. Rev. ___ (1995); Peter Schuck, *Mass Torts: An Institutional Evolutionst Perspective,* 80 Cornell L. Rev. ___ (1995); John A. Siliciano, *Mass Torts and the Rhetoric of Crisis,* 80 Cornell L. Rev. ___ (1995); Robert L. Rabin, *Continuing Tensions in the Resolution of Mass Toxic Harm Cases: A Comment,* 80 Cornell L. Rev. ___ (1995).

D. PROBLEMS IN PROFESSIONAL RESPONSIBILITY

1. SOLICITATION

MUSSLEWHITE v. THE STATE BAR OF TEXAS
Texas Court of Appeals, 1990.
786 S.W.2d 437.

Before Paul Pressler, Robertson, and Sears, JJ. Opinion by Robertson, Justice.

Benton Musslewhite appeals from a judgment revoking his probation and suspending him from the practice of law for three years. In twenty-three points of error he claims the court erred in finding he had violated a disciplinary rule and in finding he had taken on a new client during the year in which he was prohibited from doing so. Musslewhite also asserts certain procedural errors. We affirm.

[In an earlier disciplinary action, Musslewhite signed an agreed judgment first suspending him from practice, but then placing him on probation for three years. Under the terms of the probation, beginning on January 31, 1988 he was prohibited from committing professional misconduct as defined by state bar rules, and from accepting new employment until November 1, 1988. The court permitted him to refer potential clients to other attorneys. The court further ordered that "should Respondent violate any of the * * * terms or conditions of probation, the Court may revoke such probation and impose a suspension from the practice of law for a period not to exceed three years[.]" In September 1988, the State Bar of Texas filed a motion to revoke Musslewhite's probation on two grounds. The excerpted decision relates to only one of these grounds, the improper solicitation of clients.—*ed.*]

THE PIPER ALPHA ALLEGATIONS

An off-shore oil platform, known as the Piper Alpha, exploded in the North Sea on July 6, 1988. Beginning at approximately 10:30 that morning, Musslewhite began making telephone calls to Scottish solicitors to discuss a potential lawsuit. On July 15, 1988, Musslewhite made arrangements to go to Scotland to obtain cases arising out of the Piper Alpha tragedy. Before going to Scotland, Musslewhite talked with John O'Quinn about referring to O'Quinn any cases he obtained in Scotland. Musslewhite also spoke with Kelly Newman to obtain his assistance in working on the Piper Alpha cases. Musslewhite gave Newman a list of solicitors and asked him to go to Scotland and telephone them.

When Newman arrived in Scotland he began to telephone the Scottish solicitors. When talking with the solicitors, Newman identified himself as working with "some of the best trial lawyers in Houston" who were investigating the Piper Alpha tragedy. He told them he was talking to solicitors about possible referral of cases for filing in the United States. He told them Musslewhite would be there in a few days to talk with them in person. Newman did not tell the solicitors that Musslewhite was prohibited from accepting new clients until November 1, 1988, or that he would be suspended from practising law between November 1, 1988, and January 30, 1989.

When Musslewhite arrived in Scotland, two days later, he and Newman hired a public relations consultant named John MacDonald. MacDonald prepared a press release that day and issued it for Musslewhite. The press release referred to Musslewhite as the team's lead counsel, and stated that the team would be working with Scottish solicitors. The release described the unnamed members of the team as "internationally-renowned."

After the press release was issued, Musslewhite left for London while Newman stayed behind. Newman sent a letter addressed to "all victims or families of victims of the Occidental Petroleum Platform disaster." That letter said that Newman was acting on behalf of a "group of internationally renowned trial lawyers in the United States," and stated:

The purpose of this letter is to ask that if you have already retained a solicitor to let us know who that solicitor is so we can discuss the suit that we are bringing in the United States with him. If you have not retained a solicitor then we would advise that you do so as a matter of urgency and ask him to contact us so that we can discuss the action in the United States.

McDonald, the public relations consultant, prepared the letter and prepared a newspaper advertisement for Musslewhite's group. Musslewhite knew about both communications and discussed them over the telephone with Newman. The advertisement McDonald prepared stated that the team was willing to talk to "victims, families of victims, and their solicitors."

In its motion to revoke probation the State Bar claims that, by issuing the press release, the letters, and the advertisement, Musslewhite violated DR 2–101 because certain statements in those communications were false and misleading. DR 2–101 provides:

(A) A lawyer shall not make, on behalf of himself, his partner, associate, or any other lawyer, any false or misleading communication about the lawyer or the lawyer's services. A communication is false or misleading if it:

(1) Contains a material misrepresentation of fact or law, or omits a fact necessary to make the statement considered as a whole not materially misleading;

(2) Contains a statement of opinion as to the quality of legal services;

(3) Contains a representation or implication regarding the quality of legal services which is not susceptible to reasonable verification by the public;

(4) Contains predictions of future success;

(5) Contains statistical data which is not susceptible to reasonable verification by the public;

(6) Contains other information based on past performance which is not susceptible to reasonable verification by the public;

(7) Contains a testimonial about or endorsement of a lawyer;

(8) Is intended or is likely to create an unjustified expectation about results the lawyer can achieve.

SUPREME COURT OF TEXAS, RULES GOVERNING THE STATE BAR OF TEXAS art. 10, § 9 (Code of Professional Responsibility) DR 2–101 (1988).

The trial court found the press release, letters, and advertisement were false and misleading because they failed to identify the lawyers, because no team existed, because the communications suggested that Musslewhite already had Piper Alpha clients, because they did not disclose that Musslewhite could not take any cases, because Musslewhite predicted high recoveries in Texas courts, and because the advertisement did not contain a disclaimer stating that Musslewhite was not certified by the Texas Board of Legal Specialization.

In point of error one, Musslewhite contends the press release, letters, and advertisement were directed to solicitors, not the public; therefore, he did not violate DR 2–101. Musslewhite's contention is simply not true. The letters were mailed to the victims of the Piper Alpha tragedy and were addressed to "All Victims or Families of Victims of the Occidental Petroleum Platform Disaster." Further, the advertisement stated, "[W]e respectfully suggest it is in your interest to have your solicitor call us immediately or that you call us immediately and give us the name, address and phone number of your solicitor or the solicitor you propose to employ." Clearly, the press release, letters, and advertisement were directed to the victims of the tragedy, not their solicitors. Point of error one is overruled.

In points of error two and three Musslewhite claims DR 2–101 is unconstitutionally vague. A regulation that "either forbids or requires the doing of an act in terms so vague that men of common intelligence must necessarily guess at its meaning and differ as to its application, violates the first essential of due process of law." *Connally v. General Constr. Co.,* 269 U.S. 385, 391, 46 S.Ct. 126, 127, 70 L.Ed. 322 (1926). The Fourteenth Amendment's Due Process Clause insists that laws give persons of ordinary intelligence a reasonable opportunity to know what is prohibited, so that he may act accordingly. * * * This requirement applies with particular force in review of laws dealing with speech. * * * These guidelines apply fully to attorney disciplinary proceedings. In re Ruffalo, 390 U.S. 544, 550, 88 S.Ct. 1222, 1225, 20 L.Ed.2d 117 (1968).

Appellant claims that DR 2–101 is unconstitutionally vague because it does not advise the attorney that he may be prevented from advertising to other lawyers in other countries. We do not find that DR 2–101 is unconstitutionally vague. It does not forbid conduct in terms that are so vague that people of common intelligence must guess at its meaning. The rule does not regulate communication with other lawyers. Contrary to appellant's contentions, he was not disciplined for communications with other lawyers, he was disciplined for false communications to victims of the Piper Alpha tragedy. That activity is clearly prohibited by DR 2–101.

Moreover, the supreme court adopted DR 2–101 and the other State Bar rules as advertising guidelines to remove the uncertainty and confusion surrounding attorney advertising, solicitation, and trade names in the aftermath of *Bates v. State Bar of Arizona,* 433 U.S. 350, 97 S.Ct. 2691, 53 L.Ed.2d 810 (1977). We presume the court intended that DR 2–101 comply with the restraints constitutionally permitted to prevent false, deceptive, or misleading advertising. Accepting the supreme court's inherent power to adopt the rule, it is not our function as an intermediate appellate court to nullify or alter it, for once the court decides on a rule of law, the decision is, in the absence of a controlling decision by the United States Supreme Court, binding on lower courts until the court changes the rule. * * *

In points of error four through nine and eleven Musslewhite claims the evidence was insufficient to support findings that the press release, letters, and advertisement were false and misleading. He also claims that Newman acted alone in publishing the advertisement and mailing the letters. * * *

First, Musslewhite claims the evidence does not show that the press release, letters, and advertisement were false and misleading. With regard to the press release, the recitation that a "team of internationally renowned U.S. Lawyers based in Houston, Texas" is misleading because it fails to identify any of the lawyers. Further, Musslewhite admitted that anyone reading the press release would not know who the team was. The release also states that the team "would be working with United Kingdom solicitors to represent the victims or families of victims involved in the Piper Alpha tragedy." That statement is false and misleading because it suggests that Musslewhite, or the team, already had Piper Alpha clients, when they did not. The release refers to Musslewhite as the "team's lead counsel." That is misleading because the release does not disclose that the agreed judgment prevented Musslewhite from accepting new employment by clients and that he would be suspended for ninety days in the future. Finally, DR 2–101 requires a lawyer who publishes, advertises, or broadcasts with regard to any area of law to include a disclaimer stating that he is not certified by the Texas Board of Legal Specialization. The press release fails to include such a disclaimer.

The letter sent to the victims of the Piper Alpha tragedy also refers to a "group of internationally renowned trial lawyers in the United States" and is misleading because it does not identify the lawyers. Further, the statement that the team is "currently having discussions with a number of United Kingdom solicitors with a view to filing suit in the state court of Texas to obtain maximum damages" is false and misleading because it suggests that the "team" already had Piper Alpha clients when it did not.

The advertisement that was published in the local Aberdeen paper contains similar misrepresentations. Again, the reference to a "team of internationally renowned American lawyers experienced in handling damage claims in mass disaster in the United States of America and Europe" is misleading because it never identifies the lawyers and is not susceptible to reasonable verification by the public. The advertisement similarly does not contain a disclaimer. We find sufficient evidence that the press release, letters, and advertisement contained false and misleading statements.

Musslewhite also contends that Newman acted alone when in Scotland and, specifically, with regard to the running of the advertisement and the mailing of the letters to the victims. The evidence shows, however, that Musslewhite telephoned Newman and asked that Newman work with him on the project. Musslewhite provided Newman with a list of solicitors and potential clients to telephone once he arrived. Musslewhite admitted that Newman discussed the advertisement with him over the telephone and that Newman showed him the letter before it was mailed. Newman testified that MacDonald drafted the advertisement based on information provided by Newman and Musslewhite. We find the evidence sufficient to show that Newman was working with Musslewhite when he published the advertisement and mailed the letters. Points four through nine and eleven are overruled.

ERIC S. ROTH, CONFRONTING SOLICITATION OF MASS DISASTER VICTIMS *

26 Geo. L.J. 967, 971–74, 968–71 (1989).

* * *

EXAMPLES OF IMPROPER ATTORNEY CONDUCT AND INSURANCE COMPANY TACTICS

Notwithstanding the rules against in-person solicitation, some lawyers are driven by the opportunity to make money. Some mass disasters represent the potential for an attorney to earn a considerable amount of money. With recovery in these cases almost certain, often the only unknown is how much will be recovered. Thus whether it is the explosion of an oil refinery or the crash of a commercial airliner, the victims and their relatives are routinely "hustled by a whole gaggle of plaintiff's lawyers * * * [because] mere rules will not keep a lawyer without qualifications from going out and touting himself as an expert and getting retained."

The instances of direct attorney solicitation after mass disasters are numerous. Specific examples of solicitation, however, are difficult to find because of the private nature of the act of solicitation. The only witnesses of the solicitation are usually the solicitor and the solicitee. This makes in-person solicitation very hard to prove as compared to solicitation by mail, which often occurs after a mass disaster. An attorney solicits business by obtaining a list of the victims and mailing out letters to individuals or relatives detailing the lawyer's past experience in disasters. Here the letter is physical evidence of solicitation.

In 1978, after the crash of a PSA jet which had hit a private plane in San Diego, the widow of a man killed in the collision reported that she had been contacted by no less than twenty attorneys. After the recent crash of Pan Am flight 103 in Scotland, one victim's widow reported that she was solicited "by no less than 30 attorneys" within 24 hours of the crash. In the Arrow Air disaster in Gander, Newfoundland on December 12, 1985, 248 American servicemen were killed. All of the victims had been stationed at Fort Campbell, Kentucky and many lived there. The families proved to be a significant target for soliciting attorneys. One

* Reprinted with the permission of the publisher, The Georgetown Law Journal © 1989 & Georgetown University.

Washington, D.C. law firm managed to get the names of the victims and to have a non-lawyer employee of the firm call the families of the victims. He would call them and begin the conversation by saying, "Are you the wife or mother of Sgt. _____? I was sorry to learn of the accident." One widow reported she had received telephone calls from lawyers on Christmas Day, and another widow, in a radio interview, complained that she had been called at least fifty times by attorneys whom she did not know.

Perhaps the most outrageous example of solicitation occurred after the crash of a Northwest airliner in Detroit on August 16, 1987. Shortly after the accident, a man posing as a Catholic priest, Father John Irish, appeared on the scene to console the families of the victims. He "hugged crying mothers and talked with grieving fathers of God's rewards in the hereafter. He even sobbed along with dazed families. * * * Then he would pass out the business card of a Florida attorney * * * and repeatedly urge them to call the lawyer."

While many mass disasters are the result of airplane crashes, there are other types of disasters as well. Probably the most well known incident occurred in Bhopal, India at the Union Carbide chemical plant. Over 2,000 people were killed in the accident and thousands of others were injured. American lawyers rushed to India in an attempt to retain clients and in their zeal brought shame and discredit to the American bar. Many attorneys engaged in unprofessional activity using various methods of solicitation while in India. Indications are that lawyers paid claimants who signed retainer agreements, set up booths on the streets, and held receptions for the victims at which the media were present. Not only were these actions morally reprehensible, but they were contrary to the rules of professional conduct prohibiting in-person solicitation.

Another well publicized disaster occurred at the Dupont Plaza Hotel fire in San Juan, Puerto Rico on New Year's Eve, 1986, in which ninety-six people were killed. The aftermath of the hotel fire was particularly notorious for the wide range of misconduct by attorneys and the presence of insurance adjusters. A member of the Puerto Rican Bar Association likened the presence of American lawyers to that of "vultures," while a hospitalized victim complained that lawyers and hotel representatives solicited her in the hospital. One attorney on the scene said he saw numerous incidents of attorneys directly soliciting families of victims and victims themselves both at the scene and at hospitals. Guerry Thornton, an Atlanta attorney, reported that he observed another attorney directly soliciting a survivor of the fire. Thornton said that the soliciting attorney, in an effort to impress the potential client, boasted about his success in the Bhopal, India tragedy claiming that he was responsible for $380 million in settlements. Thornton noted that not only was the attorney engaging in unethical direct solicitation, but factual misrepresentation as well because American lawyers were dismissed when the case was transferred to India. He commented that attorney misrepresentation was widespread in the aftermath of the tragedy as attorneys scrambled to get clients and media exposure.

One tactic used by attorneys was to arrive at the scene and announce he had been retained by a victim to file suit and to investigate the accident when in fact he had no client. The purpose of such misrepresentation was to get media exposure which ensured the attorney that clients would contact him. In fact, one attorney had announced within twenty-four hours of the fire that he had nine cases and was preparing to file complaints using pleadings from the 1980 MGM Hotel fire in Las Vegas. In the rush to file as quickly as possible, some attorneys simply ignored Puerto Rican law and others were not even knowledgeable as to Puerto Rican law. This led some attorneys to file suits against the wrong parties as they did not yet know who was liable. Thornton also charged that some attorneys attempted to control the litigation in what he described as a monopolistic fashion. The same attorneys engaging in-person solicitation and misrepresentation were acting in concert under an agreement in an attempt to control the Multi–District Litigation Council and threatened to "cut out" any attorneys who did not cooperate with them. Moreover, some American firms hired local attorneys to refer cases to them for a fee, in direct violation of the *Model Rules*.

The Dupont Plaza fire is also notable for the actions of insurance adjusters. Representing the hotel, they sought out victims and the families of victims offering them immediate cash settlements in exchange for a waiver of their right to sue. Lawyers complained that the insurance companies were offering sums substantially less than what the individuals could expect to recover in court. The explosion at the Shell Oil refinery in Norco, Louisiana on May 5, 1988 was also the source of many complaints of attorney solicitation. Some reports claimed attorneys were roaming neighborhoods in "Lincolns and limousines" in an effort to contact potential clients. Complaints were filed with the St. Charles Parish Sheriff's Department alleging that attorneys were going door-to-door soliciting prospective clients. One attorney, after associating himself with another attorney who had a client who had been injured in the explosion, managed to get a television appearance as a part of his effort to receive publicity in order to attract clients. * * *

* * *

Rules of Attorney Conduct and Solicitation

The Model Rules of Professional Conduct expressly prohibit in-person solicitation "when a significant motive for doing so is the lawyer's pecuniary gain." Such a prohibition against in-person solicitation is based on the presumption that, whether or not actual harm results, the potential for attorneys exerting pressure on prospective clients to retain the attorney is inherent in such instances where an attorney knows a prospective client is in need of legal services. In the aftermath of a mass disaster, the potential for abuse is increased as the prospective client has likely been so shocked by the event that he is less able to reason fully or to protect his own interests, especially when confronted by an attorney, one who is trained in the art of persuasion.

The conduct of a lawyer is restrained further by the requirement that any statements a lawyer makes about his services must not be misleading or misrepresentative of the services he provides. Any statements a lawyer makes about his services should be truthful and "special care should be taken by lawyers to avoid misleading the public." Little justification is needed for such basic guidelines for professional conduct. At a very minimum, it is in the best interests of the profession to deal honestly with the public.

Although it is easy to repeat the standards of permissible solicitation, it is difficult to delineate the limits of acceptable attorney behavior following a mass disaster. Clearly, if any attorney approaches a potential client at the scene of the accident or at the hospital shortly after the event, the individual, still under the influence of the event, is susceptible to undue pressure. But is this danger so great that attorneys should be prohibited from communicating with the victims in any manner? Before answering yes, one must remember that insurance company representatives are given free reign to exert their own pressures on the survivors and the families of the victims. While one may argue whether a soliciting attorney has a potential client's best interest in mind, it is certain that an airline's insurance company has primarily its financial interest in mind when is seeks to communicate with victims or their families.

A valuable service may be rendered to the victims and their families when they are informed of their legal rights and of their legal options. Thus to prohibit attorneys from any contact with the victims may work to the victims' detriment. Conversely, to allow an attorney merely to inform the individual of his or her legal rights and then to allow the attorney to represent that individual would be improper because it is unprofessional for attorneys to solicit business for themselves. The Model Rules of Professional Conduct and the Model Code of Professional Responsibility prohibit any contact by an attorney in which a significant motive for the lawyer's conduct is pecuniary gain. Furthermore, if the attorney gives unsolicited advice that the individual should obtain legal advice or take legal action, the attorney shall not accept employment as a result of giving such advice.

Several problems exist with these rules. First, "a significant motive for pecuniary gain" is hard to identify and nearly impossible to prove. Second, the rules falsely assume that individuals are knowledgeable about legal rights. By prohibiting solicitation, the rules cut off a means by which the victims of mass disasters and their relatives can become informed of their legal rights or their legal options. If these people remain uniformed, they might be vulnerable to insurance company abuse. Lastly, varying degrees of construction of the rules makes objective determination of when a violation occurs difficult to determine. Certain conduct by one attorney may be viewed as a liberal construction or a bending of the rules while another attorney may consider the same conduct as constituting a breach of the rules.

* * *

Notes and Questions

1. Would the court's review of Mr. Musslewhite's actions in Scotland possibly have been different had he not previously been suspended and placed on probation? The trial court faulted Musslewhite for virtually every action he took: issuing a press release, sending letters, and publishing the advertisement. Was it permissible for Musslewhite to contact and discuss the possibility of litigation with the Scottish solicitors? What actions could Musslewhite permissibly have taken without violating his professional responsibilities? Could the offending press release, letters, and advertisement have been recast in an acceptable fashion? Does it make a difference that the mass accident occurred in a foreign country?

2. *Musslewhite* was decided under the Texas Code of Professional Responsibility DR 2–101, which was repealed effective November 1, 1989. The substance of that rule is now codified in the SUPREME COURT OF TEXAS, RULES GOVERNING THE STATE BAR OF TEXAS art. 10 § 9 (Rules of Professional Conduct) Rule 7.01 (1989). For comparison, Model Rule of Professional Conduct Rule 7.1 states:

A lawyer shall not make a false or misleading communication about the lawyer or the lawyer's services. A communication is false or misleading if it:

a) contains a material misrepresentation of fact or law, or omits a fact necessary to make a statement considered as a whole not materially misleading;

b) is likely to create an unjustified expectation about results the lawyer can achieve, or states or implies that the lawyer can achieve results by means that violate the Rules of Professional Conduct or other law; or

c) compares the lawyer's services with other services, unless the comparison can be factually substantiated.

In addition, Model Rule 7.3 states:

A lawyer may not solicit professional employment from a prospective client with whom the lawyer has no family or prior professional relationship, by mail, in-person or otherwise, when a significant motive for the lawyer's doing so is the lawyer's pecuniary gain. The term "solicit" includes contact in person, by telephone or telegraph, by letter or other writing, or by other communication directed to a specific recipient, but does not include letters addressed or advertising circulars distributed generally to persons not known to need legal services of the kind provided by the lawyer in a particular matter, but who are so situated that they might in general find such services useful.

The Supreme Court has ruled that states may not prohibit targeted, direct mail solicitation, see Shapero v. Kentucky Bar Association, 486 U.S. 466, 108 S.Ct. 1916, 100 L.Ed.2d 475 (1988), because such solicitation does not present the same forced or pressured situation as direct in-person solicitation. *Cf.* Ohralik v. Ohio State Bar Association, 436 U.S. 447, 98 S.Ct. 1912, 56 L.Ed.2d 444 (1978). Notwithstanding these general rules, mail solicitation of mass accident and mass tort victims and their families continues to present problematic issues relating to the permissible bounds of professional conduct. Two weeks after the crash of Pan American flight 103 over Lockerbie Scotland, but one day after the remains of a young student victim of the crash were identified, two lawyers sent the following solicitation letter to the student's father:

Dear Mr. Lowenstein:

Initially, we would like to extend our deepest sympathy for the loss of your son, Mr. Alexander Lowenstein. We know that this must be a very traumatic experience for you, and we hope that you, along with your relatives and friends, can overcome this catastrophe which has not only affected your family but has disturbed the world.

As you may already realize, you have a legal cause of action against Pan American, among others, for wrongful death due to possible negligent security maintenance. If you intend to take any legal recourse, we urge you to consider to retain our firm to prosecute your case.

Both my partner * * * and myself are experienced practitioners in the personal injury field, and feel that we can obtain a favorable outcome for you against the airline, among other possible defendants.

We would also like to inform you that if you do decide to retain our services, you will not be charged for any attorneys fees unless we collect a settlement or verdict award for you.

Before retaining any other attorney, it would be worth your while to contact us, since we will substantially reduce the customary one-third fee that most other attorneys routinely charge.

Please call us to schedule an appointment at your earliest convenience. If you are unable to come to our office, please so advise us and we will have an attorney meet you at a location suitable to your needs.

Very truly yours,

(Mr.) Magdy F. Anis

MFA/seb

P.S. There is no consultation fee.

The father filed a complaint with the New Jersey Office of Attorney Ethics. After multiple disciplinary hearings and appeals, the Supreme Court of New Jersey held that an attorney can violate the prohibition against direct solicitation of vulnerable clients even without proof that the attorney actually knew of the prospective client's inability to make a reasoned judgment about retaining counsel after the disaster. Stated the court: "The standard we attach to this Rule of Professional Conduct is an objective one. We believe that an ordinarily prudent attorney would recognize that within the hours and days following a tragic disaster, families would be particularly weak and vulnerable. * * * That some recipients might not be offended by such a letter does not rebut the generality of experience that the intrusive nature of such solicitation compounds the suffering of victims or their families." In the Matter of Magdy F. Anis, 126 N.J. 448, 599 A.2d 1265, 1269 (N.J.1992). The Court further held that the commercial speech guarantees of the First Amendment did not protect solicitation of the victim's father, and that a reprimand was appropriate for false and misleading representations in the solicitation made during a time of the father's vulnerability. *See also* In the Matter of Von Wiegen, 108 A.D.2d 1012, 485 N.Y.S.2d 399 (1985)(misleading statements in solicitation letter following the Hyatt Regency skywalk collapse directed towards disaster victims and their families warranted censure; letters represented falsely that a "litigation coordinating committee had been formed" and used trade name "The Country Lawyer"). *But see* In re Marshall I. Teichner, 75 Ill.2d 88, 25 Ill.Dec. 609, 387 N.E.2d 265 (1979)(two year sanction imposed on attorney for improper solicitation of personal injury claims after railroad derailment not involving First Amendment interests; but no sanctions allowable where attorney's activity involves associational values protected by the First Amendment). For a discussion of the solicitation problem in the context of airplane crashes, *see generally* Linda S. Althoff, *Solicitation After An Air Disaster: The Status of Professional Rules and Constitutional Limits*, 54 J. Air. L. & Com. 501 (1988).

3. As Eric Roth's piece suggests, insurance companies frequently pressure mass disaster victims soon after the traumatic events. The inverse of the lawyer solicitation letter is the so-called "Alpert Letter" that insurance companies use to attempt to get families of victims to settle for less than they might recover by filing suit. A typical Alpert letter reads, in part:

> Money can never compensate for the loss of a loved one but this is the medium recognized by the law for compensating victims and the families of victims in air disasters. * * * It is our intention to see that you receive fair compensation for the loss which you have sustained. It is also our hope that you will retain as much of the compensation as is properly due you without unnecessary diversion of large amounts of legal expenses. You may find yourselves under pressure to sign a contingent fee retainer with an attorney whereby his fee is a percentage of the final award. The rationale for such a percentage fee is that the lawyer risks getting no fee if there is no recovery. There is no such contingency in this case. There is also nothing to be gained by a precipitous lawsuit. We do suggest that it would be in your best interest to evaluate the offers which will be made to you and obtain the help of your attorney based upon a fee for the work involved rather than a percentage of the settlement award.

Jackson, *A Controversial Settlement Approach: The Alpert Letter*, 49 J. Air L. & Com. 213, 217 (1983); *see also* Eric Roth, *Confronting the Solicitation of Mass Disaster Victims, supra* at 976–77. The Alpert letter has been criticized for the same reasons as direct solicitation of mass accident victims: that the letter takes advantage of the victims' family members when they are emotionally weak, vulnerable, and unable to make a reasoned and informed decision. *See id.* Why should lawyers be held to a different standard than insurance companies? Must lawyers refrain from contacting disaster victims while insurance companies are at liberty to do so?

4. Different states have responded to the problem of solicitation of mass disaster victims in different ways. In 1990, Florida amended its rules of professional conduct to ban the mailing of letters to accident or disaster victims until thirty days after the accident occurs. *See The Florida Bar: Petition to Amend The Rules Regulating The Florida Bar—Advertising Issues,* 571 So.2d 451 (Fla.1990)(Rule 4–7.4(b)(1) forbidding targeted mail advertising to prospective clients if the cause of action relates to personal injury, wrongful death, or other accidents or disasters). Other jurisdictions have created "disaster response teams" consisting of bar members who immediately go to mass disaster sites, set up disaster response legal offices to counsel disaster victims to delay decisions about hiring counsel, and to police infractions of solicitation rules. *See generally,* Karen E. Klages, *Disaster Response: Iowa Bar Act To Prohibit Solicitation After United Crash,* 75 A.B.A.J. 24 (Oct. 1989).

5. Apart from in-person solicitation of mass disaster victims, are there other permissible means of notifying potential claimants in a nascent or developed mass tort litigation? Mass disaster cases? What ethical limitations and professional responsibility duties attach to group or aggregate representation? *See* Nancy T. Bowen, *Restrictions on Communications by Class Action Parties and Attorneys,* 1980 Duke L.J. 360 (1980); Vance G. Camisa, *The Constitutional Right to Solicit Potential Class Action Members in a Class Action,* 25 Gonz. L. Rev. 95 (1989–90); Marc C. Galanter, *Bhopals, Past and Present: The Changing Legal Response to Mass Disaster,* 10 Windsor Yearbook Access Just. 151 (1990); Herbert M. Kritzer, *Public Notification Campaigns in Mass Litigation: The Dalkon Shield Case,* 13 Justice System J. 220 (1988–89); Jeffrey R. Snyder, Comment, *Judicial Screening of Class Communications,* 55 N.Y.U.L. Rev. 671 (1980); Brian J. Waid, *Ethical Problems of the Class Action Practitioner: Continued Neglect by the Drafters of the Proposed Model Rules of Professional Conduct,* 27 Loy. L. Rev. 1047 (1981).

2. INADEQUATE REPRESENTATION

MEKDECI v. MERRELL NATIONAL LABORATORIES

United States Court of Appeals, Eleventh Circuit, 1983.
711 F.2d 1510.

Before FAY, HENDERSON and HATCHETT, CIRCUIT JUDGES. ALBERT J. HENDERSON, CIRCUIT JUDGE:

* * *

I

In 1975, Elizabeth Mekdeci gave birth to a son, David. The child suffered from a combination of birth defects, which included malformed and missing fingers and a missing pectoral muscle. Thereafter, she extensively investigated the possible origin of her son's injury and became convinced that a drug she had ingested for nausea during the pregnancy was the cause. That drug, Bendectin, is manufactured by the defendant.

Based on that conclusion, the Mekdecis, both individually and on behalf of their son, instituted the present suit against Merrell. In their complaint, they alleged Florida causes of action for strict liability, negligence, breach of warranty and fraud. At the end of a two month trial, the jury appeared to be deadlocked in its deliberations. The district court gave the jury further instruction, and soon afterward, the jury returned a verdict awarding the "plaintiff" $20,000.00, the amount stipulated by the parties as compensation for the parents' medical expenses. The verdict, however, denied any recovery on the child's individual cause of action. For that reason, the plaintiffs sought a new trial limited to a determination of damages. Declaring the jury's award to be a compromise verdict, the district court ordered a new trial on all issues.

Prior to the second trial, the plaintiffs' attorneys made several unsuccessful attempts to withdraw as counsel for the Mekdecis and to obtain a continuance. The second trial proceeded as scheduled and resulted in a verdict absolving the defendant of all liability. The district court entered a judgment in conformance with the verdict and taxed the costs incurred by Merrell in both trials against the plaintiffs. This appeal * * * followed.

* * *

III

The plaintiff's next assignment of error involves the persistent efforts of their original lawyers to withdraw as counsel for the Mekdecis. During the nine month interim between the two trials, the six attorneys of record made various attempts to abandon the case and, failing that, to obtain a continuance. Finding no compelling justification for the lawyers' requests, the district court denied the motions. In addition, the court refused to grant the six month continuance requested by another law firm, who sought to replace the recalcitrant attorneys but conditioned their entry into the case on the court's willingness to delay the proceedings. On appeal, the plaintiffs attack those rulings and urge that the presentation of their case by unwilling counsel deprived them of a fair trial.

A

The events giving rise to these allegations present an extraordinary tale. The story begins with the extensive efforts of Mrs. Mekdeci, following the birth of her son, to discover the possible cause of his defects. During the course of her investigation, she talked with many medical experts and examined numerous documents, including government studies of Bendectin. After several years, she collected sufficient information to convince her that the drug had caused David's injury. At that point, she contacted Melvin Belli in San Francisco about legal representation. Belli reviewed the materials she had assembled, and then consented to accept the case.

The agreement with Belli evidently called for him to serve as trial counsel. He also referred the Mekdecis to a Florida attorney, Gerald Tobin. Tobin brought in one of his associates, Arthur Tifford, as well as two local attorneys, Arthur Cohen and George Kokus. The arrangement contemplated that Cohen and Kokus would orchestrate the discovery, and that Belli would conduct the trial. A trial date was originally set for July, 1979. Apparently at Belli's request, the district court granted a continuance until January, 1980. However, just several weeks before the scheduled date, Belli informed the Florida attorneys that he would not appear as counsel. Consequently, the other lawyers, with the assistance of Allen Eaton, a Washington, D.C. attorney specializing in food and drug regulation, prepared to litigate the case themselves.

At a May hearing following the first trial, the judge * * * informed the parties that the second trial would begin in January, 1981. During that spring, Belli and several of the Florida attorneys capitalized on the claimed victory in the first trial in a rather obvious effort to attract other Bendectin clients. They traveled both in this country and Europe, trumpeting their participation in that trial and advertising for Bendectin mothers to contact them, ostensibly for statistical studies. Although the record does not reveal the exact number of cases they have obtained, it is clear that the attorneys now represent plaintiffs in numerous Bendectin cases, presumably as a result of this publicity.

In the summer of 1980, the first signs appeared that the lawyers might be abandoning the Mekdecis. The *London Observer* quoted Belli as saying that Mrs. Mekdeci was too difficult to work with, that her case was not that strong, and that he was turning his attention to two hundred similar cases. About the same time, on July 24, 1980, all of the attorneys of record moved to withdraw, citing an alleged "irreconcilable conflict" with the clients as the basis for the motion. The district court held a hearing on the matter on July 29, 1980. * * * There, Mrs. Mekdeci disclosed her complete surprise over the attorneys' motion as well as the allegation of an irreconcilable conflict. She denied any such disagreement. The court postponed any resolution of the issue so that the attorneys could apprise the Mekdecis of their reasons for seeking withdrawal. * * * [The Mekdecis then unsuccessfully attempted to retain successor counsel, after the court denied a continuance of the case.—ed.]

After denying the continuance, the court turned to a consideration of the motion to withdraw. In the letter of explanation requested earlier by the court, the attorneys basically cited differences of opinion between them and the Mekdecis over trial strategy. The Mekdecis informed the court that they did not consider the disagreements insurmountable, that they were willing to cooperate fully with the lawyers, and that they wished to continue with their original attorneys. Mrs. Mekdeci also suggested that the real dispute centered on her reluctance to acquiesce in the attorneys' preference to delay the trial until after the trial of another Bendectin case. Based on the plaintiffs' assurances, the district court denied the motion to withdraw, admonishing all of the parties to work together toward their common purpose.

The court's order did not even momentarily deter the attorneys' attempts to extricate themselves from the case. Less than a month later, Cohen, Kokus, Tifford and Eaton renewed their motion to withdraw. They based the request on the same conclusory allegation of an "irreconcilable conflict." They also emphasized that their motion did not include Belli, therefore leaving him to represent the plaintiffs. The Mekdecis opposed the motion. In a brief order, the district court denied the request, observing that

> [g]ood grounds have not been shown as to why it would be in the interest of justice for this Court to permit the Florida attorneys (Cohen, Kokus and Tifford) and the Washington, D.C. attorney, Allen, [sic] to abandon the plaintiffs to rely upon a California attorney who has not actively participated in this case, nor indicated a firm resolve to do so, and further, who is reported to have stated that he has no further interest in the case.

[The attorneys then petitioned the former Fifth Circuit for a writ of mandamus, which was denied.—*ed.*]

Even the district court's adherence to its original ruling and the Fifth Circuit's denial of extraordinary relief did not end the attorneys' maneuvers. On December 31, 1980, less than one month before the scheduled trial date, the attorneys renewed their request still again, this time in alternative motions to withdraw, for a continuance or stay of proceedings pending the disposition of their appeal. For the first time, they suggested that they lacked sufficient funds to finance the costs of the second trial. The court held a hearing on January 12, 1980 to consider those motions. During that hearing, Kokus asserted every conceivable basis for delaying the proceedings. He primarily attempted to convince the court that extensive discovery remained to be accomplished and that the lawyers could not afford a retrial at that time. The court noted the complete absence of any proof substantiating the lawyers' alleged inability to advance costs. Moreover, while acknowledging that the family could not cover expenses, Mrs. Mekdeci expressed her disbelief of the allegation and her determination to obtain funds to assure the presence of their chief expert witness. She also emphasized her preference to proceed to trial as scheduled, if at all possible.

The court also observed that the attorneys' assertions appeared to contradict their position in another Bendectin case pending in the United States District Court for the District of Columbia. During a hearing held only a month earlier in that case, Eaton had urged that court to set a trial date as early as June. (here, they moved for a continuance at least until October). Merrell's attorney protested that the intervening Mekdeci trial might make it impossible to complete discovery in the other case by June. In a statement that perhaps shed more light than intended on the attorneys' motivations in the Mekdeci case, Eaton recounted numerous problems in the Mekdeci lawsuit and said,

> that being the case, we have a group of people—a group of attorneys who have agreed that, in order to start afresh and develop the issues properly, that the Koller case in our opinion represents perhaps the cleanest case of all the cases and the clearest one.

> We have a nurse here who ingested Bendectin, and only Bendectin. She ingested it during the critical period. And little Anne Koller has no arms and she has only a left leg which has a club foot on it.

> We figure this was a clear case in order to litigate the issues properly.

Even though they urged an early trial date in *Koller*, the attorneys adhered to their contention that they could not afford a trial in the Florida case. In fact, they threatened the court that they would not present any live witnesses if they were unable to procure a continuance. Still, based on all of the circumstances and the plaintiffs' desire to proceed, the district court denied the request.

The second trial was the final chapter in this saga. The attorneys to some extent made good their threat, at least initially, by offering an essentially "paper" case. Midway through the proceedings, Belli sent $25,000.00 for use to pay the expenses of several live witnesses. In any event, the two witnesses which the plaintiffs primarily relied upon in the first trial did not appear in person. Several weeks into the trial, the district court learned of the brief filed * * * on behalf of the Mekdecis, in the attorneys' appeal pending before the Fifth Circuit. The brief suggested that the trial court erred in its handling of the lawyers' repeated motions, especially in its refusal to grant the last request for a continuance. Chief Judge Young was amazed, to say the least, over the plaintiffs' position, since they had consistently conveyed their preference to proceed to trial. * * *

* * *

C

After the district court denied the motion for a continuance, the Mekdecis consistently urged the court to reject the various requests by their original attorneys to withdraw from the case. Nonetheless, they now argue in this appeal that the district court erred in not granting the motion permitting the lawyers to withdraw. To justify this change in position, the plaintiffs suggest that they only opposed the motions in the trial court because that court erroneously denied a continuance for successor counsel, therefore placing them in the predicament of choosing between retaining their reluctant counsel or facing trial with the possibility of no representation. However, because we find that the district court acted within its discretion by refusing a continuance, we conclude that the choice presented them was proper. Thus, the only remaining question is whether compelling ethical considerations mandated withdrawal from the case regardless of the clients' stated preference to keep their attorneys.

Local Rule 2.03(b) of the United States District Court for the Middle District of Florida prohibits the withdrawal of counsel without the court's approval. Additionally, Local Rule 2.03(c) states that the court will not grant permission "absent compelling ethical considerations, if such withdrawal would likely cause continuance or delay." In this court, the plaintiffs advance two reasons why withdrawal was purportedly mandated under the Code of Professional Responsibility, which, if true, would obviously constitute "compelling ethical considerations" under the Local Rule.

First, they maintain that the attorney-client relationship was indeed plagued by an "irreconcilable conflict."[14] This allegation directly contradicts their repeated assurances to the district court that such enmity did not exist. Moreover, the record does not support such a claim. As the representations of Mrs. Mekdeci and the lawyers to the district court illustrated, their past disagreement basically centered on strategic choices made at the first trial. At the time they sought to be excused from the case, their only apparent dispute with the plaintiffs concerned Mrs. Mekdeci's refusal to acquiesce in their desire to obtain a continuance. Such a difference of opinion, standing alone, falls fall short of establishing an irreconcilable conflict. As the former Fifth Circuit Court of Appeals has recognized,

> [a] client by virtue of a contract with his attorney is not made an indentured servant, a puppet on counsel's string, nor a chair in the courtroom. Counsel should advise, analyze, argue, and recommend, but his role is not that of an imperator whose edicts must prevail over the client's desire.

Singleton v. Foreman, 435 F.2d 962, 970 (5th Cir.1970).[15] The record does not contain evidence of a conflict in the attorney-client relationship of such proportions as would require an ethically-mandated withdrawal of counsel.

The plaintiffs next allege that the attorneys had an improper financial stake in the outcome of the second trial, which ethically precluded their continued representation under D.R. 5–101 and 5–103. They claim that the lawyers' obligation to advance costs created such an unlawful proprietary interest. To the contrary, D.R. 5–103(B) specifically states that "a lawyer may advance or guarantee the expenses of litigation,

---

14. In this argument, the plaintiffs rely upon D.R. 2–110(C)(1)(d), which would allow an attorney to seek withdrawal if the client "renders it unreasonably difficult for the lawyer to carry out his employment effectively." Although that ground is merely a possible basis for permissive, and not mandatory, withdrawal, the Mekdecis suggest that the alleged conflict was so severe in this instance as to require withdrawal under this provision.

15. While some courts have suggested that a client's refusal to follow his attorney's advice may justify withdrawal in every instance, see, e.g., Spero v. Abbott Laboratories, 396 F.Supp. 321, 323 (N.D.Ill. 1975), we reject the implication of those decisions, as did the panel in *Singleton,* that a party must blindly acquiesce in every recommendation made by his attorney.

including court costs, expenses of investigation, expenses of medical examination, and costs of obtaining and presenting evidence, provided the client remains ultimately liable for such expenses." Hence, the attorneys' initial responsibility for trial expenses does not amount to a mandatory ground for withdrawal.[16]

In summary, the plaintiffs' lawyers did not present the court with any compelling ethical consideration demanding their withdrawal. Absent such a reason, the court had the discretion to deny the withdrawal motion. * * * When making its decision, the district court faced the emphatic insistence of the plaintiffs that it deny the withdrawal motion. The Mekdecis cannot now complain that the district court erred by assenting to their wishes.

D

Underlying each of the plaintiffs' specific contentions pertaining to the attorneys' conduct is their belief that counsel ultimately performed ineffectively at the second trial. Essentially, the fundamental premise of their argument is that they were denied a fair trial, in violation of their right to due process, because of the alleged inadequacy of the representation. Based on that perception, they suggest that the prejudice which purportedly resulted therefrom renders the trial court's rulings on the motions for a continuance and for withdrawal erroneous. While we are not unsympathetic, we find a critical flaw in their reasoning.

In effect, the plaintiffs assume that they have a protected right to competent representation in their lawsuit. Simply stated, however, "there is no constitutional or statutory right to effective assistance of counsel on a civil case." Watson v. Moss, 619 F.2d 775, 776 (8th Cir.1980); *see also* United States v. White, 589 F.2d 1283, 1285 n. 4 (5th Cir.1979); United States v. Rogers, 534 F.2d 1134, 1135 (5th Cir.), *cert. denied*, 429 U.S. 940, 97 S.Ct. 355, 50 L.Ed.2d 309 (1976). * * * The sixth amendment standards for effective counsel in criminal cases do not apply in the civil context * * * for that reason, "[a] party * * * does not have any right to a new trial in a civil suit because of inadequate counsel, but has as its remedy a suit against the attorney for malpractice." * * *

Our conclusion in no way suggests that we condone the conduct of the plaintiffs' original attorneys. On the contrary, we agree that the present record raises disturbing questions on the propriety of the lawyers' actions. The attorneys' various antics create an impression that they may have been more concerned with bettering their position in other Bendectin cases, rather than with fulfilling their professional responsibilities to the Mekdecis, who ironically made it possible for the lawyers to obtain the other cases in the first place. Additionally, there

---

16. Nor does the attorneys' professed inability to meet that responsibility somehow transform a proper contractual obligation into an impermissible financial stake. Also, based on the record before it, the district court had ample reason to share Mrs. Mekdeci's doubt about the veracity of that allegation.

are indications that several, if not all, of the attorneys may have breached their contractual obligations to the plaintiffs. Consequently, we do not necessarily discount the Mekdecis' claim that they have been aggrieved by the conduct of their lawyers. * * *

Notes and Questions

1. Of what comfort is it to the Mekdecis that the Fifth Circuit concludes by noting that it did not condone the original lawyers' "antics"? Would the Mekdecis have an action in malpractice? On what possible grounds? Were the Mekdecis indeed between the proverbial rock and a hard-place with regard to their choices? Would they have fared better by acknowledging an "irreconcilable difference" to the trial court in the first instance, and agreeing to withdrawal of their lawyers?

2. Model Rule 1.16(b)(5) of the Model Rules of Professional Conduct, like DR 2–110(C)(1)(d) of the Model Code, provides that a lawyer may permissively withdraw from representation if "the representation will result in an unreasonable financial burden on the lawyer or has been rendered unreasonably difficult by the client." For cases collected under this provision, *see* ANNOTATED MODEL RULES OF PROFESSIONAL CONDUCT (2d ed. 1992) at 274–75, citing the *Mekdeci* case.

3. Professor Joseph Sanders has described the Mekdecis' experience in the Bendectin litigation as the "first plaintiff problem." *See* Joseph Sanders, *The Bendectin Litigation: A Case Study in the Life Cycle of Mass Torts,* 43 Hastings L.J. 301, 349–54 (1992). He suggests that the first tasks in a mass tort litigation fall disproportionately on the initial plaintiff, who starts without scientific or legal resources and must marshall these resources in order to succeed. The first plaintiff must connect the injury with a defective product, amass sufficient scientific evidence to support the legal claim, and find a lawyer willing to take the case. Professor Sanders suggests that the Mekdecis' encountered multiple first plaintiff problems, including poorly prepared, inexperienced, and undercapitalized lawyers who did not devote sufficient resources to discovery and expert testimony in order to develop the case. In addition, the lawyers became drawn by the prospect of better claims where the specific causation issue would be better litigated. Did the lawyers violate any professional duties by trying to abandon the Mekdecis for better litigation prospects? Did the Mekdecis get effective assistance of counsel? How should we think about the Mekdecis' experience with their lawyers in relation to Professor Trangsrud's model of the virtues of individualized tort litigation? What about lawyers who settle their client's claims quickly? *See e.g.,* Thomas M. Burton, *The Litigator: How Stanley Chesley Settles Things Quickly in Mass Injury Suits,* Wall. St.J., June 26, 1992 at 1.

4. The Mekdecis' experience also suggests that potential mass tort litigation encourages plaintiffs' lawyers to seek out cases and to organize litigation networks. Paul D. Rheingold has noted that litigation support networks developed in mass tort litigations involving the swine flu vaccination, Dalkon Shield, Agent Orange, MER/29, birth control pills, asbestos, DES, Ford transmissions, and Bendectin. *See* Paul D. Rheingold, *The*

Development of Litigation Groups, 6 Am. J. Trial Advoc. 1 (1982). One of the earliest of these groups is described in Paul D. Rheingold, *The MER/29 Story—An Instance of Successful Mass Disaster Litigation,* 56 Cal.L.Rev. 116, 117–20 (1968). *See* Chapter IV.B.4, *infra,* on cooperative discovery. In addition, there is a great incentive for plaintiffs' lawyers to take an early lead in a potential mass tort litigation, where the prospect of consolidated treatment may require designation of a lead counsel, or a lead counsel committee. States Rheingold: "A mere 5% of the recovery in the thousands of cases filed, and to be filed, dance like sugar plums in the heads of lead counsel-to-be." Rheingold, *Litigation Groups, supra* at 3.

5. The flip side of the "first plaintiff" problem is the first defendant problem. Writes Professor Sanders:

Compared to plaintiffs, defendants generally have a substantial early advantage. Their financial resources are much greater. They can hire counsel who are experienced in the defense of defective pharmaceuticals against personal injury claims and who are well connected to governmental agencies. They have ready access to nearly all the safety data concerning their product. All these advantages inured to Merrell's benefit in the *Mekdeci* case. The company committed unlimited resources to Bendectin's defense, hiring Lawrence E. Walsh and the firm of Davis, Polk & Wardwell as defense counsel. Moreover, after its experiences with Thalidomide and MER/29, Merrell probably had as much experience as any firm in defending prescription drugs in court.

Notwithstanding these advantages, defendants may be confronted with some first case problems similar to those of the first plaintiff. The defendant, too, must confront the relative lack of evidence and the considerable uncertainty that permeates such early litigation. The defendant's legal staff most likely is not yet organized to mount a defense of the particular product. And if the firm is insured, the case might be turned over to the insurer's counsel who may lack familiarity with pharmaceutical defense and ease of access to the safety data that the defendant presumably enjoys. In sum, like plaintiffs, defendants do not begin with any particular expertise in litigating the product's safety. Indeed, in the earliest stages of mass tort litigation, the defendants may not even appreciate that they have something out of the ordinary on their hands. The first suit is not necessarily like the teacher's first occasion for sanctioning a wayward student at the beginning of the school year. The parties may not know that this is the first of a large congregation of cases. Bendectin had been on the market for nearly twenty years when litigation began, and at the time of the *Mekdeci* suit it had been nearly a decade since the Thalidomide disaster. It might well not have been immediately obvious to Merrell, upon the initial filing of the *Mekdeci* case, that this was the first of a series of cases.

See Joseph Sanders, *The Bendectin Litigation: A Case Study in the Life Cycle of Mass Torts,* 43 Hastings L.J. at 350—351 (1992).

3. ATTORNEYS' FEES

IN RE "AGENT ORANGE" PRODUCT
LIABILITY LITIGATION

United States District Court, Eastern District of New York, 1985.
611 F.Supp. 1452.

WEINSTEIN, CHIEF JUDGE:

David J. Dean, Esq., a member of the Agent Orange Plaintiffs' Management Committee ("PMC"), has moved to set aside the PMC's agreement to pay certain committee members a 300 percent return of funds they advanced to finance the litigation. The payment would be made out of all the fees awarded to the PMC attorneys by the court. The other PMC members oppose the motion and seek to compel arbitration. For reasons indicated below, Mr. Dean's motion is denied and the petition to compel arbitration is dismissed.

The issues raised by Mr. Dean's motion present new and difficult questions in the financing of major toxic tort litigations. Implicated are the boundaries of legal ethics and the legality of fee arrangements among attorneys in class actions. The instant attorneys' agreement for fee distribution will not be set aside. In any future case in this district such an agreement must be revealed to the court and members of the class as soon as possible. A "sunshine" rule is essential to protect the interests of the public, the class and the honor of the legal profession.

I. FACTS

In 1979 cases began to be transferred to this district for consolidation of pretrial proceedings in the Agent Orange multidistrict litigation. In 1980 the court tentatively certified a class and appointed Yannacone and Associates, a consortium of local lawyers, as class attorneys. Yannacone and Associates withdrew as class counsel in September 1983 because of management problems and lack of financing. They were replaced by Stephen J. Schlegel, Benton Musslewhite, and Thomas W. Henderson. Mr. Schlegel and Mr. Henderson are members of the current PMC. Mr. Musslewhite resigned in February 1985 but still considers himself bound by the PMC fee sharing agreement.

David Dean, a member of the original management committee, remained associated with the new committee. At pretrial conferences after October 1983 the court indicated that he would be expected to take the lead in preparing and trying the case. In February 1984 the court at the PMC's request approved an expansion of its membership to include Mr. Dean and other lawyers who previously had been working informally with class counsel.

The class action was settled in May 1984 on the eve of trial. Attorney fee applications were required to be submitted by the end of August 1984. The PMC submitted a joint fee award application. Only then was the court apprised of the existence of an internal management agreement among the PMC lawyers that set out the procedure for allocation of any fees awarded from a class recovery. Its provisions called for (1) a 300% return of funds advanced by certain PMC members before any other distribution, and (2) division of the remainder of the award as follows: 50% in equal shares among all committee members, 30% in proportion to hours worked, and 20% based on factors paralleling those considered by courts in granting fee award multipliers.

After the court voiced serious doubts about the legality and propriety of this arrangement at the September 26, 1984 attorney fee hearing, the PMC members renegotiated their fee-sharing agreement. The new arrangement still requires a three-fold reimbursement of monies advanced, but the remainder would be allocated to those who were awarded them by the court. This renegotiated agreement, entered into on December 13, 1984, is retroactive to October 1, 1983. It provides in pertinent part:

> When and if funds are received, either by the AOPMC or individual members thereof, the first priority distribution will be to distribute to Messrs. Brown, Chesley, Henderson, Locks, O'Quinn and Schwartz, an amount equivalent to the actual monies expended for which these six signatories were responsible toward the common advancement of the litigation up to $250,000.00 with a multiplier of three (*i.e.*, none of these six individuals will receive more than $750,000.00 each), which shall be paid to them for having secured the funds for the AOPMC and to Messrs. Dean, Schlegel and Musslewhite an amount equivalent to the actual monies expended by these three signatories toward the common advancement of the litigation up to $50,000.00 with a multiplier of three (*i.e.*, none of these three signatories will receive more than $150,000.00 each). Any additional expenses will be reimbursed without a multiplier as ordered by the Court.

> All of the expenses plus the appropriate multiplier will be deducted from the total fees and expenses awarded by the Court to all of the AOPMC firms. The remaining fees will then be distributed *pro rata* to each signatory in the proportion the individual's and/or firm's fee award bears to the total fees awarded.

The agreement also provides for mandatory arbitration of "[a]ny dispute concerning monies due a member [of the PMC] or his rights under this agreement."

Messrs. Brown, Chesley, Locks, O'Quinn and Schwartz each have advanced $250,000. Mr. Henderson has contributed a total of $200,000. The remaining three PMC members have not advanced any funds for general expenses, although they have incurred individual expenses, for which they will be individually reimbursed. * * *

According to Mr. Dean, the agreement will be interpreted to reach the results indicated in the following table taken from his motion papers. The figures given are based on the fees awarded in the January 7, 1985 order rather than the somewhat higher awards ultimately allowed on reconsideration. * * * Nevertheless, the general fee-shifting effect shown by the table remains essentially the same. Those who advanced money would be advantaged over those who gave time and skill to the enterprise.

	Court Awarded Fees	Net Fees Under Agreement	Gain or Loss	Court Awarded Rate	Net Hourly Rate
Brown	296,493.75	551,157.19	+ 254,663.44	225.00	418.26
Chesley	390,993.75	567,476.19	+ 176,482.44	225.00	326.56
Henderson	442,552.50	576,358.26	+ 133,805.76	225.00	293.03
Locks	332,268.75	562,354.76	+ 230,086.01	225.00	380.81
O'Quinn	88,305.00	515,217.00	+ 426,912.00	100.00	583.45
Schwartz	29,145.00	505,026.34	+ 475,881.34	100.00	1,732.81
Dean	1,340,437.50	331,346.75	− 1,009,090.75	225.00	55.62
Musslewhite	304,657.50	152,535.04	− 152,122.46	100.00	75.10
Schlegel	763,678.12	231,785.14	− 531,892.99	262.50	79.67

* * *

III. Law on Review of Fee Sharing Agreements

Under Rule 23(e) of the Federal Rules of Civil Procedure, the court has an obligation to protect the rights of class members. That duty requires review of the reasonableness of an internal fee-sharing agreement to ensure that it does not pose a danger of harm to the class. The court also has supervisory authority over attorneys who practice before it and thus an obligation to prevent breaches of professional ethics. * * * [The court then generally reviewed the reasonableness standard for attorney fee awards in class actions under the so-called "lodestar" formula, and indicated that class counsel could determine how a court-awarded fee would be allocated among attorneys, under fee sharing agreements. The court further concluded that "none of these cases, however, holds that a court has no power to review an internal fee allocation agreement or that it has not duty to do so when circumstances call for such an inquiry."—*ed.*]

* * *

V. Validity of the PMC Fee-Sharing Agreement

Under the terms of the renegotiated agreement now before the court, each PMC member who advanced money for general expenses of the group as distinguished from individual expenses would receive three times the amount advanced, the multiplied amount being paid out of the individual fee and expense allowances of the individual members and the expense allowance of the PMC. The question to be decided is whether this fee allocation must be stricken either as a violation of professional ethics or as a threat to the rights of the class.

The PMC fee-sharing agreement raises two potential problems of professional ethics: inappropriate division of fees between lawyers who are not members of the same firm, and acquisition of financial interest in the litigation. Ethical prohibitions in either respect are inapplicable here. In addition, no danger to the rights of the class is present under the circumstances of this case. Other considerations render undesirable a mechanical rule against fee-sharing agreements of this kind in all cases.

A. Division of Fees

The ABA Code of Professional Responsibility prohibits a lawyer from dividing a legal fee with another lawyer who is not in the same law firm, unless (1) the client consents to the arrangement, (2) the "division is made in proportion to the services performed and responsibility assumed by each," and (3) the total fee is reasonable. Code DR 2–107(A). The Model Rules of Professional Conduct adopted by the ABA in 1983 contain a more liberal provision. It allows lawyers not in the same firm to divide a fee if (1) either "the division is in proportion to the services performed by each lawyer or, by written agreement with the client, each lawyer assumes joint responsibility for the representation," (2) the client does not object to any lawyer's participation, and (3) the total fee is reasonable. Model Rule 1.5(e).

Neither provision necessarily restricts the freedom of the PMC to allocate fees among committee members. The PMC may be considered an ad hoc law firm, a joint venture formed for the purpose of prosecuting the Agent Orange multidistrict litigation.

Business realities of law practice often require that those who bring clients and capital to a law firm be better compensated than those whose talents lie in the area of preparing legal papers and arguments. * * * Rainmakers are usually better rewarded than those who labor in the back room. Given the state of the case when Yannacone and Associates found itself without funds to continue, it was clear when the PMC was organized that money was a more sought after commodity than talent.

Viewed from this perspective, the Code and Model Rule restrictions on splitting fees among lawyers of different firms do not control this joint venture. * * *

The Model Rule provision clearly reflects an increased recognition of the business realities of the legal profession. As the commentary notes, "[a] division of fee facilitates association of more than one lawyer in a matter in which neither alone could serve the client as well. * * * " Model Rule 1.5(e) comment.

The PMC agreement meets the Rule's requirements. First, each PMC member assumed joint responsibility for prosecution of the class action, and that assumption was approved by the court on behalf of the class. *Cf.* ABA Comm. on Ethics and Professional Responsibility Informal Op. 85–1514 (April 27, 1985)(Model Rule 1.5(e) requires assumption of responsibility comparable to that of a partner in a law firm under similar circumstances, including financial and ethical responsibility and responsibility for adequacy of representation and client communication), *summarized in* ABA/BNA Lawyers' Manual on Professional Conduct

766–67 (current supp.).   Second, the total fee allowed by the court is reasonable by definition.

No ethical violation can be found here on the basis of inappropriate division of fees among the lawyers not in the same firm.   Nevertheless, the provisions of Model Rule 1.5(e) and Code DR 2–107(A) on disapproval by the client of any fee splitting arrangement suggest that the class— and the court as protector of the class—has a continuing interest in being informed of any special fee arrangement as soon as possible.

B.   Acquisition of Interest in Litigation

The ABA Code of Professional Responsibility prohibits a lawyer from acquiring a proprietary interest in a case except by a lien for fees or a contingent fee arrangement.   Code DR 5–103(A).   An attorney may advance or guarantee the expenses of a litigation only if the client remains ultimately liable for payment.   *Id.* 5–103(B).   This latter provision has been held applicable to class actions, notwithstanding that it presents a formidable obstacle to the practical ability of counsel to prosecute class litigation.   *See, e.g.,* In re Mid–Atlantic Toyota Antitrust Litigation, 93 F.R.D. 485 (D.Md.1982)(denying class certification because arrangement between named plaintiffs and counsel violated DR 5– 103(B)). * * *

The Model Rules of Professional Conduct carry forward the prohibition on acquisition of a financial interest in a case.   *See* Model Rule 1.8. The Rule, however, does allow a lawyer to "advance court costs and expenses of litigation, the repayment of which may be contingent on the outcome of the matter."   *Id.* 1.8(e)(1).

The PMC agreement goes beyond the simple contingent reimbursement of expenses.   It contemplates the return of a profit on the funds advanced.   But the profit on the investment is to be paid out of the pooled fee award, not the settlement fund.   No independent interest is acquired in the litigation by the investors.   Nevertheless, to the extent that the PMC agreement creates a possible conflict of interest, it might be characterized as involving an acquisition of proprietary interest that falls within the prohibitions of the Code and Model Rules.   *Cf.* Code Canon 9 ("A Lawyer Should Avoid Even the Appearance of Professional Impropriety")(omitted from Model Rules).

The circumstances of this complex and unique class action require a more sophisticated analysis than would be appropriate in the kind of simple two-party case that furnishes the model for much of the relevant ethical guides.   *See* In re Corn Derivatives Antitrust Litigation, 748 F.2d 157, 163 (3d Cir.1984)(Adams, J. concurring).   The prohibition on acquisition of a proprietary interest in a litigation has its basis in common law concepts of champerty and maintenance.   It is a prophylactic rule intended to prevent conflicts of interest between lawyer and client that could interfere with the lawyer's exercise of free judgment on behalf of the client.   Code EC 5–3; Model Rule 1.8 comment.   Similarly, the fundamental concern in the instant case is protection of the rights of the class, in part through minimization of potentially detrimental conflicts of

interest. But it is also important to avoid creation of disincentives that in individual instances may unnecessarily discourage counsel from undertaking the expensive and protracted complex multiparty litigation often needed to vindicate the rights of a class. An ironclad requirement that class representatives remain ultimately liable for expenses incurred, for example, would prevent many meritorious cases from reaching the courts.

As more fully discussed below, a simple prohibition on advances of cash for expenses does not adequately balance these competing considerations. Moreover, because of the court's responsibility for approval of a class action settlement, it is not the only feasible alternative. A case-by-case examination is not only practical, but advances the important policies favoring class litigation in many instances.

C. *Protection of the Rights of the Class*

Under Rule 23(e) and the common fund doctrine, when a monetary settlement is reached in a class action federal courts are responsible for assessing attorney fees that are reasonable. Fee awards must reflect the actual work that benefited the class. The court's responsibility for controlling attorney fees arises from the need to safeguard the interest of the class. *See, e.g.,* In re "Agent Orange" Product Liability Litigation, 611 F.Supp. 1296, 1304–05 (E.D.N.Y. Jan. 7, 1985, as modified June 18, 1985).

When lawyers in a class action agree on allocation of their fees *inter se* that diverges from the allocation determined by the court, the court must review the reasons for an effect of that allocation to ensure that it has not and will not have an impact adverse to the interests of the class. * * * What are the dangers of a fee-splitting agreement such as that of the PMC?

Most important, an agreement of this kind may create an incentive toward early settlement that may not be in the interests of the class. An attorney who is promised a multiple of funds advanced will receive the same return whether the case is settled today or five years from now. An early settlement will maximize the investor's profit, because he or she then can reinvest the funds elsewhere immediately. A lawyer in this situation might not negotiate as hard or might decide to settle early, when holding out for a higher settlement or going to trial would be in the best interests of the class. *See generally* Coffee, *The Unfaithful Champion: The Plaintiff as Monitor in Shareholder Litigation,* Law & Contemp. Probs., Summer 1985, at 5.

The court's responsibility under Rule 23(e) for approval of a class action settlement limits to some extent the effect of this potential for premature settlement. Before approving a class action settlement, a court must find it fair, reasonable and adequate, based on a detailed analysis of the law and facts. *See, e.g.,* In re "Agent Orange" Product Liability Litigation, 597 F.Supp. 740, 758–63 (E.D.N.Y.1984). The court, however, cannot make a precise determination of the fairness of the settlement; its task is to decide whether the agreed upon settlement

falls within "the range of reasonableness." *Id.,* 597 F.Supp. at 762. Thus the court's approval process may not completely eliminate the more subtle effects of undue pressure on attorneys toward settlement.

In some cases any incentive to settle early will be counteracted by the incentive to prolong litigation created by the "lodestar" method of fee calculation. The lodestar formula rewards counsel based on the number of hours reasonably spent on a case and permits a court to award risk-of-litigation and quality-of-representation multipliers for time spent (but not expense incurred). It thus encourages attorneys to seek higher fees by delaying settlement and spending more time on a case. *See* In re "Agent Orange" Product Liability Litigation, 611 F.Supp. 1296, 1305–06 (E.D.N.Y. Jan. 7, 1985, as modified June 18, 1985).

In the instant case, the theoretical incentive to settle early appears not to have been an appreciable factor in inducing settlement. It is clear that the class action settlement was neither premature nor ill-considered, being in the best interest of the class. *Compare* In re "Agent Orange" Product Liability Litigation, 597 F.Supp. 740 (E.D.N.Y.1984)(fairness of proposed settlement) with *id., [sic]* 611 F.Supp. 1223 (E.D.N.Y.1985)(granting summary judgment in the cases of veterans who opted out of the class action). Based on the court's direct observation of counsel, the litigation and settlement negotiations, there is no reason to believe that the existence of the PMC's fee-sharing agreement had any appreciable effect on the decision to settle. Moreover, any incentive to settle would have been counteracted by the lodestar-created incentive to prolong litigation. Here, all nine PMC members worked on the case; only three invested funds without expending extensive productive hours on behalf of the class.

PETER H. SCHUCK, AGENT ORANGE ON TRIAL: MASS TOXIC DISASTERS IN THE COURTS *

The Belknap Press of Harvard University Press (1986) at 202–04.

A final significant aspect of Weinstein's initial fee opinion concerned his review of the PMC's internal fee-splitting agreement. The initial agreement [was] signed during the group's most financially desperate hours * * *; under its terms (in Weinstein's words), "those who advanced money would be advantaged to an extraordinary degree over those who gave their time and skill to the enterprise." The arrangement raised a number of important and little-explored legal and ethical issues. First, this "banker's approach" * * * might amount to champerty (the fomenting and maintenance by lawyers of litigation in which they have a proprietary interest), a practice that the courts have long regarded as unethical and illegal.

Second, * * *, the arrangement created the potential for serious conflicts of interest between the financiers and the litigators on the PMC

* Reprinted by permission of the publishers from AGENT ORANGE ON TRIAL: MASS TOXIC DISASTERS IN THE COURTS by Peter H. Schuck, Cambridge, Mass.: Harvard University Press, Copyright © 1986, 1987 by Mary Schuck Trust.

and exacerbated similar conflicts between the lawyers and their clients. A financier who knows that he will receive a profitable return on his investment "off the top" of any fee award has a strong incentive to settle the case quickly, even if the settlement amount is far below what might be obtained by holding out for a higher figure or by proceeding to trial (at the risk of losing everything). By the same token, a litigator who knows that such a settlement will siphon off the bulk of the fee award for the financiers, leaving relatively little to be divided up among the litigators, has a strong incentive to resist such a settlement. The clients' interests may well be lost in the crossfire. In such a situation mistrust flourishes; for example, some saw Chesley's eagerness to lead the settlement talks, his readiness to compromise at the $180 million figure, his assurance that even with a very small fee award he would receive a quick $600,000 on his $200,000 investment, as predictable signs of this logic at work. (Also contributing to these suspicions was Chesley's well-established reputation for settling huge class action cases, securing handsome fees in the process, and Musslewhite's allegation that Chesley had represented one of the defendants' excess insurance carriers).

Third, the PMC agreement placed the court in the awkward position of awarding fees that it knew would actually be allocated among the lawyers in an entirely different manner and without regard to the traditional, legally sanctioned criteria—work performed, professional value conferred, or responsibility assumed.

Weinstein, who learned of this agreement in the late summer of 1984, was mindful of these problems. He informed the PMC through Chesley that unless they amended their fee agreement, he would nullify it. The financiers, who desperately wanted to preserve as much of it as possible, persuaded the others to modify it, and on December 13, 1984, the PMC executed an amended agreement, which was to be retroactive to October 1, 1983. The "off the top" provision was retained—indeed, the amount that each financier might receive was increased to $750,000 (his $250,000 expenses contribution multiplied by three)—but this advantage was extended to the others (Dean, Schlegel, and Musslewhite), albeit at a lower amount ($50,000 expenses each, multiplied by three). And instead of the percentage allocation specified for the remainder of the award, the new arrangement would divide the fees remaining after the off-the-top deductions according to the proportion that each lawyer's fee award bore to the total fee award.

In his initial fee opinion, Weinstein, although clearly troubled by this renegotiated agreement, decided not to disturb it. The class would not be affected, he reasoned; only the litigators would be taxed. Furthermore, "law is a business," and lawyers should not ordinarily look to the courts to second-guess their financial decisions, especially when the litigation might not have been funded without such an agreement. Finally, no one had yet challenged it, and the judge was not going to decide so novel a question on a hypothetical basis.

This last reason was obviated in May 1985 when Dean moved to invalidate the new agreement. Conceding that he had not signed it under duress or ignorance, he pointed out that under its terms he would receive $331,000 rather than the $1.34 million that the court had awarded him, or more than 75 percent of his fee; Schlegel's reduction would be more than $530,000 and Musslewhite's more than $150,000. In contrast, Schwartz and O'Quinn would receive $475,000 more and $426,000 more, respectively, than the court had awarded them. Dean, the PMC's chief counsel, would receive an effective hourly rate of $55.62, while Schwartz, essentially a passive investor, would receive more than $1,700 per hour. This arrangement, Dean argued, constituted unethical fee-splitting, disproportionate to the services performed and responsibility assumed, and champerty; it almost amounted to a usurious loan.

Dean's arguments have some force, yet the ethical strictures they embody seem curiously anachronistic, quaint reminders of bygone attitudes toward the social functions of adjudication. The legal system cannot have it both ways. If it desires the end, then it must desire (or at least accept) the only practical means to that end. If it wishes to encourage so-called public interest tort litigation on behalf of diffuse, poorly financed interests over extremely complex issues of scientific or technical uncertainty, then it must either transform the government into a tort litigator on behalf of these interests (a solution with enormous problems of its own), or it must countenance, indeed welcome, private arrangements for securing the resources necessary for effectively prosecuting such cases. The truth is that in the fall of 1983, if the Agent Orange litigation was to go forward, the resources of the financiers were desperately needed; it is no exaggeration to say that at that critical moment and thereafter, they were needed far more than the services of the chief trial counsel, valuable as his services were. The otherwise grotesque imbalance revealed by Dean's comparisons reflected the relative value that their money and his services had for the survival of the case at that point, a value Dean obviously appreciated when he signed the agreement. Although the opportunism of investors is not a pretty or edifying sight, the prospect of meritorious cases failing for want of resources is even less appealing. Any set of principles that affirms the importance of litigating very costly cases while denying the means for doing so seems more hypocritical than ethical, more delusive than just.

On June 27, Weinstein rejected Dean's challenge to the agreement. After discussing the competing considerations, the judge chose to address the ethical problems case by case rather than announce any general rule. In this case, he observed, any conflict of interest and incentives to settle prematurely were purely hypothetical, for he had found the settlement to be fair and in the best interests of the class. In the future, however, lawyers would be required to disclose to the court the existence and terms of such a fee-sharing arrangement, so that the court could protect the class—perhaps by requiring modifications, reconsidering class certification, or notifying the class—and the lawyers could proceed accordingly.

IN RE "AGENT ORANGE" PRODUCT LIABILITY LITIGATION (Appeal of David Dean)

United States Court of Appeals, Second Circuit, 1987.
818 F.2d 216.

Before VAN GRAAFEILAND, WINTER and MINER, CIRCUIT JUDGES. MINER, CIRCUIT JUDGE:

* * * This portion of the Agent Orange appeal concerns the district court's approval of a fee sharing agreement entered into by the nine-member Plaintiffs' Management Committee ("PMC") in December of 1983. Under the agreement, each PMC member who had advanced funds to the class for general litigation expenses was to receive a three-fold return on his investment prior to the distribution of other fees awarded to individual PMC members by the district court. In result, the agreement dramatically increased the fees awarded to those PMC members who had advanced funds to the class for expenses, and concurrently decreased the fees awarded to non-investing PMC members, who performed legal services for the class.

David Dean, lead trial counsel for the plaintiff class and a non-investing member of the PMC, challenges the validity of the agreement, to which he was a signatory, contending that it violates DR 5–103 and DR 2–107(A) of the ABA Code of Professional Responsibility. * * *

* * *

Because we find that the agreement before us violates established principles governing awards of attorneys' fees in equitable fund class actions and creates a strong possibility of a conflict of interest between class counsel and those they are charged to represent, we reverse the district court's approval of the agreement. Accordingly, the fees originally allocated by the district court, based on the reasonable value of the services actually rendered, will be distributed to the members of the PMC.

* * *

The ultimate inquiry, therefore, in examining fee agreements and setting fee awards under the equitable fund doctrine and Fed.R.Civ.P. 23(e), is the effect an agreement could have on the rights of a class. Because we find that the agreement here conflicts substantially with the principles of reasonable compensation in common fund actions * * * and that it places class counsel in a potentially conflicting position in relation to the interests of the class, we reverse. * * * [The court then discussed the fee sharing agreement in light of lodestar formula precedents, and concluded that the any fee distributions must bear some relationship to services rendered—*ed.*]

* * *

In our view, fees that include a return on investment present the clear potential for a conflict of interest between class counsel and those whom they have undertaken to represent. "[W]henever an attorney is confronted with a potential for choosing between actions which may benefit himself financially and an action which may benefit the class which he represents there is a reasonable possibility that some specifically identifiable impropriety will occur. * * * The concern is not necessarily in isolating instances of major abuse, but rather is 'for those situations, short of actual abuse, in which the client's interests are somewhat encroached upon by the attorney's interests.' " *Court Awarded Attorney Fees*, Report of the Third Circuit Task Force, 108 F.R.D. 237, 266 (Oct. 8, 1985). Such conflicts are not only difficult to discern from the terms of a particular settlement, but "even the parties may not be aware that [they exist] at the time of their [settlement] discussions," *id.* This risk is magnified in the class action context, where full disclosure and consent are many times difficult and frequently impractical to obtain. * * *

The district court recognized that the agreement provided an incentive for the PMC to accept an early settlement offer not in the best interests of the class, because "[a]n attorney who is promised a multiple of funds advanced will receive the same return whether the case is settled today of five years from now." * * * Given the size and the complexity of the litigation, it seems apparent that the potential for abuse was real and should have been discouraged. Unlike the district court, however, we conclude that the risk of such an adverse effect on the settlement process provides adequate grounds for invalidating the agreement as being inconsistent with the interests of the class. The conflict obviously lies in the incentive provided to an investor-attorney to settle early and thereby avoid work for which full payment may not be authorized by the district court. Moreover, as soon as an offer of settlement to cover the promised return on investment is made, the investor-attorney will be disinclined to undertake the risks associated with the continuing litigation. The conflict was especially egregious here, since six of the nine PMC members were investing parties to the agreement.

The district court's factual finding, that the adequacy of the settlement demonstrated that the agreement had no effect on the PMC's conduct, is not dispositive. The district court's retrospective appraisal of the adequacy of the settlement cannot be the standard for review. The test to be applied is whether, at the time a fee sharing agreement is reached, class counsel are placed in a position that might endanger the fair representation of their clients and whether they will be compensated on some basis other than for legal services performed. Review based on a fairness of settlement test would not ensure the protection of the class against potential conflicts of interest, and, more important, would simply reward counsel for failing to inform the court of the existence of such an agreement until after a settlement.

We also reject the district court's finding that its authority to approve settlement offers under Fed.R.Civ.P. 23(e) acts to limit the threat to the class from a potential conflict of interest. At this late stage of the litigation, both class counsel and defendants seek approval of the settlement. The court's attention properly is directed toward the overall reasonableness of the offer and not necessarily to whether class counsel have placed themselves in a potentially conflicting position with the class. Given this focus and other administrative concerns that may come to bear, we find approval authority, in this context, to be insufficient to assure that the ongoing interests of the class are protected. * * *

Equally unpersuasive is the district court's determination that the potential incentive to settle early is offset by an incentive, fostered by he lodestar formula, to prolong the litigation. While a number of commentators have asserted that use of the lodestar formula encourages counsel to prolong litigation for the purpose of billing more hours, *e.g.,* Wolfram, *The Second Set of Players: Lawyers, Fee Shifting, and the Limit of Proportional Discipline,* 47 Law & Contemp. Probs. 293, 302 (Winter 1984), the formula's effect in this regard is far from clear, *see* Coffee, *The Unfaithful Champion: The Plaintiff As Monitor In Shareholder Litigation,* 48 Law & Contemp. Probs. 5, 34–35 ("the claim that the lodestar formula results in excessive fees is nonetheless a red herring"). * * * Moreover, the court's authority in reviewing fee petitions and approving or disapproving hours billed in an equitable fund action works as a substantial and direct check on counsel's alleged incentive to procrastinate. * * * Consequently, we do not view the lodestar system as countervailing the clear interest in early settlement created by the private agreement.

Additionally, potential conflicts of interest in class contexts are not examined solely for the actual abuse they may cause, but also for potential public misunderstanding they may cultivate in regard to the interest of class counsel. * * * While today we hold that the settlement reached here falls within the range of reasonableness permissible under Fed.R.Civ.P. 23(e), we are not insensitive to the perception of many class members and the public in general that it does not adequately compensate the individual veterans and their families for whatever harm Agent Orange may have caused. To be sure, the settlement does not provide the individual veteran or his family substantial compensation. Given the facts of this settlement, the potentially negative public perception of an agreement that awards an investing PMC member over twelve times the amount the district court has determined to be the value of his services to the class provides additional justification for invalidating the agreement and applying the lodestar formula.

We find the various additional rationales for approving the fee sharing agreement set out in the district court's decision equally unpersuasive. First, the fact that the returns on the advanced expenses did not directly affect the class fund is of little consequence, since we have already determined that the district court's responsibility under [applicable lodestar precedents], as well as under Fed.R.Civ.P. 23(e), goes beyond concern for only the overall amount of fees awarded and requires attention to the fees allocated to individual class counsel. Second, while we sympathize with counsel regarding the business decisions they must make in operating an efficient and manageable practice and agree that a certain flexibility on the court's part is essential, we are not inclined to extend this flexibility to encompass situations in which the bases for awarding fees in an equitable fund action are so clearly distorted. Third, whether this class action would have collapsed without an agreement calling for a threefold return is a matter of speculation. Any such collapse, however, would have been due to the pervasive weaknesses in the plaintiffs' case. Fourth, we find wholly unconvincing the district court's suggestion that the investors could have made a sizeable return on their funds if they had invested them in other ventures. We take note of the fact that a threefold return on one's money is a rather generous return in any market over a short period of time. Fifth, while the effect of this fee sharing agreement might have been dwarfed to the point of insignificance if the fees awarded to counsel had been much greater, this simply is too speculative to defend the agreement as not affecting the interest of the class. Finally, we do not find class counsel to have formed an ad hoc partnership. They merely are a group of individual lawyers and law firms associated in the prosecution of a single lawsuit, and they lack the ongoing relationship that is the essential element of attorneys practicing as partners.

Notes and Questions

1.   To what extent is the Second Circuit's reversal of Judge Weinstein's decision grounded in professional responsibility principles? Should litigators (or non-litigators) be able to "invest" in a mass tort litigation? Considering the "first plaintiff" problem just encountered, how should first plaintiff or early potential mass tort cases be financed? Does Professor Schuck advance a compelling argument that a modern "public law" vision of mass tort litigation should not be offended by the PMC fee agreement in *Agent Orange*? What alternative means of financing these litigations are there? Who should assume what risks? *See generally* Vincent Johnson, *Ethical Limitations on Creative Financing of Mass Tort Class Actions*, 54 Brook. L.Rev. 539 (1988)(discussing the ethical implications of representing multiple clients in the context of mass tort litigation); David Rosenberg, *The Dusting of America: A Story of Asbestos—Carnage, Coverup, and Litigation* (Book Review), 99 Harv.L.Rev. 1693 (1986)(describing attorneys' tactics as self-serving); David Rosenberg, *Toxic Tort Litigation: Crisis or Chrysalis? A Comment on Feinberg's Conceptual Problems and Proposed Solutions*, 24 Hous.L.Rev. 183 (1987)(discussing attorneys' fees as a reason for frustration of class action reform proposals).

2.   In both *Cimino v. Raymark Industries, Inc.,* 739 F.Supp.328 (E.D.Tex.1990) and *In re School Asbestos Litigation* (E.D.Pa.1983) district judges Parker and Kelly permitted early settlement awards to finance the ongoing litigation, accompanied by an interest bearing account to offset litigation expenses. For a description of the courts' handling of attorney fee issues in these litigations, as well as a description of the financing of the mass tort litigation, *see* Linda S. Mullenix, *Beyond Consolidation: Postaggre-*

gative Procedure in Asbestos Mass Tort Litigation, 32 Wm. & Mary L.Rev. 475, 528–31 (1991).

3. Professor John C. Coffee, Jr. has written a series of articles analyzing the economics of class action litigation, and the incentives and disincentives relating to adequate class representation as affected by attorneys fees. *See generally* Coffee, *Class Wars: The Dilemma of the Mass Tort Class Action,* (forthcoming 1995); Coffee, *The Regulation of Entrepreneurial Litigation: Balancing Fairness and Efficiency in the Large Class Action,* 54 U.Chi.L.Rev. 877 (1987); Coffee, *Rethinking the Class Action: A Policy Primer on Reform,* 62 Ind. L.J. 625 (1987); Coffee, *Understanding the Plaintiff's Attorney: The Implications of Economic Theory for Private Enforcement of Law Through Class and Derivative Actions,* 86 Colum.L.Rev. 669 (1986); Coffee, *The Unfaithful Champion: The Plaintiff as Monitor in Shareholder Litigation,* 48 Law & Contemp. Probs. 5 (1985).

4. There have been controversial suggestions that attorney-fee problems in class litigation might be resolved through auctions of the class counsel position. *See* Jonathan R. Macey & Geoffrey P. Miller, *Auctioning Class Action and Derivative Lawsuits: A Rejoinder,* 87 Nw. U. L. Rev. 458 (1993); Randall S. Thomas and Robert G. Hansen, *Auctioning Class Action and Derivative Lawsuits: A Critical Analysis,* 87 Nw. U. L. Rev. 423 (1993). *See also* Jonathan R. Macey and Geoffrey P. Miller, *The Plaintiffs' Attorney's Role in Class Action and Derivative Litigation: Economic Analysis and Recommendations for Reform,* 58 U. Chi. L. Rev. 1 (1991).

5. In comparing the litigation of complex mass tort cases under either Rule 23 class action procedure and Rule 42 consolidation procedure, Professor Charles Silver notes:

> The need for appropriate institutional structures is paramount, however, because the potential for agency failures in consolidated proceedings is real. Everyone, including judges, recognizes that fee arrangements affect the zealousness of representation. For this reason, flawed fee arrangements, or even arrangements that are simply poorer than others that might be devised, can cause underrepresentation in consolidated suits, either by failing to give lead counsel sufficient incentives or by discouraging other lawyers from playing watchdog roles. Inadequate monitoring devices can have the same effect. Lawyers complain and judges recognize that lead counsel are tempted both to place the interests of their own clients above those of clients represented by other lawyers and to bargain with defendants for their own advantage at other lawyers' and parties' expense. Subordinate lawyers must be able to protect themselves and their clients from such abuse.

Charles Silver, *Comparing Class Actions and Consolidations,* 10 Rev. Litig. 495, 510–511 (1991).

For additional discussions of fee problems in complex and mass tort litigation, *see generally* Christopher P. Lu, *Procedural Solutions to the Attorney's Fee Problem in Complex Litigation,* 26 U. Rich. L. Rev. 41 (1991); Judith Resnik, Dennis E. Curtis, and Deborah Hensler, *Individuals Within the Aggregate: Representation and Fees* (forthcoming 1995).

6. Apart from the problem of controversial fee-sharing agreements, a number of empirical studies conducted by the Rand Institute for Civil Justice have now documented the phenomenon of high attorney fees, as a percentage of recovery, in mass tort actions. *See generally*, James S. Kakalik, *et al.*, *Costs and Compensation Paid in Aviation Accident Litigation* (Rand, The Institute for Civil Justice 1988); Kakalik *et al.*, *Variation in Asbestos Litigation Compensation and Expenses* (Rand, The Institute for Civil Justice 1984); Kakalik, *Costs of Asbestos Litigation* (Rand, The Institute for Civil Justice 1983). The problem of determination of attorneys fees will be revisited in Chapter IV.G., *infra*.

4. FUTURE CLAIMANTS

GEORGINE v. AMCHEM PRODUCTS, INC.

United States District Court, Eastern District of Pennsylvania, 1994.
157 F.R.D. 246.

[*See also* Carlough v. Amchem Prods., Inc. at Ch. II, D., *infra—ed.*]

MEMORANDUM OPINION INCLUDING FINDINGS OF FACT AND CONCLUSIONS OF LAW

LOWELL A. REED, JR., DISTRICT JUDGE.

INTRODUCTION

This is a class action claiming damages for asbestos-related personal injuries or wrongful death. Currently before the Court is the determination of whether the proposed settlement of the class action is fair to the class.

* * *

Based upon the evidence of record and the Court's findings of fact and conclusions of law, and for the reasons discussed below, this Court concludes that all of the requirements of Fed.R.Civ.P. 23 have been met and that the settlement of this class action is fair to the class and should be approved pursuant to Fed.R.Civ.P. 23(e) as fair to the class.

* * *

After the close of discovery, written objections to the settlement were filed with the Court on February 8, 1994, and the formal fairness hearing began on February 22, 1994. Counsel for the Settling Parties, several lawyers representing various Objectors, and counsel for various Amici participated at the fairness hearing. Under the direction of the Court, the Objectors closely coordinated their activities throughout the fairness proceedings.

Because of the complexity of the issues involved, and to give all interested parties a full and fair opportunity to present their views, the fairness hearing was extensive and protracted, involving the testimony of some twenty-nine witnesses (live or by deposition) during 18 hearing days over a period of over five weeks. The Court heard testimony from participants in the settlement negotiations, several representative plaintiffs, two high-ranking officers of the [Center for Claims Resolution] CCR, medical experts, financial experts, legal ethics experts, and representative asbestos plaintiffs' attorneys. Numerous exhibits were also submitted. The substance of the testimony covered, among other things: the decades-long history of asbestos litigation in the United States; the details of the handling of asbestos litigation in the current tort system; the negotiation and operation of the proposed settlement and various objections to certain of its provisions; the competence and adequacy of Class Counsel; the medical conditions caused by exposure to asbestos and the reasonableness of the medical criteria set forth in the settlement; the ability of the CCR defendants to meet their financial obligations under the Stipulation through insurance proceeds or otherwise; and the negotiation and operation of settlements reached between Class Counsel and the CCR defendants to settle in the present tort system the inventory of pending claims of clients represented by Class Counsel and their affiliated law firms.

* * *

The Settling Parties now urge this Court, pursuant to Fed.R.Civ.P. 23, to: (1) certify the class pursuant to Fed.R.Civ.P. 23(b)(3); (2) approve the proposed stipulation of settlement as fair, adequate, and reasonable; (3) conclude that Class Counsel adequately represented the class in the negotiation of the settlement and during the pendency of this action; and (4) approve the adequacy of the notice program as implemented by the settling parties.

* * *

CONCLUSIONS OF LAW

... [T]he Court makes the following conclusions of law.

* * *

III.   ADEQUACY OF COUNSEL

A.   *Legal Standard*

58.   Fed.R.Civ.P. 23(a)(4) provides that a class action may be maintained only if "the representative parties will fairly and adequately protect the interests of the class." Fed.R.Civ.P. 23(a)(4). This prerequisite to maintenance of a class action, and ultimately the entry of a final judgment, is essential to meet the due process standards that must be satisfied at all stages of a class action. 1 H. Newberg & A. Conte, NEWBERG ON CLASS ACTIONS § 3.21, at 3–125 (3d ed. 1992).

59.   Adequacy of representation requires that "the party's attorney be qualified, experienced and generally able to conduct the proposed litigation. Additionally, it is necessary to eliminate so far as possible the likelihood that the litigants are involved in a collusive suit or that [a representative] plaintiff has interests antagonistic to those of the remainder of the class." Eisen v. Carlisle & Jacquelin, 391 F.2d 555, 562

(2d Cir.1968). *See also* In re Fine Paper Antitrust Litigation, 617 F.2d 22, 27 (3d Cir.1980).

60. In deciding whether Class Counsel adequately represented the class here, and accordingly whether the class settlement should be approved, this Court must determine whether Class Counsel were burdened by an impermissible conflict of interest as they negotiated the *Georgine* Stipulation of Settlement or whether the settlement itself was the product of collusion. *See, e.g.,* In re Corrugated Container Antitrust Litig., 643 F.2d 195, 207–09 (5th Cir.1981); Mars Steel Corp. v. Continental Illinois Nat'l Bank & Trust Co. of Chicago, 834 F.2d 677 (7th Cir.1987).

61. "The ethical standards imposed upon attorneys in federal court are a matter of federal law." Bell Atlantic Corp. v. Bolger, 2 F.3d 1304, 1316 (3d Cir.1993). In the Third Circuit, the courts look to the Model Rules of Professional Conduct to furnish the appropriate ethical standard. *Id.*

62. As many courts have recognized in a variety of different contexts, however, "courts cannot mechanically transpose to class actions the rules developed in the traditional lawyer-client setting context ..." In re Corn Derivatives Antitrust Litig., 748 F.2d 157, 163 (3d Cir.1984)(Adams, J. concurring); Rand v. Monsanto Co., 926 F.2d 596, 601 (7th Cir.1991)(vacating a district court ruling that plaintiff was an inadequate class representative because he refused to advance the costs of litigation in violation of the Model Code); In re Agent Orange Prod. Liab. Litig., 800 F.2d 14, 18 (2d Cir.1986)(refusing to disqualify two appellate attorneys who had represented parties supporting the class settlement in the district court and then represented Objectors on appeal, on the ground that "[a]utomatic application of the traditional principles governing disqualification of attorneys on grounds of conflict of interest" would have a serious adverse effect on class actions.) *See also* 3 NEWBERG ON CLASS ACTIONS, § 15.01 at 15–3 ("The class action device was designed to serve unique purposes. Categorical application of ethical precepts developed for the individual action, without accommodation of the fundamental goals of the class action rule, dilutes both the ethical standards and the effectiveness of class litigation.")

63. Thus, it is appropriate for this Court to consider the Model Rules in determining the adequacy of representation, but ultimately it is this Court's task to determine whether, in the context of this litigation, Class Counsel were vigorous and diligent in negotiating the Georgine Stipulation, unburdened by any conflicts of interest or collusion * * *.

B. *Conflict of Interest*

64. In this case, Objectors contend that Class Counsel had an impermissible conflict of interest, in violation of Model Rule 1.7(b), which adversely affected the Georgine settlement. Model Rule 1.7(b) provides: A lawyer shall not represent a client if the representation of that client may be materially limited by the lawyer's responsibilities to another client or to a third person, or by the lawyer's own interests,

unless: (1) the lawyer reasonably believes the representation will not be adversely affected; and (2) the client consents after consultation. When representation of multiple clients in a single matter is undertaken, the consultation shall include explanation of the implications of the common representation and the advantages and risks involved.

65. Model Rule 1.7(b) proscribes any concurrent representation where that representation "may be materially limited by an" ongoing representation. As set forth in the comments to the Model Rule: A possible conflict does not itself preclude the representation. The critical questions are the likelihood that a conflict will eventuate and, if it does, whether it will materially interfere with the lawyer's independent professional judgment in considering alternatives or foreclose courses of action that reasonably should be pursued on behalf of the client. Consideration should be given to whether the client wishes to accommodate the other interest involved. ABA Model Rules at 28. *See also* Hazard and Hodes, THE LAW OF LAWYERING § 1.7:301, at 246 (Supp. 1993)("[S]ince only 'material' limitations trigger operation of the bar, Rule 1.7(b) forces a case-specific inquiry into the precise effect that a particular combination of conflicting responsibilities might engender. It is for this reason that Rule 1.7(b) can be said to contemplate a balancing process, rather than a firm rule.")

66. As discussed in the above Findings of Fact, five expert witnesses have testified in this proceeding as to whether Class Counsel were burdened by any impermissible conflicts of interest in negotiating the *Georgine* settlement. Professors Hazard, Freeman, and Dash testified that there were none. Professors Cramton and Koniak testified to the contrary. * * * Because the issue is a mixed question of fact and law for the Court to decide, this Court may be guided by the expert testimony, but is not bound by it. *See, e.g.,* In re Solerwitz, 848 F.2d 1573, 1578 (Fed. Cir.1988)(in a disciplinary proceeding, court "reviewed the testimony of the three experts and their conclusions regarding the propriety of [the attorney's] conduct," but court made clear "it is this court and not [the attorney's] experts that must determine whether [the attorney's] conduct was improper.")

67. At the time that Class Counsel negotiated what became the *Georgine* settlement, there was no attorney-client relationship between Class Counsel and the unformed *Georgine* class. Class Counsel nevertheless had a fiduciary responsibility to this putative class, that is, a duty of loyalty and a duty of due care. *See* 2 NEWBERG ON CLASS ACTIONS, § 11.65, at 11–183 ("The general rule is that the named plaintiff and counsel bringing the action stand as fiduciaries for the entire class, commencing with the filing of a class complaint."). *See also* Greenfield v. Villager Industries, Inc., 483 F.2d 824, 832 (3d Cir.1973)("[C]lass action counsel possess, in a very real sense, fiduciary obligations to those not before the court."). Thus, whether or not Model Rule 1.7(b) technically applies to this Court's determination, this Court concludes that the general principles of loyalty and due care are applicable here.

68. Having carefully considered the testimony of Professors Hazard, Freeman, and Cramton, * * * and the record in this case as a whole, this Court concludes that Class Counsel's representation of the *Georgine* class was not materially limited by their representation of present clients with pending claims against the CCR defendants. Thus, the concurrent representation of present claimants, while negotiating the *Georgine* settlement, ultimately resulting in settlement terms for present clients that differed from the terms of *Georgine*, did not create an impermissible conflict of interest under Model Rule 1.7(b), or otherwise, and Class Counsel were not burdened with any such conflict throughout the negotiation of the Georgine settlement.

69. The settlement philosophy adopted by the CCR defendants in 1992 was an outgrowth of years of experience in the tort system and rational defense concerns about the growth and character of the litigation. There was nothing impermissible in the effort of CCR to reach a global solution of the asbestos litigation encompassing both present and future claims. In fact, CCR's settlement position was consistent with the urging of the federal judiciary that private parties seek to find a global solution to the litigation.

70. The settlement position of CCR was not unlike that of the defendant railroad in Holden v. Burlington Northern, Inc., 665 F.Supp. 1398 (D.Minn.1987). *Holden* was an employment discrimination class action lawsuit in which class counsel had been litigating against the defendant, in other employment litigation, for "approximately ten years." * * * There the "objectors contend[ed] the resolution of matters other than *Holden*, along with Holden, evidences a conflict of interest." * * * The *Holden* Court noted that there, as here, the fact that the defendant was interested in a global resolution of all the litigation was no secret to the parties, the Objectors, or to the Court. * * * The Court then held that it found "no necessary conflict in resolving matters other than Holden concurrently with Holden. Early on in the negotiation process the Court recognized that any settlement of Holden, if one could be attained, would have had to include a global settlement of all matters involving [class counsel] and [the defendant railroad]. . . . [A] proposed settlement consisting of anything less than a settlement of all matters . . . could never have been accomplished." * * *

71. In this case, as in *Holden,* the CCR defendants' settlement posture was well-known to the plaintiffs' and defense bars and the courts. Further, given the history of this litigation, as in *Holden,* CCR's settlement position was not unreasonable. * * * Accordingly, Class Counsel did not have an inherent conflict of interest in seeking to negotiate a futures settlement while concurrently settling their present inventory of cases with CCR provided they, as experienced asbestos litigators, reasonably believed the settlements were fair, reasonable and in the best interests of both the putative class and their present clients. This Court concludes that Class Counsel did indeed make these reasoned judgments and reasonably decided in favor of settling.

72. Class Counsel were not required to withdraw from the representation of their current clients in order to undertake the *Georgine* negotiations, as suggested by Professor Cramton. Such a step was not only not feasible, but would have prejudiced the representation of the present clients. Moreover, it was the very fact that Class Counsel represented such a substantial number of present clients, as leaders of the asbestos bar, that made them credible and appropriate counsel to negotiate on behalf of an inchoate futures class. *Cf.* Bowling v. Pfizer, Inc., 143 F.R.D. 141, 160 (S.D.Ohio 1992)(Objectors complained that class counsel had insufficient experience in litigating heart valve cases, and, as a result, additional counsel were named who had substantial experience in the litigation. On this basis the Court concluded that the interests of the class were adequately protected.).

73. The negotiations of the *Georgine* settlement and the present inventory settlements were both the product of arm's length, good faith bargaining. * * * In hindsight, those not participating in the negotiation process can always criticize specific settlement terms or assert that other terms should have been included in the settlement. The fact, however, that a settlement did not achieve all that others may have hoped for does not support the conclusion that the lawyers were burdened by an impermissible conflict of interest in negotiating that settlement. In the words of the Fifth Circuit: "It is, ultimately, in the settlement terms that the class representatives' judgment and the adequacy of their representation is either vindicated or found wanting. If the terms themselves are fair, reasonable and adequate, the district court may fairly assume that they were negotiated by competent and adequate counsel; in such cases, whether another team of negotiators might have accomplished a better settlement is a matter equally comprised of conjecture and irrelevance." In re Corrugated Container Antitrust Litig., 643 F.2d 195, 212 (5th Cir.1981).[65]

74. Thus, for example, whether the settlement might have provided an adjustment for inflation over time or revision of medical criteria based upon changes in scientific thought are issues relating to the fairness of the settlement. * * * The fact that such provisions were not included in the Stipulation is not evidence that Class Counsel had a conflict which impaired their ability to represent the class.

75. Similarly, the fact that the *Georgine* class is defined as persons with occupational exposure who had not filed claims prior to January 15, 1993 does not create an impermissible conflict of interest by permitting class counsel to prefer certain claimants over others. * * * There is no evidence in this record that Class Counsel themselves actually used their knowledge of the forthcoming class action suit to file premature claims to avoid the class, or to refrain from filing and settling appropriate cases in order to ensure the viability of the class representatives.

65. *See also In re* Chicken Antitrust Litig., 669 F.2d 228, 236 n.15 (5th Cir. Unit B 1982)("Although there may be the potential for a conflict of interest to arise, it is best to avoid second guessing the judgment of counsel in settlement negotiations absent an actual conflict of interest which renders effective representation impossible.").

76. The fact that the inventory settlements included terms that differed from the terms of the *Georgine* settlement also does not reveal an impermissible conflict of interest. Present clients in the tort system are not identically situated to future claimants. They already have engaged a lawyer, they already have made or committed to expenditures, have a place in the trial queue and have expectations of a certain course of proceedings. The relevant question is not whether the terms of the *Georgine* settlement are identical to the terms of settlements in the past, but whether, given all the circumstances, the terms of *Georgine* are fair and reasonable. *See, e.g.,* M. Berenson Co. v. Faneuil Hall Marketplace, Inc., 671 F.Supp. 819, 824 (D.Mass.1987)(approving class action settlement that provided different terms for present tenants than for former tenants, and holding that "I find that the division of the plaintiff class set out in the agreement . . . was reasonable and appropriate, and fairly reflects the reality of the business situation presented by this lawsuit.").

77. The Objectors cite to two cases in support of their contention that Class Counsel were burdened by an impermissible conflict of interest: Fiandaca v. Cunningham, 827 F.2d 825 (1st Cir.1987) and Lewis v. National Football League, 146 F.R.D. 5 (D.D.C.1992). These cases are distinguishable from this case. In *Fiandaca,* lawyers for a class of female prisoners were seeking a new facility for their incarceration. The state offered to provide a facility which was then housing another class of individuals also represented by the same counsel. It was not in the interest of the second class for the female inmates to inhabit their building, thus creating a direct conflict of interest for the class counsel. No such conflict is presented in this case where present and future claimants are both seeking compensation for their injuries from the defendants, but there is no limited fund from which this compensation is to be paid. Similarly, in *Lewis,* a law firm was found to have a conflict of interest where it sought to represent a putative class of football players while the law firm, at the same time, was representing the player's association in a lawsuit against at least 20 individual members of the plaintiff class. In *Lewis,* there was direct adversity creating the impermissible conflict. There is no such adversity here.

78. The fact that, in 1992, CCR approached Mr. Motley, Mr. Rice, and Mr. Locks to see whether they were willing to embark again on an effort to reach a global settlement, after the dissolution of the MDL negotiations, does not support the conclusion that Class Counsel had a conflict of interest. Given the history of the asbestos litigation and the prior settlement efforts, there was nothing about this procedure that created a conflict of interest here. Mr. Motley and Mr. Locks were the Co-chairs of the Plaintiffs' Steering Committee in the MDL. All three Class Counsel were unquestionably experienced, highly respected leaders of the plaintiffs' asbestos bar. * * * Indeed, counsel for Objectors forthrightly stated that they were not challenging the qualifications or experience of Class Counsel. If CCR wanted to succeed in reaching a global settlement that a Court would approve, they had no choice but to hope to negotiate with such counsel.

79. The procedure followed here was not unlike the settlement procedure reviewed by the Court of Appeals for the Third Circuit in Ace Heating & Plumbing Co. v. Crane Co., 453 F.2d 30, 33 (3d Cir.1971). *Ace Heating* involved a settlement of a nationwide class of plumbing, mechanical and general contractor claimants in antitrust litigation. The defendants there attempted to negotiate a settlement with an ad-hoc plaintiffs' committee. After that effort reached an impasse, the defendants began settlement talks with another plaintiffs' attorney. The Court recognized that this procedure, where a lawyer "unofficially represents the class during settlement negotiations," can result in plaintiffs' counsel being "under strong pressure to conform to the defendants' wishes." * * * In these circumstances, where a settlement is not negotiated by a "court designated class representative the court must be doubly careful in evaluating the fairness of the settlement to plaintiff's class." * * * In *Ace Heating,* the Court, applying this heightened scrutiny, nevertheless concluded that the plaintiffs' negotiating counsel had effectively represented the class and that the settlement was fair. * * * Thus, applying the *Ace Heating* analysis to the Georgine settlement, this Court concludes that the fact that CCR chose to negotiate with Messrs. Locks, Motley and Rice, who had not yet been designated as class counsel but who were publicly known to be accountable as co-lead counsel in the MDL proceedings or in other high profile cases, does not support a claim of ineffective representation or conflict of interest. *See also* Bowling v. Pfizer, 143 F.R.D. 141, 157 (S.D.Ohio 1992)(a settlement was not "flawed because settlement preceded class certification").

C. The Futures Provisions in the Inventory Settlements

80. Model Rule 5.6(b) provides: A lawyer shall not participate in offering or making:

. . . . .

(b) an agreement in which a restriction on the lawyer's right to practice is part of the settlement of a controversy between private parties.

81. Objectors contend that the futures provisions in the inventory settlement agreements violate this Model Rule and that this violation is evidence that Class Counsel had an impermissible conflict of interest.

82. The January 14, 1993 agreement and the August, October, and December 1992 letter agreements were superseded by the June 11, 1993 agreement and the July 9, 1993 letter agreement, respectively. * * * This Court has already found that counsel intended to act ethically and that these agreements do not violate Model Rule 5.6(b) in that they do not factually create a binding obligation on the part of Class Counsel not to represent clients who may wish to sue CCR but who did not yet meet the Georgine medical criteria. * * * Rather, the provisions represent a good faith commitment on the part of Class Counsel to recommend the Georgine medical criteria to their clients while retaining their independence to conclude otherwise in an appropriate case. * * *

83. This Court need not decide, however, whether or not a state bar disciplinary board would conclude that these provisions technically violated Rule 5.6, since that issue is not before this Court in determining the adequacy of counsel. *See, e.g.,* Rand v. Monsanto Co., 926 F.2d 596, 600, 601 (7th Cir.1991); Coles v. Marsh, 560 F.2d 186, 189 (3d Cir. 1977)(both held that while various provisions of the Model Rules are useful as guides in assessing adequacy of counsel, they should not be so rigidly applied as to subvert the use of the class action device).

84. What is significant for this proceeding is that the futures provisions did not have any adverse or improper impact on the *Georgine* class. Based on the Findings of Fact, this Court concludes that the futures provisions did not restrict Class Counsel's negotiation of the *Georgine* Stipulation, they were superseded by subsequent provisions which did not restrict Class Counsel in their practice of law in any way, and they did not create an impermissible conflict of interest for Class Counsel. * * *

* * *

F. Conclusion

91. This Court concludes that Class Counsel as highly competent, skilled and experienced members of the plaintiffs' asbestos bar, were exceedingly well qualified to serve as Class Counsel in this case and, based upon the foregoing findings of fact and conclusions of law, that they acted ethically and appropriately in negotiating the *Georgine* settlement, unburdened by any conflicting interests; that the *Georgine* settlement was not the product of fraud or deceit and, therefore, was not the product of collusion; and that Class Counsel vigorously and diligently negotiated this class action settlement in the best interests of the *Georgine* class members.

* * *

In sum, this settlement is a fair solution for these parties to a problem that left alone would cause unfair results for the asbestos victims and predictably unfortunate financial downfall for these defendants. Just as the CCR defendants have an interest in the fair compensation of all victims of asbestos disease as a result of exposure to their products, asbestos victims who are in this class have an interest in the continued financial viability of the defendant companies so that they will receive historically-based values for their claims. The settlement approved here resolves these concerns.

An appropriate Order follows.

* * *

Notes and Questions

1. ABA Model Rule of Professional Conduct 5.6 provides:

Rule 5.6 Restrictions on Right to Practice

A lawyer shall not participate in offering or making:

(a) a partnership or employment agreement that restricts the rights of a lawyer to practice after termination of the relationship, except an agreement concerning benefits upon retirement; or

(b) an agreement in which a restriction on the lawyer's right to practice is part of the settlement of a controversy between private parties.

In April 1993, the American Bar Association issued Formal Opinion 93–371, which set the stage for the ethical controversy in the *Georgine* settlement class. Was Judge Reed correct in assessing the futures conflict in *Georgine?*

Formal Opinion 93–371
Restrictions on the Right to Represent Clients in the Future
April 16, 1993

A restriction on the right of plaintiffs' counsel to represent present clients and future claimants against a defendant as part of a global settlement of some of counsel's existing clients' claims against that same defendant represents an impermissible restriction on the right to practice which may not be demanded or accepted without violating Model Rule 5.6(b).

The pressure to find creative solutions to mass tort litigation has prompted an inquiry regarding the propriety of a lawyer entering into a settlement agreement with an opposing party pursuant to which the lawyer may be obligated to refuse to represent certain present clients as well as other similarly situated individuals against the same defendant in the future. The issues raised are important ones which the Committee has never addressed in this context.

The specific facts of the present inquiry involve a defendant in mass tort litigation approaching the plaintiffs' law firm and requesting that the firm enter into a global settlement agreement that would include not only all present cases handled by the firm against that defendant, but all future cases the firm would handle against the defendant as well. The global settlement agreement would contain predetermined settlement amounts to be offered to the firm's clients depending on the severity of each client's impairment. The defendant would be required to pay the predetermined amount if the client accepted it. If the client did not accept it, the case would either proceed to litigation, or be placed in a "deferred docket." [1]

---

1. Deferred dockets are inactive dockets where cases would be filed for clients whose injuries were at a predetermined minimal level; the cases would not advance toward trial unless the client developed additional objective evidence of impairment as per the terms of the global settlement. The firm's future clients would also be subject to the conditions set forth in the global settlement regarding the deferred docket.

"Deferred docket" has been defined as follows:

[A]n inactive docket system for those plaintiffs diagnosed as having only slight evidence of asbestos related disease * * * the registry would provide a method whereby plaintiffs, who showed only some small sign of asbestos-related injury but who were forced to file a claim in

The global settlement agreement would have an "escape hatch" feature which would permit individual cases to be removed from the deferred docket and individually adjudicated. The number of such cases would be limited to a percentage of the total number of cases in the deferred docket. If the percentage of clients who refused to be placed on the deferred docket exceeded the percentage allowed under the global settlement agreement, the firm would be obligated to refuse to represent these opt-out clients whether they were clients of the firm at the time the settlement was reached or became clients of the firm thereafter.

The question presented for Committee consideration is whether, in the context of mass tort or other class action litigation, the lawyer can ethically agree, as a condition of settlement, to refrain from representing either present clients or potential future clients who would trigger the excess percentage figure.

This inquiry raises important issues regarding the intersection between a lawyer's duty to his or her present clients under Model Rule 1.2 and impermissible restrictions on the right of a lawyer to practice under Model Rule 5.6.

Restriction on the Right to Represent Clients in the Future

The question presented is whether the lawyer may accept as a condition of the global settlement a restriction on his right to represent some of his present clients who will wish to use his services for individual adjudication as well as individuals who in the future seek to become his clients against this defendant. For purposes of this discussion, we assume that a settlement offer of this sort is in the interest of some, and perhaps even most, of the lawyer's present clients * * *. Indeed, it may be that part of the reason these present clients are able to obtain particularly favorable terms is the fact that the defendant is willing to offer more consideration than it might otherwise offer in order to secure the covenant from the attorney not to represent other present clients as well as future claimants. Thus, if, as expected, most, if not all, of the present clients view the settlement offer with favor, following the injunction of Rule 1.2, the lawyer normally would be required to abide by the client's instructions to accept the settlement offer.[3]

However, Model Rule 1.2 is not dispositive of this issue. Model Rule 5.6 must also be considered. Model Rule 5.6(b) provides:

A lawyer shall not participate in offering or making:

order to preserve their rights, could defer their cause of action to such time, if ever, that their condition progressed to disability. *In Re Asbestos Cases,* 586 N.E.2d 521, 522 (Ill.App.1991).

3. Rule 1.2(a) states in relevant part:

A lawyer shall abide by a client's decision whether to accept an offer of settlement of a matter.

The Comment to the Rule states in relevant part:

Both lawyer and client have authority and responsibility in the objectives and means of representation. The client has ultimate authority to determine the purposes to be served by legal representation, within the limit imposed by law and the lawyer's professional obligations.

(b) an agreement in which a restriction on the lawyer's right to practice is part of the settlement of a controversy between private parties.

The Comment makes explicit how the rule is applicable to the present situation. Paragraph (b) prohibits a lawyer from agreeing not to represent other persons in connection with settling a claim on behalf of a client.

Disciplinary Rule DR 2–10(b) of the Model Code of Professional Responsibility similarly states as follows:

> In connection with the settlement of a controversy or suit, a lawyer shall not enter into an agreement that restricts his right to practice law.

In comparing these provisions, it is instructive to note that when Model Rule 5.6 is read in conjunction with Model Rule 8.4(a) [4] the scope of the prohibition applies, not only to a lawyer agreeing to the restriction, but also to a lawyer offering or requiring the restriction.

The rationale of Model Rule 5.6 is clear. First, permitting such agreements restricts the access of the public to lawyers who, by virtue of their background and experience, might be the very best available talent to represent these individuals. Second, the use of such agreements may provide clients with rewards that bear less relationship to the merits of their claims than they do to the desire of the defendant to "buy off" plaintiff's counsel. Third, the offering of such restrictive agreements places the plaintiff's lawyer in a situation where there is conflict between the interests of present clients and those of potential future clients. While the Model Rules generally require that the client's interests be put first, forcing a lawyer to give up future representations may be asking too much, particularly in light of the strong countervailing policy favoring the public's unfettered choice of counsel.

Given the important public policies reflected in Rule 5.6, the Committee believes that the injunction of Rule 1.2 that the lawyer shall abide a client's decision regarding settlement must be read as limited by the provisions of Rule 5.6(b) and, as a result, a lawyer cannot agree to refrain from representing present or future clients against a defendant pursuant to a settlement agreement on behalf of current clients even in the mass tort, global settlement context.

* * *

Conflicts Among Present Clients

Having addressed the issues raised by the proposed restrictions we should note that even if the restrictions on practice were permissible under the Model Rules, the hypothetical contains embedded in it a serious issue regarding conflicts of interest among present clients.

---

4. Rule 8.4 states in relevant part:

It is professional misconduct for a lawyer to:

(a) violate or attempt to violate the Rules of Professional Conduct, knowingly assist or induce another to do so, or do so through the acts of another * * *.

Under Model Rule 1.7(b) [5] a lawyer may not represent multiple co-plaintiffs under certain circumstances. The Comment to 1.7(b) provides "[a]n impermissible conflict may exist by reason of * * * the fact that there are substantially different possibilities of settlement of the claims or liabilities in question."

Certainly that situation is presented here where among the lawyer's present clients are (a) individuals who wish to accept the present settlement, (b) individuals who wish to go on the deferred docket and might be perfectly happy to accept the predetermined amount established in the proposed settlement at a later date, and (c) individuals who either now or, after being on the deferred docket a period of time, wish to have their claims individually adjudicated. There may also be a conflict simply among the lawyer's clients in category (c). There are those who, because they indicate their desire for individual adjudication early, before the trigger percentage is reached, will have an opportunity to have their claim individually adjudicated being represented by the lawyer negotiating the global settlement. There also may be a second group who, because of the trigger, will not have benefit of that lawyer's representation. Indeed, it is difficult to understand how the lawyer can resolve the dilemma into which he would place his present clients in category (c). Assuming they really want the settling lawyer to handle their individual adjudications (a not surprising wish since he is, after all, their lawyer), then solely because of the arrangement counsel has struck, they will be torn between their wish to wait for individual adjudication until their cases are ripe and their need to get to adjudication early enough to avoid the trigger which would result in the loss of the lawyer's services.

Thus, we conclude that, for this independent reason, the lawyer may not proceed with the settlement on behalf of his present clients unless he resolves this conflict among them by seeking an appropriate waiver, if that is possible, or securing, with the clients' consent, alternative counsel for those whose interests differ from those who wish to pursue that portion of the global settlement which provides predetermined settlement amounts.

* * *

2. The *Georgine* settlement class raised a furor in the practising bar and academic community. A group of over forty law professors sought to file a brief amicus curiae in opposition to the settlement, which the court refused to accept. Should the academic community have been permitted to file an amicus brief on the ethical issues? In addition to the issue relating to the

---

5. Model Rule 1.7(b) states:

A lawyer shall not represent a client if the representation of that client may be materially limited by the lawyer's responsibilities to another client or to a third person, or by the lawyer's own interests, unless:

(1) the lawyer reasonably believes the representation will not be adversely affected; and

(2) the client consents after consultation. When representation of multiple clients in a single matter is undertaken, the consultation shall include explanation of the implications of the common representation and the advantages and risks involved.

future claimants, the objectors to the settlement also raised issues, other issues of conflict of interest relating to administration of the settlement, attorneys' fees, and collusion. At the fairness hearing, Judge Reed assessed the array of ethical issues based on the testimony of competing "ethics" experts. Why should the court hear retained, paid academic experts but exclude the amicus brief of non-retained academicians? Did Judge Reed have other alternatives? How should the court determine these issues? The *Georgine* settlement class was the subject of an academic conference during fall 1994 at Cornell University, which papers will be published in volume 80 (1995) of the *Cornell Law Review*. For articles specifically relating to the ethical issues raised by the Georgine settlement class, *see e.g.,* Roger C. Cramton, *Individualized Justice, Mass Torts, and "Settlement Class Actions": An Introduction,* 80 Cornell L.Rev. __ (1995); Susan Koniak, *Feasting While the Widow Weeps: Georgine v. Amvhem Products,* 80 Cornell L.Rev. __ (1995); Carrie J. Menkel–Meadow, *Ethics and the Settlement of Mass Torts: When the Rules Meet the Road,* 80 Cornell L.Rev. __ (1995); Judith Resnik, *Aggregation, Settlement and Dismay,* 80 Cornell L.Rev. __ (1995); Charles W. Wolfram, *Mass Torts—Messy Ethics,* 80 Cornell L.Rev. __ (1995).

3. The problem of the rights and adequate representation of future claimants is one of the most compelling issues in latent injury mass torts. In thinking about the problem of future claimants, what are the interests of the current plaintiffs, the defendants, counsel, and the future claimants? What procedural mechanisms best protect future claimants? What other means could have or should have been used to protect the interests of the *Georgine* future claimants? *See* Sylvia R. Lazus, Note, *Abuse in Plaintiff Class Action Settlements: The Need for a* Guardian Ad Litem *During Pre-Trial Settlement Negotiations,* 84 Mich.L.Rev. 308 (1985); *see also* Elizabeth R. Kaczynski, Comment, *The Inclusion of Future Members in Rule 23(b)(2) Class Actions,* 85 Colum.L.Rev. 397 (1985); Alan B. Morrison and Brian Wolfman, *Representing the Unrepresented in Class Actions Seeking Monetary Relief* (forthcoming 1995).

4. Judge Jack Weinstein has published the most definitive study on ethical issues in mass tort, including a discussion of the future claimant problem and the issue of illegal "lock-out" agreements. *See* Jack B. Weinstein, *Ethical Dilemmas in Mass Tort Litigation,* 88 Nw.U.L.Rev. 469 (1994); *see also* Geoffrey C. Hazard Jr., *Reflections on Judge Weinstein's Ethical Dilemmas in Mass Tort Litigation,* 88 Nw.U.L.Rev. 569 (1994); Thomas W. Henderson & Tybe A. Brett, *A Trial Lawyer's Commentary on One Jurist's Musing of the Legal Occult: A Response to Judge Weinstein,* 88 Nw.U.L.Rev. 592 (1994); Linda S. Mullenix, *Mass Tort as Public Interest Law: Paradigm Misplaced,* 88 Nw.U.L.Rev. 579 (1994)(responding to Judge Weinstein).

5. For other discussions of ethical issues in class action litigation, *see* Paul Bergman, *Class Action Lawyers: Fools for Clients,* 4 Am.J.Trial Advoc. 243 (1980); Robert A. B. Bush, *My Brother's Keeper—Some Observations on Federal Rule 23 Mass Tort Class Actions in the United States,* 5 Civ.J.Q, 109 (1986); Theresa A. Gabaldon, *Free Riders and the Greedy Gadfly: Examining Shareholder Litigation as An Exercise in Integrating Ethical Regulation and Laws of General Applicability,* 73 Minn.L.Rev. 425 (1988); Bryant G. Garth, *Conflict and Dissent in Class Actions: A Suggested Perspective,* 77

Nw.U.L.Rev. 492 (1982); Mary Kay Kane, *Of Carrots and Sticks: Evaluating the Role of the Class Action Lawyer*, 66 Tex.L.Rev. 385 (1987); Neil L. Rock, Note, *Class Action Counsel as Named Plaintiff: Double Trouble*, 56 Forham L.Rev. 111 (1987); Marjorie A. Silver, *Giving Notice: An Argument for Notification of Putative Plaintiffs in Complex Litigation*, 66 Wash.L.Rev. 775 (1991); Joan Steinman, *The Party Status of Absent Plaintiff Class Members: Vulnerability to Counterclaims*, 69 Geo.L.J. 1171 (1981); Alan Strudler, *Mass Torts and Moral Principles*, 11 L. & Phil. 297 (1992); Richard H. Underwood, *Legal Ethics and Class Actions: Problems, Tactics, and Judicial Response*, 71 Ky.L.J. 787 (1983).

*

Part Two

MASS TORT LITIGATION AND THE FAILURE OF THE PROCEDURAL SYSTEM

Chapter II

PROBLEMS RELATING TO PRETRIAL PROCEDURE

A. THE CLASS ACTION RULE AND MASS TORTS

SUPPLEMENTARY NOTE OF THE ADVISORY COMMITTEE REGARDING THIS RULE, 1966 AMENDMENT

Subdivision (b)(3). * * * The court is required to find, as a condition of holding that a class action may be maintained under this subdivision, that the questions common to the class predominate over the questions affecting individual members. It is only where this predominance exists that economies can be achieved by means of the class-action device. In this view, a fraud perpetrated on numerous persons by the use of similar misrepresentations may be an appealing situation for a class action, and it may remain so despite the need, if liability is found, for separate determination of the damages suffered by individuals within the class. On the other hand, although having some common core, a fraud case may be unsuited for treatment as a class action if there was material variation in the representations made or in the kinds or degrees of reliance by the persons to whom they were addressed. * * * A "mass accident" resulting in injuries to numerous persons is ordinarily not appropriate for a class action because of the likelihood that significant questions, not only of damages but of liability and defenses of liability, would be present, affecting the individuals in different ways. In these circumstances an action conducted nominally as a class action would degenerate in practice into multiple lawsuits separately tried. *See* Pennsylvania R.R. v. United States, 111 F.Supp. 80 (D.N.J.1953); *cf.* Weinstein, *Revision of Procedure: Some Problems in Class Actions,* 9 Buffalo L.Rev. 433, at 469. Private damage claims by numerous individuals arising out of concerted antitrust violations may or may not involve predominating common questions. * * *

1. PROBLEMS WITH RULE 23(a) PREREQUISITES

IN RE NORTHERN DISTRICT OF CALIFORNIA, DALKON SHIELD IUD PRODUCTS LIABILITY LITIGATION

United States Court of Appeals, Ninth Circuit, 1982.
693 F.2d 847.

Before GOODWIN, ANDERSON and SCHROEDER, CIRCUIT JUDGES. GOODWIN, CIRCUIT JUDGE.

Plaintiffs appeal from a district court order conditionally certifying their claims as: (1) a nationwide class action on the issue of punitive damages pursuant to Federal Rule of Civil Procedure 23(b)(1)(B); and (2) a statewide (California) class action on the issue of liability pursuant to Rule 23(b)(3). In re Northern District of California "Dalkon Shield" IUD Products Liability Litigation, 521 F.Supp. 1188 (N.D.Cal.1981); 526 F.Supp. 887 (N.D.Cal.1981).

All plaintiffs claim to have been injured by the Dalkon Shield intrauterine device. All of those plaintiffs who have joined in this appeal challenge class certification. Defendant A.H. Robins also opposes certification of the California 23(b)(3) class. Defendant Hugh J. Davis opposes certification of both classes.

Between June 1970 and June 1974, approximately 2.2 million Dalkon Shields were inserted in women in the United States. Many users sustained injuries. Complaints include uterine perforations, infections, ectopic and uterine pregnancies, spontaneous abortions, fetal injuries and birth defects, sterility, and hysterectomies. Several deaths also were reported. On June 28, 1974, Robins withdrew the Dalkon Shield from the market.

By May 31, 1981, approximately 3,258 actions relating to the Dalkon Shield had been filed, and 1,573 claims were pending. The claims are based on various theories: negligence and negligent design, strict products liability, breach of express and implied warranty, wanton and reckless conduct, conspiracy, and fraud. Most plaintiffs seek both compensatory and punitive damages.

Some plaintiffs joined Robins, Davis, and Irwin W. Lerner as defendants, as well as their own doctors or medical practitioners who recommended and inserted the Dalkon Shield, and local suppliers. Many plaintiffs sued fewer defendants.

In 1975 all actions then pending in federal district courts alleging damages from the use of the Dalkon Shield were transferred by the Judicial Panel on Multidistrict Litigation to the District of Kansas for consolidated pretrial proceedings * * *. After four years of consolidated discovery, the Judicial Panel began vacating its conditional transfer orders and remanded the cases to their respective transferor courts. * * *

State courts have also received a number of Dalkon Shield cases. The results have been mixed. Some plaintiffs have recovered substantial verdicts. Others have recovered nothing. Many cases have been settled.

Approximately 166 Dalkon Shield cases were pending in the Northern District of California. After one jury that lasted nine weeks, Judge Williams consolidated all Dalkon Shield cases pending in that district and ordered briefing on the feasibility of a class action. All but one of California plaintiffs' counsel opposed class certification. Out-of-state plaintiffs were not notified of the briefing request and did not participate in the status conferences held to discuss the class action proposal. All defendants at that time opposed class certification.

On June 25, 1981, Judge Williams entered an order conditionally certifying a nationwide class, under Fed.R.Civ.P. 23(b)(1)(B), consisting of all persons who filed actions for punitive damages against Robins. * * * Judge Williams also conditionally certified a California statewide subclass under Rule 23(b)(3) consisting of plaintiffs who have filed actions against Robins in California. This California class is limited to the question of Robins' liability arising from the manufacture and sale of the Dalkon Shield. Any plaintiff may opt out of this class, whereas all plaintiffs in the nation would be bound by the determination on punitive damages.

Plaintiffs from California, Oregon, Ohio, Florida, and Kansas moved to decertify the punitive damages class. The district court denied the motion and certified the issues for an interlocutory appeal, pursuant to 28 U.S.C. § 1292(b). This court granted the interlocutory appeals and ordered them expedited.

THE RULE 23(b)(1)(B) NATIONWIDE PUNITIVE DAMAGES CLASS

A. Rule 23(a) Prerequisites

1. Commonality.

The district court held that the punitive damages class presented common questions about Robins' knowledge of the safety of its product at material times while the Shield was on the market. What Davis, Lerner, and Robins knew about the Dalkon Shield, when they knew it, what information they withheld from the public, and what they stated in their advertising to doctors and in their product instructions during various time periods may all be common questions. These questions are not entirely common, however, to all plaintiffs.

Moreover, as the plaintiffs correctly argue, the 50 jurisdictions in which these cases arise do not apply the same punitive damages standards. Punitive damages standards can range from gross negligence to reckless disregard to various levels of willfulness and wantonness. If commonality were the only problem in this case, it might be possible to sustain some kind of a punitive damage class. But difficulties remain with other certification requirements.

2. Typicality.

Typicality, while it may not be insurmountable, remains a significant problem. The district court order recites that representative parties have been selected. *In Re Northern District of California "Dalkon Shield" IUD Products Liability Litigation,* 526 F.Supp. at 919. However, all of the appealing plaintiffs assert that no plaintiff has accepted the role, and that no single plaintiff or group of plaintiffs could be typical of the numerous persons who might have claims. No plaintiff has appeared in this appeal in support of class certification. Again, while typicality alone might not be an insurmountable problem, it helps make the overall situation difficult to rationalize as proper for class treatment.

3. Adequacy of Representation.

The court designated lead counsel for the nationwide class, but he has resigned. New counsel has been designated but has not yet started to represent the class. Apparently none of the attorneys already involved in the case is willing to serve as class counsel. The district judge may well be better able to choose a good lawyer than some of the plaintiffs may be, but the rights of litigants to choose their own counsel is a right not lightly to be brushed aside.

The plaintiffs argue that newly appointed, even if expert counsel, may not litigate the action as vigorously as counsel selected by plaintiffs. This court is hesitant to force unwanted counsel upon plaintiffs on the assumption that appointed counsel will be adequate. Even if the class were otherwise acceptable, it would have to be certified if adequate lead counsel turned out to[ ] be unavailable.

We are not necessarily ruling out the class action tool as a means for expediting multi-party product liability actions in appropriate cases, but the combined difficulties overlapping from each of the elements of Rule 23(a) preclude certification in this case.

MERVAK v. CITY OF NIAGARA FALLS

Supreme Court of New York, 1979.
101 Misc.2d 68, 420 N.Y.S.2d 687.

JOSEPH P. KUSZYNSKI, J.

Claimants, Stephen Joseph Mervak and Catherine Mervak, Harry and Lois Gibbs, individually and as parents and natural guardians of Michael Gibbs and Melissa Gibbs, infants, on behalf of themselves and hundreds of claimants who have filed notices of claim under section 50–e of the General Municipal Law against the City of Niagara Falls, New York, the County of Niagara, New York, and the Board of Education of the City of Niagara Falls, New York, seek in this Special Term proceeding a declaration that the notices of claim have been timely filed. In the alternative, petitioners seek permission pursuant to subdivision 5 of section 50–e of the General Municipal Law for late filing *nunc pro tunc.*

Involved here are about 900 environmental disaster claims filed on behalf of infants, disabled adults and estates of deceased persons wherein damages are sought in the aggregate in excess of $2,500,000,000 for personal injuries, wrongful deaths and diminishing real estate values. Claimants included in this petition are present residents, former residents, as well as transients who had only visited the area commonly known as the "Love Canal".

In their moving papers claimants state, by way of historical background, that the "Love Canal" is an aborted canal project in the City of Niagara Falls, New York, which was abandoned in 1910. In 1920, the partially excavated channel began to be used as a disposal site for highly toxic chemical waste from local industry and as a municipal dump site by the city. About 1953, the canal was completely filled and sold to the Board of Education of the City of Niagara Falls for $1 by the antecedent companies of the present Hooker Chemical Company.

The respondent school board erected an elementary school and a playground upon the site. The balance was sold and many homes were thereafter built in this area. Claimants recite that as of mid–1978, the ownership of the location was shared by the board, the city and homeowners.

Claimants further state that in early 1978, the federal and State Governments began investigating the causes of an abnormally high number of illnesses in the "Love Canal" neighborhood and on August 2, 1978 the New York State Commissioner of Health issued an order, declaring the existence of an emergency in the area contiguous to the canal between 97th and 99th Streets.

The commissioner based his order upon findings that toxic chemicals had leaked into the basements of homes bordering the canal, that children in the 9th Street school were being exposed to toxic chemical waste and that there existed abnormally high levels of spontaneous abortion and congenitally malformed babies born. The commissioner also declared that seven chemicals found had cancer producing qualities in animals and the eighth was a known human carcinogen.

On February 8, 1979 the State Commissioner of Health issued a further supplemental order expanding the area of danger beyond the original boundary. He ordered all families with pregnant females or with children under two years of age to be relocated from the area between 93rd and 103rd Streets. The commissioner also declared that one of the most deadly substances known to man, "dioxin," was present in the canal and that it had spread to surrounding areas via underground channels.

Counsel for the claimants have consolidated the applications into one motion on behalf of all their clients maintaining "the claimants herein are all similarly situated and have filed identical claims, there was no purpose for filing separate motions for each." Claimants cite August 2, 1978, the date the commissioner declared the emergency, as being the date when their causes of action accrued pointing out that, "Until then neither [the claimants] nor their physicians knew the cause of their injuries." Claimants urge upon this court that August 2, 1978 is therefore day "zero" when the 90–day requirement concerning the serving of notices of claim upon respondents begins to run.

* * *

Several issues are raised by claimants' application to this court. The first is whether a single notice of claim for personal injuries suffices on behalf of the many claimants under the circumstances present here in this environmental tort situation. The second is whether in a class action the issues can be determined concerning the timeliness of the notices of claim as well as the requests for permission, if the notices were untimely filed, to file out of time *nunc pro tunc* * * *. Section 50–e (subd 1, par [a]) of the General Municipal Law imposes a condition precedent to a suit brought against a public corporation requiring notice "within ninety days after the claim arises, or else barring such claims * * *." [The court's opinion then describes various exceptions and tolling provisions in the statutory scheme—*ed*.]

* * *

Claimants state in their application that a notice of claim was served upon respondents on October 30, 1978 on behalf of all the litigants in a class action which included the identical allegations contained in the claims now before the court. This is the premise upon which claimants base their assertion that all notices as filed should be considered timely. It appears that, subsequently, individual notices of claim were served on October 30, 1978 through July 16, 1979, the date when their petition was placed before the court.

Claimants submit "the circumstances surrounding these claims, are practically unique as opposed to the normal tort claim, [since] no date of personal injury can be known or alleged."

Respondents contend, on the other hand, that there are some 900 separate personal injury claims before this court, each having a different starting point. They resist claimants' stance that August 2, 1978, the proclamation date of an emergency by the State Commissioner of Health, marks the beginning point of the 90–day requirement. They contend a question of fact exists when each individual claim arose, because the date of the accrual of an action must be measured from the date of injury and not the date of discovery. Respondents maintain that the "claimants have dissimilar unique injuries occurring at dissimilar times and dissimilar places with totally dissimilar exposure."

They further argue that the statute provides that a public corporation be provided in the notice of claim with the specifics of an injury sustained by a claimant. Respondents question the sufficiency of the notices of claim because, "Nowhere * * * do the claimants allege or set forth the respective times of the happening or events upon which their respective claims are based."

In essence, claimants are seeking in this proceeding a declaratory judgment validating all notices of claim encompassed by this petition.

CPLR 901 allows for a class action where a question of law or fact common to the class predominates over any question of affecting only individual members. * * * Unlike the situation of an accident, disaster which brings about an injury, with a definite starting point from which to measure the "accrual of a cause of action", the claimed basis for the injuries here is exposure over a period of time to deadly toxic chemical wastes. The facts underlying these claims, filed on behalf of many, contain variables which prevent a blanket consideration of all the claims. Some claims concern residents who became ill years ago due to the exposure, while other claims were filed by recent visitors to the site who were there only once or twice. It is safe to say that no two claimants acquired the same disease at the same time. To establish a nexus between the exposure to toxic chemical wastes and the claimed injury, the following factors are to be considered: the commencement of exposure, the nature of the malady, and the date of diagnosis.

In claims for wrongful death, the filing of notices of claim is measured from the date of appointment of a representative of the estate, while the time to commence an action begins to run from the date of death * * *. No dates of death nor the dates of the appointments of the legal representatives are before this court.

* * *

The question of "timeliness" of a notice of claim which alleges personal injuries is not a subject matter for class action but one which must be dealt with on an individual case-by-case basis since the injuries are not identical and not incurred at the same time.

When a claimant seeks to file late, *nunc pro tunc*, the statute imposes a requirement that a claimant set forth, among other facts, the reason for the delay, the specifics of the claimed injury, and under the circumstances here present, the time of the acquisition of the disease. This data is absent in the submissions by claimants before this court. A more detailed amplification of the underlying facts of a claim as to each claimant must be made in order that a proper examination may be made of it timeliness, and if untimely, to consider the granting of permission for late filing.

It is not possible to determine the dates of accrual of each of the claims filed, without the benefit of individual hearings on the circumstances concerning each claim.

With respect to notices of claim filed for diminution of real estate values, it would appear that the claimant owners in this category are on more solid footing in claiming August 2, 1978 as the date when their causes of action had accrued. There is little doubt that real estate values in the "Love Canal" area plummeted [*sic*] downward upon the commissioner's declaration of an emergency.

Notes and Questions
NOTES ON THE ORIGINAL CLASS ACTION RULE, THE 1966 REVISION, AND MASS TORT LITIGATION

1. Prior to the enactment of the Federal Rules of Civil Procedure, class actions were available in federal courts under the equity rules. With the

federal merger of law and equity in 1938, class actions became available in both law and equity. The original Rule 23 provided for three categories of class actions: the "true," "hybrid," and "spurious" classes. Generally, true class actions captured cases involving "joint" or "common" rights; hybrid class actions captured litigation involving "several" rights; and the spurious class action captured cases involving common questions of law or fact involving "several rights." Approximately 25 years experience demonstrated the vagueness and disutility of these categories, and in the early 1960s the Advisory Committee on Civil Rules began redrafting the class action rule. The purpose of the rule revision was to eliminate the rule's categorical arbitrariness and to reduce the federal court's rigidity in the rule's application.

2. The 1966 amended rule reflects the dissatisfactions of the rule drafters with the original version, and their desire to substitute functional, descriptive categories for class action lawsuits (embodied in the three Rule 23(b) categories). To what extent do the (b) categories replicate their antecedents, and to what extent did the drafters succeed in supplying functional descriptions? Have the 1966 amendments to Rule 23 rendered it more or less useful for mass accident and mass tort cases? *See* American Bar Association, *Report and Recommendations of the Special Committee on Class Action Improvements,* 110 F.R.D. 195 (1986); *see also* Bruce H. Nielson, Note, *Was The 1966 Advisory Committee Rights?: Suggested Revisions of Rule 23 to Allow More Frequent Use of Class Actions in Mass Tort Litigation,* 25 Harv. J. Legis. 461 (1988). Are the *Dalkon Shield* and *Mervak* decisions good applications of class action threshold requirements? Were these litigations suitable for class action procedure? If these individual cases are not aggregated as class actions, what options are available to the litigants? If *Mervak* is good law, is it ever possible to assemble a class action mass tort?

3. The central conceptual feature of the class action litigation is that it is *representational* in nature. In the early twentieth-century, the Supreme Court decided the seminal case relating to the binding effect of judgments in class actions, Supreme Tribe of Ben–Hur v. Cauble, 255 U.S. 356, 41 S.Ct. 338, 65 L.Ed. 673 (1921). In that decision, the Court upheld the constitutionality of making binding a decree in a federal class action upon persons who are so situated as to be appropriately foreclosed. The Court stated: "Owing to the number of interested persons and the impossibility of bringing them all before the court, the original suit was peculiarly one that could only be prosecuted by a part of those interested suing for all in a representative suit." The theory of *Ben-Hur* was that members of a class could be bound to the outcome of the action, even though they did not directly participate in the litigation, because their interests in the common right litigated were indivisible. Therefore, in protecting their own interests, the representative automatically protected the interest of the entire class. But this is sound only as long as the representatives' interests and those of the class are common, indivisible, and not adverse. To what extent do the *Dalkon Shield* and *Mervak* decisions reflect of these concerns? *See generally,* Deborah Deitsch–Perez, Note, *Mechanical and Constitutional Problems in the Certification of Mandatory Multistate Mass Tort Class Actions Under Rule 23,* 49 Brook.L.Rev. 517 (1983); Andrew C. Rose, Comment, *Federal*

Mass Tort Class Actions: A Step Towards Equity and Efficiency, 47 Alb. L.Rev. 1180 (1983); Spencer Williams, *Mass Tort Class Actions: Going, Going Gone?,* 98 F.R.D. 323 (1983).

4. In Hansberry v. Lee, 311 U.S. 32, 61 S.Ct. 115, 85 L.Ed. 22 (1940), the Supreme Court held that Illinois had denied due process under the fourteenth amendment when it gave res judicata effect to an earlier state-court class action, though some members of the "class" were actually adverse in interest to the representative and to other members of the class. The first decree, purporting to be a class action, had held valid a restrictive covenant that falsely stipulated to have been signed by 95% of the owners in a real estate development, preventing the sale of housing to persons of the "colored race." A second state-court action was brought against a black person who had purchased from signers of the agreement or descendants in title from signers. The Illinois Supreme Court held that the first decree was res judicata, though it was based on a false stipulation. The United States Supreme Court reversed, holding that those property owners who opposed the restrictive covenant were not members of the class that sought to enforce it and could not adequately be represented by those who favored such a covenant. To give the first decree res judicata effect when its opponents were not represented would be to deny due process to the non-assenting property holders and later purchasers. Does this mean that it is unconstitutional to bind a member of a class who, after the judgment has been entered, decides that on the whole he or she would prefer not to be bound?

5. Due process concerns have received renewed attention in mass tort litigation, particularly in latent injury cases involving future claimants, as well as mandatory non-opt-out (b)(1)(B) hybrid classes. Are the requirements of Rule 23(a) sufficient to protect class members? Are the devices of notice in Rule 23(c), sub-classing in Rule 23(c)(4)(A), and settlement hearings in Rule 23(e) adequate to meet due process requirements and allay fairness concerns in mass tort litigation? Does the availability of Rule 24 intervention ameliorate some of these concerns? *See generally* Bryant G. Garth, *Conflict and Dissent in Class Actions, A Suggested Perspective,* 77 Nw. U.L.Rev 492 (1982); Diane W. Hutchinson, *Class Actions: Joinder or Representational Device?,* 1983 S.Ct. Rev. 459 (1983); Deborah Rhode, *Class Conflicts in Class Actions,* 34 Stan.L.Rev. 1183 (1982). The continued vitality of due process concerns has resurfaced as class action litigation relates to personal jurisdictional requirements and non-opt-out classes. *See* Phillips Petroleum Co. v. Shutts, 472 U.S. 797, 105 S.Ct. 2965, 86 L.Ed.2d 628 (1985) and Ticor Title Insurance Co. v. Brown, ___ U.S.___, 114 S.Ct. 1359, 128 L.Ed.2d 33 (1994). *See also* section D1, *infra.*

6. The representational nature of class action litigation also implicates personal jurisdiction, diversity and amount-in-controversy requirements for diversity-based class actions. These problems (as they arise in the class action context) are discussed in II.D., *infra.*

7. Has the 1966 amended Rule 23 achieved its goals or has it created more problems? *See* the Advisory Committee's Note of 1966 to Rule 23; Benjamin Kaplan, *Continuing Work of the Civil Committee: 1966 Amendments to the Federal Rules of Civil Procedure (II),* 81 Harv.L.Rev. 591 (1968).

In the early 1990s, the Advisory Committee on Civil Rules placed revision of Rule 23 on its agenda and the Committee is proceeding with another wholesale revision of the rule. Does mass tort litigation present special problems for class action procedure? If so, should the Advisory Committee address these special requirements in revising Rule 23? What changes need to be effectuated in order to render the class action rule a fair, just, and efficient vehicle for mass tort aggregative litigation? Are these matters for the Advisory Committee on Civil Rules, or for Congressional legislation?

8. The Advisory Committee's re-examination of Rule 23 in relation to mass torts has inspired academic commentary either advocating or criticizing various reform proposals. *See e.g.,* Robert G. Bone: *Rule 23 Redux: Empowering the Federal Class Action,* 14 Rev.Litig. 79 (1994)(comments on proposed revisions to Rule 23); Edward H. Cooper: *Rule 23: Challenges to the Rulemaking Process* (forthcoming 1995); Jonathan R. Macey & Geoffrey P. Miller, *A Market Approach to Tort Reform Via Rule 23,* 80 Cornell L.Rev. ___ (1995); Richard L. Marcus, *They Can't Do That, Can They? Tort Reform Via Rule 23,* 80 Cornell L.Rev. ___ (1995); David Rosenberg, *The Individualized Case for the Collectivized Resolution of Risk–Based Claims* (forthcoming 1995); Thomas D. Rowe, Jr., *Beyond the Class Action Rule: An Inventory of Statutory Possibilities to Improve Federal Class Actions* (forthcoming 1995).

9. For discussions of class action issues in mass tort generally, *see* Myron J. Bromberg & Anastasia P. Slowinski, *Pay or Play in Mass Torts: Alleviate Backlogs With An Expanded Court System or Joinder Methods for Mass Tort Cases,* 45 Rutgers L.Rev. 371 (1993); James W. Elrod, Comment, *The Use of Federal Class Actions in Mass Toxic Pollution Torts,* 56 Tenn. L.Rev. 243 (1988); Paul D. Rheingold, *Tort Class Actions: What They Can and Cannot Achieve,* Trial at 59 (Feb. 1990); Jack B. Weinstein & Eileen B. Hershenov, *The Effect of Equity on Mass Tort Law,* 1991 U.Ill.L.Rev. 269 (1991). *See also* Bryant G. Garth, *Studying Civil Litigation Through the Class Action,* 62 Ind.L.J. 497 (1987).

2. PROBLEMS WITH RULE 23(b) CLASSIFICATIONS

YANDLE et al. v. PPG INDUSTRIES, INC.

United States District Court, Eastern District of Texas, 1974.
65 F.R.D. 566.

STEGER, DISTRICT JUDGE.

This is a massive tort action brought by former employees and survivors of former employees of the Pittsburgh Corning Corporation asbestos plant that was located in Tyler, Texas. The question before the Court is whether this case should proceed as a class action under the provisions of Rule 23(b)(3). Before passing on this question, it will be necessary for the Court to review the background of this litigation and the law on the use of class actions in mass tort cases.

By the way of history, Pittsburgh Corning purchased the plant in question from Union Asbestos and Rubber Company and began operations in 1962, producing asbestos insulation materials. The plant continued operations over a ten year period through February of 1972, when it closed its doors forever. The records of Pittsburgh Corning Corporation show that during the plant's existence some 570 employees were exposed to asbestos dust and these employees may be broken down into the following categories. . . . These persons were employed in several different positions at the plant and they were, therefore, exposed to varying concentrations of asbestos dust during their periods of employment.

Suit was brought originally against nine defendants in January, 1974, by six former employees and one survivor of a former employee of Pittsburgh Corning on behalf of themselves and others similarly situated. These plaintiffs allege that due to exposure to asbestos fibers over a lengthy period of time that they "suffer from various stages of asbestosis and/or lung cancer and/or other pulmonary disease."

Different theories of recovery were asserted against the various defendants. Negligence is attributed to PPG Industries and Corning Glass Works for failing to correct the deficiencies at the Tyler plant and in failing to warn the employees of the danger of asbestos exposure. Additionally, plaintiffs contend that Dr. Lee Grant, as an agent or employee of PPG, knew the hazards posed to the workers' health, yet he failed to advise such workers of the hazards and was therefore negligent. Essentially the same allegations are made against the Industrial Health Foundation. As to the defendant, Asbestos Textile Institute, plaintiffs claim that this unincorporated association was negligent because it impeded the flow of information about the health hazards involved in asbestos manufacturing. These plaintiffs claim that all of these actions constituted gross negligence on the part of each defendant.

The plaintiffs assert a strict liability theory against North American Asbestos, E.G.N.E.P. Limited, and Cape Asbestos Company. They allege that these defendants were in the business of mining and selling raw amosite-asbestos to Pittsburgh Corning and they failed to warn the plaintiffs of the danger, thereby rendering them strictly liable. Finally, as to the plaintiffs' employer, Pittsburgh Corning, it is alleged that they are liable for exemplary damages under the Texas Workmen's Compensation Act to all statutory beneficiaries of deceased employees who died as a result of their alleged gross negligence. Plaintiffs allege total actual and exemplary damages for the class to be at least one hundred million dollars.

* * *

In passing upon the class action question presented herein, the Court will confine its discussion to the liability issues, since the plaintiffs appear to have conceded at the December 17, 1974, hearing on this question that the damage issues are not proper for class treatment because they require individualized determination.

* * *

Class actions have had limited application in the past in mass tort cases, partially due to the recommendation of the Advisory Committee on Rules. In its 1966 revision of Rule 23, the Advisory Committee stated:

" ... A 'mass accident's resulting in injuries to numerous persons is ordinarily not appropriate for a class action because of the likelihood that significant questions, not only of damages but of liability and defenses of liability, would be present, affecting the individuals in different ways. In these circumstances an action conducted nominally as a class action would degenerate in practice into multiple lawsuits separately tried. ...' " 28 U.S.C. Rule 23, Notes of Advisory Committee on Rules, 1966 Amendment.

The policy reasons for the disallowance of class actions in mass tort cases generally fall into three categories. First of all there is the general feeling that when personal injuries are involved that each person should have the right to prosecute his own claim and be represented by the lawyer of his choice. Secondly, that the use of this procedure may encourage solicitation of business by attorneys. And finally that individual issues may predominate because the tortfeasor's defenses may depend on facts peculiar to each plaintiff. 7A Wright and Miller, FEDERAL PRACTICE AND PROCEDURE, § 1783 (1972).

There are situations where the class action device may properly be used in mass accident cases, at least for the common questions that will apply to each class member equally. Thus, in Hernandez v. Motor Vessel Skyward, 61 F.R.D. 558 (S.D.Fla.1973), the Court utilized it to try a single issue only: Whether the defendant was negligent in preparing the food and water that caused the passengers on the M/V SKYWARD to become ill. The Court found that the plaintiff's other theories, breach of contract, negligence in medical care and implied warranty of fitness, as well as the question of proximate causation were not proper for class treatment. In American Trading and Production Corp. v. Fischbach & Moore, Inc., 47 F.R.D. 155 (N.D.Ill.1969), the Court allowed a class action to be maintained on the liability issues and reserved the damage questions for individual treatment. That case involved a suit by some 1200 exhibitors of housewares who suffered losses because of a fire at the exhibition hall. The Court said that class treatment would be proper on the liability issue because identical evidence would be required to establish the origin of the fire, the parties responsible, and proximate cause. A similar opinion was expressed by the Court in Petition of Gabel, 350 F.Supp. 624 (C.D.Cal.1972), a case which involved a collision between an airliner and a military jet. In that case the Court stated that the liability issues could expeditiously be treated as a class action because there was one common set of operative facts and a single wrongful invasion of a single primary right was involved. The damage issues were to be tried separately because there was "a peculiar and different set of facts applicable to the amount of damages of each different plaintiff in the class." 350 F.Supp. at 628.

Other courts facing this question have reached contrary conclusions and have refused to allow a class action to be maintained on any of the issues in the case. In Hobbs v. Northeast Airlines, Inc., 50 F.R.D. 76 (E.D.Pa.1970), some 32 persons were killed in an air crash which also left ten survivors. In deciding that common questions of law and fact did not predominate over questions affecting the individual members, the Court said:

> "But irrespective of similarities or dissimilarities in the legal standards to be applied to a particular defendant, it is clear that each claimant in this situation may properly be regarded as having a legitimate interest in litigating independently. Not only do the claims vitally affect a significant aspect of the lives of the claimants (unlike the usual class action, where individual claims are usually somewhat peripheral to the lives of the claimants), but there is a wide range of choice of the strategy and tactics of the litigation. Some claimants may well evaluate their chances against certain potential defendants as better than against others." 50 F.R.D. at 79.

The Court went on to say that the class action device would not be superior to other available methods because persons wishing to join the litigation could intervene if they wished and the case would proceed under the Multidistrict Litigation Statute. In a case which involved the crash of a school bus, the Court in Daye v. Commonwealth of Pennsylvania, 344 F.Supp. 1337 (E.D.Pa.1972), *aff'd,* 483 F.2d 294 (3d Cir.1973), held that although liability would be a common issue, that the cause could not be maintained as a class action. After taking note of the advisory committee recommendation on the use of class actions in mass accident cases, the Court concluded that in view of the fact that there were two actions presently pending and that there would be personal injury and death claims involving different measure of damages, a class action would be improper under Rule 23(b)(3). 344 F.Supp. at 1343. *See also* Boring v. Medusa Portland Cement Co., 63 F.R.D. 78 (M.D.Pa. 1974); Wright v. McMann, 321 F.Supp. 127, 137 (N.D.N.Y.1970), *modified* 460 F.2d 126 (2d Cir.1972).

In examining the case at bar, the Court is at first troubled by the jurisdictional problems which may arise in allowing this diversity case to proceed as a class action. In Zahn v. International Paper Co., 414 U.S. 291 (1973), the Supreme Court held that not only the named but also the unnamed potential class members must satisfy the jurisdictional amount. This Court is in agreement with the District Court in *Boring v. Medusa Portland Cement Co.,* that Rule 23 may be utilized in a diversity suit for damages only when all possible potential class members can satisfy the $10,000.00 jurisdictional requirements. This Court remains unconvinced that those employees who worked at the plant for a week or a month could affirmatively show that they have been damaged in an amount exceeding the requisite jurisdictional amount.

Setting this problem aside and assuming for the purpose of argument that the plaintiffs have established the four requirements set forth in Rule 23(a), the Court is of the opinion that this case is not proper for (b)(3) class certification because the plaintiffs have not shown that the questions common to the class predominate over the questions that affect the individual members. Further, the Court is of the opinion that a class action is simply not the superior method for adjudication of this cause.

THE COMMON QUESTIONS DO NOT PREDOMINATE

As noted previously, the Pittsburgh Corning plant was in operation in Tyler for a ten year period, during which some 570 persons were employed for different periods of time. These employees worked in various positions at the plant, and some were exposed to greater concentrations of asbestos dust than were others. Of these employees it is only natural that some may have had occupational diseases when they entered their employment for Pittsburgh Corning. There are other issues that will be peculiar to each plaintiff and will predominate in this case, such as: The employee's knowledge and appreciation of the danger of breathing asbestos dust and further, whether the employee was given a respirator and whether he used it or refused to use it. Additionally, as to the defendant, Pittsburgh Corning, the only persons who could maintain an action would be the survivors of employees who were employed by that company. These are individual questions peculiar to each potential class member. Additionally, the plaintiffs have asserted various theories of recovery against the defendants, and the nine defendants have alleged differing affirmative defenses against the plaintiffs. For example, the statute of limitations may bar some plaintiffs, but not others. During the ten year period the state of medical knowledge was changing, which has a significant bearing on the defendants' duty to warn of dangers. Taking all these factors into consideration, the Court is convinced that the number of uncommon questions of law and fact would predominate over the common questions, and the case would therefore "degenerate ... into multiple lawsuits separately tried." 28 U.S.C. Rule 23, Notes of Advisory Committee on Rules, 1966 Amendment.

This case is very different from the single mass accident cases that have in the past allowed a class action to proceed on the liability issues. Those cases have normally involved a single tragic happening which caused physical harm or property damage to a group of people, and affirmative defenses are absent. Usually, one set of operative facts will establish liability. Here we have two lawsuits covering a ten year span of time in which the nine defendants acted differently at different times. The Court is in agreement with the defendant that there is not a single act of negligence or proximate cause which would apply to each potential class member and each defendant in this case.

The plaintiffs placed great reliance at the hearing on this question on the case of Biechele v. Norfolk & Western Railway Co., 309 F.Supp.

354 (N.D.Ohio 1969), which they contended was very similar to the instant case because it involved a continuing tort over a period of years. In *Biechele* a group of landowners brought an action for injunctive relief and damages against the defendant for operating its coal loading facilities as a nuisance. At the outset, it should be noted that the *Biechele* Court did not have the Supreme Court's decision in *Zahn* when it rendered its opinion. This seriously limits the precedential value of the *Biechele* case. Further, the *Biechele* case was brought under the provisions of 23(b)(1) and (2) for damages and injunctive relief, unlike the present case which is a (b)(3) damage case only. In the *Biechele* case the Court began its inquiry by first assuming that the injunctive and damage claims were both certifiable class actions. *Boring v. Medusa Portland Cement Co.* After stating this, the Court concluded that it would assume jurisdiction over the principal claim, which was injunctive in nature, and then, in the interest of judicial efficiency, the Court found that it would retain jurisdiction over the damage claims. As was pointed out by the Court in *Boring,* "... the *Biechele* precedent nevertheless is based on discretionary jurisdiction applied if the court certifies the injunction as a class action." 63 F.R.D. at 83. There is no injunctive relief requested in this case.

A Class Action Is Not the Superior Method

There are several reasons why this Court feels that a class action would not be the superior method for adjudication of this cause. A class action certification would entail costly and time consuming notice procedures and record keeping on those who would wish to "opt-out." Further, because of the nature of the injuries claimed, there may be persons that might neglect to "opt-out" of the class, and then discover some years in the future that they have contracted asbestosis, lung cancer or other pulmonary disease. These persons would be bound by decision rendered in this litigation. Finally, the Court finds that the members of the purported class have a vital interest in controlling their own litigation because it involves serious personal injuries and death in some cases. *See Hobbs v. Northeast Airlines.* This is demonstrated by the fact that there are presently four sets of plaintiffs' attorneys in two ongoing cases and the plaintiffs in the *Kay* case strongly oppose the class action certification.

Conclusion

In conclusion, the Court is of the opinion that this case should not be certified as a class action under Rule 23(b)(3), because the questions of law or fact that are common to the class as a whole do not predominate over individual questions and further because the class action device is not the superior method for adjudicating the claims presented herein. The Court is of the opinion that the superior method for adjudication of this case is to continue allowing intervention freely for those who wish to join and to maintain firm control over this litigation by utilizing the tools set forth in the MANUAL FOR COMPLEX AND MULTIDISTRICT LITIGATION.

It is, therefore, ordered that the plaintiffs' Motion for Class Action Status be, and the same is hereby in all things denied, and that the class action allegations be stricken from the plaintiffs' complaints.

IN RE "AGENT ORANGE" PRODUCT LIABILITY LITIGATION

United States District Court, Eastern District New York, 1980.
506 F.Supp. 762.

GEORGE C. PRATT, DISTRICT JUDGE.

Plaintiffs, Vietnam war veterans and members of their families claiming to have suffered damage as a result of the veterans' exposure to herbicides in Vietnam,[1] commenced these actions against the defendant chemical companies. Defendants, seeking indemnification or contribution in the event they are held liable to plaintiffs, then served third party complaints against the United States. Five motions are now considered: (1) the government's motion to dismiss the third party complaint on grounds of sovereign immunity; (2) plaintiffs' motion for class action certification; (3) defendants' motion for summary judgment; (4) plaintiffs' motion to proceed with "serial trials," and (5) plaintiffs' motion to serve and file a fifth amended verified complaint.

I. SUMMARY OF CLAIMS

There are four groups of plaintiffs: Vietnam veterans, their spouses, their parents, and their children. They assert numerous theories of liability, including strict products liability, negligence, breach of warranty, intentional tort and nuisance. Plaintiff veterans seek to recover for personal injuries caused by their exposure to Agent Orange. The family members seek to recover on various derivative claims; some of the children assert claims in their own right for genetic injury and birth defects caused by their parents' exposure to the Agent Orange; and some of the veterans' wives seek to recover in their own right for miscarriages. In their third party complaints against the government defendants allege negligence, misuse of product, post-discharge failure to warn, implied indemnity, denial of due process and failure to comply with herbicide registration laws.

* * *

III. THE CASE MANAGEMENT PLAN

There have been pending for some time motions by various parties urging the court to make various orders affecting the overall management of this action, including such matters as class action treatment, summary judgment, discovery, and division of the action into various parts for pretrial and trial purposes. The court has reserved decision on all these motions pending resolution of two major questions that greatly

---

1. Plaintiffs' complaints allege injury as a result of their exposure to a variety of herbicides including Agents Orange, Pink, Purple and Green. For convenience, the court will refer to these herbicides collectively as "Agent Orange".

affect how the case might be managed efficiently: (1) whether the United States was to be a party to the action, and (2) whether jurisdiction lies under federal common law or whether the principles and consequences of diversity jurisdiction must be considered. Now that both of these questions have been answered, it is time to get on with orderly discovery and ultimate disposition of the litigation.

In developing the case management plan described in this section, the court has weighed and considered many problems presented by this litigation. Some of them are:

1. There are a large number of plaintiffs and potential plaintiffs who claim to have been injured by exposure to Agent Orange. There are now approximately 167 suits pending in the Eastern District of New York involving over 3,400 plaintiffs. The court has been informed that there are many thousands more who have, at the court's request and pending decision of the class action motion, refrained from bringing individual actions.

2. There are numerous chemical companies named as defendants. The fact that they may have had differing degrees of involvement in manufacturing and supplying Agent Orange for the government may or may not cause differing levels of responsibility for the effects of Agent Orange on plaintiffs.

3. The present plaintiffs come from most of the 50 states and from Australia. This may require consideration of varying standards of conduct, rules of causation and principles of damages that may substantially affect the results in individual cases.

4. The causation issues are difficult and complex. Clearly this is not the "simple" type of "disaster" litigation such as an airplane crash involving a single incident, having a causation picture that is readily grasped through conventional litigation techniques, and presenting comparatively small variations among the claimants as to the effects upon them of the crash. With the Agent Orange litigation, injuries are claimed to have resulted from exposure to a chemical that was disseminated in the air over southeast Asia during a period of several years. Each veteran was exposed differently, although undoubtedly patterns of exposure will emerge. The claimed injuries vary significantly. Moreover, there is a major dispute over whether Agent Orange can cause the injuries in question, and there are separate disputes over whether the exposure claimed in each case did cause the injuries claimed. The picture is further complicated by the use in Vietnam of other chemicals and drugs that also are claimed to be capable of causing many of the injuries attributed to Agent Orange.

5. The litigation presents numerous questions of law that lie at the frontier of modern tort jurisprudence. Among them are questions of enterprise liability, strict products liability, liability for injuries that appear long after original exposure to the offending substance, and liability for so-called genetic injuries.

6. Many of the people exposed to Agent Orange may not even yet have experienced the harm it may cause.

7. Numerous scientific and medical issues are presented, and there are serious questions of whether there is adequate data to reach scientifically sound conclusions about them. There is the further question of whether legally permissible conclusions may nevertheless be reached on data that would not permit "scientific" conclusions.

8. Various agencies of the government have expressed concern but as yet have shown little tangible action about the problems claimed to have been caused by the government's use of Agent Orange.

9. There are important and conflicting public policies that run as crosscurrents through many phases of both the substantive and procedural problems of this litigation.

10. There is a wide choice available among the many procedural devices that could be used for addressing and ultimately deciding this controversy. All of these problems are compounded by the practical realities of having on one side of the litigation plaintiffs who seek damages, but who have limited resources with which to press their claims and whose plight becomes more desperate and depressing as time goes on, and having on the other side defendants who strenuously contest their liability, who have ample resources for counsel and expert witnesses to defend them, and who probably gain significantly, although immeasurably, from every delay that they can produce. Overarching the entire dispute is a feeling on both sides that whatever existing law and procedures may technically require, fairness, justice and equity in this unprecedented controversy demand that the government assume responsibility for the harm caused our soldiers and their families by its use of Agent Orange in southeast Asia.

Out of these and other problems it is this court's task as the transferee judge in this multidistrict litigation to supervise and manage the action so as to bring it to a "just, speedy and inexpensive determination", [Fed.R.Civ.P.] Rule 1, either in this court, or if that is not possible, then in the transferor courts after completion here of as much of the litigation as may fairly and reasonably be resolved under the supervision of this single judge. With the foregoing and other problems in mind, the court has considered a variety of possibilities for managing this multidistrict litigation. Each possibility has both advantages and disadvantages. Among the numerous possibilities are the following:

1. Transfer all actions to the Eastern District of New York for trial before this court.

a. *Advantages:* All parties would know precisely where they stand, and how the action would be handled. There would tend to be consistency in the results to the extent permitted by the varying applicable laws.

b. *Disadvantages:* Handling the cases would take the full time of this court, which would be able to handle no other cases, a result that would be unfair not only to the other judges in the Eastern District of New York who are already overburdened with one of the heaviest criminal workloads in the nation, but also to other civil litigants in the Eastern District, who would be further delayed in getting their cases to trial. Moreover, to separately try these actions would take far too long a time; probably neither the litigants nor this court would live long enough to see the last case tried.

2. Supervise all discovery, prepare a pretrial order, and then remand the cases for separate trials in the transferor districts around the country.

a. *Advantages:* This is by far the easiest course of action for this court to take. In many MDL cases this is an acceptable and proper technique and achieves all of the MDL benefits available to those cases. It accomplishes coordinated discovery, a single plan for processing up through the pretrial order, and a shared workload in the actual trial of the individual actions.

b. *Disadvantages:* This technique would require separate trials of each action in the transferor courts, a technique that would be repetitious and wasteful with respect to the issues that are common to all actions. Although testimony of key expert witnesses might be made available to each of the transferor courts through use of videotape so that the need for those witnesses to personally appear at each trial would thereby be eliminated, the opportunity to cross-examine the experts on special problems that relate to the individual plaintiffs would still be lost. The greatest disadvantage of this method is that it would place unnecessary burdens on each of the transferor judges, each of whom would have to struggle with identical legal and factual issues, and it would thus fail to reach the level of judicial efficiency and economy that MDL procedures were designed to achieve.

3. Coordinate discovery and other pretrial work, consolidate the actions for trial of the common issues of fact and law, and then remand to the transferor districts for separate trials of the individual issues such as specific causation and damages.

a. *Advantages:* A single trial of common issues has obvious benefits in economy and efficiency. Spreading to other courts the workload of trying individual cases at least makes a judicial solution to this litigation possible in terms of time and workloads.

b. *Disadvantages:* The consolidation technique addresses only the pending actions, that is, it involves those situations where the plaintiff has seized the initiative and brought suit. However, there are many people with valid claims who for one reason or another have not asserted them by bringing suit and who would therefore not recover for damages inflicted, including damages of which they might not yet even be aware.

4. Certify the litigation as a class action, using all the flexibility of that device, including subclasses, to determine common issues before this

court and ultimately determine the individual issues either under the direct supervision of this court or after remand to other courts.

a. Advantages: Class action treatment would give this court full control over the entire litigation. Any determinations reached in the class action would bind all defendants as well as all members of the class except those who chose to opt out, and as to them, their suits could be consolidated for joint trial with the class action. By use of subclasses to be certified as the need later arises, additional trials on issues common to identified subclasses may be conducted either here in the Eastern District of New York, or by the transferor courts after remand, or by a combination of both. This method provides the greatest flexibility and the greatest opportunity for judicial efficiency and economy of time and money.

b. Disadvantages: The disadvantages with class action treatment lie largely in technical and procedural problems that have arisen with the class action device in other contexts. Such problems have proved particularly troublesome in the context of mass tort cases. Having considered carefully the nature of those technical problems, this court is satisfied that they can be overcome by following the case management plan described in this section and the steps described under the section entitled "Class Action". After considering the submissions and arguments of the parties and after weighing all of the foregoing and many other considerations, the court has developed the following plan for management of the Agent Orange litigation assigned to it under MDL No. 381:

1. Class action. The Agent Orange litigation will be certified as a class action under Fed.R.Civ.P. 23(b)(3).

* * *

IV. Class Action

Contending that many of the issues here presented are best determined by class action to avoid duplicitous litigation by the individual members of the proposed class, plaintiffs have moved for a conditional order pursuant to Fed.R.Civ.P. 23 permitting the suit to proceed as a class action on behalf of all persons exposed to Agent Orange and various members of their families. Under Rule 23(c)(1) and 23(d), the order would be subject to such later modification as the court may find appropriate and necessary in light of future developments in the case.

Before a class action may be maintained under Rule 23, the action must meet the prerequisites of Rule 23(a) and one set of the alternate requirements of Rule 23(b). Defendants oppose class treatment, but continue to advance some outrageous arguments in the name of advocacy; detracting from whatever valid arguments they might otherwise have, they argue that plaintiffs fail to satisfy even one of the elements necessary under Rule 23. Plaintiffs, equally undiscriminating in their advocacy, argue that every element of every alternative of Rule 23 is met here.

The court has carefully read and considered the voluminous submissions of the parties and has heard and considered oral arguments of counsel on this issue. After due consideration, the court determines that plaintiffs have demonstrated that a class action is appropriate under Rule 23(b)(3). Accordingly, plaintiffs' motion for conditional class action certification is granted as herein provided. Certain specific findings are required.

A.   The Prerequisites of Rule 23(a)

1.   Numerosity

The members of the plaintiff class here are so numerous that joinder of all members of the class in the same action is impracticable. Rule 23(a)(1). Indeed, if the only members of the class were the plaintiffs in the 167 actions now pending in this court, "numerosity" would be satisfied.

2.   Commonality

Rule 23(a)(2) states that a class action may only be maintained if "there are questions of law or fact common to the class." Here, the action raises numerous questions of law and fact common to the class. Whatever may be the individual questions relating to the manner and extent of each veteran's exposure to Agent Orange, and relating to the particular effects of Agent Orange on the veteran when considered along with his/her medical history, circumstances, lifestyle and other unique conditions, all of these claims share a common ground when proceeding through the many factual and legal issues relating to the government contract defense, negligence by the defendants, whether Agent Orange was a "defective product," and the many questions embodied in the concept of "general causation." In part, the requirement of commonality is one aimed at determining whether there is a need for combined treatment and a benefit to be derived therefrom. Here the need is compelling, and the benefits are substantial.

3.   Typicality

Rule 23(a)(3) requires that in a class action "the claims or defenses of the representative parties [be] typical of the claims or defenses of the class." As already noted, plaintiffs' claims of negligence, products liability and general causation, as well as the defendants' government contract defense are not just "typical" of the entire class, they are identical. In a few areas, such as the rules governing liability and the application of various statutes of limitations, the claims may fall into groups that are "typical," but even there the different groups' claims can be efficiently managed either on a subclass basis or directly by way of separately determining the issues. Although the named plaintiffs for purposes of the class action are yet to be designated, the court is satisfied that out of the extremely large pool available representative plaintiffs can be named who will present claims typical of those of the class. As already indicated, the issues of specific causation and damages will, of course, ultimately require individual consideration, but until that point in the litigation is reached, a class action appears to be the only practicable means for managing the lawsuit.

4. Adequacy

Rule 23(a)(4) provides that a class action may only be maintained if "the representative parties will fairly and adequately protect the interests of the class." Adequacy of representation depends on the qualifications and interests of counsel for the class representatives, the absence of antagonism or conflicting interests, and a sharing of interests between class representatives and absentees. 7 Wright & Miller FEDERAL PRACTICE AND PROCEDURE §§ 1765–69 at 615–57. Here, the court will select from among the hundreds of plaintiffs representative persons who have a substantial stake in the litigation, who lack conflicts, antagonisms or reasons to be motivated by factors inconsistent with the motives of absentee class members, and who will fairly and adequately protect the interests of the class. Further the class will be represented by experienced, capable counsel, Yannacone & Associates,[32] who have shown themselves willing to undertake the considerable commitment of time, energy and money necessary for the vigorous prosecution of the claims here asserted.

5. Additional Requirements

Courts have implied two additional prerequisites to class action certification that are not specifically mentioned in Rule 23: (1) there must be an identifiable class, and (2) the class representatives must be members of the class. 7 Wright and Miller FEDERAL PRACTICE AND PROCEDURE §§ 1760, 1761 at 579–92. Here, the plaintiff class can be readily identified; they are persons who claim injury from exposure to Agent Orange and their spouses, children and parents who claim direct or derivative injury therefrom. The court has intentionally defined the class in broad terms consistent with the demands of this litigation. If we begin with the broadest possible class, the issues common to all members of that class can be resolved. It may later prove advantageous to create subclasses for various purposes, e.g., for resolving statute of limitations claims, for determining liability in "negligence" as opposed to "product liability" states, and finally, perhaps, for preserving the class action format prior to remand to the transferor judges so as to provide them with the greatest possible flexibility in ultimately determining the issues remaining after multidistrict treatment has ended.

---

32. Yannacone & Associates is a consortium of lawyers who have banded together for purposes of this lawsuit under the leadership of Victor Yannacone, who brought the initial actions and who was designated as lead counsel for the plaintiffs shortly after the cases were transferred to this court by the multidistrict panel. Some of the lawyers in the consortium represent plaintiffs in one or more of the component Agent Orange actions; others apparently have been brought into the group because of special expertise and experience. This case is too complex and too demanding for any single attorney to handle it on behalf of plaintiffs. Yannacone & Associates has already demonstrated that the combined efforts of its twenty or so members will fairly and adequately protect the interests of the class and that together they have the expertise and desire to prosecute this demanding action properly.

B. The Requirements of Rule 23(b)

Plaintiffs seek certification of a plaintiff class under Rule 23(b)(1)(A), (b)(1)(B), (b)(2) and (b)(3). For the reasons set forth below, however, the court concludes that class certification is appropriate only under Rule 23(b)(3).

1. Rule 23(b)(1)

Rule 23(b)(1), the "prejudice" class action provision, authorizes class action treatment if some prejudice would result to any party if members of the class were required to litigate their claims in a series of individual actions, and the resulting prejudice can be obviated by using a class action. The provision is broken down into two separate clauses. Rule 23(b)(1)(A) authorizes a class action when the prosecution of separate actions would create a risk of "inconsistent or varying adjudications with respect to individual members of the class which would establish incompatible standards of conduct for the party opposing the class." This section focuses on the difficulties that class action certification may visit on the party opposing the class action. It is designed to prevent situations in which different courts establish "incompatible standards of conduct" for that party. Rule 23(b)(1)(A) is not meant to apply, however, where the risk of inconsistent results in individual actions is merely the possibility that the defendants will prevail in some cases and not in others, thereby paying damages to some claimants and not others. McDonnell Douglas Corporation v. United States District Court, Central District of California, 523 F.2d 1083, 1086 (9th Cir.1975), *cert. denied sub nom.,* Flanagan v. McDonnell Douglas Corporation, 425 U.S. 911, 96 S.Ct. 1506, 47 L.Ed.2d 761 (1976). "The risk of paying money [damages] to some and not others is not what the rule-makers intended by the words 'incompatible standards of conduct.' " A. Miller, *An Overview of Federal Class Actions: Past, Present and Future* at 43 (1977). Since the only effect of inconsistent decisions here would be the payment of damages to some claimants and not others, class certification under Rule 23(b)(1)(A) would be inappropriate.

Rule 23(b)(1)(B) authorizes a class action when separate actions would create a risk of "adjudications with respect to individual members of the class which would as a practical matter be dispositive of the interest of the other members not parties to the adjudications or substantially impair or impede their ability to protect their interest." This rule emphasizes possible undesirable effects on the class members, rather than on the opposing party, and permits a class action if separate suits might have undesirable effects on the class members. "The paradigm Rule 23(b)(1)(B) case is one in which there are multiple claimants to a limited fund * * * and there is a risk that if litigants are allowed to proceed on an individual basis those who sue first will deplete the fund and leave nothing for the late-comers." A. Miller, *An Overview of Federal Class Actions: Past, Present and Future* at 45 (1977). *See also* Administrative Committee's Note, Rule 23, 39 F.R.D. 69, 101 (1966).

However large the potential damages may appear here, plaintiffs offer no evidence of the likely insolvency of defendants and apparently do not, in defendant Dow's words, "have the temerity to argue that the aggregate claims of the purported class exceed the total assets of the five named defendants." [34] ...   For good measure, Dow adds "[s]uch an argument would be ludicrous on its face."   ...   As one court has noted, "without more, numerous plaintiffs and a large *ad damnum* clause should [not] guarantee (b)(1)(B) certification." *Payton v. Abbott Labs,* 83 F.R.D. 382, 389 (D.Mass.1979).   Thus, certification under Rule 23(b)(1)(B) is not appropriate.

2.   *Rule 23(b)(2)*

Rule 23(b)(2) authorizes class action treatment where "the party opposing the class has acted or refused to act on grounds generally applicable to the class, thereby making appropriate final injunctive relief or corresponding declaratory relief with respect to the class as a whole." This subdivision "does not extend to cases in which the appropriate final relief relates exclusively or predominately to money damages," Advisory Committee's Note, Rule 23, 39 F.R.D. 69, 102 (1966); rather, it applies when injunctive relief or declaratory relief on which injunctive relief could be based is proper.   Eisen v. Carlisle & Jacquelin, 391 F.2d 555, 564 (2d Cir.1968), *vacated on other grounds,* 417 U.S. 156 (1974).   Here, the relief requested relates predominately to money damages so the class may not be certified under Rule 23(b)(2).[35]

3.   *Rule 23(b)(3)*

Rule 23(b)(3) authorizes a class action when the court finds "that the questions of law or fact common to the members of the class predominate over any questions affecting only individual members, and that a class action is superior to all other available methods for the fair and efficient adjudication of the controversy."   The rule lists four matters pertinent to a consideration of these issues:

> (A) the interest of members of the class in individually controlling the prosecution or defense of separate actions; (B) the extent and nature of any litigation concerning the controversy already commenced by or against members of the class; (C) the desirability or un-desirability of concentrating the litigation of the claims in the particular forum; (D) the difficulties likely to be encountered in the management of a class action.

Considering the circumstances of this action, and bearing in mind the manner in which the class action will proceed, the court determines that the interest of class members in individually controlling the prosecution of separate actions is minimal, especially at this early stage of the

---

34. Since that statement was made the number of named defendants has increased, ... thus rendering class certification under Rule 23(b)(1)(B) even more inappropriate.

35. The court is aware that plaintiffs have requested that a trust be established

to apply defendants' future profits for the benefit of the plaintiff class. While this possible relief has not been excluded from the case, it does not serve as a sufficient basis for class certification pursuant to Fed. R.Civ.P. 23(b)(2) litigation when the issues under consideration concern the relationship between the defendants and the government, issues that impact equally on every plaintiff's claim. Rule 23(b)(3)(A). Later stages of this litigation, especially those concerned with individual causation and damages, may require reconsideration of this element and possibly decertification, but at this stage, individual class members have almost no interest in individually controlling the prosecution of separate actions. Indeed, the problems inherent in every one of the individual actions are so great that it is doubtful if a single plaintiff represented by a single attorney pursuing an individual action could ever succeed.

With respect to the extent and nature of currently pending litigation, almost all the Agent Orange litigation currently pending is before this court under the multidistrict litigation procedures. All those cases are advancing simultaneously, and certification of a class action will serve the goals of judicial economy and reduce the possibility of multiple lawsuits. Rule 23(b)(3)(B). In addition, it will significantly expedite final resolution of this controversy. With respect to the desirability of concentrating the litigation of the claims in this forum, the actions have already been concentrated before this court through the use of MDL procedures. Allowing it to proceed as a class action will minimize the hazards of duplicate efforts and inconsistent results. Moreover, given the location of present counsel and the widely varying citizenships of the interested parties, this court is as appropriate a place to settle the controversy as any. Rule 23(b)(3)(C).

With respect to the difficulties likely to be encountered in the management of a class action, the court has carefully and humbly considered the management problems presented by an action of this magnitude and complexity, and concluded that great as they are, the difficulties likely to be encountered by managing these actions as a class action are significantly outweighed by the truly overwhelming problems that would attend any other management device chosen. While the burdens on this court might be lessened by denying class certification, those imposed collectively on the transferor courts after remand of the multidistrict cases would be increased many times. Having carefully considered the above factors and all other circumstances of this action, the court is satisfied that at this time the questions of law and fact common to the members of the class predominate over questions of law or fact affecting only individual members, and that a class action is superior to any other available method for the fair and efficient adjudication of the controversy.

Because over a year ago this court requested plaintiffs not to file actions pending decision on the class action motion, because the facts and issues in all of the pending and future cases are to a great degree identical, or at least parallel, and because this action presents a variety of questions in relatively untested areas of the law, this court sees the objectives of Fed.R.Civ.P. Rule 1 and Rule 23, as well as the interests of justice, best served by determining here, and for all parties, as many legal and factual issues as may properly be decided. To achieve those ends the court will certify this to be a class action under Fed.R.Civ.P. 23(c). Formal certification will be by separate order to be processed under the court's instructions.

IN RE FEDERAL SKYWALK CASES

United States Court of Appeals, Eighth Circuit, 1982.
680 F.2d 1175.

Before HEANEY, McMILLIAN and ARNOLD, CIRCUIT JUDGES.

McMILLIAN, CIRCUIT JUDGE.

This action challenges the validity of a mandatory class certification order rendered by the United States District Court for the Western District of Missouri during the course of litigation arising out of the collapse of two skywalks at the Hyatt Regency Hotel in Kansas City, Missouri in July, 1981. The class was certified on the issues of liability for compensatory and punitive damages and amount of punitive damages, and includes all business invitees at the hotel during the disaster.

Two objecting plaintiffs (objectors) now petition this court to vacate the order * * *.[1] * * * Alternatively, the class representative argues that the federal district judge did not abuse his discretion in certifying the class and further that the class is appropriate. For the reasons discussed below, we conclude that * * * the order must be vacated because it violates the Anti–Injunction Act, 28 U.S.C. § 2283. * * *

On July 17, 1981, two skywalks in the central lobby of the Hyatt Regency Hotel in Kansas City, Missouri, collapsed killing 114 persons and injuring hundreds of others. Following the disaster numerous individual lawsuits were filed in both the Circuit Court for Jackson County, Missouri (state court), and the United States District Court for the Western District of Missouri (district court).[2] The federal district court jurisdiction was based on 28 U.S.C. § 1332, diversity of citizenship.

The state court cases were consolidated and assigned to Judge Timothy O'Leary. The federal cases were also consolidated and assigned to Judge Scott O. Wright. Shortly after the first cases were filed, the state and district court consolidated their respective cases for discovery. Each court appointed a Plaintiffs' Liaison Committee to aid in discovery and other matters. In addition, the two courts appointed a joint state-federal Plaintiffs' Liaison Committee to aid in the consolidated discovery. * * *

Prior to the class certification, the Plaintiffs' Liaison Committee accomplished substantial discovery and trial preparation on behalf of all plaintiffs. The accomplishments included nearly completing the inter-

---

1. The class representative argues that class certification is an appropriate device to handle the claims arising out of the disaster. However, in view of our holding, we do not reach the merits of these arguments.

2. By the end of January, 1982, there were approximately 120 cases filed in state court and eighteen filed in district court. In addition, prior to the class certification, 123 claims had been settled at a total settlement cost of $18.5 million.

rogatory phase of discovery and serving requests for production upon the defendants. In addition, the committee collected approximately 300,000 documents pertaining to the litigation and had arranged for a document depository available to all plaintiffs' counsel. The committee had also arranged for the testing of the skywalk materials by the National Bureau of Standards. * * *

On October 27, 1981, Molly Riley, a district court plaintiff, filed a motion for class certification. The motion sought class certification under Fed.R.Civ.P. 23(b)(1)(B), or in the alternative under 23(b)(3), as to the issues of liability for compensatory and punitive damages and the amount of punitive damages. The basis for requesting class certification was Riley's concern that there would be inadequate funds available to pay all claims for compensatory and punitive damages. Riley also moved that her counsel be appointed as lead counsel for the class.

Several federal and state court plaintiffs filed pleadings in opposition to Riley's motion. The objecting plaintiffs challenged Riley's and her attorney's qualifications to represent the class. They also challenged the need for and desirability of class action treatment arguing that there was no evidence of insufficient funds to satisfy all claims. A hearing was held before Judge Wright on December 10, 1981.

* * *

On January 25, 1982, Judge Wright entered the order appealed from in which he (1) denied Riley's motion for class certification because her citizenship was not diverse from all defendants, (2) certified a class action under Rule 23(b)(1)(A) on the issues of liability for compensatory and punitive damages, (3) certified a class action under Rule 23(b)(1)(B) on the issues of liability for punitive damages and the amount of punitive damages * * *. In re Federal Skywalk Cases, 93 F.R.D. 415 (W.D.Mo.1982).

In support of its order the district court found that the general prerequisites for class actions prescribed by Rule 23(a) were satisfied, *id.* at 420–22, and that the specific requirements of Rule 23(b)(1) were also satisfied. The court stressed that the "interests of all parties concerned" would best be served by "the avoidance of wasteful, repetitive litigation," and that such litigation could be avoided by "trying the issues of liability for compensatory damages, liability for punitive damages and amount of punitive damages only once." *Id.* at 423. In support of the Rule 23(b)(1)(A) class the court found that individual suits on the issues of liability for compensatory and punitive damages would create a risk of inconsistent results. *Id.* at 424.

In support of the Rule 23(b)(1)(B) class the court relied on three considerations. First, the defendants held liable for punitive damages might lack the funds to pay the full amount of such damages. *Id.* at 424. Second, individual suits for punitive damages would create a risk of unfairness to the other claimants because "there is some uncertainty under Missouri law as to whether a single defendant can be liable for more than one award of punitive damages." [10] *Id.* at 424. Third, the court noted that the prosecution of individual punitive damage actions could create an ethical problem for counsel representing more than one victim in that the counsel would be forced to decide which suit to bring first. *Id.* at 425.

On February 9, 1982, the objectors filed their notice of appeal and petition for mandamus. * * *

Our initial inquiry must be whether the order is appealable. Recognizing that the order is interlocutory, we would nevertheless have appellate jurisdiction under 28 U.S.C. § 1292(a)(1) (1976) [11] if that order is injunctive in character. Therefore, resolution of this issue depends upon the nature of the order. The objectors argue that the order enjoins them from prosecuting their state court actions for punitive damages. In response the class argues that the order is not an injunction because it does not use injunction terminology and, more importantly, it does not enjoin the objectors from settling their claims. The class characterizes the order as follows:

> [t]he motion concerns only whether the defendants can use individual punitive damage settlements as evidence to defeat or diminish the recovery of punitive damages in the classwide trial on that issue. *The representative plaintiff and the class have never sought to enjoin any member of the class from entering into an individual settlement of any claim.*

* * * We do not agree with that characterization and conclude that we do have jurisdiction under 28 U.S.C. § 1292(a). * * * (1) The determination of whether an order is an injunction depends upon the substantial effect of the order rather than its terminology. * * * (2) In the present case, contrary to the class's assertion, the district court expressly prohibited class members from settling their punitive damage claims:

> Legitimate claimants may negotiate and execute settlements with those defendants who have vociferously urged this court to allow the settlement process to continue. *Those claimants who want to exact payment for allegedly punishable acts must forego the settlement process and await the trial of the punitive damage issues.*

In re Federal Skywalk Cases, at 428 (emphasis added). In addition, the substantial effect of the order also enjoined the state plaintiffs from pursuing their pending state court actions on the issues of liability for compensatory and punitive damages and the amount of punitive damages.

---

10. It appears that the main concern underlying Judge Wright's certification is that there is an uncertain question of Missouri law as to whether plaintiffs may seek to recover multiple awards of punitive damages arising from a single wrongful act of a defendant.

11. 28 U.S.C. § 1292(a)(1) provides in pertinent part: (a) The courts of appeals shall have jurisdiction of appeals from: (1) Interlocutory orders of the district courts of the United States . . ., granting, continuing, modifying, refusing or dissolving injunctions . . . .

At oral argument counsel for the class argued that 28 U.S.C. § 1292(a)(1) should not be construed to apply to class certification because the inevitable effect of a mandatory class is an injunction against state court actions on class issues. We conclude that the argument is not persuasive on the facts before us.

It is true that parties to a mandatory class are not free to initiate actions in other courts to litigate class certified issues. * * * However, in the present case the objectors had commenced their state court actions before the motion for class certification had been filed in district court. The state court cases had been filed, consolidated, and discovery had begun.[12]

* * *

Our conclusion that the order enjoins pending state proceedings necessitates an inquiry as to the propriety of that order under the Anti–Injunction Act, 28 U.S.C. § 2283. The Act provides that "[a] court of the United States may not grant an injunction to stay proceedings in a state court except as expressly authorized by Act of Congress, or where necessary in aid of its jurisdiction, or to protect or effectuate its judgment."

In Atlantic Coast Line R.R. v. Locomotive Engineers, 398 U.S. 281, 286–87, 90 S.Ct. 1739, 1742-43, 26 L.Ed.2d 234 (1970), the Supreme Court recognized that the Act imposes a flat and positive prohibition:

> On its face the present Act is an absolute prohibition against enjoining state court proceedings, unless the injunction falls within one of three specifically defined exceptions. The respondents here have intimated that the Act only establishes a "principle of comity," not a binding rule on the power of the federal courts. The argument implies that in certain circumstances a federal court may enjoin state court proceedings even if that action cannot be justified by any of the three exceptions. We cannot accept any such contention. In 1955 when this Court interpreted this statute, it stated: "This is not a statute conveying a broad general policy for appropriate ad hoc application. Legislative policy is here expressed in a clear-cut prohibition qualified only by specifically defined exceptions." Amalgamated Clothing Workers v. Richman Bros., 348 U.S. 511, 515–16, (75 S.Ct. 452, 455, 99 L.Ed. 600) (1955).

* * *

In the present case the class has an uncertain claim for punitive damages against defendants who have not conceded liability. The claim does not qualify as a limited fund which is a jurisdictional prerequisite for federal interpleader. Without the limited fund there is no analogy to

---

12. Judge O'Leary had also aided in the settlement process by convincing the insurers for Hallmark Cards, Inc., Crown Center Redevelopment Corp. and the Hyatt Corp. to commit a minimum of $151 million of the total $333 million liability insurance coverage to the settlement of the claims.

an interpleader and no reason to treat the class action as an interpleader for purposes of the Anti–Injunction Act.

The class proposes a second analogy between the order and several earlier decisions which allowed an injunction when an insurance company brought a federal suit for a declaratory judgment that a particular policy was invalid and the beneficiary subsequently sues in state court to recover under the policy. We conclude that the analogy is not persuasive. Initially we note that the most recent case cited by class was decided in 1940, long before the enactment of the current Anti–Injunction Act. We also note that even the commentator cited by the class acknowledges:

> ... it seems probable that a federal court would not be warranted in enjoining the prosecution of a pending state action [on the policy], where it is brought during the contestable period and there is an opportunity to set up the defense of fraud in the state court....

1A Moore's FEDERAL PRACTICE ¶ 910.225 at 2621.

In addition, the cited cases are distinguishable on the basis that they involved situations in which identical parties were litigating mutually exclusive theories concerning their rights in the same policy in different forums. Such is not the case here. Furthermore, as conceded by the class, the cases involved injunctions against subsequent state actions. In contrast, the injunction in the present case was against pending state actions.

Next the class argues that allowing individual actions in state court will nullify the purpose of the class. The Supreme Court has narrowly interpreted the "necessary in aid of jurisdiction" exception, and a pending state suit must truly interfere with the federal court's jurisdiction. As the objectors correctly point out, a plurality of the Supreme Court reaffirmed in *Vendo Co.* its earlier holdings that a simultaneous *in personam* state action does not interfere with the jurisdiction of a federal court in a suit involving the same subject matter.

In Toucey v. New York Life Ins. Co., 314 U.S. (118), at 134–35, (62 S.Ct. 139, 144, 86 L.Ed. 100) [(1945)], we acknowledged the existence of a historical exception to the Anti–Injunction Act in cases where the federal court has obtained jurisdiction over *res*, prior to the state-court action. Although the "necessary in aid of" exception to § 2283 may be fairly read as incorporating this historical *in rem* exception, *see* C. Wright, FEDERAL COURTS, § 47, [at] 204 (3d ed.1976), the federal and state actions here are simply *in personam*. The traditional notion is that *in personam* actions in federal and state court may proceed concurrently, without interference from either court, and there is no evidence that the exception to § 2283 was intended to alter this balance. We have never viewed parallel *in personam* actions as interfering with the jurisdiction of either court; as we stated in Kline v. Burke Construction Co., 260 U.S. 226, 43 S.Ct. 79, 67 L.Ed. 226 (1922):

"[A]n action brought to enforce [a personal liability] *does not tend to impair or defeat the jurisdiction* of the court in which a prior action for the same cause is pending. Each court is free to proceed in its own way and in its own time, without reference to the proceedings in the other court. Whenever a judgment is rendered in one of the courts and pleaded in the other, the effect of that judgment is to be determined by the application of the principles of *res adjudicata....*" *Id.* at 230 (emphasis added). 433 U.S. at 641–42....

In the present case the federal and state actions are *in personam* claims for compensatory and punitive damages. Therefore, based on the foregoing principles, we are compelled to hold that despite Judge Wright's legitimate concern for the efficient management of mass tort litigation, the class certification order must be vacated. Mr. Justice Black's concluding words in *Atlantic Coast Line* are particularly apt here:

This case is by no means an easy one. The arguments in support of the union's contentions are not insubstantial. But whatever doubts we may have are strongly affected by the general prohibition of § 2283. Any doubts as to the propriety of a federal injunction against state court proceedings should be resolved in favor of permitting the state courts to proceed in an orderly fashion to finally determine the controversy. The explicit wording of § 2283 itself implies as much, and the fundamental principle of a dual system of courts leads inevitably to that conclusion. 398 U.S. at 296–97.

* * *

The order of the district court is vacated.

IN RE BENDECTIN PRODUCTS LIABILITY LITIGATION

United States Court of Appeals, Sixth Circuit, 1984.
749 F.2d 300.

Before KEITH and MARTIN, CIRCUIT JUDGES, and JOHNSTONE, DISTRICT JUDGE.

BOYCE F. MARTIN, JR., CIRCUIT JUDGE.

Petitioners seek a writ of mandamus ordering the district court to vacate its order certifying a class action pursuant to Federal Rule of Civil Procedure 23(b)(1). 102 F.R.D. 239 (S.D.Ohio 1984). For the reasons stated below, the petition shall be granted, and the writ shall be issued.

I

This case is just one stage in a massive products liability lawsuit against Merrell Dow Pharmaceuticals, Inc., the manufacturer of the drug Bendectin. Bendectin is a prescription drug developed to relieve morning sickness in pregnant women. Numerous plaintiffs have filed claims in both federal and state court alleging that they suffer from birth defects as a result of their *in utero* exposure to Bendectin.[3]

The present controversy has its roots in a transfer order of the Judicial Panel on Multidistrict Litigation in early 1982. 533 F.Supp. 489. Pursuant to that order, all Bendectin actions pending in federal courts were transferred to the Southern District of Ohio for consolidated pretrial proceedings. Shortly after the transfer, a five-person Plaintiffs' Lead Counsel Committee was formed to coordinate discovery efforts for all plaintiffs in federal court. Over the next year, many other cases were transferred to the Southern District of Ohio, and many more cases were filed in that court as original actions.[4] In September 1983, the district judge issued an order to show cause why the cases should not be certified as a class action under Federal Rule of Civil Procedure 23 or, in the alternative, be consolidated for trial on common issues of liability pursuant to Federal Rule of Civil Procedure 42. After the parties responded to this order, the district judge held in November 1983 that the action was not appropriate for class certification and instead consolidated the cases for trial pursuant to Rule 42. The consolidation order, however, only included those cases that had been filed in Ohio federal courts, and the cases that had been transferred to the Southern District were to be returned to their original venue for trial unless the plaintiffs agreed to the consolidated trial.

The consolidated trial began June 11, 1984, and a jury was impaneled. Because of serious settlement negotiations between the Plaintiffs' Lead Counsel Committee and Merrell Dow, the district court recessed the trial on June 18 and certified a class for settlement purposes under Federal Rule of Civil Procedure 23(b). Merrell Dow has apparently made a settlement offer of $120 million, and a majority of the Plaintiffs' Lead Counsel Committee tentatively favor the settlement offer.[5] A hearing is scheduled for October 31, 1984, to determine the proper allocation of the settlement among subclasses, and a fairness hearing on the settlement is scheduled for November 30.

In the order certifying the class, the district judge found that all four requirements of Rule 23(a) were easily met. The court also found that the requirements of Rule 23(b)(1)(A) and (B) were met. * * * With respect to Rule 23(b)(1)(A), the district court stated that "continued case by case determinations will inevitably result in varying adjudications which will impose inconsistent standards of conduct upon the defendant." The district judge found 23(b)(1)(B) to have been met because "there is a risk that a limited fund may exist from which judgments can be satisfied." The district judge then certified a "non-opt out" class for settlement purposes of all persons exposed to Bendectin.

* * *

3. In 1983, Merrell Dow ceased the production and marketing of Bendectin.

4. In his order certifying a class, the district judge stated that over five hundred lawsuits concerning Bendectin were pending in the Southern District of Ohio.

5. Two of the members of the Plaintiffs' Lead Counsel Committee oppose the settlement, and one of these dissenting members appeared at argument in favor of the writ of mandamus.

II

* * *

Rule 23(b)(1)(A) provides that class actions are maintainable if a separate action would create a risk of "inconsistent or varying adjudications with respect to individual members of the class which would establish incompatible standards of conduct for the party opposing the class." The fact that some plaintiffs may be successful in their suits against a defendant while others may not is clearly not a ground for invoking Rule 23(b)(1)(A). McDonnell Douglas Corp. v. United States District Court for the Central District of California, 523 F.2d 1083, 1086 (9th Cir.1975), *cert. denied,* 425 U.S. 911, 96 S.Ct. 1506, 47 L.Ed.2d 761 (1976); In re "Agent Orange" Product Liability Litigation, 100 F.R.D. 718, 724–25 (E.D.N.Y.1983), *petition for mandamus denied sub nom.,* In re Diamond Shamrock Chemicals Co., 725 F.2d 858 (2d Cir.), *cert. denied,* 465 U.S. 1067, 104 S.Ct. 1417, 79 L.Ed.2d 743 (1984). The class certification in this case therefore cannot stand on this ground.

The district judge, however, apparently did not rely solely on the possibility of varying adjudications because he also cited Hernandez v. Motor Vessel Skyward, 61 F.R.D. 558 (S.D.Fla.1973), *aff'd mem.,* 507 F.2d 1278 (5th Cir.1975), to support his conclusion as to Rule 23(b)(1)(A). In *Hernandez,* the district judge certified a class under Rule 23(b)(1)(A) on the ground that the doctrine of collateral estoppel might bind the defendant on issues of liability if any plaintiff were to win a suit against it. Irrespective of the merits of this argument as a ground for Rule 23(b)(1)(A) certification, this concern has been eliminated by the Supreme Court's curtailment of the use of offensive collateral estoppel in Parklane Hosiery Co. v. Shore, 439 U.S. 322, 99 S.Ct. 645, 58 L.Ed.2d 552 (1979).[11] The district court therefore failed to establish any grounds for certification under Rule 23(b)(1)(A).

With respect to Rule 23(b)(1)(B), the district judge stated that there was a limited fund from which the plaintiffs could be compensated for their claims and therefore adjudications by earlier plaintiffs could "as a practical matter be dispositive of the interests of the other members [of the class] not parties to the adjudications." Fed.R.Civ.P. 23(b)(1)(B). This limited fund theory has been endorsed by several courts. In re Northern District of California, Dalkon Shield IUD Products Liability Litigation, 693 F.2d 847, 851 (9th Cir.1982), *cert. denied,* 459 U.S. 1171, 103 S.Ct. 817, 74 L.Ed.2d 1015 (1983); *In re "Agent Orange" Product Liability Litigation,* 100 F.R.D. at 725. *See also* Fed.R.Civ.P. 23 advisory committee note to 1966 amendments. The district court was therefore not clearly erroneous as a matter of law to hold that a limited fund is a justification for a class action under a Rule 23(b)(1)(B).

11. In *Parklane Hosiery,* the Supreme Court explicitly stated that offensive collateral estoppel could not be used in mass tort litigation. *Parklane Hosiery,* 439 U.S. at 330 & n.14, 99 S.Ct. at 651 & n.14.

The district court, however, was clearly erroneous as a matter of law in the method it used to determine that there was a limited fund. The certification order states without support "that there is a risk that a limited fund may exist from which judgments can be satisfied." No findings were made on the record as to this conclusion, and the petitioners in this case were given no opportunity to dispute whether there was a limited fund.[13] In deciding whether a limited fund would subvert the rights of some plaintiffs, the courts have differed over whether the proponent of the class certification must show that a limited fund will "necessarily" affect the plaintiffs' claims, *Dalkon Shield IUD Product Liability Litigation,* 693 F.2d at 852, or whether a "substantial probability" will suffice. *In re "Agent Orange" Product Liability Litigation,* 100 F.R.D. at 726. Irrespective of the proper test, the district court, as a matter of law, must have a fact-finding inquiry on this question and allow the opponents of class certification to present evidence that a limited fund does not exist. *Dalkon Shield IUD Product Liability Litigation,* 693 F.2d at 852. *See also In re "Agent Orange" Liability Litigation,* 100 F.R.D. at 727. Because the district judge in this case failed to make any such finding, the certification was clearly erroneous as a matter of law.[15]

* * *

The final guideline is whether the district court's order raises issues of first impression and creates new and important problems. Several of the issues raised by the class certification are of first impression in this Circuit. This Court has never been faced with a non-opt out class certification for settlement purposes only. Moreover, the sheer magnitude of the case makes the disposition of these issues crucial as several hundred litigants are waiting for a decision before proceeding with their cases.

Based on these guidelines, we find that the issuance of a writ of mandamus is appropriate in this case. Although we shall issue the writ, we realize that the district judge has been faced with some very difficult problems in this case, and we certainly do not fault him for attempting to use this unique and innovative certification method. On pure policy grounds, the district judge's decision may be commendable, and several commentators have argued that Rule 23 should be used in this manner. *See, e.g.,* Note, *Class Certification of Mass Accident Cases under Rule 23(b)(1),* 96 Harv.L.Rev. 1143 (1983). Because of the situation presented

---

13. If this case were on appeal, the proper remedy would be to remand the case for a finding in this regard. Because the case is before us on a petition for a writ of mandamus, our only recourse is to issue the writ.

15. For these reasons, the case is distinguishable from Union Light, Heat and Power Co. v. United States District Court, 588 F.2d 543 (6th Cir.1978), *cert. dismissed,* 443 U.S. 913, 99 S.Ct. 3103, 61 L.Ed.2d 877

(1979). . . . In that case, the district judge at least made some finding on the record as to the amount of possible claims and the net worth of the company. Coburn v. 4–R Corp., 77 F.R.D., 43, 45 (E.D.Ky.1977), *petition for mandamus denied sub nom.,* Union Light, Heat and Power Co. v. United States District Court, 588 F.2d 543 (6th Cir.1978), *cert. dismissed,* 443 U.S. 913, 99 S.Ct. 3103, 61 L.Ed.2d 877 (1979).

by this case, however, we conclude that a writ of mandamus vacating the certification order of the district court should be issued. So ordered.

Notes and Questions

1. The Advisory Committee's Note to Federal Rule of Civil Procedure 23, as amended in 1966, indicates that the class action rule is generally not a suitable procedural mechanism for adjudication of mass-accident cases. This Note, which has yet to be amended or superseded, has remained an obstacle to class certification in many mass tort cases. Does the Advisory Committee Note make sense? What continuing vitality, if any should be accorded to the Note's admonition in the face of post–1980 mass tort litigation?

2. Through the 1970s and 1980s the Advisory Committee Note frequently was cited to justify denying class certification in mass tort cases, although nothing in Rule 23 itself precludes such certification. In general, courts found that attempts to satisfy Rule 23(b)(3) class action requirements often failed to satisfy commonality, superiority, and predominance criteria, as the excerpted opinions suggest. *See, e.g.* In re Northern District of Cal., Dalkon Shield IUD Prods. Liab. Litig., 693 F.2d 847, 852 (9th Cir.1982), *cert. denied,* 459 U.S. 1171, 103 S.Ct. 817, 74 L.Ed.2d 1015 (1983)(decertifying classes in *Dalkon Shield* litigation); Ikonen v. Hartz Mountain Corp., 122 F.R.D. 258, 263 (S.D.Cal.1988)(denying class certification in flea and tick spray products liability litigation); Mertens v. Abbott Laboratories, 99 F.R.D. 38 (D.N.H.1983)(denying Rule 23(b)(3) certification in *DES* litigation); Ryan v. Eli Lilly & Co., 84 F.R.D. 230 (D.S.C.1979)(action by woman who took synthetic estrogen during pregnancy, on behalf of others similarly exposed, not suitable for class certification); Yandle v. PPG Indus., Inc., 65 F.R.D. 566 (E.D.Tex.1974)(action by employees and survivors of employees of asbestos exposure in the workplace not proper for class certification); Rosenfeld v. A.H. Robins Co., 63 A.D.2d 11, 407 N.Y.S.2d 196 (1978) (denying class certification to plaintiff purporting to represent New York women suffering from pelvic inflammatory disease), *appeal dismissed* 46 N.Y.2d 731, 413 N.Y.S.2d 374, 385 N.E.2d 1301 (1978)(denying class certification both to residents of chemical waste disposal site and to their unborn children).

3. The 1974 *Yandle* decision in the Eastern District of Texas, denying class certification to asbestos personal injury claimants, represents the early response of the federal courts to asbestos personal injury claimants. It would take a full decade after *Yandle* for the federal and state courts to realize the extent of the asbestos personal injury litigation crisis.

For comments in this period on the developing asbestos personal injury litigation, *see* Eugene A. Anderson, et al., *Asbestos Products Liability Litigation: What Can Be Done About It?,* Arb. J. at 3 (Sept.1983); Bradley M. Bingham, *Silicosis Products Liability,* 5 J. Prods. Liab. 89 (1982); John P. Burns, et al., *An Analysis of the Legal, Social and Political Issues Raised by the Asbestos Litigation,* 36 Vand.L.Rev. 573 (1983); Robert P. Glass, Comment, *The Asbestos Tragedy: Legal Issues and the Need for Reform,* 8 U. Dayton L.Rev. 353 (1983); DEBORAH R. HENSLER, ET AL., ASBESTOS IN THE COURTS: THE CHALLENGE OF MASS TOXIC TORTS (SANTA MONICA, CALIFORNIA: THE INSTITUTE FOR CIVIL JUSTICE, RAND 1985); Richard W. Kozlowski, Jr., *An Examination of*

Recurring Issues in Asbestos Litigation, 46 Alb.L.Rev. 1307 (1982); Jean A. O'Hare, Comment, *Asbestos Litigation: The Dust Has Yet to Settle,* 7 Fordham Urb. L.J. 55 (1978); Jerry J. Phillips, *Asbestos Litigation: The Test of the Tort System,* 36 Ark. L.Rev. 343 (1982); Mary K. Reeder, *Asbestos Litigation: The Insurance Coverage Question,* 15 Ind.L.Rev. 831 (1982); Samuel J. Smith & Stephen J. Birek, Jr., *Sailing the Unchartered Seas of Asbestos Litigation Under the Longshoreman's and Harbor Worker's Compensation Act,* 22 Wm & Mary L.Rev., 177 (1980); Louis Treiger, Comment, *Relief for Asbestos Victims, A Legislative Analysis,* 20 Harv. J. Legis. 179 (1983); Harry H. Wellington, *Toxic Torts: Managing the Asbestos Problem,* Yale L. Rep. at 20 (Spring 1985); THOMAS E. WILLGING, ASBESTOS CASE MANAGEMENT: PRETRIAL AND TRIAL PROCEDURES (Wash. D.C.: Federal Judicial Center 1985); Note, *Adjudicating Asbestos Insurance Liability: Alternatives to Contract Analysis,* 97 Harv.L.Rev. 739 (1984).

4. For discussions of the early Bendectin and DES cases, *see* Harlan S. Abrahams & Bobbe J. Musgrave, *The DES Labryrinth,* 33 S.C.L.Rev. 663 (1982); William B. Carter, *Comment, The DES Dilemma: An Analysis of Recent Decisions,* 52 Miss.L.J. 199 (1982); Melissa A. Turner, Comment, *Bearing the Burden of DES Exposure,* 60 Or.L.Rev. 309 (1981); *see also* Mark D. Nosacka, *Bendectin, Birth Defects, and* Brock: *A Study in Appellate Review,* 13 J.Prods.Liab. 231 (1991).

5. The Hyatt Skywalk litigation inspired critical commentary examining the problems entailed in dual system mass tort litigation. *See generally,* Robert C. Gordon, *The Optimum Management of the Skywalks Mass Disaster Litigation by the Use of the Federal Mandatory Class Action Device,* 52 UMKC L.Rev 215 (1984); Mary K. Hopkins, *et al., A Case Study in Mass Disaster Litigation: Reviewing Class Actions; Media Relations: Ethical Considerations,* 52 UMKCL.Rev. 151 (1984); Steven M. Larimore, *Exploring the Interface Between Rule 23 Class Actions in the Anti–Injunction Act,* 18 Ga.L.Rev. 259 (1984); David R. Morris & Andrew See, *The Hyatt Skywalks Litigation: The Plaintiff's Perspective,* 52 UMKCL.Rev. 246 (1984); Judith Whittaker, *Skywalk Wars,* 52 UMKC L.Rev. 296 (1984); Scott O. Wright and Joseph A. Colussi, *The Successful Use of the Class Action Device in the Management of the Skywalks Mass Tort Litigation,* 52 UMKCL.Rev. 141 (1984).

6. Judge Pratt's careful decision to certify the Agent Orange cases for class action treatment represents a somewhat "deviant" opinion in this period. To what extent does Judge's Pratt opinion in 1980 manifest the multiple procedural tensions embodied in mass tort litigation? Has Judge Pratt achieved a sensible accommodation of all competing interests and concerns? Would other procedural or administrative methods of resolving these cases have been more appropriate? *See* In re "Agent Orange" Prod. Liab. Litig., 818 F.2d 145 (2d Cir.1987)(final approval of Agent Orange settlement), *infra* at II, A.

7. Although some federal courts in the early 1980s began to consider the feasibility of (b)(3) opt-out mass tort class actions, federal courts have struggled with applying the concept of the (b)(1)(B) "limited fund" class action in the mass tort context, rarely permitting class certification under this provision. A major obstacle has been establishing, to the court's

satisfaction, the existence of the "limited fund." Who carries the burden of showing the existence of the limited fund, and how is that proof established? The Ninth Circuit supplied some helpful dictum in Green v. Occidental Petroleum Corp., 541 F.2d 1335 (9th Cir.1976):

> It is conceivable, of course, that the claims of the named plaintiffs would be so large that if the action were to proceed as an individual action the decision "would as a practical matter be dispositive of the interests of the other members not parties to the adjudications or substantially impair or impede their ability to protects their interests." Fed.R.Civ.P. 23(b)(1)(B). This would be the case where the claims of all plaintiffs exceeded the assets of the defendant and hence to allow any group of individuals to be fully compensated would impair the rights of those not in court.

Id. at 1340 n.9. However, when the Ninth Circuit next considered the *Occidental Petroleum* dictum, it rejected the certification of a (b)(1)(B) class, even for purposes of punitive damage claims. *See* In re Northern District of California, Dalkon Shield IUD Products Liability Litigation, 693 F.2d 847, 851 (9th Cir.1982). Although at least one district court has certified a (b)(1)(B) class because of the likelihood that the aggregate total of claims would render the defendant insolvent, *see* Coburn v. 4–R Corp., 77 F.R.D. 43 (E.D.Ky.1977), the Second Circuit has questioned whether such precedent supports certification of a class action to circumvent bankruptcy procedures, or to involuntarily modify creditors' rights with regard to each other. *See* In Re Joint Eastern and Southern District Asbestos Litigation, 982 F.2d 721 (2d Cir.1992), noted *infra* at II.A.6 (settlement classes).

3. INROADS AND SUCCESSES

PAYTON v. ABBOTT LABS

United States District Court, District of Massachusetts, 1979.
83 F.R.D. 382, *vacated* 100 F.R.D. 336 (D.Mass.1983).

Memorandum and Order on Class Certification

SKINNER, DISTRICT JUDGE.

The plaintiffs' motion for certification of a plaintiff class is conditionally ALLOWED to the extent and in the manner that I describe below. Their motion for certification of a defendant class is DENIED.

The plaintiff class includes all women:

1) who were exposed to diethylstilbestrol ("DES") *in utero*;

2) whose exposure occurred in Massachusetts;

3) who were born in Massachusetts;

4) who are domiciled in Massachusetts when they receive notice of this action; and

5) who have not developed uterine or vaginal cancer.[1]

---

1. The plaintiffs proposed a broader plaintiff class than the one that I have defined here. The defendants argued that members of the proposed class might be

The plaintiff class is conditionally certified under Rule 23(c)(4)(A), Fed.R.Civ.P., to permit resolution of these issues:

1) whether, in the circumstances alleged in this action, fear and anguish are, under Massachusetts law, compensable injuries;

2) whether, in the circumstances alleged in this action, having been put at an increased risk of developing cancer is, under Massachusetts law, a compensable injury;

3) whether, if without DES a class member would not have been born, she may, under Massachusetts law, maintain an action for injury from exposure to DES;

4) whether and when, in the circumstances alleged in this action, Massachusetts has recognized a cause of action for injury to a fetus;

5) whether and when the defendants were negligent in manufacturing and marketing DES for use by pregnant women to prevent miscarriages;

6) whether, under Massachusetts law, the defendants may be held strictly liable to the plaintiffs;

7) whether, under Massachusetts law, the defendants may be held absolutely liable to the plaintiffs for having allegedly tested DES on them without their consents;

8) whether a private right of action exists under the Federal Food, Drug and Cosmetic Act, 21 U.S.C. §§ 301, 331, and 352;

9) whether and when, in producing, marketing, and promoting DES as a miscarriage preventative, the defendants engaged in a joint enterprise;

10) whether and when the defendants combined and conspired in their acts and omissions relating to DES;

11) whether, if the defendants did not combine, conspire, or engage in a joint enterprise, a defendant may be held liable to a class member who cannot identify the maker of the DES to which she was exposed;

12) whether and for what periods claims of plaintiff class members under the foregoing theories of liability are barred by statutes of limitations; and

13) whether and for what periods statutes of limitations bar claims for:

capable of invoking the law of jurisdictions other than Massachusetts, that Massachusetts law was less advantageous for the plaintiffs than that of other jurisdictions, and that accordingly the named plaintiffs could not properly bind class members to Massachusetts law. The defendants contended that the choice of law problem evidenced a lack of common questions, undercut the typicality of the named plaintiffs' claims, and cast doubt on the adequacy of the named plaintiffs' representation. Members of the plaintiff class that I have defined will be bound by Massachusetts law and unable to invoke any other. As the defendants contended, other jurisdictions are more hospitable to plaintiffs than Massachusetts. The Massachusetts Supreme Judicial Court does not, for example, sanction strict liability in tort other than liability for breach of warranty under the Uniform Commercial Code.

a) breach of express warranties and representations;

b) breach of implied warranties of fitness, safety, and efficacy; and

c) fraudulent misrepresentation.

I. CERTIFICATION OF THE PLAINTIFF CLASS

A. *The Prerequisites of Rule 23(a)*

Before a class action may be maintained under Rule 23, it must meet the prerequisites of Rule 23(a) and one set of the alternative requirements in Rule 23(b). The plaintiffs bear the burden of demonstrating that a class action is appropriate. Shaw v. Mobil Oil Corporation, 60 F.R.D. 566, 568 (D.N.H.1973).

1. *Numerosity*

Rule 23(a)(1) requires that the members of a class in a class action be "so numerous that joinder of all members is impracticable." Surveys and estimates in the medical literature lead the plaintiffs to conclude that women in the United States who were exposed to DES *in utero* number between 500,000 and 2,000,000. Multiplying those figures by the percentage of the national population in Massachusetts, the plaintiffs estimate that the number of women in Massachusetts who were exposed to DES *in utero* is between 13,350 and 53,400. * * * Geographic differences in the use of DES suggest that this final range is conservative.

The plaintiffs also contacted some 25 medical projects, clinics, and practitioners in the greater Boston area treating or monitoring women who were exposed *in utero* to DES. Their search revealed a minimum of 2,339 readily identifiable women whose medical histories allegedly document exposure to DES (at least 1,441 of the total), or who believe on the basis of other evidence that they were exposed to DES (a maximum of 748, of whom some may have documentary evidence), or who show symptoms of DES exposure (at most 150, of whom some believe that they were exposed to DES).

The defendants do not contest the plaintiffs' showing of numerosity. I recognize that the plaintiffs' figures do not isolate plaintiff class members from the larger group of women in Massachusetts who were exposed to DES *in utero*. Even so, the magnitude of the plaintiffs' initial showing, 13,350 to 53,400 girls and women, makes it likely that the plaintiff class is so numerous that joinder of its members would be impracticable.

2. *Commonality*

Rule 23(a)(2) states that a class action may be maintained "[only if] ... there are questions of law or fact common to the class." The issues which this class action is designed to resolve meet that requirement.

If the plaintiffs win favorable determinations on the class issues, they will not have proved the defendants' liability to class members, but they will have established legal and factual prerequisites to it. Answers to common questions need not guarantee a determination of liability. Rule 23(c)(4)(A) explicitly authorizes class actions "with respect to particular issues."

3. Typicality

Rule 23(a)(3) requires that, in a class action, the "claims or defenses of the representative parties" be "typical of the claims or defenses of the class." With regard to the issues for which this class action has been conditionally certified, the claims and defenses of the named plaintiffs are typical of those of the class.

The Second Amended Complaint filed on July 15, 1976 listed named plaintiffs ranging then in age from eight to 29. The range and distribution of their ages make clear that they will fairly represent the class with respect to varying statutes of limitations and changes in substantive law which occurred over the period in which DES was marketed. *Cf.* 7 C. Wright & A. Miller, FEDERAL PRACTICE AND PROCEDURE § 1764 (1972 & 1979 Supp.)("varying fact patterns" do not preclude typicality; "same legal or remedial theory" sufficient); 3B Moore's FEDERAL PRACTICE ¶ 23.06–2 (1978).

There may be periods of legal significance in which no named plaintiff was exposed to DES. If it appears that there are absent class members whose interests are not being protected, I may condition continued class certification upon the joinder of additional named plaintiffs to fill chronological gaps. Class certification should not of course depend primarily on the court's evaluation of the competence and dedication of counsel for the named plaintiffs. I am impressed, however, with counsel's concern for the class as a whole, indeed for a broader class than I have certified. I doubt that "typicality" requires total identification of interests.

A more serious problem stems from the fact that many of the named plaintiffs, and probably many of the class members, will be unable to identify the brand of DES to which they were exposed. When claims of named plaintiffs and those of absent class members are against different defendants, that fact has been held to prevent class certification. La Mar v. H & B Novelty & Loan Co., 489 F.2d 461, 465 (9th Cir.1973). This careful opinion by Judge Sneed contains an important caveat against the distortion of the judicial function through imprudent extension of the class action. I have considered it both in the context of "typicality" and of "predominance," discussed *infra.*

This case falls within one of the exceptions recognized by the court in *La Mar,* in that plaintiffs allege a concerted pattern of marketing, deliberate concealment of manufacturers' identities and a conspiracy to test the product on the public. 489 F.2d at 470. Prosecution of these theories would not prejudice those plaintiff class members who can identify the manufacturer, and have the easier case. While these theories will undoubtedly complicate the trial, they would, if successfully prosecuted, provide additional potential sources of recovery or settlement for all class members.

It is also true that these asserted causes of action are novel, and their status as part of the current jurisprudence of the Commonwealth of Massachusetts is by no means clear. If they do not survive the defendants' motions to dismiss, it may be necessary to limit the class, or to create subclasses by defendant. I emphasize that certification here is conditional, and may be adjusted or terminated according to the course of the case. In the present stance of the parties, I am satisfied the class meets the requirements of *La Mar,* and that the named plaintiffs are typical.

4. Adequacy

Rule 23(a)(4) states that a class action may be maintained "only if ... the representative parties will fairly and adequately protect the interests of the class." Adequacy of representation depends on the qualifications of counsel for the representatives, on an absence of antagonism and a sharing of interests between representatives and absentees, and on the unlikelihood that the suit is collusive. Johnson v. Georgia Highway Express, Inc., 417 F.2d 1122, 1125 (5th Cir.1969). I find that the plaintiffs' counsel are capable of competent and vigorous prosecution of this action, that the action is not collusive, and that, on the issues for which I have certified this class action, the interests of the named plaintiffs and absentee class members are not antagonistic, but shared.

B. The Alternative Requirements of Rule 23(b)

The plaintiffs have moved for certification of a plaintiff class under Rule 23(b)(1)(A), (b)(1)(B), (b)(2), and (b)(3). For the reasons that follow, I conclude that certification is appropriate only under Rule 23(b)(3).

1. Rule 23(b)(1)(A)

Rule 23(b)(1)(A) is designed to prevent situations in which different courts establish "incompatible standards of conduct" for the same party. It is not meant to apply to personal injury suits for damages. McDonnell Douglas Corp. v. U.S. Dist. Ct., C.D. of Cal., 523 F.2d 1083, 1086 (9th Cir.1975), *cert. denied sub nom.,* Flanagan v. McDonnell Douglas Corp., 425 U.S. 911 (1976). *See* Advisory Committee's Note, Rule 23, 39 F.R.D. 69, 100 (1966). *Contra,* Hernandez v. Motor Vessel Skyward, 61 F.R.D. 558 (S.D.Fla.1973), *aff'd mem.,* 507 F.2d 1278 (5th Cir.1975); Petition of Gabel, 350 F.Supp. 624 (C.D.Cal.1972). I find that another court's granting declaratory or injunctive relief which would conflict with the remedies of the sort that the plaintiffs request [3] is unlikely. The plaintiffs have offered no substantial argument to the contrary.

---

3. The plaintiffs seek six remedies, of which the first four are phrased as prayers for declaratory or injunctive relief: 1) a declaratory judgment that the acts of the defendants in producing DES for use by pregnant women to prevent miscarriages were wrongful and unlawful; 2) an injunction ordering the defendants to notify girls, women, and doctors of facts about DES; 3) an injunction ordering the defendants to establish free clinics for examining plaintiff class members; 4) an injunction forbidding "mass-market testing" of drugs by the defendants; 5) monetary judgments for compensatory and punitive damages; and 6) an injunction ordering the defendants to estab-

2.   Rule 23(b)(1)(B)

Though the plaintiffs seek a group insurance fund, to be paid for by the defendants, as one of their remedies, *see* note 3, *supra,* their proposal does not require (b)(1)(B) certification. Assuming for the sake of argument that insurance is a proper form of relief, the defendants could be directed to insure individuals as well as a class.

The Advisory Committee stated that (b)(1)(B) certification was proper "when claims are made by numerous persons against a fund insufficient to satisfy all claims." Advisory Committee's Note, Rule 23, 39 F.R.D. 69, 101 (1966). The plaintiffs do not, however, offer evidence of the likely insolvency of the defendants, and I do not believe that, without more, numerous plaintiffs and a large *ad damnum* clause should guarantee (b)(1)(B) certification.

3.   Rule 23(b)(2)

Subdivision (b)(2) "does not extend to cases in which the appropriate final relief relates exclusively or predominantly to money damages." It applies instead when injunctive relief, or declaratory relief on which injunctive relief could be based, is proper. Advisory Committee's Note, Rule 23, 39 F.R.D. 69, 102 (1966). *Accord,* Eisen v. Carlisle & Jacquelin, 391 F.2d 555, 564 (2d Cir.1968). Finding that appropriate final relief in this action relates predominantly to money damages, I hold that the class may not be certified under subdivision (b)(2).

4.   Rule 23(b)(3)

For the reasons that follow, I find that the class issues, common questions of law and fact, predominate over questions affecting individual members of the plaintiff class, and that a class action is superior to other available methods for the fair and efficient adjudication of the controversy. Accordingly, I conditionally certify the plaintiff class, with regard to the common issues, under Rule 23(b)(3).

Mass marketing of potent drugs is a modern phenomenon. Traditional models of litigation, pitting one plaintiff against one defendant, were not designed to, and cannot, deal with the potential for injury to numerous and geographically dispersed persons that mass marketing presents.

The courts are faced with the choice of adapting traditional methods to the recurrent phenomenon of widespread drug litigation or leaving large numbers of people without a practical means of redress. It has been the tradition of the common law to adapt. There is a limit to a court's capacity to deal with major social problems, but this case seems to me to be still within the historical judicial function of providing private redress for violation of a legal right. *Cf.* La Mar v. H & B Novelty & Loan Co., 489 F.2d 461 (9th Cir.1973). For this litigation, in my opinion, certification under Rule 23(b)(3) offers the best means to adapt an established and tested structure to a modern phenomenon.

lish an insurance fund, or to pay a sufficiently large sum, to compensate class members who might suffer later from any cancer that DES has induced.

A fundamental aspect of justice is parity of treatment. Persons similarly situated and aggrieved should be similarly treated. The Advisory Committee wrote:

> Subdivision (b)(3) encompasses those cases in which a class action would achieve economies of time, effort, and expense, and promote *uniformity of decision as to persons similarly situated,* without sacrificing procedural fairness or bringing about other undesirable results.

Advisory Committee's Note, Rule 23, 39 F.R.D. 69, 102–03 (1966)(emphasis added). To determine whether and perhaps when the acts of the defendants were or became negligent in one proceeding is to insure that separate actions do not produce contradictory results.

The prerequisite to class certification under (b)(3) that the plaintiffs and the defendants contest most hotly is that of predominance. The defendants argue forcefully that innumerable questions would line the route from a finding that they had been negligent, or that they were strictly liable, to one that a given plaintiff was entitled to recover from them for adenosis or a risk of cancer. They say that the individual trial that would necessarily precede liability to a given plaintiff would have to encompass so many issues other than the ones that I listed above that a class action is not worth the effort. They suggest also that the individual trials would be so numerous and lengthy as to overwhelm the resources of this court. *Cf.* Windham v. American Brands, Inc., 565 F.2d 59 (4th Cir.1977), *cert. denied,* 435 U.S. 968, 98 S.Ct. 1605, 56 L.Ed.2d 58 (1978). They note the commentary of the Advisory Committee on (b)(3):

> A "mass accident" resulting in injuries to numerous persons is ordinarily not appropriate for a class action because of the likelihood that significant questions, not only of damages but of liability and defenses to liability, would be present, affecting the individuals in different ways. In these circumstances an action conducted nominally as a class action would degenerate in practice into multiple lawsuits separately tried.

Advisory Committee's Note, Rule 23, 39 F.R.D. 69, 103 (1966). Several courts have held that in personal injury suits alleging negligence or misfeasance by one or more defendants over extended periods, class certification should be denied. Ryan v. Eli Lilly & Co., No. 77–246 (D.S.C.1979); Austin v. Johns–Manville Products Corp., No. 75 754 (D.N.J.1977); Yandle v. PPG Industries, Inc., 65 F.R.D. 566 (E.D.Tex. 1974); *Tigue v. Squibb,* N.Y.L.J., May 2, 1979, at 7, col. 2 (N.Y.Sup.Ct. for N.Y. County); Ferrigno v. Eli Lilly and Co., No. L–41104–75 (Super.Ct. of N.J., L.Div., Hudson County, April 27, 1979); Rosenfeld v. A.H. Robins Co., 63 A.D.2d 11, 407 N.Y.S.2d 196 (1978).

Commentators have done little to explicate or clarify the meaning of predominance. Professor Moore states that a "quantitative test, comparing the amount of time and attention required for settlement of the common questions with that needed to conclude the individual matters, has properly been rejected...." So too, he declares, has been an "outcome-determinative" test. More important in his view are issues of how efficient class treatment will be, how significant are the common questions, and whether class certification would result in a lawsuit that was "seriously distorted." He notes that 23(c)(4) may be used to sever common issues in such a way as to insure predominance. 3B Moore's FEDERAL PRACTICE ¶ 23.45(2) (1978).

Professors Wright and Miller also reject "clockwatching" in favor of a "pragmatic" standard. They write that

> when common questions represent a significant aspect of the case and they can be resolved for all members of the class in a single adjudication, there is a clear justification for handling the dispute on a representative rather than on an individual basis.

They indicate that a complete identity of facts relating to class members is unnecessary; a "common nucleus of operative facts" will suffice. They note also that resolution of a predominating issue need not guarantee an end to the action, and cite tort liability as an issue which courts have viewed as being of "overriding significance." 7A C. Wright & A. Miller, FEDERAL PRACTICE AND PROCEDURE § 1778 (1972).

Analyzing whether mass torts were amenable to class action treatment, Judge Merhige detected a trend from wariness to acceptance. He concluded:

> On balance, it is the Court's view that under some circumstances mass accident litigation may and probably ought to be maintained as a class action. Perhaps the paradigm situation in which such treatment would be appropriate is one where: (1) the class action is limited to the issue of liability, (2) the class members support the action; and (3) the choice of law problems are minimized by the accident occurring and/or substantially all plaintiffs residing within the same jurisdiction.

Causey v. Pan American World Airways, Inc., 66 F.R.D. 392, 397 (E.D.Va.1975). This action satisfies the criteria of his paradigm as to the limited class certified.

Courts have certified (b)(3) classes in mass tort cases. *E.g.*, Bentkowski v. Marfuerza Compania Maritima, S.A., 70 F.R.D. 401 (E.D.Pa. 1976); American Trading & Pro. Corp. v. Fischbach & Moore, Inc., 47 F.R.D. 155 (N.D.Ill.1969). The defendants distinguish these cases as having dealt with contemporaneous injuries at one location. *Cf. Austin v. Johns–Manville Products Corp.; Yandle v. PPG Industries, Inc.* While I recognize that a course of injuries over time may require that I scrutinize the fairness and adequacy of class representation, I do not believe that it forecloses class treatment of the issues that I have certified. Properly framed special interrogatories, for example, would enable a jury trying class issues to establish periods of negligent conduct by one or more defendants.

Though Professors Moore, Wright, and Miller gainsay the use of a quantitative measure in determining predominance, this class action promises a likely efficiency. The plaintiffs have represented to me that "over 90% [o]f the trial time" in two individual DES suits was devoted to the question of "whether and when defendants knew or should have known of the dangers of DES exposure."

The defendants have argued that test cases offer an alternative to class certification; once one or two cases were tried, they say, the results would set the terms for settling the rest. I see no reason why the same logic should not vanquish the specter of an overwhelming onslaught of individual trials after adjudication of the class issues. In this latter case, both parties will have essential additional information with which to negotiate.

Victory for the defendants will avoid repetitive litigation asserting theories and claims that have been disposed of. Victory for the plaintiffs will go far towards bringing them recovery. And in either case, assuming that the plaintiffs have shown that they have suffered compensable injuries, the court will benefit from a determination of whether and when the defendants were negligent. A test case adjudicating the right to recover of one plaintiff alleging injury at one time could not produce that last determination.

A second alternative to this class action might have been founded on collateral estoppel. In Massachusetts, however, the party to be collaterally estopped must have been a party to the earlier action in which the issue was litigated. Rudow v. Fogel, 382 N.E.2d 1046 (Mass.1978). An action between one plaintiff and the defendants would not preclude a second plaintiff from litigating the same issues.

Rule 23(b)(3)(A)-(D) lists matters pertinent to findings of predominance and superiority. Relying on the representations of the plaintiffs and bearing in mind the form of this class action, I find that the interest of class members in individually controlling the prosecution of separate actions is minimal. Rule 23(b)(3)(A). The plaintiffs have stated that ten individual DES suits have been brought by plaintiffs who might meet the class definition. Given the estimated size of the class, that number is insignificant. The apparent interest of counsel in some of the individual cases in supporting and perhaps joining this action diminishes its significance further. Accordingly, I find that the extent and nature of existing litigation poses no bar to this class action. Rule 23(b)(3)(B). The definition of the plaintiff class makes concentrating litigation of the claims in this forum highly desirable. Rule 23(b)(3)(C). In light of the foregoing discussion, I find that this class action will probably be manageable. Rule 23(b)(3)(D).[4]

* * *

4. The defendants also object to this class action on the ground that the class is inadequately defined. They contend that the class membership of a given plaintiff will depend on evidence as to her mother's having taken DES and as to the plaintiff's

IV. Certification of a Defendant Class

The plaintiffs move for certification of a defendant class which would include all companies that manufactured DES. I deny their motion for two reasons which preclude the need for further findings. First, I find that the defenses of the representative parties are unlikely to be typical of those of the class. Rule 23(a)(3). Each defendant may have individual defenses to theories of joint or alternative liability. Second, I find that the proposed representative parties would be unlikely to protect fairly and adequately the interests of the class. Rule 23(a)(4). As representatives and absentees sought to avoid their own individual liabilities, there would be little sharing of interests and much antagonism.

JENKINS v. RAYMARK INDUSTRIES

United States Court of Appeals, Fifth Circuit, 1986.
782 F.2d 468.

Before Gee, Alvin B. Rubin and Reavley, Circuit Judges.

Reavley, Circuit Judge:

In this interlocutory appeal, the thirteen defendants challenge the decision of District Judge Robert M. Parker to certify a class of plaintiffs with asbestos-related claims. We affirm.

I. Background to Judge Parker's Plan

Experts estimate that at least 21 million American workers have been exposed to "significant" amounts of asbestos at the workplace since 1940; other millions have been exposed through environmental contact or contact with relatives who have worked with the products. R. Seltzer, *Punitive Damages in Mass Tort Litigation: Addressing the Problems of Fairness, Efficiency and Control,* 52 Fordham L.Rev. 37, 37 n.1 (1983); Note, *Mass Tort Claims and the Corporate Tortfeasor: Bankruptcy Reorganization and Legislative Compensation Versus the Common–Law Tort System,* 61 Tex.L.Rev. 1297, 1301 n.15 (1983). Because of its injurious propensities, such exposure, in human terms, has meant that literally tens of thousands of people fall ill or die from asbestos-related diseases every year. *E.g.,* Note, *Who Will Compensate the Victims of Asbestos–Related Diseases? Manville's Chapter 11 Fuels the Fire* [hereinafter, *Manville*], 14 Envtl.L. 465, 466–67 (1984). In legal terms, it has translated into thousands of lawsuits, over 20,000 as of 1983, centered mainly in industrialized areas along the country's coasts. *See* Seltzer, *supra,* at 37 n.1.

having a condition related to DES. Proving exposure to DES is analogous to, though perhaps more difficult than, proving presence at a mass accident, for which class actions have been certified. Whether exposure to DES creates a condition without gross physical symptoms that is a cogniza-ble injury is a disputed question for resolution after class certification. The definition of the plaintiff class is sufficient to allow a judgment as to the adequacy of its representation, and the provisions for notice that follow will insure that notice is adequate.

Courts, including those in our own circuit, have been ill-equipped to handle this "avalanche of litigation." *See* Note, *Manville, supra,* at 468–71. Our numerous opinions in asbestos-related cases have repeatedly recognized the dilemma confronting our trial courts, and expressed concern about the mounting backlog of cases and inevitable, lengthy trial delays. *See, e.g.,* Jackson v. Johns–Manville Sales Corp., 781 F.2d 394, 416 n.2 (5th Cir.1986)(Clark, C.J., dissenting); *Jackson,* 727 F.2d 506, 524 (5th Cir.1984); Hardy v. Johns–Manville Sales Corp., 681 F.2d 334, 348–52 (5th Cir.1982)(sympathizing with caseload and encouraging trial court innovation, such as the quoted Memorandum by Judge Parker); Migues v. Fibreboard Corp., 662 F.2d 1182, 1189 (5th Cir.1981)(calling for "new approaches to the national tragedy of asbestos-related disease").

About 5,000 asbestos-related cases are pending in this circuit. Much, though by no means all, of the litigation has centered in the Eastern District of Texas. Nearly nine hundred asbestos-related personal injury cases, involving over one thousand plaintiffs, were pending there in December of 1984. Despite innovative streamlined pretrial procedures and large-scale consolidated trials of multiple plaintiffs, the dockets of that district's courts remained alarmingly backlogged. Plaintiffs had waited years for trial, some since 1979—and new cases were (and still are) being filed every day. It is predicted that, because asbestos-related diseases will continue to manifest themselves for the next 15 years, filings will continue at a steady rate until the year 2000.

In early 1985, ten of these plaintiffs responded by moving to certify a class of all plaintiffs with asbestos-related personal injury actions pending in the Eastern District on December 31, 1984.[2] These plaintiffs hoped to determine in the class action one overarching issue—the viability of the "state of the art" defense. Because the trial of that issue consistently consumed substantial resources in every asbestos trial, and the evidence in each case was either identical or virtually so, they argued, a class determination would accelerate their cases.

II. The Plan

Following copious briefing and several hearings, the district court granted the motion. In his order of October 16, 1985, Judge Parker carefully considered the request under Rule 23(a), (b)(1) and (b)(3) of the Federal Rules of Civil Procedure. Finding a "limited fund" theory too speculative, he refused to certify the class under Rule 23(b)(1); by contrast, he found all of the elements for a 23(b)(3) action present. Drawing on his past experience, the judge concluded that evidence concerning the "state of the art" defense would vary little as to individual plaintiffs while consuming a major part of the time required for their trials. Considerable savings, both for the litigants and for the court, could thus be gained by resolving this and other defense and defense-

2. Three additional plaintiffs later moved to intervene. Proposed class counsel already represented about 80% of all members plaintiffs in their individual cases, and had tried numerous large and small asbestos cases.

related questions, including product identification, product defectiveness, gross negligence and punitive damages, in one class trial.[3] The court further found that the named representatives had "typical" claims, and that they and their attorneys would adequately represent the other class members. Accordingly, it certified the class as to the common questions, ordering them resolved for the class by a class action jury. The class jury would also decide all the individual issues in the class representatives' underlying suits; individual issues of the unnamed members would be resolved later in "mini-trials" of seven to ten plaintiffs. Although the class action jury would evaluate the culpability of defendants' conduct for a possible punitive damage award, any such damages would be awarded only after class members had won or settled their individual cases. The court subsequently appointed a special master to survey the class and prepare a report, detailing the class members and their claims, to apprise the jury of the gravity and extent of the absent members' claims and the typicality of the representatives' claims.

On appeal, defendants challenge the court's decision on three grounds: (1) the class fails to meet the requirements of Rule 23; (2) Texas law proscribes a bifurcated determination of punitive damages and actual damages; and (3) the contemplated class format is unconstitutional.

* * *

III. DISCUSSION

The purpose of class actions is to conserve "the resources of both the courts and the parties by permitting an issue potentially affecting every [class member] to be litigated in an economical fashion." General Telephone Co. of Southwest v. Falcon, 457 U.S. 147, 155 (1982)(quoting Califano v. Yamasaki, 442 U.S. 682, 701, 99 S.Ct. 2545, 2557, 61 L.Ed.2d 176 (1979)). To ensure that this purpose is served, Rule 23 demands that all class actions certified under Rule 23(b)(3) meet the requirements of both 23(a): numerosity, commonality, typicality, and adequacy of representation; and 23(b)(3): predominance and superiority. The district court has wide discretion in deciding whether or not to certify a proposed class. Assuming the court considers the Rule 23 criteria, we may reverse its decision only for abuse of discretion. Horton v. Goose Creek Independent School District, 690 F.2d 470, 483 (5th Cir.1982), *cert. denied*, 463 U.S. 1207, 103 S.Ct. 3536, 77 L.Ed.2d 1387 (1983); Boggs v. Alto Trailer Sales, Inc., 511 F.2d 114, 117 (5th Cir.1975).

---

3. The court pointed to the following general issues: (a) which products, if any, were asbestos-containing insulation products capable of producing dust that contained asbestos fibers sufficient to cause harm in its application, use, or removal; (b) which of the Defendants' products, if any, were defective as marketed and unreasonably dangerous; (c) what date each Defendant knew of should have known that insulators and their household members were at risk of contracting an asbestos-related injury or disease from the application, use, or removal of asbestos-containing insulation products; and (d) what amount of punitive damages, if any, should be awarded to the class as punishment for the Defendants' conduct.

IV. RULE 23

Defendants argue that this class meets none of the Rule 23 requirements, except "numerosity." There is no merit to this argument.

The threshold of "commonality" is not high. Aimed in part at "determining whether there is a need for combined treatment and a benefit to be derived therefrom," In re Agent Orange Product Liability Litigation, 506 F.Supp. 762, 787 (E.D.N.Y.1980), *modified,* 100 F.R.D. 718 (1983), *mandamus denied sub nom.,* In re Diamond Shamrock Chemicals Co., 725 F.2d 858 (2d Cir.), *cert. denied,* 465 U.S. 1067, 104 S.Ct. 1417, 79 L.Ed.2d 743 (1984), the rule requires only that resolution of the common questions affect all or a substantial number of the class members, Stewart v. Winter, 669 F.2d 328, 335 (5th Cir.1982). Defendants do not claim that they intend to raise a "state of the art" defense in only a few cases; the related issues are common to all class members.

The "typicality" requirement focuses less on the relative strengths of the named and unnamed plaintiffs' cases than on the similarity of the legal and remedial theories behind their claims. *E.g.,* In re Asbestos School Litigation, 104 F.R.D. 422, 429 (E.D.Pa.1984); In re Federal Skywalk Cases, 93 F.R.D. 415, 422 (W.D.Mo.), *vacated on other grounds,* 680 F.2d 1175 (8th Cir.), *cert. denied sub nom.,* Stover v. Rau, 459 U.S. 988, 103 S.Ct. 342, 74 L.Ed.2d 383 (1982); *cf.* General Telephone Co. of Southwest, 457 U.S. at 157 n.13, 102 S.Ct. at 2370 n. 13, 72 L.Ed.2d at 750 n. 13 (both commonality and typicality "serve as guideposts for determining whether . . . maintenance of a class action is economical and whether the named plaintiff's claim and the class claims are so interrelated that the interests of the class members will be fairly and adequately protected in their absence"). Defendants do not contend that the named plaintiffs' claims rest on theories different from those of the other class members.

The "adequacy" requirement looks at both the class representatives and their counsel. Defendants have not shown that the representatives are "inadequate" due to an insufficient stake in the outcome or interests antagonistic to the unnamed members.[5] *See Stewart,* 669 F.2d at 334–35; In re Asbestos School Litigation, 104 F.R.D. at 430; Wolgin v. Magic Marker Corp., 82 F.R.D. 168, 174–75 (E.D.Pa.1979). Neither do they give us reason to question the district court's finding that class counsel is "adequate" in light of counsel's past experience in asbestos cases, including trials involving multiple plaintiffs.

We similarly find no abuse in the court's determination that the certified questions "predominate," under Rule 23(b)(3). In order to "predominate," common issues must constitute a significant part of the individual cases. *See* In re Asbestos School Litigation, 104 F.R.D. at 431–32; In re Tetracycline Cases, 107 F.R.D. 719, 727 (W.D.Mo.1985); *see also* In re Asbestos School Litigation, 107 F.R.D. 215, 218–20 (E.D.Pa.1985). It is difficult to imagine that class jury findings on the

---

5. Moreover, dissatisfied members have the opportunity to "opt out" of the class.

class questions will not significantly advance the resolution of the underlying hundreds of cases.[6]

Defendants also argue that a class action is not "superior;" they say that better mechanisms, such as the Wellington Facility [7] and "reverse bifurcation," [8] exist for resolving these claims. Again, however, they have failed to show that the district court abused its discretion by reaching the contrary conclusion. We cannot find that the Wellington Facility, whose merits we do not question, is so superior that it must be used to the exclusion of other forums. Similarly, even if we were prepared to weigh the merits of other procedural mechanisms, we see no basis to conclude that this class action plan is an abuse of discretion.

Courts have usually avoided class actions in the mass accident or tort setting. Because of differences between individual plaintiffs on issues of liability and defenses of liability, as well as damages, it has been feared that separate trials would overshadow the common disposition for the class. See Advisory Committee Notes to 1966 Amendment to Fed. R.Civ.P. 23(b)(3). The courts are now being forced to rethink the alternatives and priorities by the current volume of litigation and more frequent mass disasters. *See* McGovern, *Management of Multiparty Toxic Tort Litigation: Case Law and Trends Affecting Case Management,* 19 Forum 1 (1983). If Congress leaves us to our own devices, we may be forced to abandon repetitive hearings and arguments for each claimant's attorney to the extent enjoyed by the profession in the past. Be that as time will tell, the decision at hand is driven in one direction by all the circumstances. Judge Parker's plan is clearly superior to the alternative of repeating, hundreds of times over, the litigation of the state of the art issues with, as that experienced judge says, "days of the same witnesses, exhibits and issues from trial to trial."

This assumes plaintiffs win on the critical issues of the class trial. To the extent defendants win, the elimination of issues and docket will mean a far greater saving of judicial resources. Furthermore, attorneys' fees for all parties will be greatly reduced under this plan, not only because of the elimination of so much trial time but also because the fees

---

6. Defendants argue that not all of the defendants in the underlying actions have been named in the class suit; in addition, some 70–80 potential class members have sued none of the class defendants. These arguments go nowhere, however. At worst, these latter "plaintiffs" will simply be unaffected by the class action findings. Conversely, if these "plaintiffs" do not opt out, the district court may decide to redefine the class to include only plaintiffs with claims against the named defendants. As for the plaintiffs who have sued both named and unnamed defendants, even if all class issues must be retried in the mini-trials as to all the unnamed defendants, the evidence will necessarily be significantly less than if no class findings had been made.

7. The Wellington Facility, funded by major asbestos producers, is a newly-operational center designed to resolve asbestos-related claims. The center is named for Dean Wellington of the Yale University Law School, who assisted in its organization.

8. "Reverse bifurcation" originated in the Third Circuit as a means of processing that circuit's backlog of asbestos-related cases. As its name suggests, it is a modified bifurcated trial format whereby plaintiffs in a first trial prove only that exposure to some asbestos product has caused their damages. Thereafter, either the cases are settled or remaining issues are resolved in second or third trials.

collected from all members of the plaintiff class will be controlled by the judge. From our view it seems that the defendants enjoy all of the advantages, and the plaintiffs incur the disadvantages, of the class action—with one exception: the cases are to be brought to trial. That counsel for plaintiffs would urge the class action under these circumstances is significant support for the district judge's decision.

Necessity moves us to change and invent. Both the Agent Orange and the Asbestos School courts found that specific issues could be decided in a class "mass tort" action—even on a nationwide basis. We approve of the district court's decision in finding that this "mass tort" class could be certified.

IN RE SCHOOL ASBESTOS LITIGATION

United States Court of Appeals, Third Circuit, 1986.
789 F.2d 996.

Before WEIS, HIGGINBOTHAM, and BECKER, CIRCUIT JUDGES.

WEIS, CIRCUIT JUDGE.

In an effort to reach an equitable result in these asbestos property damage cases brought by school authorities, the district court certified a nationwide mandatory class for punitive damages and an opt-out class for compensatory damages. We conclude that the mandatory class cannot be approved because of a lack of necessary findings and for the additional reason that the class, being under-inclusive, cannot in the circumstances here accomplish the objectives for which it was created. We will, however, affirm the denial of a (b)(2) class and despite misgivings on manageability, will affirm the district court's conditional certification of a Rule 23(b)(3) opt-out class on compensatory damages.

The district court invoked Fed.R.Civ.P. 23(b)(1)(B) in entering the certification order designating a mandatory class for school districts seeking punitive damages and followed Rule 23(b)(3) in forming a class for those seeking compensatory damages. A request for class certification under Rule 23(b)(2) was denied.

Pursuant to 28 U.S.C. § 1292(b), the court certified that the order constituting the 23(b)(1)(B) class raised a controlling question of law respecting possible violation of the Anti–Injunction Act, 28 U.S.C.A. § 2283. Various parties have appealed, challenging not only that phase of the case but also the propriety of the (b)(3) certification as well as the denial of the (b)(2) request.

This litigation began with the filing of class action complaints in the Eastern District of Pennsylvania by several Pennsylvania school districts and the Barnwell, South Carolina School District. The cases were consolidated soon after filing. Defendants, numbering approximately fifty, are associated with the asbestos industry as miners, bulk suppliers, brokers, assemblers, manufacturers, distributors, and at least one contractor.

As a result of federal legislation and regulation, plaintiffs are required to test for the presence of asbestos in schools.[2] The complaints seek compensatory and punitive damages as well as injunctive relief stemming from compliance with the federal legislation and the alleged need to remove or treat materials containing asbestos. The claims are based on theories of negligence, strict liability, intentional tort, breach of warranty, concert of action, and civil conspiracy.

After a group of plaintiffs presented a motion for the formation of classes under section (b)(1) and (b)(2) of Rule 23, the court issued an order certifying such classes but limited them to claims against three defendants which had agreed not to oppose that action. This ruling led to objections by various other plaintiffs and defendants, and the court later vacated the order in part. Arguments were then heard from all parties who split, not along the usual plaintiff-defendant lines, but into a number of unusual alignments as dictated by their perceived interests. The eventual certification order included the claims against all defendants.

In conditionally creating a mandatory class under (b)(1)(B) on the punitive damage claims, the court found "a substantial possibility that early awards of punitive damages in individual cases [would] impair or impede the ability of future claimants to obtain punitive damages." In re Asbestos School Litigation, 104 F.R.D. 422, 437 (E.D.Pa.1984). Although plaintiffs had advanced the argument that the defendants' funds would be exhausted before all claimants were paid, no substantive evidence was presented demonstrating that those assets would be insufficient, and accordingly the district judge declined to address that issue. *Id.* at 434 n.15.

The court believed that a mandatory class would create an opportunity for parity of treatment by bringing all injured parties into the same forum. Nevertheless, any plaintiff who opted out of the (b)(3) class would be permitted to settle a punitive damage claim with defendants. Additional support for certification was found in the strong "federal interest inherent in asbestos abatement" and the minimal intrusion on the interests of the school districts.

Class certification under 23(b)(2), however, was denied. The court commented that "despite the ingenuity of plaintiffs' claims for limited equitable remedies, this case remains at bottom, one for legal damages." 104 F.R.D. at 438. Although recognizing the possibility that at some point there might be "an incidental need for equitable relief," the court concluded that such a potential could not sustain certification under 23(b)(2).

The court directed the certification of a 23(b)(3) class, finding the numerosity requirement satisfied by estimates that friable asbestos is present in approximately 14,000 of the nation's schools, about 8,500 of

---

2. *See* The Toxic Substance Control Act, 15 U.S.C.A. § 2605 and E.P.A. regulations at 40 C.F.R. § 763.78 *et seq.* For other legislative responses to asbestos in the schools, *see* 20 U.S.C.A. § 3601 *et seq.;* 20 U.S.C.A. § 4011 *et seq.*

which have an abatement problem. Commonality existed in an underlying core of issues identified as: "(a) The general health hazards of asbestos; (b) defendants' knowledge or reason to know of the health hazards of asbestos; (c) defendants' failure to warn/test; and (d) defendant's concert of action and/or conspiracy involving formation of and adherence to industry practices." 104 F.R.D. at 429. Those elements could "be established by common proof, which, although it may be complex, does not vary from class-member school to class-member school."

The typicality requirement was satisfied because the plaintiffs' theories of liability were harmonious, and the named plaintiffs stood in a position similar to other members of the class. Some of the parties had obliquely questioned the adequacy of representation, but the court concluded that the class was represented by counsel "very experienced with class action litigation and thoroughly familiar with property damage and mass disaster litigation."

In considering the specific requirements for a (b)(3) certification, the court noted that the presence of asbestos in school buildings had a similar impact on each member of the class. Additionally, the question of proximate cause was a legal one which could be resolved on a class-wide basis without involving individualized member-by-member proof.

Addressing the requirement of superiority, the court emphasized that in resolving "at least some of the issues" on a class basis potential savings in expense would result, a consideration particularly important in asbestos litigation with its staggering costs. Moreover, because all claims were for property damage, the level of concern for the plaintiffs' right to choose individual forums and counsel was reduced.

The district judge conceded that the manageability aspect was not "wholly without difficulty," but stated "at this point I believe the management problems can be overcome." The court was convinced that although the substantive tort law of many jurisdictions might be applicable, the basic variations could be reduced to a reasonable number and subclasses could be created to accommodate those differences. Furthermore, plaintiffs represented to the trial judge that they would "direct discovery and trial briefs to meet the most stringent test of liability."

Notwithstanding the difficulties, the court determined that the class action was superior to the only existing alternative—repetitious individual litigation.

I

This appeal must be decided against the background of the asbestos scene, an unparalleled situation in American tort law. To date, more than 30,000 personal injury claims have been filed against asbestos manufacturers and producers. An estimated 180,000 additional claims of this type will be on court dockets by the year 2010. Added to those monumental figures are the claims for property damage—the cost of removing or treating asbestos-based materials used in building construction. Some indication of the magnitude of that potential liability may be gleaned from the fact that the property damage claims filed in the Johns–Manville bankruptcy proceedings stood at $69 billion as of June 1985.

The procedures of the traditional tort system proved effective in unearthing the hazards of asbestos to workers and the failure of its producers to reduce the risk. However, the undeniable limitations of the "one-on-one" approach in coping with the massive onset of claims now in the courts have caused serious and justified concern.

A report compiled by the Rand Corporation, entitled ASBESTOS IN THE COURT (1985), paints a gloomy picture. It points out the high cost and inefficiencies in handling these individual claims as well as the uneven, inconsistent, and unjust results often achieved. Perhaps the least flattering statistic is the high cost of processing these claims: "On the average, the total cost to plaintiffs and defendants of litigating a claim was considerably greater than the amount paid in compensation." REPORT at page 1.

Inefficiency results primarily from relitigation of the same basic issues in case after case. Since a different jury is empaneled in each action, it must hear the same evidence that was presented in previous trials. A clearer example of reinventing the wheel thousands of times is hard to imagine.

Apparent inconsistency of jury verdicts has often been a reflection of the ability of the system to sort out individual differences and tailor redress to precise circumstances. In the asbestos litigation field, however, the variation in jury awards has led to complaints that injustice rather than careful apportionment has resulted.

A Philadelphia Common Pleas Judge is quoted in the Rand Report:

Results of jury verdicts are capricious and uncertain. Sick people and people who died a terrible death from asbestos are being turned away from the courts, while people with minimal injuries who may never suffer severe asbestos disease are being awarded hundreds of thousands of dollars, and even in excess of a million dollars. The asbestos litigation often resembles the casinos 60 miles east of Philadelphia, more than a courtroom procedure.[3]

The problems are complicated by the variations and permutations of state law that govern tort liability. Most jurisdictions have continued, perhaps understandably, to treat the problem in a parochial and near-sighted manner. It may be that a state court does not wish to deny its litigants the benefits that are available in other jurisdictions. An attempt by a single state to impose some equitable form of apportionment to claims presently pending and to those inevitably arising in the

---

3. As an illustration, the same judge wrote about two cases in which each plaintiff had similar illnesses and symptoms: "In the case involving the man who most counsel thought to be the sicker of the two, the jury awarded $15,000. For the other plaintiff, the jury awarded $1,200,000. These results made this litigation more like roulette than jurisprudence." RAND REPORT at 42.

future is discouraged because other jurisdictions are not required to adopt a similarly enlightened viewpoint. A forum wishing to take the long-range view might find that its efforts were not only ineffective but unfair to its citizenry because claimants in the other states could drain off all the assets available for satisfaction of claims.

The national dimensions of the problem have led to calls for congressional action. Although the subject has attracted the attention of individual representatives and senators, no legislative response has garnered enough support to be enacted. Frustrated by the seemingly intractable problems inherent in the present situation, a thoughtful minority of the Court of Appeals of the Fifth Circuit would have certified to the United States Supreme Court the question of whether federal common law can apply to asbestos litigation. *See* Jackson v. Johns–Manville Sales Corp., 750 F.2d 1314 (5th Cir.1985)(*en banc*), *on reh'g*, 781 F.2d 394 (5th Cir.1986)(The original *en banc* majority certified certain questions to the state supreme court, which declined to rule on them).

Although necessarily brief, this sketch of the background of asbestos litigation is enough to show that this is not a routine class action.

* * *

III

The 23(b)(1)(B) Certification

All class actions must meet the prerequisites of Rule 23(a): numerosity, existence of questions of law or fact common to the class, typicality of claims or defenses, and adequacy of representation. Assuming the existence of these factors for present purposes, we proceed to the special elements of the (b)(1)(B) class, mindful that the most significant aspect of such a class is its mandatory character. All those who come within the description in the certification become, and must remain, members of the class because no opt-out provision exists.

In a diversity action such as this, certification of a mandatory class raises serious questions of personal jurisdiction and intrusion into the autonomous operation of state judicial systems. Another complicating factor is the Anti–Injunction Act, 28 U.S.C. § 2283, which prohibits a federal court from enjoining proceedings in a state court except with express Congressional authorization "or where necessary in aid of its jurisdiction or to protect or effectuate its judgment." By contrast, inclusion of the opt-out provision in 23(b)(3) class actions removes many of the problems raised by a mandatory procedure. Use of a voluntary class assures that only willing plaintiffs are before the court.

Rule 23(b)(1)(B) applies where there is a risk that "adjudications with respect to individual members of the class ... would as a practical matter be dispositive of the interests of the other members not parties to the adjudications or substantially impair or impede their ability to protect their interests."

Because plaintiffs had presented no evidence that the defendants' available assets would be insufficient to pay all claims, the district court did not rely on a "limited fund" theory as a basis for class certification. The proponents of the mandatory class, however, asserted "the very real possibility" that late-coming plaintiffs would be unable to receive punitive damages if a court decided in the future that defendants had been punished enough. In short, at some point punitive damages might be prohibited because they would amount to overkill, a proposition advanced in Roginsky v. Richardson–Merrell, Inc., 378 F.2d 832, 839 (2d Cir.1967). Finding a "substantial possibility" of the overkill scenario, the district court determined that creation of a (b)(1)(B) class was warranted as a measure to promote "equality of treatment for all litigants."

The demands for punitive damages have propelled this action into the controversy over awarding exemplary damages in successive mass tort cases arising from the same wrongful act. Problems in this area have been created by the failure of some courts to recognize the reasons underlying punitive damages.

*　*　*

In the era when most tort suits were "one-against-one" contests, a single act triggered a single punishment. The increasingly prevalent mass tort situation, however, exposes a defendant to repetitious punishment for the same culpable conduct. The parallels between the assessment of exemplary damages and a fine levied in criminal courts have led to suggestions that the concepts of double jeopardy and excessive punishment should be invoked in the civil field as well. *See* Aetna Life Ins. Co. v. Lavoie, 46 C.C.H.S.Ct. Bull. P. B1945 (Apr. 22, 1986); *see also* Morris, *Punitive Damages in Tort Cases*, 44 Harv.L.Rev. 1173 (1931); *cf.* Comment, *Criminal Safeguards and the Punitive Damages Defendant*, 34 U.Chi.L.Rev. 408 (1967).

Similar concerns have prompted highly respected judges to comment on the possibility that the due process clause might contain some constitutional limitation on the amount of exemplary damages to be awarded. "Unlimited multiple punishment for the same act determined in a succession of individual lawsuits and bearing no relation to the defendants' culpability or the actual injuries suffered by victims, would violate the sense of 'fundamental fairness' that is essential to constitutional due process." In re Federal Skywalk Cases, 680 F.2d 1175, 1188 (8th Cir.1982)(Heaney, J. dissenting). "There must, therefore, be some limit, either as a matter of policy or as a matter of due process, to the amount of times defendants may be punished for a single transaction." In re "Agent Orange" Product Liability Litigation, 100 F.R.D. 718, 728 (1983).

In addition to a possible federal constitutional limitation, state substantive tort law could place restraints on repetitive punitive damage awards. This concept, aimed at the prevention of "overkill" as discussed in *Roginsky*, has been labeled the "limited generosity" theory by some of the parties to this case.

In *Roginsky,* Judge Friendly speculated on the possibility of having one court assess a single punitive damage award for distribution to all successful plaintiffs. 378 F.2d at 839 n.11. *See also* Seltzer, *Punitive Damages in Mass Tort Litigation: Addressing the Problems of Fairness, Efficiency and Control,* 52 Fordham L.Rev. 37 (1983). The district court's (b)(1)(B) certification in this case is a variation on that same theme.

In a thoughtful dissertation prepared in the course of the LL.M. program for judges conducted at the University of Virginia Law School, Judge R. Barclay Surrick thoroughly reviewed the doctrine of punitive damages. He concluded that in the field of asbestos litigation, "[b]alancing the benefits to be derived from continued imposition of punitive damages against the social and economic consequences of such a course of action, it appears that the continued imposition of punitive damages cannot be justified." Surrick, *Punitive Damages and Asbestos Litigation in Pennsylvania: Punishment or Annihilation?,* 87 Dick.L.Rev. 265, 296 (1983).

Cognizant of these concerns, two federal courts of appeals have nevertheless allowed awards of punitive damages in asbestos cases on the ground that they were permitted by state law. Jackson v. Johns–Manville, 781 F.2d 394 (5th Cir.1986); Cathey v. Johns–Manville Sales Corp., 776 F.2d 1565 (6th Cir.1985). In the latter case, the court rejected the defendant's due process contention, stating that "As a matter of federal constitutional law we believe that the presence of a judicial tribunal before which to litigate the propriety of a punitive damages award provides Johns–Manville with all the procedural safeguards to which it is due." 776 F.2d at 1571.

* * *

Thus powerful arguments have been made that, as a matter of constitutional law or of substantive tort law, the courts shoulder some responsibility for preventing repeated awards of punitive damages for the same acts or series of acts. Preliminarily we will assume, without deciding, that these arguments might provide a threshold justification for the exercise of discretion in certifying a nationwide (mandatory) Rule 23(b)(1)(B) class for punitive damages. We nonetheless hold that the district court abused its discretion in certifying the 23(b)(1)(B) class here because neither the record nor the court's findings are adequate to support the procedure.

The district court made no factual findings at all as to the potential amount and scope of punitive damages. This is in sharp contrast to the detailed findings on the subject in In re Agent Orange Product Liability Litigation, 100 F.R.D. 718 (E.D.N.Y.1983), *mandamus denied,* 725 F.2d 858 (2d Cir.), *cert. denied,* 465 U.S. 1067, 104 S.Ct. 1417, 79 L.Ed.2d 743 (1984). The most the district court mustered here was its conclusion that: "It is apparent that there is a substantial possibility that early awards of punitive damages in individual cases will impair or impede the ability of future claimants to obtain punitive damages. The reality of such impairment has been recognized by commentators and courts. (citations omitted)." 104 F.R.D. at 437.

We are aware of the inherent limitations on any factual inquiry undertaken at such an early stage of the litigation, and we recognize that any record that could be developed would be inevitably predictive. Nonetheless, in our view these findings fall short of the mark.

Moreover, some basic considerations expose a critical flaw in the district court's analysis. The class certified does not even include all property damage claimants. Claims for repair of municipal buildings, for instance, are omitted, as are those of homeowners. Within a few weeks after oral argument in this appeal, a jury awarded $6 million in a property damage case brought as a result of the presence of asbestos products in a city hall. Added to the recovery was $2 million in punitive damages. City of Greenville v. W.R. Grace & Co., 640 F.Supp. 559 (D.S.C.1986).

There is some evidence that the school claims make up a significant portion of the total property damage alleged. *See* ASBESTOS LITIGATION REPORTER at 10, 243–44 (June 21, 1985). Clearly, however, this aspect of the litigation transcends the nation's classrooms and extends to municipal buildings, homes, and other structures.

Far more significant are the tens of thousands of personal injury suits in which punitive damage verdicts have been and continue to be assessed. These claims are satisfied from the same pool of assets to which the school districts now look. If a limit is ever placed on the total punitive damages to be imposed on the asbestos defendants, then that limit probably would apply to all claims whether they arise in property damage or personal injury suits. The school claims would be but a small portion of this total.

The circumstances in this case are again a decided contrast to those in the "Agent Orange" litigation where all of the claims against the defendants were concentrated in one case. In that circumstance, the court had control over all those affected and could hope to carry out the basic premise justifying the class action—parity for all victims and reduction of litigation expenses for all parties.

Assuming that the record supported the "limited generosity" theory, we would nonetheless decertify the class on the ground that it is under-inclusive. The "limited generosity" theory is a variation of the "limited fund" situation mentioned in the advisory committee note to Rule 23, the situation in which "claims are made by numerous persons against a fund insufficient to satisfy all claims." Fed.R.Civ.P. 23 advisory committee note. More precisely, "limited generosity" (or "punitive damages overkill," as some class members call it) is the functional equivalent of the limited fund in that, by operation of the limited generosity principle, only a limited amount of punitive damage funds will be available, regardless of the ability of the defendants to pay. Since the purpose of a 23(b)(1)(B) class is to avoid a judgment that "while not technically concluding the other members, might do so as a practical matter," *id.*, all persons with claims upon the "limited fund" should be included in the 23(b)(1)(B) class.

Thus, because all awards must come from the same defendants, a mandatory class predicated on a potential legal limit to punitive damages would logically include all litigants who seek such awards. From that standpoint, the (b)(1)(B) class certified here is under-inclusive with the result that separate actions by those who should properly be included in the class will go forward. However, the suppression of such separate actions is described in the advisory committee note as "the [reason] for and the principal key to the propriety and value" of a 23(b)(1) class.

* * *

The effect of the mandatory class has been to single out the school districts for special and possibly disadvantageous treatment. They have been forced to litigate in a jurisdiction and under a class procedure that many districts do not desire, and their punitive damage claims have been put "on hold" while the protracted class certification procedure runs its course. Because of this delay, this class could end up in a detrimental position if punitive damage awards are precluded because of a future judicial ruling.

Since the thousands of other claimants who seek exemplary damages from the asbestos defendants need not operate within the confines of a mandatory class procedure, the quest for punitive damages remains for them a race to the courthouse door. Consequently, if the district court proves correct in its theory that at some point a limit on all punitive damage awards will be established, the school districts may be prejudiced in their opportunity to share in the available funds in the meantime.

As noted by the district court, Rule 23(b)(1)(B) exists to protect potential claimants and provide equality of treatment. Certification of a punitive damage class under that provision here will not accomplish these objectives. In the court's pursuit of an end that is not attainable, the class designed to be protected will be burdened with hardships not imposed on any other litigants.

Nor do we see how, in the present posture of this litigation, the class could be expanded to confront effectively the punitive damage issue in the entire asbestos area. Whether a national class based on a federal constitutional challenge could accomplish that result is obviously not before us. Although we recognize and commend the district judge's attempt to grapple with the seemingly insoluble problems of punitive damages in these cases, we simply cannot find that the avenue he selected will lead to an appropriate and fair resolution.

We do not hold that under-inclusiveness is necessarily fatal to a class created under 23(b)(1)(B); [10] rather, each case requires a careful assessment of the factors mentioned in Rule 19. Courts should give particular attention to the possibility of prejudice either to those omitted from the class or to those within it. In the circumstances here, we conclude that under-inclusiveness does pose an obstacle.

A certain inherent prejudice exists when a litigant is forced to participate in an undesired mandatory class action. That result may be acceptable where the class device will serve the worthwhile goal of protecting the interests of all litigants to a potentially limited fund, but is hard to justify where only a small number of potential claimants can be included in the mandatory action.

A class action may promote efficiency by reducing repetitive testimony and evidence that otherwise would be required in individual trials. Those advantages, however, are secured at the price of delaying the disposition of individual cases that might be tried to conclusion in a number of state and district courts in the interim. In effect, a mandatory class action creates a bottleneck by concentrating the litigation, at least for a period, before one judge instead of spreading the individual cases out among many trial forums.

* * *

IV

DENIAL OF 23(b)(2) CERTIFICATION

A class may be certified under 23(b)(2) when the "party opposing the class has acted or refused to act on grounds generally applicable to the class, thereby making appropriate final injunctive relief or corresponding declaratory relief with respect to the class as a whole." Plaintiffs here seek mandatory injunctive relief in the form of certain remedial action and restitution for expenditures already incurred to ameliorate asbestos hazards.

The district court concluded that despite the plaintiffs' ingenuity the claims in this suit were essentially for damages. The judge pointed to the advisory committee notes accompanying Rule 23(b)(2), which state that it "does not extend to cases in which the appropriate final relief relates exclusively or predominantly to money damages." The district court did not rule out the possible application of equitable remedies at some stage of the proceeding but concluded that a (b)(2) certification was not appropriate at this time.

Precedent supports the district court's view that an action for money damages may not be maintained as a Rule 23(b)(2) class action. *See, e.g.,* Lukenas v. Bryce's Mountain Resort, Inc., 538 F.2d 594 (4th Cir.1976); In re Arthur Treacher's Franchise Litigation, 93 F.R.D. 590, 594 (E.D.Pa.1982). We see no justification for overturning the district judge's evaluation of the realities of the litigation before him. Counsel's

---

10. We obviously do not reach the question whether the notion of under- inclusiveness applies outside of a 23(b)(1)(B) mandatory class action.

desire to have a mandatory class is understandable, but the case for such a certification has not been established.

We find neither error of law nor abuse of discretion in the judge's ruling, and consequently will affirm the denial of a (b)(2) class.

V

THE 23(b)(3) CERTIFICATION

The advisory committee notes to (b)(3) state that a "mass accident" causing injuries to numerous persons is generally not appropriate for class action treatment because "significant questions, not only of damages but of liability and defenses of liability, would be present, affecting the individuals in different ways." If such an action were conducted as a class action, it "would degenerate in practice into multiple lawsuits separately tried."

Although that statement continues to be repeated in case law, there is growing acceptance of the notion that some mass accident situations may be good candidates for class action treatment. An airplane crash, for instance, would present the same liability questions for each passenger, although the damages would depend on individual circumstances. Determination of the liability issues in one suit may represent a substantial savings in time and resources. Even if the action thereafter "degenerates" into a series of individual damage suits, the result nevertheless works an improvement over the situation in which the same separate suits require adjudication on liability using the same evidence over and over again. *See* Hernandez v. Motor Vessel Skyward, 61 F.R.D. 558 (S.D.Fla.1973).

Reassessment of the utility of the class action in the mass tort area has come about, no doubt, because courts have realized that such an action need not resolve all issues in the litigation. See Fed.R.Civ.P. 23(c)(4)(A). If economies can be achieved by use of the class device, then its application must be given serious and sympathetic consideration.

Concentration of individual damage suits in one forum can lead to formidable problems, but the realities of litigation should not be overlooked in theoretical musings. Most tort cases settle, and the preliminary maneuverings in litigation today are designed as much, if not more, for settlement purposes than for trial. Settlements of class actions often result in savings for all concerned.

Part of the reluctance to apply the class action to mass torts is rooted in the notion that individual plaintiffs have the right to select their own counsel and forum, particularly in personal injury actions. *See* Dalkon Shield IUD Products Liability Litigation, 693 F.2d 847 (9th Cir.1982); Yandle v. PPG Indus., Inc., 65 F.R.D. 566 (E.D.Tex.1974). That factor has little, if any, relevance in this case because the claims are limited to property damage, and school districts are unlikely to have strong emotional ties to the litigation. *See* In re Three Mile Island Litigation, 87 F.R.D. 433 (M.D.Pa.1980)(certifying class action as to economic claims but not for personal injuries). Furthermore, the school districts have the right to opt out, and some have stated their intention to do so.

In short, the trend has been for courts to be more receptive to use of the class action in mass tort litigation. *See* Wright & Colussi, *The Successful Use of the Class Action Device in the Management of the Skywalk Tort Litigation,* 52 UMKC L.Rev. 141 (1984); Williams, *Mass Tort Class Actions: Going, Going, Gone?* 98 F.R.D. 323; Wright & Miller, FEDERAL PRACTICE AND PROCEDURE, § 1783; Note, *Class Certification in Mass Accident Cases Under Rule 23(b)(1),* 96 Harv.L.Rev. 114 (1983).

In reviewing the district court's (b)(3) certification, we must decide whether the criteria of Rule 23(a) are met. The requirements of numerosity, typicality, and adequacy of representation were found to be satisfied in this case, and we affirm those determinations on the basis of the district court's analysis. The only serious challenge raised to the 23(a) ruling is the argument that no "questions of law or fact common to the class" exist. *See* Rule 23(a)(2). Addressing that contention, we examine the district court's identification of the common issues involved in the plaintiffs' claims. Bogosian v. Gulf Oil Corp., 561 F.2d 434 (3d Cir.1977), *cert. denied,* 434 U.S. 1086, 98 S.Ct. 1280, 55 L.Ed.2d 791 (1978). If the district court applied the correct legal standard, its class action determination is subject to review for abuse of discretion. 561 F.2d at 448; Katz v. Carte Blanche Corp., 496 F.2d 747, 756–57 (3d Cir.1974)(*en banc*).

Noting that the complaints allege claims for damages based on negligence, strict liability, breach of warranty, intentional tort, concert of action and civil conspiracy, the district court explained that all these claims "arise out of the same common nucleus of operative facts relating to defendants' conduct and the nature of asbestos products." 104 F.R.D. at 432.

The district judge identified common factual issues as the health hazards of asbestos, the defendants' knowledge of those dangers, the failure to warn or test, and the defendants' concert of action or conspiracy in the formation of and adherence to industry practices. The court also believed that the proof of these matters would not vary widely from one class member to another. While harboring some reservations as to the breadth of the district court's analysis, we agree with its determination that Rule 23(a)(2) is satisfied.

Plaintiffs aver that low-level exposure to asbestos constitutes an excessive risk of harm, and that the presence of ambient fibers requires expensive remedial action to comply with federal legislation and regulations. Plaintiffs contend that the presence of any airborne asbestos fibers in a school presents an unacceptable hazard. Whether that is true or whether only a higher concentration creates a danger is an issue common to all members of the plaintiff class. Ascertaining the danger point is critical to the determination of whether class members have sustained a legal injury and also is pertinent in establishing the existence of a defective product.

The plaintiffs' contention that defendants knew of the dangers of asbestos and failed to warn is also common to the members of the class. The opponents assert that the defendants' knowledge cannot be proved on a common basis because medical understanding of the effects of asbestos exposure has "changed markedly" over the years. The focus, however, must be on whether the fact to be proved is common to the members of the class, not whether it is common to all the defendants. *See* Blackie v. Barrack, 524 F.2d 891 (9th Cir.1975). Similarly, proof of concert of action or conspiracy by the defendants (or some of them) involves common questions.

We find ourselves in substantial agreement with the reasoning of the Court of Appeals for the Fifth Circuit which, in upholding a (b)(3) class action of 893 asbestos personal injury claims, noted that the "threshold of commonality is not high." Jenkins v. Raymark Indus. Inc., 782 F.2d 468 (5th Cir.1986).

Once the mandates of Rule 23(a) are satisfied, certification may be upheld when common issues predominate over individual ones and the class method of adjudication is superior to existing alternatives. There may be cases in which class resolution of one issue or a small group of them will so advance the litigation that they may fairly be said to predominate. Resolution of common issues need not guarantee a conclusive finding on liability, Eisenberg v. Gagnon, 766 F.2d 770 (3d Cir. 1985), nor is it a disqualification that damages must be assessed on an individual basis. *See Bogosian,* 561 F.2d at 456.

Experience shows that in the asbestos litigation arena redundant evidence is the rule rather than the exception. In case after case, the health issues, the question of injury causation, and the knowledge of the defendants are explored, often by the same witnesses. Efforts to achieve expeditious disposition of the cases by invocation of stare decisis and collateral estoppel have been largely unsuccessful. *See* Hardy v. Johns–Manville Sales Corp., 681 F.2d 334 (5th Cir.1982); Migues v. Fibreboard Corp., 662 F.2d 1182 (5th Cir.1981).

The use of the class action device appears to offer some hope of reducing the expenditure of time and money needed to resolve the common issues which are of substantial importance. As the *Jenkins* court commented, "It is difficult to imagine that class jury findings on the class questions will not significantly advance the resolution of the underlying hundreds of cases." 782 F.2d at 472–73.

In some ways, *Jenkins* presented more difficult problems because of the complexity of the causation questions in personal injury suits; that phase of a property damage claim is more straightforward. However, the *Jenkins* class action is confined to claims arising under the law of a single state. Here the court is confronted with the substantive law of many states.

To meet the problem of diversity in applicable state law, class plaintiffs have undertaken extensive analysis of the variances in products liability among the jurisdictions. That review separates the law into four categories. Even assuming additional permutations and combinations, plaintiffs have made a creditable showing, which apparently satisfied the district court, that class certification does not present insuperable obstacles. Although we have some doubt on this score, the effort may nonetheless prove successful.[11]

We have cited only a few illustrations and have not attempted to compile a complete listing of the practical problems in this case. Some of these difficulties have already been alluded to in the order of the multi-district panel refusing to consolidate pretrial activity in some twenty school district cases. *See* In re Asbestos School Products Liability Litigation, 606 F.Supp. 713 (J.P.M.L.1985).

As we see it, at the present stage, manageability is a serious concern. In a sense, a whole industry is on trial, presenting a likelihood that defendants occupying various positions in the distribution chain could bear differing degrees of responsibility for the alleged injury to the class. For example, two of the common questions are the defendants' knowledge of the dangers of asbestos and the existence of an industry-wide conspiracy to suppress that knowledge. Although the plaintiffs' proof on those points would not differ from class member to class member, certain defendants may respond on an individual basis as to their lack of culpability. The potential for individualized defenses does not detract from the commonality of the questions as viewed from the standpoint of the class members, but the problem clearly poses significant case management concerns.

Manageability is a practical problem, one with which a district court generally has a greater degree of expertise and familiarity than does an appellate court. Link v. Mercedes–Benz, Inc., 550 F.2d at 864. Hence, a district court must necessarily enjoy wide discretion, and we are not inclined to reverse a certification before the district judge has had an opportunity to put the matter to a test. We point out the critical fact that certification is conditional. When, and if, the district court is convinced that the litigation cannot be managed, decertification is proper. *See* Payton v. Abbott Labs., 100 F.R.D. 336 (D.Mass.1983).

As the case goes forward, the district court may well find other important common issues, perhaps even more critical for resolution than those sorted out at this early stage. We are unwilling to foreclose that possibility. Nor do we limit the option of the district court to decertify if

---

11. One commentator has written: "there will be a point at which the sheer magnitude of the task of construing the various laws will compel a court not to certify the multistate class or to reduce it to a more manageable number of states. Even short of that point, choice of law may pose major problems. The first is the danger of an unwarranted intrusion into another state's legal affairs through a mistaken application of its laws. The court should thus consider its own familiarity with the other state's law, the degree to which that law is unclear or unsettled, and the extent to which it implicates important interests of the other state." Note, *Multistate Plaintiff Class Actions: Jurisdiction and Certification,* 92 Harv.L.Rev. 718, 742 (1979).

the issues it has classified as substantial later appear insufficient to justify the class procedure.

We acknowledge that our reluctance to vacate the (b)(3) certification is influenced by the highly unusual nature of asbestos litigation. The district court has demonstrated a willingness to attempt to cope with an unprecedented situation in a somewhat novel fashion, and we do not wish to foreclose an approach that might offer some possibility of improvement over the methods employed to date.

Accordingly, the order certifying a (b)(3) class will be affirmed as will the order denying a (b)(2) certification. The order granting a (b)(1)(B) class will be vacated.

IN RE "AGENT ORANGE" PRODUCT LIABILITY LITIGATION

United States Court of Appeals, Second Circuit, 1987.
818 F.2d 145.

Before VAN GRAAFEILAND, WINTER, and MINER, CIRCUIT JUDGES.

WINTER, CIRCUIT JUDGE:

This is the first of nine opinions, all filed on this date, dealing with appeals from Judge Pratt's and Chief Judge Weinstein's various decisions in this multidistrict litigation and class action. This opinion begins with a section entitled "Overview and Summary of Rulings" that summarizes the entire case and all of our decisions. The next section, "Detailed History of Proceedings," gives the background for all of the appeals. Familiarity with this section may be necessary to understand the various opinions that follow. The present opinion also contains our rulings regarding the certification of a class action and the approval of the settlement between the plaintiff class and the defendant chemical companies. Two other opinions by this author review the propriety of the distribution scheme for the resultant fund and the grant of summary judgment against those plaintiffs who opted out of the class action. Three opinions by Judge Van Graafeiland resolve issues concerning the liability of the United States to veterans, their families, and the chemical companies. A fourth opinion by Judge Van Graafeiland reviews the dismissal of actions brought by civilian plaintiffs against the United States and the chemical companies. Two opinions by Judge Miner resolve issues concerning the validity of a fee agreement among the members of the Plaintiffs' Management Committee ("PMC") and the district court's award of attorneys' fees.

* * *

I. OVERVIEW AND SUMMARY OF RULINGS

By any measure, this is an extraordinary piece of litigation. It concerns the liability of several major chemical companies and the United States government for injuries to members of the United States, Australian, and New Zealand armed forces and their families. These injuries were allegedly suffered as a result of the servicepersons' exposure to the herbicide Agent Orange while in Vietnam.

Agent Orange, which contains trace elements of the toxic by-product dioxin, was purchased by the United States government from the chemical companies and sprayed on various areas in South Vietnam on orders of United States military commanders. The spraying generally was intended to defoliate areas in order to reduce the military advantage afforded enemy forces by the jungle and to destroy enemy food supplies.

We are a court of law, and we must address and decide the issues raised as legal issues. We do take note, however, of the nationwide interest in this litigation and the strong emotions these proceedings have generated among Vietnam veterans and their families. The correspondence to the court, the extensive hearings held throughout the nation by the district court concerning the class settlement with the chemical companies, and even the arguments of counsel amply demonstrate that this litigation is viewed by many as something more than an action for damages for personal injuries. To some, it is a method of public protest at perceived national indifference to Vietnam veterans; to others, an organizational rallying point for those veterans. Thus, although the precise legal claim is one for damages for personal injuries, the district court accurately noted that the plaintiffs were also seeking "larger remedies and emotional compensation" that were beyond its power to award. In re "Agent Orange" Product Liability Litigation, 597 F.Supp. 740, 747 (E.D.N.Y.1984).

Central to the litigation are the many Vietnam veterans and their families who have encountered grievous medical problems. It is human nature for persons who face cancer in themselves or serious birth defects in their children to search for the causes of these personal tragedies. Well-publicized allegations about Agent Orange have led many such veterans and their families to believe that the herbicide is the source of their current grief. That grief is hardly assuaged by the fact that contact with the herbicide occurred while they were serving their country in circumstances that were unpleasant at best, excruciating at worst.

When the case is viewed as a legal action for personal injury sounding in tort, however—and we are bound by our oaths to so view it—the most noticeable fact is the pervasive factual and legal doubt that surrounds the plaintiffs' claims. Indeed, the clear weight of scientific evidence casts grave doubt on the capacity of Agent Orange to injure human beings. Epidemiological studies of Vietnam veterans, many of which were undertaken by the United States, Australian, and various state governments, demonstrate no greater incidence of relevant ailments among veterans or their families than among any other group. To an individual plaintiff, a serious ailment will seem highly unusual. For example, the very existence of a birth defect may persuade grieving parents as to Agent Orange's guilt. However, a trier of fact must confront the statistical probability that thousands of birth defects in children born to a group the size of the plaintiff class might not be unusual even absent exposure to Agent Orange. A trier of fact must also confront the fact that there is almost no evidence, even in studies involving animals, that exposure of males to dioxin causes birth defects in their children.

Both the Veterans' Administration and the Congress have treated the epidemiological studies as authoritative. Although such studies do not exclude the possibility of injury and settle nothing at all as to future effects, they offer little scientific basis for believing that Agent Orange caused any injury to military personnel or their families. The scientific basis for the plaintiffs' case consists of studies of animals and industrial accidents involving dioxin. Differences in the species examined and nature of exposure facially undermine the significance of these studies when compared with studies of the veterans themselves.

Proving that the ailments of a particular individual were caused by Agent Orange is also extremely difficult. Indeed, in granting summary judgment against those plaintiffs who opted out of the class action (the "optouts"), the district court essentially held that such proof was presently impossible. The first evidentiary hurdle for such an individual is to prove exposure to Agent Orange, an event years past that at the time did not carry its current significance. Such evidence generally consists only of oral testimony as to an individual's remembering having been sprayed while on the ground and/or having consumed food and water in areas where spraying took place. The second and, in the view of the district court, insurmountable hurdle is to prove that the individual's exposure to Agent Orange caused the particular ailment later encountered. Plaintiffs do not claim that Agent Orange causes ailments that are not found in the population generally and that cannot result from causes known and unknown other than exposure to dioxin. Plaintiffs' proof of causation would consist largely of inferences drawn from the existence of an ailment, exposure to Agent Orange, and medical opinion as to a causal relationship. However, the difficulties in excluding known causes, such as undetected exposure to the same or similar toxic substances in civilian life, and the conceded existence of unknown causes might make it difficult for any plaintiff to persuade a trier of fact as to Agent Orange's guilt. Causation is nevertheless an absolutely indispensable element of each plaintiff's claim.

The plaintiffs' claims are further complicated by the fact that an individual's exposure to Agent Orange cannot be traced to a particular defendant because the military mixed the Agent Orange produced by various companies in identical, unlabeled barrels. No one can determine, therefore, whether a particular instance of spraying involved a particular defendant's product. In addition, the Agent Orange produced by some defendants had a considerably higher dioxin content than that produced by others. Because the alleged ailments may be related to the amount of dioxin to which an individual was exposed, it is conceivable that if Agent Orange did cause injury, only the products of certain companies could have done so.

Difficult legal problems also arise from the considerable uncertainty as to which product liability rules and statutes of limitations apply to the various plaintiffs. The plaintiffs come from throughout the United States, Australia, and New Zealand, and each would face difficult choice of law problems that might be resolved adversely to their claims.

Finally, doubt about the strength of the plaintiffs' claims exists because of the so-called military contractor defense. The chemical companies sold Agent Orange to the United States government, which used it in waging war against enemy forces seeking control of South Vietnam. It would be anomalous for a company to be held liable by a state or federal court for selling a product ordered by the federal government, particularly when the company could not control the use of that product. Moreover, military activities involve high stakes, and common concepts of risk averseness are of no relevance. To expose private companies generally to lawsuits for injuries arising out of the deliberately risky activities of the military would greatly impair the procurement process and perhaps national security itself.

An illustration of the many factual and legal difficulties facing the plaintiffs is the dispute among their counsel as to how many "serious" or "strong" claims there are. The Plaintiffs' Management Committee ("PMC") estimates a much smaller number than do counsel for the class members who object to the settlement. Neither group has hard evidence to support its estimates. If by "serious" or "strong" one means a case likely to prevail on liability and to result in a substantial damage award, then we believe that every plaintiff would encounter difficulties in proving causation and even graver problems in overcoming the military contractor defense. If a case is considered "serious" or "strong" because the plaintiff has grave ailments or has died, then such cases do exist although their numbers remain in doubt. What is not in doubt is that the widespread publicity given allegations about Agent Orange have led to an enormous number of claims alleging a large variety of highly common ailments. The illnesses claimants now attribute to Agent Orange include not only heart disease, cancer, and birth defects, but also confusion, fatigue, anxiety, and spotty tanning.

The procedural aspects of this litigation are also extraordinary. Chief Judge Weinstein certified it as a class action at the behest of most of the plaintiffs and over the objections of all of the defendants. Certain issues, such as the damage suffered by each plaintiff, were not, of course, to be determined in the class action. Instead, they were to be left to individual trials if the outcome of the class action proceedings was favorable to the plaintiffs. Some plaintiffs opted out of the class action, but their cases remained in the Eastern District of New York as part of a multidistrict referral.

The class certification and settlement caused the number of claimants and the variety of ailments attributed to Agent Orange to climb dramatically. It also has caused disunity among the plaintiffs and increased the controversy surrounding this case. Correspondence to this court indicates that many of the original plaintiffs, most of whom joined the motions for class certification, were never advised that use of the class action device might lead to their being represented by counsel whom they did not select and who could settle the case without consulting them. In the midst of this litigation, original class counsel, Yannacone & Associates, asked to be relieved for financial reasons. Control of the class action soon passed to the PMC. Six of the nine members of the PMC advanced money for expenses at a time when the plaintiffs' case, already weak on the law and the facts, was near collapse for lack of resources. This money was furnished under an agreement that provided that three times the amount advanced by each lawyer would be repaid from an eventual fee award. These payments would have priority, moreover, over payments for legal work done on the case.

The trial date set by Chief Judge Weinstein put the parties under great pressure, and just before the trial was to start, the defendants reached a $180 million settlement with the PMC. The size of the settlement seems extraordinary. However, given the serious nature of many of the various ailments and birth defects plaintiffs attributed to Agent Orange, the understandable sympathy a jury would have for the particular plaintiffs, and the large number of claimants, 240,000, the settlement was essentially a payment of nuisance value. Although the chances of the chemical companies' ultimately having to pay any damages may have been slim, they were exposed potentially to billions of dollars in damages if liability was established and millions in attorneys' fees merely to continue the litigation.

The district judge approved the settlement. It is clear that he viewed the plaintiffs' case as so weak as to be virtually baseless. Indeed, shortly after the settlement, he granted summary judgment against the plaintiffs who opted out of the class action on the grounds that they could not prove that a particular ailment was caused by Agent Orange and that their claims were barred by the military contractor defense.

In addition, Chief Judge Weinstein awarded counsel fees in an amount that was considerably smaller than had been requested by the attorneys involved. The size of the award was clearly influenced by his skepticism about whether the case should ever have been brought.

The final extraordinary aspect of this case is the scheme adopted by Chief Judge Weinstein to distribute the class settlement award. That scheme, which is described as "compensation-based" rather than "tort-based," allows veterans who served in areas in which the herbicide was sprayed and who meet the Social Security Act's definition of disabled to collect benefits up to a ceiling of $12,000. Smaller payments are provided to the survivors of veterans who served in such areas. No proof of causation by Agent Orange is required, although benefits are available only for non-traumatic disability or death. The distribution scheme also provides for the funding of a foundation to undertake projects thought to be helpful to members of the class.

Many of the decisions of the district court were appealed, and we summarize our rulings here. In this opinion, we reject the various challenges to the certification of a class action. Although we share the prevalent skepticism about the usefulness of the class action device in mass tort litigation, we believe that its use was justified here in light of the centrality of the military contractor defense to the claims of all plaintiffs. We also approve the settlement in light of both the pervasive difficulties faced by plaintiffs in establishing liability and our conviction that the military contractor defense absolved the chemical companies of any liability. In a second opinion by this author, 818 F.2d 179, we affirm the distribution scheme's provision for disability and death benefits to veterans exposed to Agent Orange and their survivors. We reverse the scheme's establishment of a foundation; however, the district court may on remand fund and supervise particular projects it finds to be of benefit to the class. A third opinion by this author, 818 F.2d 187, affirms the grant of summary judgment against the opt-out plaintiffs based on the military contractor defense. On two grounds we hold that the chemical companies did not breach any duty to inform the government of Agent Orange's hazardous properties. First, at the times relevant here, the government had as much information about the potential hazards of dioxin as did the chemical companies. Second, the weight of present scientific evidence does not establish that Agent Orange caused injury to personnel in Vietnam. The chemical companies did not breach any duty to inform the government and are therefore not liable to the opt-outs. * * * [The court then summarizes the other opinions rendered in various appeals, and details the long procedural history of the *Agent Orange* litigation—*ed.*]

III.   Class Members' Objections to the Settlement

We now address the various objections to the maintenance and settlement of the class action made by some class members [the court first discusses objections based on subject matter and personal jurisdiction—*ed.*]

* * *

(3) Class Certification

Appellants argue that the district court erred in certifying the Rule 23(b)(3) class action. They make the same arguments made by the defendants in petitioning for a writ of mandamus seeking decertification of the class action. *See* In re Diamond Shamrock Chemicals Co., 725 F.2d 858 (2d Cir.), *cert. denied,* 465 U.S. 1067, 104 S.Ct. 1417, 79 L.Ed.2d 743 (1984). In denying the mandamus petition, we expressed doubt as to the existence of any issue of fact, let alone a common issue, regarding "general causation." *See* 725 F.2d at 860. We also stated, however, that "it seems likely that some common issues, which stem from the unique fact that the alleged damage was caused by a product sold by private manufacturers under contract to the government for use in a war, can be disposed of in a single trial. The resolution of some of these issues in defendants' favor may end the litigation entirely." *Id.* at 860–61. Therefore, we denied the petition. We stressed, however, that our scope of review in the mandamus proceeding was limited to the redress of a calculated disregard of governing rules, *id.* at 860, not the correction of ordinary error, and that the propriety of a class certification might be fully reviewed on a later appeal. *Id.* at 862. This is that appeal.

Rule 23(a) states:

One or more members of a class may sue or be sued as representative parties on behalf of all only if (1) the class is so numerous that joinder of all members is impracticable, (2) there are questions of law or fact common to the class, (3) the claims or defenses of the representative parties are typical of the claims or defenses of the class, and (4) the representative parties will fairly and adequately protect the interests of the class.

Existence of the first prerequisite in this case is undisputed. Whether there are problems regarding typicality and adequacy of representation depends upon the nature of the questions of law or fact common to the class. Our view of the existence of the third and fourth prerequisites is thus influenced by our view of the second.

We must also look to the requirements of Rule 23(b)(3) that:

the questions of law or fact common to the members of the class predominate over any questions affecting only individual members, and that a class action is superior to other available methods for the fair and efficient adjudication of the controversy.

The comment to Rule 23(b)(3) explicitly cautions against use of the class action device in mass tort cases. See Advisory Committee Note to 1966 Revision of Rule 23(b)(3)("A 'mass accident' resulting in injuries to numerous persons is ordinarily not appropriate for a class action because of the likelihood that significant questions, not only of damages but of liability and defenses of liability, would be present, affecting the individuals in different ways."). Moreover, most courts have denied certification in those circumstances. *See, e.g.,* In re Northern Dist. of Cal. Dalkon Shield IUD Products Liability Litigation, 693 F.2d 847 (9th Cir.1982), *cert. denied,* 459 U.S. 1171, 103 S.Ct. 817, 74 L.Ed.2d 1015 (1983); Payton v. Abbott Labs., 100 F.R.D. 336 (D.Mass.1983); Yandle v. PPG Industries, Inc., 65 F.R.D. 566 (E.D.Tex.1974); Boring v. Medusa Portland Cement Co., 63 F.R.D. 78, 83–85 (M.D.Pa.), *appeal dismissed,* 505 F.2d 729 (3d Cir.1974).

The present litigation justifies the prevalent skepticism over the usefulness of class actions in so-called mass tort cases and, in particular, claims for injuries resulting from toxic exposure. First, the benefits of a class action have been greatly exaggerated by its proponents in the present matter. For example, much ink has been spilled in this case over the distinction between generic causation—whether Agent Orange is harmful at all, regardless of the degree or nature of exposure, and what ailments it may cause—and individual causation—whether a particular veteran suffers from a particular ailment as a result of exposure to Agent Orange. It has been claimed that the former is an issue that might appropriately be tried in a class action, notwithstanding that individual causation must be tried separately for each plaintiff if the plaintiff class prevails.

We do not agree. The generic causation issue has three possible outcomes: 1) exposure to Agent Orange always causes harm; 2) exposure to Agent Orange never causes harm; and 3) exposure to Agent Orange may or may not cause harm depending on the kind of exposure and perhaps on other factors. It is indisputable that exposure to Agent Orange does not automatically cause harm. The so-called Ranch Hand Study of Air Force personnel who handled and sprayed the herbicide proved that much beyond a shadow of a doubt in finding no statistically significant differences between their subsequent health histories and those of similar personnel who had not been in contact with Agent Orange. Further, defendants have conceded that some kinds of exposure to Agent Orange *may* cause harm. They stated at both the argument of the mandamus petition and the argument of the appeal that Agent Orange, like anything else, including water and peanuts, may be harmful. The epidemiological studies on which defendants rely so heavily prove no more than that Vietnam veterans do not exhibit statistically significant differences in various symptoms when compared with other groups. They in no way exclude the possibility of injury, and tend at best to prove only that, if Agent Orange did cause harm, it was in isolated instances or in cases of unusual exposure.

The relevant question, therefore, is not whether Agent Orange has the capacity to cause harm, the generic causation issue, but whether it *did* cause harm and to whom. That determination is highly individualistic, and depends upon the characteristics of individual plaintiffs (*e.g.* state of health, lifestyle) and the nature of their exposure to Agent Orange. Although generic causation and individual circumstances concerning each plaintiff and his or her exposure to Agent Orange thus appear to be inextricably intertwined, the class action would have allowed generic causation to be determined without regard to those characteristics and the individual's exposure.

The second reason for our skepticism is that, with the exception of the military contractor defense, there may be few, if any, common questions of law. Although state law governs the claims of the individual veterans, *see In re "Agent Orange" Product Liability Litigation*, 635 F.2d at 993–95 (rejecting cause of action under federal common law), Chief Judge Weinstein decided that there were common questions of law because he predicted that each court faced with an Agent Orange case would resort to a national consensus of product liability law. Chief Judge Weinstein's analysis of the choice of law issues in this action, *see In re "Agent Orange" Product Liability Litigation*, 580 F.Supp. 690 (E.D.N.Y.1984), with which we assume familiarity, is bold and imaginative. However, in light of our prior holding that federal common law does not govern plaintiffs' claims, every jurisdiction would be free to render its own choice of law decision, and common experience suggests that the intellectual power of Chief Judge Weinstein's analysis alone would not be enough to prevent widespread disagreement.

Third, the dynamics of a class action in a case such as this may either impair the ability of representative parties to protect the interests of the class or cause the inefficient use of judicial resources. These undesirable results stem from the fact that potential plaintiffs in toxic tort cases do not share common interests because of differences in the strength of their claims. Before the class is certified, it is usually some of the plaintiffs who seek certification and defendants who resist. This is so because many of the plaintiffs' counsel will perceive in a class action efficiencies in discovery, legal and scientific research, and the funding of expenses. When counsel can reasonably expect to become counsel for the class and to share in a substantial award of fees, the incentive to seek certification is greatly enhanced. Defendants will resist certification, hoping to defeat the plaintiffs individually through application of their greater resources.

All plaintiffs may not desire class certification, however, because those with strong cases may well be better off going it alone. The drum-beating that accompanies a well-publicized class action claiming harm from toxic exposure and the speculative nature of the exposure issue may well attract excessive numbers of plaintiffs with weak to fanciful cases. For example, notwithstanding the grave doubt surrounding the factual basis of the plaintiffs' case, some 240,000 veterans and family members alleging hundreds of different ailments, including many that are both minor and commonplace, have filed claims for payment out of the settlement fund.

If plaintiffs with strong claims remain members of the class, they may see their claims diluted because a settlement attractive to the defendants will in all likelihood occur. Weak plaintiffs, who may exist in very large numbers, stand to gain from even a small settlement. Moreover, once a significant amount of money is on the table, the class attorneys will have an incentive to settle. They may well anticipate that the percentage of this money likely to be awarded as counsel fees will decline after a certain point. If they go to trial, on the other hand, they run the risk of losing the case and receiving no compensation for what may have been an enormous amount of work. There is thus great pressure to settle. Indeed, a settlement in a case such as the instant litigation, dramatically arrived at just before dawn on the day of trial after sleepless hours of bargaining, seems almost as inevitable as the sunrise. Such a settlement, however, is not likely to lead to a fund that can be distributed among the large number of class members who will assert claims and still compensate the strong plaintiffs for the value of their cases.

Moreover, the ability of the district court to scrutinize the fairness of the settlement is greatly impaired where the legal and factual issues to be determined in the class action are as numerous and complex as they were under the district court's order in the instant case. Similarly, the fashioning of a distribution plan that is both fair to the strong plaintiffs and efficient in adjudicating the large number of claims may be impossible. Only the weakness of the evidence of causation as to all plaintiffs and the strength of the military contractor defense enabled the district court to evaluate the settlement accurately and to fashion an appropriate distribution scheme in the instant matter. We regard those factors as largely coincidental and not to be expected in all toxic exposure cases.

If the strong plaintiffs opt out, however, the efficiencies of a class action may be negative. The class would then consist largely of plaintiffs with weak cases, many or most of which should never have been brought. The defendants would be unlikely to settle with the class because such a settlement with the class would not affect their continuing exposure to large damage awards in the individual cases brought by strong plaintiffs. Both the class action and the strong cases would then have to be tried.

Were this an action by civilians based on exposure to dioxin in the course of civilian affairs, we believe certification of a class action would have been error. However, we return to the cardinal fact we noted in denying the petition for writ of mandamus, namely that "the alleged damage was caused by a product sold by private manufacturers under contract to the government for use in a war." *In re Diamond Shamrock Chemicals Co.*, 725 F.2d at 860. In that regard, Chief Judge Weinstein noted that:

> Unlike litigations such as those involving DES, Dalkon Shield and asbestos, the trial is likely to emphasize critical common defenses applicable to the plaintiffs' class as a whole. They will include such matters as ... that if any injuries were caused by defendants' product it was because of the particular use and misuse made by the government; and that the government, not the manufacturers were wholly responsible because the former knew of all possible dangers and assumed full responsibility for any damage.... It is anticipated that a very substantial portion of a prospective four-month trial will be devoted to just those defenses. Certification would be justified if only to prevent relitigating those defenses over and over again in individual cases. *Class Certification Opinion*, 100 F.R.D. at 723.

In our view, class certification was justified under Rule 23(b)(3) due to the centrality of the military contractor defense. First, this defense is common to all of the plaintiffs' cases, and thus satisfies the commonality requirement of Rule 23(a)(2). *See* Port Authority Police Benevolent Ass'n v. Port Authority of New York & New Jersey, 698 F.2d 150, 154 (2d Cir.1983)("Since plaintiff has satisfied the requirement of *a common question* of law or fact, Rule 23(a)(2), the denial of class certification must be reversed.")(emphasis added). Second, because the military contractor defense is of central importance in the instant matter for reasons explained in our subsequent discussion of the fairness of the settlement and in our separate opinion affirming the grant of summary judgment against the opt-outs, this issue is governed by federal law, and a class trial in a federal court is a method of adjudication superior to the alternatives. Fed.R.Civ.P. 23(b)(3). If the defense succeeds, the entire litigation is disposed of. If it fails, it will not be an issue in the subsequent individual trials. In that event, moreover, the ground for its rejection, such as a failure to warn the government of a known hazard, might well be dispositive of relevant factual issues in those trials.

Appellants argue that the diverse interests of the class make adequate representation virtually impossible. We disagree. If defendants had successfully interposed the military contractor defense, they would have precluded recovery by all plaintiffs, irrespective of the strengths, weaknesses, or idiosyncrasies of their claims. Similarly, the typicality issue disappears because of the virtual identity of all of the plaintiffs' cases with respect to the military contractor defense.

It is true that some of the dynamics that generate pressure for an undesirable settlement will continue to operate in a class action limited to the military contractor defense. We believe, however, that a district court's ability to scrutinize the fairness of a class settlement is greatly enhanced by narrowing the legal and factual issues to this defense. We are confident, moreover, that such scrutiny will be informed by the court's awareness of the danger of such a settlement occurring. It is also true that the difficulty in fashioning a distribution scheme that does not overcompensate weak claimants and undercompensate strong ones is not alleviated by limiting the class certification to the military contractor defense. However, on balance we believe use of the class action was appropriate, although many potential difficulties were avoided only because all plaintiffs had very weak cases on causation and the military contractor defense was so strong.

We thus conclude that certification of the Rule 23(b)(3) class action was proper. Because our disposition of the appeals from the approval of the settlement and from the grant of summary judgment against the opt-outs excludes any possibility of an award of punitive damages, we need not address the propriety of the certification of a mandatory class under Rule 23(b)(1)(B).

CASTANO v. THE AMERICAN TOBACCO COMPANY

United States District Court, Eastern District of Louisiana, 1995.
160 F.R.D. 544.

ORDER AND REASONS

JONES, DISTRICT JUDGE.

Pending before the Court is plaintiffs' Motion for Class Certification. Having heard the oral arguments of the parties and having reviewed the briefs, the applicable law and the record, the plaintiffs' motion is GRANTED IN PART and DENIED IN PART.

BACKGROUND

Plaintiffs initially filed this "Class Action Complaint" on March 29, 1993 and filed a "First Amended Class Action Complaint" on May 9, 1993. * * * Plaintiffs Ernest R. Perry Sr. and T. George Solomon Jr. are cigarette smokers. Plaintiff Dianne A. Castano is the widow of Peter Castano, who allegedly was a cigarette smoker. Defendants are various tobacco companies as well as the Tobacco Institute, Inc. Plaintiffs allege, in essence, that defendants have fraudulently failed to inform smokers that nicotine is addictive, despite the defendants' possession of such knowledge. Plaintiffs further allege that defendants have manipulated the level of nicotine in cigarettes with the intent and purpose of creating and sustaining the addictive nature of cigarettes. According to plaintiffs, defendants have denied both the addictive nature of cigarettes and defendants' manipulation of nicotine levels in cigarettes.

The first nine causes of action are: fraud and deceit; negligent misrepresentation; intentional infliction of emotional distress; negligence and negligent infliction of emotional distress; violation of consumer protection statutes under state law; breach of express warranty; breach of implied warranty; strict product liability; and redhibition pursuant to the Louisiana Civil Code. Plaintiffs seek damages for economic loss and emotional distress as well as punitive damages. In regard to the alleged violation of consumer protection statutes, plaintiffs also seek attorneys' fees and equitable relief as requested in their tenth cause of action. Plaintiffs' tenth cause of action seeks declarations that defendants are financially responsible for notifying all class members of nicotine's addictive nature and that defendants manipulated nicotine levels with the intent to sustain the addiction of plaintiffs and the putative class members.

Plaintiffs also seek "restitution and refunds" for sums paid by plaintiffs and the putative class members to purchase cigarettes. Additionally, plaintiffs seek an order that defendants must disgorge any profits made from the sale of cigarettes and must make restitution to plaintiffs and the putative class members. Finally, plaintiffs seek establishment of a medical monitoring fund by defendants. * * * The alleged purpose of the medical monitoring fund is "to monitor the health of Plaintiffs and Class Members and to pay or reimburse Class Members for all medical expenses caused by Defendants' wrongdoing." * * * Plaintiffs do not seek recovery of personal injury damages in the form of physical pain and suffering or any related damages.[2]

Plaintiffs' proposed class representatives include plaintiffs and Gloria Scott and Denia Jackson, who are also cigarette smokers. * * * Plaintiffs' proposed class definition is:

2. "Plaintiffs' Proposed Trial Plan" makes a reference to possible expansion of this action to include personal injury damages.... The Court specifically makes no findings concerning class certification involving personal injury damages at this time, as these allegations are not before the Court.

(a) All nicotine dependent persons in the United States, its territories and possessions and the Commonwealth of Puerto Rico who have purchased and smoked cigarettes manufactured by the Tobacco Companies; (b) the estates, representatives, and administrators of these nicotine dependent cigarette smokers; and, (c) the spouses, children, relatives and "significant others" of these nicotine dependent cigarette smokers as their heirs or survivors.... In their First Amended Class Action Complaint, plaintiffs define "nicotine dependent" as referring "to persons having or had (*sic*) nicotine dependence under the criteria therefor set forth in [that] edition of the American Psychiatric Association's *Diagnostic and Statistical Manual of Mental Disorders, e.g., 3rd Ed. Revised* ('DSM IIIR')."
. . .

Plaintiffs propose the following "working definition" of "nicotine-dependent":

1. All cigarette smokers who have been diagnosed by a medical practitioner as nicotine-dependent;

2. All regular cigarette smokers who have made at least one unsuccessful effort to quit smoking; and/or

3. All regular cigarette smokers who were or have been advised by a medical practitioner that smoking has had or will have adverse health consequences who thereafter do not or have not quit smoking....

In "Plaintiffs' Answers to Defendants' Class Certification Interrogatories," plaintiffs state that their proposed class definition is consistent with and based on the *Fourth Edition of Diagnostic and Statistical Manual of Mental Disorders* (hereinafter "DSM–IV"). * * *

Plaintiffs argue that the general requirements of Fed.R.Civ.P. 23(a)(1)-(4) are easily satisfied. Plaintiffs contend that class certification is proper for their claims for damages under Fed.R.Civ.P. 23(b)(3). Plaintiffs seek class certification of their equitable claim for relief, including the medical monitoring, pursuant to Fed.R.Civ.P. 23(b)(2). Alternatively, plaintiffs seek "issue certification" under Fed.R.Civ.P. 23(c)(4). Defendants forcefully oppose class certification under any circumstances.

* * *

B. Certification Under Rule 23(b)(2)

The next issue is whether plaintiffs' claim for equitable relief can be certified under Rule 23(b)(2). In support of this argument plaintiffs principally rely on the case of Day v. NLO and the various opinions authored by Judge Spiegel in that case.[7] In Day v. NLO plaintiffs were former employees of the Feed Materials Production Center (hereinafter

---

7. Day v. NLO, Inc., 144 F.R.D. 330 (S.D.Ohio 1992), *mandamus granted in part and denied in part,* 5 F.3d 154 (6th Cir. 1993); Day v. NLO, Inc., 811 F.Supp. 1271 (S.D.Ohio 1992); and Day v. NLO, Inc., 851 F.Supp. 869 (S.D.Ohio 1994).

"FMPC") and other "independent contractors, frequenters or business invitees who frequently worked at the FMPC, and their families." Day v. NLO, 144 F.R.D. at 332. Plaintiffs claimed that the defendants, former operators of FMPC, "negligently or intentionally expose[d] the plaintiffs to dangerous levels of radioactive and hazardous materials." *Id.* They maintained that their personal property had been damaged and "that they [suffered] severe emotional distress in the form of increased fear of cancer." *Id.*

Throughout Day v. NLO, Judge Spiegel characterized plaintiffs' primary claim for relief as a "court-supervised medical monitoring program." Day v. NLO, 144 F.R.D. at 335; 811 F.Supp. at 1275; 851 F.Supp. at 885. Indeed, Judge Spiegel specifically rejected defendants' contention that plaintiffs were seeking compensatory and punitive damages and found instead that the primary relief sought was establishment of the medical-monitoring program. 811 F.Supp. at 1275.

The instant case is distinguishable from *Day v. NLO* because the medical-monitoring program sought by plaintiffs is but one type of relief sought among many. As set forth above, plaintiffs seek compensatory, statutory and punitive damages in their first nine causes of action. This is far beyond Judge Spiegel's characterization of the relief sought by plaintiffs in *Day v. NLO*. As Judge Spiegel recognized, Rule 23(b)(3) is the "preferred section [for certification] where monetary damages are the primary goal of plaintiff." *Day v. NLO*, 851 F.Supp. at 885–86. Here the Court is persuaded that plaintiffs are seeking primarily monetary damages, not equitable relief. Therefore, the Court declines to certify plaintiffs' claim for medical monitoring under Rule 23(b)(2).

The Court also finds merit in defendants' argument based on their Seventh Amendment right to a jury trial. In Thermo–Stitch, Inc. v. Chemi–Cord Processing Corp., 294 F.2d 486 (5th Cir.1961), the Fifth Circuit squarely faced the issue of whether equitable issues could be severed from issues at law for a non-jury trial. Plaintiff Chemi–Cord and one of its customers had filed suit to restrain defendant Thermo–Stitch "from interfering with its business relations and from harassing it by threats of suit" in a patent dispute. *Id.* at 487. The complaint sought injunctive relief along with a declaratory judgment that three patents held by Thermo–Stitch were invalid and not infringed. *Id.* Thermo–Stitch filed counterclaims for damages for patent infringement, fraud and anti-trust violations. *Id.* Plaintiffs moved for an immediate and separate trial on the issues of validity and infringement and sought to strike Thermo–Stitch's motion for a jury trial on those issues. *Id.* The district court granted the plaintiffs' motion, but the Fifth Circuit held "that the court below exceeded its discretion in not ordering a jury trial," following Beacon Theatres v. Westover, 359 U.S. 500, 79 S.Ct. 948, 3 L.Ed.2d 988 (1959).

Beacon Theatres holds that where the presence of legal and equitable causes in the same case requires the selection between a jury and a non-jury determination of certain common issues, the discretion of the trial court is "very narrowly limited and must, wherever possible, be exercised to preserve jury trial." Analogizing a motion for a non-jury trial of common issues to a suit for an injunction, the Court held that a showing of irreparable injury and inadequate relief at law is required. * * * While the right to trial by jury is a constitutional one, no similar importance attaches to trial by court. Under the flexible procedures of the Federal Rules [of Civil Procedure], a jury determines issues pertinent to an equitable cause of action without interruption or prejudice to the proceeding; the court decides whether equitable relief is called for on the basis of the jury's finding of fact. The mere presence of an equitable cause of action furnishes no legal justification for depriving a party to a legal action of his right to a jury trial. It is therefore immaterial that the case at bar contains a stronger basis for equitable relief than was present in *Beacon Theatres*. It would make no difference if the equitable cause of action clearly outweighed the legal cause so that the basic issue of the case taken as a whole is equitable. As long as any legal cause is involved the jury rights it creates control. This is the teaching of *Beacon Theatres,* as we construe it. *Thermo-Stitch,* 294 F.2d at 490–91 (citations and footnotes omitted).

The Court finds *Thermo-Stitch* instructive as to the issue of certification of plaintiffs' medical monitoring claim, especially in view of this Court's finding that plaintiffs' claims are not primarily for equitable relief but for damages. Certification of the medical monitoring claim in this case under Rule 23(b)(2) would infringe on the constitutional right to a jury trial. The Court cannot and will not infringe on that inviolate right.

C. Certification Under Rule 23(b)(3)

The issue that remains is whether plaintiffs' action can be certified as a class under Rule 23(b)(3). For purposes of clarity, the Court addresses the core issues of liability separate from the other issues in this matter, including those of damages.

1. Core Liability Issues

* * *

"In order to 'predominate,' common issues must constitute a significant part of the individual cases." *Jenkins*, 782 F.2d at 472, *citing In re Asbestos School Litigation*, 104 F.R.D. at 422, 431–32 (E.D.Pa.1984) and *In re Tetracycline Cases,* 107 F.R.D. 719, 727 (W.D.Mo.1985).

Like the *Jenkins* case, which involved thousands of asbestos exposure cases, the Court concludes that "[i]t is difficult to imagine that class jury findings on [the core liability issues in this case] will not significantly advance the resolution" of the thousands, if not millions, of similar issues in individual cases which have not yet been filed pending the instant ruling. * * * Thus, it is the Court's view that common factual issues include whether defendants knew cigarette smoking was addictive, failed to inform cigarette smokers of such and took actions to addict cigarette smokers. Common legal issues include fraud, negligence, breach of warranty (express or implied), strict liability, and violation of consumer protection statutes.[8]

As to the fraud allegation, the Court finds applicable the Advisory Committee Notes to the 1966 Amendment to Rule 23. In addressing the 23(b)(3) requirement of predominance, the drafters stated: [A] fraud perpetrated on numerous persons by the use of similar misrepresentations may be an appealing situation for a class action, and it may remain so despite the need, if liability is found, for separate determination of the damages suffered by individuals within the class.

The Court recognizes that the next sentence of the Advisory Notes states that "a fraud case may be unsuited for treatment as a class action if there was material variation in the misrepresentations made or in the kinds or degrees of reliance by the person to whom they were addressed." Defendants seize upon this issue, contending that the individual issues of reliance in this matter would so swamp the Court that common issues would not predominate. The Court disagrees for two reasons, both arising out of the same case on which defendants principally rely: Mirkin v. Wasserman, 5 Cal.4th 1082, 858 P.2d 568 (Cal.1993).

In that case plaintiffs' first amended complaint purported to state causes of action for deceit and negligent misrepresentation. *Id.* at 1088, 858 P.2d at 570. Plaintiffs alleged reliance in a conclusory fashion. *Id.* The trial court dismissed the complaint for an insufficient allegation of reliance, and the court of appeals sustained that decision. *Id.* The California Supreme Court first noted that the cause of action of deceit was rooted in the common law cause of action of fraud. *Id.* at 1091–92, 858 P.2d at 572. The court, also noting that its decision applied equally to deceit and negligent misrepresentation, found it well settled that a plaintiff must plead actual reliance to state such a cause of action. *Id.* at 1088–89, 868 P.2d at 570 and n.2. The issue before this Court, however, is not whether plaintiffs have stated a cause of action for fraud or negligent misrepresentation. The issue is whether the common issues so predominate over the individual issues that class certification is appropriate. Because this Court cannot prejudge the merits of this litigation, * * *, the Court holds that on the face of the pleadings before it the common issues of fraud substantially outweigh any individual issues of reliance.

Second, *Mirkin* recognized that in consumer class actions where plaintiff "specifically pled that the defendants had made identical representations to each class member," it may be appropriate to "infer that each member of a class had actually relied on the defendant's alleged misrepresentations." *Mirkin,* 5 Cal.4th at 1094, 868 P.2d at 574.

Plaintiffs here have pleaded omissions as well as commissions on the part of defendants in their various causes of action. It is true that the

---

8. Plaintiffs also alleged a cause of action under the Louisiana law of redhibition. As discussed below, this Court has not yet determined the law to be applied in this matter. Because redhibition arises only under Louisiana law, it is a common legal question as to the named plaintiffs but not, at this time, as to the proposed class.

California Supreme Court rejected the argument that actual reliance cannot be an element of deceit, or fraud, with respect to an alleged omission. However, at this point in this lawsuit, and considering the conditional nature of the certification of this class, as set forth below, the Court does not find that the issue of "omission v. commission" is so substantial a factor as to prevent a finding of predominance of class issues over individual issues. Indeed, just as the *Mirkin* court found that an inference of reliance may be available in consumer class action matters involving allegations of misrepresentations actually made, *id.* at 1095, 858 P.2d at 575, such an inference may be available in consumer class actions based on claims of misrepresentations based on omission. Moreover, as noted, this issue is more appropriate in a determination of whether plaintiffs have stated a cause of action than in a decision on a motion for class certification.

Also as to predominance, plaintiffs argue that the law applicable to each of their causes of action is so generic that individual issues will not predominate. In opposition, defendants posit that the standards for determination of each of plaintiffs' causes of action may vary from state to state and cause mass confusion such that class certification is improper. As a court sitting in diversity, this Court must apply the law of the forum concerning conflict of laws. * * * The Court is persuaded that issues of fraud, breach of warranty, negligence, intentional tort and strict liability do not vary so much from state to state as to cause individual issues to predominate. *See, e.g.,* In re Asbestos School Litigation, 104 F.R.D. 422, 434 (E.D.Pa.1984), *aff'd in part and reversed in part,* 789 F.2d 996, 1010 (1986)(discussing the similarity of negligence and strict liability in U.S. jurisdictions); "Decision and Entry ... Sustaining Plaintiffs' Motions to Conditionally Certify These Actions as a Class Action," In re Cordis Cardiac Pacemaker Product Liability Litigation, Case No. C–3–90–374 (December 23, 1992)(discussing similarities of strict liability and fraud).

Further, there has been no determination at this time of the law to be applied. The parties have only briefly addressed the conflict of laws issue in this matter, and the Court finds a determination of that issue to be premature at present. Finally, Rule 23(c)(4)(B) provides the Court with the option of dividing the class into subclasses if appropriate after the Court resolves the conflict of laws issue. In re Asbestos School Litigation, 104 F.R.D. at 434.

The same reasoning applies to application of the various consumer protection statutes. First, there has been no showing that the consumer protection statutes differ so much as to make individual issues predominate. Indeed, as with the other areas of law, the applicable statute—or statutes—has not yet been determined. The option of subclasses is available as to this issue as well.

Therefore, as to Rule 23(b)(3)'s requirement of predominance, the Court finds that plaintiffs' factual and legal allegations of liability constitute similar, common issues that would be a significant part of any individual cases that have been or may be filed. To that extent, this standard of Rule 23(b)(3) is satisfied.

The next requirement of Rule 23(b)(3) is superiority, i.e., whether a class action in this matter is superior to any other "available methods" for adjudication of the issues at hand. Once again, the Court turns to *Jenkins* for guidance on this issue. * * * [*Jenkins* discussion omitted— ed.]

* * *

This proposed class action is *sui generis*. It is not a toxic tort exposure case. *See, e.g., Day v. NLO, supra*. Neither is it a case involving exposure to a substance or product where plaintiffs claim physical injuries, such as *Jenkins*. * * * Plaintiffs do not allege physical injuries and property damage, as was alleged in In re Shell Oil Refinery, 136 F.R.D. 588 (E.D.La.1991), *aff'd sub nom*. Watson v. Shell Oil Co., 979 F.2d 1014 (5th Cir.1992), *rehearing en banc granted*, 990 F.2d 805 (5th Cir.1993). Nor is this a case involving only property damage. *See, e.g.*, In re School Asbestos Litigation, *supra*. Rather, this is a case in which plaintiffs claim that defendants' acts reached throughout the nation to addict cigarette smokers and keep them addicted.

Faced squarely with this unique action, this Court must also look forward and invent, knowing that "[t]he purpose of class actions is to conserve 'the resources of both the courts and the parties by permitting an issue potentially affecting every [class member] to be litigated in an economical fashion.'" *Jenkins*, 782 F.2d at 471, *quoting General Telephone Co. of Southwest v. Falcon*, 457 U.S. 147, 155, 102 S.Ct. 2364, 2369, 72 L.Ed.2d 740 (1982).

Rule 23(b)(3) gives guidance as to factors this Court should consider in determining predominance and superiority. In the present litigation, the most pertinent of these is its manageability as a class. While the manageability of the liability issues in this case may well prove to be difficult, the Court finds that any such difficulties pale in comparison to the specter of thousands, if not millions, of similar trials of liability proceeding in thousands of courtrooms around the nation. In addition, the common issues in this case would materially advance the resolution of the case itself. Likewise, as the *Jenkins* court pointed out, "it seems that the defendants enjoy all of the advantages, and the plaintiffs incur the disadvantages, of the class action—with one exception, the cases are brought to trial." *Jenkins*, 782 F.2d at 473.

Hence, the Court finds that plaintiffs' motion should be granted insofar as the core liability issues alleged by plaintiffs are concerned. These are the issues of fraud, breach of warranty (express or implied), intentional tort, negligence, strict liability and consumer protection.

2. *Issues of Injury-in-fact, Proximate Cause, Reliance and Affirmative Defenses*

While the core liability issues provide common ground for class certification, the foundation is not so firm regarding the issues of injury-in-fact, proximate cause, reliance [11] and affirmative defenses.

From a review of the pleadings, it is clear that all of these issues are so individually based that class certification is improper. For example, the following issues are so overwhelmingly replete with individual circumstances that they quickly outweigh predominance and superiority. First is whether a person suffered emotional injury, if any, as a result of addiction. Second is whether a person's addiction was caused by any actions of the defendants. Third is whether each plaintiff relied on defendants' representations, whether they be omissions or commissions, in beginning or continuing to smoke cigarettes.[12] Fourth is whether affirmative defenses unique to each class member preclude plaintiffs' recovery in any manner.

Thus, because individual issues, not common issues, predominate and are superior in regard to injury-in-fact, proximate cause, reliance and affirmative defenses, class certification is improper as to these issues.[13]

3. Compensatory Damages

Similarly, the Court finds that the issues of compensatory damages, including the claim for medical monitoring, are so inextricably intertwined with the issues of proximate cause and affirmative defenses that resolution of these issues would not materially advance this case. Assuming liability is found on the core liability issues, factfinders assessing the cases of individual plaintiffs would be in a much better position to determine compensatory damages, depending on whether plaintiffs can prove causation and injury and refute any affirmative defenses.

This reasoning applies equally to plaintiffs' claim for medical monitoring. In this respect, the Court finds instructive the following passage by Judge Scirica in Brown v. Southeastern Pennsylvania Transportation Authority, 1987 WL 9273, * 10 (E.D.Pa.1987). The alleged harm from [exposure to] PCBs occurred over a period of at least ten years, under a variety of circumstances and to various degrees. Some class members may have been exposed to PCBs for a few months, while others, for a

11. As stated above, the Court believes its present duty does not include a determination whether, in light of the issue of reliance, plaintiffs have stated a cause of action for fraud. At this time, the Court believes that the issues of fraud and reliance can be separated so as to certify a class for the general issue of fraud but not for the individual issue of reliance.

12. As noted above, the California Supreme Court has stated that, in appropriate circumstances, an inference of classwide reliance may pass legal muster in an action for fraud. If such an inference would be appropriate in this case, then the individual issue of reliance may be submerged into the fraud action itself. On the other hand, if the inference is not appropriate, the Court

may, for example, submit special interrogatories to the jury which require that it make findings as to all essential elements of a fraud cause of action except reliance, which might then be determined later in individual actions. However, as noted, it is premature to determine this issue, just as it would be premature to determine whether plaintiffs have stated an action for fraud.

13. Plaintiffs have only briefly mentioned in their Proposed Trial Plan that a "state of the art" defense should also be certified.... The Court finds that plaintiffs have failed to carry their burden of showing why a "state of the art" defense should be certified.

lifetime. . . .   Moreover, each plaintiff will bring a unique medical history that will provide the basis for his or her individual claim.

Here, the varying lengths of time of smoking coupled with the various medical conditions of each putative class member would overwhelm any common issues concerning medical monitoring.

4. Punitive Damages

As regard to the issues of liability for and assessment of punitive damages, plaintiffs concede that certain states "require a relationship between quantum and actual damages and that of punitive damages." * * *   Plaintiffs also concede that the states differ as to the burden of proof required of plaintiffs seeking punitive damages.   While the burden of proof in some states is by a preponderance of the evidence, the burden in others is by clear and convincing evidence.   *Id.*

However, these differences, like the differences in the law of the core liability issues among the jurisdictions, are not so substantial as to prevent certification of punitive damages under Rule 23(b)(3).   Guidance is once again found in *Jenkins, supra,* and also in Watson v. Shell Oil Company, *supra.*   * * *   [Discussion of *Jenkins,* omitted—*ed.*].

In *Watson,* the trial court identified common issues of liability as to both compensatory damages and punitive damages.   Watson, 979 F.2d at 1017.   *See also,* In re Shell Oil Refinery, 136 F.R.D. 588, 590 (E.D.La. 1991)(Mentz, J.).   The district court's trial plan provided for a determination of common issues of liability, including liability for punitive damages, in Phase 1.   Watson, 979 F.2d at 1018.   If the jury found punitive damages liability it would then perform the Phase 2 function and determine compensatory damages in 20 fully-tried sample plaintiff cases.   Based on the findings in these cases, the jury would then establish the ratio of punitive damages to compensatory damages for each class member.   If the jury finds no punitive damage liability in Phase 1, Phase 2 is to be omitted.   *Id.*   In Phase 3 a different jury would resolve issues unique to compensatory damages, such as causation and quantum, and Phase 4 provided for the district court's computing of punitive damages, if established in Phase 1, for those plaintiffs awarded actual damages.   *Id.*

The court of appeals approved the trial plan as to punitive damages for a number of reasons.   First, the court found that "the Phase 2 jury is to make a determination about punitive damages in a mass-disaster context, rather than compensatory damages in products liability litigation."   *Id.* at 1018–19.[14]   Second, because there would be "minimal variance" between plaintiffs as to the degree of culpability necessary to establish punitive damages, assessment of punitive damages on the basis of a cross-section of the class would not "require 'lift[ing] the description of the claims to a level of generality that tears them from their substan-

---

14. Thus, *Watson* was distinguishable   Cir.1990).
from In re Fibreboard, 893 F.2d 706 (5th

tially required moorings.' " *Id.*, quoting *Fibreboard.* More importantly, the Phase 2 jury is not to extrapolate punitive damages but, rather, is to determine a basis for assessment of punitive damages in the narrow form of a ratio. . . . Phases 2 and 3 appropriately enforce the Louisiana law requirement that a claimant prove both causation and damage to recover compensatory and punitive damage. Watson, 979 F.2d at 1019.

In view of the approval in both *Jenkins* and *Watson* of class certification and trial of punitive damages claims,[15] the Court finds that certification under 23(b)(3) is proper for both the issue of liability for punitive damages and assessment of punitive damages as a ratio of actual damages should punitive damages liability be found. The Court will impose the necessary safeguards at trial to ensure that jurors understand the appropriate burden or burdens of proof that plaintiffs must meet to impose punitive damages liability. The Court also will instruct the jury, in accord with *Jenkins,* that it is only assessing a ratio of punitive damages to actual damages and that some plaintiffs may not recover actual damages at all, thereby eliminating those plaintiffs' claims for punitive damages.

Viewed in light of *Jenkins* and *Watson,* the Court finds that the issues of both liability and assessment of a ratio or multiplier of punitive damages are not so individualized as to preclude class certification. Although this path may seem difficult at first, this Court believes that certification of these punitive damages issues will substantially move this litigation toward a final resolution such that class certification is proper pursuant to Rule 23(b)(3).

* * *

E. Issue Certification Under Rule 23(c)(4)

The Court's determination that only some of the issues raised by plaintiffs but not others are properly certifiable under Rule 23(b)(3) does not end the inquiry. Rule 23(c)(4) provides that, "when appropriate," not only may classes be divided into subclasses but also that "an action may be brought or maintained as a class action with respect to particular issues." The Notes of the Advisory Committee on Rules for the 1966 Amendment to Rule 23(c)(4) specifically acknowledge the applicability of issue certification as to "fraud or similar case[s]" where the class issue is liability but where individuals must prove their respective damages claims.

In accord with this rule, the Court finds that issue certification of the core liability issues set forth above is proper. Each of these core liability issues separately meets the requirements of Rule 23(a) and 23(b)(3), as discussed above and as required by 23(c)(4). *See, e.g., Central Wesleyan College v. W.R. Grace & Co.*, 6 F.3d 177, 189 (4th

---

15. The Court understands that the *Watson* judgment was vacated by the grant of rehearing en banc and that the case settled thereafter without the Fifth Circuit having an opportunity to opine on the pro-

priety of the panel decision. . . . Nevertheless, the Court finds *Watson* persuasive in light of the prior Fifth Circuit discussion in *Jenkins.*

Cir.1993). The issue of punitive damages also satisfies the requirements of Rule 23(a) and (b)(3). Further, as explained previously, while these issues will determine only liability and punitive damages, not causation, injury, reliance, compensatory damages or the applicability of affirmative defenses, the Court finds that determination of liability and punitive damages will move this litigation substantially toward an end due to its unique and far-reaching nature. As the Fifth Circuit stated in *Jenkins,* "necessity moves us to change and invent." *Jenkins,* 782 F.2d at 473. Necessity in the form of the present class action moves this Court to certify the liability issues and punitive damages on a classwide basis in order to promote judicial economy and efficiency.

F.   Conditional Certification

Finally, pursuant to Rule 23(c)(1), the Court grants plaintiffs' motion for issue certification conditionally. As this case progresses, if the Court finds that circumstances or conditions change such that, for example, individual issues predominate, alternative methods exist for fair adjudication of the liability issues or the class action becomes unmanageable, then the Court may revisit the propriety of certification.
* * *

CONCLUSION

With this decision, the Court embarks on a road certainly less traveled, if ever taken at all. *See* Edward C. Latham, THE POETRY OF ROBERT FROST, *"The Road Not Taken,"* at 105 (1969). The Court takes this first step after much thought and reflection in the hope of aiding and promoting the efficient litigation of the core liability and punitive damages issues in this massive litigation. This will be a daunting task with long, difficult days ahead. However, the Court believes that resolution of these issues now will alleviate the constant need for duplicative resolution of these issues later in hundreds of courtrooms around the nation, a task unparalleled in scope.

Notes and Questions

1. The district court's decision in *Payton v. Abbott Labs.* presaged subsequent federal court approval of class action certification for some mass tort cases. However, the *Jenkins* and *School Asbestos* decisions, announced by the Fifth and Third Circuits in 1986, represented the first two major cases in which federal appellate courts upheld class certifications in mass tort litigation. How consistent are these cases with Rule 23 requirements? Are the decisions convincing, or do they represent a pragmatic accommodation to a novel litigation problem? Have the federal courts stretched class action criteria to accommodate federal court adjudication of these cases? In what significant respects do the *Jenkins* and *School Asbestos* cases differ? The Second Circuit considered the *Agent Orange* class settlement, handing down its class certification approval in 1987. Is the *Agent Orange* class certification even more tenuous than *Jenkins* and the *School Asbestos* decisions? To what extent is the *Castano* decision consistent with *Jenkins* and the *School Asbestos* certification? Does *Castano* expand the holdings of those cases even further?

2. The asbestos property damages cases developed independently of the mass tort asbestos personal injury cases, although many of the same defendants were (and continue to be) involved in both. In what significant ways do the personal injury and property damage cases differ? Do these differences have any significance for mass tort aggregate litigation? When the Johns–Manville Corp. went into Chapter 11 bankruptcy in 1982, it set up two trust funds: one for personal injury claimants and one for property damage claimants. What relationship, if any, do these claimants have to the other? *See* discussion of the Manville bankruptcy trust funds at Chapter XIII.A, *infra*.

For discussions of asbestos property damage litigation, *see generally* J.P. Arness & Randall D. Eliason, *Insurance Coverage for "Property Damage" in Asbestos and Other Toxic Tort Cases,* 72 Va. L.Rev. 943 (1986); Lindley J. Brenza, Comment, *Asbestos in Schools and the Economic Loss Doctrine,* 54 U. Chi. L.Rev. 277 (1987); James L. Connaughton, Comment, *Recovery for Risk Comes of Age: Asbestos in Schools and the Duty to Abate a Latent Environmental Hazard,* 83 Nw. U. L.Rev. 512 (1989); Frank B. Cross, *Asbestos in the Schools: A Remonstrance Against Panic,* 11 Colum. J. Envt'l L. 73 (1986); Brent G. Curtis, Comment, *Who's Liable for Asbestos Removal Costs: Landlord or Tenant?,* 16 U. Dayton L.Rev. 695 (1991); Daniel C. Jones, Casenote, *"Property Damage" in Asbestos Litigation: The Insurer's Duty to Defend Under Comprehensive General Liability Policy,* 17 S. Ill. U.L.J. 155 (1992); John P. Kincade, *Issues in School Hazard Abatement Litigation,* 16 St. Mary's L.J. 951 (1985); Robert D. Lang, *Danger in the Classroom: Asbestos in the Public Schools,* 10 Colum. J. Envt'l L. 111 (1985); Lee S. Siegel, Note, *As the Asbestos Crumbles: A Look at New Evidentiary Issues in Asbestos–Property Damage Litigation,* 20 Hofstra L.Rev. 1139 (1992); James C. Stanley, Comment, *Asbestos in Schools: The Asbestos Hazard Emergency Response Act and School Asbestos,* 42 Vand. L.Rev. 1685 (1989); Council on Scientific Affairs, American Medical Association, *Asbestos Removal, Health Hazards, and the EPA,* 266 J. Am. Med. Assoc. 696 (1991).

3. Although in the mid–1980s some federal courts seemed receptive to aggregating mass tort cases under the class action rule, they continued to refuse to certify (b)(1) or (b)(2) classes. Do the (b)(1) and (b)(2) classes have any utility at all for mass tort litigation? Is it ever possible to establish a limited fund mass tort class action? One for injunctive or declaratory relief? *See In re Keene Corp., infra* at II.A.5. What does *Castano* add to this debate?

4. As the cases illustrate, because mass tort cases are diversity-based, they invariably implicate complicated *Erie* choice-of-law questions. How did each court handle the choice-of-law dimension to class certification? For a comprehensive examination of the choice-of-law issues in federal diversity mass torts, *see* Part Four, *infra*. Is a preferable solution for Congress to enact substantive products liability or tort legislation? Until *Jenkins* and the *School Asbestos Litigation,* lack of commonality among state tort law regimes often was a ground for denying class certification. How did the court address the choice of law question in *Jenkins*? In the *School Asbestos Litigation*? In *Castano*? Resolving choice-of-law problems in mass tort

litigation has been a major focus of reformers. *See, e.g.,* Friedrich K. Jeunger, *Mass Disasters and the Conflict of Laws,* 1989 U.Ill.L.Rev 105 (1989); Mary Kay Kane, *Drafting Choice of Law Rules For Complex Litigation: Some Preliminary Thoughts,* 10 Rev.Litig. 309 (1991); Linda S. Mullenix, *Federalizing Choice of Law For Mass Tort Litigation,* 70 Tex.L.Rev 1623 (1992); Robert A. Sedler, *Interest Analysis, State Sovereignty, and Federally Mandated Choice of Law in "Mass Tort" Cases,* 56 Alb.L.Rev 855 (1993); Robert A. Sedler and Aaron D. Twerski, *The Case Against All Encompassing Federal Mass Tort Legislation: Sacrifice Without Gain,* 73 Marq.L.Rev 76 (1989); Louise Weinberg, *Mass Torts at the Neutral Forum: A Critical Analysis of the ALI's Proposed Choice Rule,* 56 Alb.L.Rev 807 (1993); and Russell Weintraub, *Methods For Resolving Conflict-of-Law Problems in Mass Tort Litigation,* 1989 U.Ill.L.Rev 129 (1989).

5.   Does certifying a "punitive damages" class make sense? What is a "limited generosity" class? What special problems do punitive damages present in the context of mass tort litigation? *See* discussion of punitive damages at Chapter VII.B, *infra. See generally,* Kevin M. Forde, *Punitive Damages in Mass Tort Cases: Recovery on Behalf of a Class,* 15 Loyola U.Chi.L.J. 397 (1984); Nancy Morawetz, *Underinclusive Class Actions* (forthcoming 1995); Mark D. Peters, Comment, *Punitive Damages, The Common Question Class Action, and the Concept of Overkill,* 13 Pac.L.J. 1273 (1982); C. Delos Putz Jr., *et al., Punitive Damage Claims of Class Members Who Opt Out: Should They Survive?,* 16 U.S.F.L.Rev 1 (1981); Briggs L. Tobin, Comment, *The "Limited Generosity" Class Action and a Uniform Choice of Law Rule: An Approach to Fair and Effective Mass–Tort Punitive Damage Adjudication in the Federal Courts,* 38 Emory L.J. 457 (1989).

6.   The Louisiana district court in *Castano* not only relied on *Jenkins* and the *School Asbestos* decisions in support of its (b)(3) class certification, but also on the *Watson* decision, discussed *supra.* As *Castano* indicates, *Watson* technically was vacated on appeal after the parties settled. The *Watson* decision upholding class certification, in turn, was largely based on *Jenkins.* To what extent should the Louisiana district court rely on a vacated decision? What authoritative weight does the *Watson* decision have? It remains to be seen whether the *Castano* certification decision will survive appeal to the Fifth Circuit, especially in light of a 1995 Seventh Circuit decision overturning a nationwide class certification brought by claimants alleging injury from tainted blood products. *See* In the Matter of Rhone–Poulenc Rorer, Inc., 51 F.3d 1293 (7th Cir.1995), excerpted at section 5, *infra.* Nonetheless, the *Castano* class certification represents a major procedural breakthrough for plaintiffs alleging claims against tobacco companies. *See* Andrew Ready and Robert Carter, *Tobacco Litigation: Looking For Cover,* Legal Times of Washington, March 6, 1995 at S 37. In general, federal courts have not been receptive to even individualized litigation against tobacco company defendants on various liability theories. *See* Cipollone v. Liggett Group, Inc., ___ U.S. ___, 112 S.Ct. 2608, 120 L.Ed.2d 407 (1992)(liability for personal injury not established; case reversed and remanded).

4. SETBACKS AND RETREAT

CIMINO v. RAYMARK INDUSTRIES, INC.

United States District Court, East District of Texas, 1989.
December 29 Order.

JUDGE ROBERT M. PARKER:

[The facts in *Cimino* are set forth at pages 38–40, *supra—ed.*]

I. PROCEDURE

This action will proceed according to the three-phase procedure established by the Court's October 26, 1989 Memorandum and Order. Phases One and Two will be tried before the same jury. Specifically, this action will include the following:

* * *

B. *Phase One*

Phase One will proceed according to this Court's October 26, 1989 Memorandum and Order. For purposes of punitive damages, the Jury may be allowed to formulate a multiplier for each Defendant for which the Jury returns an affirmative finding on the issue of gross negligence.

C. *Phase Two*

Phase Two will proceed according to the Court's October 26, 1989 Memorandum and Order. In Phase Two, the Court will try the cases of the class representatives. In addition, the Plaintiffs and Defendants each will be allowed to introduce the testimony of the fifteen Plaintiffs chosen by the side for full depositions during discovery. Phase Two will involve classwide finds on the issues of exposure and actual damages. As explained in the Court's certification Order, the exposure and actual damages issues will involve:

> * * * [S]uch issues as (a) whether the Plaintiffs were exposed to the Defendants' products; (b) what damages, if any, the Plaintiffs suffered as a result of their exposure to the Defendants' products; and (c) what defenses, if any, the Defendants have to the Plaintiffs' claims.

* * * The Jury may be allowed to award lump sum damages in Phase Two, in place of the multiplier in Phase One, against each Defendant for which the Jury returns an affirmative finding on the issue of gross negligence.

D. *Phase Three*

In Phase Three, the Court will distribute the Jury's award of actual and punitive damages, if any, to the individual Plaintiffs. Phase Three will involve a determination by this Court of the validity of each individual Plaintiff's claim for damages. Before receiving a portion of the Jury's damage award, each individual Plaintiff will be required to provide the Court with proof of the damages suffered by that Plaintiff.

Specifically, this proof will consist of medical records, results of the medical tests performed for this action, depositions, any other evidence deemed relevant by this Court. In this manner, the Court will ensure that, before receiving a share of damages in this action, each individual Plaintiff has been exposed to defendants' asbestos products and has suffered actual damages.

The procedures embodied in the Court's plan are not deemed by the Court as revolutionary but simply as reasonable extensions of established law dictated by necessity. It has not escaped the Court's attention that portions of some of the caselaw used by the Court as authority could be read to disapprove some of the procedures while other portions form the basis for solid precedent. In this Court's view the Court's plan constitutes a good faith extension of existing law in those areas where precedent provides an inadequate methodology for resolving this controversy.

II. Objections

A. *Jenkins v. Raymark*

The Defendants argue that the Court's procedure exceeds the guidelines established in Jenkins for class action treatment of asbestos claims. *See* Jenkins v. Raymark Industries, Inc., 109 F.R.D. 269 (E.D.Tex.1985), *aff'd,* 782 F.2d 468 (5th Cir.1986). In *Jenkins*, this Court certified a class action under Fed.R.Civ.P. 23(b)(3) for resolution of the state of the art issues in 893 asbestos cases. 109 F.R.D. at 269. The Court noted that the issues of an individual's exposure to asbestos and the degree of injury resulting from that exposure were individual questions. 109 F.R.D. at 279. The Court found that the common issues of state of the art predominated over these individual questions. 109 F.R.D. at 279. Lastly, the Court found that individual questions of exposure and damages could be protected by the adoption of a procedure of mini-trials. 109 F.R.D. at 279.

The *Jenkins* decision does not preclude this Court from trying the issues of exposure and actual damages through a procedure other than the use of mini-trials. *Jenkins* merely determined that a procedure of mini-trials was an appropriate procedure, at that time, for resolution of these issues. In *Jenkins*, it was feasible to try these issues by utilizing manageable groupings. Today, it is no longer possible for the Court to try the issues of exposure and actual damages through the use of mini-trials.

The *Jenkins* decision also does not preclude this Court from finding that the exposure and actual damages issues in this action are questions common to the class. As this Court found in *Jenkins*, each asbestos case presents an issue as to an individual's exposure to asbestos and the damages resulting from that exposure. However, the issues of exposure and actual damages are also common to all the Plaintiffs in this consolidated and class action. Each case in this action involves a claim that an insulator or construction worker developed a disease as a result of his or her exposure to asbestos. All of these cases involve a workplace commonality.

As this Court has stated before, it has been this Court's experience that the testimony concerning the different diseases caused by asbestos does not differ from trial to trial. It has also been this Court's experience that the evidence concerning the effect of asbestos on the body's system is the same from case to case. As the Court explained in the certification Order, the defenses to the Plaintiff's claims, although tailored to each case, eventually will become repetitious from case to case. The Court would expect that, from these cases, the Defendants would show 1.) that a certain number of plaintiffs were smokers, 2.) that a certain number of Plaintiffs were exposed to other allegedly dangerous products, 3.) that a certain number of Plaintiffs received adequate warning regarding exposure to asbestos, and 4.) that a certain number of Plaintiffs filed cases barred by the statute of limitations. This list is not exclusive. Moreover, it is important to keep in mind that "[r]ule 23(a)(2) does not require that all issues in the litigation be common, only that common questions exist." In re Asbestos School Litigation, 104 F.R.D. 422, 429 (E.D.Pa.1984)(certification of nation-wide class of asbestos abatement from school buildings), *vacated in part, aff'd in part,* 789 F.2d 996 (3d Cir.), *cert. denied sub nom.,* Celotex Corp. v. Sch. Dist. of Lancaster, 479 U.S. 852 and, *cert. denied sub nom.,* Nat'l Gypsum Co. v. Sch. Dist. of Lancaster, 479 U.S. 915 (1986); *Hummel v. Brennan,* 83 F.R.D. 141, 145 (E.D.Pa.1979).

With regard to the commonality requirement, the Fifth Circuit has held that the "... rule requires only that the resolution of the common questions affect all or a substantial number of the class members ..." *Jenkins v. Raymark,* 782 F.2d at 472. Resolution of the exposure and actual damages issues affects all of the Plaintiffs in this action. Concerning the predominance rule, the court stated that "... common issues must constitute a significant part of the individual cases." 782 F.2d at 472. Although there are individual issues of exposure and damages in this action, it is clear that the common issues of exposure and damages constitute a significant part of the Plaintiffs' individual cases. *Accord* 782 F.2d at 472. Class Jury findings on exposure and actual damages will not only significantly advance the resolution of the underlying cases; such findings will dispose of all these cases. *Accord* 782 F.2d at 472.

The Fifth Circuit recognized that, under the caselaw at that time, only specific issues could be decided in a mass tort action. *Jenkins v. Raymark,* 782 F.2d at 473. However, the court did not foreclose the possibility that all issues in an asbestos case could be decided in a mass tort action. In fact, the court recognized that a change might be in store for the treatment of asbestos claims:

> The courts are now being forced to rethink the alternatives and priorities by the current volume of litigation and more frequent mass disasters.... If Congress leaves us to our own devices, we

may be forced to abandon repetitive hearings and arguments for each claimant's attorney to the extent enjoyed by the profession in the past.

782 F.2d at 473. The Court's procedure for this action is fully consistent with *Jenkins*.

* * *

E. *Federal Class Action Caselaw*

The Defendants contend that the Court's procedure for this action contravenes federal class action authority. In this respect, the Defendants cite a number of cases for the proposition that "federal courts have always required that awards of damages to unnamed individual plaintiffs in class action lawsuits must be based on individual proof of the amount of damages for each individual plaintiff." *E.g.* Six (6) Mexican Workers v. Arizona Citrus Growers, 641 F.Supp. 259, 267 (D.Ariz.1986); Al Barnett & Son, Inc. v. Outboard Marine Corp., 64 F.R.D. 43, 55 (D.Del.1974); and Biechele v. Norfolk & Western Railway Co., 309 F.Supp. 354, 359 (N.D.Ohio 1969). In this consolidated action and class action, the Jury will award actual damages in one lump sum for each disease category. Before receiving a share of the damages, each Plaintiff in this action will have to provide the Court with proof that he or she suffered the amount of damages allocated to that individual Plaintiff. The reasoning of the cases cited by the Defendants is that a plaintiff should not be allowed to recover on the basis of an unsubstantiated damage claim. In this action, each Plaintiff will have to substantiate his or her claims during Phase Three. Therefore, although there are factual differences between the Defendants' cases and this action, the Court's procedure does not contravene the reasoning of the cases cited by the Defendants.

A great deal of support can be found in class action law for aggregate damage awards. As stated by one authority,

> [t]here are occasions when it is feasible and reasonable to prove aggregate monetary relief for the class from an examination of the defendant's records, or by use of a common formula or measurement of damages multiplied by the number of transactions, units, or class members involved, or by reasonable approximation with proper adherence to recognized evidentiary standards.

2 H. Newberg, NEWBERG ON CLASS ACTIONS § 10.01 at p. 348 (2d ed.1985)[hereinafter cited as NEWBERG ON CLASS ACTIONS]. "Aggregate class proof of monetary relief may ... be based on sampling techniques or other reasonable estimates, under accepted rules of evidence." NEWBERG ON CLASS ACTIONS § 10.03 at 350–51. In contexts other than mass tort actions, federal courts have approved the use of aggregate proofs of damages in class actions. *E.g.,* Van Gemert v. Boeing Co., 553 F.2d 812 (2d Cir.1977)(*Van Gemert II*)(breach of contract); Samuel v. University of Pittsburgh, 538 F.2d 991, 997, 999 (3d Cir.1976)(action for illegal exaction of tuition fees); Partain v. First Nat'l Bank, 59 F.R.D. 56

(M.D.Ala.1973)(unlawful interest rate on credit cards); Roper v. Consurve, Inc., 578 F.2d 1106 (5th Cir.1978)(usury claim), *aff'd on other ground sub nom.,* Deposit Guaranty National Bank v. Roper, 445 U.S. 326 (1980). Given the procedural safeguards of the Court's Order, there is no reason that an aggregate damage award cannot be utilized in the class action at hand.

* * *

G. Mass Tort Action Caselaw

The Defendants argue that, under mass tort action caselaw, the issues of causation and damages are individual in nature. The Defendants contend further that courts addressing these issues have chosen to utilize manageable groupings of individual cases or a procedure of mini-trials. *E.g.,* Wilson v. Johns–Manville Sales Corp., 107 F.R.D. 250 (S.D.Tex.1985)(consolidation of fifty cases for a single trial for resolution of state of the art and punitive damages issues), *aff'd on other grounds,* 810 F.2d 1358 (5th Cir.), *cert. denied,* 484 U.S. 828 (1987); In re Richardson–Merrell, Inc. Bendectin Products, 624 F.Supp. 1212 (S.D.Ohio), *aff'd,* In re Bendectin Litigation, 857 F.2d (6th Cir.1988)(reviewing the propriety of trifurcating 844 consolidated cases for resolution of the issues of whether bendectin causes birth defects and for resolution of liability and damages issues), *cert. denied,* 488 U.S. 1006 (1989). The Court is aware of the cases cited by the defendants. However, none of those cases addressed the procedure established by this Court for resolving this action. Under the facts of those cases, it was appropriate to try the issues of causation and damages on an individual basis. Given the procedural safeguards of this Court's plan, this Court now finds that these issues can be tried on a common basis.

The Court is not alone in this thinking. In *Jenkins v. Raymark,* the Fifth Circuit noted that "[i]f Congress leaves us to our own devices, we may be forced to abandon repetitive hearings and arguments for each claimant's attorney to the extent enjoyed by the profession in the past." 782 F.2d at 473. Professors Wright, Miller, and Kane also support the procedure established by the Court for Phase Two:

> One possibility is to try the damages issue only once, making a single award for the class, and then develop an expeditious administrative means of dividing the lump sum among the class members. This approach has been employed in judicially approved settlements under Rule 23(e) and the courts could look for guidance to some of the procedures that have been developed in that context.

7B C. Wright, A. Miller & M. Kane, Federal Practice and Procedure Civil 2d § 1784, at 80 (1986). In a recent bankruptcy settlement case, the Fourth Circuit utilized Wright, Miller, and Kane's suggested procedure. *See* In re A.H. Robins Co., Inc., 880 F.2d 709, 743 (4th Cir.), *cert. denied,* 493 U.S. 959 (1989). In *Robins,* the court stated:

> It is interesting that this procedure for disposing of the case is not novel; it follows largely the suggestion made in 7B C. Wright, A.

Miller & M. Kane at 80 and 81, already discussed herein, and, as formulated by the courts in *Jenkins* and *Skywalk II.* The process begins under the Wright–Miller–Kane model with a trial "only once" of the damages issue, making a single award for the class, and "with the development of an expeditious administrative means of dividing the lump sum among class members."

880 F.2d at 743. The Court affirmed the certification of a class action for resolution of the issues of a Dalkon Shield manufacturer's insurer's liability as a joint tort-feasor, and approved a settlement regarding this issue. 880 F.2d at 709. Each claimant was given the opportunity to accept a settlement offer through a claims resolution facility. 880 F.2d at 743. If she chose not to accept the offer, the claimant had the option of deciding her claim by arbitration or a jury trial. 880 F.2d at 744.

As each plaintiff in the *Cimino* action has the opportunity to request exclusion from the Court's procedure, such an optional arbitration-jury procedure is not necessary in this action.

Newberg also supports the use, in mass tort litigation, of some type of procedure whereby an overall defined fund is established along with a mechanism for determining individual claims against the fund. See 3 Newberg on Class Actions § 17.23 at 399–400. In sum, the Court's Order is supported by the current trend of mass tort authorities.

* * *

IN RE FIBREBOARD CORPORATION

United States Court of Appeals, Fifth Circuit, 1990.
893 F.2d 706.

Before HIGGINBOTHAM, DAVIS and DUHÉ, Circuit Judges.

PATRICK E. HIGGINBOTHAM, CIRCUIT JUDGE:

I

On September 20, 1989, Professor Jack Ratliff of the University of Texas Law School filed his special master's report in *Cimino v. Raymark.* The special master concluded that it was "self-evident that the use of one-by-one individual trials is not an option in the asbestos cases." The master recommended four trial phases: I (classwide liability, class representatives' cases), II (classwide damages), III (apportionment) and IV (distribution). On October 26, the district court entered the first of the orders now at issue. The district court concluded that the trial of these cases in groups of 10 would take all of the Eastern District's trial time for the next three years, explaining that it was persuaded that "to apply traditional methodology to these cases is to admit failure of the federal court system to perform one of its vital roles in our society * * * an efficient, cost-effective dispute resolution process that is fair to the parties." The district court then consolidated 3,031 cases under Fed. R.Civ.P. 42(a) "for a single trial on the issues of state of the art and punitive damages and certified a class action under rule 23(b)(3) for the remaining issues of exposure and actual damages." The consolidation and certification included all pending suits in the Beaumont Division of the Eastern District of Texas filed as of February 1, 1989, by insulation workers and construction workers, survivors of deceased workers, and household members of asbestos workers who were seeking money damages for asbestos-related injury, disease, or death.

Phase I is to be a single consolidated trial proceeding under Rule 42(a). It will decide the state of the art and punitive damages issues. The district court explained that:

> the jury will be asked to decide issues such as (a) which products, if any, were asbestos-containing insulation products capable of producing dust that contained asbestos fibers sufficient to cause harm in its application, use, or removal; (b) which of the Defendants' products, if any, were defective as marketed and unreasonably dangerous; (c) when each Defendant knew or should have known that insulators or construction workers and their household members were at risk of contracting an asbestos-related injury or disease from the application, use, or removal of asbestos-containing insulation products; and (d) whether each Defendant's marketing of a defective and unreasonably dangerous product constituted gross negligence. In answering issue (d), the Jury will hear evidence of punitive conduct including any conspiracy among the Defendants to conceal the dangers (if any) of asbestos. The wording of issues (c) and (d) will depend on the applicability of the 1987 Texas Tort Reform legislation to a particular class member's individual case.

By its order of December 29, 1989, the district court explained that "the jury may be allowed to formulate a multiplier for each defendant for which the jury returns an affirmative finding on the issue of gross negligence."

The district court also described the proceedings for Phase II in its October 26 order. In Phase II the jury is to decide the percentage of plaintiffs exposed to each defendant's products, the percentage of claims barred by statutes of limitation, adequate warnings, and other affirmative defenses. The jury is to determine actual damages in a lump sum for each disease category for all plaintiffs in the class. Phase II will include a full trial of liability and damages for 11 class representatives and such evidence as the parties wish to offer from 30 illustrative plaintiffs. Defendants will choose 15 and plaintiffs will choose 15 illustrative plaintiffs, for a total of 41 plaintiffs. The jury will hear opinions of experts from plaintiffs and defendants regarding the total damage award. The basis for the jury's judgment is said to be the 41 cases plus the data supporting the calculation of the experts regarding total damages suffered by the remaining 2,990 class members.

Class members have answered questionnaires and are testifying in scheduled oral depositions now in progress. Petitioners attack the limits of discovery from the class members, but we will not reach this issue. It is sufficient to explain that defendants are allowed a total of 45 minutes to interrogate each class member in an oral deposition. These depositions will not be directly used at the trial in Phase II. Rather, the oral depositions, with the other discovery from class members, provide information for experts engaged to measure the damages suffered by the class.

II

* * *

Plaintiffs deny that Phase II would deny defendants any right. Plaintiffs argue that every plaintiff is effectively before the court; that the evidence to be offered by their experts is more the use of summary evidence under Rule 1006 of the Federal Rules of Evidence than the use of math models to extrapolate total damages from sample plaintiffs. Plaintiffs concede that the contemplated trial is extraordinary, but argue that extraordinary measures are necessary if these cases are to be tried at all. While extraordinary, the measures are no more than a change in the mode of proof, plaintiffs say. The argument continues that Rule 23 is not the necessary vehicle for the ordered trial, but will sustain it, if the "consolidation" is viewed as a class. We turn to these arguments.

* * *

The plaintiffs' answers to interrogatories and the depositions already conducted have provided enough information to show that if, as plaintiffs contend, the representative plaintiffs accurately reflect the class, it is a diverse group. The plaintiffs' "class" consists of persons claiming different diseases, different exposure periods, and different occupations. The depositions of ten tentative class representatives indicate that their diseases break down into three categories: asbestosis (pl[e]ural and pulmonary)—eight representatives; lung cancer—three representatives; and Mesothelioma—one representative. The class breaks down as follows:

Disease	#	%
Pleural cases	907	37.2%
Asbestosis cases	1184	48.6%
Lung cancer cases	219	9.0%
Other cancer cases	92	3.8%
Mesothelioma cases	33	1.4%

In addition, plaintiffs' admissions of fact show the following disparities among class members.

a. The class includes persons who do not have legal claims against Defendant ACandS, Inc. b. One or more members of the class may be barred from prosecuting claims against ACandS by virtue of their prior employment with ACandS. c. The severity and type of physical or mental injuries varies among class members. d. The nature and type of damage varies among class members. e. Not all of the Plaintiffs have been injured by the acts, omissions, conduct or fault of all of the Defendants. f. The dates of exposure to asbestos-containing products varies among class members. g. The types of products to which class members were exposed varies among class members. h. The dates that class members knew or should have known of their exposure to asbestos-containing products is not identical among class members.

We are also uncomfortable with the suggestion that a move from one-on-one "traditional" modes is little more than a move to modernity. Such traditional ways of proceeding reflect far more than habit. They reflect the very culture of the jury trial and the case and controversy requirement of Article III. It is suggested that the litigating unit is the class and, hence, we have the adversarial engagement or that all are present in a "consolidated" proceeding. But, this begs the very question of whether these 3,031 claimants are sufficiently situated for class treatment; it equally begs the question of whether they are actually before the court under Fed.R.Civ.P. Rules 23 and 42(b) in any more than a fictional sense. Ultimately, these concerns find expression in defendants' right to due process.

* * *

The 2,990 class members cannot be certified for trial as proposed under Rule 23(b)(3), Fed.R.Civ.P. Rule 23(b)(3) requires that "the questions of law or fact common to the members of the class predominate over any questions affecting individual members." There are too many disparities among the various plaintiffs for their common concerns to predominate. The plaintiffs suffer from different diseases, some of which are more likely to have been caused by asbestos than others. The plaintiffs were exposed to asbestos in various manners and to varying degrees. The plaintiffs' lifestyles differed in material respects. To create the requisite commonality for trial, the discrete components of the class members' claims and the asbestos manufacturers' defenses must be submerged. The procedures for Phase II do precisely that, but, as we have explained, do so only by reworking the substantive duty owed by the manufacturers. At the least, the enabling acts prevent that reading.

Finally, it is questionable whether defendants' right to trial by jury is being faithfully honored, but we need not explore this issue. It is sufficient now to conclude that Phase II cannot go forward without changing Texas law and usurping legislative prerogatives, a step federal courts lack authority to take.

III

We admire the work of our colleague, Judge Robert Parker, and are sympathetic with the difficulties he faces. This grant of the petition for writ of mandamus should not be taken as a rebuke of an able judge, but rather as another chapter in an ongoing struggle with the problems presented by the phenomenon of mass torts. The petitions for writ of mandamus are granted. The order for Phase II trial is vacated and the cases are remanded to the district court for further proceedings. We find no impediment to the trial of Phase I should the district court wish to proceed with that trial. We encourage the district court to continue its imaginative and innovative efforts to confront these cases. We also caution that defendants are obligated to cooperate in the common enterprise of obtaining a fair trial.

IN RE JOINT EASTERN AND SOUTHERN DISTRICT ASBESTOS LITIGATION IN RE KEENE CORPORATION

United States Court of Appeals, Second Circuit, 1993.
14 F.3d 726.

Before VAN GRAAFEILAND and WINTER, CIRCUIT JUDGES, and POLLACK, DISTRICT JUDGE.

WINTER, CIRCUIT JUDGE:

This is an appeal from Judge Weinstein's order issuing a preliminary injunction and certifying a mandatory limited-fund class action pursuant to Fed.R.Civ.P. 23(b)(1)(B). The underlying action's claim for relief is unique. It seeks a settlement with a mandatory class of all persons with present or future asbestos claims against Keene Corporation. Keene, however, does not claim that it has a right to such a settlement. Because this claim is not a case or controversy within the meaning of Article III, we vacate the district court's preliminary injunction and order the complaint dismissed.

BACKGROUND

In 1968, Keene purchased Baldwin–Ehret–Hill ("BEH"), a manufacturer of acoustical ceilings, ventilation systems, and thermal insulation products. BEH became a wholly owned subsidiary of Keene and was later merged into Keene Building Products Corporation ("KBPC"), another Keene subsidiary. From 1968 until 1972 or early 1973, BEH used asbestos in its insulation and acoustical products.

Keene's acquisition of BEH led to Keene's extensive involvement in asbestos litigation. Since 1977, Keene has been named in approximately 190,000 asbestos bodily injury claims. Keene has resolved over 95,000 of the claims, leaving roughly 98,000 claims pending against it. On average, some 2,000 new claims are filed against Keene each month, with no prospect of decline in the foreseeable future. Keene has spent $447 million on asbestos litigation so far.

As of May 31, 1993, Keene had liquid assets of $80,302,000, and non-liquid assets of $8,344,000 in the form of Keene's one operating subsidiary, Reinhold Industries, Inc. Keene has contingent assets of $25,500,000 in disputed insurance claims. Keene has current non-asbestos liabilities of $7,497,000, deferred liabilities of $2,062,000, and escrowed judgments and appeal bonds of approximately $53,225,000. Keene's net assets, therefore, are $51,362,000, including the disputed insurance claims.

Keene brought this action by filing papers styled a "Verified Class Action Complaint in Connection with Settlement" on May 13, 1993. Paragraphs 1 through 3 of the complaint claim subject matter jurisdiction based on diversity jurisdiction, 28 U.S.C. § 1332(a), admiralty and maritime jurisdiction, 28 U.S.C. § 1333, and supplemental jurisdiction, 28 U.S.C. § 1367(a). Paragraphs 4 through 16 describe the parties. The defendants are named individuals who have asserted asbestos-related claims against Keene and a mandatory class of present or future asbestos claimants. Paragraphs 17 through 28 describe Keene's history of asbestos litigation. Paragraphs 29 through 48 recount Keene's expenditures on asbestos litigation and its current assets. Paragraphs 49 through 64, entitled "Class Action Allegations" allege facts supporting class certification and recommend subclass divisions. Paragraphs 65 through 73, entitled "The Settlement," read as follows:

65. This is a settlement class action. Keene seeks court assistance, as provided by Rule 23(b)(1)(B), to negotiate and eventually approve a settlement that fairly resolves the claims with the limited funds Keene has available.

66. The Settlement Agreement will be designed to ensure that Keene complies with its obligations to the Class, but at the same time will preserve a portion of its assets for continued operations, in order that Keene may achieve an adequate balance for the protection of its shareholders.

67. Certification of the Class for settlement purposes can avoid a potential bankruptcy of Keene by allowing the asbestos-related personal injury, wrongful death, property damage and contribution litigations against Keene to come to a successful and final resolution in an expeditious and fair manner with a minimum of transaction costs.

68. Keene is presently a defendant in approximately 98,000 asbestos-related personal injury and wrongful death actions and approximately 49 property damage actions, many of which are scheduled to commence trial in the spring and summer of 1993.

69. Continued prosecutions of the approximately 98,000 pending actions against Keene nationwide will defeat the purpose of the proposed Class Action and any chance for settlement by depleting the limited fund, thereby preventing the fair, adequate, and equitable compensation of the Class.

70. The continuation of asbestos-related personal injury, wrongful death, property damage, and contribution litigations against Keene will result in irreparable harm to Keene, the Class, and the limited fund.

71. An injunction barring all pending and future asbestos-related personal injury, wrongful death, and property damage litigation against Keene is necessary to preserve this Court's jurisdiction

over the proposed class action and over the limited fund, and to protect any judgment issued herein.

72. Keene and all members of the Class, as claimants to the limited fund, are without an adequate remedy at law.

73. In the event the parties cannot reach a settlement, the order conditionally certifying the settlement class should be vacated.

Paragraphs 74 and 75 describe the "limited fund," essentially Keene's assets available to satisfy present and future asbestos claims. The remaining paragraphs, 76 through 78, specify the relief sought. In particular, paragraph 76 asks the court to "use its equitable powers to enter a declaratory judgment that Keene is not liable to defendants for any damages that relate to its manufacture and sale of products containing asbestos." Paragraph 77 asks that the court certify a class of asbestos claimants "[i]n connection with its request for a declaratory judgment." Paragraph 78 then provides: "The purpose of certifying this class is to facilitate the formation of a settlement that will mutually benefit both the claimants and Keene Corporation."

Upon filing of the complaint, Judge Weinstein referred the matter to Special Master Marvin E. Frankel for determination of the following questions: (1) Whether the financial assets of Keene Corporation are so limited that there exists substantial risk that payment for the present and prospective asbestos-related personal injury and wrongful death claims brought against the company will be placed in jeopardy? (2) Whether there is a substantial probability that if damages are awarded, the claims of earlier litigants would exhaust the defendant's available and projected assets, including any pertinent insurance proceeds? Special Master Frankel held evidentiary hearings on these questions, and at the close of the hearings, stated on the record that it was his "tentative belief" that Keene was a "limited fund." The next day, June 16, 1993, Keene requested a temporary restraining order staying all asbestos litigation then pending and thereafter commenced in which it was a defendant. Judge Weinstein heard argument on June 18 and issued an order to show cause and a temporary restraining order that day. The order also stayed execution or enforcement of judgments and settlements already obtained against Keene.

* * *

On June 29, 1993, Special Master Frankel filed a Report in which he answered both questions in the affirmative. On July 1, 1993, Judge Weinstein entered an order that adopted Special Master Frankel's report, found that Keene was a "limited fund," issued a preliminary injunction, and certified a limited-fund class pursuant to Fed.R.Civ.P. 23(b)(1)(B).

Specifically, the July 1 Order certified five subclasses of claimants and appointed counsel for each subclass. The order also appointed a Special Settlement Master "to facilitate discussions among the parties," and directed that "[s]ettlement discussions should begin immediately."

The order enjoined Keene and all class members from continuing or commencing asbestos-related litigation, except for trials already underway. The order also enjoined class members from attempting to collect judgments against Keene or its assets, and forbade Keene to make any payments other than reasonable expenses in operating its business.

The Carlisle appellants filed a notice of appeal on July 13, 1993. The Carlisle appellants also moved in the district court to stay proceedings pending the disposition of the appeal. This motion was denied on July 14. The other appellants subsequently filed notices of appeal. On August 10, 1993, we granted Carlisle's motion for a stay of all proceedings and ordered an expedited appeal.

Discussion

Appellants raise a number of challenges to the proceedings below.[1] For our purposes, however, we need consider only whether the action involves a "case" or "controversy" under Article III.

* * *

Foremost among elements of the case or controversy requirement is the requirement that the court be presented with a legal claim to adjudicate. As the Supreme Court has explained: Article III of the Constitution limits the "judicial power" of the United States to the resolution of "cases" and "controversies." The constitutional power of federal courts cannot be defined, and indeed has no substance, without reference to the necessity "to adjudge the legal rights of litigants in actual controversies." *Liverpool S.S. Co. v. Commissioners of Emigration,* 113 U.S. 33, 39, 5 S.Ct. 352, 355, 28 L.Ed. 899 (1885). Valley Forge Christian College v. Americans United for Separation of Church & State, Inc., 454 U.S. 464, 471, 102 S.Ct. 752, 758, 70 L.Ed.2d 700 (1982).

A necessary prerequisite to the exercise of judicial power, then, is the presence before a court of a claim of substantive right. Tutun v. United States, 270 U.S. 568, 577, 46 S.Ct. 425, 427, 70 L.Ed. 738 (1926). In other words, the plaintiff's complaint must allege a substantive claim that triggers the court's adjudicative function. Except when a party seeks declaratory relief, the plaintiff must assert that some conduct on the part of the defendants that has caused or is causing actual or threatened injury to the plaintiff that will be remedied or avoided by a determination of liability. Gladstone, Realtors v. Village of Bellwood, 441 U.S. 91, 99, 99 S.Ct. 1601, 1607, 60 L.Ed.2d 66 (1979).

---

1. Appellants argue that: (1) the preliminary injunction is preempted under the Supremacy Clause by the Bankruptcy Code; (2) the complaint fails to present a "case" or "controversy" within the meaning of Article III; (3) the preliminary injunction violates the Anti–Injunction Act, 28 U.S.C. § 2283 (1988); (4) the defendant class was improperly certified under Fed.R.Civ.P. 23; (5) personal jurisdiction was not obtained over absent class members; (6) the preliminary injunction denies asbestos claimants Fifth Amendment due process and equal protection rights; (7) the order violates the abstention doctrine; and (8) the preliminary injunction is not supported by the requisite findings under Fed.R.Civ.P. 65.

As described, most of Keene's complaint recounts its expenditures on asbestos litigation, its current assets, the facts that warrant class certification, and Keene's recommendations for subclasses. Paragraphs 65 through 73, entitled "The Settlement," contain what Keene considers its legal claim. As does the rest of the complaint, and Keene's brief and argument before this court, this portion alleges that a settlement between Keene and a defendant class of asbestos claimants is the most efficient and fairest means of distributing Keene's limited assets and asks for such a settlement as relief. Notably absent from this portion (or any portion of the complaint) is any allegation that any of the defendants are legally harming, or will legally harm, Keene by refusing to settle their asbestos claims. Courts do not have authority to compel parties to settle their cases, *see* Kothe v. Smith, 771 F.2d 667, 669 (2d Cir.1985), and Keene does not assert that it has a right to a settlement. Indeed, Keene requests in paragraph 73 that the class be de-certified should the parties fail to reach a settlement. There is thus no claim that, if settlement negotiations fail, Keene will be able to prove facts at a trial that would entitle it to relief.

Rather than defend the complaint as a whole, Keene seeks to rely on the assertion in one paragraph of the "Relief Sought" section of its complaint that the court should "use its equitable powers to enter a declaratory judgment that Keene is not liable to defendants for any damages that relate to its manufacture and sale of products containing asbestos." However, a request for relief in the form of a declaratory judgment does not by itself establish a case or controversy involving an adjudication of rights. Skelly Oil Co. v. Phillips Petroleum Co., 339 U.S. 667, 671–72, 70 S.Ct. 876, 879–80, 94 L.Ed. 1194 (1950). In fact, the statute authorizing the declaratory judgment remedy explicitly incorporates the Article III case or controversy limitation. *See* 28 U.S.C. § 2201 (1988)("In a case of actual controversy within its jurisdiction...."); Aetna Life Ins. Co. v. Haworth, 300 U.S. 227, 239–40, 57 S.Ct. 461, 463–64, 81 L.Ed. 617 (1937). The Declaratory Judgment Act does not expand jurisdiction. *Skelly Oil,* 339 U.S. at 671, 70 S.Ct. at 878. Nor does it provide an independent cause of action. Its operation is procedural only—to provide a form of relief previously unavailable. *Aetna Life Ins. Co.,* 300 U.S. at 240. Therefore, a court may only enter a declaratory judgment in favor of a party who has a substantive claim of right to such relief.

Keene apparently suggests that it should be declared not liable to asbestos claimants on the grounds of res judicata following the settlement it hopes to reach with the defendant class of claimants. The suggestion is of course entirely circular because the existence of the settlement is an essential element entitling Keene to a declaratory judgment of non-liability. The fact that Keene may not be liable to asbestos claimants after reaching a settlement with them does not support a legal claim triggering the court's adjudicative powers when such a settlement has not been reached.

In its brief, Keene argues that it seeks a declaration of non-liability based on some unspecified defense to the merits of the asbestos claims. Keene's request, however, is transparently pretextual. It offers no reason why it is not liable to any of the asbestos claimants. Nor, as Keene's counsel admitted at oral argument, does Keene seriously contend that a federal court might validly declare it not liable to the numerous claimant-defendants who have already obtained unexecuted but final judgments against Keene. Moreover, if Keene truly sought a declaratory judgment regarding its asbestos liabilities, Keene would have no reason to ask that the class be de-certified in the event a settlement is not reached.

Instead, it is clear that the complaint is an attempt to compel an adjustment of Keene's creditors' rights outside the Bankruptcy Code and is defended almost entirely by the argument that a mandatory class settlement of present or future asbestos claims would be better for all parties than a bankruptcy proceeding. Indeed, the process contemplated by Keene mirrors a bankruptcy proceeding. The finding of a limited fund corresponds to a finding of insolvency. The preliminary injunction serves much the same function as the automatic stay under Section 362(a) of the Bankruptcy Code. 11 U.S.C. § 362(a) (1988). The class representatives correspond to creditors' committees in Chapter 11 proceedings. *See* 11 U.S.C. § 1102 (1988). The proposed mandatory class settlement mirrors a reorganization plan and "cram-down," *see* 11 U.S.C. § 1123, 1129(b); In re Johns-Manville, 982 F.2d 721, 736 (2d Cir.1992), *modified on different grounds,* 993 F.2d 7 (2d Cir.1993), *followed by a discharge,* 11 U.S.C. § 1141(d).

Keene's argument is self-defeating, however, because it is a self-evident evasion of the exclusive legal system established by Congress for debtors to seek relief. *See In re Johns-Manville,* 982 F.2d at 735. The adoption of Keene's position would surely lead to further evasion of the Bankruptcy Code as other debtors sought relief in mandatory class actions. Keene argues that such a precedent would be limited to situations, like Keene's, of mass torts in which some plaintiffs are not known at the time of the accident. We are dubious that a limit to unknown plaintiffs is feasible. Under the limited fund theory espoused here, a class representative for a large number of trade creditors might be appointed to seek a settlement on their behalf where a company was deemed to be a limited fund because of insolvency. The argument that the company and its creditors would all be better off in such an action than in bankruptcy would be as plausible in a case involving a large number of contract creditors as it is here. Breach of warranty cases involving numerous purchasers might also fall within the theory.

Moreover, even if limited to so-called mass torts with yet unknown plaintiffs, Keene's theory would cover a large number of cases. The use of aggregative techniques and inventive legal theories are causing mass torts to become rather routine. Certainly the theory pressed here would apply to many products liability cases, *see, e.g.,* In re Silicone Gel Breast Implants Prods. Liab. Litig., 793 F.Supp. 1098 (J.P.M.L.1992), environmental torts, *see, e.g.,* In re Love Canal Actions, 92 A.D.2d 416, 460 N.Y.S.2d 850 (1983), and even physical disasters. *See, e.g.,* Phillips v. Hallmark Cards, Inc., 722 S.W.2d 86 (Mo.1986)(*en banc*)(suit by firemen against owner of hotel in which skywalks collapsed for injuries, including emotional distress, sustained while rescuing trapped victims).

Evasion of bankruptcy is also not without costs or other perils. The injunction in the instant matter has already prevented execution of final judgments on supersedeas bonds and funds in escrow that are not Keene's assets. Moreover, class members in cases such as this would have no say in the conduct of the court-appointed class representatives and, unlike creditors in bankruptcy, are not able to vote on a settlement. *See* 11 U.S.C. § 1126. For them, it would be "cram-down" from start to finish. Finally, unlike a lawyer for a creditors' committee, the class representatives in matters like the present one may not be compensated unless a settlement is reached, a situation fraught with danger to the rights of plaintiffs. *See* In re "Agent Orange" Prod. Liab. Litig., 818 F.2d 216, 222 (2d Cir.), *cert. denied,* 484 U.S. 926, 108 S.Ct. 289, 98 L.Ed.2d 249 (1987)(fee arrangement creating incentives to settle without regard to merits is void).

Keene argues passionately that bankruptcy will be a more costly route for the defendant class than this mandatory class action. It may be that the amount distributed to the class in a Keene bankruptcy will be less than in a settlement in the instant class action. Indeed, Keene has suggested that a trial be held on that issue. However, the function of federal courts is not to conduct trials over whether a statutory scheme should be ignored because a more efficient mechanism can be fashioned by judges.

* * *

Conclusion

For these reasons, we vacate the order and preliminary injunction issued by the district court and order dismissal of the complaint for lack of subject matter jurisdiction. The mandate shall issue forthwith.

IN THE MATTER OF RHONE–POULENC RORER, INC.

United States Court of Appeals, Seventh Circuit, 1995.
51 F.3d 1293.

Before Posner, Chief Judge, and Bauer and Rovner, Circuit Judges.

Posner, Chief Judge.

Drug companies that manufacture blood solids are the defendants in a nationwide class action brought on behalf of hemophiliacs infected by the AIDS virus as a consequence of using the defendants' products. The defendants have filed with us a petition for mandamus, asking us to direct the district judge to rescind his order certifying the case as a class action. We have no appellate jurisdiction over that order. An order certifying a class is not a final decision within the meaning of 28 U.S.C. § 1291; it does not wind up the litigation in the district court. * * * Mandamus has occasionally been granted to undo class certifications, *see, e.g.,* In re Fibreboard Corp., 893 F.2d 706 (5th Cir.1990), and we are not aware that any case has held that mandamus will never be granted in such cases. * * * The present case, as we shall see, is quite extraordinary when all its dimensions are apprehended. We shall also see that when mandamus is sought to protect the Seventh Amendment's right to a jury trial in federal civil cases, as in this case, the requirement of proving irreparable harm is relaxed. [Discussion of interlocutory appeal and mandamus standards omitted—*ed.*]

The suit to which the petition for mandamus relates, Wadleigh v. Rhone–Poulenc Rorer Inc., arises out of the infection of a substantial fraction of the hemophiliac population of this country by the AIDS virus because the blood supply was contaminated by the virus before the nature of the disease was well understood or adequate methods of screening the blood supply existed. The AIDS virus (HIV—human immunodeficiency virus) is transmitted by the exchange of bodily fluids, primarily semen and blood. Hemophiliacs depend on blood solids that contain the clotting factors whose absence defines their disease. These blood solids are concentrated from blood obtained from many donors. If just one of the donors is infected by the AIDS virus the probability that the blood solids manufactured in part from his blood will be infected is very high unless the blood is treated with heat to kill the virus. * * *

First identified in 1981, AIDS was diagnosed in hemophiliacs beginning in 1982, and by 1984 the medical community agreed that the virus was transmitted by blood as well as by semen. That year it was demonstrated that treatment with heat could kill the virus in the blood supply and in the following year a reliable test for the presence of the virus in blood was developed. By this time, however, a large number of hemophiliacs had become infected. Since 1984 physicians have been advised to place hemophiliacs on heat-treated blood solids, and since 1985 all blood donated for the manufacture of blood solids has been screened and supplies discovered to be HIV-positive have been discarded. Supplies that test negative are heat-treated, because the test is not infallible and in particular may fail to detect the virus in persons who became infected within six months before taking the test.

The plaintiffs have presented evidence that 2,000 hemophiliacs have died of AIDS and that half or more of the remaining U.S. hemophiliac population of 20,000 may be HIV-positive. Unless there are dramatic breakthroughs in the treatment of HIV or AIDS, all infected persons will die from the disease. The reason so many are infected even though the supply of blood for the manufacture of blood solids (as for transfusions) has been safe since the mid–80s is that the disease has a very long incubation period; the median period for hemophiliacs may be as long as 11 years. Probably most of the hemophiliacs who are now HIV-positive, or have AIDS, or have died of AIDS were infected in the early 1980s, when the blood supply was contaminated.

Some 300 lawsuits, involving some 400 plaintiffs, have been filed, 60 percent of them in state courts, 40 percent in federal district courts under the diversity jurisdiction, seeking to impose tort liability on the defendants for the transmission of HIV to hemophiliacs in blood solids manufactured by the defendants. Obviously these 400 plaintiffs represent only a small fraction of the hemophiliacs (or their next of kin, in cases in which the hemophiliac has died) who are infected by HIV or have died of AIDS. One of the 300 cases is *Wadleigh,* filed in September 1993, the case that the district judge certified as a class action. Thirteen other cases have been tried already in various courts around the country, and the defendants have won twelve of them. All the cases brought in federal court (like *Wadleigh*)—cases brought under the diversity jurisdiction—have been consolidated for pre-trial discovery in the Northern District of Illinois by the panel on multidistrict litigation.

The plaintiffs advance two principal theories of liability. The first is that before anyone had heard of AIDS or HIV, it was known that Hepatitis B, a lethal disease though less so than HIV–AIDS, could be transmitted either through blood transfusions or through injection of blood solids. The plaintiffs argue that due care with respect to the risk of infection with Hepatitis B required the defendants to take measures to purge that virus from their blood solids, whether by treating the blood they bought or by screening the donors—perhaps by refusing to deal with paid donors, known to be a class at high risk of being infected with Hepatitis B. The defendants' failure to take effective measures was, the plaintiffs claim, negligent. Had the defendants not been negligent, the plaintiffs further argue, hemophiliacs would have been protected not only against Hepatitis B but also, albeit fortuitously or as the plaintiffs put it "serendipitously," against HIV.

The plaintiffs' second theory of liability is more conventional. It is that the defendants, again negligently, dragged their heels in screening donors and taking other measures to prevent contamination of blood solids by HIV when they learned about the disease in the early 1980s. The plaintiffs have other theories of liability as well, including strict products liability, but it is not necessary for us to get into them.

The district judge did not think it feasible to certify *Wadleigh* as a class action for the adjudication of the entire controversy between the plaintiffs and the defendants. Fed.R.Civ.P. 23(b)(3). The differences in the date of infection alone of the thousands of potential class members would make such a procedure infeasible. Hemophiliacs infected before anyone knew about the contamination of blood solids by HIV could not rely on the second theory of liability, while hemophiliacs infected after the blood supply became safe (not perfectly safe, but nearly so) probably were not infected by any of the defendants' products. Instead the judge certified the suit "as a class action with respect to particular issues" only. Fed.R.Civ.P. 23(c)(4)(A). He explained this decision in an opinion which implied that he did not envisage the entry of a final judgment but rather the rendition by a jury of a special verdict that would answer a number of questions bearing, perhaps decisively, on whether the defendants are negligent under either of the theories sketched above. If the special verdict found no negligence under either theory, that presumably would be the end of all the cases unless other theories of liability proved viable. If the special verdict found negligence, individual members of the class would then file individual tort suits in state and federal district courts around the nation and would use the special verdict, in conjunction with the doctrine of collateral estoppel, to block relitigation of the issue of negligence.

With all due respect for the district judge's commendable desire to experiment with an innovative procedure for streamlining the adjudication of this "mass tort," we believe that his plan so far exceeds the permissible bounds of discretion in the management of federal litigation as to compel us to intervene and order decertification. * * *

* * *

Nevertheless we shall assume * * * that eventually there will be a final judgment to review. Only it will come too late to provide effective relief to the defendants; and this is an important consideration in relation to the first condition for mandamus, that the challenged ruling of the district court have inflicted irreparable harm, which is to say harm that cannot be rectified by an appeal from the final judgment in the lawsuit. The reason that an appeal will come to late to provide effective relief for these defendants is the sheer magnitude of the risk to which the class action, in contrast to the individual actions pending or likely, exposes them. Consider the situation that would obtain if the class had not been certified. The defendants would be facing 300 suits. More might be filed, but probably only a few more, because the statutes of limitations in the various states are rapidly expiring for potential plaintiffs. The blood supply has been safe since 1985. That is ten years ago. The risk to hemophiliacs of having become infected with HIV has been widely publicized; it is unlikely that many hemophiliacs are unaware of it. Under the usual discovery statute of limitations, they would have to have taken steps years ago to determine their infection status, and having found out file suit within the limitations period running from the date of discovery, in order to preserve their rights.

Three hundred is not a trivial number of lawsuits. The potential damages in each one are great. But the defendants have won twelve of the first thirteen, and, if this is a representative sample, they are likely to win most of the remaining ones as well. Perhaps in the end, if class-action treatment is denied (it has been denied in all the other hemophiliac HIV suits in which class certification has been sought), they will be compelled to pay damages in only 25 cases, involving a potential liability of perhaps no more than $125 million altogether. These are guesses, of course, but they are at once conservative and usable for the limited purpose of comparing the situation that will face the defendants if the class certification stands. All of a sudden they will face thousands of plaintiffs. Many may already be barred by the statute of limitations, as we have suggested, though its further running was tolled by the filing of *Wadleigh* as a class action. * * *

Suppose that 5,000 of the potential class members are not yet barred by the statute of limitations. And suppose the named plaintiffs in *Wadleigh* win the class portion of this case to the extent of establishing the defendants' liability under either of the two negligence theories. It is true that this would only be prima facie liability, that the defendants would have various defenses. But they could not be confident that the defenses would prevail. They might, therefore, easily be facing $25 billion in potential liability (conceivably more), and with it bankruptcy. They may not wish to roll these dice. That is putting it mildly. They will be under intense pressure to settle. Milton Handler, *The Shift from Substantive to Procedural Innovations in Antitrust Suits*, 71 Colum.L.Rev. 1, 8–9 (1971); William Simon, *Class Actions—Useful Tool or Engine of Destruction*, 55 F.R.D. 375 (1972); Marc Galanter, *Why the "Haves" Come Out Ahead: Speculations on the Limits of Legal Change*, 9 Law & Socy Rev. 95, 143 and n.121 (1974); Charles D. Schoor, *Class Actions: The Right to Solicit*, 16 Santa Clara L.Rev. 215, 239–40 and n.82 (1976); Joseph Grundfest, *Disimplying Private Rights of Action under the Federal Securities Laws: The Commission's Authority*, 107 Harv.L.Rev. 963, 973 n.38 (1994); Note, *Conflicts in Class Actions and Protection of Absent Class Members*, 91 Yale L.J. 590, 605 n.67 (1982). If they settle, the class certification—the ruling that will have forced them to settle—will never be reviewed. General Motors Corp. v. City of New York, 501 F.2d 639, 657–58 (2d Cir.1974)(concurring opinion); * * * Judge Friendly, who was not given to hyperbole, called settlements induced by a small probability of an immense judgment in a class action "blackmail settlements." Henry J. Friendly, FEDERAL JURISDICTION: A GENERAL VIEW 120 (1973). Judicial concern about them is legitimate, not "sociological," as it was derisively termed in In re Sugar Antitrust Litigation, 559 F.2d 481, 483 n.1 (9th Cir.1977).

* * *

. We do not want to be misunderstood as saying that class actions are bad because they place pressure on defendants to settle. That pressure is a reality, but it must be balanced against the undoubted benefits of the class action that have made it an authorized procedure for employment by federal courts. We have yet to consider the balance. All that our discussion to this point has shown is that the first condition for the grant of mandamus—that the challenged ruling not be effectively reviewable at the end of the case—is fulfilled. The ruling will inflict irreparable harm; the next question is whether the ruling can fairly be described as usurpative. We have formulated this second condition as narrowly, as stringently, as can be, but even so formulated we think it is fulfilled. We do not mean to suggest that the district judge is engaged in a deliberate power-grab. We have no reason to suppose that he wants to preside over an unwieldy class action. We believe that he was responding imaginatively and in the beast of faith to the challenge that mass torts, graphically illustrated by the avalanche of asbestos litigation, pose for the federal courts. But the plan that he has devised for the HIV-hemophilia litigation exceeds the bounds of allowable judicial discretion. Three concerns, none of them necessarily sufficient in itself but cumulatively compelling, persuade us to this conclusion.

The first is a concern with forcing these defendants to stake their companies on the outcome of a single jury trial, or be forced by fear of the risk of bankruptcy to settle even if they have no legal liability, when it is entirely feasible to allow a final, authoritative determination of their liability for the colossal misfortune that has befallen the hemophiliac population to emerge from a decentralized process of multiple trials, involving different juries, and different standards of liability, in different jurisdictions, and when, in addition, the preliminary indications are that the defendants are not liable for the grievous harm that has befallen the members of the class. These qualifications are important. In most class actions—and those the ones in which the rationale for the procedure is most compelling—individual suits are infeasible because the claim of each class member is tiny relative to the expense of litigation. That plainly is not the situation here. A notable feature of this case, and one that has not been remarked upon or encountered, so far as we are aware, in previous cases, is the demonstrated great likelihood that the plaintiffs' claims, despite their human appeal, lack legal merit. This is the inference from the defendants' having won 92.3 percent ($^{12}/_{13}$) of the cases to have gone to judgment. Granted, thirteen is a small sample and further trials, if they are held, may alter the pattern that the sample reveals. But whether they do or not, the result will be robust if these further trials are permitted to go forward, because the pattern that results will reflect a consensus, or at least a pooling of judgment, of many different tribunals.

For this consensus or maturing of judgment the district judge proposes to substitute a single trial before a single jury instructed in accordance with no actual law of any jurisdiction—a jury that will receive a kind of Esperanto instruction, merging the negligence standards of the 50 states and the District of Columbia. One jury, consisting of six persons (the standard federal civil jury nowadays consists of six regular jurors and two alternates), will hold the fate of an industry in the palm of its hand. This jury, jury number fourteen, may disagree with twelve of the previous thirteen juries—and hurl the industry into bankruptcy. That kind of thing can happen in our system of civil justice (it is not likely to happen, because the industry is likely to settle—whether or not it really is liable) without violating anyone's legal rights. But it need not be tolerated when the alternative exists of submitting an issue to multiple juries constituting in the aggregate a much larger and more diverse sample of decision-makers. That would not be a feasible option if the stakes to each class member were too slight to repay the cost of suit, even though the aggregate stakes are very large and would repay the costs of a consolidated proceeding. But this is not the case with regard to the HIV-hemophilia litigation. Each plaintiff if successful is apt to receive a judgment in the millions. With the aggregate stakes in the tens or hundreds of millions of dollars, or even in the billions, it is not a waste of judicial resources to conduct more than one trial, before more than six jurors, to determine whether a major segment of the international pharmaceutical industry is to follow the asbestos manufacturers into Chapter 11.

We have hinted at the second reason for questioning whether the district judge did not exceed the bounds of permissible judicial discretion. He proposes to have a jury determine the negligence of the defendants under a legal standard that does not actually exist anywhere in the world. One is put in mind of the concept of "general" common law that prevailed in the era of Swift v. Tyson. The assumption is that the common law of the 50 states and the District of Columbia, at least so far as bears on a claim of negligence against drug companies, is basically uniform and can be abstracted in a single instruction. It is no doubt true that at some level of generality the law of negligence is one, not only nationwide but worldwide. Negligence is a failure to take due care, and due care a function of the probability and magnitude of accident and the costs of avoiding it. A jury can be asked whether the defendants took due care. And in many cases such differences as there are among the tort rules of the different states would not affect the outcome. The Second Circuit was willing to assume dubitante that this was true of the issues certified for class determination in the *Agent Orange* litigation. In re Diamond Shamrock Chemicals Co., 725 F.2d 858, 861 (2d Cir. 1984).

We doubt that it is true in general, and we greatly doubt that it is true in a case such as this in which one of the theories pressed by the plaintiffs, the "serendipity" theory, is novel. If one instruction on negligence will serve to instruct the jury on the legal standard of every state of the United States applicable to a novel claim, implying that the claim despite its controversiality would be decided identically in all 50 states and the District of Columbia, one wonders what the Supreme Court thought it was doing in the *Erie* case when it held that it was unconstitutional for federal courts in diversity cases to apply general common law rather than the common law of the state whose law would apply if the case were being tried in state rather than federal court. Erie R. v. Tompkins, 304 U.S. 64, 78–80, 58 S.Ct. 817, 822, 82 L.Ed. 1188 (1938). The law of negligence, including subsidiary concepts such as duty of care, foreseeability, and proximate cause, may as the plaintiffs have argued forcefully to us differ among the states only in nuance, (though we think not, for a reason discussed later). But nuance can be important, and its significance is suggested by a comparison of differing state pattern instructions on negligence and differing judicial formulations of the meaning of negligence and the subordinate concepts. * * * The voices of the quasisovereigns that are the states of the United States sing negligence with a different pitch.

The "serendipity" theory advanced by the plaintiffs in *Wadleigh* is that if the defendants did not do enough to protect hemophiliacs from the risk of Hepatitis B, they are liable to hemophiliacs for any consequences—including infection by the more dangerous and at the time completely unknown AIDS virus—that proper measures against Hepatitis B would, all unexpectedly, have averted. This theory of liability, * * *, dispenses, rightly or wrongly from the standpoint of the Platonic form of negligence, with proof of foreseeability, even though a number of states, in formulating their tests for negligence, incorporate the foreseeability of the risk into the test. * * * These states follow Judge Cardozo's famous opinion in Palsgraf v. Long Island R., 248 N.Y. 339, 162 N.E. 99 (1928), under which the HIV plaintiffs might (we do not say would—we express no view on the substantive issues in this litigation) be barred from recovery on the ground that they were unforeseeable victims of the alleged failure of the defendants to take adequate precautions against infecting hemophiliacs with Hepatitis B and that therefore the drug companies had not violated any duty of care to them.

The plaintiffs' second theory focuses on the questions when the defendants should have learned about the danger of HIV in the blood supply and when, having learned about it, they should have taken steps to eliminate the danger or at least warn the hemophiliacs or their physicians of it. These questions also may be sensitive to the precise way in which a state formulates its standard of negligence. If not, one begins to wonder why this country bothers with different state legal systems.

Both theories, incidentally, may be affected by differing state views on the role of industry practice or custom in determining the existence of negligence. In some states, the standard of care for a physician, hospital, or other provider of medical services, including blood banks, is a professional standard, that is, the standard fixed by the relevant profession. In others, it is the standard of ordinary care, which may, depending on judge or jury, exceed the professional standard. * * * Which approach a state follows, and whether in those states that follow the professional-standard approach manufacturers of blood solids would be assimilated to blood banks as providers of medical services entitled to shelter under the professional standard, could make a big difference in the liability of these manufacturers. We note that persons infected by HIV through blood transfusions appear to have had little better luck suing blood banks than HIV-positive hemophiliacs have had suing the manufacturers of blood solids. * * *

The diversity jurisdiction of the federal courts is, after *Erie,* designed merely to provide an alternative forum for the litigation of state-law claims, not an alternative system of substantive law for diversity cases. But under the district judge's plan the thousands of members of the plaintiff class will have their rights determined, and the four defendant manufacturers will have their duties determined, under a law that is merely an amalgam, an averaging, of the nonidentical negligence laws of 51 jurisdictions. No one doubts that Congress could constitutionally prescribe a uniform standard of liability for manufacturers of blood solids. It might we suppose promulgate pertinent provisions of the RESTATEMENT (SECOND) OF TORTS. The point of *Erie* is that Article III of the Constitution does not empower the federal courts to create such a regime for diversity cases.

* * *

The plaintiffs argue that an equally important purpose of the class certification is to overcome the shyness or shame that many people feel at acknowledging that they have AIDS or are HIV-positive even when the source of infection is not a stigmatized act. That, the plaintiffs tell us, is why so few HIV-positive hemophiliacs have sued. We do not see how a class action limited to a handful of supposedly common issues can alleviate that problem. Any class member who wants a share in any judgment for damages or in any settlement will have to step forward at some point and identify himself as having AIDS or being HIV-positive. He will have to offer jury findings as collateral estoppel, overcome the defendants' defenses to liability (including possible efforts to show that the class member became infected with HIV through a source other than the defendants' product), and establish his damages. If the privacy of these class members in these follow-on proceedings to the class action is sought to be protected by denominating them "John Does," that is something that can equally well be done in individual lawsuits. The "John Doe" device—and with it the issue of privacy—is independent of class certification.

The third respect in which we believe that the district judge has exceeded his authority concerns the point at which his plan of action proposes to divide the trial of the issues that he has certified for class-action treatment from the other issues involved in the thousands of actual and potential claims of the representatives and members of the class. Bifurcation and even finer divisions of lawsuits into separate trials are authorized in federal district courts. Fed.R.Civ.P. 42(b); * * *. And a decision to employ the procedure is reviewed deferentially. * * * However, as we have been at pains to stress recently, the district judge must carve at the joint. * * * Of particular relevance here, the judge must not divide issues between separate trials in such a way that the same issue is reexamined by different juries. The problem is not inherent in bifurcation. It does not arise when the same jury is to try the successive phases of the litigation. But most of the separate "cases" that compose this class action will be tried, after the initial trial in the Northern District of Illinois, in different courts, scattered throughout the country. The right to a jury trial in federal civil cases, conferred by the Seventh Amendment, is a right to have juriable issues determined by the first jury impaneled to hear them (provided there are no errors warranting a new trial), and not reexamined by another finder of fact. This would be obvious if the second finder of fact were a judge. * * * But it is equally true if it is another jury. * * * In this limited sense, a jury verdict can have collateral estoppel effect. * * *

The plan of the district judge in this case is inconsistent with the principle that the findings of one jury are not to be reexamined by a second, or third, or nth jury. The first jury will not determine liability. It will determine merely whether one or more of the defendants was negligent under one of the two theories. The first jury may go on to decide these additional issues with regard to the named plaintiffs. But it will not decide them with regard to the other class members. Unless the defendants settle, a second (and third, and fourth, and hundredth, and conceivably thousandth) jury will have to decide, in individual follow-on litigation by class members not named as plaintiffs in the *Wadleigh* case, such issues as comparative negligence—if any class members knowingly continued to use unsafe blood solids after they learned or should have learned of the risk of contamination with HIV—and proximate causation. Both issues overlap the issue of the defendants' negligence. Comparative negligence entails, as the name implies, a comparison of the degree of negligence of plaintiff and defendant. * * * Proximate causation is found by determining whether the harm to the plaintiff followed in some sense naturally, uninterruptedly, and with reasonable probability from the negligent act of the defendant. It overlaps the issue of the defendants' negligence even when the state's law does not (as many states do) make the foreseeability of the risk to which the defendant subjected the plaintiff an explicit ingredient of negligence. * * * A second or subsequent jury might find that the defendants' failure to take precautions against infection with Hepatitis B could not be thought the proximate cause of the plaintiffs' infection with HIV, a different and unknown bloodborne virus. How the resulting inconsistency between juries could be prevented escapes us.

The protection of the right conferred by the Seventh Amendment to trial by jury in federal civil cases is a traditional office of the writ of mandamus. Beacon Theatres v. Westover, 359 U.S. 500, 510–11, 79 S.Ct. 948, 956–57, 3 L.Ed.2d 988 (1959); Dairy Queen, Inc. v. Wood, 369 U.S. 469, 472, 82 S.Ct. 894, 897, 8 L.Ed.2d 44 (1962); * * *. When the writ is used for that purpose, strict compliance with the stringent conditions on the availability of the writ (including the requirement of proving irreparable harm) is excused. * * * But the looming infringement of Seventh Amendment rights is only one of our grounds for believing this to be a case in which the issuance of a writ of mandamus is warranted. The others as we have said are the undue and unnecessary risk of a monumental industry-busting error in entrusting the determination of potential multi-billion dollar liabilities to a single jury when the results of the previous cases indicate that the defendants' liability is doubtful at best and the questionable constitutionality of trying a diversity case under a legal standard in force in no state. We need not consider whether any of these grounds standing by itself would warrant mandamus in this case. Together they make a compelling case.

We know that an approach similar to that proposed by Judge Grady has been approved for asbestos litigation. *See* in particular Jenkins v. Raymark Industries, Inc., 782 F.2d 468 (5th Cir.1986); In re School

Asbestos Litigation, 789 F.2d 996 (3d Cir.1986). Most federal courts, however, refuse to permit the use of the class-action device in mass-tort cases, even asbestos cases. Thomas E. Willging, Trends in Asbestos Litigation 93–98 (Federal Judicial Center 1987); *cf. In re Fibreboard Corp., supra*; In re Joint Eastern & Southern District Asbestos Litigation, 982 F.2d 721 (2d Cir.1992). Those courts that have permitted it have been criticized, and alternatives have been suggested which recognize that a sample of trials makes more sense than entrusting the fate of an industry to a single jury. *See, e.g.,* Michael J. Saks & Peter David Blanck, *Justice Improved: The Unrecognized Benefits of Aggregation and Sampling in the Trial of Mass Torts,* 44 Stan.L.Rev. 815 (1992). The number of asbestos cases was so great as to exert a well-nigh irresistible pressure to bend the normal rules. No comparable pressure is exerted by the HIV-hemophilia litigation. That litigation can be handled in the normal way without undue inconvenience to the parties or to the state or federal courts.

The defendants have pointed out other serious problems with the district judge's plan, but it is unnecessary to discuss them. The petition for a writ of mandamus is granted, and the district judge is directed to decertify the plaintiff class.

Rovner, Circuit Judge, dissenting.

The majority today takes the extraordinary step of granting defendants' petition for a writ of mandamus and directing the district court to rescind its order certifying the plaintiff class. Although certification orders like this one are not immediately appealable (*see* Coopers & Lybrand v. Livesay, 437 U.S. 463, 98 S.Ct. 2454, 57 L.Ed.2d 351 (1978)), the majority seizes upon our mandamus powers to effectively circumvent that rule. Because, in my view, our consideration of Judge Grady's decision to certify an issue class under Fed.R.Civ.P. 23(c)(4) should await an appeal from the final judgment in *Wadleigh,* I would deny the writ.

* * *

I find the majority's reasoning troubling in several respects. First, it means that the preliminary requirement for mandamus—the lack of an alternative means of obtaining relief—will be satisfied by virtually every class certification order, which then authorizes the court to assess the relative merits of the order to determine whether it is "usurpative." The majority's complaint about Judge Grady's order—that it will make a settlement more likely than if defendants' negligence were to be determined by separate juries in individual trials—is true of most every order certifying a large plaintiff class. Certification orders almost always increase the likelihood of settlement by expanding the scope of defendants' exposure. Yet that does not make the order any less reviewable if defendants resist the temptation to settle and litigate to final judgment. *See* In re Sugar Antitrust Litigation, 559 F.2d 481, 483 n.1 (9th Cir. 1977). Indeed, in concluding that certification orders are not immediately appealable under 28 U.S.C. § 1291, the Supreme Court observed that any order certifying a large plaintiff class "may so increase the defendant's potential damages liability and litigation costs that he may find it economically prudent to settle and to abandon a meritorious defense." *Coopers & Lybrand*, 437 U.S. at 476, 98 S.Ct. at 2462. Yet that did not stop the Court from finding that "orders granting class certification are interlocutory" and thus not immediately appealable as of right. *Id.* But the majority here would override *Coopers'* edict, making certification orders reviewable on mandamus simply because the likelihood of a settlement makes the order unreviewable at the end of the case. I cannot reconcile this conclusion with *Coopers & Lybrand* or with the Supreme Court's mandamus cases. * * * I thus cannot agree that the possibility of a settlement satisfies defendants' burden under the first of the two requirements for mandamus.

* * *

Furthermore, even if the possibility of a settlement were relevant to the first mandamus requirement, and even if it had been asserted by defendants in support of their petition, I still cannot agree with the majority's premise that Judge Grady's order in fact will prompt a settlement. Contrary to the clear implication of the majority's opinion* * *, the class portion of the anticipated trial in this case would not go so far as to establish defendants' liability to a class of plaintiffs; it would instead resolve only the question of whether defendants were negligent in distributing tainted clotting factor at any particular point in time. Even if defendants were faced with an adverse class verdict, then, a plaintiff still would be required to clear a number of hurdles before he would be entitled to a judgment. For example, defendants no doubt would contest at that stage whether a particular plaintiff could establish proximate causation or whether his or her claim is in any event barred by the statute of limitations. Thus, contrary to the majority's implication, a class verdict in favor of plaintiffs would not automatically entitle each member of the class to a seven-figure judgment. * * * The defendants will thus have ample opportunity to settle should they lose the class trial. And that would seem to me an advisable strategy in light of the success they have had in earlier cases. That factor distinguishes this case from a more standard class action, where a non-bifurcated trial would resolve all relevant issues and conclusively establish liability to the class. Perhaps that explains why defendants' own arguments in support of their petition are based on the assumption that a class trial would ensue, rather than on the proposition that a settlement would follow inevitably from Judge Grady's order.

Finally, although the availability of review on direct appeal after final judgment makes it unnecessary for me to discuss the merits of the certification order, the majority's arguments addressed to the propriety of forcing "defendants to stake their companies on the outcome of a single jury trial" or of allowing a single jury to "hold the fate of an industry in the palm of its hand" seem to me at odds with Fed.R.Civ.P. 23 itself. * * * That rule expressly permits class treatment of such claims when its requirements are met, regardless of the magnitude of potential liability.   And I see nothing in Rule 23, or in any of the relevant cases, that would make likelihood of success on the merits a prerequisite for class certification.   * * * The majority's preference for avoiding a class trial and for submitting the negligence issue "to multiple juries constituting in the aggregate a much larger and more diverse sample of decision-makers" * * * is a rationale for amending the rule, not for avoiding its application in a specific case. * * *

I must concede that I too have doubts about whether the class trial proposed by Judge Grady will succeed, and I sympathize with many of the apprehensions of my brothers.   But in my view, the law requires that Judge Grady's plan be given the opportunity to succeed.   Class certification orders are, after all, conditional orders subject to modification or revocation as the circumstances warrant.   Fed.R.Civ.P. 23(c)(1); * * *.   If the problems envisioned by the majority were to materialize at a class trial, Judge Grady could always modify his earlier ruling or even abandon it altogether, and his response in that regard would be reviewable by this court on direct appeal, once the actual ramifications of the certification order were evident. * * *

DAVID ROSENBERG, CLASS ACTIONS FOR MASS TORTS: DOING INDIVIDUAL JUSTICE BY COLLECTIVE MEANS *

62 Ind.L.J. 561 (1987).

INTRODUCTION

From the perspective of the common law tradition of individual justice, class actions are a necessary evil, but an evil nonetheless.   That tradition projects the private law adjudicatory ideal: the norms of right, duty, and remedy are applied according to the specific, relevant circumstances of the particular parties in the given case.   It promises the parties not only their own day in court, but a good deal of control over what is said and decided on that day.

Class actions loom as a subversive element in this context because they import the processes of bureaucratic justice mode of decision-making associated with administrative agencies, which lacks the common law's traditional commitment to party control and focus on the discrete merits of each claim.   In contrast to the party initiated and orchestrated common law trial, bureaucratic justice gives decisionmakers the controlling hand over the issue agenda as well as over the type and extent of evidence considered.   But bureaucratic justice is most strikingly antithetical to notions of individual justice because it legitimates the aggregation and averaging of circumstances and interests of affected individuals in pursuit of the collective benefits from process efficiency, outcome consistency, and the maximum production of substantive goods.

* David Rosenberg, *Class Actions for Mass Torts: Doing Individual Justice by Collective Means,* 62 Ind. L. J. 561 (1987)(Copyright 1987 by the Trustees of Indiana University.   Reprinted by permission).

These goals are implemented through "public law" procedures which combine claims for uniform and summary treatment according to classifications based on a set of salient, if partial, common variables relating to the individuals involved.

Nowhere do class actions seem a more alien force than in the torts system, which epitomizes the individual justice tradition. The hallmark of this system—at least as a formal matter—is its adherence to the "private law" mode of case-by-case, particularized adjudication. Attention is lavished on the particular details of each claim to ensure that the norms of liability and remedy are tailored to the specific facts of the defendant's conduct and its causal relationship to the plaintiff's injury. Every effort is made to avoid (or at least minimize) the erroneous redistribution of wealth that occurs when innocent defendants are held liable or deserving plaintiffs denied compensation.

In mass tort cases involving claims for personal injury, which pose daunting problems of causation and remedy, the price of individual justice is notoriously high. Because they typically involve complex factual and legal questions, mass tort claims are exceedingly, if not prohibitively, expensive to litigate. The questions of whether the defendant's conduct failed to satisfy the governing standard of liability frequently entail interrelated technological and policy issues that require extensive discovery, expertise, and preparation to present and resolve adequately. Equally demanding are the causation issues in mass tort cases, such as whether the plaintiff's condition was caused by exposure to the substance in question or to some other source of the same disease risk.

The case-by-case mode of adjudication magnifies this burden by requiring the parties and courts to reinvent the wheel for each claim. The merits of each case are determined de novo even though the major liability issues are common to every claim arising from the mass tort accident, and even though they may have been previously determined several times by full and fair trials. These costs exclude many mass tort victims from the system and sharply reduce the recovery for those who gain access. Win or lose, the system's private law process exacts a punishing surcharge from defendant firms as well as plaintiffs.

These costs of litigation, which are borne directly by the parties, also cast a broad array of shadow prices that have widespread indirect effects. The redundant adjudication of mass tort claims thus consumes vast quantities of public resources, raising the price of access for other, sporadic, types of tort claims. Moreover, even though most of the claims arising from mass accidents are eventually settled on the basis of recovery patterns projected from relatively few trials, the settlement calculus will reflect the costs of redundant, de novo, particularized adjudication, as well as the incentives of each party to increase the litigation expenses for the other. These conditions generally disadvantage claimants. Because defendant firms are in a position to spread the litigation costs over the entire class of mass accident claims, while plaintiffs, being deprived of the economies of scale afforded by class actions, cannot, the result will usually be that the firms will escape the full loss they have caused and, after deducting their attorneys' shares, the victims will receive a relatively small proportion of any recovery as compensation. As a consequence, the tort system's primary objectives of compensation and deterrence are seriously jeopardized.

Despite their potential for reducing litigation costs and burdens, and, consequently, enhancing the system's capacity to achieve its compensation and deterrence objectives, class actions have consistently received a hostile reception in mass tort cases. In opposing class actions, these decisions and supporting commentary draw upon the individual justice tradition and its rejection of the modes of bureaucratic justice. The common premise of these and similar objections to mass tort class actions is that the bureaucratic justice of class treatment—the collectivization of claims for aggregative and averaged disposition—achieves administrative goals of efficiency, consistency, and maximum substantive output by subordinating the interests of individual victims (although not of defendant firms) to the interests of the class as a whole. Under this critique, the extent to which the interests of individual victims are sacrificed is measured against the baseline of how their claims would fare in separate actions. Class actions, for example, are found unacceptable because they transfer control over the case from the individual to the class as an entity, or more accurately, the class attorney. In toxic tort cases, class actions are viewed as a device for undermining causation requirements through averaging. Instead of differentiating the "risk portfolios" applicable to each victim in the exposed population, class actions invite courts to make causal determinations on an undifferentiated basis for all members of defined reference groups or subclasses, or even for all members of the victim class as a whole.

Individual justice critiques of class actions have little power when the primary purpose of tort liability is taken to be the utilitarian objective of maximizing welfare by deterring socially inappropriate risk-taking. The aggregation and averaging techniques of bureaucratic justice are not only consistent with the social welfare justification for tort liability—at least, when defendant firms are not on the whole under or overcharged—but they also produce the positive benefits of lower administrative costs. When, however, tort liability serves to vindicate rights to personal security transgressed by a defendant's wrongful conduct, the individual justice arguments against class actions may, depending on the normative content of the rights posited, suggest the location of certain outside limitations on the use of class actions in mass tort cases. But, as I will explain below, these individual justice arguments are exaggerated. They ignore not only the realities of claimant dependency and powerlessness in individual actions, but they also fail to recognize the existence of collectivizing forces operating in the mass accident context, particularly the class-wide nature of the risk *ex ante*, which exerts a unifying influence over the security interests (deterrence) and protective responses (insurance) of the potential accident victims. A major aim of this paper is to demonstrate that, given such *ex ante* conditions, bureaucratic justice implemented through class actions provides better opportunities for achieving individual justice than does the tort system's private law, disaggregative processes.

* * *

Opposition to aggregation and averaging in mass tort class actions is in fact largely anticipatory. In the relatively few class actions which have been certified, the scope of collective adjudication has been narrowly circumscribed to preserve party control and the opportunity for individualized determinations of noncommon liability and damage questions. Most of the public law procedures which might be used in mass accident class actions—especially aggregating claims on a mandatory basis and averaging causation and damages—have been employed only in settlements, and never by coercive court order. Indeed, even when mass tort class actions have been certified for trial, the collective process is entirely elective since class members are entitled to opt out in favor of individual actions. Class treatment, moreover, has been extended solely to the common questions of law and fact concerning liability, preserving the right to an individual trial on damages. In some cases courts have gone slightly beyond the conventional bifurcation of liability and damage elements of the tort cause of action. They have instead designated certain common liability issues for class treatment, while remanding the remaining liability questions relating to the circumstances of each class member to an individual trial before, or along with, determination of damages.

A. *Potential Applications of Public Law Process: Mandatory Class Actions and Damage Scheduling*

Although contemporary class action practice generally respects the principles of individual justice by maintaining voluntary participation, critics of the procedure correctly recognize its potential to develop in more innovative public law directions. Mandatory class actions combined with damage scheduling are two changes in current practice that would have the most important applications to mass torts, especially those involving long-latency disease risks from toxic substance exposure. Class actions would be mandatory both in the sense that (i) courts could act on their own initiative to certify pending and future mass tort claims for class treatment, and (ii) there would be no opportunity to opt out in order to prosecute a separate action on the issues common to all claims as well as the issues specific to each. To achieve even greater efficiencies in the process, courts would impose damage schedules based on the average loss suffered by members of relevant subclasses or even by the class as a whole.

The choice of disaggregative over collective adjudication for mass tort accidents has profound consequences for the parties as well as the tort system's compensation and deterrence objectives. The costs of traditional disaggregative, private law processes exclude many claims from the system. The cost barriers are compounded by other prevalent conditions, such as the low income status of a significant number of the victims, and the relatively low probability of success at trial that characterizes these legally and factually complex cases. In addition, to the extent that courts begin to use proportional liability to resolve the causation issues that routinely arise in toxic tort cases, the costs of disaggregative process are magnified in the evaluation of these claims by plaintiff attorneys. Many of these claims are rendered unmarketable to competent plaintiff attorneys because the returns on their contingent fee investment, which are likely to be marginally competitive to begin with for the reasons noted above, are discounted in proportion to the probability of causation in each case. As a result, many victims not only are denied access to the system and receive no compensation, but the deterrent effects of threatened liability are significantly reduced.

In addition, the case-by-case, individualized processing of the mass tort claims that are filed confers a strategic edge upon defendant firms. While it prevents victims from deriving the benefits of concerted action, the traditional process has no similar effect on the capacity of defendant firms to spread litigation costs and prepare the common questions efficiently on a once-and-for-all basis. Most liability issues will be substantially the same for all claims arising from a given mass accident, and thus defendants can always aggregate claims to exploit (at times quite abusively) the efficiencies of a virtual class action. Because of their cost-spreading advantages, a defendant firm typically can afford not only to invest more in developing the merits of the claim than the opposing plaintiff attorney, but also to finance a "war of attrition" through costly discovery and motion practice that depletes the adversary's litigation resources. The consequences of redundantly litigating common questions thus skews the presentation of the merits, promotes abusive strategic use of procedure, needlessly consumes public resources, and ultimately drains away a large amount of the funds available to redress, by judgment or settlement, victim losses.

While defendant firms enjoy litigation cost advantages because of the system's traditional disaggregative processes, the most consistently successful beneficiaries of case-by-case adjudication are the lawyers—both for defendants and plaintiffs. A major factor in the escalating costs of the tort system is attorney fees, against which there are no presently effective market or regulatory controls. Defense lawyers contribute to the dismal ratio of litigation costs to net compensation in mass tort litigation by exploiting their hourly fee arrangements. Under such arrangements defense lawyers have every incentive to make work for themselves, particularly by grossly overstaffing multi-defendant cases, and by resisting any collective process replacement for case-by-case adjudication. Although their clients gain to some degree from these practices, because they translate into increased litigation expense for plaintiffs, the costs inflicted on the public—in terms of the needless consumption of attorney and judicial resources—by defense attorney avarice are unmitigated. For similar reasons, plaintiff attorneys, too, prefer disaggregative process. Class treatment of mass tort claims from a particular accident requires only a fraction of the legal services provided by plaintiff attorneys compared to case-by-case adjudication, which disperses claims widely over territory and time. That courts have the power in class actions to review class settlements and to determine class attorney fees helps to explain plaintiff attorney aversion to collective process.

Class treatment of these claims would produce radically different results from those generated by traditional case-by-case adjudication. Class action aggregation would very likely make the low value claims marketable to competent plaintiff attorneys, and therefore firms would be faced with liability for a much larger percentage of the compensable losses resulting from mass tort accidents. If mandatory class actions were convened by courts on their own initiative, the unnecessary costs of redundantly litigating the common questions presented in marketable mass tort claims would be eliminated. In addition, mandatory certification would substantially diminish the incentives of defendants to exploit their cost advantages in individual actions, and would negate the motivation of and eliminate the costly efforts by plaintiff and defense attorneys to oppose class actions in order to protect their fees rather than their clients' interests. The savings in administrative expense would substantially increase the proportion of the awards recovered by victims as compensation.

Damage scheduling could be used to further reduce litigation costs entailed by the individualized determination of damages. Such a procedure would greatly increase access for low value claims. Because scheduling eliminates much of the need for customized legal services, thus yielding even greater returns in compensation on relatively high value claims than would individualized determinations, it should not be used exclusively in low value class actions. Regardless of the value of the claims involved, the most dramatic cost savings could be achieved if the schedule provided compensation according to the average income loss and probability of causation for the population as a whole. Victims with above average losses or exposure might well find that their treatment at a statistical average was more than offset by the savings in litigation costs, including attorney fees.

B.   *Utilitarian Deterrence and Bureaucratic Justice*

The prevailing utilitarian justification for tort liability is to create optimal incentives for accident avoidance. Accordingly, the threat of liability should induce firms engaged in risky activities to take due or optimal care by investing in safety precautions against accidents so long as the injury loss avoided exceeds, at the margin, the expenditures on prevention. Threatened tort liability also may advance deterrence objectives by compelling firms to internalize the residual injury loss—loss which is unavoidable by optimal care—thereby inducing moderation of their levels of activity and the corresponding levels of accident risk. When administrative expenses are taken into account, the calculus becomes the extremely complicated one of maximizing the system's functional productivity in terms of the net benefits from tort liability deterrence.

Public law processes promote this social welfare maximizing function of tort liability in all phases, both by providing incentives to take optimal care and to moderate activity levels, and by achieving sharp reductions in administrative costs.   By making relatively low value claims marketable to competent plaintiff attorneys, class actions bolster the deterrent effect of threatened tort liability.   Absent class action treatment, the bulk of these claims would be excluded from the system, reducing both the firm's incentives to take precautions and its internalization of residual accident costs.   The potential for administrative cost savings is very high as well.   Mandatory class actions would radically reduce the consumption of party and public resources for redundant, case-by-case adjudication.   It would also substantially diminish the cost advantage conferred on defendant firms by the private law, disaggregative process—which in reality is disaggregative only on the plaintiff side.   Damage scheduling to replace individualized causation and injury loss determinations would not only increase the marketability of very low value claims, but also would increase the efficiency of the process overall.

* * *

Notes and Questions

1.   If the 1986 circuit court decisions in *Jenkins v. Raymark* and *School Asbestos Litigation* signaled a willingness on the part of federal courts to procedurally handle mass tort litigation using the class action rule, what then do the circuit court decisions in *Fibreboard, Keene,* and *Rhone–Poulenc* indicate?   Have the federal courts retreated from Rule 23 as a preferred mechanism for mass tort litigation?   The Fifth Circuit's mandamus decision in *Fibreboard* represented an interesting interplay between Judge Parker's decisions as a district court judge and the appellate court.   Judge Parker first provisionally certified *Cimino* as a class action during September 1989, *see Cimino v. Raymark Industries, Inc.*, 1989 WL 253889 (E.D.Tex.1989)(No. 86–0456).   After receiving a special master's report prepared by Professor Jack Ratliff of the University of Texas School of Law, Judge Parker issued his trial plan order in December 1989.   The defendants immediately challenged the trial plan and sought a mandamus in the Fifth Circuit, which they won.   Following the remand in *Fibreboard,* Judge Parker reconstituted the class action as a Rule 42 consolidated case.   On a second mandamus appeal, the Fifth Circuit affirmed Judge Parker's reformulated trial plan for *Cimino.*   The *Cimino* case was tried to conclusion during spring 1990.   *See* Cimino v. Raymark Industries, 739 F.Supp. 328 (E.D.Tex.1990); Cimino v. Raymark Industries, Inc., 751 F.Supp. 649 (E.D.Tex.1990).   *See also* Henry J. Roeke, *Asbestos Makers Lose Big Trial,* A.B.A.J. at 18 (Oct. 1992).   All but one of the representative class plaintiffs won their cases, and Judge Parker employed an extrapolation method to calculate damages for the class.   As of spring 1995, an appeal of the damages portion of *Cimino* has not yet been rendered by the Fifth Circuit.   Judge Parker was nominated and confirmed to a seat on the Fifth Circuit Court of Appeals in June 1994.

For discussion of the *Cimino* and *Fibreboard* litigation, *see generally,* Linda S. Mullenix, *Beyond Consolidation: Post–Aggregative Procedure in Asbestos Mass Tort Litigation,* 32 Wm. & Mary L.Rev 475 (1991); Jack Ratliff, *Special Master's Report in* Cimino v. Raymark Industries, Inc., 10 Rev.Litig. 521 (1991); Symposium, *Problems in Disposition of Mass Related Cases and Proposals for Change,* 10 Rev.Litig. 209 (1991).

2. In *Cimino,* Judge Parker sought to use the class action rule not only as a means of collectively aggregating individual lawsuits, but also for aggregating damage claims. Does the *Fibreboard* decision repudiate this possibility? Is *Fibreboard* limited by *Erie* doctrine? Might aggregate damages be possible in other settings? For discussion and analysis of the problem of aggregate damages in mass tort litigation, *see* Kenneth S. Abraham and Glen O. Robinson, *Aggregative Valuation of Mass Tort Claims,* 53 Law & Contemp.Probs. 137 (1990); Samuel Isacharoff, *Administering Damage Awards in Mass–Tort Litigation,* 10 Rev.Litig. 463 (1991); Michael J. Saks & Peter David Blanck, *Justice Improved: The Unrecognized Benefits of Aggregation and Sampling in the Trial of Mass Torts,* 44 Stan.L.Rev 815 (1992).

3. The possibility of utilizing class action procedure received another setback in August 1990, when a small group of federal judges attempted to certify a nationwide asbestos class action. This effort was swiftly repudiated; *see* In re Allied–Signal, Inc., 915 F.2d 190 (6th Cir.1990):

Order

This matter came before this court on petitioner Allied–Signal's petition for writ of mandamus and writ of prohibition. With respect to the petition for a writ of mandamus, Allied–Signal asks this court to direct the United States District Court for the Northern District of Ohio to vacate its orders known as *Ohio Asbestos Litigation (OAL)* Order 96, 96(a), 96(b), 96(c), and 96(d). Because Order 96(f), issued by the district court on August 13, 1990, vacates the previous orders of that court, we find that Order 96(f) moots any issue regarding the appropriateness of any class certification.

With respect to the petition for the writ of prohibition, Allied–Signal asks this court to prohibit "the 'ad hoc national coordinating committee' established by OAL Order 96 from taking any judicial action with respect to asbestos-related personal injury." Article III, Section 1 of the United States Constitution states that "[t]he judicial power of the United States shall be vested in one Supreme Court, and in such inferior courts as the Congress may from time to time ordain and establish." Unless Congress has granted jurisdiction to the courts, Article III limits the ability of district courts to act. *See* American Fire and Cas. Co. v. Finn, 341 U.S. 6, 17–18, 71 S.Ct. 534, 542, 95 L.Ed. 702 (1951). This panel acknowledges and strongly reaffirms this basic principle of limited jurisdiction and is unable to find any Congressional authority for an "ad hoc national coordinating committee" to issue orders as an Article III court.

At oral argument, Judge Lambros conceded the aforementioned. As a result, Judge Lambros has agreed to make the following modifications in his orders: (1) Order 96(f) shall be vacated, except for its vacating of the previous Orders 96 *et seq.;* (2) the *"In Re: National Asbestos Litigation Order"* of August 10, 1990, to the extent that it was filed in the Northern District of Ohio and consolidates any cases of the Northern District of Ohio, shall be considered a nullity because of the ad hoc committee's lack of Article III jurisdiction; and (3) a new order shall be issued to clarify that the September 14, 1990 hearing is not to "show cause," but rather for the purpose of addressing the five petitions for class certification pursuant to Fed.R.Civ.P. 23. The new order shall indicate that notice be sent to all other interested parties.

"The petitioners ... bear a heavy burden in showing that mandamus is the proper remedy. Mandamus is an extraordinary remedy, and it will only be granted when the petitioner shows that 'its right to issuance of the writ is clear and indisputable.'" In re Bendectin Products Liability Litigation, 749 F.2d 300, 303 (6th Cir.1984) * * *. " 'Only exceptional circumstances amounting to a judicial "usurpation of power" will justify the invocation of this extraordinary remedy.' " * * * This Court, while inclined to hold on the basis of the record that such a usurpation has occurred, will nonetheless forbear doing so in light of Judge Lambros's concessions and agreement at oral argument. Accordingly, it is unnecessary for the court to exercise our power under the All Writs Act, 28 U.S.C. § 1651. The petition for the Writ of Mandamus and Prohibition will be DENIED, effective upon the entry by the district court of the order herein described.

With this repudiation of a nationwide class certification, where did this leave asbestos litigants? What other means are available if the class action rule is not suitable for aggregating mass tort claims?

4. To what extent has Judge Posner's decision in *Rhone-Poulenc* advanced the debate over the suitability of class certification of mass tort litigation? Is Judge Posner's analysis merely consistent with the earlier trend of federal courts not to certify nascent mass torts? Has he satisfactorily distinguished the blood contamination cases from asbestos litigation? Is mass tort asbestos litigation *sui generis* among mass torts? Note that the defendants used the writ of mandamus to attack Judge Grady's grant of certification, which dissenting Judge Rovner characterizes as a circumvention of normal interlocutory appeals rules and the Supreme Court's holding in *Coopers & Lybrand v. Livesay,* 437 U.S. 463, 98 S.Ct. 2454, 57 L.Ed.2d 351 (1978)(order certifying a class action not an immediately appealable final decision within 28 U.S.C.A. § 1291). As we have seen above, mandamus has become the defendants' procedural vehicle of choice for attacking various judicial innovations in mass tort cases. Has Judge Posner expanded the standards for granting mandamus by introducing an irreparable harm principle that captures the "pressure to settle"? In his consideration of the implications of applicable law, and his reliance on *Erie* doctrine, to what extent is Judge Posner's decision consistent with the Fifth Circuit's mandamus decision in *In re Fibreboard, supra?*

5. In the *Rhone-Poulenc Rorer* decision, Judge Posner also suggests that preclusion doctrine could serve plaintiffs' interests as well as class certification of their claims:

> If in the course of individual litigations by HIV-positive hemophili-
> acs juries render special verdicts that contain findings which do not
> depend on the differing state standards of negligence—for example a
> finding concerning the date at which one or more of the defendants
> learned of the danger of HIV contamination of the blood supply—these
> findings may be given collateral estoppel effect in other lawsuits, at least
> in states that allow "offensive" use of collateral estoppel. In that way
> the essential purpose of the class action crafted by Judge Grady will be
> accomplished. If there are relevant differences in state law, findings in
> one suit will not be given collateral estoppel effect in others, Commis-
> sioner v. Sunnen, 333 U.S. 591, 599–600, 68 S.Ct. 715, 720, 92 L.Ed. 898
> (1948); Goodson v. McDonough Power Equipment, Inc., 2 Ohio St.3d
> 193, 443 N.E.2d 978, 987–88 (Ohio 1983)—and that is as it should be.

In the Matter of Rhone–Poulenc Rorer Incorporated, 51 F.3d 1293, 1302 (7th
Cir.1995). Does Judge Posner have any basis for being optimistic about the
possibility of subsequent plaintiffs being able to avail themselves of offensive
collateral estoppel to prevent relitigation of mass tort issues? For a discussion of the application of preclusion doctrine in relation to mass tort
litigation, *see* Chapter II.F, *infra*.

5. SETTLEMENT CLASSES

Review IN RE "AGENT ORANGE" PRODUCT LIABILITY LITIGATION, *supra*

IN RE A.H. ROBINS CO.

United States Court of Appeals, Fourth Circuit, 1989.
880 F.2d 709.

This diversity suit by seven individual claimants, suing on their own
behalf and as the proposed class representatives of all injured Dalkon
Shield claimants, seeks recovery against Aetna Casualty and Surety
Company (Aetna) for injuries resulting from the use of an allegedly
defective intrauterine device known as the Dalkon Shield. Aetna was
neither the manufacturer nor the vender of the device; it was the
products liability insurance carrier of A.H. Robins Company, Inc. (Robins), the manufacturer and distributor of the device. It is the theory of
the plaintiffs that Aetna's conduct, while acting in its role as insurance
carrier, was such that it rendered itself liable as a joint tortfeasor with
Robins for any injuries sustained by persons using the device. The
plaintiffs sought class certification of the suit. During consideration
whether to give final certification of the suit, the parties entered into a
settlement of the action conditioned on certification. After a duly-
noticed hearing, the District Court granted in separate orders final class
certification of the action and approval of the settlement of the action so
certified. The appeal challenges the two orders. Since the two orders
from which the appeals are taken are intimately connected, the two
appeals have been consolidated. We affirm both the class certification
and the settlement orders.

* * *

XVI

It is to be noted that a number of the decisions we have discussed involved settlements of the proposed class action. This raises the question whether class certification for settlement purposes is permissible under Rule 23. The appellants argue flatly that certification for such purposes is impermissible. However, despite this statement of appellants, certification for such purposes finds strong support in a number of various Law Review comments. Nielson, *Was the 1966 Advisory Committee Right?: Suggested Revisions of Rule 23 to Allow More Frequent Use of Class Actions in Mass Tort Litigation*, 25 Harv.J. Legislation 461, 480 (1988), for instance, recognized a "trend" in favor of such certification:

> In recent years, several federal judges have explicitly recognized the effect of class certification on the likelihood of prejudgment settlement in mass-tort suits, and have apparently allowed such recognition to influence their decision to certify class actions.

Professor Trangsrud, though he took a somewhat skeptical view of mass-tort certifications generally, felt that certification "as a pretrial joinder device to facilitate group settlements [was] both proper and desirable," adding

> Its use is proper because Federal Rule of Civil Procedure 23 provides that the court may certify a common question class action when it will prove "superior to other available methods for the fair and efficient adjudication of the controversy." A judicially supervised and approved class action settlement, like a judicially supervised trial, is a means of hearing and determining judicially, in other words, "adjudicating," the value of claims arising from a mass tort. As a result, if conditional certification of the case as a common question class action for settlement purposes would enhance the prospects for a group settlement, then Rule 23 authorizes certification.

Trangsrud, *Joinder Alternatives in Mass Tort Litigation*, 70 Cornell L.Rev 779, 835 (1985).

Recent court decisions have also spoken approvingly of the class certification of mass-tort actions for purposes of settlement in conformity with these academic comments. These decisions confirm that the promotion of settlement may well be a factor in resolving the issue of certification. Thus, in *Agent Orange*, Chief Judge Weinstein wrote, (100 F.R.D. at 723):

> Finally, the court may not ignore the real world of dispute resolution. As already noted, a classwide finding of causation may serve to resolve the claims of individual members, in a way that determinations in individual cases would not, by enhancing the possibility of settlement among the parties and with the federal government.

Similarly, in *In re School Asbestos Litigation*, 789 F.2d at 1009, the Court said:

Concentration of individual damage suits in one forum can lead to formidable problems, but the realities of litigation should not be overlooked in theoretical musings. Most tort cases settle, and the preliminary maneuverings in litigation today are designed as much, if not more, for settlement purposes than for trial. Settlements of class actions often result in savings for all concerned.

The only federal court decision which has actually granted class certification for settlement purposes in a mass-tort action is In re Bendectin, 102 F.R.D. 239, 240 (S.D.Ohio 1984). In that case, Judge Rubin, in granting certification for settlement purposes, said:

> The *Bendectin* litigation is but one example of massive product liability lawsuits involving large numbers of plaintiffs, protracted trials and substantial litigation costs. The traditional court system is simply unequipped to handle such [mass tort] litigation in a conventional manner without materially depleting the judicial resources available for all other litigation. It is theoretically possible to assign sufficient judicial time to hear these cases promptly but only at the cost of further delay in an already overburdened system. The cost to the parties of litigating these cases under current procedures is such that few plaintiffs could afford the expense or the delay. Justice is not served by erecting tollgates at the courthouse door.
>
> There is a solution. The resolution of disputes does not necessarily require trial. Within the judicial authority of this Court is a means whereby the parties might be assisted in reaching a prompt and equitable disposition of the entire problem. That solution involves limited use of Rule 23 of the Federal Rules of Civil Procedure. A class certification would enable any proposed settlement to be presented to all class members and by them either accepted or rejected.

On appeal, the certification was invalidated, 749 F.2d 300 (6th Cir.1984). The ground for denial was that the action failed to qualify for certification under (b)(1) because of the limitation in the use of the class action decision stated in *McDonnell Douglas,* and under the "limited fund" doctrine. The Court, however, was careful to point out that it was not determining that class certification for settlement purposes of the mass tort in that case was impermissible. To emphasize this fact, the Court declared at p. 305, n.10:

> We do note that there is precedent for the proposition that a class can be certified for settlement purposes only. *See, e.g.,* In re Beef Industry Antitrust Litigation, 607 F.2d 167 (5th Cir.1979), *cert. denied,* 452 U.S. 905, 101 S.Ct. 3029, 69 L.Ed.2d 405 (1981). The *Beef Industry* case involved the certification of a temporary settlement class prior to certification of a class for trial. In this case, the District Judge certified a class for settlement purposes after having rejected the same class for trial purposes. The District Judge therefore implicitly held that the standards for certifying a class are different depending on whether the class is for settlement or wheth-

er it is for trial.   Because we decide the case on other grounds, we do not consider whether this holding is correct. . . .

As *Bendectin* had recognized, courts in cases involving numerous parties, though not mass-tort cases, had granted class certification for settlement purposes.   Judge Wisdom in In re Beef Industry Antitrust Litigation, 607 F.2d 167 (5th Cir.1979), *cert. denied,* 452 U.S. 905, 101 S.Ct. 3029, 69 L.Ed.2d 405 (1981), carefully considered all angles of the question of class certification to promote settlement and, in his convincing opinion, found certification under proper circumstances to be in order.   That decision has been followed in other cases, perhaps the most notable one being Weinberger v. Kendrick, 698 F.2d 61, 72–73 (2d Cir.1982), in which Judge Friendly, speaking for the court, said:

> The hallmark of Rule 23 is the flexibility it affords to the courts to utilize the class device in a particular case to best serve the ends of justice for the affected parties and to promote judicial efficiencies. Temporary settlement classes have proved to be quite useful in resolving major class action disputes.   While their use may still be controversial, most Courts have recognized their utility and have authorized the parties to seek to compromise their differences, including class action issues through this means.

See also In re Mid–Atlantic Toyota Antitrust Litigation, 564 F.Supp. 1379, 1388–90 (D.Md.1983); In re First Commodity Corp. of Boston, 119 F.R.D. 301, 306–08 (D.Mass.1987).

Though, as we have said, these cases were not mass-tort suits, there seems to be no real reason why the precedent established by the cases, just cited, should not be equally applicable to the mass-tort.   If not a ground for certification per se, certainly settlement should be a factor, and an important factor, to be considered when determining certification.   That is all the District Court did in this case.   Its action in considering this circumstance would appear to have been appropriate.

XVII

In summary, we take it as the lessons to be gleaned from the authorities already cited and discussed to be (a) that the "trend" is once again to give Rule 23 a liberal rather than a restrictive construction, adopting a standard of flexibility in application which will in the particular case "best serve the ends of justice for the affected parties and promote judicial efficiency;" (b) that the Advisory Committee's Note suggestion that suit for damages is "not appropriate" for class certification has proved unworkable and is now increasingly disregarded; (c) that the theory that the Rule should be constrained by establishing judicially, without support in the Rule itself, limitations on its use such as were stated in *La Mar, Green,* and *McDonnell Douglas* has been outdated by the increasing phenomenon of the mass products tort action and by the growing body of recent class action decisions and comments favoring class actions in the mass tort context; (d) that, in order to promote the use of the class device and to reduce the range of disputed issues, courts should take full advantage of the provision in subsection (c)(4) permitting class treatment of separate issues in the case and, if such separate issues predominate sufficiently (i.e., is the central issue), to certify the entire controversy as in *Agent Orange;* and (e) that it is "proper" in determining certification to consider whether such certification will foster settlement of the case with advantage to the parties and with great saving in judicial time and services; and (f) that the mass tort action for damages may in a proper case be appropriate for class action, either partially on in whole.

We accordingly now turn to an attempt to apply these lessons to the facts of this case.

* * *

GEORGINE v. AMCHEM PRODUCTS, INC.

United States District Court, Eastern District of Pennsylvania, 1994.
157 F.R.D. 246.

[See Text and Discussion of *Georgine* at Ch. 1, D.4.]

* * *

CLOSING DISCUSSION

No one disputes the notion that settlement is a preferred alternative to costly time-consuming litigation. This Court has been presented with an intricate comprehensive settlement plan on behalf of a nationwide opt-out class. The members of the class total conservatively in the tens of thousands and possibly as many as several hundred thousand or more. They are defined as workers or their family members who have been occupationally or secondarily exposed to asbestos products manufactured by at least one of the twenty settling defendants.

Unlike the tort system, the settlement provides certain and prompt cash compensation to all class members who have suffered impairment or death as a result of their exposure to asbestos. The [Center for Claims Resolution] CCR defendants, in exchange, have waived all liability defenses except proof of exposure to one of their asbestos products. To all those class members who do not suffer an impairing asbestos-related disease, the settlement provides certain benefits, including the right to certain cash compensation if and when they become sick.

Also unlike the tort system, the claim procedures under the Stipulation are essentially non-adversarial; most qualifying claims of persons actually disabled from demonstrable asbestos disease will be settled for sums within a range of dollar values similar to the historical values paid by CCR over recent years. These settlements will include limitations on claimants' counsel fees and binding arbitration for most exceptional and extraordinary claims. A small number of unusually exceptional and difficult claims will be allowed to return to the tort system.

The CCR defendants have committed to the payment of a likely $1.289 billion (plus $317 million in costs) to settle anticipated claims under the Stipulation over the first ten years of its operation. And, because CCR was able to reach the settlement in this class action, it has further committed an additional $1.626 billion over the next four years to settle the inventory of cases presently pending in the tort system.

This case has received a great deal of attention from the press and from the asbestos bar and has been the subject of much debate. However, this Court has been determined to decide the fairness and jurisdictional issues assigned to it fairly and objectively and to stay removed from the fray. This Court has been constantly aware of whose interests are ultimately at stake in this lawsuit: the class members and the defendants. And, this Court has been deliberate in its case management, allowing unprecedented discovery and pre-hearing procedures to take place over many months in preparation for the fairness hearing and has been appropriately expansive in the receipt of evidence.

The competent, comprehensive and hard-pressed advocacy of all of the objectors' counsel has indeed aided and improved this Court's analysis of the fairness of the settlement. The absence of such advocacy might have prevented this Court's thorough review of the objectors' concerns. This advocacy has been especially important because this settlement is not conventional but rather is innovative and seeks a partial solution to a crisis that has plagued and overextended the Courts.

The extensive analysis by prestigious scholars and quasi-judicial bodies of the problem with asbestos litigation in the tort system, as well as the research and writing all outlined in the findings of fact above, have convinced this Court that the usually adequate conventional tort system, state and federal, must adopt far from conventional methods to compensate victims of disease and death as a result of asbestos exposure. These methods, of course, must protect the rights of the parties concerned. The thoughtful distinguished authors, groups, panels, committees and the Judicial Panel on Multidistrict Litigation itself, have all encouraged the parties to proffer forms of all-encompassing settlement methods for present and future claims. This Court has concluded that the settlement plan presented to it in this case is fair and goes a long way toward meeting the goals sought to be achieved.

The inadequate tort system has demonstrated that the lawyers are well paid for their services but the victims are not receiving speedy and reasonably inexpensive resolution of their claims. Rather, the victims' recoveries are delayed, excessively reduced by transaction costs and relegated to the impersonal group trials and mass consolidations. The sickest of victims often go uncompensated for years while valuable funds go to others who remain unimpaired by their mild asbestos disease. Indeed, these unimpaired victims have, in many states, been forced to assert their claims prematurely or risk giving up all rights to future compensation for any future lung cancer or mesothelioma. The plan which this Court approves today will correct that unfair result for the class members and the CCR defendants.

It might appear, as the objectors argue, that the financial stability and potential future profitability of the settling defendants in this case would augur against the need for, or approval of, any group settlement of the future claims of the asbestos victims exposed to their products. This Court has concluded to the contrary because of the series of bankruptcies of similarly viable companies which have succumbed to the onslaught of asbestos claims. The time to prevent bankruptcies is before they occur. This settlement allows reliable business and financial planning by the CCR defendants, designed to reasonably assure the availability of funds for the payment of these claims in the future. This not only benefits the businesses but assures the victims that their claims will be paid.

This Court is convinced that the terms of the settlement before it were the result of arms-length adversarial negotiations by extraordinarily competent and experienced attorneys. The attorneys for the plaintiff class are highly respected members of the plaintiffs' asbestos bar, and it is clear to this Court that they intended to negotiate this settlement in compliance with the ethical rules governing the conduct of attorneys. This determination is based upon the evidence of the negotiations themselves, the testimony of the ethics experts and the legal conclusions recited above. Furthermore, the result of the negotiations, that is the settlement itself, is evidence that the attorneys involved were competent representatives of the class. This Court has determined that the terms of the settlement are fair and reasonable to the class and that the settlement itself is an innovative solution to a long-standing problem. The settlement calls for non-adversarial claims resolution procedures, sophisticated recognition of discrete asbestos-related diseases, and has been determined by some of the best medical experts in the field to cover almost all victims who are disabled or die as a result of their exposure to CCR asbestos products.[67]

This Court is also satisfied that the claims resolution procedures will be carried out fairly. While it is true that representatives of CCR will receive the medical data and make the settlement offers, liability has been virtually conceded and there is no basis for CCR to reject a qualified claim and no routine procedures for medical rebuttal by CCR. Under the Stipulation, if CCR does dispute a medical claim, it must meet a heavy burden of proving that the diagnosis was "clearly erroneous." CCR will be motivated to administer the plan fairly because CCR's performance is subject to audit by unencumbered separate class counsel and leaders of the AFL–CIO. CCR has agreed that these same auditors shall also have influence over the appointment of arbitrators and medical panel members. Beyond internal oversight, the incentive to act fairly is strong because of CCR's interest that the settlement succeed. Their

67. This Court has recited in its findings of fact the detailed terms of the large sums of money which CCR has agreed to pay in settlement of Class Counsel's inventory of pending claims. Since CCR had determined to settle these claims for historical values, Class Counsel had a duty to their existing clients to resolve those claims. There is no persuasive evidence that these settlement agreements influenced the substance of the settlement presently before this Court for consideration.

plan to extend the settlement terms into the future as authorized by the Stipulation will be for naught if it does not. Finally, this Court will retain jurisdiction over the settlement by its approval of the settlement and incorporation of its terms into the final Order of this Court. Accordingly, the Court will have supervisory power to enforce the agreement.

This Court is confident that due process has been and will be given to the class victims covered by this settlement. As a result of the extensive and expensive notice procedure carried out by the settling parties and cooperating union leaders, over six million union members and retirees and members of the general population received actual notice materials. A national television and print media campaign costing millions of dollars reached millions more people. In short, a very large class received notice of this class action and of the settlement by a massive effort.

Those class members who were either disinterested in the settlement or who opposed the settlement, were given the opportunity to opt out of the class. Those persons who have properly opted out of this class will no longer be a concern of this settlement and their rights and remedies are not changed.[68] Another group, the unimpaired class members, do not currently impact significantly upon the case flow predictions under this settlement. While many of them may qualify for benefits in the future, their deferral from entry into the case flow procedures unless and until they become ill will tend to insure that the case flow predictions and maximums will be achieved. Thus this Court is convinced that the large numbers of cases settled by or commenced against the CCR defendants since 1992 is in no way a prediction of the numbers of claims which will be made under this settlement and any argument to the contrary is not supported by the record.

In sum, this settlement is a fair solution for these parties to a problem that left alone would cause unfair results for the asbestos victims and predictably unfortunate financial downfall for these defendants. Just as the CCR defendants have an interest in the fair compensation of all victims of asbestos disease as a result of exposure to their products, asbestos victims who are in this class have an interest in the continued financial viability of the defendant companies so that they will receive historically-based values for their claims. The settlement approved here resolves these concerns.

An appropriate Order follows.

* * *

68. Although over two hundred thousand opt-out requests were received, the record is silent as to whether these persons are actually members of the class, are or ever will be qualified for damages in the tort system, or thus will ever enter the tort system.

IN RE GENERAL MOTORS CORPORATION PICK–UP TRUCK FUEL TANK PRODUCTS LIABILITY LITIGATION

United States Court of Appeals, Third Circuit, 1995.
55 F.3d 768.

Before: BECKER, ALITO, and GIBSON, CIRCUIT JUDGES.

BECKER, CIRCUIT JUDGE.

This is an appeal from an order of the District Court for the Eastern District of Pennsylvania approving the settlement of a large class action following its certification of a so-called settlement class. Numerous objectors challenge the fairness and reasonableness of the settlement. The objectors also challenge: (1) the district court's failure to certify the class formally; (2) its denial of discovery concerning the settlement negotiations; (3) the adequacy of the notice as it pertained to the fee request; and (4) its approval of the attorneys' fee agreement between the defendants and the attorneys for the class, which the class notice did not fully disclose, thereby (allegedly) depriving the class of the practical opportunity to object to the proposed fee award at the fairness hearing.

The class members are purchasers, over a 15 year period, of mid-and full-sized General Motors pick-up trucks with model C, K, R, or V chassis, which, it was subsequently determined, may have had a design defect in their location of the fuel tank. Objectors claim that the side-saddle tanks rendered the trucks especially vulnerable to fuel fires in side collisions. Many of the class members are individual owners (i.e., own a single truck), while others are "fleet owners," who own a number of trucks. Many of the fleet owners are governmental agencies. As will become apparent, the negotiated settlement treats fleet owners quite differently from individual owners, a fact with serious implications for the fairness of the settlement and the adequacy of representation of the class.

While all the issues we have mentioned are significant (except for the discovery issue), the threshold and most important issue concerns the propriety and prerequisites of settlement classes. The settlement class device is not mentioned in the class action rule, Federal Rule of Civil Procedure 23. Rather it is a judicially crafted procedure. Usually, the request for a settlement class is presented to the court by both plaintiff(s) and defendant(s); having provisionally settled the case before seeking certification, the parties move for simultaneous class certification and settlement approval. Because this process is removed from the normal, adversarial, litigation mode, the class is certified for settlement purposes only, not for litigation. Sometimes, as here, the parties reach a settlement while the case is in litigation posture, only then moving the court, with the defendants' stipulation as to the class's compliance with the Rule 23 requisites, for class certification and settlement approval. In any event, the court disseminates notice of the proposed settlement and fairness hearing at the same time it notifies class members of the pendency of class action determination. Only when the settlement is about to be finally approved does the court formally certify the class, thus binding the interests of its members by the settlement.

The first MANUAL FOR COMPLEX LITIGATION [hereinafter MCL] strongly disapproved of settlement classes. Nevertheless, courts have increasingly used the device in recent years, and subsequent manuals (MCL 2d and MCL 3d (in draft)) have relented, endorsing settlement classes under carefully controlled circumstances, but continuing to warn of the potential for abuse. This increased use of settlement classes has proven extremely valuable for disposing of major and complex national and international class actions in a variety of substantive areas ranging from toxic torts (Agent Orange) and medical devices (Dalkon Shield, breast implant), to antitrust cases (the beef or cardboard container industries). But their use has not been problem free, provoking a barrage of criticism that the device is a vehicle for collusive settlements that primarily serve the interests of defendants—by granting expansive protection from law suits—and of plaintiffs' counsel—by generating large fees gladly paid by defendants as a quid pro quo for finally disposing of many troublesome claims.

After reflection upon these concerns, we conclude that Rule 23 permits courts to achieve the significant benefits created by settlement classes so long as these courts abide by all of the fundaments of the Rule. Settlement classes must satisfy the Rule 23(a) requirements of numerosity, commonality, typicality, and adequacy of representation, as well as the relevant 23(b) requirements, usually (as in this case) the (b)(3) superiority and predominance standards. We also hold that settlement class status (on which settlement approval depends) should not be sustained unless the record establishes, by findings of the district judge, that the same requisites of the Rule are satisfied. Additionally, we hold that a finding that the settlement was fair and reasonable does not serve as a surrogate for the class findings, and also that there is no lower standard for the certification of settlement classes than there is for litigation classes. But so long as the four requirements of 23(a) and the appropriate requirement(s) of 23(b) are met, a court may legitimately certify the class under the Rule.

In this case the district judge made no Rule 23 findings, and significant questions remain as to whether the class could have met the requisites of the rule had the district court applied them. Principally at issue is adequacy of representation. In particular, the objectors contend that there is a conflict between the positions of individual owners on the one hand and fleet owners on the other hand. The disparity in settlement benefits enjoyed by these different groups, objectors argue, creates an intra-class conflict that precludes the finding of adequacy of representation required by the rule. Moreover, they submit, the large number of different defenses available under the laws of the several states involved also creates a potentially serious commonality and typicality problem.

We conclude that the objectors' adequacy of representation claim probably has merit. At all events, the district court did not properly evaluate the differential impact of the settlement on individual fleet owners, and should determine on remand whether the conflicts among class members are so great as to preclude certification (or at least sufficient to require the creation of subclasses). The district court should also focus on the commonality and typicality problems, to determine whether the national scope of the class litigation and the plethora of defenses available in different jurisdictions prevent these requirements from being met.

For the reasons that follow at some length, we conclude that, although settlement classes are valid generally, this settlement class was not properly certified. We also conclude that the settlement is not fair and adequate; more precisely, we hold that the district court abused its discretion in determining that it was, primarily because the district court erred in accepting plaintiffs' unreasonably high estimate of the settlement's worth, in over-estimating the risk of maintaining class status and of establishing liability and damages, and in misinterpreting the reaction of the class. Finally, although our disposition of the foregoing issues makes it unnecessary for us to pass on the approval of the attorneys fees, we clarify the governing standards for these fee awards to guide the district court on remand. We therefore reverse the challenged order of the district court and remand for further proceedings.

* * *

C. Arguments Favoring Settlement Classes

Although settlement classes are vulnerable to potent criticisms, some important dynamics militate in favor of a judge's delaying or even substantially avoiding class certification determinations. Because certification so dramatically increases the potential value of the suit to the plaintiffs and their attorneys as well as the potential liability of the defendant, the parties will frequently contest certification vigorously. As a result, a defendant considering a settlement may resist agreeing to class certification because, if the settlement negotiations should fail, it would be left exposed to major litigation. *See* In re Beef Indus. Antitrust Litig., 607 F.2d 167, 177–78 (5th Cir.1979)("[A blanket rule against settlement classes] may render it virtually impossible for the parties to compromise class issues and reach a proposed class settlement before a class certification...."); In re Baldwin—United, 105 F.R.D. 475 (S.D.N.Y.1984).

In mass tort cases, in particular, use of a settlement class can help overcome certain elements of these actions that otherwise can considerably complicate efforts to settle. These hurdles include "the large number of individual plaintiffs and lawyers; * * * the existence of unfiled claims by putative plaintiffs; and ... the inability of any single plaintiff to offer the settling defendant reliable indemnity protection...." Trangsrud, 70 Cornell L.Rev. at 835. By using the courts to overcome some of the collective action problems particularly acute in mass tort cases, the settlement class device can make settlement feasible. The use of settlement classes can thus enable both parties to realize substantial savings in litigation expenses by compromising the action before formal certification. *See* 2 Newberg & Conte § 11.09 at 11–13. Through settlement class certification, courts have fostered settlement of some very large, complex cases that might otherwise never have yielded deserving plaintiffs any substantial renumeration.

Settlement classes also increase the number of actions that are amenable to settlement by increasing the rewards of a negotiated solution, in at least four ways. First, the prospect of class certification increases a defendant's incentive to settle because the settlement would then bind the class members and prevent further suits against the defendant. Second, settlement classes may reduce litigation costs by allowing defendants to stipulate to class certification without forfeiting any of their legal arguments against certification should the negotiations fail. Third, because the payment of settlement proceeds, even relatively small amounts, may palliate class members, settlement can reduce differences among class members, and thus make class certification more likely, increasing the value of settlement to the defendant, since a larger number of potential claims can thus be resolved.

Fourth, the use of settlement classes reduces the probability of a successful subsequent challenge to the class-wide settlement. By treating the class as valid pending settlement, a temporary class facilitates notice to those persons whom the court might consider part of the class. The expanded notice afforded by access to the customary class action notification process protects both the absentees and the defendants by eliminating negotiations between the defendants and the named plaintiffs with respect to the class definition that could leave the defendant vulnerable to additional suits by absentees whose interests, a court later determines, were not adequately served or protected. 2 Newberg & Conte § 11.27 at 11–40 * * *. Increasing the certainty that the settlement will be upheld augments the value of settling to the defendant and consequently the amount defendants will be willing to pay. Thus, delaying certification, in contravention of a strict reading of Rule 23, encourages settlement, an important judicial policy, by increasing the prospective gains to the defendant (and thus potentially to the plaintiffs as well) from exploring a negotiated solution.

Moreover, critics of settlement classes may underestimate the safeguards that still inhere. Although courts are often certifying settlement classes with sub-optimal amounts of information, and without the full benefit of the processes meant to protect the absentees' interests, the provisional certification of a settlement class does not finally determine the absentees' rights. When the simultaneous notice of the class and the settlement is distributed to the proposed class, objecting class members can still challenge the class on commonality, typicality, adequacy of representation, superiority, and predominance grounds—they are not limited to objections based strictly on the settlement's terms. 2 Newberg & Conte § 11.27 at 11–40 * * *

Furthermore, the view that, in settlement class cases, the court lacks the information necessary to fulfill its role as protector of the absentees, may reflect an assumption that the court's approval always comes early in the case. *See* 2 Newberg & Conte § 11.27 at 11–43 to 11–44. While it often does, the certification decision is sometimes made later in the case, when the parties have presumably developed the merits more fully (in discovery or in the course of wrangling over the settlement terms) and when prior governmental procedures or investigations might have also yielded helpful information. *Id.* Whatever the timing of the certification ruling, the judge has the duty of passing on the fairness and adequacy of the settlement under Rule 23(e) and also of determining whether the class meets the Rule's requisites under 23(a). Whether or not the court certifies the class before settlement discussions, these duties are the same. * * *

Although a judge cannot presume that the putative class counsel actively represented the absentees' interests, the court can still monitor the negotiation process itself to assure that both counsel and the settlement adequately vindicate the absentees' interests. Thus, there is no reason to inflexibly limit the use of settlement classes to any specified categories of cases (for example, those cases with few objectors, those which do not involve partial settlements, or those which do not involve an expanded class). Even apparently troublesome litigation activity, such as expanding the class just before settlement approval at the defendant's request, is no more free from judicial scrutiny in a settlement class context than it would be otherwise. The court still must give notice to the now-expanded class and satisfy itself that the requisites of class certification are met. * * * Since the party advocating certification bears the burden of proving appropriateness of class treatment, * * *, where the procedural posture is such that the court lacks adequate information to make those determinations, it can and should withhold the relevant approvals. * * *

But even if the use of settlement classes did reduce a judge's capacity to safeguard the class's interests, it does not necessarily impair the ability of absentees to protect their own interests. Individual class members retain the right to opt out of the class and settlement, preserving the right to pursue their own litigation. *See* Premier Elec. Const. Co. v. N.E.C.A., Inc., 814 F.2d 358 (7th Cir.1987)(criticizing settlement classes because they create opportunities for one-way intervention). In fact, the use of the settlement class in some sense enhances plaintiffs' right to opt out. Since the plaintiff is offered the opportunity to opt out of the class simultaneously with the opportunity to accept or reject the settlement offer, which is supposed to be accompanied by all information on settlement, the plaintiff knows exactly what result he or she sacrifices when opting out. * * * *See* In re Beef Industry Antitrust Litigation, 607 F.2d at 174.

In sum, settlement classes clearly offer substantial benefits. However, the very flexibility required to achieve these gains strains the bounds of Rule 23 and comes at the expense of some of the protections the Rule-writers intended to construct. As Judge Schwarzer has explained: "one way to see [the settlement class] is as a commendable example of the law's adaptability to meet the needs of the time-in the best tradition of the Anglo–American common law. But another interpretation might be that it is an unprincipled subversion of the Federal Rules of Civil Procedure. True, if it is a subversion, it is done with good intentions to help courts cope with burgeoning dockets, to enable claimants at the end of the line of litigants to recover compensation, and to allow defendants to manage the staggering liabilities many face. But as experience seems to show, good intentions are not always enough to ensure that all relevant private and public interests are protected. The siren song of Rule 23 can lead lawyers, parties and courts into rough waters where their ethical compass offers only uncertain guidance." William W. Schwarzer, *Settlement of Mass Tort Class Actions: Order Out of Chaos,* Cornell L.Rev. (forthcoming).

D. Are Settlement Classes Cognizable Under Rule 23?

Although not specifically authorized by Rule 23, settlement classes are not specifically precluded by it either; indeed, Judge Brieant has read subsection (d), giving the court power to manage the class action, as authorizing the creation of "tentative", "provisional", or "conditional" classes through its grant of power to modify or decertify classes as necessary. *See, e.g.,* In re Baldwin–United Corp., 105 F.R.D. 475, 478–79 (S.D.N.Y.1984). And because of the broad grant of authority in Rule 23(d), at least one commentator has noted that the validity of temporary settlement classes is usually not questioned. 2 Newberg & Conte § 11.22 at 11–31. Courts apparently share this confidence. Indeed, one court believed that "[i]t is clear that the Court may provisionally certify the Class for settlement purposes." South Carolina Nat'l Bank v. Stone, 749 F.Supp. 1419, (D.S.C.1990).

We believe that the "provisional" or "conditional" conception of the settlement class device finds at least a colorable textual basis in the Rule. Rule 23(d) enables a court to certify a class, if it complies with its duty to assure that the class meets the rule's requisites by making appropriate Rule 23 findings * * *. Some courts appear to have concluded that the built-in flexibility of the Rule, which enables the court to revisit the requisites and modify or decertify the class should its nature change dramatically during the negotiation process, renders it acceptable to determine class status after settlement and thus avoid scrutinizing and adjudicating class status at an earlier stage when the outcome is unknown. *See, e.g.,* In re Baldwin–United, 105 F.R.D. at 483; In re Beef Antitrust Litig., 607 F.2d at 177 ("[T]he Court finds that a conditional class should be certified for the purpose of considering the proposed settlements.")

Alternatively, some courts have conceived of settlement classes as a "temporary assumption" by the court to facilitate settlement. *See Mars Steel,* 834 F.2d at 680; *In re Beef Indus. Antitrust Litig.,* 607 F.2d at 177; 2 Newberg & Conte § 11.27 at 11–50. The arguments of the late

Herbert Newberg, one of the leading advocates of settlement classes, reflect an assumption that the Rule 23 determinations are merely postponed, not eliminated: "On analysis, however, it would appear that this argument [that courts using settlement classes circumvent the need to test the propriety of the class action according to the specific criteria of Rule 23] may be rebutted by perceiving the temporary settlement class as nothing more than a tentative assumption indulged in by the court. * * * The actual class ruling is deferred in these circumstances until after hearing on the settlement approval. * * * At that time, the court in fact applies the class action requirements to determine whether the action should be maintained as a class action." * * * 2 Newberg & Conte § 11.27 at 11–50. Newberg posits, therefore, that the temporary assumption conception of the settlement needs no special authorization since the court eventually follows the ordinary certification process, only deferring it until the settlement approval stage.

Courts have also relied on the more general policies of Rule 23–promoting justice and realizing judicial efficiencies—to justify this arguable departure from the rule. [T]he hallmark of Rule 23 is flexibility. * * * Temporary settlement classes have proved to be quite useful in resolving major class action disputes. While their use may still be controversial, most Courts have recognized their utility and have authorized the parties to compromise their differences, including class action issues through this means. * * * One commentator found implicit authorization for settlement classes under a settlement-oriented interpretation of Rule 23:

> [Rule 23] provides that a court may certify a common question class action when it will prove "superior to other available methods for the fair and efficient adjudication of the controversy."

> A judicially supervised and approved class action settlement, like a judicially supervised trial, is a means of hearing and determining judicially, in other words "adjudicating," the value of claims arising from a mass tort. As a result, if conditional certification of the case as a common question class action for settlement purposes would enhance the prospects for a group settlement, then Rule 23 authorizes certification.

Roger H. Trangsrud, *Joinder Alternatives in Mass Tort Litig.,* 70 Cornell L.Rev. 779, 835 (1985)(footnotes omitted).

It is noteworthy that resistance to more flexible applications of Rule 23 has diminished over time. *See* In re Taxable Mun. Bond Secur. Litig., 1994 WL 643142, *4 (E.D.La.1994)(commenting upon this trend). The evolution of the reception accorded settlement classes has manifested itself in the successive versions of the MANUAL FOR COMPLEX LITIGATION. The first edition of the MANUAL criticized the initiation of settlement negotiations before certification, and discouraged all such negotiations. See MCL 1st § 1.46. The second edition recognizes the potential benefits of settlement classes but still cautioned that "the court should be wary of presenting the settlement to the class." MCL § 30.45 at 243.

The (draft) third version acknowledges that "[s]ettlement classes offer a commonly used vehicle for the settlement of complex litigation" and aims only to supervise rather than discourage their use. *See* MCL § 30.45 at 192.

A survey of the caselaw confirms the impression that resistance to settlement classes has diminished: few cases since the late 1970's and early 1980's even bother to squarely address the propriety of settlement classes. Moreover, no court of appeals that has had the opportunity to comment on the propriety of settlement classes has held that they constitute a per se violation of Rule 23. *See, e.g.,* Ace Heating & Plumbing Co. v. Crane Co., 453 F.2d 30, 33 (3d Cir.1971)(finding no prohibition but granting absentees standing to appeal settlement approval); Marshall v. Holiday Magic, Inc., 550 F.2d 1173, 1176 (9th Cir.1977)(describing how court approved combined notice of the pendency of the class and the terms of the proposed settlement); In re Beef Antitrust Litig., 607 F.2d 167 (5th Cir.1979); Corrugated Container Antitrust Litig., 643 F.2d 195, 223 (5th Cir.1981)(upholding settlement despite pre-certification negotiations with some defendants); Weinberger v. Kendrick, 698 F.2d 61 (2d Cir.1982); Mars Steel, 834 F.2d 677, 681 (7th Cir.1987)(criticizing settlement classes but ultimately approving settlement). But some courts recognize that this practice represents a significant departure from the usual Rule 23 scenario and thereby counsel that courts should scrutinize these settlements even more closely.

We acknowledge that settlement classes, conceived of either as provisional or conditional certifications, represent a practical construction of the class action rule. Such construction affords considerable economies to both the litigants and the judiciary and is also fully consistent with the flexibility integral to Rule 23. A number of other jurisdictions have already accepted settlement classes as a reasonable interpretation of Rule 23 and thereby achieved these substantial benefits. Although we appreciate the concerns raised about the device, we are confident that they can be addressed by the rigorous applications of the Rule 23 requisites by the courts at the approval stages, as we discuss at greater length herein. For these reasons, we hold that settlement classes are cognizable under Rule 23.

* * *

PETER H. SCHUCK, THE ROLE OF JUDGES IN SETTLING COMPLEX CASES: THE AGENT ORANGE EXAMPLE

53 U.Chi.LRev 337 (1986).

In the vast literature on the contemporary judiciary, the judge's role in settling civil cases receives little attention. This neglect is striking for several reasons. The vast majority of civil cases are settled before trial and an even higher percentage are settled before verdict. Moreover, judges routinely—indeed, often mandatorily—involve themselves in the settlement process, and there is at least anecdotal evidence that this involvement is increasing. As a purely statistical matter, then, judicial settlement activity bulks very large. Finally, the legal, philosophical, and policy issues raised by judge-contrived or judge-approved settlements are difficult and profoundly important. As my colleague Owen Fiss has recently reminded us, we cannot assume that a settlement is legitimate simply because the parties' lawyers voluntarily subscribe to it. Whether or not settlements are (as Fiss believes) the civil litigation equivalent of criminal plea bargaining, one's view of the propriety of the judge's role in fashioning them must surely be an important element in one's own evaluation of our court procedures.

* * *

On April 10, less than three weeks before [the Agent Orange] trial, Weinstein appointed three special masters for settlement. Feinberg and David I. Shapiro, a prominent class action expert and skillful negotiator, would work with the lawyers. Leonard Garment, a Washington political insider, would explore what resources the government might contribute to a settlement. Feinberg and Shapiro immediately identified three major obstacles to settlement: the parties were more than a quarter of *a billion dollars apart*; each side was deeply divided internally over whether and on what terms to settle (and in defendants' case, how to allocate liability); and the government was manifestly unwilling to contribute toward a settlement fund or even to participate in settlement negotiations.

The judge and special masters decided to convene an around-the-clock negotiating marathon at the courthouse during the weekend before the trial. The lawyers were ordered to appear on Saturday morning, May 5, with their "toothbrushes and full negotiating authority." On that morning, while preliminary jury selection work was proceeding in another room, Weinstein met with the lawyers and gave them a "pep talk" about settlement. Then the special masters undertook a grueling two-day course of shuttle diplomacy, holding separate meetings with each side interspersed with private conferences with Judge Weinstein. On several occasions, the judge met privately with each side.

Several features of the discussion were particularly salient in generating the settlement agreement. First, the court did not permit the two sides to meet face-to-face until the very end, after the terms of the deal had been defined. This strategy preserved the court's control over the negotiations and prevented them from fragmenting. In particular, it stymied the plaintiffs' lawyers in their last-ditch effort to improve on the deal by settling with five of the defendants and isolating Monsanto and Diamond Shamrock, the two companies they thought most vulnerable to liability and punitive damages.

Second, the masters attempted to break log-jams in the negotiations by helping the lawyers to predict the consequences of the various approaches under consideration, and by proposing alternative solutions.

For example, when the chemical companies' lawyers expressed the fear that a settlement would be rendered worthless if a large number of veterans decided to opt out of the class and sue on their own, Shapiro devised a "walk-away" provision that would minimize those concerns. The tax implications of a settlement were also questions that the masters helped to clarify.

Third, when especially difficult issues arose that threatened to derail the settlement, the parties agreed to be bound by the judge's decision. The most important example of the judge acting as arbitrator involved perhaps the most difficult question facing the defendants—how to allocate liability among themselves. Another example involved the question of one of the defendants' "ability to pay" its share.

Fourth, the judge and his special masters, while being careful not to be duplicitous, did emphasize different things to each side. In their discussions with plaintiffs' lawyers, they stressed the weakness of the evidence on causation, the novelty of many questions of law in the case, the consequent risk of reversal on appeal of a favorable verdict, the prospect that they might lose everything if they rejected settlement, and the enormous costs of continued litigation. To the defendants' lawyers, they stressed the presumed pro-plaintiff sympathies of Brooklyn juries, the reputational damage that protracted litigation and unfavorable publicity would cause their clients, and the high costs of the trial and of the inevitable appeals.

Fifth, a common theme in all discussions was the pervasive *uncertainty* that surrounded the law, the facts, the duration and ultimate outcome of the litigation, and the damages likely to be awarded. By almost all accounts, it was this uncertainty that proved to be the decisive inducement to settlement. On one count, however, Judge Weinstein left little doubt in the lawyers' minds: the court, having crafted and taken responsibility for the settlement, was in a position to make it stick.

Sixth, the imminence and ineluctability of trial "concentrated the minds" of the lawyers as nothing else could have done. This deadline imparted to their deliberations an urgency and a seriousness that swept aside objections that might have undermined negotiations in less compelling circumstances. The lawyers' growing physical and mental exhaustion during that weekend of feverish intensity abetted the conciliatory effect. As one plaintiff's lawyer later complained in his challenge to the validity of the settlement, "the Judge wore us all down with that tactic."

Seventh, the judge and special masters displayed a degree of skill, sophistication, imagination, and artistry in fashioning the settlement that almost all the participants viewed as highly unusual. But even this would not have availed had Judge Weinstein not inspired an extraordinary measure of respect, even awe, in the lawyers, and had the special masters not been viewed as enjoying the authority to speak and make commitments for him.

Eighth, the settlement was negotiated without any agreement (or even any serious discussion) of how the settlement fund would be distributed among the claimants, and without reliable information as to the number of claims that would be filed. The first, of course, was of great interest to the plaintiffs and a matter of indifference to the defendants. The second, however, was significant to both sides. It is not at all certain that settlement could have been reached had the parties been required to resolve these issues in advance. The problem was not simply that preparation of a distribution plan required an immense amount of analysis. A protracted process of political compromise and education was also needed to gain support for the plan, a process whose results even now remain doubtful and perhaps legally vulnerable.

Ninth, the lawyers on the PMC at the time of the settlement possessed very different personalities, ideologies, and incentives than those of the group of lawyers that had launched the case and carried it through its first five years. These differences likely affected the lawyers' disposition to settle. The veterans' passionate desire for vindication at trial, quite apart from their wish for compensation, had strongly driven their chosen lawyer, Victor Yannacone, during the earlier stages of the litigation. Yet the PMC's deliberations concerning the settlement were strongly influenced by lawyers who had only the most attenuated relationship to the veterans. And under the terms of an internal fee-sharing agreement, these lawyers would be secured financially by even a "low" settlement.

Finally, the court was prepared to allocate substantial resources to the quest for a settlement. Judge Weinstein devoted a great deal of his own time to thinking through and implementing a settlement strategy. His three special masters for settlement commanded high compensation and worked long hours. Their billings to the court totaled hundreds of thousands of dollars, even excluding the massive amount of work they later invested in connection with the distribution plan.

According to virtually all of the lawyers who participated in the negotiation of the Agent Orange settlement, Judge Weinstein's distinctive intervention was essential to the settlement. It is possible, of course, that the lawyers are wrong, and that a pretrial settlement would have been reached even without Weinstein's intervention—or, at the very least, that a settlement would have been reached after some witnesses had testified and "blood" had been drawn. But the court's settlement activity was regarded as crucial by those in the best position to know.

II

Why might it be necessary or desirable for a judge to play any role *at all* in the settlement of a complex case? If one subscribes to the dominant law-and-economics model of the decision to litigate or to settle, the answer to this question is not at all obvious.

For present purposes, two of the model's central assumptions are most interesting. First, it assumes that settlement is a two-person, party-exclusive bargaining process, one in which the judge plays no *distinctive* role. To be sure, he or she can provide information that may assist the attorneys to perform their cost and benefit calculations. But on the face of the model, the judge is no different in that respect from a newspaper account, a law book, or a deposition. Second, it assumes that the litigating attorneys possess perfect information about the magnitudes of their own and their opponents' litigation and settlement costs and their stakes in the case, and that each forms an estimate of plaintiff's probability of success on the basis of that information.

It seems likely that these assumptions more or less accurately characterize the decision to litigate or to settle in the vast majority of lawsuits. The judge, of course, will never know as much as the parties do about their settlement and litigation costs. The lawyers hardly need a judge to remind them that their *financial* incentives to settle cases are already great. The costs of trial (and appeal) are ordinarily quite high compared to the costs of pretrial litigation and settlement. The all-or-nothing aspect of most civil cases (comparative negligence is an important exception) presumably further encourages settlement by all but the risk-preferring lawyer and client. And the contingent fee arrangements of most plaintiffs' lawyers, at least in tort cases, usually provide strong incentives for the lawyers to settle rather than to litigate. Even a lawyer's fidelity to the client's interests, which may diverge from the lawyer's, cannot wholly eliminate the lawyer's powerful motive to settle.

Moreover, the judge will seldom know as much as the parties do about the plaintiff's probability of success or the likely size of a damage award, at least prior to trial. That is not to deny, however, that the judge sometimes has special knowledge that is relevant to the decision to litigate or to settle. Typically, the judge enjoys some discretion with respect to defining the outcome-relevant facts and law. If the manner in which the judge will exercise that discretion is important to the outcome, and if the parties' estimates of how it will be exercised are sufficiently divergent, they may not be able to negotiate a settlement on their own. A judge who informs the parties of the likely result of these discretionary decisions can, by helping the parties' estimates to converge, strongly influence their choice between litigation and settlement.

Although this possibility of superior judicial information certainly exists, one should not exaggerate its magnitude. First, unless the judge has participated extensively in resolving numerous discovery disputes in the case (a kind of participation that the growing use of special masters and magistrates makes increasingly unlikely), or has otherwise become immersed in the details of the litigation, the judge will probably not acquire more than a generalized understanding of the nature of a case until the parties file their trial briefs, or perhaps even until the trial is well under way. Indeed, a conscientious judge will strive (not always successfully) to avoid forming a settled view of the merits of the case as long as possible. The same scruples about detachment are likely to deter judges from early resolution of the kinds of ''discretionary'' issues that, as we have seen, may be highly relevant to the decision to litigate or to settle. Second, even if the judge knows a great deal about the case, its significance may only "come together" for him or her during the synthetic, focused process of trial. Finally, whatever the judge thinks of the case, the jury may think differently and the jury, in the end, usually has the decisive voice.

If lawyers already possess both the economic incentive to settle and the information (to the extent that *anyone* possesses it) that the Landes–Posner model deems relevant to making a rational decision, then the growing judicial role in settlement poses a genuine puzzle: under those conditions, after all, that role would seem to be superfluous. If judges are increasingly active in settlement activity, the model suggests, they are taking on an unnecessary burden—unless the model omits certain important features of the actual settlement process. Since it is demonstrable that trial lawyers emphatically do *not* regard an active judicial role in settlement as superfluous, the latter explanation appears to be the correct one. As we shall see, the Agent Orange experience strongly supports that view.

In fact, a judge controls four distinct kinds of resources that may facilitate or even be indispensable to settlement, especially in complex cases. Typically, these resources are inaccessible to the lawyers except insofar as the judge decides to make them available. They include control over the disposition of certain issues; knowledge about other factors relevant to settlement of the case; the judge's reputation for fairness; and control over certain inducements and administrative supports. These resources, of course, are not equally important in any particular case, and some of them may actually conflict with others. Taken together, however, they go far towards explaining why judges sometimes play a key role in settlement and why the decision to litigate or to settle is often more properly viewed as a bargaining process involving three parties rather than two.

A.   The Judge's Control Over Particular Issues

I have already indicated that in many cases, especially complex ones, the judge will know little about the case prior to trial and thus will not be able to influence settlement negotiations by indicating in advance how he or she will rule on crucial issues. Occasionally, however, a judge will master the essentials of the case quickly enough to have a major impact. Agent Orange was such a case.

In Judge Weinstein's initial meeting with the lawyers, only days after he was assigned to the case, he displayed a mastery of the important features of the five-year-old Agent Orange litigation that was quite remarkable and much remarked upon. For present purposes, the question of how he acquired this knowledge so quickly is less interesting than the question of how he used it. He immediately took charge of the case, which had stalled for many months, and not only propelled it toward trial but self-consciously reshaped it, substantively and strategically, in ways that proved to be highly relevant to the case's eventual settlement.

Several examples must suffice. First, Judge Weinstein decided that while *Feres v. United States* barred tort claims against the government by veterans, that bar did not apply to the independent claims of members of the veterans' families. This novel proposition provided him with a reason (not to say a pretext) for restoring the government to the case—a crucial ingredient of the settlement that he hoped to fashion. Second, he suspected that the plaintiffs' causation evidence was weak. As the trial date approached, this suspicion ripened into a firm conviction, which the judge used as the essential premise and prod for goading the plaintiffs into a settlement. Finally, he made several so-called "preliminary" rulings that unmistakably signaled to the lawyers—especially plaintiffs' counsel—that they would probably not achieve certain hoped-for outcomes at the trial court level. His expressed intention to preclude the jury from awarding punitive damages eliminated what was probably the single greatest source of the parties' uncertainty as to the stakes of the case. On the other hand, by indicating that he would apply "national consensus law" principles to resolve choice-of-law questions, and by declining to indicate what those principles were, Weinstein maximized his own discretion, rendering the applicable law on a host of issues essentially indeterminate until such time as he should rule on each of them.

Two important points about Weinstein's signaling should be emphasized. First, he increased the parties' uncertainty in some respects and reduced it in others. There is no reason to believe, however, that these effects simply canceled one another out in the lawyers' calculations. The crucial consideration would seem to be that the uncertainty-reducing effect, especially as to causation and punitive damages, predominated. These rulings also favored the defendants, of course, and that fact strongly influenced the specific terms of the eventual settlement. For present purposes, however, the more important observation is that, as the Priest–Klein elaboration of the economic model predicts, Weinstein's rulings also increased the *probability* of settlement. This was not because of their substantive content, which was equally known and presumably taken into account by each side, but because, on balance, they reduced uncertainty and thus caused the parties' estimates of the probable outcome to converge.

Second, although Weinstein's rulings did reduce uncertainty, they did not wholly eliminate it. A great deal of uncertainty remained, both as to liability and as to damages. The lawyers on both sides believed that if the case went to a jury, a plaintiffs' verdict was quite possible and the damages, given uncertainty about the number and quality of claims and about the size of pain and suffering awards, would be unpredictable. Despite his expressed doubts about the causation evidence, Weinstein was careful not to state whether he viewed the plaintiffs' case as sufficiently weak to justify granting summary judgment in favor of the defendants, or whether he was prepared to enter judgment notwithstanding a pro-plaintiff jury verdict. In short, despite the judge's substantial control over the outcome and his willingness to signal his intentions with some clarity, the residual uncertainty was great.

In the end, this residual uncertainty proved to be an important motive for settlement. The reason is that *both sides seemed to become more pessimistic about the likely outcome at trial.* In terms of the economic model, judicial intervention will encourage settlement if both parties can be induced to reduce their estimates of their probable chances of winning at trial. The difficulty is that under ordinary circumstances, a given piece of information would be expected to make only one party more pessimistic; that information should cause the other party to become more optimistic. Judge Weinstein took two steps, however, that may have caused both sides to become more pessimistic, albeit for different reasons. First, he and his masters isolated the parties during the crucial stage of settlement negotiations and acted as an intermediary in all communications that passed between them. This stratagem enabled him to stress different aspects of the case to each side. In particular, he was able simultaneously to arouse plaintiffs' fear that the case would not even reach the jury and defendants' fear that it would. Second, by clearly signaling how he was likely to rule on some issues, he suggested that he saw the remaining issues as very close ones, thus magnifying uncertainty and possibly reducing optimism on both sides.

B. *Knowledge About Other Factors Relevant to Settlement*

In the Agent Orange case, the judge who fashioned the settlement also had the power to decide the case on the merits should settlement fail. As we have just seen, having one judge wield both of these powers was instrumental in producing the settlement. But this merging of roles is neither logically nor legally required, and some courts and most lawyers have rejected it. Indeed, in a case like Agent Orange, this identity raises serious questions of judicial propriety, a point to which I turn in Part III. But even a "settlement judge" (or judicial adjunct) who lacks any power to rule on the merits acquires two types of knowledge that may be used to encourage settlement: knowledge about the social benefits and costs of a decision to litigate or to settle, and knowledge about barriers to settlement.

1. *Knowledge about Externalities.* The costs and benefits of litigation, especially in complex cases, do not accrue entirely to the parties and their lawyers. The parties have little or no incentive to attend to these external costs and benefits, and their decisions to litigate or to settle do not take them into account. The judge, in contrast, not only knows about certain externalities but is in a position to consider them when deciding whether and how to influence the parties' decisions. Indeed, in class actions certified under rule 23, the court is *obliged* to consider these social effects (among other considerations) in deciding whether to approve a settlement proffered by the parties.

The Agent Orange case suggests that the range and magnitude of externalities from the decision to litigate or to settle may be substantial.

On the cost-of-litigation side, I have already described the burdens that the massive pretrial proceedings imposed on the court system; the administrative costs of the anticipated lengthy trial would have been even more formidable. To these costs, the value of judicial, lawyer, client, witness, and juror time and resources—only some of which the parties internalize—must be added. On the other hand, litigation can generate some important social benefits. By establishing and refining authoritative legal rules, litigation can minimize future disputes and litigation by informing the public about norms for conduct and the likely judicial application of those norms. In the Agent Orange case, such guidance would have especially benefited those concerned with the manufacture, transportation, disposal, and storage of toxic substances. Litigation also serves important symbolic functions, using the evocative forms of narrative and combat to affirm certain fundamental communal values. The veterans' desire to use the courts to tell their story to an uninformed public and to win vindication for their sacrifices is a classic example of that symbolic function.

For present purposes, it matters neither whether the judge *should* consider these externalities in deciding whether and how to seek to influence the parties' decision, nor whether these externalities were on balance positive or negative in the Agent Orange case. The important points are that they can be significant, and that only the "settlement judge," as the larger society's representative in the dispute, is in a position to take them into account.

2. *Knowledge About Barriers to Settlement.* According to the Landes–Posner model, the choice of whether to settle is a purely rational, resource-maximizing decision in which there are no barriers to communication between the lawyers, and in which the costs and benefits of the alternative courses of action are objective and verifiable. The Agent Orange case, however, suggests that the negotiation process is sometimes impeded by distorted perceptions, perhaps psychologically induced, that only a neutral third party can correct, and by strategic behavior that only such a third party can overcome.

As the inexorable Agent Orange trial date approached in early 1984, a "trial mentality" took hold. This mind-set had several notable features. First, although their financial incentives strongly favored settling the case, plaintiffs' lawyers—particularly those designated to try the case—nevertheless resisted broaching the subject of settlement with their adversaries. The defendants' lawyers were reluctant as well. Both sides feared that to initiate discussions would be to betray a lack of confidence in their case. They also feared that to enter into settlement negotiations while preparing for trial on an extremely tight schedule would sap the martial energy and interrupt the momentum thought to be essential to successful trial work in high-stakes litigation.

It is certainly not the case that the robust financial incentives to settle invariably bow to these psychological and strategic obstacles; obviously, the statistics on the frequency of settlement imply that the reverse is more likely to be true. Rather, the point is only that such obstacles sometimes do exist, and that in certain cases, the intervention of a judge may be necessary to surmount them. The judge's role becomes one of opening and centrally coordinating a blocked communication system—convening the parties, defining the agenda, and saying what the parties know but are afraid to admit.

A second feature of the lawyers' "trial mentality" was a tendency to exaggerate both the strengths of their own case and the weaknesses of their adversaries' case. The Posner–Landes model does not consider how such perceptions might confound and distort the lawyers' evaluation of the parameters they face and thereby discourage certain settlement options that more accurate appraisals might commend to them. Judge Weinstein and his settlement masters, by furnishing the lawyers with an informed "outsider's" view, helped to counterbalance this tendency.

C. Reputation for Fairness

The judge's power over the disposition of particular issues, knowledge about externalities, and aid in overcoming barriers to bargaining can only be useful to the parties' search for settlement if they view the judge as fair. For the court to be serviceable, they need not think it indifferent as to the case's mode of disposition or even its outcome. The parties may suspect, for example, that the judge strongly desires a settlement in the case, yet believe that no recrimination will occur should they decide instead to litigate. They may even know that the judge has formed some opinion as to the merits. What is crucial is not that the judge be seen as a tabula rasa but that the parties view him or her as objective and fairminded.

In the Agent Orange case, most of the lawyers who negotiated the settlement viewed Judge Weinstein as disinterested in this special sense. All were well aware, of course, that he wanted to settle the case—he had made his intentions unmistakably clear—but none believed that his desire for settlement was animated by personal bias, ideology, or anything other than his conception of what justice in the case required. Similarly, although his view of the merits, especially on the causation issue, was one with which plaintiffs' lawyers profoundly disagreed, most were convinced that he had come to his view in a detached, intellectually honest fashion. Moreover, because they respected his acuity, his views influenced their own to some degree.

The judge's reputation for fairness can have an additional, more substantive effect on settlement. In any complex negotiation, certain issues will arise that are especially difficult to resolve and that threaten to derail the discussions. Sometimes only a trusted third party can resolve these "deal-breaker" issues. As Part I indicated, the Agent Orange settlement almost foundered on several disputes of this kind, most notably problems of allocating liability among defendants and of insurance coverage. The parties' confidence in Judge Weinstein's wisdom and fairness enabled them to submit these issues to him for authoritative resolution.

D.   Special Resources and Inducements

Two other kinds of resources can be used to encourage and shape settlements. I shall call them administrative resources and bargaining inducements. In terms of the economic model, they can be viewed as factors that reduce settlement costs and increase litigation costs. The important point that the model ignores, however, is that these resources, although valuable to the parties and their lawyers, are controlled by judges and thus can be manipulated by them to influence the decision to litigate or to settle.

1.   *Administrative Resources.* A judge—especially, as in Agent Orange, the chief judge of a court—controls physical facilities, specialized personnel and support staff, a bureaucratic organization, a communications apparatus, and the litigation calendar. In the Agent Orange case, Judge Weinstein conspicuously and effectively wielded these and other trappings of judicial power first to facilitate and then to legitimate the settlement. For example, he convened intensive negotiations in the federal courthouse itself; appointed magistrates and special masters; presided over an unprecedented series of "fairness hearings" held in cities throughout the nation to elicit the comments of class members on the proposed settlement; ordered unusual forms of class notice; and prepared, disseminated, and administered what may be the most complex distribution plan ever adopted by a court. His skillful deployment of these resources was probably essential to the negotiation, approval, and implementation of a settlement in so complex a case.

2.   *Bargaining Inducements.* In addition to controlling administrative resources that facilitate settlement, a judge can create and manipulate incentives to which the lawyers are likely to respond, orchestrating those responses into a settlement agreement that might not otherwise be reached. The essential, unvarnished fact is this: The lawyers know—and the judge knows that the lawyers know—that the judge is in a position to make many decisions of vital concern to them and their clients in the future, both in this case and in subsequent cases in which they will appear before that judge. Many of these decisions entail the exercise of some judicial discretion. Some, like the pace and nature of discovery, the time of trial, and the admissibility of expert testimony, are almost wholly discretionary. Especially in a complex case, even those decisions that are in principle not discretionary are often not appealable as a legal or practical matter. Some of the most important decisions from the lawyer's selfish point of view—class certification, appointment of lead class counsel, and award of attorneys' fees and costs—may turn upon the judge's perception of a particular lawyer's ability and performance. Rightly or wrongly, lawyers believe that these decisions are more likely to be favorable, at least at the margin, if the judge regards the lawyers as reasonable and cooperative. It would be astonishing, under these circumstances, if lawyers did not seek to present themselves as conciliatory actors who are anxious to please the court.

None of this suggests either that judges threaten lawyers with retribution if they are unwilling to settle on terms that the court proposes, or that lawyers sacrifice their clients' interests in a fulsome display of obeisance. The pattern of influence in the Agent Orange case was far more subtle. Much of Judge Weinstein's leverage over the lawyers was implicit rather than explicit; whatever force it exerted derived from the fact that it was felt, anticipated, and internalized without having to be discussed or justified. Its outward manifestations—the lawyers' deference, even obsequiousness, towards the judge throughout the settlement process—were so conventional as to almost escape notice. To be sure, their responsiveness to his wishes partly reflected the unusual degree of admiration with which almost all of the lawyers regarded Judge Weinstein. But much of it seems more systematic, more deeply embedded in professional norms and strategic concerns.

III

The analysis presented in Part II emphasizes that an active judicial role in the settlement of complex cases like Agent Orange may have several previously unsuspected or at least unarticulated features. Although there evidently is widespread support for such a role among lawyers, judges, and even clients, the reason for this support seems to be little more than an undefined sense that judicial involvement "works" in producing settlements that are regarded as acceptable. If the analysis is accurate, we now have a better idea of *why* and in *what respect* it works. Judicial involvement in settlement may tend to "perfect" the lawyer-centered bargaining process envisioned by the Landes–Posner model by introducing a third party who can correct for certain "market failures." To put the point another way, the existing model identifies the variables relevant to the decision to litigate or to settle—settlement costs, litigation costs, stakes in the case, and estimated probability of success—but it ignores the judge's role in influencing the magnitude and salience of those variables and thus the outcome of the decision.

The analysis also suggests, however, that there are risks to justice, and to the appearance of justice, when judges—especially those who are in a position to rule on the merits and thus control the outcome of a case—actively involve themselves in settlement. These risks exist even when settlement is thought to be a good thing, either in general or in a particular case. Even if the risks of judicial involvement are outweighed by the advantages, as I think they were in the Agent Orange case, they merit profound concern. These risks seem to me to be of three main types: judicial overreaching, judicial over-commitment, and procedural unfairness.

A. *Judicial Overreaching*

As noted in Part II, judges control inducements that they can manipulate in order to influence lawyers' behavior. Even if judges scrupulously avoid rewarding or punishing lawyers who do or do not cooperate in effecting settlement, the danger remains that lawyers will interpret judicial involvement as thinly-veiled coercion or will conform their behavior to what they believe the judge is demanding rather than to the needs of their clients. In the Agent Orange case, for example, several plaintiffs' lawyers alleged in their challenge to the settlement that Judge Weinstein improperly pressured them to settle. Consider one lawyer's account (in a sworn deposition) of the judge's behavior:

> He would say: "Now, I am not going to hold it against you if you don't settle. I am not going to penalize you. I am going to conduct this trial on a fair basis to everybody," and then came the "but".....

> "But," he would say, "I have carried you plaintiffs all this time. I have decided a lot of questions in your favor I could have decided the other way. And I want you to know that at nine o'clock Monday morning [when the trial was to begin] I am through carrying you. You are on your own. I will do my duty as a Judge."

> Then a little conversation would take place and then he would come back and say: "You know, remember, I just don't think you have got a case on medical causation. I don't think you have a case on punitive damages."

The question for present purposes is not whether this account of the exchange is accurate, or if so, how the judge's words were said and how they were understood by the lawyers. Such questions are probably impossible to resolve on the basis of the available evidence. Instead, two points seem especially pertinent. First, settlement discussions in such cases take place unrecorded, behind closed doors, in a highly-charged emotional environment. Under such circumstances, ambiguity and misunderstanding flourish. After-the-fact recrimination is a constant temptation. Second, except perhaps at the extremes, there is no consensus on what constitutes "judicial impropriety" in such a situation, much less the "appearance" of impropriety. The facts that a judge as conscientious and sophisticated as Judge Weinstein could be accused of overreaching (although the lawyer hesitated to call it "duress") and that other judges have occasionally been found guilty of it suggest that the risk is not a trivial one.

B. Judicial Over–Commitment

Judges, like other people, do not like to invest a great deal in a project without receiving the anticipated return. The Agent Orange experience suggests that fashioning a settlement in that kind of case requires an enormous judicial investment, and that a judge who makes such an investment is unlikely to remain indifferent as to the outcome of the negotiations. The risk is that the judge's commitment may become excessive, compromising the appearance or reality of the judge's fairness as to whether the case will be litigated or settled, and possibly even with regard to the merits.

The Agent Orange case exemplifies this risk. Under rule 23(e), Judge Weinstein was obliged to decide whether the settlement was "fair, reasonable and adequate." Consider whether the reality of the situation permitted him to do so in a disinterested fashion. The settlement, after all, was not an agreement that the lawyers had negotiated and drafted by themselves and brought to the court for its evaluation and approval. Judge Weinstein had invested an enormous amount of the court's resources in the effort and had placed his considerable personal and judicial reputation on the line in extracting concessions and accommodations from both sides in the interests of securing an agreement. Finally, he had, quite literally, dictated its principal terms—the settlement amount, the trigger date on interest, the opt-out walkaway provision, the preservation of claims against the government—and had cajoled the lawyers into accepting them. Had he not contrived the settlement, it would by all accounts not have occurred when and in the form that it did; indeed, it may not have occurred at all. His broad conception of the lawsuit's structure and significance, and his architectonic strategy for settling it, had guided his every action and decision in the case. His hand (and that of his special masters) appeared in every provision, every detail of the settlement document.

The judge was deeply committed to the settlement in another sense. He had made many innovative rulings that might well be reversed on appeal if the case were to continue. To that extent, he had staked his reputation and authority upon his ability to craft a settlement that would terminate the dispute.

Given his firm commitment to a settlement almost entirely of his own creation, it was virtually inconceivable that Judge Weinstein would fail to find that the agreement was "fair, reasonable and adequate." Again, the issue is not whether the settlement met the standards implicit in [R]ule 23; in my view, it clearly did. For present purposes, the more relevant and interesting question is whether Judge Weinstein at some point became so much the author of the settlement that he lost the ability to be the disinterested appraiser envisioned by [R]ule 23(e). Again, in my view, he clearly did. He could not dispassionately evaluate the terms of a settlement that he had, with such difficulty and investment, personally wrought. He could not fairly act as a judge in what, in a real sense, had come to be his own case.

C. Procedural Unfairness

Settlement negotiations are necessarily informal, secretive, rapidly changing affairs, and are ill-suited to the conventional forms of procedural due process. Moreover, the settlement process in complex class actions like Agent Orange may be quite protracted, involving a variety of distinct phases: the negotiations themselves, "fairness hearings," a "fairness decision," preparation of a distribution plan, public consideration and court approval of a plan, and implementation of the plan. Some of the procedural short-cuts or compromises that are appropriate for one phase, such as negotiation, may be quite troubling when applied to another phase, such as approval of the distribution plan. The risk of procedural unfairness—the threat to procedural values such as accuracy, individual dignity, participation, openness of decisionmaking, and the like—magnifies the risks of judicial overreaching and overcommitment.

Again, the Agent Orange case exemplifies this risk, despite Judge Weinstein's energetic and sensitive efforts to minimize it. During both the negotiation and the distribution plan phases, numerous *ex parte* communications passed between the judge and the special masters and between the special masters and the lawyers; in effect, then, these communications occurred between the lawyers and the judge. This problem was compounded by the decision to keep the two sides separate during negotiations and to channel all communications between them through the court. Whether or not this procedure violated Canon 3 of the Code of Judicial Conduct, it clearly merits concern. Similarly, the distribution plan—the "bottom line" of the litigation for the veterans—was prepared and approved with few if any of the procedural protections that surround even the most trivial discovery motion—such as the right to a decision based on findings of fact derived from a record compiled through adversarial processes. Moreover, the distribution plan is an integral part of the settlement, and must be reviewed by the court before the settlement can be approved. Weinstein's decision to approve the settlement without such a plan seems improper. Again, the point is neither to disparage the results reached by Judge Weinstein and Special Master Feinberg nor to argue that different procedures would have yielded different outcomes. Rather, it is to suggest the dangers that the lack of procedural protections could pose in the less capable hands that more typically administer such matters.

If one assumes, as I think one should, that genuinely voluntary settlement of civil disputes short of trial is generally a good thing, then the emerging judicial role in settlement would seem to be a valuable instrument for reaching that objective. Judges may actually be able to facilitate some settlements, especially in complex cases, that are "better"—in the sense of more accurately reflecting what the parties would negotiate if they were fully informed about the relevant variables, including likely outcomes—than those that the litigation market would otherwise generate.

But that value, as the Agent Orange case suggests, can be obtained only at some risk of judicial overreaching, over-commitment, and procedural unfairness. It is impossible to know how great that risk actually is, for the only people in a position to identify and appraise it—the lawyers who interact with the settlement judge—cannot always be counted on to blow the whistle. For example, the lawyer may have a personal financial or professional stake in a settlement that the client, if fully informed, would reject. The lawyer may not be sufficiently strong or independent to resist an oppressive judge bent upon settlement.

Although the risk of abuse cannot be quantified, there are several procedural reforms that might, at low cost, reduce it. First, the judge who is to preside over the litigation of the merits can be barred from participating in settlement negotiations. This procedure is already standard practice in certain judicial districts and apparently enjoys widespread support among attorneys. Although the advantages of this approach are obvious, its limitations should not be ignored. The risk of over-commitment may simply shift from "merits" judges to "settlement" judges; in fact, a judge whose only task with regard to a case is to settle it may have even stronger reasons to "force" settlement. In addition, the proposal could impose additional demands on scarce judicial resources. When applied to complex cases like Agent Orange, for a second judge (who is already busy with his or her own docket) to invest the considerable time and study required to learn what the "merits" judge already knows (or must eventually learn) would be costly. The use of special masters for settlement could reduce the drain on judges' time, of course, but that resource is also costly—and the use of special masters creates its own problems.

Another procedural reform would be to bar the judge who fashioned a class action settlement from evaluating the fairness of that settlement. Since there are some advantages in cost and quality of decision in having the judge who is most knowledgeable about the case evaluate the fairness of the settlement, this change should ideally be limited to those cases in which the court played an active role in designing or negotiating the settlement. Those cases must be distinguished from the presumably far more common situations in which the settlement was essentially produced by the parties and merely presented to the judge. An important question, then, is how such a distinction would be defined and how difficult its application would be in practice. Moreover, this reform would affect only settlements in the relatively small percentage of cases that are class actions. A novel requirement that all settlements be judicially approved—and further, that they be approved by a judge not previously involved with the case—would be cost-effective only if a significant fraction of civil settlements are coerced or reflect improper judicial behavior.

Such an assumption is plainly unwarranted on the basis of the existing evidence. Until stronger contrary evidence appears, we should seek to meet concerns about judicial overreaching, over-commitment, and procedural unfairness in settlements by tailoring the limited procedural reforms suggested above. More important, we must seek to strengthen the normative and institutional safeguards upon which any judicial system must principally rely: the self-consciousness of judges, the vigilance and assertiveness of advocates, the probing suspicions of journalists, and the fastidious carping of scholars.

Notes and Questions

1. As *In re A.H. Robins* indicates, the procedural phenomenon of the "settlement class" is a relatively recent innovation in the federal court settlement arsenal. Although class actions typically are certified "as soon as practicable after the commencement of an action," *see* Fed.R.Civ.P. 23 (c)(1), courts also are permitted to conditionally or provisionally certify actions under this provision. The "settlement class" represents a further extension

of this procedure: the litigants negotiate a settlement, of which class certification is part of the deal. What problems are present in this mode of proceeding? How does it deviate from usual class action procedure? For a book-length treatments of the Dalkon Shield litigation, *see* Ronald J. Bacigal, THE LIMITS OF LITIGATION: THE DALKON SHIELD CONTROVERSY (1990); Sheldon D. Engelmayer & Robert Wagman, LORD'S JUSTICE: ONE JUDGE'S BATTLE TO EXPOSE THE DEADLY DALKON SHIELD I.U.D. (1985); Karen M. Hicks, SURVIVING THE DALKON SHIELD IUD: WOMEN V. THE PHARMACEUTICAL INDUSTRY (1994); Morton Mintz, AT ANY COST: CORPORATE GREED, WOMEN, AND THE DALKON SHIELD (1985); Susan Perry & Jim Dawson, NIGHTMARE: WOMEN AND THE DALKON SHIELD (1985); *see also* Emily Couric, *The A.H. Robins Saga,* A.B.A.J. 56 (July 1986); Paul Marcotte, *$2.48 Billion Trust Fund: A.H. Robins Faces Claimants, Bankruptcy, Takeover Agreement,* A.B.A.J. 24 (March 1988); Joseph A. Page, *Asbestos and the Dalkon Shield: Corporate America on Trial,* 85 Mich.L.Rev 1324 (1987).

2. The development of the procedural device of the "settlement class" has renewed the debate surrounding the nature and limits of managerial judging. *See generally* Judith Resnik, *Managerial Judging,* 96 Harv.L.Rev 374 (1982). To what extent may a judge supervise a class action or aggregate settlement of mass tort or other complex litigation? *See generally* Federal Rule of Civil Procedure 16; *see also* MANUAL FOR COMPLEX LITIGATION (2d ed.1985) at § 20.1 (judicial supervision) and § 23.1 (settlement, role of court). Some federal judges have been highly criticized for judicial overreaching in the settlement of certain mass tort cases. *See generally,* Peter Schuck, AGENT ORANGE ON TRIAL (1986). *See also* Allan Ashman, *Court Rebukes Judge Lord's Interference in Settlement,* A.B.A.J. at 166 (April 1985)(Dalkon Shield settlement); Valle S. Dutcher, Comment, *The Asbestos Dragon: The Ramifications of Creative Judicial Management of Asbestos Cases,* 10 Pace Envt'l L.Rev. 955 (1993); Eric D. Green, *et al., Settling Large Case Litigation: An Alternative Approach,* 11 Loy.L.A.L.Rev. 493 (1978); Patrick F. Harrigan, *Affirmative Judicial Case Management: A Viable Solution to the Toxic Product Liability Litigation Crisis,* 38 Me.L.Rev. 339 (1986); Leroy J. Tornquist, *The Active Judge in Pretrial Settlement: Inherent Authority Gone Awry,* 25 Williamette L.Rev. 743 (1989); Jack B. Weinstein, *A View From the Judiciary,* 13 Cardozo L.Rev. 1957 (1992).

Portions of Judge Weinstein's settlement of the *Agent Orange* Litigation subsequently were overturned on appeal, *see* In re "Agent Orange" Prod. Liab. Litig., 818 F.2d 216 (2d Cir.1987), *reversing* 611 F.Supp. 1452 (E.D.N.Y.1985)(overturning Judge Weinstein's approval of fee arrangement in the Agent Orange class settlement). Other portions of Judge Weinstein's settlement were subsequently upheld, *see, e.g.,* In re "Agent Orange" Prod. Liab. Litig., 818 F.2d 179 (2d Cir.1987)(approving distribution plan that did not require proof that claimant's death or disability resulted from exposure to Agent Orange, but rejecting provision to establish a foundation to fund projects and services that would benefit the entire class).

Judge Weinstein has written that "positive law no longer functions well in the modern context of mass tort cases," and that "[m]ass tort cases are akin to public litigations involving court-ordered restructuring of institutions to protect constitutional rights." Therefore, he believes that judges ought to assume expansive managerial roles in supervising the resolution of mass tort cases, based on what he deems "communitarian-communicatarian" ethics. *See* Jack B. Weinstein, *Ethical Dilemmas in Mass Tort Litigation,* 88 Nw.U.L.Rev 469, 472, 484–93 (1994). In response, two practicing members of the bar have argued:

> * * * We simply differ with him on the fundamentals of his new jurisprudence. The fundamentals of our system of justice, including the adversarial process (where lawyers are highly relevant), separation of powers (where judges' powers are circumscribed and for good reason), and the Bill of Rights, serve important purposes that would be undercut or even decimated by adopting Judge Weinstein's arguments that a so-called "communitarian/communicatarian approach" is required in mass tort cases, that lawyers are too greedy to advance such a public-minded approach, and that judges must therefore take on the role of guardian as a "substitute for traditional ethical roles."
>
> Constitutionally mandated limitations prevent a judge, however well meaning, from imposing on individuals his own view of the proper result. There are mechanisms in place to assure that mass tort law and law in general develop consonant with the public interest. There are sound reasons why some new branch of government, for example, the communitarian/communicatarian judge, should not replace the adversarial model.

See Thomas W. Henderson and Tybe A. Brett, *A Trial Lawyer's Commentary On One Jurist's Musing of the Legal Occult: A Response to Judge Weinstein,* 88 Nw.U.L.Rev 592, 593–94 (1994). *Cf.* Daniel J. Meador, *Inherent Judicial Authority in the Conduct of Civil Litigation,* 73 Texas L.Rev. 1805 (1995).

3. The use of settlement classes in mass tort litigation also has focused attention on the potential for lawyer overreaching and unethical conduct. What opportunities are there for attorney overreaching in settlement classes? Who is the client in class action litigation, and how is the client protected in this representational litigation? Does the device of the settlement class in any way exacerbate the professional responsibility problems in class action litigation? For discussions of the problems relating to class representation and professional responsibility *see generally* Jules Coleman & Charles Silver, *Justice in Settlements,* 4 Soc Phil & Pol'y 102 (1986); Michael D. Ricciuti, *Equity and Accountability in the Reform of Settlement Procedures in Mass Tort Cases: The Ethical Duty to Consult,* 1 Geo.J. Legal Ethics 817 (1988); Deborah Rhode, *Class Conflicts in Class Actions,* 34 Stan.L.Rev 1183 (1982); Jack B. Weinstein, *Ethical Dilemmas, supra. See also* Symposium, *Mass Tortes: Serving Up Just Desserts,* 80 Cornell L.Rev. ___ (forthcoming 1995)(focus on ethical issues in mass tort settlement classes).

As Judge Weinstein has amply detailed in his study, a major source of problems in aggregate mass tort class settlements involve lawyer financing and fee arrangements, conflicts of interest, buyouts, and sweetheart deals. Professor John C. Coffee, Jr. also has explored these problems as they relate to class action procedure. *See generally* Coffee, *Class Wars: The Dilemma of the Mass Tort Class Action* (forthcoming 1995); Coffee, *The Regulation of Entrepreneurial Litigation: Balancing Fairness and Efficiency in the Large Class Action,* 54 U.Chi.L.Rev. 877 (1987); Coffee, *Rethinking the Class*

Action: A Policy Primer on Reform, 62 Ind.L.J. 625 (1986–87); Coffee, *Understanding the Plaintiff's Attorney: The Implications of Economic Theory For Private Enforcement of Law Through Class and Derivative Actions,* 86 Colum.L.Rev. 669 (1986); Coffee, *The Unfaithful Champion: The Plaintiff As Monitor in Shareholder Litigation,* Law & Contemp. Probs. 5 (Summer 1985). *See also* Richard M. Shusterman, *et al., Use of Judgment/Settlement Sharing Agreements in Multi–Party Mass Disaster Litigation,* 42 Fed.Ins. Corp.Couns.Q. 79 (1991).

4.   Since *A.H. Robins,* the use of settlement classes has been uneven. Can a federal court use a "limited fund" settlement class to resolve the claims of present and future mass tort claimants when a defendant's trust fund in a bankruptcy becomes insolvent?   In 1990 Judge Weinstein was given judicial authority to attempt to settle asbestos claims in his jurisdiction, in coordination with the federal bankruptcy court overseeing the Manville Trust.   Soon after assuming this authority, Judge Weinstein *sua sponte* issued several orders, including one urging "all those involved to make recommendations for 'a Rule 23(b)(1)(B) global settlement' and he warned, '[f]ailure to do so will leave this Court no alternative but to consider other available options.'"   After a special master's report found the Manville Trust substantially insolvent, Judge Weinstein certified a (b)(1)(B) settlement class to prioritize present and future claimants.   The Second Circuit rejected this settlement class.   *See* In re Joint Eastern And Southern District Asbestos Litigation, 982 F.2d 721 (2d Cir.1992)(judgment approving the settlement must be vacated because, to the extent that the judgment rests on diversity jurisdiction, the use of a mandatory non-opt-out class action without proper subclasses violates the requirements of Rule 23 of the Federal Rules of Civil Procedure, and, to the extent that the judgment rests on bankruptcy jurisdiction, it represents an impermissible modification of a confirmed and substantially consummated plan of reorganization in violation of section 1127(b) of the Bankruptcy Code).   *But see* In re Drexel Burnham Lambert Group, Inc., 960 F.2d 285 (2d Cir.), *cert. dismissed sub nom.* Hart Holding Co. v. Drexel Burnham Lambert Group, ___ U.S. ___, 113 S.Ct. 1070, 122 L.Ed.2d 497 (1993) approving class action settlement to make a non-uniform adjustment of creditors' rights against an insolvent entity).

For discussions of the issues relating to mandatory non-opt-out mass tort class actions, *see* Linda S. Mullenix, *Class Actions, Personal Jurisdiction, and Plaintiffs' Due Process: The Implications for Mass Tort Litigation,* 28 U.C. Davis L.Rev. 871 (1995); Kent D. Syverud, *Mandatory Class Actions* (forthcoming 1995).

5.   The *Joint Asbestos Litigation, supra,* raised questions relating to the limits of the federal courts to resolve mass tort cases, either as a matter of bankruptcy law or aggregative, adjudicative procedure.   The use of bankruptcy by defendant corporations to solve their mass tort liability exposure has proved highly controversial, as the history of the Manville Trust has demonstrated.   Does the failure of the Manville Trust justify federal court intervention into bankruptcy proceedings?   For discussions of the role of bankruptcy in resolving mass tort litigation, *see, e.g.,* Anne Hardiman, Recent Developments, *Toxic Torts and Chapter 11 Reorganization: The Problem of Future Claims,* 38 Vand.L.Rev 1369 (1985); Harvey J. Kesner, *Future Asbestos Related Litigants as Holders of Statutory Claims Under*

Chapter 11 of the Bankruptcy Code and Their Place in the Johns–Manville Reorganization, 62 Am.Bank.L.J. 69 (1988); Margaret I. Lyle, Note, *Mass Tort Claims and the Corporate Tortfeasor: Bankruptcy Reorganization and Legislative Compensation Versus the Common–Law Tort System,* 61 Tex. L.Rev. 1297 (1983); Paul Marcotte, *$2.48 Billion Trust Fund: A.H. Robins Faces Claimants, Bankruptcy, Takeover Agreement,* A.B.A.J. 24 (March 1988); Mark J. Roe, *Bankruptcy and Mass Tort,* 84 Colum.L.Rev. 846 (1984); Mark J. Roe, *Corporate Strategic Reaction to Mass Tort,* 72 Va. L.Rev. 1 (1986); Steven L. Schultz, In re Joint Eastern and Southern District Asbestos Litigation: *Bankrupt and Backlogged—A Proposal For the Use of Federal Common Law in Mass Tort Class Actions,* 58 Brook.L.Rev. 553 (1992); Note, *The Manville Bankruptcy: Treating Mass Tort Claims in Chapter 11 Proceedings,* 96 Harv.L.Rev. 1121 (1983); Note, *Strategic Bankruptcies: Class Actions, Classification and the Dalkon Shield Cases,* 7 Cardozo L.Rev. 817 (1986).

6. Will the Third Circuit's decision in the *General Motors Corp. Pick–Up Truck Fuel Tank Products Liability Litigation, supra,* provide a sound appellate basis for approving mass tort settlement classes under Rule 23? Will it provide the basis for approving *Georgine* on appeal? Although the Third Circuit gave its qualified approval to use of settlement classes under Rule 23, the court nonetheless invalidated the specific settlement agreement negotiated by the parties, deeming the $1000 rebate coupon remedy unfair to class claimants. Note that the *GMC* class action was based on federal claims arising under the Magnuson–Moss Act and Lanham Trademark Act; common law and statutory claims, including negligence and breach of warranty; and violations of state consumer statutes. In this regard, the *GMC* litigation more resembled the *School Asbestos Litigation* than other mass torts based on aggregated personal injury claims. Judge Becker, in portions of the *GMC* decision not excerpted here, was very aware of the developing use of the settlement class in the context of mass tort litigation, especially in relation to ethical issues. The Third Circuit's *GMC* decision, running more than eighty pages, provides the most through-going close textual and doctrinal analysis of the settlement class device.

The underlying *GMC* MDL litigation consisted of pick-up truck owners in every state but Texas. *See* In re General Motors Corp. Pickup Truck Fuel Tank Products Liab. Litig., 846 F.Supp. 330 (E.D.Pa.1993), reversed 55 F.3d 768 (3d Cir.1995). A Texas trial court approved an identical settlement applicable only to Texans, but the Texas Court of Appeals reversed. *See* Bloyed v. General Motors Corp., 881 S.W.2d 422 (Tex Ct.App.1994).

7. Apart from the various ethical issues relating to settlement classes, academic commentators have raised various substantive and procedural issues relating to the use of settlement classes as device for resolving mass tort litigation. While some commentators view the settlement class as a desirable mechanism for achieving global peace, other critics have questioned whether Rule 23 authorizes settlement classes, as well as the scope and limits of federal courts in approving such agreements. *See generally* James A. Henderson Jr., *Comment: Settlement Class Actions and the Limits of Adjudication,* 80 Cornell L.Rev. ___ (1995); John Leubsdorf, *Co-Opting the Class Action,* 80 Cornell L.Rev. ___ (1995); William W. Schwarzer, *Settle-*

ment of Mass Tort Class Actions: Order Out of Chaos, 80 Cornell L.Rev. ___ (1995).

B. MULTIDISTRICT LITIGATION AND MASS TORTS

1. MDL TRANSFER DENIED

IN RE ASBESTOS AND ASBESTOS INSULATION MATERIAL PRODUCTS LIABILITY LITIGATION

Judicial Panel on Multidistrict Litigation, 1977.
431 F.Supp. 906.

Before JOHN MINOR WISDOM, CHAIRMAN, and EDWARD WEINFELD, EDWIN A. ROBSON, WILLIAM H. BECKER, JOSEPH S. LORD, III, STANLEY A. WEIGEL and ANDREW A. CAFFREY, JUDGES OF THE PANEL.

OPINION AND ORDER

PER CURIAM

This litigation consists of 103 actions pending in nineteen districts. The distribution of these actions is as follows:

Northern District of Ohio	23
Southern District of Texas	20
District of Connecticut	16
Eastern District of Texas	12
District of South Carolina	7
District of New Jersey	6
Southern District of Florida	4
Eastern District of Illinois	2
Eastern District of Michigan	2
District of Montana	2
Eastern District of Tennessee	1
Western District of Pennsylvania	1
Eastern District of Pennsylvania	1
Eastern District of Missouri	1
Eastern District of Louisiana	1
District of Rhode Island	1
Southern District of Indiana	1
District of Maryland	1
Southern District of West Virginia	1

The 103 actions have been brought by workers who were exposed to asbestos dust in the course of their employment, or by persons associated with those workers, either as co-workers or as members of the family. Many diverse types of vocational exposure are involved in these actions. Plaintiffs in most of the actions are or were workers at plants which produce asbestos products (the factory worker actions), or tradesmen who work with a variety of asbestos products (the tradesman actions).

A majority of the tradesmen are installers of insulation products containing asbestos. Ninety-four of the actions are tradesman actions and nine of the actions are factory worker actions.

Six of the actions were brought as class actions on behalf of employees at three different plants that manufacture or once manufactured asbestos products. Three of the actions in the Eastern District of Texas were brought as class actions on behalf of employees at a PPG Industries plant in Tyler, Texas. Class certification has been denied in these three actions. The other three purported class actions are pending in the District of New Jersey * * *. Two are brought on behalf of employees of Raybestos Manhattan, Inc. at a now defunct plant in Passaic, New Jersey. The other action is brought on behalf of employees at a Johns–Manville, Inc. plant in Manville, New Jersey. Class certification is still pending in the New Jersey actions.

There are a total of 80 defendants in the 103 actions. The majority of the defendants are manufacturers or distributors of various asbestos products. Johns–Manville is a defendant in 91 of the actions. Seven other defendant corporations are named in more than 50 actions, seven others are named in more than 30 actions, and ten others are named in ten or more actions.

The complaints in the actions generally allege that the defendants wrongfully caused the plaintiffs to be exposed to asbestos dust and asbestos fibers over a period of time, as a result of which the plaintiffs have contracted or are in danger of contracting asbestosis, mesothelioma, or other disorders. Alleged liability is based on the principles of strict liability, negligence, and/or breach of warranties of merchantability and/or fitness. It is also alleged that the defendants knew or should have known of the dangers to persons exposed to asbestos products, but that defendants failed to warn the plaintiffs of these dangers; failed to provide adequate precautions, safety devices, or wearing apparel to prevent exposure; and/or failed to establish reasonable standards for exposure.

Pursuant to 28 U.S.C. § 1407(c)(i) and Rule 8, R.P.J.P.M.L., 65 F.R.D. 253, 258–59 (1975), the Panel issued an order to show cause why all these actions should not be transferred to a single district for coordinated or consolidated pretrial proceedings. All except one of the 55 respondents to the Panel's order to show cause oppose transfer in this litigation. The primary arguments presented by the parties in opposition to transfer are the following:

(1) Many of the actions have been pending for several years and are well advanced in discovery. In several actions a discovery cutoff date or a trial date has been set. Transfer would merely delay the progress of discovery or the trial of those actions.

(2) In several districts, arrangements for voluntarily sharing the common aspects of discovery have been made among the parties to the actions pending within those districts. Transfer would cause unneces-

sary additional expenses which can be avoided by voluntary coordination of efforts among the parties.

(3) There is a lack of commonality among the parties in these actions. (a) There is considerable variation in named defendants from action to action. No defendant or category of defendants is a party to all actions. Defendants include manufacturers of asbestos products, distributors of asbestos products, insurance companies, doctors, suppliers of raw asbestos fibers, trade associations, trade unions, and the United States of America. (b) The plaintiffs are not a homogeneous group. They include insulation workers involved in the installation or removal of insulation products, workers in factories manufacturing asbestos products, co-workers, members of workers' families, and persons living in the proximity of asbestos manufacturing facilities.

(4) Although a common thread among these actions is exposure to some type of asbestos or asbestos product, the circumstances of exposure are predominantly individual to each action. The variables include the following: (a) type of vocational exposure (e.g. miner, transporter, factory worker, or tradesman); (b) products to which exposed; (c) conditions of exposure; (d) duration and intensity of exposure; (e) safety precautions taken by the worker; (f) medical, personal, employment, and family history of the worker over the long periods of exposure involved (up to 50 years).

Regarding the factory workers and tradesmen, the two basic types of vocational exposure involved, the exposure of factory workers was to 100% raw asbestos, while the exposure of tradesmen was to products which generally contain about 15% asbestos.

(5) The question of causation is an individual issue. Several different types of disorders are alleged, including asbestosis, lung cancer, peritoneal mesothelioma, mesothelioma of the lining of the stomach or gastric organs, cancer of the esophagus, cancer of the colon, and cancer of the rectum. The question of whether particular disorders may be attributable to exposure to a particular type of asbestos is a matter of dispute among medical authorities. Causation of an individual's disability by asbestos exposure will necessarily be related to the individual factors of length, intensity, and type of vocational exposure, and to the physical characteristics of the person. A considerable amount of technical medical evidence such as diagnoses, x-rays and tissue microscopies will be involved in each action. This evidence is of an individual nature.

Significant differences in causation will exist between the factory worker actions and the tradesman actions. Medical and scientific knowledge concerning the two types of exposure is different. The tradesmen will have been exposed to a wider variety of asbestos products, and will need to prove which products caused their disabilities.

(6) The liability of each defendant in each action is predominantly an individual question. The variables will include the defendants' knowledge at a particular time of the health risks involved in exposure to asbestos, the adequacy of any product testing by the defendant

manufacturers, the sufficiency of any warnings or directions for use of products, and the issue of assumption of risk by the plaintiffs. Other variables will include the materials used, the method of manufacture, and the period of production.

(7) Although a common aspect among these actions is the state of medical and scientific knowledge at a particular time regarding the health hazards posed by exposure to asbestos, this knowledge can be readily discerned from literature which is easily available in most medical libraries. The common need for this literature is therefore not a significant justification for transfer.

(8) Local issues will predominate in the discovery process. The medical, personnel, and product use records of each individual will be found locally. Liability in these actions will be based on state substantive law. As a result, transfer would not promote the parties' and witnesses' convenience regarding discovery.

(9) There is not a significant possibility of inconsistent or overlapping class action determinations since any certifiable class could include only those persons who were exposed to asbestos in a specific plant or in the service of a particular employer. The classes alleged to date are properly restricted, and do not overlap in any respect.

Although we recognize the existence of some common questions of fact among these actions, we find that transfer under Section 1407 would not necessarily serve the convenience of the parties and witnesses or promote the just and efficient conduct of the litigation. Accordingly, the order to show cause is vacated.

The virtually unanimous opposition of the parties to transfer, though a very persuasive factor in our decision to deny transfer in this litigation, is not by itself determinative of the question of transfer under Section 1407. In an appropriate situation, the Panel has the power to order transfer in multidistrict litigation even if all parties are opposed to transfer.

We are, however, persuaded by the parties' arguments in this particular litigation. On the basis of the record before us, the only questions of fact common to all actions relate to the state of scientific and medical knowledge at different points in time concerning the risks of exposure to asbestos. The pertinent literature on this subject is readily available. *See generally,* Borel v. Fibreboard Paper Products Corp., * * * 493 F.2d at 1083–86. Many factual questions unique to each action or to a group of actions already pending in a single district clearly predominate, and therefore transfer is unwarranted. *See* In re Fotomat Franchisee Litigation, 394 F.Supp. 798, 799 (J.P.M.L.1975). Furthermore, many of these actions already are well advanced. Some of the actions have been pending for up to four years, and trial dates or discovery cutoff dates have been set in several actions. Under these circumstances, transfer would not further the purposes of Section 1407. *See* In re Braniff Airways, Inc. Employment Practices Litigation, 411 F.Supp. 798, 800 (J.P.M.L.1976).

It is therefore ordered that the order to show cause regarding the actions listed on the following Schedule A be, and the same hereby is, vacated.

IN RE ORTHO PHARMACEUTICAL "LIPPES LOOP" PRODUCTS LIABILITY LITIGATION

Judicial Panel on Multidistrict Litigation, 1978.
447 F.Supp. 1073.

OPINION AND ORDER

Before JOHN MINOR WISDOM, CHAIRMAN, and EDWARD WEINFELD, EDWIN A. ROBSON, JOSEPH S. LORD, III , STANLEY A. WEIGEL, ANDREW A. CAFFREY, and ROY W. HARPER, JUDGES OF THE PANEL.

PER CURIAM.

This litigation consists of five actions pending in different federal districts one each in the Middle District of Pennsylvania, the Eastern District of Michigan, the Southern District of Texas, the District of New Mexico, and the District of New Jersey. All these actions involve alleged personal injuries resulting from use of an intrauterine contraceptive device known as the "Lippes Loop." Ortho Pharmaceutical Corp., the manufacturer of the Lippes Loop, is named as a defendant in all five actions. Two of the actions also name plaintiffs' doctors as defendants. Liability is asserted against the defendants on principles of, *inter alia*, strict liability, breach of express and implied warranties and/or negligence, including inadequate designing, manufacturing and testing of the Lippes Loops and failure to warn adequately of the risks involved in its use.

Pursuant to 28 U.S.C. § 1407(c)(i) and Rule 8, R.P.J.P.M.L., 65 F.R.D. 253, 258–59 (1975), the Panel ordered the parties to show cause why these actions should not be transferred to a single district for coordinated or consolidated pretrial proceedings. All parties that have responded defendant Ortho, one of the defendant physicians, and plaintiffs in three actions oppose transfer.

Although we are of the view that these actions involve some common questions of fact, *see generally,* In re A.H. Robins Co., Inc. "Dalkon Shield" IUD Products Liability Litigation, 406 F.Supp. 540, 542 (J.P.M.L.1975), we find that transfer under Section 1407 would not at the present time serve the convenience of the parties and witnesses or promote the just and efficient conduct of the litigation. Accordingly, we vacate the show cause order.

Plaintiff and defendant Ortho in the New Mexico action represent that pretrial proceedings have been completed and trial is imminent in that action. In the Michigan action we are advised that a discovery cutoff date of June 1, 1978, and a trial date in August of this year have been set. Because these two actions are so advanced, we believe that they should be excluded from transfer under Section 1407. *See* In re Celotex Corporation "Technifoam" Products Liability Litigation, 68

F.R.D. 502, 505 (J.P.M.L.1975). Since only three actions remain, we are not convinced that the common factual issues are sufficiently complex and the accompanying discovery time consuming enough to justify transfer. *See* In re Scotch Whiskey Antitrust Litigation, 299 F.Supp. 543, 544 (J.P.M.L.1969).

It is therefore ordered that the order to show cause regarding the actions listed on the following Schedule A be, and the same hereby is, vacated, without prejudice to the right of any party to move for transfer under Section 1407 at a later date if additional actions are filed or if any party believes that future circumstances otherwise warrant transfer.

IN RE ASBESTOS SCHOOL PRODUCTS LIABILITY LITIGATION

Judicial Panel on Multidistrict Litigation, 1985.
606 F.Supp. 713.

Before ANDREW A. CAFFREY, CHAIRMAN, ROBERT H. SCHNACKE, FRED DAUGHERTY, SAM C. POINTER, JR., S. HUGH DILLIN, MILTON POLLACK, and LOUIS H. POLLAK, JUDGES OF THE PANEL.

ORDER DENYING TRANSFER

PER CURIAM.

Presently before the Panel is a motion, pursuant to 28 U.S.C. § 1407, filed by three defendants in actions in this docket, to centralize in the Eastern District of Pennsylvania for coordinated or consolidated pretrial proceedings the twenty actions listed on the following Schedule A.

On the basis of the papers filed and the hearing held, we find that Section 1407 transfer would neither serve the convenience of the parties and witnesses nor further the just and efficient conduct of the litigation. Although we recognize that the actions in this litigation involve some common questions of fact, we are not persuaded that these common questions of fact will predominate over individual questions of fact present in each action. Moreover, we note that the common questions of fact involved in these actions have been extensively litigated for the past ten years in connection with thousands of personal injury actions arising from alleged asbestos exposure. We further note that 1) one action included in the Section 1407 motion has already been tried, and several other actions have been scheduled for trial within the next six months; and 2) the great majority of parties responding to the Section 1407 motion opposes centralization. The Panel concludes that centralization of these actions is inappropriate for many of the reasons expressed by the Panel in its previous rulings denying transfer of asbestos-related actions. *See* In re Asbestos and Asbestos Insulation Material Products Liability Litigation, 431 F.Supp. 906 (J.P.M.L.1977); In re Asbestos Products Liability Litigation (No. II), MDL–416 (J.P.M.L., March 13, 1980)(unpublished order).

It is therefore ordered that the motion for transfer, pursuant to 28 U.S.C. § 1407, be, and the same hereby is, denied.

IN RE A.H. ROBINS CO., "DALKON SHIELD" IUD PRODUCTS LIABILITY LITIGATION (NO. II).

Judicial Panel on Multidistrict Litigation, 1985.
610 F.Supp. 1099.

Before ANDREW A. CAFFREY, CHAIRMAN, ROBERT H. SCHNACKE, FRED DAUGHERTY, SAM C. POINTER, JR., S. HUGH DILLIN, MILTON POLLACK, and LOUIS H. POLLAK, JUDGES OF THE PANEL.

OPINION AND ORDER

PER CURIAM.

Presently before the Panel is a motion, pursuant to 28 U.S.C. § 1407, brought by defendant A.H. Robins Co., Inc., (Robins) to centralize the more than 1700 Dalkon Shield actions listed on the following Schedule A (including some actions that have been or are presently pending in MDL–211) in the Eastern District of Virginia for coordinated or consolidated pretrial proceedings. Also before the Panel is a motion by plaintiffs in three actions (that are or have been included in the MDL–211 proceedings in the District of Kansas) who have intervened in the Eastern District of Virginia in order to oppose Robins' motion pending in that district to certify a nationwide class on the issue of punitive damages for plaintiffs who have allegedly been injured through use of Robins' intrauterine device. This second group of movants has filed a Section 1407 motion in MDL–211 seeking transfer of their actions and the class certification issues in Virginia to the District of Kansas, where MDL–211 is pending before Judge Frank G. Theis.

On the basis of the papers filed and the hearing held, we find that both motions must be denied, because granting either of them would neither serve the convenience of the parties and witnesses nor further the just and efficient conduct of the litigation.

We recognize that the actions subject to Robins' motion share questions of fact, but we are not persuaded that transfer under Section 1407 is appropriate. MDL–211 has been pending for over ten years, and common discovery in the District of Kansas has been closed, reopened once, and, recently, reopened one more time for limited purposes. The bulk of the completed Dalkon Shield common discovery, along with the remaining discovery in the process of being completed in MDL–211 in the District of Kansas, can be made available to the parties in the actions before the Panel without recourse to Section 1407 and without the need for disrupting the many Dalkon Shield actions subject to Robins' motion that are currently proceeding apace in their respective districts. As we noted in 1981, when it then appeared that all common discovery in MDL–211 had been completed: [T]he judges to whom the ... actions are assigned could issue orders to show cause why all discovery heretofore completed in the transferee district should not be made applicable to the actions. *See* MANUAL FOR COMPLEX LITIGATION, Parts I and II, §§ 3.11 (rev.ed.19[81]). Judge Theis, as transferee judge, has also prepared a final pretrial order which has been entered in the actions which have already been remanded in this docket. This order is available to the parties, counsel and judges involved in these ... actions, can provide a convenient expression of the conclusions of the transferee judge which have been reached through his familiarity with the litigation, and can serve as an aid in avoiding duplication of discovery and preventing inconsistent pretrial rulings. *See* In re Seeburg–Commonwealth United Merger Litigation, 415 F.Supp. 393, 396 (J.P.M.L.1976). In re A.H. Robins Co., Inc., "Dalkon Shield" IUD Products Liability Litigation, 505 F.Supp. 221, 223 (J.P.M.L.1981)(footnote omitted).

Robins has been candid in stating to the Panel that it seeks transfer of these actions under Section 1407 to the Eastern District of Virginia (a district other than the original MDL–211 transferee district, and also the district in which Robins is headquartered) as part of an overall effort to secure a universal resolution of all Dalkon Shield actions. Such a goal is certainly not inimical to the principles underlying Section 1407, but Section 1407 transfer can only be a tool in such an effort if the statutory criteria for transfer under Section 1407 have been satisfied. This simply has not been done in regard to the Robins motion.

The motion of the MDL–211 plaintiffs who have intervened in the Eastern District of Virginia suffers from a lack of precision. To the extent, however, that the motion essentially seeks transfer of certain class action issues now pending in the Eastern District of Virginia to the District of Kansas, the motion must be denied. The Panel does not have power to separate issues in civil actions, assigning one or more to the transferee court and one or more to transferor courts. In re Plumbing Fixture Cases, 298 F.Supp. 484, 489–90 (J.P.M.L.1968).

IT IS THEREFORE ORDERED that the motions for transfer, pursuant to 28 U.S.C. § 1407, be, and the same hereby are, DENIED.

Notes and Questions

1. It was not until mid-century that federal courts began to become seriously concerned with the problems relating to complex litigation. This concern prompted Chief Justice Vinson to appoint a committee to investigate the procedures for handling complex litigation, which resulted in the so-called "Prettyman Report" adopted by the Judicial Conference of the United States. *See Report on Procedure in Anti-trust and Other Protracted Cases,* 13 F.R.D. 62 (1951). In 1960 the Judicial Conference adopted the HANDBOOK OF RECOMMENDED PROCEDURES FOR THE TRIAL OF PROTRACTED CASES, a manual of recommendations to federal judges for managing complex litigation. In the 1960s, federal court experience in adjudicating a series of complex electrical equipment conspiracy suits prompted two further initiatives concerning complex litigation. The first was the publication of a MANUAL ON COMPLEX AND MULTIDISTRICT LITIGATION (1968), now in its third draft (forthcoming). *See* Andrew J. Simons, *The Manual for Complex Litigation: More Rules of Mere Recommendation?,* 62 St. John's L.Rev. 493 (1988); Comment, *Observations*

on the Manual for Complex Litigation and Multidistrict Litigation, 68 Mich.L.Rev. 303 (1969).

The second initiative was Congressional enactment in 1968 of a new venue provision, 28 U.S.C.A. § 1407, which authorizes the temporary transfer of cases filed in different federal courts to a single district for the coordination of pretrial proceedings. The statute also authorizes a Judicial Panel on Multidistrict Litigation (*see* 28 U.S.C.A. § 1407(d) to determine whether a series of cases should be accorded MDL status, and to determine what district to transfer the cases). For discussion of early experience with the multidistrict litigation procedures *see generally* Robert A. Cahn, *A Look at the Judicial Panel on Multidistrict Litigation,* 72 F.R.D. 211 (1976); George T. Conway III, Note, *Consolidation and Transfer in the Federal Courts: 28 U.S.C.A. Section 1407 Viewed in Light of Rule 42(a) and 28 U.S.C.A. Section 1404(a),* 22 Hastings L.J. 1289 (1971); John F. Cooney, Comment, *The Experience of Transferee Courts Under the Multidistrict Litigation Act,* 39 U.Chi.L.Rev. 588 (1972); Thomas B. Goodbody, *Complex Litigation and Multidistrict Litigation,* 3 Class Act. Rptr. 71 (1974); Wilson Herndon, *Section 1407 and Antitrust Multidistrict Litigation—The First Decade,* 47 Antitrust L.J. 1161 (1979); Wilson Herndon & Ernest R. Higginbotham, *Complex Multidistrict Litigation—An Overview of 28 U.S.C.A. Sec. 1407,* 31 Baylor L.Rev. 33 (1979); Patricia D. Howard, *A Guide to Multidistrict Litigation,* 75 F.R.D. 577 (1977); Stanley J. Levy, *Complex Multidistrict Litigation and the Federal Courts,* 40 Fordham L.Rev. 41 (1971); John T. McDermott, *The Judicial Panel on Multidistrict Litigation,* 57 F.R.D. 215 (1973); O'Connor & Kukankos, *Estoppel by Verdict, the Multidistrict Litigation Act, and Constitutional Rights of Litigants—Can They Coexist?,* 20 Trial Law. Guide 249 (1976); Note, *The Judicial Panel and the Conduct of Multidistrict Litigation,* 87 Harv.L.Rev. 1001 (1974).

2. In May 1993 the Judicial Panel on Multidistrict Litigation adopted new rules of procedure under 28 U.S.C.A. § 1407, which became effective on July 1, 1993. These new rules are set out at 15 Wright, Miller, and Cooper, FEDERAL PRACTICE AND PROCEDURE § 3865 (1994 Supp.). For a recent discussion of MDL procedure *see generally* David F. Herr, MULTIDISTRICT LITIGATION: HANDLING CASES BEFORE THE JUDICIAL PANEL ON MULTIDISTRICT LITIGATION (1986).

3. In the 1970s and 1980s, federal courts generally followed the same reluctant pattern with regard to the multidistrict litigation statute as with the class action rule as a method to aggregate mass tort cases. Is the multidistrict litigation statute a more suitable procedural means of aggregating mass tort litigation? Does the Judicial Panel's refusal to certify mass tort cases for MDL treatment make sense? Even if the Judicial Panel did certify a mass tort case for MDL transfer, what limitations does the statute embody that might impair or impede the resolution of mass tort cases? What advantages does the MDL statute have over other means of aggregation? *See* John W. Beatty, *The Impact of Consolidated Multidistrict Proceedings on Plaintiffs in Mass Disaster Litigation,* 38 J. Air & Com. 183 (1972).

2. CHANGING TIDES: MDL TRANSFER APPROVED

IN RE ASBESTOS PRODUCTS LIABILITY LITIGATION

Judicial Panel on Multidistrict Litigation, 1991.
771 F.Supp. 415.

OPINION AND ORDER

JUDGES POLLAK, WOODWARD, MERHIGE and ENRIGHT joined.

On January 17, 1991, the Panel issued an order to show cause why all pending federal district court actions not then in trial involving allegations of personal injury or wrongful death caused by asbestos should not be centralized in a single forum under 28 U.S.C. § 1407. Because of the difficulty in serving this order on the enormous number of parties in this docket, the Panel relied on the clerks of all district courts to serve the parties to actions in their respective districts.[1] As a result, the parties to the 26,639 actions pending in 87 federal districts and listed on the following Schedule A are subject to the Panel's order.[2] More than 180 pleadings have been filed in response to the Panel's order, and a four hour hearing on the question of transfer was held on May 30, 1991 in New York City, at which time 37 counsel presented oral argument. In many instances the attorneys filing these pleadings or participating in oral argument were representing the views of large groups of parties.

Supporting transfer are plaintiffs in approximately 17,000 actions (including a core group of more than 14,000 plaintiffs represented by over 50 law firms) and 30 defendants (24 of which are named in more than 20,000 actions). Opposing transfer are plaintiffs in at least 5,200 actions and 454 defendants. The positions of those parties that have expressed a preference with respect to transferee district are varied. Many parties suggest centralization in what amounts to their home forum. The Eastern District of Pennsylvania is the district either expressly favored or not objected to in the greatest number of pleadings. The Eastern District of Texas, which is the choice of the aforementioned core group of 14,000 plaintiffs, is also the district that has generated the most opposition from defendants. Other suggested districts that go beyond the home forum approach are the District of the District of

---

1. It appears that the only districts with pending asbestos actions that did not effect service of the Panel's order are the Eastern District of Wisconsin and the District of Rhode Island. In view of the Panel's disposition of this docket, the actions pending there will be treated as potential tag-along actions in accordance with the Panel's Rules. *See* Rules 12 and 13, R.P.J.P.M.L., 120 F.R.D. 251, 258–59 (1988).

2. The Statistical Division of the Administrative Office of the United States Courts reports that as of March 31, 1991, nearly 31,000 actions were pending in federal districts. Based on Panel communications with courts throughout the country, the approximately 4,000 pending actions not embraced by the present order likely include actions that, as of January 17, 1991, were overlooked, in trial or already at least partially tried but not yet statistically closed because, *inter alia*, claims against one or more defendants were stayed under the Bankruptcy Code.

Columbia, the Eastern District of Louisiana, the Northern District of Ohio, and the Eastern District of New York. Some parties' forum recommendations are expressed in the forum of a suggested individual transferee judge or transferee judge structure.

On the basis of the papers filed and the hearing held, the Panel finds that the actions in this litigation involve common questions of fact relating to injuries or wrongful death allegedly caused by exposure to asbestos or asbestos containing products, and that centralization under § 1407 in the Eastern District of Pennsylvania will best serve the convenience of the parties and witnesses and promote the just and efficient conduct of this litigation.

DISCUSSION

Any discussion of § 1407 transfer in this docket must begin with the recognition that the question does not arise in a vacuum. Indeed, the impetus for the Panel's order to show cause was a November 21, 1990 letter signed by eight federal district judges responsible for many asbestos actions in their respective districts.[3] These judges, citing the serious problem that asbestos personal injury litigation continues to be for the federal judiciary, requested that the Panel act on its own initiative to address the question of § 1407 transfer. Furthermore, as the title of this docket suggests, this is the sixth time that the Panel has considered transfer of asbestos litigation. On the five previous occasions (1977, 1980, 1985, 1986 and 1987) that the Panel considered the question, it denied transfer in each instance.[4]

The Panel's constancy is not as dramatic as a mere recitation of the denials might suggest, however. The 1986 and 1987 dockets considered by the Panel involved only five and two actions, respectively. The 1985 Panel decision pertained not to personal injury/wrongful death asbestos actions but rather to property damage claims of school districts that incurred significant costs in removing asbestos products from school buildings. The denial in the 1980 Panel docket was based almost exclusively on the movants' failure to offer any distinctions that would warrant a disposition different from the Panel's first asbestos decision in 1977.

It is only in the 1977 decision, pertaining to 103 actions in nineteen districts, that the Panel offered any detailed analysis of its asbestos

---

3. The signatories to this letter are Judges Walter J. Gex, III (S.D.Miss.), Thomas D. Lambros (N.D.Ohio), Alan H. Nevas (D.Conn.), Richard A. Schell (E.D.Tx.), Charles Schwartz, Jr. (E.D.La.), Charles R. Weiner (E.D.Pa.), Charles R. Wolle (S.D.Iowa) and Rya W. Zobel (D.Mass.). Additionally, Judge Jack B. Weinstein (E.D.N.Y.) has contacted the Panel staff and requested that he also be considered a signatory to the letter.

4. In re Asbestos and Asbestos Insulation Material Products Liability Litigation,

431 F.Supp. 906 (J.P.M.L.1977); In re Asbestos Products Liability Litigation (No. II), MDL–416 (J.P.M.L. March 13, 1980) (unpublished order); In re Asbestos School Products Liability Litigation, 606 F.Supp. 713 (J.P.M.L.1985); In re Ship Asbestos Products Liability Litigation, MDL–676 (J.P.M.L. Feb. 4, 1986)(unpublished order); and In re Leon Blair Asbestos Products Liability Litigation, MDL–702 (J.P.M.L. Feb. 6, 1987)(unpublished order).

litigation reasoning with respect to asbestos personal injury/wrongful death actions. In that decision, the Panel first listed the primary arguments of the responding parties that unanimously opposed transfer: advanced stage of proceedings in many of the actions; use of voluntary coordinating arrangements in several districts; lack of commonality among defendants and plaintiffs; circumstances of exposure predominantly unique to each action; individual questions of causation in each action; predominantly individual questions of the liability of each defendant in each action; local issues predominating in the discovery process; absence of possibility of inconsistent or overlapping class certifications; and the readily discernible nature of the principal area common to all actions, the state of medical and scientific knowledge at a particular time regarding the health hazards posed by exposure to asbestos.

In denying transfer in the 1977 decision, the Panel recognized the existence of some common questions of fact among the actions. For in that docket, as in the matter currently before the Panel, all actions contained allegations of personal injury or death as a result of exposure to asbestos or asbestos containing products. The Panel nevertheless held that the other criteria for § 1407 transfer were not satisfied. In relevant part, the Panel stated:

> Many factual questions unique to each action or to a group of actions already pending in a single district clearly predominate, and therefore transfer is unwarranted.... Furthermore, many of these actions already are well advanced. Some of the actions have been pending for up to four years, and trial dates or discovery cutoff dates have been set in several actions. Under these circumstances, transfer would not further the purposes of Section 1407.

In re Asbestos and Asbestos Insulation Material Products Liability Litigation, 431 F.Supp. 906, 910 (J.P.M.L.1977).

Many of the parties presently opposing transfer in this docket rely on the facts and reasoning of the Panel's 1977 transfer decision. They insist that the situation that warranted denial then not only still prevails but has been magnified by the greatly increased number of actions and parties in federal asbestos personal injury/wrongful death litigation— more than 30,000 pending federal actions now, as opposed to the 103 actions subject to the Panel's 1977 decision. In our view, it is precisely this change that now leads us to conclude that centralization of all federal asbestos personal injury/wrongful death actions, in the words of 28 U.S.C. § 1407(a), "will be for the convenience of parties and witnesses and will promote the just and efficient conduct of such actions." In short, we are persuaded that this litigation has reached a magnitude, not contemplated in the record before us in 1977, that threatens the administration of justice and that requires a new, streamlined approach.

The Panel is not the first to reach such a conclusion. Just this past March 1991, the Judicial Conference Ad Hoc Committee on Asbestos Litigation, whose members were appointed by Chief Justice William H. Rehnquist, stated as follows:

The committee has struggled with the problems confronting the courts of this nation arising from death and disease attributable to airborne asbestos industrial materials and products. The committee has concluded that the situation has reached critical dimensions and is getting worse. What has been a frustrating problem is becoming a disaster of major proportions to both the victims and the producers of asbestos products, which the courts are ill-equipped to meet effectively.

After extensive study, the Institute for Civil Justice of the Rand Corporation in 1985 observed, with respect to how the civil justice system handles asbestos claims, that—

The picture is not a pretty one. Decisions concerning thousands of deaths, millions of injuries, and billions of dollars are entangled in a litigation system whose strengths have increasingly been overshadowed by its weaknesses.

The ensuing five years have seen the picture worsen: increased filings, larger backlogs, higher costs, more bankruptcies and poorer prospects that judgments—if ever obtained—can be collected.

It is a tale of danger known in the 1930s, exposure inflicted upon millions of Americans in the 1940s and 1950s, injuries that began to take their toll in the 1960s, and a flood of lawsuits beginning in the 1970s. On the basis of past and current filing data, and because of a latency period that may last as long as 40 years for some asbestos related diseases, a continuing stream of claims can be expected. The final toll of asbestos related injuries is unknown. Predictions have been made of 200,000 asbestos disease deaths before the year 2000 and as many as 265,000 by the year 2015.

The most objectionable aspects of asbestos litigation can be briefly summarized: dockets in both federal and state courts continue to grow; long delays are routine; trials are too long; the same issues are litigated over and over; transaction costs exceed the victims' recovery by nearly two to one; exhaustion of assets threatens and distorts the process; and future claimants may lose altogether. REPORT OF THE JUDICIAL CONFERENCE AD HOC COMMITTEE ON ASBESTOS LITIGATION, 1–3 (1991)(footnote omitted)(hereinafter ASBESTOS COMMITTEE REPORT). The Committee pointed out that presently in the federal system nearly two new asbestos actions are being filed for every action terminated, and that at the current rate, there will be more than 48,000 actions pending in the federal courts at the end of three years....

The Committee also discussed the ongoing change in the demographics of asbestos litigation in the federal courts:

In 1984, when the Federal Judicial Center held its first asbestos conference, asbestos litigation in the federal courts was largely concentrated in only four district courts. Since that time, however, asbestos cases have infiltrated virtually every federal district. Asbestos litigation must therefore be viewed as a national problem rather than merely a local or regional one, especially with the number of Americans affected.

ASBESTOS COMMITTEE REPORT, *supra* at 9 (footnote omitted).

Conclusions similar to those of the Judicial Conference Asbestos Committee have also been reached by judges actively involved in asbestos litigation. In perhaps the most recent comprehensive review of asbestos litigation, Judge Jack B. Weinstein (E.D.N.Y.) observed:

> The large number of asbestos lawsuits pending throughout the country threatens to overwhelm the courts and deprive all litigants, in asbestos suits as well as other civil cases, of meaningful resolution of their claims.... Several commentators have recounted the inefficiencies and inequities of case-by-case adjudication in the context of mass tort disasters. *See, e.g.,* Rosenberg, *Class Actions for Mass Torts: Doing Individual Justice by Collective Means,* 62 Ind.L.J. 561 (1987); *Trends in Asbestos Litigation* (Federal Judicial Center 1987); Rubin, *Mass Torts and Litigation Disasters,* 20 Ga.L.Rev. 429 (1986); Note, *Class Certification in Mass Accident Cases Under Rule 23(b)(1),* 96 Harv.L.Rev. 1143 (1983); Comment, *Federal Mass Tort Class Actions: A Step Toward Equity and Efficiency,* 47 Alb. L.Rev. 1180 (1983).

The heyday of individual adjudication of asbestos mass tort lawsuits has long passed. *See* [ASBESTOS COMMITTEE REPORT], *supra* at 7 ("one point on which plaintiffs' counsel, defense counsel and the judiciary can agree is that the present way in which we have attempted to resolve asbestos cases has failed"). The reasons are obvious: the complexity of asbestos cases makes them expensive to litigate; costs are exacerbated when each individual has to prove his or her claim de novo; high transaction costs reduce the recovery available to successful plaintiffs; and the sheer number of asbestos cases pending nationwide threatens to deny justice and compensation to many deserving claimants if each claim is handled individually. The backlog is eroding a fundamental aspiration of our judicial system to provide equality of treatment for similarly situated persons. *Cf. Asbestos in the Courts: The Challenge of Mass Toxic Torts* (RAND, Inst. of Social Justice 1985), *supra* at 12 (recent wave of asbestos litigation marked by high concentration of claims, dominance of characteristics of individual asbestos cases, behavior of parties, lawyers and the attributes of judges "created a situation in which dispositions are slow, costs are high, and outcomes are variable").

Overhanging this massive failure of the present system is the reality that there is not enough available from traditional defendants to pay for current and future claims. Even the most conservative estimates of future claims, if realistically estimated on the books of many present defendants, would lead to a declaration of insolvency—as in the case of some dozen manufacturers already in bankruptcy. In re Johns–Manville Corporation, No. 90–3973, slip op. at 61–63, 1991 WL 86304 (E.D.N.Y. May 16, 1991).

Given the dimensions of the perceived problem in federal asbestos litigation, it is not surprising that no ready solution has emerged. The Judicial Conference Asbestos Committee concluded that the only true solution lies in Congressional legislation. Nevertheless, it stressed that "at the same time, or failing congressional action, the federal judiciary must itself act now to achieve the best performance possible from system under current law." ASBESTOS COMMITTEE REPORT, *supra* at 4. The Committee also noted that the Panel's order to show cause was pending at the time of the issuance of the Committee's report. The Committee observed that "this committee, by its recommendations, does not intend to affect or restrict in any way the actions of the Panel under 28 U.S.C. § 1407 or reduce the Panel's jurisdiction or authority." *Id.* at 22.[5]

It is against this backdrop that the Panel's decision and role in this litigation must be understood. First of all, our decision to order transfer is not unmindful of the fact that the impact of asbestos litigation varies from district to district, and that in some courts asbestos personal injury actions are being resolved in a fashion indistinguishable from other civil actions. It is not surprising, therefore, that parties and courts involved in such actions might urge that inclusion of their actions in multidistrict proceedings is inappropriate. The Panel, however, must weigh the interests of all the plaintiffs and all the defendants, and must consider multiple litigation as a whole in the light of the purposes of the law. In re Multidistrict Private Civil Treble Damage Litigation Involving Library Editions of Children's Books, 297 F.Supp. 385, 386 (J.P.M.L.1968). It is this perspective that leads us to conclude that centralization in a single district of all pending federal personal injury and wrongful death asbestos actions is necessary.

Much of the argument presented to the Panel in response to its order to show cause is devoted to parties' differing (and often inconsistent) visions of § 1407 proceedings: 1) some plaintiffs see centralized pretrial proceedings as a vehicle leading to a single national class action trial or other types of consolidated trials on product defect, state of the art and punitive damages, while many defendants staunchly oppose such a trial, favor a reverse bifurcation procedure where actual damages and individual causation are tried before liability, and hope to use § 1407 proceedings to effect the severance of claims for punitive damages through a transferee court order directing that, upon the return of any case to its transferor district, such claims not be tried until claims for compensatory damages have been resolved in all federal cases; 2) some parties hope to persuade the transferee court to establish case deferral programs for plaintiffs who are not critically ill, or who have been exposed to asbestos but do not presently show any signs of impairment (i.e., pleural registries), while many plaintiffs assert that such procedures are unfair or unconstitutional; 3) in response to the pressing concern

---

5. The Committee also observed that, in the interest of centralizing asbestos claims to the greatest extent possible, the Panel's authority "could be expanded to allow the Panel to transfer actions for trial as well as for pretrial proceedings." ASBESTOS COMMITTEE REPORT, *supra* at 31.

about transaction costs in this litigation, some defendants consider § 1407 transfer necessary in order to provide a single federal forum in which limits on plaintiffs' contingent fees can be addressed, while some plaintiffs maintain that transfer is necessary to prevent the depletion of defendants' limited insurance coverage by defense costs incurred in multiple districts; 4) some plaintiffs and defendants urge that transfer is necessary in order to develop through discovery proceedings nationwide product data bases on all asbestos products and corporate histories of all asbestos defendants, while other plaintiffs and defendants contend that such efforts would be of no utility and are simply designed to shift liability; 5) some plaintiffs are suggesting that defendants' finances are so fragile as to require limited fund class action determinations pursuant to Fed.R.Civ.P. 23(b)(1)(B), while other plaintiffs resist any attempt to restrict their right to pursue punitive damages; 6) some parties anticipate that a single transferee court would speed up case disposition and purge meritless claims, while others expect a system of spacing out claims so as not to overwhelm currently solvent defendants' cash flow and drive them into bankruptcy; and 7) some parties contend that single transferee court is necessary for the purpose of exploring the opportunities for global settlements or alternative dispute resolution mechanisms, while other parties assert that such hopes are utopian at best as long as i) more than twice as many asbestos cases remain pending in state courts as in federal courts, and ii) currently stayed claims against bankrupt defendants cannot be addressed by the transferee court.[6]

* * *

6. There appears to be some confusion among the parties concerning the interaction of the provisions of the Bankruptcy Code and § 1407. Transfer under § 1407 of an action containing claims against a defendant in bankruptcy has no effect on the automatic stay provisions of the Bankruptcy Code (11 U.S.C. § 362). Claims that have been stayed in the transferor court remain stayed in the transferee court. The Panel, however, has never considered the pendency of such stayed claims in an action to be an impediment to transfer of the action. 28 U.S.C. § 1407(a) authorizes the Panel to transfer only "civil actions" and not claims. The complex multidistrict litigations before the Panel have often included actions brought against multiple defendants, the claims against one or more of which have been stayed as a result of bankruptcy. To have allowed the pendency of claims against a single bankrupt defendant to preclude the transfer of actions containing claims actively being litigated against common nonbankrupt defendants would have frustrated the essential purpose of § 1407.

Some parties have urged the Panel to treat the bankruptcy reorganizations themselves as "civil actions" appropriate for transfer under § 1407 to the transferee district. The reorganization proceedings are not subject to our order to show cause, and this question is therefore not ripe for a Panel decision. We have not addressed this question before and would be reluctant to do so until: 1) the transferee court determines that other alternatives, such as coordination with the concerned bankruptcy courts, are insufficient to accomplish the goals of § 1407; and 2) other suggested means of transferring the bankruptcy reorganizations or relevant portions thereof have been fully explored by the transferee court and the concerned bankruptcy courts.

Finally, we note that to the extent that state court actions and bankruptcy proceedings are excluded from the ambit of the Panel's transfer decision, transfer will nonetheless have the salutary effect of creating one federal court with which such proceedings can be coordinated, to the extent deemed desirable by the concerned courts. Indeed, state court judges have communicated to the Panel that coordination among state courts and a single transferee court for the federal actions is an objective worthy of pursuit.

We cite these issues only as illustrations of 1) the types of pretrial matters that need to be addressed by a single transferee court in order to avoid duplication of effort (with concomitant unnecessary expenses) by the parties and witnesses, their counsel, and the judiciary, and in order to prevent inconsistent decisions; * * * and 2) why, at least initially, all pending federal personal injury or wrongful death asbestos actions not yet in trial must be included in § 1407 proceedings. For example, if, as some courts, parties and commentators have suggested, there are insufficient funds to fairly compensate all deserving claimants, this should be determined before plaintiffs in lightly impacted districts go to trial and secure recoveries (often including punitive damages) at the possible expense of deserving plaintiffs litigating in districts where speedy trial dates have not been available. Similarly, if there are economies to be achieved with respect to remaining national discovery, pretrial rulings or efforts at settlement, these should be secured before claims against distinct types or groups of defendants are separated out of the litigation. Finally, because many of the arguments of parties seeking exclusion from transfer are intertwined with the merits of their claims or defenses and affect the overall management of this litigation, we are unwilling, on the basis of the record presently before us, to carve out exceptions to transfer. We prefer instead to give the transferee court the opportunity to conduct a substantive review of such contentions and how they affect the whole proceedings.

It may well be that on further refinement of the issues and close scrutiny by the transferee court, some claims or actions can be remanded in advance of the other actions in the transferee district. Should the transferee court deem remand of any claims or actions appropriate, the transferee court can communicate this to the Panel, and the Panel will accomplish remand with a minimum of delay. *See* Rule 14, R.P.J.P.M.L., 120 F.R.D. 251, 259–61 (1988). * * * We add that for those parties urging that resolution of this litigation lies primarily in the setting of firm, credible trial dates, § 1407 transfer may serve as a mechanism enabling the transferee court to develop a nationwide roster of senior district and other judges available to follow actions remanded back to heavily impacted districts, for trials in advance of when such districts' overburdened judges may have otherwise been able to schedule them.

We remain sensitive to the concerns of some parties that § 1407 transfer will be burdensome or inconvenient. We note that since § 1407 transfer is primarily for pretrial, there is usually no need for the parties and witnesses to travel to the transferee district for depositions or otherwise. *See, e.g.,* Fed.R.Civ.P. 45(d)(2). Furthermore, the judicious use of liaison counsel, lead counsel and steering committees will eliminate the need for most counsel ever to travel to the transferee district. *See* MANUAL FOR COMPLEX LITIGATION, Second, § 20.22 (1985). * * * And it is most logical to assume that prudent counsel will combine their forces and apportion their workload in order to streamline the efforts of the parties and witnesses, their counsel, and the judiciary, thereby effectuating an overall savings of cost and a reduction of inconvenience to all concerned. *See* In re Nissan Motor Corporation Antitrust Litigation, 385 F.Supp. 1253, 1255 (J.P.M.L.1974). Hopefully, combining such practices with a uniform case management approach will, in fact, lead to sizeable reductions in transaction costs (and especially in attorneys' fees).

In a docket of this size and scope, no district emerges as the clear nexus where centralized pretrial proceedings should be conducted. The Panel has decided to centralize this litigation in the Eastern District of Pennsylvania before Judge Charles R. Weiner. We note that: 1) more asbestos personal injury or wrongful death actions are pending in that district than any other; 2) the court there has extensive experience in complex litigation in general and asbestos litigation in particular; and 3) the court has graciously expressed its willingness to assume the responsibility for this massive undertaking. Furthermore, in the person of Judge Weiner the Panel finds a judge thoroughly familiar with the issues in asbestos litigation, a track record of accomplishment and successful innovation,[10] and, on the basis of the pleadings before the Panel in which an opinion was expressed, a selection to which the majority of responding plaintiffs and defendants either expressly agree or are not opposed.

Many parties have suggested that the dynamics of this litigation make it impractical, if not impossible, for one single judge to discharge the responsibilities of transferee judge, while other parties have emphasized that more than a single transferee judge would dilute the judicial control needed to effectively manage the litigation. Varying suggestions have been made that the Panel appoint additional transferee judges to

---

10. The ASBESTOS COMMITTEE REPORT, *supra,* noted at 15:

Judge Charles Weiner, the asbestos case manager in the Eastern District of Pennsylvania, is able to call upon over 20 active and senior judges in the district to handle asbestos cases on a priority basis. In addition to mandating standard, abbreviated pleadings, such as complaint, answer, and discovery requests, Judge Weiner meets regularly with counsel and handles on a regular basis all motions and discovery requests. Applying these sophisticated case management techniques, Judge Weiner and his colleagues have disposed of more than 2,000 cases through 1990.

Another testament to Judge Weiner's techniques comes from the Panel pleading of certain plaintiffs already before him in the Pennsylvania district:

The Eastern District of Pennsylvania may be unique in another respect, and that again is due to the involvement of the Court. Perhaps no other jurisdiction has had the mutual cooperation of liaison counsel who have been instrumental, to-

gether with the Court in attempting to resolve the asbestos problem. The adversary system remains, but the Court has eliminated the usual posturing of the litigants and has encouraged them to come up with programs and solutions. The classic example is the unique program established by counsel with the Court of binding arbitration through stipulated percentage of defendants' liability. The arbitrators are experts in asbestos litigation, and the medical issues are tried by submission on report. The average disposition rate is four cases in one day without judicial time.

Our reference to these passages is not meant to be an endorsement of any pretrial techniques to the exclusion of others, and in no way should be viewed as limiting Judge Weiner in his assessment of the appropriate tools to be used now that all federal personal injury/wrongful death asbestos actions will be before him for pretrial proceedings. We do consider such passages to be helpful, however, in allaying the fears of parties not familiar with Judge Weiner that § 1407 transfer will result in their actions entering some black hole, never to be seen again.

handle specific issues (e.g., class or limited fund determinations, discovery, settlement, claims administration, etc.), to deal with separate types of claims or defendants (e.g., maritime asbestos actions, railroad worker actions, friction materials actions, tire workers actions, etc.), or to divide the litigation along regional or circuit lines (helping to insure uniformity of decisions within each circuit pertaining, inter alia, to state law questions involved in the actions). Each of these suggestions has merit, as long as one judge has the opportunity to maintain overall control.

Section 1407(b) contemplates that multidistrict litigation may be conducted by "a judge or judges." It further expressly provides that "upon request of the panel, a circuit judge or a district judge may be designated and assigned temporarily for service in the transferee district by the Chief Justice of the United States of the United States or the chief judge of the circuit, as may be required, in accordance with the provisions of chapter 13 of this title." And the Panel has long expressed its willingness to appoint additional transferee judges in litigants whose size and complexity make it difficulty for the original transferee judge to handle § 1407 proceedings alone. *See In re Multidistrict Civil Antitrust Actions Involving Antibiotic Drugs*, 320 F.Supp. 586, 588 (J.P.M.L.1970). We emphasize our intention to do everything without our power to provide such assistance in this docket. Before making any specific appointments, however, we deem it advisable to allow the transferee judge to make his own assessment of the needs of this docket and communicate his preferences to us.

The Panel is under no illusion that centralization will, of itself, markedly relieve the critical asbestos situation. It offers no panacea. Only through the combined and determined efforts of the transferee judge and his judicial colleagues, of the many attorneys involved in asbestos matters, and of the parties, can true progress be made toward solving the "asbestos mess." This order does offer a great opportunity to all participants who sincerely wish to resolve these asbestos matters fairly and with as little unnecessary expense as possible.

* * *

THOMAS D. ROWE, JR. AND KENNETH D. SIBLEY, BEYOND DIVERSITY: FEDERAL MULTIPARTY, MULTIFORUM JURISDICTION

135 U.Pa.L.Rev. 7 (1986) at 9.

* * * The problem is the unavailability of any single forum in which to consolidate scattered, related litigation—a difficulty that is becoming more and more common given the increasing number of complex tort actions, such as those growing out of mass accidents and product liability claims. As a result of the statutory limitations on the authority of the federal courts and the constitutional bounds imposed on state systems by *World-Wide Volkswagen*, related proceedings arising out of the same events are often conducted as a multi-ring circus in two or more forums.

It is possible to provide a single forum much more frequently than is now done. Often, however, such consolidation cannot take place in the courts of any one state because of the due process holding against state court jurisdiction in *World-Wide Volkswagen*. In the wake of that case, use of the article III authority for federal diversity of citizenship jurisdiction must be a major part of any effective, comprehensive solution.

* * *

The problem of scattered, related actions is a multifaceted one, upon which many types of procedural devices and developments have a bearing. The most common responses to the problem have been actual or proposed changes in jurisdiction and joinder. Choice of law, federal venue transfer and consolidation provisions, and former adjudication principles have also come into play. In this century, perceptions of the problem and prescriptions for its solution have varied as our procedural systems and litigation patterns have evolved.

* * *

Resolving problems in complex litigation, however, can be like severing heads of the Hydra: at least two more may grow when one is lopped off. In the 1960's two main responses to such problems were Congress's adoption in 1968 of section 1407 of the Judicial Code and the ALI's never-enacted proposal of a dispersed necessary parties jurisdiction for the federal courts. Both, however, attempted to deal only with discrete parts of the scattered-litigation problem. Section 1407 took federal court jurisdiction as it found it and provided only for consolidated pretrial proceedings; it made no provision for consolidated trials without the consent of the parties. The ALI proposal focused solely on necessary parties not joinable in the courts of a single state. The proposal was criticized as a cumbersome device responding to a theoretical problem encountered infrequently, if at all, in reality. To the extent the problem was genuine, moreover, it existed largely because of limitations on state court service of process; the general spread of state long-arm provisions has at least considerably reduced that difficulty. The present lack of a single forum available to join all necessary parties causes probably no more than a small fraction of the difficulties engendered by the availability and use of several forums for related litigation.

* * *

Our discussion thus far has focused on scattered litigation problems arising in state law or diversity cases. But just as an ordinary federal question case today may happen also to satisfy the requirements for diversity jurisdiction, dispersed federal question actions could similarly meet the criteria for the new federal jurisdiction. If and only if such a case did so, it could qualify for the new jurisdiction and make use of its provisions without regard to the source or sources of law upon which the claims in the case rested. If the new jurisdiction were defined with a careful eye to the purpose of a federal action-consolidating device—making it possible to gather scattered, related litigation—the substantive law involved should be irrelevant to the availability of the federal forum. If a federal question case did not satisfy the criteria, it would not have enough need for the new jurisdiction; if it did meet the jurisdictional standards, it could use the mechanisms afforded by the jurisdiction regardless of its federal question nature.

A precedent for such an approach to federal question matters is the current section 1407 of the Judicial Code, which authorized transfer for pretrial proceedings in civil actions involving common questions of fact pending in different federal districts. Such transfers are available without regard to the source of the right claimed and are used in diversity and federal question matters alike. To a considerable extent, existing section 1407, especially if used in combination with authority under section 1404 to transfer some cases for trial, handles for federal question cases the problems to which our proposal responds. It cannot do so entirely, however, at least for federal question cases over which state courts have concurrent jurisdiction. Even if section 1407 were expanded to allow for trial as well as pretrial proceedings, as long as it remains the rule that all defendants must join in a removal petition under section 1441 some defendants may find themselves stuck in state courts even though they face scattered federal question claims and wish to remove. The primary need for a multiparty, multiforum jurisdiction, of course, exists in state law matters, which can sometimes be brought only in state courts or—given the present structure of the general diversity jurisdiction—must be split between state and federal courts.

* * *

Those who favor retaining the present general diversity jurisdiction sometimes contend that it plays the sort of role we propose for a federal multiparty, multiforum jurisdiction, by making possible at least consolidated pretrial proceedings via the use of section 1407 when diversity cases are initially dispersed among federal courts. The argument is that the valuable function of permitting consolidation of related state law cases scattered among federal courts in litigation over such matters as airline crashes, now performed by the diversity jurisdiction, would be lost if it were abolished. The point is technically correct as far as it goes, but it could fairly count against abolition only if diversity were not replaced with a jurisdiction that would itself permit the same or greater consolidation. The argument also ignores the extent to which present diversity jurisdiction fails to serve its ostensible purposes and, in fact, is part of the scattered litigation problem.

* * *

Notes and Questions

1. Recall *In re Allied–Signal Inc.*, (discussed *supra* at pages 2–3, 224–225) that the Sixth Circuit in August 1990 repudiated the efforts of a group of federal district court judges to certify a nationwide asbestos class action on the grounds that such certification constituted impermissible legislative action on the part of Article III judges. Yet only six months later, another

group of judges comprising the Panel on Multidistrict Litigation granted MDL status to all asbestos cases nationwide, to be transferred and consolidated in the Eastern District of Pennsylvania. Why were the judges in *Allied Signal* acting any less pursuant to their authority than the MDL judges in *In re Asbestos Litigation*? In their decision to consolidate asbestos cases under the MDL statute, Judge Nangle notes that all five previous attempts to seek MDL status in asbestos litigation had been rejected by previous MDL panels. Is this MDL panel convincing in its explanation for its reversal? To what extent was this decision motivated by other than legal considerations?

2. To what extent does the 1991 MDL decision to consolidate the nationwide asbestos cases signal a receptivity of the MDL panel to use the MDL procedure to resolve other mass tort cases? How successful has the asbestos MDL been in resolving the asbestos litigation crisis? For post-MDL asbestos developments, *see* Andrew Blum, *Asbestos Confusion Continues,* Nat'l L.J., March 9, 1992 at 1; Alex Dominguez, *Nation's Largest Asbestos Trial Opens,* Chi. Daily Bull., March 10, 1992 at 1; Gordon Hunter, *Asbestos Deal Brewing in Tyler, Texas,* Tex. Lawyer, March 29, 1993 at 1 (the *Ahearn* settlement class); Lori J. Khan, *Untangling the Insurance Fibers in Asbestos Litigation: Toward a National Solution to the Asbestos Injury Crisis,* 68 Tul. L.Rev. 195 (1993); Michael J. Levy & Marguerite L. Brown, *Asbestos Coverage Wars Continue: Report From the Front,* 59 Def.Couns.J. 574 (1992); Peter H. Schuck, *The Worst Should Go First: Deferral Registries in Asbestos Litigation,* 75 Judicature 318 (1992); Richard A. Solomon, Comment, *Clearing the Air: Resolving the Asbestos Personal Injury Crisis,* 2 Fordham Envt'l.L.Rep. 125 (1991).

3. Prior to the Panel's approval of MDL consolidation for asbestos cases, MDL procedure had been and continues to be the most frequently used consolidation mechanism in airplane crash disaster cases. *See, e.g.,* In re Air Crash Disaster at Sioux City, Iowa, on July 19, 1989, 128 F.R.D. 131 (J.P.M.L.1989); In re Air Disaster at Lockerbie, Scotland, on December 21, 1988 709 F.Supp. 231 (J.P.M.L.1989); In re Air Crash Disaster at Stapleton Int'l Airport, Denver, Colorado on November 15, 1987, 683 F.Supp. 266 (J.P.M.L.1988); In re Air Crash Disaster at Detroit Metropolitan Airport on August 16, 1987, 674 F.Supp. 27 (J.P.M.L.1987); In re Air Crash Disaster at Gander, Newfoundland, on December 12, 1985, 633 F.Supp. 50 (J.P.M.L. 1986); and In re Air Crash at Dallas/Fort Worth Airport on August 2, 1985, 623 F.Supp. 634 (J.P.M.L.1985); and similar single-site railroad crashes, *see* In re Rail Collision Near Chase, Maryland on January 4, 1987, 661 F.Supp. 69 (J.P.M.L.1987). *See generally* Kyle Brackin, Comment, *Salvaging the Wreckage: Multidistrict Litigation and Aviation,* 57 J. Air L. & Com. 655 (1992); George E. Farrell, *Multidistrict Litigation in Aviation Accident Cases,* 38 J. Air L. & Com. 159 (1972); John H. Lowrie, Note, *Air Crash Litigation and 28 U.S.C.A. § 1407: Experience Suggests a Solution,* 1981 U.Ill.L.Rev. 927 (1981).

Although MDL status has been granted in some mass tort cases, *see, e.g.,* In re Silicone Gel Breast Implants Prods. Liability Litigation, 793 F.Supp. 1098 (J.P.M.L.1992); In re San Juan Dupont Plaza Hotel Fire Litigation, 789 F.Supp. 1212 (D.C. Puerto Rico 1992); In re Union Carbide Corp. Gas Plant Disaster at Bhopal, India in December, 1984, 601 F.Supp.

1035 (J.P.M.L.1985), *dismissed with conditions*, 634 F.Supp. 842 (D.C.N.Y.)(*see also supra* for Second Circuit *forum non conveniens* decision); MDL consolidation has been denied in others, *see, e.g.*, In re Repetitive Stress Injury Products Liability Litigation, 1992 WL 403023 (J.P.M.L.1992)(reporting on denial of MDL status to this litigation by the JMDL Panel).

A third litigation category where MDL status has been found appropriate involves securities litigation. *See e.g.*, In re Integrated Resources Real Estate Ltd. Partnerships Secs. Litigation, 815 F.Supp. 620 (S.D.N.Y.1993); In re Computervision Corp. Secs. Litigation, 814 F.Supp. 85 (J.P.M.L.1993); In re Alert Income Partners Sec. Litigation, 788 F.Supp. 1230 (J.P.M.L. 1992); In re American Continental Corp./Lincoln Sav. & Loan Secs. Litigation, 130 F.R.D. 475 (J.P.M.L.1990); In re General Motors Class E Stock Buyout Secs. Litigation, 696 F.Supp. 1546 (J.P.M.L.1988).

Why is MDL procedure suitable for transferring and consolidating some types of litigation, but not others? How do the standards of § 1407 differ from the standards for aggregation cases or claims under Rules 23 or 42?

4. In order to improve and expand multidistrict litigation procedure, the American Law Institute in its COMPLEX LITIGATION PROJECT recommended a series of proposals to build upon current multidistrict litigation experience under § 1407. The standard for the new multidistrict procedure is set forth in § 3.01:

§ 3.01. Standard For Consolidation

(a) Actions commenced in two or more United States District Courts may be transferred and consolidated if:

(1) they involve one or more common questions of fact, and,

(2) transfer and consolidation will promote the just, efficient, and fair conduct of actions.

(b) Factors to be considered in deciding whether the standard set forth in subsection (a) is met include

(1) the extent to which transfer and consolidation will reduce duplicative litigation, the relative costs of individual and consolidated litigation, the likelihood of inconsistent adjudications, and the comparative burdens on the judiciary, and

(2) whether transfer and consolidation can be accomplished in a way that is fair to the parties and does not result in undue inconvenience to them and the witnesses. In considering those factors, account may be taken of matter such as

a. the number of parties and actions involved;

b. the geographic dispersion of the actions;

c. the existence and significance of local concerns;

d. the subject matter of the dispute;

e. the amount in controversy;

    f. the significance and number of common issues involved; including whether multiple laws will have to be applied to those issues;

    g. the likelihood of additional related actions being commenced in the future;

    h. the wishes of the parties;

    i. the stages to which the actions already have progressed.

    (c) When the United States is exempted by Act of Congress from participating in consolidated proceedings in actions under the antitrust or securities laws, it shall have the right to be exempted from transfer and consolidation under this section.

    (d) Transfer and consolidation need not be denied simply because one or more of the issues are not common so that consolidated treatment of all parts of the dispersed actions cannot be achieved. The interests of particular individual litigants can be considered when determining whether they have shown cause to be excluded from the consolidated proceeding, as provided in § 3.05.

See American Law Institute, COMPLEX LITIGATION: STATUTORY RECOMMENDATIONS AND ANALYSIS § 3.01 (1994). How does this proposal compare with § 1407? The recommendations also include elaborate provisions relating to a new Complex Litigation Panel (§ 3.02); timing of transfer and consolidation of cases (§ 3.03); standards for determining where to transfer MDL cases (§ 3.04); procedures to be followed by the new Complex Litigation Panel (§ 3.05); powers of the transferee court (§ 3.06); review of MDL decisions (§ 3.07); and personal jurisdiction in the transferee court (§ 3.08). For various discusses and criticisms of the COMPLEX LITIGATION recommendations, *see Symposium, American Law Institute Complex Litigation Project,* 54 La.L.Rev. 835 (1994).

    5. Congress also has attempted, several times, to modify § 1407 to accommodate the particular problems relating to aggregate litigation, but this legislation has yet to pass both houses. It is interesting to compare this proposed legislation with the American Law Institute's more elaborate proposals. *See* Court Reform and Access to Justice Act of 1988, H.R. 3152, 100th Cong., 1st Sess. (1987); Multiparty, Multiforum Jurisdiction Act of 1989, H.R. 3406, 101st. Cong., 1st Sess. (1989); Multiparty, Multiforum Jurisdiction Act of 1990, H.R. 3406, 101st Cong., 2d Sess. (1990); Multiparty, Multiforum Jurisdiction Act of 1991, H.R. 2450, 102nd Cong., 1st Sess. (1991); Multiparty, Multiforum Jurisdiction Act of 1993, H.R. 1100, 103rd Cong., 1st Sess. (1993). *See generally* Charles G. Geyh, *Complex Litigation Reform and the Legislative Process,* 10 Rev.Litig. 410 (1991); Robert W. Kastenmeier and Charles G. Geyh, *The Case in Support of Legislation Facilitating the Consolidation of Mass–Accident Litigation: A View From the Legislature,* 73 Marq.L.Rev. 535 (1990).

    6. During the 1980s and 1990s, particularly with the rise of mass tort litigation as a distinct federal court litigation phenomenon, the possible uses of multidistrict litigation procedure under 28 U.S.C.A. § 1407 generated a sizeable body of critical commentary, as well as recommendations for amendment of this statute. To what extent do Professor Rowe and Mr. Sibley

believe that § 1407 can provide a sensible basis for federal court aggregation of mass tort cases?   The commentary on § 1407 and Professor Rowe's and Sibley's recommendations figured largely in reform proposals generated by the American Bar Association, the American Law Institute, and Congress. *See generally,* Arthur R. Miller & Price Ainsworth, *Resolving the Asbestos Personal–Injury Litigation Crisis,* 10 Rev.Litig. 419 (1991); Linda S. Mullenix, *Beyond Consolidation: Post-Aggregative Procedure in Asbestos Mass Tort Litigation,* 32 Wm. & Mary L.Rev. 475 (1991); Diana E. Murphy, *Unified and Consolidated Complaints in Multidistrict Litigation,* 132 F.R.D. 597 (1990); Blake M. Rhodes, Comment, *The Judicial Panel on Multidistrict Litigation in State and Federal Courts,* 78 Va.L.Rev. 1689 (1992); Roger Trangsrud, *Joinder Alternatives in Mass Tort Litigation,* 70 Cornell L.Rev. 779 (1985); William Schwarzer, Alan Hirsch & Edward Sussman, *Judicial Federalism: A Proposal to Amend the Multidistrict Litigation Statute to Permit Discovery Coordination of Large–Scale Litigation Pending in State and Federal Courts,* 73 Tex.L.Rev. 1529 (1995); William W. Schwarzer, *et al., Judicial Federalism in Action: Coordination of Litigation in State and Federal Courts,* 78 Va.L.Rev. 1689 (1992).   *See also* Thomas D. Rowe, *Jurisdictional and Transfer Proposals for Complex Litigation,* 10 Rev.Litig. 325 (1991); Standing Committee on Federal Judicial Improvements, American Bar Association, *Report to the House of Delegates on H.R. 3406* (Multiparty, Multiforum Jurisdiction Act of 1990).

7.   The Federal Courts Study Committee, in its *Report,* recommended that "Congress should amend the multi-district litigation statute to permit consolidated trials as well as pretrial proceedings and should create a special federal diversity jurisdiction, based on the minimal diversity authority conferred by Article III, to make possible the consolidation of major multi-party, multi-forum litigation." *See Report of the Federal Courts Study Committee* at 44 (April 2, 1990).   The Committee also recommended that the MANUAL FOR COMPLEX LITIGATION should be revised to include guidelines for consolidation and severance of cases.

8.   Once the Judicial Panel on Multidistrict Litigation approves MDL status for a set of independent cases, what happens?   How is the MDL case handled?   What limitations are imposed by § 1407?   What are the powers of the transferee court under 28 U.S.C.A. § 1407?   The statute says that actions pending in different district may be transferred to the designated MDL forum for the purpose of "coordinated or consolidated pretrial proceedings."   What authority is encompassed by this language?   Professors Wright, Miller, and Cooper indicate that MDL courts, under § 1407 authority, have ruled on an array of preliminary legal and factual questions, including motions to amend under Rule 15, motions to dismiss for lack of jurisdiction, venue, failure to state a claim, and motions for summary judgment.   Obviously, MDL courts also have jurisdiction to supervise all discovery-related activity.   For collected cases, *see* 15 Wright, Miller and Cooper, FEDERAL PRACTICE AND PROCEDURE § 3866 (2d ed. 1986 and Supp.).   *See also* Stanley A. Weigel, *The Judicial Panel on Multidistrict Litigation, Transferor Courts and Transferee Courts,* 78 F.R.D. 575 (1978).

9.   What law applies in an aggregated MDL case?   Most federal courts conducting MDL proceedings have agreed that the MDL transferee court must follow the *Van Dusen/Ferens* rules, requiring application of state

substantive law; *see, e.g.,* Menowitz v. Brown, 991 F.2d 36 (2d Cir.1993); In re Lou Levy & Sons Fashions, Inc., 988 F.2d 311 (2d Cir.1993). However, MDL courts have rejected these rules where the transferee court must determine an issue of applicable federal law. *See e.g.,* In re Pan American Corp., 950 F.2d 839 (2d Cir.1991); In re Litigation Involving Alleged Loss of Cargo, 772 F.Supp. 707 (D. Puerto Rico 1991); *cf.* In Re Integrated Resources Real Estate Ltd. Partnerships Secs. Litigation, 815 F.Supp. 620 (D.N.Y.1993). *See generally* Joan Steinman, *Law of the Case: A Judicial Puzzle in Consolidated and Transferred Cases and in Multidistrict Litigation,* 135 U.Pa.L.Rev. 595 (1987).

10. The American Law Institute has proposed federalizing choice-of-law principles for state-created actions consolidated pursuant to its proposed multidistrict litigation statute. *See* American Law Institute, COMPLEX LITIGATION: STATUTORY RECOMMENDATIONS AND ANALYSIS at §§ 6.01–6.08 (1994). For critical commentary on these proposals *see generally, Symposium, American Law Institute Complex Litigation Project,* 54 La.L.Rev. 835 (1994). Each of Congress's proposed Multiparty, Multiforum Jurisdiction Acts also have included proposals for federalizing choice-of-law criteria for multidistrict consolidated litigation. *See* proposed statutes, *supra* Note 4, and Chapter X.B., *infra.*

C. CONSOLIDATION AND MASS TORTS

1. CONSOLIDATION AS A CLASS ACTION SUBSTITUTE

CIMINO v. RAYMARK INDUSTRIES, INC.

[Review Judge Parker's class certification and consolidation order, *supra.*]

IN RE REPETITIVE STRESS INJURY LITIGATION

United States Court of Appeals, Second Circuit, 1993.
11 F.3d 368.

Before: MESKILL, WINTER and PRATT, CIRCUIT JUDGES.

WINTER, CIRCUIT JUDGE:

Defendants-appellants International Business Machines Corporation ("IBM") and Wang Laboratories, Inc. ("Wang") appeal from Judge Weinstein's order ("Weinstein Order"), In re Repetitive Stress Injury Cases, 142 F.R.D. 584 (E.D.N.Y.1992), granting the plaintiffs-appellees' motion to consolidate the forty-four cases in the Eastern District of New York that assert a claim for damages for "repetitive stress injuries." Defendants-appellants the NEC companies ("NEC"), Xerox Corporation ("Xerox"), Sony Corporation of America ("Sony"), Stenograph Corporation, Quixote Corporation, and Data General Corporation and defendant-intervenor Compaq Computer Corporation appeal from Judge Hurley's subsequent order ("Hurley Order"), In re Repetitive Stress Injury Litig., No. 91–CV–2079 (E.D.N.Y. Aug. 10, 1992), that extended the Weinstein

Order to include all actions filed thereafter in the Eastern District claiming "repetitive stress injuries." Defendant-intervenor Zenith Data Systems, Incorporated appeals from both the Weinstein Order and the Hurley Order.

Plaintiffs-appellees move to dismiss these appeals for lack of jurisdiction. We grant the motion and dismiss the appeals. However, we treat the attempted appeals as petitions for writs of mandamus and grant the petitions. We vacate the consolidation orders and remand to the district court for further proceedings consistent with this decision.

BACKGROUND

Plaintiffs are individuals who have brought actions alleging injuries resulting from "repetitive stress" encountered in the use of equipment manufactured or distributed by various defendants. These so-called "repetitive stress injuries" ("RSI") include "carpal tunnel" syndrome, a malady of the hands and wrists, and a diverse array of other ailments including de Quervain's disease, Raynaud's Syndrome, synovitis, stenosing tenosynovitis crepitans, tendinitis, tenosynovitis, and epicondylitis, commonly known as "tennis elbow." Some plaintiffs also allege that they suffer from rotator cuff tears, lumbosacral sprain, degenerative disc disease, cervical sprain, muscle spasms, "trigger finger," neck pain, and back pain. The claimed afflictions do not have a single cause and, defendants argue, may result, inter alia, from hereditary factors, vascular disorders, obesity, metabolic disorders, high blood cholesterol levels, connective tissue disorders, primary pulmonary hypertension, and prior trauma.

Defendants are companies that manufacture, and in some cases distribute, various types of equipment, including keyboards, keypunches, alphanumeric machines, video display terminals, cash registers, supermarket workstations, stenographic machines, and computer "mouse" devices. Each plaintiff alleges that a device of this sort caused his or her injury.

On May 12, 1992, plaintiffs applied to Judge Weinstein, sitting as Miscellaneous Part Judge, for an Order to Show Cause why their forty-four separate actions pending before seven judges of the Eastern District should not be consolidated. On June 2, 1992, Judge Weinstein consolidated the forty-four pending "RSI" cases before Judge Hurley as the judge with the earliest-filed RSI case on his docket, pursuant to the usual practice of the district court. In re Repetitive Stress Injury Cases, 142 F.R.D. 584 (E.D.N.Y.1992). Although Judge Weinstein's opinion seemed at times to recognize that the factual or legal issues of the various cases were not identical and might subsequently lead to the subdividing of proceedings by classes of issues, he ordered full consolidation with the result that, as matters presently stand, all counsel must attend all discovery and all court proceedings.

On July 14, 1992, Judge Hurley established preliminary discovery procedures and solicited from the parties their suggestions for composing relevant "subgroups" for purposes of discovery, as suggested by Judge

Weinstein. In re Repetitive Stress Injury Litig., No. 91–CV–2079, slip op. at 4 (E.D.N.Y. July 14, 1992). On August 10, 1992, Judge Hurley issued an order extending the Weinstein Order to all subsequent RSI actions. The Hurley Order gave leave to the defendants in the newly consolidated actions to file letter motions with the court seeking severance, but threatened movants who made "frivolous or ill-conceived" applications with Rule 11 sanctions.

Appellants appealed from the consolidation orders. Soon after both sets of appellants filed appeals, appellees moved to dismiss the appeals for lack of jurisdiction because the interlocutory appeals had not been certified by the district court under 28 U.S.C. § 1292(b). Other panels referred the motions to us, the panel hearing the appeal.

Pursuant to 28 U.S.C. § 1407, appellees have also moved before the Judicial Panel on Multidistrict Litigation ("MDL") for an order consolidating all RSI cases pending nationwide in the Eastern District of New York. The MDL Panel denied appellees' motion because it was not persuaded that "the degree of common questions of fact among these actions rises to the level that transfer under Section 1407 would best serve the overall convenience of the parties and witnesses and promote the just and efficient conduct of this entire litigation." In re Repetitive Stress Injury Products Liability Litig., 61 U.S.L.W. 2376, 2376, 1992 WL 403023 (J.P.M.L.1992).

Discussion

[The court first held that an order for consolidation was not appealable as a final order under 28 U.S.C. § 1291, nor as a "collateral order" under the *Cohen* doctrine.—*ed.*]

* * *

We may, however, treat an attempted appeal as a petition for leave to file a writ of mandamus. In re Hooker Investments, Inc., 937 F.2d 833, 837 (2d Cir.1991); Richardson Greenshields Securities, Inc. v. Lau, 825 F.2d 647, 652 (2d Cir.1987). The granting of a writ of mandamus is an extraordinary measure and should be done sparingly, to redress a "clear abuse of discretion," *Richardson Greenshields,* 825 F.2d at 652, or "to confine an inferior court to a lawful exercise of its prescribed authority...." Moses H. Cone Memorial Hospital v. Mercury Constr. Corp., 460 U.S. 1, 18, 103 S.Ct. 927, 938, 74 L.Ed.2d 765 (1983). *See also* Chase Manhattan Bank, N.A. v. Turner & Newall, PLC, 964 F.2d 159, 163 (2d Cir.1992)(overturning a discovery order violating attorney-client privilege); In re von Bulow, 828 F.2d 94 (2d Cir.1987)(same).

A party moving for consolidation must bear the burden of showing the commonality of factual and legal issues in different actions, MacAlister v. Guterma, 263 F.2d 65, 70 (2d Cir.1958), and a district court must examine "the special underlying facts" with "close attention" before ordering a consolidation. Katz v. Realty Equities Corp., 521 F.2d 1354, 1361 (2d Cir.1975). The allegations of the complaints afford no support to the district courts' conclusion that these cases are sufficiently related to warrant consolidation. Indeed, the district court substituted a discussion of so-called mass torts for precise findings as to what are the "common question[s] of law or fact" justifying consolidation pursuant to Fed.R.Civ.P. 42.

We believe that consolidation here was a sufficiently clear abuse of discretion to warrant mandamus relief. At this stage of the litigation, the sole common fact among these cases is a claim of injury of such generality that it covers a number of different ailments for each of which there are numerous possible causes other than the tortious conduct of one of the defendants. As a class, the plaintiffs presumably have the usual wide variety of individual health conditions and problems that are found in any similar sample of persons and that might be relevant to the claimed injuries. The defendants manufacture or distribute a variety of mechanical devices with differing propensities, if any, to cause the harm alleged. With regard to issues of law, the plaintiffs come from a variety of jurisdictions and rely for their claims on the laws of different states. An order that merges all discovery and court proceedings and requires the participation of all counsel simply has no basis in Rule 42.

Although consolidation may enhance judicial efficiency, "[c]onsiderations of convenience and economy must yield to a paramount concern for a fair and impartial trial." Johnson v. Celotex Corp., 899 F.2d 1281, 1285 (2d Cir.), *cert. denied*, 498 U.S. 920, 111 S.Ct. 297, 112 L.Ed.2d 250 (1990). As we have recently cautioned, "The systemic urge to aggregate litigation must not be allowed to trump our dedication to individual justice, and we must take care that each individual plaintiff's—and defendant's—cause not be lost in the shadow of a towering mass litigation." In re Brooklyn Navy Yard Asbestos Litig., 971 F.2d 831, 853 (2d Cir.1992).

In Johnson, we enumerated the factors to consider in ordering consolidation in the context of analogous claims involving asbestos. They are, in relevant part: " '(1) common worksite; (2) similar occupation; (3) similar time of exposure; (4) type of disease ...; (6) status of discovery in each case; (7) whether all plaintiffs were represented by the same counsel....' " *Johnson,* 899 F.2d at 1285, quoting In re All Asbestos Cases Pending in the United States District Court for the District of Maryland, (D.Md. Dec. 16, 1983)(*en banc*)(unreported). Although the majority of the plaintiffs are represented by the same counsel and discovery had not yet begun in any of the cases, the other factors strongly militate against consolidation. The plaintiffs are employed at different worksites and in different occupations, ranging from word processor, to key puncher, to stenographer. They report different conditions relating to the alleged ailments and disparate ailments themselves. Moreover, each of the ailments alleged may have a cause other than the tortious conduct of an individual defendant much less all the defendants. Finally, factors 1–4 are far more important than identity of counsel and progress of discovery. *Johnson* factors 1–4 go to the central issue of commonality, while factors 6–7 go solely to convenience, and here the convenience of only one side. As we recently stated, "it is possible to go too far in the interests of expediency and to sacrifice basic fairness in the process." Malcolm v. National Gypsum Co., 995 F.2d 346, 353 (2d Cir.1993).

When entering the consolidation orders, the district court contemplated the subdividing of discovery or other proceedings and even the severance of some cases as the litigation proceeds. Because the question of whether there are common issues of law or fact in these cases is open, there is no doubt some discovery that is applicable to a group of, or all, cases. The district judges' approach, however, reverses the proper process. The burden is on the party seeking aggregation to show common issues of law or fact; the burden is not on the party opposing aggregation to show divergences. *MacAlister*, 263 F.2d at 70. This is so even in the case of the so-called mass tort, where a shifting of this burden is likely to render the label mass tort into a self-fulfilling prophecy.

We emphasize, however, that we see nothing wrong with assigning all RSI cases in a district to a single district judge who may order that particular proceedings or certain discovery requests relate to defined groups of RSI cases or, when appropriate, all the RSI cases in the district. Our differences with the district court are more than philosophical. The burden is on the party seeking aggregation of discovery or other proceedings to show common factual or legal issues warranting it. A party may not use aggregation as a method of increasing the costs of its adversaries—whether plaintiffs or defendants—by forcing them to participate in discovery or other proceedings that are irrelevant to their case. It may be that such increased costs would make settlement easier to achieve, but that would occur only at the cost of elemental fairness.

CONCLUSION

We dismiss the appeals. We treat the attempted appeals as petitions for writs of mandamus. We grant the petitions and vacate the consolidation orders.

Notes and Questions

1. The general purpose of Rule 42 is to allow federal courts some control over how similar cases spread across the federal docket may be tried in an economical and efficient manner, consistent with justice for the parties. Thus, Rule 42(a) permits multiple cases (or issues within those cases) filed in a judicial district to be consolidated for a single trial. Rule 42(b), on the other hand, allows a court to order the separate trial of issues within a single case. To what extent, then, does Rule 42(b) undermine the general purposes of 42(a)? What purposes are served by Rule 42(b), and how does it also serve the interests of judicial efficiency and economy?

2. In *Cimino v. Raymark*, Judge Parker reformulated the class action as a Rule 42 consolidated (after the Fifth Circuit's mandamus of the trial plan). What is the relationship of Rule 42 consolidation to the class action rule? Can a federal judge simply re-label a failed consolidation as a class action? Can a federal judge reconstitute a failed class action as a consolidat-

ed case? What is the consequence of the Second Circuit's rejection of a consolidated action in the repetitive stress injury litigation?

3. Rule 42 consolidation often is used in tandem with an MDL transfer pursuant to 28 U.S.C.A. § 1407. For a discussion of the relationship of these transfer-and-consolidation rules, *see generally,* Gregory R. Harris, Note, *Consolidation and Transfer in the Federal Courts: 28 U.S.C. Section 1407 Viewed in Light of Rule 42(a) and 28 U.S.C. Section 1404(a),* 22 Hastings L.Rev. 1289 (1971). *See also* Joan Steinman, *The Effects of Case Consolidation and the Procedural Rights of Litigants: What They Are, What They Might Be, Part I, Justiciability and Jurisdiction,* 42 U.C.L.A. L. Rev. 717 (1995).

4. For general discussion of the utility of consolidations in mass tort litigation, *see generally,* Richard A. Epstein, *The Consolidation of Complex Litigation: A Critical Evaluation of the ALI Proposal,* 10 J.L. & Com. 1 (1990); Theodore Goldberg & Tybe A. Brett, *Consolidation of Individual Plaintiff Personal–Injury Toxic Tort Actions,* 11 J.L. & Com. 59 (1991); Thomas W. Henderson & Ernest R. Higginbotham, *Class Actions and Consolidations in Mass Tort Cases, in* 1 American Bar Ass'n, Managing Modern Litigation: Learning to Live with New Judicial Controls and New Trial Tools (1991); Robert W. Kastenmeier & Charles G. Geyh, *The Case in Support of Legislation Facilitating the Consolidation of Mass–Accident Litigation: A View From the Legislature,* 73 Marq.L.Rev. 535 (1990).

5. Are the repetitive stress injury cases a "nascent" mass tort? What will it take to turn the RSI cases into a "mature" mass tort? Soon after Judge Winter's decision, an individual plaintiff tried the first RSI injury case against IBM Corporation in a jury trial in Minneapolis, Minnesota during spring 1995. The plaintiff lost. Does this jury verdict vindicate Judge Winter's decision not to consolidate the RSI cases? Does it support Judge Posner's rationale for not certifying the hemophiliac tainted-blood products cases in *Rhone-Poulenc Rorer, supra?* On the RSI litigation, *see generally* Barnaby J. Feder, *As Hand Injuries Mount, So Do The Lawsuits,* N.Y. Times, June 8, 1992 at D1. What do the RSI cases tell us about the development of mass tort litigation? *Cf.* Edmund J. Ferdinand III, Comment, *Asbestos Revisited: Lead–Based Paint Toxic Tort Litigation in the 1990s,* 5 Tul. Envtl. L.J. 581 (1992).

2. SPECIAL PROBLEMS WITH CONSOLIDATED MASS TORTS

MALCOLM v. NATIONAL GYPSUM CO.

United States Court of Appeals, Second Circuit, 1993.
995 F.2d 346.

Before: Timbers, Walker, and McLaughlin, Circuit Judges.

McLaughlin, Circuit Judge:

Keene Corporation appeals from a final judgment of the United States District Courts for the Eastern and Southern Districts of New York (Charles P. Sifton, Judge) awarding plaintiff Roberta Kranz, as the executrix of the estate of Lee Lewis, $226,038.49 for personal injury, wrongful death, and loss of consortium. In re Joint E. & S. Dists. Asbestos Litig., 798 F.Supp. 925 & 798 F.Supp. 940 (E. & S.D.N.Y.1992). The claims arose from Lewis's exposure to asbestos products manufactured by Keene's subsidiary, the Baldwin–Ehret–Hill Company ("BEH"). For the reasons stated below, we reverse and remand for a new trial.

BACKGROUND

The Explosion of Asbestos Litigation

One of the greatest challenges facing both state and federal courts is the crush of tort suits arising from the extensive use of asbestos as flame-retardant insulation throughout much of this century. Asbestos litigation today constitutes the largest mass toxic tort in the United States. *See* In re Joint E. & S. Dists. Asbestos Litig., 125 F.R.D. 60, 63 (E.D.N.Y.1989)(hereinafter *Drago*). To date, more than 200,000 asbestos cases have been filed by injured persons and their heirs, and as many as 250,000 additional cases may be filed in years to come. *See* Stefan Fatsis, *Fallout from Asbestos Crises Still Clogs Court, Defies Solutions,* L.A. Times, August 2, 1992 at A1.

Asbestos fibers—which contain highly toxic carcinogens—have debilitated and killed many workers. Asbestos-related injuries are characterized by prolonged latency periods and typically do not become apparent until years, and in some cases decades, after exposure. Thus, many potential plaintiffs were unable to recover from the manufacturers and distributors of such products because of statutes of limitations that started running from exposure to asbestos rather than from manifestation of disease.

Recognizing the inequity, New York amended its statute of limitations in 1986 to provide some recourse to asbestos victims. The new legislation triggered the limitations period from discovery of the disease, New York Toxic Tort Reform Act of 1986, L.1986 ch. 682, § 2 (codified at N.Y.C.P.L.R. § 214–c (McKinney 1990)), and explicitly revived previously time-barred asbestos actions. L.1986, ch. 682, § 4, reprinted after N.Y.C.P.L.R. § 214–c (McKinney 1990).

Because of these changes, both the state and federal courts were swamped with asbestos suits. In response, the federal courts tried several innovative procedures. For example, recognizing that "[t]he heyday of individual adjudication of asbestos mass tort lawsuits has long passed," the Judicial Panel on Multidistrict Litigation ordered the pretrial consolidation of 26,639 pending asbestos cases in July 1991. In re Asbestos Prods. Liab. Litig. (No. VI), 771 F.Supp. 415, 419 (J.P.M.L. 1991).

In New York, the Chief Judges of the Second Circuit, the Southern District, and the Eastern District transferred all cases filed in either district to the district judge in this action for purposes of discovery. 798 F.Supp. at 944. We commend Judge Sifton for his masterful stewardship of these cases. Eventually, the cases approached the Rubicon of either settling or going to trial. To facilitate settlements and provide for manageable trials, the cases were "subdivided by the location in which the plaintiff suffered primary exposure." *Id.*

The Consolidation Here

In the instant action, 600 cases were consolidated. The thread upon which all 600 cases hung was that each plaintiff had been exposed to asbestos in one or more of over 40 power-generating stations, or "power-houses" as they are called, in New York State.

Forty-eight were selected from the 600 cases for trial on a reverse-bifurcated basis, i.e. damages to be tried first and then liability. The damages trial began on April 1, 1991. Each of the 48 plaintiffs had named as defendants between 14 and 42 manufacturers or distributors of asbestos-containing products. Of these, 25 appeared at trial as direct defendants. Several of the defendants impleaded third-party defendants. For example, on March 18, 1991, 13 days before the trial began, Judge Sifton allowed defendant Owens–Corning Fiberglas Corporation to implead over 200 companies. Some of the third-party defendants, in turn, impleaded fourth-party defendants.

During the four-month damages trial, evidence of the debilitating diseases and/or deaths of all 48 plaintiffs was presented to the jury. Often, the plaintiffs themselves would testify to the devastating consequences suffered as a result of asbestos-related disease. Where, as in Kranz–Lewis's case, a particular victim had died prior to trial, evidence regarding his disease and death was presented by family members. A parade of medical doctors testified on the etiologies and pathologies of the asbestos-related diseases suffered by each of the plaintiffs. Economists testified concerning the present value of past and future income streams, and the dollar value of ordinary household services.

In addition, detailed testimony for each victim was necessary concerning his degree of impairment, specific medical history, emotional state, and medical prognosis. Further complicating matters, the jury had to sift through each victim's medical history to determine whether factors other than asbestos, such as smoking, were responsible, in whole or part, for his physical complaints. For example, Mr. Lewis's son testified that his father smoked cigarettes until the mid–1950's, suffered episodes of chronic coughing and hoarseness, switched to pipes and cigars, switched back to cigarettes, experienced a scare after an episode of hoarseness, and ultimately quit after developing a polyp on his voice box in the early 1960's. Claims by spouses and children presented extensive plaintiff-specific evidence.

After four months of such evidence, the jury returned verdicts for 45 of the plaintiffs for an aggregate of over $94 million. Kranz–Lewis's damages were calculated as $1,682,795, including $1,250,000 for "Pain, Suffering and Other Non–Economic Losses to Decedent."

The liability portion of the trial began on September 11, 1991. During this phase, the jury was presented with a dizzying amount of evidence regarding each victim's work history. Where a victim, like

Lewis, had died before trial, the sites where he had worked during his career, the types of asbestos-containing products with which he had been involved, and the identity of the manufacturers or distributors of the asbestos products to which he may have been exposed were reconstructed through the testimony of family members and co-workers.

The testimony of just one plaintiff illustrates the cosmic sweep of the factual data that the jury had to absorb. That plaintiff, Hubert Feeley, testified that from 1953 until 1974, he worked in "hundreds of" buildings; "could not keep track of all of them;" used "[p]ipe covering, block cement, asbestos cloth, all different sorts of cement;" worked for "[t]wenty-five or so" employers; traveled as an asbestos worker to Alaska, Egypt, Wyoming, Minnesota, West Virginia, Connecticut, White Plains and New Jersey; worked in "[o]ffice buildings, high-rises, shopping centers, [and] state office buildings" including the Chase Manhattan Building, the Exxon Building and the Holiday Inn; and worked in at least seven powerhouses throughout the greater New York area. He also testified that he used at least ten different products while working for one of his many employers. He candidly testified on direct examination that "of the hundreds of buildings [he had] worked on," "[m]aybe eight or nine were powerhouses." Finally, the longest period that he could recall working at any one powerhouse was "about six months." (It should be remembered that the common thread supporting consolidation of all these cases was asbestos-exposure in a powerhouse.).

After three months, plaintiffs rested on December 4, 1991. For the next three months, the defendants presented their case. The district court and the lawyers valiantly attempted to maintain the identity of each claim throughout the trial. The jury was instructed on several occasions to consider each case separately and each juror was given a notebook for this purpose. Thanks to the effective settlement techniques of the district judge and a special master, only two plaintiffs remained by the time the jury rendered its liability verdict. It concluded that appellant Keene Corporation was 9% liable for the Kranz–Lewis damages.

Following the verdict, Keene moved for judgment as a matter of law, a new trial, or other post-verdict relief, contending, *inter alia*, that the district court's decision to consolidate the 48 cases for trial constituted prejudicial error. The district judge rejected this argument without extended discussion; and, after molding the verdict in accordance with various New York statutes to add interest and to reflect different degrees of fault among defendants, entered a judgment for Kranz against Keene for $226,038.29.

Discussion

Addressing the complaints of hundreds of thousands of severely injured asbestos plaintiffs, while safeguarding the rights of the defendants, all the while searching for equitable resolutions in each case, is a herculean task. Many of the asbestos victims suffered exposure for decades and at many different worksites. Finding an appropriate forum to resolve all these claims with minimal delay is the goal. Faced with this challenge, district judges throughout the country have reacted with commendable ingenuity. Pre-trial consolidation for the purposes of discovery, the appointment of special masters to expedite settlement, and, especially, the liberal use of consolidated trials have ameliorated what might otherwise be a sclerotic backlog of cases.

Federal Rule of Civil Procedure 42(a) provides that "[w]hen actions involving a common question of law or fact are pending before the court, it may order a joint hearing or trial of any or all the matters in issue in the action...." As we recently noted, consolidation of tort actions sharing common questions of law and fact is commonplace. This is true of asbestos-related personal injury cases as well. The trial court has broad discretion to determine whether consolidation is appropriate. In the exercise of discretion, courts have taken the view that considerations of judicial economy favor consolidation. However, the discretion to consolidate is not unfettered. Considerations of convenience and economy must yield to a paramount concern for a fair and impartial trial. Johnson v. Celotex Corp., 899 F.2d 1281, 1284–85 (2d Cir.)(citations omitted), *cert. denied,* 498 U.S. 920, 111 S.Ct. 297, 112 L.Ed.2d 250 (1990); *see also* Flintkote Co. v. Allis–Chalmers Corp., 73 F.R.D. 463, 464 (S.D.N.Y.1977)("consolidation should not be ordered if it would prejudice defendant"). In *Johnson,* we noted that a court considering a consolidation must consider:

> [W]hether the specific risks of prejudice and possible confusion [are] overborne by the risk of inconsistent adjudications of common factual and legal issues, the burden on parties, witnesses, and available judicial resources posed by multiple lawsuits, the length of time required to conclude multiple suits as against a single one, and the relative expense to all concerned of the single-trial, multiple-trial alternatives.

899 F.2d at 1285 (alteration in original)(quoting Hendrix v. Raybestos–Manhattan, Inc., 776 F.2d 1492, 1495 (11th Cir.1985)(citation omitted)).

The benefits of efficiency can never be purchased at the cost of fairness. As we recently stated:

> [W]e are mindful of the dangers of a streamlined trial process in which testimony must be curtailed and jurors must assimilate vast amounts of information. The systemic urge to aggregate litigation must not be allowed to trump our dedication to individual justice, and we must take care that each individual plaintiff's—and defendant's—cause not be lost in the shadow of a towering mass litigation.

In re Brooklyn Navy Yard Asbestos Litig., 971 F.2d 831, 853 (2d Cir.1992); *see also* Arnold v. Eastern Air Lines, Inc., 712 F.2d 899, 906 (4th Cir.1983)(*en banc*)("considerations of convenience may not prevail where the inevitable consequence to another party is harmful and serious prejudice"), *cert. denied,* 464 U.S. 1040, 104 S.Ct. 703, 79 L.Ed.2d 168 (1984); Baker v. Waterman S.S. Corp., 11 F.R.D. 440, 441

(S.D.N.Y.1951)("a fair and impartial trial to all litigants" is the foremost concern when considering consolidation); Cain v. Armstrong World Indus., 785 F.Supp. 1448, 1457 (S.D.Ala.1992)(new trial warranted where "[a]s the evidence unfolded ... it became more and more obvious ... that a process had been unleashed that left the jury the impossible task of being able to carefully sort out and distinguish the facts and law of thirteen plaintiffs' cases that varied greatly in so many critical aspects").

To strike the appropriate balance as to consolidation *vel non*, "[c]ourts in the Southern and Eastern Districts of New York have used [a standard set of] criteria ... as a guideline in determining whether to consolidate asbestos exposure cases." *Johnson*, 899 F.2d at 1285. These criteria include:

> (1) common worksite; (2) similar occupation; (3) similar time of exposure; (4) type of disease; (5) whether plaintiffs were living or deceased; (6) status of discovery in each case; (7) whether all plaintiffs were represented by the same counsel; and (8) type of cancer alleged....

Id. (quoting In re All Asbestos Cases Pending in the United States District Court for the District of Maryland, slip op. at 3 (D.Md. Dec. 16, 1983)(*en banc*)). As in *Johnson*, we again conclude that the test furnishes a useful guideline to evaluate consolidation of asbestos cases.

(1) Worksite

Plaintiffs did not all work at the same worksite. Rather, their only worksite similarity was that each was alleged to have suffered some part of his asbestos exposure at one or more of over 40 power-generating plants throughout New York State. Judge Sifton apparently selected the 48 cases based on his conclusion that, in each case, the plaintiff had suffered "primary" exposure in such powerhouses. The basis for this conclusion is unclear. For example, Lewis's exposure to asbestos came at thirteen worksites, only two of which were powerhouses. Additionally, the work history which his executrix introduced at trial belies any contention that more than 50% of his asbestos exposure occurred at powerhouses. The testimony of Mr. Feeley, discussed above, presents another good example of a plaintiff who spent only a small percentage of his time at power plants. Significantly, he never testified to spending more than a matter of months at any one of the eight or nine plants where he worked during a twenty-one year period.

The work history evidence of other plaintiffs similarly dispels the notion that they shared primary exposure at the 40-odd power plants. Indeed, the record contains evidence of over 250 worksites. Thus, not only was there no common worksite in this case, but any contention that there was a common type of worksite must be viewed with a skeptical eye.

(2) Similar Occupation

This inquiry is significant because a worker's exposure to asbestos must depend mainly on his occupation. For example, insulators, who actually applied the asbestos, suffered from direct asbestos exposure, whereas sheet-metal workers, like Mr. Lewis, suffered from asbestos exposure in a bystander capacity. The occupations of the plaintiffs in this case ranged from plumbers to machinists to carpenters to boiler-makers to sheet-metal workers.

(3) Times of Exposure

The third factor similarly does not support a finding of commonality. The time frame that the jury was required to consider was enormous: a period involving exposures in intervals that began as early as the 1940's and ended as late as the 1970's. While some plaintiffs suffered asbestos exposure over periods of up to 30 years, others had much shorter periods of exposure, undercutting the benefit of efficiency, and increasing the likelihood of prejudice, particularly concerning "state-of-the-art" evidence.

(4) Disease Type

Not all plaintiffs alleged the same type of disease. Rather, of the 48 plaintiffs, 28 suffered from asbestosis, 10 suffered from lung cancer, and 10 from mesothelioma. The significance of this disparity is obvious. When the plaintiffs suffer from the same disease, the economy derived by not rehashing the etiology and pathology of the particular disease will be great, while the concomitant prejudice will be minimal. Here, by contrast, the jury was required to hear testimony about three different diseases. The opportunity for prejudice is particularly troubling where, as here, asbestosis sufferers, who may under certain circumstances expect close to normal life spans, are paired for trial with those suffering from terminal cancers, such as mesothelioma and lung cancer.

(5) The Living & the Dead

Some victims in this case were still living during trial. Others had already died. Lewis died in 1985 at the age of 75. The significance of this factor is evident. *Drago*, 125 F.R.D. at 65–66 ("[T]he presence of wrongful death claims and personal injury actions in a consolidated trial is somewhat troublesome.... [T]he dead plaintiffs may present the jury with a powerful demonstration of the fate that awaits those claimants who are still living.").

(6) Discovery Status

Keene does not argue that any of the 48 cases was not ready for trial. We note however, the absence of any express finding of readiness in the district court's decision rejecting a challenge to consolidation. Query: were the 200 third-party defendants that were impleaded two weeks before the trial ready for the trial?

(7) Counsel

Plaintiffs were represented by five law firms, each of which played an active role throughout the trial.

(8) Cancer

Two different types of cancer were alleged: lung cancer, and mesothelioma, a cancer of the lining of the wall of the chest. Each required distinct testimony regarding its etiology, pathology, and consequences.

In addition to the foregoing eight factors, courts contemplating consolidation must also take into account the number of cases affected. In re New York Asbestos Litig., 145 F.R.D. 644, 653 (S.D.N.Y.1993)(consolidating twelve cases). Here, the maelstrom of facts, figures, and witnesses, with 48 plaintiffs, 25 direct defendants, numerous third-and-fourth party defendants, and evidence regarding culpable non-parties and over 250 worksites throughout the world was likely to lead to jury confusion. Kranz quite properly emphasizes the number of precautions the district court took to assure that each case maintained its identity. *See Johnson,* 899 F.2d at 1285. We conclude, however, that the sheer breadth of the evidence made these precautions feckless in preventing jury confusion.

Plaintiff contends that even if the consolidation was not warranted, the decision below should nevertheless be affirmed because Keene can show no prejudice arising from it. We disagree. At trial, Keene did not dispute that Lewis was exposed to a wide array of asbestos-containing products; rather, Keene disputed exposure to its products. Also, Keene readily conceded that it was known early on that massive, prolonged, and direct exposure to pure asbestos dust was dangerous; but Keene vehemently disputed that bystander exposure, such as that suffered by Mr. Lewis, was known to be dangerous when Lewis was allegedly exposed to Keene's products.

We are concerned that the jury's ability to focus on this distinction may have been compromised in this case. While the evidence regarding Lewis's exposure to Keene's products was vague, minimal, and heavily circumstantial when compared to the extensive evidence regarding the products of defendant Owens–Corning Fiberglas, the jury apportioned an equal 9% liability to each defendant. This is hard to explain. We conclude that under the unique circumstances of this case, there is an unacceptably strong chance that the equal apportionment of liability amounted to the jury throwing up its hands in the face of a torrent of evidence. *Cf. Arnold,* 712 F.2d at 907 ("[w]hile peculiar characteristics of the ... cases might afford an explanation" for an apparently incongruous result, reversal of consolidation was appropriate where "the other possibility [that the prejudice arising from an improper consolidation led to the result] simply could not be eliminated"); *Cain,* 785 F.Supp. at 1455 (ordering a new trial following the consolidated trial of thirteen asbestos-related cases where "[i]t appear[ed] that the jury simply lumped ... plaintiffs into two categories and gave plaintiffs in each category the same amount of compensatory damages no matter what their injuries'').

Kranz argues that we cannot reverse on the consolidation issue here without turning our back on In re E. & S. Dists. Asbestos Litig. (*Brooklyn Navy Yard*), 772 F.Supp. 1380 (E. & S.D.N.Y.1991), *aff'd in part, rev'd in part*, In re Brooklyn Navy Yard Asbestos Litig., 971 F.2d 831 (2d Cir.1992). There, Judge Weinstein was confronted with a number of cases arising from asbestos exposure to workers at the Brooklyn Navy Yard from World War II through the mid–1970's. Judge Weinstein first divided the case into three phases: "Phase I consisted of cases in which over 90% of plaintiffs' exposure to asbestos occurred in the Yard; Phase II encompassed cases in which between 50% and 90% of plaintiffs' exposure took place in the Yard; Phase III covered all remaining cases involving Yard exposure to asbestos." 772 F.Supp. at 1386. 64 Phase I cases were then tried jointly. Subsequently, 15 cases from Phase II and Phase III were also tried together. The second trial involved only three defendants.

After the two trials, Judge Weinstein rejected a challenge by the defendants to the propriety of the consolidation. He noted our opinion in *Johnson*, and also referred to the Maryland Factors test: "Several of these criteria are present in the *Brooklyn Navy Yard* cases. A strong geographic nexus tied these asbestos cases together through plaintiffs' exposure at one worksite, the Brooklyn Navy Yard. The plaintiffs were represented by a few law firms and sued the same former manufacturers and distributors of asbestos-containing products. Extensive overlap in witnesses, primarily former co-workers attesting to product identification at this worksite and medical and epidemiological experts, saved litigants time and money. The years of exposure spanned the period during which asbestos was utilized at the Navy Yard, beginning in the 1930's through the early 1970's." 772 F.Supp. at 1388. The defendants elected not to appeal on the consolidation issue, and accordingly we did not consider its propriety. *In re Brooklyn Navy Yard,* 971 F.2d at 836 n.1. We did applaud Judge Weinstein "for his innovative managerial skills," and indeed, the consolidation in *Brooklyn Navy Yard* is a chiaroscuro study in contrast with the instant case.

The Brooklyn Navy Yard was owned and operated for the entire relevant time period by one entity, the United States government. Because uniformity is a way of life with the military, the commonality of the 64 Phase I cases cannot be overstated. Presumably, asbestos-containing products were purchased by government contract from the same manufacturers and distributors. Determining the identities of those parties at a particular time was a relatively simple endeavor. Thus, the goal of efficiency was attained. Because the yard was used exclusively to build naval warships, and because such ships were regularly produced pursuant to uniform practices, the overlap in testimony relevant to the cases was obvious. Additionally, workers performing similar occupations on different ships during similar time frames were likely to experience exposure in similar ways. Judge Weinstein recognized that 64 cases where over 90% of asbestos exposure had occurred in a common worksite—subject to the uniformity in procurement and practice typical of the Navy—could be jointly tried without confusing or distracting the jury. The efficiency of the consolidated *Brooklyn Navy Yard* trial is evident from the fact that it lasted only four months, with an additional four weeks for jury deliberations. This stands in stark contrast with the ten-month trial here—particularly when one remembers that this trial involved 25% fewer cases.

The crucial difference between the *Brooklyn Navy Yard* case and Keene is that here there simply was no primary worksite. Rather there was an alleged primary type of worksite: powerhouses. Thus, instead of one locus where each plaintiff had worked for most of his career, consolidation was premised on the fact that each plaintiff had spent some part of his career at one or more powerhouses. There was no showing that the powerhouses that served as the focal point for consolidation provided anything like the uniformity at the Brooklyn Navy Yard. There was no finding of common ownership, common suppliers or common practices. It should also be noted that at least one of the powerhouses, Indian Point, is a nuclear facility, and, surely, the construction of such facilities must differ dramatically from that of conventional power-generating stations.

Kranz contends that even if the "strong geographic nexus" distinguishes the first *Brooklyn Navy Yard* trial, the second trial—involving plaintiffs who had less than 90% of their exposure at the yard—is not distinguishable on that basis. This contention is difficult to assess without knowledge of the facts of the plaintiffs' exposure in the second trial. We note that the second *Brooklyn Navy Yard* trial had only 12 plaintiffs and three defendants. Here, by contrast, there were 48 plaintiffs, 25 direct defendants, and hundreds of third-party defendants.

The distinctions between *Brooklyn Navy Yard* and the instant case lie at the very heart of our holding today. While district courts need not perform any specific rituals or recite any incantations before ordering cases to be consolidated, they must in every instance consider whether the "actions involv[e] a common question of law or fact." Only then can all be assured that innovative and creative efforts to provide compensation to deserving plaintiffs do not violate Federal Rule of Civil Procedure 42(a), which is designed to achieve efficiency without compromising a litigant's right under the Seventh Amendment to a jury trial.

We do not wish to be understood as condemning all consolidations of asbestos cases. Our holding today is narrow and amounts to little more than a caution that it is possible to go too far in the interests of expediency and to sacrifice basic fairness in the process. In ordering consolidation we repeat the counsel of Talleyrand, *"Pas trop de zele"*— not too much zeal.

Accordingly, the judgment of the district court is reversed, and the matter remanded for a new trial.

WALKER, CIRCUIT JUDGE, dissenting:

Although the majority states that its holding is "narrow," the implications of its decision are very broad. In disapproving the consolidated trial challenged here, this court is sending a message that will have a serious impact upon products liability litigation in this Circuit and other jurisdictions.

Notwithstanding statements to the contrary, the majority's opinion overturns a consolidated trial of cases "involving a common question of law or fact," Fed.R.Civ.P. 42(a), without any meaningful showing of prejudice. As far as I am aware, no other court has reached such a result.

The majority relies in part upon Cain v. Armstrong World Indus., 785 F.Supp. 1448 (S.D.Ala.1992), wherein an Alabama District Court granted a new trial motion after a consolidated trial of 13 asbestos cases. However, the differences between the two trials are striking. The *Cain* court had strong evidence that the jury failed to consider each claim separately, noting that "confusion and prejudice is manifest in the identical damages awarded in the non-cancer personal injury cases and in the cancer personal injury cases, the relatively short deliberation time as well as in the inflated amounts of many of the damage awards and the lack of evidence supporting some of the damages in several cases." *Id.* at 1455. In this case, by contrast, there is no substantial evidence of prejudice to defendant Keene Corporation arising from the consolidation.

The majority questions why Keene was apportioned the same percentage of liability as settling defendant Owens–Corning Fiberglas Corporation, given that—looking at the cold record—the evidence against this defendant appears stronger. However, there is evidence that Lewis was exposed to various Keene products in several worksites, making the jury's findings far from unsupported. I also note that Keene's trial strategy was to deny that decedent Lewis was exposed to its products at all, not to contest its share of liability. Any disproportionality in the jury's findings is as likely the product of the failure of this strategy, as the product of prejudice resulting from the consolidation.

The majority also speculates that Keene may have been prejudiced by the jury's inability to focus upon its claim that, at the time of Lewis' exposure, it reasonably believed that asbestos was dangerous only to persons working in asbestos manufacturing plants. However, Keene had ample opportunity to present evidence in support of this contention at trial, and emphasized it in its summation, at which point it was the sole remaining defendant in the Lewis case. * * *

Adherence to the court's reasoning in these consolidated cases would likely compel the post-trial reversal of most large-scale consolidated trials of product liability claims. For example, despite the majority's assertions to the contrary, a fair application of its holding would necessitate reversal of Judge Weinstein's consolidated trials of *Brooklyn Navy Yard* asbestos cases in In re E. & S. Dists. Asbestos Litig., 772 F.Supp.

1380 (E. & S.D.N.Y.1991)(*BNY*), *aff'd in part, rev'd in part,* 971 F.2d 831 (2d Cir.1992). In reversing the district court, the majority states that the asbestos victims in these cases: "did not all share identical occupations, were exposed to asbestos at different times, were both living and dead, were represented by more than one law firm, and suffered different ailments." But each of these factors cut the same way in the *BNY* consolidations. Attempting to distinguish *BNY*, the majority emphasizes that the victims here were exposed to asbestos in different worksites, while the largest *BNY* trial involved workers who suffered their primary asbestos exposure at a single worksite, the Navy Yard. However, the Navy Yard was a vast worksite where different ships were often built simultaneously, and within which workers engaged in different tasks were exposed to asbestos under different circumstances. Moreover, like these cases, the *BNY* cases involved exposures over a period of some four decades. I find it hard to believe that working conditions in the Navy Yard did not vary during that period.

Plainly, the common issues of fact and law that linked the *BNY* cases are substantially similar to the common issues that justified consolidation of these cases. With respect to the *BNY* cases, the majority states that "workers performing similar occupations on different ships during similar time frames were likely to experience exposure in similar ways." * * * But the same is true for workers belonging to the same trades who worked in different powerhouses and other construction sites; and the time frame involved in this trial was virtually the same as that at issue in *BNY*. The workers at issue in this trial, like those in *BNY*, also suffered from many of the same ailments, such as lung cancer and mesothelioma, creating substantial overlap with respect to the relevant medical and epidemiological evidence. Finally, given that many of the plaintiffs asserted claims against the same groups of defendants, the relevant "state-of-the-art" evidence, concerning manufacturers' knowledge of the dangers of asbestos, substantially overlapped.

Consolidated trials are an indispensable means of resolving the thousands of asbestos claims flooding our state and federal courts, as well as claims arising from other types of mass torts. I agree that trial courts should not employ consolidated trials where they pose substantial risks of prejudice, and that to do so when the risks are manifest and prejudice results amounts to an abuse of the considerable discretion the law accords to trial courts in deciding whether to consolidate. However, by overturning the consolidated trial here, where indisputably substantial common issues of fact and law prevailed, without a substantial showing of prejudice, I think the majority errs, while sending the wrong message to courts faced with the difficult task of administering such claims in a manner that is fair to all parties involved.

I respectfully dissent.

IN RE AIR CRASH DISASTER AT DETROIT METRO. AIRPORT ON AUGUST 16, 1987

United States District Court, Eastern District of Michigan, 1989.
737 F.Supp. 391.

JULIAN ABELE COOK, JR., CHIEF UNITED STATES DISTRICT JUDGE

The instant multidistrict litigation arose as a result of the crash of Northwest Flight 255 on August 16, 1987. Less than two weeks later (August 28, 1987), the first case was filed in the Eastern District of Michigan. * * * On December 9, 1987, the Judicial Panel on Multidistrict Litigation determined that all federal cases arising from the Flight 255 accident should be consolidated in this judicial district for pretrial purposes. *See* 28 U.S.C. § 1407.

Since that time, this Court has presided over all of the pretrial proceedings in this matter. As of this date, one hundred fifty-six (156) cases are under the jurisdiction of this Court for pretrial purposes.

This Order is intended to establish guidelines for the trial on the issues of liability which is scheduled to begin on October 2, 1989. * * *

I

On July 5, 1989, this Court identified a case, *Johnson v. Northwest Airlines, Inc.,* * * * which would serve as an exemplar case for a trial as to liability issues. This Court also designated four (4) other cases which would serve as alternate exemplar cases in the event that *Johnson* does not proceed to a liability trial on October 2, 1989.

It is the desire of this Court and all of the parties in this litigation to resolve all liability issues, which involve essentially identical proofs, as expeditiously and efficiently as possible. While the presentation of the Plaintiffs' claims may involve different substantive standards, the evidence which will be offered at trial on these issues is substantially the same for all claimants. Therefore, this Court concludes that these goals will not be met by conducting a single exemplar trial which does not resolve all of the liability claims arising from the air crash.

The MANUAL ON COMPLEX LITIGATION (SECOND) reads:

> Pretrial proceedings in complex litigation are often focused upon a lead or primary case; the failure to explore fully the possibilities of consolidation of other cases for trial has sometimes necessitated additional trials that could have been avoided. Utilizing Fed. R.Civ.P. 42(a), the court should consider consolidating all cases pending in (or transferable to) the court for a joint trial of those issues on which essentially the same evidence probably will be presented. * * *

Whether consolidation is permissible or desirable will depend upon the nature and extent of the non-common evidence to be presented at such a trial. Fed.R.Civ.P. 42(b) may often be used to isolate for an initial joint trial particular issues on which all or most of the evidence will be common to all cases, while reserving non-common issues for subsequent individual trials. MANUAL ON COMPLEX LITIGATION (SECOND) § 21.631, at 109 (1985)(footnotes omitted).

Therefore, rather than preside over the claims of an individual plaintiff, as was previously scheduled, this Court has determined that it is in the best interests of all of the parties to (1) transfer and consolidate all cases in this multidistrict litigation, (2) bifurcate the issue of liability from the issue of damages, and (3) commence joint trial that will resolve all liability issues which remain as of the first day of trial. * * *

* * *

III

This Court has broad discretion to determine whether to consolidate separate actions that are pending before it pursuant to Federal Rule of Civil procedure 42(a), which provides:

> When actions involving a common question of law or fact are pending before the court, it may order a joint hearing or trial of any or all matters in issue in the actions; it may order all the actions consolidated; and it may make such orders concerning proceedings therein as may tend to avoid unnecessary costs or delay.

Fed.R.Civ.P. 42(a); *see* Vincent v. Hughes Air West, Inc., 557 F.2d 759, 773–74 (9th Cir.1977); Atlantic States Legal Foundation v. Koch Refining Co., 681 F.Supp. 609, 615 (D.Minn.1988)(quoting C. Wright & A. Miller, FEDERAL PRACTICE & PROCEDURE CIVIL § 2382 (1971)). In addition, this Court may issue an order of consolidation despite the protestations of the parties in interest. C. Wright & A. Miller, FEDERAL PRACTICE & PROCEDURE CIVIL § 2383 (1971); *see also* Mutual Life Insurance Co. v. Hillmon, 145 U.S. 285, 293, 12 S.Ct. 909, 911, 36 L.Ed. 706 (1892). The MANUAL ON COMPLEX LITIGATION recommends that, in the multidistrict litigation context in which the same evidence will be presented by each Plaintiff with regard to one or both of the Defendants' alleged culpability, the trial judge should attempt to consolidate all pending cases for a joint liability trial. *See* MANUAL ON COMPLEX LITIGATION (SECOND) §§ 21.631, 33.23.

It is the belief of this Court that the consolidation of all pending cases for a joint trial on all liability issues, including those cases originating in other judicial districts,[4] will best comport with the spirit of

---

4. Numerous other courts have transferred and consolidated cases originating in another forum for trial purposes. See In re Fine Paper Antitrust Litigation, 685 F.2d 810, 820 (3d Cir.1982), *cert. denied,* 459 U.S. 1156, 103 S.Ct. 801, 74 L.Ed.2d 1003 (1983); Winbourne v. Eastern Air Lines, Inc., 632 F.2d 219 (2d Cir.1980); Pfizer, Inc. v. Lord, 447 F.2d 122, 124–25 (2d Cir. 1971); In re Air Crash Disaster at Stapleton International Airport, Denver, Colorado, on November 15, 1987, 720 F.Supp. 1455 (D.Colo.1988); In re Longhorn Securities Litigation, 573 F.Supp. 274, 276 (W.D.Okl.1983); In re Bristol Bay, Alaska, Salmon Fishery Antitrust Litigation, 424 F.Supp. 504, 507 (J.P.M.L.1976)(per curiam); In re Multidistrict Civil Actions Involving the Air Crash Disaster Near Hanover, New Hampshire, on October 25, 1968, 342 F.Supp. 907 (D.N.H.1971). Section 1404(a) and Rule 14(b) of the Rules on Multidistrict Litigation, which explicitly

the Federal Rules of Civil Procedure which mandate that the Rules "be construed to secure the just, speedy, and inexpensive determination of every action." Fed.R.Civ.P. 1. In the case *sub judice,* the complexity of the issues presented, the substantial number of common questions of fact relating to liability, and the potential for resolving all of the numerous claims in this case in a uniform and consistent manner mandate a consolidation of this litigation under Rule 42(a).

Therefore, all currently pending multidistrict cases which arise from the Flight 255 air crash shall be consolidated for a joint trial on the issues of liability.

IV

This Court has the authority to try issues of liability and damages separately pursuant to Federal Rule of Civil Procedure 42(b), which provides:

> The court, in furtherance of convenience or to avoid prejudice, or when separate trials will be conducive to expedition and economy, may order a separate trial of any claim, cross-claim, counterclaim, or third-party claim, or of any separate issue or of any number of claims, cross-claims, counterclaims, third-party claims, or issues, always preserving inviolate the right of trial by jury as declared by the Seventh Amendment to the Constitution or as given by a statute of the United States.

Fed.R.Civ.P. 42(b). It is well settled within the Sixth Circuit that " 'the district court has broad discretion to order separate trials.' " In re Bendectin Litigation, 857 F.2d 290, 307 (6th Cir.1988)(quotation omitted), *cert. denied* * * *, 488 U.S. 1006, 109 S.Ct. 788, 102 L.Ed.2d 779 (1989); *see also* Moss v. Associated Transport, 344 F.2d 23 (6th Cir. 1965). In deciding whether to sever particular issues for a separate trial, the court must consider the "potential prejudice to the parties, potential confusion to the jury, and the relative convenience and economy which would result." In re Beverly Hills Fire Litigation, 695 F.2d 207, 216 (6th Cir.1982)(footnote omitted); *see also Bendectin,* 857 F.2d at 307–08. The Sixth Circuit Court of Appeals has warned that by severing liability issues from damages issues, "there is a danger that bifurcation may deprive the plaintiffs of their legitimate right to place before the jury the circumstances and atmosphere of the entire cause of action which they have brought into court, replacing it with a sterile or laboratory atmosphere in which causation is parted from the reality of injury." *Beverly Hills,* 695 F.2d at 217. The MANUAL ON COMPLEX LITIGATION contemplates that a court, which presides over multidistrict actions that sound in tort, should sever liability issues from damages issues. *See* MANUAL ON COMPLEX LITIGATION (SECOND) § 33.26.

empower a transferee court to transfer cases to itself for trial, would essentially have no purpose if the transferee court was not permitted to transfer and consolidate for trial those cases that had been filed in a foreign judicial district.

In this multidistrict litigation, bifurcation of liability issues from damages concerns is appropriate for the following reasons: (1) bifurcation allows the consolidation of all pending cases for a joint trial addressing all liability issues, (2) bifurcation may simplify the jury's task in deciding liability issues, (3) bifurcation will not prejudice the respective positions of the Plaintiffs or the Defendants, (4) bifurcation may obviate the need for considering damages claims, thereby minimizing expense and expediting the resolution of these proceedings, (5) the proofs regarding liability and damages are not necessarily intertwined, and (6) no party in interest has objected to such bifurcation as of this date.

Accordingly, the issues regarding an award of compensatory and punitive damages, if available, are severed from the liability issues and are reserved for a subsequent determination, if necessary. Should the Plaintiffs prevail in the joint liability trial, those claimants who originally filed their cases in a transferor court may move to remand the issue of damages to the transferor district for a final determination.

V

If the joint liability trial results in a verdict in favor of the Plaintiffs, the damages issues shall be tried before the same jury that resolved the liability issues. *See* Manual For Complex litigation (Second) § 21.6323 (1985). By adopting this approach, the Court can protect against the possibility that bifurcation may create "a sterile or laboratory atmosphere in which causation is parted from the reality of injury." *Beverly Hills,* 695 F.2d at 217. If the jury determines that one or both of the Defendants are liable to the Plaintiffs for the air crash, the issue of damages will be presented separately and consecutively to the same trier of fact three weeks following the conclusion of the joint liability trial. * * *

VI

It is the intention of this Court to appoint the Plaintiffs' Steering Committee (PSC) to serve as the trial counsel for the purposes of prosecuting the joint liability trial on behalf of all the Plaintiffs. *See* Manual For Complex Litigation (Second) § 22.22 (1985)(in multi-party cases "the court should insist that appropriate arrangements be made, whether formally by designating one or more attorneys to serve as lead counsel or members of a trial team, or informally by the attorneys deciding who will be chiefly responsible for the examination of particular witnesses"). All objections, and the basis for such objections, to the designation of the PSC to act as the trial counsel in the joint liability trial shall be filed on or before August 28, 1989.

* * *

It is so ordered.

Notes and Questions

1. What are the limitations on the utility of consolidation as an aggregative device? At least one major limitation is suggested by the *Detroit*

Airport air crash litigation. Rule 42(a) permits consolidation only of cases "pending before the court." This language effectively limits consolidation in the federal system to cases filed in one judicial district. In order to make more efficient use of the consolidation rule, federal litigants frequently use Rule 42 in coordination with the federal transfer provisions, 28 U.S.C.A. §§ 1404 and 1406, as well as the multi-district litigation statute, 28 U.S.C.A. § 1407. As the *Detroit Airport* opinion illustrates, cases filed and pending before other courts may be transferred to another federal forum, and then consolidated pursuant to Rule 42(a) for multidistrict pretrial proceedings under the multidistrict litigation statute. The "pending cases" language also frustrates the ability of federal courts to join parties who possess related claims but who have not filed suit as of the date of the consolidation. *See, e.g.,* Pan Am. World Airways, Inc. v. United States District Ct. for Cent. Dist. of Cal., 523 F.2d 1073, 1080 (9th Cir.1975)(denying authority of court to notify victims of airplane crash who had not yet sued that they could join in pending consolidated case on ground that "Rule 42 may be invoked only to consolidate actions already pending"); *cf.* In re Air Crash Disaster at Fla. Everglades on Dec. 29, 1972, 549 F.2d 1006, 1009 (5th Cir.1977) and Vincent v. Hughes Air West, Inc., 557 F.2d 759, 762 (9th Cir.1977)(opt-in notices sent to air disaster claimants who had not previously filed). Professor Charles Silver has noted that "In this respect, Rule 42(a) is weaker than Rule 23(b)(3), which, as an alternative to permissive joinder, enables judges to bind all people who have similar claims, including those who have not sued." *See* Charles Silver, *Comparing Class Actions and Consolidations,* 10 Rev.Litig. 495, 502 (1991).

Notwithstanding these limitations, federal judges have frequently resorted to Rule 42 as a means of consolidating mass tort litigation. *See generally* Roger Trangsrud, *Mass Trials in Mass Tort Cases: A Dissent,* 1989 U.Ill.L.Rev. 69 (1989); Roger Trangsrud, *Joinder Alternatives in Mass Tort Litigation,* 70 Cornell L.Rev. 779 (1985)(discussing cases).

2. To what extent is Rule 42(b) consistent or inconsistent with the purpose of the consolidation rule? Note that Rule 42(b) provides that a federal court can order a separate trial of any claims or issues "in furtherance of convenience or to avoid prejudice, or when separate trials will be conducive to expedition and economy." Compare this provision with the possibility of "severance" under Rule 21. What are the legal differences between the two provisions? What constitutes "prejudice" sufficient under the rule to permit a separate trial? *See generally,* Jacqueline Gerson, Comment, *The Appealability of Partial Judgments in Consolidated Cases,* 57 U.Chi.L.Rev. 169 (1990).

Rule 42(b), as illustrated in the *Detroit Airport* case, is most often invoked in personal injury litigation in order to separate trial of the issues of liability from those relating to damages, a procedure known as "bifurcation." Although the bifurcation procedure has been used in other litigation contexts, as well as to order separate trials on threshold issues such as jurisdiction or venue—or affirmative defenses—its most controversial application has been in federal diversity tort litigation. In some complex cases, federal judges have expanded use of Rule 42(b) innovatively to create procedures denoted as "trifurcation" and "polyfurcation," or reversed the usual sequence of trial issues, a procedure known as "reverse bifurcation."

What are the main justifications for bifurcation in personal injury litigation, and what are the criticisms of this procedure? *See generally,* Warren F. Schwartz, *Severance—A Means of Minimizing The Role of Burden and Expense in Determining the Outcome of Litigation,* 20 Vand.L.Rev. 1197 (1967); Jack B. Weinstein, *Routine Bifurcation of Jury Negligence Trials: An Example of the Questionable Use of Rule Making Power,* 14 Vand.L.Rev. 831 (1961); Hans Zeisel & Thomas Callahan, *Split Trials and Time Saving: A Statistical Analysis,* 76 Harv.L.Rev. 1606 (1963).

Federal courts have adjudicated mass tort claims using bifurcated or polyfurcated trial procedures in hotel fire litigation, the *Agent Orange* case, Bendectin litigation, and asbestos cases, although this use of Rule 42(b) has been highly controversial. *See* Linda S. Mullenix, *Beyond Consolidation: PostAggregative Procedure in Asbestos Mass Tort Litigation,* 32 Wm. & Mary L.Rev. 475, 557 (1991)(discussing bifurcation and polyfurcation, and objections to these procedures). *See also* Susan E. Abitanta, Comment, *Bifurcation of Liability and Damages and Rule 23(b)(3) Class Actions: History, Policy, Problems and a Solution,* 36 Sw.L.J. 743, 746–47 , 758–59 (1982); Albert P. Bedecarre, *Rule 42(b) Bifurcation at an Extreme: Polyfurcation of Liability Issues in Environmental Tort Cases,* 17 B.C.Envtl.Aff.L.Rev. 123, 139–47 (1989).

3. Is the Second Circuit's reversal of the consolidated asbestos trial in *Malcolm,* after a jury verdict, a draconian result? Why didn't the court vacate the consolidation decision earlier? What does the *Malcolm* decision indicate about the utility of Rule 42 consolidations for mass tort litigation? Is *Malcolm* significantly distinguishable on its facts so as not to represent a broad-sweeping precedent for other attempted mass tort consolidations?

As the *Repetitive Stress Injury* and *Malcolm* decisions suggest, the possibility of mass tort consolidation in federal court has had a mixed reception. *Cf.* In re Paoli R.R. Yard PCB Litigation, 35 F.3d 717 (3d Cir.1994)(consolidation of 38 lawsuits for exposure to PCBs in railyard); In re New York Asbestos Litigation, 149 F.R.D. 490 (S.D.N.Y.1993)(consolidation of 6 asbestos actions against 12 defendants); In re New York Asbestos Litigation, 145 F.R.D. 644 (S.D.N.Y.1993)(consolidation of 13 asbestos tort actions against 88 defendants); In re Joint Eastern and Southern Districts Asbestos Litigation, 769 F.Supp. 85 (E.D.N.Y.1991)(consolidation of asbestos cases promotes efficiency); In re Shell Oil Refinery, 136 F.R.D. 588 (E.D.La. 1991), *aff'd sub nom.,* Watson v. Shell Oil Co., 979 F.2d 1014 (5th Cir.1992), *r'hrg granted,* 990 F.2d 805 (5th Cir.1993)(consolidation of opt-out cases with class action for single trial on damages does not violate due process). *See also* Hopkins v. Dow Corning, 1992 WL 176560 (N.D.Cal.1992)(plaintiffs' motion to consolidate silicone breast implant cases under Fed.R.Civ.P. 42(a) must await decision of Judicial Panel on Multidistrict Litigation).

4. Consolidated actions also raise difficult problems relating to conduct of the consolidated cases, representation, and attorneys fees. For a lengthy discussion and resolution of these issues, *see In re Air Crash Disaster at Florida Everglades on December 29, 1972, supra. See also* Gaylord A. Virden, *Consolidation Under Rule 42 of the Federal Rules of Civil Procedure: The U.S. Courts of Appeal Disagree on Whether Consolidation Merges the*

Separate Cases and Whether the Cases Remain Separately Final for the Purposes of Appeal, 141 F.R.D. 169 (1992).

D. JURISDICTIONAL PROBLEMS

1. PERSONAL JURISDICTION

CARLOUGH v. AMCHEM PRODUCTS, INC.

United States Court of Appeals, Third Circuit, 1993.
10 F.3d 189.

Before: MANSMANN, GREENBERG and LEWIS, CIRCUIT JUDGES.

OPINION OF THE COURT

MANSMANN, CIRCUIT JUDGE.

The appellants, the *"Gore* plaintiffs"*,* are absent members of a purported federal plaintiff class in an action brought pursuant to Federal Rule of Civil Procedure 23(b)(3) for asbestos-related tort damages in the United States District Court for the Eastern District of Pennsylvania. Simultaneously with the federal class action, but prior to the establishment of an opt out period in the federal suit, the *Gore* plaintiffs initiated a class action in the State Circuit Court of Monongalia County, West Virginia, against the same defendants named in the federal class action. The federal district court issued a preliminary injunction pursuant to the Anti–Injunction Act and the All–Writs Act, enjoining the *Gore* plaintiffs from prosecuting their state claims on the ground that the injunction was "necessary in aid" of the federal court's jurisdiction. The *Gore* plaintiffs appeal that injunction.

The *Gore* plaintiffs first asserted that the injunction was not binding on them because it purported to be effective outside of the jurisdictional reach of the federal district court. Essentially, the *Gore* plaintiffs claimed that unresolved jurisdictional challenges to the federal district court's subject matter jurisdiction in the action *sub judice* deprived the district court of authority to issue the injunction. The *Gore* plaintiffs further claimed, among other things, that the district court failed to observe the basic requisite of obtaining personal jurisdiction over the absent class members whom it purported to bind under the injunction. The injunction was issued prior to notice to the *Gore* plaintiffs of the commencement of the federal class action, prior to the establishment of the "opt out" period, without the *Gore* plaintiffs' consent to the jurisdiction of the federal court, and without some of the *Gore* plaintiffs having minimum contacts with the Eastern District of Pennsylvania. These claims have since been vitiated by a belated October 6, 1993 order of the district court finding that it indeed had subject matter jurisdiction over the *Carlough* action, and an even more belated October 27, 1993 order of the district court approving notice to be disseminated to the *Carlough* class. Nevertheless, we find that the *Gore* appeal continues to be viable because the question remains whether the injunction, which is still operative over the pending *Gore* action in the state court, is permitted under the "necessary in aid" exception to the interdicts of the Anti–Injunction Act, 28 U.S.C. § 2283, and the All Writs Act, 28 U.S.C. § 1651.

The appellees, numerous asbestos producers jointly represented by the Center For Claims Resolution (the "CCR") and named as defendants in both actions, assert that the district court may consider the merits of the proposed settlement agreement filed simultaneously with the federal class action complaint before the state court entertains the *Gore* plaintiffs' request for declaratory judgment, when such a declaration allegedly would threaten to undermine the district court's oversight of the settlement. Thus they argue that the injunction must continue to be maintained in aid of the district court's jurisdiction. Prior to the elimination of the *Gore* appellants' jurisdictional challenges, the CCR defendants had asserted that because the federal class action was going to afford the *Gore* plaintiffs an opportunity to "opt out," the *Gore* plaintiffs were required to await the establishment and commencement of the "opt out" period and to exercise that option before prosecuting their related state action. The future, but certain, opportunity to "opt out," they argued, dispelled any concerns of comity and federalism.

* * *

I

A

On January 15, 1993, a class action complaint pursuant to Fed. R.Civ.P. 23(b)(3), an answer and a stipulation of settlement were simultaneously filed in the United States District Court for the Eastern District of Pennsylvania. The complaint was brought on behalf of Edward M. Carlough and other named plaintiffs on behalf of a class consisting of:

> (a) All persons ... who have been exposed in the United States ..., either occupationally or through the occupational exposure of a spouse or household member, to asbestos or to asbestos-containing products for which one or more of the Defendants may bear legal liability and who, as of January 15, 1993, reside in the United States ..., and who have not, as of January 15, 1993, filed a lawsuit for asbestos-related personal injury, or damage, or death in any state or federal court against the Defendant(s).... (b) All spouses, parents, children, and other relatives ... of the class members ... who have not, as of January 15, 1993, filed a lawsuit for the asbestos-related personal injury, or damage, or death of a class member ... in any state or federal court against the Defendant(s). * * *

The "*Carlough* plaintiffs" seek recovery for asbestos-related personal injury caused by the exposure of members of the putative class to the asbestos and asbestos-containing products of the defendants, who are miners, manufacturers, distributors, and suppliers of asbestos or asbestos-containing products, and their predecessors-in-interest, jointly represented by the Center For Claims Resolution. Upon the joint motions of the named plaintiffs and the CCR members, the district court issued a conditional class certification order for the class defined in the complaint for purposes of settlement on January 29, 1993. The certification order further indicated that notice to absent class members would be given as to the pendency of the federal class action and of their rights to exclude themselves from the class.

On March 1, 1993, the district court issued a Rule to Show Cause and ordered a preliminary hearing on whether the action should be finally certified as a Rule 23(b)(3) class and whether the settlement was "fair, adequate and reasonable." The parties were directed to file with the Clerk memoranda of law and any other documents in support of their respective positions no later than March 19, 1993. Among the various motions and objections filed in response to the Rule to Show Cause were challenges to the district court's subject matter jurisdiction under Article III of the United States Constitution and under the federal diversity statute, 28 U.S.C. § 1332, as well as challenges to the district court's personal jurisdiction over the parties. Although these issues were resolved in the interim between the filing of the present appeal and the entering of our opinion and order in this matter, they were pending when the present appeal was taken.

On March 17, 1993, Gregory Gore, a resident of West Virginia, William Ferrel, a resident of Ohio, and Michael and Lynn Conley, residents of Pennsylvania, filed a related asbestos class action complaint, in the state court of West Virginia, under West Virginia law on behalf of themselves and as representatives of a putative class of plaintiffs similarly situated. *Gore v. Amchem Products, Inc.*, C.A. No. 93–C–195 (Circuit Court of Monongalia County, West Virginia). This state class action, which names the same CCR defendants as in the *Carlough* federal class action, was commenced prior to the impending "opt out" period of the federal action and prior to the district court's determination of its subject matter and personal jurisdiction, and seeks as relief a declaration that the proposed *Carlough* settlement is unenforceable and not entitled to full faith and credit in the West Virginia courts and is not binding on members of the purported West Virginia class. It further seeks a declaration that the *Gore* plaintiffs are adequate representatives of the purported West Virginia class and are authorized to "opt out" of the purported federal class in *Carlough* on behalf of the entire West Virginia class. Finally, the *Gore* action seeks compensatory damages for each member of the West Virginia class for injury caused by the defendants' conduct in violation of West Virginia law, as well as punitive damages. The class of persons defined in the West Virginia suit parallels that defined in the federal *Carlough* suit, except that the West Virginia class is limited to persons whose claims are based on asbestos exposure occurring in West Virginia and is further limited to persons "who do not presently have a diagnosed medical condition related to asbestos."

On April 12, 1993, the defendant members of the CCR sought a temporary restraining order and preliminary injunction enjoining the

West Virginia plaintiffs, their attorneys, agents and employees, and the class they purport to represent, from taking any steps in the further prosecution of their state claim or from pursuing similar "duplicative" litigation in any other forum. A telephonic hearing was held two days later concerning CCR's motion, and a temporary restraining order was granted the following day, April 15, valid until April 25, 1993. In issuing the temporary restraining order, the court found that [T]he CCR Defendants may suffer irreparable harm in the prosecution of the *Gore* action as the relief prayed for is substantially preemptive in nature as it relates to the present [*Carlough*] case. Further, the court finds CCR Defendants have established a reasonable probability of success on the merits of their request for an injunction and that a [*sic*] there is a substantial possibility of harm to a multitude of other potential class members, and that the public interest favors the issuance of this temporary restraining order.

Upon the expiration of the terms of the temporary restraining order, and upon a renewed motion for preliminary injunction, the district court extended the temporary restraining order through April 30, 1993 and scheduled a hearing on that date. After the hearing, the court further extended the temporary restraining order through May 5, 1993. When the extension expired, the district court granted a preliminary injunction, restraining and enjoining the *Gore* plaintiffs, their attorneys, agents and employees, and the class they purport to represent "from taking any steps in the prosecution of the [*Gore*] action and from initiating similar litigation in any other forum." The *Gore* plaintiffs appealed this order. During the pendency of this appeal, the district court resolved the challenges to its subject matter jurisdiction, ruling in an October 6, 1993 opinion that it had Article III and 28 U.S.C. § 1332 subject matter jurisdiction over the *Carlough* class action. Shortly thereafter, on October 27, 1993, the district court approved the plan for dissemination and content of notice of the commencement of the federal action to all putative members of the *Carlough* plaintiff class.

B

* * *

* * * [T]he district court rejected the *Gore* plaintiffs' contentions that the federal court lacked personal jurisdiction, finding that the Federal Rules of Civil Procedure allow federal courts to bind absent class members in opt out class actions, even without minimum contacts, without impinging federal due process protections, and concluding that the injunction was "necessary to protect [its] jurisdiction" under the All–Writs Act and the Anti–Injunction Act.

II

* * *

We discuss first the jurisdictional issues which we find resolved by the two orders of the district court entered subsequent both to the issuance of the preliminary injunction and to the appeal taken from that injunction. We note that neither the Anti–Injunction Act, 28 U.S.C. § 2283 (1970), nor the All–Writs Act, 28 U.S.C. § 1651 (1988), dispels the federal court's jurisdictional requisite or divests the West Virginia court of its jurisdiction to adjudicate the *Gore* action, but rather the judicial authority extended by the Acts is wholly derivative in nature. Thus the application of the Anti–Injunction and All–Writs Acts should have been preceded by the satisfaction of jurisdictional prerequisites. *See* Atlantic Coast Line R.R. Co. v. Brotherhood of Locomotive Engineers, 398 U.S. 281, 287, 90 S.Ct. 1739, 1743, 26 L.Ed.2d 234 (1970)(exceptions to § 2283 should not be enlarged by liberal statutory construction). Nevertheless, we will recognize the district court's jurisdiction over the *Carlough* action and the *Gore* plaintiffs in light of its belated October orders.

Turning to the question of personal jurisdiction over the *Gore* plaintiffs, we recognize that it is a fundament of personal jurisdiction in a court of law that a defendant be actually domiciled or present within the territory of the forum court, without which the court would lack authority to bind that defendant. International Shoe Co. v. Washington, 326 U.S. 310, 316, 66 S.Ct. 154, 158, 90 L.Ed. 95 (1945). Though this standard has been elaborated, and to some extent relaxed, particularly to befit the practical realities of the modern corporate entity and to reflect the replacement of the *capias ad respondendum* with personal service of process and modern forms of notice, it remains beyond cavil, as a general principle of jurisdictional authority, that "in order to subject a defendant to a judgment in personam, if he be not present within the territory of the forum, he have certain minimum contacts with it such that the maintenance of the suit does not offend 'traditional notions of fair play and substantial justice.' " *Id.* (citations omitted). *International Shoe* arose in the state court system and the opinion expressed the due process guarantees of the Fourteenth Amendment; nonetheless, the minimum contacts requirement for personal jurisdiction applies to federal courts having subject matter jurisdiction on the basis of diversity of citizenship as well as cases brought on the basis of a federal claim. *See* In re Real Estate Title, 869 F.2d 760, 766 n.6 (3d Cir.1989). Thus, it would offend the Fifth Amendment's guarantee of due process for a federal court to enjoin an absentee class member whose minimum contacts with the forum have not been established or, in lieu of minimum contacts, who has not consented to the court's jurisdiction, explicitly or inferentially.

In Phillips Petroleum Co. v. Shutts, 472 U.S. 797, 105 S.Ct. 2965, 86 L.Ed.2d 628 (1985), the Supreme Court held that a court may bind an absent plaintiff class member to a class action damages judgment, despite the absentee's lack of minimum contacts with the forum, without abrogating minimal due process protection. 472 U.S. 797 at 811–12, 105 S.Ct. at 2974-75. The absentee plaintiff class member's due process rights would be satisfied if the plaintiff received reasonable notice, an opportunity to be heard and to meaningfully partake in the litigation, adequate representation, and "at a minimum ... an opportunity to remove himself from the class by executing and returning an 'opt out' or 'request for exclusion' form to the court." *Id.* at 812, 105 S.Ct. at 2975. The Court justified the relaxation of the minimum contacts standard for personal jurisdiction as applied to absent plaintiffs by adverting to the relatively less onerous burdens placed by a state on an absent plaintiff class member as compared to those placed on an absent defendant. *Id.* at 808, 105 S.Ct. at 2973. A plaintiff class member who is afforded an opportunity to opt out, but who fails to exercise that option, may be deemed to have consented to jurisdiction. *Id.* at 812, 105 S.Ct. at 2975. As we noted in *In re Real Estate Title,* "[t]he procedural protections of Fed.R.Civ.P. 23 replace the rigid rules of personal jurisdiction in this context and are all that is needed to meet the requirements of due process." 869 F.2d 760, 766 (3d Cir.1989)(footnote omitted.)

In re Real Estate Title afforded us an opportunity to examine *Shutts* and to reaffirm the critical importance of the right to opt out in drawing any inference of consent to jurisdiction by absent plaintiff class members who otherwise would have no affiliation with the forum. We held that

> [i]f the member has not been given the opportunity to opt out in a class action involving both important injunctive relief and damage claims, the member must either have minimum contacts with the forum or consent to jurisdiction in order to be enjoined by the district court that entertained the class action.

In re Real Estate Title, 869 F.2d at 769. Because neither the opportunity to opt out (or any indicia of consent) nor minimum contacts were present, we held that the federal district court was not authorized to enjoin a state court damages suit brought by two state school boards, the absent plaintiffs in the related federal multi-district class action, against title insurance companies, the defendants in both the federal and state actions, for violations of state antitrust law.[7] We confirmed that the traditional minimum contacts requirement applies to enjoining a plaintiff who has not been allowed to opt out of a class action. *See also* Compagnie des Bauxites de Guinea v. Insurance Company of North America, 651 F.2d 877, 880 (3d Cir.1981)(district court must have personal jurisdiction over party before it can enjoin actions)(citing Zenith Radio Corp. v. Hazeltine Research, Inc., 395 U.S. 100, 112, 89 S.Ct. 1562, 1570, 23 L.Ed.2d 129 (1969)), *aff'd sub nom.,* Insurance Corp. of Ireland,

---

7. We further noted in *In re Real Estate Title* that, despite the federal court's inability to enjoin the state action, the settlement of the federal class action would still have value to the title companies. We noted that the settlement afforded the title companies the defense that the school boards were precluded from proceeding with the state court on the ground that they were bound to the settlement. In turn, we noted that the school boards could claim inadequate representation in the federal class action, or perhaps raise other due process claims which would invalidate the settlement as to themselves. If the school boards could demonstrate either that they were not members of the federal class, or that the federal proceeding did not comply with due process guarantees, then the state court action would not be prohibited by the terms of the federal class action settlement.

Ltd. v. Compagnie des Bauxites de Guinee, 456 U.S. 694, 102 S.Ct. 2099, 72 L.Ed.2d 492 (1982).

As in *In re Real Estate Title,* the present case was distinguishable from *Shutts* during the interim when the absent class plaintiffs had not yet been notified and the opt out period had not yet been established in that the *Gore* plaintiffs had not yet been afforded the opportunity to opt out—an essential component of personal jurisdiction in lieu of the more traditional minimum contacts. The lack of personal jurisdiction over the *Gore* plaintiffs at that time is further evidenced in the record by clear indications that the *Gore* plaintiffs did not consent to the district court's jurisdiction. Not only did the *Gore* complaint expressly indicate the desire to be excluded from the federal action, but the *Gore* plaintiffs had not received notice of the Carlough proceedings prior to the motions to enjoin their state court actions. *Cf.* Battle v. Liberty Nat. Life Ins. Co., 877 F.2d 877, 883 (11th Cir.1989)(after Fed.R.Civ.P. 23(b)(3) notice had been effected on about 90% of class, district court properly issued injunctive order pursuant to Anti–Injunction Act). Although an inference of consent might have been drawn from silence or inaction after notice and the running of the opt out period, *Shutts,* 472 U.S. at 806–14, 105 S.Ct. at 2971-75, we find no precedent for assuming consent prior to notice and the commencement of the opt out period.[8] Thus, with neither express or inferred consent, nor minimum contacts, and prior to notice and the commencement of the opt out period, the district court did not have personal jurisdiction over the *Gore* plaintiffs and did not have authority to bind their actions when it issued the injunction. In short, the district court's pre-notice, pre-opt out period injunction was premature.

We do not believe that the mere promise, even certain eventuality, that the opportunity to opt out of the class will be offered to absent class plaintiffs satisfies the requirements of due process as defined by *Shutts.* There the Supreme Court specifically required that "an absent plaintiff be provided with an opportunity to remove himself from the class by executing and returning an 'opt out' or 'request for exclusion' form to the court." 472 U.S. at 812, 105 S.Ct. at 2974. Because of this emphasis by the Supreme Court on the receipt of the opt out forms, we reject the district court's implication here that the opt out requirement is satisfied in all cases where a class action will provide for the opportunity to opt out.

Thus, prior to notice and the opt out period, and absent minimum contacts with the Pennsylvania forum or consent to its jurisdiction, a

---

8. It might have been persuasive, as we conjectured in *In re Real Estate Title,* that "in a hybrid class action that involves important injunctive and damage components, a defendant need only consent to a class certification that allows for opt outs in order to avoid due process challenges to the settlement in multiple fora, as long as the court approves that certification." *In re* *Real Estate Title,* 869 F.2d at 770. But facing the issue squarely in the present case, we find no reason to relax the jurisdictional requisite to a binding in personam judgment beyond *Shutts* and other precedent, which allow an inference of consent to jurisdiction where an absent plaintiff class member is notified and fails to exercise the opt out prerogative.

federal injunction enjoining state action would violate due process. *See In re Real Estate Title*, 869 F.2d at 762. Strictly and narrowly enforcing the requisite opportunity to opt out for Rule 23 class plaintiffs before exerting personal jurisdiction comports with the overall class action mechanism and is derived from policy considerations bearing upon comity and federalism. Here the district court's premature issuance of the injunction threatened to compromise these principles. Nevertheless, once the district court approved the dissemination of notice and commenced the opt out period pursuant to its October 27, 1993 order, the jurisdictional problem was resolved. Thus, despite the district court's initial jurisdictional overreach, we will recognize its legitimate exercise of personal jurisdiction over the *Gore* appellants.

* * *

V

The order of the district court of May 6, 1993 enjoining the Gore plaintiffs, their attorneys, agents and employees, and the class they purport to represent from taking any further steps in the prosecution of their claims in the Circuit Court of Monongalia County, West Virginia, or from initiating similar litigation in any other forum, is affirmed.

IN RE DES CASES

United States District Court, Eastern District of New York, 1992.
789 F.Supp. 552, *appeal dismissed* 7 F.3d 20 (2d Cir.1993).

MEMORANDUM AND ORDER

WEINSTEIN, DISTRICT JUDGE:

I. INTRODUCTION

This diversity case presents a classic illustration of why traditional limits on personal jurisdiction must be modified for mass torts. The torts alleged here involve numerous claims of injury from exposure *in utero* to diethylstilbestrol (DES). DES was developed and tested in laboratories throughout the country and the world. Permission to use it was sought and obtained from the federal Food and Drug Administration by pharmaceutical companies scattered across the nation. Some companies conducted national advertising and a national corps of salespersons hawked the drug in doctors' offices in every part of the country. Discussions among medical specialists and word-of-mouth information traded among doctors and patients led to national acceptance of the drug as useful for the prevention of miscarriages. Even companies producing exclusively for local markets relied on the nationally developed understanding and consensus about DES and used knowledge and chemicals from all parts of the United States and the world. Thousands of persons in hamlets and cities across the country are now claiming to have been adversely affected by exposure to the drug. In short, the technology, marketing, sociology, and possible ill effects of DES knew no state

boundaries.   The national nature of the resulting toxic tort litigation
must be reflected in the law's treatment of jurisdictional issues.

Motions to dismiss for lack of jurisdiction raise the following questions: Do the complaints against the moving defendants state a claim
under New York's substantive laws?   Are those laws constitutional?
Are New York's substantive laws applicable under New York's choice-of-
law rules?   Are those choice-of-law rules constitutional?   Do New York's
jurisdictional statutes provide for jurisdiction over a successor corporation licensed to do business in New York for causes of action relating to
the activities of its predecessor corporation, which never sold DES in
New York and was never present in New York?   Does New York's long
arm statute provide for jurisdiction over a manufacturing corporation
which never sold DES in the New York market and was never present in
New York?   Are New York's jurisdictional statutes constitutional?   In
light of the specific characteristics and history of the moving defendants,
and of all the parties and the suit, would requiring the defendants to
litigate in New York be fair so that jurisdiction is not barred by the
Constitution and should not be declined under a prudential theory akin
to *forum non conveniens*?   All must be answered "yes."

II.   FACTS

A.   *Background*

DES, a synthetic estrogen, was developed in the late 1930s.   It was
thought to be useful in treating symptoms of certain cancers and
menopause, among other things.   In 1941, twelve companies formed a
committee to oversee submissions in support of a joint New Drug
Application for DES to the Food and Drug Administration.   On the basis
of these submissions, the FDA approved DES for certain uses, not
including the prevention of miscarriages.

Researchers were simultaneously discovering that miscarriages were
often accompanied by low levels of natural estrogen.   In theory, the
administration of natural or synthetic estrogen would improve a woman's ability to carry the pregnancy to term.   In 1947 and 1948 several of
the twelve DES manufacturers sought and were granted permission by
the FDA to market DES to prevent miscarriage and fetal death.   By
1952 the FDA considered DES proven safe.   Hundreds of additional
manufacturers then entered the market.   Millions of pregnant women
ingested DES during the 1950s and 1960s.

In 1971, doctors in Boston concluded that DES was a teratogen
responsible for the appearance of adenocarcinoma, a rare form of vaginal
cancer, in eight young women who had been exposed to DES in the
womb.   The FDA soon thereafter disapproved the continued marketing
of DES for pregnancy use.   There is some evidence that doctors nonetheless continued to prescribe DES through the early 1970s.

Women exposed to DES *in utero* may develop adenosis, a precancerous cell change which can be treated by cauterization or surgery.
DES is said to cause a variety of other more serious disorders, including

miscarriage, uterine deformities, ectopic pregnancy, and breast cancer. Male fetuses exposed to DES may be at risk of developing undescended testicles, sterility, and deformities. As persons exposed to DES *in utero* age, other medical problems may be linked to DES. There is also evidence that DES daughters pass on defects to their own female children. Whether permanent inheritable genetic damage will be spread more widely in future generations is uncertain.

DES was sold as a generic drug. It was produced in tablets of various dosages according to the same formula by all manufacturers and marketed nationally under a generic description. Pharmacists filled prescriptions by using DES manufactured by different companies interchangeably. Each of the many manufacturers produced and sold DES for different periods between 1949 and 1971. Some of the companies that made and sold DES no longer exist.

Litigation concerning alleged DES-related injuries has occupied courts around the country since the mid–1970s. In New York state alone, more than 500 DES cases against scores of defendants are pending in state and federal courts. In January of this year, a joint special master/referee was appointed by this court and by New York Supreme Court Justice Ira Gammerman to coordinate settlement negotiations with respect to these cases. *See* In re DES Cases, 142 F.R.D. 58 (E.D.N.Y.1992).

B. *Present Actions*

In *Ashley v. Abbott Laboratories,* No. 91–3784, and *Silveri v. Abbott Laboratories,* No. 91–4986, plaintiffs claim injuries from their exposure (or their spouses' exposure) *in utero* to DES. Plaintiff Angela Silveri is a New York resident, as are approximately half of the *Ashley* plaintiffs. The remaining *Ashley* plaintiffs each reside in another state or a foreign country. All plaintiffs allege causes of action sounding in warranty, negligence and strict liability and seek compensatory and punitive damages. Defendants are companies that manufactured and distributed DES or are successors to such companies. Subject matter jurisdiction in each case is predicated on diversity of citizenship.

Defendant Boehringer Ingelheim Pharmaceuticals, Inc. ("Boehringer") has never produced or sold DES, but it is alleged to be responsible for Stayner Corporation, a company that did. Boehringer was incorporated in 1971. In 1979 Stayner was merged into Boehringer. Between 1949 and 1971 Stayner obtained its supply of DES from chemical companies located in California, Tennessee and Ohio, manufactured DES tablets at a plant in California and sold the tablets in California, Oregon, Washington and Montana; undoubtedly the California, Tennessee and Ohio plants obtained some of their supplies from other states. Available figures for the years 1949–56 indicated that Stayner's DES revenues averaged a little over $5,000 per year during that period. Affidavits from senior Stayner employees indicate that the company never was licensed to do business in New York, never maintained an office or agent in New York, never solicited business in New York and never shipped

DES to New York. By contrast, Boehringer, a Delaware corporation with its principal place of business in Connecticut, has been authorized to do business in New York since its inception. Boehringer markets its products (which do not include DES) in all states and is licensed to do business in several other states besides New York.

Boyle & Co. ("Boyle") is a closely held California corporation. At oral argument, counsel for Boyle indicated that the company manufactured and sold DES between 1949 and 1960 in California and other states west of the Mississippi River. Sales of DES tablets peaked in 1950, when Boyle sold about 157,000 tablets in packages of 100 and 1,000. Total revenues from all company business reached their highest point in the late 1950s and are now minimal. Boyle claims never to have shipped DES to New York or sold it here. Employee affidavits attest that the company has never been licensed to do business in New York, never maintained an office or agents in New York and never advertised in New York.

* * *

V. PERSONAL JURISDICTION

Personal jurisdiction must be determined in the first instance according to the jurisdictional law of the forum—New York Arrowsmith v. United Press Int'l, 320 F.2d 219 (2d Cir.1963)(*en banc*). The application of New York law must then be measured against due process limits. *See, e.g.,* International Shoe Co. v. Washington, 326 U.S. 310, 66 S.Ct. 154, 90 L.Ed. 95 (1945).

* * *

A. New York Jurisdictional Statutes

Possible state law bases for jurisdiction over the moving defendants are found in sections 301 and 302(a)(3) of the New York C.P.L.R.

1. C.P.L.R. § 301

Section 301 incorporates common law bases for jurisdiction existing at the time of the section's enactment in 1962. It provides simply that "[a] court may exercise such jurisdiction over persons, property, or status as might have been exercised heretofore." One established basis for jurisdiction is consent. Under New York case law from before and after 1962, "[w]hen a foreign corporation is licensed to do business in New York, it consents to be sued on causes of action arising within and without the State." LeVine v. Isoserve, Inc., 70 Misc.2d 747, 334 N.Y.S.2d 796, 799 (1972)(citing, *inter alia*, Bagdon v. Philadelphia & Reading Coal & Iron Co., 217 N.Y. 432, 111 N.E. 1075 (1916)). A defendant's engagement in "a continuous and systematic course of 'doing business' " in New York is another basis for general jurisdiction incorporated into section 301. Simonson v. International Bank, 14 N.Y.2d 281, 285, 251 N.Y.S.2d 433, 200 N.E.2d 427 (1964).

2. C.P.L.R. § 302

By contrast, section 302 is a long arm provision. Section 302(a)(3) allows, under certain conditions, jurisdiction over non-residents for tortious acts occurring outside New York. The section was not intended to reach the limits of long arm jurisdiction allowed under the federal Constitution. Banco Ambrosiano v. Artoc Bank & Trust, Ltd., 62 N.Y.2d 65, 71, 476 N.Y.S.2d 64, 464 N.E.2d 432 (1984).

Section 302(a)(3)(ii) is the provision which applies to the activity of companies alleged not to have conducted any business in New York. It provides for jurisdiction over defendants whose out-of-state tortious acts cause injury to a person within the state, so long as the tortfeasor should have expected its act to have consequences in the state and it derives substantial revenue from interstate or international commerce. It reads:

> (a) As to a cause of action arising from any of the acts enumerated in this section, a court may exercise personal jurisdiction over any non-domiciliary ... who in person or through an agent ... (3) commits a tortious act without the state causing injury to person or property within the state ... if he ... (ii) expects or should reasonably expect the act to have consequences in the state and derives substantial revenue from interstate or international commerce....

There is a developed body of case law interpreting the scope and meaning of the "injury within the state," "reasonable expectation of consequences," and "substantial revenue" conditions on the exercise of jurisdiction under section 302(a)(3)(ii).

Establishing that an out-of-state defendant's revenue from interstate commerce is "substantial" requires examination of either the percentage of a defendant's revenues that is derived from interstate commerce or the absolute amount of revenue generated by interstate commercial activities. Ronar, Inc. v. Wallace, 649 F.Supp. 310, 316 (S.D.N.Y.1986). The actual numbers that have sustained or failed to sustain a claim of substantial revenue vary considerably, making it difficult to define the point at which revenue becomes "substantial." *See id.* at 317. This element is not at issue in the present case since, during the period when the movants were selling DES, both received substantial revenues from commerce in several states.

With respect to the existence of an in-state injury, the general rule is that " 'the situs of the injury is the location of the original event which caused the injury, not the location where the resultant damages are subsequently felt by the plaintiff.' " Carte v. Parkoff, 152 A.D.2d 615, 543 N.Y.S.2d 718, 719 (1989)(citations omitted). Most of the complexities in this element concern the locus of a commercial injury such as loss of business. *See, e.g.,* Cooperstein v. Pan–Oceanic Marine, Inc., 124 A.D.2d 632, 507 N.Y.S.2d 893, 895 (1986)(plaintiff alleging economic injury based on transactions with Virginia and Florida cannot claim injury occurred in New York), *appeal denied,* 69 N.Y.2d 611, 517

N.Y.S.2d 1025, 511 N.E.2d 84 (1987). As applied to non-commercial tort cases, the situs rule is meant to prevent parties from carrying injuries that occurred out of state back to New York in order to bring suit. *See, e.g.,* Twine v. Levy, 746 F.Supp. 1202, 1206 (E.D.N.Y.1990)(where malpractice suit is based on treatment in defendant's out-of-state office, injury occurred out of state); *Carte,* 543 N.Y.S.2d at 719 (same); Hermann v. Sharon Hosp., Inc., 135 A.D.2d 682, 522 N.Y.S.2d 581, 583 (1987)(same); Black v. Oberle Rentals, Inc., 55 Misc.2d 398, 285 N.Y.S.2d 226, 228–29 (1967)(in suit based on car accident in Massachusetts, injuries occurred in Massachusetts).

Where, as here, an allegedly harmful drug is ingested in New York, or acts upon a resident of the state while the resident is in the state or upon her progeny when they are in the state, the situs of the injury is New York: there is no sense in which plaintiffs have merely carried their injuries into the state for the purpose of bringing suit. Moreover, to construe plaintiffs' injuries as having occurred at the place of manufacture rather than the place of exposure would defeat the purpose of section 302(a)(3)(ii) by making its reach co-extensive with that of section 302(a)(2), which covers only torts committed within the state. *See* Friedr. Zoellner (New York) Corp. v. Tex Metals Co., 278 F.Supp. 52, 56 (S.D.N.Y.1967)(section 302(a)(3)(ii) "was designed ... to cover cases where products purchased or manufactured in another jurisdiction caused injury in New York") * * *, *aff'd,* 396 F.2d 300 (2d Cir.1968).

The "reasonable expectation" element of section 302(a)(3)(ii) requires that a defendant foresee that its tortious act will have some consequences in New York, although not necessarily the exact consequences that occurred. Allen v. Auto Specialties Mfg. Co., 45 A.D.2d 331, 357 N.Y.S.2d 547, 550 (3d Dep't 1974); Tracy v. Paragon Contact Lens Lab., Inc., 44 A.D.2d 455, 355 N.Y.S.2d 650, 652–53 (3d Dep't 1974).

As to this element, the lower New York courts have been particularly concerned to avoid any potential conflict with federal constitutional due process limits on state court jurisdiction as set out in cases like World–Wide Volkswagen Corp. v. Woodson, 444 U.S. 286, 100 S.Ct. 559, 62 L.Ed.2d 490 (1980). They have thus asserted that the mere likelihood that a defendant's product will find its way into New York does not satisfy this element, and that purposeful availment of the benefits of the laws of New York such that the defendant may reasonably anticipate being haled into New York court is required. *See* Martinez v. American Standard, 91 A.D.2d 652, 457 N.Y.S.2d 97, 98–99 (1982), *aff'd,* 60 N.Y.2d 873, 470 N.Y.S.2d 367, 458 N.E.2d 826 (1983); *see also* Schaadt v. T.W. Kutter, Inc., 169 A.D.2d 969, 564 N.Y.S.2d 865, 866 (3d Dep't 1991)("foreseeability must be coupled with evidence of a purposeful New York affiliation, for example, a discernible effort to directly or indirectly serve the New York market"); Murdock v. Arenson Int'l USA, Inc., 157 A.D.2d 110, 554 N.Y.S.2d 887, 889 (1st Dep't 1990)(same); Cooperstein v. Pan–Oceanic Marine, Inc., 124 A.D.2d 632, 507 N.Y.S.2d 893, 895 (1986)(same), *appeal denied,* 69 N.Y.2d 611, 517 N.Y.S.2d 1025, 511

N.E.2d 84 (1987); Prentice v. Demag Material Handling Ltd., 80 A.D.2d 741, 437 N.Y.S.2d 173, 175 (4th Dep't 1981)(same); Tracy v. Paragon Contact Lens Lab., Inc., 44 A.D.2d 455, 355 N.Y.S.2d 650, 653 (3d Dep't 1974)(same).

Requiring that a defendant reasonably expect to be haled into New York court is not a workable basis for determining jurisdiction since the test itself is circular. The reasonableness of that expectation, unlike the expectation that out-of-state acts will have forum consequences, depends entirely on the content of New York's jurisdictional laws. *See* Redish, *Due Process, Federalism, and Personal Jurisdiction: A Theoretical Evaluation,* 75 Nw.U.L.Rev. 1112, 1134 (1981)(because reasonable expectation of being haled into a forum is determined by the forum's jurisdictional law, it cannot provide the standard for determining reasonableness of jurisdiction); Stephens, *Sovereignty and Personal Jurisdiction Doctrine: Up the Stream of Commerce Without a Paddle,* 19 Fla.St. L.Rev. 105, 139–40 (1991)(same). As written, rather than as interpreted in the non-mass tort context, the statute provides a framework within which the jurisdictional problems of traditional and mass torts and other new forms of litigation may be efficiently resolved.

Cases holding that jurisdiction cannot be asserted where a product's contact with New York was only through the stream of national commerce and unintended by the manufacturer are not relevant to the present case. Each involved traditional tort suits by individual plaintiffs against individual providers of goods and services. *See, e.g., Schaadt,* 564 N.Y.S.2d at 865 (action by individual against manufacturer and distributor of meat packing machine); *Murdock,* 554 N.Y.S.2d at 888 (action by individual against retailer of defective chair); *Martinez,* 457 N.Y.S.2d at 98 (action on behalf of individual decedent against manufacturer and installer of air conditioner); *Prentice,* 437 N.Y.S.2d at 174 (action by individual and spouse against manufacturer of chain hoist); *Tracy,* 355 N.Y.S.2d at 651 (action on behalf of individual against manufacturer of contact lenses). *Hymowitz* is not a traditional tort case. It is the New York courts' response to what would otherwise be the intractable nature of the DES mass tort. Local businesses, or foreign businesses whose products normally have no contact with the United States, may arguably rely on the fact that they never expected to have any dealings that affect New Yorkers. But the same is not true of manufacturers of generic goods participating in a national industry and market.

Existing case law on section 302(a)(3)(ii) thus offers no direct guidance on the application of the "reasonable expectation" element to mass DES torts; precedent is here only a slight inhibitant against rational decisionmaking. *See* E. Hanks & S. Nemerson, THE LEGAL PROCESS: CASES AND MATERIALS Ch. 3, at 1–2 (temporary ed. 1992); *cf.* Goldberg, Note: *Community and the Common Law Judge: Reconstructing Cardozo's Theoretical Writings,* 65 N.Y.U.L.Rev. 1324, 1352 (1990)(describing Cardozo's concern that *stare decisis* not degenerate into "the tyranny of concepts"). The issue must instead be resolved in a manner consistent with the court's informed prediction of what the New York Court of Appeals would do when faced with the same issue. DeWeerth v. Baldinger, 836 F.2d 103, 108 (2d Cir.1987), *cert. denied,* 486 U.S. 1056, 108 S.Ct. 2823, 100 L.Ed.2d 924 (1988); In re E. & S. Dists. Asbestos Litig., 772 F.Supp. 1380, 1390 (E. & S.D.N.Y.1991). That court has already gone to considerable lengths to adapt state substantive law to the particular circumstances of the DES cases. Moreover, *Hymowitz* itself drew a direct link between the jurisdictional and substantive components of DES litigation by imposing several, rather than joint and several, liability. *See Hymowitz,* 73 N.Y.2d at 512–13, 541 N.Y.S.2d 941, 539 N.E.2d 1069. New York law favors fully compensating plaintiffs for losses sustained. *See In re E. & S. Dists. Asbestos Litig.,* 772 F.Supp. at 1401. For mass torts involving numerous defendants, this result is usually achieved by the imposition of joint and several liability. *Id.* at 1400–03 (to fully compensate plaintiffs, New York General Obligations Law holds non-settling defendants jointly and severally liable for damages attributable to unreachable defendants). Given the *Hymowitz* court's decision to forgo joint and several liability, a DES plaintiff's full recovery would be frustrated if all manufacturers for pregnancy use could not be brought into court. *See Hymowitz,* 73 N.Y.2d at 521, 541 N.Y.S.2d 941, 539 N.E.2d 1069 (Mollen, J., dissenting).

Hymowitz and the New York Civil Practice Law and Rules as well as legislative policy must thus be read as favoring a jurisdictional reach consistent with the national market share rationale and the adoption of several liability. A consonant interpretation of C.P.L.R. § 302(a)(3)(ii) supports the conclusion that any manufacturer of DES, by its participation in the national marketing of a generic drug, should "reasonably expect" its act of selling in the national market "to have," as C.P.L.R. 302(a)(3)(ii) puts it, "consequences in the state."

Even before *Hymowitz,* all DES manufacturers knew that their acts were having forum consequences in New York. All were competing to carve out local spheres of influence within the national DES market. Since the product was a generic, perfectly fungible consumer item, each manufacturer and distributor secured its market niche knowing that, by occupying this territory, other suppliers would have cause to look elsewhere to sell the same product. Moreover, the existence of the local markets depended upon the creation of a national DES market. Defendants' engagement in the national DES industry alerted them to the fact that their conduct in marketing generic DES in one part of the country would have economic and trade flow consequences in every other part, including New York. There was here a true national market encouraged and protected by the Commerce Clause of the federal Constitution and national drug regulations, not a series of discrete inward-looking and unrelated markets. Sales in any part of the national market had a necessary impact on every other part. *Hymowitz* simply marked the Court of Appeals' recognition that these features of the DES economy were relevant to the apportionment of liability among defendants.

The fact that DES manufacturers did not anticipate *Hymowitz* or the jurisdictional consequences flowing from that decision is not significant. The parties in this suit are governed by the substantive common law and jurisdictional law in effect at the time of the suit. Linkletter v. Walker, 381 U.S. 618, 626 n.10, 85 S.Ct. 1731, 1736 n. 10, 14 L.Ed.2d 601 (1965)("'A federal court sitting in a diversity case must ... apply the most recent state court decision, even if it came after the operative events....'")(citing Note, *Prospective Overruling and Retroactive Application in the Federal Courts,* 71 Yale L.J. 907, 915 (1962)). To the extent any defendant actually tailors its primary conduct to avoid appearing in certain fora, legal innovations like *Hymowitz* may undermine such efforts. The same holds true, however, of defendants' attempts to conform their primary conduct to substantive common law. Our legal system is at least as solicitous of defendants' attempts to comply with substantive law as it is of their ability to plan their activities so as to avoid jurisdiction. Yet changes in substantive common law routinely defy parties' expectations. *See, e.g.,* Great N. Ry. v. Sunburst Oil & Refining Co., 287 U.S. 358, 364, 53 S.Ct. 145, 148, 77 L.Ed. 360 (1932)(state court has discretion to determine whether to apply innovative decisions only prospectively or to the parties before it). Jurisdictional legislation is likewise exempt from the general rule that statutes be applied only prospectively. McGee v. International Life Ins. Co., 355 U.S. 220, 224, 78 S.Ct. 199, 201, 2 L.Ed.2d 223 (1957)(jurisdictional legislation is remedial and does not affect substantive rights; it may thus be applied to cases whose operative facts occurred prior to its passage); Simonson v. International Bank, 14 N.Y.2d 281, 290, 251 N.Y.S.2d 433, 200 N.E.2d 427 (1964)(C.P.L.R. § 302 must be applied retroactively; question of retroactivity determined exclusively by reference to legislative design).

In finding a reasonable expectation of forum consequences for all manufacturers of DES for pregnancy use, the law need not attribute a co-conspirator, agency or concerted action relationship among the manufacturers. *See* In re North Dakota Personal Injury Asbestos Litig. No. 1, 737 F.Supp. 1087, 1095–98 (D.N.D.1990)(out-of-state defendant amenable to jurisdiction where it was allegedly a member of a trade association that knowingly suppressed information about asbestos hazards in furtherance of a conspiracy to commit deceit and other members of the association sold asbestos in the jurisdiction); Gudaitis v. Adomonis, 643 F.Supp. 383 (E.D.N.Y.1986)(court may assert jurisdiction over defendant by attributing co-conspirator's acts in the forum to defendant); Allen v. Auto Specialties Mfg. Co., 45 A.D.2d 331, 357 N.Y.S.2d 547, 550 (3d Dep't 1974)(defendant that by itself and through agents solicited business in New York should reasonably expect forum consequences). *But cf.* Sage v. Fairchild–Swearingen Corp., 70 N.Y.2d 579, 587, 523 N.Y.S.2d 418, 517 N.E.2d 1304 (1987)(manufacturer of defectively designed product is liable for injuries caused by duplicate where (1) duplicate adheres to design of original and (2) plaintiff's use of duplicate was foreseeable).

The language of *Hymowitz* in fact bars this attribution. There the court noted that the

> drug companies were engaged in extensive parallel conduct in developing and marketing DES. There is nothing in the record, however, beyond this similar conduct to show any agreement, tacit or otherwise, to market DES for pregnancy use without taking proper steps to ensure the drug's safety.

73 N.Y.2d at 506, 541 N.Y.S.2d 941, 539 N.E.2d 1069 (citation omitted). It is too late for plaintiffs to controvert this finding. The Court of Appeals reaffirmed *Hymowitz* in two recent opinions. Rastelli v. Goodyear Tire & Rubber Co., 79 N.Y.2d 289, 582 N.Y.S.2d 373, 591 N.E.2d 222 (1992); In re DES Market Share Litig., 79 N.Y.2d 299, 582 N.Y.S.2d 377, 591 N.E.2d 226 (1992). Even if factually unfounded—as plaintiffs contend—the policy is now settled New York law and all New York law must be adjusted to that policy. *See* In re DES Cases, 789 F.Supp. 548 (E.D.N.Y.1992).

B.   *Constitutionality of New York Statutes*

C.P.L.R. §§ 301 and 302(a)(3)(ii) must be applied in a manner that does not violate the federal Constitution. The issue is whether the Constitution limits the ability of New York state to provide full compensation to residents injured by a product sold in the national DES market.

1.   *Current Due Process Doctrine and Problems Raised by Its Application to Mass Torts*

There is considerable doubt about the current existence of a unitary, coherent jurisdictional due process standard. *See* Burger King Corp. v. Rudzewicz, 471 U.S. 462, 471–78, 105 S.Ct. 2174, 2181-85, 85 L.Ed.2d 528 (1985)(listing alternative formulations); *see also, e.g.,* Borchers, *The Death of the Constitutional Law of Personal Jurisdiction: From* Pennoyer *to* Burnham *and Back Again,* 24 U.C. Davis L.Rev. 19, 73 (1990)(describing formulations in *Burger King* as "unwieldy"); Korn, *The Implications of* Burnham v. Superior Court *for the DeConstitutionalization of Judicial Jurisdiction, Address to the Faculty of Columbia Law School,* Feb. 27, 1992 (on file)(discussing contradictions in current cases); McDougal, *Judicial Jurisdiction: From a Contacts to an Interest Analysis,* 35 Vand.L.Rev. 1, 8–13 (1982)(criticizing "minimum contacts" approach); Murphy, *Personal Jurisdiction and the Stream of Commerce Theory: a Reappraisal and a Revised Approach,* 77 Ky.L.J. 243, 270–72 (1988)(noting tensions in recent decisions); Stephens, *Sovereignty and Personal Jurisdiction, supra,* at 105–06, 122–23 (arguing that "stream of commerce" cases have created confusion).

One common feature of recent Supreme Court formulations is that a defendant must reasonably expect that its activity could result in litigation in the forum state. *See, e.g., Burger King,* 471 U.S. at 474 (defendant must "purposefully establish[   ] 'minimum contacts' in the forum State" so that " 'the defendant's conduct and connection with the forum State are such that he should reasonably anticipate being haled into court there' ")(*quoting* World–Wide Volkswagen Corp. v. Woodson, 444 U.S. 286, 297, 100 S.Ct. 559, 567, 62 L.Ed.2d 490 (1980)). The Court has emphasized that this standard is ultimately designed to protect the liberty interests of defendants. Insurance Corp. of Ireland, Ltd. v. Compagnie des Bauxites de Guinee, 456 U.S. 694, 702–03 n.10, 102 S.Ct. 2099, 2104-05 n. 10, 72 L.Ed.2d 492 (1982).

The Court has, however, acknowledged other interests besides (1) the interest of a defendant in being able to predict the location of future litigation, namely (2) the forum state's interest in providing a convenient forum to its residents, (3) the plaintiff's interest in obtaining relief, (4) the state courts' interest in efficient resolution of disputes, and (5) the shared interests of the several states. These other interests have been described as "surrogate[s]" of defendants' underlying liberty interests. Keeton v. Hustler Magazine, Inc., 465 U.S. 770, 776, 104 S.Ct. 1473, 1479, 79 L.Ed.2d 790 (1984). Introduction of the "surrogate" interests into due process analysis complicates matters. Thus,

> [a] State generally has a "manifest interest" in providing its residents with a convenient forum for redressing injuries inflicted by out-of-state actors. Moreover, where individuals "purposefully derive benefit" from their interstate activities, it may well be unfair to allow them to escape having to account in other States for consequences that arise proximately from such activities; the Due Process Clause may not readily be wielded as a territorial shield to avoid interstate obligations that have been voluntarily assumed.

Burger King, 471 U.S. at 473–74, 105 S.Ct. at 2182-83 (citations omitted). Likewise,

> the determination of the reasonableness of the exercise of jurisdiction in each case will depend on an evaluation of several factors. A court must consider the burden on the defendant, the interests of the forum State, and the plaintiff's interest in obtaining relief. It also must weigh in its determination "the interstate judicial system's interest in obtaining the most efficient resolution of controversies; and the shared interests of the several States in furthering fundamental substantive social policies."

Asahi Metal Indus. Co. v. Superior Court, 480 U.S. 102, 113, 107 S.Ct. 1026, 1033, 94 L.Ed.2d 92 (1987)(plurality opinion)(*quoting* World–Wide Volkswagen Corp. v. Woodson, 444 U.S. 286, 292, 100 S.Ct. 559, 564, 62 L.Ed.2d 490 (1980)).

The Supreme Court has never had occasion to balance this multiplicity of factors in a mass tort case involving parties from across the nation. The so-called "stream of commerce" cases—*World-Wide Volkswagen* and *Asahi*—appear to prevent the assertion of jurisdiction in traditional tort cases solely on the grounds that it was foreseeable to a defendant that its product might travel through the national or international economy and therefore might surface in any given jurisdiction. *See Asahi* 480 U.S. at 112 (plurality opinion). While some have suggested that *Asahi* is limited in applicability because it involved an indemnification action between two foreign corporations, the case has been given more general application. *See, e.g.,* Wiles v. Morita Iron Works Co., 125 Ill.2d 144, 125 Ill. D[ec]. 812, 816–17, 530 N.E.2d 1382, 1386–87 (1988)(under *Asahi,* jurisdiction lacking in tort suit against foreign manufacturer of "air cell former" machine); Kohn v. La Manufacture Francaise Des Pneumatiques Michelin, 476 N.W.2d 184, 187 (Minn.Ct App.1991)(jurisdiction lacking in tort suit against foreign tire manufacturer); Graham v. Machinery Distribution, Inc., 410 Pa. Super. 267, 599 A.2d 984, 987–88 (Pa.Sup.Ct.1991)(jurisdiction lacking in tort suit against foreign manufacturer of forklift); Parry v. Ernst Home Center Corp., 779 P.2d 659, 668 (Utah 1989)(jurisdiction lacking in tort suit against foreign tool manufacturer); *cf.* Humble v. Toyota Motor Co., 727 F.2d 709 (8th Cir.1984)(jurisdiction lacking over foreign car seat manufacturer). Thus applied, *Asahi* 's plurality rule is of dubious utility even in traditional litigation. *See, e.g.,* Stephens, *Sovereignty and Personal Jurisdiction, supra,* at 106; Weintraub, Asahi *Sends Personal Jurisdiction Down the Tubes,* 56 Tex. Int'l L.J. 55, 56 (1988).

The *Asahi-Volkswagen* approach is particularly pernicious in the advantage it gives to foreign producers whose goods enter the American common market. These firms can organize themselves to avoid jurisdiction in any state or federal court. *See Kohn,* 476 N.E.2d at 188 ("We recognize . . . that denying jurisdiction allows a corporation to structure itself to avoid suit in foreign jurisdictions."). What should be an issue of venue—where in the United States a foreign manufacturer can be sued—is turned into a jurisdictional barrier to suit anywhere in the country. *But cf.* Bulova Watch Co. v. K. Hattori & Co., 508 F.Supp. 1322 (E.D.N.Y.1981)(asserting jurisdiction over Japanese company because of loyalty between company managers and management of United States subsidiary). Because jurisdictional due process allows many foreign manufacturers to circumvent the American courts altogether, United States residents often will be unable to avail themselves of the strong protections of American tort law. Foreign manufacturers also gain a competitive advantage.

In any event, neither *Volkswagen* nor *Asahi,* which both involved conventional product liability claims by individual plaintiffs, are controlling in DES mass torts brought under *Hymowitz* for the same reasons that the traditional New York tort cases interpreting the "reasonable expectation" element of C.P.L.R. 302(a)(3)(ii) are unhelpful in applying that statute to mass tort cases such as this one. As was pointed out above, mass torts raise unique problems of substantive, quasi-substantive, and procedural law that have just begun to receive the attention they require in federal and state courts and legislatures. The wooden application of inapt precedent will not effectively resolve these cases. As both *Burger King* and *Asahi* indicate, a careful weighing of the interests of the parties, the forum states, and the interstate system is required.

In their jurisdictional cast, DES mass tort cases perhaps most resemble Keeton v. Hustler Magazine, Inc., 465 U.S. 770, 104 S.Ct. 1473, 79 L.Ed.2d 790 (1984). Keeton, a New York resident, sued Hustler magazine for libel in New Hampshire. Jurisdiction in New Hampshire was predicated in the first instance on the defendant's distributing a small percentage of the allegedly offending publications in that state. Noting that the plaintiff had alleged injuries occurring in every state in the country, the Court focused its minimum contacts analysis on the issue of whether it would be " 'fair' to compel [Hustler] to defend a multistate lawsuit in New Hampshire seeking nationwide damages ... even though only a small portion of ... [the allegedly libelous] copies were distributed in New Hampshire." *Id.* at 775, 104 S.Ct. 1778-79. In light of New Hampshire's interest in redressing the small percentage of national injuries that occurred in its state, *id.* at 776, 104 S.Ct. at 1479, and the several states' interest in the efficient adjudication of a national claim in a single forum, *id.* at 777, 104 S.Ct. at 1479, the Court found an assertion of jurisdiction constitutional despite the fact that the defendant had *de minimis* contacts and the plaintiff no connection to the forum other than the lawsuit. *Id.* at 780, 104 S.Ct. at 1481.

Like considerations favor a finding that jurisdiction over the defendants in this case can be constitutionally asserted. *Hymowitz, Besser,* and the legislative modifications to New York's statutes of limitations for DES plaintiffs evince New York's intent to provide as full a recovery as is practicable to those of its residents injured by DES. New York and its residents therefore have a strong interest in the assertion of jurisdiction. Likewise, the several states share an interest in the efficient resolution of DES cases.

The fit with *Keeton* is not exact. In the present case, for example, some of the DES manufacturers cannot be said to have directly availed themselves of the forum state's market, whereas Hustler clearly did, albeit to a trivial extent. Still, by competing to establish a territorial niche within the national DES market, every manufacturer directly or indirectly benefited from the Commerce Clause of the federal Constitution and the laws of every state in the nation by participating in the national market for a generic good. In a sense, then, each DES manufacturer did "purposefully derive benefit from [its] interstate activities," such that none may be entitled to rely on the Due Process Clause "as a territorial shield to avoid interstate obligations that have been voluntarily assumed." *Burger King,* 471 U.S. at 473–74, 105 S.Ct. at 2183. Under the federal Commerce Clause and the substantive law of *Hymowitz,* the United States constitutes a common economic pond that knows no state boundaries. A substantial interjection of products at any point of the national market has ripple effects in all parts of the market.

The strain created in trying to accommodate jurisdictional issues raised by mass torts into the literal requirements of accepted formulations like "purposeful availment" suggests that modifications of jurisdictional law may be no less appropriate than modifications of substantive and quasi-substantive law already undertaken by state courts and legislatures. The standard jurisdictional formulations are, after all, the product of traditional cases which were not decided with mass litigation in mind. In this instance, at least, where substantive law has undergone significant development to accommodate socioeconomic change, it is necessary to interpret jurisdictional law so that it meets the demands of the subject matter of the litigation. *See, e.g.,* Erichson, Note: *Nationwide Personal Jurisdiction, supra,* at 1158 & n.265 (noting recent scholarship discussing advantages of linking substantive and procedural law). The need for adaptation in this case is clearly indicated by the fact that, without it, these New York plaintiffs would likely be barred from recovering from these defendants in any court. If, for example, plaintiffs sought out the defendants in the California courts, California choice-of-law rules would probably call for the application of California substantive law. *See* Bernhard v. Harrah's Club, 16 Cal.3d 313, 128 Cal.Rptr. 215, 546 P.2d 719 (*en banc*)(adopting "comparative impairment of state interests" approach to choice-of-law issues), *cert. denied,* 429 U.S. 859, 97 S.Ct. 159, 50 L.Ed.2d 136 (1976). The defendants could then obtain a dismissal under *Sindell* by proving that they did not market DES in New York.

The Supreme Court itself has suggested the need for modified jurisdictional analysis in the special context of mass litigation. In the *Shutts* case, the Court confronted the issue of whether the Kansas state court had jurisdiction to bind each of the almost 30,000 plaintiff class members located around the country without requiring a showing of minimum contacts between each member and Kansas. Phillips Petroleum Co. v. Shutts, 472 U.S. 797, 105 S.Ct. 2965, 86 L.Ed.2d 628 (1985). Noting the necessity of the national class action device to provide relief where it might otherwise be unattainable, Chief Justice Rehnquist wrote that "minimum contacts" analysis was inapplicable and that, instead, a lower standard of "minimal procedural due process protection" was sufficient. *Id.* at 811–12. This standard requires only (1) best practicable notice and an opportunity to be heard, as defined by Mullane v. Central Hanover Bank & Trust Co., 339 U.S. 306, 70 S.Ct. 652, 94 L.Ed. 865 (1950); (2) a right to opt out of the litigation and (3) a showing that the named plaintiff(s) adequately represent absent class members. *Id.* 472 U.S. at 812. By this formula, the Court essentially employed the time-honored jurisdiction-stretching technique of implied consent to cope with the special problem of jurisdiction in mass class actions: plaintiffs who received notice and did not opt-out were deemed to have implicitly consented to jurisdiction. *See* Miller & Crump, *Jurisdiction and Choice of Law in Multistate Class Actions After* Phillips Petroleum Co. v. Shutts, 96 Yale L.J. 1, 16–17 (noting Court's reliance on fiction of implied consent).

Similar modifications are necessary in the DES context. Although the *Shutts* opinion stressed that its treatment of the plaintiff class did not necessarily apply to defendants or defendant classes, *see Shutts,* 472 U.S. at 808–11 & 811–12 n.3, the difficulties raised by mass litigation and the present case warrant a restatement of jurisdictional due process law that can function in this and other mass torts.

[Judge Weinstein next canvasses, at length, the history of personal jurisdiction due process in non-mass tort cases, beginning with *Pennoyer v. Neff* through *International Shoe* and its progeny—*ed.*]

3. Sovereignty and Fairness in Mass Torts

Two aspects of the constitutional case law of personal jurisdiction must be re-emphasized.

The first is that the cases continue to rely on two distinct inquiries—sovereignty and fairness. Furthermore, both the sovereignty and fairness inquiries have required some connection between the forum state and the defendant. The Supreme Court's fairness inquiries have retained the traditional requirement of a physical, *territorial* nexus: a non-resident defendant will be constitutionally subject to state assertions of jurisdiction only if it voluntarily commits acts within the state. By contrast, the Court's sovereignty inquiry now requires only an *interest* nexus: so long as the non-resident defendant's acts give rise to a forum interest, the state has authority to assert jurisdiction.

The second feature of note is that this jurisprudence of jurisdictional due process has been developed in cases almost all of which involved one or a few parties on each side. The Supreme Court's two-pronged inquiry has never been articulated in the context of a mass tort case arising out of the national (or international) marketing of a product. Only in *Shutts* has the Court dealt with this type of case, and there it was prepared to stretch prevailing jurisdictional standards by reliance on an implied consent theory.

This pair of considerations bears directly on the Due Process Clause standard appropriate to mass torts. The issue is whether the sovereignty and fairness inquiries legitimately can be adapted to such cases.

* * *

The oddity of the territorial nexus requirement will only become more evident in time. In the first place, the development of transportation and particularly communications technology—which, for example, allows courts to receive voluminous briefs in minutes by facsimile machine and to conduct hearings by telephone and soon by satellite video transmissions—continues to "shrink" the country.

Second, it seems likely that the phenomenon of mass litigations will continue to grow, and it is in these cases that the irrationality of the territorial nexus requirement is arguably most evident and the need for an improved approach most urgent. Mass tort suits typically are brought against groups of corporate defendants. In these cases the intuition linking territorial and convenience concerns—that a defendant in a civil case must travel to the forum to defend him-, her-or itself—is factually least plausible. As a rule, local counsel rather than defendants appear for motion and trial practice. Discovery need not and often will not take place in the forum. In federal court, moreover, discovery is subject to Federal Rule of Civil Procedure 26(b)(1)(iii), which now requires the district courts to take account of burdens on the parties in setting discovery parameters. As of the Rule's amendment in 1983, the courts must consider "the needs of the case, the amount in controversy, limitations on the parties' resources, and the importance of the issues at stake in the litigation."

The actual litigation costs per case of defendants in mass cases is also likely to be lower than the costs to defendants appearing alone. To the extent permitted by professional ethical rules, defendants often can cooperate to defray costs by effecting a division of labor. Even where defendants do not explicitly cooperate, in many mass cases some defendants will rely on the work of the defendants with the greatest potential exposure in the case and therefore the greatest interest in litigating effectively. In almost all mass torts, much of the cost of litigation is eventually paid by national insurance companies.

While the need for territorial nexus-based protections of defendants is arguably least pressing in mass torts, the continued reliance on such protections creates significant obstacles to their resolution. This is particularly evident in a case such as the instant one, where New York substantive law empowers plaintiffs to bring in all industry participants to achieve a full and economical resolution of their lawsuits, yet jurisdictional law may prevent the very result envisioned by the state's substantive, remedial and procedural laws.

4. Due Process Standard for Mass DES Torts

Given that New York law has evolved to promote the efficient resolution of mass DES torts, and given the problems of applying prevailing traditional jurisdictional concepts to such cases, a modification of established standards to determine the constitutionality of jurisdictional statutes that incorporates an interest nexus inquiry but not a territorial nexus inquiry is necessary in the DES context—and perhaps in other mass tort cases. The following pair of principles results from a conservative view of precedents. (Obviously, a more radical position eliminating the state interest requirement, thus allowing a neutral forum to accept jurisdiction, could be developed were the Supreme Court to revisit precedent.)

I.   The court must first determine if the forum state has an appreciable interest in the litigation, i.e., whether the litigation raises issues whose resolution would be affected by, or have a probable impact on the vindication of, policies expressed in the substantive, procedural or remedial laws of the forum. If there is an appreciable state interest, the assertion of jurisdiction is prima facie constitutional.

II.   Once a *prima facie* case is made, the assertion of jurisdiction will be considered constitutional unless, given the actual circumstances of the case, the defendant is unable to mount a defense in the forum state without suffering relatively substantial hardship. Evidence to be considered in determining the defendant's relative hardship includes, *inter alia*, (1) the defendant's available assets; (2) whether the defendant has or is engaged in substantial interstate commerce; (3) whether the defendant is being represented by an indemnitor or is sharing the cost of the defense with an indemnitor or co-defendant; (4) the comparative hardship defendant will incur in defending the suit in another forum; and (5) the comparative hardship to the plaintiff if the case were dismissed or transferred for lack of jurisdiction.

It must be emphasized that this standard is designed only to establish the minimum due process requirements for assertions of jurisdiction absent a defendant's consent. Considerations such as parties' and witnesses' convenience, administrative practicalities, and interstate comity concerns may still counsel against exercising that jurisdiction. Convenience and administrative feasibility are, of course, standard criteria for deciding motions to transfer or dismiss for improper venue or *forum non conveniens*. Interstate comity concerns would be raised, for example, if a state court has jurisdiction over a product liability case when a large number of related cases are pending in another state; courts or litigants may wish in such circumstances to seek consolidation in the other state. Ideally, such consolidations would be coordinated under a compact among the states or by authority of federal legislation. *See, e.g.,* American Law Institute, COMPLEX LITIGATION PROJECT, *Tentative Draft No. 3,* Ch. 4 (March 31, 1992)(proposing methods of case consolidation among state courts). At present, state courts can use doctrines such as *forum non conveniens* to protect interstate comity interests by dismissing cases outright or on condition that the defendant submit to jurisdiction in a more appropriate forum.

The mass tort standard does incorporate several factors acknowledged in Supreme Court case law and by academic commentators as relevant to the constitutional-jurisdictional inquiry. They include the size and type of litigation, the relative financial condition of the parties, other burdens on plaintiff and defendant, the forum's interest in the litigation, whether the litigation will involve only two parties or several parties or indemnitors, and whether the operation of the forum's choice-of-law rules or substantive laws impose a hardship on the defendant, favor the interests of the plaintiff, or both. *Cf.* Gottlieb, *In Search of the Link Between Due Process and Jurisdiction,* 60 Wash.U.L.Q. 1291, 1327–34 (1983)(constitutionality should turn on type of litigation and resources of parties); Redish, *Due Process, Federalism, and Personal Jurisdiction, supra,* at 1138–42 (assertion of jurisdiction that causes defendant "meaningful inconvenience" is unconstitutional unless inconvenience is outweighed by potential burdens on the plaintiff or by the forum state's interest in the litigation); Weintraub, *Due Process Limitations on the Personal Jurisdiction of State Courts: Time for a Change,* 63 Or.L.Rev. 485, 522–26 (1984)(if defendant demonstrates that assertion of jurisdiction works an unfairness, plaintiff may establish the propriety of jurisdiction "because of something that defendant has done in the forum or caused to occur in the forum").

Principle I incorporates the "interest" nexus requirement of cases like *Keeton, Burger King* and *Asahi.* By necessitating an appreciable interest, it also incorporates a proximate cause inquiry, thus imposing some limitations on the causal chain between a particular litigation and the state's interest. In keeping with current law, the burden of proving the existence of an interest is the plaintiff's.

* * *

After a *prima facie* case for the constitutionality of jurisdiction is made based on the court's authority to hear the case, the court must next inquire under the second principle whether the assertion of jurisdiction will be unfair to the defendant. The factors indicated in the second principle measure, among other things, the defendant's present ability to mount a reasonable defense as compared with the hardship plaintiff may suffer in having to bring its case elsewhere. The analysis will in some respects parallel the flexible analysis applied in controlling discovery under Rule 26(b)(1)(iii), * * * and in considering forum non conveniens motions. *See, e.g.,* Piper Aircraft Co. v. Reyno, 454 U.S. 235, 249, 102 S.Ct. 252, 262, 70 L.Ed.2d 419 (1981) (hallmark of *forum non conveniens* is its flexible application to facts of each case); *see also* Hodson v. A.H. Robins Co., 528 F.Supp. 809 (E.D.Va.1981) (in suit by English citizens against American manufacturer and distributor of allegedly defective contraceptive device for injuries occurring in England, *forum non conveniens* motion to dismiss denied in light of public and private interests favoring trial in American forum), *aff'd,* 715 F.2d 142 (4th Cir.1983); *cf.* In re Union Carbide Corp. Gas Plant Disaster at Bhopal, India in December, 1984, 809 F.2d 195 (2d Cir.)(suit by Indian plaintiffs against American corporation for mass industrial accident in India rightly dismissed on *forum non conveniens* grounds given plaintiffs' Indian citizenship, competence of Indian courts to handle case centered on Indian regulatory law, location of evidence and witnesses and fact that plant was run exclusively by Indian citizens), *cert. denied,* 484 U.S. 871, 108 S.Ct. 199, 98 L.Ed.2d 150 (1987); Union Carbide Corp. v. Union of India, ___ S.C.R. ___ (Sup.Ct.India Oct. 22, 1991)(upholding settlement of Bhopal claims except for that portion dismissing parallel criminal case). Since the issue is jurisdiction, however, the focus is on the particular hardships to defendant, and the showing of hardship required would be greater than that necessary to support transfer or dismissal under *forum non conveniens* doctrine.

Although the test under Principle II does not shift the burden of persuasion to defendants, the court will, as under current practice, assume fairness unless the defendant informs it of potential litigation burdens and the desirability of transfer or dismissal.

* * *

Notes and Questions

1. With regard to federal class action procedure and the parameters of due process, *Phillips Petroleum Co. v. Shutts,* left many questions unanswered. *Shutts* involved due process standards as they related to personal jurisdictional in a state-based class action. To what extent are the standards

articulated in *Shutts* applicable to federal class actions? Would it be possible for the Supreme Court to determine that due process requirements in federal nationwide class action lawsuits permit or require different due process requirements? For a general discussion of these questions, *see* John E. Kennedy, *The Supreme Court Meets the Bride of Frankenstein,* Phillips Petroleum Co. v. Shutts *and the State Multistate Class Action,* 34 Kan. L. Rev. 255 (1985); Rebecca K. Michalek, Note, Phillips Petroleum Co. v. Shutts: *Multistate Plaintiff Class Actions: A Definite Forum, But Is It Proper?,* 19 Marshall L.Rev. 483 (1986); Arthur Miller & David Crump, *Jurisdiction and Choice of Law in Multistate Class Actions After* Phillips Petroleum Co. v. Shutts, 96 Yale L.J. 1 (1986); Patricia M. Noonan, *State Personal Jurisdictional Requirements and the Non–Aggregation Rule in Class Actions,* 1987 U. Ill. L. Rev. 445 (1987); Kurt A. Schwartz, Note, *Due Process and Equitable Relief in State Multistate Class Actions After* Phillips Petroleum Co. v. Shutts, 68 Tex.L.Rev. 415 (1989); Bob Wenbourne, Comment, Phillips Petroleum Co. v. Shutts, *Procedural Due Process, and Absent Class Plaintiffs: Minimum Contact Is Out—Is Individual Notice In?,* 13 Hastings Const.L.Q. 817 (1986); Barbara A. Winters, Comment, *Jurisdiction Over Unnamed Plaintiffs in Multistate Class Actions,* 73 Cal.L.Rev. 181 (1985).

2. Assuming that *Shutts* is applicable to federal class actions, how broad or restricted are its due requirements for different categories of class actions? Do the *Shutts* criteria apply only to Rule 23(b)(3) class actions? What, if anything, does *Shutts* require in actions seeking injunctive or other equitable relief? In so-called "hybrid" actions seeking both injunctive and compensatory relief. What about actions seeking damages from a limited fund under Rule 23(b)(1)? *See* Linda S. Mullenix, *Class Actions, Personal Jurisdiction, and Plaintiffs' Due Process: Implications for Mass Tort Litigation,* ___ U.C. Davis L. Rev. ___ (1995); Kent D. Syverud, *Mandatory Class Actions* (forthcoming 1995); Mark Weber, *Preclusion and Procedural Due Process in Rule 23(b)(2) Class Actions,* 21 U.Mich.J.L.Ref. 347 (1988).

Why does the Constitution require notice and a right to opt-out only in damages cases? As Professors Wright, Miller, and Kane have questioned: " ... why should class members have a constitutional right to exclude themselves just because they are in a damages class action? If the Court is suggesting that parties should not be bound unless they impliedly consent by not excluding themselves, then that notion seems just as pertinent to injunction suits." Is the Court's rationale for rejecting an opt-in requirement sound? What arguments support an affirmative requirement that class members opt-in, rather than opt-out of a class action? *See* George A. Rutherglen, *Better Late Than Never: Notice and Opt-out at the Remedy Stage of Class Actions* (forthcoming 1995); for a discussion of *Shutts* and the questions it left open, *see* Wright, Miller, and Kane, 7B Federal Practice and Procedure § 1789, *supra.*

3. In Walter Thomas Brown v. Ticor Title Insurance Company, 982 F.2d 386 (9th Cir.1992), the Ninth Circuit held:

> Brown also argues that minimal procedural due process must be provided in a class action lawsuit in order "to bind known plaintiffs concerning claims wholly or predominately" for monetary damages. *See*

Phillips Petroleum Co. v. Shutts, 472 U.S. 797 n.3, 105 S.Ct. 2965, 86 L.Ed.2d 628 (1985). Brown asserts that certifying the MDL 633 class pursuant to Federal Rules of Civil Procedure 23(b)(1) and (b)(2), which do not provide for the right to opt out, would be a violation of minimum due process if the class judgment precluded future recovery of damages, and therefore res judicata is not applicable to his case.

In order to bind an absent plaintiff concerning a claim for monetary damages, the court must provide minimal due process. * * * *Shutts* is limited to claims "wholly or predominately for money judgments." * * * The Third Circuit held that the MDL 633 litigation was a "hybrid suit that involved the foreclosure of substantial damage claims." * * * We follow the Third Circuit's holding.

According to *Shutts,* minimal due process requires that "an absent plaintiff be provided with an opportunity to remove himself from the class by executing and returning an 'opt out' or 'request for exclusion' form to the court," if monetary claims are involved. * * * Because Brown had no opportunity to opt out of the MDL 633 litigation, we hold there would be a violation of minimal due process if Brown's damage claims were held barred by res judicata. Brown will be bound by the injunctive relief provided by the settlement in MDL 633, and foreclosed from seeking other or further injunctive relief in this case, but res judicata will not bar Brown's claims for monetary damages against Ticor.

On appeal of the Ninth Circuit's decision in *Ticor Title,* the Supreme Court granted certiorari to consider the question: "Whether a federal court may refuse to enforce a prior class action judgment, properly certified under Rule 23, on grounds that absent class members have a constitutional due process right to opt out of any class action which asserts monetary claims on their behalf." On the day the writ was granted, the parties settled and requested the Court dismiss the appeal. The Court refused and required the parties brief and argue the case, which they did.

After oral argument, the Court dismissed the writ as having been improvidently granted on the ground that "deciding this case would require us to resolve a constitutional question that may be entirely hypothetical." The Court concluded:

That certified question is of no general consequence if, whether or not absent class members have a constitutional right to opt out of such actions, they have a right to do so under the Federal Rules of Civil procedure. Such a right would exist if, in actions seeking monetary damages, classes can be certified only under Rule 23(b)(3), which permits opt-out, and not under Rules 23(b)(1) and (b)(2), which do not. * * * That is at least a substantial possibility—and we would normally resolve the preliminary nonconstitutional question before proceeding to the constitutional claim. * * * The law of res judicata, however, prevents that question from being litigated here. It was conclusively determined in the MDL No. 633 litigation that respondents' class fit within Rules 23(b)(1)(A) and (b)(2); even though that determination may have been wrong, it is conclusive upon these parties, and the alternative of using the Federal Rules instead of the Constitution as the means of imposing an opt-out requirement for this settlement is no longer available.

See Ticor Title Insurance Co. v. Brown, ___ U.S. ___, ___, 114 S.Ct. 1359, 1361, 128 L.Ed.2d 33 (1994).

4. In federal courts, at least, what is the status of opt-out rights with regard to hybrid and non-damage cases after *Ticor Title*? Are there different rules in the Third and Ninth Circuits? In a dissent from the dismissal, Justice O'Connor joined by the Chief Justice and Justice Kennedy argued that the Court's prudential rule avoiding constitutional questions had no application to *Ticor's* appeal. Refuting the majority's assertion that a resolution of the constitutional question would have no practical consequence, the dissenters pointed out that lower federal courts consistently have certified damage class actions under Rules 23(b)(1)(A) and (b)(2). "Under the Ninth Circuit's rationale in this case, every one of them [class members] has the right to go into federal court and relitigate their claims against the defendants in the original action." Furthermore, since federal courts will continue to certify (b)(1) and (b)(2) classes notwithstanding the presence of damage claims, "the constitutional opt-out right announced by the court below will be implicated in every such action, at least in the Ninth Circuit." Hence, the dissenters concluded that "[t]he resolution of a constitutional issue with such broad-ranging consequences is both necessary and appropriate." *See Ticor Title,* ___ U.S. at ___, 114 S.Ct. at 1363 (J. Rehnquist, O'Connor, and Kennedy dissenting).

Does *Ticor Title* apply to state class actions, as well? The dissenters believe so, arguing that the Ninth Circuit's decision was based on the Due Process Clause, and therefore it "presumably applies to the States." Does this interpretation conflict with *Phillips Petroleum Co. v. Shutts?*

5. *Phillips Petroleum* and *Carlough v. Amchem* involved (b)(3) opt out class actions. The lower federal courts will have an opportunity to revisit the minimum contacts-due process issue left unanswered by the Supreme Court in *Ticor Title,* in a mass tort asbestos settlement class negotiated in the Eastern District of Texas, Ahearn v. Fibreboard Corp., CV No. 6:93CV526 (E.D.Tex.1994) *Ahearn* is a Rule 23(b)(1)(B) limited fund, non-opt out, compensatory damages class action settlement. The fairness hearing in Ahearn was held in February 1995. For a discussion of the problems relating to mandatory non-opt-out class actions, *see* Linda S. Mullenix, *Class Actions, Personal Jurisdiction and Plaintiffs' Due Process: Implications for Mass Tort Litigation,* ___ U.C. Davis L. Rev. ___ (forthcoming 1995).

6. Judge Weinstein's opinion in the *DES Cases* represents a more conventional consideration of personal jurisdiction problems, only in a mass tort context. To what extent is Judge Weinstein's decision tied to New York state substantive law, particularly the *Hymowitz* decisions? For a discussion of the *Hymowitz* decision, *see infra* Part Three, Chapter V. C. *See generally,* Paul D. Rheingold, *The* Hymowitz *Decision—Practical Aspects of New York DES Litigation,* 55 Brook.L.Rev. 883 (1989). Is Judge Weinstein correct in suggesting that mass tort cases need a different set of standards for determination of the due process component of personal jurisdiction? Why are existing standards inadequate to this task, and why should mass tort cases be treated differently than any other multiparty cases? Are Judge

Weinstein's proposed standards more suitable? For a discussion of the substantive choice-of-law implications of dispersed mass torts, *see* Georffrey P. Miller, *Competing Classes and Conflicting Jurisdictions* (forthcoming 1995).

2. SUBJECT MATTER JURISDICTION

CARLOUGH v. AMCHEM PRODUCTS, INC.

United States District Court, Eastern District of Pennsylvania, 1993.
834 F.Supp. 1437.

[*See also* Georgine v. Amchem Products, Inc. at Ch. 1.D.4, *supra*]

MEMORANDUM

LOWELL A. REED, JR., DISTRICT JUDGE.

This lawsuit is a class action for asbestos-related personal injuries. This memorandum opinion addresses whether this Court has subject matter jurisdiction over this case.

I. BACKGROUND

On January 15, 1993, counsel for the plaintiff class (or the "*Carlough* class") filed the complaint in this action along with motions for class certification and for approval of a proposed settlement agreement ("proposed settlement" or "settlement") between the plaintiff class and the defendants. The complaint alleges that the defendants, members of the Center for Claims Resolution ("the CCR defendants"), are liable to the plaintiff class under the legal theories of (1) negligent failure to warn, (2) strict liability, (3) breach of express and implied warranty, (4) negligent infliction of emotional distress, (5) enhanced risk of disease, (6) medical monitoring, and (7) civil conspiracy. In their complaint, the named plaintiffs allege that jurisdiction is based upon diversity of citizenship and that the amount in controversy for each member of the plaintiff class exceeds $100,000.

On the same day as the complaint was filed, the CCR defendants answered the complaint and joined in plaintiffs' request that the class be certified and the settlement agreement approved.

On January 29, 1993, the Honorable Charles R. Weiner of this Court conditionally certified an opt-out class consisting of:

> 1. All persons (or their legal representatives) who have been exposed in the United States or its territories (or while working aboard U.S. military, merchant or passenger ships), either occupationally or through occupational exposure of a spouse or household member, to asbestos or to asbestos containing products for which one or more of the defendants may bear legal liability and who, as of January 15, 1993, reside in the United States or its territories, and who have not, as of January 15, 1993, filed a lawsuit for asbestos-related personal injury or damage, or death in any state or federal

court against the defendant(s)(or against entities for whose actions or omissions the defendant(s) bear legal liability).

2. All spouses, parents, children, and other relatives (or their legal representatives) of the class members described in paragraph 1 above who have not, as of January 15, 1993, filed a lawsuit for the asbestos-related personal injury, or damage, or death of a class member described in paragraph 1 above in any state or federal court against the defendant(s)(or against entities for whose actions or omissions the defendant(s) bear legal liability).

* * *

This memorandum addresses the four principal threshold issues raised by the objectors: standing, collusion, mootness and satisfaction of the amount in controversy for purposes of diversity jurisdiction. * * *

II. DISCUSSION

A. *Standing*

It is fundamental that a federal court lacks jurisdiction to hear any matter that is not a justiciable case or controversy under Article III of the U.S. Constitution, and that an action is not justiciable if the plaintiff does not have standing to sue. Bender v. Williamsport Area School District, 475 U.S. 534, 541–42, 106 S.Ct. 1326, 1331, 89 L.Ed.2d 501 (1986). "In essence the question of standing is whether the litigant is entitled to have the court decide the merits of the dispute or of particular issues." Warth v. Seldin, 422 U.S. 490, 498, 95 S.Ct. 2197, 2205, 45 L.Ed.2d 343 (1975). This question is answered by determining whether the plaintiff has a "personal stake in the outcome of the controversy." *Id.* at 498–99. Such a personal stake assures " 'concrete adverseness which sharpens the presentation of the issues.' " Phillips Petroleum Co. v. Shutts, 472 U.S. 797, 804, 105 S.Ct. 2965, 2970, 86 L.Ed.2d 628 (1985)(*quoting* Baker v. Carr, 369 U.S. 186, 204, 82 S.Ct. 691, 703, 7 L.Ed.2d 663 (1962)). The Supreme Court has held that a party has the requisite personal stake if s/he can demonstrate that: (1) s/he personally has suffered a concrete injury in fact, (2) the injury is fairly traceable to the challenged conduct, and (3) the injury is likely to be redressed by a favorable decision. Allen v. Wright, 468 U.S. 737, 751, 104 S.Ct. 3315, 3324, 82 L.Ed.2d 556 (1984)(citing Valley Forge Christian College v. Americans United for Separation of Church and State, Inc., 454 U.S. 464, 472, 102 S.Ct. 752, 758, 70 L.Ed.2d 700 (1982)).

* * *

Although these three elements appear straightforward, the Supreme Court has more than once acknowledged that "the concept of 'Article III standing' has not been defined with complete consistency in all of the various cases decided by [the] Court which have discussed it[.]" Whitmore v. Arkansas, 495 U.S. 149, 155, 110 S.Ct. 1717, 1723, 109 L.Ed.2d 135 (1990)(*quoting Valley Forge*, 454 U.S. at 475, 102 S.Ct. at 760). * * *

In this lawsuit, the objectors claim that many of the members of the *Carlough* class do not have Article III standing because they have not sustained an "injury in fact." The objectors note that the *Carlough* class includes those who have been occupationally exposed to asbestos but who do not manifest any asbestos-related condition (hereinafter "the exposure-only plaintiffs"). And, in their memoranda of law, the objectors point to several state and federal cases which have held that "subclinical injury resulting from exposure to asbestos is insufficient to constitute actual loss or damage to a plaintiff's interest required to sustain a cause of action under generally applicable principles of tort law." ... The objectors argue that the lack of a cause of action under applicable state tort law mandates a finding that the exposure-only plaintiffs have alleged no injury in fact for purposes of Article III standing.[2]

In response, the settling parties argue that exposure to a toxic substance is sufficient injury in fact and that, for purposes of Article III standing, it is irrelevant whether the plaintiffs' injuries support a valid legal claim.

It is true that prior to 1970, the test for Article III standing was the so-called "legal interest" test. *See* Alabama Power Co. v. Ickes, 302 U.S. 464, 478–80, 58 S.Ct. 300 303–04, 82 L.Ed. 374 (1938); G. Nichol, *Injury and The Disintegration of Article III*, 74 Calif.L.Rev. 1915, 1920 (1986). Under that test, a plaintiff only had Article III standing "if the actions of the defendant harmed a 'legal interest' of the plaintiff." *Alabama Power Co.*, 302 U.S. at 478–80, 58 S.Ct. at 303-04. In other words, plaintiffs had to show injury sufficient to sustain a valid cause of action to have standing to sue in federal court.

In Association of Data Processing Service Organizations, Inc. v. Camp, 397 U.S. 150, 90 S.Ct. 827, 25 L.Ed.2d 184 (1970), however, the Supreme Court jettisoned the "legal interest" test and adopted the "injury in fact" test. According to the Supreme Court in *Camp*, "[t]he 'legal interest' test goes to the merits" and is thus "quite distinct from the problem of standing." *Id.* at 152–53 & n.1, 90 S.Ct. at 829-30 & n.1 . With the adoption of the injury in fact test, the Supreme Court "intended the injury standard to insulate the case or controversy determination from the sway of the claim on the merits." Nichol, *supra,* at 1923–24. In the years since the *Camp* decision, the Supreme Court has stressed that the requirement of standing "focuses on the party seeking to get his [or her] complaint before a federal court and *not on the issues [s/]he wishes to have adjudicated.*" *Valley Forge,* 454 U.S. at 484, 102 S.Ct. at 765 (*quoting* Flast v. Cohen, 392 U.S. 83, 99, 88 S.Ct. 1942, 1952, 20 L.Ed.2d 947 (1968)(emphasis added)).[3]

---

2. The objectors concede, and I agree, that those members of the plaintiff class who already manifest an asbestos-related condition have Article III standing to bring this lawsuit.

3. Many other courts have recognized that standing looks only to the existence of a factual injury and not the magnitude or legal significance of that injury. National Wildlife Fed'n v. Burford, 871 F.2d 849, 852

In sum, the Supreme Court has made clear that the Article III determination "in no way depends on the merits of the plaintiff's [claim]." *Whitmore*, 495 U.S. at 155, 110 S.Ct. at 1723 (quoting *Warth*, 422 U.S. at 500, 95 S.Ct. at 2206).

... This Court has expressly recognized this principle in the context of another nationwide asbestos case:

> Standing, which derives from the article III case or controversy requirement, is met when the plaintiff can demonstrate "injury in fact." To what extent that injury is legally cognizable under the laws of the various jurisdictions is a separate inquiry.

In re Asbestos School Litigation, 104 F.R.D. 422, 425 n.1 (E.D.Pa.1984)(citation omitted), *amended in other respects*, 107 F.R.D. 215 (E.D.Pa.1985), *aff'd in part and rev'd in part on other grounds*, 789 F.2d 996 (3d Cir.1986).

Other lower courts have also recognized the distinction between the existence of an "injury in fact" and the legal significance of that injury by holding that, for purposes of determining Article III standing, the plaintiff's legal theories must be accepted as valid. *See* Chiles v. Thornburgh, 865 F.2d 1197, 1202 (11th Cir.1989)("just as we accept the validity of the plaintiff's factual assertions, we must also accept the validity of the plaintiff's theory of a cause of action"); Goldwater v. Carter, 617 F.2d 697, 701–02 (D.C.Cir.)("For purposes of the standing issue, we accept, as we must [plaintiff's] pleaded theories as valid."), *vacated on other grounds*, 444 U.S. 996, 100 S.Ct. 533, 62 L.Ed.2d 428 (1979); *see also* United States v. Nichols, 841 F.2d 1485, 1498 (10th Cir.1988). *But see* Robinson v. Vaughn, 1992 WL 368461 1992 U.S. Dist. LEXIS 19518 (E.D.Pa.Dec. 2, 1992)(court cited to Pennsylvania tort law and held that prisoner exposed to asbestos did not have injury in fact).

* * *

Almost directly on point is Bowling v. Pfizer, Inc., 143 F.R.D. 141 (S.D.Ohio 1992). In that case, the defendants were manufacturers of heart valves that later proved faulty. The plaintiff class included those implanted with a heart valve that had not fractured. Those plaintiffs wished to recover for their fear or anxiety that their heart valves might fracture in the future. In its decision approving the proposed settlement, the district court held that these class members might not have had a valid cause of action under applicable tort law. *Id.* at 147–48. Indeed, before the settlement was reached, the defendants had moved to dismiss the claims of these plaintiffs for failure to state a claim upon which relief could be granted. However, because the district court was informed of the settlement negotiations, it delayed ruling on the defen-

(9th Cir.1989); Consolidated Gold Fields PLC v. Minorco, S.A., 871 F.2d 252, 258 n.5 (2d Cir.1989), *opinion modified on other grounds*, 890 F.2d 569 (2d Cir.1989); Haskell v. Washington Township, 864 F.2d 1266, 1275 (6th Cir.1988); Coalition for Environment v. Volpe, 504 F.2d 156, 168 (8th Cir.1974); Boggs v. Divested Atomic Corp., 141 F.R.D. 58, 61 (S.D.Ohio 1991); Honey v. George Hyman Constr. Co., 63 F.R.D. 443, 446–47 (D.D.C.1974).

dants' motion. *Id.* Ultimately, the court approved the settlement and never ruled on the motion to dismiss.

The *Bowling* court was under a duty, as are all federal courts, to satisfy itself that those plaintiffs with properly functioning heart valves had standing to sue for damages. The fear and anxiety of those plaintiffs along with the medical expenses involved with monitoring their heart valves was enough to satisfy the injury in fact requirement. This is true even though they might not have stated a valid legal claim. And, as long as the plaintiffs had standing to bring their action in federal court, the court had subject matter jurisdiction to decide whether the proposed settlement was fair.

Going beyond the case law, it is easy to understand the logic behind the change from the "legal interest" test to the "injury in fact" test. If federal courts must look to whether plaintiffs in federal court under diversity jurisdiction have stated a valid cause of action in order to find that they have standing to sue in federal court, state law and not federal law would control the scope of Article III standing. Indeed, the same factual injury might be sufficient to confer standing in the federal courts of one state but not in the federal courts of another. Federal standing law, therefore, would not only depend on state law, it would vary from state to state. Because standing is a question of federal constitutional law, *Phillips Petroleum Co.,* 472 U.S. at 804, 105 S.Ct. at 2970, such a lack of uniformity would be undesirable. Also, if a plaintiff had to show a valid cause of action to confer Article III jurisdiction, federal courts could never entertain diversity cases where the existence of the asserted claim under state law was unclear. This is so because standing to sue must clearly exist before a federal court is permitted to reach the merits of a case. Of course, federal courts are often called upon to decide unsettled issues of state law. *See, e.g.,* Silver v. Mendel, 894 F.2d 598, 606 (3d Cir.), *cert. denied,* 496 U.S. 926, 110 S.Ct. 2620, 110 L.Ed.2d 641 (1990).

Therefore, I conclude that the applicable legal precedent requires that the question of whether the exposure-only plaintiffs have standing to bring this lawsuit in federal court does not depend on whether they have stated a valid cause of action under applicable tort law. The standing analysis does not end here, however. I must still determine whether, pursuant to federal precedent, the harm alleged by the exposure-only plaintiffs, namely exposure to asbestos, constitutes injury in fact which is fairly traceable to the defendants' conduct and is likely to be redressed by a favorable decision.

1. *Injury in Fact*

To satisfy the first requirement of standing, the exposure-only plaintiffs must demonstrate that they have suffered an injury in fact which is concrete and particularized, and actual or imminent rather than merely conjectural or hypothetical. *Lujan,* ___ U.S. at ___, 112 S.Ct. at 2136. By this the Supreme Court means "that the injury must affect the plaintiff in a personal and individual way." *Lujan,* ___ U.S. at ___ n.

1, 112 S.Ct. at 2136 n. 1. Put another way, "an interest need only be expressible in terms of the individual's satisfaction or experiences; but such satisfaction or experiences need not be unique to the litigant." L. Tribe, AMERICAN CONSTITUTIONAL LAW § 3–16, at 117 (2d ed.1988)(emphasis omitted).

The severity of the injury is immaterial. The Supreme Court and the Court of Appeals for the Third Circuit have explained that "[t]hese injuries need not be large, an 'identifiable trifle' will suffice." Public Interest Research Group, Inc. v. Powell Duffryn Terminals Inc., 913 F.2d 64, 71 (3d Cir.1990)(quoting United States v. Students Challenging Regulatory Agency Procedures, 412 U.S. 669, 689 n.14, 93 S.Ct. 2405, 2416 n. 14, 37 L.Ed.2d 254 (1973)), *cert. denied,* 498 U.S. 1109, 111 S.Ct. 1018, 112 L.Ed.2d 1100 (1991). Indeed, other kinds of non-economic harm have been accepted as Article III injury in fact, including aesthetic harm and emotional distress. Sierra Club v. Morton, 405 U.S. 727, 734–41, 92 S.Ct. 1361, 1366–69, 31 L.Ed.2d 636 (1972)(non-quantifiable aesthetic and environmental injuries); Clayton v. White Hall School Dist., 875 F.2d 676, 679 (8th Cir.1989)(emotional and psychological distress).

In *Duke Power,* the Supreme Court addressed the issue of whether exposure to a toxin is sufficient to confer Article III standing. In that case, the plaintiffs claimed that the future exposure to radiation from two nuclear power plants under construction constituted injury in fact entitling them to challenge the constitutionality of a statute which limited the liability for accidents at nuclear power plants. At the time the suit was brought, the plants were still under construction, and, therefore, plaintiffs had sustained no radiation-related diseases as a result of future emissions. The district court found "immediate" injury to the plaintiffs in "the production of small quantities of non-natural radiation which would invade the air and water" and "a 'sharp increase' in the temperature of two lakes presently used for recreational purposes...." *Duke Power,* 438 U.S. at 73–74, 98 S.Ct. at 2630-31. The Supreme Court agreed that *each* of these effects constituted injury in fact for purposes of Article III standing analysis:

> It is enough that several of the "immediate" adverse effects were found to harm appellees. Certainly the environmental and aesthetic consequences of the thermal pollution of the two lakes in the vicinity of the disputed power plants is the type of harmful effect which has been deemed adequate in prior cases to satisfy the "injury in fact" standard. *And* the emission of non-natural radiation into appellees environment would also seem a direct and present injury, given our generalized concern about exposure to radiation and the apprehension flowing from the uncertainty about the health and genetic consequences of even small emissions like those concededly emitted by nuclear power plants.

Id. at 73–74, 98 S.Ct. at 2630-31 (emphasis added, citations omitted).

The objectors point to language in *Duke Power* which appears to limit its holding on standing. At the beginning of the above-cited paragraph, the Supreme Court cautioned that it:

> need not determine whether all the putative injuries identified by the District Court, particularly those based on the possibility of a nuclear accident and the present apprehension generated by this future uncertainty, are sufficiently concrete to satisfy constitutional requirements. It is enough that several of the "immediate" adverse effects were found to harm appellees.

Id. at 73, 98 S.Ct. at 2630. However, the Court went on to select two of the injuries identified by the district court upon which to base its holding that the plaintiffs did indeed have standing: 1) the environmental and aesthetic consequences of the thermal pollution of the two lakes, and 2) the health and genetic consequences of exposure to small emissions of radiation. *Id.* at 73–74, 98 S.Ct. at 2630-31. Because the settling parties rely on the Court's holding only as to the second injury, I conclude that the Court's failure to rule on the concreteness of the other putative injuries is irrelevant.

* * *

Finally, the objectors argue that *Duke Power* is an old case and that Supreme Court decisions concerning standing have become more stringent in the fifteen years since. The objectors claim that since its holding in *Duke Power,* the Supreme Court has added another element to the injury in fact analysis: that the harm be not only concrete and particularized, but also "actual or imminent, not conjectural or hypothetical." *Lujan,* ___ U.S. at ___, 112 S.Ct. at 2136; *Whitmore,* 495 U.S. at 155, 110 S.Ct. at 1723; Los Angeles v. Lyons, 461 U.S. 95, 102, 103 S.Ct. 1660, 1665, 75 L.Ed.2d 675(1983). However, the holding in *Duke Power* is in line with the requirement that the injury be actual or imminent. The Court expressly held that exposure to radiation constituted "direct and present injury[.]" *Duke Power,* 438 U.S. at 74, 98 S.Ct. at 2631. This it held in spite of the fact that the construction of the nuclear power plants was not yet completed. In this case, the exposure-only plaintiffs have already been exposed to a toxin. Thus, even if *Duke Power* represents the most permissive end of the Supreme Court's spectrum of standing decisions, this case still falls within its holding.

Moreover, the objectors' argument that *Duke Power* is no longer good law is odd in the face of the Supreme Court's recent decision in Helling v. McKinney, ___ U.S. ___, 113 S.Ct. 2475, 125 L.Ed.2d 22 (1993). In *Helling,* the Supreme Court held that an allegation of intentional exposure of a prisoner to second-hand tobacco smoke, without present injury, states a valid claim for relief under the Eighth Amendment. *Helling* suggests that prisoners exposed to second-hand tobacco smoke may now have a valid cause of action. And, a necessary predicate to the Supreme Court's reaching the merits of the plaintiff's case in *Helling* was the implicit conclusion that mere exposure to second-hand smoke satisfied the injury in fact test of Article III.

Even before *Helling,* other courts had specifically held that exposure to a toxin constitutes injury in fact under Article III. *See, e.g.,* In re "Agent Orange" Prod. Liab. Litig. (Ivy v. Diamond Shamrock Chemicals Co.), 996 F.2d 1425 (2d Cir.1993); Ashton v. Pierce, 541 F.Supp. 635, 637 (D.D.C.1982), *aff'd,* 716 F.2d 56 and 723 F.2d 70 (D.C. Cir.1983). Indeed, the Second Circuit's recent decision in the *Agent Orange* litigation is directly on point here. *Ivy,* 996 F.2d at 1433–35. *Ivy* turned on the effect of the settlement of a prior Agent Orange class action lawsuit in which the class had included "future claimants," that is, persons who had been exposed to Agent Orange but did not yet manifest any disease. Subsequently, several individuals whose disease manifested itself after the settlement filed new lawsuits. In seeking to avoid the binding effect of the class action settlement, they argued that, at the time of the class action, they lacked injury in fact for purposes of Article III standing because they manifested no disease as a result of their exposure to Agent Orange. They argued that, because of their lack of standing, their claims were not within the Article III jurisdiction of the court that approved the class action settlement and, therefore, could not have been settled. *Id.* at 1433–35.

The Second Circuit rejected that argument. It held that " 'some types of injury to the body occur prior to the appearance of any symptoms; thus, the manifestation of the injury may well occur after the injury itself,' " and rejected the argument that " 'injury in fact' means injury that is manifest, diagnosable or compensable." *Id.* at 1434 (citations omitted). Instead, the Second Circuit agreed that the plaintiffs' injury in fact occurred at the time of exposure. *Id.* at 1434 (citing *Duke Power,* 438 U.S. at 74, 98 S.Ct. at 2631).

In another case involving a settlement in an asbestos class action, objectors argued that those members of the class who had not yet manifested an asbestos-related illness did not allege Article III injury in fact. In re Joint Eastern & Southern Dist. Asbestos Litig. (In re Johns–Manville Corp.), 129 B.R. 710, 834 (E. & S.D.N.Y.1991). In response to these objections, the Honorable Jack B. Weinstein held: ["]Since asbestos-related illnesses progress over time, the injury can be presumed to have occurred though the victim may not be aware of it.["] *Id.* Judge Weinstein found that "[t]he question of whether compensable injury has occurred is not subject to doubt by any court[,]" because latent injury has been recognized throughout the law (including in statutes of limitation decisions, in medical monitoring claims, in bankruptcy proceedings, and in insurance cases). After reviewing various areas of the law regarding the factual injury of asbestos exposure, Judge Weinstein reasoned:

> If persons exposed to asbestos fibers have a sufficient injury to warrant insurance coverage, they must have suffered a quantum of harm adequate to satisfy the constitutional case or controversy minimum injury-in-fact. ... Early status for Article III standing to be heard is particularly necessary in mass-tort-latent-disease cases. Often settlements and alternate dispute resolution techniques will

be instituted even before litigation is threatened to provide protection against a looming storm cloud of future controversies. The courts need to be in a position to intervene as necessary.

Id. at 835–36.

Finally, in *Ashton,* the district court held that persons exposed to lead-based paint, but who did not yet manifest disease, had standing because their "alleged exposure to the risk of lead poisoning as a result of the continued presence of lead-based paint in [Washington,] D.C. public housing clearly constitutes a sufficient claim of injury in fact." *Ashton,* 541 F.Supp. at 637 (citing *Duke Power,* 438 U.S. at 74, 98 S.Ct. at 2631). In fact, many federal class action cases have involved a class that included persons who had been exposed to a toxin but manifested no disease. *See, e.g.,* In re Paoli R.R. Yard PCB Litig., 916 F.2d 829, 861 (3d Cir.1990), *cert. denied,* 499 U.S. 961, 111 S.Ct. 1584, 113 L.Ed.2d 649 (1991)(holding that persons who had been exposed to PCBs could sue for medical monitoring expenses because "regardless of whether all plaintiffs alleged demonstrable physical injury, they all clearly alleged monetary injury"); In re A.H. Robins Co., 880 F.2d 694, 709 (4th Cir.1989)(affirming district court's settlement of claims by class of persons with potential future injuries caused by use of Dalkon Shield contraceptive device).[10] Although in many of those cases there is no express finding as to Article III standing, it is clear to me that the courts were satisfied as to their Article III jurisdiction because a finding of such jurisdiction is a necessary predicate to taking action on the merits.

Based upon the foregoing analysis, I conclude that exposure to a toxic substance constitutes sufficient injury in fact to give a plaintiff standing to sue in federal court. The objectors do not dispute, nor could they, that asbestos is a toxin. *See In re Joint Asbestos Litig.,* 129 B.R. at 739 ("The capacity of asbestos fibers to cause serious injuries is no longer disputed."). In this case, the class consists of persons who have been exposed to asbestos either occupationally or through the occupational exposure of a spouse or household member. Accordingly, by definition, each class member sues on the basis of *actual* exposure and not future exposure to asbestos. Without more, the exposure-only plaintiffs have alleged sufficient injury in fact.

Apart from the authority dealing with exposure to a toxin as Article III injury in fact, I conclude that the available medical data on the health

---

10. *See also* Bowling v. Pfizer, Inc., 143 F.R.D. 141, 147–48 (S.D.Ohio 1992)(approving settlement of emotional distress claims on behalf of a 51,000–person class composed of individuals with "properly functioning ... heart valves" who feared that these valves might fracture in future), *appeal dismissed without op.,* 995 F.2d 1066 (6th Cir. 1993); Boggs v. Divested Atomic Corp., 141 F.R.D. 58, 60–62 (S.D.Ohio 1991)(the court certified the class based on the class members' actual exposure to radiation and hazardous waste); In re Fernald Litig., 1989 WL 267039, 1989 U.S. Dist. LEXIS 17764 (S.D.Ohio 1989)(approving settlement on behalf of class of persons exposed to radiation from uranium processing plant who had not yet manifested disease); *Pearl,* 566 F.Supp. at 401 (denying motion to dismiss class action complaint of persons exposed to urea formaldehyde insulation, notwithstanding claim that class members suffered no detectable harm).

consequences of exposure to asbestos also require a conclusion that the exposure-only plaintiffs have alleged a demonstrable physical injury which satisfies the Article III injury in fact requirement.

The Pennsylvania Supreme Court recently characterized the immediate consequences of exposure to asbestos as a "direct injury." J.H. France Refractories Co. v. Allstate Ins. Co., 626 A.2d 502, 505–6 (Pa. 1993). The court summarized current medical evidence which shows that:

> asbestos fibers in the respiratory tract interact with the membranes of the cells lining the trachea and cause the release of enzymes and superoxides which either damage or kill individual cells. If sufficient cells are damaged, tissue (an accumulation of cells) is damaged or destroyed. This injury occurs within minutes after asbestos fibers enter the cells.

Id. The court went on to hold that, for purposes of triggering an insurer's duty to indemnify, "the medical evidence of discrete cellular injuries occurring upon exposure to asbestos justifies the conclusion that exposure to asbestos causes immediate 'bodily injury' . . .", even if disease is not manifested until much later. *Id.* at 506. Judge Weinstein in *In re Joint Asbestos Litig.* agreed: ["]Since asbestos-related illnesses progress over time, the injury can be presumed to have occurred though the victim may not be aware of it.["] *In re Joint Asbestos Litig.*, 129 B.R. at 834. Thus, to show injury in fact, the exposure-only plaintiffs are not relying on speculative future harm, but on their *present* injuries resulting from exposure to asbestos.

In sum, the weight of recognized medical research on asbestos-related diseases shows that exposure to asbestos causes immediate cellular changes. And, only those who have been exposed to asbestos are members of the plaintiff class. They have been personally affected by defendants' conduct in a concrete and particular way whether or not they ever develop a serious medical condition. This is exactly the type of personal stake the Article III injury-in-fact requirement demands. Therefore, I conclude that the exposure-only plaintiffs have alleged Article III injury in fact.

2. *Traceability*

The second requirement of standing is that the plaintiff show that there is some causal connection between the injury and the conduct complained of, i.e., the injury has to be fairly traceable to the challenged action of the defendants and not the result of the independent action of some third party. *Lujan,* ___ U.S. at ___, 112 S.Ct. at 2136.

In their complaint, plaintiffs allege that their injuries are the proximate result of exposure to the CCR defendants' asbestos products. It is clear that they have been exposed to asbestos, and it is clear that the CCR defendants manufactured asbestos and asbestos-containing products. Therefore, I conclude that plaintiffs have shown, for purposes of Article III standing, that their injuries are fairly traceable to the defendants' conduct.

3.   Redressability

To satisfy the final requirement of standing, a federal plaintiff must show that his or her injury is likely to be redressed by a favorable decision. *Lujan,* ___ U.S. at ___, 112 S.Ct. at 2136. Because of this requirement, "the form of relief sought is often critical in determining whether the plaintiff has standing." Brown v. Fauver, 819 F.2d 395, 400 (3d Cir.1987).

The redressability requirement has been problematic only in cases requesting declaratory or injunctive relief. For example, in Linda R.S. v. Richard D., 410 U.S. 614, 93 S.Ct. 1146, 35 L.Ed.2d 536 (1973), the plaintiff claimed that the Texas policy of not prosecuting the fathers of illegitimate children for failure to pay child support was unconstitutionally discriminatory. The plaintiff, an unwed mother, asked the district court to issue an injunction forcing state officials to prosecute the father of her child. The Supreme Court, however, held that the plaintiff did not have Article III standing to bring the suit. The Court reasoned that an injunction commanding state prosecutions would not ensure that the mother would receive any additional support money. The Court explained that if the plaintiff "were granted the requested relief, it would result only in the jailing of the child's father. The prospect that prosecution will . . . result in payment of support can, at best, be termed only speculative." *Id.* at 618, 93 S.Ct. at 1149. In other words, the plaintiff lacked standing because her injury was not likely to be redressed by the relief she requested.

Similarly, in Warth v. Seldin, 422 U.S. 490, 95 S.Ct. 2197, 45 L.Ed.2d 343 (1975), several plaintiffs challenged the constitutionality of a suburb's exclusionary zoning practices. They claimed that the zoning practices prevented construction of multifamily dwellings and low-income housing and, therefore, effectively excluded them from the neighborhood. The Supreme Court held that these plaintiffs lacked standing because they could not demonstrate that appropriate housing would be constructed without the exclusionary zoning ordinances. The Court felt that overturning the zoning ordinances would not guarantee that builders would choose to construct new housing in the area, or that low-income residents would be able to afford to live there. *Id.* at 505–07, 98 S.Ct. at 2208–09; *see also* Simon v. E. Ky. Welfare Rights Org., 426 U.S. 26, 45–46, 96 S.Ct. 1917, 1928, 48 L.Ed.2d 450 (1976).

In this case, it is self-evident that the very conventional remedy sought by the plaintiffs—money damages—would do much to redress their injuries. Unlike claims for injunctive or declaratory relief, as in the above-cited cases, "[a] damage claim, by definition, presents a means to redress an injury." Cardenas v. Smith, 733 F.2d 909, 914 (D.C.Cir. 1984). Therefore, I conclude that the exposure-only plaintiffs have shown that their injuries are likely to be redressed by the relief requested in their complaint.

4. Conclusion

The exposure-only plaintiffs have satisfied the three requirements of Article III standing. Beyond that, a reexamination of the policies served by the standing requirement convinces me of the propriety of this finding. * * * First, this is not a case where the courts are being "called upon to decide abstract questions of wide public significance ..." *Warth,* 422 U.S. at 500, 95 S.Ct. at 2206. Here, the plaintiffs have particular, concrete and individual claims of injury. That there are many victims of asbestos does not change the individual and personal stake each plaintiff has in the outcome of this litigation. Judicial intervention is, therefore, appropriate and necessary.

Second, this case provides the type of factual setting which is necessary for judicial review to be effective. Because the claims of the exposure-only plaintiffs are based on their personal experiences and involve particularized concrete injuries, there is no risk of ruling on an ill-defined or abstract controversy.

Finally, the exposure-only plaintiffs have been directly affected by the CCR defendants' conduct. They are not merely concerned bystanders. Therefore, this case serves the Article III policy of reserving the federal courts for parties whose lives will be directly affected by the outcome of specific litigation.

Having reviewed the applicable case law and the Article III policies which have guided the courts in their decisions, it is clear to me that the claims of the exposure-only plaintiffs are precisely the type which confer standing to sue in federal court. I conclude, therefore, that the exposure-only plaintiffs have Article III standing to bring this lawsuit.

B. Diversity Jurisdiction—Amount in Controversy

The plaintiff class seeks to invoke the subject matter jurisdiction of this Court based on the federal diversity statute, 28 U.S.C. § 1332. That statute authorizes federal courts to exercise subject matter jurisdiction over actions "between citizens of different States" so long as "the matter in controversy exceeds the sum or value of $50,000, exclusive of interest and costs." 28 U.S.C. § 1332. In class actions, each class member must on his or her own meet the amount in controversy requirement. Zahn v. International Paper Co., 414 U.S. 291, 301, 94 S.Ct. 505, 512, 38 L.Ed.2d 511 (1973).

* * *

The plaintiffs allege that jurisdiction is based upon diversity of citizenship and an amount in controversy for each member of the plaintiff class which exceeds $100,000. The objectors, on the other hand, argue that the exposure-only plaintiffs cannot in good faith allege damages in excess of the jurisdictional minimum.

... courts in class action personal injury cases seeking unliquidated damages have uniformly held that it cannot be said to a "legal certainty" that any class member's claim is for less than the jurisdictional amount.

For example, in the class action brought on behalf of asbestos personal injury plaintiffs against the Manville Settlement Trust, both Judge Weinstein and the Second Circuit rejected the argument that some members of the class did not meet the amount in controversy requirement, even though the class included those who had not yet manifested an asbestos-related condition, and even though the settlement imposed a cap on some claimants below the $50,000 level. *In re Joint Asbestos Litig.,* 129 B.R. at 793–94, 982 F.2d at 734. The class in that case consisted of "all beneficiaries of the [Manville] Trust who now have *or in the future may have* (a) any unliquidated claims for death or injury resulting from exposure to Manville asbestos...." 982 F.2d at 729 (emphasis added). Nevertheless, Judge Weinstein, relying on his own experience and on cases from other courts, took "judicial notice of the fact that the value of every claim in the complaint can in good faith be said to exceed $50,000 for the purpose of pleading." 129 B.R. at 793–94. Also, under the proposed stipulation of settlement—which was filed simultaneously with the complaint—the maximum possible award to certain kinds of claimants was $30,000. 982 F.2d at 730. With respect to the settlement cap, Judge Weinstein noted that "[w]hile any plaintiff is free to settle a claim for less than the amount sought in the complaint, the amount that controls for jurisdictional purposes is what the claimant in good faith pleads." 129 B.R. at 793. On appeal, the Second Circuit summarily rejected the challenge to these rulings, specifically agreeing that the settlement cap below $50,000 did not affect the Court's jurisdiction. 982 F.2d at 734.

The same conclusions have been reached in other class action product liability cases. The Second Circuit twice rejected an amount in controversy challenge in the *Agent Orange* litigation, even though (1) the class included "future claimants," i.e., those who did not yet manifest a disease as a result of exposure to Agent Orange, and (2) the settlement provided no payment to many members of the class. *Ivy,* 996 F.2d at 1434; In re Agent Orange Prod. Liab. Litig., 818 F.2d 145, 157–58, 163 (2d Cir.1987). In the *Ivy* case, several class members who were classified as "future claimants" when the initial class action was settled in 1984 asserted that they had subsequently suffered injury as a result of their Agent Orange exposure and that they were not bound by the 1984 class action settlement. As with the standing issue, the *Ivy* plaintiffs argued that they could not be bound by the original settlement on the theory that their individual claims in 1984 (for not-yet manifested conditions) could not have satisfied the amount in controversy requirement. The Second Circuit disagreed, holding that it did not appear to a legal certainty that the claims of the plaintiff class, including the claims of the exposure-only plaintiffs, were really for less than the jurisdictional amount.

Likewise, in a case involving the drug DES, a district court certified a class of women who had been exposed to DES in utero but had not developed cancer. The court rejected a challenge to the jurisdictional amount requirement as follows:

Plaintiffs' claimed damages are unliquidated and subject to a jury's evaluation of many subjective factors. I cannot now find to a legal certainty that the claim of any member of the plaintiff class is less than the jurisdictional amount.

Payton v. Abbott Labs, 83 F.R.D. 382, 395 (D.Mass.1979), *vacated on other grounds,* 100 F.R.D. 336 (D.Mass.1983).

Similarly, in the Dalkon Shield litigation, the certified class included women "who had used the Dalkon Shield but had not yet manifested an injury" from that use. [ ] In re A.H. Robins Co., 88 B.R. 742, 745 (E.D.Va.1988). Nevertheless, the Fourth Circuit rejected a challenge to the amount in controversy, noting that such personal injury claimants always sought an amount in excess of the jurisdictional amount and holding that it is "indisputable that it cannot be said to a 'legal certainty' that the jurisdictional amount herein was not satisfied." In re A.H. Robins Co., 880 F.2d 709, 723–25 (4th Cir.1989).

Finally, in the *Bowling* case discussed above, the court, in approving a class action settlement, rejected the argument that not all members of the plaintiff class met the $50,000 requirement, even though the heart valves implanted in several of the class members were, at the time of settlement, still functioning properly. The court stated that, "[a]lthough it is unlikely that the Plaintiffs would have made it to trial and then prevailed, had they done so, the Plaintiffs can assert in good faith that they would have received more than $50,000 each from a jury." *Bowling,* 143 F.R.D. at 167. This the court held even though, had the parties not settled, the claims of these plaintiffs would probably have been dismissed for failure to state a claim upon which relief could be granted.

The objectors argue that in spite of the holdings in the above-cited cases the exposure-only plaintiffs in this case have not met the amount in controversy requirement: (1) without a presently diagnosed asbestos-related condition, the exposure-only plaintiffs only have a cause of action for medical monitoring, if anything, and hence cannot recover more than $50,000, and (2) the proposed settlement itself shows that the amount in controversy does not exceed $50,000.[16]

I do not find it necessary to make a claim-by-claim analysis of the causes of action available to diversity plaintiffs in order to determine whether the plaintiffs have alleged the jurisdictional minimum. I conclude that it is enough that the kind of factual injuries alleged by the exposure-only plaintiffs—physical, monetary, and emotional injuries—plainly support a claim to more than $50,000. The *Manville Trust,*

---

16. The objectors also attempt to distinguish many of the above-cited cases on the ground that, in those cases, "each of the named plaintiffs specifically alleged that they had sustained physical injury as a result of the defendant's conduct." * * * That argument fails because (1) the amount in controversy requirement applies to class members as well as to class representatives, *Zahn,* 414 U.S. at 301, 94 S.Ct. at 512, and (2) in this case, the plaintiffs, including those with no manifested asbestos-related condition, do allege physical injury as a result of exposure to defendants' products—adverse cellular changes.

Agent Orange, DES, Dalkon Shield, and *Heart Valve* cases discussed above included persons who had been exposed to the hazardous substance or product but manifested no compensable disease or condition, and the courts nonetheless found that the plaintiffs all met the jurisdictional minimum. None of those courts found it necessary or appropriate to make a detailed examination of the causes of action available to such persons for purposes of the jurisdictional amount requirement.

Even those claims that would not be recognized under applicable law must still be counted for jurisdictional purposes. This is evident from the recent Third Circuit decision in Angus v. Shiley, Inc., 989 F.2d 142 (3d Cir.1993). In that case, the plaintiff alleged that she was suffering extreme anxiety and emotional distress as a result of learning that her implanted heart valve, which had been manufactured by the defendant, might fracture in a fashion that could cause death or serious injury. Her suit seeking compensatory damages for emotional distress and punitive damages was brought in Pennsylvania state court and removed by defendant to federal district court. The district judge rejected plaintiff's motion to remand the case to state court and dismissed the case on the merits for failure to state a claim.

On appeal, the plaintiff first contended that the district court had lacked diversity jurisdiction because her claims did not satisfy the amount in controversy requirement. The Third Circuit rejected this contention:

> Given that the complaint does not limit its request for damages to a precise monetary amount, the district court properly made an independent appraisal of the value of the claim, ... and reasonably found that the actual amount in controversy exceeded $50,000 *for there can be no doubt that a reasonable jury likely could have valued Angus' losses at over $50,000.*

Id. at 146 (footnote omitted, emphasis added). Turning to the merits, the court upheld the dismissal of Angus' complaint for failure to state a claim, finding that Pennsylvania would not allow a cause of action for emotional distress under the circumstances. *Id.* at 147.

With its decision in *Angus,* the Third Circuit in essence held that claims for damages for emotional distress in product liability cases should be included in determining whether the jurisdictional amount is met, even when those claims ultimately must be dismissed for failure to state a valid claim.[18] *See also Bowling,* 143 F.R.D. at 167. The settling parties argue that the "lesson" from *Angus* was in fact required by the general rule that a court does not lose jurisdiction even when "the complaint discloses the existence of a valid defense to the claim." *St. Paul Mercury Indem. Co.,* 303 U.S. at 289, 58 S.Ct. at 590.

---

18. *Angus* cannot be distinguished on the ground that it is a heart valve case and this is an asbestos case. The availability of damages for emotional distress obviously does not turn on the type of product involved. In fact, *Angus* expressly relied upon asbestos cases in deciding that the case should be dismissed.

Alternatively, even if a claim-by-claim examination is necessary, the exposure-only plaintiffs have alleged a cognizable claim for medical monitoring and punitive damages. On this point most of the objectors concede, and I agree, that the claim for medical monitoring is not frivolous. Those objectors assert, however, that damages for medical monitoring cannot exceed approximately $500 per year, or approximately $10,000 per claimant.

But the plaintiffs also seek punitive damages. As noted above, claims for punitive damages must be counted in determining whether the jurisdictional amount has been satisfied unless they are "patently frivolous and without foundation." *Packard,* 994 F.2d at 1046. Conceding this, one of the objectors contends that punitive damages are not available at all when only medical monitoring damages can be sought, arguing that:

> there is *no* authority to suggest that the "exposure only" plaintiffs' nominal claims for medical surveillance—without more—would support an award of punitive damages. Indeed, it appears that no court in any jurisdiction has ever upheld such an award. Accordingly, the punitive claims must be stricken from the amount in controversy. . . .

* * * The objectors suggest, in effect, that if no known or reported decision has upheld an award of punitive damages in such circumstances, I must conclude to a "legal certainty" that punitive damages could never be awarded. This, however, is not the law. The "legal certainty" test requires that such a claim be *unavailable* as a matter of law. *Packard,* 994 F.2d at 1046. In other words, controlling adverse precedent is required to show that a claim would certainly fail.

In any event, it is not uncommon for plaintiffs to join claims for punitive damages with claims for medical monitoring. The potential substantiality of such claims is shown by In re Fernald Litig., 1989 WL 267039, 1989 U.S. Dist. LEXIS 17764 (S.D.Ohio 1989). There the court approved a class action settlement of claims brought by owners of property adjacent to a nuclear facility and certain current and former employees of the facility. In evaluating the settlement, the court noted that, to facilitate settlement, it had conducted an advisory summary jury trial in which the non-binding verdict included "$1,000,000 for diminution of property values, $80,000,000 for a medical monitoring fund, and $55,000,000 for punitive damages." *Id.,* 1989 WL 267039, at *2, 1989 U.S. Dist. LEXIS 17764, at *4.

* * *

The objectors also contend that punitive damages could not be awarded in a sufficient amount to exceed $50,000 when combined with the award for medical monitoring damages because "in Pennsylvania punitive damages must be reasonably related, and not disproportionate, to the amount of compensatory damages." * * * The objector's argument mistakenly invokes the law of only one state, and also misstates that law. This is a nationwide class action in diversity jurisdiction, and the class members' claims are subject to the laws of the various states, not just Pennsylvania. In any event, this Court recently noted in applying Pennsylvania law that "punitive damages need not bear a reasonable relationship to compensatory damages." Fine v. State Farm Fire & Cas. Co., 1993 WL 196888, *1, 1993 U.S. Dist. LEXIS 7682, at *4 (E.D.Pa. June 11, 1993)(citing Kirkbride v. Lisbon Contractors, Inc., 521 Pa. 97, 555 A.2d 800 (1989)). And, in light of the recent Supreme Court decision of TXO Production Corp. v. Alliance Resources Corp., ___ U.S. ___, 113 S.Ct. 2711, 125 L.Ed.2d 366 (1993), where a punitive award 526 times greater than the compensatory award was upheld, it cannot be argued with legal certainty that the Constitution imposes any requirement that punitive damages bear a reasonable relationship to compensatory damages. In short, there is no mathematically certain limit on the amount of punitive damages that might be awarded to the plaintiffs in this case.

In fact, there have been many large punitive damage awards in prior asbestos cases. Just recently, a majority of the Third Circuit, sitting en banc, approved a $1 million award of punitive damages on behalf of a single plaintiff against a former manufacturer of asbestos-containing insulation. Dunn v. HOVIC, 1 F.3d 1371, 1383 (3d Cir.1993). In so doing, the court noted that: "[a] multi-million dollar punitive damages award is not unique in products liability cases. See, e.g., Glasscock v. Armstrong Cork Co., 946 F.2d 1085 (5th Cir.1991)($6.1 million in asbestos case); ... Cathey v. Johns–Manville Sales Corp., 776 F.2d 1565 (6th Cir.1985)($1.5 million in asbestos case)...." Id. at 1383.

The objectors rely heavily on Packard v. Provident Nat'l Bank, 994 F.2d 1039 (3d Cir.1993), for their argument that the exposure-only plaintiffs cannot satisfy the jurisdictional minimum with their claims for medical monitoring and punitive damages. In Packard, the plaintiffs sought recovery of quantifiable "sweep fees" that defendant trustee banks had charged to trusts. Those liquidated sums were far less than $50,000 per class member, with the named plaintiff seeking recovery of only about $4,000 in such fees. Id. at 1046. This case, however, is much different. The complaint here seeks unliquidated damages that would be subject to a jury's subjective evaluation. It cannot be said with legal certainty that a jury would not award the exposure-only plaintiffs unliquidated, compensatory damages and punitive damages for medical monitoring in excess of the jurisdictional amount. In other words, Packard dealt only with the counting of punitive damages where the compensatory damages were liquidated at a level far less than $50,000. The Packard holding does not apply to cases like this one where the plaintiffs seek unliquidated compensatory damages.

Furthermore, because the level of liquidated compensatory damages in Packard was so low, the plaintiffs were necessarily trying to satisfy the jurisdictional amount almost entirely through their punitive damages claim. The court stated that "when it appears that [a punitive damages] claim comprises the bulk of the amount in controversy and may have been colorably asserted solely or primarily for the purpose of conferring jurisdiction, that claim should be given particularly close scrutiny." *Id.* at 1046. The court then examined whether plaintiffs in *Packard* could possibly state a viable claim for punitive damages under Pennsylvania law and concluded that that law foreclosed the award of punitive damages against a trustee. *See id.* at 1047–49. It accordingly determined that there was a legal certainty that the plaintiffs' claims in that case could not satisfy the jurisdictional amount and it ordered that the action be dismissed. *Id.* at 1050.

It cannot be said in this case that punitive damages are unavailable as a matter of law. Nor can it be said with legal certainty that there is a strict mathematical limit on the amount of such damages that might be awarded. *See, e.g., Fine,* 1993 WL 196888, at *1, 1993 U.S. Dist. LEXIS 7682, at *3 n.2 (without commenting on the ultimate merits of plaintiffs' claim for punitive damages, the court noted that, from the face of the complaint, it was not patently frivolous and thus could be considered in assessing the amount in controversy).

In light of the foregoing I find that, even if only the claims for medical monitoring and punitive damages are considered, the exposure-only plaintiffs' claims exceed the jurisdictional minimum. In other words, I cannot find to a legal certainty that a jury could not award the exposure-only plaintiffs more than $50,000 in compensatory and punitive damages on their medical monitoring claims.

* * *

It is widely known that asbestos personal injury claimants invariably seek—and often obtain—damages well in excess of $50,000. Therefore, there is no basis on which to conclude that the damage calculation was inflated here to create federal jurisdiction. Because the "[p]laintiffs' claimed damages are unliquidated and subject to a jury's evaluation of many subjective factors," *Payton,* 83 F.R.D. at 395, I conclude that it is impossible to establish "to a legal certainty" that the claims of the exposure-only plaintiffs are for less than the jurisdictional amount. Therefore, I necessarily conclude that the plaintiff class has satisfied the amount in controversy requirements of 28 U.S.C. § 1332.

C. Collusion

Because of the "case or controversy" requirement in Article III, "federal courts will not entertain friendly suits, or those which are feigned or collusive in nature." *Flast,* 392 U.S. at 100. The Constitution demands a "honest and actual antagonistic assertion of rights." United States v. Johnson, 319 U.S. 302, 305, 63 S.Ct. 1075, 1077, 87 L.Ed. 1413 (1943)(quoting Chicago & Grand Trunk R. Co. v. Wellman, 143 U.S. 339, 345, 12 S.Ct. 400, 402, 36 L.Ed. 176 (1892)). "[I]f two litigants commence a suit with the same goals in mind, no controversy exists to give the district court jurisdiction[.]" Pennsylvania Ass'n for Retarded Children v. Pennsylvania, 343 F.Supp. 279, 290 (E.D.Pa.1972).

The objectors argue that this class action is collusive, or "friendly," because (1) the complaint and the proposed settlement were filed simultaneously, and (2) a provision of the proposed settlement provides that the CCR defendants will pay class counsel's fees.

* * *

The settling parties do not dispute that this class action was settled before the complaint was filed. They claim, however, that the CCR defendants, as asbestos manufacturers, and the plaintiffs, as asbestos victims, have diametrically opposed legal interests in this lawsuit just as they have throughout the twenty-year history of asbestos litigation. The settling parties claim, and the objectors do not dispute, that the negotiations leading to the proposed settlement were long, arduous, complex and arms-length. This type of controversy, the settling parties argue, is the opposite of the type banned from the federal courts for lack of a genuine dispute.

The recent decisions in *In re Joint Asbestos Litig.* support the argument that pre-filing negotiations do not evidence a "friendly" lawsuit. In that case, the complaint was filed on the same day as the proposed settlement. 982 F.2d at 728. Neither Judge Weinstein nor the Second Circuit saw any problem with the justiciability of the lawsuit resulting from that fact. Also, other federal courts have held that the simultaneous filing of the complaint and the proposed settlement does not show a collusive suit or undermine the court's jurisdiction. SEC v. Randolph, 736 F.2d 525 (9th Cir.1984); Rodgers v. United States Steel Corp., 536 F.2d 1001 (3d Cir.1976); United States v. Allegheny–Ludlum Indus., Inc., 517 F.2d 826 (5th Cir.1975); United States v. TW Servs., Inc., 1993 U.S. Dist. LEXIS 7882 (N.D.Cal. Apr. 1, 1993); Colorado Environmental Coalition v. Romer, 796 F.Supp. 457, 458 (D.Colo.1992); West Virginia ex rel. Tompkins v. Coca–Cola Bottling Co., 1990 WL 17541, 1990 U.S. Dist. LEXIS 5304 (S.D.W.Va. Jan. 16, 1990); United States v. Acton Corp., 131 F.R.D. 431 (D.N.J.1990).

* * *

The objectors contend that there is no need to resort to the courts in this case to settle the claims of the named plaintiffs against the CCR defendants, i.e., there is no need for judicial approval. They claim that the parties can do so by contract. Instead, the objectors argue, this suit was brought by cooperating interests for the sole purpose of affecting the rights of others. The objectors find collusion in the presentation of this lawsuit as a class action. The class action form, they claim, is used solely for the purpose of "rop[ing] millions of future asbestos claimants into [the] settlement [.]" * * * The objectors argue that when class actions are settled prior to filing the complaint, they are necessarily brought solely to enforce a settlement on others.

The objectors' argument on this point is without merit. As I see it, *all* class actions are brought to affect the rights of class members. "The purpose of a class action is to dispose of the claims of numerous parties in one proceeding." King v. South Cent. Bell Tel. & Tel. Co., 790 F.2d 524, 528 (6th Cir.1986); *see also* EEOC v. American Tel. & Tel. Co., 556 F.2d 167, 173–74 (3d Cir.1977), *cert. denied,* 438 U.S. 915, 98 S.Ct. 3145, 57 L.Ed.2d 1161 (1978). It follows that class action settlements are reached for the same reason—regardless of their timing. This is precisely why Rule 23 requires judicial scrutiny of class action settlements to determine whether they are fair to the class members. Presentation of this lawsuit as a class action, therefore, is not evidence of collusion.

Looking to the nature of the controversy, and not the timing of the settlement agreement, it is clear that the plaintiffs and the CCR defendants are true adversaries. The proposed settlement simply represents a compromise of a genuine dispute. *See, e.g.,* In re Joint E. & S. Dist. Asbestos Litig., 982 F.2d 721, 739 (2d Cir.1992), *modified in other respects,* 993 F.2d 7 (2d Cir.1993)(asbestos claimants and defendant companies cannot be put in same subclass because their interests are "profoundly adverse to each other.").

I conclude that this case is one involving genuinely adverse interests, but, because of the settlement, it lacks a dispute as to the remedy. I conclude, therefore, that the simultaneous filing of the complaint and the proposed settlement does not require a conclusion that the case is collusive or lacks a genuine dispute. A contrary rule would unwisely discourage pre-litigation negotiations and, by encouraging parties to wait an "appropriate" period of time after filing suit to file a proposed settlement, elevate form over substance.

The objectors' second collusion argument is that the CCR defendants' agreement in the settlement to pay class counsel's fees is evidence that this lawsuit is "friendly." A review of class action cases, however, quickly reveals that such agreements are standard practice.... Such a provision was expressly approved by the court as "preferable and proper" in In re A.H. Robins Co., 88 B.R. 755, 761 (E.D.Va.1988), *aff'd,* 880 F.2d 709 (4th Cir.1989). Because in those cases, as in this case, the *amount* of class counsel's fees is to be fixed by the court, the fee agreements do not support an allegation of collusion.

In light of the foregoing, I conclude that this case is not a collusive or "friendly" suit.

D. Mootness

To satisfy the Article III case or controversy requirement, the parties must not only present a "honest and actual antagonistic assertion of rights," *Johnson,* 319 U.S. at 305, 63 S.Ct. at 1077, but the controversy must continue to exist at all stages of the federal proceedings. If events subsequent to the filing of the complaint resolve the dispute, the case should be dismissed as moot. United States Parole Com. v. Geraghty, 445 U.S. 388, 397, 100 S.Ct. 1202, 1209, 63 L.Ed.2d 479 (1980). Generally, if the parties reach a settlement, the case is no longer justiciable as an Article III controversy. There is, however, an exception to this rule: a case does not become moot when the parties reach a *proposed* settlement that is contingent on the approval of the court. *Havens Realty Corp.,* 455 U.S. at 371 n.10; Coopers & Lybrand v. Livesay, 437 U.S. 463, 465 n.3, 98 S.Ct. 2454, 2456 n. 3, 57 L.Ed.2d 351 (1978). And, as discussed above in the context of collusion, a class action settlement requires judicial approval pursuant to Rule 23 to be binding on the class members. Thus, the objectors' first argument, that the proposed settlement moots the case, is without merit.

The objectors also argue, however, that certain "side agreements" between class counsel and the CCR defendants effectively settle the claims of the named or representative plaintiffs. The objectors claim that because of these side agreements, the individual claims of the named plaintiffs and the entire class action are moot.

The objectors point to the existence of certain side agreements between the CCR defendants and various law firms who represent asbestos victims, including class counsel, as requiring a finding that this lawsuit is moot. * * * The agreements are an attempt by the CCR defendants to provide an alternative dispute resolution ("ADR") procedure with respect to future asbestos claims in the event that the proposed settlement in this case fails to be approved and implemented. Under the terms of the side agreements, the signatory law firms will recommend to their future asbestos clients that they defer filing suit against the CCR defendants until any asbestos-related disease is manifested. By deferring their claims, these clients would be accepting the criteria in the CCR defendants' ADR procedure which is virtually identical to the criteria in the proposed settlement. The clients are free to reject the recommendation of counsel, however, and sue the CCR defendants at any time. If the clients accept class counsel's recommendation, the statute of limitations is, by the terms of the agreement, tolled.

These side agreements superseded a prior agreement with one of the two law firms representing the plaintiff class. In the original agreement, if a future asbestos client did not wish to defer filing suit against the CCR defendants until an asbestos-related condition is manifested, the law firm could not represent him or her in a suit against the CCR defendants. However, in light of the recent opinion of the American Bar Association Standing Committee on Ethics and Professional Responsibility (Formal Opinion 93–371), the parties changed this agreement so as to avoid a possible violation of Model Rule of Professional Conduct 5.6(b) which prohibits restrictions on a lawyer's right to practice law.

The objectors claim that these side agreements require dismissal of this class action as moot under the recent Third Circuit case of Lusardi v. Xerox Corp., 975 F.2d 964, 983 (3d Cir.1992). In *Lusardi,* former employees brought an age discrimination class action case against their employer. After the case was filed and while no class certification motion was yet pending, the named plaintiffs fully and unconditionally settled their own claims against their employer. The claims of the rest of the putative class remained unsettled, and the named plaintiffs wished to reserve their right to act as class representatives. The Third Circuit held that because the named plaintiffs settled their claims before class certification, the class action was moot. *Id.* at 974. The court stated: In such a situation, "there is no plaintiff (either named or unnamed) who can assert a justiciable claim against any defendant and consequently there is no longer a 'case or controversy' within the meaning of Article III of the Constitution." *Id.* (quoting Zeidman v. J. Ray McDermott & Co., 651 F.2d 1030, 1041 (5th Cir.1981)).

The objectors claim that, as in *Lusardi,* the named plaintiffs in this case have, through the existence of the side agreements, effectively settled their claims against the CCR defendants whether or not the proposed settlement is approved. * * * This statement is factually untrue. The side agreements do not settle any claims with any asbestos victims. The side agreements only bind the signatory law firms, not their individual clients. Thus, in the event that the proposed settlement is not approved, the claims of the named plaintiffs are not settled. They, and all future asbestos claimants, remain free to sue the CCR defendants, and the various signatory law firms can still represent them in their suit. Therefore, *Lusardi* is inapplicable here because, unlike the named plaintiffs in that case, the named plaintiffs in this class action have not definitively settled their claims.

The objectors further claim that the obvious intent of the parties was to have class counsel agree, on behalf of all their clients (i.e., the named plaintiffs), to process claims using the same criteria and procedures as those detailed in the proposed settlement in the event that the settlement is not approved. However, I find that if the claims of the named plaintiffs are not actually settled by the side agreements because these individual plaintiffs themselves are not bound by the side agreements, then the "true" intention of the parties is not important. *Cf.* Parks v. Pavkovic, 753 F.2d 1397, 1404 (7th Cir.), *cert. denied,* 473 U.S. 906, 105 S.Ct. 3529, 87 L.Ed.2d 653 (1985)(case does not become moot because one of the parties, while continuing to take all the steps that a live adversary would take to assert his rights, has secretly concluded that come what may he will give his opponent everything the opponent seeks). In other words, whether or not the named plaintiffs have, as the objectors state, committed themselves to the *Carlough* criteria and procedures, is irrelevant if their current claims are not yet settled and thus are not moot.

I conclude, therefore, that this class action is not moot.

III. CONCLUSION

Federal courts are under a continuing duty to satisfy themselves of their jurisdiction before proceeding to the merits of any case. Having done so here, I find that this Court has subject matter jurisdiction over this case. For the reasons discussed above, I find that this class action is a non-collusive justiciable case or controversy in which plaintiffs have standing pursuant to Article III of the Constitution. I also find that it cannot be concluded to a legal certainty that the amount in controversy for each class member does not exceed $50,000 in accordance with 28

U.S.C. § 1332. Accordingly, the objections to this Court's subject matter jurisdiction are overruled.

Notes and Questions

1.   Class action procedure involves complex problems relating to the applicability of standing and mootness doctrines, and these doctrines have interesting implications for latent injury mass torts, as the *Carlough* decision suggests. Who must possess the requisite standing: the class representatives, class members, or as in *Phillips,* the defendants? What happens to the class if the representative's claim is mooted? Class action procedure often stretches the Art. III actual case or controversy requirement, as well as the prudential concern that the class plaintiff be sufficiently interested to fully litigate the interests or claims involved in the action. In particular, the standing requirement of "actual injury" sometimes may be loosely construed in the class action context, and standing may be satisfied where a plaintiff can show a possibility that he or she may manifest injury in the future. *See e.g.,* Washington v. Lee, 263 F.Supp. 327 (D.Ala.1966). However, other federal courts have found standing lacking where class representatives did not hold a sufficiently direct interest or where class members had not sustained any direct injuries. Has the *Carlough* decision stretched the injury component of standing to its outer limits?

In addition to satisfying the Rule 23(a) and (b) requirements for class certification, standing and mootness are threshold determinations at the outset of class litigation. Many courts have adopted the view that standing is satisfied if the class representative is a member of the class, and is an adequate representative with claims typical of class members. "As long as the representative parties have a direct and substantial interest, they have standing; the question whether they may be allowed to present claims on behalf of others who have similar, but not identical, interests depends not on standing, but on an assessment of typicality and adequacy of representation." Also, special standing problems are raised when a plaintiff class attempts to sue a defendant class. In many instances, courts have held that class plaintiffs lack standing to sue class defendants who have not directly injured them. *See, e.g.,* La Mar v. H & B Novelty & Loan Co., 489 F.2d 461 (9th Cir.1973). For a discussion of standing and mootness requirements as they relate to class actions, *see* Charles Alan Wright, Arthur R. Miller, and Mary Kay Kane, 7B FEDERAL PRACTICE AND PROCEDURE § 1785.1 (2d ed.1986 & 1993 Supp.).

2.   The requirement of diverse parties generally has not been a ground for challenging a federal court's subject matter jurisdiction in mass tort cases, but challenges based failure to satisfy the amount-in-controversy requirement has been a renewed objection in many mass tort cases. Generally these challenges have not been successful. *See, e.g.,* Watson v. Shell Oil Co., 979 F.2d 1014 (5th Cir.1992), *rehearing granted* 990 F.2d 805 (5th Cir.1993), *affirming* In re Shell Oil Refinery, 136 F.R.D. 588 (E.D.La. 1991)(18,000 class members satisfied amount-in-controversy requirement for federal diversity jurisdiction); *but see* Herlihy v. Ply—Gem Industries, Inc., 752 F.Supp. 1282 (D.Md.1990)(homeowner actions against fire-retardant plywood manufacturer do not meet amount-in-controversy requirements; claims cannot be aggregated for diversity purposes in class action).

3. Judge Reed also rejected the objectors' collusion challenge to the federal courts' subject matter jurisdiction. The objectors' collusion challenge was re-asserted during the fairness hearing, which the court again rejected. *See Georgine v. Amchem Products, Inc.,* Part I, Chapter I. D.4.

4. For a thorough-going analysis of the problems of both personal jurisdiction and subject matter jurisdiction relating to mass torts, *see generally* Thomas D. Rowe, Jr. & Kenneth D. Sibley, *Beyond Diversity: Federal Multiparty, Multiforum Jurisdiction,* 135 U.Pa.L.Rev. 7 (1986). *Cf.* Allan R. Kamp, *The Shrinking Forum: The Supreme Court's Limitation of Jurisdiction—An Argument for a Federal Forum in Multi–Party, Multi–State Litigation,* 21 Wm & Mary L. Rev. 161 (1979).

5. Some asbestos cases have been brought in the federal courts' admiralty jurisdiction because of claimants' shipboard asbestos exposure. Does federal admiralty jurisdiction provide a better basis for resolving mass tort litigation? Does the admiralty-jurisdiction approach suggest that federalization of mass tort subject matter jurisdiction is a better way of dealing with mass torts? *See generally* Jonathan Gutoff, Note, *Admiralty Jurisdiction Over Asbestos Torts: Unknotting the Tangled Fibers,* 54 U. Chi. L. Rev. 312 (1987).

3. MINIMAL DIVERSITY PROPOSALS

AMERICAN LAW INSTITUTE, COMPLEX LITIGATION PROJECT, PRELIMINARY DRAFT NO. 2

(September 13, 1989).

§ 5.01. Jurisdiction for Multiparty, Multiforum Litigation

(a) Subject to the requirements of subdivision (b), the district courts shall have original jurisdiction of civil actions arising out of the same transaction, occurrence, or series of related transactions or occurrences, if

(1) [the matter in controversy exceeds the sum or value of $25,000 for each of any twenty-five actual or prospective plaintiffs,] [the sum or value of the injury alleged in good faith to have been incurred by any twenty-five persons exceeds $25,000 per person], exclusive of interest and costs, and if at least one of the actions [may be filed] [is likely to be filed] or has been filed in a court of a state other than that of any other action; or

(2) [the matter in controversy exceeds the sum or value of $5,000 for each of any five actual or prospective plaintiffs,] [the sum or value of the injury alleged in good faith to have been incurred by any five persons exceeds $5,000 per person,] exclusive of interest and costs, and if:

(A) all of the defendants cannot be joined in the courts of any one state but can be joined in a single district court under the provisions of subdivision (c); or

(B) all of the defendants to the action cannot be joined in the courts of a state in which a substantial part of the acts or omissions giving rise to the action occurred, and all of the defendants can be joined in a single district court under the provisions of subdivision (c); or

(C) a substantial part of the acts or omissions giving rise to the action occurred in two or more states.

(b) An action may be brought under subdivision (a) only if a party is a citizen of a state and any actual or prospective adverse party is—

(1) a citizen of another state,

(2) a citizen or subject of a foreign state, or

(3) a foreign state, as defined in § 1603(a) of title 28.

(c) An action may be brought under subdivision(a) in any district in which any defendant resides or in which a substantial part of the acts or omissions giving rise to the action occurred.

(d) A district court may exercise jurisdiction over parties to an action brought under subdivision (a) to the full extent of the power of a federal court under the United States Constitution and shall apply choice of law rules a authorized by federal statute.

a. General purpose and scope. This section envisions a federal subject matter jurisdiction statute that would provide a federal forum for the adjudication of those multiparty actions that cannot be resolved efficiently or effectively in the state courts. Original subject matter jurisdiction is set out in § 5.01(a) and (b). Venue is controlled by § 5.01(c) and thus would be proper not only in districts where any defendant resides, but also in districts where a substantial part of the acts or omissions giving rise to the action occurred. Finally, as is true for actions transferred and consolidated under § 3.01, a court exercising jurisdiction under this section would be able to exert nationwide personal jurisdiction and the actions would benefit from the application of a single federal choice of law rule provided in § 5.01(d). . . . In this way, a federal district court is provided in which all the plaintiffs are able to file their claims [sic] consolidate their actions themselves. By allowing the plaintiffs to file together in a single district court, the grant of original jurisdiction therefore decreases the likelihood that a plaintiff's choice of forum will need to be overridden in order to resolve the dispute effectively and efficiently. Moreover, by giving the plaintiffs the option of suing together in a single district court, this jurisdictional grant allows the parties themselves to weigh the benefits and disadvantages of consolidation. Dispersed litigation will result from party choice and not from jurisdictional necessity.

This proposal is intended to promote fairness and efficiency. Specifically, its aim is to reduce the possibility that one or more parties will have to litigate the same issue in multiple jurisdictions by authorizing a single federal court to assume jurisdiction over the entire controversy. Consolidation is encouraged because it should decrease the litigation costs for parties who otherwise might be engaged in multiple and dispersed lawsuits, as well as reduce the likelihood that a party will be subject to conflicting resolutions of the same basic issues. Consolidation also should inhibit the dissipation or exhaustion of litigation capability that may result if a party is required to defend or prosecute multiple cases simultaneously or successively. The possibility that some parties will be involved in litigation for inordinate periods of time or will have to wait unduly long for other suits to be resolved before their own can begin also should be reduced.... Thus, expansion of federal jurisdiction here allows the benefits of proceeding in a consolidated fashion to be extended to multiparty, multiforum cases currently confined to state courts because they fail to meet existing federal jurisdiction requirements.

MULTIPARTY, MULTIFORUM JURISDICTION ACT OF 1991

H.R. Rep. No. 373, 102nd Cong., 1st Sess. 1991, 1991 WL 255971.

HOUSE REPORT NO. 102–373

November 25, 1991.
[To accompany H.R. 2450].

The Committee on the Judiciary, to whom was referred the bill (H.R. 2450) to amend title 28, United States Code, to provide for Federal jurisdiction of certain multiparty, multiform civil actions, having considered the same, report favorably thereon with an amendment and recommend that the bill as amended do pass. The amendment is as follows: Strike out all after the enacting clause and insert in lieu thereof the following:

Section 1. Short Title.

This Act may be cited as the "Multiparty, Multiforum Jurisdiction Act of 1991".

Sec. 2. Jurisdiction of District Courts.

(a) Basis of Jurisdiction.—Chapter 85 of title 28, United States Code, is amended by adding at the end of the following new section:

"§ 1368. Multiparty, multiforum jurisdiction

"(a) The district courts shall have original jurisdiction of any civil action involving minimal diversity between adverse parties that arises from a single accident, where at least 25 natural persons have either died or incurred injury in the accident at a discrete location and, in the case of injury, the injury has resulted in damages which exceed $50,000 per person, exclusive of interest and costs, if—

"(1) a defendant resides in a State and a substantial part of the accident took place in another State or other location, regardless of whether that defendant is also a resident of the State where a substantial part of the accident took place;

"(2) any two defendants reside in different States, regardless of whether such defendants are also residents of the same State or States; or

"(3) substantial parts of the accident took place in different States.

"(b) For purposes of this section—

"(1) minimal diversity exists between adverse parties if any party is a citizen of a State and any adverse party is a citizen of another State, a citizen or subject of a foreign state, or a foreign state as defined in section 1603(a) of this title;

"(2) a corporation is deemed to be a citizen of any State, and a citizen or subject of any foreign state, in which it is incorporated or has its principal place of business, and is deemed to be a resident of any State in which it is incorporated or licensed to do business or is doing business;

"(3) the term 'injury' means—

"(A) physical harm to a natural person; and

"(B) physical damage to or destruction of tangible property, but only if physical harm described in subparagraph (A) exists;

"(4) the term 'accident' means a sudden accident, or a natural event culminating in an accident, that results in death or injury incurred at a discrete location by at least 25 natural persons; and

"(5) the term 'State' includes the District of Columbia, the Commonwealth of Puerto Rico, and the territories or possessions of the United States.

"(c) In any action in a district court which is or could have been brought, in whole, or in part, under this section, any person with a claim arising from the accident described in subsection (a) shall be permitted to intervene as a party plaintiff in the action, even if that person could not have brought an action in a district court as an original matter.

"(d) A district court in which an action under this section is pending shall promptly notify the judicial panel on multidistrict litigation of the pendency of the action.".

* * *

Sec. 3. Venue.

Section 1391 of title 28, United States Code, is amended by adding at the end the following:

"(g) A civil action in which jurisdiction of the district court is based upon section 1368 of this title may be brought in any district in which any defendant resides or in which a substantial part of the accident giving rise to the action took place.".

Sec. 4.   Multidistrict Litigation.

Section 1407 of title 28, United States Code, is amended by adding at the end the following:

"(i)(1) In actions transferred under this section when jurisdiction is or could have been based, in whole or in part, on section 1368 of this title, the transferee district court may, notwithstanding any other provision of this section, retain actions so transferred for the determination of liability and punitive damages. An action retained for the determination of liability shall be remanded to the district court from which the action was transferred, or to the State court from which the action was removed, for the determination of damages, other than punitive damages, unless the court finds, for the convenience of parties and witnesses and in the interest of justice, that the action should be retained for the determination of damages.

"(2) Any remand under paragraph (1) shall not be effective until 60 days after the transferee court has issued an order determining liability and has certified its intention to remand some or all of the transferred actions for the determination of damages. An appeal with respect to the liability determination and the choice of law determination of the transferee court may be taken during that 60–day period to the court of appeals with appellate jurisdiction over the transferee court. In the event a party files such an appeal, the remand shall not be effective until the appeal has been finally disposed of. Once the remand has become effective, the liability determination and the choice of law determination shall not be subject to further review by appeal or otherwise.

"(3) An appeal with respect to a determination of punitive damages by the transferee court may be taken, during the 60–day period beginning on the date the order making the determination is issued, to the court of appeals with jurisdiction over the transferee court.

"(4) Any decision under this subsection concerning remand for the determination of damages shall not be reviewable by appeal or otherwise.

"(5) Nothing in this subsection shall restrict the authority of the transferee court to transfer or dismiss an action on the ground of inconvenient forum.".

Sec. 5.   Removal of Actions.

Section 1441 of title 28, United States Code, is amended—

(1) in subsection (e) by striking out "(e) The court to which such civil action is removed" and inserting in lieu thereof "(f) The court to which a civil action is removed under this section"; and

(2) by inserting after subsection (d) the following new subsection:

"(e)(1) Notwithstanding the provisions of subsection (b) of this section, a defendant in a civil action in a State court may remove the action to the district court of the United States for the district and division embracing the place where the action is pending if—

"(A) the action could have been brought in a United States district court under section 1368 of this title, or

"(B) the defendant is a party to an action which is or could have been brought, in whole or in part, under section 1368 in a United States district court and arises from the same accident as the action in State court, even if the action to be removed could not have been brought in a district court as an original matter. The removal of an action under this subsection shall be made in accordance with section 1446 of this title, except that a notice of removal may also be filed before trial of the action in State court within 30 days after the date on which the defendant first becomes a party to an action under section 1368 in a United States district court that arises from the same accident as the action in State court, or at a later time with leave of the district court.

"(2) Whenever an action is removed under this subsection and the district court to which it is removed or transferred under section 1407(i) has made a liability determination requiring further proceedings as to damages, the district court shall remand the action to the State court from which it had been removed for the determination of damages, unless the court finds that, for the convenience of parties and witnesses and in the interest of justice, the action should be retained for the determination of damages.

"(3) Any remand under paragraph (2) shall not be effective until 60 days after the district court has issued an order determining liability and has certified its intention to remand the removed action for the determination of damages. An appeal with respect to the liability determination and the choice of law determination of the district court may be taken during that 60–day period to the court of appeals with appellate jurisdiction over the district court. In the event a party files such an appeal, the remand shall not be effective until the appeal has been finally disposed of. Once the remand has become effective, the liability determination and the choice of law determination shall not be subject to further review by appeal or otherwise.

"(4) Any decision under this subsection concerning remand for the determination of damages shall not be reviewable by appeal or otherwise.

"(5) An action removed under this subsection shall be deemed to be an action under section 1368 and an action in which jurisdiction is based on section 1368 of this title for purposes of this section and sections 1407, 1659, 1697, and 1785 of this title.

"(6) Nothing in this subsection shall restrict the authority of the district to transfer or dismiss an action on the ground of inconvenient forum.".

* * *

[Sections relating to choice of law have been omitted; *see* Ch. X.A., *infra—ed.*]

* * *

Summary and Purpose

The purpose of H.R. 2450—the Multiparty, Multiforum Jurisdiction Act of 1991—is to improve the efficiency with which Federal Courts are able to handle certain complex, multidistrict litigation. This bill would amend several portions of the Judicial Code, creating Federal court jurisdiction to deal with problems of dispersed and complex litigation arising out of airline accidents, hotel fires and other disasters in which many people are killed or seriously injured in a single accident. Accidents of this nature can give rise to a multitude of suits in Federal and State courts. Under existing law, a variety of impediments exist to effective consolidation of these closely related cases. As a consequence, identical issues of liability must, in some cases, be tried by a number of courts, thereby wasting judicial resources, increasing litigation costs, heightening the risk of inconsistent results, and delaying the dispensation of justice. This bill removes certain impediments to consolidation of these cases, and in so doing improves the fairness and efficiency of the process by which these cases are resolved.

Legislative History

* * *

Discussion

Background

Under existing law, an array of barriers prevent consolidation of related litigation in either the State or the Federal courts. In the case of State court systems, the main impediments to effective consolidation are constitutional in nature. The due process clause of the Fourteenth Amendment has been construed to require a minimum threshold of contact between a person and a State, before the courts of that State may properly assert personal jurisdiction over the person in question. Consequently, in any given case, there may be no single State forum in which the contacts with all relevant parties are sufficient to permit consolidation of all related litigation. Federal courts, on the other hand, can constitutionally exercise broader personal jurisdiction, and therefore can, if authorized, bring scattered parties together in one forum when that is desirable. At present, though, several statutory impediments often make such consolidation impossible. The requirement of complete diversity among the parties will frequently prevent all parties from getting into Federal court. Among the cases that can be filed in Federal court, venue restrictions further limit efforts to gather related litigation together in a single forum. And even to the extent consolidation in a single forum is possible, existing multidistrict litigation procedures limit the authority of the court to which cases have been transferred, to resolving pretrial matters only. The Federal courts therefore are unable to perform as well as they might a valuable function for which the Federal judicial forum would be uniquely suited. The problems presented by scattered, related litigation prompted the American Bar Association and the American Law Institute, among others, to undertake studies of the procedures for consolidation of related proceedings in mass tort cases. H.R. 2450 would remove the barriers that impede consolidation or related litigation in the Federal court system, in the limited context of cases arising out of single accidents in which many people are killed or injured. The bill takes its inspiration from a proposal first made by the Department of Justice in 1979.[2] It would create a new Federal court jurisdiction over cases in which 25 or more people are killed or incur injury in a single accident, based on minimal diversity of citizenship of parties as authorized by Article III of the Constitution. Earlier incarnations of the bill in previous Congresses were drafted so as to apply not only to multiple suits arising out of single accidents, such as airplane crashes or bridge collapses, but also to multiple suits arising out of multiple events, such as repeated exposures to toxic substances or a series of incidents in which people are injured by defectively designed or manufactured products. The Department of Justice, the Judicial Conference and others, in the past have expressed concern over application of the consolidation procedures provided for in this bill, to products liability or toxic exposure cases. Their concerns were at least three-fold: first, that enlarging Federal jurisdiction to include products liability or toxic exposure litigation could cause too dramatic a rise in Federal court caseload, given that the total volume of such cases in State and Federal courts far exceeds that for single accident cases; second, that consolidation of thousands of suits in a single forum—which would not be unusual in products liability of toxic exposure cases—could give rise to serious case management problems both for judges, who may have an unwieldy number of cases to resolve, and for litigants, particularly plaintiffs, who may lose too much control over their individual suits; and third, that products liability or toxic exposure cases, which typically concern injuries occurring in separate incidents, can give rise to multiple issues of fact requiring case-by-case resolution, thereby diminishing the efficiencies created by consolidation.[3] Accordingly, H.R. 2450, following the lead of H.R. 3406 in the last Congress, is limited to suits arising out of single accidents. At first glance, a bill that expands the jurisdiction of the Federal courts over a subset diversity of citizenship actions would appear at odds with the ongoing efforts of this Committee to relieve Federal court congestion generally and to better accommodate dramatic increases in caseload resulting from heightened efforts to prosecute drug related

---

2. The Department of Justice's proposal was more fully developed in a 1986 article by Professor Thomas Rowe and Mr. Kenneth Sibley, published in the University of Pennsylvania Law Review. *See,* Rowe & Sibley, *"Beyond Diversity: Federal Multiparty, Multiform Jurisdiction,"* 135 U.Pa. L.Rev. 7 (1986).

3. Such cases commonly turn on conditions that are unique to the injured person's own conduct and life history. Such issues are less frequent in an airplane crash or hotel fire. Given concerns relating to plaintiff-specific issues, as well as the other concerns identified above, products liability and toxic exposure cases are excluded from the scope of the bill.

crimes. As both the Judicial Conference, which represents the judges burdened by Federal caseload pressures, and the Department of Justice, which prosecutes the increasing number of criminal cases, testified, however, the proposal would be unlikely to have a significant effect on Federal court caseload. First, as noted above, the expanded jurisdiction is limited to suits arising out of single accidents. Second, in most cases, the new jurisdiction would not bring entirely new, large actions before the Federal courts, but rather would simply permit consolidation in a single Federal forum of scattered litigation, part of which was already in or destined for Federal court. Third, whatever increase in new actions might occur would be offset by efficiencies created by the consolidation of multiple State and Federal courts. Under the present rules, cases arising from a single-event mass disaster that are filed or removed to different Federal district courts may be consolidated for purposes of pretrial proceedings but then are returned to the district court from which they came. In cases arising from single-event mass disasters, the interest of efficiency and fairness dictate that liability for compensatory and punitive damages be determined in a single, consolidated trail. Such consolidated treatment would avoid both inconsistent results and the possibility that multiple punitive damages awards would be assessed against a defendant for the same conduct. This bill is not an invasion of a domain of State courts, but rather is a narrowly focused use of the Federal judicial forum to employ its unique capabilities to deal with dispersed, related actions. The proposal rests squarely on the constitutional authorization of minimal diversity jurisdiction in Article III and meets a need that State court systems are constitutionally unable to fulfill. The limited new jurisdiction creates no Federal substantive law and can be invoked only at the initiative of litigants. Moreover, it establishes a presumption in favor of a novel measure—remand for damage determinations from Federal to State courts—when a claim was originally filed in State court but then removed to Federal court under the new jurisdiction, and a decision reached upholding liability. The proposal is, in short, in the best tradition of a cooperative and voluntary federalism, respecting State authority in a Federal jurisdiction that should improve economy and uniformity in the administration of the law.

SECTION-BY-SECTION ANALYSIS

Section 1. Short Title

Section 1 of the bill identifies the short title as the "Multiparty, Multiforum Jurisdiction Act of 1991".

Section 2. Jurisdiction of the District Courts

Section 2 of the bill establishes the proposed special jurisdiction by adding a new section 1368 at the end of the existing Federal district court jurisdictional provisions of title 28 of the United States Code. Its subsection (a) defines the basic requirements for the jurisdiction: (1) Minimal diversity of citizenship among adversaries; (2) at least 25 persons have suffered substantial injury or death in a single accident;

and (3) dispersion of events or defendants. The first requirement is constitutionally required under Article III for Federal court jurisdiction based on citizenship of the parties. The second requirement limits the availability of the jurisdiction to mass torts in which substantial injuries to a significant number of persons are caused in a single accident. The third requirement isolates the circumstances in which geographically scattered litigation can arise, making the jurisdiction necessary. Section 1368 does not directly address claims in the alternative. For example, in the case of a train accident, passengers may allege that their injuries were caused by the accident, by medical malpractice afterward, or both. While it would not be desirable to clog the Federal courts with large numbers of satellite claims, neither would it be desirable to fragment such litigation when plaintiffs otherwise could have used Rule 20 of the Federal Rules of Civil Procedures, or a State counterpart, to avoid pursuing such claims separately. While the legislation does not directly address this complex issue, it is not intended to limit the court's development and use of discretionary pendent claim and party jurisdiction to deal with such alternative claims. Subsection (b) of section 1368 contains definitions, for purposes of this section, of minimal diversity, corporate citizenship and residence, injury, and accident.

"Accident": As defined in this section, "accident" must be sudden in nature, may include natural events culminating in accidents, and must occur in a discrete location. Thus, the bill is intended to apply to those events in which 25 or more persons are killed or injured together in a single, catastrophic accident, such as a hotel fire, a railroad, airplane or bus accident, or a bridge collapse. The reference to natural events is inserted to ensure that an accident such as a bridge collapse qualifies as an accident within the scope of the bill, notwithstanding that the collapse was caused by long-term flooding, foundation shifting or other natural events that precipitate a sudden accident, but arguably are not "sudden" in and of themselves. Given this definition of accident, the bill does not apply to ordinary product liability actions, including failure to warn actions and design defect cases involving multiple, identically manufactured units, because the injuries in such actions do not usually occur in a large number together in a single accident. Therefore, the term "accident" does not include the act of or a decision relating to designing, manufacturing, labeling, packaging, testing or filing reports with Federal agencies with respect to any product. Of course, defectively manufactured, designed or labeled products may cause an "accident" within the meaning of the bill. For example, a defectively designed sprinkler system may fail to put out a hotel fire. To that limited extent the bill would reach suits raising product liability issues. The Committee has, however, strived to limit the scope of this bill so that it could be interpreted to apply to ordinary product liability actions, and believes that language of the bill is now sufficiently clear in that regard.

"Injury": The bill defines injury to mean bodily injury, as well as injury to property provided that property injury is accompanied by some bodily injury. Accordingly, at least 25 people must have sustained some bodily injury before the Federal jurisdiction created by this bill would apply. The bill is structured, however, so that as long as at least 25 people have sustained some bodily injury, the jurisdiction created would be available to others who have sustained only property damage in the same accident, as in the case of hotel guests who escape a hotel fire but lose their belongings. In order to make the new mass tort jurisdiction broadly available, the definition of corporate citizenship, for purposes of section 1368, is drawn from current law. Subsection (c) of section 1368 furthers the policy of allowing joinder of related matters by permitting someone not a party to the action as originally filed in or removed to Federal court to intervene, whether or not that person could have invoked the new Federal jurisdiction as an original matter. Thus, if a prospective plaintiff with no claim under Federal law was a citizen of the same State as all defendants, such a party could not sue on his or her own in Federal court as an original matter for lack of the constitutionally required minimal diversity; but if others brought a section 1368 suit in or removed it to a Federal court, it would defeat the action-consolidating purposes of the jurisdiction if the outsider could not now join the litigation. For cases within the jurisdiction, this subsection also provides the requirement of existing law that each plaintiff in most Federal actions to which a jurisdictional amount requirement applies must have a claim for the needed amount in controversy. Again, if the action is large enough for the jurisdiction to be invoked under subsection (b), it would defeat the purpose of the jurisdiction if parties with related but smaller claims could not join. Subsection (d) of section 1368, facilitates coordination of related actions by requiring that any district court in which an action under section 1368 is pending promptly notify the Judicial Panel on Multidistrict Litigation.

Section 3.　Venue

Section 3 of the bill amends section 1391 of title 28 of the United States Code, by adding a new subsection (g), which provides a venue provision for cases brought under section 1368. Venue is authorized in any judicial district where any defendant resides or where a substantial part of the accident occurred. In the words of the 1979 Justice Department commentary: This provision is similar to, but slightly broader than, the current venue provision for actions not founded on diversity of citizenship in section 1391(b) of title 28, United States Code. They differ mainly in that existing section 1391(b) creates venue where "all defendants" reside. The broader venue scope that the language "any defendant" provides, along with nationwide service of process provision . . . , will allow potential defendants not living in the State where the action is filed to be brought in at the action's inception, thus avoiding a multiplicity of suits in different States. The provision authorizing venue in any district where a "substantial part" of an accident occurred (as opposed to the district where the accident occurred) is intended to address only the unusual circumstance in which an accident covered by the legislation would occur in more than one district, such as a mid-air plane collision that occurs above the border of two States. The language is not intended to expand the meaning of the term "accident".

Section 4. Multidistrict Litigation

For cases within the new jurisdiction, section 4 of the bill amends section 1407 of title 28, United States Code, to expand present district court authority over transferred actions, which formally covers pretrial proceedings, to permits joint trial of liability issues. In the words of the 1979 Justice Department explanation: The existing provision of the multidistrict litigation statute, section 1407 of title 28, United States Code, permits consolidation and transfer of cases pending in different judicial districts in which there are common questions of fact. Transfer is currently authorized for pretrial proceedings only. This amendment would add a new subsection, (i), to section 1407 * * * which would apply only to cases transferred involving multi-person injuries. * * * Expanding the power of the transferee judge to include conducting a trial on the merits is preferable in several respects to the current requirement of a remand to the transferor court following pre-trial proceedings. First, having presided over complicated and protracted discovery proceedings and pretrial motions and transferee judge has already attained a degree of expertise in a complex matter that is wasteful to disregard. Second, experience has shown that many transferee judges currently manage to retain actions for trial by transferring the cases to themselves at the conclusion of pre-trial proceedings through the change of venue provision in section 1404(a) of title 28, United States Code. This provision, however, restricts transfer to a district where the action could originally have been brought. By allowing the transferee judge to retain multiperson injury actions for trial, we merely codify current practice and eliminate the restrictions imposed by the 1404(a) transfer device. For similar reasons, the bill permits joint trial of punitive damage issues. Whereas case-to-case variations in facts relevant to resolving compensatory damage issues will ordinarily be such that there is no net gain to having those issues tried by a single court, that is not the case with punitive damage issues; moreover, by consolidating punitive damage determinations, the risk of inappropriate, multiple punitive damage awards is reduced. Revised section 1407 calls for remand, however, of damage determinations (other than punitive damages), including the possibility of remand to State courts in which actions were originally filed, unless the Federal court finds that it would serve the convenience of parties and witnesses and the interests of justice to retain the damages phase as well. That section also provides that if the Federal transferee court is sending cases back for damage determinations, a party may appeal the courts' liability determination (and its choice of law determination) before the remand. Once all such appeals have been disposed of (or if no such appeal is taken), the section provides that the liability determination and the choice of law determination shall not be subject to further review (either in remanded or retained proceedings), and the remand shall take effect. In addition, the section bars appellate review of the decision whether or not to remand for the determination of damages.

Section 5. Removal of Actions

Section 5 of the bill redesignates subsection (e) of 28 U.S.C. 1441 as subsection (f), and adds a new subsection (e) to those general removal provisions. New subsection (e) would permit removal both to invoke the proposed jurisdiction (as by a defendant sued on related matters in the courts of two or more States) and to join actions within the jurisdiction pending in the Federal court (as by a defendant sued in State court after the filing in Federal court of a section 1368 action). Any defendant meeting the requirements of subsection (e)(1) may effect the removal, whether or not any of the defendants is a citizen of the State in which the action is brought. Thus, the general all-defendants requirement for removal contained in subsection (a) of section 1441, and the instate defendant limitation in subsection (b), would not apply to the removal of such actions. To avoid making actions unremovable from State court when joinder to a later-filed Federal section 1368 action is sought, subsection (e) authorizes removal before trial within thirty days of a defendant's becoming a party to a section 1368 suit, or at a later time with leave of the district court. The additional 30–day period reflects the fact that removal may be impossible for jurisdictional reasons within the normal removal period of section 1446. For example, if the initial suits brought in State court against a defendant all involved nondiverse plaintiffs, it might not be able to remove them until some other plaintiff initiated a section 1368 suit against it in State court. The subsection also allows removal beyond the extended time period with leave of the district court because consolidated adjudication of mass tort cases may further important systemic interests, even if a defendant does not consider it in its self-interest to remove the State actions against it at an early point in the litigation. The new subsection (e) also establishes a presumption in favor of discretionary remand to State courts, or "reverse removal," for damages determinations after rulings on liability. This provision both respects State adjudication and limits the burden from the new jurisdiction on the Federal judiciary. If the Federal district court is sending cases back for damage determinations, a party may appeal the court's liability determination (and its choice of law determination) before the remand. Once all such appeals have been disposed of (or if no such appeal is taken), the section provides that the liability choice of law determinations shall not be subject to further review (either in remanded or retained proceedings), and the remand shall take effect. In addition, the subsection bars appellate review of the decision whether or not to remand for the determination of damages. Paragraph (5) of subsection (e) makes clear that an action removed pursuant to that subsection is to be considered a section 1368 suit for such purposes as intervention (section 1368(c)), notification of the multi-district litigation panel (section 1368(d)), transfer and consolidation (section 1407(i)), removal of related action in State court (section 1441(e)), choice of law (section 1659), and service of process and subpoenas (sections 1697, 1785).   Nothing in subsection (e) is intended to restrict the district court's ability, at any time, to transfer an action under section 1404(a) or dismiss an action under the doctrine of forum on conveniens.

* * *

ROBERT A. SEDLER AND AARON D. TWERSKI, THE CASE AGAINST ALL ENCOMPASSING FEDERAL MASS TORT LEGISLATION: SACRIFICE WITHOUT GAIN

73 Marq.L.Rev. 76 (1989).

BE IT RESOLVED that the American Bar Association, recognizing that separate adjudication of individual tort claims arising from a single accident or use of or exposure to the same product or substance is inefficient and wasteful, seriously burdens both state and federal judicial systems, poses unacceptably high risks of inconsistent results, and contributes to public dissatisfaction with the tort law system and the legal profession, adopts the following recommendations of the Commission on Mass Torts. . . .

With this preamble as its factual predicate, the American Bar Association Commission on Mass Torts has undertaken to restructure the litigation of mass torts in the United States.   It has proposed legislation which would empower federal courts to consolidate the litigation of mass torts in a single court utilizing the law of a single state. Legislation similar to that proposed by the ABA commission is now under serious consideration by Congress.   The Multiparty, Multiforum Jurisdiction Act of 1989 (H.R. 3406), though different in many particulars from the ABA proposal, is driven by the same concern for litigation efficiency.   Though the motives behind these legislative initiatives are laudable, these objectives cannot be achieved in our federal system with its constitutional constraints, without doing serious violence to longstanding principles of state sovereignty and progressive trends in choice of law.   We believe that their goals can only be accomplished by riding roughshod over important federalism principles while concomitantly reviving regressive and thoroughly discredited choice of law rules.

* * *

II.   THE ASSAULT ON FEDERALISM

A.   Respecting State Sovereignty

Fundamental federalism considerations strongly militate against a federally required consolidation of "mass tort" cases, a federally imposed "single jurisdiction choice of law rule," and the resulting displacement of state conflicts law in such cases.   Both the ABA Report and H.R. 3406 fail to give sufficient consideration to the impact of consolidation, and of the "single jurisdiction choice of law rule" on the traditional sovereignty exercised by the states in our constitutional system. The focus of both the Report and the bill is solely upon "efficiency and judicial economy," and upon the purported undesirability of "inconsistent results" in the adjudication of claims arising from the same "mass tort." There is little, if any, concern that the price to be paid for such "efficiency and consistency" is an improper intrusion on state sovereignty, by depriving the states of their power to promulgate the rules governing disputes between private parties in "mass tort" cases, and to adjudicate such disputes in their courts.

In American constitutional theory, the sovereignty formerly possessed by the British Crown over domestic matters evolved upon each of the states at the time of independence; therefore, the states have the primary responsibility for developing legal rules that govern disputes between private persons, and adjudicating such disputes in their courts. As the Supreme Court noted in holding that the full faith and credit clause generally does not compel one state to displace its own law in favor of that of another state:

> [T]he very nature of the federal union of states, to which are reserved some of the attributes of sovereignty, precludes resort to the full faith and credit clause as the means for compelling a state to substitute the statutes of other states for its own statutes dealing with a subject matter concerning which it is competent to legislate.

Congress, of course, has the power, as a matter of federal supremacy, to override or displace state law in any area coming within the federal legislative power. Since the federal legislative power, particularly the power of Congress over interstate commerce, has been broadly construed, Congress has the affirmative power to override or displace state law in "mass tort" cases. However, as we shall demonstrate, the drafters of the mass tort proposals have gone about displacing state law in mass tort cases in a manner that raises serious constitutional concerns. In any event, the measure of Congress' constitutional power is not the measure of a proper exercise of that power. Congress itself has recognized that any exercise of federal power should be undertaken with due regard for the traditional sovereignty of the states and their role in our federal system.

Nowhere does Congress' regard for the traditional sovereignty of the states appear more clearly than in the matter of the states' power to develop legal rules governing disputes between private persons, and to adjudicate such disputes in their courts. Congress has recognized the primacy of state law in disputes between private persons by requiring the application of state law in diversity cases under the Rules of Decision Act. The Supreme Court's holding in *Erie R.R. Co. v. Tompkins*, that "state law" means the common law of the state as declared by the highest state court, and its "*Klaxon* holding," that this includes the application of state conflict of laws and rules, coupled with the Court's expansive interpretation of what is "substantive" for *Erie* purposes, all reinforce Congressional recognition of the primacy of state law in governing disputes between private persons.

Congress has also recognized the primary responsibility of the state courts to adjudicate disputes between private persons, including persons residing in different states.   The exercise of diversity jurisdiction in the federal courts has been carefully limited by requiring complete diversity, instead of the constitutionally permissible "minimal diversity."   Diversity jurisdiction in suits involving corporations is further restricted by the fact that, as subsection 1332(c) specifically provides, a corporation is a citizen both of the state where it is incorporated, and the state where it has its principal place of business.   Furthermore, in 1988, Congress increased fivefold the jurisdictional amount in diversity cases, from $10,000 to $50,000.

Congressional respect for state sovereignty in this area is also reflected in the Court's extreme reluctance to allow federal preemption of the state's power to promulgate legal rules governing the disputes between private persons.   Thus, the Court has held that, although federal law controls the radiological safety aspects of nuclear power, it does not preempt state tort law remedies, including an award of punitive damages, for harm caused by the escape of hazardous nuclear energy materials.   Moreover, in the labor law area, where preemption is often found, the Court has held that in certain circumstances federal labor law does not preempt state tort law remedies in suits involving employers, employees, and unions.

The foregoing illustrations demonstrate that under our federal system the states have the primary responsibility for promulgating the law governing disputes between private persons, and for adjudicating such disputes in their courts.   Congress has traditionally been solicitous of the responsibility of the states in this regard.   This being the case, proponents of a "federal solution" to the purported problems of "mass tort" litigation, through the displacement of state law and the role of the state courts in resolving these cases, should properly bear a heavy burden of justification.   They should be required to demonstrate an overriding necessity for such a radical subversion of state sovereignty. In light of the values of our constitutional system, state sovereignty should not be lightly cast aside in the name of "efficiency and uniformity."

Unfortunately, this is exactly what would be done under the ABA proposal, as well as H.R. 3406.   We will use the terms of H.R. 3406 as the focal point for our discussion.   This bill would radically subvert state sovereignty in "mass tort" cases, first by establishing minimal diversity, and more significantly, by overruling *Klaxon,* and displacing state choice of law in favor of a federally-imposed solution.   Section 1658 directs the federal courts to "designat[e] a single jurisdiction whose substantive law is to be applied in all other actions under section 1367 arising from the same event of [sic] occurrence." In addition, the federal courts are not "bound by the choice of law rules of any State." The purpose and effect of the Bill, then, is to destroy the authority of the state courts to decide "mass tort" cases, and to determine what substantive law shall apply to the resolution of those cases.

We do not argue that it is improper in all circumstances for Congress to modify state law applicable to the resolution of disputes between private persons. In certain limited circumstances, Congress may conclude that national interests require displacement of state law, and that diverse or cumulative imposition of liability in cases with interstate or international ramifications impose an "undue burden" on interstate commerce. Indeed, one of the authors of this Article has been a proponent of federal products liability legislation which is specifically targeted to resolve certain problems that he thinks need resolution at the national level. Whatever may be one's views as to the wisdom of federal substantive tort legislation, the ABA proposal and H.R. 3406 do not seek to establish a national substantive norm. Where Congress legislates by creating substantive law to resolve a problem of national significance, it presumably has done so after having weighed the merits of the issue, and chosen a national solution to it. By relying on state substantive law as the measure of the rights of the parties, the ABA proposal and H.R. 3406 look to a body of the law that is not national in character. The legislation, in effect, declares the mass tort problem to be a matter of overreaching federal concern, while still presuming that a "one state solution" is rational. In addition, when the law chosen is based on irrational choice of law methodology, the affront to federalism is profound.

B. Sacrificing State Interests

1. Single Disaster Cases

The radical subversion of state sovereignty effected by H.R. 3406 is dramatically illustrated by the following example. Twenty members of the Elks Club in Denver, Colorado, charter a bus for a trip to Arizona for an Elks Convention. The bus company, Colorado Coaches, Inc., is a Colorado corporation doing business mostly within the state. In Phoenix, thirty Arizona Elks members board the bus for a local sightseeing trip. Due to the negligence of the bus driver, the bus hits a culvert, causing the bus to overturn. All the passengers suffer serious and debilitating injuries. A Colorado statute adopted in 1987 limits recovery for non-economic loss to $250,000 for each plaintiff. There is no such limitation under Arizona law.

Both the cases of the Colorado plaintiffs and the Arizona plaintiffs give rise to a conflict of laws problem. This is because in both cases the parties are not residents of the same state and/or all the legally significant facts did not occur in the same state. In addition, the laws of the involved states differ on the point in issue. In the case of the Colorado plaintiffs, although both the plaintiffs and the defendant are Colorado residents, the accident occurred in another state, Arizona. In the case of the Arizona plaintiffs, although the accident occurred in Arizona, the defendant is a resident of a different state, Colorado. The laws of the involved states differ on the point in issue, in that Arizona allows unlimited recovery for non-economic loss, while Colorado limits recovery for non-economic loss to $250,000.

It is submitted that in these cases a functionally sound result is for the Arizona plaintiffs to obtain unlimited recovery under Arizona law, but for the Colorado plaintiffs to be limited to the $250,000 limitation on non-economic loss in accordance with Colorado law. In an interstate accident situation, the primarily interested states are the parties' home states, where the consequences of the accident and of allowing or denying recovery will be felt by the parties. The Arizona policy of allowing unlimited recovery thus will always be advanced when the victims are residents of Arizona. The application of Arizona law to determine liability in the claim of the Arizona plaintiffs against Colorado Coaches, Inc., is fully fair to the defendant, since the accident occurred in Arizona on a local sightseeing trip. There is no doubt that the Arizona plaintiffs will be able to obtain unlimited recovery there. They will bring suit against Colorado Coaches, Inc. in Arizona, where the defendant is subject to jurisdiction under the Arizona "long-arm" act, and Arizona will apply its own law, thus allowing unlimited recovery.

In the suit between the Colorado plaintiffs and the Colorado defendant, Colorado law, limiting recovery to $250,000 for non-economic loss, should likewise apply to determine the rights of the Colorado parties. The Colorado legislature has made this determination as to the proper measure of recovery for non-economic loss. Therefore, Colorado is the only state that has a real interest in having its law applied to the issue in this case because the social and economic consequences of the accident, and of imposing or denying liability, will be felt by the parties there. Thus, Colorado will apply its own law in the event that suit is brought there, and it is likely that if suit were brought in Arizona, its courts would apply Colorado law in this case as well.

The result in this situation, then, is that the Colorado plaintiffs would be limited to $250,000 in damages for non-economic loss in accordance with Colorado law, because both the plaintiffs and the defendant are residents of Colorado, and the social and economic consequences of the accident and of allowing or denying recovery will be felt by the parties in Colorado. The Arizona plaintiffs, however, would obtain unlimited recovery in accordance with Arizona law, since they were injured in their home state on a purely local trip. Such a result (the Colorado plaintiffs being denied unlimited recovery in accordance with Colorado law, and the Arizona plaintiffs obtaining unlimited recovery in accordance with Arizona law) is functionally sound and fair to all the parties involved. It is irrelevant that the parties were victims in the same "mass tort." The "mass" nature of the tort has nothing to do with the consequences of that tort for the individual victims and with the interest of the victims' home states in applying their law to determine the rights of the victims. The consequences of this "mass tort" will be felt by the victims in their home states, and it is the law of their respective home states that should determine the amount of damages they will each recover for this "mass tort."

The intrusion of a federally imposed "single designated jurisdiction" rule, however, would require the federal court to either deny the Arizona plaintiffs unlimited recovery or, more likely, grant the Colorado plaintiffs a "windfall." This would not be permitted according to the law of their home state. There exists no reason to deny the Colorado defendant the protection of the law which the Colorado legislature sought to bestow upon it while granting to Colorado plaintiffs a "windfall" denied to them by the legislature of their home state. The application of the "single designated jurisdiction" rule in this case, therefore, not only runs counter to progressive trends in choice of law, but unjustifiably defeats the strong policy of Colorado, in the case of the Colorado parties, without advancing any legitimate policy of Arizona. Again, if the Arizona courts were permitted to retain control over this case, they would likely respect the legitimate policy and interest of Colorado and displace Arizona law in favor of Colorado law on the point in issue.

We submit, therefore, that proper regard for the traditional sovereignty of the states in our federal system dictates that Colorado law govern the rights of the Colorado plaintiffs and the Colorado defendant, while Arizona law govern the rights of the Arizona plaintiffs and Colorado defendant arising out of an Arizona accident. This regard for state sovereignty is thwarted, however, by the "designated single jurisdiction" rule of H.R. 3406.

In arguing for the consolidation of "mass tort" litigation and the application of a federally imposed "single designated jurisdiction" rule to govern all the cases arising from the "mass tort," the American Bar Association Commission on Mass Torts has stated that:

> [S]eparate adjudication of individual tort claims arising from a single accident or use of or exposure to the same product or substance is inefficient and wasteful, seriously burdens both state and federal judicial systems, poses unacceptably high risks of inconsistent results, and contributes to public dissatisfaction with the tort law system and the legal profession.

The Report, however, fails to demonstrate empirical evidence that the present system of "mass tort" litigation produces any of these claimed harmful effects. Rather, the Report focuses on the difficulty of consolidating the "mass tort" cases in a single court to be governed by a single law, and simply assumes that all of these alleged harmful effects result from this difficulty. In addition, nowhere in the Report is there consideration of the effect consolidation and resolution of the "mass tort" cases under a federally imposed "single designated jurisdiction" rule would have on the traditional sovereignty of the states in our federal system, and the longstanding function of the states to develop the legal rules that govern disputes between private persons and to adjudicate such disputes in their courts. It is simply assumed that state sovereignty must be shunted aside in the name of "efficiency and uniformity of result" in "mass tort" litigation.

Let us now look at the Colorado–Arizona bus trip "mass tort" case and examine how the cases would be handled under the present system of tort litigation. This system relies primarily on state law and the state courts to determine the rights and liabilities of the parties involved in interstate accidents, "mass tort" or otherwise. The Arizona plaintiffs would doubtless file their suits against the Colorado defendant in the Arizona courts, where that defendant is subject to jurisdiction under the Arizona "long-arm" act. They will not file their suits in Colorado, not only because of possible inconvenience in doing so, but because there is a real possibility that Colorado would apply its own law in order to protect the Colorado defendant. If the plaintiffs file separate actions, the Arizona courts would have the power to consolidate them, so the "efficiency" problem is rectified.

The Colorado plaintiffs are also likely to sue in Arizona, hoping to obtain the application of Arizona law as the law of the state of injury instead of the less favorable law of their home state. Again, all of their cases could be consolidated with the cases of the Arizona plaintiffs, and there could be a single trial on the issue of liability. [   ] Therefore, the "efficiency" concern is satisfied. If liability is established, there would have to be separate trials on the issue of damages for each plaintiff as there is under H.R. 3406. Consequently, the Colorado plaintiffs would be limited to $250,000 for non-economic loss in accordance with Colorado law.

The fact that the Arizona plaintiffs would recover greater damages than the Colorado plaintiffs for harm arising out of the same accident would mean that there would be "inconsistent results" in the recovery arising from the same "mass tort." It is difficult to understand why this creates any kind of problem. The "inconsistent results" are due to the fact that the parties' home states have different rules as to the amount of damages recoverable. These are also the states where the consequences of the accident and of imposing or denying liability will be felt by the parties. Once the reason for the "inconsistent results" is understood, it cannot be said to be "unacceptable" to limit each victim to the measure of recovery afforded by the law of the victim's home state. Surely, such a result is preferable to imposing a "choice of law straightjacket" that would improperly intrude on the power of Arizona to apply its substantive law for the benefit of the Arizona victims. This would also impair Colorado's ability to implement the rule of the

Colorado Legislature: recovery for non-economic loss should be limited in a case involving Colorado plaintiffs and a Colorado defendant.

In the Arizona–Colorado bus trip example, the present system achieves substantially the same "efficiency" that would be achieved under H.R. 3406 without intruding upon the power of each state to apply its own law to determine the rights of its resident plaintiffs.

* * *

Notes and Questions

1. The American Law Institute's proposed jurisdictional provision, set forth in *Preliminary Draft No. 2* at § 5.01, *supra*, did not survive successive re-draftings of the COMPLEX LITIGATION PROJECT, and ultimately was omitted from the final draft. Is it possible to procedurally resolve federal mass tort cases without formulating a subject-matter provision? What problems were entailed with the ALI proposal? How does it differ from the jurisdictional provision drafted by Congress in the Multiparty, Multiforum Jurisdiction Act? For a discussion of the ALI proposed jurisdiction provision, *see generally,* Linda S. Mullenix, *Complex Litigation Reform and Article III Jurisdiction,* 59 Ford.L.Rev. 169 (1990); Linda S. Mullenix, *Unfinished Symphony: The Complex Litigation Project Rests,* 54 La.L.Rev. 977 (1994).

2. Some version of the Multiparty, Multiforum Jurisdiction Act has been introduced in the House of Representatives since 1988, but none have passed both houses of Congress yet. *See* PREFACE, *supra,* describing institutional law reform efforts in relation to mass tort litigation. Is the Multiparty, Multiforum Jurisdiction Act an improvement on the ALI's proposal?

Professors Sedler and Twerski have been leading opponents in the jurisdictional debate surrounding promulgation of a federal jurisdictional statutory scheme to handle mass torts, although much of their furor has been directed at the proposed single choice-of-law proposals. *See also* Robert A. Sedler, *The Complex Litigation Project's Proposal for Federally–Mandated Choice of Law in Mass Tort Cases: Another Assault on State Sovereignty,* 54 La.L.Rev. 1085 (1994); Robert A. Sedler, *Interest Analysis, State Sovereignty, and Federally–Mandated Choice of Law in "Mass Tort" Cases,* 56 Alb.L.Rev. 855 (1993); Robert A. Sedler & Aaron Twerski, *State Choice of Law in Mass Tort Cases: A Response to "A View From the Legislature,"* 73 Marq.L.Rev. 625 (1990).

3. For other discussions of the jurisdictional proposals for mass tort cases, *see generally,* Charles Gardner Geyh, *Complex-Litigation Reform and the Legislative Process,* 10 Rev.Litig. 401 (1991); Robert W. Kastenmeier, *The Case in Support of Legislation Facilitating the Consolidation of Mass–Accident Litigation: A View From the Legislature,* 73 Marq.L.Rev. 535 (1990); Linda S. Mullenix, *Problems in Complex Litigation,* 10 Rev.Litig. 213 (1991); Thomas D. Rowe, *Jurisdictional and Transfer Proposals for Complex Litigation,* 10 Rev.Litig. 325 (1991).

E. TRANSFER AND *FORUM NON CONVENIENS*

1. TRANSFER UNDER 28 U.S.C.A. § 1404

IN RE EASTERN DISTRICT REPETITIVE STRESS INJURY LITIGATION

United States District Court. Eastern District of New York, 1994.
850 F.Supp. 188.

MEMORANDUM

HURLEY, DISTRICT JUDGE.

Defendants seek to transfer all or part of 78 cases in which plaintiffs allege repetitive stress injuries to the districts around the United States in which plaintiffs' claims arose. Defendants also seek severance of individual plaintiffs' claims to the extent necessary to effectuate transfer.

BACKGROUND

[See facts set forth in *In re Repetitive Stress Injury Cases, supra* Part C.2—*ed.*]

By orders dated June 2, 1992 and July 14, 1992, all RSI cases in the Eastern District of New York were consolidated before this court. Thereafter, Messrs. Phillips and Ponterio, as the attorneys for plaintiffs in the 119 cases then pending in the Eastern District of New York, moved pursuant to 28 U.S.C. § 1407, for an order transferring 40 RSI cases in other federal courts to this district for "coordinated or consolidated pretrial proceedings." That application was denied by the Judicial Panel on Multidistrict Litigation, by order filed on November 27, 1992, as the Panel was "not persuaded ... that the degree of common questions of fact among these actions rises to the level that transfer under Section 1407 would best serve the overall convenience of the parties and witnesses and promote the just and efficient conduct of this entire litigation."

While plaintiffs were unsuccessfully seeking multi-district consolidation, defendants were pursuing an appeal of the consolidation orders within this district. By decision dated December 9, 1993, In re Repetitive Stress Injury Litigation, 11 F.3d 368 (2d Cir.1993), the Second Circuit vacated the two consolidation orders, concluding that their issuance constituted an "abuse of discretion" [summarizing Second Circuit's holdings; *see* decision at C.2, *supra*—*ed.*]

Defendants' motions to transfer venue were made while their appeal to the Second Circuit of the consolidation orders was pending. Accordingly, those motions have been held in abeyance awaiting a decision, and guidance, from the appellate court. Now in receipt of both, and for the reasons stated below and in orders entered this date in each individual case, defendants' motions are granted in 75 cases and denied in three cases whose particular facts justify retention by this court.

DISCUSSION

I. Transfer of Venue

A federal district court may transfer a civil action "to any other district or division where it might have been brought" when transfer will serve "the convenience of parties and witnesses" or furthers "the interest of justice." 28 U.S.C. § 1404(a).

On a motion to transfer, the movant bears the burden of establishing that the motion should be granted. Factors Etc., Inc. v. Pro Arts Inc., 579 F.2d 215, 218 (2d Cir.1978), *cert. denied,* 440 U.S. 908, 99 S.Ct. 1215, 59 L.Ed.2d 455 (1979).

Defendants must establish both (1) that the actions could have been brought in the proposed transferee districts and (2) that transfer serves the convenience of parties and witnesses or is in the interests of justice.

The issue of whether a particular action might have been brought in the proposed transferee district requires individualized treatment and is addressed in the orders entered this date in each individual case. The issue of whether transfer will serve the convenience of the parties and witnesses or serves the interest of justice is addressed below.

Plaintiff's Choice of Forum

A plaintiff's choice of forum is generally entitled to "great weight." Helfant v. Louisiana & Southern Life Ins. Co., 82 F.R.D. 53, 57 (E.D.N.Y.1979). However, when a plaintiff's chosen forum has no connection to the events which gave rise to the claim for relief, "plaintiff's choice of forum is a less weighty consideration." *Helfant,* 82 F.R.D. at 57; *see also* Hernandez v. Graebel Van Lines, 761 F.Supp. 983, 990–91 (E.D.N.Y.1991).

In the cases at bar, the events giving rise to plaintiffs' claims occurred outside the Eastern District of New York. A primary goal of plaintiffs in suing in this district was apparently to effect a *de facto* multidistrict consolidation. Therefore, little deference need be shown to their choice of forum.

Convenience of Witnesses

Convenience of witnesses is the most powerful factor governing the decision to transfer a case. Saminsky v. Occidental Petroleum Corp., 373 F.Supp. 257, 259 (S.D.N.Y.1974). Courts consider the convenience of witnesses both to minimize the burden they must face, and to secure live testimony at trial. In the present cases, convenience of witnesses strongly favors transfer to the districts where the claims arose.

Minimizing Witnesses' Burdens. Defendants have shown, at least preliminarily, that individual plaintiffs' work histories, circumstances of employment, day-to-day habits, practices outside the workplace, and medical histories may have caused the injuries plaintiffs allege. As a result, trials will require testimony from treating physicians, coworkers, and persons familiar with individual plaintiffs' lifestyles. Most or all of these witnesses reside in the proposed transferee districts. Trial in the transferee districts will therefore benefit witnesses.

Securing Live Testimony. Absent transfer, most witnesses will not be subject to this court's subpoena power. *See* Fed.R.Civ.P. 45(b)(2). Even if witnesses were willing to testify, the long-distance travel required could impede trial in this district and would impose substantial expense on witnesses or the parties calling them. Transfer will allow live trials at lesser expense, an important factor in determining whether to transfer a case. *See Hernandez,* 761 F.Supp. at 990; *see also* Kreisner v. Hilton Hotel Corp., 468 F.Supp. 176, 178 (E.D.N.Y.1979).

Plaintiffs suggest that the problem of securing the appearance of witnesses at trial can be mitigated by use of *de bene esse* depositions at trial. Depositions, however, even when videotaped, are no substitute for live testimony. Ledingham v. Parke–Davis Div. of Warner–Lambert Co., 628 F.Supp. 1447, 1451 (E.D.N.Y.1986). *See also* Gulf Oil v. Gilbert, 330 U.S. 501, 511, 67 S.Ct. 839, 844, 91 L.Ed. 1055 (1947)("to fix the place of trial at a point where litigants cannot compel personal attendance and may be forced to try their case on deposition, is to create a condition not satisfactory to court, jury or most litigants.")

Location of Books and Records. The location of books and records is entitled to some weight when determining whether a case should be transferred. Mobil Oil Corp. v. SEC, 550 F.Supp. 67, 71 (S.D.N.Y.1982). In the case at bar, plaintiffs' medical records, work records, insurance records, workers' compensation records and accident reports will generally be located in the transferee districts. At the same time, the books and records of some defendants are located in the New York area. In sum, the location of books and records favors neither transfer nor denial of transfer.

Convenience of Parties

Transfer will, on balance, be more convenient for all parties. Transfer will minimize travel for testifying plaintiffs, who work and/or reside in the transferee districts. While some moving defendants are incorporated in New York or have their principal place of business in this district, employees with knowledge relevant to a plaintiff's claims likely reside near where the plaintiff works.

Interest of Justice

Access to the Courts. Plaintiffs argue that transfer will deprive them of their day in court because they have limited resources and transfer would destroy the "economies of scale" which they now enjoy by litigating together in the Eastern District of New York.

While plaintiffs clearly lack the resources of defendants, they overstate the benefits of litigating in this district.

First, in light of the Second Circuit's decision reversing consolidation, each case is now a separate case. As the litigation progresses, some type of subgrouping for discovery purposes may become appropriate should—as noted by the Second Circuit—a "party seeking aggregation [so move, showing] * * * common factual or legal issues warranting it." 11 F.3d at 374. However, at this juncture, there are no discernable "economies of scale" to be realized from retaining cases which have minimal contact with this district, and any future benefits that might result from retention are speculative, would be limited in scope, and would be more than outweighed by the factors favoring transfer.

Second, were plaintiffs' claims litigated in this district, defendants would still be entitled to discovery in the districts where plaintiffs' claims arose. Thus, denying transfer would not relieve plaintiffs' counsel of the need to retain local counsel or bear the expense of travelling to distant locales.

Third, litigation in this district will proceed whether or not this court grants defendants' motions. Relevant information obtained here by plaintiffs' counsel may be used in the transferee courts, thus reducing the costs of preparing those cases.

In sum, the court rejects the argument that meritorious RSI claims from distant locales will not be pursued absent access to the Eastern District of New York.

Judicial Economy. Plaintiffs argue that the economies derived from having a few judges in this district develop expertise in RSI cases will be lost if cases are transferred to districts around the nation.

Plaintiffs again overstate the benefits to be derived from denying transfer.

They err, first, by supposing that this court's decision to retain jurisdiction would relieve other courts of the burden of becoming familiar with RSI cases. Assuming plaintiffs' claims have merit, other plaintiffs, represented by other attorneys, will likely file suit in other districts. At the present time, actions are already pending or have been litigated to judgment in a number of districts.

Plaintiffs also overstate the expertise required to deal with RSI cases. This court has developed some familiarity with the science of soft tissue injuries. In essence, however, RSI cases are products liability cases, a class of cases with which every district in the country has considerable familiarity.

Local Adjudication of Local Controversies. The public interest in the local adjudication of local controversies also supports transfer. A lawsuit is not purely a matter of private concern. When an action involves injuries sustained in a particular locale, the public interest supports adjudication of the controversy in that locale, where it may be a matter of local attention, rather than in a remote location where it will be learned of only by report. *Gulf Oil,* 330 U.S. at 509; *see also* Kolko v. Holiday Inns, Inc., 672 F.Supp. 713, 716 (S.D.N.Y.1987)(interest in local resolution of dispute supported view that personal injury action should be tried where tort allegedly occurred).

Forum Court's Familiarity with the Governing Law. Federal courts have generally favored adjudication of a controversy by the court which sits in the state whose law will provide the rules of decision. *Hernandez,* 761 F.Supp. at 991; *see also Gulf Oil,* 330 U.S. at 509 ("There is an appropriateness, too, in having the trial of a diversity case in a forum that is at home with the state law that must govern the case"). Under the New York choice of law rules governing these diversity actions, the law of the states in which the transferee courts sit will generally provide the rules of decision in these actions. *See* Miller v. Miller, 22 N.Y.2d 12, 290 N.Y.S.2d 734, 737, 237 N.E.2d 877, 880 (1968). In that regard, the law of products liability varies significantly among jurisdictions. *See* Henderson & Twerski, *A Proposed Revision of Section 402A of the Restatement (Second) of Torts,* 77 Cornell L.Rev. 1512 (1992). Under such circumstances, the federal court for the district where the alleged wrong occurred is clearly the more appropriate forum. This factor therefore supports transfer.

Docket Congestion. The congestion of this court's docket also dictates transfer. Justice delayed is justice denied, and transfer to districts elsewhere in the United States will help secure the parties the prompt trials to which they are entitled. *See* A. Olinick & Sons v. Dempster Bros., Inc., 365 F.2d 439, 445 (2d Cir.1966)(docket congestion a factor); *see also Hernandez,* 761 F.Supp. at 991.

In the cases at bar, virtually all transferee districts are less congested than the Eastern District of New York, both in terms of total cases per judge and in terms of time from joinder of issue to trial.

Cases Located in the Northeast

Finally, plaintiffs argue that transfer is particularly inappropriate for cases to be transferred to other districts in the Northeast because of their close proximity to this courthouse. While the inconvenience to witnesses and parties may be somewhat diminished by close proximity, most parts of the Northeast lie outside the range of this court's subpoena power. Fed.R.Civ.P. 45(b)(2). Further, this court finds no basis for subjecting witnesses and parties in other districts to the requirement that they appear in this district when federal courthouses much closer at hand are available. Some courts have refused to transfer on the basis of convenience when two courts were close to each other. *E.g.,* De Moraes v. American Export Isbrandtsen Lines, Inc., 289 F.Supp. 861 (E.D.Pa.1968)(transfer from Philadelphia to New York City denied); Wellington Computer Graphics, Inc. v. Modell, 315 F.Supp. 24, 28 (S.D.N.Y.1970)(transfer from Newark to New York denied). None of the cases cited by plaintiffs, however, involved facts which argued as strongly for transfer as the facts of the cases at bar.

* * *

CONCLUSION

Defendants' motions for severance and transfer are granted in 75 cases and denied in three cases, as provided in the orders rendered this date in each individual case.

2. MASS TORTS AND EXTRATERRITORIALITY

IN RE UNION CARBIDE CORPORATION GAS PLANT DISASTER AT BHOPAL, INDIA, DECEMBER, 1984

United States Court of Appeals, Second Circuit, 1987.
809 F.2d 195.

Before MANSFIELD, PRATT and ALTIMARI, CIRCUIT JUDGES.

MANSFIELD, CIRCUIT JUDGE

This appeal raises the question of whether thousands of claims by citizens of India and the Government of India arising out of the most devastating industrial disaster in history—the deaths of over 2,000 persons and injuries of over 200,000 caused by lethal gas known as methyl isocyanate which was released from a chemical plant operated by Union Carbide India Limited (UCIL) in Bhopal, India—should be tried in the United States or in India. The Southern District of New York, John F. Keenan, Judge, granted the motion of Union Carbide Corporation (UCC), a defendant in some 145 actions commenced in federal courts in the United States, to dismiss these actions on grounds of *forum non conveniens* so that the claims may be tried in India, subject to certain conditions. The individual plaintiffs appeal from the order and the court's denial of their motion for a fairness hearing on a proposed settlement. UCC and the Union of India (UOI), a plaintiff, cross-appeal. We eliminate two of the conditions imposed by the district court and in all other respects affirm that court's orders.

The accident occurred on the night of December 2–3, 1984, when winds blew the deadly gas from the plant operated by UCIL into densely occupied parts of the city of Bhopal. UCIL is incorporated under the laws of India. Fifty and nine-tenths percent of its stock is owned by UCC, 22% is owned or controlled by the government of India, and the balance is held by approximately 23,500 Indian citizens. The stock is publicly traded on the Bombay Stock Exchange. The company is engaged in the manufacture of a variety of products, including chemicals, plastics, fertilizers and insecticides, at 14 plants in India and employs over 9,000 Indian citizens. It is managed and operated entirely by Indians in India.

Four days after the Bhopal accident, on December 7, 1984, the first of some 145 purported class actions in federal district courts in the United States was commenced on behalf of victims of the disaster. On January 2, 1985, the Judicial Panel on Multidistrict Litigation assigned the actions to the Southern District of New York where they became the subject of a consolidated complaint filed on June 28, 1985.

In the meantime, on March 29, 1985, India enacted the Bhopal Gas Leak Disaster (Processing of Claims) Act, granting to its government, the UOI, the exclusive right to represent the victims in India or elsewhere. Thereupon the UOI, purporting to act in the capacity of *parens patriae*, and with retainers executed by many of the victims, on April 8, 1985, filed a complaint in the Southern District of New York on behalf of all victims of the Bhopal disaster, similar to the purported class action complaints already filed by individuals in the United States. The UOI's decision to bring suit in the United States was attributed to the fact that, although numerous lawsuits (by now, some 6,500) had been instituted by victims in India against UCIL, the Indian courts did not have jurisdiction over UCC, the parent company, which is a defendant in the United States actions. The actions in India asserted claims not only against UCIL but also against the UOI, the State of Madhya Pradesh, and the Municipality of Bhopal, and were consolidated in the District Court of Bhopal.

By order dated April 25, 1985, Judge Keenan appointed a three-person Executive Committee to represent all plaintiffs in the pre-trial proceedings. It consisted of two lawyers representing the individual plaintiffs and one representing the UOI. On July 31, 1985, UCC moved to dismiss the complaints on grounds of *forum non conveniens*, the plaintiffs' lack of standing to bring the actions in the United States, and their purported attorneys' lack of authority to represent them. After several months of discovery related to *forum non conveniens*, * * * the individual plaintiffs and the UOI opposed UCC's motion. After hearing argument on January 3, 1986, the district court, on May 12, 1986, in a thoroughly reasoned 63–page opinion granted the motion, dismissing the lawsuits before it on condition that UCC:

(1) consent to the jurisdiction of the courts of India and continue to waive defenses based on the statute of limitations,

(2) agree to satisfy any judgment rendered by an Indian court against it and upheld on appeal, provided the judgment and affirmance "comport with minimal requirements of due process," and

(3) be subject to discovery under the Federal Rules of Civil Procedure of the United States.

On June 12, 1986, UCC accepted these conditions subject to its right to appeal them; and on June 24, 1986, the district court entered its order of dismissal. In September 1986 the UOI, acting pursuant to its authority under the Bhopal Act, brought suit on behalf of all claimants against UCC and UCIL in the District Court of Bhopal, where many individuals suits by victims of the disaster were then pending.

In its opinion dismissing the actions the district court analyzed the *forum non conveniens* issues, applying the standards and weighing the factors suggested by the Supreme Court in Gulf Oil Corp. v. Gilbert, 330

U.S. 501, 67 S.Ct. 839, 91 L.Ed. 1055 (1947), and Piper Aircraft Co. v. Reyno, 454 U.S. 235, 102 S.Ct. 252, 70 L.Ed.2d 419 (1981). At the outset Judge Keenan concluded, in accordance with the Court's expressed views in *Piper* that, since the plaintiffs were not residents of the United States but of a foreign country, their choice of the United States as a forum would not be given the deference to which it would be entitled if this country were their home. * * * Following the dictates of *Piper,* the district court declined to compare the advantages and disadvantages to the respective parties of American versus Indian Laws or to determine the impact upon plaintiffs' claims of the laws of India, where UCC had acknowledged that it would make itself amenable to process, except to ascertain whether India provided an adequate alternative forum, as distinguished from no remedy at all. Judge Keenan reviewed thoroughly the affidavits of experts on India's law and legal system, which described in detail its procedural and substantive aspects, and concluded that, despite some of the Indian system's disadvantages, it afforded an adequate alternative forum for the enforcement of plaintiffs' claims.

The Indian judiciary was found by the court to be a developed, independent and progressive one, which has demonstrated its capability of circumventing long delays and backlogs prevalent in the Indian courts' handling of ordinary cases by devising special expediting procedures in extraordinary cases, such as by directing its High Court to hear them on a daily basis, appointing special tribunals to handle them, and assigning daily hearing duties to a single judge. He found that Indian courts have competently dealt with complex technological issues. Since the Bhopal Act provides that the case may be treated speedily, effectively and to the best advantage of the claimants, and since the Union of India represents the claimants, the prosecution of the claims is expected to be adequately staffed by the Attorney General or Solicitor General of India.

The tort law of India, which is derived from common law and British precedent, was found to be suitable for resolution of legal issues arising in cases involving highly complex technology. Moreover, Indian courts would be in a superior position to construe and apply applicable Indian laws and standards than would courts of the United States. Third parties may be interpleaded under Order 1, Rule 10(2) of the Indian Code of Civil Procedure, and defendants may seek contribution from third parties. The absence in India of a class action procedure comparable to that in federal courts here was found not to deprive the plaintiffs of a remedy, in view of existing Indian legal authorization for "representative" suits under Order 1, Rule 8 of the Indian Code of Civil Procedure, which would permit an Indian court to create representative classes. Judge Keenan further found that the absence of juries and contingent fee arrangements in India would not deprive the claimants of an adequate remedy.

In two areas bearing upon the adequacy of the Indian forum the district court decided to impose somewhat unusual conditions on the transfer of the American cases to India. One condition dealt with pretrial discovery. Indian courts, following the British pattern, permit parties to have pre-trial discovery of each other through written interrogatories, liberal inspection of documents and requests for admission. Non-party witnesses can be interviewed and summoned to appear at trial or to produce documents. *See* India Code Civ. Proc., Order 16, Rule 6. Witnesses unable to appear at trial are sometimes permitted to give evidence by means of affidavits. * * * Discovery in India, however, as in Britain, is limited to evidence that may be admitted at trial. Litigants are not permitted to engage in wide-ranging discovery of the type authorized by Fed.R.Civ.P. 26(b), which allows inquiry into any unprivileged matter that could reasonably lead to the discovery of admissible evidence.

Judge Keenan, concluding that the Indian system might limit the victims' access to sources of proof, directed that dismissal of the actions on grounds of *forum non conveniens* must be conditioned on UCC's consent to discovery of it in accordance with the Federal Rule of Civil Procedure after the cases were transferred to India. He added, "While the Court feels that it would be fair to bind the plaintiffs to American discovery rules, too, it has no authority to do so."

Another condition imposed by the district court upon dismissal on grounds of *forum non conveniens* dealt with the enforceability in the United States of any judgment rendered by an Indian court in the cases. Judge Keenan, expressing the view that an Indian judgment might possibly not be enforceable in the United States, provided in his order that UCC must "agree to satisfy any judgment rendered by an Indian court, and if applicable, upheld by an appellate court in that country, where such judgment and affirmance comport with the minimum requirements of due process."

As the district court found, the record shows that the private interests of the respective parties weigh heavily in favor of dismissal on grounds of *forum non conveniens*. The many witnesses and sources of proof are almost entirely located in India, where the accident occurred, and could not be compelled to appear for trial in the United States. The Bhopal plant at the time of the accident was operated by some 193 Indian nationals, including the managers of seven operating units employed by the Agricultural Products Division of UCC, who reported to Indian Works Managers in Bhopal. The plant was maintained by seven functional departments employing over 200 more Indian nationals. UCIL kept at the plant daily, weekly and monthly records of plant operations and records of maintenance as well as records of the plant's Quality Control, Purchasing and Stores branches, all operated by Indian employees. The great majority of documents bearing on the design, safety, start-up and operation of the plant, as well as the safety training of the plant's employees, is located in India. * * * Proof to be offered at trial would be derived from interviews of these witnesses in India and study of the records located there to determine whether the accident was caused by negligence on the part of the management or employees in the operation of the plant, by fault in its design, or by sabotage. In short, India has greater ease of access to the proof than does the United States.

The plaintiffs seek to prove that the accident was caused by negligence on the part of UCC in originally contributing to the design of the plant and its provision for storage of excessive amounts of the gas at the plant. As Judge Keenan found, however, UCC's participation was limited and its involvement in plant operations terminated long before the accident. Under 1973 agreements negotiated at arm's-length with UCIL, UCC did provide a summary "process design package" for construction of the plant and the services of some of its technicians to monitor the progress of UCIL in detailing the design and erecting the plant. However, the UOI controlled the terms of the agreements and precluded UCC from exercising any authority to "detail design, erect and commission the plant," which was done independently over the period from 1972 to 1980 by UCIL process design engineers who supervised, among many others, some 55 to 60 Indian engineers employed by the Bombay engineering firm of Humphreys and Glasgow. The preliminary process design information furnished by UCC could not have been used to construct the plant. Construction required the detailed process design and engineering data prepared by hundreds of Indian engineers, process designers and sub-contractors. During the ten years spent constructing the plant, its design and configuration underwent many changes.

The vital parts of the Bhopal plant, including its storage tank, monitoring instrumentation, and vent gas scrubber, were manufactured by Indians in India. Although some 40 UCIL employees were given some safety training at UCC's plant in West Virginia, they represented a small fraction of the Bhopal plant's employees. The vast majority of plant employees were selected and trained by UCIL in Bhopal. The manual for start-up of the Bhopal plant was prepared by Indians employed by UCIL.

In short, the plant has been constructed and managed by Indians in India. No Americans were employed at the plant at the time of the accident. In the five years from 1980 to 1984, although more than 1,000 Indians were employed at the plant, only one American was employed there and he left in 1982. No Americans visited the plant for more than one year prior to the accident, and during the 5–year period before the accident the communications between the plant and the United States were almost non-existent.

The vast majority of material witnesses and documentary proof bearing on causation of and liability for the accident is located in India, not the United States, and would be more accessible to an Indian court than to a United States court. The records are almost entirely in Hindi or other Indian languages, understandable to an Indian court without translation. The witnesses for the most part do not speak English but Indian languages understood by an Indian court but not by an American court. These witnesses could be required to appear in an Indian court but not in a court of the United States. Although witnesses in the United States could not be subpoenaed to appear in India, they are comparatively few in number and most are employed by UCC which, as a party, would produce them in India, with lower overall transportation costs than it the parties were to attempt to bring hundreds of Indian witnesses to the United States. Lastly, Judge Keenan properly concluded that an Indian court would be in a better position to direct and supervise a viewing of the Bhopal plant, which was sealed after the accident. Such a viewing could be of help to a court in determining liability issues.

After a thorough review, the district court concluded that the public interest concerns, like the private ones, also weigh heavily in favor of India as the situs for trial and disposition of the cases. The accident and all relevant events occurred in India. The victims, over 200,000 in number, are citizens of India and located there. The witnesses are almost entirely Indian citizens. The Union of India has a greater interest than does the United States in facilitating the trial and adjudication of the victims' claims. Despite the contentions of plaintiffs and amici that it would be in the public interest to avoid a "double standard" by requiring an American parent corporation (UCC) to submit to the jurisdiction of American courts, India has a stronger countervailing interest in adjudicating the claims in its courts according to its standards rather than having American values and standards of care imposed upon it.

India's interest is increased by the fact that it has for hears treated UCIL as an Indian national, subjecting it to intensive regulations and governmental supervision of the construction, development and operation of the Bhopal plant, its emissions, water and air pollution, and safety precautions. Numerous Indian government officials have regularly conducted on-site inspections of the plant and approved its machinery and equipment, including its facilities for storage of the lethal methyl isocyanate gas that escaped and caused the disaster giving rise to the claims. Thus India has considered the plant to be an Indian one and the disaster to be an Indian problem. It therefore has a deep interest in ensuring compliance with its safety standards. Moreover, plaintiffs have conceded that in view of India's strong interest and its greater contacts with the plant, its operations, its employees, and the victims of the accident, the law of India, as the place where the tort occurred, will undoubtedly govern. In contrast, the American interests are relatively minor. Indeed, a long trial of the 145 cases here would unduly burden an already overburdened court, involving both jury hardship and heavy expense. It would face the court with numerous practical difficulties, including the most impossible task of attempting to understand extensive relevant Indian regulations published in a foreign language and the slow process of receiving testimony of scores of witnesses through interpreters.

Having made the foregoing findings, Judge Keenan dismissed the actions against UCC on grounds of *forum non conveniens* upon the conditions indicated above, after obtaining UCC's consent to those conditions subject to its right to appeal the order. After the plaintiffs filed their notice of appeal, UCC and the Union of India filed cross appeals.

Upon these appeals, the plaintiffs continue to oppose the dismissal. The Union of India, however, has changed its position and now supports the district court's order. UCC, as it did in the district court, opposes as unfair the condition that it submit to discovery pursuant to the Federal Rules of Civil Procedure without reciprocally obligating the plaintiffs and Union of India to be subject to discovery on the same basis so that both sides might be treated equally, giving each the same access to the facts in the others' possession.

Upon argument of the appeal, UCC also took the position that the district court's order requiring it to satisfy any Indian court judgment was unfair unless some method were provided, such as continued availability of the district court as a forum, to ensure that any denial of due process by the Indian courts could be remedied promptly by the federal court here rather than delay resolution of the issue until termination of the Indian court proceedings and appeal, which might take several years. UCC's argument in this respect was based on the sudden issuance by the Indian court in Bhopal of a temporary order freezing all of UCC's assets, which could have caused it irreparable injury if it had been continued indefinitely, * * * and by the conflict of interest posed by the UOI's position in the Indian courts where, since the UOI would appear both as a plaintiff and a defendant, it might as a plaintiff voluntarily dismiss its claims against itself as a defendant or, as a co-defendant with UCC, be tempted to shed all blame upon UCC even though the UOI had in fact been responsible for supervision, regulation and safety of UCIL's Bhopal plant.

DISCUSSION

The standard to be applied in reviewing the district court's *forum non conveniens* dismissal was clearly expressed by the Supreme Court in *Piper Aircraft Co.,* 454 U.S. at 257, 102 S.Ct. at 266, as follows:

> The *forum non conveniens* determination is committed to the sound discretion of the trial court. It may be reversed only when there has been a clear abuse of discretion; where the court has considered all relevant public and private interest factors, and where its balancing of these factors is reasonable, its decision deserves substantial deference.

Having reviewed Judge Keenan's detailed decision, in which he thoroughly considered the comparative adequacy of the forums and the public and private interests involved, we are satisfied that there was no abuse of discretion in his granting dismissal of the action. On the contrary, it might reasonably be concluded that it would have been an abuse of discretion to deny a *forum non conveniens* dismissal. *See* Schertenleib v. Traum, 589 F.2d 1156, 1164 (2d Cir.1978); De Oliveira v. Delta Marine Drilling Co., 707 F.2d 843 (5th Cir.1983)(per curiam).

Practically all relevant factors demonstrate that transfer of the cases to India for trial and adjudication is both fair and just to the parties.

Plaintiffs' principal contentions in favor of retention of the cases by the district court are that deference to the plaintiffs' choice of forum has been inadequate, that the Indian courts are insufficiently equipped for the task, that UCC has its principal place of business here, that the most probative evidence regarding negligence and causation is to be found here, that federal courts are much better equipped through experience and procedures to handle such complex actions efficiently than are Indian courts, and that a transfer of the cases to India will jeopardize a $350 million settlement being negotiated by plaintiffs' counsel. All of these arguments, however, must be rejected.

Little or no deference can be paid to the plaintiffs' choice of a United States forum when all but a few of the 200,000 plaintiffs are Indian citizens located in India who, according to the UOI, have revoked the authorizations of American counsel to represent them here and have substituted the UOI, which now prefers Indian courts. The finding of our district court, after exhaustive analysis of the evidence, that the Indian courts provide a reasonably adequate alternative forum cannot be labelled clearly erroneous or an abuse of discretion.

The emphasis placed by plaintiffs on UCC's having its domicile here, where personal jurisdiction over it exists, is robbed of significance by its consent to Indian jurisdiction. Plaintiffs' contention that the most crucial and probative evidence is located in the United States is simply not in accord with the record or the district court's findings. Although basic design programs were prepared in the United States and some assistance furnished to UCIL at the outset of the 10–year period during which the Bhopal plant was constructed, the proof bearing on the issues to be tried is almost entirely located in India. This includes the principal witnesses and documents bearing on the development and construction of the plant, the detailed designs, the implementation of plans, the operation and regulation of the plant, its safety precautions, the facts with respect to the accident itself, and the deaths and injuries attributable to the accident.

Although the plaintiffs' American counsel may at one time have been close to reaching a $350 million settlement of the cases, no such settlement was ever finalized. No draft joint stipulation in writing or settlement agreement appears to have been prepared, much less approved by the parties. No petition for certification of a settlement class under Fed.R.Civ.P. 23 has ever been presented. * * * Most important, the UOI, which is itself a plaintiff and states that it now represents the Indian plaintiffs formerly represented by American counsel, is firmly opposed to the $350 million "settlement" as inadequate. Under these circumstances, to order a Rule 23 "fairness" hearing would be futile. The district court's denial of the American counsels' motion for such a hearing must accordingly be affirmed.

The conditions imposed by the district court upon its *forum non conveniens* dismissal stand on a different footing. Plaintiffs and the UOI, however, contend that UCC, having been granted the *forum non conveniens* dismissal that it sought and having consented to the district court's order, has waived its right to appellate review of these conditions. We disagree. UCC expressly reserved its right to appeal Judge Keenan's order. Moreover, it has made a sufficient showing of prejudice from the second and third conditions of the court's order to entitle it to seek appellate review. UCC's position is comparable to that of a prevailing party which, upon being granted injunctive relief, is permitted to challenge by appeal conditions attaching to the injunction that are found to be objectionable. * * * Similarly, conditions imposed by the court upon dismissals without prejudice under Fed.R.Civ.P. 41(a)(2) may be appealed by the plaintiff when they prejudice the plaintiff. * * *

All three conditions of the dismissal are reviewable since plaintiffs have appealed the district court's order and UCC has cross-appealed "from each judgment and order appealed in whole or part by any plaintiff." We therefore have jurisdiction over the entire case and may in the interests of justice modify the district court's order. * * *

The first condition, that UCC consent to the Indian court's personal jurisdiction over it and waive the statute of limitations as a defense, are not unusual and have been imposed in numerous cases where the foreign court would not provide an adequate alternative in the absence of such a condition. * * * The remaining two conditions, however, pose problems.

In requiring that UCC consent to enforceability of an Indian judgment against it, the district court proceeded at least in part on the erroneous assumption that, absent such a requirement, the plaintiffs, if they should succeed in obtaining an Indian judgment against UCC, might not be able to enforce it against UCC in the United States. The law, however, is to the contrary. Under New York law, which governs actions brought in New York to enforce foreign judgments, * * *, a foreign-country judgment that is final, conclusive and enforceable where rendered must be recognized and will be enforced as "conclusive between the parties to the extent that it grants or denies recovery of a sum of money" except that it is not deemed to be conclusive if:

> "1. the judgment was rendered under a system which does not provide impartial tribunals or procedures compatible with the requirements of due process of law;

> "2. the foreign court did not have personal jurisdiction over the defendant."

Art. 53, Recognition of Foreign Country Money Judgments, 7B N.Y.Civ. Prac L. & R. §§ 5301–09 (McKinney 1978). Although § 5304 further provides that under certain specified conditions a foreign country judgment need not be recognized, * * * none of these conditions would apply to the present cases except for the possibility of failure to provide UCC with sufficient notice of proceedings or the existence of fraud in obtaining the judgment, which do not presently exist but conceivably could occur in the future.

UCC, as a New York business corporation, would be subject to personal jurisdiction in a court sitting in New York. An Indian money judgment could be enforced against UCC in New York by means of either an action on the judgment or a motion for summary judgment in lieu of complaint. * * * In either case, once converted into a New York judgment, the judgment would be enforceable as a New York judgment, and thus entitled to the full faith and credit of New York's sister states.

UCC contends that Indian courts, while providing an adequate alternative forum, do not observe due process standards that would be required as a matter of course in this country. As evidence of this apprehension it points to the haste with which the Indian court in Bhopal issued a temporary order freezing its assets throughout the world and the possibility of serious prejudice to it if the UOI is permitted to have the double and conflicting status of both plaintiff and co-defendant in the Indian court proceedings. It argues that we should protect it against such denial of due process by authorizing Judge Keenan to retain the authority, after *forum non conveniens* dismissal of the cases here, to monitor the Indian court proceedings and be available on call to rectify in some undefined way any abuses of UCC's right to due process as they might occur in India.

UCC's proposed remedy is not only impractical but evidences an abysmal ignorance of basic jurisdictional principles, so much so that it borders on the frivolous. The district court's jurisdiction is limited to proceedings before it in this country. Once it dismisses those proceedings on grounds of *forum non conveniens* it ceases to have any further jurisdiction over the matter unless and until a proceeding may some day be brought to enforce here a final and conclusive Indian money judgment. Nor could we, even if we attempted to retain some sort of supervisory jurisdiction, impose our due process requirements upon Indian courts, which are governed by their laws, not ours. The concept of shared jurisdictions is both illusory and unrealistic. The parties cannot simultaneously submit to both jurisdictions the resolution of the pre-trial and trial issues when there is only one consolidated case pending in one court. Any denial by the Indian courts of due process can be raised by UCC as a defense to the plaintiffs' later attempt to enforce a resulting judgment against UCC in this country.

We are concerned, however, that as it is written the district court's requirement that UCC consent to the enforcement of a final Indian judgment, which was imposed on the erroneous assumption that such a judgment might not otherwise be enforceable in the United States, may create misunderstandings and problems of construction. Although the order's provision that the judgment "comport with *minimal* requirements of due process" (emphasis supplied) probably is intended to refer to "due process" as used in the New York Foreign Country Money Judgments Law and others like it, there is the risk that it may also be interpreted as providing for a lesser standard than we would otherwise require. Since the court's condition with respect to enforceability of any final Indian judgment is predicated on an erroneous legal assumption and its "due process" language is ambiguous, and since the district court's purpose is fully served by New York's statute providing for recognition of foreign-country money judgments, it was error to impose this condition upon the parties.

We also believe that the district court erred in requiring UCC to consent (which UCC did under protest and subject to its right of appeal) to broad discovery of it by the plaintiffs under the Federal Rules of Civil Procedure when UCC is confined to the more limited discovery authorized under Indian law. We recognize that under some circumstances, such as when a moving defendant unconditionally consents thereto or no undiscovered evidence of consequence is believed to be under the control of a plaintiff or co-defendant, it may be appropriate to condition a *forum non conveniens* dismissal on the moving defendant's submission to discovery under the Federal Rules without requiring reciprocal discovery by it of the plaintiff. *See, e.g.,* Piper Aircraft v. Reyno, 454 U.S. at 257 n. 25, 102 S.Ct. at 267 n. 25 (suggesting that district courts can condition dismissal upon a defendant's agreeing to provide all relevant records); Ali v. Offshore Co., 753 F.2d 1327, 1334 n.16 (5th Cir.1985)(same); Boskoff v. Transportes Aereos Portugueses, 17 Av.Cas. (CCH) 18,613, at 18,616 (N.D.Ill.1983)(accepting defendant's involuntary commitment to provide discovery in foreign forum according to Federal Rules). Basic justice dictates that both sides be treated equally, with each having equal access to the evidence in the possession or under the control of the other. Application of this fundamental principle in the present case is especially appropriate since the UOI, as the sovereign government of India, is expected to be a party to the Indian litigation, possibly on both sides.

For these reasons we direct that the condition with respect to the discovery of UCC under the Federal Rules of Civil Procedure be deleted without prejudice to the right of the parties to have reciprocal discovery of each other on equal terms under the Federal Rules, subject to such approval as may be required of the Indian court in which the case will be pending. If, for instance, Indian authorities will permit mutual discovery pursuant to the Federal Rules, the district court's order, as modified in accordance with this opinion, should not be construed to bar such procedure. In the absence of such a court-sanctioned agreement, however, the parties will be limited by the applicable discovery rules of the Indian court in which the claims will be pending.

As so modified the district court's order is affirmed.

Notes and Questions

1. In general, the federal venue and transfer provisions are protections for defendants against being sued in inconvenient places. While state-court venue provisions are generally geared to counties, in the federal district court venue is geared to the "federal district." Venue is a defense that may

be waived, and is waived if objection is not made in a timely fashion. *See* 28 U.S.C.A. § 1406(b); Rule 12(b) of the Federal Rules of Civil Procedure. *See generally,* Wright, Miller, and Cooper, 15 FEDERAL PRACTICE AND PROCEDURE §§ 3801 *et seq.* (2d ed.1986 & Supp.).

In response to recommendations of the Federal Courts Study Committee, Congress in 1990 substantially revamped the general venue provisions contained in 28 U.S.C.A. §§ 1391(a) & (b). *See* § 311 of the Judicial Improvements Act of 1990, Pub. L. 101–650, 104 Stat. 5089. In Section 504 of the Federal Courts Administration Act of 1992, Congress additionally amended 28 U.S.C.A. § 1391(a)(3) to correct an interpretative problem that developed under the 1990 amendments, illustrated in U.S. Fidelity & Guaranty Co. v. Mayberry, 789 F.Supp. 901 (E.D.Tenn.1992).

2. The recently amended venue provisions have been extensively analyzed and critiqued. *See generally,* John Oakley, *Recent Statutory Changes in the Law of Federal Jurisdiction and Venue: The Judicial Improvements Acts of 1988 and 1990,* 24 U.C. Davis L.Rev. 735 (1991); David Siegel, *Changes in Federal Jurisdiction and Practice Under the New Judicial Improvements and Access to Justice Act,* 123 F.R.D. 399 (1989). *See also* REPORT OF THE FEDERAL COURTS STUDY COMMITTEE at 94 (1990); Note, *Here Today, Gone Tomorrow: The Timing of Contacts for Jurisdiction and Venue Under 28 U.S.C.A. § 1391,* 78 Cornell L.Rev. 707 (1993).

With regard to cases involving multiple defendants, Section 1392(a) provides that "[a]ny civil action, not of a local nature, against defendants residing in different districts in the same State, may be brought in any of such districts." It is believed that the 1990 amendments to § 1391 have rendered this separate provision largely superfluous. *See* 15 Wright, Miller, and Cooper, FEDERAL PRACTICE AND PROCEDURE § 3807 (1994 Supp.). *See also* Note, *Federal Venue Under Section 1392(a): The Problem of the Multidistrict Defendant,* 85 Mich.L.Rev. 330 (1986).

3. The doctrine of *forum non conveniens* was endorsed for the federal courts by the Supreme Court's 1947 holding in Gulf Oil Corp. v. Gilbert, 330 U.S. 501, 67 S.Ct. 839, 91 L.Ed. 1055 (1947), and subsequently affirmed in Piper Aircraft Co. v. Reyno, 454 U.S. 235, 102 S.Ct. 252, 70 L.Ed.2d 419 (1981). The application of the doctrine, which results in dismissal of an action otherwise within the district court's jurisdiction, usually is limited to situations where there is another available and far more convenient forum.

The doctrine of *forum non conveniens* and its interpretation in *Gulf Oil* were the bases for § 1404(a) of the Judicial Code, which was added in 1948. Section 1404(a) reads:

> For the convenience of parties and witnesses, in the interest of justice, a district court may transfer any civil action to any other district or division where it might have been brought.

At least one commentator has suggested that § 1404(a) was proposed well in advance of the Supreme Court's endorsement of the doctrine of *forum non conveniens* in *Gulf Oil,* and therefore the Reviser's Note to that section represents "a creative bit of retroactive legislative history." *See* Allan Stein,

Forum Non Conveniens *and the Redundancy of Court Access Doctrine,* 133 U. Pa.L.Rev. 781, 807 (1985).

Under § 1404(a), the criteria for transfer from one judicial district in the United States to another are broader and the plaintiff's choice of forum is entitled to less weight, than in a *forum non conveniens* situation. Section 1404(a) uses the criteria defined in *Gulf Oil*; transfer must be warranted by the "convenience of the parties and witnesses and in the interest of justice." Nonetheless, because § 1404(a) does not specify the weight to be accorded the factors for transfer, in reality federal judges have great discretion in making this determination, and often grant the motion. For a criticism of this modern trend, see Note, *"Adrift on an Uncharted Sea:" A Survey of Section 1404(a) Transfer in the Federal System,* 67 N.Y.U.L.Rev. 612 (1992):

> This unchecked district court discretion has resulted in several problems. First, the transfer motion has become a common, almost reactive defendant response to a lawsuit. Because § 1404(a) embraces so many different factors as relevant to a transfer motion, defendants almost always have grounds to argue in good faith that transfer is appropriate, if not desirable. Second, because district courts weigh the many applicable factors inconsistently, it is hard to predict whether a transfer motion will be successful. Third, lack of defined standards allows parties to utilize statutory transfer for purely strategic purposes, such as raising the stakes of litigation and manipulating the applicable law. Because the 1990 venue legislation increased the number of fora to which transfer can be sought, it may have exacerbated these problems.

Id. 67 N.Y.U.L.Rev. at 615–617.

4. Under the language of § 1404(a), transfer is limited to a district "where it might have been brought." In Hoffman v. Blaski, 363 U.S. 335, 80 S.Ct. 1084, 4 L.Ed.2d 1254 (1960), these words were interpreted by the Court to preclude transfer, on defendant's motion, to a district where, at the outset of the case, venue was lacking and jurisdiction over the person could not have been obtained without the waiver or the consent of the defendant. This interpretation of the Congressional enactment has somewhat limited the utility of transfer at defendant's behest. On the other hand, at least one federal court has found that the fact that a statute of limitations in a transferee district would have barred suit does not preclude a finding that the transferee district is a district where the action "might have been brought," and therefore transfer is possible to such a district. *See, e.g.,* Packer v. Kaiser Foundation Health Plan of Mid–Atlantic States, Inc., 728 F.Supp. 8 (D.D.C.1989).

5. In addition to § 1404(a), Congress in 1948 added § 1406(a) to the Code, providing for transfer as an alternative to dismissal when defendant has made a conclusive showing that venue is lacking in the forum in which the action was brought. Section 1406(a) states:

> The district court of a district in which is filed a case laying venue in the wrong division or district shall dismiss, or if it be in the interest of justice, transfer such case to any district or division in which it could have been brought.

6. In the *Repetitive Stress Injury* case, the court briefly considered the problem of applicable law on the proposed transfer, concluding that the better applicable law was that of the district where the alleged wrong occurred. Was that a sound decision? The only decision? May litigants use the venue transfer provisions to gain an advantage as to the applicable law? What law applies to cases transferred within the federal system? Does it matter which party initiates the transfer? Should transfer within the federal system provide an opportunity to gain an applicable law advantage to either party?

In Van Dusen v. Barrack, 376 U.S. 612, 84 S.Ct. 805, 11 L.Ed.2d 945 (1964), the Court held that where a defendant's motion to transfer an action under § 1404(a) is granted, the transferee federal district court is to apply the substantive law that would have been applied in the transferor forum. In a diversity case, this is the substantive law of the state in which the transferor district sits, including that state's conflicts of laws rules, under *Erie R.R. v. Tompkins* and *Klaxon*, discussed *infra* Part Four, Ch. VIII. The transfer is, under these circumstances, "but a change in courtrooms," so far as substantive law is concerned. Is this a fair rule? Should the same rule apply to plaintiff-initiated transfers? Why or why not?

The Supreme Court resisted resolving the plaintiff-initiated transfer issue until 1990. In a controversial 5–4 decision, the Court in Ferens v. John Deere Co., 494 U.S. 516, 110 S.Ct. 1274, 108 L.Ed.2d 443 (1990) announced that even in plaintiff-initiated transfers, the transferee court must apply the law of the transferor court: "A transfer under § 1404(a), in other words, does not change the law applicable to a diversity case." For criticisms of the *Ferens* rule, *see* Linda S. Mullenix, *Badly Fractured Decisions Muddy Cases on Venue,* Nat'l L.J. S9, S17 (Aug. 13, 1990); David Seidelson, *1(*Wortman*) + 1(*Ferens*) = 6 (years): That Can't Be Right—Can It? Statutes of Limitations and Supreme Court Inconsistency,* 57 Brook. L.Rev. 787 (1991).

Does the *Van Dusen/Ferens* doctrine apply to federal as well as state-based claims? Must a federal district court follow the interpretive law of a transferor district? While some courts follow the *Van Dusen* rule in federal claim cases and defer to the transferor court's interpretation of federal law, *see, e.g.,* In re Rospatch Securities Litig., 760 F.Supp. 1239, 1256–57 (D.Mich. 1991), other federal courts have not followed the *Van Dusen* rule in federal claim cases and have instead exercised their independent judgment. *See, e.g.,* In re Pan American Corp., 950 F.2d 839, 847 (2d Cir.1991); In re Korean Air Lines Disaster, 829 F.2d 1171 (D.C.Cir.1987), *affirmed on other grounds,* 490 U.S. 122, 109 S.Ct. 1676, 104 L.Ed.2d 113 (1989). *See generally,* Richard Marcus, *Conflict Among Circuits and Transfers Within the Federal Judicial System,* 93 Yale L.J. 677 (1984); Fini, *The Scope of the* Van Dusen *Rule in Federal–Question Transfers,* 1992–93 Ann.Surv.Am.L. 49 (1993).

7. The Bhopal disaster raised troubling questions relating to client solicitation in mass tort cases, *see supra* Part One, Ch. 1, D1. Should such ethical or professional responsibility issues play any part in a federal court's jurisdiction, venue, or *forum non conveniens* determinations? For a discus-

sion of the ethical issues relating to client solicitation in the Bhopal disaster, *see* David T. Austern, *Is Lawyer Solicitation of Bhopal' Clients Ethical?*, Legal Times, Jan. 21, 1985 at 16; Tim Covell, *The Bhopal Disaster Litigation: It's Not Over Yet,* 16 N.C.J. Int'l L. & Com. Reg. 279 (1991); Monroe Freedman, *Ambulance Chasing in the Public Interest,* Legal Times, July 16, 1990 at 16 (critical of bar's attempts to promulgate ethical rule prohibiting trial lawyers from going to scene of disaster without invitation, inspired by Bhopal and DuPont Plaza hotel fire disasters); Peter Huber, *Bhopalization of U.S. Tort Law,* Issues Sci. & Tech., Fall 1985 at 73; Deborah L. Rhode, *Solicitation,* 36 J. Legal Educ. 317 (1986)(California trial lawyers vote to censure attorneys who solicited clients in wake of Bhopal disaster); *Bhopal Censure,* Nat'l L.J., Jan. 28, 1985 at 3. *See generally,* Jack B. Weinstein, *Ethical Dilemmas in Mass Tort Litigation,* 88 Nw.U.L.Rev. 469 (1994).

8. Should foreign plaintiffs have access to American federal courts to litigate their grievances? Under what circumstances? What about litigation that involves both foreign plaintiffs and foreign defendants? Do American jurisdictional and venue rules adequately meet the problems raised by a global economy and international trade? For discussions of the doctrine of *forum non conveniens* in relation to the globalization of litigation, *see* Sheila Birnbaum & Douglas W. Dunham, *Foreign Plaintiffs and* Forum Non Conveniens, 16 Brook.J.Int'l.L. 241 (1990); David Boyce, Note, *Foreign Plaintiffs and* Forum Non Conveniens: *Going Beyond* Reyno, 64 Tex.L.Rev. 193 (1985); Jacqueline Duval–Major, Note, *One-Way Ticket Home: The Federal Doctrine of* Forum Non Conveniens *and the International Plaintiff,* 77 Cornell L.Rev. 650 (1992); Hanson Hosein, *Unsettling: Bhopal and the Resolution of International Disputes Involving an Environmental Disaster,* 16 B.C. Int'l & Comp. L.Rev.285 (1993); R.R. Jesperson, *The Bhopal Decision: A* Forum Non Conveniens *Perspective,* 18 Lincoln L.Rev. 73 (1988); Peter McAllen, *Deference to the Plaintiff in* Forum Non Conveniens, 13 S.Ill.U.L.J. 192 (1989); Laurel E. Miller, Comment, Forum Non Conveniens *and State Control of Foreign Plaintiff Access to U.S. Courts in International Tort Actions,* 58 U.Chi.L.Rev. 1369 (1991); William L. Reynolds, *The Proper Forum For a Suit: Transnational* Forum Non Conveniens *and Counter–Suit Injunctions in the Federal Courts,* 70 Tex.L.Rev. 1664 (1992); Margaret G. Stewart, Forum Non Conveniens: *A Doctrine in Search of a Role,* 74 Calif.L.Rev. 1259 (1986); Note, *International Mass Tort Litigation:* Forum Non Conveniens *and the Adequate Alternative Forum in Light of the Bhopal Disaster,* 16 Ga.J.Int'l.L. 109 (1986).

9. Many states have different concepts of the doctrine of *forum non conveniens*—indeed, some do not recognize it—than do federal courts. Does federal *forum non conveniens* doctrine pre-empt conflicting state principles? *Cf.* Chick Kam Choo v. Exxon Corp., 486 U.S. 140, 108 S.Ct. 1684, 100 L.Ed.2d 127 (1988) in which the Supreme Court suggested but did not decide whether the federal rules of *forum non conveniens* in an admiralty case preempted state law under reverse-*Erie* doctrine, *with* Ikospentakis v. Thalassic S.S. Agency, 915 F.2d 176 (5th Cir.1990)(holding federal *forum non conveniens* doctrine supreme in maritime cases over Texas state law not recognizing the doctrine; federal court had discretion to issue injunction to

prevent relitigation of the choice-of-law determination made pursuant to a *forum non-conveniens* dismissal).

In American Dredging Co. v. Miller, ___ U.S.___, 114 S.Ct. 981, 127 L.Ed.2d 285 (1994) the Supreme Court laid this issue to rest by determining that in admiralty cases originally filed in state court under the Jones Act and invoking a "savings to suitors clause," federal law did not pre-empt Louisiana state law regarding the doctrine of *forum non conveniens*. The Supreme Court indicated that *forum non conveniens* is different in two significant respects from other matters where the Court has held that state law is preempted by federal admiralty law. First, federal *forum non conveniens* doctrine is a "sort of venue rule" that is procedural in nature, rather than substantive, and therefore unlikely to create any expectancies in the parties. Second, because it is a discretionary doctrine applying multiple relevant factors, application of the federal doctrine is unlikely to produce uniform results. In addition, the Jones Act permits states to apply their local *forum non conveniens* rules.

How broad is the *American Dredging* holding with regard to federal preemption doctrine and state *forum non conveniens*? Does is apply just to maritime cases, or more broadly to other federally-based claims? In a two-tier court system, what are the implication of *American Dredging* for litigants' choice-of-forum?

Texas has been dubbed the "world's forum of last resort" as a state hospitable to foreign plaintiffs who are able to allege some arguable connection to Texas in order to pursue litigation in an American forum. In 1983 eighty-three plantation workers in Costa Rica brought suit against Shell Oil Company and Dow Chemical Co. for personal injuries, including sterility, allegedly caused by exposure to chemical pesticides manufactured by the two companies. The plaintiffs filed suits in Florida, California, and Texas; the Florida and California cases were dismissed on state *forum non conveniens* grounds. In Dow Chem. Co. v. Castro Alfaro, 786 S.W.2d 674 (Tex.1990), *cert. denied,* 498 U.S. 1024, 111 S.Ct. 671, 112 L.Ed.2d 663 (1991), the Texas Supreme Court, however, determined that Texas law prohibited a *forum non conveniens* dismissal. In commenting on the *Alfaro* case and related jurisdictional decisions, Professor Alex Albright has commented that "Understandably, *Alfaro* [and related decisions] terrify defendants sued in Texas by alien plaintiffs alleging claims arising overseas. * * * " *See* Alex Wilson Albright, *In Personam Jurisdiction: A Confused and Inappropriate Substitute For* Forum Non Conveniens, 71 Tex.L.Rev. 351 (1992). *See also* Friedrich Juenger, *Forum Shopping, Domestic and International,* 63 Tul. L.Rev. 553 (1989); William L. Reynolds, *The Proper Forum For a Suit: Transnational* Forum Non Conveniens *and Counter–Suit Injunctions in the Federal Courts,* 70 Tex.L.Rev. 1663 (1992); David W. Robertson & Paula K. Speck, *Access to State Courts in Transnational Personal Injury Cases:* Forum Non Conveniens *and AntiSuit Injunctions,* 68 Tex.L.Rev. 937 (1990); Russell J. Weintraub, *The Need for* Forum Non Conveniens *Legislation in Texas,* 55 Tex.B.J. 346 (1992).

F. PRECLUSION DOCTRINE

1. COLLATERAL ESTOPPEL APPLIED

FLATT v. JOHNS MANVILLE SALES CORPORATION

United States District Court, Eastern District of Texas, 1980.
488 F.Supp. 836.

MEMORANDUM OPINION AND ORDER

ROBERT M. PARKER, DISTRICT JUDGE.

Plaintiffs have brought this products liability action contending that exposure to cement pipes which contained asbestos was a producing cause of Alvin Flatt's incapacity and ultimate death due to mesothelioma, a cancerous tumor of the membrane which lines the chest cavity. The cement pipes in question were manufactured by defendants Johns Manville and Certain–Teed and sold to East Texas Salt Water Disposal Company, decedent's employer from the mid 1940's until 1978. Plaintiffs contend that the cement pipes containing asbestos as manufactured, marketed, sold, or distributed by defendants Johns Manville and Certain–Teed were defective and unreasonably dangerous to users of such products under Section 402A of the RESTATEMENT (SECOND) OF TORTS (1965). Defendants deny that their products were defective as manufactured and distributed, and defendants contend their products were accompanied by adequate warnings which made their use safe. Plaintiffs have moved the Court to grant a partial summary judgment on the issue of whether the cement pipes in question were defective and unreasonably dangerous. In support of their position that cement pipes containing asbestos are unreasonably dangerous as a matter of law, plaintiffs cite Borel v. Fibreboard Paper Products Corporation, 493 F.2d 1076 (5th Cir.), *cert. denied,* 419 U.S. 869, 95 S.Ct. 127, 42 L.Ed.2d 107 (1974). Defendants oppose the application of collateral estoppel to the cement pipe in question, contending that *Borel* is limited to a holding that insulation products containing asbestos are unreasonably dangerous to users of such products. Further, defendants assert that it is inappropriate for the Court to invoke offensive collateral estoppel on the issue of whether cement pipe containing asbestos is unreasonably dangerous.

In this strict liability action, plaintiffs have the burden of proving by a preponderance of the evidence the following elements: 1. Defendants manufactured, marketed, sold, distributed, or placed in the stream of commerce products containing asbestos. 2. Products containing asbestos are unreasonably dangerous. 3. Asbestos dust is a competent producing cause of mesothelioma. 4. Decedent was exposed to defendant's products. 5. The exposure was sufficient to be a producing cause of mesothelioma. 6. Decedent contracted mesothelioma. 7. Plaintiffs suffered damages. *See* RESTATEMENT (SECOND) OF TORTS § 402A(1)(1965). In moving for partial summary judgment, plaintiffs contend that *Borel* established as a matter of law that defendant Johns Manville manufactured and distributed products containing asbestos and that such products are unreasonably dangerous and defective. Plaintiffs argue that collateral estoppel should be invoked so as to preclude relitigation of elements # 1, 2, and 3. Defendant Johns Manville asserts that the differences in the products involved, cement pipe containing asbestos in the present case and insulation products containing asbestos in *Borel*, make the application of collateral estoppel in this case unfair. Defendant Certain–Teed argues that due process considerations prevent application of collateral estoppel to products it has manufactured because Certain–Teed was not a party to the judgment entered in *Borel*.

The Court is of the opinion that federal law governs the issue of collateral estoppel application in this diversity of citizenship action. The Court is persuaded that the reasoning underlying the decision in Aerojet–General Corporation v. Askew, 511 F.2d 710 (5th Cir.1975), holding that federal law controls the res judicata effect to be given a prior diversity judgment in a federal question lawsuit, is equally applicable to the issue of which law controls the issue of collateral estoppel effect in a diversity lawsuit.

Borel was a diversity lawsuit in which another plaintiff successfully contended that Johns Manville's insulation products containing asbestos were unreasonably dangerous and defective. The theory of plaintiff's lawsuit in *Borel* was that the products with which Clarence Borel worked were not accompanied by an adequate warning of the dangers associated with inhalation of asbestos dust so as to make the product unreasonably dangerous to users. Liability in *Borel* was predicated upon the following rationale:

> "In *Borel*, manufacturers of insulation products were held strictly liable to an insulation worker who developed asbestosis and mesothelioma and ultimately died because of their failure to warn of the dangers of inhaling asbestos dust. Our holding in that case however, was predicated on our conclusion that the dangers of inhaling asbestos dust were not sufficiently obvious to insulation workers to relieve the manufacturers of the duty to warn. *See* 493 F.2d at 1093. The relation of asbestos dust inhalation to asbestosis and mesothelioma was well documented in medical journals during most if not all of the period of Borel's exposure, but Borel, an insulation worker since 1936, was understandably unaware of these technical medical findings." Martinez v. Dixie Carriers, 529 F.2d 457, 466 (5th Cir.1976).

The Fifth Circuit affirmed the jury's finding that products containing asbestos were unreasonably dangerous because of a marketing defect; *Borel* established that asbestos products introduced into the stream of commerce since the mid 1930's were not accompanied by warnings sufficient to allow users to make an intelligent choice about exposure. *Ibid.*, p. 1089.

There are three threshold requirements for the application of collateral estoppel. First, the issue to be concluded must be identical to that involved in the prior action; second, the issue must have been actually litigated in the prior action; and finally, the determination made of the issues in the prior action must have been necessary and essential to the resulting judgment. James Talcott, Inc. v. Allahabad Bank, Ltd., 444 F.2d 451, 458 (5th Cir.1971).

After being under attack by commentators and courts for many years, the mutuality of estoppel doctrine, which required both parties to have been parties to the prior judgment before estoppel could be used to foreclose subsequent litigation on an issue, was discarded by the Supreme Court in Blonder–Tongue Laboratories v. University of Illinois Foundation, 402 U.S. 313 (1971). In abandoning mutuality of estoppel, the *Blonder-Tongue* Court held that collateral estoppel could be used defensively by a defendant in a patent infringement action where the prior judgment had declared the same patent invalid. *Id.* p. 347. Eight years after the *Blonder-Tongue* decision, the Supreme Court sanctioned the use of offensive collateral estoppel by a plaintiff in appropriate circumstances. Parklane Hosiery v. Shore, 439 U.S. 322, 99 S.Ct. 645, 58 L.Ed.2d 552 (1979).

Holding that a plaintiff stockholder's class could collaterally estop the defendant from relitigating the factual issue of a false, misleading proxy on the basis of a prior declaratory judgment obtained by the Securities and Exchange Commission, the Supreme Court ruled that application of offensive collateral estoppel is a discretionary matter with the trial judge. *Id. at* 331, 99 S.Ct. p. 651. Contrary to the position of Johns Manville, Justice Stewart relied heavily upon *Blonder-Tongue* in concluding that offensive use of collateral estoppel is not precluded; specifically, *Parklane Hosiery* adopted the *Blonder-Tongue* reasoning that "repeated litigation of the same issue...." is a waste of judicial resources. *Ibid.* The distinctions that *Parklane Hosiery* did draw between defensive and offensive collateral estoppel mandate that trial court consider notions of fairness to the defendant and whether plaintiff could have joined in the earlier action where a plaintiff seeks to invoke offensive collateral estoppel, in addition to the traditional threshold requirements. *Parklane Hosiery* distinguished promotion of judicial economy in the two situations by explaining that "defensive collateral estoppel gives a plaintiff a strong incentive to join all potential defendants in the first action if possible", while in offensive collateral estoppel situations "the plaintiff has every incentive to adopt a 'wait and see' attitude, in the hope that the first action by another plaintiff will result in a favorable judgment." *Id,* at 329–30, 99 S.Ct. at pp. 650-51. Thus, if plaintiff could have easily joined the earlier lawsuit, offensive collateral estoppel should not be applied. Offensive collateral estoppel results in unfairness to the defendant if the first action was not vigorously defended, either because plaintiff sued for small damages or future lawsuits were not foreseeable, or if procedural opportunities are available in the subsequent action for the first time. *Ibid.*

The Court is persuaded that the traditional requirements of collateral estoppel are met in the case at bar. The factual issue of whether asbestos products were defective as marketed was litigated and concluded in *Borel*. *See also,* Karjala v. Johns–Manville, 523 F.2d 155 (8th Cir.1975). Defendant Johns Manville argues that the issue of whether cement pipe containing asbestos was defectively marketed is not identical to the *Borel* conclusion that asbestos insulation products are unreasonably dangerous to users. The Court rejects defendant's contention that insulation products and cement pipe are entirely different; both products contain asbestos and produce asbestos dust upon use. The position of the defendants that adequacy of warning and dangerousness of asbestos dust inhalation should be relitigated for every different type of asbestos product manufactured during the last fifty years reflects "the aura of the gaming table" that was laid to rest in *Blonder-Tongue*. *Borel* established that asbestos products were distributed without proper warnings; foreseeability and knowledge at the time of manufacture are not at issue in a products liability lawsuit. *See* Green, *Strict Liability Under Sections 402A and 402B: A Decade of Litigation,* 54 Tex.L.Rev. 1185 (1976).

Differences in the end uses of cement pipes and insulation products, percentage of asbestos content of the products, and environmental conditions present when the products were used are all factors which relate to the issue of whether there was sufficient exposure to asbestos dust to be a producing cause of mesothelioma. Insufficient exposure is a defense which is preserved under this collateral estoppel order preventing relitigation of whether products containing asbestos are defective and whether asbestos dust can be a producing cause of mesothelioma.

Plaintiffs' wrongful death cause of action is alleged to have accrued in 1977–1978 when Alvin Flatt contracted mesothelioma and died; obviously, plaintiffs could not have joined in *Borel*. Plaintiffs did not know of their claim during the period when *Borel* was being litigated. Johns Manville was not sued for nominal damages by Clarence Borel's survivors, and the procedural rules currently in effect in the federal courts are the same as the rules that governed the trial of *Borel*. The Court is convinced that the estoppel effect of the *Borel* judgment was foreseeable to Johns Manville; furthermore, the Court finds that the *Borel* opinion relates to all products which contain asbestos and is not limited to the particular products to which Clarence Borel was exposed.

Johns Manville has successfully defended several asbestos lawsuits in the recent past. Campbell v. Johns Manville, No. 3–78–185 (E.D.Tenn.1978); Starnes v. Johns Manville, No. 2075–122 (E.D.Tenn. 1977); Carpenter v. Johns Manville, No. C–78–224 (N.D.Ohio1979). The Court notes that Johns Manville had a judgment entered in its favor in Mooney v. Fibreboard Corp., 485 F.Supp. 242 (E.D.Tex.1980), a case in which Chief Judge Fisher collaterally estopped relitigation of the issue of whether products containing asbestos are unreasonably dangerous and held that asbestos dust is a competent producing cause of mesothelioma and asbestosis. These previous judgments in favor of Johns Manville are not inconsistent with the conclusion reached in *Borel* that asbestos products were defectively marketed without an adequate warning because "inhaling asbestos dust in industrial conditions, even with relatively light exposure, can produce the disease of asbestosis." *Ibid.* at 1083. Rather, lawsuits in which Johns Manville has prevailed have been decided on the basis that there was insufficient exposure to asbestos dust, or alternatively, the plaintiff, or decedent, did not contract asbestosis or mesothelioma.

The Court holds that as a matter of law products containing asbestos are defective and unreasonably dangerous within the meaning of section 402A of the RESTATEMENT. As a matter of law asbestos dust is a producing cause of certain lung diseases, including asbestosis and mesothelioma. The Court grants plaintiffs' motion for partial summary judgment as relates to whether cement pipes containing asbestos as manufactured, marketed, sold, or distributed by defendant Johns Manville were defective and unreasonably dangerous; the Court precludes defendants from relitigating this issue.

Defendant Certain–Teed was not a party to *Borel* and has never been a party to an adverse judgment in an asbestos lawsuit. *Borel* established that any products containing asbestos which were distributed since the mid 1930's are unreasonably dangerous; therefore, the Court grants partial summary judgment in favor of the plaintiffs and against defendant Certain–Teed on the issue of whether products containing asbestos are defective and unreasonably dangerous. However, due process considerations require the Court to deny plaintiffs' motion for partial summary judgment as it relates to whether defendant Certain–Teed manufactured, sold, marketed, or distributed products containing asbestos.

Defendants Johns Manville and Certain–Teed are precluded from relitigating the issue of whether their asbestos products which were manufactured by each of said defendants were defective and unreasonably dangerous, under the provisions of the RESTATEMENT (SECOND) OF TORTS (1965). The Court directs that each defendant be collaterally estopped from raising said issue in the course of this trial.

The Court finds as a matter of law that products placed in the stream of commerce containing asbestos are defective for the reason that the same are unreasonably dangerous to the users of such products. *Borel*. The Court holds as a matter of law that asbestos dust is a competent producing cause of certain lung diseases, including asbestosis and mesothelioma.

The Court holds that the defendants are not entitled to and will not present evidence on the "state of the art" defense, as such evidence is immaterial on the issues remaining to be tried in this cause. Evidence relating to the state of the art at the time of manufacture is relevant only to the issue of due care in the manufacturing process, a negligence concept not at issue in this strict liability action. *Borel* conclusively determined that asbestos products are defective because of the lack of an adequate warning. Regardless of what was reasonably foreseeable to the defendants at the time of manufacture, asbestos products should have been accompanied by adequate warnings; the nature of this strict liability action makes the defendants' state of knowledge at the time of manufacture irrelevant. The product and warnings attached thereto are in issue, not the defendants' conduct. Gonzales v. Caterpillar Tractor, 571 S.W.2d 867, 871 (Tex.1978).

The Court directs that the following issues will be tried to a jury in this cause: (1) whether defendant Certain–Teed introduced products containing asbestos into the stream of commerce; (2) whether Alvin Flatt was exposed to any particular defendant's product containing asbestos, and if so, whether the degree of such exposure to such defendant's product was sufficient to be a producing cause of decedent's death; (3) whether decedent contracted mesothelioma; (4) plaintiffs' damages, if any; (5) defendants' affirmative defenses, if any.

The Court is of the opinion that judicial economy will be served by the submission of any excluded evidence after the jury has retired for deliberation.

HARDY v. JOHNS–MANVILLE SALES CORPORATION

United States District Court, Eastern District of Texas, 1981.
509 F.Supp. 1353, reversed in part info 681 F.2d 334 (5th Cir.1982).

MEMORANDUM OPINION AND ORDER

ROBERT M. PARKER, DISTRICT JUDGE.

In these asbestos-related cases, three motions are before the Court. The Defendant Forty–Eight Insulations has moved for an order permitting discovery and for leave to file cross-actions based upon a contribution theory of market share apportionment. Sixteen defendants have joined in a motion for reconsideration of the collateral estoppel order entered pursuant to Flatt v. Johns–Manville Sales Corporation, 488 F.Supp. 836 (E.D.Tex.1980). Alternatively, the sixteen defendants request the Court to certify the question of collateral estoppel for interlocutory appeal to the Fifth Circuit as provided for in 28 U.S.C. § 1292(b).

By separate order, the Court shall grant the two motions of Defendant Forty–Eight Insulations. The motion for reconsideration is denied; a contemporaneous order shall grant the interlocutory appeal certification.

I

The Marshall cases represent a variety of asbestos-related claims. Some of the plaintiffs were insulation workers, while others claim exposure as pipefitters, carpenters and factory workers. Absolute identity of defendants does not exist on a case by case basis. That is, complaints may name Johns–Manville alone or include as many as twenty asbestos manufacturers. At latest tally, fifty-seven such cases were assigned to the docket of the undersigned in the Marshall division alone. By two separate orders, the cases are consolidated for pretrial purposes and captioned collectively *Hardy v. Johns–Manville Sales Corporation.* * * *

Ten years ago the widow of Clarence Borel tried her case to a favorable jury verdict before the Honorable Joe J. Fisher. Borel v. Fibreboard Paper Products Corporation, 493 F.2d 1076 (5th Cir.1973), *cert. denied,* 419 U.S. 869, 95 S.Ct. 127, 42 L.Ed.2d 107 (1974), affirmed Judge Fisher's judgment entered on the jury findings. Since that time, the Eastern District of Texas has become inundated with asbestos-related litigation. Huge oil refineries and petrochemical plants in the southern end of the district have partially accounted for the existence of over three thousand plaintiffs within the Eastern District alone. The shipyards on the coastline and the presence of an asbestos manufacturing plant in Tyler, Texas, add to our burgeoning asbestos-related docket. In short, Judge Fisher's pioneering *Borel* trial and the industrial environment of the district have tended to contribute to the large number of asbestos-related filings.

Ten years after *Borel,* it cannot be seriously argued that asbestos exposure causes disease. So comfortable are we with that assertion, that a former Secretary of Health, Education and Welfare estimated that more than 67,000 human lives are taken each year by asbestos-related cancers. Thus far in the litigation, asbestos has been found to be a competent producing cause of asbestosis and mesothelioma. *Borel.*

Pulmonary asbestosis can best be described as a nonmalignant scarring of the lungs. Asbestosis is generally cumulative; the continued exposure to asbestos dust and fibres increases both the risk and the severity of the disease. *Borel.* Its latent period makes it legally and medically impossible to state with certainty when asbestosis was first contracted or which exposure to asbestos caused or contributed to the disease. Knowledge of the danger can be attributed to the industry as early as the mid–1930's, and the conduct throughout the industry despite the danger has been summarized as one of indifferent silence. *Borel.*

The industry was also silent with respect to the dangerous relationship between asbestos and cancer. Mesothelioma is a form of malignant tumor of the chest and lungs; it may also effect the abdomen. Extraordinarily painful and always fatal, it is a relatively rare form of cancer whose relationship to asbestos has been generally known since the late 1930's. Like asbestosis, mesothelioma has a long latent period. *Borel.* Rather unlike asbestosis, mesothelioma may result from one exposure to asbestos dust or fibres.

Yet, products containing asbestos fibres have great utility in an industrial society. The heat resistant property of asbestos has made it important in insulation and pipe covering. Each year in the U.S. alone industry consumes one million tons of asbestos.

Asbestos-related cases provide the courts with a classic utility versus danger evaluation. The Fifth Circuit has spoken with respect to marketing defects in insulation products. *Borel.* Ten years after the verdict in *Borel,* considerable dispute exists with respect to its holding, and this Court's interpretation of that decision. The questions before the Court in the consolidated cases require serious consideration. The gravity of the issues raised and their interrelationship have prompted a rather lengthy response. While this Court may be accused of re-inventing the *Borel* wheel, the issues deserve more than a perfunctory response in a vacuum. With the brief review of the history of the litigation together with examination of the generic substance and its relationship to disease as a context, the Court may address the issues of market share liability and collateral estoppel [discussion of applicability of market share liability omitted—*ed.*].

* * *

III

Collateral estoppel means issue preclusion. In the motion for reconsideration filed on behalf of sixteen defendants in these consolidated cases, the Court has had occasion to consider the extent of issue preclusion which the June 9, 1980, order affects. The breadth of preclusion, as it relates to the specific objections raised by the defendants, warrants some clarification. Let it be understood at the outset that the Court adheres to its original position. *Flatt,* speaks for itself in that regard. For that reason, the motion for reconsideration is overruled, and the June 9, 1980, order remains in effect with the following modification.

The objections which have prompted the Court to postscript *Flatt* are essentially four in number. The defendants argue that in applying federal law, the Court has erred. Secondly, they assert that Texas law adheres strictly to the doctrine of mutuality such that collateral estoppel is inappropriate as to any non-*Borel* defendant. Further, the defendants maintain the identity of issues requirement is not met in the non-insulator cases, and, therefore, collateral estoppel in those cases is inappropriate. In the end, they make a catch-all argument that the Court's order of June 8, 1980, violates due process because it tramples on the rights of corporate defendants in the name of judicial economy.

The universal thread running through all the arguments brought on behalf of the defendants is that the Court has incorrectly interpreted *Borel.* Therefore, it seems to be a prerequisite that the Court review its reading of the landmark decision, referred to by one writer as the "Magna Carta for widows of insulation workers." If *Borel* provides any guidance to the lower courts, it certainly must be that the standard of conduct in the asbestos insulation industry was inconsistent with its duty to warn at least prior to 1964, when the first warning was placed on insulation containing asbestos fibres. Implicit in that determination is the apparent finding by the *Borel* court that insulation products containing asbestos are "unavoidably unsafe products." *Borel,* at 1088. Reaching that conclusion, the court readily accepts the proposition; i.e., that asbestos is a competent producing cause of mesothelioma and asbestosis. The *Borel* court relied extensively on the medical literature to reach that conclusion. *Id.* 1083–87. Finding the danger to be grave and the utility of the product to be unparalleled, the Court concluded that the only way for insulation products which contained asbestos to escape the strict liability conclusion that the products were unreasonably dangerous as marketed was for such products to have been marketed with an adequate warning. *Id.* 1089. The warning standard was not met by the industry pre–1964 or for the *Borel* defendants post–1964 to 1969. *Id.*, 1104, 1106. With respect to insulation, the uncontroverted evidence is that there were no warnings prior to 1964 by any manufacturer. With the *Borel* framework adequately constructed, the Court may evaluate the specific arguments raised in support of the motion for reconsideration.

First and foremost, the Court continues to be persuaded that the choice of law made in *Flatt* is correct. That is, under any standard, federal law applies. Aerojet–General Corporation v. Askew, 511 F.2d 710 (5th Cir.1975); Willis v. Fournier, 418 F.Supp. 265 (M.D.Ga.) *aff'd without comment,* 537 F.2d 1142 (5th Cir.1976). Because of that, the Court is convinced that the application of collateral estoppel in these cases is correct. Parklane Hosiery Co. v. Shore, 439 U.S. 322, 99 S.Ct. 645, 58 L.Ed.2d 552 (1979); *see also* Mooney v. Fibreboard Corporation, 485 F.Supp. 242 (D.C.Tex.1980); and *Flatt.*

Assuming, arguendo, that the application of federal law is incorrect, the mutuality arguments raised by the Defendants are without merit as a matter of state law. Strict mutuality, or an absolute mirroring of parties, is a legal concept subject to constant erosion and qualification. Comment, *"Collateral Estoppel: The Changing Role of Mutuality,"* 41 Missouri L.E. 521 (1976). The demise of mutuality began with the concept of respondeat superior, and the effect given to prior adjudications against employees on employers. Consequently, the courts search for the familiar exception to the rule of mutuality privity.

Texas has joined the other jurisdictions in taking a more liberal view of mutuality through the privity exception. The Corpus Christi Court of Appeals recently summarized the development in the Texas courts: "Originally, mutuality was essential to the invocation of collateral estoppel. However, the Texas Courts have apparently abandoned the requirement of mutuality and have retained the requirement of privity only to the party against whom the plea of collateral estoppel is made. * * * So long as an essential issue of fact has been determined and adjudicated, the judgment therein will estop the parties or their privies from relitigating the same issues in a subsequent suit." * * * Olivarez v. Broadway Hardware, Inc., 564 S.W.2d 195 (Tex.Civ.App. Corpus Christi 1978, no writ)(citations omitted.)

* * *

Under the law of Texas, there can be no objection to a non-party invoking a plea of collateral estoppel. *Olivarez.* Therefore, the Defendant's objection with respect to the plaintiffs is without merit. Collateral estoppel as a matter of state law may only be invoked against 1) a party, or 2) one in privity with a party to a prior adjudication. Therefore, for the non-*Borel* defendants the essential issue is a question of privity.

Texas recognizes the "identity of interest" rule of privity as set forth in RESTATEMENT OF JUDGMENTS § 83(2). *Olivarez,* at 200. If the non-*Borel* defendants share sufficient identity of interests with *Borel* defendants, mutuality cannot bar the application of collateral estoppel. For reasons stated in ... the foregoing opinion, as well as those articulated in *Borel,* the Court holds that the non-*Borel* defendants share sufficient identity of interest such that the application of collateral estoppel would not conflict with the state standard.

As far as the insulation cases are concerned, the non-*Borel* defendants share precisely the same interests as do the *Borel* defendants, at least for the pre–1964 period. If exposure to any product occurs in a case prior to 1964, there can be no serious challenge to a claim of collateral estoppel on the ultimate issue of marketing an unreasonably dangerous product without an adequate warning, provided it is asserted by one exposed to insulation products.

The pre–1964 exposure insulation cases are the cases in which collateral estoppel may be entered in its broadest form and without serious objection. Included within the consolidated cases is at least one case in which the product at issue is not insulation but is insulated pipe, the *Flatt* case. Assuming federal law applies, the ruling in *Flatt* remains correct. Because it has come to the attention of the Court that at least one of my brethren on the trial bench in this circuit disagrees with the application of federal law, it may very well be that a considerable difference of judicial opinion could exist on that issue.

If *Flatt* is incorrect on the choice of law, collateral estoppel in its broadest terms may be incorrect in cases in which the claimed exposure is not related to an insulation product. This is so because the standard of conduct with respect to warning in the insulation industry was determined in *Borel*. The practice with respect to warnings on other products containing asbestos was not at issue in *Borel*; the conclusion with respect to the adequacy of the warnings is not identical. Therefore, collateral estoppel on the ultimate issue of marketing a product which was unreasonably dangerous to the ultimate user may be inappropriate as a matter of state law. *Benson; Hardy.* This does not mean that issue preclusion on inquiries necessary to the ultimate issue would be inappropriate. That is, *Borel* under any concept of privity would support collateral estoppel of the issue that asbestos is a competent producing cause of asbestosis and mesothelioma. The danger of the generic ingredient is the same irrespective of the finished product. The degree of danger may vary with the finished product, and, consequently, the duty to warn may vary.

Yet, under any standard, it would be a clear abuse of process in the courts to relitigate the issue of whether asbestos causes mesothelioma or asbestosis. This is the "can it" question versus the "did it" question in a particular case. Under any collateral estoppel application, the "did it" question is always litigated. The danger of the generic ingredient of the defendants products to the human user cannot be seriously questioned. To do so would unduly burden the plaintiff and slow the Eastern District to a standstill.

* * *

The due process arguments espoused by the defendants relate chiefly to verdicts which have resulted in victory for the manufacturers subsequent to *Borel*. The argument with respect to inconsistency as violative of a standard of fundamental fairness is adequately dealt with in *Flatt,* and does not warrant repetition of the Court's position. *See also Mooney,* at 247–48. If there is a fundamental fairness issue, it relates to the non-insulation defendant for reasons stated above. On balance, that issue is cured by a paring down of the collateral estoppel issue to the question of disease-relation of the generic ingredient. Even so, the Federal Rules of Evidence provide a means to reach this bottom line result if by another vehicle judicial notice of adjudicative fact. Fed.R.Ev. 201(b)(2) and (c). Relying upon the wealth of authority on this issue which is not subject to question,[23] judicial notice may be taken of the disease-relation as an alternative to collateral estoppel.

Asbestos-related litigation is an appropriate candidate for collateral estoppel because it is a mass tort, a tort against a large undefinable group of people by industry. *See* Comment, *"Asbestos Litigation: The Dust Has Yet to Settle," supra.* * * * Because of differences in products within the industry, the application of collateral estoppel may vary somewhat with the product at issue. Yet, if *Parklane* is to be followed by this Court, its discretion to invoke collateral estoppel should not be questioned. For reasons first articulated in *Flatt,* justice as well as judicial economy requires that collateral estoppel be imposed. The defendants should not be allowed to litigate the plaintiffs to death on an issue which can best be described as a dead horse.

For the foregoing reasons and those previously articulated by the Court, the motion for reconsideration is DENIED. Contemporaneous to the entry of this opinion the Court shall enter an amended collateral estoppel order, and it shall enter an order with the appropriate findings for certification of the collateral estoppel issue to the Fifth Circuit Court of Appeals pursuant to 28 U.S.C. § 1292(b).

* * *

23. For use of Rule 201 as it relates to medical facts not subject to rational dispute, *see* Franklin Life Insurance Co. v. William J. Champion & Co., 350 F.2d 115, 130 (6th Cir.1965), *cert. denied,* 384 U.S. 928, 86 S.Ct. 1445, 16 L.Ed.2d 531 (1966) and Golaris v. Jewel Tea Co., 22 F.R.D. 16, 19 (N.D.Ill.1958).

2. COLLATERAL ESTOPPEL REPUDIATED

MIGUES v. FIBREBOARD CORP.

United States Court of Appeals, Fifth Circuit, 1981.
662 F.2d 1182.

In Borel v. Fibreboard Paper Products Corporation, 493 F.2d 1076 (5th Cir.1973) this Court provided an extensive analysis of Texas product liability law as it is to be applied in suits brought against manufacturers of asbestos products. Now we are called upon to determine whether *Borel* can serve as precedential authority for the proposition that all asbestos products are unreasonably dangerous as a matter of law. We conclude that it cannot.

I. BACKGROUND

Mr. Russell Migues worked as an insulator at Texaco, Incorporated from 1944 until 1977. According to the testimony of his co-workers, Mr. Migues' job as an insulator involved cutting asbestos insulating products. The cutting process produced asbestos dust which Mr. Migues and the other insulators inhaled. In September 1977, a medical biopsy revealed that Mr. Migues was suffering from mesothelioma, a fatal form of lung cancer. According to plaintiff's expert medical witnesses, mesothelioma is caused by asbestos inhalation. Mr. Migues died soon after the 1977 diagnosis.

Mrs. Migues brought suit in the federal district court for the Eastern District of Texas against fourteen asbestos manufacturers, charging that the asbestos products manufactured by defendants were unreasonably dangerous and that exposure to these products caused her husband's death.

Prior to trial, Judge Parker granted plaintiff's Motion for Partial Summary Judgment on the issue of whether asbestos-containing products were unreasonably dangerous to users or consumers under Texas products liability law. According to Judge Parker, the only issues for the jury to decide were: (1) whether defendants manufactured asbestos, (2) if so, whether the decedent Russell Migues was exposed to any individual defendant's products, (3) whether such exposure, if any, was a producing cause of his death, (4) whether Mr. Migues contracted mesothelioma, and finally, (5) the amount of plaintiff's damages, if any.

Following the District Court's order, thirteen defendants settled with plaintiff prior to trial for a total amount of $400,000. The case then went to trial against the remaining defendant, Nicolet Industries, Inc. (hereinafter "Nicolet"). The jury found in favor of Mrs. Migues, and awarded her damages of three million dollars. In response to specific interrogatories by the Court, the jury found that Mr. Migues had been exposed to the thirteen settling defendants' asbestos products in addition to those of Nicolet, and that all of these products were producing causes of Mr. Migues' death.

Defendant Nicolet's Motions for Directed Verdict and for Judgment Notwithstanding the Verdict were denied. Judge Parker did, however, reduce Mrs. Migues' award, via remittitur, to $1.5 Million. He then credited Nicolet with the $400,000 paid in settlement by the other defendants, and entered judgment, 493 F.Supp. 61, against Nicolet for the remainder.

Defendant Nicolet brought this appeal, alleging several reasons for reversal. Appellant first suggests that this Court must reverse the District Court's denial of Nicolet's Motions for Directed Verdict and for Judgment Notwithstanding the Verdict. Nicolet argues that even if we assume, as did the District Court, that asbestos is unreasonably dangerous as a matter of law, plaintiff did not meet her burden of proving that the products of this particular defendant, Nicolet, were a producing cause of her husband's death. Alternatively, Nicolet asks that we remand this case for a new trial, citing several alleged errors made by the District Court in the proceedings below. Foremost among these arguments is Nicolet's claim that the District Court's order granting partial summary judgment to plaintiff on the issue of the unreasonably dangerous nature of asbestos products violates Nicolet's rights to due process and to a jury trial under the Fourteenth and the Seventh Amendments. * * *

III. COLLATERAL ESTOPPEL

A great deal of sound and fury has been generated over the question of whether Nicolet could be precluded from litigating the unreasonably dangerous nature of its asbestos-containing products based on the collateral estoppel effect of a case—*Borel v. Fibreboard*—to which Nicolet was not a party. We decline to reach this question for the simple reason that it is not presented in the case before us. The District Court's order granting plaintiff's Motion for Partial Summary Judgment, makes it clear that appellant herein—Nicolet—was precluded from litigating the dangerousness of asbestos products on the basis of what the District Court thought to be the *stare decisis* effect of *Borel's* holdings of law and not on the grounds that Nicolet was collaterally estopped by any issue of fact decided in *Borel*.

In his pre-trial order precluding all fourteen original defendants from litigating the unreasonably dangerous character of asbestos, Judge Parker clearly distinguished between two groups of defendants: one group was precluded on the basis of collateral estoppel; and the other group, which included appellant Nicolet, was precluded on the basis of *Borel's* stare decisis effect. The order lists eleven defendants who had been parties to one or both of two prior asbestos cases: *Borel,* and Condray v. Fibreboard, B–76–108–CA (E.D.Tex.1977). In both cases, it was determined that the asbestos products manufactured by these eleven defendants were unreasonably dangerous to users or consumers under Texas products liability law. Therefore, concluded Judge Parker, these eleven defendants were collaterally estopped from relitigating both the issue of whether they manufactured asbestos products, and the issue of whether these products were unreasonably dangerous.

Appellant Nicolet, however, was not included in the list of eleven defendants who were collaterally estopped, because Nicolet, along with two other defendants, had not been parties to either *Borel* or *Condray*. As to these three defendants, Judge Parker cited *Borel* and held "as a matter of law," that products containing asbestos were defective and unreasonably dangerous to consumers or users of the product, and that asbestos was a producing cause of such lung diseases as asbestosis and mesothelioma. However, unlike the eleven defendants who were collaterally estopped by prior cases, Nicolet and the other two defendants had never been found in any prior proceeding to have manufactured and sold asbestos products. Therefore, in order to prevail against these three defendants, Judge Parker ordered that plaintiffs would be required to introduce evidence that the defendants manufactured and sold asbestos products. Thus, it is apparent that Judge Parker distinguished between preclusion on the grounds of collateral estoppel, which included preclusion as to matters of "fact" found in prior cases; and preclusion on the grounds of what the District Court thought to be the *stare decisis* effect of *Borel,* which did not extend to issues of "fact." And it is the latter theory—*stare decisis*—which formed the basis for Judge Parker's pretrial order as to appellant Nicolet.

[The court next summarizes Judge Parker's holdings in *Flatt—ed.*]

* * *

It is true that in a recent case, Hardy v. Johns–Manville Sales Corp., 509 F.Supp. 1353 (E.D.Tex.1981), Judge Parker appears to have taken a new approach toward collaterally estopping asbestos manufacturers who were not parties to *Borel* and thereby precluding them from litigating the unreasonably dangerous nature of their products. However, *Hardy* and the collateral theories set forth therein, are not before us on appeal today. The sole issue presented by the case which is before us concerns the *stare decisis* effect of *Borel*. Accordingly, we express no opinion as to whether *Borel* may be used to collaterally estop either asbestos manufacturers who were parties to that case, or those who were not, in future cases arising out of asbestos-related diseases. Latent within this litigation, we realize, is the need to redefine the doctrine of collateral estoppel spawned by Blonder–Tongue Laboratories, Inc. v. University of Illinois Foundation, 402 U.S. 313, 91 S.Ct. 1434, 28 L.Ed.2d 788 (1971) and Parklane Hosiery Co. v. Shore, 439 U.S. 322, 99 S.Ct. 645, 58 L.Ed.2d 552 (1979). This task, however, we must bequeath to our brethren in future cases which squarely present the issue of collateral estoppel.

IV. THE *Stare Decisis* EFFECT OF *Borel*

In its order granting plaintiff's Motion for Partial Summary Judgment, the District Court construed the *Borel* case as establishing "as a matter of law" that asbestos products cause lung cancers, and that such products are unreasonably dangerous to consumers or users under Texas

standards of strict products liability. This "holding of law" was found
to control all product liability actions involving asbestos through the
operation of stare decisis principles. Accordingly, the District Court held
that insofar as the unreasonably dangerous nature of asbestos had
already been established as a matter of law, that issue need not be tried
to the jury in this case. We find, however, that the District Court's
interpretation of *Borel* is erroneous. The District Court may have
thought that *Borel* stands for the proposition that all asbestos products
are unreasonably dangerous as a matter of law, but upon reviewing
Borel, we must conclude that there is no such *decisis* in *Borel* to *stare*.

In *Borel*, this Court examined both the District Court's instructions
to the jury on Texas products liability law, and its denial of defendants'
Motions for Directed Verdict and for JNOV. In reviewing the jury
instructions, we set out the elements of a cause of action in strict
products liability under Texas law. *Borel's* explanation of products
liability law under the RESTATEMENT (SECOND) OF TORTS has been affirmed
by this Court upon numerous occasions, *see* Burks v. Firestone Tire &
Rubber Co., 633 F.2d 1152, 1155 (5th Cir.1981) . . . [other citations
omitted–*ed.*] Nothing in today's opinion should be construed as impugn-
ing the integrity of those holdings of law which are stated in *Borel*.
However, no amount of maneuvering or interpretation will allow us to
add to these holding, and to affirm the District Court's conclusion that
Borel holds, "as a matter of law," that all asbestos products are unreasonably dangerous.

In addition to its discussion of products liability law, the *Borel* Court
also examined the lower court's denial of defendants' Motions for Directed Verdict and for JNOV. In doing so, this Court applied products
liability law to the specific facts of the Borel case. The central question
was whether there was substantial evidence to support a jury finding in
favor of plaintiff. *Boeing v. Shipman.* We concluded that the evidence
was indeed sufficient to support a finding of liability. The only determination made by this court in *Borel* was that, based upon the evidence in
that case, the jury's findings could not be said to be incorrect as a matter
of law. But this Court certainly did not decide that every jury presented
with the same facts would be compelled to reach the conclusion reached
by the *Borel* jury: that asbestos was unreasonably dangerous. Such a
holding would have been not only unnecessary, it would also have been
unwarranted.

In *Borel*, this Court said: "the jury was *entitled* to find that the
danger to Borel and other insulation workers from inhaling asbestos
dust was foreseeable to the defendants at the time the products causing
Borel's injuries were sold," 493 F.2d at 1093 (emphasis added). We did
not say that the jury was compelled, as a matter of law to reach this
result, or that it could not have reached another result. On the issue of
plaintiff Borel's possible voluntary assumption of risk, this Court stated
"we cannot say that, as a matter of law, the danger (of asbestos
inhalation) was sufficiently obvious to asbestos installation workers to
relieve the defendants of the duty to warn." *Id.* This Court did not say

that, as a matter of law, the danger of asbestos inhalation was so hidden from every asbestos worker in every situation as to create a duty to warn on the part of all asbestos manufacturers. On rehearing, this Court held that although some asbestos products used by plaintiff Borel contained warnings, there was sufficient evidence that the warnings were inadequate to inform workers of the actual dangers posed by asbestos inhalation to justify submission of that issue to the jury. 493 F.2d at 1105. This Court did not state that every jury would be required, as a matter of law, to find such warnings inadequate.

In sum, this Court held in *Borel* only that the *Borel* jury, on the evidence presented to it, could have found that asbestos products unaccompanied by adequate warnings were unreasonably dangerous. The proposition that all juries presented with similar evidence regarding asbestos products would be compelled to find those products unreasonably dangerous was not presented in *Borel*, and therefore, this Court did not reach it. Since *stare decisis* is accorded only those issues necessarily decided by a court in reaching its result, the District Court erred in overreading the holding of our opinion in *Borel*.

V. CONCLUSION

This is not the first, nor will it be the last, asbestos case confronting this Court. At recent count, there were over three thousand asbestos plaintiffs in the Eastern District of Texas alone. Hardy v. Johns–Manville Sales Corp., 509 F.Supp. 1353, 1354 (E.D.Tex.1981). It is understandable that the district courts will seek ways of eliminating the need to continuously reinvent the asbestos liability wheel in every one of these cases. Considerations of judicial economy demand a more streamlined mechanism for compensating asbestos victims and apportioning liability among those responsible for causing injury. Nevertheless, we hold today that this result cannot be accomplished by reading *Borel v. Fibreboard Paper Products Corp.* to stand for the proposition that in all cases, asbestos products are unreasonably dangerous as a matter of law.

There may be alternative methods for adjudicating the thousands of asbestos cases facing the courts in a manner that conserves the resources of both the courts and the parties. Nothing in our opinion today should be read as foreclosing these alternatives. Some judicial constructions, such as the enterprise liability theory of collateral estoppel set forth by Judge Parker in *Hardy v. Johns–Manville Sales Corp.* may appear at first glance to be novel, startling, or even revolutionary. We express no opinion as to the wisdom or propriety of such theories, as they did not form the basis for the District Court's decision in the instant case. However, we do note that the juggernaut of modern technology has repeatedly given rise to new concepts in our torts jurisprudence and procedure. Changes have come about both through expansion of the common-law and through legislative enactments. Illustrative of this development are the doctrines of strict products liability, comparative negligence, workmen's compensation, no-fault insurance, consumer protection, and the class action device—doctrines which, at the time they were first introduced, also seemed novel, startling and revolutionary. Old citadels of jurisprudence have [been] demolished, modified and redefined to meet the needs of a rapidly changing industrial society; one which confers on its members both benefits and burdens previously unimaginable.

Whether through judge-made common-law or legislative enactment, there is an urgent need for new approaches to the national tragedy of asbestos-related disease. But, we must reiterate, the approach taken by the District Court in this case: reliance on the *stare decisis* effect of *Borel* to prevent defendant Nicolet from litigating the unreasonably dangerous nature of asbestos products, cannot be sustained. We therefore reverse the District Court's order granting plaintiff's Motion for Partial Summary Judgment on the issue of the unreasonably dangerous nature of asbestos products under Texas law, and remand this case for further proceedings in accordance with this decision.

Reversed in part and remanded.

HARDY v. JOHNS–MANVILLE SALES CORP.

United States Court of Appeals, Fifth Circuit, 1982.
681 F.2d 334.

Before GEE and JOHNSON, CIRCUIT JUDGES, and VAN PELT, DISTRICT JUDGE.

GEE, CIRCUIT JUDGE:

This appeal arises out of a diversity action brought by various plaintiffs—insulators, pipefitters, carpenters, and other factory workers—against various manufacturers, sellers, and distributors of asbestos-containing products. The plaintiffs, alleging exposure to the products and consequent disease, assert various causes of action, including negligence, breach of implied warranty, and strict liability. The pleadings in each of the cases are substantially the same. No plaintiff names a particular defendant on a case-by-case basis but, instead, includes several—often as many as twenty asbestos manufacturers—in his individual complaint. The rationale offered for this unusual pleading practice is that, given the long latent period of the diseases in question, it is impossible for plaintiffs to isolate the precise exposure period or to identify the particular manufacturer's product responsible. The trial court accepted this rationale and opted for a theory of enterprise or industry-wide liability. * * * This ruling is not on appeal here.

Defendants' interlocutory appeal under 28 U.S.C. § 1292(b) is directed instead at the district court's amended omnibus order dated March 13, 1981, which applies collateral estoppel to this mass tort.

* * *

Because we conclude that the trial court abused its discretion in applying collateral estoppel and judicial notice, we reverse.... [The court first determines that federal law of collateral estoppel governs.— *ed.*]

* * *

THE NON-*Borel* DEFENDANTS

This is the first and, in our view, insurmountable problem with the trial court's application of collateral estoppel in the case *sub judice*. The omnibus order under review here does not distinguish between defendants who were parties to *Borel* and those who were not; it purports to estop all defendants because all purportedly share an "identity of interests" sufficient to constitute privity. The trial court's action stretches "privity" beyond meaningful limits. While we acknowledge the manipulability of the notion of "privity," *see, e.g., Collateral Estoppel of Nonparties,* 87 Harv.L.Rev. 1485, 1490, 1494–95 & n.66 (1974), this has not prevented courts from establishing guidelines on the permissibility of binding nonparties through res judicata or collateral estoppel. Without such guidelines, the due process guarantee of a full and fair opportunity to litigate disappears. Thus, we noted in Southwest Airlines Co. v. Texas International Airlines, 546 F.2d 84, 95 (5th Cir.1977):

> Federal courts have deemed several types of relationships "sufficiently close" to justify preclusion. First, a nonparty who has succeeded to a party's interest in property is bound by any prior judgments against that party. ... Second, a nonparty who controlled the original suit will be bound by the resulting judgment. ...Third, federal courts will bind a nonparty whose interests were represented adequately by a party in the original suit.

(Citations omitted). The rationale for these exceptions—all derived from RESTATEMENT (SECOND) OF JUDGMENTS §§ 30, 31, 34, 39–41 (1982)—is obviously that in these instances the nonparty has in effect had his day in court. In this case, the exceptions elaborated in Southwest Airlines and in the RESTATEMENT are inapplicable. First, the *Borel* litigation did not involve any property interests. Second, none of the non-*Borel* defendants have succeeded to any property interest held by the *Borel* defendants. Finally, the plaintiffs did not show that any non-*Borel* defendant had any control whatever over the *Borel* litigation. "To have control of litigation requires that a person have effective choice as to the legal theories and proofs to be advanced in behalf of the party to the action. He must also have control over the opportunity to obtain review." RESTATEMENT (SECOND) OF JUDGMENTS § 39, comment c (1982). *Accord, e.g.,* MOORE'S ¶ 0.411(6) at 1564–67. In, for example, Sea–Land Services v. Gaudet, 414 U.S. 573, 94 S.Ct. 806, 39 L.Ed.2d 9 (1974), the Supreme Court held that a nonparty may be collaterally estopped from relitigating issues necessarily decided in a suit by a party who acted as a fiduciary responsible for the beneficial interests of the nonparties. Even in this context, however, the Court placed the exception within strict confines: "In such cases, 'the beneficiaries are bound by the judgment with respect to the interest which was the subject of the fiduciary relationship....' " *Id.* at 593–94, 94 S.Ct. at 819, *quoting* F. James,

CIVIL PROCEDURE § 11.28 at 592 (1965). Many of our circuit's cases evince a similar concern with keeping the nonparties' exceptions to res judicata and collateral estoppel within strict confines. *See, e.g., Southwest Airlines Co. v. Texas International Airlines.*

The fact that all the non-*Borel* defendants, like the *Borel* defendants, are engaged in the manufacture of asbestos-containing products does not evince privity among the parties. The plaintiffs did not demonstrate that any of the non-*Borel* defendants participated in any capacity in the *Borel* litigation—whether directly or even through a trade representative—or were even part of a trustee-beneficiary relationship with any *Borel* defendant.[5] On the contrary, several of the defendants indicate on appeal that they were not even aware of the *Borel* litigation until those proceedings were over and that they were not even members of industry or trade associations composed of asbestos product manufacturers.

Plaintiffs can draw little support from the doctrine of "virtual representation" of cases such as *Aerojet-General Corp. v. Askew* in which we stated that "[u]nder the federal law of res judicata, a person may be bound by a judgment even though not a party if one of the parties to the suit is so closely aligned with his interests as to be his virtual representative" and that "the question whether a party's interests in a case are virtually representative of the interests of a nonparty is one of fact for the trial court." 511 F.2d at 719. In that case we approved a district court's determination that the interests of two government entities were so closely aligned that a prior judgment against one entity bound the other. The proposition that governments may represent private interests in litigation, thereby precluding relitigation, while uncertain at the margin, appears to be an unexceptional special instance of the examples noted in RESTATEMENT (SECOND) OF JUDGMENTS § 41(1)(1982). The facts here permit no inference of virtual representation of interest. As we explained in Pollard v. Cockrell, 578 F.2d 1002, 1008–09 (5th Cir.1978):

> Virtual representation demands the existence of an express or implied legal relationship in which parties to the first suit are accountable to nonparties who file a subsequent suit raising identical issues.... In the instant case ... the [first] plaintiffs were in no sense legally accountable to the [second] plaintiffs; they shared only an abstract interest in enjoining enforcement of the ordinance. The [first] plaintiffs sued in their individual capacities and not as representatives of a judicially certified class. Representation by the same attorneys cannot furnish the requisite alignment of interest.

Thus, in *Pollard* we rejected the contention that one group of massage parlor owners were bound by a judgment in a prior lawsuit brought by another group. Virtual representation was rejected despite nearly identical pleadings filed by the groups and representation by common attorneys. The court's omnibus order here amounts to collater-

---

5. Indeed, the plaintiffs were compelled to prove little, since the trial court entered its omnibus order on its own motion without any evidentiary hearing.

al estoppel based on similar legal positions—a proposition that has been properly rejected by at least one other district court that considered the identical issue. Mooney v. Fibreboard Corp., 485 F.Supp. 242, 249 (E.D.Tex.1980). We agree with the Texas Supreme Court that "privity is not established by the mere fact that persons may happen to be interested in the same question or in proving the same state of facts," Benson v. Wanda Petroleum Co., 468 S.W.2d 361, 363 (Tex.1971), and hold that the trial court's actions here transgress the bounds of due process.

Our conclusion likewise pertains to those defendants who, while originally parties to the *Borel* litigation, settled before trial. * * * The plaintiffs here did not show that any of these defendants settled out of the *Borel* litigation after the entire trial had run its course and only the judicial act of signing a final known adverse judgment remained. Such action would suggest settlement precisely to avoid offensive collateral estoppel and, in an appropriate case, might preclude relitigation. All the indications here are, however, that the defendants in question settled out of the case early because of, for example, lack of product identification. Like the non-*Borel* defendants, these defendants have likewise been deprived of their day in court by the trial court's omnibus order.

The *Borel* Defendants

The propriety of estopping the six defendants in this case who were parties to *Borel* poses more difficult questions. In ascertaining the precise preclusive effect of a prior judgment on a particular issue, we have often referred to the requirements set out, *inter alia,* in International Association of Machinists & Aerospace Workers v. Nix, 512 F.2d 125, 132 (5th Cir.1975), and cases cited therein. The party asserting the estoppel must show that: (1) the issue to be concluded is identical to that involved in the prior action; (2) in the prior action the issue was "actually litigated"; and (3) the determination made of the issue in the prior action must have been necessary and essential to the resulting judgment. If it appears that a judgment may have been based on more than one of several distinctive matters in litigation and there is no indication which issue it was based on or which issue was fully litigated, such judgment will not preclude, under the doctrine of collateral estoppel, relitigation of any of the issues. FEDERAL PROCEDURE, LAWYERS ED. § 51.218 at 151 (1981)(citations omitted). *See also, e.g.,* MOORE'S ¶ 0.442; RESTATEMENT (SECOND) JUDGMENTS § 29, comment a (1982).

Appellants argue that *Borel* did not necessarily decide that asbestos-containing insulation products were unreasonably dangerous because of failure to warn. According to appellants, the general *Borel* verdict, based on general instructions and special interrogatories, permitted the jury to ground strict liability on the bases of failures to test, of unsafeness for intended use, of failures to inspect, or of unsafeness of the product. Strict liability on the basis of failure to warn, although argued to the jury by trial counsel for the plaintiff in *Borel,* was, in the view of the appellants, never formally presented in the jury instructions and therefore was not essential to the *Borel* jury verdict.

Appellants' view has some plausibility. The special interrogatories answered by the *Borel* jury were general and not specifically directed to failure to warn. Indeed, as we discussed at length in our review of the *Borel* judgment, the jury was instructed in terms of "breach of warranty." 493 F.2d at 1091. Although the jury was accurately instructed as to "strict liability in tort" as defined in section 402A of the RESTATEMENT (SECOND) OF TORTS, that phrase was never specifically mentioned in the jury's interrogatories. It is also true that the general instructions to the *Borel* jury on the plaintiff's causes of action did not charge on failure to warn, except in connection with negligence. Yet appellants' argument in its broadest form must ultimately fail. We concluded in *Borel*:

> The jury found that the unreasonably dangerous condition of the defendants' product was the proximate cause of Borel's injury. This necessarily included a finding that, had adequate warnings been provided, Borel would have chosen to avoid the danger.

493 F.2d at 1093. As the appellants at times concede in their briefs, "if *Borel* stands for any rule at all, it is that defendants have a duty to warn the users of their products of the long-term dangers attendant upon its use, including the danger of an occupational disease." Indeed, the first sentence in our *Borel* opinion states that that case involved "the scope of an asbestos manufacturer's duty to warn industrial insulation workers of dangers associated with the use of asbestos." *Id.* at 1081. *See also* 493 F.2d at 1105 (*on reh'g*). Our conclusion in *Borel* was grounded in that trial court's jury instructions concerning proximate cause and defective product.... Close reading of these instructions convinced our panel in *Borel* that a failure to warn was necessarily implicit in the jury's verdict. While the parties invite us to reconsider our holding in *Borel* that failure to warn grounded the jury's strict liability finding in that case, we cannot, even if we were so inclined, displace a prior decision of this court absent reconsideration *en banc*. Further, there is authority for the proposition that once an appellate court has disposed of a case on the basis of one of several alternative issues that may have grounded a trial court's judgment, the issue decided on appeal is conclusively established for purposes of issue preclusion. *See* MOORE'S ¶ 0.416(2) at 2231, ¶ 443(5) at 3921 n.10; IRO v. Republic SS Corp., 189 F.2d 858, 862 (4th Cir.1951). Nonetheless, we must ultimately conclude that the judgment in *Borel* cannot estop even the *Borel* defendants in this case for three interrelated reasons.

First, after review of the issues decided in *Borel,* we conclude that *Borel,* while conclusive as to the general matter of a duty to warn on the part of manufacturers of asbestos-containing insulation products, is ultimately ambiguous as to certain key issues. As the authors of the RESTATEMENT (SECOND)-JUDGMENTS § 29, comment g (1982), have noted, collateral estoppel is inappropriate where the prior judgment is ambivalent:

The circumstances attending the determination of an issue in the first action may indicate that it could reasonably have been resolved otherwise if those circumstances were absent. Resolution of the issue in question may have entailed reference to such matters as the intention, knowledge, or comparative responsibility of the parties in relation to each other.... In these and similar situations, taking the prior determination at face value for purposes of the second action would extend the effects of imperfections in the adjudicative process beyond the limits of the first adjudication, within which they are accepted only because of the practical necessity of achieving finality.

The *Borel* jury decided that Borel, an industrial insulation worker who was exposed to fibers from his employer's insulation products over a 33–year period (from 1936 to 1969), was entitled to have been given fair warning that asbestos dust may lead to asbestosis, mesothelioma, and other cancers. The jury dismissed the argument that the danger was obvious and regarded as conclusive the fact that Borel testified that he did not know that inhaling asbestos dust could cause serious injuries until his doctor so advised him in 1969. The jury necessarily found "that, had adequate warnings been provided, Borel would have chosen to avoid the danger." 493 F.2d at 1093. In *Borel,* the evidence was that the industry as a whole issued no warnings at all concerning its insulation products prior to 1964, that Johns–Manville placed a warnings label on packages of its products in 1964, and that Fibreboard and Rubberoid placed warnings on their products in 1966. *Id.* at 1104.

Given these facts, it is impossible to determine what the *Borel* jury decided about when a duty to warn attached. Did the jury find the defendants liable because their warnings after 1966, when they acknowledged that they knew the dangers of asbestosis, were insufficiently explicit as to the grave risks involved? If so, as appellants here point out, the jury may have accepted the state of the art arguments provided by the defendants in *Borel*—i.e., that the defendants were not aware of the danger of asbestosis until the 1960's. Even under this view, there is a second ambiguity: was strict liability grounded on the fact that the warnings issued, while otherwise sufficient, never reached the insulator in the field? If so, perhaps the warnings, while insufficient as to insulation workers like Borel, were sufficient to alert workers further down the production line who may have seen the warnings—such as the carpenters and pipefitters in this case. Alternatively, even if the *Borel* jury decided that failure to warn before 1966 grounded strict liability, did the duty attach in the 1930's when the "hazard of asbestosis as a pneumoconiotic dust was universally accepted," *id.* at 1083, or in 1965, when documentary evidence was presented of the hazard of asbestos insulation products to the installers of these products?

As we noted in *Borel*, strict liability because of failure to warn is based on a determination of the manufacturer's reasonable knowledge:

[I]n cases such as the instant case, the manufacturer is held to the knowledge and skill of an expert. This is relevant in determining (1) whether the manufacturer knew or should have known the danger, and (2) whether the manufacturer was negligent in failing to communicate this superior knowledge to the user or consumer of its product.... The manufacturer's status as expert means that at a minimum he must keep abreast of scientific knowledge, discoveries, and advances and is presumed to know what is imparted thereby.

493 F.2d at 1089. Thus, the trial judge in *Borel* instructed the jury that the danger "must have been reasonably foreseen by the manufacturer." *Id.* at 1090. As both this instruction and the ambiguities in the *Borel* verdict demonstrate, a determination that a particular product is so unreasonably hazardous as to require a warning of its dangers is not an absolute. Such a determination is necessarily relative to the scientific knowledge generally known or available to the manufacturer at the time the product in question was sold or otherwise placed in the stream of commerce.

Not all the plaintiffs in this case were exposed to asbestos-containing insulation products over the same 30–year period as plaintiff Borel. Not all plaintiffs here are insulation workers isolated from the warnings issued by some of the defendants in 1964 and 1966. Some of the products may be different from those involved in *Borel*. Our opinion in *Borel*, "limited to determining whether there [was] a conflict in substantial evidence sufficient to create a jury question," did not resolve that as a matter of fact all manufacturers of asbestos-containing insulation products had a duty to warn as of 1936, and all failed to warn adequately after 1964. Although we determined that the jury must have found a violation of the manufacturers' duty to warn, we held only that the jury could have grounded strict liability on the absence of a warning prior to 1964 or "could have concluded that the [post–1964 and post–1966] 'cautions' were not warnings in the sense that they adequately communicated to Borel and other insulation workers knowledge of the dangers to which they were exposed so as to give them a choice of working or not working with a dangerous product." 493 F.2d at 1104. As we have already had occasion to point out in *Migues v. Fibreboard Corp.*, 662 F.2d at 1188–89, our opinion in *Borel* merely approved of the various ways the jury could have come to a conclusion concerning strict liability for failure to warn. We did not say that any of the specific alternatives that the jury had before it were necessary or essential to its verdict.

The *only* determination made by this court in *Borel* was that, based upon the evidence in that case, the jury's findings could not be said to be incorrect as a matter of law. But this Court certainly did not decide that every jury presented with the same facts would be compelled to reach the conclusion reached by the *Borel* jury: that asbestos was unreasonably dangerous. Such a holding would have been not only unnecessary, it would also have been unwarranted.

In *Borel,* this Court said: "the jury was *entitled* to find that the danger to Borel and other insulation workers from inhaling asbestos dust was foreseeable to the defendants at the time the products causing Borel's injuries were sold," 493 F.2d at 1093 (emphasis added).... This Court did not say that, as a matter of law, the danger of asbestos inhalation was so hidden from every asbestos worker in every situation as to create a duty to warn on the part of all asbestos manufacturers. On rehearing, this Court held that although some asbestos products used by plaintiff Borel contained warnings, there was sufficient evidence that the warnings were inadequate to inform workers of the actual dangers posed by asbestos inhalation to justify submission of that issue to the jury. 493 F.2d at 1105. This Court did not state that every jury would be required, as a matter of law, to find such warnings inadequate.

In sum, this Court held in *Borel* only that the *Borel* jury, on the evidence presented to it, could have found that asbestos products unaccompanied by adequate warnings were unreasonably dangerous. The proposition that all juries presented with similar evidence regarding asbestos products would be compelled to find those products unreasonably dangerous was not presented in *Borel,* and therefore, this Court did not reach it. Since *stare decisis* is accorded only those issues necessarily decided by a court in reaching its result, the District Court erred in overreading the holding of our opinion in *Borel.*

Id. (emphasis in original). Like *stare decisis,* collateral estoppel applies only to issues of fact or law necessarily decided by a prior court. Since we cannot say that *Borel* necessarily decided, as a matter of fact, that all manufacturers of asbestos-containing insulation products knew or should have known of the dangers of their particular products at all relevant times, we cannot justify the trial court's collaterally estopping the defendants from presenting evidence as to the state of the art.

Even if we are wrong as to the ambiguities of the *Borel* judgment, there is a second, equally important, reason to deny collateral estoppel effect to it: the presence of inconsistent verdicts. In *Parklane Hosiery,* 439 U.S. at 330–31, the Court noted that collateral estoppel is improper and "unfair" to a defendant "if the judgment relied upon as a basis for the estoppel is itself inconsistent with one or more previous judgments in favor of the defendant." *Id.* at 330. *Accord* RESTATEMENT (SECOND) JUDGMENTS § 29(4)(1982).[13] Not only does issue preclusion in such cases appear arbitrary to a defendant who has had favorable judgments on the same issue, it also undermines the premise that different juries reach

---

13. The injustice of applying collateral estoppel in cases involving mass torts is especially obvious. Thus, in *Parklane* the Court cited Prof. Currie's "familiar example": "A railroad collision injures 50 passengers all of whom bring separate actions against the railroad. After the railroad wins the first 25 suits, a plaintiff wins in suit 26. Professor Currie argues that offensive use of collateral estoppel should not be applied so as to allow plaintiffs 27 through 50 automatically to recover." 439 U.S. at 331 n.14, 99 S.Ct. at 651 n.14, *citing* Currie, *Mutuality of Estoppel: Limits of the* Bernhard *Doctrine,* 9 Stan.L.Rev. 281, 304 (1957).

equally valid verdicts. *See* RESTATEMENT (SECOND) JUDGMENTS § 29, comment f (1982). One jury's determination should not, merely because it comes later in time, bind another jury's determination of an issue over which there are equally reasonable resolutions of doubt.

The trial court was aware of the problem and referred to *Flatt v. Johns Manville Sales Corp.*, 488 F.Supp. at 841, a prior opinion by the same court. In *Flatt* the court admitted that Johns–Manville had "successfully defended several asbestos lawsuits in the recent past" but stated that "lawsuits in which Johns–Manville has prevailed have been decided on the basis that there was insufficient exposure to asbestos dust, or alternatively, the plaintiff, or decedent, did not contract asbestosis or mesothelioma." *Id.* Given the information made available to us in this appeal, we must conclude that the trial court in *Flatt* and in the proceeding below was inadequately informed about the nature of former asbestos litigation. On appeal, the parties inform us that there have been approximately 70 similar asbestos cases thus far tried around the country. Approximately half of these seem to have been decided in favor of the defendants.[14] A court able to say that the approximately 35 suits decided in favor of asbestos manufacturers were all decided on the basis of insufficient exposure on the part of the plaintiff or failure to demonstrate an asbestos-related disease would be clairvoyant. Indeed, the appellants inform us of several products liability cases in which the state of the art question was fully litigated, yet the asbestos manufacturers were found not liable. Although it is usually not possible to say with certainty what these juries based their verdicts on, in at least some of the cases the verdict for the defendant was not based on failure to prove exposure or failure to show an asbestos-related disease. In Starnes v. Johns–Manville Corp., No. 2075–122 (E.D.Tenn.1977), one of the cases cited in *Flatt v. Johns Manville Sales Corp.*, the court's charge to the jury stated that it was "undisputed that as a result of inhaling materials containing asbestos, Mr. Starnes contracted the disease known as asbestosis." The verdict for the defendant in Starnes must mean, *inter alia,* that the jury found the insulation products involved in that case not unreasonably dangerous. This court takes judicial notice of these inconsistent or ambiguous verdicts pursuant to Fed.R.Evid. 201(d). We conclude that the court erred in arbitrarily choosing one of these verdicts, that in Borel, as the bellwether.

Finally, we conclude that even if the *Borel* verdict had been unambiguous and the sole verdict issued on point, application of collateral estoppel would still be unfair with regard to the *Borel* defendants because it is very doubtful that these defendants could have foreseen that their $68,000 liability to plaintiff Borel would foreshadow multimillion dollar asbestos liability. As noted in *Parklane,* it would be unfair to apply collateral estoppel "if a defendant in the first action is sued for small or nominal damages (since) he may have little incentive to defend vigorously, particularly if future lawsuits are not foreseeable." 439 U.S.

---

14. The parties also inform us that there are at least seven judgments in favor of several of the defendants in this case alone.

at 330, 99 S.Ct. at 651. While in absolute terms a judgment for $68,000 hardly appears nominal, the Supreme Court's citation of Berner v. British Commonwealth Pacific Airlines, 346 F.2d 532 (2d Cir.1965), *cert. denied,* 382 U.S. 983, 86 S.Ct. 559, 15 L.Ed.2d 472 (1966)(application of collateral estoppel denied where defendant did not appeal an adverse judgment awarding damages of $35,000 and defendant was later sued for over $7 million), suggests that the matter is relative. The reason the district court here applied collateral estoppel is precisely because early cases like *Borel* have opened the floodgates to an enormous, unprecedented volume of asbestos litigation. According to a recent estimate, there are over 3,000 asbestos plaintiffs in the Eastern District of Texas alone and between 7,500 and 10,000 asbestos cases pending in United States District Courts around the country. The omnibus order here involves 58 pending cases, and the many plaintiffs involved in this case are each seeking $2.5 million in damages. Such a staggering potential liability could not have been foreseen by the *Borel* defendants. *See* McCarty v. Johns–Manville Sales Corp., 502 F.Supp. 335, 339 (S.D.Miss. 1980).

The trial court's application of issue preclusion to the "fact" that asbestos is in all cases a competent producing cause of mesothelioma and asbestosis involves similar problems. *Borel* dealt with the disease-causing aspects of asbestos dust generated by insulation materials. That case did not determine as a matter of fact that because airborne asbestos dust and fibers from thermal insulation materials are hazardous, all products containing asbestos—in whatever quantity or however encapsulated—are hazardous. The injustice in precluding the "fact" that the generic ingredient asbestos invariably and in every use or mode causes cancer is clearest in the case of appellant Garlock. Garlock points out that its products, unlike the loosely woven thermal insulation materials in *Borel* that, when merely handled, emitted large quantities of airborne asbestos dust and fibers, are linoleum-type products in which the asbestos is encapsulated in a rubber-like coating. According to Garlock, its gasket products do not release significant amounts of dust or fibers into the air and have never been demonstrated to be dangerous in installation, use, or removal. Certainly, defendants ought to be free, even after *Borel,* to present evidence of the scientific knowledge associated with their particular product without being prejudiced by a conclusive presumption that asbestos in all forms causes cancer. The court regarded collateral estoppel in this context as precluding merely the "can it" question rather than the "did it" question. 509 F.Supp. at 1362. The problem is that the "can it" and "did it" questions cannot in this instance be so easily segregated, and a determination that asbestos generally is hazardous threatens to undermine a defendant's possibly legitimate defense that its product was not scientifically known to be hazardous, now or at relevant times in the past. If the trial court's application of issue preclusion on the generic danger of asbestos is not meant to burden a defendant's ability to present such evidence, then we fail to see the intended usefulness of the court's action.

For much the same reasons, the court's alternative justification for this aspect of its omnibus order—relying upon judicial notice of adjudicative fact under Fed.R.Evid. 201(b)(2) and (c)—is likewise improper. As the court itself concedes, Rule 201 relates to medical facts not subject to reasonable dispute. In Franklin Life Insurance Co. v. William J. Champion & Co., 350 F.2d 115, 130 (6th Cir.1965), *cert. denied,* 384 U.S. 928, 86 S.Ct. 1445, 16 L.Ed.2d 531 (1966), the court took judicial notice of the fact that cancer does not manifest itself quickly but lies dormant, typically for long periods. As in *Franklin,* judicial notice applies to self-evident truths that no reasonable person could question, truisms that approach platitudes or banalities. The proposition that asbestos causes cancer, because it is inextricably linked to a host of disputed issues—*e.g.,* can mesothelioma arise without exposure to asbestos, is the sale of asbestos insulation products definitely linked to carcinoma in the general population, was this manufacturer reasonably unaware of the asbestos hazards in 1964—is not at present so self-evident a proposition as to be subject to judicial notice. The rule of judicial notice "contemplates there is to be no evidence before the jury in disproof." Fed.R.Evid. 201, Adv. Comm. Note g (1975). Surely where there is evidence on both sides of an issue the matter is subject to reasonable dispute. Judicial notice was therefore inappropriate here.

Like the court in *Migues,* we too sympathize with the district court's efforts to streamline the enormous asbestos caseload it faces. None of what we say here is meant to cast doubt on any possible alternative ways to avoid reinventing the asbestos liability wheel. We reiterate the *Migues* court's invitation to district courts to attempt innovative methods for trying these cases. We hold today only that courts cannot read *Borel* to stand for the proposition that, as matters of fact, asbestos products are unreasonably dangerous or that asbestos as a generic element is in all products a competent producing cause of cancer. To do otherwise would be to elevate judicial expedience over considerations of justice and fair play.

Reversed.

LYNCH v. MERRELL–NATIONAL LABORATORIES

United States Court of Appeals, First Circuit, 1987.
830 F.2d 1190.

Before CAMPBELL, CHIEF JUDGE, TORRUELLA and NOONAN, CIRCUIT JUDGES.

NOONAN, CIRCUIT JUDGE.

Margo Lynch, the minor daughter of Dennis and Margaret Lynch, and her parents, all citizens of Massachusetts, sue Merrell–National Laboratories, Division of Richardson–Merrell, Inc., an Ohio corporation. Jurisdiction is based on diversity of citizenship; Massachusetts law applies. The case is one of a number which have arisen in which the drug Bendectin is alleged to have caused a birth defect. The district court gave judgment for the defendant. Lynch v. Merrell–National

Laboratories, 646 F.Supp. 856 (D.Mass.1986). We affirm the district court.

FACTS

Bendectin, as originally designed, was a combination of three components: dicyclomine hydrochloride, an antispasmodic drug, earlier marketed under the name Bentyl; doxylamine succinate, an antihistamine, earlier marketed under the name Decapryn; and pyridoxine (Vitamin B6). The composite was approved by the Food and Drug Administration for sale in the United States in 1956 for use in alleviating morning sickness in pregnancy. In 1976 the composition was altered to omit Bentyl. The defendant was its manufacturer. In 1983, in the face of a host of lawsuits and some congressional criticism, the defendant withdrew it from the market.

In the fourth week of her pregnancy, in the last week of June 1974, Margaret Lynch began experiencing severe 24–hour-a-day morning sickness. Her physician, Ambler Garnett, Jr. of Newburyport, prescribed Bendectin, which she then took for the remainder of her term.

On February 17, 1975, Margaret's daughter Margo was born. She was born without a right hand and without the lower portion of her right forearm. She needed special medical care, which her parents provided. Her losses were, of course, permanent. She and her parents suffered from the cruel injury.

William J. Driscoll III, the obstetrician-gynecologist who delivered Margo, had no opinion as to the cause. Eventually, however, the Lynches came to the conclusion that Bendectin was the cause. On February 10, 1985 they brought suit against its maker, alleging that the manufacturer had negligently designed, developed, selected materials for, manufactured, assembled, tested, inspected, advertised, sold, promoted and distributed the drug; had negligently failed to warn its users; had falsely and misleadingly advertised it; had breached both express and implied warranties of safety; and had put on the market a drug dangerous and defective in design. They sought total damages of $7.5 million.

PROCEEDINGS

The Lynches' case was transferred to the Southern District of Ohio where since 1982 similar cases had been brought for pre-trial proceedings under Judge Carl Rubin. Over 1,000 cases were consolidated for this purpose under the authority of 28 U.S.C. § 1407. The Lynches stipulated to be bound by the pretrial discovery in these proceedings. Given the option, however, of joining in the trial or having their case remanded to the district court in Massachusetts, the Lynches elected the latter course.

The consolidated cases proceeded to trial before Judge Rubin in Cincinnati. Just as trial began, he certified the plaintiffs as a class for settlement; the certification was reversed by mandamus. In re Bendectin Products Liability Litigation, 749 F.2d 300 (6th Cir.1984). After a trial on the merits, the jury found for the defendant, Merrell–National Laboratories. In re Richardson–Merrell, Inc. "Bendectin" Products Liability Litigation, 624 F.Supp. 1212 (S.D.Ohio 1985), *appeal pending*.

In Boston in 1986 the defendant moved for summary judgment against the Lynches. The district court granted the motion, ruling that the Lynches were collaterally estopped by the judgment in the multi-district litigation and that in any event they had presented insufficient proof of causation to permit a reasonable trier of fact to conclude that Bendectin had caused the birth defect of Margo Lynch. * * * The Lynches appealed. [portions of the opinion dealing with the admissibility of expert witness testimony have been omitted—*ed.*]

* * *

ANALYSIS

I. *Collateral estoppel.* The question is close and the thoughtful analysis by the district court all but compelling. A preliminary question is whether, in litigation based on diversity of citizenship, the doctrine of estoppel to be applied is federal or state. *See Burbank, "Interjurisdictional Preclusion, Full Faith and Credit and Federal Common Law: A General Approach"* 71 Corn.L.R. 733 (1986); Degnan, *"Federalized Res Judicata,"* 85 Yale L.J. 741 (1976). The parties and the district court have assumed that the law is federal. But the teaching of Erie R. Co. v. Tompkins, 304 U.S. 64, 58 S.Ct. 817, 82 L.Ed. 1188 (1938) is clear as to the law to be applied in diversity:

> Except in matters governed by the Federal Constitution or by Acts of Congress, the law to be applied in any case is the law of the State ... There is no federal general common law.

The law on collateral estoppel is as substantive in its effect as the law of contracts or torts. It is not a law created by the Constitution or an Act of Congress. This court has applied Massachusetts law on collateral estoppel in a case where jurisdiction rested on diversity and an earlier case, relied on by the defendant, had been decided in a Massachusetts court. Standard Accident Ins. Co. v. Doiron, 170 F.2d 206, 207 (1st Cir.1948). On the other hand, the argument must be considered that the federal system has the power and duty to protect its own judgments, and that when the effect of a federal judgment is at issue, even in a diversity action, federal law must govern. Kern v. Hettinger, 303 F.2d 333, 340 (2d Cir.1962); *cf.* Byrd v. Blue Ridge Cooperative, 356 U.S. 525, 537, 78 S.Ct. 893, 900, 2 L.Ed.2d 953 (1958).

We need not resolve the question for every possible context. In this case involving the effect of multi-district litigation in a federal court, we believe the same result would follow under either federal or state law. Massachusetts has abandoned the old requirement of strict mutuality and permits a defendant to bind a plaintiff by the plaintiff's previous defeat in another case presenting the same issue, Home Owners Federal

Sav. & Loan Ass'n v. Northwestern Fire & Marine Insurance Co., 354 Mass. 448, 238 N.E.2d 55 (1968); and Massachusetts permits a plaintiff to bind a defendant by a previous criminal conviction. Aetna Casualty and Surety Co. v. Niziolek, 395 Mass. 737, 481 N.E.2d 1356, 1361 (1985). But so far Massachusetts has not permitted a defendant to bind a plaintiff by the defendant's previous victory in another case presenting the same issue. Federally, the traditional requirement of mutuality has been eliminated to permit a defendant to invoke estoppel against a plaintiff who lost on the same issue to an earlier defendant, Blonder-Tongue Laboratories, Inc. v. University of Illinois Foundation, 402 U.S. 313, 91 S.Ct. 1434, 28 L.Ed.2d 788 (1971), and to permit a plaintiff to invoke estoppel against a defendant who lost to a prior plaintiff. Parklane Hosiery Co. v. Shore, 439 U.S. 322, 99 S.Ct. 645, 58 L.Ed.2d 552 (1979).

The preference of both state and federal decisions for judicial economy might well be read as the district court read the federal cases, to indicate that mutuality should also be dispensed with where, as here, a plaintiff presents precisely the issue on which the defendant has prevailed against a prior plaintiff. Such an extension of estoppel has additional appeal where, as here, the plaintiffs had ample opportunity to join the multi-district litigation and chose not to do so, perhaps believing that if the defendant lost in Cincinnati the plaintiffs would avail themselves of that victory while if the defendant won, the plaintiffs would have a second shot in Boston.

Nonetheless we do not believe that either federal or state law would warrant the application of collateral estoppel in the present context. In rejecting certification of the class, the Sixth Circuit noted the teaching of *Parklane Hosiery,* 439 U.S. at 330, 99 S.Ct. at 651, that later plaintiffs could not invoke to their benefit a favorable result in mass tort litigation. *In re Bendectin Products Liability Litigation,* 749 F.2d at 305. If later plaintiffs could not, why should the defendant? Judge Rubin himself, dealing with plaintiffs who had opted out of the multi-district litigation, refused to give estoppel effect to the ultimate result in favor of the defendant. In re Bendectin Cases, No. 85–0996 (E.D.Mich.1986). Estoppel should not be applied unless the plaintiffs had a fair and full opportunity to litigate. *Parklane Hosiery,* at 327, n. 7, 99 S.Ct. at 649, n. 7, *citing Blonder–Tongue* at 329, 91 S.Ct. at 1443. But the plaintiffs were allowed to think that they could withdraw from Cincinnati and lose nothing. They did not have a fair opportunity when they understood that their withdrawal would not prejudice them. If they were now bound, the multi-district litigation would in effect have been a class action leaving the Lynches no true option. We believe that their freedom to withdraw and come back to Boston was not illusory.

IN RE BENDECTIN PRODUCTS LIABILITY LITIGATION

United States District Court, Eastern District of Michigan, 1990.
732 F.Supp. 744.

Order

Carl B. Rubin, Chief Judge.

This matter is before the Court on a motion for summary judgment pursuant to Fed.R.Civ.P. 56 filed by defendant Merrell Dow Pharmaceuticals, Inc. (Merrell Dow). Plaintiffs have filed an opposing memorandum and the defendant has subsequently replied.

Plaintiffs filed these products liability cases, now consolidated for trial before this Court, seeking damages for birth defects allegedly sustained by the minor plaintiffs as a result of their mothers' ingestion of the drug, Bendectin, during pregnancy. Merrell Dow, the manufacturer of Bendectin, moves for summary judgment of these cases on the theory that plaintiffs should be collaterally estopped from litigating the issue of whether Bendectin causes birth defects. Merrell Dow further argues that plaintiffs, as a matter of law, cannot demonstrate that a genuine issue of material fact exists as to the element of causation.

* * *

Merrell Dow contends that the principles of collateral estoppel bar plaintiffs from litigating their claims. Defendant asserts that the consolidated trial held before this Court in February and March, 1985 ("the MDL Common Issues Trial") provided plaintiffs with a fair opportunity to be heard on the issue of whether Bendectin causes birth defects.[2] [ ] Merrell Dow further contends that based on the extensive history of the Bendectin litigation in which juries have returned verdicts in favor of Merrell Dow, or in the alternative, judges have granted defendant's motions for JNOV, relitigation of the causation issue is "fruitless." Since the vast majority of these trials have resulted in final verdicts or judgments for Merrell Dow, the defendant submits that the causation issue has been "exhaustively" litigated and "overwhelmingly" decided in the defendant's favor.

The Defensive Use of Collateral Estoppel

The doctrine of collateral estoppel provides that an actual and necessary determination of an issue by a court of competent jurisdiction is conclusive in subsequent cases based upon a different cause of action but involving a party to the prior litigation. Parklane Hosiery Co. v.

2. The MDL Common Issues Trial was held before this Court and tried on the sole issue of whether Bendectin causes birth defects. The jury returned a verdict in favor of Merrell Dow. In re Richardson–Merrell, Inc., "Bendectin Products Litigation," 624 F.Supp. 1212 (S.D.Ohio 1985), aff'd, 857 F.2d 290 (6th Cir.1988), cert. denied, Hoffman v. Merrell Dow Pharmaceuticals, Inc., 488 U.S. 1006, 109 S.Ct. 788, 102 L.Ed.2d 779 (1989).

Shore, 439 U.S. 322, 326 n.5, 99 S.Ct. 645, 649, n. 5, 58 L.Ed.2d 552 (1979). Federal law not state law governs the inquiry of whether a prior federal court judgment collaterally estops the adjudication of a subsequent federal diversity action involving identical issues. Cemer v. Marathon Oil Co., 583 F.2d 830, 831 (6th Cir.1978). Previously, the scope of collateral estoppel was limited by the doctrine of mutuality which precluded either party from using a prior judgment as an estoppel against the other unless both parties were bound by that judgment. Bigelow v. Old Dominion Copper Co., 225 U.S. 111, 32 S.Ct. 641, 56 L.Ed. 1009 (1912). The doctrine of mutuality has been eroded, Blonder–Tongue Laboratories, Inc. v. University of Illinois Foundation, 402 U.S. 313, 91 S.Ct. 1434, 28 L.Ed.2d 788 (1971), and a defendant may now preclude a nonparty to the previous suit from contesting an issue a plaintiff in the prior suit has already litigated and lost if the nonparty plaintiff has had a full and fair opportunity to be heard on the issue. *Id.* at 329.

Nonparties to a prior action have had a "full and fair opportunity" to litigate if they:

> [A]ssume control over litigation in which they have a direct financial or proprietary interest and then seek to redetermine issues previously resolved ... [T]he persons for whose benefit and at whose direction a cause of action is litigated cannot be said to be "strangers to the cause ... [O]ne who prosecutes or defends a suit in the name of another to establish and protect his own right, or who assists in the prosecution or defense of an action in aid of some interest of his own ... is as much bound ... as he would be if he had been a party to the record."

Montana v. United States, 440 U.S. 147, 99 S.Ct. 970, 59 L.Ed.2d 210 (1979). The rule derived from the Supreme Court's examination of this issue is that a nonparty may be estopped if (1) he had a direct financial or proprietary interest in the prior litigation; and (2) he assumed control over the prior litigation. Virginia Hosp. Ass'n. v. Baliles, 830 F.2d 1308, 1312 (4th Cir.1987); *see also* Alman v. Danin, 801 F.2d 1, 4–5 (1st Cir.1986); 1B J. Moore, J. Lucas and T. Currier, MOORE'S FEDERAL PRACTICE ¶ 0.411[6], at 445 (2d ed.1984). The *Montana* rule ensures that the nonparty was afforded his right to due process. Hardy v. Johns–Manville Sales Corp., 681 F.2d 334, 338 (5th Cir.1982). If a nonparty had a direct financial or proprietary interest in the prior litigation, he had an incentive to litigate the issues raised in the previous suit fully. *Virginia Hosp. Ass'n,* at 1312. If the nonparty also had control over the prior litigation, he had the ability to ensure that the issues were fully litigated at that time. *Id.*

Merrell Dow recites a different standard to be employed when courts examine the collateral estoppel effect of a prior judgment on nonparties,[4]

---

4. Merrell Dow asserts that a nonparty may be held bound by the results of prior litigation where (1) the prior litigation was conducted on a representative basis; (2) a common interest is involved in both the prior and current action; or (3) the nonpar-

ignoring the Supreme Court precedent pronounced in *Montana* and its progeny. Nonetheless, the Court must evaluate the appropriateness of the application of collateral estoppel to plaintiffs in this consolidated action using the *Montana* rule.

Plaintiffs in these cases had no direct financial or proprietary interest in the outcome of the MDL Common Issues Trial or in any subsequent individual Bendectin action against Merrell Dow. To the contrary, those plaintiffs who specifically opted out of the MDL Common Issues Trial withdrew precisely so that they would not be bound by its outcome. Upon their withdrawal, plaintiffs severed any financial interest they previously had in the outcome of that consolidated trial. *See* Lynch v. Merrell–National Laboratories, 830 F.2d 1190, 1193 (1st Cir. 1987); *see also* In re Bendectin Cases, No. 85–0996, 1986 WL 20466 (E.D.Mich.1986). Plaintiffs' undeniable concern for a favorable outcome to the MDL Common Issues Trial or to other *Bendectin* trials does not constitute a financial or proprietary interest in the outcome. Mere academic interest in the determination of a question of law in a prior suit, or even a substantial interest in establishing favorable precedent under the doctrine of *stare decisis,* simply does not give rise to the presumption of financial or proprietary interest. *Virginia Hosp. Ass'n,* at 1313 *quoting* 1B J. Moore, J. Lucas, & T. Currier, Moore's Federal Practice ¶ 0.411[6], at 446. Plaintiffs in this consolidated action had no financial stake in any previous *Bendectin* case and therefore cannot be estopped from litigating their claims on that basis.

The second inquiry, whether plaintiffs assumed control over any previous *Bendectin* lawsuit, dictates the same finding. Merrell Dow argues that plaintiffs in these cases participated in discovery in the MDL Common Issues Trial, rely on the same evidence presented in that action, and seek to prove the same contention litigated in that consolidated proceeding. This type of participation, however, does not amount to an exercise of control over the prior lawsuit. To have control over litigation, a party must have effective choice over which legal theories and proofs are advanced. Benson and Ford, Inc. v. Wanda Petroleum Co., 833 F.2d 1172, 1174 (5th Cir.1987). Examples of such control are: a president and sole shareholder controls his company; a parent corporation controls its subsidiary; and a liability insurer assumes control of the defense of the insured. *Id.* at 1174; Freeman v. Lester Coggins Trucking, Inc., 771 F.2d 860, 864 n.3 (5th Cir.1985). It is simply not enough that a nonparty supplied an attorney to the previous plaintiff or is represented by the same law firm; participated in consolidated pretrial proceedings; urges the same facts or the same issues; or otherwise participated in the prior action in a limited way. *Benson and Ford, Inc.,* at 1174.

ty has intentionally declined an opportunity to participate as a matter of litigation strategy.

Moreover, plaintiffs in this consolidated action were not adequately represented in the MDL Common Issues Trial because their counsel participated in that proceeding. In the absence of an express or implied legal relationship between plaintiffs in this consolidated action and plaintiffs in the MDL Common Issues Trial, as a matter of law, adequate representation cannot be established. *Id.* at 1175.

Finally, plaintiffs may not be estopped from litigating their claims on the grounds that they had an opportunity to join in the MDL Common Issues Trial. A nonparty is not obliged to seize an available opportunity to participate in pending litigation which addresses a question of concern to the nonparty. *Id.* at 1176. Merrell Dow fails to demonstrate how plaintiffs in these consolidated cases had a direct financial or proprietary interest in the prior *Bendectin* litigation or how they assumed control over previous *Bendectin* cases. Consequently, plaintiffs may not be estopped from litigating their claims in this consolidated action.

* * *

In sum, Merrell Dow fails to advance an adequate basis to support entry of summary judgment in its favor. Plaintiffs may not be collaterally estopped from litigating their claims in this consolidated action. Accordingly, it is hereby ordered that Merrell Dow's motion for summary judgment under Fed.R.Civ.P. 56 is hereby denied.

It is so ordered.

Notes and Questions

1. What is the difference between res judicata (claim preclusion) and collateral estoppel (issue preclusion)? Between defensive collateral estoppel and offensive collateral estoppel? The doctrine of *stare decisis*? With regard to collateral estoppel, what does the doctrine of mutuality require?

The doctrines of collateral estoppel, in particular, present an interesting tension between two normative values: judicial efficiency versus litigant fairness. Until mid-century, most state courts adhered to a strict mutuality requirement in order for either a plaintiff or a defendant to assert collateral estoppel. Justice Roger Traynor of the California Supreme Court accomplished the first inroad on the mutuality doctrine in Bernhard v. Bank of America Nat. Trust & Sav. Ass'n, 19 Cal.2d 807, 122 P.2d 892 (1942), which indicated that a lack of mutuality might not be required for a defensive assertion of collateral estoppel. Notwithstanding Justice Traynor's decision and subsequent inroads on the mutuality requirement in federal court, some states still adhere to the mutuality requirement for assertions of collateral estoppel. In states that still recognize the mutuality rule, what impact does this have on mass tort litigants' ability to avail themselves of preclusion doctrine to relitigate issues previously litigated in similar mass tort cases?

2. The federal courts abandoned the mutuality requirement for defensive assertions of collateral estoppel, *see* Blonder–Tongue Lab., Inc. v. University of Ill. Foundation, 402 U.S. 313, 91 S.Ct. 1434, 28 L.Ed.2d 788 (1971), and in limited circumstances for offensive collateral estoppel, *see*

Parklane Hosiery Co. v. Shore, 439 U.S. 322, 99 S.Ct. 645, 58 L.Ed.2d 552 (1979). What due process and Seventh Amendment concerns does offensive assertion of collateral estoppel entail? In *Parklane Hosiery* the Supreme Court suggested that plaintiffs could take advantage of offensive collateral estoppel provided that certain standards were met for assertion of the offensive preclusion. What concerns do those factors involve? For discussion of the problems entailed in collateral estoppel doctrine, *see generally*, Michael A. Berch, *A Proposal to Permit Collateral Estoppel of Nonparties Seeking Affirmative Relief*, 1979 Ariz.St.L.J. 511 (1979); Lawrence C. George, *Sweet Uses of Adversity:* Parklane Hosiery *and the Collateral Class Action*, 32 Stan.L.Rev. 655 (1980); Aaron Gershonowitz, *Issue Preclusion: The Return of the Multiple Claimant Anomaly*, 14 U.Balt.L.Rev. 227 (1985); Geoffrey C. Hazard, Jr., *Preclusion as to Issues of Law: The Legal System's Interest*, 70 Iowa L.Rev. 81 (1984); Michael C. Sachs, Comment, *Mandatory Intervention: Expansion of Collateral Estoppel in Favor of Single Defendants Against Multiple Plaintiffs in Federal Civil Litigation*, 14 J. Marshall L.Rev. 441 (1981); Jack Ratliff, *Offensive Collateral Estoppel and the Option Effect*, 67 Tex.L.Rev. 63 (1988); and Elinor P. Schroeder, *Relitigation of Common Issues: The Failure of Nonparty Preclusion and an Alternative Proposal*, 67 Iowa L.Rev. 917 (1982).

3. Judge Parker's decisions in *Flatt* and *Hardy* represent an interesting attempt to utilize preclusion doctrine in asbestos mass tort litigation, subsequently repudiated by the Fifth Circuit in *Migues* and *Hardy*. Are the Fifth Circuit's opinions disallowing collateral estoppel convincing? Did Judge Parker suspect that he might be on shaky ground in seeking to apply collateral estoppel to prevent relitigation of certain asbestos issues? What about Judge Parker's alternative theories based on *stare decisis*, and even judicial notice under the evidence rules? *See generally*, Michael D. Green, *The Inability of Offensive Collateral Estoppel to Fulfill Its Promise: An Examination of Estoppel in Asbestos Litigation*, 70 Iowa L.Rev. 141 (1984); Michael A. Pope & Maryann C. Hayes, *The Proper Application of Collateral Estoppel in Toxic Tort Litigation, in* Preparation of a Complex Toxic Tort Chemical or Hazardous Waste Case 127 (1986); and Michael Weinberger, *Collateral Estoppel and the Mass Produced Product: A Proposal*, 15 New Eng.L.Rev. 1 (1980).

4. As the cases demonstrate, attempts to invoke preclusion doctrine to streamline or prevent relitigation have generally met with resistance in the federal courts. Is there no set of facts upon which a plaintiff or defendant might be able to successfully invoke preclusion doctrine in the context of a mass tort case? Doesn't preclusion doctrine seem precisely tailored as an efficient doctrinal means of accomplishing judicial economy in mass tort cases? For discussion of the uses and limitations of preclusion doctrine in the class action context, *see generally*, Roger Furman, Note, *Offensive Assertion of Collateral Estoppel by Persons Opting Out of Class Actions*, 31 Hast.L.J. 1189 (1980); Mark C. Weber, *Preclusion and Procedural Due Process in Rule 23(b) Class Actions*, 21 U.Mich.J.L.Ref. 347 (1988).

Chapter III

MASS TORTS AND FEDERALISM

A. DUAL SYSTEM MASS TORTS: FEDERAL–STATE ISSUES

AMERICAN LAW INSTITUTE, COMPLEX LITIGATION: STATUTORY RECOMMENDATIONS AND ANALYSIS

(1994)

CHAPTER 4: CONSOLIDATION IN STATE COURTS, INTRODUCTORY NOTE

a. *Complex litigation in state courts.* State courts, like federal courts, increasingly are called upon to handle complex cases. For example, many of the thousands of suits filed against the manufacturers of asbestos, DES, and the Dalkon shield have been filed in state courts. To a significant degree this is because joining separate individual related actions in federal courts may be prevented by a lack of complete diversity or the jurisdictional amount requirement. * * *

Reporter's Notes to Comment a

* * *

2. For examples of complex cases that have been filed in state courts, *see, e.g.,* Brown v. Superior Court (Abbott Laboratories), 44 Cal.3d 1049, 245 Cal.Rptr. 412, 751 P.2d 470 (1988)(DES case involving approximately sixty-nine plaintiffs and 170 drug company defendants); Sindell v. Abbott Labs., 26 Cal.3d 588, 163 Cal.Rptr. 132, 607 P.2d 924 (1980), *cert. denied* 449 U.S. 912, 101 S.Ct. 285, 66 L.Ed.2d 140 (1980)(DES case); Kaufman v. Eli Lilly & Co., 65 N.Y.2d 449, 492 N.Y.S.2d 584, 482 N.E.2d 63 (1985)(DES); Martin v. Johns–Manville Corp., 322 Pa.Super. 348, 469 A.2d 655 (1983)(asbestos); Fischer v. Johns–Manville Corp., 103 N.J. 643, 512 A.2d 466 (1986)(asbestos). *See also* In re Bendectin Litigation, 857 F.2d 290 (6th Cir.1988), *cert. denied* 488 U.S. 1006, 109 S.Ct. 788, 102 L.Ed.2d 779 (1989); In re "Agent Orange" Prods. Liability Litigation, 565 F.Supp. 1263 (E.D.N.Y.1983). *See generally,* Sanders, *The Bendectin Litigation: A Case Study in the Life Cycle of Mass Torts,*

43 Hast.L.J. 301 (1992); Schuck, *The Role of Judges in Settling Complex Cases: The* Agent Orange *Example,* 53 U.Chi.L.Rev. 337 (1986); Tannenbaum, *The Pratt–Weinstein Approach to Mass Tort Litigation,* 52 Brook.L.Rev. 455 (1986)(history of *Agent Orange* suit).

Nearly two-thirds of the asbestos cases brought against Johns–Manville in 1984 were in state courts. *See* Parrish, *Asbestos Litigation—The Dimensions of the Problem,* 1984 State Ct. J. 5, *cited in* Note, *The Consolidation of Multistate Litigation in State Courts,* 96 Yale L.J. 1099, 1104 (1987). More than 8,500 asbestos cases were consolidated for trial under Judge Marshall A. Levin of the Baltimore City Circuit Court; jury verdicts in test cases have been rendered on questions of liability and punitive damages, finding liability for three of the six sample plaintiffs against six asbestos manufacturers. *See* A.B.A.J. 18 (Oct. 1992).

* * *

b. *State courts as forums for complex litigation.* Even when diversity jurisdiction limitations are not a bar, litigation in federal courts may not always be the most desirable means of handling complex litigation. First, some believe that federal courts should focus their attention and resources on those cases that involve federal interests, which federal courts are uniquely qualified to hear. When substantive state interests are at issue, forcing all actions regardless of where they were filed into a consolidated federal court action might be thought to raise federalism concerns. * * *

* * *

Examples of cases that particularly lend themselves to adjudication in state courts involve "single disaster" events, area pollution cases, and insurance coverage litigation. Illustratively, following the 1981 collapse of the Hyatt skywalks in Kansas City, lawsuits were filed in both Missouri state and federal courts. Because all discovery would be concentrated in Missouri, witnesses were located there, and Missouri law would be applied to most, if not all, of the cases, a Missouri state court was the appropriate forum for this litigation. In re Federal Skywalk Cases, 680 F.2d 1175 (8th Cir.1982). Similarly, although area pollution litigation may involve parties from many states, the most reasonable forum may be in a court of the state where the injured land is located.

Consolidation in state court may be more problematic in those situations in which a clearly preferred single forum cannot be identified because the parties and events are scattered. Examples include products liability and toxic tort suits, such as DES and asbestos. In these cases a single, clearly ideal forum to handle all the litigation may not exist. Nonetheless, it is important that in those instances in which significant numbers of cases are filed in various state and federal courts across the nation procedures be available to allow the state courts to function effectively in cooperation with their federal and state counterparts in trying to resolve these crises because the federal courts cannot handle them alone.

1. INTERSYSTEM COOPERATION AND FEDERAL ABSTENTION

SCHOMBER v. JEWEL

United States District Court, Northern District of Illinois, 1985.
614 F.Supp. 210.

MEMORANDUM OPINION AND ORDER

GETZENDANNER, DISTRICT JUDGE:

This class action complaint for personal injuries arises out of the 1985 salmonellosis outbreak in the greater Chicago metropolitan area. Plaintiff and named class representative Allison Schomber is an Indiana resident. Defendant Jewel Companies, Inc. ("Jewel") is a New York corporation with its principal place of business in Illinois. Jurisdiction is predicated on diversity of citizenship, 28 U.S.C. § 1332, and the amount in controversy exceeds $10,000 exclusive of interest and costs. The matter is currently before the court on the motion of defendants to dismiss, or alternatively, to stay the action, and the motion of numerous putative class members to intervene as co-plaintiffs.

Facts

Defendant Jewel is engaged in the processing, manufacture, and distribution of food products for resale, including the sale of milk under the brand names Hillfarm and Bluebrook. In 1985, a substantial amount of Hillfarm and Bluebrook 2% Low–Fat Milk was discovered to be contaminated by salmonella bacteria. Plaintiff and other class members are individuals who drank the contaminated milk or are members of the household of those who contracted salmonellosis from drinking the contaminated milk.

The present complaint was filed on May 3, 1985. By that time, approximately 143 individual lawsuits had been filed in the Circuit Court of Cook County, Illinois, and other state courts in both Indiana and Illinois, including a number of putative class actions. All of the Cook County cases have been "consolidated" for pre-trial and discovery purposes before Judge William Quinlan in *In re Salmonella Litigation*, Master File No. 85 L 000000, with all discovery and other pretrial matters to be handled by a Committee of plaintiffs' attorneys. A motion for class certification is also pending before Judge Quinlan. While the present motions were being briefed, the Illinois Supreme Court further consolidated all state cases for discovery purposes, thus in effect "multi-districting" the Illinois cases.

* * *

Motion to Dismiss or Stay

Defendant argues that this court should abstain from deciding this case, or at least plaintiff Schomber's class claims, out of deference to the pending proceedings in the Illinois state courts. This motion depends for its support on the principles developed in Colorado River Water Conservation District v. United States, 424 U.S. 800, 96 S.Ct. 1236, 47 L.Ed.2d 483 (1976), and its progeny. In *Colorado River,* the Supreme Court noted that, despite the "virtually unflagging obligation of the federal courts to exercise the jurisdiction given them," 424 U.S. at 817, 96 S.Ct. at 1246, considerations of judicial economy and federal-state comity may justify abstention in situations involving the contemporaneous exercise of jurisdiction by state and federal courts. *Id.* Although the Court stated that only "exceptional circumstances" would justify a stay of jurisdiction, *id.,* the court upheld the stay in the case at bar, and identified the considerations relevant to such decisions. Those considerations include the desirability of avoiding piecemeal adjudication, the inconvenience of the federal forum, and the order in which jurisdiction was obtained by the respective forums. *Id.* at 818. In Moses H. Cone Memorial Hospital v. Mercury Construction Corp., 460 U.S. 1, 103 S.Ct. 927, 74 L.Ed.2d 765 (1983), the Court additionally stressed the presence or absence of federal law issues and the adequacy of the parallel state court litigation as other factors to be weighed. 460 U.S. at 23, 26, 103 S.Ct. at 941.

As explained in *Moses H. Cone,* a decision to abstain on the basis of parallel state proceedings "does not rest on a mechanical checklist [of the factors identified in *Colorado River*] but on a careful balancing of the important factors as they apply in a given case with the balance heavily weighted in favor of the exercise of jurisdiction." 460 U.S. at 16, 103 S.Ct. at 937. The *Moses H. Cone* Court further stressed that the weight to be given any one factor may vary greatly, depending on the particular factual or legal setting of the action. *Id.* The decision to abstain is within the discretion of the district court. Will v. Calvert Fire Insurance Co., 437 U.S. 655, 663, 98 S.Ct. 2552, 2557, 57 L.Ed.2d 504 (1978).

The balancing encompassed by these two decisions can be best summarized by noting the different results of the two cases. In *Colorado River,* a suit involving federal government claims to water rights, the Court upheld a federal court's deference to state judicial proceedings based on the peculiarly local nature of the matters at stake, and on federal policy, as expressed in the McCarran Amendments, in favor of state court adjudication under such circumstances. In *Moses H. Cone,* by contrast, the Court held it error to stay an action to compel arbitration in deference to a state court contract suit. The court noted that the case involved federal law, that the federal suit had been promptly filed despite the prior initiation of the state court litigation, and that the issue to be decided in federal court—arbitrability—was severable from the larger dispute.

The Seventh Circuit has had numerous opportunities since *Colorado River* to define the scope of the "exceptional circumstances" which justify federal court deference to parallel state proceedings. In Illinois Bell Telephone Co. v. Illinois Commerce Commission, 740 F.2d 566 (7th Cir.1984), the Court affirmed a district court decision not to abstain where the suit involved federal law issues and the state court suit, although initiated first, was no closer to resolution than the federal action. In Microsoftware Computer Systems v. Ontel Corp., 686 F.2d 531 (7th Cir.1982), by contrast, the Court held that the district court abused discretion in not staying suit where the defendant in a New York state court action filed an identical diversity suit in the Northern District of Illinois more than one year after the state court suit was underway. The Court stressed the absence of federal questions and the grand waste of effort that would come from parallel suits in geographically distinct fora. The Court also noted that the New York defendant could have removed the state court suit to federal court, and therefore that granting the stay would cause no diminishment of that party's right to a federal forum. In Board of Education v. Bosworth, 713 F.2d 1316 (7th Cir.1983), the Court upheld abstention where the state court suit was well underway, and the rights to be enforced were local in nature, even though no factor of geographic inconvenience was at stake.

These cases, while adhering to the language of *Colorado River* requiring "exceptional circumstances," indicate that the matter of abstention is largely within the district court's discretion. *Microsoftware Computer Systems*, 686 F.2d at 537. The underlying inquiry is intended to "prevent duplication of judicial effort in two separate court systems and to confine the litigation to the forum able to make the most comprehensive disposition." Calvert Fire Insurance Co. v. American Mutual Reinsurance Co., 600 F.2d 1228 (7th Cir.1979). Accordingly, the courts have implicitly required a finding that the state court is better equipped to deal with the matter at hand, usually because of the extent of progress before granting a stay in deference to state proceedings. For example, where a diversity suit involved special problems in supervising international discovery, the Court upheld the district court decision not to abstain despite the absence of federal issues. Voktas, Inc. v. Central Soya Co., Inc., 689 F.2d 103 (7th Cir.1982). Not always, however, is an implicit finding of state court expertise required. In *Calvert Fire Insurance Co.*, the Court noted that the "vexatious nature of the federal suit" may be properly relied on as a factor compelling deference, despite the presence of securities law claims which were within the exclusive jurisdiction of the federal court. 600 F.2d at 1234.

Plaintiff argues that the above line of cases are irrelevant since neither Schomber herself nor the intervenors are presently parties to the state court litigation. According to plaintiff, the cases are therefore not "parallel" for the doctrine of *Colorado River* to apply. While this argument has some force with respect to Schomber's individual claim, the class allegations in this suit are identical to those pending in state court except for the names of the class representatives. Moreover, in *Colorado River* the federal court plaintiff had only been joined as a party to the state court after its lawsuit had been filed. In this case, plaintiff may herself become bound by the state court class and seeks to represent litigants who are presently before Judge Quinlan. The doctrine of *Colorado River* is therefore fully applicable to plaintiff's action.

Having surveyed the case law, and having found the state and federal suits to be "parallel," the court now applies the factors of *Colorado River* and *Moses H. Cone* to the present case. First is the avoidance of piecemeal litigation. Plaintiff's counsel seeks to certify a class of all consumers injured by the presence of salmonella in defendant's milk products, despite the pendency of similar class proceedings in the Illinois state courts and around 200 individual lawsuits in Illinois and two other states brought by putative class members. The burden imposed on defendant in litigating this class action in two fora would be great; indeed, the very arguments plaintiff makes for class certification support defendant's argument that the claims should be confined to a single forum as far as possible.

The second factor, inconvenience of the federal forum, is not an issue here, as the state and federal courthouses in Chicago are only a few blocks away from each other. *See* Arkwright–Boston Manufacturers Mutual Insurance Co. v. City of New York, 762 F.2d 205, 210 (2d Cir.1985). The court will therefore turn to the third factor, namely the order in which jurisdiction was obtained. As noted in *Moses H. Cone,* this factor should not be determined by a race to the courthouse but instead by the extent of progress in the respective forums. 460 U.S. at 21, 103 S.Ct. at 940.

The earliest of the state court suits predates Schomber's complaint by approximately one month. Although the state case has not advanced very far and no class has yet been certified, the state court has undertaken complex administrative procedures to oversee the action. All state court complaints have been consolidated under one number and assigned to one judge, who will oversee all pretrial matters on a consolidated basis. At present, according to the amicus brief of the state court litigants, over 200 lawsuits, including twelve class actions, have been filed. A committee of plaintiffs' attorneys has been elected to effectuate the organization and accommodation of all discovery and other pretrial matters.

Although both cases are in early stages of discovery, the state court litigation is significantly further along in this respect than the proceedings in this court. Extensive protective orders were entered in early April (before this suit was filed) to ensure the retention of milk samples and documents regarding the salmonella outbreak. Several contested hearings have been held relative to these orders, and sanctions have been obtained against defendant for the alleged failure to preserve contaminated milk in violation of the protective order.

Other discovery matters are also well underway in the state court litigation. The state court attorneys for plaintiffs have undertaken searches at defendant's Hillfarm Dairy with microbiologists to obtain samples of the contaminated milk and have visited Silliker Laboratories, a private lab retained by defendant for the purpose of analyzing those samples. The state attorneys have met with Silliker's counsel several times, have obtained document production from defendant, Silliker, and the Illinois Department of Public Health, and have filed Freedom of Information Act requests with the Food and Drug Administration and the Center for Disease Control. Finally, the Supreme Court of Illinois on June 27 ordered that the depositions of Jewel employees, witnesses and experts on the liability issue be telecast and videotaped, at Jewel's expense, to one location in each of the circuits in which such cases are pending. By contrast, almost no pretrial discovery—in terms of content or procedures—has been initiated in this court.

With respect to the issue of class certification, the difference between the two fora is less substantial. The state court plaintiffs recently filed a consolidated class action complaint. Defendants filed an answer on July 5, 1985, and a motion to strike the class allegations on July 8th. Depositions of thirty potential class representatives are scheduled to commence this month and to conclude in early August. While some of this activity appears to have been prompted by the threat of parallel federal proceedings, and is therefore tainted by an arguably improper motive, the fact remains that early class certification is more likely to occur in the state court than here. Therefore, despite the limited gap of time between the filing of the two lawsuits, the greater progress in the state court, combined with the fact that most of the litigants are currently proceeding before Judge Quinlan, make that court a "distinctly more convenient and competent forum" for resolving the present dispute. In re Special March, 1981 Grand Jury, 753 F.2d 575, 580 (7th Cir.1985).

The next factor is the absence of federal law issues. This factor does not weigh in favor of abstention, but is nonetheless important since "the presence of federal-law issues must always be a major consideration weighing against surrender." *Moses H. Cone,* 103 S.Ct. at 942. In a similar vein, the Seventh Circuit has admonished that the diversity litigant is entitled to a federal forum and therefore cannot be relegated to state court on a lesser showing of judicial economy than would be required in a federal question case. Evans Transportation Co. v. Scullin Steel Co., 693 F.2d 715, 717 (7th Cir.1982). Having determined that the Magnuson–Moss claims asserted by the intervenors are without merit, the court finds that the absence of federal law issues removes one countervailing factor which might otherwise override the concerns of avoiding piecemeal litigation.

The final factor articulated in *Moses H. Cone*—adequacy of the state forum—similarly presents no reason to weigh against abstention. The Illinois class action statute allows for certification over out of state plaintiffs, Miner v. Gillette Co., 87 Ill.2d 7, 428 N.E.2d 478 (1981), *cert. dismissed,* 459 U.S. 86, 103 S.Ct. 484, 74 L.Ed.2d 249 (1982), and the Supreme Court just recently upheld the constitutionality of such a procedure. Phillips Petroleum Co. v. Shutts, [472] U.S. [797], 105 S.Ct. 2965, 86 L.Ed.2d 628 (1985). Plaintiff suggests that only this court can provide "total oversight and judicial relief for all of the class members" but fails to identify any particulars in which the Illinois state courts are deficient. The plaintiff also suggests that only this court can preclude parallel class action certifications in other states, in disregard of the fact that this court has no power to enjoin state court litigation except under limited circumstances which would not be applicable here.

Plaintiff finally suggests that what is needed for the putative class is prompt certification, and that a class certified by the state court may be substantially different from the class which plaintiff seeks to certify in this case. For the reasons stated earlier, however, the possibility of prompt certification is greater in the state court than here. Moreover, the class which the state court litigants seeks to certify is in all material respects identical to the class described in plaintiff's complaint, except that this court only has jurisdiction over class members whose claims exceed $10,000. Zahn v. International Paper Co., 414 U.S. 291, 301, 94 S.Ct. 505, 512, 38 L.Ed.2d 511 (1973); 394 U.S. 332, 340, 89 S.Ct. 1053, 1058, 22 L.Ed.2d 319 (1969). Obviously, the chief beneficiaries of class certification in this action would be plaintiff's counsel, and not the putative class, whose interests would be more expeditiously served by certification in the litigation which is more advanced.

Given the complexity of this litigation and of the extraordinary steps already taken by the state court to supervise the consolidated cases, "exceptional circumstances" exist so as to justify federal court abstention. The court takes special note that the Second Circuit recently affirmed a decision to abstain under similar but even less compelling facts. Arkwright–Boston Manufacturers Mutual Insurance Co. v. City of New York, 762 F.2d 205 (2d Cir.1985). That case arose out of the electrical blackout occurring in midtown Manhattan in 1983 and in particular involved business losses suffered by Gimbel Brothers, Inc. On the same day that Gimbel filed a state court suit for its uninsured losses, Gimbel's insurers, who had become subrogated to Gimbel's rights in the amount of covered losses, filed a diversity action raising identical allegations. Like the case at bar, Arkwright involved hundreds of claims and numerous parties; the case concerned significant local interests; and the state litigation had been consolidated and assigned to a single state court judge. The case is significant since, at the time of the abstention decision, the motion for consolidation of the state court actions was only pending and almost no discovery had been undertaken. The Second Circuit nonetheless held the abstention proper based almost solely on considerations of avoiding piecemeal litigation. 762 F.2d at 211.

Having determined that abstention is appropriate, the court now addresses the question of relief. Defendant argues that dismissal is appropriate since the difference between stay and dismissal would be "academic" under the facts of the case. In the Matter of Special March, 1981 Grand Jury, 753 F.2d 575, 581 (7th Cir.1985). The Seventh Circuit has repeatedly held, however, that a federal court which declines to exercise jurisdiction because of the pendency of parallel state proceedings should stay rather than dismiss the case because of the possible collateral consequences of characterizing the action as a dismissal. Failure to do so is reversible error. Ohio River Co. v. Carrillo, 754 F.2d 236, 238 (7th Cir.1985); Board of Education v. Bosworth, 713 F.2d 1316, 1322

(7th Cir.1983); Evans Transportation Co. Scullin Steel Co., 693 F.2d 715, 717–18 (7th Cir.1982). A stay rather than dismissal is especially appropriate in the present case since plaintiff Schomber is at present only a putative party to the state court proceeding, may never become a party if class certification is denied or limited to in-state parties, and may in any event have the right to opt out of state class action proceedings to pursue her individual diversity claim here.

Accordingly, the court concludes that abstention is appropriate, but that it would be an abuse of discretion to dismiss the present case. The court therefore stays the present action pending resolution of the state court suit. This decision is, of course, subject to reconsideration if the state court denies class certification or certifies a class which would exclude Schomber. Since defendant has not filed an answer, plaintiff remains free to file a voluntary dismissal under Rule 41(a)(1) and refile in state court if she wishes.

CONCLUSION

Defendant's motion to dismiss is denied, but the motion to stay the proceedings is granted. * * *

It is so ordered.

2. ANTI–SUIT INJUNCTIONS

[Review *In re Federal Skywalk Cases, supra* Part Two, Chapter II, A. 3]

CARLOUGH v. AMCHEM PRODS.

United States Court of Appeals, Third Circuit, 1993.
10 F.3d 189.

Before: MANSMANN, GREENBERG and LEWIS, CIRCUIT JUDGES.

OPINION OF THE COURT

MANSMANN, CIRCUIT JUDGE.

[Review Facts at *Carlough v. Amchem,* Part Two, Chapter II, D.1, *supra*]

B

The district court grounded its authority for granting the preliminary injunction in the Anti–Injunction Act, 28 U.S.C. § 2283 (1970), and the All-Writs Act, 28 U.S.C. § 1651 (1988). The Anti–Injunction Act provides that:

> A court of the United States may not grant an injunction to stay proceedings in a State court except as expressly authorized by Act of Congress, or where necessary in aid of its jurisdiction, or to protect or effectuate its judgments.

The All–Writs Act in part provides that:

Congress may issue all writs necessary or appropriate in aid of their respective jurisdictions and agreeable to the usages and principles of law.

In granting the injunction, the district court relied on the parallel "necessary in aid of jurisdiction" language of the two Acts and cited several cases in which federal courts have enjoined or upheld injunctions against absent class members who have initiated a duplicative state court suit, derived from the same matters pending in the federal district court. *See, e.g.,* In re Asbestos School Litigation, 1991 WL 61156, 1991 U.S.Dist. LEXIS 5142 (E.D.Pa. April 16, 1991)(construing All–Writs Act and Anti–Injunction Act similarly, and holding that stay of state proceeding is "necessary in aid of jurisdiction" when parallel action would seriously impair federal court's flexibility and authority or opportunity to adjudicate as to the *res*), *aff'd mem.,* 950 F.2d 723 (3d Cir.1991); In re Baldwin–United Corp. (Single Premium Deferred Annuities Ins. Litigation), 770 F.2d 328 (2d Cir.1985)(injunction proper when multi-defendant opt out class action is so far advanced that it is equivalent to a *res* over which district court requires control, and potential for onslaught of duplicative state proceedings would seriously impair federal court's flexibility and authority); *see also* In re Corrugated Container Antitrust Litigation, 659 F.2d 1332 (5th Cir.1981), *cert. denied,* 456 U.S. 936, 102 S.Ct. 1993, 72 L.Ed.2d 456 (1982).

The district court rejected the *Gore* plaintiffs' reliance on our prior holdings in In re Real Estate Title and Settlement Services Antitrust Litigation, 869 F.2d 760 (3d Cir.) *cert. denied,* 493 U.S. 821, 110 S.Ct. 77, 107 L.Ed.2d 44 (1989) and in In re Glenn W. Turner Enterprises Litigation, 521 F.2d 775 (3d Cir.1975). The court distinguished our reversal of the injunction in *In re Real Estate Title* on the ground that it involved an absent class member who was denied the opportunity to opt out and who also had never consented to jurisdiction, whereas the *Gore* plaintiffs were going to be afforded an opportunity to opt out of the *Carlough* action. With regard to *In re Glenn Turner,* the district court's decision again turned on the state court plaintiffs' ability to opt out of the federal action. In *In re Glenn Turner,* the successful appeal from the injunction order was brought by the State Attorney General, who as a non-class member, was not eligible to opt out of the federal action. We thus permitted him to maintain a collection suit in state court, which was commenced subsequent to a restitution judgment in state court, but prior to class certification in the related federal action. We held, however, that the injunction as against class members, who could opt out, was valid as a directive facilitating the efficient management of the federal class action. By analogy, the district court reasoned that once the opt out period is commenced in the *Carlough* action, an unrealized but future certainty at the time the district court issued its order, the *Gore* plaintiffs would then be able to individually opt out of *Carlough* and file claims for asbestos-related injuries against the *Carlough* defendants in the forum of their choice, safeguarding policies of federalism and making the *Gore* action unnecessary. The court characterized the sole purpose of the *Gore* action as "preemptive" of the federal class action.

In addition, the district court rejected the *Gore* plaintiffs' contentions that the federal court lacked personal jurisdiction, finding that the Federal Rules of Civil Procedure allow federal courts to bind absent class members in opt out class actions, even without minimum contacts, without impinging federal due process protections, and concluding that the injunction was "necessary to protect [its] jurisdiction" under the All–Writs Act and the Anti–Injunction Act.

Finally, the court held that issuance of the injunction enjoining absent class members was proper notwithstanding pending jurisdictional motions. *Citing* In re Asbestos School Litigation, 1991 WL 61156, 1991 U.S.Dist. LEXIS 5142 (E.D.Pa. April 16, 1991)(presumption against injunction overcome despite pending jurisdictional issues where time and expense incurred by parties and court on settlement is great and absent class member failed to opt out). Without any preliminary discussion of its jurisdiction, the district court summarily stated that "if it is finally determined that this Court lacks jurisdiction, the injunction over the *Gore* suit will be lifted." * * *

* * *

IV

Having determined that the district court satisfactorily, albeit belatedly, ascertained its jurisdictional authority, we turn now to the remaining question of the propriety of the court's application of the "necessary in aid" exception to the Anti–Injunction and All–Writs Acts.

The All–Writs Act, 28 U.S.C. § 1651, provides:

(a) The Supreme Court and all courts established by Act of Congress may issue all writs necessary or appropriate in aid of their respective jurisdictions and agreeable to the usages and principles of law.

The Anti–Injunction Act, 28 U.S.C. § 2283, states that:

A court of the United States may not grant an injunction to stay proceedings in a state court except as expressly authorized by Act of Congress, or where necessary in aid of its jurisdiction, or to protect or effectuate its judgments.

The two statutes act in concert to permit issuance of an injunction. While the Anti–Injunction Act does not provide positive authority for issuance of injunctions, it describes those situations where injunctions are not permitted. The All–Writs Act, by contrast, grants the federal courts the authority to issue injunctions where necessary in aid of their jurisdiction. The parallel "necessary in aid of jurisdiction" language is construed similarly in both the All–Writs Act and the Anti–Injunction Act. *See* In re Asbestos School Litigation, 1991 WL 61156, 1991 U.S. Dist. LEXIS 5142 (E.D.Pa. April 16, 1991), *aff'd mem.,* 950 F.2d 723 (3d Cir.1991).

In In re Glenn Turner, 521 F.2d 775 (3d Cir.1975), we examined the "necessary in aid of the court's jurisdiction" exception to the Anti–

Injunction Act. There the Attorney General instituted a collection suit in a state court following a money judgment and just days after the federal district court had certified the federal class action. Nevertheless, execution upon the state court judgment was effectively enjoined by order of the district court, purportedly by authority of the Anti–Injunction Act. In reversing the injunction of the district court, we reiterated that for the "necessary in aid of jurisdiction" exception to apply, "it is not enough that the requested injunction is related to that jurisdiction, but it must be 'necessary in aid' of 'that jurisdiction.'" In re Glenn Turner, 521 F.2d at 780 (*citing* Atlantic Coast Line R.R. Co., 398 U.S. 281, 90 S.Ct. 1739, 26 L.Ed.2d 234 (1970)). We noted that the exception authorizing injunctions necessary in aid of the court's jurisdiction applies only " 'to prevent a state court from so interfering with a federal court's consideration or disposition of a case as to seriously impair the federal court's flexibility and authority to decide that case.' " *Id.* Finally, we held that Fed.R.Civ.P. 23(b)(3) does not prohibit state proceedings when an action for the same cause is pending in federal court. In recognition of the independence and equivalent stature of the state and federal courts, we held that actions derived from the same cause against the same defendants may be maintained simultaneously in federal and state court. The effect of a judgment in one would be determined by the principle of res judicata. *In re Glenn Turner,* 521 F.2d at 780–81 (*citing* Kline v. Burke Constr. Co., 260 U.S. 226, 43 S.Ct. 79, 67 L.Ed. 226 (1922); Jos. L. Muscarelle, Inc. v. Central Iron Mfg. Co., 328 F.2d 791 (3d Cir.1964)). Moreover, we held that the state citizens on whose behalf judgment was entered in state court "were not proper members of the [federal] class by virtue of the state judgment, rendering unnecessary their opting out before the district court finally determined the class membership." *In re Glenn Turner,* 521 F.2d at 781.

Thus, simultaneous federal and state adjudications of the same *in personam* cause of action do not of themselves trigger the necessary in aid exception, and the letter and spirit of the Anti–Injunction Act and All–Writs Act counsel a restrictive application of that exception. The Supreme Court has cautioned, in deference to principles of federalism, that [a]ny doubts as to the propriety of a federal injunction against state court proceedings should be resolved in favor of permitting the state courts to proceed in an orderly fashion to finally determine the controversy. The explicit wording of § 2283 itself implies as much, and the fundamental principle of a dual system of courts leads inevitably to that conclusion. Atlantic Coast Line R. Co., 398 U.S. 281, 297, 90 S.Ct. 1739, 1748, 26 L.Ed.2d 234 (1970).

Despite the deference paid to the independence of the state courts and principles of comity, there are instances in which courts of appeals have determined that state actions must be enjoined to allow the federal court to proceed ably with pending matters. We find the standard enunciated in these cases in which the courts have upheld issuance of "necessary in aid of" injunctions persuasive and relevant here.

In In re Asbestos School Litigation, 1991 WL 61156, 1991 U.S.Dist. LEXIS 5142 (E.D.Pa. April 16, 1991), *aff'd mem.*, 950 F.2d 723 (3d Cir.1991), we affirmed without an opinion, a district court's issuance of an injunction prohibiting absent class members from pursuing a state court asbestos property damage suit which duplicated a federal school property class action. There, after an absent member in the federal class action failed to opt out, it filed a state court suit against a group of defendants seeking relief corresponding to that in the action pending in federal court. Several of the defendants requested that maintenance of the state court suit be enjoined. Adverting to the complexity of the federal class action and its impending settlement, the court granted the injunction on the ground that the state action so impeded the prosecution of the federal action as to warrant resort to the "necessary in aid" exception.

Our sister circuits have also identified impending and finalized settlements in federal actions as justifying "necessary in aid of jurisdiction" injunctions of duplicative state actions. In In re Baldwin—United Corp., 770 F.2d 328 (2d Cir.1985), a consolidated MDL proceeding, over 100 lawsuits were brought against 26 defendants by holders of securities. After years of negotiations, many defendants agreed to a settlement and signed stipulations to that effect. Prior to the entry of final judgment approving the settlements, the attorneys general of several states made known their intent to commence enforcement suits in their state courts seeking restitution and other damages against some of the defendants. The district court enjoined the imminent state proceedings under the necessary in aid exception to the All–Writs Act, explaining:

> that the existence of actions in the state court would jeopardize its ability to rule on the settlements, would substantially increase the cost of litigation, would create a risk of conflicting results, and would prevent the plaintiffs from benefitting from any settlement already negotiated or from reaching a new and improved settlement in federal court.

Id. at 333.

The Court of Appeals for the Second Circuit affirmed, adding that, [t]he existence of multiple and harassing actions by the states could only serve to frustrate the district court's efforts to craft a settlement in the multi-district litigation before it.

* * *

Under the circumstances we conclude that the injunction * * * was * * * unquestionably "necessary or appropriate in aid of" the federal court's jurisdiction. *Id.* at 337–38. *See also* In re Corrugated Container Antitrust Litigation, 659 F.2d 1332 (5th Cir.1981), *cert. denied,* 456 U.S. 936, 102 S.Ct. 1993, 72 L.Ed.2d 456 (1982)(state court proceeding halted to protect federal jurisdiction over imminent settlement); Battle v. Liberty National Life Ins., 877 F.2d 877, 882 (11th Cir.1989)(collateral state proceedings enjoined under necessary in aid exception); James v.

Bellotti, 733 F.2d 989, 994 (1st Cir.1984)(provisionally improved settlement may justify protective injunction against state court suits).

Here the prospect of settlement was indeed imminent, as in other cases in which federal courts have issued injunctions. Additionally, as the district court found, the nature of the *Gore* suit provides further justification for the injunction. The *Gore* plaintiffs are not requesting relief strictly parallel to that sought in the federal forum. Rather than requesting damages for exposure to asbestos, the stated purpose of the *Gore* suit is to challenge the propriety of the federal class action, which the district court characterized as a preemptive strike against the viability of the federal suit, and to obtain rulings from the West Virginia state court regarding the West Virginia class members' right to opt out of the federal action. In addition, *Carlough* is an opt out federal class action posing no impediment to the *Gore* plaintiffs' individual exercise of their opt out right and option to commence their own respective lawsuits in the forum of their choice. *Cf.* In re Real Estate Title, 869 F.2d 760, 769 (injunction not proper where no opportunity to opt out); In re Glenn Turner, 521 F.2d 775, 778–79 (injunction precluded for non-class members but not precluded as against members of an opt out class where necessary to orderly and efficient federal class management). Thus, we agree with the district court findings that judicial precedent as well as the preemptive cast of the *Gore* suit and the recent establishment of the opt out period overcome the reluctant disposition of the courts to issue a necessary in aid injunction.

We hold that given the establishment of an opt out period and the *Gore* plaintiffs' ability to opt out, it is within the sound discretion of the district court to enjoin their action in state court. The *Gore* plaintiffs individually are at liberty to pursue litigation of their asbestos-related injury claims in the forum of their choice. This ability abrogates any argument of the *Gore* plaintiffs that their West Virginia rights are not adequately addressed by the federal court settlement. Injunction of that portion of the *Gore* suit seeking a ruling from the West Virginia court permitting a mass opting out of all West Virginia plaintiffs is also necessary in aid of the district court's jurisdiction. At this mature phase of the settlement proceedings and after years of pre-trial negotiation, a mass opting out of West Virginia plaintiffs clearly would be disruptive to the district court's ongoing settlement management and would jeopardize the settlement's fruition. In addition, a mass opting out presents a likelihood that the members of the West Virginia class will be confused as to their membership status in the dueling lawsuits. All members of the *Gore* class are only now receiving notice of the federal suit. A declaration by the West Virginia court at this time that all West Virginia members of the federal class are now in the West Virginia suit (and we make no comment as to the legal authority of the West Virginia court to so rule) could cause havoc.

We note also that litigating the propriety of the federal settlement in West Virginia would subject the CCR defendants to unnecessarily duplicative and costly efforts when a fairness hearing has already been scheduled in the district court. Although there is no prohibition against related causes of action being adjudicated in both state and federal forums, two actions here would unduly burden the defendants.

We find it difficult to imagine a more detrimental effect upon the district court's ability to effectuate the settlement of this complex and far-reaching matter than would occur if the West Virginia state court was permitted to make a determination regarding the validity of the federal settlement. Challenges that the settlement violates West Virginia law can be presented to the district court, and those plaintiffs wishing to preserve their claims for West Virginia adjudication may opt out of the federal class.

Given the concerns of the district court to finalize the settlement and given the time invested in reaching that goal, we find that the district court did not abuse its discretion in determining that the injunction should issue. We will, therefore, affirm the order of the district court granting preliminary relief in favor of the defendants.

V

The order of the district court of May 6, 1993 enjoining the *Gore* plaintiffs, their attorneys, agents and employees, and the class they purport to represent from taking any further steps in the prosecution of their claims in the Circuit Court of Monongalia County, West Virginia, or from initiating similar litigation in any other forum, is affirmed.

IN RE JOINT EASTERN AND SOUTHERN DISTRICT ASBESTOS LITIGATION

United States Distict Courts, Eastern & Southern Districts of New York, 1990.
134 F.R.D. 32.

MEMORANDUM ON STAYS

WEINSTEIN, DISTRICT JUDGE:

This Memorandum describes the authority of a federal court to stay proceedings in all other courts to prevent the inequitable distribution of a limited pool of assets after a "limited fund" class action has been conditionally certified in accordance with a proposed settlement agreement. Part One briefly describes the current status of asbestos litigation in the courts. Part Two outlines the procedural background of the current proceedings [this portion has been omitted—*ed.*]. Part Three provides the legal basis for enjoining all proceedings against Eagle–Picher Industries, Inc. ("Eagle–Picher").

I. ASBESTOS LITIGATION

Asbestos litigation in the federal and state courts has reached crisis proportions. Over 100,000 pending asbestos personal injury and wrongful death cases have backlogged the courts—preventing many injured persons from obtaining much needed compensation in a timely and efficient manner. Even more troubling is the current realization that each day, as more judgments are paid, the possibility that similarly situated claimants will not receive the full value of their claims becomes increasingly likely. A fundamental tenet of our legal system—equal treatment—no longer exists for asbestos victims.

The national war over asbestos has produced unnecessary casualties. Many of the persons harmed by asbestos-containing products have been injured once again by our legal system's method of litigating tort cases. Case-by-case adjudications for each injured person has both delayed payment and consumed the bulk of the monies available for those injured. Less than 40% of every asbestos-litigation dollar goes to pay asbestos victims—the persons who actually suffered the injury. *See, e.g.*, INSTITUTE OF CIVIL JUSTICE, ANNUAL REPORT, APRIL 1, 1990–MARCH 31, 1991 (RAND). Much of the billions of dollars in transaction costs going to attorneys could be used to compensate the suffering and injured. Judicial resources now unnecessarily tied up in these cases could be used for other pressing needs.

Amatex Corporation, Brunswick Fabricators, Celotex Corporation, 48 Insulations, Inc., Johns–Manville Corporation, National Gypsum Company, Nicolet Inc., Pacor, Inc., Raytech Corporation, Standard Insulations, Inc. and Unarco Industries have all filed for bankruptcy protection in the face of a deluge of asbestos-related damage claims and mounting asbestos litigation expenses. The transaction costs and attorneys fees associated with these bankruptcy proceedings have further reduced the total funds available to compensate those injured by asbestos. The bankruptcies have also generally delayed payments for many years.

It has become impossible to ignore this challenge to our justice system. A compensation scheme geared towards victims' needs that is fair and equitable and maximizes their recovery is desirable. The circumstances of this case provide an appropriate method of accomplishing this result through a class action pursuant to Rule 23(b)(1)(B) of the Federal Rules of Civil Procedure.

* * *

III. LEGAL ANALYSIS

Asbestos litigation has generated unprecedented challenges to both state and federal court systems. A limited fund class action—seeking to end the repetitious, wasteful and burdensome litigation that has become a hallmark of asbestos proceedings—may provide one tool to assist in resolving all present and future asbestos claims expeditiously and equitably. *See* In re Joint Eastern and Southern Districts Asbestos Litigation (Johns–Manville), 120 B.R. 648 (E. & S.D.N.Y.1990)(parallel litigation involving Manville Personal Injury Settlement Trust).

A. *Effect of Class Certification*

Conditional certification of a national mandatory class action pursuant to Rule 23(b)(1)(B) of the Federal Rules of Civil Procedure will supercede all litigation against Eagle–Picher pending in federal and state forums. *See* In re Federal Skywalk Cases, 680 F.2d 1175, 1180–82 (8th Cir.), *cert. denied,* 459 U.S. 988, 103 S.Ct. 342, 74 L.Ed.2d 383 (1982)(certification order will enjoin prosecution of pending state court actions); In re Joint Eastern and Southern Districts Asbestos Litigation (Johns–Manville), 120 B.R. 648 (E. & S.D.N.Y.1990)(same). The effect of conditional class certification will be for all pending state and federal cases to become part of the mandatory class and cease to exist as independent cases. If the settlement agreement is approved by the court, all pending actions will be adjudicated according to the settlement's terms—saving scarce funds for distribution among all class members.

To permit pending actions against Eagle–Picher to proceed in their present form would substantially impair or impede the interests of other asbestos claimants and would significantly deplete the assets available to resolve all pending and future cases. These pending cases, if allowed to continue independently, will seriously hinder the ability of the court to evaluate the adequacy and fairness of the proposed settlement of the class action by constantly depleting Eagle–Picher's assets. The need to end this drain of Eagle–Picher's assets is especially acute in view of Special Master Frankel's limited fund findings and the rate at which new claims are being filed.

The court was informed that no cases are actually on trial. Halting present litigation will save a great deal of legal expenses. It is also efficient and reflects the growing cooperation among federal and state courts in adjudicating asbestos cases. *See* In re Joint Eastern and Southern Districts Asbestos Litigation (Johns–Manville), 120 B.R. 648 (E. & S.D.N.Y.1990). Should any court, for special circumstances, desire to continue with scheduled trials or hearings, an application for an exception may be made.

B. *Operation of Anti–Injunction Act*

Since the certification of a mandatory national class action will enjoin all pending cases including those filed in state courts, the court considers the implications of the Anti–Injunction Act. 28 U.S.C. § 2283 (1988); *see* In re Dennis Greenman Sec. Litig., 829 F.2d 1539, 1544 (11th Cir.1987). The Anti–Injunction Act precludes a federal court from staying existing proceedings in state court "except as expressly authorized by Act of Congress, or when necessary in aid of its jurisdiction, or to protect or effectuate its judgments." 28 U.S.C. § 2283 (1988); *see* Standard Microsystems Corp. v. Texas Instruments, Inc., 916 F.2d 58, 60 (2d Cir.1990).

The Anti–Injunction Act only prohibits a federal court from staying pending state court proceedings and does not affect a federal court's power to enjoin future state actions or any actions in other federal courts. *See* Dombrowski v. Pfister, 380 U.S. 479, 484 n.2, 85 S.Ct. 1116, 1119 n. 2, 14 L.Ed.2d 22 (1965)(Anti–Injunction Act does "not preclude injunctions against the institution of state court proceedings, but only bar[s] stays of suits already instituted") * * * While the policy underlying the Anti–Injunction Act is avoidance of "disharmony between federal and state systems, the exception in Section 2283 reflects congressional recognition that injunctions may sometimes be necessary in order to avoid that disharmony." Amalgamated Sugar Co. v. NL Industries, 825 F.2d 634, 639 (2d Cir.), *cert. denied,* 484 U.S. 992, 108 S.Ct. 511, 98 L.Ed.2d 511 (1987). Under the present circumstances, the power to enjoin the pending state cases falls within the "necessary in aid of jurisdiction" exception to the Anti-Injunction Act.

Courts have interpreted the "necessary in aid of jurisdiction" exception liberally "to prevent a state court from * * * interfering with a federal court's flexibility and authority" to decide the case before it. Atlantic Coast Line R. v. Brotherhood of Locomotive Eng'rs, 398 U.S. 281, 295, 90 S.Ct. 1739, 1747, 26 L.Ed.2d 234 (1970); *see* In re Baldwin–United Corp., 770 F.2d 328, 337 (2d Cir.1985)(same); In re Corrugated Container Antitrust Litig., 659 F.2d 1332, 1334 (5th Cir.1981), *cert. denied,* 456 U.S. 936, 102 S.Ct. 1993, 72 L.Ed.2d 456 (1982)(same); *see also* Redish, *The Anti–Injunction Statute Reconsidered,* 44 U.Chi.L.Rev. 717, 754 (1977)("necessary in aid of jurisdiction" exception should be construed "to empower the federal court to enjoin a concurrent state proceeding that might render the exercise of the federal court's jurisdiction nugatory.").

The Second Circuit has recognized that a stay of proceedings in state court is appropriate under the "necessary in aid of jurisdiction" exception "where a federal court is on the verge of settling a complex matter, and state court proceedings undermine its ability to achieve that objective." Standard Microsystems Corp. v. Texas Instruments Inc., 916 F.2d 58, 60 (2d Cir.1990); *see* United States v. International Brotherhood of Teamsters, 907 F.2d 277, 281 (2d Cir.1990)(stay is appropriate to allow district judge to "legitimately assert comprehensive control over complex litigation"); In re Baldwin-United Corp., 770 F.2d 328, 337 (2d Cir.1985)(court can issue injunction against actions in state court that would "frustrate the district court's efforts to craft a settlement"); *see also* James v. Bellotti, 733 F.2d 989, 994 (1st Cir.1984)(provisionally approved settlement may justify injunction against state court actions).

A mandatory national class action certified pursuant to Rule 23(b)(1)(B) falls squarely within the rationale of these controlling Second Circuit precedents. The court is in the process of reviewing the settlement agreement of the proposed class action encompassing all asbestos-related claims against Eagle–Picher. At this critical juncture, the court can only continue its evaluation if the assets available to settle the case remain intact. An injunction of all proceedings is necessary to implement the terms of the settlement and to protect the court's jurisdiction over the class action.

The All–Writs Act furnishes additional authority to certify the class action and to stay all pending proceedings. It empowers a federal court to issue "all writs necessary or appropriate in aid of their respective jurisdictions...." 28 U.S.C. § 1651 (1988). The Second Circuit has held that cases interpreting the "necessary in aid of jurisdiction" exception in the Anti–Injunction Act are "helpful in understanding the meaning of the All–Writs Act." *See* In re Baldwin–United Corp., 770 F.2d 328, 335 (2d Cir.1985); *see also* United States v. District of Columbia, 654 F.2d 802, 809 n.16 (D.C.Cir.), *cert. denied,* 454 U.S. 1082, 102 S.Ct. 637, 70 L.Ed.2d 616 (1981)(same); * * *. Whether viewed as an affirmative grant of power to the courts or an exception to the Anti–Injunction Act, the All–Writs Act permits courts to certify a national class action and to stay pending federal and state cases brought on behalf of class members.

The All–Writs Act empowers a federal court to issue an injunction against actions in state court "even before a federal judgment is reached...." In re Baldwin–United Corp., 770 F.2d 328, 335 (2d Cir.1985). Such an injunction allows the court to protect its settlement efforts. * * *

The court has before it a settlement agreement purporting to resolve all present and future asbestos-related claims asserted against Eagle–Picher. Conditional certification of the class is a necessary first step on the road to its possible approval and implementation. Rule 23 of the Federal Rules of Civil Procedure mandates exercise of power to maintain the status quo during the trial and appellate process. Fairness hearings, for example, must now be conducted. A stay of all proceedings must be entered now to protect Eagle–Picher's assets during these hearings— assets the settlement assumes will be available—and to ensure an equitable result for all present and future persons injured by asbestos-containing products. Thus, the rationale of *Baldwin-United* requires interpretation of the Anti–Injunction Act to permit operation of Rule 23. *See* Standard Microsystems Corp. v. Texas Instruments Inc., 916 F.2d 58, 60–61 (2d Cir.1990).

The "in aid of jurisdiction" exception would also authorize a stay of state court proceedings when the "federal court's jurisdiction is in rem and the state court action may effectively deprive the federal court of the opportunity to adjudicate as to the *res*...." Standard Microsystems Corp. v. Texas Instruments Inc., 916 F.2d 58, 60 (2d Cir.1990); Mitchum v. Foster, 407 U.S. 225, 235–37, 92 S.Ct. 2151, 2158–59, 32 L.Ed.2d 705 (1972)(same).

Several courts have considered class action litigation analogous to *in rem* actions given their magnitude and complexity. In *Baldwin-United* the class action proceeding was "so far advanced that it was the virtual equivalent of a res over which the district judge required full control." In re Baldwin-United Corp., 770 F.2d 328, 337 (2d Cir.1985); *see* Battle v. Liberty National Life Ins. Co., 877 F.2d 877, 882 (11th Cir. 1989)("makes sense to consider this case, involving years of litigation and mountains of paperwork, as similar to a res to be administered").

It is readily apparent, in view of Special Master Frankel's report, that parallel court proceedings may produce inconsistent and inequitable results. Some judgments may be paid in full while others will receive nothing or less than full value. Under these circumstances, the *in rem* nature of the court's jurisdiction over the class action and the limited fund provides an additional ground for concluding that a stay of all existing proceedings is consistent with the Anti–Injunction Act.

Federal courts have also relied upon the "in aid of jurisdiction" exception to the Anti–Injunction Act to justify a stay of existing state proceedings in interpleader actions pursuant to Rule 22 of the Federal Rules of Civil Procedure. *See, e.g.,* United States v. Major Oil Corp., 583 F.2d 1152, 1158 (10th Cir.1978)(stay of state proceedings in Rule 22 interpleader is in aid of the court's jurisdiction); Emmco Ins. Co. v. Frankford Trust Co., 352 F.Supp. 130, 132–33 (E.D.Pa.1972)(same); Pan American Fire & Casualty Co. v. Revere, 188 F.Supp. 474, 484–85 (E.D.La.1960)(same). Interpleader is traditionally employed when two or more persons claim an interest in a fund, and the claims to the fund may exceed the total value of that fund. *See* State Farm Fire & Casualty Co. v. Tashire, 386 U.S. 523, 533 n. 15, 87 S.Ct. 1199, 1205 n. 15, 18 L.Ed.2d 270 (1967).

Limited fund class actions closely resemble an interpleader action. *Cf.* In re Federal Skywalk Cases, 680 F.2d 1175, 1182–83 (8th Cir.), *cert. denied,* 459 U.S. 988, 103 S.Ct. 342, 74 L.Ed.2d 383 (1982)(implying that a limited fund is analogous to interpleader). In light of the severely limited assets of Eagle–Picher, the class members here are virtually identical to interpleader claimants. The class members, like interpleader claimants, must recover from Eagle–Picher's limited assets or not recover at all.

Given the similarity of the present class action to an interpleader action, a stay of state proceedings would be warranted under the "necessary in aid of jurisdiction" exception. Only by staying all other proceedings can the class action achieve the goal of adjudicating all asbestos claims against Eagle–Picher in one action and preventing recovery from its assets in an inequitable or inconsistent manner.

Under the circumstances of this case, it seems apparent that the Anti–Injunction Act would permit certification of a mandatory class action. Nevertheless, two courts, In re Temple (Raymark Industries), 851 F.2d 1269, 1272 (11th Cir.1988) and Waldron v. Raymark Indus., Inc., 124 F.R.D. 235 (N.D.Ga.1989), have denied certification of mandatory class actions relying in part on dicta in In re Federal Skywalk Cases, 680 F.2d 1175, 1182–83 (8th Cir.), *cert. denied,* 459 U.S. 988, 103 S.Ct. 342, 74 L.Ed.2d 383 (1982). While these cases are contrary to controlling Second Circuit precedent, they have sparked significant commentary and merit discussion.

In *Skywalk,* the Eighth Circuit vacated certification of a limited fund class action primarily on the ground that the finding of a limited fund was inadequate and unsupported as a matter of law. * * * The Eleventh Circuit, in dicta, has construed the *Skywalk* decision as holding that the Anti–Injunction Act bars certification of a mandatory class action if state cases have been started. *See* In re Temple (Raymark

Industries), 851 F.2d 1269, 1272 (11th Cir.1988), *on remand*, Waldron v. Raymark Indus., Inc., 124 F.R.D. 235 (N.D.Ga.1989). The district court, on remand, never reached the "in aid of jurisdiction" exception to the Anti–Injunction Act because it summarily concluded that the *Temple* dicta precluded certification of a non-opt-out class action when state cases are pending. * * *

The *Temple* court's interpretation of *Skywalk* and its subsequent application in *Waldron*, however, ignore the fact that the basis for vacating certification in *Skywalk* was the absence of a limited fund. Without the limited fund—such as exists in the present case—as a jurisdictional predicate, a court cannot proceed with a limited fund class action as a basis for enjoining existing state actions. The "necessary in aid of jurisdiction" exception to the Anti–Injunction Act would not apply because the court is without jurisdiction to aid. Properly construed, *Skywalk* stands only for the proposition that where class certification is improper because no limited fund exists, a court cannot rely upon the "necessary in aid of jurisdiction" exception to the Anti–Injunction Act to justify a stay of existing state proceedings.

The dicta contained in the *Skywalk* decision and its subsequent interpretation by other courts have generated considerable criticism. *See, e.g.,* In re Dennis Greenman Sec. Litig., 829 F.2d 1539, 1544 (11th Cir.1987)("inclined to hold the [Anti–Injunction] Act not a bar to class certification"); In re Federal Skywalk Cases, 680 F.2d 1175, 1192 (8th Cir.), *cert. denied,* 459 U.S. 988, 103 S.Ct. 342, 74 L.Ed.2d 383 (1982)(Heaney, J., dissenting)("It seems self-evident that an injunction to protect the ordinary scope of a mandatory class action is 'necessary in aid of' the federal jurisdiction over such a class."); In re Asbestos School Litigation, 104 F.R.D. 422, 436 (E.D.Pa.1984), *modified on other grounds,* 789 F.2d 996 (3d Cir.1986)(same); In re Dennis Greenman Sec. Litig., 622 F.Supp. 1430, 1449–50 & n.15 (S.D.Fla.1985), *rev'd on other grounds,* 829 F.2d 1539 (11th Cir.1987)(disagreeing with reasoning of *Skywalk* majority and certifying class for settlement); Gordon, *The Optimum Management of the Skywalks Mass Disaster Litigation by Use of the Federal Mandatory Class Action Device,* 52 UMKC L.Rev. 215, 231–32 (1984)(noting that several articles have described the Eighth Circuit's decision as "unreasonable," "untenable," "arcane," "obscure," "unnecessarily narrow" and "inequitable"); Note, *Class Certification in Mass Accident Cases Under Rule 23(b)(1),* 96 Harv.L.Rev. 1143, 1159–61 (1983)(certification of mandatory class comes within "necessary in aid" of jurisdiction exception to Anti–Injunction Act); Note, *Mechanical and Constitutional Problems in the Certification of Mandatory Multistate Mass Tort Class Actions Under Rule 23,* 49 Brook.L.Rev. 517 (1983)(compelling reasons support finding that "necessary in aid of jurisdiction" exception allows mandatory class certification).

The *Skywalk* dicta is also contrary to the presumption of validity enjoyed by the Federal Rules of Civil Procedure, which requires effective means for the enforcement of Rule 23. *See Hanna v. Plumer,* 380 U.S. 460, 471, 85 S.Ct. 1136, 1143, 14 L.Ed.2d 8 (1965).

IV. Conclusion

The United States District Court for the Southern and Eastern Districts of New York has by its orders dated December 11, 1990 properly enjoined all asbestos litigation pending against Eagle–Picher, with exceptions, and restrained any new proceedings from being instituted against the company.

So ordered.

Notes and Questions

1. Two possible methods of dealing with parallel duplicative federal and state mass tort actions are either through federal injunctive power or abstention doctrine. Since the power of federal courts to enjoin or stay state proceedings is severely circumscribed by the Anti–Injunction Act, abstention doctrine offers the other procedural means of avoiding duplicative litigation. In general, the Supreme Court has articulated at least four discrete abstention doctrines: *see* Railroad Comm'n. of Texas v. Pullman Co., 312 U.S. 496, 61 S.Ct. 643, 85 L.Ed. 971 (1941)(abstention to avoid federal court constitutional rulings); Louisiana Power and Light Co. v. City of Thibodaux, 360 U.S. 25, 79 S.Ct. 1070, 3 L.Ed.2d 1058 (1959)(abstention because of unclear state law in diversity cases); Burford v. Sun Oil Co., 319 U.S. 315, 63 S.Ct. 1098, 87 L.Ed. 1424 (1943)(abstention to defer complex state administrative procedures); and Younger v. Harris, 401 U.S. 37, 91 S.Ct. 746, 27 L.Ed.2d 669 (1971)(prohibition against enjoining state criminal proceedings). *See generally,* Erwin Chemerinsky, Federal Jurisdiction §§ 12.1–13.4 (2d ed.1994)(discussing various abstention doctrines). *See also* Michael T. Gibson, *Private Concurrent Litigation in Light of* Younger, Pennzoil, *and* Colorado River, 14 Okla. C.U.L.Rev. 185 (1989); Martin Redish, *Abstention, Separation of Powers, and the Limits of the Judicial Function,* 94 Yale L.J. 71 (1984).

2. In Colorado River Water Conservation Dist. v. United States, 424 U.S. 800, 96 S.Ct. 1236, 47 L.Ed.2d 483 (1976), discussed in *Schomber,* the Supreme Court articulated yet another ground for federal court abstention, to avoid duplicative litigation in the interests of "sound judicial administration." *See also* Moses H. Cone Memorial Hosp. v. Mercury Constr. Corp., 460 U.S. 1, 103 S.Ct. 927, 74 L.Ed.2d 765 (1983). In addition to *Colorado River* abstention, do any of the other abstention doctrines supply a reasonable ground for federal courts to defer to parallel state mass tort actions? Has the court in *Schomber* well-applied the doctrine of *Colorado River* abstention?

Colorado River abstention has proved somewhat controversial as a basis for a federal court to decline its validly conferred jurisdiction. In mass tort litigation, why should federal litigants be made to defer to parallel state proceedings? Why shouldn't federal litigants have the benefit of their preferred federal forum? For discussions of the problems with *Colorado River* abstention, *see generally,* Erwin Chemerinsky, Federal Jurisdiction §§ 14.1–14.4, *supra*; Howard A. Davis, *Slowing the Flow of* Colorado River: *The Doctrine of Abstention to Promote Judicial Administration,* 77 Ill.Bar.J. 648 (1989); David A. Sonenshein, *Abstention: The Crooked Course of* Colorado River, 59 Tul.L.Rev. 651 (1985); Linda S. Mullenix, *A Branch Too Far:*

Pruning the Abstention Doctrine, 75 Geo.L.J. 99 (1986); Comment, *Federal Court Stays and Dismissals in Deference to Parallel State Court Proceedings: The Impact of* Colorado River, 44 U.Chi.L.Rev. 641 (1977).

3. The Anti–Injunction Act contains three exceptions, indicated in the decisions. The first exception to the general prohibition against federal district courts enjoining pending state-court proceedings was incorporated in § 2283 in 1948 in the phrase "as expressly authorized by Act of Congress." This was a congressional recognition that a number of federal statutes had been interpreted as legislative exceptions to the original absolute prohibition contained in the Act of 1793. If an action is removed to the federal district court, for example, § 1446(e) of the Judicial Code, echoing language in the removal acts since 1789, states: "the State court shall proceed no further unless and until the case is remanded." This has been recognized as statutory authority for the district court, if necessary, to enjoin a state court that continues to consider the action after removal and before it is remanded. Similarly, the federal court can enjoin state courts in connection with limitation-of-liability proceedings in admiralty, 46 U.S.C.A. §§ 181–185; interpleader, 28 U.S.C.A. § 2361; the bankruptcy act, 11 U.S.C.A. § 362 (*see* Kalb v. Feuerstein, 308 U.S. 433, 60 S.Ct. 343, 84 L.Ed. 370 (1940)); and habeas corpus proceedings, 28 U.S.C.A. § 2251.

4. The second exception contained in § 2283, "where necessary in aid of its jurisdiction," was a recognition by Congress in 1948 that court decisions had forged exceptions to the Act of 1793 that went beyond those postulated upon a theory of subsequent congressional enactment. The most prominent of these was the rule that a federal court can enjoin a state court proceeding that interferes with its prior *in rem* jurisdiction, *i.e.*, that disturbs a *res* over which that federal court has taken control. In Kline v. Burke Construction Co., 260 U.S. 226, 229, 43 S.Ct. 79, 81, 67 L.Ed. 226 (1922), the Court has stated:

> Where the action is *in rem,* the effect is to draw to the federal court the possession or control, actual or potential, of the *res,* and the exercise by the state court of jurisdiction over the same *res* necessarily impairs, and may defeat, the jurisdiction of the Federal court already attached. The converse of the rule is equally true, that where the jurisdiction of the state court has first attached, the Federal court is precluded from exercising its jurisdiction over the same *res* to defeat or impair the state court's jurisdiction.

Thus, the rule is that the court, state or federal, which first acquires jurisdiction over a *res* can enjoin interference with its *in rem* jurisdiction. *See* 1A Moore's FEDERAL PRACTICE ¶¶ 0.214–0.216, for detailed discussion of what constitutes possession of the *res* and what constitutes a *res* for these purposes; *see also* 17 Wright, Miller, and Cooper, FEDERAL PRACTICE AND PROCEDURE § 4225 (2d ed.1988 & Supp.). Do these concepts of a *"res"* apply to limited fund mass tort class actions?

5. In contrast to the rule with regard to *in rem* jurisdiction, it has long been held that two *in personam* cases on the same cause of action and between the same parties can be brought, one in federal court and one in state court, so long as there is concurrent jurisdiction over the subject matter in the federal courts. *Kline v. Burke Constr. Co.* Section 2283 would

prevent a federal court from enjoining the state-court action merely on the ground that it is a competing *in personam* action. In *Toucey v. Life Ins. Co.,* 314 U.S. 118, 62 S.Ct. 139, 86 L.Ed. 100 (1941), the Supreme Court interpreted the then-existing anti-injunction statute to prohibit a federal court from enjoining the relitigation in state court of a cause of action between the same parties that had gone to judgment in the federal court. The 1948 amendment rejected *Toucey* and created the third exception to § 2283 that permits the federal court to enjoin a pending state-court action "to protect or effectuate its judgment." Thus once a federal action has been fully litigated and gone to judgment, not only does it become a basis for the defense of res judicata in the state-court action, but the further prosecution of the state-court action can be enjoined by the federal court which rendered the judgment. *See, e.g.,* Woods Exploration & Producing Co. v. Aluminum Co. of Am., 438 F.2d 1286 (5th Cir.1971), *cert. denied,* 404 U.S. 1047, 92 S.Ct. 701, 30 L.Ed.2d 736 (1972).

6. Despite Congress' rejection of the *Toucey* case in drafting the 1948 version of the Anti–Injunction Act, the exception "in aid of its jurisdiction" has been narrowly construed. In Amalgamated Clothing Workers v. Richman Brothers, 348 U.S. 511, 75 S.Ct. 452, 99 L.Ed. 600 (1955), the Supreme Court held that § 2283 prohibited an injunction by a federal district court against a state-court injunction barring peaceful picketing in a labor dispute. Though it is apparent that the state court did not have jurisdiction with regard to a dispute involving interstate commerce, neither would the district court. Exclusive jurisdiction with regard to such dispute was vested in the National Labor Relations Board. Thus it might seem that an employer could thwart peaceful picketing by resort to a state-court action. However, if an unfair labor practice complaint is before the National Labor Relations Board, the Board can seek an injunction in federal court against state-court actions. Capital Service v. National Labor Relations Board, 347 U.S. 501, 74 S.Ct. 699, 98 L.Ed. 887 (1954). *See also* In re Federal Skywalk Cases, 680 F.2d 1175 (8th Cir.1982)(injunction against competing state actions vacated). The bar of § 2283 applies to injunctions against state court "proceedings." It does not bar an injunction against the *institution* of a state court proceeding. *See* Dombrowski v. Pfister, 380 U.S. 479, 85 S.Ct. 1116, 14 L.Ed.2d 22 (1965).

7. Do class actions have any claim to special consideration for application of the Anti–Injunction Act to stay parallel state proceedings, as the court in the *Joint Asbestos Litigation* seems to suggest? Does it make a difference how the class is certified? Is the court's analogizing the (b)(1)(B) "limited fund" to a *res* (necessary to bring this type of class action within the second exception) plausible? Legally sound? What about the rule that federal courts may not issue injunctions to restrain parallel *in personam* state actions? Does the decision in the *Joint Asbestos Litigation* violate this well-established rule? Does the *Joint Asbestos Litigation* decision merely represent another pragmatic accommodation of an activist judge to a perceived crisis in the federal courts?

As the opinion indicates, not all federal courts have agreed that the Anti–Injunction Act may be utilized to enjoin parallel state proceedings where there is a pending federal class action, adhering to a limited view of the *"in rem "* exception. However, many critics have suggested that the second exception to the Anti–Injunction Act (along with the third exception) ought to be more liberally construed to prevent state courts from impairing or impeding a federal court's ability to decide a case. *See generally,* Larimore, *Exploring the Interface Between Rule 23 Class Actions and the Anti–Injunction Act,* 18 Ga.L.Rev. 259 (1984); Mayton, *Ersatz Federalism Under the Anti–Injunction Statute,* 78 Col.L.Rev. 330 (1978); and Martin Redish, *The Anti–Injunction Statute Reconsidered,* 44 U.Chi.L.Rev. 717 (1977); Edward Sherman, *Class Actions and Duplicative Litigation,* 62 Ind.L.J. 507 (1986).

8. Can defendants use removal procedure to escape the consequences of the Anti–Injunction Act? At least one federal court has held that the Anti–Injunction Act does not apply to a state action after it has been removed; *see* Hyde Park Partners, L.P. v. Connolly, 839 F.2d 837 (1st Cir.1988), *citing* Bondurant v. Watson, 103 U.S. (13 Otto) 281, 26 L.Ed. 447 (1880) for the principle that removal is proper even if it is done to escape the Anti–Injunction Act. Similarly, in In re "Agent Orange" Product Liability Litigation, 996 F.2d 1425 (2d Cir.1993), Circuit Judge Van Graafeiland held that the removal of state-based tort actions for damages arising out of exposure to Agent Orange did not violate the Anti–Injunction Act, and that the district court's removal was necessary in aid of its continuing jurisdiction over the *Agent Orange* federal class action settlement fund. The district court also invoked the third exception, as well. In reaching this conclusion, the court stated:

> Assuming without deciding that removal of a case from state court to federal court is sufficiently akin to an injunction to come within the Act's ambit, the facts of the instant case bring it squarely within the above-mentioned exceptions to the Act. First, the district court's removal was "necessary in aid of its jurisdiction." Judge Weinstein has continuing jurisdiction over the *Agent Orange I* class action, not only to administer the settlement fund, ... but also to ensure that the Settlement Agreement as a whole is enforced according to its terms.... "In a class action, the district court has a duty to class members to see that any settlement it approves is completed, and not merely to approve a promise...." In re Corrugated Container Antitrust Litig., 752 F.2d 137, 141 (5th Cir.), *cert. denied,* 473 U.S. 911, 105 S.Ct. 3536, 87 L.Ed.2d 660 (1985). Second, removal was needed "to protect or effectuate" the district court's *Agent Orange I* judgment. This exception in the statute authorizes a federal court to proscribe state litigation of an issue that actually has been previously presented to and decided by the federal court. *See* Chick Kam Choo v. Exxon Corp., 486 U.S. 140, 147, 108 S.Ct. 1684, 1689, 100 L.Ed.2d 127 (1988). A review of the arguments, orders and judgment in *Agent Orange I* makes it crystal clear that the court in fact did determine the central issue of class membership raised here, i.e., that persons who had yet to manifest injury were class members. * * *

9. In the *Joint Asbestos Litigation* decision, Judge Weinstein relied both on the All Writs Act, 28 U.S.C.A. § 1651, and the "necessary in aid of its jurisdiction" exception to the Anti–Injunction Act. What is the relationship of these two provisions? Are they redundant? If relief is expansively available under the All Writs Act, should we be concerned about narrow

interpretations of the second exception to the Anti–Injunction Act? The Second Circuit, in its *Agent Orange* decision, *id.*, similarly relied on its jurisdiction powers authorized in the All Writs Act:

> Alternatively, the district court found authority for removal in its power under the All Writs Act to issue writs "necessary or appropriate" in aid of its jurisdiction. 28 U.S.C. § 1651. Here, the district court was on sounder ground. A district court, in exceptional circumstances, may use its All Writs authority to remove an otherwise unremovable state court case in order to "effectuate and prevent the frustration of orders it has previously issued in its exercise of jurisdiction otherwise obtained." United States v. New York Tel. Co., 434 U.S. 159, 172, 98 S.Ct. 364, 372, 54 L.Ed.2d 376 (1977).

> If Agent Orange victims were allowed to maintain separate actions in state court, the deleterious effect on the *Agent Orange I* settlement mechanism would be substantial. The parties to the settlement implicitly recognized this when they agreed that all future suits by class members would be permanently barred. It is difficult to conceive of any state court properly addressing a victim's tort claim without first deciding the scope of the *Agent Orange I* class action and settlement. The court best situated to make this determination is the court that approved the settlement and entered the judgment enforcing it. Removal in the instant case was an appropriate use of federal judicial power under 28 U.S.C. § 1651. *See* United States v. City of New York, 972 F.2d 464, 469 (2d Cir.1992); Yonkers Racing Corp. v. City of Yonkers, 858 F.2d 855, 863–64 (2d Cir.1988), *cert. denied*, 489 U.S. 1077, 109 S.Ct. 1527, 103 L.Ed.2d 833 (1989). In so holding, we are not unmindful of the fact that the All Writs Act is not a jurisdictional blank check which district courts may use whenever they deem it advisable. "Although that Act empowers federal courts to fashion extraordinary remedies when the need arises, it does not authorize them to issue ad hoc writs whenever compliance with statutory procedures appears inconvenient or less appropriate." Pennsylvania Bureau of Correction v. United States Marshals Serv., 474 U.S. 34, 43, 106 S.Ct. 355, 361, 88 L.Ed.2d 189 (1985). Given the "exceptional circumstances" surrounding the instant case, issuance was a proper exercise of judicial discretion. The district court was not determining simply the preclusive effect of a prior final judgment on claims or issues expected to be raised in subsequent collateral proceedings; it was enforcing an explicit, ongoing order against relitigation of matters it already had decided, and guarding the integrity of its rulings in complex multidistrict litigation over which it had retained jurisdiction.

For a discussion of removal generally, *see* Marilyn J. Ireland, *Entire Case Removal Under 1441(c): Toward a Unified Theory of Additional Parties and Claims in Federal Courts*, 11 Ind. L.Rev. 556 (1978).

10. To what extent does application of the Anti–Injunction Act exceptions in the *Joint Asbestos Litigation* and the *Agent Orange* decision violate *Younger* doctrine? In response to such a challenge raised in the Agent Orange removal case, the Second Circuit decided:

Appellants contend that Younger v. Harris, 401 U.S. 37, 91 S.Ct. 746, 27 L.Ed.2d 669 (1971), and its progeny, particularly Pennzoil Co. v. Texaco, Inc., 481 U.S. 1, 107 S.Ct. 1519, 95 L.Ed.2d 1 (1987), require that the district court abstain from exercising jurisdiction in deference to the Texas state courts. This argument stands the *Younger* doctrine on its head. *Younger* teaches us to recognize the interest of the states in protecting the authority of their judicial system so that their orders and judgments are not rendered nugatory. *Pennzoil,* 481 U.S. at 14 n.12 (*quoting* Juidice v. Vail, 430 U.S. 327, 336 n. 12, 97 S.Ct. 1211, 1217 n. 12, 51 L.Ed.2d 376 (1977)). The application of *Younger,* as advocated by appellants, would threaten the authority of the federal judicial system and potentially nullify the federal courts' orders and judgments. This result is not the sort of federal-state comity envisioned in *Younger* and *Pennzoil. See* Town of Lockport v. Citizens for Community Action at the Local Level, Inc., 430 U.S. 259, 264 n. 8, 97 S.Ct. 1047, 1051 n. 8, 51 L.Ed.2d 313 (1977).

11. In addition to academic commentators who individually have suggested liberalizing the application of exceptions to the Anti–Injunction Act, the American Law Institute, in COMPLEX LITIGATION: STATUTORY RECOMMENDATIONS AND ANALYSIS (1994), recommended a modified Anti–Injunction Statute to enable the transferee court in federal consolidated complex litigation to stay parallel state proceedings. The proposed statute provides:

§ 5.04. Antisuit Injunctions

(a) When actions are transferred and consolidated pursuant to § 3.01 or § 5.01, the transferee court may enjoin transactionally related proceedings, or portions thereof, pending in any state or federal court whenever it determines that the continuation of those actions substantially impairs or interferes with the consolidated actions and that an injunction would promote the just, efficient, and fair resolution of the actions before it.

(b) Factors to be considered in deciding whether an injunction should issue under subsection (a) include

(1) how far the actions to be enjoined have progressed;

(2) the degree to which the actions to be enjoined share common questions with and are duplicative of the consolidated actions;

(3) the extent to which the actions to be enjoined involve issues or claims of federal law; and

(4) whether parties to the action to be enjoined were permitted to exclude themselves from the consolidated proceeding under § 3.05(a) or § 5.01(b).

American Law Institute, COMPLEX LITIGATION: STATUTORY RECOMMENDATIONS AND ANALYSIS at § 5.04 (1994).

In contrast, the Federal Courts Study Committee recommended further study, but took no position on, modification of the Anti–Injunction Act. *See* REPORT OF THE FEDERAL COURTS STUDY COMMITTEE at 48 (April 2, 1990).

12.   Does the Anti–Injunction Act apply to permit federal courts to stay or enjoin parallel foreign litigation?   At least one federal court has held that the Anti–Injunction Act has no application to lawsuits in foreign countries. *See* China Trade & Development Corp. v. M.V. Choong Yong, 837 F.2d 33 (2d Cir.1987), *noted in* Brian W. Riley, *Civil Procedure—Antisuit Injunction Held Invalid Against Parallel Suit in Foreign Country,* 22 Suffolk U.L.Rev. 1234 (1988).   For other discussions of the possible international implications of the Anti–Injunction Act, *see generally,* Vaughan Black, *The Antisuit Injunction Comes to Canada,* 13 Queen's L.J. 103 (1988);   Thomas E. Burck, *What Should Be The Role of International Comity in the Issuance of Antisuit Injunctions?,* 18 N.C.J.Int'l.L. & Comm.Reg. 475 (1993);   Trevor C. Hartley, *Comity and the Use of Antisuit Injunctions in International Litigation,* 35 Am.J.Comp.L. 487 (1987);   and Richard W. Raushenbush, *Antisuit Injunctions and International Comity,* 71 Va.L.Rev. 1039 (1985).

B.   MASS TORTS AND STATE SOVEREIGNTY

AMERICAN LAW INSTITUTE, COMPLEX LITIGATION: STATUTORY RECOMMENDATIONS AND ANALYSIS

(1994).

§ 4.01   Designating a State Court as a Transferee Forum for Federal Actions

(a) Subject to the exceptions in subsection (c), when determining under § 3.04 where to transfer and consolidate actions, the Complex Litigation Panel may designate a state court as the transferee court if the Panel determines

(1) that the events giving rise to the controversy are centered in a single state and a significant portion of the existing litigation is lodged in the courts of that state;

(2) that fairness to the parties and the interests of justice will be materially advanced by transfer and consolidation of the federal actions with other suits pending in the state court;   and

(3) that the state court is superior to other possible transferee courts.

The Complex Litigation Panel may designate a state court as the transferee court solely for pretrial proceedings, including discovery and motion practice, or for the full or partial adjudication of the controversy. The consent of the appropriate judicial authority in the state in which the designated transferee court is located must be obtained.   Once transfer is approved, a state transferee court shall have the same powers and responsibilities as a federal transferee court under [other sections omitted—*ed.*]

(b) When determining whether the requirements in subsection (a) are met, the Complex Litigation Panel should consider factors such as

(1) the number of the individual cases that initially were filed or are pending in state courts relative to the number of actions pending in federal courts;

(2) the number of states in which the state and federal cases are located;

(3) whether the procedures or law to be applied in the state transferee court differ from that which would have been applied by a federal transferee court to a sufficient degree that designation of the state transferee court creates a risk of prejudice to some of the parties to be transferred there; and

(4) any other factor indicating the need to accommodate a particular state or federal interest.

(c) The Complex Litigation Panel shall not transfer to a state court any action that is within the exclusive jurisdiction of the federal courts, or any action that has been removed to a federal court under any provisions of 28 U.S.C. § 1441(d), 28 U.S.C. § 442, or 28 U.S.C. § 1443, or brought in a federal court under the provisions of 42 U.S.C. § 1983. In any action brought by the United States under 28 U.S.C. § 1345, or removed by it under 28 U.S.C. § 1444, the government shall have the right to be exempted from transfer to state court.

(d) Other than as provide in § 3.07(b), appellate review in federal actions transferred for consolidation to a state court pursuant to this section shall be in the appellate courts of the state in which the transferee court sits.

§ 4.02 Formulation of an Interstate Complex Litigation Compact or a Uniform Complex Litigation Act

In order to facilitate the transfer and consolidation of related litigation pending in the courts of different states and to promote the just, efficient, and economical resolution thereof, consideration should be given to the formulation of an Interstate Complex Litigation Compact or a Uniform Complex Litigation Act.

AMERICAN LAW INSTITUTE, COMPLEX LITIGATION: STATUTORY RECOMMENDATION AND ANALYSIS

(1994).

APPENDIX B. REPORTER'S STUDY

A MODEL SYSTEM FOR STATE TO STATE TRANSFER AND CONSOLIDATION

§ 1. Standard for Transfer and Consolidation

(a) The Interstate Complex Litigation Panel established in § 2 may transfer and consolidate actions commenced in the courts of two or more states if:

(1) common questions of fact predominate, and

(2) transfer and consolidation will promote substantially the just, efficient, and fair conduct of the actions and is superior to their separate adjudication.

(b) Factors to be considered in deciding whether the standard set forth in subsection (a) is met include

(1) the extent to which transfer and consolidation will reduce duplicative litigation, the relative costs of individual and consolidated litigation, the likelihood of inconsistent adjudications, and the comparative burdens on the judiciary, and

(2) whether transfer and consolidation can be accomplished in a way that is fair and does not result in undue inconvenience to the parties and witnesses.

In considering those factors, account my be taken of matters such as:

    a.   the number of parties and actions involved;

    b.   The geographic dispersion of the actions;

    c.   the existence and significance of local concerns;

    d.   the subject matter of the dispute;

    e.   the amount in controversy;

    f.   the significance and number of common issues that are involved, including whether multiple laws will have to be applied to those issues;

    g.   the likelihood of additional related state actions being commenced in the future;

    h.   the wishes of the parties;

    i.   the stages to which the actions already commenced have progressed.

(c) Transfer and consolidation need not be denied simply because one or more of the issues are not so common that consolidated treatment of all parts of the dispersed actions cannot be achieved. Although the Panel typically shall transfer and consolidate entire cases, in special circumstances it may transfer and consolidate one or more common issues, rather than entire cases.

* * *

NATIONAL CONFERENCE ON COMMISSIONERS ON UNIFORM STATE LAWS, TRANSFER OF LITIGATION ACT

(1991).

§ 101. Power to Transfer

A [designate] court of this State may transfer an action or any part of an action to a court not of this State pursuant to Sections 102 to 110.

COMMENT

Section 101 establishes the basic authority to transfer. Transfer can be made to a court in a jurisdiction that has not enacted this act as well as to courts in jurisdictions that have. States that wish to limit authority to transfer to specified courts can identify the appropriate courts by name in the brackets provided in Sections 101, 102, and 103. Sections 102 to 109 set out the occasions and criteria for transfer, the procedures for transfer, the consequences of transfer, the duty to accept return, and the rules for appellate review.

The Act is not designed for transfer between courts of a single state. Section 101, as well as Sections 102 and 103, authorizes transfer only to a court "not of this State." The problems of intrastate transfer are quite different from the problems of interstate transfer, and the provisions of the Act should not take the place of specific state procedures adapted to the local court system.

There is no explicit limit in the Act on the nature of the actions that may be transferred. Limits are most likely to arise from concepts of subject matter jurisdiction. Ordinary civil actions, including those seeking equitable relief, are routine candidates for transfer. The Act is not drafted in terms that limit transfer to civil actions, however, because of the prospect that transfer may be appropriate as to proceedings that some courts may not characterize as civil actions. Domestic relations disputes, for example, may prove suitable for transfer, particularly as the parties move away from the state of the initial forum. Transfer also may prove appropriate as to some part of a probate proceeding. Criminal prosecutions, on the other hand, are not covered by the Act. Transfer of a criminal prosecution would entail all of the practical problems and theoretical difficulties that underlie the traditional rule that prosecution for an offense against one sovereign cannot be maintained in the courts of another sovereign.

The power to transfer part of an action includes power to transfer any matter that is usefully transferred. There are no technical or conceptual restrictions on what may be treated as "part" of an action. A single proceeding or issue may be transferred. Issues of liability might be transferred for consolidated proceedings, retaining damages issues for determination in the transferring court. Transfer for purposes of consolidated discovery on specified issues would be another example. Transfer for purposes of enforcing an equity decree would be a less obvious but potentially useful example.

Transfer confers broad powers on the receiving court, particularly under Sections 203, 208, 212, and 218. Transfer of part of a case might lead to consequences that were not intended by the transferring court. Protection against this possibility can be achieved by formally severing the case into separate actions and transferring only those parts of the original case that the court is willing to put beyond its control. Severance may be especially suitable if the transferring court has finally disposed of one or more claims or of all claims involving one or more parties. Severance in such circumstances ordinarily would be followed by entry of final judgment and appeal in the state of the transferring court.

The potential limitation that transfer can be made only to a court of record is included as an optional term. Some states may feel it necessary to safeguard against improvident transfer to a court that could assert subject matter jurisdiction but that operates informally.

§ 102. Transfer by Court Having Jurisdiction

A [designate] court of this State which has jurisdiction of the subject matter of an action and the parties may transfer all or part of the action to a court not of this State which consents to the transfer and can exercise jurisdiction over the matters transferred.

COMMENT

Section 102 authorizes transfer from a court that has jurisdiction of the subject matter and parties to a court that consents to the transfer and that has jurisdiction of the subject matter. Subject matter jurisdiction is controlled by the law of the receiving court, if a particular limitation is characterized as one of subject matter jurisdiction by the receiving court, the fact that the transferring court may adopt a different characterization in unavailing. It is not required that the receiving court be able to establish personal jurisdiction as an independent matter under its own law. Under the provisions of Section 203, the receiving court can assert personal jurisdiction over any party that was subject to personal jurisdiction in the transferring court, subject only to constitutional constraints. These provisions reflect the view that a court with personal jurisdiction should be able to exercise sufficient control over a case to determine that the litigation is better handled in a court that could not command personal jurisdiction over all parties had the action first been brought there. The receiving court cannot exercise personal jurisdiction over any party beyond the limits of due process or other constitutional constraints. Application of the underlying constitutional concepts, however, may be affected by the transfer process.

The requirement in Sections 102 and 103 that the receiving court consent to the transfer is a central part of the Act. The need to convince both courts that transfer is sensible affords strong protection against the danger of improvident or unfair transfer. The consent of the receiving court protects the parties and the receiving court itself. Consent can be refused if the grounds stated for transfer or the terms of transfer seem mistaken. The receiving court, moreover, has better knowledge of its own ability to handle the litigation; this knowledge of conditions in the receiving court may be especially important when transfer is ordered in an effort to achieve consolidation of parallel cases.

Consideration of the factors that warrant transfer may at times show that it is best to transfer an action to a court that could not establish personal jurisdiction over all parties if the action had initially been brought in that court. Section 203 supplements the long-arm statutes of the receiving state to provide a statutory basis for personal jurisdiction. Constitutional limits may be satisfied because the balance of advantages is so great that the parties who would be beyond the jurisdiction of the receiving court consent to transfer. A party who seeks transfer to another court from a court that has personal jurisdiction should be held to consent to personal jurisdiction in the receiving court unless for extraordinary reasons the transferring court agrees to allow preservation of a personal jurisdiction challenge. Transfer should not be ordered unless the party who seeks transfer agrees to submit to the personal jurisdiction of the receiving court as to at least part of the matters transferred.

Transfer should be available, however, even though one or more nonmoving parties do not consent to personal jurisdiction in the receiving state. In simple cases, transfer may be appropriate as a means of filling in gaps in the long-arm statutes of the receiving state. Some state long-arm statutes do not reach to the full extent permitted by constitutional limits; if both transferring and receiving courts conclude that a particular case is best tried in the receiving court, this additional long-arm power is easily justified.

Transfer also justifies expansion of the receiving court's personal jurisdiction in circumstances that do not involve gaps in local long-arm statutes. The constitutional rules that limit personal jurisdiction necessarily are cast in general terms that not only prevent untoward overreaching but also occasionally prohibit litigation in a court that in fact would be more convenient than another court that has jurisdiction. If both courts agree to a transfer, there is sufficient assurance of fairness to go beyond the general limits. The determination of the transferring court that it is fair for the receiving court to decide the case provides a neutral and valuable protection against overreaching.

More complex considerations are presented by multiparty litigation, and particularly by litigation that parallels other litigation arising out of the same events. Ordinary rules of personal jurisdiction are cast in broad general terms that treat each party as if the action involved only one plaintiff and one defendant. Actions involving multiple parties require a different jurisdictional calculus. So long as there is a sufficient relationship between the forum, the events giving rise to the litigation, and all the parties as a group, due process concerns may be satisfied as to parties who would not be subject to personal jurisdiction in a simple two party action. The Act does not attempt a specific formulation of the due process test; whatever words might be chosen to reflect contemporary Supreme Court decisions might be superseded in the continuing evolution of constitutional doctrine. The need for limits is met by the substantial protections against overreaching that are built into the Act. The initial determination that it is fair to proceed in the receiving court is made by the transferring court, which can be trusted to take a neutral view of the matter. The receiving court too must be persuaded that it is a fair forum for the entire litigation.

At some point, however, fairness to individual parties—plaintiffs as well as defendants—may override the advantages of transfer, both in relatively simple and in clearly complex litigation. Constitutional limits on the personal jurisdiction of the receiving court may be implemented by return to the transferring court under Section 214 if the transferring court had personal jurisdiction, and otherwise may be enforced by dismissal or transfer to another court. These protections can be ensured on appeal in the receiving state, and in an extreme case can be reviewed in the transferring state before transfer is effected.

Transferring personal jurisdiction from the transferring court to the receiving court does not address all the jurisdictional questions surrounding transfer. Traditional views of jurisdiction and allied matters also should be adjusted to recognize the opportunities created by transfer. The archaic local action rule, for example, has restrained some courts from entertaining claims that relate to real property in another jurisdiction. The local action rule should be disregarded entirely in deciding on transfer. A proceeding to foreclose a mortgage on real property in one state, for example, could easily involve questions related to litigation pending in another state; transfer of part of the action could be as useful in this setting as in any other, without encountering any of the difficulties that might be imagined in other circumstances.

§ 103. Transfer by Court Lacking Jurisdiction

A [designate] court of this State which lacks jurisdiction of the subject matter of an action or part of an action or which lacks personal jurisdiction of a party may transfer all or part of the action to a court not of this State which consents to the transfer and can exercise jurisdiction over the matters transferred and the parties.

COMMENT

Section 103 authorizes transfer from a court that lacks jurisdiction to a court that has jurisdiction. Transfer can be more efficient than dismissal, particularly if significant actions have been taken before the lack of jurisdiction is recognized. Transfer also may help avoid statute of limitations problems that might impede filing a new action in a court that has jurisdiction; Section 210 carries the date of filing in the transferring court forward to the receiving court.

Transfer from a court that lacks personal jurisdiction to a court that has personal jurisdiction does not violate the rules limiting personal jurisdiction. A lack of personal jurisdiction deprives the court of power to enter judgment on the merits, but the court has other powers. Discovery of facts bearing on the jurisdiction issue can be required. In states that have a final judgment rule, a trial court can proceed through trial. If the defendant appears without objecting to jurisdiction, the objection is lost. If the defendant raises the jurisdiction issue, a ruling that jurisdiction exists is binding by way of res judicata. The power to transfer to a court that does have personal jurisdiction is properly added to this list.

Problems arising from a lack of property jurisdiction are treated in the same way as problems arising from a lack of subject matter jurisdiction or personal jurisdiction. In some situations a state court may believe that lack of authority with respect to property defeats subject matter jurisdiction. If the court concludes that it has subject matter jurisdiction but lacks property jurisdiction, it has the same power to transfer that it has when there is no personal jurisdiction. For this purpose, a lack of property jurisdiction is described as a lack of personal jurisdiction.

Transfer may be requested before the court determines whether it has jurisdiction, and indeed transfer may be a useful means of avoiding difficult questions of jurisdiction. If the court orders transfer without determining whether it has jurisdiction, however, it must act under Section 103—transfer can be made only to a court that has both subject matter and personal jurisdiction. Transfer also may be ordered after the court has concluded that it lacks jurisdiction. A request for transfer is timely so long as it is made during the period provided by local practice for reconsidering a judgment of dismissal.

§ 104. Reasons for Transfer

A court may order a transfer to serve the fair, effective, and efficient administration of justice and the convenience of the parties and witnesses. In deciding whether to order a transfer, the court shall consider all relevant factors, including the interest of each plaintiff in selecting a forum and the public interest in securing a single litigation and disposition of related matters.

COMMENT

Section 104 states the general criteria for transfer. Many different factors may be considered in determining whether transfer will advance the fair, effective, and efficient administration of justice and the convenience of the parties and witnesses. All of these factors must be weighed together in a process that depends on the broad discretion of the transferring court to reach a wise decision based on the specific circumstances of each case. It is not possible to list all of the factors that may prove relevant, much less to prescribe a weighing process. The only factors specifically identified by the Act are the plaintiff's interest in selecting a forum and the public interest in securing a single litigation and disposition of related matters. These factors have been enumerated to ensure that courts reach uniform results as to fundamental matters that could easily generate disagreement. A list of other potentially relevant factors is set out at the end of this Comment. Many of these factors bear on the determination whether transfer is consistent with constitutional limits on receiving court jurisdiction over the parties.

One major issue that must be resolved by the Act is the weight to be given the plaintiff's interest in selecting the forum. Courts traditionally have given substantial weight to the plaintiff's interest, although some recent cases have questioned this tradition. There are substantial arguments in favor of giving equal weight to the interests of all parties in choosing a forum. Rules of jurisdiction and venue are drawn in general terms that may provide access to courts chosen for reasons of strategic advantage or even harassment. Perhaps more important, it is difficult to find any coherent standard to define the circumstances in which deference to the plaintiff's choice should outweigh a conclusion that another forum is more fair for all parties. Nonetheless, the Act directs that consideration be given the plaintiff's interest in selecting a forum. This traditional rule reflects the fact that it is the plaintiff who is responsible for initiating suit and a belief that a party who must carry the burdens of production and persuasion should enjoy some compensating advantage in selecting the forum. In adopting the traditional rule, the Act does not specify the weight to be given the plaintiff's interest. The determination will be affected by many of the general factors that go into the transfer decision—plaintiffs who would be at a significant disadvantage in a distant forum deserve more protection than those who seek only strategic advantage, perhaps in a court that otherwise is less convenient for all parties. Very little deference would be due a declaratory plaintiff who has anticipated the declaratory defendant's suit for coercive relief by racing to a favorable forum. And if the plaintiff seeks transfer from a forum initially selected by the plaintiff, the court must protect the defendant against deliberate manipulation by the plaintiff and the additional costs that may result from transfer.

The Act also addresses the issue whether public interests can be considered in addition to the private interests of the parties. Transfer is permitted to serve not only the convenience of the parties but also the fair and efficient administration of justice and the convenience of witnesses. Public interests can overcome the convenience of the parties considered alone. The most common reason for transfer in the public interest will be the need to consolidate related litigation. Most often consolidation will serve the convenience and private interests of the parties as well as the public interests in promoting efficient use of judicial resources and securing a single, uniform and coherent disposition of related matters. All parties to all consolidated actions benefit from shared discovery, joint pretrial, and the like. Significant inconvenience to some parties, moreover, often can be reconciled with the advantages of consolidation by securing consolidation of many related actions without insisting on consolidation of all parts of every one. Private disadvantage often will be more a matter of strategic opportunity than a matter of unfair or inconvenient litigation. In the end, however, consolidation may be ordered even though it would not be ordered if the only consideration were the interests of the parties to a particular action.

By allowing consideration of the interest in securing a single litigation and disposition of related matters, this Act establishes a starting point for consolidation in state court systems of multiparty, multiforum disputes. As courts become familiar with the opportunities created by the statute, they should be able to go a long way toward reducing the costs of conducting multiple parallel proceedings in two or more different states. In some situations there will be an obvious forum for consolidation—the court at the scene of an air crash, hotel fire, building collapse, or like single event provides a clear example. Another clear example is the court that has the largest share of the related cases. The statute, however, does not provide any means for taking cases from courts that are unwilling to let go, nor for transferring cases to courts that are unwilling to accept. Transfer and consolidation will depend on the joint cooperation and consent of transferring and receiving courts. In some situations the mass of litigation may be too large to be managed in a single court; despite the obvious problems of coordination, transfer and consolidation may be achieved in a relatively small number of courts on a regional or functional basis.

Many factors beyond the plaintiff's interest in selecting a forum and the public interest in consolidation could be considered in deciding on transfer. The Act does not attempt to provide a complete list of all these factors. Among the factors that have been considered in transferring cases between federal courts or in resolving *forum non conveniens* questions are:

- The residence of the parties and the distance of each party from the relevant courts.

- The locations of the events giving rise to the action.

- The distance between transferring and receiving courts.

- The comparative costs to each party of litigating in each court, including the ability of each party to bear those costs and the possibility of conditioning transfer on payments by the moving party.

- The amount of damages and the importance of the principles involved.

- Whether transfer will limit the ability of present counsel to conduct the litigation, and whether retaining new counsel will impose untoward costs on any party.

- Any agreement among the parties as to the place of litigation.

- The law that will apply to the action or any part of it.

- The locations of witnesses.

- The places in which discovery will occur.

- The desirability of facilitating joinder of additional claims or parties.

- The opportunity to achieve consolidation of related matters or to transfer to a court that is familiar with the underlying transaction, occurrence, or series of transactions or occurrences.

- The progress of the action up to the time of transfer.

- Whether transfer will delay or expedite further progress of the action.

- If part of an action is transferred, the impact of transfer on disposition of the parts not transferred.

- The interest of the forum and of the receiving court in adjudicating the action.

- The desires of the parties.

- The public interest in the consistent resolution of related disputes.

- The availability of jury trial; the impact of transfer of part of an action on the character of jury trial; the possibility of community prejudice or interest that may affect a jury verdict; and the importance of trial before a jury familiar with the community standards relevant to the case.

- Differences in available procedures, including rules of discovery and privilege and reliance on alternate dispute resolution methods.

- The nature of the claims.

- The degree of involvement of each party with the merits of the suit.

- The prospect that transfer may avoid difficult questions of jurisdiction in the transferring court.

- The foreseeability of litigation in the forum and in each court considered for transfer.

- The extent to which the parties were involved in a commercial capacity with the events underlying the action.

- Ease of enforcing the judgment, whether for monetary or specific relief.

* * *

Notes and Questions

1. The American Law Institute's COMPLEX LITIGATION: STATUTORY RECOMMENDATIONS AND ANALYSIS (1994) has taken different approaches towards dealing with the problems involved with dual system mass tort litigation. With regard to transferring and consolidating state cases in federal court, the ALI COMPLEX LITIGATION recommendations (in sections not reproduced here), has proposed various provisions for removal jurisdiction (§§ 5.01 and 5.02) and for federal court supplemental jurisdiction of state court claims (§ 5.03). As indicated, the COMPLEX LITIGATION project also has proposed a modified Anti–Injunction Statute to enhance the ability of federal courts to handle consolidated federal mass torts in their jurisdiction (§ 5.04), and also proposed provisions relating to court-ordered mandatory intervention and the operation of preclusion doctrine (§ 5.05). For a criticism of some of

these proposals, *see* Linda S. Mullenix, *Complex Litigation Reform and Article III Jurisdiction,* 59 Ford.L.Rev. 169 (1990).

2. A second method for dealing with dual system mass torts is to devise procedures for permitting federal courts to transfer mass tort cases to the state courts. Section 4.01, reproduced *supra,* represents the ALI's proposal for intersystem transfer from federal to state courts. What constitutional or statutory problems are involved with such transfer? *See generally,* George T. Conway, III, *The Consolidation of Multistate Litigation in State Courts,* 96 Yale L.J. 1099 (1987); Thomas D. Rowe Jr. & Kenneth D. Sibley, *Beyond Diversity: Federal Multiparty. Multiforum Jurisdiction,* 135 U.Pa.L.Rev. 9 (1987); Mark C. Weber, *Complex Litigation and the State Courts: Constitutional and Practical Advantages of the State Forum Over the Federal Forum in Mass Tort Cases,* 21 Hast.Const.L.Q. 215 (1994).

3. A third possible method for enhanced state resolution of mass torts is embodied in § 4.02, recommending the formulation of interstate compacts among groups of states to handle mass tort cases. The "Compact Clause" of the Constitution is found at art. I, § 10, cl.3: "[n]o State shall, without the consent of Congress, * * * enter into any Agreement or Compact with another State, or with a foreign Power * * *." Is the possibility of interstate compacts a feasible idea for interstate resolution of mass tort litigation? What might such an interstate compact accomplish? What limitations are there on interstate compacts? For a discussion of the problems entailed in interstate compacts with regard to mass tort litigation, *see generally,* Leonard J. Feldman, *The Interstate Compact: A Cooperative Solution to Complex Litigation in State Courts,* 12 Rev.Litig. 137 (1992). *See also* Reporter's Notes and Comments to § 4.02, COMPLEX LITIGATION: STATUTORY RECOMMENDATIONS AND ANALYSIS (1994).

4. The Uniform State Transfer of Litigation Act has finally been adopted by the National Conference of Commissioners on Uniform State Laws, and it must now be adopted by individual states. The initial sections of the Act are excerpted, *supra.* Does promulgation of a Uniform State Transfer of Litigation Act provide a more promising vehicle for interstate cooperation in resolving multistate mass tort litigation? How does it differ from the ALI interstate transfer-and-consolidation proposals? For a discussion of the Uniform Transfer of Litigation Act, *see generally,* Edward H. Cooper, *Interstate Consolidation: A Comparison of the ALI Project with the Uniform Transfer of Litigation Act,* 54 La.L.Rev. 897 (1994), and Chapter XIV, B, *infra.*

Chapter IV

PROBLEMS RELATING TO POST–AGGREGATIVE PROCEDURE

A. TRIAL STRUCTURE: BIFURCATED, TRIFURCATED AND MULTIPHASE PROCEEDINGS

IN RE BEVERLY HILLS FIRE LITIGATION

United States Court of Appeals, Sixth Circuit, 1982.
695 F.2d 207.

JUDGES: EDWARDS, CHIEF JUDGE, ENGEL, CIRCUIT JUDGE, and WEICK, SENIOR CIRCUIT JUDGE.

OPINION: ENGEL, CIRCUIT JUDGE.

On the evening of May 28, 1977, fire destroyed the Beverly Hills Supper Club in Southgate, Kentucky. One hundred sixty-five patrons and employees perished in the fire and many others were injured. Extensive litigation followed in both the State and Federal courts. Underlying this appeal is a class action commenced in the United States District Court for the Eastern District of Kentucky, based on diversity of citizenship. The class consists of the legal representatives of the persons killed and approximately thirty-five individuals who claimed to have been injured in the fire. Plaintiffs named as defendants several manufacturers of "old technology" aluminum branch circuit wiring, claiming those materials had been installed in the supper club and had caused the fire.[1]

Shortly before the trial was scheduled to begin, the trial judge ordered that it be bifurcated. The jury first would consider the question of "causation in fact." If aluminum wiring were found to be a cause of the fire, the jury would then determine questions of liability and damages. Plaintiffs' theory at trial was that the fire began in a "dead" or

---

1. Plaintiffs alleged three theories of liability in their complaint: concert of action, alternative liability, and enterprise liability. The trial judge granted summary judgment in favor of defendants on the issues of alternative and enterprise liability, stating that Kentucky recognized neither theory as a basis for liability. He allowed plaintiffs to go forward on a theory of concerted action. In re Beverly Hills Fire Litigation, C. No. 77–79 (E.D.Ky. Nov. 14, 1979). * * *

empty space within the north wall of a cubbyhole next to the Zebra Room, located on the first floor of the Supper Club. Plaintiffs asserted that the fire originated at an aluminum duplex receptacle. The receptacle, a standard electrical outlet into which electrical appliances are plugged, was allegedly located in the cubbyhole and connected to aluminum branch circuit wiring. Plaintiffs claimed that, due to a number of physical characteristics of old technology wiring, heat developed at the connection of the aluminum branch circuit wiring to the receptacle, and that this heat eventually ignited the wooden studs and other building materials in the wall. Plaintiffs claimed that the heat finally caused an open flame which spread undetected within the wall for approximately one to one and one-half hours before flame broke through the wall and directly engaged the Zebra Room itself.

Defendants responded that the receptacle in the cubbyhole was not proved to have been wired with aluminum branch circuit wiring. They claimed that the fire more likely began due to copper wiring of an electrical pump that was connected to a water fountain located in front of a staircase on the north side of the north wall. The defendants also suggested that the fire started as a result of numerous fire code violations found to have existed in the club. After twenty-two days of trial over a period of eleven weeks, the jury returned a special verdict answering in the negative the question whether the connection of old technology aluminum wired to an electrical device caused the fire at the Supper Club.

Based upon that finding, the trial judge entered a general judgment in favor of the defendants. Plaintiffs moved for a mistrial, for judgment notwithstanding the verdict and for a new trial. The trial judge denied all motions. These appeals followed.

* * *

II

Two claimed errors concern the severance of causation from other issues in the trial.

Plaintiffs first assert that the trial judge had no authority to isolate the issue of causation. It is well settled that the ordering of separate trials is within the sound discretion of the trial judge. Kosters v. Seven–Up Co., 595 F.2d 347 (6th Cir.1979); Crummett v. Corbin, 475 F.2d 816 (6th Cir.1973); Moss v. Associated Transport, 344 F.2d 23 (6th Cir. 1965). Plaintiffs argue, however, that no case law supports severance of the issue of causation; rather, only severance of liability and damages has been allowed. This view-point is inconsistent with the language of Fed.R.Civ.P. 42(b), which provides in part:

> *Separate Trials.* The court, in furtherance of convenience or to avoid prejudice, or when separate trials will be conducive to expedition and economy, may order a separate trial ... of *any* separate issue.... (emphasis added).

There is thus no reason to adopt a different standard with regard to severing causation. As the Rule indicates, and as our circuit has recognized, the court in ordering separate trials must consider several issues such as potential prejudice to the parties, potential confusion to the jury, and the relative convenience and economy which would result.[13] *See, e.g.*, Koster[s], 595 F.2d at 355–56. A balance of these concerns led the Eighth Circuit to approve bifurcation of the causation issue in Beeck v. Aquaslide 'N' Dive Corp., 562 F.2d 537 (8th Cir.1977). The court observed:

> Evidence of plaintiffs' injuries and damages would clearly have taken up several days of trial time, and because of the severity of the injuries, may have been prejudicial to the defendant's claim [that it did not manufacture the product that injured plaintiff].... Judicial economy, beneficial to all the parties, was obviously served by the trial court's grant of a separate trial.

* * *

The *Beeck* court also recognized that whether resolution of a single issue would likely be dispositive of an entire claim is highly relevant in determining the efficacy of bifurcation. The trial judge in the present case considered both the projected length of the trial and the likelihood that a resolution of the causation issue could shorten it.[14]

The conclusion of the trial judge has support in the record. The trial on causation alone took thirty-two days. Proof regarding the further issues of liability among the numerous defendants and of damages would be extensive and expensive.[15] It therefore was reasonable for the trial judge to conclude that litigation of those issues should be

---

13. Plaintiffs also claim they were prejudiced by the lateness of a decision to bifurcate the proceedings. We admit some sympathy with this complaint, but we cannot say that any prejudice to the plaintiffs was not outweighed by other considerations of efficiency and convenience. In any event, it is not likely to recur.

14. The trial judge described the potential advantages as follows:

This is a class action on behalf of approximately 200 persons against 23 defendants who have been grouped together as the "Aluminum Wire and Device Group." The parties estimate that approximately 40 trial days will be required for the presentation of several hundred witnesses. Critical to plaintiffs' case is the issue of causation. Before any determination of liability upon any of these defendants can be made, it must be established that "old technology" aluminum wire either caused or contributed to the fire at the Beverly Hills Supper Club May 28, 1977. While such establishment does not in and of itself determine liability of

any or all of the defendants, a negative determination would free them from such liability. There is reason to believe that a determination of this issue would materially reduce the time required to try this case. While a determination for the defendants would as a matter of law end the proceedings, it is entirely possible that an affirmative determination might enhance the likelihood of settlement.

In re Beverly Hills Fire Litigation, C. No. 77–79 (E.D.Ky.Dec. 12, 1979).

15. Certainly evidence regarding whether defendants breached a legal standard of care will be extensive. Moreover, because each of several defendants could insulate itself from liability by proving it was not part of any express or tacit agreement to produce defective wiring, it is anticipated that much evidence would be submitted regarding this issue. * * * A defendant further may offer evidence tending to show its wiring, because of inherent metallurgical or other differences, would perform differently from that of other companies. Additionally, the damages issue remains unresolved.

avoided if they might be mooted by an adverse finding on the causation issue. The value of severance in expediting this case has already been proved. Had the juror experiment required a mistrial after the *entire* case had been tried, many more weeks of effort would have to be repeated.

A strong argument can, it is true, be made against the bifurcation of a trial limited to the issue of causation. There is a danger that bifurcation may deprive plaintiffs of their legitimate right to place before the jury the circumstances and atmosphere of the entire cause of action which they have brought into the court, replacing it with a sterile or laboratory atmosphere in which causation is parted from the reality of injury. In a litigation of lesser complexity, such considerations might well have prompted the trial judge to reject such a procedure. Here, however, it is only necessary for us to observe that the occurrence of the fire itself, a major disaster in Kentucky history by all standards, was generally known to the jurors from the outset. Further, the proofs themselves, although limited, were nonetheless fully adequate to apprise the jury of the general circumstances of the tragedy and the environment in which the fire arose. As a result, we hold that the trial judge did not abuse his discretion in severing the issue of causation here. In so ruling, however, we emphasize that the decision whether to proceed in the same manner on any retrial is within the discretion of the trial judge, who will undoubtedly be benefitted from the experiences in the first trial as he makes his decision.

The plaintiffs next claim that severance, even if not in itself error, nonetheless resulted in the improper exclusion of evidence relevant to the issue of causation. Plaintiffs offered several documents as evidence supporting their contentions that aluminum wiring has a greater propensity to cause fires and that some defendants knew of this propensity. The trial judge excluded some documents in their entirety, and allowed certain evidence admitted upon deletion of references to individual defendants. In re Beverly Hills Fire Litigation, C. No. 77–79 (E.D.Ky. Jan. 7, 1980). In reviewing the documents at issue, the trial judge determined that several documents, though admissions as to some defendants, were hearsay as applied to other defendants. *See* Fed.R.Evid. 802; 801(d)(2). He determined further that documents indicating knowledge of some defendants were perhaps relevant to liability but were not relevant to causation, which alone was before the jury. *See* Fed.R.Evid. 401. Finally, he determined that those documents which were relevant to the issue of propensity of aluminum to cause fires were nonetheless inadmissible because their probative value was outweighed by the potential for prejudice if a specifically identified defendant were singled out. *See* Fed.R.Evid. 403. Evidence is not admissible in all cases where it is relevant. Fed.R.Evid. 403 provides:

> Although relevant, evidence may be excluded if its probative value is substantially outweighed by the danger of unfair prejudice, confusion of the issues, or misleading the jury, or by considerations of

undue delay, waste of time, or needless presentation of cumulative evidence.

Under this rule, admission of such evidence is placed within the sound discretion of the trial court. United States v. Brady, 595 F.2d 359 (6th Cir.1979). We have reviewed the documents deemed inadmissible by the trial judge and find that he did not abuse his discretion in excluding them. To the extent that the documents did not refer only to the knowledge of the defendants but also to the propensity of aluminum to cause fires, they were relevant. They were, however, largely cumulative of plaintiffs' evidence respecting the characteristics of aluminum wire. Moreover, as the trial judge observed, they may have improperly prejudiced the jury.

The trial judge on remand may decide not to isolate causation from liability. In that case, the evidence could in the trial court's discretion be offered against some defendants with an appropriate limiting instruction. *See* Fed.R.Evid. 105. If the case is again bifurcated, it again will be within the trial judge's discretion whether and under what circumstances to admit the documents. Although we see the dilemma caused by these exhibits as one argument working against the employment of bifurcation here, it does not constitute a basis for denying it altogether, if in the discretion of the trial judge it remains the most efficient method of managing this complex litigation on remand.

* * *

IN RE BENDECTIN LITIGATION

United States Court of Appeals, Sixth Circuit, 1988.
857 F.2d 290.

Before ENGEL, CHIEF JUDGE, and JONES and NELSON, CIRCUIT JUDGES.

ENGEL, CHIEF JUDGE.

These actions were brought on behalf of children with birth defects against Merrell Dow Pharmaceuticals, Inc., alleging that their birth defects were caused by their mothers' ingestion during pregnancy of defendant's anti-nausea drug Bendectin. Immediately involved are eleven hundred eighty claims in approximately eight hundred forty-four multidistrict cases. These cases represent only a part of the Bendectin cases which have been brought in numerous federal and state courts around the nation. Although there are some differences among the complaints, most are virtually identical, requesting relief on the grounds of negligence, breach of warranty, strict liability, fraud, and gross negligence, and asserting a rebuttable presumption of negligence per se for defendant's alleged violation of the misbranding provisions of the federal Food, Drug and Cosmetic Act (FDCA), 21 U.S.C. § 301 *et seq*.

After twenty-two days of trial on the sole question of causation, the jury answered the following interrogatory in the negative: "Have the plaintiffs established by a preponderance of the evidence that ingestion of Bendectin at therapeutic doses during the period of fetal organogenesis is is a proximate cause of human birth defects?" In re Richardson–Merrell, Inc., Bendectin Products, 624 F.Supp. 1212, 1269 (S.D.Ohio 1985). Had the jury answered this question in the affirmative, it then would have answered a second question concerning the particular categories of birth defects that Bendectin caused when administered at therapeutic doses: musculoskceletal defects, central nervous system defects, heart and circulatory defects, head defects, respiratory defects, gastrointestinal defects, genitourinary defects, and death. * * * Accordingly, the district judge entered judgment for defendant.

* * *

I. Background of the Case

The unusually large number of individual cases involved here found their way to the United States District Court for the Southern District of Ohio in a variety of ways. Eight hundred thirty-four of these claims were filed either in the Northern or Southern Districts of Ohio, while seventy-three claims, originally filed in Ohio state courts, were removed to Ohio federal courts. Only twenty-nine of the cases were initially filed in Ohio by Ohio citizens. The remainder included sixty-two plaintiffs from California, five from Texas, six from Pennsylvania, and sixty-six from other states or foreign countries. Two hundred seventy-three claims were filed or removed to federal district courts outside Ohio and were transferred to the Southern District of Ohio by the Judicial Panel on Multidistrict Litigation. In addition to these cases, the Judicial Panel on Multidistrict Litigation referred, pursuant to 28 U.S.C. § 1407, forty-seven cases under MDL 486 for consolidated pretrial discovery. Between 1982 and the completion of the trial in 1985, 582 additional cases were referred by the panel and 557 cases were filed in the Southern District of Ohio.

The court designated a five-member Plaintiffs' Lead Counsel Committee to act as the counsel for all plaintiffs. After the completion of discovery, on November 16, 1983, the district court consolidated under Rule 42(a) of the Federal Rules of Civil Procedure all Bendectin cases originally filed in the Southern District of Ohio or transferred in MDL 486 from the Northern District of Ohio and set those cases for trial beginning June 4, 1984 on all common issues of liability. The original decision was to bifurcate the trial, and if the plaintiffs were successful in obtaining a verdict finding liability, the court would schedule individual damages trials. While consolidation for trial was mandated for all cases pending in federal court in Ohio, the trial judge also permitted consolidation upon the liability issues for any case which had been transferred to the Southern District of Ohio under MDL 486. 28 U.S.C. § 1404. Those cases would be returned to the originating district if the verdict in the first portion of the bifurcated trial was for the plaintiffs.

* * *

The district court asked counsel to stipulate as to all common issues of liability that could be tried during the first phase of the trial. Defendant suggested a trial only on the issue of whether Bendectin was an unreasonably dangerous product imposing upon Merrell Dow a duty to warn about such dangers. It argued that substantive law differences among the various jurisdictions represented by plaintiffs prevented consolidation as to any other issue, regardless of whether the cases had been originally filed in Ohio or had been subsequently transferred there. The plaintiffs requested a trial of all common interrelated issues of law and fact, including whether Bendectin increased the risk of birth defects in the children of pregnant mothers who ingested the drug. They also indicated that the liability issues were inextricably interwoven and needed to be tried together with causation. Because the parties could not agree which issues should be tried during the first phase of trial, the court itself decided that the common issues to be tried beginning on June 11, 1984, would be whether: (1) taken as prescribed, Bendectin caused any of a list of birth defects; (2) Bendectin was unreasonably dangerous as defined by Ohio courts; and (3) Merrell Dow provided to the medical profession adequate warnings of the danger of the product. On April 12, 1984, the district court amended this order. Rather than bifurcating the trial on issues of liability and damages, the court instead decided to trifurcate the case, or bifurcate the liability question into liability and causation. Initially, a jury determination would be made on the causation question. If plaintiffs prevailed on the causation question, the jury would then consider the other liability questions. Conversely, if defendant received a favorable verdict on the causation issue, the trial would cease. * * *

* * *

The trifurcated trial commenced in February, 1985. Fearing undue prejudice to defendant, the trial judge, without actually viewing any plaintiffs, granted defendant's motion in limine to exclude all visibly deformed plaintiffs as well as all plaintiffs below the age of ten, whether or not they displayed birth defects. In another room in the courthouse, the court provided video arrangements to enable any excluded plaintiff to view the course of trial, as well as communications equipment so that plaintiffs could assist counsel. Further, the jurors and the deformed plaintiffs used different elevator banks so as to preclude the possibility of even accidental contact. Following trial, judgment was entered for defendant upon the jury's negative answer to the question whether plaintiffs had proven that ingestion of Bendectin proximately causes birth defects.

* * *

IV. TRIFURCATION

The plaintiffs challenge the district judge's decision to trifurcate this case by trying only the issue of proximate causation. They maintain that trifurcation violates their due process rights and Seventh Amendment right to trial by jury, and thus renders the decision an abuse of discretion. While defendant argues that the plaintiffs cannot raise this challenge on appeal because they made no objection to trifurcation at trial, the record supports a finding that plaintiffs timely preserved their objection to this procedure.

Plaintiffs raise many different arguments to support their claim that the district court judge abused his discretion in ordering trifurcation. First, they maintain that under the law of proximate causation as applied in this case, causation is not an issue capable of separation from issues of defendant's fraud, wrongful conduct, or negligence. Second, they object to the ruling because: the court's trifurcation decision came as a surprise and only after discovery had been completed; a different jury would have heard later stages of trial; proximate cause was a particularly difficult and improper issue to be independently decided by a lay jury; and trifurcation resulted in a sterile trial removed from plaintiffs' actual injuries. Third and finally, plaintiffs assert that the trifurcation ruling resulted in the exclusion of evidence that was vital to the determination of the single, causation issue.

Of all the issues on appeal, the validity of the trifurcation ruling has been most troubling to us. We reiterate that the standard of review is abuse of discretion. "[T]he district court ha[s] broad discretion to order separate trials; the exercise of that discretion will be set aside only if clearly abused." United States v. 1,071.08 Acres of Land, 564 F.2d 1350, 1352 (9th Cir.1977). *See also* Parmer v. National Cash Register Co., 503 F.2d 275, 277 (6th Cir.1974)(per curiam). "The decision whether to try issues separately is within the sound discretion of the court. . . . Abuse of discretion exists only where there is 'definite and firm conviction that the court below committed a clear error of judgment in the conclusion it reached upon a weighing of the relevant factors.' " Yung v. Raymark Industries, 789 F.2d 397, 400 (6th Cir.1986)(citation omitted).

The standards for separating issues is set forth in the language of Fed.R.Civ.P. 42(b): "The court, in furtherance of convenience or to avoid prejudice, or when separate trials will be conducive to expedition and economy, may order a separate trial of any claim, cross-claim, counterclaim, or third-party claim, or of any separate issue or of any number of claims, cross-claims counterclaims, third-party claims, or issues, always preserving inviolate the right of trial by jury as declared by the Seventh Amendment to the Constitution or as given by a statute of the United States." "The Advisory Committee Note to the 1966 amendment, though cryptic, suggests that . . . the changes in Rule 42 were intended to give rather delphic encouragement to trial of liability issues separately from those of damages, while warning against routine bifurcation of the ordinary negligence case." 9 C. Wright, A. Miller & F. Elliott, FEDERAL PRACTICE & PROCEDURE, § 2388 at 280 (1971 & Supp.1987). It cannot seriously be argued that this is a routine case.

The principal purpose of the rule is to enable the trial judge to dispose of a case in a way that both advances judicial efficiency and is fair to the parties. The provision for separate trials in Rule 42(b) is intended to further convenience, avoid delay and prejudice, and serve the ends of justice. It is the interest of efficient judicial administration that is to be controlling, rather than the wishes of the parties. The piecemeal trial of separate issues in a single suit is not to be the usual course. It should be resorted to only in the exercise of informed discretion when the court believes that separation will achieve the purposes of the rule. * * * Neither Rule 42(b) nor the textual elaboration cited gives any precise guidelines for the trial judge in considering the propriety of ordering separate trials, probably because of the wide variety of circumstances in which it might come into play. Consequently, courts have adopted a case-by-case approach. "Essentially, the question is one that seems to depend on the facts of each case, a matter to be determined by the trial judge exercising a sound discretion." Southern Ry. Co. v. Tennessee Valley Authority, 294 F.2d 491, 494 (5th Cir.1961). "In deciding whether one trial or separate trials will best serve the convenience of the parties and the court, avoid prejudice, and minimize expense and delay, the major consideration is directed toward the choice most likely to result in a just final disposition of the litigation." In re Innotron Diagnostics, 800 F.2d 1077, 1084 (Fed.Cir.1986). * * *

In our case this same test applies to whether the decision is to try only one or more than one issue separately. Our opinion in In re Beverly Hills Fire Litigation, 695 F.2d 207 (6th Cir.1982), approving trifurcation on the causation question, did not indicate any different standard of review than that applicable to bifurcation nor has our research led us to authority suggesting such a distinction. While few cases appear to have been trifurcated on the issue of causation,[12] there are nonetheless numerous cases that have tried an individual issue separately under circumstances that, had the issue been decided in favor of the plaintiff, the trial would have had more than two phases to it.[13] In affirming a trial solely on the issue of the defense of statute of limitations, *Yung v. Raymark,* 789 F.2d at 400, we quoted Wright & Miller and held that "Rule 42(b) is sweeping in its terms and allows the court, in its discretion, to grant a separate trial of any kind of issue in any kind of case." C. Wright, A. Miller & F. Elliott, *supra,* § 2389 at 284. It follows, therefore, that a decision to try an issue separately will be affirmed unless the potential for prejudice to the parties is such as to clearly demonstrate an abuse of discretion. *Beverly Hills,* 695 F.2d at 216.

* * *

12. *See* Marder v. G.D. Searle & Co., 630 F.Supp. 1087 (D.Md.1986), *aff'd sub. nom.,* Wheelahan v. G.D. Searle and Co., 814 F.2d 655 (4th Cir.1987); *Beverly Hills,* 695 F.2d at 207.

13. Beeck v. Aquaslide 'N' Dive Corp., 562 F.2d 537 (8th Cir.1977)(trial limited to whether defendant had manufactured the product); Rossano v. Blue Plate Foods, Inc., 314 F.2d 174, 176 (5th Cir.1963)(separate trial on issue of agency in negligence case); Bowie v. Sorrell, 209 F.2d 49 (4th Cir.1953)(separate trial on question of validity of release; tried before two juries).

A. *Proximate Causation as a Separable Issue*

Fundamental to plaintiffs' challenge of the trifurcation decision is their argument that the causation question in this case was not an issue which could be tried separately. In support of their claim, plaintiffs rely heavily on Gasoline Products Co. v. Champlin Refining Co., 283 U.S. 494, 500 (1931). There, the Court held that "[w]here the practice permits a partial new trial, it may not properly be resorted to unless it clearly appears that the issue to be retried is so distinct and separable from the others that a trial of it alone may be had without injustice." The Court noted that the issue in that case could not be submitted independently of the others without creating jury confusion and uncertainty that would "amount to a denial of a fair trial." *Id.* Many courts consider the issue's ability to be tried separately, and without injustice, to be the standard for determining whether the Seventh Amendment has been violated by conducting a trial only on that one issue. Thus, they apply the *Gasoline Products* standard to initial determinations whether a district judge properly ordered a separate trial in the first instance. Franchi Construction Co. v. Combined Insurance Co. of America, 580 F.2d 1, 7 (1st Cir.1978). While *Beverly Hills* did not cite *Gasoline Products,* our court in Helminski v. Ayerst Laboratories, 766 F.2d 208, 212 (6th Cir.1985), cited *Gasoline Products* as the standard for determining whether the issues of liability and damages in that case were sufficiently separable to justify a separate trial. *See also In re Innotron Diagnostics,* 800 F.2d at 1086 (separate jury trials appropriate where issues to be tried are "distinct and separable"). We affirm the appropriateness of the *Gasoline Products* standard to the context of Rule 42(b).

Under this standard, many courts have upheld cases bifurcated between liability and damages because the evidence pertinent to the two issues is wholly unrelated, and as a logical matter, liability must be resolved before the question of damages. *See* C. Wright, A. Miller & F. Elliott, *supra,* § 2390 at 296–97. By the same token, courts have refused to permit even bifurcation of liability and damages where these issues could not be tried separately. In C.W. Regan, Inc. v. Parsons, 411 F.2d 1379, 1388 (4th Cir.1969), the court disapproved bifurcation because under the law of Virginia, liability and damages could not be divided when the separate and unconnected actions of several people may have produced the total damage.

In the present case, plaintiffs argue that the *Gasoline Products* standard is violated because under the current standards and presumptions set forth in Ohio law, the issue of causation cannot be separated from the issue of defendant's tortious conduct. In their assertion of the nonseparability of these two issues, plaintiffs cite various tort theories that shift the burden of proof to defendants before causation has been proven more probable than not or weaken plaintiffs' burden of proof with regard to causation.

First, plaintiffs contend that in cases involving multiple possible causes, the courts must abandon any "but for" causation test in favor of the "substantial factor" test to be applied where plaintiff seeks to prove that the defendant's wrongful act is only one of several substantial factors bringing about the injury.   Thus, it is argued, because the determination of wrongdoing affects which standard plaintiffs need prove, liability must be tried either before or contemporaneously with the determination of causation.   Moreover, plaintiffs argue that the court should have charged the jury that the plaintiff need only show that Bendectin is a substantial contributing factor in causing birth defects and the burden of proof would then shift to the defendant to prove that Bendectin was not such a substantial factor.

In his decision denying plaintiffs' motion for judgment NOV or new trial, however, Judge Rubin held that the "substantial factor" test was not recognized in Ohio and refused to apply it under *Erie*.   Instead, Judge Rubin instructed the jury in the following language:

> The question you must answer is whether the plaintiffs established by a preponderance of the evidence that the ingestion of Bendectin at therapeutic doses during the period of fetal organogenesis is a proximate cause of birth defects?   The term "proximate cause" is defined as that which in a natural and continuous sequence produces an injury which would not have otherwise occurred.   This does not mean that the law recognizes only one proximate cause of an injury.   Thee [sic] may be more than one proximate cause. There may be other factors that operate at the same time, either independently or together, to cause an injury.   In such a case, each factor may be a proximate cause.   In order to conclude that Bendectin in therapeutic doses caused a specific category of birth defects, it is not necessary for you to find that all women who ingested Bendectin delivered children with birth defects.   The ingestion of Bendectin by a pregnant women [sic] in therapeutic doses and the subsequent delivery of a child with a specific birth defect standing alone is not evidence that Bendectin caused that defect.   At all times in your deliberations on causation, you must assume that Bendectin was ingested only in doses prescribed by physicians. . . .

In arguing that Judge Rubin's instructions were erroneous and that the substantial factor test should have been applied to the causation issue, plaintiffs cite various cases which they assert support the use of the test by Ohio courts, such as Cascone v. Herb Kay Co., 6 Ohio St.3d 155, 451 N.E.2d 815 (1983).   However, *Cascone* does not address the "but for" versus "substantial contributing factor" issue, but the quite different question whether an initial actor should be held liable for injuries caused by an intervening or superseding actor.   The court there held that the initial actor could still be held liable if his conduct remained a substantial contributing factor to the injury.   In this context, that is all "substantial contributing legal cause" refers to.   Thropp v. Bache Halsey Stuart Shields, Inc., 650 F.2d 817, 821 (6th Cir.1981). Under *Cascone*, even where there is an intervening actor, however, the first step of the proximate cause analysis is whether the original tortfeasor's negligence was an actual cause or a "cause in fact" of the injury.

* * * Plaintiffs also cite Utzinger v. United States, 432 F.2d 485 (6th Cir.1970), but again that case states the rule for an intervening agent. *Cf.* Hupp v. United States, 563 F.Supp. 25, 30 (S.D.Ohio 1982). To this we must add the observation that the plaintiffs never argued that Merrell Dow was an initial tortfeasor whose drug Bendectin caused birth defects because of the act of any intervening third party. The plaintiffs affirmatively alleged in their complaint and argued at trial that the drug itself was a direct cause of birth defects without the interference of any third party. Insofar as we can ascertain, the district judge's denial of plaintiffs' proposed instruction would have been proper under the law of any state.

Plaintiffs also point to the substantial factor theory in section 432(2) of the RESTATEMENT (SECOND) OF TORTS, which holds that when "two forces are actively operating, one because of the actor's negligence, the other not because of any misconduct on his part, and each of itself is sufficient to bring about harm to another, the actor's negligence may be found to be a substantial factor in bringing it about." Prosser and Keeton describe the substantial factor test as applied to two actors: "When the conduct of two or more actors is so related to an event that their combined conduct, viewed as a whole, is a but-for cause of the event, and application of the but-for rule to them individually would absolve all of them, the conduct of each is a cause in fact of the event." W. Prosser & R. Keeton, THE LAW OF TORTS, § 41 at 268 (5th ed.1984)(footnotes omitted). A review of the RESTATEMENT's own comment to section 432(2) indicates that it has no application here, however. The third illustration of that section's comment concerns two fires negligently set by the separate acts of two railroads. The two fires coalesced before reaching and subsequently setting fire to a third party's property. The normal spread of either fire would have been sufficient to burn the property, and the third party barely escaped from his house. Although in that situation the plaintiff would not need to prove "but for" causation, because he could not definitely say which of the railroads had caused the fire that damaged his house, he would have to prove that both fires could have caused the damage. In fact, the requirement under the substantial factor test of section 432(2) that plaintiff first prove that the conduct of each defendant, acting alone, was sufficient to be a possible proximate cause of the injury was set forth clearly in an Ohio case cited by plaintiffs themselves. Minnich v. Ashland Oil Co., 15 Ohio St.3d 396, 398, 473 N.E.2d 1199, 1201 (1984)("no determination has been made as to whether either defendant committed a tortious act, or whether either defendant's act was the proximate cause of appellant's injuries. These issues must be decided by a trier of fact in order to apply the RESTATEMENT rule [433B].").

Here, plaintiffs' witness, Dr. Swan, testified that in some cases, a woman might have taken Bendectin while exposed to another agent that independently causes birth defects. Although this other agent might have been present, she testified that would not mean that the contribution of Bendectin to that birth defect would have been any less. She also testified that Bendectin might act synergistically with other drugs to produce birth defects. However, section 432(2) has no relevance to the case unless the plaintiffs can show that Bendectin by itself caused birth defects, which the jury verdict indicates they did not do. Had it been established that Bendectin could bring about the harm individually and had there been cases in which Bendectin had been administered while other independent causes of birth defects were operating, then section 432(2) could apply.[14]

We conclude therefore that even if the cited Ohio cases were applied to the present case, plaintiffs would still have to prove "but for" causation rather than some weaker "substantial factor" standard. The substantial factor standard applies only to initial negligent actors in determining their liability in the face of action by a subsequent actor, or in determining causation between simultaneous actors, both of whose acts could have been "but for" causes of plaintiffs' injuries. For the same reasons that the plaintiffs' complaint would not have justified this instruction under the law of Ohio, it also would not have justified this instruction under the law of any other state, and we have been led to no other persuasive authority to the contrary.

* * *

At oral argument on appeal, counsel raised yet another argument: that the trifurcation order prevented the plaintiffs from showing alternate causation. Under alternate causation, the burden would have shifted to the defendant to prove that its negligence was not a proximate cause of the birth defects. If this argument applies, the district judge would have been bound to instruct the jury that defendant had the burden of proof, since a federal court in a diversity case must apply the state court's burden of proof rules. Palmer v. Hoffman, 318 U.S. 109, 117, 63 S.Ct. 477, 482, 87 L.Ed. 645 (1943). According to the plaintiffs' complaints, however, not only would plaintiffs not have been entitled to an alternate liability instruction with the shifted burden of proof in a trifurcated trial; they would not have been entitled to such an instruction even at a unitary trial. The doctrine of alternate liability simply does not apply to the facts alleged here. Cases that apply this doctrine, such as Sindell v. Abbott Laboratories, 26 Cal.3d 588, 163 Cal.Rptr. 132 (1980), and Summers v. Tice, 33 Cal.2d 80, 199 P.2d 1 (1948), do so only when two or more defendants have been at fault, and one and only one caused the injury. Rather than dismissing for plaintiff's inability to show causation by a preponderance of evidence against any individual plaintiff, courts in this situation shift the burden of proof to the defendant to prove that he was not the negligent actor that caused the injury. This is codified in section 433B(3) of the RESTATEMENT: "Where the conduct of two or more actors is tortious, and it is proved that harm

---

14. While we agree with the trial judge that Dr. Swan's testimony would not support application of section 432(2), it was nevertheless consistent with the court's instruction as given. It is important to observe that the jury, if it credited Dr. Swan's testimony, would plainly have understood that it could return a verdict for the plaintiffs where Bendectin was one of the proximate causes of the defects.

has been caused to the plaintiff by only one of them, but there is uncertainty as to which one has caused it, the burden is upon each such actor to prove that he has not caused the harm." As the RESTATEMENT'S comments to this subsection show, see for example comment (g), the rule is not applicable unless more than one defendant has been negligent. Here, however, the plaintiffs have sued only one defendant, Merrell Dow. That is the only actor whose conduct was alleged to have been negligent. Therefore, the doctrine of alternate liability, even if it has been adopted in states such as Texas, as Wood's attorney contends, does not apply to the one-defendant case.

Plaintiffs raise an additional argument for shifting the burden of proof to defendant regarding proximate cause. They claim that proof of a violation of the FDCA would give rise to negligence per se under Toole v. Richardson–Merrell, 251 Cal.App.2d 689, 60 Cal.Rptr. 398 (1967), and shift the burden to defendant to prove that Bendectin did not cause their injuries. Without trifurcation, they allege that some plaintiffs could have demonstrated negligence per se which would have enabled them to rely on a rebuttable presumption of causation based upon the violation of a statute designed to protect their safety. A cited example in support of this negligence per se argument is Haft v. Lone Palm Hotel, 3 Cal.3d 756, 91 Cal.Rptr. 745, 478 P.2d 465 (1970), in which a father and son drowned in a motel swimming pool, cause unknown. Contrary to the requirements of a California statute, the motel owner had failed either to place a lifeguard on duty at the pool, or post a sign indicating that no lifeguard was on duty. The court allowed plaintiffs to sustain their initial burden of proof on the issue of causation by proving that the violation of the statutory lifeguard requirement had occurred. Then, the burden shifted to the defendant to show that its violation did not proximately cause the death. Since defendant had been negligent by violating the statute, and since the failure to provide a lifeguard greatly increased the chances that the drownings would occur, and since the facts suggested that a competent lifeguard would have prevented the deaths, the plaintiffs according to the court, had done all that they could to prove the requisite causal connection between the negligence and the accidents. When there exists a substantial probability that a defendant's negligence caused an accident, and "when the defendant's negligence makes it impossible, as a practical matter, for plaintiff to prove 'proximate causation' conclusively, it is more appropriate to hold the defendant liable than to deny an innocent plaintiff recovery, unless the defendant can prove that his negligence was not a cause of the injury." * * *

Once again, the negligence per se argument is inapplicable to the facts of this case. The case law and legal commentary on application of the negligence per se standard in similar cases reveal that to shift the burden of proof to defendants plaintiffs must not only prove that defendant violated a statute, but also must prove that plaintiff's harm fell within the risk proscribed by the statute, or that there is a substantial probability (not necessarily more probable than not, but at least reasonably conceivable) that the violation and injuries are causally related.[17] In the present case we find that the plaintiffs' proof of causation between certain types of birth defects and defendant's misrepresentations and/or omissions in conducting research and labelling Bendectin is beyond the realm of common experience,[18] and thus plaintiffs would have been unable to shift the burden under the negligence per se standard even if violation of the FDCA was proved. While it is theoretically possible to envision a case where fraudulent research and mislabelling of a drug could, within the realm of common experience, be seen to cause serious injuries to purchasers following consumption, plaintiffs here have simply failed to present sufficient evidence to indicate substantial probability of a causal link between ingestion of the mislabelled drug and plaintiffs' injuries.

* * *

B. Trifurcation as a Potential Source of Unfair Prejudice

Plaintiffs also argue that the decision to trifurcate the trial was an abuse of discretion because the ruling unfairly prejudiced presentation of their case in a variety of ways. First, one of the plaintiffs' attorneys alleges that the decision to trifurcate was rendered after discovery had been completed and allowed him only two months to reorganize depositions and videotape testimony for a trial limited to the issue of proximate causation. Factually, this claim is inaccurate. Plaintiffs actually had ten months to revise the videotape depositions. The trial was postponed from June 1984, two months after the decision to trifurcate, to February 1985 because of the settlement negotiations. Plaintiffs argue that not all of this additional eight months could be used to reorganize the materials for trial, due to the settlement negotiations. While settlement discussions often dull the edge of advocacy, they do not provide a legal excuse for failure to continue preparations for trial. Had counsel for plaintiffs genuinely feared prejudice, they could have made a request to reopen discovery. While they claim on appeal that they did make such a

17. See, e.g., Wright, CAUSATION IN TORT LAW, 73 Cal.L.Rev. 1735, 1772–74 (1985). In Stanton by Brooks v. Astra Pharmaceutical Products, Inc., 718 F.2d 553 (3d Cir. 1983), the court applied the negligence per se standard specially [sic—ed.] to a claim of violation of the FDCA. Although in that case the court permitted plaintiffs to rely on negligence per se for defendant's violation of the FDCA and then shifted the burden of proof to defendant, it was already resolved that the cardiac arrest that plaintiff suffered was in fact caused by the drug which defendant manufactured. The question was whether defendant was liable for plaintiff's injury for failing to provide the FDA with information on the drug after the agency had approved it. In this case, even if the doctors would have considered Merrell Dow's wrongful withholding of information from the FDA to be sufficient to stop them from prescribing Bendectin, the fact that they continued to do so despite the statutory violation would be irrelevant if Bendectin does not in fact cause birth defects. The Fourth Circuit has also allowed negligence per se upon proof of a violation of the FDCA, even though it admitted that there was no express private civil remedy. Orthopedic Equipment Co. v. Eutsler, 276 F.2d 455, 460–61 (4th Cir.1960).

18. At trial, the proof adduced by plaintiffs to prove causation consisted of highly technical scientific studies, including toxicity studies on laboratory animals, chemical studies of the biochemical properties of Bendectin, and epidemiological studies or case histories of persons exposed to the drug.

request, the record does not support it. The plaintiffs further argue on appeal that the testimony of their witness, Theirsch, became unintelligible as a result of the removal of noncausation liability evidence. Our examination of Theirsch's testimony, including the specific page references cited to us, satisfies us that his testimony was intelligible despite its editing to eliminate references to liability. Plaintiffs had ample time in which to rearrange their proof, and they never requested more. The care and legal skill demonstrated in their advocacy leads us to conclude that they perceived no prejudice in fact from the amount of time available to them to reform their strategy. Neither do we.

The plaintiffs also challenge the trifurcation order because even had they won this stage of the trial, the court gave no assurance that the same jury that heard the evidence on causation, and rendered them a favorable verdict, would decide the question of liability. Plaintiffs' attorney Chesley specifically repeated this assertion at oral argument. The facts are otherwise. In Mr. Chesley's presence, the district judge indicated "that if the plaintiffs prevailed * * * the same jury [would] be used for the next phase of the trial." Judge Rubin did, however, offer to impanel a new jury if both sides so requested. No objection was raised to either comment, and, in fact Mr. Chesley explicitly indicated that it would "not [be] impossible to seat a new jury." Even had such a procedure been contemplated, and we emphasize that it was not, the party challenging such a procedure was willing to accept it below. In his argument on behalf of plaintiffs on appeal, Professor Arthur Miller acknowledged that there is no constitutional prohibition against trying these issues before different juries. *Cf.* 9 C. Wright, A. Miller & F. Elliott, *supra,* § 2391 at 302.

Plaintiffs' next challenge the decision to trifurcate on the proximate causation question because the issue trifurcated was the one which a lay jury would be least qualified to understand, evaluate, and decide. The district judge offered to try the case before a blue ribbon jury, but the plaintiffs rejected the idea. This was, of course, their right. In any event we conclude that if the issues were indeed difficult, their resolution was not rendered more difficult due to trifurcation. If anything, the narrowing of the range of inquiry through trifurcation substantially improved the manageability of the presentation of proofs by both sides and enhanced the jury's ability to comprehend the causation issue.

Plaintiffs' primary argument against trifurcation as unfairly prejudicial is that trying the question alone prejudiced plaintiffs by creating a sterile trial atmosphere. In *Beverly Hills,* we addressed similar concerns that trifurcation could possibly prevent the plaintiffs from exercising their right to present to the jury the full atmosphere of their cause of action, including the reality of injury: "A strong argument can, it is true, be made against the bifurcation of a trial limited to the issue of causation. There is a danger that bifurcation may deprive plaintiffs of their legitimate right to place before the jury the circumstances and atmosphere of the entire cause of action which they have brought into the court, replacing it with a sterile or laboratory atmosphere in which causation is parted from the reality of injury. In a litigation of lesser complexity, such considerations might well have prompted the trial judge to reject such a procedure. Here, however, it is only necessary for us to observe that the occurrence of the fire itself, a major disaster in Kentucky history by all standards, was generally known to the jurors from the outset. Further, the proofs themselves, although limited, were nonetheless fully adequate to apprise the jury of the general circumstances of the tragedy and the environment in which the fire arose. As a result, we hold that the trial judge did not abuse his discretion in severing the issue of causation here." *Beverly Hills,* 695 F.2d at 217. Judge Rubin considered this language when he denied the plaintiffs' motion for a new trial. On appeal plaintiffs also rely heavily on the same language.[19] Sterility is not necessarily the inevitable consequence in a trifurcated trial merely because the jury may not hear the full evidence of defendant's alleged wrongdoing. It more properly refers to the potential danger that the jury may decide the causation question without appreciating the scope of the injury that defendant supposedly caused and without the realization that their duties involve the resolution of an important, lively and human controversy. It is with respect to this latter concern that the plaintiffs urge that they were unfairly prejudiced by the trifurcation. The record reveals that the district judge consciously worked to avoid the potential for unfair prejudice. . . .

The court was not alone in efforts to avoid the dangers of sterility. In his final argument, plaintiffs' attorney Eaton told the jury that the trial was not an academic exercise, and that the case involved many real people who sought justice, and who would, as children, be affected by the jury's verdict well into the next century.

Finally, plaintiffs argue that Judge Rubin failed to consider the caveats of Rule 42(b) in his trifurcation decision, and instead justified trifurcation only upon unsubstantiated claims of judicial efficiency, thus unduly prejudicing plaintiffs' case without good reason. We believe, however, that the district judge carefully made the necessary inquiry. In his final order the trial judge noted that Bendectin litigation could "substantially immobiliz[e] the entire Federal Judiciary. There have been only four cases involving Bendectin which have been individually tried. They required an average of 38 trial days." *In re Bendectin,* 624 F.Supp. at 1221. Judge Rubin calculated that if all 1100 cases were tried at that average length on an individual basis, they would be able to keep 182 judges occupied for one year. * * * Contrary to the plaintiffs' claims that Judge Rubin never considered the language of Rule 42(b), he did correctly require plaintiffs to prove that the defendant's drug caused their injury, and would not allow plaintiffs to buttress a weak causation case with a strong negligence case. Thus, in line with the language of

19. Plaintiffs maintain that the exclusion of all visibly deformed plaintiffs from the courtroom, as well as all children under ten, whether or not visibly deformed, also contributed to sterile or laboratory conditions.

Rule 42(b), the trial judge considered the causation question to be a separate issue.

* * *

C. Claims of Prejudice Resulting From Exclusion of Evidence Bearing on Causation

While we have held that proximate causation is a separate legal question, that trifurcation did not unfairly prejudice more general aspects of plaintiffs' case, and that trifurcation furthered economy in this case, we must still consider whether trifurcation unduly prejudiced plaintiffs by restricting the evidence they could bring forth in proving the proximate causation issue.

First, plaintiffs argue that this format prejudiced them because it precluded them from introducing evidence about the individual circumstances of different plaintiffs concerning their ingestion of the drug. Although the record on this point is not completely free of doubt, the court did not exclude all evidence of the effect of the drug on individual plaintiffs. The plaintiffs stated that they intended to have Dr. Done testify about individual cases, and it is significant in our view that the court denied the defendant's motion to preclude such testimony. The plaintiffs never offered such testimony, and they were not precluded from doing so. Thus, there was no evidence offered that individual circumstances in ingesting Bendectin had any causal relationship to birth defects, even though the district judge allowed plaintiffs to introduce evidence of individual differences. Plaintiffs' argument, asserted repeatedly at oral argument and in their briefs, that the district judge precluded factual testimony is also not supported by the record. Factual testimony was permitted on rebuttal, and plaintiffs chose to subpoena only one factual witness. We can only conclude that their decision was tactical. We perceive no reversible error in this regard.

Plaintiffs also assert on appeal that they were unable to argue that there was a genetic susceptibility to Bendectin that varied among individuals, and that the jury should have been so instructed. The plaintiffs were not precluded from arguing that there was an individual susceptibility to Bendectin, but all their witnesses testified only that there were individual genetic susceptibilities to drugs in general. No one testified that there was such a susceptibility to Bendectin. Judge Rubin therefore correctly advised counsel that if the plaintiffs argued to the jury that there was such an individual susceptibility to Bendectin, he would have to instruct the jury that there was no evidence to that effect.

Probably the plaintiffs' most serious charge is that the trifurcation format prevented them from challenging the validity of various studies that the defendant relied on in support of its position that Bendectin did not cause birth defects. For example, at oral argument plaintiffs' counsel represented that while plaintiffs could attack part of the Bunde–Bowles study defendant had used to justify the safety of Bendectin, most of the study could not be criticized because of limitations placed upon counsel by the court. Also, co-counsel alleged at oral argument that when the defendants relied on a particular study, the plaintiffs tried to cross-examine these studies' methodology and biases, but the district judge prevented this line of inquiry because of the trial's limitation to causation. These assertions would be potentially serious except that they are not supported by the record.

For example, the plaintiffs complain that they could not show criminal conduct and fraud in the preparation of the Bunde–Bowles study. It is true that the district judge would not allow testimony going to the fraudulent preparation of this study, but he did not preclude proof affecting the accuracy of test results indicating that Bendectin did not cause birth defects. Although a fraudulent motive might be more dispositive of the value of a study, it is also in most cases a prejudicial and inaccurate gauge of how incomplete a scientific study actually is. Instead the most effective way to discredit these studies is through a critique of their technical flaws, as was done here. [other examples omitted—*ed.*]

D. Conclusion

To summarize, the three considerations we apply in reviewing a decision to try an issue separately are (1) whether the issue was indeed a separate issue, (2) whether it could be tried separately without injustice or prejudice, and (3) whether the separate trial would be conducive to judicial economy, especially if a decision regarding that question would be dispositive of the case and would obviate the necessity of trying any other issues. We hold that since the initial trial on the proximate causation issue was a separate issue, promoted efficiency, and did not unduly prejudice plaintiffs, trifurcating this case on the separate issue of proximate causation was proper. We need not decide whether this was the best or even the only good method of trying this case. We need only determine whether, under all of the circumstances before him, the trial judge's decision to trifurcate was an abuse of discretion.

* * *

CONCLUSION

In reviewing the record and in making the determination as to the extent to which the decisions of the district court should be upheld or reversed, it is helpful to the perspective to realize, as we observed earlier, that the jury verdict following trial here might have been for the plaintiffs instead of for the defendant. Thus, where judicial discretion is to be reviewed, it must be from the perspective of a trial judge faced with many difficult choices and without the benefit of hindsight. Likewise, where there have been issues which are purely legal in nature, their resolution requires an objective adherence to sound legal and constitutional principles. In a trial of this length and complexity, it is virtually certain that at specific points of the trial one or all of us might have ruled differently on a certain procedure or on the admissibility or inadmissibility of a certain piece of evidence. It is with this realization in mind that we defer in large part to the wisdom and discretion of the trial judge who is provided with a superior vantage point from which he is able to exercise this discretion in organizing the course of trial in a meaningful and practical way. In upholding the result here to the extent we have, it is at least deserving of note that a careful examination of the trial record itself reveals the management of the trial by a judge who does not appear at any time throughout to have sought consciously or unconsciously to have unfairly tipped the scales in favor of one side or the other, but who instead in his rulings appeared to be genuinely concerned with producing a trial that was as fair and free from error as human endeavor could make it. While we must always be conscious of the potential danger of making the trial a sterile exercise of scientific investigation by limiting issues and evidence too narrowly, it is quite evident, through several thousand pages of testimony, that the jury was presented with and bound to appreciate the seriousness of a very real issue of great importance to the parties at suit. In fact, to have broadened the issues beyond that of causation would have occasioned a real risk of overencumbering the jurors and impairing their ability to reach a knowledgeable and intelligent verdict based upon the evidence and upon the law applicable under the appropriate instructions. The result of these proceedings, and of our decision here, will of course mean that for some parties the litigation is concluded, but that for others it may be resumed and continued elsewhere. The reasons for this we have already set forth at length in this opinion and to those we can only observe that such would have been the case in any event had efforts at joinder and then trifurcation not been attempted. This litigation has been substantially advanced by the efforts of the district judge and, we hope, by this decision. We can expect no more at this juncture.

* * *

NATHANIEL R. JONES, CIRCUIT JUDGE, concurring in part and dissenting in part.

I write separately today for two reasons. First, I write to point out my disagreement with the majority on the exclusion, by the district court, of certain plaintiffs from the courtroom during the twenty-two day jury trial on causation. Secondly, I write to express a few of my concerns regarding the district court's trifurcation order. My opinion, however, is both narrow and focused as I examine only these two issues; issues which possess both great value and import in the functioning of our judicial system. As to all remaining issues raised by this appeal, I concur in the very thorough and well-written majority opinion.

I

Although I concur in the final result of the majority opinion with regard to the district court's trifurcation order, I do so reluctantly and with serious reservation. However, pursuant to the applicable standard of review, i.e., an abuse of discretion standard which favors the district court's ability and judgment to fairly and expeditiously handle its docket, and to case law within this circuit where such a procedure has previously been approved, i.e., In re Beverly Hills Fire Litigation, 695 F.2d 207 (6th Cir.1982), I agree with the majority that, in this instance, the district court did not abuse its discretion in trifurcating the issues of causation, liability and damages. However, I do express my concerns about the fairness of this mechanism as a tool for handling complex cases such as this. In so doing, I do not re-analyze all of the relevant factors to which courts look in making their decisions as to trifurcation; Chief Judge Engel has quite thoroughly analyzed those factors. * * * Instead, I point out potential problems and prejudices that can arise by the use of this procedure.

While it is clear that a trifurcation order such as the one here is not unprecedented, it is equally clear that trifurcated trials are a rarity and have only been approved in the most extreme cases. The fact that trifurcation has rarely taken place, however, does not mean that it is without merit. Rather, since so many potential prejudices loom, trifurcation of issues is limited to rare occasions.

Although I have no problem with the approved trifurcation order in this court's *Beverly Hills* decision, I do become hesitant when that decision is applied, seemingly without reservation, to a case, such as this one, which is complex in nature. Because I find several distinctions between this case and *Beverly Hills,* I am reluctant to apply such reasoning wholesale. Thus, I find that if *Beverly Hills* is narrowly construed, several problems become apparent with the majority opinion.

First, all of the victims in the *Beverly Hills* litigation were affected by the same event, a disastrous and tragic fire. Thus, the issue of causation could, quite competently, be tried separately from the issues of liability and damages with only a small chance that the plaintiffs would be prejudiced. This was simply because all plaintiffs were affected in the same manner by a unique, single event. Individual facts about the individual plaintiffs would therefore, have had little significance in regard to the question of causation.

The Bendectin litigation, however, is quite different. Over eight hundred plaintiffs, whose mothers took the drug at different times and places and under different circumstances, are involved. As such, a single, unique event such as a fire is replaced by over eight hundred distinct events that, in all likelihood, affected the individual plaintiffs in different ways. Although each distinct event involved the ingesting of the same drug, it is hard to believe that all eight hundred plus claims can be tied neatly into one package and satisfactorily resolved by the answering of one question, i.e., did Bendectin cause the relevant birth defects? In tying all of these claims together, an argument could certainly be made as to prejudice. That is, by not allowing the plaintiffs to present evidence as to how they were individually affected by the drug could have resulted in prejudice to them in their attempt to establish the required elements of their case. Indeed, although I concur in the majority's end result, I disagree with the language used in reaching the conclusion. The majority opinion refers to the fact that the plaintiffs were not "unduly" prejudiced by the court's trifurcation order. I do not agree that this is the burden plaintiffs must meet to establish an abuse of discretion by the lower court with regard to a trifurcation order. Rather, my suggestion is that any prejudice to a plaintiff in the litigation of his or her case should be enough to hold that the lower court has abused its discretion. I do not agree with the majority that absent a showing of unduly or excessive prejudice, the court's order should be upheld. Indeed, this court should define the amount of prejudice that must be demonstrated to establish that a trifurcation order was an abuse of discretion. Such a discussion in this case, however, is without utility. Plaintiffs here simply failed to meet their burden to demonstrate any prejudice. That is, plaintiffs lost their case because they failed to establish any link between their birth defects and the drug Bendectin, not because of any prejudice to them resulting from the trifurcation order.

In conclusion, trifurcation orders present fundamental problems of fairness simply because the typical procedure in litigation does not involve the splitting up of a case, element by element, and trying each point to the jury separately. Rather, the plaintiff's entire case is presented to the jury at once, thereby preventing the isolation of issues in a sterile atmosphere. Simply because a litigant shares his complaint with eight hundred other claimants is not a reason to deprive him of the day in court he would have enjoyed had he been the sole plaintiff. However, as the majority points out, a trifurcation order is authorized and necessitated at some point so as to allow a district court to manage and control the complexities and massive size of a case. The duty of this court, however, is to prevent such a case-management tool from becoming a penalty to injured plaintiffs seeking relief via the legal system.

In this case, after all of these concerns have been considered and accounted for, I agree with the majority that the district court did not abuse its discretion in trifurcating the issue of causation.

Notes and Questions

1. In the *Beverly Hills Fire Litigation* and the *Bendectin* case, plaintiffs appealed the bifurcation and trifurcation orders after unsuccessful trials. Who determines whether a mass tort case will be bifurcated or trifurcated? Does polyfurcation favor one side of the litigation or another? In what way? Can a plaintiff or defendant request a certain type of trial plan? May the court order a multiphase trial over the objections of either or both sides of the litigation? Does the judicial system have independent interests in the phasing of the trial? May those interests override those of the litigants? How is the Seventh Amendment implicated in trial staging? Due process?

2. In both cases above, the circuit courts upheld the lower courts' trial phasing. In the *Bendectin* litigation, the court extensively canvassed the relationship of Ohio state substantive tort law to possible prejudice that might result from the lower court's trifurcation procedure. Is the Sixth Circuit's decision persuasive? Is it possible to envision state substantive tort law that would vitiate against a bifurcated or trifurcated trial? In dissent

Judge Jones argues that the *Beverly Hills Fire Litigation,* as a single site mass disaster, is sufficiently distinguishable from the *Bendectin* cases as to raise troubling doubts about the trifurcated trial procedure used by Judge Rubin. Isn't Judge Jones correct in distinguishing types of mass torts and the consequential prejudicial effects of polyfurcated trial proceedings?

3. In *Yung v. Raymark,* 789 F.2d 397 (6th Cir.1986)(an asbestos case), cited by the court in *Bendectin,* the court upheld the separate trial of the defendants' affirmative statute of limitations defense over the plaintiffs' objection based on prejudice. Citing to *Beverly Hills,* the court suggested that "Whether resolution of a single issue would likely dispose of an entire claim is extremely relevant in determining the usefulness of a separate trial on the issue. * * * This procedure should be encouraged because court time and litigation expenses are minimized." *Id.* at 401. What other issues, either as part of the plaintiffs' claims or the defendants' defenses, are likely to dispose of an entire claim? How is the court to determine this?

4. In *Cimino v. Raymark,* Judge Robert Parker of the Eastern District of Texas formulated another version of a trifurcated trial plan consisting of (1) presentation of common defenses and liability for punitive damages, (2) exposure, and (3) compensatory damages. *See* Linda S. Mullenix, *Beyond Consolidation: Post Aggregative Procedure in Asbestos Mass Tort Litigation,* 32 Wm. & Mary L.Rev. 475, 557–65 (1991)(describing *Cimino* trial plans as well as bifurcated trial plan for *In re School Asbestos Litigation*). What is reverse bifurcation? Reverse trifurcation? What does the court hope to accomplish by reversing or re-ordering the trial of issues? *See also Watson v. Shell Oil Co.,* 979 F.2d 1014 (5th Cir.1992), *aff'g,* In re Shell Oil Refinery, 136 F.R.D. 588 (E.D.La.1991)(approving trial plan based on *Cimino*).

5. The use of polyfurcated trial procedure has proven controversial. For discussion of the constitutional and practical problems relating to multiphase trial procedure, *see generally* Albert P. Bedecarre, *Rule 42(b) Bifurcation at an Extreme: Polyfurcation of Liability Issues in Environmental Tort Cases,* 17 B.C.Envtl.Aff.L.Rev. 123 (1989); Kenneth S. Bordens & Irwin A. Horowitz, *Mass Tort Civil Litigation: The Impact of Procedural Changes on Jury Decisions,* Judicature, June–July 1989, at 22; Susan E. Abitanta, Comment, *Bifurcation of Liability and Damages in Rule 23(b)(3) Class Actions: History, Policy, and a Solution,* 36 Sw.L.J. 743 (1982); Thomas E. Willging, Trends in Asbestos Litigation at 102–04 (1987)(bifurcation and trifurcation in asbestos litigation).

B. DISCOVERY IN MASS TORT LITIGATION

1. TIME, PLACE, AND MANNER RESTRICTIONS
IN THE UNITED STATES DISTRICT COURT FOR
THE EASTERN DISTRICT OF TEXAS
BEAUMONT DIVISION

CLAUDE CIMINO, *et al.*   *

                                            *

vs.   *   NUMBER B–86–0456–CA

                                            *

RAYMARK INDUSTRIES, INC. *et al.*   *

DISCOVERY PLAN AND SCHEDULE FOR DEPOSITIONS AND MEDICAL EXAMINATIONS OF PLAINTIFFS

In this action, 3,031 individual asbestos cases have been consolidated for trial on the issues of state of the art and punitive damages. Additionally, the issues of exposure, actual damages, affirmative defenses and contributions have been certified as a class action. The court has determined that trial will commence on February 5, 1990. Approximately three months remain before trial.

Although most cases involved in this consolidated trial/class action have been pending for a substantial amount of time, defendants have deferred discovery concerning the individual claimants until now. Additionally, the court's suggestion that the parties limit discovery to a statistically significant sample of plaintiffs has been rejected. Defendants insist on individualized discovery regarding each claimant. Specifically, the defendants seek to depose all plaintiffs and to conduct full medical examinations of most plaintiffs.

The sheer number of cases, the limited physical resources of counsel, the abbreviated number of discovery days remaining before trial, and consideration of human factors affecting the individual plaintiffs require that the court develop specialized procedures in order to enable defendants to obtain reasonable and adequate discovery without delaying or otherwise hampering the trial of this action.

It is, therefore, ORDERED that defendants' discovery, regarding individual plaintiffs, shall consist of the following:

1. Discovery provided to the defendants under provisions of the court's standing order relating to asbestos cases.

2. An oral deposition or interview (at defendants' option).

Oral depositions shall occur generally in accordance with "Attachment C" of the Feasibility Report submitted by Ms. Dianne Dwight to the Honorable Robert M. Parker, November 3, 1989. * * * Depositions shall commence no later than November 17, 1989, and shall occur in the plaintiffs' counsel's offices in Beaumont, Texas, or any other mutually agreed locations.

Depositions shall occur according to the following schedule:

CALENDAR OF WORK DAYS

NOVEMBER:

11/17–11/18	9 DAYS (INCLUDES ONE SATURDAY,
11/20–11/22	[11/18], EXCLUDES THANKSGIVING
11/27–11/30	HOLIDAYS)

DECEMBER:

12/01–12/02	22 DAYS (INCLUDES THREE SATURDAYS,
12/04–12/09	[12/2, 12/9, 12/16], EXCLUDES
12/11–12/16	CHRISTMAS)

12/18–12/21
12/26–12/29

JANUARY:

1/02–1/06   26 DAYS (INCLUDES ALL SATURDAYS,
1/08–1/13   EXCLUDES NEW YEAR'S DAY)
1/15–1/20
1/22–1/27
1/29–1/31

FEBRUARY:

2/01–2/03   3 DAYS (INCLUDES 1 SATURDAY)

PERFORMANCE: 3144

Within three days from the entry of this order, plaintiffs' counsel shall specify to defendant's counsel the various locations for the depositions.

Defendants shall arrange for and provide court reports.

Plaintiffs' counsel shall be responsible for securing the individual plaintiffs' presence at the appointed times and designated places. Plaintiffs' counsel shall have sole discretion to determine the order in which any given plaintiff's deposition shall be taken. Plaintiffs' counsel's responsibility is to ensure that the depositions proceed according to the forty-five (45) minute plan (See "Attachment C"). Plaintiffs' counsel has no obligation to schedule the individual deponents in any particular order or location so long as all plaintiffs are made available for deposition or interview according to schedule.

3. A medical examination for every plaintiff.

Individual medical examinations may be conducted by defendants generally in accordance with the four-phase procedure proposed by Mr. George Shipley in his letter to Honorable Robert M. Parker, dated November 2, 1989.... The examinations may consist of any medically acceptable procedure determined to be reasonable, necessary and appropriate by physicians selected by the defendants to perform the examinations. All phases of the examination shall occur in Beaumont, Texas, on the same day and shall be completed within eight (8) hours from the time any given individual's appointment is scheduled to begin.

Defense counsel shall, within seven (7) days from entry of this order, supply plaintiffs' counsel with a list of those plaintiffs defendants desire to examine. Defense counsel shall further specify the location(s) for the examinations and provide the court and plaintiffs' counsel with a calendar of examination days not to exceed thirty to commence no later than November 27, 1989, and to terminate no later than January 10, 1990.

Thereafter, plaintiffs' counsel shall be responsible for securing the presence of the individual plaintiffs at the designated times and places for the examinations. As with the depositions, plaintiffs' counsel's responsibility is limited to insuring that individual plaintiffs are present for examination in the aggregate daily numbers contemplated under the defendants' plan. Plaintiffs' counsel have no obligation to present the plaintiffs for medical examinations in any particular order, unless mutual agreement between counsel so provides.

It is further ordered that the parties shall confer and agree on the details required to implement this discovery plan. If problems are encountered, the parties may contact the court for further guidance under the provisions of Fed.R.Civ.P. 26(f).

SIGNED this 9 day of November, 1989

EARL S. HINES
UNITED STATES MAGISTRATE

ATTACHMENT C
45–MINUTE PLAN

MONDAY–THURSDAY-   One depo every 45 minutes from 8 a.m. to 11:45 a.m.; 1 p.m. to 5:30; and 7 p.m. to 9:15 p.m.

FRIDAY AND SATURDAY–One depo every 45 minutes from 8 a.m. to 11:45 a.m.; 1 p.m. to 5:30 p.m.

Performance based upon calendar (Attachment A) and four groups:

November	704
December	1160
January	1360
	3224 (Excess allows for "no shows" and resets)

With four groups, plan yields:

Monday–Thursday = 14 per group x 4 groups = 56 per day

Friday and Saturday = 11 per group x 4 groups = 44 per day

**IN THE UNITED STATES DISTRICT COURT,
EASTERN DISTRICT OF TEXAS
BEAUMONT DIVISION**

CLAUDE CIMINO, *et al.*	*	
	*	
vs.	*	CIVIL ACTION NO. B–86–0456–CA
	*	
RAYMARK INDUSTRIES, INC., *et al.*	*	

ORDER

Pursuant to 28 U.S.C. 636(b)(1), this Court referred to United States Magistrate Earl S. Hines the task of formulating a discovery plan for this consolidated action and class action. Before formulating such a plan, the Magistrate met with and heard from liaison counsel for the Plaintiffs and Defendants. On November 9, 1989, the Magistrate filed his Discovery Plan and Schedule for Depositions and Medical Examinations of Plaintiffs. Since that time, a number of Defendants have filed objections to the Discovery Plan and Schedule. The Defendants contend that the Discovery Plan and Schedule impairs their ability to obtain full discovery in this action.

The Court agrees with the Magistrate that the "defendants have deferred discovery concerning the individual claimants until now." In light of the procedure for this action, the Court suggested that the parties limit discovery to a statistically significant sample of Plaintiffs. However, the Defendants rejected this suggestion, insisting on individualized discovery regarding each claimant.

The cost of individualized discovery, including attorneys' fees, would be astronomical. In addition, given the large number of cases in this action, such a discovery procedure clearly would not be feasible. Most of these cases have been pending for a substantial amount of time. As this Court has stated before, many of the Plaintiffs are ill; some of them have died since the filing of this action. An extended discovery schedule would only serve to put off what the Defendants have avoided for so long: trial of this action. This Court finds that the Magistrate's Discovery Plan and Schedule provides the Defendants with reasonable and adequate opportunity to obtain discovery in this action.

The Court's decision to allow depositions and medical examinations of all the Plaintiffs in this action was made solely for the benefit of the Defendants. These procedural safeguards are not available in the typical class action. In the usual class action, a group of class members are allowed to represent the interests of the entire class of plaintiffs. Rather than limit the Defendants' discovery to a representative group of class members, however, this Court has allowed the Defendants to conduct discovery relative to each and every Plaintiff in this action. Given that the Defendants chose to take advantage of these additional procedural safeguards, the Defendants can hardly complain about the abbreviated nature of the discovery in this action.

Having made a de novo determination of the objections raised by the Defendants, the Court is of the opinion that the objections are without merit. The Court hereby adopts the Discovery Plan and Schedule of the United States Magistrate as the Discovery Plan and Schedule of this Court.

It is ORDERED that Defendants Pittsburgh Corning Corporation's motion to set aside the Magistrate's Report or in the alternative to allow an interlocutory appeal is DENIED. It is FURTHER ORDERED that

Defendants Celotex Corp. and Carey Canada, Inc.'s request for modification of the Discovery Plan and Schedule is DENIED. Lastly, it is ORDERED that Defendant AC and S, Inc.'s motion for a protective order and motion to continue trial date is DENIED.

SIGNED this 3rd day of January, 1990.

> ROBERT M. PARKER
> UNITED STATES DISTRICT
> JUDGE

IN THE UNITED STATES DISTRICT COURT FOR THE EASTERN DISTRICT OF PENNSYLVANIA

IN RE ASBESTOS SCHOOL LITIGATION	: MASTER FILE NO. 83–0268
	:
	:
	:
THIS DOCUMENT RELATES TO:	:
ALL ACTIONS	:
	:

PRETRIAL ORDER NO. 249

AND NOW, this 16th day of July, 1990, in consideration of the parties' submission pursuant to Pretrial Order No. 239 of a joint proposal governing a schedule and procedures for expert discovery and the date for the submission of a final joint pretrial order, and;

WHEREAS the parties were ordered (Order 169) on January 27, 1989 to depose expert witnesses between January 1, 1990 and March 1, 1990 and submit a joint pretrial order on or before May 1, 1990; and;

WHEREAS the parties were ordered (Order 207) on January 26, 1990 that plaintiffs were to provide a list of their expert witnesses by February 9, 1990 and defendants were to provide a list within thirty (30) days thereafter and;

WHEREAS plaintiffs' list of expert witnesses on common issues was filed on February 13, 1990 and a majority of defendants have filed their list of expert witness on or before April 12, 1990 and;

WHEREAS no party filed a request for an extension of the May 1, 1990 deadline for filing a joint pre-trial memorandum pursuant to Order No. 169 despite knowing of the deadline for seventeen (17) months and;

WHEREAS the parties have subsequently been on notice to negotiate the proposed pre-trial order and related issues since Order No. 235 was entered on May 17, 1990, it is ORDERED that:

1. Prior to July 27, 1990 plaintiffs will serve their final list of expert witnesses they intend to present at trial, and prior to August 10, 1990, defendants will serve their final list of expert witnesses they intend to present at trial. Thereafter, supplementation shall be by

agreement of counsel or upon approval of the Court upon a showing of good cause.

2. Plaintiffs and defendants shall designate no more than two expert discovery coordinating counsel (coordinating counsel) for the limited purpose of arranging for expert depositions, including dates, times, and locations.

3. Expert witness documentary discovery shall be conducted as follows:

a. No subpoena duces tecum will be served on any expert witness identified by any party as a witness expected to be called to testify at trial.

b. Prior to August 22, 1990, the parties proffering each expert witness shall produce:

i. a current curriculum vitae of the expert;

ii. a complete list of all publications of the expert, including those submitted for publication;

iii. all unpublished papers, prepared by the expert himself, which report information on which the expert intends to rely in proffering his opinion; and

iv. all data, both compiled and raw, developed or prepared or assembled by the expert himself, on which the expert intends to rely in proffering his opinion, if that data has not been the subject of an article published in a medical or scientific publication.

c. At least fourteen (14) days in advance of the expert's deposition, the parties proffering each expert witness shall produce:

i. all other unpublished papers which report information not otherwise published in a medical or scientific publication, within the possession, custody or control of the expert and on which the expert intends to rely in proffering his opinion;

ii. all other data, both compiled and raw, within the possession, custody or control of the expert and on which the expert intends to rely in proffering his opinion, if that data has not yet been the subject of an article published in a medical or scientific publication.

d. Recognizing that experts may engage in additional investigations and studies following the production of the unpublished material, any unpublished material subject to production as described above (on which an expert intends to rely) developed following such production shall be produced to coordinating counsel at least fourteen (14) days in advance of the expert's deposition. If such unpublished material is developed and produced less than fourteen (14) days in advance of the expert's deposition, and the primary interrogating counsel does not have sufficient time to prepare his examination of the expert regarding unpublished material, and does not, in fact, question the expert about such unpublished material, the expert shall be made available for a supplemental nonrepetitive deposition limited to the additional unpublished material and any opinions formulated in reliance thereon. If such additional unpublished material is developed following the completion of the expert's deposition, the expert shall be made available for a supplemental nonrepetitive deposition limited to the additional unpublished material and any opinions formulated in reliance thereon.

e. An expert witness will be precluded from proffering any opinion in direct testimony formulated in reliance on unpublished material required to be produced in accordance with the requirements of this paragraph unless the unpublished material has been provided to opposing counsel in accordance with the requirements of this paragraph.

f. It is understood that this order does not resolve the issues of discovery of or preclusion of any opinion rendered in reliance on unpublished articles and data where such articles and data have not been produced because they are not in the possession, custody, or control of the expert witness seeking to rely thereon; nor does this order affirmatively determine that any testimony will be admissible.

g. Copies of the documents described in paragraphs 3.b.i-iii shall be served on all opposing counsel. Five copies of the data described in paragraphs 3.b.iv. and 3,c shall be served on coordinating counsel at addresses to be supplied pursuant to this order.

4. Expert witnesses shall be deposed during a four month period commencing on September 10, 1990. In order to facilitate the scheduling of depositions of expert witnesses, plaintiffs and defendants shall make each of their expert witnesses available for deposition, for up to three days, during the four month expert deposition period on the following schedule, except by agreement of coordinating counsel or order of court upon good cause shown:

a. All depositions of plaintiffs' experts shall be conducted during the weeks beginning with Monday, September 10, October 8, November 5, and December 3.

b. All depositions of defendants' experts shall be conducted during the subsequent three weeks;

c. No depositions will be taken on Saturday or Sunday unless insisted upon by the expert because of the expert's schedule;

d. During each month of the expert discovery period, the proffering parties shall produce all of their experts for deposition in a single city selected by the proffering parties;

e. The proffering parties shall produce each expert for deposition during the four month period in an order that will accommodate their experts' schedules, provided that by the end of the four month period all experts will have been deposed;

f. The proffering parties shall make each expert available for up to three days, consecutively, with each coordinating counsel for the interrogating party advising coordinating counsel for the proffering party, starting August 10, 1990, and no later than August 27, 1990, of how much time is reasonably expected to be needed, and what depositions cannot be taken at the same time because the same attorney is assigned primary responsibility for the depositions;

g. Starting on August 27, 1990, and on the days listed in 4(a), coordinating counsel shall circulate to all parties the then-current schedule of expert depositions;

h. Up to thirty percent (30%) of the experts listed by plaintiffs or defendants may be proffered for deposition during the same four week period, provided that on no day does the number of experts proffered exceed the proportion of days available divided by the number of experts increased by fifty percent (50%)[1] unless agreed to by coordinating counsel.

i. No depositions shall be conducted on November 22, 1990, December 25–26, 1990 and January 1, 1991.

j. Any remaining depositions of plaintiffs' experts shall be conducted during the week of December 31, 1990. Any remaining depositions of defendants' experts shall be conducted during the week of January 7, 1991.

5. The interrogating parties shall pay the experts' fees for time spent at the deposition. All other fees and expenses, including all travel and lodging expenses and time spent in preparation for, and review of signing of, the deposition shall be paid by the proffering parties.

6. All counsel are directed to cooperate fully in scheduling and facilitating expert discovery.

7. Nothing herein shall be construed to prohibit any party from seeking such additional relief with regard to discovery as such party deems appropriate.

8. The parties shall submit a proposed joint pretrial order in accordance with Local Rule of Civil Procedure 21(d) on or before March 4, 1991. The plaintiffs shall initiate the procedures for preparation of the order by providing counsel for the defendants with the written draft of the proposed order on or before February 8, 1991. The defendants shall provide counsel for the plaintiffs with written drafts of the proposed order on or before February 22, 1991.

9. The parties are advised that preliminary work on the joint pretrial order should take place contemporaneously with expert discovery. Any further requests for extensions of time in which to file the joint pretrial order shall be viewed unfavorably by the Court.

BY THE COURT:
JAMES McGIRR KELLY, J.

---

1. Experts/days × 1.5. Fractions shall be rounded to the nearest whole number.

IN THE UNITED STATES DISTRICT COURT FOR THE EASTERN DISTRICT OF PENNSYLVANIA

IN RE ASBESTOS SCHOOL LITIGATION	: MASTER FILE NO. 83–0268
	:
	:
THIS DOCUMENT RELATES TO: ALL ACTIONS	:
	:

MEMORANDUM OF CERTAIN DEFENDANTS REGARDING PRETRIAL ORDER NO. 249

Certain defendants submit this memorandum in response to Pretrial Order No. 249, in order to apprise the Court of the status of certain discovery matters that are collateral to that Order.

While the defendants listed below believe that Pretrial Order No. 249 will allow the parties to attempt to complete expert witness discovery in an orderly fashion, it does not address a separate discovery scheduling issue which may arise in the future. Specifically, the Pretrial Order does not address what will invariably be certain defendants' need for building-specific discovery to the extent that the named plaintiffs' claims survive pending or soon-to-be filed summary judgment motions. (The basis for these motions is (1) the named plaintiffs' failure to make threshold evidentiary showing that the products of certain individual defendants are actually present in plaintiffs' buildings, and (2) that *all* of Memphis' claims are barred by the statute of limitations).

As the Court is aware, building-specific discovery essentially has not taken place (particularly with regard to the largest named plaintiff, Memphis City Schools), because of several factors. In a general sense, all discovery was interrupted (or at least delayed) by this Court's dismissal of the Class Action complaints, with leave to amend, and the Court's related stay of all motions practice (a stay remained in effect for approximately 6 months while plaintiffs attempted to cure jurisdictional defects * * *). More particularly, building-specific discovery was a practical impossibility because of the named plaintiffs' refusal, despite repeated Court orders * * * to provide the necessary building-specific information or evidence linking particular defendants' products with particular buildings.[1] These factors combined to preclude any meaning-

---

1. The Court has been regularly advised of the status of building-specific discovery as it relates to plaintiffs' repeated failure to produce product identification evidence. For example, in order to initiate building-specific discovery (which plaintiffs had re-sisted), Defendants' moved to compel the production of product identification evidence as early as April 1988 (a request which this Court granted in Pretrial Order No. 134). Because plaintiffs still refused to produce this evidence defendants moved to

ful ability of defendants to comply with the discovery schedule set forth in Pretrial Order No. 169, at least as to building-specific fact discovery. Memphis, for example, did not even begin notifying defendants of the specific products allegedly present in any of its buildings (notwithstanding this Court's clear orders on the subject) until March 15, 1990. Even at that late date it identified products alleged to be present in only 5 of its 162 buildings.

Because of plaintiffs' failure to identify the alleged presence of certain defendants' products in the named plaintiffs' buildings, and for separate reasons associated with the applicable statute of limitations, a number of defendants have sought, or will shortly seek, summary judgment on their behalf regarding the claims of the named plaintiffs. Depending upon the resolution of these motions, any defendant then still remaining in the case will need an opportunity too take building-specific discovery regarding buildings in which its products have been specifically identified. Nothing contained in Pretrial Order No. 249 should be construed as a waiver of any defendant's right, at the appropriate time, to take building-specific discovery.

Respectfully submitted,
[Defense counsel omitted—*ed.*]

Notes and Questions

1. As the court orders in the *Cimino* and *School Asbestos* cases illustrate, mass tort litigation often raises difficult issues relating to the conduct of discovery. Both orders reflect the tension between the judicial system's desire to accomplish aggregate justice versus the defendants' interest in obtaining individualized proof of claims. Do these discovery orders adequately and fairly balance these concerns? Do plaintiffs also have an interest in individualized discovery? Doesn't the demand for individualized discovery subvert the desire for speedy and efficient resolution of claims?

2. Magistrate Hines' discovery order limited plaintiff depositions to forty-five minutes each, on an expedited calendar schedule. What could the defendants hope to discover on this schedule? Do litigants have a right to unrestricted discovery? Does the *Cimino* order violate either due process or the litigants' Seventh Amendment right to a trial by jury? On mandamus appeal to the Fifth Circuit, the defendants again challenged Magistrate Hine's and Judge Parker's discovery order. The Fifth Circuit affirmed, without discussing the defendants' objections to the discovery order. *See* In re Fibreboard Corp., 893 F.2d 706, 709 (5th Cir.1990)("Petitioners attack the limits of discovery from the class members, but we will not reach this issue."). *See also* Linda S. Mullenix, *Beyond Consolidation: Post Aggregative Procedure in Asbestos Mass Tort Litigation,* 32 Wm. & Mary L.Rev. 531–

enforce Pretrial Order No. 134 in July 1988 (a request granted in Pretrial Order No. 173 and confirmed in February 1990 by issuance of Pretrial Order No. 210.). At each stage of this process, defendants' specifically informed the Court that (1) production of this crucial evidence was a predicate to defendants' ability to conduct building-specific discovery, and (2) plaintiffs' continuing failure to produce this evidence prejudiced defendants' ability to pursue building-specific discovery. * * *

37 (1991)(discussing discovery procedures in *Cimino v. Raymark* and the *School Asbestos Litigation*).

3. Judge Parker noted that the defendants had rejected an earlier court proposal to conduct full discovery on a sample of representative plaintiffs. Would such discovery provide an adequate and reasonable alternative to over 3,000 45–minute depositions? Were the defendant manufacturers in the *School Asbestos Litigation* entitled to building-specific discovery? The plaintiff class included over 35,000 school districts nationwide, involving hundreds-of-thousands of school buildings. How should the court handle discovery in such instances? Would a sampling technique be more appropriate in the context of a mass tort litigation such as the *School Asbestos* case?

4. In both *Cimino* and the *School Asbestos Litigation,* the court expressed dissatisfaction with the defendants' delay in pursuing discovery of the claimants' class. Whose fault was this? Should the defendants discovery be limited because of prior procrastination in pursuing discovery? In general, judges have great leeway in controlling discovery in complex cases, either through standing orders or through use of procedures recommended in the MANUAL FOR COMPLEX LITIGATION (2d Ed.1985). *See also* Danny P. Richey, *Document Control and Management in Complex Litigation,* 38 Def. L.J. 593 (1989).

2. PROTECTIVE ORDERS

IN RE "AGENT ORANGE" PRODUCT LIABILITY LITIGATION

United States Court of Appeals, Second Circuit, 1987.
821 F.2d 139.

Before VAN GRAAFEILAND, KEARSE and MINER, CIRCUIT JUDGES.

MINER, CIRCUIT JUDGE:

Defendants-appellants Dow Chemical Company, Diamond Shamrock Chemicals Company, Hercules Incorporated, Monsanto Company, TH Agriculture & Nutrition Company, Inc., Thompson Chemicals Corporation and Uniroyal, Inc. (collectively the "chemical companies") appeal from an order of the United States District Court for the Eastern District of New York (Weinstein, Ch. J.) unsealing materials produced or generated during discovery in the Agent Orange litigation. The materials in question had been sealed pursuant to two prior protective orders of the district court.

In ordering the documents unsealed, the district court relied on the findings of Magistrate Scheindlin, who concluded that intervenor-appellee Vietnam Veterans of America ("VVA") and intervenor Victor J. Yannacone, as well as the Agent Orange Plaintiffs' Management Committee, which filed a brief in support of the VVA's motion, had a statutory right of access to the subject discovery materials by virtue of Fed.R.Civ.P. 26(c) and Fed.R.Civ.P. 5(d). In balancing the interests of the parties, Magistrate Scheindlin determined that the chemical companies should be required to demonstrate good cause for continuing the protective order as to any particular document or category of documents. Appellants contest the magistrate's determination and argue that the blanket protective orders should remain in force absent a showing of extraordinary circumstances or compelling need. We affirm.

BACKGROUND

The extensive procedural history and general background of the Agent Orange litigation is reported in In re "Agent Orange" Product Liability Litigation MDL No. 381, 818 F.2d 145 (2d Cir.1987), familiarity with which is assumed. Only those facts relevant to the protective orders at issue will be discussed here.

On February 6, 1981, Judge Pratt, then supervising the *Agent Orange* litigation, issued an order allowing the defendant chemical companies to designate as "confidential" any records that, in their estimation, contained "confidential developmental, business, research or commercial information." Any party receiving documents designated as "confidential" was required to refrain from disclosing them and to file them with the district court under seal, if filing was required. The documents were to be returned or destroyed at the end of the litigation. * * * Initial discovery involving the chemical companies took place pursuant to the February 6, 1981 order.

In May 1982, Special Master Schreiber, then supervising discovery in the litigation, orally issued a blanket protective order on all records produced or generated in discovery by any party, including the chemical companies and the government. The order provided that all documents and depositions were to be treated confidentially. In response to a motion filed on July 29, 1982, by CBS, Inc., the special master on October 14, 1982 signed a protective order incorporating procedures for dissemination of the discovery material, *see* In re "Agent Orange" Product Liability Litigation, 96 F.R.D. 582, 585–87 (E.D.N.Y.1983)(Special Master's Protective Order), and submitted a memorandum in support of the order to the district court.

The October 14, 1982 protective order provided that only "designated persons," e.g., parties, their attorneys, expert witnesses, and witnesses to depositions, would have unrestricted access to the discovery material. Under the terms of the order, those persons could disseminate discovery material to undesignated people only upon the authorization of the special master, following a review procedure. The party seeking to prevent dissemination had the burden of showing that good cause existed for continuation of the order with respect to the discovery material in question. *See* Fed.R.Civ.P. 26(c). The order also included a clause indicating that the October 14, 1982 order did not supersede the February 6, 1981 order regarding production of confidential documents.

In his supporting memorandum, the special master noted that good cause for his order existed because of the "complexity of this litigation, the emotionalism surrounding the issues, the number of documents yet to be reviewed and the desirability of moving discovery expeditiously in order to meet the June 1983 trial date." 96 F.R.D. at 583. He also concluded that the protective order did not unduly restrain first amendment rights. Finally, he noted that, "as discovery progresses and fundamental disputes are resolved, it may become desirable to lift this order." * * * Judge Pratt approved and adopted the special master's protective order. 96 F.R.D. at 585.

The October 14, 1982 protective order subsequently was modified on two occasions. First, on May 12, 1983, Judge Pratt granted summary judgment in favor of four of the chemical companies based on the government limit contractor defense. Judge Pratt directed the special master to consider whether the blanket protective order should be modified to permit disclosure of papers and exhibits filed in connection with the summary judgment motion. In re "Agent Orange" Product Liability Litigation, 565 F.Supp. 1263, 1277–78 (E.D.N.Y.1983). The special master recommended that the October 14, 1982 protective order be lifted insofar as it related to "the material submitted with and referred to in the parties' summary judgment papers." In re "Agent Orange" Product Liability Litigation, 98 F.R.D. 539, 548 (E.D.N.Y.1983)(Special Master's Recommendation). Judge Pratt accepted and adopted the recommendation. *Id.* at 541. A further modification of the October 14, 1982 order, pursuant to a recommendation by the special master, was adopted by Chief Judge Weinstein, who had assumed responsibility for supervision of the Agent Orange litigation. In re "Agent Orange" Product Liability Litigation, 99 F.R.D. 645, 646 (E.D.N.Y.1983). That modification permitted release, with the consent of the government, of both its employees' depositions and documents it had produced that were not otherwise subject to specific protective orders filed in the litigation.[2]

On April 23, 1984, two weeks before the trial was scheduled to commence, the parties filed their pretrial orders with the clerk, attaching all of the documents and depositions they intended to offer at trial. The orders and exhibit lists were filed publicly, and the sealed exhibits were filed in a locked room at the courthouse.

On May 7, 1984, several hours before the trial was to begin, the parties agreed to a tentative settlement, subject to the approval of the court. On June 11, 1984, a formal settlement agreement was filed. This agreement set forth in detail the terms of the settlement negotiated by the parties, subject to the approval of the district court. Paragraph 12 of the settlement agreement provided that [t]he attorneys for the Class shall return to each defendant, respectively, all documents in their possession or control produced by that defendant, including microfilm and all copies, within 30 days after final judgment is entered in this action and is no longer subject to appeal or review, or if plaintiffs pursue

---

2. At various times, the district court has entered specific protective orders designed to limit disclosure of particular categories of documents produced by the government, including medical files and records of the Veterans Administration, documents from a particular file of the United States Department of Agriculture, and certain documents produced by the Environmental Protection Agency. *See* In re "Agent Orange" Product Liability Litigation, 99 F.R.D. 645, 649 (E.D.N.Y.1983).

claims against the United States within one year after the date of this Agreement, within 30 days after final adjudication of those claims, whichever is later. * * *

Before approving the settlement, Chief Judge Weinstein held Rule 23(b) fairness hearings throughout the United States. At a hearing held in New York on August 9, 1984, a representative of the VVA requested access to all of the *Agent Orange* discovery materials still subject to the protective orders. At the district court's direction, the VVA filed a motion returnable before Magistrate Scheindlin on August 31, 1984. Subsequently, the Agent Orange Plaintiffs' Management Committee and Victor Yannacone, Jr., counsel for certain plaintiffs in this litigation, joined in the VVA's motion.

Before the VVA's motion was argued, the district court issued a preliminary order on September 25, 1984, tentatively approving the settlement. In re "Agent Orange" Product Liability Litigation, 597 F.Supp. 740 (E.D.N.Y.1984)("Settlement Opinion"). Chief Judge Weinstein addressed a number of concerns raised during the course of the fairness hearings, including the concern that there be no "cover-up" of information contained in the sealed files. *Id.* at 769–70. He observed that the veterans' concern about non-disclosure, "while understandable, is not an appropriate reason for rejecting the settlement." *Id.* at 770. The district court noted that it retained the power to order documents released despite the fact that they were sealed as part of a settlement. The court directed that until the *Agent Orange* litigation was completed, no documents should be destroyed. In addition, Chief Judge Weinstein directed that the parties "file all depositions and other papers obtained in discovery in a depository at the courthouse in accordance with directions to be provided by a Magistrate who will determine sealing and disposition subject to appeal to the court." *Id.*

The VVA's motion subsequently was argued before Magistrate Scheindlin, who ordered that non-privileged records subject to the February 6, 1981 and October 14, 1982 protective orders be unsealed. In re "Agent Orange" Product Liability Litigation, 104 F.R.D. 559, 562 (E.D.N.Y.1985)(Magistrate's Pretrial Order No. 33, dated December 17, 1984)("Protective Orders Opinion"). Magistrate Scheindlin noted that the records at issue fell within two categories: records accompanying the parties' pretrial orders, which were filed with the clerk, stored in the courthouse, and later removed by the parties when the settlement was announced, and all other records produced during discovery, which the parties were required to file with the district court pursuant to the court's September 25, 1984 order. Judge Weinstein adopted Magistrate Scheindlin's order, *id.* at 562, but issued a stay pending final disposition of appeals from the district court's approval of the Agent Orange settlement. This appeal followed.

DISCUSSION

Appellants raise three arguments on appeal. First, they contend that the order unsealing the discovery materials improperly alters an integral term of the settlement agreement reached with the plaintiff class. Second, they claim that the public has no right of access to the discovery materials at issue. Finally, they argue that once a protective order has been entered and relied on, it can be modified only if extraordinary circumstances or compelling needs warrant the requested modification. We discuss appellants' contentions seriatim.

A. *Alteration of the Settlement Agreement*

Appellants contend that paragraph 12 of the settlement agreement, providing for return to appellants of documents obtained during discovery, was an integral part of the agreement, and that the district court's order unsealing the discovery materials improperly alters a term of the settlement agreement. We disagree.

When Judge Pratt entered the February 6, 1981 order, he specifically limited its applicability to the pretrial stages of the litigation and indicated that the issue of confidentiality would again be addressed once the trial was scheduled to commence.... As to the October 14, 1982 protective order, appellants were on notice virtually from the time it was issued that the district court's order might be lifted or modified. In his memorandum in support of the order, the special master noted that it might be desirable to lift the order "as discovery progresses and fundamental issues are resolved." ... Later, when questions were raised during the fairness hearings regarding whether veterans and the public would have access to all discovery materials, Chief Judge Weinstein directed the VVA to move to have the protective orders lifted. At the time he tentatively approved the settlement agreement, Chief Judge Weinstein emphasized the court's inherent power to order documents released, and he directed the parties to file all discovery materials at the courthouse. *Settlement Opinion*, 597 F.Supp. at 770.

Despite ample indications that the protective orders might be lifted, appellants never sought to be released from the settlement agreement, nor do they seek that relief here. Moreover, the terms of paragraph 12 contemplated that some of the protected materials eventually might be introduced into evidence during the plaintiff class' then-pending suit against the United States, and therefore would become part of the public record. Appellants also were aware that the materials, once discovered, could be introduced into evidence in many non-class suits then pending. More importantly, appellants doubtless were aware that, regardless of the terms of the settlement agreement reached between the chemical companies and the plaintiff class, such an agreement could not prevent interested non-class member parties from intervening to seek access to the discovery materials. We therefore have difficulty accepting appellants' assertion that "maintenance of the protective orders was a sine qua non of the settlement and was central to resolution of the litigation." * * *

We recognize that the district judge generally should not dictate the terms of a settlement agreement in a class action. Rather, "he should approve or disapprove a proposed agreement as it is placed before him and should not take it upon himself to modify its terms," In re Warner Communications Securities Litigation, 798 F.2d 35, 37 (2d Cir.1986)(*citing* Plummer v. Chemical Bank, 668 F.2d 654, 655 n.1 (2d Cir.1982)), subject to certain limited exceptions, *see, e.g.,* Jones v. Amalgamated Warbasse Houses, Inc., 721 F.2d 881, 884–85 (2d Cir.1983)(district court has discretion to modify attorneys' fee agreement submitted as part of proposed settlement of class action civil rights suit), *cert. denied,* 466 U.S. 944, 104 S.Ct. 1929, 80 L.Ed.2d 474 (1984); Beecher v. Able, 575 F.2d 1010, 1016 (2d Cir.1978)(district court has discretion to modify settlement agreement with respect to allocation of settlement proceeds when use of formula for allocation under agreement would lead to inequitable results). However, the language of the settlement agreement to which appellants direct our attention contains no reference to maintaining the confidentiality of the discovery materials, and our independent review of the agreement reveals no such clause. By its express terms, paragraph 12 mandates only that attorneys for the class must return to appellants any documents produced during discovery. Therefore, appellants did not bargain for or procure the continued confidentiality of the discovery materials by private agreement; rather, the confidentiality of those documents was ensured solely by independent judicial acts, i.e., the protective orders.

It is undisputed that a district court retains the power to modify or lift protective orders that it has entered. *See* Palmieri v. New York, 779 F.2d 861, 864–65 (2d Cir.1985); United States v. GAF Corp., 596 F.2d 10, 16 (2d Cir.1979); *see also* 8 C. Wright, A. Miller & F. Elliot, FEDERAL PRACTICE AND PROCEDURE § 2043, at 143–44 (Supp.1986); *cf.* United States v. Davis, 702 F.2d 418, 422–23 (2d Cir.)(informal understanding of confidentiality), *cert. denied,* 463 U.S. 1215, 103 S.Ct. 3554, 77 L.Ed.2d 1400 (1983). Therefore, appellants can claim only that, by lifting the protective orders in this case, the district court effectively modified paragraph 12 in that counsel for the plaintiff class no longer are able to return the discovery materials to appellants once those documents become part of the public record. However, to the extent that the district court "modified" the settlement agreement, we hold that such an incidental modification was not an abuse of the district court's discretion under the circumstances of this case, *cf. Beecher,* 575 F.2d at 1016; Zients v. LaMorte, 459 F.2d 628, 629–30 (2d Cir.1972)(district court overseeing settlement distribution has inherent power to accept late claims despite contrary terms of agreement), and we note that, despite this "modification," appellants have not sought rescission of the settlement agreement.

B. *Right of Access*

Magistrate Scheindlin, in an opinion adopted by the district court, determined that both Rule 26(c) and Rule 5(d) of the Federal Rules of Civil Procedure "require that discovery is presumptively open to public scrutiny unless a valid protective order directs otherwise," *Protective Orders Opinion,* 104 F.R.D. at 568, and that, as a result, appellee had a statutory right of access to the subject discovery materials. Appellee, joined by amici curiae, urges us to affirm the district court's order on constitutional, common law and statutory grounds. Because we hold that the statutory right of access relied on by the district court sufficiently supports the court's order, we need not discuss the other grounds raised on appeal.

Rule 26(c) provides, in pertinent part, that "[u]pon motion by a party or by the person from whom discovery is sought, and for good cause shown, the court ... may make any order which justice requires to protect a party or person from annoyance, embarrassment, oppression, or undue burden or expense...." Fed.R.Civ.P. 26(c). A plain reading of the language of Rule 26(c) demonstrates that the party seeking a protective order has the burden of showing that good cause exists for issuance of that order. It is equally apparent that the obverse also is true, i.e., if good cause is not shown, the discovery materials in question should not receive judicial protection and therefore would be open to the public for inspection. *Cf.* Seattle Times Co. v. Rhinehart, 467 U.S. 20, 37, 104 S.Ct. 2199, 2209, 81 L.Ed.2d 17 (1984)(approving trial court's finding, under Washington state statute identical to Rule 26(c), that party seeking protective order had shown good cause for issuance of order; implicit conclusion that information would have been available to public absent demonstration of good cause). Any other conclusion effectively would negate the good cause requirement of Rule 26(c): Unless the public has a presumptive right of access to discovery materials, the party seeking to protect the materials would have no need for a judicial order since the public would not be allowed to examine the materials in any event.

Fed.R.Civ.P. 5(d) requires that all discovery materials must be filed with the district court, unless the court orders otherwise. However, due to the volume of discovery materials in the Southern and Eastern Districts of New York, this requirement has been altered by local rule, which provides that "depositions, interrogatories, requests for documents, requests for admissions, and answers and responses shall not be filed with the Clerk's Office except by order of the court." SDNY, EDNY Civ. R. 18(a). *See Scheindlin, Discovering the Discoverable: A Bird's Eye View of Discovery in a Complex Multi-district Class Action Litigation,* 52 Brook.L.Rev. 397, 407 n.35 (1986). Appellants disparage Rule 5(d) as merely a housekeeping rule, but an examination of the notes accompanying Rule 5(d) reveals substantive policy considerations underlying the Rule.

The Advisory Committee note accompanying Rule 5(d) discloses that the Committee originally had contemplated incorporating into Rule 5(d) a procedure similar to that now in effect in the Southern and Eastern Districts, but decided instead to require filing of discovery materials because "such materials are sometimes of interest to those who may have no access to them except by a requirement of filing, such as members of a class, litigants similarly situated, or the public generally." Fed.R.Civ.P. 5(d) advisory committee note. As Judge Mansfield, then Chairman of the Advisory Committee on Civil Rules, noted at the time of the Rule's amendment, the drafters of Rule 5(d) anticipate[d] (and so stated in our committee notes accompanying the proposal) that a judge would not be expected to excuse parties from filing materials in any case in which the public or the press has an interest, such as a Watergate or similar scandal. Moreover, should the public importance of the material not appear until after filing has been excused, it is expected that the judge, upon motion of the press or other interested persons, would order the parties to file the documents for inspection. N.Y. Times, Aug. 2, 1980, at 20, col. 4 (letter to the Editor). Moreover, when the Advisory Committee proposed amending Rule 5(d) in 1978 so that it would function similarly to Local Rule 18(a), it offered the following caveat: "any party may request that designated materials be filed, and the court may require filing on its own motion. It is intended that the court may order filing on its own motion at the request of a person who is not a party who desires access to public records, subject to the provisions of Rule 26(c)". Fed.R.Civ.P. 5(d) advisory committee note (1978 proposed amendments), *reprinted in* 77 F.R.D. 613, 623 (1978). The Advisory Committee notes make clear that Rule 5(d), far from being a housekeeping rule, embodies the Committee's concern that class action litigants and the general public be afforded access to discovery materials whenever possible. Moreover, we note that access is particularly appropriate when the subject matter of the litigation is of especial public interest, which certainly is true of the *Agent Orange* litigation. Therefore, we agree with Magistrate Scheindlin's determination, adopted by the district court, that Rule 5(d) and Rule 26(c) provide a statutory right of access to the discovery materials in question.

Appellants raise an additional point regarding the scope of the district court's Rule 5(d) order, which required appellants to file all discovery materials with the court. They assert that documents produced for discovery and inspection in response to Rule 34 document requests are not "papers" within the meaning of Rule 5(d). Rule 34, unlike other rules governing discovery, does not provide that responsive material be filed with the court and made part of the public record. *See* In re Halkin, 598 F.2d 176, 191 n.26 (D.C.Cir.1979). However, the district court's order clearly required the filing of all discovery materials, including those made available for inspection. While such documents technically may not fall within the terms of Rule 5(d), we find no abuse of discretion in the district court's order in light of the district court's broad supervisory authority in class actions. It would make little sense to allow access to documents requesting inspection of discovery materials and documents facilitating the inspection of discovery materials, without allowing access to the discovery materials themselves. We emphasize that Magistrate Scheindlin set forth a procedure whereby appellants can seek continued protection for any discovery materials in the *Agent Orange* litigation. Appellants thereby can ameliorate the effect of the district court's order requiring the filing of all discovery materials and its subsequent order unsealing those materials.

C. *Standard for Modifying Protective Orders*

As discussed above, there is no question that a Rule 26(c) protective order is subject to modification. Whether to lift or modify a protective order is a decision committed to the sound discretion of the trial court. Krause v. Rhodes, 671 F.2d 212, 219 (6th Cir.), *cert. denied,* 459 U.S. 823, 103 S.Ct. 54, 74 L.Ed.2d 59 (1982). Appellants contend that this circuit requires that "[o]nce a confidentiality order has been entered and relied upon, it can only be modified if an 'extraordinary circumstance' or 'compelling need' warrants the requested modification." Federal Deposit Ins. Corp. v. Ernst & Ernst, 677 F.2d 230, 232 (2d Cir.1982)(per curiam)(citation omitted); *see* Palmieri v. New York, 779 F.2d 861, 865 (2d Cir.1985); Martindell v. International Tel. & Tel. Corp., 594 F.2d 291, 295 (2d Cir.1979). Magistrate Scheindlin determined, however, that the cases cited by appellants were inapplicable to the *Agent Orange* litigation, and concluded that the burden of proof should remain with the proponents of continued protection. We need not reach that issue, however, because, assuming without deciding that the *Ernst & Ernst* standard applies, appellee has demonstrated both that appellants reasonably could not have relied on the protective orders and that extraordinary circumstances warrant modification.

In each of the cases cited by appellants, the parties seeking the protective order relied on the permanence of that order. In *Martindell,* the parties entered a stipulation of confidentiality ensuring that the material provided would not be used for any purpose other than preparing for and conducting the litigation between them. *Martindell,* 594 F.2d at 293. In *Palmieri,* the protective order specifically was entered to prevent subsequent inquiry by a government agency, thereby encouraging settlement negotiations. *Palmieri,* 779 F.2d at 863. In *Ernst & Ernst,* the settlement expressly was made contingent upon a court order ensuring the confidentiality of the settlement terms. *Ernst & Ernst,* 677 F.2d at 231. In contrast, as discussed above, appellants in the *Agent Orange* litigation could not have relied on the permanence of the protective order. The February 6, 1981 order by its very terms was applicable solely to the pretrial stages of the litigation. Judge Pratt specifically indicated that the confidentiality issue would be reconsidered upon commencement of the trial. The fact that the litigation resulted in a settlement rather than a trial does not alter the temporary nature of the February 6, 1981 order. Similarly, appellants had ample warning that the October 14, 1982 order was of a temporary nature: Any reliance on such a sweeping, temporary protective order simply was misplaced.

More significantly, appellants never have been required to demonstrate good cause for shielding any document from public view. Under the February 6, 1981 order, appellants needed only to designate discovery materials as confidential to protect them. Under the October 14, 1982 order, all materials were protected regardless of whether appellants themselves considered protection to be necessary. We conclude that the exceptionally pervasive protection granted appellants during the pretrial stages of this litigation, coupled with the fact that appellants never were required to show good cause as mandated by Rule 26(c), amounts to the type of extraordinary circumstances contemplated in our prior decisions. Although we believe that the unusual scope of the *Agent Orange* litigation warranted imposition of the protective orders at issue, we note that, had the district court not lifted the orders, we would be compelled to find that the orders had been improvidently granted because the district court never required appellants to make the requisite good cause showing. Improvidence in the granting of a protective order is yet another justification for lifting or modifying the order. *See Martindell,* 594 F.2d at 296. We are satisfied, however, that the district court properly entered the orders initially as temporary measures, and properly lifted them thereafter.

Appellants argue that the cost of poring through the voluminous discovery materials in the *Agent Orange* litigation would be prohibitive. However, appellants would have had to bear that cost during the pretrial stages of the litigation except for the protective orders. The orders merely delayed a document-by-document assessment; they did not obviate the need for such an assessment. Moreover, appellants' assertion is somewhat disingenuous in that many of the discovery materials previously had been designated as confidential, and many more were examined and catalogued in preparation for trial. Any inconvenience to which appellants are subjected certainly is outweighed by the enormous public interest in the *Agent Orange* litigation and the compelling need for class members and non-class members alike to evaluate fully the efficacy of settling this litigation. Under the circumstances, we hold that the district court was well within its discretion to lift the protective orders at issue, subject to a showing, on an individualized basis, of good cause for continued protection.

CONCLUSION

Based on the foregoing, the order of the district court lifting the protective orders in the Agent Orange litigation is affirmed.

MIRAK v. McGHAN MEDICAL CORPORATION

United States District Court, District of Massachusetts, 1992.
142 F.R.D. 34.

MEMORANDUM OF DECISION

LAWRENCE P. COHEN, UNITED STATES MAGISTRATE JUDGE.

After hearing, the Motion of Command Trust Network, Inc., for Leave to Intervene, to Vacate the Protective Order, and to Require Filing of Discovery in Court (# 101) is allowed to the extent that Command Trust Network, Inc., seeks to intervene for the purpose of moving to vacate the protective order heretofore entered into by the parties, and for the purpose of seeking an order requiring filing of discovery in court.

To the extent, however, that Command Trust Network, Inc., seeks substantive relief—i.e., vacation of that protective order, and the filing of discovery, that motion is—at this time—denied without prejudice for the reasons set forth below.

Plaintiffs' Motion for Relief from Confidentiality Stipulation and Protective Order (# 93) is allowed in part and denied in part.

I. THE MOTION FILED BY COMMAND TRUST NETWORK, INC.

A. *Procedural Posture*

On or about December 21, 1989, plaintiffs filed their complaint in this court alleging claims in the nature of products liability—i.e., that defendants negligently designed and/or manufactured breast implants. On or about June 15, the case was referred to this court for Rule 16(b) proceedings. An initial conference was held on July 31, 1991. During the course of that first conference, this court, and counsel for the parties, generally discussed impending discovery matters which might require judicial intervention. This court directed the filing of appropriate motions to compel, and conditioned the filing of the amendments to pleadings to a period of three months after ruling on the anticipated motions to compel (# 64). In addition, following that conference, this court entered a Rule 16(b) discovery order which, among other things, consistent with the provisions of Rule 5(d), Fed R Civ. P., and Rule 16(g) of the Local Rules of this Court, prohibited the filing of discovery materials except to the extent permitted by Rule 16(g).

Thereafter, the parties appeared for a hearing vis a vis cross-motions to compel. Many of the matters briefly addressed at the first conference had been rendered moot by virtue of the fact that plaintiffs and defendant McGhan had entered into a confidentiality agreement and stipulated protective order (# 80)—approved by this court—which obviated most, if not all, concerns raised by defendant McGhan.

Because of that protective order, discovery then proceeded without incident. Defendant McGhan established a document depository of sorts and permitted counsel for plaintiffs to simply peruse through any and all documents—and to make copies of any and all documents plaintiffs chose. Pursuant to this agreement, counsel for plaintiffs copied—and currently has possession of—some thirteen thousand documents, more or less, most of which, if not all, were marked confidential by defendant McGhan, and the relevance and/or discoverability of which have not been challenged by the defendant McGhan prior to the motions currently pending before this court.

B. *The Intervenor*

Command Trust Network, Inc. ("Command Trust") is a nonprofit organization co-founded by Sybil N. Goldrich. The purpose of that organization is—among other things—to educate women about the potential health hazards associated with silicone breast implants.[7] By its motion (# 101), Command Trust seeks vacation of the confidentiality

---

7. Ms. Goldrich was a plaintiff in an action against silicone breast suppliers and/or manufacturers in a case filed in the Superior Court in California. Judgment was entered against her in that case on the basis of a motion for summary judgment.

agreement and protective order, filing of *all* discovery materials, and access to *all* discovery materials.[8] Command Trust says that this is necessary to its mission of educating women as to the health hazards associated with silicone breast implants, and to educate the Food and Drug Administration as to those hazards at further hearings presently scheduled for April 20, 1992.[9]

* * *

D. Discussion

In the circumstances, assuming proper grounds for intervention,[11] the intervenor's motion, as drafted, seeking *all* documents, in the present procedural posture, is denied without prejudice.

8. It is not entirely clear precisely what discovery—beyond documents actually copied by plaintiffs and currently in the possession of counsel for plaintiffs, and, perhaps [but again not clear], documents to which counsel for plaintiffs had access in selecting those from which copies were made—Command Trust seeks. Since the bulk—if not the entirety—of the discovery from McGhan to date consists of documents, this action is currently taken in that context.

9. As this court understands from the position of the parties, a majority of the documents marked confidential consists of (1) trade secret or proprietary information; and (2) Medical Device Reports ("MDR's") submitted by defendant McGhan to the Food and Drug Administration and related complaints which provide identifying data with respect to persons who had received surgical implants. Despite its all inclusive request for all documents, Command Trust has not, in its moving papers or otherwise, indicated the need—in terms of its mission—for the trade secret and proprietary information. With respect to the MDR's, even if Command Trust testifies at hearing scheduled before the Food and Drug Administration, although redacted summaries of the MDR's are available to Command Trust, or anyone else for that matter, under the Freedom of Information Act, *see* 21 C.F.R. § 803.9, Command Trust would not be entitled to the actual unredacted MDR's. Thus, in a sense, Command Trust seeks to obtain from this court that which it could not from the Federal Food and Drug Administration—despite the fact that that agency has struck the balance between legitimate privacy concerns, on the one hand, and the public's need to know, on the other.

11. Command Trust points to Public Citizen v. Liggett Group, Inc., 858 F.2d 775 (1st Cir.1988), as authority for its position on intervention. Significantly, however,

Command Trust has pretermitted a potential caveat carved out by that Court. There that court observed—

> We have uncovered only one access case where standing was found lacking, but that case is clearly distinguishable. Oklahoma Hospital Ass'n v. Oklahoma Publishing Co., 748 F.2d 1421 (10th Cir. 1984), *cert. denied,* 473 U.S. 905, 105 S.Ct. 3528, 87 L.Ed.2d 652 (1985), involved a protective order entered by stipulation covering documents solely in the hands of the parties. The court found that a third party lacked standing to attack the protective order because, even if the protective order were modified, the parties in possession of the documents would not, and could not be compelled to, disseminate the documents to the third party. * * *

Here, however, far from agreeing to the protective order, the plaintiffs to this action have opposed the protective order at every stage. Moreover, the plaintiffs have indicated clearly that they will disseminate the documents if permitted to do so. Because obtaining a modification of the protective order will, as a practical matter, guarantee Public Citizen access to documents in the plaintiffs' possession, Public Citizen has standing to seek the modification. This case is far closer to that presented to the Tenth Circuit than that presented to the First Circuit in *Public Citizen.* In this case, precisely like that in *Oklahoma Hospital Ass'n,* the documents which the intervenor seeks are in the custody of the parties based on a confidentiality agreement freely entered into by all parties. And in this case, like in *Oklahoma Hospital Ass'n,* plaintiffs did not oppose the protective order; to the contrary, plaintiffs executed the very stipulated confidentiality agreement which formed the basis for the protective order. And finally, in this case, again like in *Okla-*

In contending that it is entitled to the relief sought, Command Trust, relying on the holding in *Public Citizen* simply contends: (1) Discovery documents need not be filed [and hence, access, as a practical matter, denied] only by virtue of the second clause of Rule 5(d), Fed. R.Civ.P., and Rule 33–36(f) [formerly Local Rule 16(g), . . .] of the Local Rules of this Court; and (2) defendant has not made a showing of "good cause" for continued confidentiality of those *discovery* documents.[13] In the circumstances, however, this court finds and concludes that Command Trust is not entitled to the relief sought for two reasons:

1. First and foremost, the Court in *Public Citizen* assumed, apparently without objection by any parties to that case, that Rule 5(d), Fed.R.Civ.P., and Local Rule 16(g) governed the documents there in issue.[14] In this court's view, however, neither rule so governs:

Rule 5(d) provides:

> (d) Filing. All papers after the complaint *required to be served upon a party* shall be filed with the court either before service or within a reasonable time thereafter, but the court may on motion of a party or on its own initiative order that depositions upon oral examination and interrogatories, requests for documents, requests for admission, and answers, and *responses thereto* not be filed unless on order of the court or for use in the proceeding.

And Local Rule 16(g) [currently Local Rule 33–36(f)] provides:

> (f) Nonfiling of Discovery Materials. Depositions upon oral examinations and notices thereof, interrogatories, requests for documents, requests for admissions, and answers and *responses thereto*, shall not be filed unless so ordered by the court or for use in the proceeding. The party taking a deposition or obtaining any material through discovery is responsible for its preservation and delivery to the court if needed or so ordered. If for any reason a party or concerned citizen believes that any of the named documents should

---

homa Hospital Ass'n, apart from some six categories of documents, discussed *infra,* plaintiffs do not seek vacation of the protective order to which they previously agreed. Thus, for this reason, and one other—*i.e.,* all the documents to which Command Trust seeks access here will be made available to the very community which it represents in the action currently pending in the Southern District of Ohio—it is not entirely clear that Command Trust is entitled to, or should be permitted to, intervene under Rule 24(a) or Rule 24(b), Fed.R.Civ.P. But since this court reaches the merits on the relief sought, there is no occasion to further explore that issue at this time.

13. Insofar as this court can determine, Command Trust does not contend that it has a common law or first amendment right to inspect those documents. And it is clear that it does not. *See, e.g.,* Seattle Times v. Rhinehart, 467 U.S. 20, 104 S.Ct. 2199, 81 L.Ed.2d 17 (1984); *Public Citizen,* 858 F.2d at 788.

14. Acknowledging—as apparently conceded by Command Trust, *see* footnote 13, *supra*—that intervenors do not have a common law or constitutional right of access to discovery documents, the Court in Public Citizen based its holding solely on compliance with the Federal Rules of Civil Procedure. *Id.,* at 788–89 ("Rather, Public Citizen has based its claim on [emphasis in original] the federal rules. . . . Public Citizen asks for no more than compliance with the legislative scheme as embodied in the federal rules . . . But nothing in those opinions [rejecting a common law or constitutional right of access] purported to elevate privacy and efficiency as factors to be considered over and above compliance with the federal rules.")

be filed, an *ex parte* request may be made that such document be filed, stating the reasons therefor. The court may also order filing *sua sponte*. If relief is sought under Fed.R.Civ.P. 26(c) or 37, copies of the relevant portions of disputed documents shall be filed with the court contemporaneously with any motion. If the moving party under Fed.R.Civ.P. 56 or the opponent relies on discovery documents, copies of the pertinent parts thereof shall be filed with the motion or opposition. (Emphasis added in first sentence.)

Rule 5(d)—and, derivatively, Local Rule 16(g)—by its very terms, applies only to pleadings *required to be served upon a party*. That is to say, Rule 5(d) must be read in conjunction with Rule 5(a), Fed.R.Civ.P. That rule, in turn, only requires service when required by the Federal Rules of Civil Procedure in general, or, in particular vis a vis discovery, "...every paper relating to discovery *required to be served upon a party* ...". (Emphasis added.)

Nothing in the Federal Rules of Civil Procedure in general, and nothing in those rules relating to discovery in particular, *require service* of documents on the adversaries.

Discovery of documents under the Federal Rules of Civil Procedure is governed by Rule 34. That rule provides, in pertinent part:

> (a) Scope. Any party may serve on any other party a request (1) to produce and permit the party making the request ... to inspect and copy, any designated documents....

> (b) Procedure.

> . . . . .

> The party upon whom the request is served shall *serve a written response* within 30 days after the service of the request.... *The response shall state, with respect to each item or category, that inspection and related activities will be permitted as requested, unless the request is objected to, in which event the reasons for objection shall be stated.* (Emphasis added).

Accordingly, under the Federal Rules of Civil Procedure generally, and under Rule 34 of those Rules in particular, defendant McGhan, upon receipt of plaintiff's request for production of documents, was required only to serve on counsel for plaintiffs (and hence, file under Rule 5(d)) a *written response which "shall state, with respect to each item or category, that inspection and related activities will be permitted as requested, unless the request is objected to, in which event the reasons for objection shall be stated"*—nothing more, and nothing less.

In this case, defendant McGhan fully complied with Rules 5(a) and 34. Plaintiffs served their request for production of documents on defendant McGhan on February 26, 1990. Defendant McGhan, in turn, served its response to that request on plaintiffs on April 9, 1990. ... And, indeed, that response was subsequently filed with the court, has been spread upon the public record, and is available to all.

Accordingly, this court finds and concludes that—with deference to the holding in *Public Citizen,* a holding limited to the matters raised by the parties in that particular case—neither Rule 5(a), Rule 5(d), Rule 34(b), nor any other rule of the Federal Rules of Civil Procedure, *requires service* or *filing* of documents made available for inspection and/or copying pursuant to a request made under Rule 34(a), Fed. R.Civ.P.[16] That being the case, Local Rule 16(g), and its requirement of "good cause", is simply beside the point.

2. Secondly, and equally as important, even without gainsaying the holding in *Public Citizen,* the chink in the intervenor's position is that, in the present posture of this case, it simply puts the cart before the horse. That is because the argument assumes that the documents currently in the possession of counsel for the plaintiffs, and the documents to which counsel had access in the depository provided by defendant McGhan are, indeed, *discovery* documents.

In the circumstances, that threshold showing has not been made. It is clear that *discovery* documents, as that term is used in Rule 5(d) and Local Rule 16(g), means something more than *any* document which might be in the possession of one party or another, or *any* document which, apart from the discovery rules set forth in the Federal Rules of Civil Procedure, one party tenders or shows to another party. It is clear that, in context, *discovery* documents within the meaning of those rules must mean documents which, over the objection of one party or the other, must be provided to the adversary under Rules 26 through 37 of the Federal Rules of Civil Procedure, and particularly Rule 34, that is, documents (and/or other discovery information) which is *relevant* and not otherwise *privileged.* See Rule 26(b)(1), Fed.R.Civ.P.

In its present posture, this case is like that presented in Oklahoma Hospital Ass'n v. Oklahoma Publishing Co., 748 F.2d 1421 (10th Cir. 1984), *cert. denied,* 473 U.S. 905, 105 S.Ct. 3528, 87 L.Ed.2d 652 (1985). There, in denying a claim for access to documents by an intervenor—albeit on grounds of "standing"—that Court observed:

> Such is the case here. The district court entered protective orders in order to expedite a discovery process involving literally hundreds of thousands of documents, many of which were subject to claims of privilege. At that stage in the litigation, *those documents had not been filed with the court and certainly had not satisfied threshold tests of relevancy and admissibility.* They therefore were not available to the public generally, and OPUBCO does not have standing to complain about the existence of the protective order.

So too, here. Based on the stipulation of confidentiality entered into by the plaintiffs, defendant McGhan opened its doors to freewheeling

---

16. And that, of course, assumes that the documents made available to counsel for plaintiffs were pursuant to their Rule 34 request. For the reasons that follow in the text * * *, however, that may well not be, inasmuch as plaintiffs were apparently given free rein to peruse through defendant McGhan's entire document depository, culling and copying whatever fit their fancy.

document inspection, permitting plaintiffs to pick and choose as they desired, without reference to the issue of relevancy, privilege, and/or admissibility. It may be, but has not been shown, that any or all of the documents [none of which have been particularized by the intervenor—even in a general sense] are relevant and non-privileged; that is, that the documents to which Command Trust seeks access are *discovery* documents within the meaning of *Public Citizen*. The motion of the Command Trust Network, Inc.—to the extent that Command Trust seeks substantive relief—is accordingly denied without prejudice.

II. THE MOTION FILED BY PLAINTIFF

To the extent that plaintiffs, by way of their Motion for Relief from Confidentiality Stipulation and Protective Order (# 93), seek relief from that stipulation and protective order for the purpose of submitting the six exhibits referred to in that motion to the Food and Drug Administration, that motion is—with the assent of defendant McGhan—allowed.

To the extent that plaintiffs seek to disclose those documents generally, or even to other counsel, the motion is denied.

In support of their position, counsel for plaintiffs, at the hearing before this court, suggested that disclosure to other counsel was necessary for preparation of plaintiffs' case before this court. The Confidentiality Stipulation and Protective Order, however, does not preclude that preparation. To the contrary, Section 4 of that Confidentiality Agreement and Protective Order specifically provides:

4. Counsel for Plaintiffs shall not disclose or permit the disclosure of any material or information designated as confidential under this Stipulation and Protective Order to any other person or entity except in the following circumstances:

(a) Disclosure may be made to employees of counsel who have direct functional responsibility for the preparation and trial of this action or in the appeal herein. Any employee to whom disclosure is made shall be advised of, and become subject to, the provisions of this Stipulation and Protective Order requiring that the material and information be held in confidence.

(b) Disclosure may be made to consultants or experts (hereinafter "expert") employed by counsel to assist in the preparation and trial of this litigation. Prior to disclosure to Plaintiff and any expert, they must agree to be bound by the terms of this Stipulation and Protective Order by executing the confidentiality Agreement annexed hereto as Exhibit A. A copy of each executed Confidentiality Agreement shall be delivered to counsel for Defendant at the time the Plaintiff lists its experts which it intends to call at trial. If disclosure is made to persons employed by competitors or to consultants hired by competitors of Defendant, McGhan Medical Corporation, then such persons must agree to not use such information for competitive purposes.

5.   Counsel for Plaintiff shall keep all material or information designated as confidential which is received under this Stipulation and Protective Order in a secure and locked file with access limited to those persons with a need to know for the purpose of preparation of the case.

Section 4 clearly permits counsel for plaintiffs to use the material in preparation of their case before this court.   Plaintiffs have proffered no valid reason to excuse them from the terms of their prior agreement.

JACK B. WEINSTEIN, ETHICAL DILEMMAS IN MASS TORT LITIGATION

88 Nw.U.L.Rev. 469, 512–17 (1994).

* * *

C.   Secrecy

Let us turn now to examine how the lawyer's obligation to maintain client confidences, and other ethical duties, are implicated by secrecy agreements in mass tort cases.   In this area it becomes impossible to discuss the lawyer's obligations without also considering the role of the judge.

Many, if not all, mass tort cases involve serious public concerns in terms of safety and the prevention of future injuries from the same harm.   And yet, many of these cases terminate in some form of secrecy agreement.   Historically, the private litigant has not been required to take into account public safety in vindicating his or her rights.   More significantly, the plaintiffs' attorney's duty of loyalty requires him or her to put the client's interests ahead of all others.   In traditional theory, the lawyer has no ethical obligation to consider the interests of third parties.   Likewise, the defendant's attorney, according to the ethical rules, is to maintain the client's confidences.   There is an affirmative duty not to reveal information.

Some plaintiffs' and defendants' attorneys tell me that it is almost impossible to settle many mass tort cases without a secrecy agreement. This has been my own experience in helping to settle thousands of cases.

Secrecy often has been, in fact, the price of settlement.   It is not unusual for a defendant to "sweeten" the settlement offer to plaintiffs on condition of secrecy.   The defendant may threaten the plaintiff with a lengthy and expensive trial to coerce confidentiality.   Some court cases can be brought and settled without the filing of a single revelatory document.   Others are settled on just the threat of legal action with no public record.   Since the ethical rules require that attorneys obtain a swift and optimal recovery for their clients, the plaintiffs' attorney seems to have little choice but to accept a favorable settlement offer on secrecy terms.

Three categories of secrecy should be considered separately: secrecy as to documents that appear to reveal a defendant's negligent or otherwise wrongful conduct, such as an engineer's report during the early development of a product indicating incipient dangers; secrecy as to the amount of a settlement or terms of payment; and secrecy as to conversations among attorneys on either plaintiff's or defendant's side, or even between plaintiff and defense counsel.

1. Documents and Oral Admissions Relating to Merits.—The most damaging of this information are "smoking gun" documents that indicate defendants knew of the danger but suppressed the information. Oral material obtained in depositions is also often highly useful to plaintiffs and devastating to defendants. Documents showing cover-ups or early knowledge by defendants of defects can lead to billions of dollars in punitive damages as well as extensive liability for ordinary damages, so there is strong reason for defendants to try to keep them secret. Plaintiffs' attorneys' threats to reveal them can be a powerful lever for higher settlements.

The societal interest in knowing what went wrong and why is great. Yet, there is some basis for the points made by defendants' counsel that first, the cost and time to explain a single document taken out of context by a plaintiffs' lawyer creates an incentive not to write things down, and, second, what appears damning may, in context after difficult proof, be shown to be neutral or even favorable to the defendant.

Courts have broad discretion in entering protective orders and sealing records. Most agreements are uncontested, and crowded calendars put great pressure on judges to move cases. As a result, judges routinely approve sealing and secrecy orders. Settlement agreements are filed under seal as a matter of course. It has been my practice to append a note to such approvals that "this order is subject to modification by the court in the public interest." In the *Agent Orange* case I set one of these orders aside after settlement because the public needed to know the facts.

Ultimately, if the court is faced with the question of whether to seal documents, it should engage in a balancing test, weighing the interest of the plaintiff against the interests in keeping the information confidential. In addition, judges should consider the interests of litigants in other suits, the needs of regulatory agencies to have access to information, concerns of public interest groups, and the interests of future plaintiffs.

In cases dealing with sociopolitical problems, the court must look to the effect on the community. The individual litigant's needs cannot be the court's sole concern. The mass tort case is, as already noted, similar to an institutional reform case in its impact. The public, which created and funds our judicial institutions, depends upon those institutions to protect it. Sometimes the needs of individual members of the community must yield to those of the community as a whole.

Should we be satisfied with a system that requires officers of the court to remain silent for years while more and more women suffer from what they think was harm caused by breast implants? If this silence is "a price we must pay," what do we receive in return?

Currently a national campaign is underway, in the name of public safety, to create a presumption of public access to all information produced in litigation. Advocates claim that protective orders are being used to hide product defects and public hazards and they have been pressing for legislation to restrict the courts' discretion to issue protective and sealing orders. These plaintiffs' attorneys have a selfish interest in opening the files for other litigations. Yet, much can be said in favor of the public's right to know.

Arguably, even out-of-court procedures such as arbitration and the like affect the public interest. A federal statute supports our national arbitration scheme. Should attorneys have an ethical obligation to inform the public, or at least the appropriate government body, of dangers revealed in private arbitrations? Is this sound as a matter of public policy? I think it is, under adequate judicial control.

While legislation to limit protective orders has been defeated in most jurisdictions, two states, Florida and Texas, have enacted sweeping reforms to restrict the courts' ability to seal documents. Both provisions are facing constitutional challenges. The Florida statute prohibits a court from issuing a protective order that conceals "information concerning a public hazard." A public hazard is broadly defined as "a product that has or is likely to cause injury."

The Texas rule establishes a presumption that civil records be open. To obtain a protective order, a party has the heavy burden of showing a "specific, serious and substantial interest which clearly outweighs a presumption of openness to the general public." A court can seal the records only after deciding that the interest at stake outweighs the public interest in access. The order, however, can always be contested after it is granted. The Texas rule is being challenged in product liability cases involving the sleep-inducing drug Halcion, the antidepressant Prozac, and the Ford Bronco II.

In 1993 at least fifteen states are likely to consider proposals to change their rules about protective orders, and action is sought at the federal level as well. This "sunshine" approach is not without its critics. One defense attorney from a large firm who testified before a California legislative committee investigating protective orders and the public safety asserted that troops in the Persian Gulf War were fighting to prevent the type of privacy invasion that such a rule would effect. Another likened forcing defense attorneys to consider the public interest in revelation of potential dangers to asking a criminal defense attorney who knows his client is guilty to turn the client over to the authorities.

The knowledge that secrecy cannot be depended on may discourage engineers and others from expressing doubts about a policy in written reports. There is thus a possibility that less secrecy may increase dangers to society. Even some attorneys for plaintiffs admit that rules limiting protective orders make them nervous, because they "inject a wild card into the settlement equation."

Protective orders may have a legitimate role when there is no public impact or when true trade secrets are involved. But we can strike a fairer balance between privacy interests and the health and safety of the public. A publicly maintained legal system ought not protect those who engage in misconduct, conceal the cause of injury from the victims, or render future victims vulnerable. Moreover, this sort of secrecy defeats the deterrent function of the justice system.

The balance, it is submitted, must involve the exercise of some judicial discretion. Yet, even judges have a conflict. They are under great pressure to clear their calendars. They will tend, therefore, to approve secrecy agreements that encourage settlement. One law professor suggested that a remedy might be for the court to employ an ombudsperson to weigh the secrecy issue independently of the trial judge. In the federal courts a magistrate judge might do the job, although even this official probably would want to see the court's calendar reduced.

Whatever the method chosen, it should be a national approach whenever cases are consolidated on a national basis. It is not possible to control the litigation effectively if each state's privileges and secrecy laws are applied. Such laws should, for purposes of mass torts, be deemed procedural so that, under *Erie,* the federal court does not have to apply the laws of fifty states.

Notes and Questions

1. Is Judge Weinstein correct? Are mass tort cases like public interest litigation that therefore justify different or relaxed confidentiality rules? Judge Weinstein's lengthy opinion adopting the magistrate's modification of the confidentiality agreement is reported at In re Agent Orange Prod. Liab. Litig., 104 F.R.D. 559 (E.D.N.Y.1985). For an extensive discussion of the discovery order, *see* Shira A. Scheindlin, *Discovering the Discoverable: A Bird's Eye View of Discovery in a Complex Multi–District Class Action Litigation,* 52 Brook.L.Rev. 397 (1986). For views sympathetic to Judge Weinstein's position concerning secrecy and protective orders, *see* Andrew Blum, *Protective Order Battle Continues,* Nat'l L.J., Jan. 11, 1993, at 3; Teresa M. Hendricks & Joseph W. Moch, *Protective Orders Assault Consumers,* Nat'l L.J., Feb. 8, 1993, at 15; Michael J. Mucchetti, *Public Access to Public Courts: Discouraging Secrecy in the Public Interest,* 69 Tex.L.Rev. 643 (1991)(discussing Tex.R.Civ.P. 76(a) open records rule). For arguments against presumptive public access *see generally* Arthur R. Miller, *Confidentiality, Protective Orders, and Public Access to the Courts,* 105 Harv.L.Rev. 427 (1991); Alan Morrison, *Protective Orders, Plaintiffs, Defendants and Public Interest Disclosure: Where Does the Balance Lie?,* 24 U.Rich.L.Rev. 109 (1989).

2. The district court in *Mirak,* reviewing almost the same set of procedural provisions in the Agent Orange litigation, nonetheless refused to permit broader access to discovery materials. Do factual differences be-

tween the two cases account for the different results? Does it make a crucial difference that the party seeking disclosure was an intervenor in the case? What of Judge Weinstein's public interest argument? Isn't it just as compelling in the silicone breast implant litigation as the *Agent Orange* litigation?

3. PRIVILEGES AND IMMUNITIES

IN RE SAN JUAN DUPONT PLAZA HOTEL FIRE LITIGATION

United States Court of Appeals, First Circuit, 1988.
859 F.2d 1007.

Before CAMPBELL, CHIEF JUDGE, TORRUELLA and SELYA, CIRCUIT JUDGES.

SELYA, CIRCUIT JUDGE.

This matter arises on an infrastructure of important concerns involving the prophylaxis to be accorded to attorneys' work product and the scope of trial judges' authority to confront case management exigencies in complex multi-district litigation. The critical question is somewhat novel. We delve rather deeply into the doctrinal underpinnings of the work product rule and the emergent need for increased judicial intervention in the early stages of the adjudicative process in explaining our affirmance of the challenged district court order.

I. BACKGROUND

On New Year's Eve 1986, a conflagration engulfed the San Juan Dupont Plaza Hotel. The blaze resulted in ninety-six deaths, numerous personal injuries, and extensive property damage. Upwards of 2,000 persons sued. Many of the suits were brought in, or removed to, federal district courts. Under the aegis of the Judicial Panel on Multi–District Litigation, those actions were consolidated for discovery purposes in the United States District Court for the District of Puerto Rico. The litigation has attained heroic proportions: there are roughly two hundred defendants and ten times that number of plaintiffs.

Pretrial discovery has proven to be a gargantuan undertaking. More than 2,000,000 documents have been produced; countless interrogatories have been served; and depositions are proceeding daily along fourteen simultaneous tracks. The trial judge recently estimated that over 2,000 depositions would be required before discovery closed. Due to the immensity of the litigation, the district court has necessarily assumed an active managerial role. As the linchpin of that endeavor, the court entered an elaborate forty-five page case management order (CMO). We described certain facets of the CMO in a recent opinion, In re Recticel Foam Corp., 859 F.2d 1000, 1001 (1st Cir.1988), and will not repastinate that ground. It suffices for today to state that, *inter alia,* the CMO set out general discovery guidelines, established a phased schedule for pretrial preparation, and ordered formation of a joint discovery committee (JDC). From time to time, as appropriate, the court has supplemented the CMO with additional orders and refinements, whilst repeatedly imploring counsel "to explore novel methods of discovery that would ensure expeditious progress of the litigation." *Recticel,* 859 F.2d at 1001.

Not surprisingly, discovery disputes occurred with monotonous regularity. On February 24, 1988, the magistrate who the judge had appointed to oversee discovery held a hearing anent one such dispute. The defense representatives on the JDC sought to require parties taking depositions to identify, five days beforehand, the exhibits which they intended to utilize at deposition. Plaintiffs' representatives complained that such a paradigm, if sanctioned, would require disclosure of attorney work product. The magistrate turned a deaf ear to the protest and adopted the identification protocol.

Upon entry of the magistrate's order, the plaintiffs' steering committee (PSC), a coterie of lawyers representing the shared interests of all of the claimants, prosecuted an appeal to the district judge. *See* Fed. R.Civ.P. 72(a). The judge upheld the magistrate. In essence, the district court concluded that a document list of the type required was not attorney work product; that, even if such a list could be so categorized, it was at most qualifiedly privileged—and the privilege was overborne in this instance by the special needs of the sprawling litigation; and that, therefore, the order was not clearly erroneous or contrary to law. The judge appended to his affirmance a set of guidelines aimed at easing application of the identification protocol. The guidelines modified the order slightly by requiring all parties who wished to examine at the deposition to prepare and submit document lists. Yet the PSC's basic grievance was not mollified.

After the district court certified its order for interlocutory appeal under 28 U.S.C. § 1292(b), the PSC requested that we hear the matter, and we agreed.

II. DISCUSSION

Appellant makes a well-constructed four-part argument which runs along the following lines: (1) PSC members sifted through millions of pieces of paper in order to locate and identify approximately 70,000 documents which they thought relevant to the litigation; (2) although the documents themselves are not protected work product, the identification protocol requires plaintiffs' lawyers to reveal to their opponents the mental processes, impressions, and opinions of the attorneys who culled the wheat from the chaff; (3) these mental processes, impressions, and opinions constitute "opinion" work product which—unlike its poor relation, "ordinary" work product—should enjoy absolute protection; and (4) inasmuch as preidentification of relevant documents necessarily divulges the results of the attorneys' selection process, the work product doctrine interdicts the challenged order.

* * *

B. The Identification Protocol. Before we can define the actual limitations which, in this case, impinge upon the district court's adoption of the identification protocol, we must determine more specifically the source of the court's power to enter the challenged order. Neither the district judge nor the magistrate attempted to elucidate this point, so we must look to the nature of the order itself, and the circumstances of its interposition, for guidance.

By its terms, the order establishes "rules ... for prior identification and production of ... exhibits." Appendix to Pretrial Order No. 57, at 1. Its text tells us that these rules were formulated by the district court "[i]n the interest of expediting the taking of depositions and to afford the parties the opportunity adequately to prepare for discovery...." *Id.* The key provision of the protocol states in relevant part:

> Any party wishing to use exhibits during the questioning of a deponent ... shall place a list of all exhibits which it intends to use during the taking of said deposition in the Joint Document Depository, at least five (5) working days before the commencement date for said deposition.

Id. The rules constrain all parties: plaintiffs and defendants, those who notice depositions and those who receive deposition notices. They prohibit counsel referring to unlisted documents during a deposition unless their usage "could not have been reasonably anticipated." *Id.* at 2.

It is readily apparent that this decree is not a discovery order of the genre to which we are accustomed. Traditionally, discovery orders resolve conflicts arising when a party, through the use of one of the enumerated discovery devices, seeks to gain information from an adverse party or a third person. A, for example, propounds an interrogatory to B; dissatisfied with the response—it seems incomplete, or evasive, or simply never materializes—A asks the judge to order that a proper response be served. In that sort of situation, litigant initiative mobilizes and drives the discovery engine. The trial court acts as an umpire: the judge resolves the immediate dispute between the parties and fashions relief, usually grounded in Rule 26's oversight powers, based on the nature and circumstances of the discovery requests. But the order here at issue is not cut from this staple cloth. It is unconventional, perhaps because "[t]he art of our necessities is strange." W. Shakespeare, KING LEAR (1606).

The protocol presently in dispute is not so much a discovery order as a case management order. Litigant initiative is of no moment: the identification protocol is a product of judicial action, not judicial reaction. Notwithstanding the PSC's insinuations to the contrary, it seems to us crystal clear that the district court crafted the challenged decree with care to serve the overall needs of the litigation rather than the individual interests of any particular party or group of parties. The resultant order is temporally and substantively pervasive; that is to say, it will guide the entire discovery phase of the litigation and leave its mark upon the taking of an estimated 2,000 depositions. It affects the parties' abilities effectively to depose persons thought to possess relevant information. It changes the plane of the playing field, but leaves the field level in that its impact is felt equally by plaintiffs and defendants.[4]

This focus on the systemic needs of the litigation, combined with the pervasive scope of the ensuing guidelines, persuades us that the order derives not from the district court's familiar Rule 26 "scope-of-discovery" power, but from the court's newly-augmented authority to control and manage the litigation and the course of discovery. *See* Fed.R.Civ.P. 16(e), 26(f). The question then becomes whether the work product doctrine limits a court's case management powers—and if so, to what extent. Asking such a question, we think, is materially different from asking how the work product doctrine restricts a court's traditional power to compel discovery from Litigant A and cause the fruits to be delivered to Litigant B.

C. The Work Product Doctrine. The work product doctrine, first recognized by the Supreme Court in Hickman v. Taylor, 329 U.S. 495, 67 S.Ct. 385, 91 L.Ed. 451 (1947), has most frequently acted as a "limitation on the nonevidentiary material which may be the subject of pretrial discovery...." United States v. Nobles, 422 U.S. 225, 243, 95 S.Ct. 2160, 2172, 45 L.Ed.2d 141 (1975)(White, J., concurring). Although the Court has approached the doctrine in terms reminiscent of qualified privilege, its scope and effect outside the civil discovery context is largely undefined. 422 U.S. at 238. Fed.R.Civ.P. 26(b)(3), for example, partially codifies the work product doctrine as recognized in *Hickman,* but is narrowly drawn to confine its scope to its historical origins.[5] Read literally, the rule applies only where a civil litigant seeks production of tangible information in another's possession. So, it is on its face inapplicable to the district court's order. Nonetheless, because the challenged decree governs the litigation's discovery phase and operates in a manner somewhat analogous to a stock discovery order—it forces one party involuntarily to disclose information to other parties—the spirit of Rule 26(b)(3), at least, should have pertinency. To assume that

---

4. We recognize, of course, that the actual burden of the order has to date fallen principally on the plaintiffs—but only because they happen to have noticed, thus far, the majority of depositions. This fact does not, however, alter the order's neutrality, nor is it of moment with regard to the work product issue which the PSC has raised.

5. The rule provides in pertinent part as follows: Subject to the provisions of subdivision (b)(4) of this rule, a party may obtain discovery of documents and tangible things otherwise discoverable ... and prepared in anticipation of litigation or for trial by or for another party['s attorney] ... only upon a showing that the party seeking discovery has substantial need of the materials in the preparation of the party's case and that the

party is unable without undue hardship to obtain the substantial equivalent of the materials by other means. In ordering discovery of such materials when the required showing has been made, the court shall protect against disclosure of the mental impressions, conclusions, opinions, or legal theories of an attorney or other representative of a party concerning the litigation. Fed.R.Civ.P. 26(b)(3). Rule 26(b)(4), referred to in the first sentence of Rule 26(b)(3), deals with discovery of expert opinions developed in anticipation of litigation or for trial. Inasmuch as this case does not involve depositions of experts as a separate class, we put Rule 26(b)(4) aside for the time being.

the work product doctrine does not apply at all when a court's order transcends the conventional discovery model would be to ignore the evolution of discovery.

It is, therefore, not surprising that the work product doctrine has found application beyond the prototypical civil discovery realm. The Supreme Court has recently recognized that the doctrine's underlying rationales are apposite in other, analogous, contexts. *See* Upjohn Co. v. United States, 449 U.S. 383, 397–402, 101 S.Ct. 677, 686–89, 66 L.Ed.2d 584 (1981)(work product doctrine applicable to Internal Revenue Service summonses); *United States v. Nobles*, 422 U.S. at 236, 101 S.Ct. at 686 (recognizing work product doctrine in criminal matters). Our adversarial system of justice cannot function properly unless an attorney is given a zone of privacy within which to prepare the client's case and plan strategy, without undue interference. *See Upjohn Co. v. United States*, 449 U.S. at 397–98, 101 S.Ct. at 686; *United States v. Nobles*, 422 U.S. at 238, 95 S.Ct. at 2170; *Hickman v. Taylor*, 329 U.S. at 511, 67 S.Ct. at 393; In re Grand Jury Subpoena, 622 F.2d 933, 935 (6th Cir.1980); Coastal States Gas Corp. v. Department of Energy, 617 F.2d 854, 864 (D.C.Cir.1980); *see also* Special Project, *The Work Product Doctrine*, 68 Cornell L.Rev. 760, 784–87 (1983)(explaining need for zone of privacy). To preserve this quiet and secluded corner for the use and benefit of attorneys in complex civil litigation, the work product doctrine must also act to some degree as a brake on the court's power to manage the discovery and pretrial phases of such litigation. *Cf. Nobles*, 422 U.S. at 238, 95 S.Ct. at 2170 (styling work product doctrine as "an intensely practical one, grounded in the realities of litigation in our adversary system"). But to posit applicability of the doctrine "to some degree" is not tantamount to plotting the intersecting lines; to say that some limitation exists is merely to refocus the question rather than to answer it. Because the nature and extent of such a limitation is not necessarily coterminous with those work product restrictions which accrue in the conventional discovery context, we must take a fresh look at the doctrinal infrastructure of the work product rule and the interests which shape it.

D. Obtaining Work Product. In *Hickman v. Taylor,* the Supreme Court ruled that materials prepared "with an eye towards litigation" were not freely discoverable without some showing of necessity. 329 U.S. at 511, 67 S.Ct. at 394. *See also* Fed.R.Civ.P. 26(b)(3), quoted *supra* at note 5. The boundaries of the doctrine were mapped, originally, by balancing the systemic interest in providing lawyers with "a certain degree of privacy, free from unnecessary intrusion by opposing parties and their counsel," 329 U.S. at 510–11, 67 S.Ct. at 393, against the societal interest in ensuring that the parties obtain "[m]utual knowledge of all the relevant facts gathered...." *Id.* at 507. *See generally,* S. Cohn, *The Work Product Doctrine: Protection, Not Privilege,* 71 Geo.L.J. 917, 918–22 (1983).

Although the substantial need/undue hardship standard was soon accepted as basic to the work product calculus, the standard has never been applied across the board. The *Hickman* Court hinted broadly that some materials prepared in anticipation of litigation merited a greater degree of protection than might routinely be accorded to others. 329 U.S. at 512–13, 67 S.Ct. at 394. The draftsmen of Fed.R.Civ.P. 26(b)(3) also recognized a distinction between types of work product: even where the need/hardship hurdle has been cleared, the court must continue to afford "protect[ion] against disclosure of the mental impressions, conclusions, opinions or legal theories of an attorney. . . ." *Id.* Striations of this kind have led courts to distinguish between "opinion" work product and "ordinary" work product—the former category encompassing materials that contain the mental impressions, conclusions, opinions or legal theories of an attorney, the latter category embracing the residue. *See, e.g.,* Sporck v. Peil, 759 F.2d 312, 316 (3d Cir.), *cert. denied,* 474 U.S. 903, 106 S.Ct. 232, 88 L.Ed.2d 230 (1985); In Re Murphy, 560 F.2d 326, 329 n.1 (8th Cir.1977); Duplan Corp. v. Moulinage et Retorderie de Chavanoz, 509 F.2d 730, 732 (4th Cir.1974), *cert. denied,* 420 U.S. 997, 95 S.Ct. 1438, 43 L.Ed.2d 680 (1975). The dichotomy—or some form of it—has now seemingly been recognized by the Court, *see Upjohn Co. v. United States,* 449 U.S. at 399–400, 101 S.Ct. at 687-688 , but the exact import and dimensions of the approach remains tenebrous. Courts typically afford ordinary work product only a qualified immunity, subject to a showing of substantial need and undue hardship, while requiring a hardier showing to justify the production of opinion work product. *See, e.g.,* In Re Grand Jury Investigation, 599 F.2d 1224, 1231 (3d Cir.1979). Indeed, some courts have seemingly concluded that the protection for certain types of opinion work product is ironclad. *See, e.g.,* In Re Grand Jury Proceedings, 473 F.2d 840, 848 (8th Cir.1973)(lawyer's personal recollections, notes, and memoranda pertaining to witness interviews safeguarded absolutely). The Supreme Court, however, has made no commitment concerning the correct standard for revelation of opinion work product. *See Upjohn Co. v. United States,* 449 U.S. at 401, 101 S.Ct. at 688 (specifically reserving question).

For today we merely note—but do not address—this distinction. For the reasons mentioned below, *see infra* Part II(E), we are satisfied that only ordinary work product is involved in the identification protocol. The standard for disclosure, therefore, would seem at first blush to be that of balancing substantial need against undue hardship. Yet even that standard, useful as it may be in the discovery context, appears maladroit when the source of the intrusion is not a discovery order but a case management order. The evolution of the work product doctrine—which sprouted and grew in the fruited plains of pretrial discovery—explains what we see as a lacuna: the need/hardship balance, such as is precisely enunciated in Rule 26(b)(3), has traditionally been a barometer only of the relative interests of the opposing litigants. This makes abundant good sense for the resolution of discovery rhubarbs, but leaves the circle unclosed in the Rule 16 milieu. Insofar as we can tell, concerns for maximizing the efficient use of judicial and litigant resources (such as are served by broadening judicial management powers) have never heretofore been a relevant consideration in formulating the work product doctrine. Given the rigors of modern-day litigation, and the increased emphasis on case management, the omission looms as intolerable.

When case management, rather than conventional discovery, becomes the hammer which bangs against the work product anvil, logic demands that the district judge must be given greater latitude than provided by the routine striking of the need/hardship balance. Because of "the taxing demands of modern-day case management," *Recticel,* at 1007, the requirements of the litigation and the court must, we think, be weighed in determining whether a management technique impermissibly impinges upon the protected zone of work product privacy. In this context, the vista is not exclusively head-to-head, A against B, plaintiff versus defendant; the relationship is triangular, with the court itself as a third, important, player. There is no reason, then, why the crying need for efficient use of scarce judicial resources cannot—and should not—be factored into the equation. We hold that it must.

E. Classification of the Lists. Having refashioned the geometry of the weighbeam, we turn to an evaluation of the work product interest which the PSC asks us to place on the scales. We begin with an abecedarian verity: not every item which may reveal some inkling of a lawyer's mental impressions, conclusions, opinions, or legal theories is protected as opinion work product. Were the doctrine to sweep so massively, the exception would hungrily swallow up the rule. *See Sporck v. Peil,* 759 F.2d at 319 (Seitz, J., dissenting)("[e]very act by a litigant or his attorney gives rise to ... vague inferences" as to strategy and counsel's thought processes). Whatever heightened protection may be conferred upon opinion work product, that level of protection is not triggered unless disclosure creates a real, nonspeculative danger of revealing the lawyer's thoughts. *See Gould, Inc. v. Mitsui Mining & Smelting Co.,* 825 F.2d 676, 680 (2d Cir.1987); Research Institute for Medicine and Chemistry, Inc. v. Wisconsin Alumni Research Foundation, 114 F.R.D. 672, 680 (W.D.Wis.1987). There is, moreover, a second line of demarcation. Some materials do not merit heightened protection because, despite the revelations they contain as to an attorney's thought processes, the lawyer has had no justifiable expectation that the mental impressions revealed by the materials will remain private.[6]

* * *

On the other hand, efficacious operation of the judicial system has much to gain by expedition of the disclosure in such circumstances.

---

6. The principle, we think, is analogous to the expectation of privacy which may (or may not) be inherent in the attorney-client relationship itself. All depends on the circumstances surrounding a given communication. Absent an expectation of confidentiality, none accrues. As one leading commentator has noted:

The [attorney-client] privilege assumes, of course, that the communications are made with the intention of confidentiality.... 'The moment confidence ceases,' said Lord Eldon, 'privilege ceases.' This much is universally conceded....

8 J. Wigmore, EVIDENCE § 2311 (McNaughton rev. 1961)(citations omitted).

Time and effort are conserved, and no meaningful intrusion takes place. Thus, the overall balance of equities plainly favors making what amounts to a timing adjustment, in the process treating such materials as something less than fully-protected opinion work product. *Cf.* Fed. R.Civ.P. 26(b)(3) advisory committee note (although party required to divulge mental impressions and conclusions, lawyer remains "entitled to keep confidential documents containing such matters *prepared for internal use*")(emphasis supplied).

A reconstructed balance of this kind is equally adaptable to the looming collision between legitimate work product concerns and modern case management techniques. Courts, pursuant to the powers granted by Rule 16, routinely require parties to file pretrial memoranda or otherwise to identify witnesses, pre-mark exhibits, define contentions, and spell out their legal theories. *See, e.g.,* Spray–Rite Service Corp. v. Monsanto Co., 684 F.2d 1226, 1245 (7th Cir.1982)(compilation and exchange of witness lists), *aff'd,* 465 U.S. 752, 104 S.Ct. 1464, 79 L.Ed.2d 775 (1984); Elliott v. Louisiana Power & Light Co., 671 F.2d 865, 868–69 (5th Cir.1982)(same; exhibit lists); *cf.* Hernandez v. Alexander, 671 F.2d 402, 407 (10th Cir.1982)(legal theory not elucidated in agreed pretrial order not cognizable thereafter). *See also* Note, *Pretrial Conference: A Critical Examination of Local Rules Adopted by Federal District Courts,* 64 Va.L.Rev. 467, 469 (1978). Like the provisions of the Civil Rules anent discovery, such case management devices do not decide *whether* certain aspects of the attorney's thought processes will be disclosed, but simply determine *when* the disclosure will occur. In other words, they do little more than change the timing, expediting revelations which would ultimately be made during the normal course of pretrial proceedings or trial itself. Since these incursions into the attorney's mental impressions are inevitable, any violation of the zone of privacy is marginal, and the sturdier prophylaxis given to opinion work product is neither needed nor warranted.

In our view, the exhibit lists demanded by the district court's identification protocol fall well within this less-shielded category. The PSC concedes that the documents themselves are nonprivileged and that, apart from work product connotations, the lists are not otherwise eligible for special swaddling. More to the point, the challenged order does not result in the evulgation of matters which would otherwise remain perpetually hidden. When the deposition is held and examination commences, the questioner's document selection, and the stratagems it reveals, will become obvious to all. Requiring preidentification merely moves up the schedule, accelerating disclosures which would inevitably take place. Consequently, the resultant lists cannot validly aspire to the stature of opinion work product, nor can they command the correlative degree of (heightened) protection.

We recognize, of course, that the process of selecting relevant documents for use in depositions "is often more crucial than legal research." Shelton v. American Motors Corp., 805 F.2d 1323, 1329 (8th Cir.1986). But as we have already pointed out, the information spotlighted by such lists (including whatever insights may be gleaned from the choice of exhibits) will undeniably be gained during the course of the deposition. Like requiring pleadings, answers to contention interrogatories, pretrial exhibit and witness lists, and trial memoranda, the district court's identification protocol merely adjusts the timing of disclosure. The situation is not remotely analogous to the situation where a party seeks an attorney's personal notes and memoranda which contain his confidential assessments of the testimony of prospective witnesses. *See Hickman*, 329 U.S. at 512–13. Such notes and memoranda are usually prepared solely for the attorney's own use—or at most, for confidential consideration between attorney, client, and their privies (*e.g.,* junior counsel, investigators, retained experts). Under ordinary circumstances, the lawyer can expect that such materials will never be subject to his opponents' scrutiny—or at least, that he can effectively control whether or not such dissemination will occur. In contrast, no lawyer can be so sanguine as to expect that the opposition will not become privy to his choice of deposition exhibits; the exhibits are integral to the taking of the deposition and will, by definition, have to be revealed during the session.

* * *

F. Calibrating the Scales. Notwithstanding our conclusion that the exhibit lists do not comprise opinion work product, we recognize that attorneys and their staffs sorted and segregated the documents in anticipation of litigation. We do not deny that a glimpse of the selection process's yield provides insight into opposing counsel's understanding of his case. Forced production of an exhibit list makes some incursion into the attorney's quiet and secluded corner and consequently implicates the work product rule to an extent—but treating the lists as ordinary work product fully safeguards whatever legitimate privacy concerns are at stake. Adopting this taxonomy, we find, as did the court below, that the warranted degree of protection was clearly overbalanced by the exigencies of the case.

* * *

We can conclude this aspect of our inquiry with little added ado. Mindful of the enormity of the litigation, and of its complexity, the fashioning of a more serviceable judicial handle on the case seems a consummation devoutly to be wished. Thus, we deem it important that no other, less intrusive means of reaping the benefits which inhere in the identification protocol come readily to mind. (Certainly, the PSC has suggested none.) All in all, we have no reason to second-guess the trial court's reasoned conclusion that the balance of relevant equities counsels in favor of the identification protocol: as the district judge supportably found, the parties have a substantial need to obtain the materials; equivalent information is unobtainable through other means without undue hardship; and the court's ability successfully to manage the litigation will be hampered in the absence of the protocol. Appellant has pointed out no relevant factor which the district court failed to consider, nor any factor which it improperly included in the mix. The record leaves us with a firm and abiding conviction that, given the unusual dimensions of this behemoth, the disputed order makes eminently good sense. The PSC has failed to demonstrate any misuse of judicial discretion.

III. CONCLUSION

We need go no further. The district court had adequate power pursuant to Rules 16(e) and 26(f) to order those choosing to take part in a given discovery deposition to provide, five days prior to the deposition, a list of exhibits to be utilized during the questioning. Although the work product rule can truncate the usual sweep of a court's powers, there is no requirement that case management orders which impinge upon work product be barred absolutely.

In this instance, work product considerations do not interdict the district judge's order. The information provided to opposing parties by the order's operation is ordinary work product, not opinion work product. In the context of a complex case, the court, if the needs of the litigation and the litigants reasonably so dictate, has broad discretion to command production of materials constituting ordinary work product. Given the special requirements of this mammoth collection of consolidated suits and the particularized findings which were made below, we conclude that the district court's calibration of the scales should not be disturbed. The court had power, authority, and sound reason to impose the preidentification condition.

Affirmed.

Notes and Questions

1. Can Rule 16, used in combination with "inherent judicial power" and case management authority be used to abridge traditional attorney-client privilege and work product immunity in mass tort cases? Does the magnitude of a litigation or complex discovery justify encroaching on existing privileges and immunities? Is Judge Selya's opinion, that his ruling is consistent with existing rules and doctrine, convincing?

2. Do mass tort cases, consistent with Judge Weinstein's public interest theory, justify relaxation of the traditional protections afforded by attorney-client privilege and work product immunity? Why? Is the justification the same as for a more expansive view of protective orders? For a discussion of a defendant's unsuccessful invocation of privilege to prevent disclosure in asbestos litigation, *see* Andrew Blum, *Westinghouse Loses on Paper: Asbestos Memos at Issue,* Nat'l L.J., Mar. 22, 1993, at 1 (discussing three court orders denying application of privilege for internal corporate memoranda); *see also* Brad N. Friedman, Note, *Mass Products Liability Litigation: A Proposal for Dissemination of Discovered Material Covered by a Protective Order,* 60 N.Y.U.L. Rev. 1137 (1985).

3. In 1993, Congress enacted a package of federal rules amendments, which included amended Fed.R.Civ.P. 26(a), requiring mandatory disclosure of certain information at the outset of trial. Some writers have suggested

that the new mandatory disclosure provisions will impair existing privileges and immunities. *See, e.g.,* Griffin B. Bell *et al., Automatic Disclosure in Discovery—The Rush to Reform,* 27 Ga.L.Rev. 1 (1992); William H. Erickson, *Limited Discovery and the Use of Alternative Procedures for Dispute Resolution,* 71 Denv.U.L.Rev. 303 (1994); Paul R. Sugarman & Marc C. Perlin, *Proposed Changes to Discovery Rules in Aid of "Tort Reform": Has the Case Been Made?,* 42 Am.U.L.Rev. 1465 (1993). For a contrary view, *see* Linda S. Mullenix, *Adversarial Justice, Professional Responsibility, and the New Federal Discovery Rules,* 14 Rev.Litig. 13 (1994). Will the new mandatory disclosure rules effect mass tort discovery?

4. COOPERATIVE DISCOVERY

WILLIAM W. SCHWARZER, *et al.,* JUDICIAL FEDERALISM IN ACTION: COORDINATION OF LITIGATION IN STATE AND FEDERAL COURTS

78 Va.L.Rev. 1689, 1700–13 (1992).

* * *

III. Case Studies in Informal Intersystem Coordination

We have studied various cases in which state and federal judges coordinated proceedings before them. In this Part, we draw on these case studies to analyze what kinds of coordination at what stages of litigation are most promising. To set the stage for that analysis, we offer a brief summary (in chronological order) of each instance of litigation we have studied in depth. Details of these and other cases will emerge in the following discussion of the nature of coordination that has been achieved at each stage of litigation.

A. *Illustrative Cases*

1. *Florida Everglades Air Crash*

On December 29, 1972, a jet aircraft flying from New York to Miami crashed in the Florida Everglades, killing ninety-six passengers and injuring many others. Lawsuits were filed in Florida state courts and in federal courts in Florida and New York. Eventually, the JPML transferred all the federal cases to the docket of Judge Peter T. Fay, then a District Judge for the Southern District of Florida, for coordinated pretrial proceedings. The Florida state cases were all assigned to Judge Harvie S. DuVal. Judges Fay and DuVal coordinated discovery extensively. They considered a joint state federal trial on liability, but instead opted for the trial of two federal test cases, with many of the state parties agreeing to be bound by the results. Ten days before trial, the parties settled on the liability issue. Disputes over damages were tried or settled by the judges within their own jurisdictions, without coordination.

2. *Beverly Hills Supper Club Fire*

On May 28, 1977, a fire destroyed a nightclub in Kentucky, killing or injuring over 300 persons. Numerous lawsuits were filed in both the

United States District Court for the Eastern District of Kentucky and in Kentucky state court. Because of a backlog in the Eastern District of Kentucky, Judge Carl B. Rubin of the Southern District of Ohio volunteered to hear the federal cases. He was designated to sit in the Eastern District of Kentucky and was assigned the cases. The state cases were before Judge John A. Diskin. The two judges coordinated all scheduling and pretrial activity. Judges Rubin and Diskin eventually divided the cases into groups, some to be tried in federal court, others in state court. Judge Rubin certified a federal class action involving the claims against most defendants, and Judge Diskin certified a state class action involving the remaining defendants. The cases proceeded to trials and verdicts in the two courts.

3. Chicago Air Crash

On May 25, 1979, a DC–10 aircraft departing O'Hare International Airport in Chicago en route to Los Angeles crashed shortly after takeoff, killing 273 people and injuring several others. Eventually more than 150 wrongful death and personal injury suits were either filed in or removed to federal court, all based on diversity jurisdiction. The JPML transferred all the cases to Judges Edwin A. Robson and Hubert L. Will of the Northern District of Illinois for consolidated pretrial proceedings. A number of suits remained in the state courts, including a cluster of seventy that were assigned to Judge Rafael H. Galceran in the Superior Court of Los Angeles County. The state and federal judges devised a joint discovery program, and exchanged information pertaining to settlement efforts. The cases that did not settle were tried in their respective systems, with the federal cases remanded to the district in which they had been originally filed or to which they had been removed.

4. Hyatt Skywalk Cases

On June 17, 1981, two walkways in the Hyatt Regency Hotel in Kansas City, Missouri collapsed, killing more than 100 people and injuring over 200. Roughly twenty cases were filed in the United States District Court for the Western District of Missouri and over 100 in Missouri state court. The state cases were assigned to Judge Timothy D. O'Leary and the federal cases to Judge Scott O. Wright. The two judges coordinated discovery and discussed, but eventually abandoned, the idea of a joint state-federal trial. Judge Wright certified a mandatory federal class action. His order was vacated by the Eighth Circuit, but he later certified an opt-out class. Separate trials were scheduled in state and federal courts. Eventually, separate class-wide settlements of both the state and federal cases were reached.

5. Ohio Asbestos Litigation

During the early 1980s, asbestos claims were beginning to crowd a number of federal and state court dockets. Two judges in Ohio, Thomas D. Lambros of the United States District Court for the Northern District of Ohio and James J. McMonagle of the Cuyahoga County Court of Common Pleas, determined that coordinating their asbestos cases would reduce cost and delay. In June 1983, all eighty asbestos cases in the

Northern District were transferred to Judge Lambros' docket; approximately fifty cases were pending before Judge McMonagle at that time. The two judges decided to coordinate every stage of litigation, with the state court tracking the federal court's formal case management plan. Judge McMonagle grouped and moved his cases to correspond to the treatment of the federal cases in order to facilitate simultaneous settlement. The two judges participated in joint settlement sessions in both courts, and held joint scheduling sessions and pretrial hearings. They also coordinated discovery efforts. Coordination proceeded until Judge McMonagle's retirement in August 1990, and continued thereafter with some of the judges who took over his asbestos caseload.

6. MGM Grand Hotel Fire

On November 21, 1980, a fire in a Las Vegas hotel/casino killed eighty-four people and injured over 1000. Cases were filed in federal courts around the country, and in California and Nevada state courts. In May 1981, the JPML transferred all federal cases to the United States District Court for the District of Nevada for consolidated pretrial proceedings. Judge Louis C. Bechtle, of the Eastern District of Pennsylvania, volunteered to sit in Nevada and was assigned the cases. All of the cases in Nevada state courts had been consolidated before Judge J. Charles Thompson. The two judges engaged in extensive coordination of discovery proceedings. Their coordination extended to the settlement process as well, with an eye toward a "global settlement," which they eventually achieved.

7. Technical Equities Fraud

In 1986, Technical Equities Corporation, a San Jose real estate and investment firm, went bankrupt, leaving 1200 investors with losses of over $150 million on investments in stocks, partnership interests, and short-term notes. Several hundred lawsuits were filed alleging fraud by the corporation's officers and directors. Additional suits were filed against accounting firms, banks, and insurance companies for aiding and abetting the alleged fraudulent conduct. Most of the cases were brought in California state court and eventually consolidated before Judge Conrad Rushing. A handful of cases were filed in federal court, and assigned to Judge William A. Ingram of the Northern District of California.

Judge Rushing appointed a settlement master for the state cases. The master enlisted the cooperation of Judge Ingram and Bankruptcy Judge Lloyd King (along with Judge Rushing) in an effort to achieve a global settlement. Judge Rushing also appointed a state discovery master. Later, Judge Ingram appointed the same special discovery master for the federal cases. As a result, the two courts coordinated discovery. Two groups of state cases, using test-group plaintiffs and applying the findings to similarly situated plaintiffs, have been tried— one in 1988, the other in 1990. A settlement of the federal cases was reached in July 1991.

8. L'Ambiance Plaza Collapse

On April 23, 1987, L'Ambiance Plaza, a high-rise building under construction in Bridgeport, Connecticut, collapsed, killing twenty-eight people and injuring sixteen. Five cases were filed in federal court and assigned to Judge Warren W. Eginton, and others were filed in state court. Judge Eginton approached Federal Judge Robert C. Zampano, an alternative dispute resolution (ADR) specialist, about the possibility of using ADR. Believing that any settlement would have to include both the state and the federal cases, Judge Zampano formulated a plan for coordinated settlement of all cases. The state cases were assigned for discovery to Judge James T. Healey and for settlement to Judge Frank S. Meadow. Judges Zampano and Meadow put in place a mediation procedure for both the state and federal cases, while Judges Eginton and Healey coordinated discovery and held joint hearings. Eventually a global settlement was achieved.

9. Brooklyn Navy Yard Asbestos Litigation

After New York enacted two statutory changes in 1986, its state and federal courts were inundated with asbestos-related lawsuits. By February 1988, over 5000 asbestos cases were pending in state and federal courts, many of them identical suits involving the same parties. The federal cases filed in the Eastern and Southern Districts of New York were all consolidated before Judge Charles P. Sifton of the Eastern District of New York. The cases filed in the state courts in the five counties of the City of New York were eventually consolidated before Justice Helen E. Freedman. By that time Judge Sifton had a management plan in place. Justice Freedman issued a management plan for the state cases modeled on the federal plan. The two judges made sure that they and the litigants were kept abreast of related actions pending in each other's court system. They also coordinated their motion rulings, with each court sending a copy of its memoranda and orders to the other court, which would often follow the outcome and reasoning when ruling on similar motions.

As the cases were proceeding to trial in the separate systems, Federal Judge Jack B. Weinstein suggested a consolidated state and federal court trial, presided over by Justice Freedman and himself, involving all cases that arose from exposure to asbestos at the Brooklyn Navy Yard. In January 1990, the *Brooklyn Navy Yard* cases on Judge Sifton's docket, and those of other federal judges, were transferred to Judge Weinstein. Judge Weinstein and Justice Freedman coordinated all pretrial matters, including settlement negotiations. They considered holding a joint state-federal trial, but eventually decided to try the cases separately, in part because most of the cases had already settled.

10. The Exxon–Valdez Oil Spill

On March 24, 1989, the tanker Exxon–Valdez ran aground and ruptured on Bligh Reef (approximately twenty-five miles from the southern end of the Trans–Alaska Pipeline), releasing over eleven million gallons of crude oil into the waters of Prince William Sound. During the ensuing months, the oil spread widely, contaminating waters, killing fish and other animals, and affecting the livelihood of many people. The spill led to assorted criminal and civil actions brought by the federal government, the State of Alaska, and the Native Alaskan Villages. In addition, private citizens filed hundreds of suits in both state and federal courts. The private claims were based on common law and on the Trans–Alaska Pipeline Authorization Act and parallel state legislation. The majority of the federal actions were consolidated before Judge H. Russel Holland of the United States District Court for the District of Alaska. The state actions were consolidated before Judge Brian Shortell.

Judges Shortell and Holland have engaged in extensive coordination of all pretrial matters, sometimes conducting joint hearings, and are currently developing a schedule to coordinate the state and federal cases in the trial phase.

11.   Sioux City Air Crash

On July 19, 1989, a United Airlines flight from Denver to Chicago crashed at Sioux City, Iowa, killing 112 people. Cases were filed in state and federal courts around the country. Many were filed in Illinois state courts, and these were assigned to Judge Donald P. O'Connell. The JPML transferred all federal cases to Judge Suzanne B. Conlon of the Northern District of Illinois for consolidated pretrial proceedings. That court was chosen, in part, to "facilitate coordination among the federal and Illinois state court actions." The two courts coordinated discovery, kept one another updated on all activity in their respective courts, and aimed for consistent rulings. The cases eventually settled or were remanded to the districts in which they were originally filed.

A number of factors motivated the judges in these cases to coordinate their proceedings. Some sought to prevent the "great duplication of effort and money" that would result "if both court systems were going to conduct discovery and hold hearings and * * * settlement negotiations." Other judges worried that if the cases proceeded separately, scheduling conflicts or other tensions between the court systems would impede their progress. Still others were motivated by a desire for consistency in the state and federal treatment of the cases in order to ensure comparable outcomes for similarly situated parties. Finally, a few judges believed that coordination would help them take charge of their cases. Mass litigation can present an awesome managerial task, and when judges work together they can jointly develop strategies to manage the litigation and can reinforce each other's strategies.

The discussion that follows confirms these views; coordinating state and federal cases accomplished important objectives. What follows is a description of how coordination was implemented and how it fared at each stage.

B.   Discovery

Discovery creates the greatest need and presents the greatest opportunity for coordination. Virtually all judges and attorneys who have participated in cases involving intersystem coordination agree that duplicative discovery—serving the same interrogatories on the same parties, taking depositions on the same matters of the same witnesses, and producing the same documents and physical evidence in two courts rather than a common depository—is enormously wasteful. Thus, judges who want to streamline the litigation process frequently agree that they will "first and foremost" coordinate discovery proceedings, and most attorneys are eager to assist. Intersystem coordination of discovery can be achieved in various ways. Though treated separately below, the different methods of coordination are by no means mutually exclusive.

1. Joint Scheduling

The most basic form of coordination, which took place in the early stages of many of the cases we studied, involves scheduling discovery to proceed in tandem. This enables lawyers to prepare simultaneously for discovery in both courts, and gives judges an opportunity to exchange information and discuss discovery matters. Joint scheduling may also extend to other kinds of coordination, such as sharing resources, including special masters and document depositories. Such an arrangement also enhances the chances of a global settlement, because all the parties are at the same stage of discovery and privy to the same information, and thus are more likely to make similar assessments about their prospects.

In the *Exxon-Valdez* litigation, the state and federal judges together met with all the attorneys involved in the civil cases to discuss the organization of the litigation and the potential for state-federal coordination. Following the initial conference, the judges entered identical orders in which they noted that scheduling and planning for the state and federal cases "should, to the maximum degree feasible, proceed in tandem." Similarly, in the *Sioux City* air crash cases, Judge Conlon developed a discovery schedule that was later adopted by the state court.

Joint scheduling is not a one-time occurrence. Because the progress of litigation cannot be fully anticipated at the outset, ongoing attention and scheduling adjustments will generally be necessary.

2. Joint Discovery Plan

In some instances joint state-federal discovery plans have been developed. This gives a common structure to the discovery process and paves the way for extensive coordination. The courts can either craft a discovery plan themselves or, as in the *Exxon-Valdez* litigation, direct counsel to do so. In the Ohio asbestos litigation, Judge Lambros appointed two special masters to develop a management plan for the federal cases. This plan provided for truncated discovery to gather information necessary for individual case evaluation and settlement negotiations. Although the state court did not formally adopt this plan, Judge McMonagle issued an order announcing the state court's commitment to cooperate fully with it. In a jointly issued federal-state memorandum of accord, Judges Lambros and McMonagle expressed their "desire that there be a coordinated and uniform treatment of the asbestos cases pending before [their] two courts, and that the approach developed by the Special Masters will aid in the resolution of cases on both dockets."

Even without adopting a full-fledged common plan, state and federal courts can issue orders establishing a degree of coordination during discovery. In the *Florida Everglades* litigation, the courts created a master list of all litigants involved in the state and federal cases, and developed a procedure to allow each party to participate in all discovery proceedings. Similarly, in the *Brooklyn Navy Yard* litigation, the state and federal judges required litigants to inform each other of related actions pending in the other system, and provided for joint listing of and attendance at depositions.

3. Common Discovery Master

State and federal courts may make a joint appointment of a special master to supervise discovery in both state and federal cases. A common discovery master can help reduce duplicative discovery and ensure consistency by establishing common standards and procedures for the state and federal cases. This, in turn, reduces the incentive for forum shopping and provides guidance on how future matters will be handled.

Federal magistrates have often been chosen to serve in this capacity. In the *Brooklyn Navy Yard* litigation, Judge Weinstein and Justice Freedman designated a federal magistrate to settle discovery disputes for both courts. In the *MGM Hotel* litigation, prior to state-federal coordination, the federal judge appointed a federal magistrate to hear discovery matters. Later, when the state and federal cases were coordinated, the federal magistrate ruled on both state and federal matters.

Separate appointments of a common discovery master can achieve many of the benefits of a joint appointment. In the *Technical Equities* litigation, the state and federal judges, at separate times, appointed the same individual to oversee discovery matters in their respective courts. The master developed common procedures for both state and federal discovery, and also provided other valuable services. He had contact with both the state and federal judges and acted as a liaison between them. In addition, because the master was aware of the discovery undertaken in both the state and federal litigation, if a witness had already been deposed, the master would so inform any other party seeking to depose that witness. In general, he encouraged all counsel to read and familiarize themselves with the record in an effort to avoid plowing the same ground. The discovery master helped coordinate the proceedings of the state and federal courts even when more extensive coordination between the judges was not feasible.

The appointment of a joint special master is often difficult. Rule 53(b) of the Federal Rules of Civil Procedure states that appointment of a master "shall be the exception and not the rule" and specifies the only instances in which such an appointment is justified: 1) in a jury trial if "the issues are complicated"; 2) in a bench trial "upon a showing that some exceptional condition requires it"; or 3) in any cases where the parties consent to having a federal magistrate serve as master. Despite the textual limitations, use of special masters "has proliferated in a wide variety of situations, only a few of which are expressly contemplated by the Rule." Furthermore, differences among federal courts' and state courts' authority to appoint masters may frustrate a joint state-federal appointment. In the Ohio asbestos litigation, for example, no joint appointment was made because State Judge McMonagle did not think he had the authority to appoint a special master.

4. Joint Use of Discovery Materials

Regardless of whether the cases are proceeding in accordance with coordinated schedules, under a common plan, or using a common special master, the courts can ensure that material discovered in one case can be used in companion cases. Courts may simply accept discovery initially (or concurrently) developed in other cases. Several courts have issued orders providing that discovery taken in another court's case could be used in the proceedings of the court issuing the order. These orders can apply to all forms of discovery or be limited in scope. In the Chicago air crash litigation, for example, the state and federal courts agreed to accept discovery material developed in the other court pertaining to liability.

Judges generally have been willing to allow depositions taken in a case in one court system to be used in related cases pending in the other. In some instances, such as the *Beverly Hills Supper Club* litigation, the courts suggested, but did not insist on, joint depositions. Other courts have prohibited litigants from duplicating depositions in companion cases. In the *Brooklyn Navy Yard* litigation, the judges experimented with each of these methods. State defendants were originally given the option of attending depositions conducted by federal defendants or deposing the same parties at another time. Justice Freedman later ordered all state defendants to appear for federal depositions in all cases filed in both courts, however, stating that failure of counsel to participate in those depositions would be deemed a waiver of discovery.

Attorneys tend to approve of joint depositions and sometimes agree to them even when not required. In the *Exxon-Valdez* litigation, the attorneys' discovery plan specifically provided for common depositions. In the *Hyatt Skywalk* litigation, a State–Federal Liaison Committee, composed of lawyers, voluntarily coordinated the taking of depositions for both the state and federal cases. Similarly, in the *Beverly Hills Supper Club* litigation, the attorneys agreed that all depositions could be used in both the federal and state actions, and conducted some joint state-federal depositions.

State and federal courts have also coordinated the use of interrogatories. In the *Brooklyn Navy Yard* litigation, for example, the state court's case management plan provided that interrogatories filed in the federal court would apply to all cases pending in the state court. In the *Hyatt Skywalk* cases, the State–Federal Liaison Committee was given the task of drafting interrogatories applicable to cases pending in both the state and federal systems.

In some instances, state and federal courts have created common document and physical evidence retention plans. These plans generally provide for joint depositories accessible to all federal and state counsel and parties. These depositories can be supervised by both the state and federal courts or can be maintained by one court with the other making use of the facilities.

5. Joint Discovery Hearings

Some judges have recognized that although not all aspects of the related cases could be aggregated in one court, important matters could be heard in a single proceeding. In the *Beverly Hills Supper Club* litigation, for example, Judges Rubin and Diskin frequently sat "together on the bench" and heard discovery motions. They sat together every two or three months to dispose of all disputes. In the *L'Ambiance Plaza* litigation, Judge Zampano recognized the importance of having a state counterpart for Judge Eginton, who was handling discovery for the federal cases. He communicated this view to the Chief Court Administrator for the State of Connecticut, and subsequently all state cases were assigned for discovery purposes to Superior Court Judge James T. Healey. Alternating between the state and federal courts, Judges Healey and Eginton met with attorneys and conducted joint discovery hearings. More recently, in the *Brooklyn Navy Yard* litigation, Judge Weinstein and Justice Freedman, along with the federal magistrate appointed to handle discovery disputes, sat together on numerous occasions.

These discovery hearings are discussed below in connection with joint pretrial hearings generally. Here, it is sufficient to note that because the discovery issues that arise in state and federal courts are generally similar, joint hearings are possible and can help dispose of matters expeditiously.

6. Resolving Differences

Although state and federal procedural and evidentiary rules sometimes differ, these differences have generally not impeded coordination of discovery. Judges who coordinate proceedings find that state and federal discovery rules are usually compatible. In the *Exxon-Valdez* litigation, for example, Judge Holland found it easy to have one special master handle discovery for both courts because the federal and the Alaska state rules are essentially the same. In the *L'Ambiance Plaza* litigation, Judges Eginton and Healey found that carefully wording texts and exchanging drafts enabled them to formulate orders that satisfied both the state and federal rules.

At times, judges have avoided conflict by maintaining an "open" discovery policy. As one judge involved in the *Florida Everglades* litigation recalls, "what went on in discovery wasn't going to have a thing to do with whether [material] was admissible as evidence [in court]."

Differences in procedures and rules were thus glossed over early in the litigation and differences in interpretation or application of rules were rare. One judge involved in a cooperative scheme remarked that most decisions were so "obvious" that anyone would have decided them the same way.

When conflicts did arise, judges employed a variety of mechanisms to resolve them. Where federal procedures differed significantly from state procedures, some courts agreed to apply federal law to all discovery matters, presumably because the federal rules tend to be more liberal.

A policy of deference often forestalls possible conflict. In the Sioux City litigation, a dispute arose over whether certain documents sought during discovery were protected by the attorney-client privilege or work product rule. The issue was raised first in the federal court and decided by a federal magistrate. Perceiving the need for consistency, State Judge O'Connell issued an order similar to the one issued by the federal court. Similarly, during the early stages of the *Brooklyn Navy Yard* litigation, State Supreme Court Justice Freedman often deferred to the discovery rulings issued by the federal court, which was further along in the litigation. (She did, however, remain involved in the decisionmaking process—the state and federal judges maintained contact and conferred about these matters prior to several federal court rulings.)

In some cases, especially the earlier ones, the federal court took the lead in handling all discovery matters. In the *MGM Hotel Fire* litigation, all discovery was supervised by Federal Judge Bechtle. State Judge Thompson issued an order providing that discovery pertaining to liability issues in the state cases be "made in, conducted through, and governed by" the federal litigation. He ruled that all depositions and documents generated from state cases had to be filed in the federal court rather than the state court. All motions were heard by the federal judge. A similar situation developed in the *Florida Everglades* litigation. Because the federal cases were proceeding at a faster pace than those in the state court, Federal Judge Fay heard all motions regarding discovery matters; the state court automatically ratified his orders unless counsel objected. As discussed below, federal courts often have institutional advantages, greater resources, and more flexible tools for aggregating their own cases that may make it advisable for them to take the lead in discovery.

Conflicts can also be avoided through specialization rather than deference. Judge O'Leary recounts that during the *Hyatt Skywalk* litigation, the federal judge would rule on matters raised by the federal case attorneys, and the state judge would rule on matters raised by state case attorneys. The judges and attorneys in that litigation also developed a "golden rule": before attorneys could raise a discovery matter with the judges, the attorneys had to try to resolve it among themselves. As a result, Judge O'Leary recalls, few discovery disputes reached the judges.

Note and Questions

Cooperative federal-state discovery procedures have become a norm in inter-system mass tort litigation, and much effort has been made in recent years to educate federal and state judges to opportunities for federal-state cooperation in handling mass tort cases. To what extent does such judicial management override or encroach on the traditional litigation model that places the conduct of discovery in the litigants' hands? Cooperative discovery clearly benefits the judicial system. Does it benefit the litigants? In what ways? Judge Schwarzer's article amply describes the positive aspects of cooperative discovery. Are there any drawbacks? For discussion of one of the earliest efforts at coordinated discovery in mass tort litigation, *see* Paul D. Rheingold, *The MER/29 Story—An Instance of Successful Mass Disaster Litigation,* 56 Cal.L.Rev. 116 (1968).

C. SPECIAL EVIDENTIARY PROBLEMS IN MASS TORT: THE PROBLEM OF PROBABILISTIC PROOF

IN RE AGENT ORANGE PROD. LIAB. LITIG.

United States District Court, Eastern District of New York, 1984.
597 F.Supp. 740.

* * *

The preceding discussion assumed that although a plaintiff would be unable to identify the manufacturer of the Agent Orange to which the veteran was exposed he or she would be able to prove, by a preponderance of the evidence, that the specific injuries he or she suffers were caused by Agent Orange. It is likely, however, that even if plaintiffs as a class could prove that they were injured by Agent Orange, no individual class member would be able to prove that his or her injuries were caused by Agent Orange. For example, plaintiffs as a class may be able to show that statistically, X% of the population not exposed to Agent Orange could have been expected to develop soft-tissue sarcoma, but that among those veterans who were exposed to Agent Orange, X + Y% suffer from soft-tissue sarcoma. If Y is equal to or less than X and there is no meaningful "particularistic" or anecdotal proof as to the vast majority of plaintiffs, virtually no plaintiff would be able to show by a preponderance of the evidence that his or her cancer is attributable to the Agent Orange rather than being part of the "background" level of cancer in the population as a whole. The probability of specific cause would necessarily be less than 50% based upon the evidence submitted.

(1) SCOPE OF THE PROBLEM

The problem just noted is one that has received a significant amount of scholarly discussion as well as some attention from the United States Congress. *See, e.g.,* Rosenberg, The *Causal Connection in Mass Exposure Cases: A "Public Law" Vision of the Tort System,* 97 Harv.L.Rev. 849 (1984); Black and Lilienfeld, *Epidemiological Proof in Toxic Tort Litigation,* 52 Ford.L.Rev. 732, 782–83 (1984); Dore, *A Commentary on the Use of Epidemiological Evidence in Demonstrating Cause-in-Fact,* 7 Harv.Envtl.L.Rev. 429 (1983); Delgado, *Beyond* Sindell: *Relaxation of Cause-in-Fact Rules for Indeterminate Plaintiffs,* 70 Cal.L.Rev. 881

(1982); Proposed Radiogenic Cancer Compensation Act of 1983, S.921, 98th Cong., 1st Sess., 129 Cong.Rec. S.3918 (daily ed. March 24, 1983), introduced by Senator Hatch (1983). Because of the rarity of the situation until recently scant attention has been given to the issue by the courts. There has apparently been only one other mass exposure decision that has discussed the indeterminate plaintiff problem explicitly, *viz,* Allen v. United States, 588 F.Supp. 247 (D.Utah 1984), a case where injury was claimed as a result of radiation exposure from testing of atomic explosive devices.

In our complex industrialized society it is unfortunately possible that some products used on a widespread scale will cause significant harm to the public. While it may be possible to prove, through the use of such proof as laboratory tests on animals and epidemiological evidence, that such harm—for example cancer—can be "caused" by a particular substance, it may be impossible to pinpoint which particular person's cancer would have occurred naturally and which would not have occurred but for exposure to the substance. Epidemiological statistics, which constitute the best (if not the sole) available evidence in mass exposure cases, can only attribute a proportion of the disease incidence in the population to each potential source. * * * But * * * it is impossible to pinpoint the actual source of the disease afflicting any specific member of the exposed population. Rosenberg, *The Causal Connection in Mass Exposure Cases: A "Public Law" Vision of the Tort System,* 97 Harv.L.Rev. 849, 856–57 (1984)(footnotes omitted).

In two of the largest and most widely publicized mass tort litigations, those involving DES and asbestos, the problem outlined above does not pose a serious obstacle since at least some of the damage caused by the harmful substance was, it has been claimed, unique to that substance. Adenosis and clear cell adenocarcinoma of the vagina and uterus, the conditions associated with DES, are, it is said, almost unknown among women whose mothers had not taken DES. Note, *DES and a Proposed Theory of Enterprise Liability,* 46 Ford.L.Rev. 963, 965 (1978). The situation is similar, in the asbestos litigation, albeit to a lesser extent. Although lung cancer is associated with cigarette smoking and other factors as well as asbestos exposure and mesothelioma may have causes other than asbestos, *see* Stanton & Wrench, Mechanisms of *Mesothelioma Induction With Asbestos and Fibrous Glass,* 48 J. Nat'l Cancer Inst. 797, 811–15 (1972), asbestosis is alleged to be uniquely associated with asbestos exposure. Borel v. Fibreboard Paper Products Corp., 493 F.2d 1076, 1083 (5th Cir.1973), *cert. denied,* 419 U.S. 869, 95 S.Ct. 127, 42 L.Ed.2d 107 (1974). In most other mass exposure cases, however, the harm caused by the toxic substance is indistinguishable from the naturally occurring disease or condition. *See* Dore, *A Commentary on the Use of Epidemiological Evidence in Demonstrating Cause-in-Fact,* 7 Harv.Envtl.L.Rev. 429, 437 (1983); Solomons, *Workers' Compensation for Occupational Disease Victims: Federal Standards and Threshold Problems,* 41 Alb.L.Rev. 195, 199 (1977).

The recent case of Allen v. United States, 588 F.Supp. 247 (D.Utah 1984), illustrates the problem well. Plaintiffs claimed that they developed various forms of cancer as a result of their exposure to radiation from nuclear explosions. While some forms of cancer can, it is contended, with some certainty be attributed to factors other than exposure to radiation, many others "cannot be distinguished from cancer of the same organ arising from . . . unknown causes", i.e., the "background" cancers. J. Gofman, RADIATION AND HUMAN HEALTH 59 (1981), quoted in *Allen v. United States,* 588 F.Supp. at 406. The statistical evidence in *Allen* apparently made it clear that there was a strong positive association between exposure to low-level ionizing radiation, presumably the result of atomic explosions, and various forms of cancer suffered by plaintiffs. Thus, the *Allen* case has some of the characteristics of the DES and asbestos cases in addition to persuasive statistical correlations.

(2) PREPONDERANCE RULE

Even if there were near certainty as to general causation, if there were significant uncertainty as to individual causation, traditional tort principles would dictate that causation be determined on a case-by-case basis using the preponderance-of-the-evidence rule. Santosky v. Kramer, 455 U.S. 745, 755, 102 S.Ct. 1388, 1395, 71 L.Ed.2d 599 (1982); W. Prosser, HANDBOOK OF THE LAW OF TORTS, 208–09 (1971); Kaplan, *Decision Theory and the Fact Finding Process,* 20 Stan. L.Rev. 1065, 1072 (1968). The rule provides an " 'all or nothing' approach, whereby [assuming all other elements of the cause of action are proven], the plaintiff becomes entitled to full compensation for those . . . damages that are proved to be 'probable' (a greater than 50 percent chance), but is not entitled to any compensation if the proof does not establish a greater than 50 percent chance." Jackson v. Johns–Manville Sales Corp., 727 F.2d 506, 516 (5th Cir.1984).

Under the "strong" version of the preponderance rule, statistical correlations alone indicating that the probability of causation exceeds fifty percent are insufficient; some "particularistic" or anecdotal evidence, that is, "proof that can provide direct and actual knowledge of the causal relationship between the defendant's tortious conduct and the plaintiff's injury," is required. Rosenberg, *supra,* 97 Harv.L.Rev. at 857, 870. *See* Ryan v. Eli Lilly & Co., 514 F.Supp. 1004 (D.S.C.1981); Namm v. Charles E. Frosst & Co., 178 N.J.Super. 19, 427 A.2d 1121 (App.Div. 1981). As Professor Jaffee has put it,

> If all that can be said is that there are 55 chances of negligence out of 100, that is not enough. There must be a rational, i.e., evidentiary basis on which the jury can choose the competing probabilities. If there is not, the finding will be based . . . on mere speculation and conjecture.

Jaffee, *Res Ipsa Loquitur Vindicated,* 1 Buff.L.Rev. 1, 4 (1951). The "weak" version of the preponderance rule would allow a verdict solely on statistical evidence; the "all-or-nothing" approach converts the statistical probability into a legally absolute finding that the causal connection did or did not exist in the case. C. McCormick, HANDBOOK ON THE LAW OF DAMAGES, 118 (1935). The justification for not requiring "particularistic" or anecdotal evidence is trenchantly and accurately stated by Professor Rosenberg:

> [T]he entire notion that "particularistic" evidence differs in some significant qualitative way from statistical evidence must be questioned. The concept of "particularistic" evidence suggests that there exists a form of proof that can provide direct and actual knowledge of the causal relationship between the defendant's tortious conduct and the plaintiff's injury. "Particularistic" evidence, however, is in fact no less probabilistic than is the statistical evidence that courts purport to shun.... "Particularistic" evidence offers nothing more than a basis for conclusions about a perceived balance of probabilities.

Rosenberg, *supra,* 97 Harv. L.Rev. at 870 (footnotes omitted). Except where it appears that the absence of anecdotal evidence may be due to spoliation, probabilities based upon quantitative analysis should support a recovery. *See, e.g.,* E.M. Morgan & J.M. Maguire, CASES AND MATERIALS ON EVIDENCE, 39 (7th ed.1983).

There would appear to be little harm in retaining the requirement for "particularistic" evidence of causation in sporadic accident cases since such evidence is almost always available in such litigation. In mass exposure cases, however, where the chance that there would be particularistic evidence is in most cases quite small, the consequence of retaining the requirement might be to allow defendants who, it is virtually certain, have injured thousands of people and caused billions of dollars in damages, to escape liability. Because of this fact and the fact that "particularistic evidence ... is ... no less probabilistic than ... statistical evidence," the "weak" version of the preponderance rule appears to be the preferable standard to apply in mass exposure cases— particularly where, as here, all claimants and defendants are joined in one suit.

(a) Application of the Preponderance Rule to Mass Exposure Cases

Conventional application of the "weak" version of the preponderance rule would dictate that, if the toxic substance caused the incidence of the injury to rise more than 100% above the "background" level, each plaintiff exposed to the substance could recover if he or she is suffering from that type of injury. If, however, to put it in somewhat graphic, albeit artificial terms, the incidence rose only 100% or less, no plaintiff could recover—i.e., the probability of specific causation would not be more than 50%.

Where a plaintiff's injuries result from a series of unrelated sporadic accidents, this "all-or-nothing" rule is justifiably rationalized on the ground that it is the fairest and most efficient result. In mass exposure cases, however, this all-or-nothing rule results in either a tortious defendant being relieved of all liability or overcompensation to many plaintiffs and a crushing liability on the defendant. These results are especially troublesome because, unlike the sporadic accident cases, it may be possible to ascertain with a fair degree of assurance that the defendant did cause damage, and, albeit with somewhat less certainty, the total amount of that damage.

The problem is both illustrated and further compounded by the fact that lack of precision in the data and models used may cause the range of the probabilities estimated by the statistical proof to lie on either or both sides of the 100% line. Because the statistical proof will almost never be as complete or as free from confounding factors as desirable, it may be possible to infer, for example, that the toxic substance caused the incidence to rise over the background level somewhere between 80 and 120%. *See, e.g.,* Allen v. United States, 588 F.Supp. 247, 438, 439 n.197 (D.Utah 1984)(noting significant variation in experts' interpretations of statistical evidence relating to the likelihood that plaintiff's cancer was caused by exposure to radiation). Moreover, issues of credibility and varying inferences drawn by the trier based upon varying assessments of probative force may cause reasonable people to assess these percentages in a range from almost zero to well over 120. *See, e.g.,* E.M. Morgan & J.M. Maguire, CASES AND MATERIALS ON EVIDENCE, ch. 1 (7th ed.1983).

Under the traditional application of the preponderance rule, whether individual plaintiffs recover will depend on where the probability percentage line is drawn despite the fact that a reasonable trier would conclude that a large proportion of the plaintiffs were injured by the defendant and a large number were not. Even if the statistical increase attributed to the substance in question is just a few percentage points, if statistical theory supports a finding of correlation there is no reason why the industry as a whole should not pay for the damages it probably caused.

A simple hypothetical will illustrate why too heavy a burden should not be placed on plaintiffs by requiring a high percentage or incidence of a disease to be attributable to a particular product. Let us assume that there are 10 manufacturers and a population of 10 million persons exposed to their product. Assume that among this population 1,000 cancers of a certain type could be expected, but that 1,100 exist, and that this increase is "statistically significant," permitting a reasonable conclusion that 100 cancers are due to the product of the manufacturers. In the absence of other evidence, it might be argued that as to any one of the 1,100 there is only a chance of about 9% (100/1,100) that the product caused the cancer. Under traditional tort principles no plaintiff could recover.

(b) Inadequacy of Individualized Solutions

Any attempt to resolve the problem on a plaintiff-by-plaintiff basis cannot be fully satisfactory. The solution that would most readily suggest itself is a burden shifting approach, analogous to that used in the indeterminate defendant situation .... *Allen v. United States* provides a good example of how burden-shifting would be applied in an indeterminate plaintiff case. A plaintiff must show that the defendant, in that case the United States, negligently put "an identifiable population group" of which he was a member at "increased risk" and that his injury is consistent with having been caused by the hazard to which he has been negligently subjected, such consistency having been demonstrated by substantial, appropriate, persuasive and connecting factors. * * * *Allen,* 588 F.Supp. at 415. At that point, the burden shifts to the defendant which will be held liable unless it can offer "persuasive proof" of noncausation. *Id.*

Generally courts have shifted the burden to the defendant to prove that it was not responsible for plaintiff's injury only in sporadic accident cases where it was certain that one of a very limited number of defendants injured the plaintiff, *see, e.g.,* Summers v. Tice, 33 Cal.2d 80, 199 P.2d 1 (1948); Ybarra v. Spangard, 25 Cal.2d 486, 154 P.2d 687 (1944), or in mass exposure cases where general causation was certain and liability was apportioned in accordance with some market-share theory. *See, e.g.,* Sindell v. Abbott Laboratories, 26 Cal.3d 588, 607 P.2d 924, 163 Cal.Rptr. 132, *cert. denied,* 449 U.S. 912, 101 S.Ct. 285, 66 L.Ed.2d 140 (1980); Copeland v. Celotex Corp., 447 So.2d 908 (Fla.App. 1984). *But see* Abel v. Eli Lilly & Co., 418 Mich. 311, 343 N.W.2d 164 (1984)(joint and several liability in DES cases).

Shifting the burden of proof in such cases will, at least theoretically, not result in crushing liability for the defendant either because the litigation only involves a sporadic accident, as in *Summers* and *Ybarra,* or because the defendant will only be held liable for the amount of damage it caused based on market share—although as indicated above, there may be practical problems in defining market share. By contrast, shifting the burden of proof in the indeterminate plaintiff situation could result in liability far out of proportion to damage caused. It is not helpful in most situations to say that the defendant will not be liable for "those harms which [he] can reasonably prove were not in fact a consequence of his risk-creating, negligent conduct," *Allen,* 588 F.Supp. at 415, since, were such individualized proof available, there would have been no need to shift the burden.

(3) POSSIBLE SOLUTION IN CLASS ACTION

Since the problem results from a plaintiff-by-plaintiff method of adjudication, one solution is to try all plaintiffs' claims together in a class action thereby arriving at a single, class-wide determination of the total harm to the community of plaintiffs. Given the necessarily heavy reliance on statistical evidence in mass exposure cases, such a determination seems feasible. The defendant would then be liable to each exposed plaintiff for a pro rata share of that plaintiff's injuries.

This approach can be illustrated using the hypothetical given above. Suppose all 1,100 of those who were exposed to the harmful substance and who developed the cancer in the example join in a class action against all 10 manufacturers. Let us say that damages average $1,000,-000 per cancer. A recovery of $100,000,000 (100 x $1,000,000) in favor of the class would be allowed with the percentage of the award to be paid by each manufacturer depending on the toxicity of its product. For example, if a company produced only 20% of the substance in question but, because of the greater toxicity of its product, likely caused 60% of the harm, it would contribute 60% of the total amount. If accurate records are available on the composition of each defendant's product, that analysis should be possible.

Since no plaintiff can show that his or her cancer was caused by any one of the defendants, they should divide the $100,000,000 by 1,100, giving each a recovery of about $90,000. While any plaintiff might feel that his or her recovery denigrated the degree of harm, the alternative of receiving nothing is far worse. The latter is, of course, the necessary result in any plaintiff's individual suit. Moreover, the deterrent effect of this result on producers would be significant. *See* Delgado, *Beyond Sindell: Relaxation of Cause-in-Fact Rules for Indeterminate Plaintiffs,* 70 Cal.L.Rev. 881, 893 (1982).

If the number of cases were only 1,050, most statisticians would say the difference was not statistically significant and a court using the pro rata approach might find that the defendant is not legally responsible for any of the increased incidence. *But see* Allen v. United States, 588 F.Supp. at 416–17 (noting that although increased incidence might be deemed "insignificant" by a scientist or statistician, it may well be that it "is still far more likely than not" that "the observed increase is related to its hypothetical cause rather than mere chance"). (In the numbers used, the standard deviation could be computed by square root as square root $1000 = 31.6$.) Two standard deviations—a rough test of statistical significance often used in the law—is 63.2; 50 is less than two standard deviations. Yet, assuming the 100 variation of the hypothetical (more than 3 standard deviations), the law should nonetheless attribute to the defendants all 100 additional cancers, not just $100 +{-}63$ or 37 (the total variation less two standard deviations). As a matter of rough justice, once legal responsibility for the increased incidence is found, it is sounder to attribute all 100 cases to the defendant, even though a substantial number of these cases may be random variations with no reasonable assurance that they are attributable to the defendants' activities. There is, of course, also the possibility that more than 100 cases were "caused by" defendant's activities since the figure properly attributable to background cancer incidence might have been less than 1,000. We are in a different world of proof than that of the archetypical smoking gun. We must make the best estimates of probability that we can using the help of experts such as statisticians and our own common sense and experience with the real universe.

Putting a dollar amount on the damages suffered by individual plaintiffs is, from a real-world standpoint, a critical part of the solution. If the judicial and monetary economies of the class action are not to be lost through lengthy and expensive individual trials on damages, some mechanism must be devised to decide damage claims without the need for a full-fledged trial for each plaintiff. As Professor Rosenberg points out, "[p]ossibly the greatest source of litigation expense [in mass exposure tort litigation] is the individual assessment and distribution of damages that must follow trial of common liability questions." Rosenberg, *supra,* 97 Harv.L.Rev. at 916.

How individualized such a mechanism would have to be depends on (1) the size of the individual claim and (2) what the variations between plaintiffs are in the nature of the claims: the smaller the individual claim and the less the variation, the more generalized the process can be. If the claims are for one type of injury, a compensation schedule to calculate average loss could be developed based on sampling techniques. *See* MANUAL FOR COMPLEX LITIGATION § 2.712 at 116–18 (1982). If a number of different injuries are to be compensated, the process could be made somewhat more sophisticated.

Every effort should be made to reduce questions of fact to a bare minimum. A preferred solution is to pay claims on a fixed and somewhat arbitrary schedule using a ministerial agency as is done with the Medicaid and Medicare programs where disbursements are made by insurance agencies acting for the United States.

No matter what system is used the purpose is to hold a defendant liable for no more than the aggregate loss fairly attributable to its tortious conduct. As long as that goal is met a defendant can have no valid objection that its rights have been violated.

IN RE JOINT EASTERN AND SOUTHERN DISTRICT ASBESTOS LITIGATION

United States District Court, Southern District of New York, 1991.
758 F.Supp. 199.

SWEET, DISTRICT JUDGE.

Defendants Owens–Corning Fiberglass Corporation ("OCF"), United States Mineral Products Company ("USMP"), Pittsburgh Corning Corporation ("PCC"), Fibreboard Corporation ("FC") and Combustion Engineering, Inc. ("CEI") move for summary judgment dismissing the complaint of plaintiff Arlene Maiorana ("Maiorana"), which alleges product liability arising out of exposure to asbestos, on the grounds that Maiorana cannot establish that her husband's colon cancer was caused by exposure to asbestos. For the following reasons, the motion is granted.

THE PARTIES

Maiorana is the widow of John Maiorana, a sheetmetal worker who died of colon cancer on June 16, 1983. She asserts that her husband's cancer was caused by his exposure to asbestos and asbestos-containing products during his construction career.

The defendants are manufacturers of various asbestos-containing products to which Mr. Maiorana is alleged to have been exposed. [discussion of prior proceedings omitted—*ed.*]

THE FACTS

The defendants assert that summary judgment is warranted here because Maiorana has not and can not set forth evidence from which a jury could conclude that her husband's colon cancer was more probably than not caused by exposure to asbestos. They contend that, aside from the colon cancer itself, Maiorana has presented no clinical evidence indicating that her husband suffered from any asbestos-related infirmities and that therefore her case is based solely on epidemiological data indicating an increased risk of colon cancer among people exposed to asbestos. While the defendants do not, for purposes of the present motion, contest the existence of a causal relationship between asbestos and colon cancer,[2] it is their position that Maiorana must prove not only that her husband's contact with asbestos increased his chances of contracting colon cancer, but also that the increase in probability was such that the disease was more probably than not caused by asbestos exposure.

In opposition, Maiorana has relied principally on affidavits from Mr. Maiorana's personal physician Dr. Nathan Rothman ("Rothman"), from two medical experts, Drs. Steven B. Markowitz ("Markowitz") and Carl M. Shy ("Shy"), and from Maiorana herself. Rothman states that he treated Mr. Maiorana, that he was told that his patient had been exposed to asbestos, and that "[b]ased upon my knowledge and my particular experience in caring for and treating John Maiorana, it is my opinion, to a reasonable degree of medical certainty that Mr. Maiorana's exposure to asbestos while a sheetmetal worker was more likely than not and probably was a contributing factor to his developing colon cancer."

Markowitz, a specialist in internal medicine and in occupational medicine, relies on a review of Mr. Maiorana's health records and "[n]umerous epidemiological studies [which] show elevated rates of colon cancer among the asbestos exposed groups", none of which he identifies, to conclude "to a reasonable degree of medical certainty that Mr. Maiorana's occupational exposure to asbestos was a significant factor in the cause and development of his colon cancer and death." Shy, a professor of epidemiology and a clinical physician, reaches a similar conclusion, namely "to a reasonable medical certainty that Mr. Maiorana's occupational exposure to asbestos was a proximate cause, and a substantial factor in his development of colon cancer and of his death." He bases this conclusion on review of Mr. Maiorana's medical records and on the results of several epidemiological studies, which he describes in more detail than Markowitz, relating the incidence of colon cancer to asbestos exposure.

Both Markowitz and Shy expressly condition their conclusions on the assumption that Mr. Maiorana did not possess any other characteristics which would have increased his risk of colon cancer, such as a family

---

2. However, the defendants have on occasion referred to studies which might dis- prove such relationship.

history of colon cancer, an unusually high diet of red meat, or a history of ulcerative colitis or multiple polyposis.

Finally, Maiorana's affidavit states that to her knowledge her husband had no family history of colon cancer, that he had no history of ulcerative colitis or polyposis, and that he "did not eat a diet of unusually high fat content but rather had and consumed a balanced diet."

DISCUSSION

1. The Standard for Summary Judgment

Summary judgment is appropriate where no genuine issue of material fact exists and the moving party is entitled to judgment as a matter of law. Fed.R.Civ.P. 56(c). In deciding a motion for summary judgment, the court is not expected to resolve disputed issues of fact, Donahue v. Windsor Locks Board of Fire Commissioners, 834 F.2d 54, 57 (2d Cir.1987), but to determine whether there are any factual issues which require a trial. Matsushita Electric Industrial Co. v. Zenith Radio Corp., 475 U.S. 574, 585–87, 106 S.Ct. 1348, 1355–56, 89 L.Ed.2d 538 (1986). However, the non-moving party "must do more than simply show that there is some metaphysical doubt as to the material facts." *Id.* at 586. This is particularly true when the issue is one on which the opponent of summary judgment would bear the burden of proof at trial. Celotex Corp. v. Catrett, 477 U.S. 317, 322–23, 106 S.Ct. 2548, 2552–53, 91 L.Ed.2d 265 (1986). "Summary judgment is appropriate when, after drawing all reasonable inferences in favor of the party against whom summary judgment is sought, no reasonable trier of fact could find in favor of the nonmoving party." Lund's, Inc. v. Chemical Bank, 870 F.2d 840, 844 (2d Cir.1989).

2. Maiorana Must Do More Than Show That Asbestos
Exposure Increases the Risk of Colon Cancer

A significant portion of Maiorana's opposition to the defendants' motion consists of discussion of the fact that exposure to asbestos increases a person's chances of contracting colon cancer. As discussed *supra* at note 2, the defendants do not presently contest this fact. Their motion is based on the contention that Maiorana must prove not simply that asbestos exposure increased her husband's chances of contracting cancer, but that it is more probable than not that the disease was caused by exposure, citing "the tort law requirement that a plaintiff establish a probability of more than fifty percent that the defendant's action injured him." In re Agent Orange Product Liability Litigation, 597 F.Supp. 740, 785 (E.D.N.Y.1984).

3. Epidemiological Data

Maiorana's claim against the defendants rests principally on epidemiological evidence. Epidemiology is the study of the distribution of disease in human populations to detect unusual patterns of disease and to associate those patterns with environmental or biological risk factors. The raw data consists of health surveys, studies of causes of death, medical records and examinations. Epidemiologists analyze this data by statistical methods to discover disease trends which are due to factors other than random chance.

Because of its statistical foundations, epidemiology is useful in recognizing increased rates of affliction in different groups of individuals, rather than to identify the cause of a disease in a particular individual. At most, an epidemiologist can calculate the likelihood that an individual will contract a particular disease. "Risk factors" for a disease are identified by comparing the incidence of the disease in different populations or "cohorts," then studying the different characteristics of the cohorts.

For example, an epidemiologist studying the effects of asbestos exposure might select two cohorts, one comprised of a random sampling of people who had been exposed to asbestos and the other containing individuals who had not been exposed. If the exposed cohort experienced a statistically significant increase in the incidence of any particular disease—that is, an increase which is not likely to have been due to random differences between the cohorts—then the researcher would be likely to conclude that asbestos exposure was a risk factor for that particular disease.[3]

For any risk factor, the epidemiologist also attempts to determine the magnitude of the risk: how much that factor will increase an individual's probability of contracting the disease. The magnitude is commonly expressed in terms of "relative risk," the ratio of the number of occurrences of the disease in an exposed cohort to the number of occurrences in an unexposed one. Thus if a given factor does not affect the rate of a disease at all, its relative risk would be 1.0, while a factor which doubled an individual's chances of being afflicted would have a relative risk of 2.0. Only when the risk level exceeds 2.0 can it be said that the one risk factor is more likely to cause the disease than any other factor affecting the unexposed cohort.

As an example, if it is the case that in a random sample of 5,000 people 100 are likely to contract colon cancer, and in a random sample of 5,000 people who have been exposed to asbestos 150 are likely to develop the disease,[4] then asbestos exposure would have a relative risk of 1.5 for this disease. However, only one third of the afflicted people in the exposed cohort could be said to have contracted colon cancer as a result of their exposure, because on average 100 would have developed it anyway. Epidemiology alone would offer no way to identify which 50 victims were attributable to asbestos. In the absence of any other evidence, the strongest conclusion which could be drawn would be that

3. One important point is that this type of statistical analysis is incapable of identifying a true causal relationship between the risk factor and the disease. In the example above, there would be no way to know whether the disease was biologically "caused" by asbestos, or whether some oth-er characteristic shared by the members of the exposed cohort might be responsible.

4. For the purposes of the example, it is assumed that the population size is large enough to generate statistically meaningful data and that the difference in results between cohorts is statistically significant.

for each of the 150 afflicted individuals there was a one in three chance that the disease was caused by asbestos. As this probability is less than fifty percent, none of the victims could satisfy the legal standard of showing that it was more probable than not that the cancer was due to asbestos exposure. Without any direct evidence of causation, a plaintiff can only meet the "preponderance of the evidence" standard if the relative risk is greater than 2.0. *In re Agent Orange,* 597 F.Supp. at 785 ("[A]t least a two-fold increase in incidence of the disease attributable to . . . exposure is required to permit recovery if epidemiological studies alone are relied upon.").

Although this result might appear inequitable, it is important to note that it applies only to those victims who are unable to adduce direct evidence of excessive asbestos exposure. A plaintiff who could show such direct evidence might be able to support an inference that the probability that the disease was attributable to the exposure was greater than that suggested by the epidemiological data, and thus might create a triable issue of fact even in the absence of conclusive epidemiological studies. Moreover, the apparent harshness in the example would be reversed if instead of 150 victims in the exposed cohort there were 250. In that case, only the 150 additional cases could be attributed to asbestos, but all 250 of the victims could, by relying on epidemiology alone, show that their afflictions were more probably than not caused by exposure, and thus collect from the parties responsible for that exposure.[5]

4. *Maiorana Has Not Shown a Relative Risk Greater Than 2.0 for Asbestos and Colon Cancer*

Regrettably, application of the preceding concepts here will deprive Maiorana of an opportunity to prove that her husband's illness was the result of his occupational exposure to asbestos. Simply put, she has failed to adduce admissible epidemiological evidence indicating that asbestos exposure has a relative risk greater than 2.0 for colon cancer. The strongest result discussed in any of her papers is the one identified by Shy as a study published by Frumkin and Berlin in 1988, which concluded that for certain individuals with significant levels of asbestos exposure,[6] the relative risk of colon cancer was 1.68, with a 95% confidence range of between 1.34 and 2.09. Even accepting the extreme value of 2.09, Maiorana has failed to adduce any evidence to indicate that

---

5. Of course, before applying any epidemiological result to an individual case, it is necessary to prove that the particular risk factor applies to the afflicted person:

the fact that people exposed to asbestos have an increased risk of developing colon cancer is of no use in the case of a person who never came into contact with asbestos. Thus a plaintiff might not prevail even after presenting epidemiological data establishing a relative risk of greater than 2.0, having failed to convince the

factfinder that the victim was exposed to the risk factor.

6. The study distinguished between those people whose exposure to asbestos placed them in the category of people with a 2.0 relative risk of lung cancer and those with lower levels of exposure. Surprisingly, the relative risk of colon cancer for the less-exposed group was less than 1.0, suggesting that this population actually had a lower-than-average rate of contracting the disease.

her husband's asbestos exposure level was great enough to place him in this high risk group, so the results of this study are simply inapplicable.

Shy also mentions but does not discuss in detail a recent study from Sweden suggesting a relative risk of 3.4 for colon cancer from asbestos exposure. However, this study applies, by Shy's own testimony, to "workers exposed to the highest cumulative dose of asbestos." Shy Aff. P 11. Again the lack of any evidence that Mr. Maiorana belonged to this category means this study is inapplicable as well.

In summary, none of the epidemiological data set forth by Maiorana establishes the requisite relative risk level between asbestos exposure and colon cancer to support a finding—in the absence of any other evidence of causation—that Mr. Maiorana's disease was more probably than not due to asbestos.

5. *Maiorana Has Not Adduced Evidence to Overcome the Insufficiency of the Epidemiological Data*

a. Rothman Does Not Qualify as an Expert on Colon Cancer or Asbestos Exposure.

Rothman's affidavit offers little more than his opinion that "Mr. Maiorana's exposure to asbestos was more likely than not and probably was a contributing factor to his developing colon cancer." Beyond the threshold question of whether this statement even satisfies the requirement that Maiorana prove that the exposure was more probably than not the cause of the disease,[7] Rothman offers no evidence from which to conclude that he is an expert on colon cancer or occupational asbestos exposure, but rather states simply that he is an expert in treating Mr. Maiorana. Under Federal Rule of Evidence 702, "a witness, qualified as an expert by knowledge, skill, experience training, or education, may testify thereto in the form of an opinion or otherwise." The failure to demonstrate that Rothman possessed the requisite expertise here renders his conclusion inadmissible. *See also* Maddy v. Vulcan Materials Co., 737 F.Supp. 1528 (D.Kan.1990)(summary judgment appropriate where plaintiff's witness had not demonstrated sufficient expertise to make conclusion admissible); *cf.* Washington v. Armstrong World Industries, Inc., 839 F.2d at 1123; Viterbo v. Dow Chemical Co., 826 F.2d 420, 422 (5th Cir.1987)("If an opinion is fundamentally unsupported, then it offers no expert assistance to the jury.").

b. The Ultimate Conclusions of Markowitz and Shy Concerning Causation Are Not Adequately Supported.

Both Markowitz and Shy also offer ambiguous opinions on the ultimate question of whether asbestos exposure more probably than not

---

7. The statement could be construed to state that more probably than not Mr. Maiorana's asbestos exposure increased, by some undetermined amount, his chances of contracting colon cancer. If this interpretation were applied, the statement would be of no help in satisfying Maiorana's burden of proof. *See* Washington v. Armstrong World Industries, Inc., 839 F.2d 1121, 1123 (5th Cir.1988)(granting summary judgment against plaintiff on grounds that medical expert never actually concluded that decedent's colon cancer was caused by asbestos, but merely stated that such a link was probable).

caused Mr. Maiorana's cancer: Markowitz concludes that the exposure "was a significant factor" in the disease, Shy that it "was a proximate cause, and a substantial factor." However, as with Rothman's opinion, it is unnecessary to determine whether these two opinions could help Maiorana to satisfy her burden of proof, because both are inadmissible, as the underlying assumptions are not adequately supported in the record.

As discussed *supra,* both experts condition their opinions on the assumption that Mr. Maiorana had no family history of colon cancer or polyps, had no personal history of ulcerative colitis or multiple polyposis, and that he did not eat an unusually high meat diet. Markowitz Aff. P 20, Shy Aff. P 15. Maiorana herself attempts to support these assumptions in her affidavit testimony. Maiorana Aff. PP 4–6. However, she does not testify that her husband had no family history of colon cancer, but only that "to [her] knowledge" that is the case. Significantly, Rothman offers no testimony relating to Mr. Maiorana's personal or family medical history, a topic on which he would appear to have had more knowledge than Maiorana. In addition, on the one subject which might be considered to be peculiarly within Maiorana's expertise, she does not state that her husband's diet was not high in meat content, but only that it was not high in fat. The failure to support the experts' underlying assumptions renders their ultimate conclusions as to the cause of Mr. Maiorana's cancer inadmissible.

c. Maiorana Has Presented No Clinical Evidence That Her Husband's Asbestos Exposure Had Any Effect on His Health.

Maiorana concedes that her husband's medical records offer no indication—aside from his colon cancer itself—that he was exposed to asbestos. In his affidavit, Markowitz characterizes this fact as irrelevant, because there is no medical linkage between colon cancer and other asbestos-related diseases: a person exposed to asbestos could contract colon cancer without ever suffering from another asbestos-related affliction. However, the point is not that the absence of clinical evidence of exposure proves that Mr. Maiorana's cancer was not caused by asbestos, but rather that the lack of any direct evidence of excessive exposure leaves Maiorana with only epidemiological evidence to prove her case. Because, as discussed *supra,* the epidemiological data is insufficient to meet the "more probable than not" standard, Maiorana's claim must be dismissed.

CONCLUSION

As causation is an issue on which Maiorana would bear the burden of proof at trial, her inability to present any clinical evidence that her husband showed any signs of any asbestos-related health problems, coupled with her failure to produce any epidemiological data which could support a finding that he had a relative risk greater than 2.0 for colon cancer as a result of his occupational exposure to asbestos, warrants granting the defendants' motion for summary judgment.

It is so ordered.

Notes and Questions

1. Mass tort litigation, especially involving latent-injury torts, raise interesting and difficult evidentiary problems. One of these problems may relate to plaintiffs' inability to identify the manufacturer of the product allegedly causing the injury. This is the problem of the indeterminate defendant, and it is addressed by various theories of substantive tort liability. *See* Part Three, Chapter V. B., *infra*. An equally vexing problem concerns the inability of some plaintiffs to establish general causation, an evidentiary problem sometimes captured by the designation of "indeterminate plaintiff." *See* Part Three, Chapter V. A., *infra*. As the decisions above suggest, courts handling mass tort litigation have dealt with this problem through interpretation of substantive tort principles and evidentiary rules.

The *Agent Orange* litigation presented Judge Weinstein with almost a paradigmatic mass tort involving indeterminate plaintiffs, indeterminate defendants, and a lack of epidemiological evidence sufficient to establish a causal link between the veterans' injuries and Agent Orange. The excerpted portion of Judge Weinstein's decision articulates his solution to the indeterminate plaintiff problem, adopting a standard of probabilistic proof. In light of Southern District's opinion in the *John Maiorana* decision, above, it is interesting to note that Judge Weinstein in *Agent Orange* believed that most asbestos claims did not suffer from the problem of lack of epidemiological proof. And as the two decision suggest, mass tort cases may involve problematic issues relating to scientific proof. These questions are discussed in Part Three, Chapter V.F., *infra*. *See also* Charles Nesson, *Agent Orange Meets the Blue Bus: Factfinding at the Frontiers of Knowledge*, 66 B.U.L. Rev. 521 (1986).

2. Should judges exploit plaintiffs' evidentiary problems to leverage a settlement? In the *Agent Orange* litigation, Judge Weinstein did precisely that. *See* Peter H. Shuck, AGENT ORANGE ON TRIAL (1986); *see also* Jack B. Weinstein, *Ethical Issues in Mass Tort Litigation*, 88 Nw.U.L.Rev. 469, 550–51 (1994). At least one commentator has suggested that Judge Weinstein's approach to the evidentiary defects and lack of scientific proof in the *Agent Orange* case has led to academic studies that are "scientific sham[s], perpetrated solely for political reasons." *See* Dorothy J. Howell, SCIENTIFIC LITERACY AND ENVIRONMENTAL POLICY at 35 (1992). How true is this statement, in light of the silicone breast implant litigation?

3. In a portion of Judge Weinstein's decision not reproduced here, Judge Weinstein suggests that the statistical approach to causal indeterminacy that he proposes for the *Agent Orange* litigation is analogous to that used by other federal courts in litigation relating to employment discrimination cases and consumer class actions. *See supra*, 597 F.Supp. at 839–41. Are the analogies Judge Weinstein seeks to draw apt? What differences are there between class employment discrimination claims, class consumer fraud claims, and aggregate personal injury tort actions? Do any of these distinctions vitiate the authority of analogous statistical assessment of claims?

4. Is the *Maiorana* decision especially harsh since it is reached on a summary judgment motion? Or is this rather an efficient method of dismissing a problematic case? Shouldn't the plaintiff be entitled to his or

her day in court to permit the jury to draw permissible inferences and assess problematic proof? What evidentiary standards apply at summary judgment? *See* Anderson v. Liberty Lobby, Inc., 477 U.S. 242, 106 S.Ct. 2505, 91 L.Ed.2d 202 (1986). Will the Court's decision in *Anderson* make summary judgment dismissals of certain mass tort cases more likely?

5. There is a substantial literature relating to the problems of scientific evidence, causation, and probabilistic proof in mass tort litigation, suggesting the complexity and dimensions of this problem for the courts. *See generally* Kenneth S. Abraham, *What Is a Tort Claim?, An Interpretation of Contemporary Tort Reform*, 51 Md. L. Rev. 172 (1992); Troyen A. Brennan, *Causal Chains and Statistical Links: The Role of Scientific Uncertainty in Hazardous–Substance Litigation*, 73 Cornell L.Rev. 469 (1988); Neil B. Cohen, *Confidence in Probability: Burdens of Persuasion in a World of Imperfect Knowledge*, 60 N.Y.U.L.Rev. 385 (1985); Daniel A. Farber, *Toxic Causation*, 71 Minn. L. Rev. 1219 (1987); Steve Gold, *Causation in Toxic Torts: Burdens of Proof, Standards of Persuasion, and Statistical Evidence*, 96 Yale L.J. 376 (1986); Michael D. Green, *Expert Witnesses and Sufficiency of Evidence in Toxic Substances Litigation: The Legacy of Agent Orange and Bendectin Litigation*, 86 Nw.U.L.Rev. 643 (1992); Ora F. Harris, *Toxic Tort Litigation and the Causation Element*, 40 Sw. U. L. Rev. 909 (1986); Paul D. Rheingold, *New Frontiers in Causation and Damages: Compensating Clients Injured by Toxic Torts*, Trial, Oct. 1985 at 42; Glen O. Robinson, *Probabilistic Causation and Compensation for Tortious Risk*, 14 J. Legal Stud. 779 (1985); David Rosenberg, *The Causal Connection in Mass Exposure Cases: A "Public Law" Vision of the Tort System*, 97 Harv.L.Rev. 849 (1984); Peter H. Schuck, *Legal Complexity: Some Causes, Consequences, and Cures*, 42 Duke L.J. 1 (1992); Peter H. Schuck, *Two Causation Conundrums: Mass Exposures and Social Causes*, 1 Cts. Health Sci. & L. 305 (1991); Melissa M. Thompson, Comment, *Causal Inference in Epidemiology: Implications for Toxic Tort Litigation*, 71 N.C.L.Rev. 247 (1992); Jack B. Weinstein, *Litigation and Statistics*, 3 Stat.Sci. 286 (1988); Richard W. Wright, *Actual Causation vs. Probabilistic Linkage: The Bane of Economic Analysis*, 14 J. Legal Stud. 435 (1985); Richard W. Wright, *Causation, Responsibility, Risk, Probability, Naked Statistics, and Proof: Pruning the Bramble Bush by Clarifying the Concepts*, 73 Iowa L.Rev. 1001 (1988).

D. AGGREGATE DAMAGES

JACK RATLIFF, SPECIAL MASTER'S REPORT IN *CIMINO v. RAYMARK INDUSTRIES, INC.**

10 Rev. Litig. 521–523, 524–28, 532–535 (1991).

After *Cimino v. Raymark Industries, Inc.* was certified as a class action, Judge Robert Parker asked me to serve as Special Master to assist in finding a way to break through the asbestos litigation impasse. * * * *Cimino* was to follow the guidance of *Jenkins v. Raymark Industries, Inc.*, which had approved, at least in part, a format for the first

* Reproduced from 10 Rev.Litig. 521 (1991).

phase of a mass-tort class action.[2] My charge was to recommend procedural approaches for the remaining phases. * * *

* * *

The award of "shares" in the lump sum damages fund (if there should be one) is essential to avoid the risk of a shortfall. Because the fund is finite, early claimants in the distribution phase might recover too much, leaving nothing for later claimants. Consequently, under our proposal the ratable share of each class member would be decided before any payments were made, with an allowance for possible hardship exceptions.

Awards based on increased risk of contracting cancer would likely be handled as "cancerophobia" claims. The effect of the "one injury" limitations rule is such that cancerophobia is the practical way a plaintiff recovers for an increased risk of cancer which has not yet risen to the level of probability.

* * *

20 September 1989

MASTER'S REPORT IN *CIMINO V. RAYMARK*

TO: Hon. Robert Parker
         U.S. District Court, Eastern District of Texas
         221 W. Ferguson, Suite 100
         Tyler, TX 75702
FROM: Jack Ratliff
RE: *Cimino et al. v. Raymark Industries, Inc. et al.*

I. SUMMARY OF RECOMMENDATIONS

As we noted earlier, it is now self-evident that the use of one-by-one individual trials is not an option in the asbestos cases. Taking its lead from *Jenkins,* this Court has decided on class action handling. The *Hardy* opinions have curtailed the use of collateral estoppel (though the doctrine may yet have a more limited role in these cases). The best prospect for unitary disposition is the class action and the asbestos cases are good candidates. Unlike many mass tort cases, these do not raise choice of law, jurisdictional, or unusual management problems: the class consists of cases already on file so that class members have been identified; the cases are controlled by a few law firms, making communication and choice of lead counsel easy; the litigants are already gathered in a single court; and the governing law will be that of Texas. If a class action cannot be used here it seems unlikely that it can ever be used for toxic torts. Because this case will break new ground, we have set a high priority on simplicity and have tried to avoid undue fragmentation. We have concluded that it would be better, if possible, for the same jury or juries to hear all phases of the case because of the need to avoid

---

2.   782 F.2d 468, 473 (5th Cir.1986).

repetition and because of the close connection between the liability and causation questions. * * * [W]e supplement and modify our earlier report of May 1, 1989 and recommended that the case be tried (following a carefully planned pre-trial phase) in four trial phases: I (classwide liability, class representatives' cases), II (classwide damages), III (apportionment) and IV (distribution). We further recommend, in summary, as follows:

1. That the trial of this case should follow the pattern suggested by *A.H. Robins Co., Inc.,* and endorsed by Wright, Miller, and Kane and by Newberg: a jury trial on liability (including punitive damages conduct), followed by a jury trial in which classwide damages are considered and awarded or not, followed by a Court-supervised non-jury distribution of any proceeds.[6]

2. That the non-conforming settlers be excluded from the class, and that (absent indication or evidence to the contrary) the Court accept Plaintiffs' Counsels' assurance that collection of judgments will not be a problem and that no conflicts between disease categories require the designation of subclasses.

3. That, contrary to our original recommendation, construction workers may be included in Plaintiffs' class because we are now persuaded that the "workplace share liability" approach is unnecessary in determining joint and several liability.

4. That Plaintiffs claiming mesothelioma damages may be feasibly retained as part of the class despite the existence of the "chrysotile" defense, though there are persuasive reasons for dropping those cases from the class if the Court should so decide.

5. That non-mesothelioma cancers (lung cancers, "other" cancers) should be excluded from the class and tried in another proceeding.

6. That individualized proofs of exposure, causation, damages, and affirmative defenses should be permitted only in the Phase I cases of individual class representatives and in the Phase IV distribution of proceeds, and that the proof in Phase II (classwide damages) should be confined to expert and statistical proof of aggregate damages to the class as a whole.

7. That an initial submission of proof-of-claim or other summary is desirable as a way of providing information necessary to insure the typicality of the claims of class representatives and to provide the data for the experts' Phase II analysis of damages.

8. That the Plaintiffs have no standing nor interest which would permit their participation in the Phase III allocation of percentages of responsibility between Defendants and that the Defendants have no standing nor interest which would permit their participation in Phase IV (distribution of award to individual class members).

6. We leave open the possibility (but do not recommend) that a trial on the sole questions of individual exposures (causation) might precede the four phases we suggest.

9. That in the Phase IV distribution of the classwide damages award (if any), the Court can and should make individual awards through a Master and/or claims facility after consultation with Plaintiffs' Counsel and without the involvement of a Jury.

10. That, with the addition of conspiracy claims added in this case, Phase I should track *Jenkins v. Raymark* as closely as possible, resolving completely the individual claims of the class representatives, except that the amount of classwide punitive damages should be found in a lump sum in Phase II after the Jury has found lump sum compensatory damages and then heard net worth evidence.

11. That the Court should permit interim argument as the case proceeds.

12. That the class action opt-out notice should summarize in considerable detail the four-phase procedure (leaving open the possibility that any of the phases might be modified by appellate direction), and making clear that distribution of classwide damages of proceeds will be made by the Court (through a Master or claims facility) and not by a Jury.

13. That in the Phase II trial regarding classwide damages the Court should permit experts to consider and to testify about the existence of settlement practices and formulas, along with results reached in similar cases if the Court is satisfied that such testimony is relevant.

14. That the dates on which individual class representatives filed suit (not the date of class certification) should govern the case respecting tort reform and that the representatives should be selected so that the filings are consistent with that approach, unless the Court concludes that the case law is to the contrary or that substantive rights will be impaired, in which event the Court should consider having the entire case heard by two juries (one of which would vote only on issues affected by tort reform). At the appropriate time, Jury #1 (pre-tort reform) could answer all generally applicable questions and those based on the earlier law, while Jury #2 (post-tort reform) would answer only questions arising from tort reform changes in the law. It would be preferable, though not absolutely essential, for all Juries to be present during Phase I and to use the same Jury for as many issues as possible.

15. That the Court should appoint early its own trial master and/or panel of experts (medical, legal, statistical) whose conclusions will be used to assist in the final selection of class representatives in the Pretrial Phase and with the Jury award in Phase II.

16. That the Court, after hearing counsel's time estimates, should leave a substantial period of time for the preparation of statistical evidence and expert testimony before Phase I so that an extended time interval will not be required between Phase I and II.

17. That no permanent or ongoing fund be established but that all net proceeds, if any, be distributed to claimants. (This means that each claimant's damages may include, if the Court finds it appropriate, an

amount related to his/her chances of contracting asbestosis-pleural cancer and, if appropriate, related phobias.) The alternative, which we do not recommend, is an ongoing fund for those who later contract cancer.

18. That, except for the class representative, the Court use the certification process to handle the threshold matter of individual exposures to specific products so that the only evidence for the Jury regarding members of the class will be statistical and not claimant specific.

II. SUMMARY OF RECOMMENDED TRIAL PHASES

[Recommendations for Pre-trial and Phase I Omitted—*ed.*]

Phase II

We recommend as desirable, though not absolutely essential, that the Court appoint a panel of experts and/or a Special Master (as recommended by Professor McGovern and the ABA Commission Report). Plaintiffs and Defendants will themselves have such experts.

Each of three teams of experts (Plaintiffs' team, Defendants' team, the Court's team) will have made a statistical profile of the Plaintiff's class. A "team" of experts might include one or more persons as the parties elect but would likely include at least one doctor, one lawyer, and one statistician. The evidence and cross-examination in Phase II will be almost entirely related to experts' conclusions about the class "profile" and what amount of actual damages has likely been incurred by the Plaintiffs' class as a whole. This testimony may appropriately be keyed to the Jury's damages finding on the class representatives. It would assist the Jury to have characteristics of segments of the class compared by the experts to the class representatives: "like Mr. X, the class representative" or "a combination of Mr. X and Mr. Y." By applying the Phase I findings (through extrapolation) to a classwide profile, the experts will reach conclusions about the total damages and testify about those conclusions to the Jury. The same process (involving attorney experts) would be used to assist the Jury in calculating an average percentage reduction of damages for typical classwide contributory fault and for the percentage of cases which will be barred by limitations. The Court-appointed experts must be selected with care as they will be seen as neutral by the Jury and their recommendations will carry great weight. They should undergo limited (and carefully supervised) deposition and in-trial cross-examination by the parties so that their premises and conclusions may be tested. The Court's experts do not usurp the Jury's function, as the Jury will make the final decision as to which (if any) of the various experts is persuasive.

The Court may wish to give the experts a more limited role. They could be directed to make no independent findings, but to review the conclusions of the partisan experts and comment to the Jury about which experts, if any, have gone outside the acceptable boundaries of good faith professional difference of opinion. The Court's experts could assist the Jury by assessing which of the partisan experts, in their opinion, is more credible or accurate on a given issue. This approach should help to "channel" the testimony of partisan experts (particularly in the difficult and sometimes confusing area of statistics) and serve to keep all experts within the limits of legitimate professional dispute.

Under the approach suggested here we do not think it necessary to have the Jury award damages by disease category as we originally suggested. Such compartmentalization could increase the likelihood that the aggregate claims will be greater or less than the total available for distribution within a given category and might give rise to the need for subclasses with separate representation because of asserted conflicts of interest affecting the class plaintiffs' attorneys. The conflicts problem is minimized by the Phase IV procedure which distributes a common fund.

We recommend that, in Phase II, the Jury (1) hear evidence on classwide compensatory damages and make a lump sum award; then (if required), (2) hear evidence on Defendants' net worth and then (3) make a punitive damages lump sum (not a multiple) award.

Phase III

The Defendants will try to a Jury the issues related to apportionment of Plaintiffs' damages, if any. It is difficult to see how Defendants can deal with these issues without resort to some approach such as market share liability. For reasons set out in the Discussion section, however, we now conclude that a workplace or market share liability theory is not required in Phase I, II or IV, given the potential existence of classwide joint and several liability. Each Defendant will be required to develop its own theory of apportionment and the supporting evidence and it is likely that some will rely on some form of market share evidence. Some Defendants may seek to have damages sorted by workplace in Phase III in order to advance a given theory of contribution or indemnity. That could be done through information elicited in the claims forms.

Unless the Phase III apportionment somehow affects collectability of a Plaintiffs' judgment—and it is hard to see how it could—Plaintiffs should have no standing or interest nor participation in Phase III.

Phase IV

Using the class damages fund for expenses as necessary, the Court would, under our proposal, appoint a master or claims-handling facility (patterned in part after the Johns–Manville Trust and other such facilities) to divide the proceeds among the Plaintiffs' class. The awards should be by way of "shares" in the fund (compensatory and punitive damages combined) until substantially all claims have been processed. Each claimant's share would represent a ratable claim to the total funds available after expenses and attorneys' fees. This procedure would avoid the hazard of "overspending" on early claimants. (If significant delay is contemplated, the Court might authorize partial awards or "advances" in hardship cases or other unusual circumstances).

Defendants urge that they have a right to participate in Phase IV, resist claims, and take any balance left in the fund after all awards are made (though with no obligation to add to the fund if it is inadequate to cover the aggregate established claims established in Phase IV). We disagree. Once a Jury makes a lump sum award following a fair class action trial consistent with due process, Defendants should have no more claim on how it should be divided among the class members than they do in the case of a class action settlement. Our recommendations regarding Phase IV follow the course suggested by Wright, Miller and Kane. These authorities, by the way, reinforce our view that a court-directed non-jury division of proceeds is consistent with Seventh Amendment guarantees, particularly in light of an opt-out process which enables a plaintiffs' class member to avoid this procedure if he wants his own individual jury trial on causation and damages.

IN THE UNITED STATES DISTRICT COURT FOR THE EASTERN DISTRICT OF TEXAS BEAUMONT DIVISION

CLAUDE CIMINO, *et al.*   :
                                 :
vs.   :   CIVIL ACTION NO. B–86–0456–CA
                                 :
RAYMARK INDUSTRIES, INC., *et al.* :

ORDER

On October 26, 1989, this Court consolidated 3031 cases for resolution of the state of the art and punitive damages. The Court also certified, under Fed.R.Civ.P. 23(b)(3), a class of plaintiffs in personal injury asbestos cases pending in the Beaumont Division of the Eastern District of Texas as of February 1, 1989, for a determination of the exposure and actual damage issues. The Defendants informed the Court of their desire to respond to the certification Order. Subsequently, the Defendants filed numerous objections and requests for modification of the Order as well as numerous requests for certification of issues pursuant to 28 U.S.C. 1292(b). For reasons given below, the Defendants' objections are overruled; the requests for modification of the Court's Order are denied and the requests for certification of the Court's Order are denied and the requests for certification of issues pursuant to 28 U.S.C. 1292(b) are denied.

This memorandum will discuss, in more detail, the procedure set out in the Court's October 26, 1989, Order for the trial of this action and, then, will discuss the Defendants' objections to the Court's Order.

I. Procedure

This action will proceed according to the three-phase procedure established by the Court's October 26, 1989, Memorandum and Order. Phases One and Two will be tried before the same Jury. Specifically, this action will include the following:

A. Discovery

The discovery in this action will continue to proceed according to Magistrate Hines' Discovery Plan and Schedule for Depositions and Medical Examinations of Plaintiffs, filed November 9, 1989. In addition, the parties shall be allowed to take full depositions of thirty (30) Plaintiffs, fifteen (15) of which shall be chosen by each side. Testimony from these Plaintiffs will be heard during Phase Two. Both sides will be allowed to take these depositions with the aid of video equipment.

B. Phase One

Phase One will proceed according to this Court's October 26, 1989 Memorandum and Order. For purposes of punitive damages, the Jury may be allowed to formulate a multiplier for each Defendant for which the Jury returns an affirmative finding on the issue of gross negligence.

C. Phase Two

Phase Two will proceed according to the Court's October 26, 1989, Memorandum and Order. In Phase Two, the Court will try the cases of the class representatives. In addition, the Plaintiffs and Defendants each will be allowed to introduce the testimony of the fifteen Plaintiffs chosen by that side for full depositions during discovery. Phase Two will involve classwide findings on the issues of exposure and actual damages. As explained in the Court's certification Order, the exposure and actual damages issues will involve:

> ... such issues as: (a) whether the Plaintiffs were exposed to the Defendants' products; (b) what damages, if any, the Plaintiffs suffered as a result of their exposure to the Defendants' products; and (c) what defenses, if any, the Defendants have to the Plaintiffs' claims.

... The Jury may be allowed to award lump sum punitive damages in Phase Two, in place of the multiplier in Phase One, against each Defendant for which the Jury returns an affirmative finding on the issue of gross negligence.

* * *

II. OBJECTIONS

* * *

C. Use of Statistical Evidence

The Defendants contend that the Court's use of statistics in Phase Two of this action is inappropriate and violates Defendants' right to a jury trial. If Phase Two consisted only of statistical evidence, the Defendants' arguments might carry some weight. However, the procedure envisioned by this Court for Phase Two will include more than statistical evidence. It will include the cases of the eleven class representatives as well as testimonial evidence from thirty Plaintiffs, fifteen of which will be chosen by the Defendants. Lastly, in Phase Three of this action, each Plaintiff will be required to submit to the Court proof of individual damages before receiving any portion of the Jury's damage award.

The underlying principle of the class action is that it is representative in nature. It is a mechanism by which a portion of the plaintiffs in the action are allowed to represent the entire body of plaintiffs where the subject matter of the suit is common to all the plaintiffs. *See* Supreme Tribe of Ben Hur v. Cauble, 255 U.S. 356, 41 S.Ct. 338, 65 L.Ed. 673 (1921). Under the basic principle of the class action, then, it is appropriate for the eleven class representatives, as well as the thirty illustrative Plaintiffs, to represent the interests of all the Plaintiffs in this action. In this action, the Jury will listen to evidence concerning the issues of exposure and actual damages as it applies to the cases of each one of the eleven class representatives and the additional thirty plaintiffs. The Jury will determine actual damages for each one of the eleven representatives. Using the expert testimony concerning all the Plaintiffs as well as the testimony of the eleven representatives and the thirty illustrative Plaintiffs, the Jury will then be able to award actual damages for the class as a whole. The Jury's award will be binding on the entire class of plaintiffs. The binding nature of this procedure is the very essence of a class action.

MICHAEL J. SAKS & PETER DAVID BLANCK, JUSTICE IMPROVED: THE UNRECOGNIZED BENEFITS OF AGGREGATION AND SAMPLING IN THE TRIAL OF MASS TORTS *

44 Stan. L.Rev. 815, 815–16, 821–51 (1992).

Commentators of every persuasion agree that mass torts, particularly trials of asbestos-induced diseases, confront the justice system with serious problems for which it has yet to find solutions. While merely disposing of these cases has proven a formidable burden to courts, actually doing justice in them seems daunting. A procedure is evolving in the trial of these cases whereby samples of cases are tried and the resulting damages are then applied to the remaining population of cases.

In this article, we discuss two aspects of this issue. First, we evaluate collective trials of mass torts under several theories of justice. Though the use of aggregation and sampling is sometimes criticized for failing to approximate the justice afforded by traditional case-by-case determinations, we conclude that the perception that aggregation provides inferior adjudication is largely illusory. The perception proceeds from relying on the traditional bilateral trial as the touchstone of due process. In fact, aggregation adds an important layer of process which, when done well, can produce more precise and reliable outcomes. Paradoxically, the procedural innovation of aggregation provides a quality of justice that surpasses what courts have, until now, been capable of in any kind of case.

Second, using sampling theory and inferential statistics, we discuss a number of factors the ideal aggregation procedure should consider to achieve its potential and minimize its pitfalls.

* * *

II. An Illustration of Aggregation: *Cimino v. Raymark*

* * *

B. The Statistical "Solution" in Cimino

Under Federal Rule of Civil Procedure 23(b)(3), the court certified a class consisting of 3031 members with existing asbestos cases in the Eastern District of Texas. All the plaintiffs claimed asbestos-related injury or disease resulting from exposure to defendants' asbestos-containing insulation products. After the settlement and dismissal of some 700 cases, the remaining class consisted of 2298 plaintiffs.

Cimino was tried in three phases. Phase I used the procedures approved by the Fifth Circuit in *Jenkins* to resolve all common issues of law and fact. Phase II required a jury determination for each of the worksites, crafts, and relevant time periods as to whether asbestos-containing insulation products were used, as well as which groups were sufficiently exposed to such asbestos products to cause the alleged injuries. This phase also included an apportionment of responsibility among the defendants. In addition, asbestos exposure issues submitted to the court were further specified as to time, place, craft, and amounts of exposure.

Phase III assessed damages and provides the main focus of our analysis. All of the *Cimino* plaintiffs waived their right to an individualized verdict and agreed to the following sampling procedures. The 2298 class members were divided into five disease categories based on the plaintiffs' injury claims. From each of the five disease categories the court selected a random sample, distributed as follows:

	Sample Size	Disease Category Population
Mesothelioma	15	32
Lung Cancer	25	186
Other Cancer	20	58
Asbestosis	50	1050
Pleural Disease	50	972
Totals	160	2298

The damage portion of each sampled case was submitted to a jury and those plaintiffs were awarded the actual individual verdicts, subject to remittiturs or new trial orders. Then, the average verdict after remittiturs, within each of the five disease categories, was awarded to each nonsample group member.

The verdict for Phase I was returned in March, 1990. Two new juries were selected for Phases II and III in July, 1990. These two juries sat together for the first five trial days, which were devoted primarily to medical testimony. Next, the two juries were divided and each began hearing testimony on its share of the 160 sampled plaintiffs. The juries then began returning damage verdicts; the last verdict was received in early October, 1990, some eight months after the trial had begun.

Phase II was designed to resolve the issue of plaintiffs' exposure to defendants' products on a class-wide basis. The court concluded that the resolution of the issues in Phase II was facilitated by the "homogeneous nature" of these plaintiffs' work histories. After the juries reached their verdicts for the nine class representatives and the 160 trial sample plaintiffs, the court ordered remittiturs in thirty-four of the pulmonary and pleural cases and in one mesothelioma case.

In Phase I, the initial jury had found the defendants grossly negligent, holding them liable for punitive damages. This jury had also assessed a punitive damages multiplier for each dollar of actual damages in varying amounts for each of the non-settling defendants. The court then would apply the multipliers set for a defendant to that defendant's allocated share of actual damages.

During Phase III, the defendants introduced evidence of plaintiffs' contributory negligence. The two new juries were instructed to consider the plaintiffs' contributory negligence, for example from smoking, only if the plaintiff was suffering from an asbestos-related disease linked to smoking, and only if the plaintiff had knowledge and appreciation of the danger of the product. As a result, some plaintiffs received awards of zero, which were factored into the average amounts awarded to the nonsample plaintiffs.

Phase III of the court's solution used inferential statistics to resolve damages for the nontrial sample. Using this procedure, damages were computed for the 2138 cases other than the 160 actually tried. In support of the use of sampling, the court quoted a Sixth Circuit decision, *E.K. Hardison Seed Co. v. Jones,* which held samples to be admissible "to show the quality or condition of the entire lot or mass from which they are taken." The *Hardison* court had found two prerequisites necessary to admit samples. First, the total population of cases should be substantially uniform with reference to the quality of the sample in question. Second, the sample should be representative of the total population.

Defendants asserted that the use of these statistical methods was inappropriate. The court rejected this claim, pointing out the use of statistics and extrapolation by the defendants in their own evidence during the trial. The court then gave examples of the use of statistics in medical research, testing of new products, standardized educational testing, the political arena, and in the courts. The court described the use of statistics as "commonplace," with applications in employment discrimination, antitrust, trademark infringement, civil rights, and tort cases (e.g., to prove liability and damages).

When the class was certified, the court considered two options for allocating damages. One was to provide a lump sum award to the plaintiffs as a group. Under the lump sum approach, typical plaintiffs would be chosen for a jury's benefit in determining a single lump sum damage award for the entire class. However, this approach was rejected by the Fifth Circuit in *In re Fibreboard Corp.*

Instead, the *Cimino* court decided to try a representative sample of cases and then extrapolate those awards to the nonsample cases. The sampling option, in contrast to the lump sum award procedure, included the allocation of damages to the 160 randomly sampled plaintiffs. When the court adopted the random sampling approach to damages, it deferred a decision on the "representativeness" of the sample until after the actual trials for the 160 plaintiffs. The court later concluded that the impact of the 160 cases was of sufficient importance that it had to determine whether the sample was in fact representative. This required that the randomly drawn samples be comparable to the population of each disease category.

To address this issue, the court held a post-trial hearing. At the post-trial hearing, the court concluded that the samples within each disease category were representative of the larger population of nontrial cases. In setting the sample size for each disease category, the court sought a confidence level of 95 percent. Expert testimony indicated that the actual precision level achieved by the samples exceeded that sought by the court. In addition, this testimony revealed that, with two minor exceptions, the samples on the whole achieved a 99 percent confidence level. Defendants presented no evidence at the post-trial hearing attacking the methodology for comparing the sample to the entire class population. The court concluded, therefore, that the distributions of numerous variables were comparable between the samples and their respective subclasses of the population of cases. It found that because the goodness-of-fit exceeded the acceptable limits it had articulated, no further cases needed to be tried prior to extrapolation of the damage awards to the nontrial sample.

In summary, the court found no methodological reason why the average damage verdicts for the 160 sampled cases in each disease category should not be applied to the non-sample class members. The average damages were calculated after remittitur and took into account those cases in which plaintiffs failed to prove the existence of an asbestos-related disease, resulting in a zero verdict. The court concluded:

> Individual members of a disease category who will receive an award that might be different from one they would have received had their individual case been decided by a jury have waived any objections, and the defendants cannot show that the total amount of damages would be greater under the court's method compared to

individual trials of these cases. Indeed, the millions of dollars saved in reduced transaction costs inure to defendants' benefit.

The court was sensitive to the view that statistical models cannot replace completely the traditional values embodied in our notions of due process. Nevertheless, it concluded that science had assumed its proper role in the dispute resolution process in this mass tort situation. The court asserted that it could not be said that the solution in *Cimino* was not a "trial"; the orders entered were a product of judicial opinion, and the liability verdicts and 160 damage awards for the randomly sampled cases were made by juries.

As mentioned earlier, the plaintiffs stipulated to the use of aggregation, thereby waiving all objections to the procedure. In contrast, the defendants objected to the solution, asserting that even in mass tort asbestos litigation, due process entitles defendants to a traditional individual trial in each of the 2298 cases. Defendants argued that no common issues existed and that the damages elements varied among plaintiffs. The court found, however, that: (1) it was undisputed that the product list submitted during Phase I comprised insulation products manufactured by the defendants, (2) the jury found these products to be defective, and (3) these factors would not vary from plaintiff to plaintiff. Although the degree of exposure varied for each plaintiff, the court concluded these factors had been set by the stipulations in Phase II of the trial. The court opined that the essential elements of damages in personal injury tort cases were tried, and that it had ascertained the appropriate damages in Phase III.

In the end, the court reasoned that unless its solution were used, these cases would not be tried, which would be the ultimate failure of due process:

> Defendants complain about the 1% likelihood that the result would be significantly different. However, plaintiffs are facing a 100% confidence level of being denied access to the courts. The Court will leave it to academicians and legal scholars to debate whether our notion of due process has room for balancing these competing interests.

III. THE JUSTICE OF SAMPLING AND AGGREGATION

In this section, we examine the constitutional, psychological, and societal values that aggregated trial procedures may serve. First, we review broadly both the instrumental and noninstrumental values procedural due process is thought to express and to support. Then, we probe more deeply into two value domains where aggregation appears to raise the greatest concern: distributive justice and procedural justice.

A. *Instrumental and Noninstrumental Values in Procedural Due Process*

Assuming that aggregation is capable of ameliorating the numbers problem that mass tort litigation presents, the procedure still must meet the constitutional test of due process. Defendants involved in aggregated trials like *Cimino* claim that aggregated procedures deny them their constitutional due process right to a one-on-one trial. But a closer look at the aggregated trial, at least in the mass tort context, suggests that this procedure does not necessarily violate traditional notions of due process under the Fifth and Fourteenth Amendments. In fact, the absence of such procedures is tantamount to denying many litigants their due process trial rights altogether.

Two basic points are made in this subsection: (1) traditional notions of procedural due process are, in fact, met in the aggregated context, and (2) alternative procedures, such as aggregated trials, may be necessary for vindicating due process values in the context of mass tort litigation. The discussion that follows considers what types of procedures may be necessary to meet due process requirements in aggregating trials in mass tort litigation. We conclude that the argument that due process requirements, traditional or otherwise, are not met in the aggregated trial process has little merit. Indeed, we will show that the aggregated trial is, in some vital respects, superior to the individual trial.

In the past twenty years considerable analysis has been done on the requirements of due process. The analysis here reviews the issue from the vantage point of the litigant—both plaintiff and defendant—in mass tort litigation who may invoke the clause. As others have put the question, what process is due when it is recognized that the guarantee already applies in a particular case? Professors Redish and Marshall have provided a useful framework for analysis of what procedures are necessary to meet the requirements of due process in aggregated mass tort litigation. They describe the Supreme Court's flexible conception of due process that is to be applied on a case-by-case basis, and analyze core values of the procedural due process requirement. Their work supports the view that "due process, unlike some legal rules, is not a technical conception with a fixed content unrelated to time, place and circumstances."

The Supreme Court has applied a balancing approach, weighing procedural safeguards against the State's burden in providing such protections. In *Mathews v. Eldridge,* the Court identified the three factors that shape the balancing process: (1) the private interest affected, (2) the risk of erroneous deprivation of the interest through the procedures used, and (3) the Government's interest, including all fiscal and administrative burdens that the additional procedure would require. The *Mathews* test attempts to ensure the accuracy of outcome from the process. It is relatively less focused on the fairness or perceived fairness of the procedures themselves.

Recently, in *Connecticut v. Doehr,* the Supreme Court has refined the third prong of the *Mathews* test for disputes involving only private parties. In *Doehr,* the Court found unconstitutional a Connecticut statute that allowed prejudgment attachment of real estate without prior notice or a hearing (e.g., without a trial). A plaintiff merely had to verify that there was probable cause to sustain the attachment's validity.

Although the Court followed the first two factors in *Mathews,* it altered the third factor to focus principally on the interest of the party seeking its prejudgment remedy, with "due regard for any ancillary interest the government may have in providing the procedure or foregoing the added burden of providing greater protections." The ultimate outcome in *Doehr,* like that in *Cimino,* hinges on the due process interests of both the plaintiffs and the defendants. But in *Doehr,* the Court underscored the importance of the plaintiffs' interest in the modified *Mathews* test by suggesting that a showing by the plaintiff of some exigent circumstance may be enough to allow a pre-hearing attachment. In *Cimino,* the class members are faced with just such exigent circumstances.

The aggregation procedure is not necessarily inconsistent with the *Mathews* test. First, the private interest affected principally involves the compensation defendants would have to pay plaintiffs, including both those in actual trials and those receiving the extrapolated damage awards. But this prong does not address the relationship between the procedure afforded the parties and the interest at stake. One could argue that in the aggregated trial, the defendants' total liability almost certainly does not significantly exceed what they would have to pay after individual trials, attorney fees and other transaction costs. However, the *Mathews* test as applied to the aggregated trial clearly does not suggest a mere assessment of plaintiffs' and defendants' monetary compensation, regardless of the trial procedures used.

Under the second prong of the *Mathews* test there may be little or no risk of erroneous deprivation of the defendants' property through aggregation procedures. In the aggregated trial, a determination of liability occurs, with judicial orders subject to objection and appeal. Each plaintiff still must prove medical status, liability, and all other components of the traditional tort claim (e.g., in *Cimino,* during Phases I and II). The only issue decided in the aggregate is how the damages are to be allocated from defendants to particular plaintiffs based on their individual circumstances (e.g., in *Cimino,* during Phase III).

The third prong of the *Mathews* test is really not a factor at all in the mass tort litigation context. No one can argue rationally that the procedure creates additional fiscal or administrative burdens for the defendants that come close to those resulting from the traditional one-on-one trial context. Again, one need only consider the enormous transaction costs involved in trying the huge and growing backlog of cases pending in the courts to appreciate this point. *Doehr* lends support to the view that the *Cimino* class members' interests in the aggregation procedure are compelling because, in the absence of such procedures, they would not receive their day in court, which would be the ultimate failure of due process.

Although the flexible structure of the *Mathews* test seems by itself to support the constitutionality of aggregation procedures in mass tort litigation, hypothesized "instrumental" and "noninstrumental" values embodied in procedural due process implicate the psychological and societal benefits of the procedure and warrant brief analysis. This analysis supports the conclusion that the due process values embodied in *Mathews* and its progeny are constitutionally satisfied in the aggregated mass tort trial.

Instrumentalists argue that the constitutional purpose of the due process clause is to ensure the most accurate decision possible. The rights to notice, hearing, and counsel each contribute to the goal of accuracy. These procedures allow litigants to argue their case fairly before the decisionmaker and, as Justice Frankfurter stated, "generat[e] the feeling, so important to a popular government, that justice has been done."

In some circumstances it is possible "to fashion a hearing that meets the requirements of due process, even though one or another of these procedural elements is absent." For example, cases on appeal regularly are decided on written briefs without oral argument. Another example arises in small claims trials, where participation by counsel is neither required nor customary. Thus, in certain circumstances, traditional elements of due process have been omitted "without adversely affecting the factfinding process." Likewise, the instrumental conception may be applied to aggregated trials. In the properly conducted aggregated trial, parties receive adequate and fair notice of the proceedings. The entire process is conducted as a judicial proceeding before an independent adjudicator. Parties whose property rights are implicated have the opportunity to be represented and heard unless they stipulate otherwise, as did the *Cimino* class members.

Additionally, in the aggregated trial, parties present written briefs and the right to counsel is no more limited than in an ordinary class action. Evidence and witnesses are examined and cross-examined, and motions are argued. When well done, the aggregated trial does not deny any of the instrumental values of due process, particularly from the viewpoint of defendants. Moreover, the value of procedural participation, central to legitimate judicial process, is not necessarily compromised in aggregated trials for either class members or defendants. Of course, as the Fifth Circuit concluded in *In re Fibreboard*, there is some point at which changes in procedure affect the parties' substantive legal rights and duties.

Legal scholars have also asserted "noninstrumental" values that are said to be embodied in procedural due process, particularly in civil litigation. One noninstrumental value is the "appearance" of justice and fairness in the courtroom. These scholars argue that due process requires trial judges to be not only fair and impartial; they also must satisfy the appearance of justice. The instrumental value of being fair cannot be realized fully unless the noninstrumental value of appearing fair is also achieved. The appearance of judicial impartiality and independence is not necessarily undermined by aggregation procedures. To the contrary, the aggregation procedure may even minimize, for example, incentives for trial judges to develop preconceived notions about individual trial outcomes. Judge Newman has taken the argument one step further, suggesting that traditional conceptions of fairness in our system of justice are related to "many of the undesirable aspects of our modern process of litigation," such as a narrow emphasis on individual case results.

Another noninstrumental value that has been suggested is equality before the law. In principle, procedural rules in aggregated trials should be "equal" for all plaintiffs and defendants. But in reality, equality sometimes does not prevail. For example, in *Cimino* all class members should probably have received the average damage award, regardless of whether or not their particular award was determined by a jury, and yet only 160 class members received jury awards.

Predictability, transparency, and rationality have also been asserted as noninstrumental values. These values relate to the litigants' ability to plan and make rational and informed choices about their case, and require the court's decision to be based on relevant factors. In the aggregated trial, predictability, transparency, and rationality require that the procedures produce results that are valid (e.g., that may be properly extrapolated) and repeatable (e.g., that the methodologies employed be applied in other contexts in similar cases). These issues are further explored in Part IV below, where we consider some of the principles that affect how aggregation serves the goals and values of procedural due process.

Another noninstrumental value, participation, relates to the litigants' right to communicate their views and feelings to their adversaries and to the court (as opposed to the instrumental conception of participation). Participation is important to the litigants on both a psychological level (e.g., to give the perception that they are playing a meaningful part in the litigation process) and on a societal level (e.g., to give the perception that the decisionmaking system works). A related noninstrumental value, "revelation," also provides psychological and societal benefits, but is distinct from procedural methods affecting the outcome of a case. Simply put, revelation embodies the litigants' desire to know the grounds on which their cases were decided and to receive a fair explanation of the result. Like participation, revelation affords litigants and others the ability to develop future litigation strategies in similar cases. Again, in principle, the value of revelation would not necessarily be thwarted by aggregated procedures.

Our brief review of the values of procedure suggests that, on balance, the aggregated trial serves these values as well as traditional one-on-one trials. Aggregated trials in mass tort litigation do not, by their nature, deprive litigants of the interests embodied in due process. Likewise, the instrumental values relating to procedure actually are realized more fully in a well conducted aggregated trial than in the individual trial. The picture is less clear with respect to noninstrumental values, however.

While the values of equality, predictability, transparency, rationality, and revelation may be quite well served by aggregation, other related values may not be. For example, the "appearance" of justice and fairness may fare well if aggregation procedures are considered carefully, but on superficial examination they may seem inferior to the individual trial. The right of a defendant to communicate his or her views is largely preserved in the aggregated trial, despite being not so well preserved in relation to each individual plaintiff. Finally, although autonomy and dignity seem to suffer in the aggregated trial, both are vindicated largely by comparing the relative losses to plaintiffs versus defendants as to the various realistic alternatives for adjudication in mass injury situations. These points are further developed in the next two sections, in which we analyze the impact of aggregate trials on some of the most crucial values at stake in procedural due process.

B. *Distributive Justice: Instrumental Values*

A major—perhaps the major—due process concern in an aggregated trial is the validity of the outcome. That is, as we have said, one important instrumental function of the legal process is ensuring rational, reasonable, accurate, and non-arbitrary outcomes. A fair process ought to result in plaintiffs receiving, within reasonable tolerances, the proper amount in damages. Similarly, corrective justice may require that the process extract from defendants only the amount they owe to the particular plaintiff to whom they are liable, no more than that amount and no less.

The main argument against trial by aggregation and sampling asserts that such trials cannot give the parties as accurate a result as they would obtain through traditional bilateral trials. Indeed, the intuitive plausibility of this argument is almost irresistible: How could a damage award, arrived at by extrapolation from an average of other, though similar, cases, possibly be as accurate as the verdict of a jury that hears the particulars of an individual case? Yet, paradoxically perhaps, this intuition is incorrect. Aggregation, properly conducted, will provide awards that are more accurate, not less.

Most might assume that each plaintiff who receives a sample's average as an award is receiving an estimate that likely constitutes over- or under-compensation. An individual award, however, is also an estimate-in fact, a less accurate estimate. Consider the archetypal single case more carefully. To regard an individualized damages determination as the correct amount is nothing more than a potent—and often desirable—illusion resulting largely from the fact that more is invisible than evident about the measurement process that underlies the legal process.

Let us consider one important nonobvious feature of the process. Every verdict is itself merely a sample from the large population of potential verdicts. That "population of verdicts" consists of all the awards that would result from trying the same case repeatedly for an infinite number of times. We can remind ourselves that the exact same case could have been tried repeatedly in different contexts: before the same jury; before different juries; or by different lawyers using exactly the same facts. Or, the case could have been tried using different permutations of the same facts or different facts and arguments that could have been assembled out of the same basic case. Clearly, any given trial of a case is but a single instance from among thousands of possible trials of that same basic case. It makes more sense, then, to think of the "true" award as the average of the population of possible awards. The fact that we normally obtain only one award from one trial of each case obscures the population of possible awards from which that one was drawn.

The large skewed distribution in Figure 1 depicts the damage awards from a typical court's docket. However, each of the individual awards which compose this distribution is itself just one from among that individual award's potential range of outcomes.

Imagine a case were tried 100 times. Then the verdicts are arrayed on a frequency distribution. (This distribution is depicted as the small shaded one in Figure 1.) It should be apparent that any single verdict is just one from among those. Many of the possible single verdicts constitute over-or under-compensation compared to the mean of that distribution, and that mean is the best estimate of the "true" award. Thus, to find the true award for a case, we would need to retry each case numerous times and take the mean of the resulting awards. By taking just the one award that results from a single trial we are accepting the likelihood of some error. With traditional individualized cases the legal process always accepts this error, and it always has.

In turn, any array of damage awards conceals the underlying variation due to the measurement error associated with each of the individual awards, as shown in Figure 1. A distribution of damage awards really consists of a set of mini-distributions reflecting the error in measurement around some "true" award for each case. The "correct" award can be made visible by certain procedural devices, such as repeated trials of the same case, or aggregation.

Try another thought experiment. Suppose that in an aggregation of cases, every one of 1000 were identical, and from those, 100 were drawn at random for trial. By trying these 100 cases and taking the average award, the court will have done the equivalent of our first thought experiment and will have far more accurately measured the correct damages than is usually done in individualized cases. By granting the mean award to each of the 100 cases, the court awards a more nearly correct amount than if each case received the award assigned by its jury. By awarding that same amount to each of the remaining 900 plaintiffs, the court also does better, in terms of accuracy of award, than it would if it conducted 900 individualized trials. The goals of corrective justice are better achieved: defendants pay to each plaintiff an amount that is better correct than could otherwise be accomplished.

Figure 1
Hypothetical Distribution of Damage
Awards in a Court's Docket

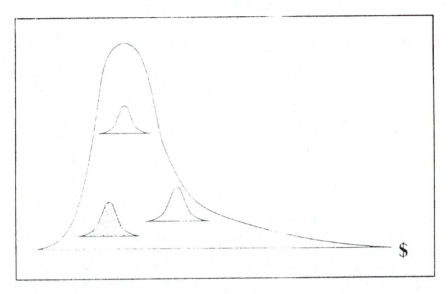

Upon closer examination, then, any given award in a traditional trial is likely to be an over-or under-award relative to the true, or population, mean of awards for that trial. The aggregation approach is capable of surmounting this defect. For one thing, in aggregated trials people recognize that the problem exists and they begin to think about how to minimize it. The structure of traditional trials blinds us to their jurimetrics. More importantly, the aggregation procedure itself provides a device for minimizing the problem and producing a more accurate estimate of the true award.

Another benefit is that aggregation will refine out some of the random and systematic error (that is, irrationality and bias) of jury decisions, while preserving the rational core of the jury's logic. Individual awards vary due to legally relevant differences among cases, but also due to random noise in decisionmaking as well as to larger biases and smaller nuances. The aggregation process refines the decision by averaging out of existence the undesirable variations and bringing the systematic and legally relevant relationships into sharper relief.

Of course, the cases composing *Cimino,* or any other collection of cases, are not identical. The more they vary from each other in legally relevant ways, the more we move away from aggregation's accuracy-producing benefits and move toward its error-producing harms. Thus, one needs to know how hetero-or homogeneous are the subgroups from which the cases were sampled and to which extrapolations are later made. At some point along the heterogeneity-homogeneity continuum, aggregation ceases to improve the accuracy of traditional trials and becomes a vitiation. The court in *Cimino* may have improved on conventional trials or may have introduced more error. We could determine that with precision only by comparing the homogeneity of the strata with the measurement error in individual cases.

In practical terms, from the standpoint of distributive justice, this problem does not matter. Assume that the aggregation procedure inadvertently brought together heterogeneous subgroups. Those who would have a serious potential objection about distributive injustice would be the plaintiffs, who get a single bite at the compensation apple. Whether they receive the correct amount, a windfall, or are seriously undercompensated, they have had their day in court. From the view-point of defendants, even if there are relatively large errors, with numerous over-and under-awards, all of those differences will cancel each other out and the average award will be the same in the collective trial as it would have been with the individualized determinations.

From the defendant's perspective, it is hard to conceive of a reasonably well done aggregation procedure that would not deliver equally or more accurate outcomes. The people to whom heterogeneity problems can make a real difference are the individual plaintiffs, for whom the situation is more complicated. The more heterogeneous the subgroups, the greater the error involved. Either the subgroups need to be composed of sufficiently similar cases to insure reduction rather than magnification of error, or the plaintiffs would have to waive their right to more accurate determinations.

C. Procedural Justice: Noninstrumental Goals

A considerable amount of research has shown that parties to judicial procedures are not concerned merely with distributive justice. Participants care a great deal about the process. The more the process affords party control of the presentation of evidence, and insures that third party decisionmakers pay serious attention to the particulars of the case, the more satisfied participants are with the process. Indeed, parties are more accepting of undesired outcomes when the process affords procedural justice.

The proposed aggregation procedure may seem to violate much of what we have learned about the importance of procedural justice. After all, in aggregation thousands of plaintiffs in thousands of cases would be deprived of their day in court and their chance to present their case. Furthermore, although all defendants would have an opportunity to present their evidence and arguments, they would not get to do so in response to every plaintiff, but only to a sample of them.

Several answers may be offered to the objection that aggregation denies parties procedural justice. One answer is that aggregation has never been compared empirically with traditional procedures. It may be that when a party has a vicarious day in court, represented by other litigants whose circumstances are very similar to his own, this would approximate, in terms of procedural justice, what the traditional adversary procedure provides.

Another answer comes from asking the question, "Compared to what?" For asbestos defendants, the choice is between a day in court in each and every case, on the one hand, or being denied a day in court for the majority of cases, on the other. Undoubtedly they would receive more occasions for procedural justice with traditional case-by-case litigation. On the other hand, with aggregation, they never will be shut out of trial opportunities altogether. They will always get to represent themselves, if only in a subset of cases. Moreover, the differences in procedural justice for defendants are far less pronounced than those facing plaintiffs.

The practical alternatives faced by asbestos plaintiffs are: (a) individualized damage determinations which, for some large number of plaintiffs, will occur after they have already died of their diseases; (b) bilateral settlements which, in class actions or mass consolidations, involve plaintiff-lawyer to defendant-lawyer negotiations with little or no involvement by the actual parties; or (c) aggregation and sampling. We see no way around a frankly utilitarian judgment here. How much satisfaction, in total, will be produced by these three options? The first holds little promise. A few plaintiffs will get their day in court and enjoy the full panoply of procedural rights. But most will have no day in court, no participation, and will die without knowing what became of their cases. The second option is the *Agent Orange* situation, and many of those plaintiffs are not just dissatisfied, they are furious. The third option, aggregation, offers an opportunity to be heard through representatives from a potentially cohesive group of fellow victims speaking on behalf of the whole group.

Although it is an empirical question as to which option affords the greatest procedural justice, our reflections lead us to conclude that of the realistic options available to asbestos plaintiffs, aggregation would provide more procedural justice than the alternatives. Indeed, it may well afford the most procedural justice that possibly can be provided under the circumstances.

D. Bidding Farewell to the Illusion of Individualized Justice

We already have noted one flaw in the imagery of the archetypal civil trial: The verdict appears precise and individualized, but in reality it is only a sample of one from a wider population of possible outcomes. The illusion that individualized adjudication provides a precision that aggregation lacks is nothing more than that, an illusion. Individualized trials substitute one form of error for another. Therefore, their results actually may be less accurate than those of a well-conducted aggregated trial.

In an article cited by Judge Parker in *Cimino* and by the report of the Judicial Conference Ad Hoc Committee, Deborah Hensler identifies other conceptions about the traditional trial that have not withstood empirical examination. Hensler reports the findings of studies on three myths about litigation: lawyer-client relations and litigant control, opportunities for adjudication, and substantive outcomes. The findings show that tort lawyers and their clients in mass tort cases communicate remarkably little about their cases and that clients have little control over the course of the litigation. Even in the absence of formal aggregative procedures, lawyers informally aggregate cases by representing hundreds or thousands of clients and meeting with them in large groups. Settlement discussions often are conducted about large groups of claimants, sometimes under pressure from judges.

Such informal aggregation is dangerous because it lacks the procedural safeguards of formal aggregation. No effort is made to ensure that the groups are homogeneous or that the cases discussed are representative. Moreover, no one checks to make sure the plaintiffs consent to the aggregation. According to Hensler's article, some lawyers could not even locate their clients, much less inform them or take direction from them. While the full-fledged trial is the standard about which debates over procedural reforms inevitably are conducted, trials are rare occurrences, especially when mass torts are involved.

Finally, damage awards in traditional settlements and trials are not models of accuracy or equity. Some plaintiffs enjoy windfalls, but these are usually those plaintiffs with the lowest losses. Most plaintiffs, particularly those with serious injuries, recover only a fraction of their actual losses. In product liability cases generally, those with losses under $10,000 recovered $7.27 per dollar of actual losses, while those with losses over $1,000,000 recovered only $0.25. This pattern of low end over-compensation and high end under-compensation is a well-replicated phenomenon. One study of asbestos workers' widows found that they recovered an average of $0.31 cents per dollar of loss.

For opponents of aggregation or bilateral adjudication idealists, these studies do not really undercut traditional trials. Even if conventional procedures in mass tort cases fall short of the ideals so venerated in the traditional vision of the trial, opponents of aggregation still can argue that formal aggregation makes matters worse. In their view, approving formal aggregative procedures would give plaintiffs even shorter shrift than at present. By demanding that the litigation system strive toward an unattainable ideal, they would argue, a greater degree of justice and fairness is attained than would otherwise be realized.

This article, however, argues that formal aggregative procedures offer important affirmative advantages over traditional trials. The data Hensler reports show that there is considerable room for improvement; one can at least hope that aggregation will produce some of those improvements. Put simply, at least as much reason exists to expect aggregation to improve matters as to expect it to enlarge further the gap between what the justice system promises and what it delivers.

IV. AGGREGATING WELL

Providing a manual of statistical and methodological procedures for conducting aggregated trials is far beyond the scope of this article. Nevertheless, we need to consider some of the principles that will affect how well or poorly aggregation will serve the goals and values of procedure. For aggregation to be a realistic solution, the courts must conduct it in such a way that its benefits are most likely to be maximized and its potential harms minimized. In this section, we discuss the major methodological and statistical issues that must be considered in developing aggregative procedures.

A. Sampling Cases for Trials

Mass torts represent a sampling theorist's dream. The population of cases from which the sample is to be drawn is known with unusual completeness. This provides the sampling frame from which any type of case sampling proceeds. In addition, many details are known or can be learned about each member of the population. Thus, the degree to which the sample is representative of the population can be known with near certainty—a great improvement over most sampling situations. Representativeness is the touchstone of good sampling.

One must be on guard against one problem in particular: Samples that are representative when first drawn may grow less so over time. Attention must be paid to possible changes that could render a previously representative sample unrepresentative. When that occurs, sampling will not accurately reflect what needs to be known about the population. If over time cases are added to the docket by new filings or removed through settlement, a sample already drawn may grow increasingly unrepresentative. This problem can be minimized by prohibiting new cases from entering the aggregation once the sample is drawn, and by not authorizing settlements.

Rather than drawing from the population of cases as a whole, samples can be drawn from subgroups, or stratifications, of the population. For example, the population of cases in *Cimino* was divided into five groups based on the asbestos-related disease from which the plaintiff was suffering. Such subgrouping helps to insure that a sufficient number of cases are sampled from each subgroup in order to obtain a reliable estimate of that subgroup's awards. It also creates more homogeneous subpopulations.

How many cases need to be sampled? This depends in large part on the variability of the population. The more diverse the population, the larger the sample must be in order to reflect the population accurately. The more homogeneous the population, the fewer cases that need to be sampled. Thus, dividing the population of cases into homogeneous subgroups not only serves the important goal of improving the accuracy of outcomes as required by distributive justice, but also allows for more efficient sampling.

In general, the larger the sample, the more likely it will reflect the population; the smaller the sample, the less likely it is to do so—for any given degree of heterogeneity. How do we know whether the sample is large enough, under the given circumstances, to faithfully reflect the population parameters? This question requires both a descriptive statistical answer and a normative legal answer.

The statistical answer provided in *Cimino* was to compute confidence limits around a sample statistic. That court concluded that on a wide variety of background factors, the population means and proportions fell within a 99 percent confidence interval of the sample's means and proportions.

Confidence limits normally are drawn around a sample's mean when the population mean is not known, in order to infer a zone within which the population mean exists at a specified level of probability. But in *Cimino* the relevant population parameters were known, they did not have to be inferred. The question, rather, was whether the sample represented the population accurately enough.

What was needed was a test of whether the sample statistics differed from the population parameters to a degree that would raise doubts about the sample's representativeness. One straightforward approach to this would be to test each sample mean against an exact hypothesis of its corresponding population mean, while setting the critical level for that test at something far higher than a conventional p-level of .05 or .01. This is because conventional significance testing aims to be conservative about erroneous rejection of the presumption of no differences. Thus, one would reject the presumption of no-difference only if the probability of that decision being erroneous was smaller than, say, one percent. That is, we make it hard to find significance and easy to walk away empty handed. But in the situation of sampling from known aggregations the reverse is true. The error we want to guard against is erroneously concluding that the sample means equal the population mean. We should, therefore, make it easy to reject the presumption that the sample and the population are alike, and hard to conclude that they are alike. That can be accomplished by setting the p-level for the proposed significance tests at .20 or higher.

The normative answer requires deciding what is a sufficiently large and representative sample. How close a fit is close enough for the law's purposes is a legal judgment that eventually will have to be made by the courts or Congress, and requires a balancing of the costs of greater accuracy against the consequences of error.

B. Achieving Within–Group Homogeneity and Between–Group Heterogeneity

We discussed earlier the critical importance of sampling from relatively homogeneous groups in order to attain the increased accuracy that aggregation makes possible. We now consider how homogeneity can be maximized, and the cost of failing to do so.

In *Cimino*, the court created subgroups by stratifying the population into disease categories. Presumably, the cases within disease categories are more similar to each other (and more different from those in the other groups) than cases in the intact population. This strategy implies that the cases can be lined up on a single dimension for assessing similarity, such as severity of disease. Again, because data on the entire population of cases are available, we need not guess at this.

In selecting variables for stratifying the cases, courts can be guided by empirical research studying the determinants of jury awards in conventional asbestos cases or by the findings of other courts as they acquire experience with aggregation. Such sources can tell a court which differences among plaintiffs are likely to have an impact on the awards. On the basis of those important differences, population subgroups can be formed. This approach implies that cases differ on a substantial number of different variables on which cases will be profiled.

Other techniques might refine the effort further. For example, by using cluster analysis on data describing the case population, subgroupings could be defined that maximize the ratio of between-group variation to within-group variation. In other words, cases could be grouped so that the cases within a group are most like each other, while the subgroups themselves are most different from each other. Cases that do not fit into a cluster could be deemed too sui generis to be included in the aggregations and could be tried individually. Samples could then be drawn from these highly homogeneous clusters.

A tradeoff has to be made between the number and size of the subgroups. The more subgroups formed, the more homogeneous they will be. The more of them, the smaller they will be. The smaller the subgroups are, the less reliable and less efficient sampling will be. At some point a line has to be drawn where it is judged that further refinement into subgroups will cost more in lost reliability than it gains in increased homogeneity. This, too, requires the exercise of judicial wisdom informed by statistical information.

We noted earlier that a continuum exists between the circumstances in which aggregation increases accuracy of outcomes and the circumstances in which aggregation reduces accuracy. At the beneficial end of that continuum, subgroups are relatively pure and homogeneous. As the number of cases counted into that subpopulation is enlarged, the sample gains the advantage shrinking error, along with the risk of greater heterogeneity. At the point where the increased error due to increased heterogeneity overtakes the decreased error due to larger size, the overall error begins to increase.

Figure 2 depicts the situation at both the desirable and the undesirable ends of that continuum. In Figure 2a, measurement error for individual cases is large and the standard error of the sampling distribution is small. In this situation, aggregation would achieve a greater accuracy in assigning awards to cases than if they were tried individually. But in Figure 2b, measurement error is small and the standard error of the sampling distribution is large. In this situation, aggregation and sampling would assign awards that are an unacceptable departure from the true awards that should be received.

Figure 2
Hypothetical Distribution of Damage Awards
in a Subgroup of Cases

2a. Homogeneous Subgroup with Large Measurement Error per Case

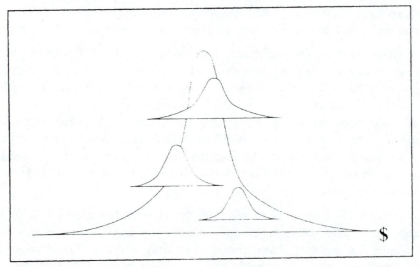

2b. Heterogeneous subgroup with Small Measurement Error per Case

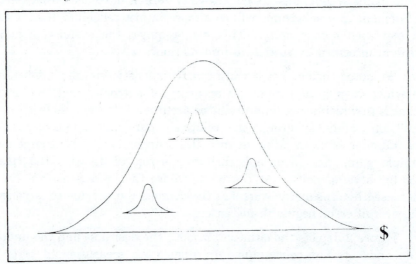

The reliability of juries becomes visible only when their decisions are aggregated and correlated with predictor variables. But when the decisions of different juries seeing the same or similar cases are compared to each other, a high degree of error variation becomes apparent. This variability has given rise to the familiar belief that jury verdicts are unpredictable. But despite the unpredictable nature of individual jury decisions, there is an underlying consistency and predictability, which becomes apparent through statistical aggregation. By carefully harnessing the power of aggregation in actual trials, the strengths of jury decisionmaking can be more fully realized.

C.   Juries

The ways in which juries are employed can make a difference in the consistency and accuracy of outcomes. In *Cimino*, two juries decided eighty cases each. The opinion does not tell us the order in which cases from the various subgroups were presented to each jury.

Think of the jury as a measuring instrument, like a thermometer or a bathroom scale. The problems associated with measuring instruments are to a great extent mirror images of those encountered by the aggregation procedure. The degree of homogeneity of the population of cases has its parallel in the degree of reliability of the measuring instrument. The more heterogeneous the population, the more cases that must be sampled from it in order to faithfully reflect it. Similarly, the more unreliable a type of measuring instrument is, the more variation in measurement it produces, and the more of them must be employed in order to consistently reflect what they are measuring. For example, if we have a reliable thermometer, a single one will suffice to give consistent measures of the temperature. The more unreliable our thermometers are—the more they err in random amounts, over-or-understating the real temperature—the more of them we would need in order to increase the reliability of the measurements being taken.

In addition to reliability, psychometricians and others interested in the theory and practice of measurement are concerned with validity—that is, the accuracy of measurement. A bathroom scale may reliably (consistently) report weight as seventeen pounds greater than it really is. For the most part the law sets aside the problem of validity. The law assumes that the proper verdict is a social judgment, with no external criterion of correctness other than that which the community (of which the jury is a representative) would find appropriate. This is most clearly exemplified in cases where the jury must place a dollar value on pain and suffering. Thus, juries that treat like cases alike are considered reliable, and that is as far as the law takes the measurement problem. In short, the law takes reliability to be validity as well.

In order to know how few or how many juries are needed, we must know how reliable juries are. Although conventional wisdom holds that juries are of doubtful reliability—in terms of unpredictability of verdicts or awards—systematic empirical research has uncovered a rather different picture. For example, studies of juries assessing damages find awards to be predictable once certain key information about the cases being decided becomes known. These findings suggest that juries are considerably more reliable than is commonly assumed.

On the other hand, juries are not so reliable as to justify using one or a few of them to decide a large number of cases. Take the extreme situation: If one jury is used and it tends to be much too high or too low in its estimations—compared with the population of juries from which it was drawn—then the verdicts in the tried cases would under or overstate the damage amounts for the tried cases. Those systematic inaccuracies would then be extrapolated to the untried cases as well.

In principle, we could determine the optimal number of juries by developing data that produced a curve relating gains in reliability to increases in the number of juries. We could then identify the point where the marginal increase in reliability was so modest that the use of additional juries was not worth the cost and effort. Again, this calls for a judicial judgment based on the intelligence provided by the data. In the absence of such data, the safest way to avoid this risk is to use as many juries as practicable. Then, when the means are calculated and applied to the untried cases, the errors will cancel each other out.

The problems described above are also present, though usually ignored, in the determination of awards in conventional trials. As we have noted, the advantage of aggregation is that it offers the means for overcoming these problems. It would be regrettable to lose the advantages of aggregating cases by failing to appreciate the need for a similar sort of aggregating of the "measuring instruments" as well.

So far we have spoken of juries as thermometers or scales, as if they were fairly stable instruments whose errors were themselves relatively stable. But with human measuring instruments, the sources of unreliability are more complex and, unfortunately, more systematic than random. Consider the following additional complications. All measuring instruments change with use, perhaps especially humans. Thus, by the time a jury is hearing its 80th case on similar issues, it likely is not making decisions in the same way it did in its first decision of that series. More particularly, when the same decision-makers see a series of cases, they become increasingly sensitized to subtle differences that would not be detected by different decisionmakers deciding one case each. Moreover, we might wonder whether jurors deciding a series of highly similar cases do not become excessively, "unnaturally," consistent in their treatment of cases or try to balance out errors they feel they made in one direction by deliberately erring in subsequent cases in the opposite direction. Courts may want to consider whether to regard such changes as a distortion or as an improvement due to experience. On the other hand, the law may consider it sufficient cause for concern that these juries may grow increasingly different from the typical jury.

Courts must think about how such problems could be avoided. The risk to untried cases is that if cases sampled from one type of subgroup are decided early and those from another subgroup are decided later, the differences between the average awards for the two groups might be the product, not only of the cases' inherent differences, but also of systematic changes that developed in the jury over time. Protection from this potential problem could come from having numerous juries decide the tried cases. If each of several juries is to hear multiple cases, then cases should be assigned to juries randomly so that the mix of cases early in the series is no different from the mix of cases later in the series.

Randomization of assignment would help to minimize potential bias to tried cases, putting them in much the position they would be in a conventional trial situation. The best protection, however, would actually come from giving even tried cases the mean aggregate award rather than the one arrived at for it by the jury that heard that particular case.

Aggregation helps to eliminate another problem that has crept into the civil justice system due to the use of smaller juries. As the size of the jury decreases, the error variation in awards increases. The use of the mean award from multiple juries would reduce or eliminate those errors. Thus, in the context of aggregation, the use of smaller juries would be both efficient and accurate, while in the traditional trial setting we give up some reliability in verdicts in order to acquire some additional efficiency.

D. *Extrapolating From Sample to Finite Population*

One way to apply the awards from a group of tried cases to the remaining population of untried cases is simply to take the subgroup sample mean, after adjusting for remittiturs granted, and award that amount to each untried case in that subgroup. A more refined approach would take into account additional differences among the cases within each subgroup.

For example, suppose a subgroup is homogeneous in every way except that the plaintiffs vary with respect to the number of future work years they will lose. Such a variable ought to affect the amount of damages awarded. Creating subgroups for each year (or ranges of years) of lost work might create too many subgroups that are too small. The pattern of verdicts in tried cases almost certainly would reflect that the jury took into account the effects of the years of work lost. Within a subgroup, the effect of this variable could be captured by developing a mathematical model of the jury decisions. The model would permit additional variables (including but not limited to number of working years lost) to be taken into account and permit more precise awards to be made among untried cases within subgroups.

In addition, the courts might want to build in a procedure whereby a judge could consider unusual factors in certain of the untried cases, a kind of routinized remittitur review. The number of such cases would be small, owing to the cluster analysis which grouped together only like cases and removed oddball cases from the aggregation altogether, and to the mathematical modeling, which would already have taken into account certain important systematic differences among cases within the same subgroup.

The approach we have been suggesting—clustering cases into homogeneous subgroups—is a refinement of that which was employed in *Cimino*. We have selected this more "physical" approach largely because it would make the procedures more transparent and be more intuitively comprehensible to nonstatisticians (that is, most judges, lawyers, litigants, and citizens). Nevertheless, completely statistical modeling would be a perfectly sensible alternative approach. In essence, this approach takes the mathematical modeling refinement suggested above and replaces the clusters with more variables in the model. That is, juries would decide a representative sample of cases, the characteristics of the cases and the juries' responses to them would be captured in a mathematical model, and the mathematical model would be used to extrapolate damages for the rest of the finite population of cases. Such an approach gains the benefit of jury judgments about how different case facts (variables) affect decisions in the cases and permits tailoring to the particulars of each case.

V. CONCLUSION

Necessity is the mother of invention. And sometimes inventions work better than the devices they have been modeled after. Such is the case with aggregation and sampling in the determination of damages in mass torts. While most commentators debate whether aggregated trials preserve enough of the features of procedural due process to be judged constitutional, we have suggested that aggregated trials have the potential to achieve a level of justice that simply is not possible in traditional individual trials.

Done well, aggregation not only can increase efficiency, it can systematically increase accuracy, reduce bias, and still provide meaningful individualization of awards—all based on jury judgments of the meaning various case characteristics have for case outcomes.

Although a variety of methodological and statistical considerations need to be taken into account in deciding just how aggregated trials can best be conducted, our fundamental conclusion is that they can be carried out in ways that satisfy the norms of procedural due process—and then some.

Notes and Questions

1. Have Professors Saks and Blanck adequately analyzed and answered all the legal and practical problems relating to statistical sampling and aggregate damages in mass tort litigation? Have they adequately refuted Professor Trangsrud and others who assert a right to individualized justice? The due process standard they use, from *Mathews v. Eldridge* and *Connecticut v. Doehr,* were cases dealing with pre-judgment seizure (provisional remedies). Do these cases supply the appropriate due process standard for trial-on-the merits? What of the defendants' Seventh Amendment arguments, also asserted in *Cimino*? What if the plaintiffs had not assented to an aggregate damages plan? Is it fair that some plaintiffs who might have received no damages at trial will receive compensation as a result of an aggregative distribution of damages?

2. For an in-depth assessment of sampling schemes in the context of mass tort litigation, including a review of Judge Parker's techniques in *Cimino* and a detailed critique of the Saks and Blanck defense of the sampling methodology, *see generally* Robert G. Bone, *Statistical Adjudication: Rights, Justice, and Utility in a World of Process Scarcity,* 46 Vand. L.Rev. 561 (1993). Commenting on the Saks and Blanck analysis, Professor Bone suggests:

> Professors Saks and Blanck have recently argued, in defense of *Cimino,* that the average of sample case verdicts is likely to be more accurate than an individual trial verdict for many mass tort cases. If this argument is correct, it should allay much of the concern about sampling. Unfortunately, however, the argument is flawed . . . The fact is that, in many mass tort aggregations, an individual trial will give a more accurate verdict than sampling for at least some cases. . . . But it is also true for the more powerful—and more expensive technique of regression analysis . . . , since any cost-effective regression procedure has to ignore many damage-related variables.

Id. at 577. Professor Bone concludes: " Because it distributes by lottery, random sampling is justifiable on process-oriented grounds only if a lottery is a fair distributional scheme. This requires some argument, and the argument shows that sampling creates a much greater tension between process and outcome values than previous commentators realized." *Id.* at 568.

3. Judge Parker's sampling and aggregative damages techniques were subsequently adopted by the Louisiana federal district court as the method for assessing classwide punitive damages in an oil refinery mass accident case. *See* In re Shell Oil Refinery, 136 F.R.D. 588 (E.D.La.1991), *aff'd sub nom.,* Watson v. Shell Oil Co., 979 F.2d 1014 (5th Cir.1992). Judge Parker's methodology has yet to be reviewed on appeal to the Fifth Circuit. For a discussion of Judge Parker's damage scheme in *Cimino* and its application to other mass tort cases, *see* Samuel Isaacharoff, *Administering Damage Awards in Mass–Tort Litigation,* 10 Rev.Litig. 463 (1991).

4. Other academic commentators have proposed other sampling methodologies for mass tort litigation. *See, e.g.,* Kenneth S. Abraham & Glen O. Robinson, *Aggregative Valuation of Mass Tort Claims,* 53 L. & Contemp. Probs. 137 (Autumn 1990); James F. Blumstein, *et al., Beyond Tort Reform: Developing Better Tools for Assessing Damages for Personal Injury,* 8 Yale J. Reg. 171 (Winter 1991); Glen O. Robinson & Kenneth S. Abraham, *Collective Justice in Tort Law,* 78 Va.L.Rev. 1481 (1992); David Rosenberg, *The Causal Connection in Mass Exposure Cases: A Public Law Vision of the Tort System,* 97 Harv.L.Rev. 849 (184); David Rosenberg, *Class Actions for Mass Torts: Doing Individual Justice by Collective Means,* 62 Ind.L.J. 561 (1987). *Cf.* Kenneth R. Cone & James E. Laurence, *How Accurate are the Estimates of Aggregate Damages in Securities Fraud Cases?,* 49 Bus. Law 505 (1994).

E. JURY COMPETENCE

DAN DRAZAN, THE CASE FOR SPECIAL JURIES IN TOXIC TORT LITIGATION

72 Judicature 292 (February/March, 1989).

The complexities of toxic tort cases are beyond the lay jury's "practical abilities and limitations." Specially qualified expert juries that can better understand and evaluate technical concepts are needed.

The common sense of the common man ... cannot be brought to bear unless there is comprehension of the facts and the law.[1]

Special juries do not exist, as many people seem to suppose, by the authority of a modern statute; on the contrary, they are as ancient as the law itself.[2]

The post-World War II industrialization which has raised our standing of living has also generated products and byproducts gravely dangerous to human health. Toxic substances in our homes, our factories and in the environment are the cause for many diseases, including cancer. The U.S. Environmental Protection Agency (EPA) estimated that in 1980 alone 57 million metric tons of hazardous waste were generated throughout the nation. Almost 90 per cent was improperly disposed, creating "significant imminent hazards" to the public's health. Environmentally-induced cancer and disease are now considered a public health problem. The scientific community holds that between 60 and 90 per cent of all cancers are caused by exposure to man-made chemicals released into the environment.

Armed with scientific and medical data linking human diseases with exposure to toxic substances, thousands of persons have filed toxic tort claims against the federal government and private industry. Claims against the federal government include those made by plaintiffs with injuries stemming from radiation exposure caused by the testing of atomic bombs and from the government-sponsored swine flue vaccination program. In the private sector, thousands of claims have been brought for injuries stemming from exposure to asbestos, the drug diethylstilbestrol (DES), the intrauterine device (IUD), the defoliant agent orange and for injuries stemming from exposure to such hazardous substances in the environment as dioxin, lead, benzene and arsenic.

The extensive documentation of toxic substances, ironically, has also made it very difficult for many victims to recover under existing common tort law. Scientific data suggests there may be many sources for an

---

1. Note, *The Case for Special Juries in Complex Litigation,* 89 Yale L.J. 1134 (1980), citing former Chief Justice Warren Burger in a speech to the Conference of State Chief Justices, Nat'l L.J., Aug. 13, 1979.

2. Oldham, *The Origins of the Special Jury,* 50 U.Chi.L.Rev. 137 (1983), *citing Thomas Erskine, Esq., November 15, 1793. The Case of Libel,* The King v. John Lambert and Others, Printer and Proprietors of the Morning Chronicle 16 (2 ed. London, 1794).

individual's injury. It is precisely this uncertainty, due to factors unique to toxic exposure, which make toxic torts fundamentally different from traditional tort cases. Unlike traditional tort cases where there is an immediate wrong and injury, the typical toxic tort claim stems from chronic misconduct, and the injury/disease only manifests itself many years after exposure. This long latency period makes it very difficult for the plaintiff to show that the defendant's conduct caused his or her injuries and not such other factors as ambient toxic substances, diet, lifestyle and smoking. Determining the cause of latent injury is "one of the major obstacles facing the plaintiff in a court action for exposure to hazardous waste." There is widespread agreement that proving causation is the largest barrier to recovery in toxic tort cases.

Briefly stated, the plaintiff must prove by a preponderance of the evidence that the defendant's conduct caused the injury. To satisfy this test, it must be shown that the injury was caused, not by the multitude of toxic chemicals to which the defendant was exposed over the latency period, but by the exposure to the toxic substance under the defendant's control or responsibility. To help tackle the causation issue, lawyers for both sides have turned to scientific data. Such documents as epidemiological studies and their respective mathematical models are now a necessity for toxic tort litigation. Courts recognize that these studies are important to resolving the causation issue and are increasingly admitting them into evidence. But, can judges, and particularly lay juries, comprehend and properly evaluate this complex and technical evidence? Unfortunately, there is scant data on jury performance in civil actions. However, as society and its legal issues become more complex, jury duty also becomes more difficult. For example, uncertainties, probabilities and competing expert opinions are inherent to epidemiological evidence. One lawyer who has studied the role of such studies in the courtroom warns they can prejudice and overly confuse the jury.[14] For example, a study's finding that the defendant's conduct increased the plaintiff's risk of injury may cause the jury to improperly conclude that the defendant's actions actually caused the injuries. This concern is compounded by the belief that jurors often rely on their instincts of right and wrong, and not the facts and law, to decide complex cases.

Courts have held that certain kinds of litigation and the issues they present, on a case-by-case basis, may be too complex and difficult for the jury.[17] Antitrust and securities litigation are two such kinds of cases. As shown below, toxic tort litigation presents many of the same kinds of problems for jurors as antitrust and securities litigation; thus, it may also be too complex for juries.

14. Dore, *A Commentary on the Use of Epidemiological Evidence in Demonstrating Cause–In–Fact,* 7 Harv.Envtl.L.Rev. 428, 437 (1983).

17. *See* In re Japanese Electronic Products Antitrust Litigation, 631 F.2d 1069 (3d Cir.1980); In re Boise Cascade Securities Litigation, 420 F.Supp. 99 (W.D.Wash. 1976); In re United States Financial Securities Litigation, 75 F.R.D. 702 (S.D.Cal. 1977), *rev'd* 609 F.2d 411 (9th Cir.1979), *cert denied,* 446 U.S. 929 (1980); and Berstein v. United Pictures Inc., 79 F.R.D. 59 (S.D.N.Y.1978).

The purpose of this article is to add an issue to the ongoing debate of toxic tort reform—whether toxic tort litigation is too complex for lay jurors. Toxic torts are unique and complex litigation. Little is gained from the debate if jury incompetence is ignored and is subsequently found to be the weak link in toxic tort litigation.

The article concludes that complex scientific and medical evidence, coupled with the voluminous discovery necessary to account for the latency period, are beyond the jury's reach. It proposes that special juries made up of scientific and medical experts from many fields be used in complex toxic tort cases. The special jury, while not widely practiced in the United States, has historical precedent in England dating back to the 1600s. Of course, a special jury would need to pass constitutional muster and not violate the Seventh Amendment's guarantee of a trial by jury or the due process clause of both the Fifth and Fourteenth Amendments. As discussed below, the due process concern is procedural and centers around ensuring that the jury represents an impartial cross-section of the community. A carefully tailored program for selecting and using special juries can satisfy these concerns.

It is often said that litigation is the best way for discovering the truth and ensuring justice. Presently, plaintiffs who have been injured from exposure to toxic substances face many legal obstacles to establishing their case. Courts are easing these burdens by permitting the use of epidemiological studies and statistical analyses. In return, jurors trained in the sciences can ensure this valuable information is given fair treatment and that informed decisions result.

This article first discusses how toxic tort cases are unlike other tort cases: the differences between legal and medical causation and the use of epidemiological studies to show causation. It then examines why these studies are too difficult for jurors to understand and compares the complexities of toxic tort cases to antitrust and securities litigation. Finally, it examines the historical use of special juries in both England and the United States, discussing the constitutional issues they raise and proposes using special juries in toxic tort litigation.

UNIQUE LEGAL CHALLENGES

In the typical personal injury tort case, the tortious behavior and resulting injury are almost simultaneous. If a person is injured by a malfunctioning piece of equipment or from acute chemical exposure, there is little doubt what caused the immediate injury and who was responsible. The plaintiff can quickly identify the cause of her injury, gather the necessary evidence on how the event occurred and easily name the responsible defendant.

Toxic tort cases are fundamentally different, especially environmental exposure claims for toxic waste injuries. The most obvious difference is that the tortious behavior and resulting injury are never contemporaneous. First, exposure to the toxic substance is chronic and often extends over many years. The resulting disease or cancer does not manifest itself until many years later after exposure has ceased. Cancer, for instance, typically does not appear until 7 to 20 years after exposure to a carcinogen. In toxic waste cases, there is an estimated 20–30 year latency period between exposure and manifestation of injury. The long latency period makes it very difficult for the plaintiff to prove causation. Since injury does not immediately result from toxic exposure, the exposure creates only a risk that a disease or cancer may manifest itself many years later. However, during this latency period the plaintiff is exposed to multiple environmental chemicals which may be injurious. These chemicals interact with each other and have synergistic effects on the plaintiff. As a result, the plaintiff often is prevented from isolating a single responsible pollutant. Yet, the traditional tort system requires that the plaintiff isolate a specific toxic agent and satisfy a "but-for" test of causation: but for the defendant's conduct, the injury would not have occurred. In other words, the plaintiff's burden of proof requires the following:

- identifying the toxic substances which substantially caused the injury;

- showing that exposure to this toxic substance was in the duration and concentration which scientists believe can cause injury;

- identifying the party or parties responsible for the exposure; and,

- eliminating ambient toxic substances, lifestyle, diet and other "background risks" as substantial factors.

Medical vs. Legal Causation

The preceding section examined the plaintiff's burden of proving legal causation. One component of this test is proving by medical standards that the chemical in question caused the plaintiff's injury. This medical causation test requires the plaintiff show that such other factors as background chemicals, lifestyle, smoking and diet did not substantially cause the injury. However, when scientists determine medical "causes," they do not rely on the same rigid standards used for showing legal proof. Scientific proof is essentially based on consensus judgment of possibilities. Yet the tort system requires showings of probabilities based on direct causal relationships. Therefore, a valid showing of medical causation is frequently inadequate for satisfying the legal causation standard. Legal causation requires that the plaintiff introduce expert testimony based on "reasonable medical certainty" that the alleged injury was caused by the defendant's conduct. Despite its legal shortcomings, medical causation may be our best understanding of what "causes" diseases from environmental exposure. Epidemiological studies play a very important role in the expert testimony of medical causation.

To bridge the gap between medical causation and legal causation, courts have relaxed evidentiary requirements and now widely rely on epidemiological studies. These studies are used in many kinds of toxic tort claims, and have emerged as a necessity in toxic tort litigation. Epidemiology is the statistical study of incidence, prevalence and distribution of disease in human populations. Epidemiological studies examine high incidences of disease in a community and associate this disease rate with unusual exposures to environmental factors. They involve extensive use of mathematical and statistical measurements such as comparative ratios, distributions, means, standard deviations, quantiles and correlation coefficients. The studies explain the level of risk of injury that confronts a given community. They do not, however, suggest the level of risk facing the individual plaintiff. For example, they answer such questions as; "Does exposure to this chemical increase the incidence of cancer in the community?" Proponents contend that these studies often are the best, if not the only, proof of causation in toxic tort claims.

Despite their promise, these studies have limitations. First, they are purely statistical in nature and study only populations and not individuals. Second, they provide only correlations between exposure and injury and do not establish cause and effect relationships for the individual plaintiff. For example, they do not answer the question whether exposure to a given chemical caused the plaintiff's injuries. Last, and perhaps most important, there are serious doubts whether lay juries are capable of understanding this complex information and handling it in an informed and impartial manner. The jury's limitation is discussed below.

COMPLEX LITIGATION AND LAY JURIES

Mathematical models and such statistical concepts as comparative ratios, quantiles and correlation coefficients are the nuts and bolts of epidemiological studies. Ambiguities and competing health surveys and expert opinion are also inherent to these studies. However, the trier of fact is typically a jury—lay persons with no specialized background or training. The typical juror has, at best, a high school education. Therefore, the trier of fact is being asked to analyze very complex and technical statistical and medical evidence that is outside lay competence. It is believed that since lay juries lack the training and experience needed to independently assess this evidence, they often simply elect to ignore it. Instead, lay jurors look to their individual attitudes, beliefs and experiences for guidance. For example, many jurors are unable to comprehend the principle that exposure to a toxic chemical dosage of one part-per-billion produces a different biological effect than exposure to the same chemical at one part-per-million. Instead, their common sense leads them to believe that "a poison, is a poison, is a poison."

The morality issues associated with toxic torts also demonstrate how juries rely on their emotions and may disregard the medical and scientific evidence. Juries intuitively feel that it is wrong for chemicals to leach from a landfill into one's drinking water. It is immaterial that scientists cannot "prove" to the legal standard that the chemicals caused the plaintiff's injuries. For many, the fact that the plaintiff was exposed to a risk to which he or she did not consent is very troubling. As a result, they may rely on their sympathies and decide for the plaintiff, regardless of the scientific and medical evidence. Commenting on juries generally, the respected trial lawyer Louis Nizer has said, "Although juries are extraordinarily right in their conclusion, it is usually based upon common sense 'instincts' about right and wrong, and not on sophisticated evaluations of complicated testimony."

Toxic tort litigation is very complex and technical for additional reasons. The litigants need to account for their conduct during the long latency period and this results in reams of evidence. The jury then must digest hundreds of documents and thousands of pages of transcripts. In addition, typically, there are large numbers of litigants and the trial can take between six months to more than a year. A recent dioxin exposure case lasted more than four years.

DATA ON JURIES

There exists little data on jury performance. This stems, in part, from federal and local statutes designed to prevent jury tampering and maintain secrecy. The most extensive study in jury behavior was conducted by Harry Kalven, Jr. at the University of Chicago more than 20 years ago. The Kalven study found that in ordinary personal injury cases, judge and jury agreed on the liability question 79 per cent of the time. However, the study did not involve complex toxic tort suits, or such similar complex cases as antitrust or securities litigation. The study, however, is often cited by jury proponents to support their belief that juries perform as well as judges in deciding liability issues.

Judge Jack Weinstein of the U.S. District Court for the Eastern District of New York has expressed faith in the jury system in recent writings. He suggests that better control of the Federal Rules of Evidence can help make factfinding more accurate and improve jury performance.[52] Nevertheless, Judge Weinstein recognizes that mass tort actions involving delayed causation and injury, such as asbestos or environmental injury need special treatment. Noting that "compensation is delayed, expensive and erratic," Judge Weinstein has proposed a National Disaster Court. While the National Disaster Court seems aimed at procedural reforms, the proposal does underscore the belief that toxic torts is inherently different from other tort litigation.

TOXIC TORT COMPLEXITIES

Despite the sparse data on jury competence, federal courts have held that selected complex antitrust and securities suits are beyond the jury's capabilities. The juries were dismissed and bench trials were held. Each case relied on the Supreme Court's famous footnote ten in *Ross v. Berhard,* which said that courts may consider the "practical abilities and limitations of juries" to determine the "legal nature of an issue."

The courts cited the following reasons for concluding that the cases were too complex for juries: the presence of highly technical facts, huge

---

52. Weinstein, *The Role of the Court in Toxic Tort Litigation,* 73 Geo.L.J. 1389 (1985), *Preliminary Reflections on the* *Law's Reaction to Disasters,* 11 Colum.J.Envtl.L.1 (1986)

volumes of documentary evidence, numerous parties and claims, accountability of many years of conduct and the prospects that the trial would last many months or even years. These concerns are strikingly similar to toxic tort litigation. Therefore, certain toxic tort cases may also be considered too complex for the jury. Numerous commentators have questioned whether the jury is competent to evaluate the complex and technical evidence in toxic tort cases.

* * *

This section has argued that the complexities of toxic tort cases are of similar magnitude to antitrust and securities litigation, and thus are beyond the lay jury's "practical abilities and limitations." However, it is not suggested that in these instances that bench trials be conducted. The bench, while it has access to more resources than the jury, still has its own limitations. A judge may simply be no more qualified to understand and handle complex and technical litigation than a lay jury. Moreover, only a jury truly ensures that the community's values are reflected in the court's decision. However, a jury composed of particularly qualified persons could understand and evaluate complex concepts that may be beyond either a judge or lay jury.

SPECIALLY-QUALIFIED EXPERT JURIES

One alternative to lay juries is using "special" juries composed of individuals who are qualified experts in the fields of science and medicine. These "blue ribbon" juries would better understand the complex and technical concepts present in many toxic tort claims. They could evaluate the evidence in an impartial and competent manner, thereby increasing the likelihood of fair and logical decisions.

Special juries have strong historical support. Their use in civil trials in England during the seventeenth and eighteenth centuries is well documented.[63] Juries composed of "men of particular trades" were commonly used because "they might have a better knowledge of matters in difference which was to be tried, then [sic] others could who were not of the profession." Special juries included merchants, cooks, "fishmongers," booksellers and printers, clerks and attorneys.

In America, 16 states have expressly provided for special juries by statute. Some states have repealed these statutes and others have simply discontinued using special juries. A common test for invoking special juries was whether the facts of the case were "intricate and important" or "of exceptional difficulty or importance." Special juries have been used in such cases as a contested will involving over 135 witnesses and voluminous documentary evidence, a railroad company's reorganization and litigation involving stocks and bonds or banking institutions. They have not, however, been used in toxic tort cases.

---

63. Oldham, *supra* n.2, at 137, Luneburg and Nordenberg, *Specially Qualified Juries and Expert Non–Jury Tribunals: Alternatives for Coping with the Complexities* *of Modern Civil Litigation,* 67 Va.L.Rev. 887, 902 (1981), *citing* Thayer, *The Jury and Its Development,* 5 Harv.L.Rev. 295 (1892).

New York once employed a system of selecting jurors of above-average intelligence for complex cases. These jurors were selected on the basis of written answers to a juror questionnaire and an interview with a jury commissioner. During the personal interview the prospective juror gave testimony under oath pertaining to his qualifications and fitness for jury duty. (New York eventually repealed its special jury system in 1965, even though it was held constitutional by the Supreme Court.)

Even though special juries have been used in the United States, they provide little guidance for their proposed use in toxic tort cases. Many of the special juries were designed merely to attract persons of above-average intelligence and did not require that jurors be trained in the technical subject matter of the case. Further, the cases in which special juries were used are not as complex and difficult as today's antitrust, securities and toxic tort litigation.

Special Juries and the Constitution

The special jury can only be employed if it satisfies the Constitution's requirements for a jury trial. The Seventh Amendment and the due process clause of the Fifth and Fourteenth Amendments are the controlling standards.

The Seventh Amendment requires that in "suits in common law . . . the right of trial by jury shall be preserved." Beginning with Justice Story's 1812 circuit opinion in *United States v. Wonson,* courts have generally decided that the right to a jury trial is guaranteed in all those civil cases that would have gone to a jury under English practice in 1791.[75] Since special juries were part of English procedure by 1791 as shown above, they satisfy the Seventh Amendment's historical test.

The procedural due process issue raised by special juries centers around the litigants' right to an impartial and capable jury. To ensure this protection, the Supreme Court has ruled that a litigant is constitutionally entitled to a jury drawn from a cross-section of the community. The Court said:

> The American tradition of trial by jury . . . [is] an impartial jury drawn from a cross-section of the community. This does not mean, of course, that every jury must contain representatives of all the economic, social, religious, racial, political and geographical groups of the community . . .

See also Taylor v. Louisiana, where the Court stated that the jury need not be a mirror image of the community. The purpose of the cross-section requirement is to ensure that the constitutional standards of due process and equal protection are met.

The cross-section requirement is not a knockout punch for special juries for two reasons. First, the intent behind the cross-section require-

---

75. *The Case for Special Juries, supra* n.1, at 1160–61; *Comment, Complex Civil Litigation and the Seventh Amendment's* *Right to a Jury Trial,* 51 U.Chi.L.Rev. 581 (1984).

ment is distinguishable. The cases behind the cross-section requirement were concerned primarily with the discriminatory practice of excluding minorities and others for reasons unrelated to their capabilities as jurors. The Court believed that such discriminatory practices prevented impartial and rational proceedings. Special juries would not require the invidious discrimination of minorities and would be more closely aligned with the "constitutional ideals of fairness, competence, and impartiality than the traditional jury." Second, the cross-section standard itself can be limited by the state. The state may exclude from jury duty those individuals who are unable to perform the duties efficiently and intelligently. Similarly, the Federal Jury Selection and Service Act of 1968 disqualifies from jury duty persons who are: not United States citizens; unable to read, write, speak or understand English; charged with or convicted of a felony; and persons whose physical or mental disabilities make it impossible to provide satisfactory jury service. Further, despite the cross-section requirement, courts may require that juries be able "to decide the facts in an informed and capable manner." Courts have also indicated that there is a due process right to a competent and rational fact finder. Finally, recent court decisions have recognized that lay jurors may be incapable of deciding complex cases within the spirit of the due process clause. Therefore, special juries, as proposed below, do not present the kind of vice which the due process clause sought to remedy. Rather, they uphold the due process requirement for jury competence and therefore are a constitutional alternative to lay juries in complex litigation like toxic torts.

SPECIAL JURIES FOR TOXIC TORT CASES

Special juries raise concerns of elitism, bias and manipulation. These fears in part led to passage of the Federal Jury Selection and Service Act, which requires that jurors be "selected at random from a fair cross section of the community ..." In fact, a 1970 amendment specifically prohibited blue-ribbon or special juries. But, as shown above, the cross-section requirement was intended to eliminate the discriminatory practice of excluding persons for reasons unrelated to their abilities as jurors. Special juries, as proposed here, do not present this kind of vice. Therefore, this article suggests the Act be amended and allow the use of special juries in toxic tort litigation. Such an amendment has been proposed for complex antitrust and securities litigation by law commentators.

The special jury would be composed of experts within the medical and scientific professions. The first question which arises is from where will these expert jurors be selected. The pool of potential experts can be generated from consultations with such objective institutions as government agencies and research centers, scientific and medical societies, academia and retired persons from the business community. Second, what criteria would be used to generate this pool of potential jurors? It is unnecessary that the experts be trained in and intimately familiar with the legal and technical issues specific to each case. The pool, for example, should not be limited to only epidemiologists, persons trained in cancer research and pollution control experts. Rather, the pool would consist of individuals capable of understanding and assessing technical medical and scientific issues. They would be chosen from a broad spectrum of specialties. Further, since scientific decisionmaking is often based on consensus, a broad distribution of opinion from these fields is essential.

The final question, and perhaps the most important in light of the due process requirements, is how would the individual jurors be selected from this pool of experts? Two possible selection procedures are proposed. The least controversial approach is to retain most of the traditional features of jury selection. The experts would be contacted randomly from the pool. The opposing attorneys would also retain their power to examine the potential jurors and dismiss those not wanted.

A more ambitious selection procedure could be fashioned after a procedure commonly used to select arbitrators. Each side would nominate a person to select the panel, and the two would choose a third person. The three representatives would select jurors from the standing pool of qualified experts. To ensure objectivity, the judge could review the prospective panel for signs of bias, or other improper criteria such as race or gender discrimination.

Finally, and most importantly, it is emphasized that the special jury would function like a regular jury. Its powers and responsibilities would be no different from lay juries. Procedural and evidentiary rules governing both the trial and jury instructions would remain unchanged to every extent possible.

Once a new phenomenon, toxic tort litigation is growing and here to stay. Difficult and technical issues of law and fact typify this untraditional tort claim. Lay jurors are being asked to digest information that is beyond their reach. Alternatively, specially-qualified juries can provide a constitutional solution which ensures more competent, impartial and reasoned decisions.

KENNETH S. BORDENS & IRWIN A. HOROWITZ, MASS TORT CIVIL LITIGATION: THE IMPACT OF PROCEDURAL CHANGES ON JURY DECISIONS

73 Judicature 22 (June/July, 1989).

In an effort to help juries deal with complex cases, judges are using such innovations as bifurcation of trial issues and consolidation of plaintiffs. Recent research suggests that such techniques, when compared to traditional trial formats, may alter outcomes.

In the past decade we have witnessed a fundamental change in the type of civil case that courts must manage and resolve. The frequency and number of lawsuits filed to redress injuries caused by a product or agent manufactured on a national level has increased dramatically.

Many of these cases involve claims for similar injuries among many thousands of plaintiffs and include a variety of insidious diseases that are carcinogenic, mutagenic or teratogenic in nature. These cases have posed an unprecedented challenge for the tort system.

This expansion of products liability litigation is now a common theme and need not be catalogued. Trials dealing with products such as Bendectin, formaldehyde or groundwater pollutants frequently involve multiple plaintiffs and defendants, as well as multiple forums. The litigation is complex, the victims many and the total losses are unprecedented. Given the inherent complexity of the modern mass tort case, it is not surprising to find that many commentators have expressed concern about the civil jury's ability to adjudicate complex cases. These concerns, however, have not resulted in empirical answers to the many questions raised about the competence of civil juries. Most attempts at answering questions surrounding the civil jury have been anecdotal and speculative. In this article, we will report the results of a series of experimental studies concerning the performance of juries in mass tort cases.

Mass tort cases pose problems for the judicial system in at least two intertwined areas: case management and jury competence. The first problem centers on how to deal with cases involving many plaintiffs, defendants and trial issues. The second problem addresses the ability of the lay jury to comprehend the many issues presented in a mass tort case and reach a fair, just verdict. Ideally, a case management procedure is identified that enhances the ability of the jury to comprehend the evidence.

* * *

Cognitive Problems

As cognitive social psychologists, we were particularly concerned with the abilities of jurors to deal with complex information in the contexts of these procedural changes. We know from other contexts that jurors have difficulty in keeping related issues separate for the purposes of decisionmaking. For example, when multiple criminal offenses are joined for trial, despite explicit instructions to keep the evidence separate and distinct for each offense and to deliver a separate and independent verdict on each, jurors are unable to follow these instructions.

Jurors do not keep these issues separate because they may make the perfectly rational decision that multiple charges suggest that the defendant has a "criminal personality" and it is illogical to disregard this pattern of behavior. There is more involved, however. Jurors simply do not have the cognitive ability to keep such evidence separate. They tend to confuse evidence and when asked to recall the facts, jurors make a large number of "intrusive errors," recalling evidence pertaining to one charge when it properly related to another offense.

While the research on criminal joinder may argue for separation of trial issues in the context of a complex trial, other research suggests that decisionmakers need the entire fabric of the evidence to come to a decision. Pennington and Hastie have recently indicated that jurors' explanations of legal evidence in complex criminal trials take the form of a coherent narrative or story in which intentional and causal interrelationships among the episodes of the story are prominent. Pennington and Hastie suggest that more than one story will be considered by the jurors as an explanatory narrative, but the story with the greatest coherence (completeness, consistency and plausibility) will be accepted. If more than one coherent narrative is generated, uncertainty will result.

This explanation-based model of decisionmaking suggests that jurors process evidence as a narrative organization of the trial data in which causal and intentional relations are informed by the availability of experiences in their lives which may help jurors "explain" the trial scenario. The more complex the trial and the more foreign the trial facts are to the jurors' everyday experiences, the less likely jurors will have available a scenario that will satisfactorily capture the theme of the case. Separation of trial issues would make it most difficult to establish the kind of narrative that jurors commonly use to decide complex cases. Jurors may then be left to devices that may have less logic than the story narratives they usually utilize.

EMPIRICAL RESEARCH

To date, researchers have not paid much research attention to the problems facing civil courts. Instead, the bulk of research in psychology and law has focused on criminal trials. We have, however, recently completed two experiments that put to test the validity of procedural changes in mass tort civil litigation.

In our first jury simulation experiment [14] we investigated the impact the size of the plaintiff population and the presence or absence of a severely injured plaintiff (outlier) on jury decisionmaking.

The major objectives of this first experiment were:

- To compare the juries' decisions when given different information as to the size of non-trial plaintiff population of which the trial plaintiffs were representatives ("bellwethers"). Three levels of information were given: Juries were told that the trial plaintiffs (there were four) represented 26 other victims, hundreds of others or were not given any information as to the population of non-trial victims.

- To ascertain the impact of a plaintiff whose injuries are significantly more severe (an outlier) than the others. Some juries, therefore, heard a trial which included an outlier while others did not.

14. Horowitz & Bordens, *The Effects of Outlier Presence, Plaintiff Population Size, and Aggregation of Plaintiffs on Stimulated* *Jury Decisions,* 12 L. & Human Behavior 209–29 (1988).

- To determine the effect of consolidating plaintiffs for trial as compared to having a separate trial for each plaintiff.

Sixty-six juries, each consisting of six persons, listened to a four-hour toxic tort trial [16] in which either one or four plaintiffs were presented in the trial. All jurors in this research program were drawn from the jury rolls and were paid for their services. The jurors were brought to a moot courtroom for the experimental sessions.

The 66 juries were randomly assigned to the experimental conditions. Juries that heard a trial involving four (trial) plaintiffs were told that these individuals were representative of other people who had similar claims against the defendant. That is, juries were informed by the trial judge that the four were representative ("bellwethers") of 26 other plaintiffs, (or) hundreds of others or provided with no information about the size of the non-trial plaintiff population. The juries that heard the trial containing only one plaintiff were not given any information about the non-trial plaintiff population.

One-half of these juries heard a case that involved a plaintiff (the outlier) who had very severe injuries (liver cancer), whereas the remainder were exposed to the same plaintiff with less severe injuries. Therefore, half of the juries that heard a trial containing four plaintiffs confronted a situation in which one of the plaintiffs sustained injuries substantially more severe than the remaining three parties. The other juries confronted four individuals who had injuries similar in severity. Each of the four plaintiffs went through an individual trial (before separate juries) without the three other parties.

The design of this experiment allowed us to determine the effects of consolidation of plaintiffs by comparing verdicts from conditions in which one or four plaintiffs were presented (the outcome for each plaintiff tried individually was compared with the results of the consolidated trial), the impact of size of the plaintiff population that the bellwether plaintiffs represented and the impact of the presence or absence of an outlier plaintiff.

The mock juries provided decisions, after deliberation, on the four general issues adjudicated in mass tort civil cases: general causation (a yes/no verdict), liability (a yes/no verdict), compensatory damages and punitive damages (both in dollars). In addition, juries completed measures indicating how much the plaintiffs were responsible for their own injuries and rated the credibility and importance of each trial witness.

The most interesting result of this first study was that the punitive damages awarded to the plaintiffs were significantly affected by the size of the plaintiff population and the presence of an outlier. Figure 1

---

16. The mock trial was based upon an actual mass tort trial, Wilhoit v. Olin Corp. (No. CV–83–5021 NE)(N.D.Ala.1985). Professional actors played the various roles. The mock juries heard an audiotape of the trial, and a coordinated slide show presented photographs of each of the 14 expert witnesses, four plaintiffs, two lawyers and the judge. All of our experiments were conducted in a moot courtroom of a college of law.

shows the average amount of money awarded as punitive damages as a function of plaintiff population size and outlier presence for each individual plaintiff. The connected points show the data for plaintiffs when they were aggregated with the other plaintiffs (consolidated trial), whereas the disconnected points the data for the disaggregated individual plaintiffs (on the "No Outlier Present" graph, the means for both Lamont and Bessant are represented by the filled circle because the means were so close to one another).

Figure 1

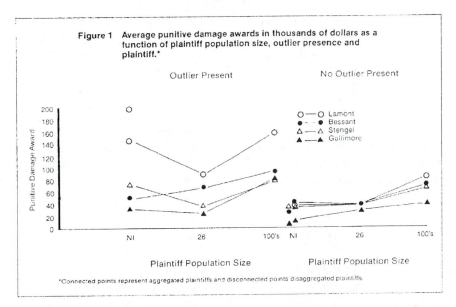

The findings with respect to the overall effect of consolidating plaintiffs show that the outlier, the plaintiff with the most severe injuries, received higher awards in the context of an individual trial. The outlier tended to pull up the awards of the less severely injured. The plaintiff who had the weakest case was best served by being yoked to an outlier. Jurors reported that the severity of the outlier's injuries suggested that all the plaintiffs would eventually share that fate.

When we evaluated the juries' assignment of fault, we found that as the size of the non-trial plaintiff population increased, so did the amount of responsibility assigned to the defendant. Hence, as the number of (non-trial) plaintiffs represented by those plaintiffs presented at trial increased, juries were more likely to blame the defendant for the injuries. In turn, we found that the increased blame that was attached to the defendant was significantly and positively related to the size of the damage award made to the plaintiffs.

Finally, there was a rather significant amount of inter-jury disagreement. Juries exposed to precisely the same evidence and experimental manipulations rendered highly divergent decisions. In some of the experimental conditions, the range of punitive damage awards, for example, was from zero to $500,000 for individual plaintiffs. The monetary awards in this latent injury case tended to be erratic.

Taken together, the results from our first experiment suggest that creative case management techniques centered around consolidating plaintiffs significantly affect the outcome of this trial. The presence of the outlier augments the amount of money awarded to the other plaintiffs, especially the plaintiff with the weakest case.

Additionally, the use of "bellwether" plaintiffs at trial to represent larger groups of plaintiffs also appeared to have a substantial impact. When the jury was informed that other plaintiffs existed, the defendant was seen as responsible for the plaintiffs' injuries significantly more than if the jury believed that the only plaintiffs involved were the ones presented at trial.

BIFURCATION

The second experiment explored the impact of separating issues for purposes of the trial. We wanted to study the impact of this case management technique on both the outcome of trials and the process by which juries reached decisions.

Our strategy was to design a study in which we compared the performance of juries in trials in which, as is customary, all issues are presented in a single unitary setting, to the performance of juries that dealt with the trial issues in a contingent, separated manner.

One-half of the 128 six-person juries listened to the four-hour trial and then decided each of the four trial issues (unitary trial). The remaining juries heard the same trial with the issues bifurcated or trifurcated according to Rule 42A (separated trial). Within each trial type (unitary v. separated), half of the juries heard general causation evidence first while the remaining juries heard liability evidence first.

As in the first study, juries deliberated to verdicts on general causation and liability, and assigned dollar awards for compensatory and punitive damages (depending on the trial condition to which they were assigned).

The results showed that significantly more liability verdicts against the defendant occurred in the unitary trial condition (100 per cent) than in the separated trial condition (72 per cent). The distribution of liability verdicts across conditions is shown in Table 1. Also, when liability was judged before causation, fewer juries found the defendant liable (83 per cent) than if liability was judged after causation (97 per cent). Additionally, there was an effect of trial type on general causation verdicts. More juries in the unitary trial condition (85.7 per cent) found in favor of the plaintiffs than in the separated trial condition (56.5 per cent). The distribution of general causation verdicts is shown in Table 2.

Table 1
Liability verdicts for bifurcation experiment

	Number of decisions			
Order of decisions	4	3	2	1
Unitary trial				
Liability first	8(8)	8(8)	8(8)	8(8)
Causation first	7(7)	7(7)	6(6)	NA
Separated trial				
Liability first	5(8)	5(8)	6(8)	5(8)
Causation first	3(3)	3(4)	4(4)	NA

Note. Numbers in parentheses indicate the number of juries in each condition which decided on the issue of liability. Some juries did not decide liability because a previous decision went against the plaintiffs.

Table 2
Causation verdicts for bifurcation experiment

	Number of decisions			
Order of decisions	4	3	2	1
Unitary trial				
Liability first	7(8)	8(8)	6(8)	NA
Causation first	7(8)	7(8)	6(8)	7(8)
Separated trial				
Liability first	4(5)	4(5)	5(5)	NA
Causation first	3(8)	4(8)	4(8)	2(7)

Note. Numbers in parentheses indicate the number of juries in each condition which decided on the issue of causation. Some juries did not decide causation because a previous decision went against the plaintiffs.

We also found that compensatory damages were affected by bifurcation of trial issues. These results are displayed in Figure 2. An examination of the average compensatory damages award for those juries that found in favor of the plaintiffs shows that damages awarded to the plaintiffs were lower in the unitary trial (M = 275.8)[19] than in the separated trial (M = 458.62). Additionally, when three decisions were required, the average compensatory damage award was higher when trial issues were separated than if unified.

When we evaluated the assignment of responsibility to the defendant and plaintiffs, we found that, overall, more responsibility was assigned to the plaintiffs in the separated trial condition than in the unitary trial condition when the juries find for the defendant. Finally, as we reported above, there was a high degree of interjury inconsistency. Once again, the range of awards made by juries exposed to identical evidence varied widely. There was, however, a high degree of intrajury consistency in terms of the dollar awards made to each of the four

19. All means represent thousands of dollars.

Figure 2

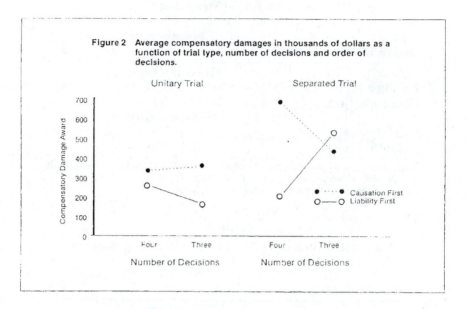

Figure 2   Average compensatory damages in thousands of dollars as a function of trial type, number of decisions and order of decisions.

plaintiffs presented at trial. Evidently, once a jury decides to award one plaintiff a given amount, it followed suit for the other plaintiffs. Juries tended to treat the four plaintiffs alike with respect to awards.

Once again, our results show that procedural innovations, driven by the complexities of the modern tort trial, significantly affect the outcome of those trials. The "traditional" unitary trial yields significantly more liability verdicts favoring the plaintiffs. The plaintiffs, however, suffer to an extent when issues are separated.

A second consequence of bifurcation is that if the jury does find for the plaintiffs in the separated trial, the compensatory damage award to the plaintiffs is higher than the damages awarded by juries in the unitary trial.

Manipulating the order in which general causation and liability are presented also significantly influenced the juries' decisions. When juries were asked to consider evidence [20] concerning general causation, they were less likely to decide for the plaintiffs than if liability was considered first. If juries evaluated liability before causation, the data indicate more pro-plaintiff decisions (substance X causes harm Y) than if causation is judged first.

It appeared that in the evidentiary configuration of this mock trial, in which the evidence for general causation was the most difficult and ambiguous, the juries' evaluation of this issue was the critical determi-

20. All evidence for each of the four trial issues was carefully calibrated. The evidence for all issues except general causa- tion was rated as "somewhat ambiguous," general causation evidence was rated as moderate to high in ambiguity.

nant of the fate of the remaining trial issues. Once juries passed the evidentiary threshold on general causation, they were highly likely to find the defendant liable for damages. There appeared to be a cascading effect. Once a difficult decision is rendered against the defendant, subsequent anti-defendant decisions are more easily made.

While we are now in the process of analyzing the audiotapes made during the jury deliberations, one observation concerning the differences between unitary and separated trial juries may be made: unitary trial juries do tend to use some version of the Pennington and Hastie story model to decide the issues. They utilize all the trial evidence while deciding each individual trial issue. Indeed, the initial analysis of the deliberations indicate that unitary trial juries often do not decide liability or causation until they hear evidence concerning damages.

Juries in separated trials appear to employ other, perhaps less sophisticated, heuristics to decide the issues. These latter juries tend to use more extreme heuristics: corporate-capitalist versus the little guy; good guy versus bad guy rhetoric dominates these deliberations. The bifurcation of general causation in the separated trial condition produces greater disbelief about causation yielding fewer verdicts for the plaintiffs. It may be that only more extreme pro-plaintiff juries who appeal to the good guy-bad guy rhetoric remain in the separated trial condition to vote for the plaintiffs. This is because the evidence for general causation, heard without the context of the other trial issues, is most ambiguous. Therefore, only the very strongly pro-plaintiff juries remain. These more "extreme" juries in turn give higher awards to the plaintiffs than the larger sample of unitary trial juries that decided for the plaintiffs.

As in our previous study, we found that there was a significant amount of interjury disagreement, even when juries heard the same evidence under the same trial conditions. These data suggest that in a representative complex tort case in which the evidence is high in volume and technically difficult to comprehend, unpredictable verdicts emerge. There was, once again, however, considerable intrajury consistency. Once a jury sets on a course of action for one plaintiff they follow suit for any other plaintiffs included in the action.

Tentative Conclusions

The experimental studies we have carried out over the past three years suggest that several of the procedural techniques used to manage mass tort cases alter the outcomes when compared to the traditional unitary trial format. In addition, the consolidation of plaintiffs for trial purposes yields outcomes that differ from those obtained when each individual received a separate trial.

Additional evidence from other research venues is needed at this point to add support to these findings. For example, systematic field research exploring juror reactions to different types of trials (consolidated, bifurcated, etc.) would help reinforce our findings. While the two studies described in this paper utilized 194 juries, the research employed one mass toxic tort trial that may not be entirely representative of such cases. Additionally, further research is needed to delineate the cognitive processes jurors and juries use when processing evidence from complex trials.

Comments with respect to the competence of the juries must be quite indefinite. The extant empirical data are, at this point, relatively tentative. What is certainly clear from our research is that the task facing the juror and jury in a mass tort trial is formidable. Large quantities of technically complex and often ambiguous information must be processed effectively. Unfortunately, juries have a great deal of difficulty comprehending complex trial evidence and also have difficulty compartmentalizing evidence from the different trial issues. The net effect is that evidence for one trial issue contaminates the judgment of the other trial issues.

The difficulty is that these Rule 42 procedures appear to alter the outcomes and may affect both the perception and reality of justice. Furthermore, use of Rule 42 assumes that causation and liability can be separated logically and cognitively. There is a danger of uncritical acceptance of bifurcation or trifurcation in all types of complex cases. Further research is needed to specify the kinds of evidentiary dimensions that make bifurcation a viable logical and psychological option.

In the first study, the juries quite rationally concluded that when a great many people claimed injuries the defendant was more likely to have been culpable. This effect only occurred, however, when juries were informed that at least hundreds of individuals were involved.

In the second study involving the separation of trial issues, juries not unreasonably used all the trial evidence to decide liability, causation and damages. The variability we observed in the decision-making of the juries resided primarily in the assignment of damages, the ultimate "black box" of the tort trial. Juries, by and large, were consistent within the various experimental contexts—number of plaintiffs, separated versus unitary trials, *etc.*—with respect to liability and general causation decisions. It seems to us that a careful reading of our data thus far suggests that juries, given the complexities of the trial evidence and the cognitive limits of people, performed relatively competently and rationally. This is not to say that these jurors understood most of the issues or could accurately recall the majority of the evidence. Our data thus far suggest that they cannot. It must be noted that judges are likely to be just as prone as jurors to the same cognitive infirmities.

It is likely however, that as the interest in the civil jury increases, we will soon have a better sense of what precisely makes evidence difficult to comprehend and to use in decisionmaking. It may then be possible to enhance the performance of the civil jury.

Notes and Questions

1. Molly Selvin and Larry Pincus of RAND, the Institute for Civil Justice, conducted one of the few empirical studies of jury competence in a

mass tort trial. See Molly Selvin & Larry Pincus, *The Debate Over Jury Performance: Observations From a Recent Asbestos Case* (RAND, The Institute for Civil Justice 1987). The trial they studied was *Charles Newman v. Johns–Manville* (E.D.Tex.1984) involving four plaintiffs suing ten asbestos manufacturers. After one day of deliberation, the jury found each defendant liable for the plaintiffs' injuries and awarded the plaintiffs $3.9 million in compensatory damages and $4 million in punitive damages. The *Newman* case was part of a larger consolidation of thirty asbestos cases, of which Judge Robert M. Parker had selected four claimants to be tried first. Judge Parker's goal was that verdicts in the first group would induce the defendants to settle the remaining claims, which the defendants subsequently did. *See id.* at 3–4.

Selvin and Pincus interviewed the jurors two months after the trial. Among other points, they learned that (1) the jury's recollection of specific scientific and medical facts, as well as their understanding of the medical issues, contained several errors; (2) the jurors formed opinions as to the merits of witness testimony based more on perceptions of personality and behavior, rather than the substance of the witness's testimony; (3) the jurors were skeptical and negatively disposed to many of the medical experts; (4) the jurors reacted negatively to the plaintiff's lawyers attempts to draw sympathy to the individual defendants; (5) the jurors reacted negatively to the number and tactics of the defense attorneys; (6) the jurors began their deliberations with a tentative belief that asbestos manufacturers had ignored the results of scientific research demonstrating the hazards of asbestos exposure; and (7) that the jurors had difficulty in at least three instances remembering and following the judge's instructions. *See id.* at 24–35

In the concluding portions of their study, Selvin and Pincus observe:

> Although complaints about the performance of lay juries are as old as the Republic itself, the increasing incidence of toxic tort and other types of complex litigation has prompted a resurgence of criticism of the jury system. Our review of the *Newman* trial and deliberation and our previous research on the processing of claims * * * indicate that asbestos litigation in particular and toxic tort litigation more generally may present special challenges to juries. Moreover, rather than diminishing, the number of toxic tort cases—involving a growing number of substances—is multiplying. Estimates of the number of current and future claims for damages resulting from the removal of asbestos from public and private buildings, the use of the Dalkon Shield, and from exposure to DES, Bendectin, and a host of other potentially toxic agents threaten to dwarf the number of asbestos cases already filed.

* * *

> * * * Much of the debate over the performance of juries in complex civil cases centers not just on the outcomes of deliberations but rather on those outcomes as a function of the process of deliberation. Criticism that the size of a jury's damage award is "too high" or "too low" is often criticism of the process of understanding and decisionmaking that led the jury to a finding of liability and a calculation of damages. Yet the standards we have reviewed focus on outcome alone—the amount of compensation awarded, the extent to which the outcome reflects or

deviates from both public opinion and the judge's instructions, or the extent to which the jury verdict is consistent with a judge's probable decision in that same case. The courts have rendered few affirmative edicts regarding the process of jury deliberation, instead examining issues that precede deliberation itself—including jury representation, jury selection, juror impartiality, and how and when a case can be taken away from a jury.

Problems of measurement abound in the discussion of any criteria against which to gauge jury performance. How do we measure whether the *Newman* jury's deliberation of the evidence was "fair and reasonable" as the Third Circuit dictated in the *Japanese Electronics* case? Judicial decisions are not generally instructive on this issue; and some existing empirical research, such as that comparing jury decisions with those of a "judge-baseline," is methodologically flawed.

Without consensus as to the criteria by which we assess or compare jury verdicts the debate over jury performance will continue. Some observers call for greater restrictions on the right to jury trial, including perhaps the use of panels of "neutral" or scientific experts in cases arising from exposure to toxic substances, or the removal of these claims from the tort system altogether * * * Others have criticized judges for withholding particular issues in toxic tort cases from juries and advocate providing additional assistance to jurors, particularly in the deliberation of complex cases, rather than imposing further restrictions on the right to jury trial. * * *

The adoption of any particular plan devised to address the perceived deficiencies of the existing jury system implies we have reached some broader societal consensus about "standards." We found no evidence for such consensus.

Id. at 63–65.

2. Recall that most federal courts will uphold bifurcated and trifurcated trial plans as against litigant challenges based on alleged due process and Seventh Amendment violations. *See* Ch. IV. A, *supra.* What weight, if any, should courts give to such empirical studies of the impact of trial procedure as the Bordens and Horowitz study? Does that study make you rethink the legal issues and conclusions relating to polyfurcated trial procedure?

3. For discussions of the problems of jury competence in mass tort litigation and complex litigation generally, *see* JOE S. CECIL, ET AL., JURY SERVICE IN LENGTHY CIVIL TRIALS (Washington D.C.: Federal Judicial Center 1987); Committee on Federal Courts of the New York State Bar Association, *Improving Jury Comprehension in Complex Civil Litigation,* 62 St. John's L.Rev. 549 (1988); Charles W. Fournier, Note, *The Case for Special Juries in Complex Litigation,* 89 Yale L.J. 1155 (1980); Douglas King, Comment, *Complex Civil Litigation and the Seventh Amendment Right to a Jury Trial,* 51 U.Chi.L.Rev. 581 (1984); Richard O. Lempert, *Civil Juries and Complex Cases: Let's Not Rush to Judgment,* 80 Mich.L.Rev. 68 (1981); Lisa S. Meyer, Note, *Taking the "Complexity" Out of Complex Litigation: Preserving the Constitutional Right to a Civil Jury Trial,* 28 Val.U.L.Rev. 337 (1993); William V. Nordenberg & Mark A. Nordenberg, *Specially Qualified Juries and Expert Non Jury Tribunals: Alternatives to Coping with the*

Complexities of Modern Civil Litigation, 67 Va.L.Rev. 887 (1981); Note, *The Right to Jury Trial in Complex Civil Litigation*, 92 Harv.L.Rev. 898 (1979). *Cf.* Patrick Devlin, *Equity, Due Process, and the Seventh Amendment: A Commentary on the* Zenith Case, 81 Mich. L. Rev. 1571 (1983).

F. JURY INSTRUCTIONS AND SPECIAL VERDICTS

Review *Hardy v. Johns–Manville* at Chapter II, section F.2, *supra*.

MOLLY SELVIN & LARRY PINCUS, THE DEBATE OVER JURY PERFORMANCE—OBSERVATIONS FROM A RECENT ASBESTOS CASE

(RAND, The Institute for Civil Justice 1987) at 12, 19–21, 35, 80–85, 93.

* * *

At the beginning of the trial (*see Charles Newman v. Johns–Manville*), Judge Parker gave each juror a notebook containing a list of all the asbestos products manufactured by each of the defendants and the dates of manufacture. In addition, the notebook contained copies of the warnings defendants placed on the products and the dates these warnings were first used.[12] Judge Parker allowed the jurors to use the notebooks for reference both during the trial and in their deliberations. Judge Parker also allowed the jurors to take notes during the trial.

* * *

JUDGE PARKER'S INSTRUCTIONS TO THE JURY

The judge took over an hour to instruct the jury. He repeated his earlier instruction that the jurors were to use the preponderance of the evidence as the standard in determining whether an allegation had been proven. He defined this standard as "whether it's more likely so than not. In other words, * * * such evidence when compared and considered, compared with the evidence against it produces in your minds that what is sought to be true is more likely true than not true, tipping of the scales, one way or the other." * * *

Judge Parker then told the jury that under Texas products liability law, it is the duty and responsibility of the manufacturer to inform and warn users of the dangers of using their product. He amplified his pretrial discussion of warnings, advising the jury that in deciding whether a warning is necessary, the manufacturer is assumed to have the "knowledge and skill level of an expert, which means at a minimum the manufacturer must keep abreast of the relative, technical and scientific knowledge, discoveries and advances relating to the product." In addition, if a warning is determined to be necessary, it must be timely,

---

12. The judge's staff prepared these notebooks from the defendants' answers to interrogatories before the trial. Each defendant had an opportunity before distribution to correct information in the notebook.

sufficiently emphatic to convey a fair indication of the danger or risk involved in use of the product, and it must be "conspicuous, comprehensible and understandable to the mind of the average user and reasonably calculated to reach those likely to use the product[.]" * * *

The judge then told the jury that if they found for the plaintiffs, they would be asked to rule on the question of assumption of risk. If they determined that the plaintiffs should have known about the dangers of working with asbestos, they could reduce the award by an appropriate percentage.

At this point, Judge Parker handed out four verdict forms; the jurors were asked to decide:

- **Question 1:** Whether any of the products manufactured by two of the defendants, Raymark and Celotex, was "an asbestos-containing insulation product capable of producing dust containing asbestos fibers sufficient to cause harm in its application, use or removal.[23]

- **Question 2:** Whether any of the defendants' manufactured products were defective as marketed and unreasonably dangerous because of the manufacturer's failure to provide adequate warnings. The verdict form provided a definition of adequate warnings and allowed the jury to decide either that all of the defendants' products were defective or than only the products of certain manufacturers were defective in this manner.

- **Question 3:** From the preponderance of the evidence, the date upon which each defendant knew or should have known that insulators were at risk of contracting an asbestos-related injury or disease from the application, use, or removal of asbestos-containing products.

- **Question 4:** From the preponderance of the evidence, what date the manufacturers knew or should have known that household members of insulation workers were at risk of contracting an asbestos-related disease.

Finally, the judge discussed the components of the damages awards. If the jury found the defendants liable, it could award compensatory damages for past and future lost income, future medical expenses, pain and suffering of the plaintiff, and loss of consortium for Mrs. Newman and Mrs. Goodson. The judge specifically instructed the jurors not to award damages for past medical expenses because the plaintiffs had made no claim for nor introduced evidence as to those expenses but allowed them to award compensation for future medical expenses. * * * The judge also described the standard of proof that the jury was to use in deciding whether to award punitive damages. "The Plaintiff must prove

---

23. This question resulted from the disagreement between plaintiff and defense attorneys as to whether these products, which the manufacturers claimed were textiles products and not insulation products, caused a level of dust sufficient to be a hazard to insulators.

that the Defendant demonstrated a conscious indifference to the rights of insulators ... in a callous and intentional, reckless disregard for their well-being." * * * Judge Parker also told the jury that if they decided to award punitive damages, there must be a reasonable relationship between the actual and punitive damages awarded.[26]

* * *

DEVIATIONS FROM THE LAW

The *Newman* jurors had difficulty in three instances remembering and following the judge's instructions. They applied evidence incorrectly, awarded compensation for expenses they were not supposed to consider, and considered extralegal factors in determining liability and punitive awards. The jurors did not have a copy of the judge's instructions during deliberation; however, they did receive additional oral instructions from him on the issue of punitive damages.

The *Newman* jury applied crucial documentary evidence incorrectly in determining whether to award punitive damages. Judge Parker specifically instructed the jury to consider the evidence presented against each of the four defendants only with regard to the punitive damages claim against that defendant. * * * Yet the jurors told us that they considered the Summer Simpson papers, which were only to be used as evidence against Owens–Illinois, to be the most important pieces of evidence against Raymark, and the Saranac Lake report, which was only to be used as evidence against Owens–Illinois, to be the most important pieces of evidence in determining that all ten defendants were liable for damages to the plaintiffs.

The *Newman* jurors also deviated from the language and intent of Judge Parker's instructions in their compensatory awards. They awarded legal fees to each plaintiff as part of the compensatory damage award. In general, juries are not supposed to consider legal fees in determining an award and judges frequently instruct juries specifically not to consider them. * * * Although Judge Parker's instructions are silent on the subject of legal fees, he instructed the jury to "consider the following elements of damage and none other." Judge Parker then specified the permissible components of the jury's compensatory award. * * * The *Newman* jury also awarded each of the plaintiffs compensation for past medical expenses * * * even though Judge Parker specifically instructed them to award future but not past medical expenses.

Finally, in determining Flotte's award, they considered extralegal factors such as his ethnicity.

* * *

---

26. Judge Parker said, "exactly what the relationship is * * * will be * * * exclusively for you to determine * * * The general requirement is that punitive damages must not so greatly exceed the actual damages as to indicate * * * that the Jury has been guided by passion or prejudice rather than by reason." * * *

Notes and Questions

1. *Newman v. Raymark Industries* was tried subsequent to the Fifth Circuit's decision in *Hardy v. Johns–Manville.* In what ways do Judge Parker's special verdict forms and jury instructions attempt to deal with the problems identified in *Hardy?* How useful or successful are special verdict forms in light of Selvin and Pincus's observations drawn from their study of the *Newman* deliberations? Are there any other possible corrective or ameliorative measures a judge might take in order to avoid the problems identified by the Fifth Circuit in *Hardy?*

2. Judge Parker and other federal judges have continued to utilize jury notebooks, interim argument, detailed jury instructions and special verdict forms to assist jury comprehension and deliberation in complex mass tort litigation. *See generally* Linda S. Mullenix, *Beyond Consolidation: Post-Aggregative Procedure in Asbestos Mass Tort Litigation,* 32 Wm. & Mary L.Rev. 475, 565–68 (1991); Robert M. Parker, *Streamlining Complex Cases,* 10 Rev.Litig. 547 (1991). *See also* Larry Heuer & Stephen Penrod, *Increasing Jurors' Participation in Trials: A Field Experiment with Jury Notetaking and Question Asking,* 12 L. & Hum.Behav. 231 (1988).

3. Annother innovative method for dealing with complex litigation is through the use of the summary jury trial. Does the summary jury trial offer a possible alternative method for resolving mass tort litigation? *See generally* Thomas D. Lambros, *The Summary Jury Trial and Other Alternative Methods of Dispute Resolution: A Report to the Judicial Conference of the United States Committee on the Operation of the Jury System,* 103 F.R.D. 461 (1984); Thomas D. Lambros & Thomas H. Shunk, *The Summary Jury Trial,* 29 Clev. St. L. Rev. 43 (1980); *but cf.* Richard A. Posner, *The Summary Jury Trial and Other Methods of Alternative Dispute Resolution: Some Cautionary Observations,* 53 U. Chi. L. Rev. 366 (1986); Charles F. Webber, *Mandatory Summary Jury Trials: Playing by the Rules?,* 56 U. Chi. L. Rev. 1495 (1989).

G. ATTORNEY'S FEES

RICHARD B. SOBOL, BENDING THE LAW: THE STORY OF THE DALKON SHIELD BANKRUPTCY

(University of Chicago Press 1991) at 111–112, 266, 267–268.

Shortly after his appointment [as legal representative of future tort claimants] [Stanley K.] Joynes took steps to obtain expert assistance. Seeing that all the other parties in the case were represented by teams of bankruptcy experts from major law firms, Joynes contacted Vern Countryman, a professor at the Harvard Law School who is widely recognized as one of this country's leading experts and writers in the field of bankruptcy law. Because of his interest in the issue, Countryman agreed to serve as special bankruptcy counsel to Joynes. On May 1, 1986, Joynes filed an application for approval of his retention of Countryman, reciting Countryman's credentials and stating that Countryman would assist him "with the issue of the Future Tort Claimants' due process rights and the related issues of whether the Future Tort Claimants are 'creditors' and hold 'claims' within the intendment of the Bankruptcy Code."

In his application, Joynes explained that Countryman had agreed to work at a rate of $125 per hour, or whatever lower amount might be set by the court. This is extraordinarily low; large law firms charge more for first-year associates. And, because Countryman would work as an individual and not part of a law firm with partners, associates, law clerks, and paralegals to involve in the project, his fees for the entire case probably would not have amounted to $50,000.

Joynes's application was quickly denied in an order signed by Judge Shelley. The order stated:

> It appears to the Court that Joynes and other members of his firm ... are lawyers, duly qualified and admitted to practice in this Court and have appeared in this case and that sufficient cause has not been demonstrated to justify this Court authorizing additional counsel, and it further appears that said Future Tort Claimants are currently represented by counsel and there may be a substantial likelihood of unnecessary duplication of effort and expense.

The court's power of the purse is an unusual feature of bankruptcy proceedings. Particularly in a large, complicated case, it enables the court to decide who participates, what issues are raised, and what expenses can be incurred. In the Robins bankruptcy, the court's concern over "unnecessary duplication of effort and expense" did not prevent Robins from retaining one of the largest law firms in the United States, in addition to a major Richmond law firm. During certain months, more than twenty-five lawyers in the two firms did work for Robins, generating bills for the month of several hundred thousand dollars. Ultimately, counsel and other professionals (investment advisers and accountants) for Robins alone would be paid fees and expenses in excess of $28 million. Additional millions were spent on counsel and other professionals for the equity committee, an official committee composed of large Robins shareholders outside the Robins family whose interest in minimizing liability to women injured by the Dalkon Shield was the same as that of the company. Yet cost was cited as the ground to prevent Joynes from consulting with Professor Countryman.

* * *

Judge Merhige issued his opinion approving the *Breland* settlement on July 26, 1988, the day after he issued his decision confirming the plan of reorganization. * * *

* * * In the *Breland* settlement, Aetna had agreed to pay attorney fees to Friedberg and his colleagues, above the consideration for the settlement, in the amount "awarded by order of the Court." The settlement agreement provided that "[i]n advance of the hearing at which final approval by the Court of the Settlement is sought * * *

plaintiffs shall file petitions for allowance of their litigation expenses, including attorneys' fees and costs."

Friedberg did not file such a petition in advance of the fairness hearing. On June 20, 1988, when he told Joe McDowell that he would not produce the documents showing how much time he and his colleagues had expended in the litigation, because they "are available only in raw form," Friedberg added, "Since counsel anticipates a separate hearing on the issue of counsel fees in the event that this settlement is approved, those will be available prior to such hearing."

At the fairness hearing, John Harkins explained Aetna's position on Friedberg's fees:

> McDowell: Now, who is going to pay the Friedberg group's legal fee * * *?

> Harkins: Aetna will pay such amount as Judge Mehrige orders, if anything. And that was one of the things I learned in class actions long ago. Don't bargain on a fee because I believe there is a conflict. What you do is say, we will settle this case and let the judge decide what the fee is. We simply said that whatever fee the judge decides to set, we will pay that separately so it doesn't diminish that which is going to the claimants, and it won't take money away from them.

The *Breland* settlement became final on December 6, 1989, after it had been upheld by the court of appeals and review of that decision had been denied by the Supreme Court. On December 9, 1989, Friedberg filed a petition asking Merhige to approve an agreement he had reached with Aetna by which Aetna would pay Friedberg and his colleagues $8.575 million.

The proceedings in *Breland* had been quite limited, and the services performed by counsel for the plaintiffs hardly seemed to justify a fee of $8.575 million. The case had been stayed for much of the twenty months it was pending before the settlement. Until the settlement, all the pleadings filed in the case fitted into a single file folder in the clerk of court's office. While the *Breland* case was pending, Friedberg was twice admonished by Judge Merhige for failing to attend relevant proceedings. Friedberg did not even go to New York in January 1988 to attend the meetings at which the final agreements were reached. The *Breland* case was settled by telephone. After the settlement was approved, counsel for the class did not file a separate brief in the appeal, instead joining in the brief filed on behalf of Aetna. The major activity of plaintiff's counsel in the litigation was examining the documents Aetna had made available in Hartford.

Friedberg did not submit in support of his petition any records or itemized listings of the time expended by the attorneys for the class or of the nature of the work they had performed. Instead, each of the nine attorneys in the seven law offices that formed the Friedberg group submitted affidavits setting forth the total number of hours that he had worked on the case, often in round numbers, and a statement of his customary hourly rates. The hours of work reported in the various affidavits came to a total of 20,210 hours, the equivalent of twelve full years of full time for one hard-working attorney. The hours spent in preparing the class action that Friedberg filed against Robins on August 2, 1985, and again in the bankruptcy proceeding on August 22, 1985, were included. The rates claimed ranged up to $300 per hour.

All of these hours multiplied by the hourly rates claimed by each attorney came to $3.755 million. Aetna did not question the number of hours or rates. To the contrary, it agreed to multiply $3.755 million by a factor of 2.2 in consideration of the "very high risk" of the litigation, to reach a total of $8.261 million. (The extra $314,000 was for expenses and to cover future legal services in the case.). Of the total, $1.25 million was allocable to Judge Mehrige's former law firm in Richmond for the services as local counsel rendered by the judge's friend Murray Janus and his associate Theodore Brenner.

On December 9, 1989, the same day Friedberg's petition was filed, Judge Merhige signed an order finding that the fees requested were fair and reasonable, and approving their payment.

IN RE "AGENT ORANGE" PRODUCT LIABILITY LITIGATION
(APPEAL OF ATTORNEYS' FEE AWARDS)

United States Court of Appeals, Second Circuit, 1987.
818 F.2d 226.

Before VAN GRAAFEILAND, WINTER and MINER, CIRCUIT JUDGES.

MINER, CIRCUIT JUDGE:

Our discussion of the background and procedural history of this litigation appears in Judge Winter's lead opinion, 818 F.2d 145. The nine members of the Plaintiffs' Management Committee ("PMC") and various outside counsel appeal, on a number of grounds, the district court's decision setting attorneys' fees. On June 18, 1985, the district court issued an amended order, awarding over seven million dollars in fees and three million dollars in expenses to eighty-eight attorneys and law firms involved in the action. In re "Agent Orange" Product Liability Litigation, 611 F.Supp. 1296 (E.D.N.Y.1985)(*Agent Orange*). The nine members of the PMC, individually and as a group, challenge the district court's use of a national hourly rate in calculating the fee awards under the lodestar formula set forth in City of Detroit v. Grinnell Corp., 495 F.2d 448 (2d Cir.1974)(*Grinnell I*), and City of Detroit v. Grinnell Corp., 560 F.2d 1093 (2d Cir.1977)(*Grinnell II*), the level of the quality multipliers it set, and its failure to apply a risk multiplier to the fee awards and to credit certain hours and expenses. Four outside counsel challenge the district court's findings as to the value of their work to the class and the decision to abrogate various contingency fee arrangements between counsel and certain class members. For the reasons set forth below, we affirm in part and reverse in part.

I. Background

In May of 1984, on the eve of trial, a settlement was reached with the chemical company defendants, calling for the establishment of a $180 million dollar fund for the benefit of the class. By order dated June 11, 1984, the district court required fee petitions to be filed no later than August 31, 1984, and scheduled hearings on the petitions for the early fall. Notice of Proposed Settlement of Class Action, reprinted in In re "Agent Orange" Product Liability Litigation, 597 F.Supp. 740, 867 (E.D.N.Y.1984). Pursuant to this procedure, well over 100 attorneys and law firms filed petitions, claiming tens of thousands of hours of work performed for the benefit of the class. The fee petitions fell into three categories: those filed by the nine members of the PMC; those filed by members of Yannacone and Associates, the original consortium of attorneys in charge of the action; and those filed by attorneys not connected with any court-appointed entity representing the class.

In reviewing fee petitions, the district court developed guidelines falling into two categories—one covering the hours to be credited for work performed and the other covering the expenses to be reimbursed. The hourly guidelines were as follows:

1. *Court Time:* One-half of the time requested for review of court orders was permitted on the ground that the majority of court orders were made in open court or after extensive briefing. Telephone conference time with court personnel was awarded in full, except that no time was awarded for conferences relating to internal management difficulties of the PMC. Attendance at, and preparation for, court hearings was awarded in full. Review of hearing transcripts was awarded in full for those attorneys attending the hearing. Nonattending attorneys were awarded for only half such time. Travel to and from hearings and court appearances also was awarded on a fifty percent basis.

2. *Management Committee Meetings:* All time for PMC meetings on substantive issues was permitted. Travel to and from such meetings was awarded on a fifty percent basis. No time was awarded for meetings on nonsubstantive topics. The same division was made for telephone conferences among PMC members.

3. *Educational Reading:* Time for review of scientific materials relating to the causation issue and other issues in the case was awarded on a fifty percent basis on the ground that such knowledge could be used by counsel in future cases.

4. *Depositions:* Half of the time was awarded for travel to and from depositions, for attendance by nonparticipating attorneys, and for review and reading. All time for preparing and sum-

marizing depositions was granted. No limit on the length of depositions was enforced.

5. *Document Preparation:* All time for review and preparation of legal documents was awarded, except that those hours used to prepare documents concerning internal PMC organizational issues were not credited.

6. *Mail:* If a short period of time for review of a substantial amount of mail was requested, no time was awarded under the assumption that counsel simply was opening the mail. If a lengthy period of time was claimed for review of only a few letters, all time was credited under the assumption that counsel was reviewing a letter brief.

7. *Intra-Firm Conferences:* This time was credited on a fifty percent basis when related to substantive issues.

Agent Orange, 611 F.Supp. at 1320–21, 1350–51. The expense guidelines were as follows:

1. *Travel:* Documented expenses for hotels were reimbursed at ninety dollars per day. Meals were reimbursed at fifty dollars per day and twenty dollars per day if the attorney was in his home city.

2. *Paralegal Time:* Paralegals were treated as an expense and reimbursed at a rate of twenty dollars per hour.

3. *Out-of-Pocket Expenses:* Telephone, mailing, duplication and similar expenses were reimbursed in full if adequately documented.

4. *Percentage Approval:* When counsel submitted adequate documentation to prove expenses but were unable to establish that those expenses were all related to compensable activity, expenses were reimbursed on a percentage basis.

5. *Fees for Non–Causation Experts:* A cap of $5,000 per expert was set on the ground that their input was not substantial and not reasonably related to class interests.

Id. at 1321–22, 1351.

Following these guidelines and applying the lodestar formula for calculating attorneys' fees in an equitable fund action, *see Grinnell I,* 495 F.2d at 471, the district court awarded $10,767,443.63 in individual fees and expenses to various counsel who, in the court's view, had performed work beneficial to the class. In arriving at the lodestar figure, the court employed national hourly rates of $150 for the work of a partner, $100 for the work of an associate, and $125 for the work of a law professor. *Agent Orange,* 611 F.Supp. at 1326. The court, in its discretion, further applied quality multipliers, ranging from 1.50 to 1.75, to the fees allowed various members of the PMC and other counsel who had exhibited exceptional skill in the litigation and settlement negotiations. * * * The district judge, however, declined to apply a risk multiplier to the lodestar figure. * * *

Not satisfied with these awards, two groups of attorneys, including the PMC, now raise numerous objections on appeal.

II. DISCUSSION

A. *PMC Members*

The district court awarded the individual members of the PMC an aggregate of $4,713,635.50 in fees and $650,356.97 in individual expenses. In addition, the court awarded the PMC, as a whole, expenses in the sum of $1,711,155.87. These attorneys now raise four specific challenges to their individual awards.

1. *National Hourly Rates*

Faced with a flood of fee petitions from counsel located in all regions of the country, the district court utilized national hourly rates for calculating the fee awards for each attorney. While it recognized that the general rule for fee calculation in this circuit requires the use of "the hourly rate normally charged for similar work by attorneys of like skill in the area," *Grinnell II,* 560 F.2d at 1098, the district court noted that special problems arise "in applying this general standard in a complex multidistrict litigation that is national in scope, involves counsel from all over the country and extends over many years during which the rates for particular lawyers and classes of lawyers are changing," *Agent Orange,* 611 F.Supp. at 1308.

Specifically, the court pointed out that if the general rule were interpreted to require imposition of the rates normally imposed within the district, the rule would make little sense in the context of this action, given that the vast majority of counsel involved were non-local. Alternatively, if the rule were interpreted to require imposition of varying rates depending upon the location of each counsel's practice, the district judge perceived that such a rule would minimize the court's familiarity with the rates to be awarded, require an almost unworkable case-by-case review of such rates, and consistently benefit non-local counsel at the expense of the class fund. The district judge concluded that in large multiparty litigation, where substantial numbers of specialized non-local attorneys are involved, utilization of a national hourly rate is appropriate because it "recognizes the national character of the lawsuit and of class counsel while retaining a vitally important administrative simplicity together with an essential neutrality of result as between fee applicants and fund beneficiaries." * * *

Relying on five separate sources, the district court developed the national rates to be applied in this action. First, the court considered data compiled in the NATIONAL LAW JOURNAL DIRECTORY OF THE LEGAL PROFESSION (B. Gerson, M. Liss & P. Cunningham eds. 1984), a periodical that provided rate information concerning law firms of fifty or more attorneys throughout the country as of March 1983. Second, the court reviewed the submissions of counsel, in particular the defendants' Memorandum Concerning Plaintiffs' Lawyers' Applications for Attorneys' Fees and for Reimbursement of Expenses, which provided further information on national rates. Third, the court reviewed various surveys of law firm economics, dated 1980 through 1984, and other periodicals relating to the manner in which firms bill their clients. Fourth, the court took notice of its own experience in setting fee awards in class actions. Finally, the district judge reviewed recent fee awards by other courts to understand more fully the manner in which other jurisdictions set appropriate rates. *Agent Orange,* 611 F.Supp. at 1325–28 (citing, *inter alia,* In re Fine Paper Antitrust Litigation, 751 F.2d 562, 590 n.22 (3d Cir.1984); Grendel's Den, Inc. v. Larkin, 749 F.2d 945, 955–56 (1st Cir.1984)). From an analysis of this data, the district court arrived at national hourly rates of $150 for partners, $100 for associates and $125 for law professors.

The members of the PMC challenge the use of national rates on the ground that they do not comport with the principles governing attorneys' fee awards in equitable fund actions. They assert that the practice in this and other circuits required the court to review independently the hourly rate for each attorney in order to ensure that he was compensated at a level commensurate with that of other counsel of like skill in the area in which he practices. *See, e.g.,* In re Fine Paper, 751 F.2d at 590–91 (classifying application of national hourly rates as legal error on the grounds that the district court presented no evidentiary basis for their establishment and such rates ignored the market rates that the attorneys would command in their respective communities). Relying on large class action cases in other circuits where courts have awarded varying rates to counsel from different localities, *e.g.,* In re Equity Funding Corp. of America Securities Litigation, 438 F.Supp. 1303 (C.D.Cal.1977), they argue that, while the task may be a difficult one, other jurisdictions routinely undertake it.

In passing on the efficacy of national hourly rates, we note that fees in this action were awarded under the equitable fund doctrine, which seeks to ensure that counsel who have performed services beneficial to the class receive fair and just compensation for their respective efforts. Trustees v. Greenough, 105 U.S. (15 Otto) 527, 536 (1882). In order to provide counsel with such compensation and, at the same time, temper these awards to prevent windfalls, we have adopted a lodestar formula for calculating fees in equitable fund and statutory fee contexts. *Grinnell II,* 560 F.2d at 1099; *Grinnell I,* 495 F.2d at 469–71. Under the formula, the district court initially multiplies the number of hours reasonably billed by the hourly rate normally charged for equivalent work by similarly-skilled attorneys in the area. *Grinnell II,* 560 F.2d at 1098. Once calculated, the district court then may, in its discretion, upwardly or downwardly adjust this figure by considering such factors as the quality of counsel's work, the probability of success of the litigation and the complexity of the issues. * * *

While at least one circuit looks to the rates employed in the area in which the attorney practices, Cunningham v. City of McKeesport, 753

F.2d 262, 267 (3d Cir.1985), we traditionally have interpreted *Grinnell I* and *Grinnell II* as requiring use of the hourly rates employed in the district in which the reviewing court sits, Polk v. New York State Department of Correctional Services, 722 F.2d 23, 25 (2d Cir.1983). We generally have adhered to this rule whether the attorney involved was local or non-local. *Id.; accord* Donnell v. United States, 682 F.2d 240, 251–52 (D.C.Cir.1982), *cert. denied,* 459 U.S. 1204 , 103 S.Ct. 1190, 75 L.Ed.2d 436(1983); Chrapliwy v. Uniroyal, Inc., 670 F.2d 760, 768–69 (7th Cir.1982), *cert. denied,* 461 U.S. 956, 103 S.Ct. 2428, 77 L.Ed.2d 1315 (1983); Avalon Cinema Corp. v. Thompson, 689 F.2d 137, 140–41 (8th Cir.1982)(*en banc*). We and other circuits have strayed from this rule only in the rare case where the "special expertise" of non-local counsel was essential to the case, it was clearly shown that local counsel was unwilling to take the case, or other special circumstances existed. *Polk,* 722 F.2d at 25; *Avalon Cinema,* 689 F.2d at 140–41.

Accordingly, the issue for review here is whether the district court erred in deviating from this established precedent. While we concede that such conduct in the ordinary case would constitute legal error and require recalculation of the lodestar, we conclude that, in an exceptional multiparty case such as this, where dozens of non-local counsel from all parts of the country are involved, public policy and administrative concerns call for the district court to be given the necessary flexibility to impose a national hourly rate when an adequate factual basis for calculating the rate exists.

An examination of the alternatives to the use of national rates in large multiparty class actions of this sort readily establishes the necessity for affording district courts this discretion. Use of our forum rule would distort dramatically the purposes of the lodestar calculation itself—to ensure fair and just compensation to counsel and to prevent the award of windfall fees. This distortion would occur because, in cases in which the vast majority of attorneys involved are non-local, the forum rule necessarily will either overcompensate or undercompensate a substantial number of non-local attorneys. Undercompensation could deny counsel their right to fair and just fees; overcompensation would not be consistent with the need to prevent windfalls. Adherence to the forum rule in cases in which the inherent limitations of the rule are magnified, i.e., where few local counsel and vast numbers of non-local counsel are involved, therefore, makes little sense.

Resort to a varying approach, depending upon the area in which the individual practices, fares no better. In an action of the magnitude of *Agent Orange,* in which well over one hundred fee petitions were filed by counsel throughout the country, such an approach would pose an administrative nightmare for the district court. As the district judge here noted, "[s]implicity becomes an especially important goal in a complex case involving a hundred or more fee applications and tens of thousands of pages of supporting documentation and requiring a number of years for prosecution during which rates for particular attorneys and geographic locations change in different ways." *Agent Orange,* 611 F.Supp.

at 1308. While administrative interests normally should not be the primary concern of a court in formulating substantive rules of review, we observe that the attorney-by-attorney approach recommended by the PMC simply would over-tax the capacity of a district court to review fee petitions adequately. *Cf.* New York Association for Retarded Children v. Carey, 711 F.2d 1136, 1146 (2d Cir.1983)(burden-saving measures may be taken by district court in light of voluminous fee petitions).

Although not a panacea, the use of national hourly rates in exceptional multiparty cases of national scope, where dozens of non-local counsel are involved, appears to be the best available method of ensuring adherence to the principles of the lodestar analysis. The risk of over-compensation or undercompensation on a large scale, apparent under the forum rule, is somewhat neutralized, while, at the same time, the administrative burden on the district court, apparent under the varying rate rule, is reduced to a manageable level. In granting the district court this discretion, however, we caution that such rates should be employed only in the exceptional case presenting problems similar to those presented here. We further caution that, even in similar cases, national hourly rates should be employed only when the district court is presented with an adequate evidentiary basis on which to fix such rates. Once the court is satisfied with the evidence, it should make clear, factual findings that support its determination.

We are aware that at least one circuit has rejected the imposition of national hourly rates on the ground that they do not comport with the lodestar principle. *In re Fine Paper,* 751 F.2d at 591. To the extent, however, that the Third Circuit's decision was based upon the fact that the national rates employed did not comport with that circuit's rule requiring the hourly rate to reflect the rate normally charged in the locale in which counsel practices, we already have rejected its analysis by following a forum rate rule. *See Polk,* 722 F.2d at 25. In addition, *In re Fine Paper,* though not entirely clear on this point, may be read to condemn only national hourly rates not based on an adequate evidentiary record. The Third Circuit, in reversing the district court's adoption of such rates, indicated that the district court there had not referred to any evidence supporting the existence of such rates, 751 F.2d at 590, and noted that "the subject is not one on which judicial notice is appropriate," *id.* If read in that context, our decision is in accord with that of the Third Circuit, since we limit the utilization of national rates to those instances in which an adequate evidentiary basis exists. Finally, even assuming that *In re Fine Paper* stands for an absolute prohibition on the imposition of national hourly rates, we note that, subsequent to that decision, the Third Circuit Task Force on Court Awarded Attorney Fees, organized at the behest of the Chief Judge of that Circuit, recommended that the court permit the utilization of such rates in exceptional cases. *Court Awarded Attorney Fees,* Third Circuit Task Force, 108 F.R.D. 237, 260–62 (Oct. 8, 1985).

Given our determination that the utilization of national hourly rates in limited circumstances is proper, we further conclude that the district court did not abuse its discretion in calculating the specific hourly rates in the present case. In its decision, the court set forth the five bases upon which it computed these rates. The PMC does not challenge specifically those bases and we find little reason to question them. Hourly rates for counsel in this action were difficult to calculate because the majority of attorneys involved normally would have been compensated through contingency fee arrangements rather than on an hourly basis. Difficulties aside, however, the district judge, in our view, took adequate steps to ensure a fair and just hourly rate of compensation. We therefore hold that the national hourly rates of $150 for partners, $100 for associates and $125 for law professors constituted an element of fair and just compensation for counsel in the context of this case.

2.   *Quality Multipliers*

Having computed the initial lodestar figure, the district court awarded discretionary quality multipliers of 1.5, and in one case 1.75, to six members of the PMC on the ground that these attorneys had exhibited exceptional skills in the litigation and settlement negotiations. The six PMC recipients now challenge the level of the multipliers as being unjustifiably low and further challenge the district court's failure to award quality multipliers in connection with the fees of the three other PMC members.

The decision to allow a quality multiplier rests in the sound discretion of the district court, Hensley v. Eckerhart, 461 U.S. 424, 437 (1983); *Grinnell II,* 560 F.2d at 1098, due to "the district court's superior understanding of the litigation and the desirability of avoiding frequent appellate review of what essentially are factual matters." *Hensley,* 461 U.S. at 437. The Supreme Court, however, in Blum v. Stenson, 465 U.S. 886, 899, 104 S.Ct. 1541, 1549, 79 L.Ed.2d 891 (1984), and more recently in Pennsylvania v. Delaware Valley Citizens' Council for Clean Air, 478 U.S. 546, 106 S.Ct. 3088, 92 L.Ed.2d 439 (1986), has severely restricted those instances in which a district court may allow such a multiplier.[2]

In *Blum,* a decision concerning application of the lodestar analysis to a fee award under 42 U.S.C. § 1988, the Court determined that factors such as quality of representation are *presumed* to be fully reflected in the initial lodestar figure, derived by multiplying the number of hours reasonably billed by the court-established hourly rate. *Blum,* 465 U.S. at 899, 104 S.Ct. at 1549. Accordingly, the Court concluded that an adjustment to the lodestar figure for such a factor would only be proper in "the rare case where the fee applicant offers specific evidence to show that the quality of service rendered was superior to that one reasonably should expect in light of the hourly rates charged and that the success was 'exceptional.'" *Id.* (emphasis added). In *Delaware Valley Citizens' Council,* a decision concerning application of the lodestar analysis to a

---

2. Blum and Delaware Valley Citizens' Council are statutory fee cases whereas here fees were awarded under the equitable fund doctrine. While the lodestar formula applies to both types of cases, equitable fund cases may afford courts more leeway in enhancing the lodestar, given the absence of any legislative directive.

fee award under section 304(d) of the Clean Air Act, 42 U.S.C.A. § 7604(d)(West 1983), the Court reaffirmed the narrow approach taken in *Blum,* declaring that calculating fee awards under the lodestar analysis "leaves very little room for enhancing the award based on [counsel's] post-engagement performance." *Delaware Valley Citizens' Council,* 106 S.Ct. at 3098.

Given these pronouncements, the issue, in our view, is not whether the quality multipliers awarded by the district court here were set too low, but rather whether they should have been awarded at all. In what we consider to be a close case, we conclude that the district court did not abuse its discretion in awarding the multipliers for quality to six of the PMC members, or in failing to award them to the other three members.

The district court specifically found that these six attorneys, as well as several outside counsel who have not appealed, deserved to be awarded quality multipliers at various rates because each had "demonstrated an unusual degree of skill in presenting complex and often novel issues to the court," *Agent Orange,* 611 F.Supp. at 1328, or had "shown a level of organization and efficiency that goes beyond what is usually expected," *id.* Under ordinary circumstances, even assuming the high level of work performed by counsel here, we would be constrained to reverse the district court's award in light of the severe restrictions set forth in *Blum* and *Delaware Valley Citizens' Council.* While the work indeed may have been of high quality, the presumption is that such factors already are reflected in the initial lodestar figure.

In this case, however, we find that the use of a national hourly rate skews the normal lodestar analysis enough to require consideration of quality factors in order to satisfy the requirements of just and fair compensation. While we affirm the use of national rates in the present case, we realize that such rates inherently cannot be calculated as precisely as those under the forum rule, or those under the varying locale rule. Consequently, the *Blum* and *Delaware Valley Citizens' Council* presumption of inclusion of quality factors within the initial lodestar figure should not, in our view, apply to those instances in which the district court utilizes this less precise analysis.

3. Risk Multiplier

The district court declined to award a risk multiplier to any attorney involved in the case. It reasoned that risk of success should not be judged solely from the vantage point of whether a complete recovery at the conclusion of the action is viable, but also should include an evaluation of the likelihood that the parties will reach a settlement. In this regard, the court noted that it was probable that the defendant chemical companies would settle the case "to avoid the further burden of litigation and to improve their respective financial pictures." *Agent Orange,* 611 F.Supp. at 1311. The court also recognized that awarding risk multipliers in a case such as *Agent Orange,* which held out little chance for a victory on the merits but a significant chance of settlement, would fuel the filing of nuisance litigation "in which settlement becomes the main object and attorney fee awards an overpowering motivating force." *Id.*

Furthermore, the court indicated that strict application of inversely proportionate risk multipliers to cases such as *Agent Orange,* which it described as a high-risk case of highly questionable merit, would lead to a confounding disparity in the treatment of cases falling just above and just below the standard for frivolousness under Fed.R.Civ.P. 11. Attorneys in successful cases bordering on the frivolous, yet falling just above the proscriptions of Rule 11, would be awarded the highest risk multipliers, since the risk of success in such cases obviously would be great. In contrast, counsel in similar cases falling just below Rule 11's proscriptions, would not only receive no risk multiplier, but also would be subject to court-imposed sanctions for having brought such a case.

Finally, the court took note that, as a matter of public policy, the need to utilize a risk multiplier in a given case must be viewed in relation to the equally important concerns of judicial administration and legal morality. To this end, the refusal to allow a multiplier here would force the legal community "to think at least twice before initiating sprawling, complicated cases of highly questionable merit that will consume time, expense and effort on the part of all concerned, including the courts, in a degree vastly disproportionate to the results eventually obtainable." Id. at 1312. While such a policy would not reward the filing of these questionable cases, the court did note that counsel's entitlement to a lodestar award without a multiplier would nonetheless serve adequately to encourage attorneys to represent plaintiffs in cases of this nature.

The PMC challenges the district court's failure to allow a risk multiplier on the ground that it does not comport with principles of just and fair compensation. While conceding that plaintiffs' case would have been difficult to prove, the PMC members strongly take exception to the district court's description of the action as being of dubious or questionable merit. As to the probability of the parties reaching a settlement in the action, the PMC members point to the fact that such a settlement was not reached until the eve of trial, and label as "economic suicide" the notion that they advanced funds and spent thousands of hours working on the case with some inner assurance that defendants would make a reasonable settlement proposal because of the bothersome nature of the litigation.

We have labeled the risk-of-success factor as "perhaps the foremost" factor to be considered under the second prong of the lodestar analysis. *Grinnell I,* 495 F.2d at 471. The multiplier takes into account the realities of a legal practice by rewarding counsel for those successful cases in which the probability of success was slight and yet the time invested in the case was substantial. *Id.; see* 7B C. Wright, A. Miller & M. Kane, FEDERAL PRACTICE AND PROCEDURE § 1803, at 524–27 (1986). As the chance of success on the merits or by settlement increases, the justification for using a risk multiplier decreases. *Grinnell I,* 495 F.2d at 471. The need for this type of multiplier is magnified when the "diminutive character of the individual claims" forces counsel to bring the action on a class basis. 7B C. Wright, A. Miller & M. Kane, *supra*, § 1803, at 527. Without the prospect of some consideration for the risks and uncertainties of the action, "the necessary incentive [for prosecuting such a suit] would be lacking and a major weapon for enforcing various public policies would be blunted." *Id.*

The problem with risk multipliers, however, is that they tend to reward counsel for bringing actions of dubious merit. If such multipliers are awarded on a perfectly proportionate basis, *i.e.,* the greater the chance that the case would not succeed the higher the multiplier, "the net effect . . . would be to make a marginal case as attractive to bring as a very strong case." Laffey v. Northwest Airlines, Inc., 746 F.2d 4, 27 (D.C.Cir.1984), *cert. denied,* 472 U.S. 1021, 105 S.Ct. 3488, 87 L.Ed.2d 622 (1985). This, in turn, would provide an incentive for counsel to flood "the courts with unmeritorious litigation," McKinnon v. City of Berwyn, 750 F.2d 1383, 1392 (7th Cir.1984), "leading . . . to a situation in which every conceivable claim would be litigated, subject only to the ability of the courts to handle the burden," *Laffey,* 746 F.2d at 27; *accord* Leubsdorf, *The Contingency Factor in Attorney Fee Awards,* 90 Yale L.J. 473, 491 (1981). The net result, of course, would be a dilution of the judiciary's ability to handle those cases with potentially meritorious claims.

A court, therefore, in adjudging whether to award a risk multiplier, should examine closely the nature of the action in order to determine whether, as a matter of public policy, it is the type of case worthy of judicial encouragement. In our view, the case here clearly is not and, consequently, we agree with the district court's decision not to impose a risk multiplier.

From the outset, the factual and legal difficulties hindering the successful prosecution of plaintiffs' case have been staggering. Factual evidence of causation has been at best tenuous and, if not for the last-minute settlement, the military contractor defense would have prevented class members from realizing any recovery at all. When these significant weaknesses in plaintiffs' case are viewed in light of the sheer magnitude of the action and the thousands of hours of court time that this type of action requires, it becomes clear that the federal courts should not actively encourage the bar to file such dubious actions in the future.

Besides matters of public policy, the settlement itself presents a rationale for denying counsel's request. While today we hold that the settlement falls within the range of reasonableness under Fed.R.Civ.P. 23, we are aware that the $180 million settlement provides a very small return to the class in light of the claims asserted. In our estimation, the relatively small size of the settlement reflects class counsel's realization of the extreme difficulty they would incur in overcoming the inherent weaknesses of their case, in particular the military contractor defense, and the defendant chemical companies' realization that they could end a burdensome litigation at very low cost. Award of a risk multiplier in such circumstances, as the district court reasoned, only would further the unwelcome prospect of nuisance litigation being brought in federal courts.

In denying class counsel their requested multiplier, we note that each attorney has received the fair value of his services to the class under the lodestar analysis. An additional award of a risk multiplier not only would provide excessive compensation but would encourage counsel to accept similar matters for litigation in the future. We find no reason to do more to encourage litigation that could substantially occupy the federal judiciary in matters of little merit.

4. Hours and Expenses

The PMC members challenge the district court's guidelines on the grounds that they improperly failed to credit certain hours and reimburse certain expenses. Specifically, they challenge the court's decision to disallow fifty percent of the time spent on reading scientific literature, to disallow fifty percent of the time spent on travel, to disallow a portion of the time spent reviewing mail and on the telephone, to disallow fifty percent of the time spent reviewing depositions, and to disallow a substantial amount of post-settlement work. As to expenses, they challenge the court's decision to reduce expenses by a percentage when such expenses could not be connected with compensable activity, to set a maximum fee for noncausation expert witnesses, and to treat paralegals as a cost. In sum, they allege that, taken together, if not separately, such radical deductions in their hours and expenses billed constituted an abuse of the court's discretion.

The district court is given broad discretion in setting fee awards. *Hensley,* 461 U.S. at 437, 103 S.Ct. at 1941; *Carey,* 711 F.2d at 1146. We cannot reverse a district court's finding in this regard merely because we might have weighed the information provided in the fee petitions differently or might have found more of the hours billed as being beneficial to the class. *Cf.* Anderson v. Bessemer City, 470 U.S. 564, 573–74, 105 S.Ct. 1504, 1511–12, 84 L.Ed.2d 518 (1985). The district judge is in the best position to weigh the respective input of counsel, considering its "superior understanding of the litigation." *Hensley,* 461 U.S. at 437, 103 S.Ct. at 1941. Accordingly, we will reverse a district court's findings as to which hours to compensate "only when it is apparent that the size of the award is out of line with the degree of effort reasonably needed to prevail in the litigation." *Carey,* 711 F.2d at 1146.

We find no abuse of discretion here. The critical inquiry when reviewing hours billed to the common fund in a class action is whether the work performed resulted in a benefit to the class. *See Grinnell II,* 560 F.2d at 1099. In determining which hours were beneficial, we note that there "are no hard-and-fast rules," Seigal v. Merrick, 619 F.2d 160, 164 n.9 (2d Cir.1980), but that "[a]mple authority supports reduction in the lodestar figure for overstaffing as well as for other forms of duplicative or inefficient work," *id.* Moreover, we and other circuits have held that in cases in which substantial numbers of voluminous fee petitions are filed, the district court has the authority to make across-the-board percentage cuts in hours "as a practical means of trimming fat from a fee application." *Carey,* 711 F.2d at 1146; *accord* Ohio–Sealy Mattress Manufacturing Co. v. Sealy Inc., 776 F.2d 646, 657 (7th Cir.1985); Copeland v. Marshall, 641 F.2d 880, 903 (D.C.Cir.1980)(*en banc*). *But see In re Fine Paper,* 751 F.2d at 596 (court must identify with some specificity any disallowed hours). Under such circumstances, no item-by-item accounting of the hours disallowed is necessary or desirable. *Ohio-Sealy,* 776 F.2d at 658.

Here, the fee petitions, to say the least, were voluminous, consisting of tens of thousands of pages of billing sheets and other exhibits. To suggest that the district court could not take advantage of percentage reductions in such a context would be absurd. In reviewing these across-the-board cuts, we find nothing that we could classify as an abuse of discretion. Moreover, it is not unusual for hours of travel time, deposition time and other quasi-administrative items to be compensated at lower rates. *E.g.,* Sun Publishing Co. v. Mecklenburg News, Inc., 594 F.Supp. 1512, 1520 (E.D.Va.1984); Steinberg v. Carey, 470 F.Supp. 471, 479–80 (S.D.N.Y.1979). *But see* Crumbaker v. Merit Systems Protection Board, 781 F.2d 191, 193–94 (Fed.Cir.1986)(reasonable travel time should be compensated at the same rate as other working time). The district judge gave reasons, though somewhat generalized, for each percentage cut that he made. We find these to be an adequate reflection of the benefit that the class derived from counsel's work.

We also find no abuse of discretion in the district court's guidelines for expenses. Counsel are entitled to reimbursement only for those expenses incurred in the course of work that benefitted the class. In re Armored Car Antitrust Litigation, 472 F.Supp. 1357, 1388–89 (N.D.Ga. 1979), *modified and remanded on other grounds,* 645 F.2d 488 (5th Cir.1981). Overstaffing and other extravagances are not recoverable. *Id.*

Given this standard, the district court's finding that the reports of the non-causation witnesses were of only marginal use to the class and were "uniformly inadequate" suggests that the court in fact was generous in setting the cap for fees to these experts at $5,000 each. *Report and Recommendation of United States Magistrate, Re: Fee Petitions,* appendixed to and incorporated in *Agent Orange,* 611 F.Supp. at 1351. We also find no abuse of discretion in the district court's determination that expenses connected with those hours disallowed as not being beneficial to the class should not be reimbursed. *See* In re Fine Paper Antitrust Litigation, 98 F.R.D. 48, 85 (E.D.Pa.1983), *rev'd on other grounds,* 751 F.2d 562 (3d Cir.1984). Finally, although we concede that under certain circumstances it may be appropriate not to treat paralegal time as an expense in a large class action, *see* Dorfman v. First Boston Corp., 70 F.R.D. 366, 374–75 (E.D.Pa.1976), we note that the district court in so doing was simply following our prior directive, *see Grinnell I,* 495 F.2d at 473. We decline to reevaluate that rule here.

* * *

IN RE NINETEEN APPEALS ARISING OUT OF THE SAN JUAN DUPONT PLAZA HOTEL FIRE LITIGATION

United States Court of Appeals, First Circuit, 1992.
982 F.2d 603.

Before SELYA, CIRCUIT JUDGE, LAY, SENIOR CIRCUIT JUDGE, O'SCANNLAIN, CIRCUIT JUDGE.

SELYA, CIRCUIT JUDGE.

These appeals call upon us to descend once more into the belly of a beast previously (and accurately) described as a "litigatory monster." In re Recticel Foam Corp., 859 F.2d 1000, 1001 (1st Cir.1988). On this occasion, we are involved less with the litigants than with their champions. One group of lawyers, appellants here, contend that the procedures followed by the district court in awarding attorneys' fees and directing cost reimbursement were fundamentally unfair, ignored the requirements of procedural due process, and constituted an abuse of discretion. Another group of lawyers, appellees here, vehemently deny these charges and seek to uphold the award. Because we agree that the proceedings in question were profoundly flawed, we vacate the district court's order.

I. BACKGROUND

Given the narrow purview of these appeals, we need not dwell upon the tragic facts of the incendiary fire that claimed nearly one hundred lives at the San Juan Dupont Plaza Hotel on December 31, 1986. For our purposes, a bareboned preface serves to place the instant appeals into workable perspective.[1]

A

In 1987, the Judicial Panel on Multidistrict Litigation consolidated over two hundred seventy cases, involving approximately twenty-three hundred plaintiffs, and placed them under the aegis of the Honorable Raymond L. Acosta in the District of Puerto Rico. *See* In re Fire Disaster at Dupont Plaza Hotel, 660 F.Supp. 982 (J.P.M.L.1987)(per curiam). Shortly thereafter, the Chief Justice appointed the Honorable Louis C. Bechtle as a "settlement judge." While the litigation moved toward trial in Judge Acosta's court, Judge Bechtle endeavored to advance settlement prospects by determining individual and aggregate values for the cases.

---

1. We refer readers interested in the arson and the course of the ensuing litigation to the plethora of opinions which grace the federal reports. *See, e.g.,* In re San Juan Dupont Plaza Hotel Fire Litig., 888 F.2d 940 (1st Cir.1989); S.C., 789 F.Supp. 1212 (D.P.R.1992); S.C., 768 F.Supp. 912 (D.P.R.1991); S.C., 745 F.Supp. 79 (D.P.R. 1990); *see also Recticel,* 859 F.2d 1000.

In an effort to organize the plaintiffs' side of the litigation, Judge Acosta appointed a steering committee (the PSC) to act as lead and liaison counsel for the plaintiffs. Because PSC members would exert the lion's share of control over the direction of the litigation and would, therefore, likely lay claim to a larger slice of the fee pie than their non-member colleagues, appointment to the PSC was much coveted; only attorneys who had been retained by individual plaintiffs were eligible to apply, and more than forty of the fifty-six individually retained plaintiffs' attorneys (IRPAs) declared their candidacies. Judge Acosta initially chose nine members and, in June 1988, increased the complement by two.[2]

By dint of the PSC's role, a rough division of labor emerged. The PSC members looked after the big picture: mapping the overarching discovery, trial, and settlement strategies and coordinating the implementation of those strategies. The IRPAs handled individual client communication and other case-specific tasks such as answering interrogatories addressed to particular plaintiffs, preparing and attending the depositions of their clients, and taking depositions which bore on damages. The IRPAs also worked with Judge Bechtle on a case-by-case basis in his efforts to identify and/or negotiate appropriate settlement values for individual claims. When Judge Acosta determined that the plaintiffs should try twelve representative claims as a means of facilitating settlement, a collaborative composed of three PSC members and four IRPAs bent their backs to the task.

For the most part, Judge Acosta's work on this massive litigation has been a model of judicial craftsmanship and practical ingenuity. The exigencies of these appeals do not demand that we describe the judge's many innovations. We do note, however, that he wisely segmented the liability inquiry into phases. The first two phases, now concluded, established the liability of the hotel's owners and certain suppliers, respectively; when the results of these phases were integrated with the representative trial outcomes and with Judge Bechtle's handiwork, the combination generated an aggregate settlement fund of approximately $220,000,000.

At the close of the second phase, Judge Acosta opted to disburse the settlement fund because, in his words, "the Phase III litigation will not affect the results of the previous phases in any way and consequently [there is] no reason why distribution of the settlement fund to the victims and their attorneys should not go forward at this time." In re San Juan Dupont Plaza Hotel Fire Litig., 768 F.Supp. 912, 936 (D.P.R.1991)(hereinafter "Fees Op. "). The parties to these appeals—who agree on little else—do not dispute this assessment of the situation.

---

2. To prevent down time during the selection process, Judge Acosta appointed an interim plaintiffs' steering committee (the IPIC). Certain IPIC members were not appointed to the PSC but were ultimately awarded fees and costs for IPIC-related work. In addition, Judge Acosta named an alternate member of the PSC.

B

The IRPAs were originally retained under a variety of contingent-fee agreements, most of which were capped at the legal maxima: twenty-five percent for minors or incompetents; thirty-three and one-third percent for adults. In addition, the plaintiffs agreed to pay certain costs. Thus, the amount available for legal fees was a fixed percentage of the overall recovery pool and the only figures which the court needed to compute prior to distributing the settlement fund were (1) the amount of PSC fees to be deducted from the attorneys' fund (a fund comprising the portion of the settlement reserved for legal fees) and (2) the amount of costs to be deducted from the plaintiffs' fund (a fund comprising the portion of the settlement reserved for the victims, excluding counsel fees).

Before discussing the former computation, some introductory comments are in order. Under standard "American rule" practice, each litigant pays his or her own attorneys' fees. *See, e.g.,* Alyeska Pipeline Serv. Co. v. Wilderness Soc'y, 421 U.S. 240, 245, 95 S.Ct. 1612, 1615, 44 L.Ed.2d 141 (1975). Yet, there are times when the rule must give way. For example, when a court consolidates a large number of cases, stony adherence to the American rule invites a serious free-rider problem. *See generally* Mancur Olson, THE LOGIC OF COLLECTIVE ACTION (1971). If a court hews woodenly to the American rule under such circumstances, each attorney, rather than toiling for the common good and bearing the cost alone, will have an incentive to rely on others to do the needed work, letting those others bear all the costs of attaining the parties' congruent goals.

A court supervising mass disaster litigation may intervene to prevent or minimize an incipient free-rider problem and, to that end, may employ measures reasonably calculated to avoid "unjust enrichment of persons who benefit from a lawsuit without shouldering its costs." Catullo v. Metzner, 834 F.2d 1075, 1083 (1st Cir.1987). Such courts will most often address the problem by specially compensating those who work for the collective good, chiefly through invocation of the so-called common fund doctrine. In its paradigmatic formulation, the common fund doctrine permits the trustee of a fund, or a person preserving or recovering a fund for the benefit of others in addition to himself, to recover his costs, including counsel fees, from the fund itself, or alternatively, from the other beneficiaries. *See* Boeing Co. v. Van Gemert, 444 U.S. 472, 478 (1980); *Alyeska,* 421 U.S. at 257; Catullo, 834 F.2d at 1083.[5] Although common fund cases are *sui generis,* they typically evince certain characteristics. These include ease in identifying the persons, or classes of persons, benefitted by the recovery; ease in tracking the benefit flow; the ability to trace benefits with enough accuracy that, in the end, the flow chart inspires confidence; and the

---

5. The district court's power to award attorneys' fees through an application of the common fund doctrine is derived from its traditional power to do equity. *See Boe-* *ing,* 444 U.S. at 478, 100 S.Ct. 749; Weinberger v. Great N. Nekoosa Corp., 925 F.2d 518, 523 (1st Cir.1991).

ability to shift litigation costs with enough precision and reliability that cost and benefit are fairly proportionate to one another. See *Boeing,* 444 U.S. at 478–79; *Alyeska,* 421 U.S. at 265 n.39.

Here, Judge Acosta's decision to use a steering committee created an occasion for departure from the American rule. In apparent recognition of the free-rider problem, the judge served notice from the beginning that he would eventually make what he, relying in part on appellees' counsel, *see Fees Op.,* 768 F.Supp. at 924 n.42, later termed a "common fund fee award" to remunerate PSC members for their efforts on behalf of communal interests. This was a proper exercise of judicial power. *See* Mills v. Electric Auto–Lite Co., 396 U.S. 375, 392 (1970); *see also* In re "Agent Orange" Prod. Liab. Litig., 818 F.2d 226, 240 (2d Cir.1987)(upholding a fee award to a plaintiffs' steering committee under the equitable fund doctrine); Bebchick v. Washington Metro. Area Transit Comm'n, 805 F.2d 396, 402 (D.C.Cir.1986)(collecting cases); In re MGM Grand Hotel Fire Litig., 660 F.Supp. 522, 526 (D.Nev.1987).

C

After Phase III ended and court-appointed accountants determined that the attorneys' fund was in the approximate amount of $66,000,000, Judge Acosta held a two-day hearing addressed to the method and amount of compensation to be awarded to PSC members for their efforts on behalf of the whole. In the course of the hearing, five of the eleven PSC members broke rank and proposed that PSC fees should be calculated on a lodestar basis, not as a percentage of the settlement fund. A prominent law professor outlined this position on behalf of the five insurgents.[6] The majority of the PSC members repudiated the insurgents' proposal and asked the court to award PSC fees as a percentage of the settlement fund, in line with Judge Acosta's stated intent when forming the PSC.

This intramural dispute was not so much motivated by principle as by profit. Although each PSC member was in some sense an IRPA— each member had been retained by at least one plaintiff—there was a wide disparity in the number of clients that each lawyer represented. One consequence of this disparity was that a large PSC award stood to benefit PSC members who had few clients and to disadvantage PSC members who had many clients.[7] The interests of the PSC members and the non-PSC IRPAs diverged even more starkly; after all, each dollar that went to the former was a full dollar less that would otherwise be divided among the latter.

Despite this adversariness, however, Judge Acosta severely limited the IRPAs' participation throughout the fee-determination process. For

---

6. The district court characterized the professor's presentation as akin to the testimony of a friend of the court. We find this characterization to be wholly insupportable. The hearing transcript makes it clear that the professor appeared as a paid advocate of the PSC minority's parochial interests.

7. The former would anticipate receiving the bulk of their compensation from PSC fees while the latter would anticipate receiving most of their compensation from their clients' cases.

instance, the judge's ground rules barred any non-PSC members from testifying at the hearing. Moreover, the IRPAs were told that they had to file their objections to the insurgents' fee proposal on a one-page form designed by the court. The form * * * allotted only seven lines for substantive comment, i.e., "reason[s] for opposition" to the fee proposal. The court stressed that longer submissions would be ignored.

When the fee-determination hearing began, Judge Acosta flatly refused to permit the IRPAs, either individually or through a designated representative, to examine the witnesses. The IRPAs were not allowed to offer oral argument. After the hearings ended, Judge Acosta gave the IRPAs leave to file any written objections which were not foreseeable beforehand, but he restricted these filings to the same one-page form. The court again admonished the IRPAs that, if they deviated from the mandated format, the court would not consider their objections.

On the basis of the insurgents' fee proposal, the testimony at the fee hearing, and those objections filed in accordance with the form, Judge Acosta awarded some $36,000,000 of the $66,000,000 attorneys' fee fund to PSC members for their services in that capacity. The court asserted that the fee calculation was the composite product of the percentage and lodestar methods. *See* Fees Op., 768 F.Supp. at 926–27 ("[T]he Court finds that the use of both the percentage and the lodestar approach is both logical and practical and will lead to a fair and reasonable result because one method serves to check the other."). The court also awarded costs of approximately $10,000,000 to PSC members, chargeable against the plaintiffs' fund.[8]

Two members of the PSC majority, the PSC alternate, a number of IRPAs, and several individual plaintiffs then prosecuted the instant appeals. The five insurgent PSC members appear as appellees.

* * *

[Portion of decision relating to appellate jurisdiction under finality rule, omitted—*ed.*]

III. DUE PROCESS CONSIDERATIONS

The gravamen of appellants' claim is that Judge Acosta's ruling tapped the settlement funds, in which appellants had a constitutionally protected property interest, without affording them the process that was due. We canvass the controlling legal principles and then inspect the particulars of the proceedings below.

A

The Supreme Court "consistently has held that some form of hearing is required before an individual is finally deprived of a property

---

8. Insofar as costs are concerned, the total charge-back to the plaintiffs' fund was in excess of $16,000,000. Of this amount, however, $3,563,575 represented a contingency set-aside reserved for future allocation; slightly over $1,500,000 represented trustees' fees; $766,700 represented reimbursement of cost assessments previously levied by the court to fund ongoing expenses of the litigation; and close to $900,-000 represented miscellaneous charges, such as PSC office expenses and local taxes.

interest." Mathews v. Eldridge, 424 U.S. 319, 333, 96 S.Ct. 893, 902, 47 L.Ed.2d 18 (1976); *accord* Wolff v. McDonnell, 418 U.S. 539, 557–58, 94 S.Ct. 2963, 2975, 41 L.Ed.2d 935 (1974). Perfunctory gestures will not suffice. At bedrock, "[t]he fundamental requirement of due process is the opportunity to be heard at a meaningful time and in a meaningful manner." *Mathews,* 424 U.S. at 333 (citation and internal quotation marks omitted).

The Court has not forged a boilerplate standard for determining what process is due in all circumstances, but, instead, has articulated three areas of particular importance: "[T]he specific dictates of due process generally require[ ] consideration of three distinct factors: First, the private interest that will be affected by the official action; second, the risk of an erroneous deprivation of such interest through the procedures used, and the probable value, if any, of additional or substitute procedural safeguards; and finally, the Government's interest, including the function involved and the fiscal and administrative burdens that the additional or substitute procedural requirement would entail." *Id.* at 335, 96 S.Ct. at 903; *see also* Connecticut v. Doehr, 501 U.S. 1, ___, 111 S.Ct. 2105, 2112, 115 L.Ed.2d 1 (1991); Reardon v. United States, 947 F.2d 1509, 1518 (1st Cir.1991)(*en banc*). The Court's language in *Mathews* explicates what is essentially a constitutional balancing test. *See* Amsden v. Moran, 904 F.2d 748, 753 (1st Cir.1990), *cert. denied,* 498 U.S. 1041, 111 S.Ct. 713, 112 L.Ed.2d 702 (1991); Needleman v. Bohlen, 602 F.2d 1, 5 (1st Cir.1979).

We do not approach the *Mathews* factors in a vacuum. Rather, we sally forth mindful that, in many, if not most, instances, due process does not require a full-scale trial, or even a hearing strictly conforming to the rules of evidence. *See Mathews,* 424 U.S. at 348; Doyle v. Secretary of HHS, 848 F.2d 296, 301 (1st Cir.1988). Due process is malleable, calling "for such procedural protections as the particular situation demands." Morrissey v. Brewer, 408 U.S. 471, 481, 92 S.Ct. 2593, 2600, 33 L.Ed.2d 484 (1972). A court may hand-tailor procedures to account for the nature of the affected interests and the circumstances of the threatened deprivation. *See* Neron v. Tierney, 841 F.2d 1197, 1201 (1st Cir.1988), *cert. denied,* 488 U.S. 832, 109 S.Ct. 90, 102 L.Ed.2d 66 (1988).

"As the rubric itself implies, 'procedural due process' is simply 'a guarantee of fair procedure.' " *Amsden,* 904 F.2d at 753 (quoting Zinermon v. Burch, 494 U.S. 113, 125, 110 S.Ct. 975, 983, 108 L.Ed.2d 100 (1990)); *see also* Newman v. Burgin, 930 F.2d 955, 961 (1st Cir. 1991). Hence, we review cases involving adversarial hearings to determine whether, under the specific facts and circumstances of a given situation, the affected individual has had a fundamentally fair chance to present his or her side of the story. Gorman v. University of R.I., 837 F.2d 7, 14 (1st Cir.1988). Throughout, we resist bright line rules and mechanical tests, mindful that a nisi prius court may use its sound discretion to assemble an appropriate process by choosing from among a multitude of available methods, so long as the end product stays within the four corners of that discretion and satisfies the rigors of the Due Process Clause.

B

With this flexible standard in mind, we focus the lens of our inquiry on whether the procedures employed below satisfied the constitutional imperative. In so doing, we follow the *Mathews* framework.

1. *The Private Interest.* In this instance, the affected private interest is the monetary share of the funds due each IRPA.[13] The district court necessarily deprived the appellants of money when it invaded the attorneys' fund to pay PSC fees. Not only do the appellants have a property interest in escrowed funds, *see* Reed v. Commissioner, 723 F.2d 138, 146 (1st Cir.1983), but the amounts involved are substantial and the deprivation is complete. For these reasons, we find the affected interest to be an important one.

2. *Risk of Error.* During the four years preceding the filing of the insurgents' lodestar proposal in February 1991, the district court engendered the assumption that it would calculate PSC fees as a percentage of the total fee award—"probably less than 10%." Order 2 (March 18, 1987).[14] Judge Acosta reiterated his intention a year and one-half later in Order 127, In re Dupont Plaza Hotel Fire Litig., MDL 721, 1989 WL 168401, at *15, 1988 U.S. Dist. Lexis 17332, at *40 (D.P.R. Dec. 2, 1988). Although these orders did not bind the district court to a ten percent cap, they did induce the IRPAs to rely on the percentage mechanism. This reliance manifested itself in two ways. Because the court led the IRPAs to believe that it would calculate the PSC's fees as a percentage of the settlement fund, the IRPAs had virtually no incentive to monitor the PSC members' time sheets (which were regularly filed with the court). Similarly, because the IRPAs were working under contingent-fee agreements and had every reason to assume that time records would not be material in deciding what portion of the attorneys' fund would be diverted to remunerate the PSC, they were ill prepared to supply the type of documentation necessary to counter the late-blooming lodestar proposal advanced by the PSC minority.[15]

The initial indication that PSC fees might be determined by anything other than a percentage approach surfaced on January 31, 1991,

---

13. For simplicity's sake, we refer here only to the IRPAs' stake and the differences of opinion concerning fees (as opposed to costs). Nevertheless, the same analysis applies to the individual plaintiffs and the lower court's subtraction of costs from the plaintiffs' fund. See *infra* Part III(C).

14. Judge Acosta's initial estimate of a ten percent ceiling for PSC compensation did not itself appear unusual. *See, e.g.,* In re MGM Grand Hotel Fire Litig., 660 F.Supp. at 529 (awarding seven percent of the recovery pool as steering committee compensation).

15. The proposal suggested that the court use the lodestar method, a time-and-rate-based framework for setting counsel fees. The specifics of the lodestar method have been frequently recounted elsewhere, *see, e.g.,* Blum v. Stenson, 465 U.S. 886, 896–902, 104 S.Ct. 1541, 1547–50, 79 L.Ed.2d 891 (1984); Lipsett v. Blanco, 975 F.2d 934, 937 (1st Cir.1992); *Metropolitan Dist. Comm'n,* 847 F.2d at 19, and need not be rehearsed here.

when the PSC submitted a petition for a fee award together with a motion for partial distribution of funds. In the petition, the PSC discussed the need for a hearing to determine the hours spent by PSC members and consider appropriate multipliers. The petition's import was clouded, however, by the contemporaneous motion for partial distribution, in which the PSC suggested a hearing to establish a percentage allotment to be withheld from the attorneys' fund for PSC fees and a percentage allotment to be withheld from the plaintiffs' fund for PSC costs. On February 5, 1991, the district court notified the parties in interest that it would convene a fee-determination hearing on February 20. Although the order, Order 305 (February 5, 1991), indicated that the court would entertain proposals anent the amount of fees and method of fee calculation, it was not until the deadline date for applications (February 15, 1991) that a filing by an insurgent member of the PSC gave appellants the first clear notice that any PSC member would actively campaign for the lodestar method.

In a nutshell, after four years of justifiable reliance on the district court's stated intent to calculate fees for PSC members on a percentage basis, probably not to exceed ten percent, the IRPAs had only a few days to consider the ramifications of a possible switch to the lodestar method, reconstruct their own hours in order to protect their interest in the funds,[16] and sift the hours claimed by PSC members. To compound the problem, the court required the IRPAs to confine their objections to a one-page form.

In the ordinary course, due process might have been expected to mitigate the IRPAs' concerns, because "when a person has an opportunity to speak up in his own defense, and when the [decisionmaker] must listen to what he has to say, substantively unfair and simply mistaken deprivations of property interests can be prevented." Fuentes v. Shevin, 407 U.S. 67, 81, 92 S.Ct. 1983, 1994, 32 L.Ed.2d 556 (1972). But here, that expectation never blossomed into actuality. Cf. John McGahern, *The Leavetaking,* pt. II (1974)("[w]e have to learn never to expect anything"). The hearing procedures outlined by the district court in Order 310 became part of the problem, not part of the solution.

To be blunt, the protocol that governed the hearing hogtied the IRPAs, severely restricting their ability to participate in the fee-determination process. The court summarily abrogated the PSC's "majority decision" rule without prior notice, allowing the insurgents' proposal to go forward. The court then stated, in Order 310, that "[t]he role of [the IRPAs] at the hearing will be limited to that of spectators, that is, they may not interrogate the witnesses, raise objections or otherwise address the Court." Even the PSC members were admonished to testify only as to their participation as PSC members and not to recount their services in their dual capacity as IRPAs. As a final indignity, the court limited

---

16. The standard form promulgated by the district court, reproduced in the appendix, required each objecting IRPA to specify the total number of hours he had worked on his clients' cases.

the IRPAs' posthearing objections to matters which could not have been foreseen prior to the hearing and confined them to the same tourniqueted form used for prehearing objections.

Such miserly process is certainly not sufficient to meet constitutional minima. While "[n]otice and an opportunity to be heard have traditionally and consistently been held to be the essential requisites of procedural due process," *Gorman,* 837 F.2d at 12, a last-minute warning of a fundamental change in the fee structure is not constitutionally adequate notice [17] and a rigid limitation of one affected group's input into the hearing while giving members of the other affected group a much broader array of participatory rights does not comprise a constitutionally adequate chance to be heard. Appellants were entitled to reasonable forewarning and an opportunity to present their side of the controversy in a meaningful manner. They received neither. Hence, the risk that appellants would be erroneously deprived of their property was intolerably great.[18]

3. *The Public Interest.* We do not gainsay the substantial governmental interest in conserving scarce judicial resources. Particularly in mass disaster litigation, courts must run tight ships to ensure that litigation stays on course. We recognize that Judge Acosta imposed the restrictions about which appellants complain in a well-intentioned effort to keep the case velivolant. His renitency was understandable in light of the number of lawyers involved, the four-year life span of the litigation, and the Supreme Court's admonition that "[a] request for attorney's fees should not result in a second major litigation." Hensley v. Eckerhart, 461 U.S. 424, 437, 103 S.Ct. 1933, 1941, 76 L.Ed.2d 40 (1983).

Nonetheless, the court was not faced with an all-or-nothing choice between allowing the IRPAs free rein and unfairly hobbling them. There were a wide range of procedures available which, in any one of

---

17. Appellees argue that any failure of notice was inconsequential because Judge Acosta eventually couched the PSC fee award in terms of a percentage. We agree that, after calculating the award by using lodestar techniques, Judge Acosta then translated it into a percentage. Notwithstanding this effort to touch all bases, it is pellucid that the court relied on the lodestar method to reach a dollar figure, see *Fees Op.,* 768 F.Supp. at 929 n.49 (rejecting percentage suggestions on the ground that they did not encompass "the number of hours, value for various tasks performed, etc."), and then paid lip service to the percentage method. It beggars credulity to argue that this bit of adroit wordplay fulfilled the court's original promise to set the PSC's fees on a percentage basis. Form cannot be allowed to triumph over substance. Because the court posted a different menu when the PSC was formed, due process precludes the court from effectively scrapping the menu by the simple expedient

of preparing a lodestar stew and serving it up under another name.

18. The strictures on IRPA participation also likely contributed to Judge Acosta's failure to compensate those IRPAs who conducted the representative trials for their work in that capacity. Although Judge Acosta did ask for, and receive, an accounting from these IRPAs, he did not allow them to participate in the fee hearing. In the end, despite the evident contributions made by these IRPAs in undertaking the representative trials, the judge "tacitly denied" them special fees, splitting the attorneys' fund between the PSC and the IRPAs generally. Order 402 (Oct. 16, 1991). Moreover, Judge Acosta awarded those counsels' costs to the PSC as part of the PSC cost award. *Fees Op.,* 768 F.Supp. at 934 n.74. The fate that befell these IRPAs is illustrative of the hazards that an adjudicator faces in listening to only one side of a multi-sided story.

several possible combinations, could have brought a sense of fundamental fairness to the fee-determination hearing while at the same time husbanding the court's resources. The court could, for example, have granted the IRPAs more latitude in making written submissions, heard some testimony on their behalf, allowed them to designate one or more representatives for purposes of cross-examination, and/or given them a right to participate in oral argument. To be sure, the court was free to pick and choose from among these (and other) alternatives or to impose reasonable restrictions—but the court was not free to construct a set of ground rules that largely ignored the IRPAs' substantial stake in the controversy.[19] While we do not suggest that a full-scale evidentiary hearing was essential, the court, having opted for one (wisely, we think, considering the stakes), should at the very least have permitted the IRPAs to make submissions of a reasonable length—certainly, more than seven lines—and should have allowed the IRPAs to appear or to designate a prolocutor to question witnesses and address the court. After all, the root purpose of the fee-determination proceeding was to decide upon an equitable allocation of fees between the IRPAs and the PSC—a purpose which could scarcely be achieved by hearing only one side of a long, complicated story.[20]

Let us be perfectly clear. We do not hold today that the Due Process Clause requires the district court to convene an evidentiary hearing for all attorneys' fee disputes. *See* Weinberger v. Great N. Nekoosa Corp., 925 F.2d 518, 528 (1st Cir.1991)(stating that hearings are not always obligatory in connection with fee awards). Nor do we hold that a district court must always take live testimony or afford adversarial discovery in such matters. We do rule, however, that, once Judge Acosta elected to convene a fee-determination hearing, the hearing format itself had to be fair. In other words, when a judge constructs a process for setting fees, the process must contain at least the procedural minima that the Due Process Clause requires; and, moreover, those

---

19. Although we do not reach the question of whether the district court abused its discretion in the particulars of its fee award, we note that the court's belated shift from a percentage approach to a lodestar approach raises serious questions in this respect. In justifiable reliance on the court's original declaration that it would calculate PSC fees on a percentage basis, see Order 2 (March 18, 1987), the majority of the IRPAs did not maintain time records. Thus, despite our brother's contrary view, ... we cannot see a practical method by which to compare PSC members' time to IRPAs' time on the paper record alone. In view of this seemingly unavoidable impasse, we think that the lower court, at the very least, should have heard the IRPAs' views on the advisability of so basic a change in the method of PSC compensation.

20. There are indications in the record below that the district court viewed its task solely in terms of fixing suitable compensation for the PSC. Judge Lay seemingly falls into the same trap. ... In our view, such a focus distorts the reality of the situation. Because the total amount available for counsel fees was limited, the court necessarily determined the amount due to the IRPAs when it determined the amount due to the PSC members. Indeed, a trier who attempted punctiliously to follow the classic lodestar formula, to the exclusion of all else, could theoretically wind up awarding the entire fee pool to the PSC, leaving nothing for the IRPAs. Surely, that result is completely indefensible.

procedures must apply in a fair and evenhanded manner to the parties in interest, without preferring one group of disputants over another.

In this instance, we cannot see how the court could fairly adjudicate this dispute unless it afforded the IRPAs a viable means (comparable to the means afforded the PSC) of describing their contribution to the litigation, contrasting their contribution with the PSC's contribution, and questioning the PSC members regarding their work. *See* Briscoe v. LaHue, 460 U.S. 325, 333–34, 103 S.Ct. 1108, 1114–15, 75 L.Ed.2d 96 (1983); California v. Green, 399 U.S. 149, 158, 90 S.Ct. 1930, 1935, 26 L.Ed.2d 489 (1970); Kennerly v. United States, 721 F.2d 1252, 1257–58 (9th Cir.1983)(reversing district court award of funds where interested party did not receive a hearing); *see also Weinberger,* 925 F.2d at 525 ("The court's role as the guarantor of fairness obligates it not to accept uncritically what lawyers self-servingly suggest is reasonable compensation for their services."); In re Air Crash Disaster at Fla. Everglades, 549 F.2d 1006, 1021 (5th Cir.1977)(requiring plaintiffs' committee and counsel to offer evidence and submit to cross-examination at fee-determination hearing). Although using such a model would have prolonged the hearing, it would not have created an unreasonable or intolerable burden on the district court. Given the panoply of available alternatives, the public interest in the integrity of court proceedings demanded considerably more.

4. *Recapitulation.* After assessing the relevant criteria and giving proper weight to the litigation's great complexity and the size of the pecuniary stakes, we find the process afforded appellants as unbalanced as a two-legged stool. The IRPAs' important property interests and the inversely limited means that the lower court afforded for representing and protecting those interests were not counterbalanced by any sufficient governmental interest. Contrary to our concurring brother, we do not see how a district court's "equitable judgment," . . . no matter how familiar the judge may be with the underlying litigation or how laudable his intentions, can displace the Due Process Clause. We are thus constrained to conclude that the IRPAs received too short shrift. In sum, the court below employed constitutionally inadequate process.

C

Although our discussion to this point focuses on the attorneys' fund, we have other concerns as well. Certain individual plaintiffs also appealed and appellants' consolidated brief limns a fully developed due process claim on their behalf. In that wise, appellants contend that the district court taxed the plaintiffs' fund for PSC costs, amounting to more than $10,000,000, *see supra* note 8 and accompanying text, without providing a meaningful process through which individual plaintiffs could air their concerns.

It would serve no useful purpose to repastinate ground that has already been thoroughly ploughed. Suffice to say that the same analysis we have used in connection with the IRPAs' claims applies *ex proprio vigore* to the plaintiffs' claims. First, the affected private interest is significant: each individual plaintiff has an independent pecuniary inter- est in the monies contained in the plaintiffs' fund; because the district court decreed that various expenses should be recouped by deductions from the plaintiffs' fund, the plaintiffs' loss of their property interest is complete; and the amount of the loss is substantial. Second, the risk of an erroneous deprivation is fairly steep: because the court relegated plaintiffs' lawyers (the IRPAs) to the sidelines, the plaintiffs' interests were, for all practical purposes, unrepresented in the hearing which determined cost reimbursement; the plaintiffs were given virtually no chance to be heard on the subject at a meaningful time and in a meaningful manner; and, moreover, some of the costs for which reim- bursement was sought (and granted) were at least arguably unreimburs- able. Third, muting the plaintiffs' voices served no countervailing public interest.

The short of it is that the hearing procedures devised by the district court deprived the individual plaintiffs of meaningful input into the decisionmaking process by which the court decided what costs were properly to be charged against the plaintiffs' fund. Hence, because the plaintiffs, like the IRPAs, did not receive due process of law, the costs, as well as the fees, must be determined afresh.

IV. Conclusion

We need go no further. We admire the district court for its unflagging efforts, effective stewardship, and mastery of the unwieldy dimensions of this massive piece of litigation. We appreciate that the court struggled doggedly to confront an increasingly contentious and fragmented dispute over the allocation of sizable attorneys' fees and substantial costs. Even so, challenging circumstances cannot excuse fundamental flaws. Because the district court, in an excess of zeal, impermissibly abridged appellants' due process rights as to the distribu- tion of both the attorneys' and the plaintiffs' funds, we must vacate the district court's order.

The order appealed from is vacated and the cause is remanded to the district court for further proceedings consistent herewith. Costs in favor of appellants.

GEORGINE v. AMCHEM PRODUCTS, INC.

United States District Court, Eastern District of Pennsylvania, 1994.
157 F.R.D. 246.

* * *

(4) Attorneys' Fees

* * * Under Part XIX, the CCR defendants will pay the attorneys' fees incurred by Class Counsel in their role as Class Counsel, with the amount to be approved by this Court. ... Any claimant who submits a claim for compensation under the Stipulation may proceed without an attorney or may be represented by his or her own attorney, including

Messrs. Motley, Locks and Rice, if they so choose; provided, however, that, ... the fee that may be charged by such attorney will be limited to 25% of the compensation award received by the claimant (and 20% of any amount received by the claimant above the maximum award under the individualized payment procedures for that claimant's medical category).

* * * Testimony at the fairness hearing demonstrated the benefit to claimants from the 20–25% limitation on attorneys' fees under Part XX for representing an individual claimant seeking compensation under the Stipulation. This testimony reliably proved that the fee arrangements used by most plaintiffs' attorneys in the asbestos litigation have provided for a 33–40% contingency. ... Furthermore, the availability of counsel to class members, based upon traditional considerations, is improved when counsel are adequately compensated. This provision was negotiated by well-experienced lawyers who are obliged to consider the availability of counsel to the class members, and there were no persuasive objections to the stipulated rate of compensation.

* * * Based on the foregoing, the Court finds that the provisions regarding attorneys' fees in the Stipulation are reasonable and fair to the class.

Notes and Questions

1.   We have already seen that attorneys' fees can raise troubling ethical issues in mass tort litigation, especially in the context of class actions. *See* Part I.D.3, *supra.* Are attorney fee problems in mass tort any different than in other litigation? What attributes of the mass tort litigation phenomenon give rise to difficult fee determination problems? The cases and commentary excerpted above suggest a variety of methods for allocating attorney fees. Are any methods better than others? Would the problem of mass tort attorney fees be better dealt with by statute? How? Would the possibility of a fee-shifting rule effect the conduct of mass tort litigation? *See generally* John J. Donohue III, *The Effects of Fee Shifting on the Settlement Rate: Theoretical Observations on Costs, Conflicts, and Contingency Fees,* 54 Law & Contemp. Probs. 195 (1991); *see also* Danny Boggs, *Comment on* Donohue, 54 Law & Contemp. Probs. 223 (1991); Christopher P. Lu, *Procedural Solutions to the Attorney's Fee Problem in Complex Litigation,* 26 U.Rich. L.Rev. 41 (1991) and Thomas E. Willging, JUDICIAL REGULATION OF ATTORNEYS' FEES: BEGINNING THE PROCESS AT PRETRIAL (Federal Judicial Center 1984).

2.   As tort litigation, most mass torts are structured on some contingency-fee basis. If the mass tort is aggregated under the class action rule, then Rule 23 provides a basis for judicial scrutiny of the fee arrangements. If a mass tort is not aggregated under Rule 23, do the courts have any authority for regulating attorney fees? For discussion of problems of contingency-fee arrangements in the context of mass tort litigation, *see* In re Joint E. & S. Dist. Asbestos Litig., 129 B.R. 710, 863–64 (E. & S.D.N.Y.1991); Lester Brickman, *The Asbestos Litigation Crisis: Is There a Need for an Administrative Alternative?,* 13 Cardozo L.Rev. 1819 (1992); Lester Brickman, *Contingent Fees Without Contingencies: Hamlet Without the Prince of Denmark?,* 37 U.C.L.A.L.Rev. 29 (1989). For a discussion of attorney fee

arrangements in *The School Asbestos Litigation* and *Cimino v. Raymark, see* Linda S. Mullenix, *Beyond Consolidation: Post Aggregative Procedure in Asbestos Mass Tort Litigation,* 32 Wm. & Mary L. Rev. 526–31 (1991).

3. Because of the size and complex nature of aggregated mass tort cases, class counsel designation often is awarded by the court to a particular law firm or set of attorneys, even though the mass tort may have begun as hundreds of individual cases. How can the judicial system fairly award lead counsel position to attorneys in mass tort litigation? Even if the court orders a committee structure for the litigation, how should attorney fees be distributed among counsel? Should representation in mass tort cases be auctioned to the lowest bidder, a procedure used in the Northern District of California to designate lead counsel in a securities case? *See* In re Oracle Sec. Litig., 131 F.R.D. 688 (N.D.Cal.1990). For commentary on auctioning the lead counsel function, *see generally* Beverly C. Moore, Jr., *Going Once, Going Twice: Bidding for Work,* Legal Times, Dec. 17, 1990, at 27; Jonathan R. Macey & Geoffrey P. Miller, *The Plaintiffs' Attorney's Role in Class Action and Derivative Litigation: Economic Analysis and Recommendations for Reform,* 58 U.Chi.L.Rev. 1 (1991); Jack B. Weinstein, *Ethical Dilemmas in Mass Tort Litigation,* 88 Nw.U.L.Rev. 527–32 (1994).

4. To what extent does the award of substantial attorney fees in highly publicized mass tort litigation undermine the public's confidence in the justice system? Are the award of such large fees justified? The high transactions costs of mass tort litigation, relative to claimant compensation, has been well documented by numerous studies. *See generally,* Michel F. Baumeister, *Latent Toxic Injury and Compensation Schemes: Response to Schuck and Rosenberg,* 1 Cts. Health Sci. & L. 360 (1991); Harvey P. Berman, *The Agent Orange Veteran Payment Program,* 53 Law & Contemp. Probs. 49 (Autumn 1990); Andrew T. Berry, *Asbestos Personal Injury Compensation and the Tort System: Beyond "Fix It 'Cause It's Broke,"* 13 Cardozo L.Rev. 1949 (1992); A. Leo Levin & Denise D. Colliers, *Containing the Cost of Litigation,* 37 Rutgers L.Rev. 219 (1985); Samuel Isaacharoff, *Administering Damage Awards in Mass Tort Litigation,* 10 Rev.Litig. 463 (1991); James S. Kakalik & Nicholas M. Pace, Costs and Compensation Paid in Tort Litigation (Santa Monica, California: The Institute for Civil Justice, RAND 1986); James S. Kakalik, *et al.,* Variation in Asbestos Litigation Compensation (Santa Monica, California: The Institute for Civil Justice, RAND 1984); Allan Kanner, *Critique of Compensation Schemes: Response to Rosenberg,* 1 Cts. Health Sci. & L. 352 (1991); Robert L. Rabin, *Some Thoughts on the Efficacy of a Mass Toxics Administrative Scheme,* 52 Md.L.Rev. 951 (1993); Paul D. Rheingold, *New Frontiers in Causation and Damages: Compensating Clients Injured by Toxic Torts,* Trial, Oct. 1986, at 42; Glen O. Robinson, *Probabilistic Causation and Compensation for Tortious Risk,* 14 J. Legal Stud. 779 (1985); David Rosenberg, *The Uncertainties of Assigned Shares Tort Compensation: What We Don't Know Can Hurt Us,* 6 Risk Analysis (1986); and David Rosenberg, *Damage Scheduling in Mass Exposure Cases,* 1 Cts. Health Sci. & L. 335 (1991).

*

Part Three

SUBSTANTIVE LAW ISSUES IN MASS TORT LITIGATION

Chapter V

SPECIAL SUBSTANTIVE ISSUES IN MASS TORT LITIGATION

INTRODUCTORY NOTES ON THE TORT LITIGATION CRISIS

1. The debate surrounding mass tort litigation needs to be understood against the backdrop of a larger debate concerning a perceived crisis in the American tort liability system. During the 1980s and 1990s, a number of lawyers, reform groups, and academicians have studied the tort and product liability system. Have the resulting studies and reports supported claims to a crisis in the liability system? *See generally* Commission to Improve the Tort Liability System, American Bar Association, *Report and Recommendations to the House of Delegates* (1987); Conference, *Catastrophic Personal Injuries,* 13 J. Legal Stud. 425 (1984); Patricia M. Danzon, *Tort Reform and the Role of Government in Private Insurance Markets,* 13 J. Legal Stud. 517 (1984); Theodore Eisenberg & James A. Henderson, *Inside the Quiet Revolution in Products Liability,* 39 U.C.L.A. L. Rev. 731 (1992); Allan Kanner, *Future Trends in Toxic Tort Litigation,* 20 Rutgers L.J. 667 (1989); Richard Pierce, *Institutional Aspects of Tort Reform,* 73 Cal. L. Rev. 917 (1985); Michael J. Saks, *Do We Really Know Anything About the Behavior of the Tort Litigation System—And Why Not?,* 140 U. Pa. L. Rev. 1147 (1992); Joseph Sanders & Craig Joyce, *"Off to the Races:" The 1980s Tort Crisis and the Law Reform Process,* 27 Hous. L. Rev. 207 (1990); Symposium, *Tort Reform,* 27 Gonz. L. Rev. 147 (1992). *Cf.* Richard L. Abel, *The Real Tort Crisis: Too Few Claims,* 48 Ohio St. L.J. 443 (1987).

2. For discussions of various proposals for reform of the tort system, *see generally* Richard A. Chesley & Kathleen W. Kolodgy, Note, *Mass Exposure Torts: An Efficient Solution to a Complex Problem,* 54 U. Cin. L. Rev. 467 (1985); Alan Schwartz, *Proposals for Products Liability Reform: A Theoretical Synthesis,* 97 Yale L.J. 353 (1988); Victor E. Schwartz & Barbara H. Bares, *Federal Reform of Products Liability Law: A Solution That Will Work,* 13 Cap. U.L. Rev. 351 (1984); Alan D. Twerski, *A Moderate and Restrained Products Liability Bill: Targeting the Crisis Areas for Resolution,* 18 U. Mich. J.L. Ref. 575 (1985);

Symposium, *Toxic Torts: Judicial and Legislative Responses,* 28 Vill. L. Rev. 1083 (1983); Tort Policy Working Group, United States Dept. of Justice, *An Update on the Liability Crisis* (1987).

3. A comprehensive products liability statute was introduced in Congress in February 1995. *See* Common Sense Product Liability and Legal Reform Act of 1995, H.R. 956, 104th Cong., 1st Sess. (1995). Among other provisions, this legislation would limit punitive damages to three times the amount of economic loss, or $250,000, which ever is greater.

A. INDETERMINATE PLAINTIFFS

Review *In Re "Agent Orange" Prods. Liab. Litig.,* at Part Two, Chapter IV. C, *supra.*

1. THE PROBLEM OF LATENT INJURY

IN RE THREE MILE ISLAND LITIGATION
United States District Court, Middle District Pennsylvania, 1980.
87 F.R.D. 433.

* * *

III.   CERTIFICATION OF CLASS III

The proposed Class III definition submitted to the court includes a request for medical detection services to monitor for future manifestations of injury. The request is essentially one for money to provide the services and is a remedy rather than a cause of action.

Defendants argue that there is no legal basis for granting the relief because it is unsupported by a claim. A class certification ruling is not the appropriate vehicle for determining whether plaintiffs have stated a claim upon which relief can be granted. Eisen v. Carlisle & Jacquelin, 417 U.S. 156, 177–78, 94 S.Ct. 2140, 2152–53, 40 L.Ed.2d 732 (1974). Exhibit A, accompanying plaintiffs' motion for certification of Class III, is a statement of the claims of the named plaintiffs. Many of the plaintiffs mention emotional distress and the possibility of latent injury. The justiciability of a latent injury claim is a question which will not be decided here.

The court is aware that there has been widespread concern among the population within a twenty-five mile radius of TMI over the possibility that there may be future physical problems caused by exposure to deleterious emissions from TMI. It believes that, if there is any legal basis for the claim or merit in it, the issues are susceptible to class treatment. The class, when limited to the claimed need for medical monitoring, meets the criteria of Rule 23(a). The potential plaintiffs number in the tens of thousands, making joinder of all members of the class impracticable. As discussed below, there are numerous common factual issues, and the same legal issues concerning liability as exist for

Classes I and II. The limited claim of the representative parties that their exposure to emissions from TMI warrants an award of damages for medical monitoring will be identical to those of the class. No apparent divergence of interest exists between the representatives and the proposed class.

The predominance of common issues required by Rule 23(b)(3) also exists. Beyond the question of causation there will be factual issues concerning the kinds and amounts of substances emitted during the accident, the likely pattern of their dispersal under the prevailing meteorological conditions, and what future physical effect the exposed population might expect. Since the facts and data will be the same for people residing in the same areas, a saving of time and expense can be realized by litigating this question as a class issue. A class action will be the superior method of deciding whether there is any basis for granting the damages for medical detection services.

CARLOUGH v. AMCHEM PRODUCTS, INC.

United States District Court, Eastern District of Pennsylvania, 1993.
834 F.Supp. 1437.

Review Judge Reed's "standing" analysis in relation to future claimants in the *Carlough* settlement class, at Part Two, Chapter II. D. 2, *supra*.

Notes and Questions

1. One of the signal characteristics of mass tort litigation is the problem of latent injury. Although issues relating to latent injury arise in simple products liability litigation, most often with reference to statute of limitations problems, issues relating to latent-injury claimants have complicated mass tort litigation in interesting ways. The excerpt from the *Three Mile Island Litigation* suggests an early approach of some courts to certify "medical monitoring" subclasses to provide some recompense for future claimants. Other attempts to certify medical monitoring subclasses for persons suffering from latent injury have been less successful. *See e.g.,* Brown v. Southeastern Pennsylvania Transportation Authority, 1987 WL 9273 (E.D.Pa.1987)(denying class certification to medical monitoring subclass for persons exposed to polychlorinated biphenyls ("PCBs") at the Paoli Railyard in Paoli, Pennsylvania). *See also* Kuhn v. Skyline Corp., C.A. 83–0942 (M.D.Pa.1984)(reconsidering *Three Mile Island* medical monitoring class certification). For an early discussion of the substantive tort issues raised by the indeterminate plaintiff problem, *see generally* Richard Delagdo, *Beyond Sindell: Relaxation of Cause-in-Fact Rules for Indeterminate Plaintiffs,* 70 Cal. L.Rev. 881 (1982); *see also* William H. Armstrong, *Tort Damages for Personal Injuries Not Yet Suffered,* Natl. Resources & Envt'l, Spring 1988, at 26.

2. Judge Reed's lengthy analysis of the standing issue relating to future claimants in the *Carlough* case illustrates at least two central problems relating to latent-injury claimants in the context of mass tort litigation. The first issue concerns whether exposure-only claimants may

join actual-injury claimants in an aggregate action, and whether such latent-injury claimants possess standing to assert claims. The second issue concerns the interests of latent-injury claimants in class action settlements.

In *Carlough,* the court goes to great lengths to interpret current standing doctrine to legitimate the standing of latent-injury claimants. Is the court's interpretation of standing doctrine convincing? Was the court correct in divorcing federal standing doctrine from underlying state tort law requirements? In the latter portion of his analysis, the Judge Reed concludes that exposure-only claimants meet the "injury-in-fact" requirement, suggesting that no disease manifestation is necessary to satisfy this standing criterion. Is this a satisfactory conclusion? If, as the medical data suggests, cellular alteration occurs at the moment of exposure to asbestos, does Judge Reed need to discuss the lack of disease manifestation?

In addition to standing problems, latent injury also complicates class action settlements that include both present and future claimants. In one of the many subsequent actions brought as a consequence of the lengthy *Agent Orange Litigation,* Judge Weinstein held that exposure-only plaintiffs were bound by the *Agent Orange* class settlement, even though the latency of their injuries prevented them from knowing definitively whether they were or were not included in the class at the time of the first deadline for opting out of the class action. *See* Ryan v. Dow Chemical, 781 F.Supp. 902 (E.D.N.Y.1991), *affirmed* In re "Agent Orange" Prod. Liab. Litig. (Ivy v. Diamond Shamrock Chemicals Co.), 996 F.2d 1425 (2d Cir.1993)(cited by Judge Reed). In reaching this conclusion, Judge Weinstein stated:

> Nevertheless, a representative suit can work unfairness, particularly when the representation binds persons who only become aware that they are class members after settlement rather than persons who, at the time the action is brought and decided, can definitively determine whether they are in the class. One can imagine many genuine conflicts of interest between two such groups within a class action. *See* In re Joint Eastern & Southern Dist. Asbestos Litig., 129 B.R. at 771–73. For example, current litigants might be willing to achieve a settlement even if it leaves funds inadequate to compensate future victims. Alternatively, future claimants might, in retrospect, disagree with prior litigation strategy or find new evidence in support of their claims.

> Although Federal Rule of Civil Procedure 23(a) and (b) sets out criteria designed to ensure that all class members are being properly represented, for Rule 23(b)(3) actions, the "best practicable notice" requirement of Rule 23(c) is intended to provide additional protection of "the interests of individuals in pursuing their own litigations." *See* Fed.R.Civ.P. 23(c)(2) Advisory Committee's Note to 1966 Amendments. Yet, a plaintiff with a latent injury may even have actual notice and still not receive this additional protection because he or she may not have reason to believe the injury will appear.

> Courts are authorized to take steps to alleviate these problems in the interest of fairness. As in the Manville bankruptcy actions, courts can oversee the appointment of a guardian to represent the interests of future claimants in class action litigations and settlements. *See* In re Joint E. & S. Dist. Asbestos Litig., 129 B.R. at 773. Such a guardian

was not necessary in the Agent Orange Settlement because of the way it was structured to cover future claimants. All of the courts which considered the Agent Orange Settlement were fully cognizant of the conflict arguments now hypothesized by the plaintiffs and took steps to minimize the problem in the way they arranged for long-term administration of the Settlement Fund.

In many cases the conflict between the interests of present and future claimants is more imagined than real. In the instant case, for example, the injustice wrought upon the plaintiffs is nonexistent. These plaintiffs, like all class members who suffer death or disability before the end of 1994, are eligible for compensation from the Agent Orange Payment Fund. The relevant latency periods and the age of the veterans ensure that almost all valid claims will be revealed before that time.

Does Judge Weinstein's analysis provide comfort to those Agent Orange latent-injury claimants who might have desired to opt-out of the settlement?

3. The problem of mass tort latent injury also intersects with third-party insurance coverage of such claims. In many jurisdictions, courts have variously interpreted policy "occurrence" terms necessary or sufficient to trigger policy coverage. *See e.g.,* Stonewall Insurance Co. v. Nat'l Gypsum Co., 1992 WL 123144 (S.D.N.Y.1992)(analyzing what constitutes "occurrence" for purposes of policy deductibles in asbestos abatement and removal litigation); Uniroyal Inc. v. The Home Insurance, 707 F.Supp. 1368 (E.D.N.Y.1988)("occurrence" triggering policy coverage consisted of manufacturer's delivery of Agent Orange chemicals to military); American Home Products Corp. v. Liberty Mutual Ins. Co., 565 F.Supp. 1485 (S.D.N.Y. 1983)(in DES litigation, "occurrence" triggering policy coverage must be injury in fact, not exposure to harmful substance or actual manifestation of injury). *See generally* American Law Institute, *Reporter's Study,* ENTERPRISE RESPONSIBILITY FOR PERSONAL INJURY 66–76 (1991)(describing the liability insurance system).

4. The most common issues related to latent injury in mass tort cases involve state "discovery" rules, tolling provisions, and applicable statutes of limitation. *See* Chapter VI, section A, *infra.* Latent injury claimants often run afoul of various timing provisions for asserting claims or joining actions. *See e.g.,* Roth v. G.D. Searle Co., 27 F.3d 1303 (8th Cir.1994)(injury claims by IUD user not timely filed and state discovery rule did not apply; manufacturer not equitably estopped from asserting statute of limitations defenses); Renfroe v. Eli Lilly Co., 541 F.Supp. 805 (E.D.Mo.1982)(plaintiff's DES claim did not arise or accrue until plaintiff suffered reasonably discoverable injuries and plaintiff knew or in the exercise of reasonable diligence should have known, whichever occurred first, that injuries were caused by DES exposure).

5. Latent injury mass torts also may implicate claims for current or future psychic injuries. How does substantive tort law view such claims? *See* Irwin N. Perr, *Asbestos Exposure and Psychic Injury—A Review of 48 Claims,* 20 Bull. Am. Acad. Psychiatry L. 383 (1992) and Adam P. Rosen, Comment, *Emotional Distress Damages in Toxic Tort Litigation: The Move Towards Foreseeability,* 3 Vill. Envt'l L.J. 113 (1992).

2. FUTURE CLAIMANTS

GRADY v. A.H. ROBINS COMPANY, INC.
LEGAL REPRESENTATIVE FOR THE FUTURE TORT
CLAIMANTS v. A.H. ROBINS COMPANY, INC.

United States Court of Appeals, Fourth Circuit, 1988.
839 F.2d 198.

Before RUSSELL, WIDENER and CHAPMAN, CIRCUIT JUDGES.

WIDENER, CIRCUIT JUDGE:

Rebecca Grady and the Legal Representative of the Future Claimants appeal an order of the district court deciding that Mrs. Grady's claim against A.H. Robins Co., Inc. (Robins) arose prior to the date Robins sought protection under the Bankruptcy Code and therefore was subject to the automatic stay provision of 11 U.S.C. § 362(a)(1). In re A.H. Robins Co., Inc., 63 B.R. 986 (Bkrtcy. E.D.Va.1986). We affirm.[1]

Robins, a pharmaceutical company, was the manufacturer and marketer of the Dalkon Shield, an interuterine contraceptive device, from 1971 to 1974. Production was discontinued in 1974 because of mounting concerns about the device's safety. See A.H. Robins Co., Inc. v. Piccinin, 788 F.2d 994 (4th Cir.1986). Because of the overwhelming number of claims filed against it because of the Dalkon Shield, Robins filed a petition for reorganization under Chapter 11 of the Bankruptcy Code, 11 U.S.C. § 1101 et seq., on August 21, 1985.

Mrs. Grady had had inserted a Dalkon Shield some years before but thought that the device had fallen out. On August 21, 1985, she was admitted to Salinas Valley Memorial Hospital, Salinas, California, complaining of abdominal pain, fever and chills. X-rays and sonograms revealed the presence of the Dalkon Shield. On August 28, 1985, the Dalkon Shield was surgically removed. Mrs. Grady was discharged from the hospital but not long after returned to her physician, complaining of persistent pain, fever and chills. She was again admitted to the hospital on November 14, 1985, on which admission she was diagnosed as having pelvic inflammatory disease, and underwent a hysterectomy. She blames the Dalkon Shield for those injuries.

On October 15, 1985 (almost two months after Robins filed its petition for reorganization), Mrs. Grady filed a civil action against Robins in the United States District Court for the Northern District of California. * * * The case was subsequently transferred to the Eastern District of Virginia. * * *

Mrs. Grady then filed a motion in the bankruptcy court, seeking a decision that her claim did not arise before the filing of the petition so

1. We use the terms district court and bankruptcy court interchangeably in our opinion. The district court did not refer this proceeding to a bankruptcy judge under 28 U.S.C. § 157.

that it would not be stayed by the automatic stay provision of the Code. If the claim arose when the Dalkon Shield was inserted into her, the district court reasoned, then it would be considered a claim under the Bankruptcy Code and its prosecution would be stayed by the provisions of 11 U.S.C. § 362(a)(1). If, however, the claim was found to arise when the injuries became apparent, then it might not be a claim for bankruptcy purposes and the automatic stay provision would be inapplicable.

The bankruptcy court determined that Mrs. Grady's claim against Robins arose when the acts giving rise to Robins' liability were performed, not when the harm caused by those acts was manifested. * * * The court rejected Mrs. Grady's contention that the court must look to state law to determine when her cause of action accrued and equate that with a right to payment. It concluded that the court must follow federal law in determining when the claim arose. * * * It held that the right to payment under 11 U.S.C. § 101(4)(A) of Mrs. Grady's claim arose when the acts giving rise to the liability were performed and thus the claim was pre-petition under 11 U.S.C.§ 362(a)(1).

We emphasize the narrowness of the district court's holding. It held only that the automatic stay provision of 11 U.S.C. § 362 applied, and we have recited its reasoning to arrive at that conclusion. It did not decide whether or not Mrs. Grady's claim would constitute an administrative expense under 11 U.S.C. § 503(b)(1)(A), and it also did not decide whether or not the Future Tort Claimants would have a dischargeable claim within the reorganization case. * * * We affirm, although our reasoning may vary somewhat from that of the district court.

Section 362 of the Bankruptcy Code, 11 U.S.C. § 362, provides in part:

> (a) Except as provided in subsection (b) of this section, a petition filed under section §§ 301, 302, or 303 of this title, ... operates as a stay, applicable to all entities, of—
>
> > (1) the commencement or continuation, including the issuance of employment of process, of a judicial, administrative, or other action or proceeding against the debtor that was or could have been commenced before the commencement of the case under this title, or to recover a claim against the debtor that arose before the commencement of the case under this title;
>
> > * * *
>
> The legislative history of the Code reveals the importance of § 362 stay provision: The automatic stay is one of the fundamental debtor protections provided by the bankruptcy laws. It gives the debtor a breathing spell from his creditors. It stops all collection efforts, all harassment, and all foreclosure actions. It permits the debtor to attempt a repayment or reorganization plan, or simply to be relieved of the financial pressures that drove him into bankruptcy.

House Report No. 95–595, 95th Cong. 1st Sess. 340–1 (1977); Senate Report No. 95–989, 95th Cong. 2d Sess. 54–55 (1978); *reprinted in* 1978 U.S. Code Cong. & Adm. News 5787 at 5840 and 6296–97.

The district court correctly noted that the automatic stay is particularly critical to a debtor seeking to reorganize under Chapter 11 because he needs breathing room to restructure his affairs. *Robins,* 63 B.R. at 988, *citing* Matter of Baldwin–United Corp., 48 B.R. 901, 902 (Bkrtcy. S.D. Ohio 1985). While the importance of § 362 cannot be overemphasized, its coverage extends only to claims against the debtor that arose prior to the filing of its petition.

11 U.S.C. § 101(4), as pertinent, defines a claim to be a

> (A) right to a payment, whether or not such right is reduced to judgment, liquidated, unliquidated, fixed, contingent, matured, unmatured, disputed, undisputed, legal, equitable, secured or unsecured;

Congress intended that the definition of claim in the Code be as broad as possible, noting that "the bill contemplates that all legal obligations of the debtor, no matter how remote or contingent, will be able to be dealt with in the bankruptcy. It permits the broadest possible relief in the bankruptcy court." H.R. Rep. No. 595, 95th Cong., 1st Sess. 309 (1977), S. Rep. No. 989, 95th Cong., 2d Sess. 21–22 (1978), *reprinted in* 1978 U.S. Code Cong. & Adm. News, 5787 at 5807–08 and 6266. The courts have consistently recognized the very broad definition to be given to claims. *E.g.* Ohio v. Kovacs, 469 U.S. 274, 279, 105 S.Ct. 705, 707, 83 L.Ed.2d 649 (1985); Robinson v. McGuigan, 776 F.2d 30, 34 (2d Cir. 1985), *rev'd on other grounds sub. nom.,* Kelly v. Robinson, 479 U.S. 36, 107 S.Ct. 353, 93 L.Ed.2d 216 (1986); Matter of M. Frenville Co., Inc., 744 F.2d 332, 336 (3d Cir.1984), *cert. den.* 469 U.S. 1160, 105 S.Ct. 911, 83 L.Ed.2d 925 (1985); In re Edge, 60 B.R. 690, 692–94 (Bkrtcy. M.D.Tenn.1986); In re Johns–Manville Corp., 57 B.R. 680, 686–88 (Bkrtcy. S.D.N.Y.1986).

While the parties agree that the term claim is broadly defined under the Bankruptcy Code, they disagree over whether Mrs. Grady's suit falls within that definition. Mrs. Grady primarily relies upon *Matter of M. Frenville Co.* to support her contention that her claim falls outside the protection of the automatic stay.

Prior to filing its petition, Frenville, an independent auditing firm, had employed Avellina and Bienes (A & B), an accounting firm, to prepare its financial statement. After the bankruptcy petition was filed, several banks which had received the financial statement sued A & B, claiming that the statement was negligently prepared. A & B moved for relief from the automatic stay in order that it could bring Frenville into those lawsuits as a third-party defendant for their indemnification.

The court concluded that a pre-petition act by a debtor giving rise to later liability is not enough to bring an action within the definition of a claim. It held that the right to payment must exist pre-petition before a claim can exist. *Frenville,* 744 F.2d at 335–36. Because the Bankruptcy Code does not provide when a right to payment arises, the court turned to state law for its answer.[3] Because A & B had had no right under state law to seek indemnification from Frenville before the banks filed their suit, the claim was held to arise post-petition and therefore was not barred by the automatic stay provision of s 362(a)(1).

Mrs. Grady argues that her cause of action against Robins did not accrue until after Robins had filed its reorganization petition and therefore the stay provision is inapplicable. Under California law, she argues that she could not have sued Robins until she knew the nature of her injuries.[4] The argument goes that because she had no right to payment from Robins under state law until she was injured, and since that injury occurred after the reorganization petition was filed, the stay provision of § 362 should not bar her case from its prosecution. While not agreeing that state law necessarily controls, the Future Tort Claimants agree that Mrs. Grady had no pre-petition right of payment from Robins and therefore no claim under the Bankruptcy Code.

Robins argues that the district court was correct in declining to apply the reasoning of *Frenville* and in its conclusion that Mrs. Grady's claim falls within the definition set out in § 101 (4)(A) because the tortious conduct occurred prior to the filing of the petition. Robins relies primarily upon In re Black, 70 B.R. 645 (Bkrtcy. D. Utah 1986); *In re Edge*; In re Baldwin–United Corp., 57 B.R. 759 (S.D. Ohio 1985); and *In re Johns–Manville Corp.* These cases decline to apply the reasoning in *Frenville* and conclude that claim accrual for bankruptcy purposes must be determined in light of bankruptcy law and not state law.

We have found no court outside the Third Circuit which has followed the reasoning and holding of *Frenville.* All of the cases coming to our attention which have considered the issue have declined to follow *Frenville's* limiting definition of claim. *In re Black*; Acevedo v. Van Dorn Plastic Machinery Co., 68 B.R. 495 (Bkrtcy. E.D.N.Y.1986); *In re Edge*; *In re Johns–Manville; In re Baldwin–United Corp.;* In re Yanks, 49 B.R. 56 (Bkrtcy. S.D.Fla.1985); In re Baldwin–United Corp., 48 B.R. 901 (Bkrtcy. S.D. Ohio 1985). *See also* In re Baldwin–United Corp. Litigation, 765 F.2d 343, 348 n.4 (2d Cir.1985)(in which the court declines to routinely accept *Frenville*); In re Riso, 58 B.R. 978 (Bkrtcy. D.N.H.1986). We likewise decline to follow *Frenville,* and our reasoning follows.

---

3. The court did comment that application of federal law might be appropriate in instances where the bankruptcy stems from a mass tort. *Frenville,* 744 F.2d at 337 n. 8.

4. Mrs. Grady takes the position that, under California law, a cause of action does not accrue until the injured person knows or by the exercise of reasonable diligence should have discovered the cause of the injury when that injury results without perceptible trauma. Warrington v. Charles Pfizer & Co., 274 Cal.App.2d 564, 567, 80 Cal.Rptr. 130, 132 (1969). Since Mrs. Grady's injuries manifested themselves the same day as the filing of Robins' petition, we are far from certain that her claim should not be treated as pre-petition in all events. We will assume, however, for the purposes of this case that they manifested themselves under California law a few days later when her Dalkon Shield was discovered to be in place.

We commence with the proposition that " ... except where federal law, fully apart from bankruptcy, has created obligations by the exercise of power granted to the federal government, a claim implies the existence of an obligation created by State law." Vanston Committee v. Green, 329 U.S. 156, 167, 170, 67 S.Ct. 237, 242, 243, 91 L.Ed. 162 (1946)(Justice Frankfurter concurring), and further, from that concurring opinion, that "[b]ankruptcy legislation is superimposed upon rights and obligations created by the laws of the States." 329 U.S. at 171, 67 S.Ct. at 244. The opinion of the court in *Vanston* further stands for the proposition that "In determining what claims are allowable and how a debtor's assets are to be distributed, a bankruptcy court does not apply the law of the State where it sits." 329 U.S. at 162, 67 S.Ct. at 240. So, the bankruptcy Code is superimposed upon the law of the State which has created the obligation. Congress has the undoubted power under the bankruptcy article, U.S. Const. Art. I, § 8 cl. 4, to define and classify claims against the estate of a bankrupt. *See* Carpenter v. Wabash Ry. Co., 309 U.S. 23, 28, 60 S.Ct. 416, 418, 84 L.Ed. 558 (1940); Kuehner v. Irving Trust Co., 299 U.S. 445, 450, 57 S.Ct. 298, 300, 81 L.Ed. 340 (1937). In the case of a claim as noted above, the legislative history shows that Congress intended that all legal obligations of the debtor, no matter how remote or contingent, will be able to be dealt with in bankruptcy. The Code contemplates the broadest possible relief in the bankruptcy court. Also, that history tells us that the automatic stay is one of the fundamental debtor protections provided by the bankruptcy laws. It provides a breathing spell to the debtor to restructure his affairs, which could hardly be done with hundreds or thousands of creditors persevering in different courts all over the country for a first share of a debtor's assets. Absent a stay of litigation against the debtor, dismemberment rather than reorganization would, in many or even most cases, be the inevitable result.

With those thoughts in mind, we turn to the pertinent parts of the statutes at hand. Section 362(a)(1) provides for an automatic stay of, among other things, judicial action against the debtor " ... contingent, matured, unmatured, disputed, undisputed, legal, equitable, secured or unsecured."

The *Frenville* case, in construing these two sections, identified the crucial issue as "when did [the] right to payment arise." It found that a right to payment must exist prior to the filing of the petition, and by that the court obviously meant the right to the payment of money immediately, for it distinguished cases involving sureties which it reasoned involved a right to payment immediately upon the signing of a contract of suretyship, but contingent upon the occurrence of a future event. The court obviously was of the view, which is that espoused by Mrs. Grady and the Future Tort Claimants, that, so far as § 362 is concerned, there is no such thing as a contingent tort claim.

While we do not dispute that the result obtained in *Frenville* is not irrational, with respect, we decline to follow it, and while the numerous cases which have declined to follow *Frenville,* many of which we have referred to above, have done so for a variety of reasons, we draw our conclusion largely from the words of the statute.

Shortly after the commencement of this case, the bankruptcy court created a class of claimants called "Future Tort Claimants." While we have been unable to find an order precisely describing the class created, the notices which have been sent out by the multiplied thousands by the bankruptcy court and which were approved by order of the bankruptcy court, to which exception has not been taken, describe this class as follows: "Though not aware of any injury, I may have been injured by my use or another's use of the Dalkon Shield."

Code § 101(4)(A) provides for a "right to payment" whether or not "such right" is "contingent."

BLACK'S LAW DICTIONARY, 5th Ed., 1979, defines "contingent" as follows, and we adopt this definition, there being no indication that Congress meant to use the word in any other sense:

> **Contingent.** Possible, but not assured; doubtful or uncertain; conditioned upon the occurrence of some future event which is itself uncertain, or questionable. Synonymous with provisional. This term, when applied to a use, remainder, devise, bequest, or other legal right or interest, implies that no present interest exists, and that whether such interest or right ever will exist depends upon a future uncertain event.

Mrs. Grady's claim, as well as whatever rights the other Future Tort Claimants have, is undoubtedly "contingent." It depends upon a future uncertain event, that event being the manifestation of injury from use of the Dalkon Shield. We do not believe that there must be a right to the immediate payment of money in the case of a tort or allied breach of warranty or like claim, as present here, when the acts constituting the tort or breach of warranty have occurred prior to the filing of the petition, to constitute a claim under § 362(a)(1). It is at once apparent that there can be no right to the immediate payment of money on account of a claim, the existence of which depends upon a future uncertain event. But it is also apparent that Congress has created a contingent right to payment as it has the power to create a contingent tort or like claim within the protection of § 362(a)(1). We are of opinion that it has done so.

Not only do we think that a literal reading of the statute requires the result we have reached, our reading is fortified by other considerations. The broad reading of the word "claim" required by the legislative history and the cases, *see, e.g.,* Ohio v. Kovacs, is considerable support. That the legislative history contemplates "the broadest possible relief in the bankruptcy court" also enters our reasoning. If Mrs. Grady and the Future Tort Claimants, who had no right to the immediate payment of money at the time of the filing of the petition, were participants in a Chapter 7 proceeding, the chances are that they would receive nothing, for no compensable result had manifested itself prior to the filing of the petition.

We also find persuasive the fact that the district court probably had authority to achieve the same result by staying Mrs. Grady's suit under 11 U.S.C. § 105(a) in the use of its equitable powers to assure the orderly conduct of reorganization proceedings. *See* A.H. Robins Co. Inc. v. Piccinin, 788 F.2d 994, 1002–03 (4th Cir.1986); In re Baldwin—United Corp. Litigation, 765 F.2d 343, 347–48 (2d Cir.1985); 2 COLLIER ON BANKRUPTCY (1987) ¶ 105.02.

We emphasize, as did the district court, that we do not decide whether or not Mrs. Grady's claim or those of the Future Tort Claimants are dischargeable in this case. Neither do we decide whether or not post-petition claims constitute an administrative expense. We hold only that the Dalkon Shield claim in the case before us, when the Dalkon Shield was inserted in the claimant prior to the time of filing of the petition, constitutes a "claim" "that arose before the commencement of the case" within the meaning of 11 U.S.C. § 362(a)(1).

The order appealed from is

AFFIRMED.

GEORGINE v. AMCHEM PRODUCTS, INC.

United States District Court, Eastern District of Pennsylvania, 1994.
157 F.R.D. 246.

[Review *Georgine v. Amchem Products,* Part One, Chapter 1.D.4, *supra—ed.*]

* * *

Notes and Questions

1. In the *Georgine* settlement class, the parties sought to provide some prospective relief for exposure-only claimants through a "futures" provision that permit persons who manifested disease or injury at some future date, according to specified medical criteria, to make a claim under the agreement. Such future claimants, however, could not receive any current award for exposure-only injury. In this respect the futures provision departed from a usual global class settlement where some exposure-only claimants might have received some current value for their claims. As we have already seen, this controversial "futures" provision engendered a heated debate surrounding ethical issues in negotiating and implementing the provision. Apart from the ethical issues involved, is the *Georgine* "futures" provision a sound approach—as a matter of substantive law—to handling exposure-only future claimants? Why shouldn't defendants be able to condition payment on a manifestation of injury? Clearly, the CCR defendants desired this formulation of a futures provision. How do the defendants benefit from such a provision? What, if anything, have the future claimants received in exchange?

2. *Grady v. A.H. Robins* embodies an alternative approach to dealing with latent-injury future claimants through the auspices of bankruptcy law, and illustrates the intersection of substantive tort, bankruptcy, and proce-

dural law. Are the federal bankruptcy provisions a better procedural vehicle for handling mass tort claims, especially future claimants? The issues and problems involved in a bankruptcy approach to mass tort cases is discussed more fully in Chapter XIII, *infra*.

Federal courts have exclusive jurisdiction over bankruptcy proceedings (28 U.S.C.A. § 1334) and special bankruptcy judges handle proceedings under the bankruptcy code. Individuals or entities typically seek bankruptcy protection under either Chapter 7 (liquidation) or Chapter 11 (reorganization). In bankruptcy liquidations, the court will appoint a trustee to conduct the debtor's estate; under Chapter 11 reorganizations, an entity need not be totally insolvent to seek the protection of the bankruptcy court. In general, the filing of a bankruptcy petition affects or involves all persons or entities having a claim against the debtor's assets; the *Grady* case illustrates the intersection of state and federal substantive law in defining what constitutes a claim for the purposes of bankruptcy proceedings. The Johns–Manville bankruptcy, deriving from that corporation's exposure to asbestos litigation, gave rise to a series of cases construing the ability of the bankruptcy court to assess contingent liability as against the debtor corporation. *See e.g.* Roberts v. Johns–Manville Corp., 45 B.R. 823 (S.D.N.Y.1984); In re UNR Industries, Inc., 45 B.R. 322 (N.D.Ill.1984).

As *Grady* also suggests, in addition to ordering or prioritizing claims against an estate or entity, bankruptcy proceedings also provide for an automatic stay or injunction against other litigation. *See* 11 U.S.C.A. § 362. Since the presence of other proceedings is a problem that complicates many mass tort cases, are bankruptcy proceedings a superior procedural framework within which to handle some mass torts? For a related case dealing with the injunctive power in the A.H. Robins Dalkon Shield bankruptcy proceedings, *see* A.H. Robins Co., Inc. v. Piccinin, 788 F.2d 994 (4th Cir. 1986).

B. INDETERMINATE DEFENDANTS
SINDELL v. ABBOTT LABORATORIES
Supreme Court of California, 1980.
26 Cal.3d 588, 163 Cal.Rptr. 132, 607 P.2d 924.

MOSK, JUSTICE.

This case involves a complex problem both timely and significant: may a plaintiff, injured as the result of a drug administered to her mother during pregnancy, who knows the type of drug involved but cannot identify the manufacturer of the precise product, hold liable for her injuries a maker of a drug produced from an identical formula?

Plaintiff Judith Sindell brought an action against eleven drug companies and Does 1 through 100, on behalf of herself and other women similarly situated. The complaint alleges as follows:

> Between 1941 and 1971, defendants were engaged in the business of manufacturing, promoting, and marketing diethylstilbesterol (DES), a drug which is a synthetic compound of the female hormone estrogen. The drug was administered to plaintiff's mother and the

mothers of the class she represents,[1] for the purpose of preventing miscarriage. In 1947, the Food and Drug Administration authorized the marketing of DES as a miscarriage preventative, but only on an experimental basis, with a requirement that the drug contain a warning label to that effect.

DES may cause cancerous vaginal and cervical growths in the daughters exposed to it before birth, because their mothers took the drug during pregnancy. The form of cancer from which these daughters suffer is known as adenocarcinoma, and it manifests itself after a minimum latent period of 10 or 12 years. It is a fast-spreading and deadly disease, and radical surgery is required to prevent it from spreading. DES also causes adenosis, precancerous vaginal and cervical growths which may spread to other areas of the body. The treatment for adenosis is cauterization, surgery, or cryosurgery. Women who suffer from this condition must be monitored by biopsy or colposcopic examination twice a year, a painful and expensive procedure. Thousands of women whose mothers received DES during pregnancy are unaware of the effects of the drug.

In 1971, the Food and Drug Administration ordered defendants to cease marketing and promoting DES for the purpose of preventing miscarriages, and to warn physicians and the public that the drug should not be used by pregnant women because of the danger to their unborn children.

During the period defendants marketed DES, they knew or should have known that it was a carcinogenic substance, that there was a grave danger after varying periods of latency it would cause cancerous and precancerous growths in the daughters of the mothers who took it, and that it was ineffective to prevent miscarriage. Nevertheless, defendants continued to advertise and market the drug as a miscarriage preventative. They failed to test DES for efficacy and safety; the tests performed by others, upon which they relied, indicated that it was not safe or effective. In violation of the authorization of the Food and Drug Administration, defendants marketed DES on an unlimited basis rather than as an experimental drug, and they failed to warn of its potential danger.

Because of defendants' advertised assurances that DES was safe and effective to prevent miscarriage, plaintiff was exposed to the drug prior to her birth. She became aware of the danger from such exposure within one year of the time she filed her complaint. As a result of the DES ingested by her mother, plaintiff developed a malignant bladder tumor which was removed by surgery. She suffers from adenosis and must constantly be monitored by biopsy or colposcopy to insure early warning of further malignancy.

---

1. The plaintiff class alleged consists of "girls and women who are residents of California and who have been exposed to DES before birth and who may or may not know that fact or the dangers" to which they were exposed. Defendants are also sued as representatives of a class of drug manufacturers which sold DES after 1941.

The first cause of action alleges that defendants were jointly and individually negligent in that they manufactured, marketed and promoted DES as a safe and efficacious drug to prevent miscarriage, without adequate testing or warning, and without monitoring or reporting its effects.

A separate cause of action alleges that defendants are jointly liable regardless of which particular brand of DES was ingested by plaintiff's mother because defendants collaborated in marketing, promoting and testing the drug, relied upon each other's tests, and adhered to an industry-wide safety standard. DES was produced from a common and mutually agreed upon formula as a fungible drug interchangeable with other brands of the same product; defendants knew or should have known that it was customary for doctors to prescribe the drug by its generic rather than its brand name and that pharmacists filled prescriptions from whatever brand of the drug happened to be in stock.

Other causes of action are based upon theories of strict liability, violation of express and implied warranties, false and fraudulent representations, misbranding of drugs in violation of federal law, conspiracy and "lack of consent."

Each cause of action alleges that defendants are jointly liable because they acted in concert, on the basis of express and implied agreements, and in reliance upon and ratification and exploitation of each other's testing and marketing methods.

Plaintiff seeks compensatory damages of $1 million and punitive damages of $10 million for herself. For the members of her class, she prays for equitable relief in the form of an order that defendants warn physicians and others of the danger of DES and the necessity of performing certain tests to determine the presence of disease caused by the drug, and that they establish free clinics in California to perform such tests.

Defendants demurred to the complaint. While the complaint did not expressly allege that plaintiff could not identify the manufacturer of the precise drug ingested by her mother, she stated in her points and authorities in opposition to the demurrers filed by some of the defendants that she was unable to make the identification, and the trial court sustained the demurrers of these defendants without leave to amend on the ground that plaintiff did not and stated she could not identify which defendant had manufactured the drug responsible for her injuries. Thereupon, the court dismissed the action. This appeal involves only five of ten defendants named in the complaint.

* * *

This case is but one of a number filed throughout the country seeking to hold drug manufacturers liable for injuries allegedly resulting from DES prescribed to the plaintiffs' mothers since 1947.[6] According

---

6. DES was marketed under many different trade names.

to a note in the Fordham Law Review, estimates of the number of women who took the drug during pregnancy range from 1½ million to 3 million. Hundreds, perhaps thousands, of the daughters of these women suffer from adenocarcinoma, and the incidence of vaginal adenosis among them is 30 to 90 percent. (Comment, *DES and a Proposed Theory of Enterprise Liability* (1978) 46 Fordham L.Rev. 963, 964–967 (hereafter Fordham *Comment*).) Most of the cases are still pending. With two exceptions,[7] those that have been decided resulted in judgments in favor of the drug company defendants because of the failure of the plaintiffs to identify the manufacturer of the DES prescribed to their mothers.[8] The same result was reached in a recent California case. (McCreery v. Eli Lilly & Co. (1978) 87 Cal.App.3d 77, 82–84, 150 Cal.Rptr. 730.) The present action is another attempt to overcome this obstacle to recovery.

We begin with the proposition that, as a general rule, the imposition of liability depends upon a showing by the plaintiff that his or her injuries were caused by the act of the defendant or by an instrumentality under the defendant's control. The rule applies whether the injury resulted from an accidental event (*e.g.*, Shunk v. Bosworth (6th Cir.1964) 334 F.2d 309) or from the use of a defective product. (*E.g.*, Wetzel v. Eaton Corporation (D.Minn.1973) 62 F.R.D. 22, 29–30; Garcia v. Joseph Vince Co. (1978) 84 Cal.App.3d 868, 873–875, 148 Cal.Rptr. 843; and *see* annot. collection of cases in 51 A.L.R.3d 1344, 1351; 1 Hursh and Bailey, AMERICAN LAW OF PRODUCTS LIABILITY 2d (1974) p. 125.)

There are, however, exceptions to this rule. Plaintiff's complaint suggests several bases upon which defendants may be held liable for her injuries even though she cannot demonstrate the name of the manufacturer which produced the DES actually taken by her mother. The first of these theories, classically illustrated by Summers v. Tice (1948) 33 Cal.2d 80, 199 P.2d 1, places the burden of proof of causation upon tortious defendants in certain circumstances. The second basis of liability emerging from the complaint is that defendants acted in concert to cause injury to plaintiff. There is a third and novel approach to the problem, sometimes called the theory of "enterprise liability," but which we prefer to designate by the more accurate term of "industry-wide" liability,[9] which might obviate the necessity for identifying the manufacturer of the injury-causing drug. We shall conclude that these doctrines,

---

7. In a recent New York case a jury found in the plaintiff's favor in spite of her inability to identify a specific manufacturer of DES. An appeal is pending. (Bichler v. Eli Lilly and Co. (Sup.Ct.N.Y.1979).) A Michigan appellate court recently held that plaintiffs had stated a cause of action against several manufacturers of DES even though identification could not be made. (Abel v. Eli Lilly and Co. (decided Dec. 5, 1979) Docket No. 60497.) That decision is on appeal to the Supreme Court of Michigan.

8. *E.g.*, Gray v. United States (S.D.Tex. 1978) 445 F.Supp. 337. In their briefs, defendants refer to a number of other cases in which trial courts have dismissed actions in DES cases on the ground stated above.

9. The term "enterprise liability" is sometimes used broadly to mean that losses caused by an enterprise should be borne by it. (Klemme Enterprise Liability (1976) 47 Colo.L.Rev. 153, 158.)

as previously interpreted, may not be applied to hold defendants liable under the allegations of this complaint. However, we shall propose and adopt a fourth basis for permitting the action to be tried, grounded upon an extension of the Summers doctrine.

IN RE "AGENT ORANGE" PRODUCT LIABILITY LITIGATION MDL NO. 381

United States Court of Appeals, Second Circuit, 1987.
818 F.2d 145.

Review discussion of the problem of indeterminate defendants in *In Re "Agent Orange" Products Liability Litigation,* at Chapter II, Part A.4, *supra.*

Notes and Questions

1. *Sindell* is the landmark case that provides an analytical description of the problem of the indeterminate defendant; subsequent mass tort cases, such as *Agent Orange,* have elaborated on the variations of the problem of the indeterminate defendant. For our purposes, the problem of the indeterminate defendant is significant because it implicates substantive tort law theories of joint and several liability. As the subsequent materials suggests, mass tort cases have pushed the boundaries of joint liability theory, building on simple theories developed in less-complex cases.

The American Law Institute's *Reporter's Study* of ENTERPRISE RESPONSIBILITY FOR PERSONAL INJURY (1991) described the problem of the indeterminate defendant:

> Finally, it may be far more difficult to identify the particular contribution of an alleged source of harm than in a classic accident case. In some instances the problem may be that a large number of manufacturers marketed an essentially fungible product, and the victim cannot identify the source to which he or she was exposed. In other situations, such as hazardous waste dump exposure, the victim may be suffering from the consequences of synergistic effects resulting from the commingling of a large number of toxic substances. Whatever the case, mass tort episodes frequently raise issues of joint and several responsibility—again posing enormous problems of *ex ante* predictability and *ex post* proof—that are a striking contrast to the simple issues of co-responsibility found in multiple defendant, common law tort cases.

Id. at 387–388 (footnote omitted).

2. For a discussion of the indeterminate defendant problem, *see* Rebecca J. Greenberg, *The Indeterminate Defendant in Products Liability Litigation and a Suggested Approach for Ohio,* 39 Clev.St.L.Rev. 207 (1991).

C. JOINT LIABILITY

1. MASS TOXIC TORT LITIGATION

SINDELL v. ABBOTT LABORATORIES

Supreme Court of California, 1980.
26 Cal.3d 588, 163 Cal.Rptr. 132, 607 P.2d 924.

MOSK, JUSTICE

* * *

I

Plaintiff places primary reliance upon cases which hold that if a party cannot identify which of two or more defendants caused an injury, the burden of proof may shift to the defendants to show that they were not responsible for the harm. This principle is sometimes referred to as the "alternative liability" theory.

The celebrated case of Summers v. Tice, 33 Cal.2d 80, 199 P.2d 1, a unanimous opinion of this court, best exemplifies the rule. In *Summers,* the plaintiff was injured when two hunters negligently shot in his direction. It could not be determined which of them had fired the shot which actually caused the injury to the plaintiff's eye, but both defendants were nevertheless held jointly and severally liable for the whole of the damages. We reasoned that both were wrongdoers, both were negligent toward the plaintiff, and that it would be unfair to require plaintiff to isolate the defendant responsible, because if the one pointed out were to escape liability, the other might also, and the plaintiff-victim would be shorn of any remedy. In these circumstances, we held, the burden of proof shifted to the defendants, "each to absolve himself if he can." * * * We stated that under these or similar circumstances a defendant is ordinarily in a "far better position" to offer evidence to determine whether he or another defendant caused the injury.

In *Summers,* we relied upon Ybarra v. Spangard (1944) 25 Cal.2d 486, 154 P.2d 687. There, the plaintiff was injured while he was unconscious during the course of surgery. He sought damages against several doctors and a nurse who attended him while he was unconscious. We held that it would be unreasonable to require him to identify the particular defendant who had performed the alleged negligent act because he was unconscious at the time of the injury and the defendants exercised control over the instrumentalities which caused the harm. Therefore, under the doctrine of res ipsa loquitur, an inference of negligence arose that defendants were required to meet by explaining their conduct.

The rule developed in *Summers* has been embodied in the RESTATEMENT OF TORTS. (REST. 2D TORTS, § 433B, subsec. (3).) [11] Indeed, the *Summers* facts are used as an illustration ....

---

11. Section 433B, subsection (3) of the RESTATEMENT provides: "Where the conduct   of two or more actors is tortious, and it is proved that harm has been caused to the

Defendants assert that these principles are inapplicable here. First, they insist that a predicate to shifting the burden of proof under *Summers-Ybarra* is that the defendants must have greater access to information regarding the cause of the injuries than the plaintiff, whereas in the present case the reverse appears.

Plaintiff does not claim that defendants are in a better position than she to identify the manufacturer of the drug taken by her mother or, indeed, that they have the ability to do so at all, but argues, rather, that *Summers* does not impose such a requirement as a condition to the shifting of the burden of proof. In this respect we believe plaintiff is correct.

In *Summers*, the circumstances of the accident themselves precluded an explanation of its cause. To be sure, *Summers* states that defendants are "[o]rdinarily ... in a far better position to offer evidence to determine which one caused the injury" than a plaintiff ..., but the decision does not determine that this "ordinary" situation was present. Neither the facts nor the language of the opinion indicate that the two defendants, simultaneously shooting in the same direction, were in a better position than the plaintiff to ascertain whose shot caused the injury. As the opinion acknowledges, it was impossible for the trial court to determine whether the shot which entered the plaintiff's eye came from the gun of one defendant or the other. Nevertheless, burden of proof was shifted to the defendants.

Here, as in *Summers*, the circumstances of the injury appear to render identification of the manufacturer of the drug ingested by plaintiff's mother impossible by either plaintiff or defendants, and it cannot reasonably be said that one is in a better position than the other to make the identification. Because many years elapsed between the time the drug was taken and the manifestation of plaintiff's injuries she, and many other daughters of mothers who took DES, are unable to make such identification. Certainly there can be no implication that plaintiff is at fault in failing to do so [when] the event occurred while plaintiff was in utero, a generation ago.[13]

On the other hand, it cannot be said with assurance that defendants have the means to make the identification. In this connection, they

plaintiff by only one of them, but there is uncertainty as to which one has caused it, the burden is upon each such actor to prove that he has not caused the harm." The reason underlying the rule is "the injustice of permitting proved wrongdoers, who among them have inflicted an injury upon the entirely innocent plaintiff, to escape liability merely because the nature of their conduct and the resulting harm has made it difficult or impossible to prove which of them has caused the harm." (REST. 2D TORTS, § 433B, com. f, p. 446.)

13. Defendants maintain that plaintiff is in a better position than they are to identify the manufacturer because her mother might recall the name of the prescribing physician or the hospital or pharmacy where the drug originated, and might know the brand and strength of dosage, the appearance of the medication, or other details from which the manufacturer might be identified, whereas they possess none of this information. ..., we assume for purposes of this appeal that plaintiff cannot point to any particular manufacturer as the producer of the DES taken by her mother.

point out that drug manufacturers ordinarily have no direct contact with the patients who take a drug prescribed by their doctors. Defendants sell to wholesalers, who in turn supply the product to physicians and pharmacies. Manufacturers do not maintain records of the persons who take the drugs they produce, and the selection of the medication is made by the physician rather than the manufacturer. Nor do we conclude that the absence of evidence on this subject is due to the fault of defendants. While it is alleged that they produced a defective product with delayed effects and without adequate warnings, the difficulty or impossibility of identification results primarily from the passage of time rather than from their allegedly negligent acts of failing to provide adequate warnings. Thus Haft v. Lone Palm Hotel (1970) 3 Cal.3d 756, 91 Cal.Rptr. 745, 478 P.2d 465, upon which plaintiff relies, is distinguishable.[14]

It is important to observe, however, that while defendants do not have means superior to plaintiff to identify the maker of the precise drug taken by her mother, they may in some instances be able to prove that they did not manufacture the injury-causing substance. In the present case, for example, one of the original defendants was dismissed from the action upon proof that it did not manufacture DES until after plaintiff was born.

Thus we conclude that the fact defendants do not have greater access to information which might establish the identity of the manufacturer of the DES which injured plaintiff does not *per se* prevent application of the *Summers* rule.

Nevertheless, plaintiff may not prevail in her claim that the *Summers* rationale should be employed to fix the whole liability for her injuries upon defendants, at least as those principles have previously been applied. There is an important difference between the situation involved in *Summers* and the present case. There, all the parties who were or could have been responsible for the harm to the plaintiff were joined as defendants. Here, by contrast, there are approximately 200 drug companies which made DES, any of which might have manufac-

---

14. In *Haft,* a father and his young son drowned in defendants' swimming pool. There were no witnesses to the accident. Defendants were negligent in failing to provide a lifeguard, as required by law. We held that the absence of evidence of causation was a direct and foreseeable result of the defendants' negligence, and that, therefore, the burden of proof on the issue of causation was upon defendants. Plaintiff attempts to bring herself within this holding. She asserts that defendants' failure to discover or warn of the dangers of DES and to label the drug as experimental caused her mother to fail to keep records or remember the brand name of the drug pre-

scribed to her "since she was unaware of any reason to do so for a period of 10 to 20 years." There is no proper analogy to *Haft* here. While in *Haft* the presence of a lifeguard on the scene would have provided a witness to the accident and probably prevented it, plaintiff asks us to speculate that if the DES taken by her mother had been labelled as an experimental drug, she would have recalled or recorded the name of the manufacturer and passed this information on to her daughter. It cannot be said here that the absence of evidence of causation was a "direct and foreseeable result" of defendants' failure to provide a warning label.

tured the injury-producing drug.[16]

Defendants maintain that, while in *Summers* there was a 50 percent chance that one of the two defendants was responsible for the plaintiff's injuries, here since any one of 200 companies which manufactured DES might have made the product which harmed plaintiff, there is no rational basis upon which to infer that any defendant in this action caused plaintiff's injuries, nor even a reasonable possibility that they were responsible.[17]

These arguments are persuasive if we measure the chance that any one of the defendants supplied the injury-causing drug by the number of possible tortfeasors. In such a context, the possibility that any of the five defendants supplied the DES to plaintiff's mother is so remote that it would be unfair to require each defendant to exonerate itself. There may be a substantial likelihood that none of the five defendants joined in the action made the DES which caused the injury, and that the offending producer not named would escape liability altogether. While we propose, *infra,* an adaptation of the rule in *Summers* which will substantially overcome these difficulties, defendants appear to be correct that the rule, as previously applied, cannot relieve plaintiff of the burden of proving the identity of the manufacturer which made the drug causing her injuries.

II

The second principle upon which plaintiff relies is the so-called "concert of action" theory. Preliminarily, we briefly describe the procedure a drug manufacturer must follow before placing a drug on the market. Under federal law as it read prior to 1962, a new drug was defined as one "not generally recognized as . . . safe." * * * Such a substance could be marketed only if a new drug application had been filed with the Food and Drug Administration and had become "effective." If the agency determined that a product was no longer a "new drug," *i.e.,* that it was "generally recognized as . . . safe," (21 U.S.C.A. § 321, subd. (p)(1)) it could be manufactured by any drug company without submitting an application to the agency. According to defendants, 123 new drug applications for DES had been approved by 1952, and in that year DES was declared not to be a "new drug," thus allowing any manufacturer to produce it without prior testing and

16. According to the RESTATEMENT, the burden of proof shifts to the defendants only if the plaintiff can demonstrate that all defendants acted tortiously and that the harm resulted from the conduct of one of them. (REST. 2D TORTS, § 433B, com. g, p. 446.) It goes on to state that the rule thus far has been applied only where all the actors involved are joined as defendants and where the conduct of all is simultaneous in time, but cases might arise in which some modification of the rule would be necessary if one of the actors is or cannot be joined, or because of the effects of lapse of time, or other circumstances.

17. Defendants claim further that the effect of shifting the burden of proof to them to demonstrate that they did not manufacture the DES which caused the injury would create a rebuttable presumption that one of them made the drug taken by plaintiff's mother, and that this presumption would deny them due process because there is no rational basis for the inference.

without submitting a new drug application to the Food and Drug Administration.

With this background we consider whether the complaint states a claim based upon "concert of action" among defendants. The elements of this doctrine are prescribed in section 876 of the RESTATEMENT OF TORTS. The section provides, "For harm resulting to a third person from the tortious conduct of another, one is subject to liability if he (a) does a tortious act in concert with the other or pursuant to a common design with him, or (b) knows that the other's conduct constitutes a breach of duty and gives substantial assistance or encouragement to the other so to conduct himself, or (c) gives substantial assistance to the other in accomplishing a tortious result and his own conduct, separately considered, constitutes a breach of duty to the third person." With respect to this doctrine, Prosser states that "those who, in pursuance of a common plan or design to commit a tortious act, actively take part in it, or further it by cooperation or request, or who lend aid or encouragement to the wrongdoer, or ratify and adopt his acts done for their benefit, are equally liable with him. Express agreement is not necessary, and all that is required is that there be a tacit understanding...." (Prosser, LAW OF TORTS (4th ed.1971), sec. 46, p. 292.)

Plaintiff contends that her complaint states a cause of action under these principles. She alleges that defendants' wrongful conduct "is the result of planned and concerted action, express and implied agreements, collaboration in, reliance upon, acquiescence in and ratification, exploitation and adoption of each other's testing, marketing methods, lack of warnings ... and other acts or omissions ..." and that "acting individually and in concert, (defendants) promoted, approved, authorized, acquiesced in, and reaped profits from sales" of DES. These allegations, plaintiff claims, state a "tacit understanding" among defendants to commit a tortious act against her.

In our view, this litany of charges is insufficient to allege a cause of action under the rules stated above. The gravamen of the charge of concert is that defendants failed to adequately test the drug or to give sufficient warning of its dangers and that they relied upon the tests performed by one another and took advantage of each others' promotional and marketing techniques. These allegations do not amount to a charge that there was a tacit understanding or a common plan among defendants to fail to conduct adequate tests or give sufficient warnings, and that they substantially aided and encouraged one another in these omissions.

The complaint charges also that defendants produced DES from a "common and mutually agreed upon formula," allowing pharmacists to treat the drug as a "fungible commodity" and to fill prescriptions from whatever brand of DES they had on hand at the time. It is difficult to understand how these allegations can form the basis of a cause of action for wrongful conduct by defendants, acting in concert. The formula for DES is a scientific constant. It is set forth in the United States

Pharmacopoeia, and any manufacturer producing that drug must, with exceptions not relevant here, utilize the formula set forth in that compendium. (21 U.S.C.A. § 351, subd. (b).)

What the complaint appears to charge is defendants' parallel or imitative conduct in that they relied upon each others' testing and promotion methods. But such conduct describes a common practice in industry: a producer avails himself of the experience and methods of others making the same or similar products. Application of the concept of concert of action to this situation would expand the doctrine far beyond its intended scope and would render virtually any manufacturer liable for the defective products of an entire industry, even if it could be demonstrated that the product which caused the injury was not made by the defendant.

None of the cases cited by plaintiff supports a conclusion that defendants may be held liable for concerted tortious acts. They involve conduct by a small number of individuals whose actions resulted in a tort against a single plaintiff, usually over a short span of time, and the defendant held liable was either a direct participant in the acts which caused damage, or encouraged and assisted the person who directly caused the injuries by participating in a joint activity.

* * *

III

A third theory upon which plaintiff relies is the concept of industry-wide liability, or according to the terminology of the parties, "enterprise liability." This theory was suggested in Hall v. E. I. Du Pont De Nemours & Co., Inc. (E.D.N.Y.1972) 345 F.Supp. 353. In that case, plaintiffs were 13 children injured by the explosion of blasting caps in 12 separate incidents which occurred in 10 different states between 1955 and 1959. The defendants were six blasting cap manufacturers, comprising virtually the entire blasting cap industry in the United States, and their trade association. There were, however, a number of Canadian blasting cap manufacturers which could have supplied the caps. The gravamen of the complaint was that the practice of the industry of omitting a warning on individual blasting caps and of failing to take other safety measures created an unreasonable risk of harm, resulting in the plaintiffs' injuries. The complaint did not identify a particular manufacturer of a cap which caused a particular injury.

The court reasoned as follows: there was evidence that defendants, acting independently, had adhered to an industry-wide standard with regard to the safety features of blasting caps, that they had in effect delegated some functions of safety investigation and design, such as labelling, to their trade association, and that there was industry-wide cooperation in the manufacture and design of blasting caps. In these circumstances, the evidence supported a conclusion that all the defendants jointly controlled the risk. Thus, if plaintiffs could establish by a preponderance of the evidence that the caps were manufactured by one of the defendants, the burden of proof as to causation would shift to all the defendants. The court noted that this theory of liability applied to industries composed of a small number of units, and that what would be fair and reasonable with regard to an industry of five or ten producers might be manifestly unreasonable if applied to a decentralized industry composed of countless small producers.[23]

Plaintiff attempts to state a cause of action under the rationale of *Hall*. She alleges joint enterprise and collaboration among defendants in the production, marketing, promotion and testing of DES, and "concerted promulgation and adherence to industry-wide testing, safety, warning and efficacy standards" for the drug. We have concluded above that allegations that defendants relied upon one another's testing and promotion methods do not state a cause of action for concerted conduct to commit a tortious act. Under the theory of industry-wide liability, however, each manufacturer could be liable for all injuries caused by DES by virtue of adherence to an industry-wide standard of safety.

* * *

We decline to apply this theory in the present case. At least 200 manufacturers produced DES; *Hall,* which involved 6 manufacturers representing the entire blasting cap industry in the United States, cautioned against application of the doctrine espoused therein to a large number of producers. * * * Moreover, in *Hall,* the conclusion that the defendants jointly controlled the risk was based upon allegations that they had delegated some functions relating to safety to a trade association. There are no such allegations here, and we have concluded above that plaintiff has failed to allege liability on a concert of action theory.

Equally important, the drug industry is closely regulated by the Food and Drug Administration, which actively controls the testing and manufacture of drugs and the method by which they are marketed, including the contents of warning labels. To a considerable degree, therefore, the standards followed by drug manufacturers are suggested or compelled by the government. Adherence to those standards cannot, of course, absolve a manufacturer of liability to which it would otherwise be subject. * * * But since the government plays such a pervasive role in formulating the criteria for the testing and marketing of drugs, it would be unfair to impose upon a manufacturer liability for injuries resulting from the use of a drug which it did not supply simply because it followed the standards of the industry.

IV

If we were confined to the theories of *Summers* and *Hall,* we would be constrained to hold that the judgment must be sustained. Should we require that plaintiff identify the manufacturer which supplied the DES

---

23. In discussing strict liability, the *Hall* court mentioned the drug industry, stating, "In cases where manufacturers have more experience, more information, and more control over the risky properties of their products than do drug manufacturers, courts have applied a broader concept of foreseeability which approaches the enterprise liability rationale." (345 F.Supp. 353 at p. 370.)

used by her mother or that all DES manufacturers be joined in the
action, she would effectively be precluded from any recovery. As defendants candidly admit, there is little likelihood that all the manufacturers
who made DES at the time in question are still in business or that they
are subject to the jurisdiction of the California courts. There are,
however, forceful arguments in favor of holding that plaintiff has a cause
of action.

In our contemporary complex industrialized society, advances in
science and technology create fungible goods which may harm consumers
and which cannot be traced to any specific producer. The response of
the courts can be either to adhere rigidly to prior doctrine, denying
recovery to those injured by such products, or to fashion remedies to
meet these changing needs. Just as Justice Traynor in his landmark
concurring opinion in Escola v. Coca-Cola Bottling Company (1944) 24
Cal.2d 453, 467–468, 150 P.2d 436, recognized that in an era of mass
production and complex marketing methods the traditional standard of
negligence was insufficient to govern the obligations of manufacturer to
consumer, so should we acknowledge that some adaptation of the rules
of causation and liability may be appropriate in these recurring circumstances. The RESTATEMENT comments that modification of the *Summers*
rule may be necessary in a situation like that before us.

The most persuasive reason for finding plaintiff states a cause of
action is that advanced in *Summers*: as between an innocent plaintiff
and negligent defendants, the latter should bear the cost of the injury.
Here, as in *Summers*, plaintiff is not at fault in failing to provide
evidence of causation, and although the absence of such evidence is not
attributable to the defendants either, their conduct in marketing a drug
the effects of which are delayed for many years played a significant role
in creating the unavailability of proof.

From a broader policy standpoint, defendants are better able to bear
the cost of injury resulting from the manufacture of a defective product.
As was said by Justice Traynor in *Escola,* "(t)he cost of an injury and the
loss of time or health may be an overwhelming misfortune to the person
injured, and a needless one, for the risk of injury can be insured by the
manufacturer and distributed among the public as a cost of doing
business." * * * The manufacturer is in the best position to discover
and guard against defects in its products and to warn of harmful effects;
thus, holding it liable for defects and failure to warn of harmful effects
will provide an incentive to product safety. * * * These considerations
are particularly significant where medication is involved, for the consumer is virtually helpless to protect himself from serious, sometimes permanent, sometimes fatal, injuries caused by deleterious drugs.

Where, as here, all defendants produced a drug from an identical
formula and the manufacturer of the DES which caused plaintiff's
injuries cannot be identified through no fault of plaintiff, a modification
of the rule of *Summers* is warranted. As we have seen, an undiluted
Summers rationale is inappropriate to shift the burden of proof of

causation to defendants because if we measure the chance that any particular manufacturer supplied the injury-causing product by the number of producers of DES, there is a possibility that none of the five defendants in this case produced the offending substance and that the responsible manufacturer, not named in the action, will escape liability.

But we approach the issue of causation from a different perspective: we hold it to be reasonable in the present context to measure the likelihood that any of the defendants supplied the product which allegedly injured plaintiff by the percentage which the DES sold by each of them for the purpose of preventing miscarriage bears to the entire production of the drug sold by all for that purpose. Plaintiff asserts in her briefs that Eli Lilly and Company and 5 or 6 other companies produced 90 percent of the DES marketed. If at trial this is established to be the fact, then there is a corresponding likelihood that this comparative handful of producers manufactured the DES which caused plaintiff's injuries, and only a 10 percent likelihood that the offending producer would escape liability.

If plaintiff joins in the action the manufacturers of a substantial share of the DES which her mother might have taken, the injustice of shifting the burden of proof to defendants to demonstrate that they could not have made the substance which injured plaintiff is significantly diminished. While 75 to 80 percent of the market is suggested as the requirement by the Fordham *Comment* * * *, we hold only that a substantial percentage is required.

The presence in the action of a substantial share of the appropriate market also provides a ready means to apportion damages among the defendants. Each defendant will be held liable for the proportion of the judgment represented by its share of that market unless it demonstrates that it could not have made the product which caused plaintiff's injuries. In the present case, as we have see, one DES manufacturer was dismissed from the action upon filing a declaration that it had not manufactured DES until after plaintiff was born. Once plaintiff has met her burden of joining the required defendants, they in turn may cross-complaint against other DES manufacturers, not joined in the action, which they can allege might have supplied the injury-causing product.

Under this approach, each manufacturer's liability would approximate its responsibility for the injuries caused by its own products. Some minor discrepancy in the correlation between market share and liability is inevitable; therefore, a defendant may be held liable for a somewhat different percentage of the damage than its share of the appropriate market would justify. It is probably impossible, with the passage of time, to determine market share with mathematical exactitude. But just as a jury cannot be expected to determine the precise relationship between fault and liability in applying the doctrine of comparative fault * * * or partial indemnity * * *, the difficulty of apportioning damages among the defendant producers in exact relation to their market share does not seriously militate against the rule we adopt. As we said in

Summers with regard to the liability of independent tortfeasors, where a correct division of liability cannot be made "the trier of fact may make it the best it can." * * *

We are not unmindful of the practical problems involved in defining the market and determining market share,[29] but these are largely matters of proof which properly cannot be determined at the pleading stage of these proceedings. Defendants urge that it would be both unfair and contrary to public policy to hold them liable for plaintiff's injuries in the absence of proof that one of them supplied the drug responsible for the damage. Most of their arguments, however, are based upon the assumption that one manufacturer would be held responsible for the products of another or for those of all other manufacturers if plaintiff ultimately prevails. But under the rule we adopt, each manufacturer's liability for an injury would be approximately equivalent to the damages caused by the DES it manufactured.[30]

The judgments are reversed.

BIRD, C. J., and NEWMAN and WHITE, JJ., concur.

RICHARDSON, JUSTICE, dissenting.

I respectfully dissent. In these consolidated cases the majority adopts a wholly new theory which contains these ingredients: The plaintiffs were not alive at the time of the commission of the tortious acts. They sue a generation later. They are permitted to receive substantial damages from multiple defendants without any proof that any defendant caused or even probably caused plaintiffs' injuries.

Although the majority purports to change only the required burden of proof by shifting it from plaintiffs to defendants, the effect of its holding is to guarantee that plaintiffs will prevail on the causation issue because defendants are no more capable of disproving factual causation than plaintiffs are of proving it. "Market share" liability thus represents a new high water mark in tort law. The ramifications seem almost limitless, a fact which prompted one recent commentator, in criticizing a substantially identical theory, to conclude that "Elimination of the burden of proof as to identification (of the manufacturer whose drug injured plaintiff) would impose a liability which would exceed absolute liability." (Coggins, *Industry-Wide Liability* (1979) 13 Suffolk L.Rev. 980, 998, fn. omitted; * * *) In my view, the majority's departure from traditional tort doctrine is unwise.

---

29. Defendants assert that there are no figures available to determine market share, that DES was provided for a number of uses other than to prevent miscarriage and it would be difficult to ascertain what proportion of the drug was used as a miscarriage preventative, and that the establishment of a time frame and area for market share would pose problems.

30. The dissent concludes by implying the problem will disappear if the Legislature appropriates funds "for the education, identification, and screening of persons exposed to DES." While such a measure may arguably be helpful in the abstract, it does not address the issue involved here: damages for injuries which have been or will be suffered. Nor, as a principle, do we see any justification for shifting the financial burden for such damages from drug manufacturers to the taxpayers of California.

The applicable principles of causation are very well established. A leading torts scholar, Dean Prosser, has authoritatively put it this way: "An essential element of the plaintiff's cause of action for negligence, or for that matter for any other tort, is that there be some reasonable connection between the act or omission of the defendant and the damage which the plaintiff has suffered." (Prosser, TORTS (4th ed.1971) § 41, p. 236, * * *). With particular reference to the matter before us, and in the context of products liability, the requirement of a causation element has been recognized as equally fundamental. "It is clear that any holding that a producer, manufacturer, seller, or a person in a similar position, is liable for injury caused by a particular product, must necessarily be predicated upon proof that the product in question was one for whose condition the defendant was in some way responsible. Thus, for example, if recovery is sought from a manufacturer, it must be shown that he actually was the manufacturer of the product which caused the injury; . . ." * * * Indeed, an inability to prove this causal link between defendant's conduct and plaintiff's injury has proven fatal in prior cases brought against manufacturers of DES by persons who were situated in positions identical to those of plaintiffs herein. * * *

The majority now expressly abandons the foregoing traditional requirement of some causal connection between defendants' act and plaintiffs' injury in the creation of its new modified industry-wide tort. Conceptually, the doctrine of absolute liability which heretofore in negligence law has substituted only for the requirement of a breach of defendant's duty of care, under the majority's hand now subsumes the additional necessity of a causal relationship.

According to the majority, in the present case plaintiffs have openly conceded that they are unable to identify the particular entity which manufactured the drug consumed by their mothers. In fact, plaintiffs have joined only five of the approximately two hundred drug companies which manufactured DES. Thus, the case constitutes far more than a mere factual variant upon the theme composed in Summers v. Tice (1948) 33 Cal.2d 80, 199 P.2d 1, wherein plaintiff joined as codefendants the only two persons who could have injured him. As the majority must acknowledge, our *Summers* rule applies only to cases in which ". . . it is proved that harm has been caused to the plaintiff by . . . one of (the named defendants), but there is uncertainty as to which one has caused it, . . ." (REST. 2D TORTS, § 433B, subd. (3).) In the present case, in stark contrast, it remains wholly speculative and conjectural whether any of the five named defendants actually caused plaintiffs' injuries.

The fact that plaintiffs cannot tie defendants to the injury-producing drug does not trouble the majority for it declares that the *Summers* requirement of proof of actual causation by a named defendant is satisfied by a joinder of those defendants who have together manufactured "a substantial percentage "of the DES which has been marketed. Notably lacking from the majority's expression of its new rule, unfortunately, is any definition or guidance as to what should constitute a "substantial" share of the relevant market. The issue is entirely open-ended and the answer, presumably, is anyone's guess.

Much more significant, however, is the consequence of this unprecedented extension of liability. Recovery is permitted from a handful of defendants each of whom individually may account for a comparatively small share of the relevant market, so long as the aggregate business of those who have been sued is deemed "substantial." In other words, a particular defendant may be held proportionately liable even though mathematically it is much more likely than not that it played no role whatever in causing plaintiffs' injuries. Plaintiffs have strikingly capsulated their reasoning by insisting ". . . that while one manufacturer's product may not have injured a particular plaintiff, we can assume that it injured a different plaintiff and all we are talking about is a mere matching of plaintiffs and defendants." * * * In adopting the foregoing rationale the majority rejects over 100 years of tort law which required that before tort liability was imposed a "matching" of defendant's conduct and plaintiff's injury was absolutely essential. Furthermore, in bestowing on plaintiffs this new largess the majority sprinkles the rain of liability upon all the joined defendants alike those who may be tortfeasors and those who may have had nothing at all to do with plaintiffs' injury and an added bonus is conferred. Plaintiffs are free to pick and choose their targets.

The "market share" thesis may be paraphrased. Plaintiffs have been hurt by someone who made DES. Because of the lapse of time no one can prove who made it. Perhaps it was not the named defendants who made it, but they did make some. Although DES was apparently safe at the time it was used, it was subsequently proven unsafe as to some daughters of some users. Plaintiffs have suffered injury and defendants are wealthy. There should be a remedy. Strict products liability is unavailable because the element of causation is lacking. Strike that requirement and label what remains "alternative" liability, "industry-wide" liability, or "market share" liability, proving thereby that if you hit the square peg hard and often enough the round holes will really become square, although you may splinter the board in the process.

The foregoing result is directly contrary to long established tort principles. Once again, in the words of Dean Prosser, the applicable rule is: "[Plaintiff] must introduce evidence which affords a reasonable basis for the conclusion that it is more likely than not that the conduct of the defendant was a substantial factor in bringing about the result. A mere possibility of such causation is not enough; and when the matter remains one of pure speculation or conjecture, or the probabilities are at best evenly balanced, it becomes the duty of the court to direct a verdict for the defendant." * * * Under the majority's new reasoning, however, a defendant is fair game if it happens to be engaged in a similar business and causation is possible, even though remote.

In passing, I note the majority's dubious use of market share data. It is perfectly proper to use such information to assist in proving, circumstantially, that a particular defendant probably caused plaintiffs' injuries. Circumstantial evidence may be used as a basis for proving the requisite probable causation. * * * The majority, however, authorizes the use of such evidence for an entirely different purpose, namely, to impose and allocate liability among multiple defendants only one of whom may have produced the drug which injured plaintiffs. Because this use of market share evidence does not implicate any particular defendant, I believe such data are entirely irrelevant and inadmissible, and that the majority errs in such use. In the absence of some statutory authority there is no legal basis for such use.

Although seeming to acknowledge that imposition of liability upon defendants who probably did not cause plaintiffs' injuries is unfair, the majority justifies this inequity on the ground that "each manufacturer's liability for an injury would be approximately equivalent to the damages caused by the DES it manufactured." * * * In other words, because each defendant's liability is proportionate to its market share, supposedly "each manufacturer's liability would approximate its responsibility for the injuries caused by his own products." * * * The majority dodges the "practical problems" thereby presented, choosing to describe them as "matters of proof." However, the difficulties, in my view, are not so easily ducked, for they relate not to evidentiary matters but to the fundamental question of liability itself.

Additionally, it is readily apparent that "market share" liability will fall unevenly and disproportionately upon those manufacturers who are amenable to suit in California. On the assumption that no other state will adopt so radical a departure from traditional tort principles, it may be concluded that under the majority's reasoning those defendants who are brought to trial in this state will bear effective joint responsibility for 100 percent of plaintiffs' injuries despite the fact that their "substantial" aggregate market share may be considerably less. This undeniable fact forces the majority to concede that, "a defendant may be held liable for a somewhat different percentage of the damage than its share of the appropriate market would justify." * * * With due deference, I suggest that the complete unfairness of such a result in a case involving only five of two hundred manufacturers is readily manifest.

Furthermore, several other important policy considerations persuade me that the majority holding is both inequitable and improper. The injustice inherent in the majority's new theory of liability is compounded by the fact that plaintiffs who use it are treated far more favorably than are the plaintiffs in routine tort actions. In most tort cases plaintiff knows the identity of the person who has caused his injuries. In such a case, plaintiff, of course, has no option to seek recovery from an entire industry or a "substantial" segment thereof, but in the usual instance can recover, if at all, only from the particular defendant causing injury. Such a defendant may or may not be either solvent or amenable to process. Plaintiff in the ordinary tort case must take a chance that defendant can be reached and can respond financially. On what principle should those plaintiffs who wholly fail to prove any causation, an essential element of the traditional tort cause of action, be rewarded by being offered both a wider selection of potential defendants and a greater opportunity for recovery?

The majority attempts to justify its new liability on the ground that defendants herein are "better able to bear the cost of injury resulting from the manufacture of a defective product." * * * This "deep pocket" theory of liability, fastening liability on defendants presumably because they are rich, has understandable popular appeal and might be tolerable in a case disclosing substantially stronger evidence of causation than herein appears. But as a general proposition, a defendant's wealth is an unreliable indicator of fault, and should play no part, at least consciously, in the legal analysis of the problem. In the absence of proof that a particular defendant caused or at least probably caused plaintiff's injuries, a defendant's ability to bear the cost thereof is no more pertinent to the underlying issue of liability than its "substantial" share of the relevant market. A system priding itself on "equal justice under law" does not flower when the liability as well as the damage aspect of a tort action is determined by a defendant's wealth. The inevitable consequence of such a result is to create and perpetuate two rules of law one applicable to wealthy defendants, and another standard pertaining to defendants who are poor or who have modest means. Moreover, considerable doubts have been expressed regarding the ability of the drug industry, and especially its smaller members, to bear the substantial economic costs (from both damage awards and high insurance premiums) inherent in imposing an industry-wide liability. * * *

An important and substantial countervailing public policy in defendants' favor was very recently expressed in a similar DES case, *McCreery v. Eli Lilly & Co.* Although the majority herein impliedly rejects the appellate court's holding, in my opinion pertinent language of the *McCreery* court, based upon the RESTATEMENT OF TORTS and bearing on the majority's "market share" theory, is well worth repeating:

> Application of the comments to the RESTATEMENT SECOND OF TORTS, section 402A, to this situation compels a rejection of the imposition of liability. As the comment states, ". . . It is also true in particular of many new or experimental drugs as to which, because of lack of time and opportunity for sufficient medical experience, there can be no assurance of safety, or perhaps even of purity of ingredients, but such experience as there is justifies the marketing and use of the drug notwithstanding a medically recognizable risk. The seller of such products, again, with the qualification that they are properly prepared and marketed, and proper warning is given, where the situation calls for it, is not to be held to strict liability for unfortunate consequences attending their use, merely because he has undertaken to supply the public with an apparently useful and desirable product, attended with a known but apparently reasonable risk." (REST. 2D TORTS, § 402A, comment k.) This section implicitly

recognizes the social policy behind the development of new pharmaceutical preparations. As one commentator states, "(t)he social and economic benefits from mobilizing the industry's resources in the war against disease and in reducing the costs of medical care are potentially enormous. The development of new drugs in the last three decades has already resulted in great social benefits. The potential gains from further advances remain large. To risk such gains is unwise. Our major objective should be to encourage a continued high level of industry investment in pharmaceutical R & D (research and development)." ...

In the present case the majority imposes liability more than 20 years after ingestion of drugs which at the time they were used, after careful testing, had the full approval of the United States Food and Drug Administration. It seems to me that liability in the manner created by the majority must inevitably inhibit, if not the research or development, at least the dissemination of new pharmaceutical drugs. Such a result, as explained by the RESTATEMENT, is wholly inconsistent with traditional tort theory.

I also suggest that imposition of so sweeping a liability may well prove to be extremely shortsighted from the standpoint of broad social policy. Who is to say whether, and at what time and in what form, the drug industry upon which the majority now fastens this blanket liability, may develop a miracle drug critical to the diagnosis, treatment, or, indeed, cure of the very disease in question? It is counterproductive to inflict civil damages upon all manufacturers for the side effects and medical complications which surface in the children of the users a generation after ingestion of the drugs, particularly when, at the time of their use, the drugs met every fair test and medical standard then available and applicable. Such a result requires of the pharmaceutical industry a foresight, prescience and anticipation far beyond the most exacting standards of the relevant scientific disciplines. In effect, the majority requires the pharmaceutical research laboratory to install a piece of new equipment—the psychic's crystal ball.

I am not unmindful of the serious medical consequences of plaintiffs' injuries, and the equally serious implications to the class which she purports to represent. In balancing the various policy considerations, however, I also observe that the incidence of vaginal cancer among "DES daughters" has been variously estimated at one-tenth of 1 percent to four-tenths of 1 percent. * * * These facts raise some penetrating questions. Ninety-nine plus percent of "DES daughters" have never developed cancer. Must a drug manufacturer to escape this blanket liability wait for a generation of testing before it may disseminate drugs? If a drug has beneficial purposes for the majority of users but harmful side effects are later revealed for a small fraction of consumers, will the manufacturer be absolutely liable? If adverse medical consequences, wholly unknown to the most careful and meticulous of present scientists, surface in two or three generations, will similar liability be imposed? In my opinion, common sense and reality combine to warn that a "market share" theory goes too far. Legally, it expects too much.

I believe that the scales of justice tip against imposition of this new liability because of the foregoing elements of unfairness to some defendants who may have had nothing whatever to do with causing any injury, the unwarranted preference created for this particular class of plaintiffs, the violence done to traditional tort principles by the drastic expansion of liability proposed, the injury threatened to the public interest in continued unrestricted basic medical research as stressed by the RESTATEMENT, and the other reasons heretofore expressed.

The majority's decision effectively makes the entire drug industry (or at least its California members) an insurer of all injuries attributable to defective drugs of uncertain or unprovable origin, including those injuries manifesting themselves a generation later, and regardless of whether particular defendants had any part whatever in causing the claimed injury. Respectfully, I think this is unreasonable overreaction for the purpose of achieving what is perceived to be a socially satisfying result.

Finally, I am disturbed by the broad and ominous ramifications of the majority's holding. The law review comment, which is the well-spring of the majority's new theory, conceding the widespread consequences of industry-wide liability, openly acknowledges that "The DES cases are only the tip of an iceberg." (Comment, *DES and a Proposed Theory of Enterprise Liability* (1978) 46 Fordham L.Rev. 963, 1007.) Although the pharmaceutical drug industry may be the first target of this new sanction, the majority's reasoning has equally threatening application to many other areas of business and commercial activities.

Given the grave and sweeping economic, social, and medical effects of "market share" liability, the policy decision to introduce and define it should rest not with us, but with the Legislature which is currently considering not only major statutory reform of California product liability law in general, but the DES problem in particular. (*See* Sen. Bill No. 1392 (1979–1980 Reg. Sess.), which would establish and appropriate funds for the education, identification, and screening of persons exposed to DES, and would prohibit health care and hospital service plans from excluding or limiting coverage to persons exposed to DES.) An alternative proposal for administrative compensation, described as "a limited version of no-fault products liability" has been suggested by one commentator.... Compensation under such a plan would be awarded by an administrative tribunal from funds collected "via a tax paid by all manufacturers." * * * In any event, the problem invites a legislative rather than an attempted judicial solution.

I would affirm the judgments of dismissal.

CLARK AND MANUEL, JJ., concur.

IN RE RELATED ASBESTOS CASES

United States District Court, Northern District of California, 1982.
543 F.Supp. 1152.

ORDER

PECKHAM, CHIEF JUDGE.

* * *

ON MOTION FOR USE OF MARKET SHARE THEORY

Plaintiffs' motion for use of the market share theory of liability in the present litigation, and defendants' opposition thereto, came before this court for hearing on March 16, 1982. The court having reviewed the memoranda submitted in support of and in opposition to this motion, and having heard argument of counsel, denies plaintiffs' motion as follows.

The market share theory of liability was created by the California Supreme Court in Sindell v. Abbott Laboratories, et al., 26 Cal.3d 588, 163 Cal.Rptr. 132, 607 P.2d 924 (1980), *cert. denied,* 449 U.S. 912, 101 S.Ct. 285, 66 L.Ed.2d 140 (1980). *Sindell* was a personal injury action arising from the plaintiff's prenatal exposure to the drug DES. Since the plaintiff was suing years later as an adult, it was impossible for her to prove which defendant manufactured the drug her mother had taken. Accordingly, the court shifted the burden of proof to the defendants to prove that each could not have manufactured the product which caused the plaintiff's injuries. Each defendant which could not make that exculpatory showing would be held liable for the proportion of the judgment corresponding to its share of the DES market.

After careful consideration of the issue, it is concluded that the market share liability theory was not intended to be applied in a context such as the one which is before the court. Where asbestos is the product in question, numerous factors would make it exceedingly difficult to ascertain an accurate division of liability along market share lines. For example, unlike DES, which is a fungible commodity, asbestos fibers are of several varieties, each used in varying quantities by defendants in their products, and each differing in its harmful effects. Second, defining the relevant product and geographic markets would be an extremely complex task due to the numerous uses to which asbestos is put, and to the fact that some of the products to which the plaintiffs were exposed were undoubtedly purchased out of state sometime prior to the plaintiffs' exposure. A third factor contributing to the difficulty in calculating market shares is the fact that some plaintiffs were exposed to asbestos over a period of many years, during which time some defendants began or discontinued making asbestos products.

Perhaps more important than the practical difficulty in ascertaining shares here is the fact that, unlike the plaintiff in *Sindell,* who was completely unable to identify which defendant had manufactured the product which her mother had ingested, plaintiffs in the present case apparently plan to call as witnesses individuals who will testify that plaintiffs were exposed to asbestos products manufactured by defendants. Where a plaintiff does have information as to the identity of the defendants who caused his alleged injury, the rationale for shifting the burden of proof in Sindell is simply not present. *See generally,* Prelick v. Johns–Manville Corporation, 531 F.Supp. 96 (W.D.Pa.1982); Starling v. Seaboard Coast Line Railroad Co., 533 F.Supp. 183 (S.D.Ga.1982).

Accordingly, each plaintiff is precluded from relying upon the market share theory of liability in the present action.

This order will apply to all related asbestos cases in the Northern District of California, where counsel have had notice and an opportunity to participate in the hearings on these issues, subject to new developments in the law, or to factual inapplicability of our rulings to specific asbestos cases.

SO ORDERED.

On Motion to Dismiss

Defendants' motion to dismiss plaintiffs' concert of action claims on the ground that each fails to state a claim upon which relief can be granted came before this court for hearing on March 16, 1982. The court, having reviewed the memoranda submitted in support of and in opposition to this motion, and having heard argument of counsel denies this motion as follows.

Under the liberal standards of federal pleading, it is found that plaintiffs have met the requirements for stating a claim for concert of action. Plaintiffs will thus be permitted to produce evidence of concert of action, within the meaning ascribed to that term by the California Supreme Court.

For guidance, it is noted that any plaintiff's evidence of concert of action, in order to be relevant, must tend to establish that defendants, in pursuance of a common plan or design to commit a tortious act, actively took part in that act, or furthered it by cooperation or request, or lent aid or encouragement to a wrongdoer, or ratified and adopted wrongful acts done for their benefit. *See* Sindell v. Abbott Laboratories, 26 Cal.3d 588, 604, 163 Cal.Rptr. 132, 607 P.2d 924 (1980), *cert. denied,* 449 U.S. 912, 101 S.Ct. 285, 66 L.Ed.2d 140 (1980); Prosser, Law of Torts, Section 46, p. 292 (4th ed.1971). It is not enough for a plaintiff's evidence to establish that the defendants' conduct was merely "parallel or imitative . . . in that (defendants) . . . relied upon each others' testing and promotion methods." Sindell v. Abbott Laboratories, 26 Cal.3d at 605, 163 Cal.Rptr. 132, 607 P.2d 924. Nor is it enough that defendants "assisted and encouraged one another to inadequately test (the asbestos products in question) . . . and to provide inadequate warnings." * * *

Accordingly, each plaintiff shall abstain from any reference, comment, or offer of evidence, either by way of documents or testimony, or any concert of inaction or non-feasance or of any suppression or cover-up on the part of defendants, without first obtaining permission of the court outside the presence and hearing of the jury.

Plaintiff's counsel shall also inform all of the plaintiff's witnesses not to make any references to any documents which refer to the topics just mentioned, and shall themselves not make any such references without first obtaining permission of the court outside the presence of the jury. Furthermore, in order to preclude any possibility of prejudice to defendants in the event that plaintiff is unable to meet his burden of proof on the concert of action issue, plaintiff shall likewise abstain from any use of the terms "conspiracy" and "concert of action" except under the conditions set forth.

This order will apply to all related asbestos cases in the Northern District of California, where counsel have had notice and an opportunity to participate in the hearings on these issues, subject to new developments in the law, or to factual inapplicability of our rulings to specific asbestos cases.

SO ORDERED.

HYMOWITZ v. ELI LILLY AND COMPANY

New York Court of Appeals, 1989.
73 N.Y.2d 487, 541 N.Y.S.2d 941, 539 N.E.2d 1069, *cert. denied*
493 U.S. 944, 110 S.Ct. 350, 107 L.Ed.2d 338 (1989).

OPINION OF THE COURT

WACHTLER, CHIEF JUDGE.

Plaintiffs in these appeals allege that they were injured by the drug diethylstilbestrol (DES) ingested by their mothers during pregnancy. They seek relief against defendant DES manufacturers. While not class actions, these cases are representative of nearly 500 similar actions pending in the courts in this State; the rules articulated by the court here, therefore, must do justice and be administratively feasible in the context of this mass litigation. With this in mind, we now resolve the issue twice expressly left open by this court, and adopt a market share theory, using a national market, for determining liability and apportioning damages in DES cases in which identification of the manufacturer of the drug that injured the plaintiff is impossible (*see,* Kaufman v. Lilly & Co., 65 N.Y.2d 449, 456, 492 N.Y.S.2d 584, 482 N.E.2d 63; Bichler v. Lilly & Co., 55 N.Y.2d 571, 580, 450 N.Y.S.2d 776, 436 N.E.2d 182).
* * *

I.

The history of the development of DES and its marketing in this country has been repeatedly chronicled (*see, e.g., Bichler v. Lilly & Co.;* Martin v. Abbott Labs., 102 Wash.2d 581, 689 P.2d 368; Sindell v. Abbott Labs., 26 Cal.3d 588, 163 Cal.Rptr. 132, 607 P.2d 924, *cert. denied* 449 U.S. 912, 101 S.Ct. 285, 66 L.Ed.2d 140. Sheiner, *DES and a Proposed Theory of Enterprise Liability,* 46 Fordham L.Rev. 963). Briefly, DES is a synthetic substance that mimics the effect of estrogen, the naturally formed female hormone. It was invented in 1937 by British researchers, but never patented.

In 1941, the Food and Drug Administration (FDA) approved the new drug applications (NDA) of 12 manufacturers to market DES for the treatment of various maladies, not directly involving pregnancy. In 1947, the FDA began approving the NDAs of manufacturers to market DES for the purpose of preventing human miscarriages; by 1951, the FDA had concluded that DES was generally safe for pregnancy use, and stopped requiring the filing of NDAs when new manufacturers sought to produce the drug for this purpose. In 1971, however, the FDA banned the use of DES as a miscarriage preventative, when studies established the harmful latent effects of DES upon the offspring of mothers who took the drug. Specifically, tests indicated that DES caused vaginal adenocarcinoma, a form of cancer, and adenosis, a precancerous vaginal or cervical growth.

Although strong evidence links prenatal DES exposure to later development of serious medical problems, plaintiffs seeking relief in court for their injuries faced two formidable and fundamental barriers to recovery in this State; not only is identification of the manufacturer of the DES ingested in a particular case generally impossible, but, due to the latent nature of DES injuries, many claims were barred by the Statute of Limitations before the injury was discovered.

The identification problem has many causes. All DES was of identical chemical composition. Druggists usually filled prescriptions from whatever was on hand. Approximately 300 manufacturers produced the drug, with companies entering and leaving the market continuously during the 24 years that DES was sold for pregnancy use. The long latency period of a DES injury compounds the identification problem; memories fade, records are lost or destroyed, and witnesses die. Thus the pregnant women who took DES generally never knew who produced the drug they took, and there was no reason to attempt to discover this fact until many years after ingestion, at which time the information is not available.

We recognized this predicament in *Bichler v. Lilly & Co.* * * *, where the court stated that in DES cases it is a "practical impossibility for most victims [to] pinpoint * * * the manufacturer directly responsible for their particular injury". We allowed plaintiff's recovery in that case, however, notwithstanding the failure of the plaintiff to identify the manufacturer of the injurious DES, on the limited basis that "the evidence was legally sufficient to support the jury verdict for the plaintiff" on the law as charged to the jury, and unobjected to by the defendant (*see,* Kaufman v. Lilly & Co., 65 N.Y.2d 449, 456, 492 N.Y.S.2d 584, 482 N.E.2d 63). The question, therefore, of whether nonidentification of the manufacturer precludes plaintiffs from recovering for DES caused injuries, remained unresolved after *Bichler v. Lilly & Co.*

* * *

A.

As we noted in Bichler v. Lilly & Co. * * *, the accepted tort doctrines of alternative liability and concerted action are available in some personal injury cases to permit recovery where the precise identification of a wrongdoer is impossible. However, we agree with the near unanimous views of the high State courts that have considered the matter that these doctrines in their unaltered common-law forms do not permit recovery in DES cases (*see, e.g., Sindell v. Abbott Labs.;* Collins v. Lilly & Co., 116 Wis.2d 166, 342 N.W.2d 37; *Martin v. Abbott Labs.; but see,* Abel v. Lilly & Co., 418 Mich. 311, 343 N.W.2d 164 [held that there was a question of fact presented as to alternative liability and concerted action]).

The paradigm of alternative liability is found in the case of Summers v. Tice, (33 Cal.2d 80, 199 P.2d 1). In *Summers,* plaintiff and the two defendants were hunting, and defendants carried identical shotguns and ammunition. During the hunt, defendants shot simultaneously at the same bird, and plaintiff was struck by bird shot from one of the defendants' guns. The court held that where two defendants breach a duty to the plaintiff, but there is uncertainty regarding which one caused the injury, "the burden is upon each such actor to prove that he has not caused the harm" (RESTATEMENT [SECOND] OF TORTS § 433B[3]; *Bichler v. Lilly & Co.; cf.,* Ravo v. Rogatnick, 70 N.Y.2d 305, 520 N.Y.S.2d 533, 514 N.E.2d 1104 [successive tort-feasors may be held jointly and severally liable for an indivisible injury to the plaintiff]). The central rationale for shifting the burden of proof in such a situation is that without this device both defendants will be silent, and plaintiff will not recover; with alternative liability, however, defendants will be forced to speak, and reveal the culpable party, or else be held jointly and severally liable themselves. Consequently, use of the alternative liability doctrine generally requires that the defendants have better access to information than does the plaintiff, and that all possible tort-feasors be before the court (see, Summers v. Tice, *supra,* at 86, 199 P.2d 1; RESTATEMENT [SECOND] OF TORTS § 433B, comment h). It is also recognized that alternative liability rests on the notion that where there is a small number of possible wrongdoers, all of whom breached a duty to the plaintiff, the likelihood that any one of them injured the plaintiff is relatively high, so that forcing them to exonerate themselves, or be held liable, is not unfair (*see,* Sindell v. Abbott Labs., *supra,* . . .).

In DES cases, however, there is a great number of possible wrongdoers, who entered and left the market at different times, and some of whom no longer exist. Additionally, in DES cases many years elapse between the ingestion of the drug and injury. Consequently, DES defendants are not in any better position than are plaintiffs to identify the manufacturer of the DES ingested in any given case, nor is there any real prospect of having all the possible producers before the court. Finally, while it may be fair to employ alternative liability in cases involving only a small number of potential wrongdoers, that fairness disappears with the decreasing probability that any one of the defendants actually caused the injury. This is particularly true when applied to DES where the chance that a particular producer caused the injury is often very remote (*Sindell v. Abbott Labs.*, at 603, 163 Cal.Rptr. 132, 607 P.2d 924; *Collins v. Lilly & Co.*, 116 Wis.2d at 184, 342 N.W.2d 37). Alternative liability, therefore, provides DES plaintiffs no relief.

Nor does the theory of concerted action, in its pure form, supply a basis for recovery. This doctrine, seen in drag racing cases, provides for joint and several liability on the part of all defendants having an understanding, express or tacit, to participate in "a common plan or design to commit a tortious act" (Prosser and Keeton, Torts § 46, at 323 [5th ed.]; *see, Bichler v. Lilly & Co.*, 55 N.Y.2d at 580–581; De Carvalho v. Brunner, 223 N.Y. 284, 119 N.E. 563). As we noted in *Bichler v. Lilly & Co.*, and as the present record reflects, drug companies were engaged in extensive parallel conduct in developing and marketing DES (*see, id.*, 55 N.Y.2d at 585, * * *). There is nothing in the record, however, beyond this similar conduct to show any agreement, tacit or otherwise, to market DES for pregnancy use without taking proper steps to ensure the drug's safety. Parallel activity, without more, is insufficient to establish the agreement element necessary to maintain a concerted action claim (*Sindell v. Abbott Labs.*, 26 Cal.3d at 605; *Collins v. Lilly & Co.*, 116 Wis.2d at 185, 342 N.W.2d 37; *Martin v. Abbott Labs.*, 102 Wash.2d at 599, 689 P.2d 368). Thus this theory also fails in supporting an action by DES plaintiffs.

In short, extant common-law doctrines, unmodified, provide no relief for the DES plaintiff unable to identify the manufacturer of the drug that injured her. This is not a novel conclusion; in the last decade a number of courts in other jurisdictions also have concluded that present theories do not support a cause of action in DES cases. Some courts, upon reaching this conclusion, have declined to find any judicial remedy for the DES plaintiffs who cannot identify the particular manufacturer of the DES ingested by their mothers (*see,* Zafft v. Lilly & Co., 676 S.W.2d 241 [Mo] [*en banc*]; Mulcahy v. Lilly & Co., 386 N.W.2d 67 [Iowa] [stating that any change in the law to allow for recovery in nonidentification DES cases should come from the Legislature]). Other courts, however, have found that some modification of existing doctrine is appropriate to allow for relief for those injured by DES of unknown manufacture (*e.g., Sindell v. Abbott Labs.; Collins v. Lilly & Co.; Martin v. Abbott Labs.*).

We conclude that the present circumstances call for recognition of a realistic avenue of relief for plaintiffs injured by DES. These appeals present many of the same considerations that have prompted this court in the past to modify the rules of personal injury liability, in order "to achieve the ends of justice in a more modern context" (*see,* People v. Hobson, 39 N.Y.2d 479, 489, 384 N.Y.S.2d 419, 348 N.E.2d 894; Codling v. Paglia, 32 N.Y.2d 330, 341, 345 N.Y.S.2d 461, 298 N.E.2d 622), and we perceive that here judicial action is again required to overcome the " 'inordinately difficult problems of proof' "caused by contemporary products and marketing techniques (*see, Bichler v. Lilly & Co.*, 55

N.Y.2d at 579–580, * * * [*quoting* Caprara v. Chrysler Corp., 52 N.Y.2d 114, 123, 436 N.Y.S.2d 251, 417 N.E.2d 545]).

Indeed, it would be inconsistent with the reasonable expectations of a modern society to say to these plaintiffs that because of the insidious nature of an injury that long remains dormant, and because so many manufacturers, each behind a curtain, contributed to the devastation, the cost of injury should be borne by the innocent and not the wrong-doers. This is particularly so where the Legislature consciously created these expectations by reviving hundreds of DES cases. Consequently, the ever-evolving dictates of justice and fairness, which are the heart of our common-law system, require formation of a remedy for injuries caused by DES (*see,* Woods v. Lancet, 303 N.Y. 349, 355, 102 N.E.2d 691; *see, also,* Kaye, *The Human Dimension in Appellate Judging: A Brief Reflection on a Timeless Concern,* 73 Cornell L.Rev. 1004).

We stress, however, that the DES situation is a singular case, with manufacturers acting in a parallel manner to produce an identical, generically marketed product, which causes injury many years later, and which has evoked a legislative response reviving previously barred actions. Given this unusual scenario, it is more appropriate that the loss be borne by those that produced the drug for use during pregnancy, rather than by those who were injured by the use, even where the precise manufacturer of the drug cannot be identified in a particular action. We turn then to the question of how to fairly and equitably apportion the loss occasioned by DES, in a case where the exact manufacturer of the drug that caused the injury is unknown.

B.

The past decade of DES litigation has produced a number of alternative approaches to resolve this question. Thus, in a sense, we are now in an enviable position; the efforts of other courts provided examples for contending with this difficult issue, and enough time has passed so that the actual administration and real effects of these solutions now can be observed. With these useful guides in hand, a path may be struck for our own conclusion.

First, this court's opinion in *Bichler v. Lilly & Co.* must be considered. There the jury was instructed on a modified version of concerted action, which, in effect, substituted the fact of conscious parallel activity by manufacturers for the usual common-law requirement that there be proof of an actual agreement between actors to jointly act tortiously (*id.,* 55 N.Y.2d at 584). The defendant in *Bichler* did not object to this instruction, and the modified concerted action theory became the law applicable to that particular case (*id.,* at 583–584).

Now given the opportunity to assess the merits of this theory, we decline to adopt it as the law of this State. Parallel behavior, the major justification for visiting liability caused by the product of one manufacturer upon the head of another under this analysis, is a common occurrence in industry generally. We believe, therefore, that inferring agreement from the fact of parallel activity alone improperly expands the concept of concerted action beyond a rational or fair limit; among other things, it potentially renders small manufacturers, in the case of DES and in countless other industries, jointly liable for all damages stemming from the defective products of an entire industry (*accord, Sindell v. Abbott Labs.*, 26 Cal.3d at 605, 163 Cal.Rptr. 132, 607 P.2d 924).

A narrower basis for liability, tailored more closely to the varying culpableness of individual DES producers, is the market share concept. First judicially articulated by the California Supreme Court in *Sindell v. Abbott Labs.* variations upon this theme have been adopted by other courts (*see, Collins v. Lilly & Co.; Martin v. Abbott Labs.*). In *Sindell v. Abbott Labs*, the court synthesized the market share concept by modifying the *Summers v. Tice* alternative liability rationale in two ways. It first loosened the requirement that all possible wrongdoers be before the court, and instead made a "substantial share" sufficient. The court then held that each defendant who could not prove that it did not actually injure plaintiff would be liable according to that manufacturer's market share. The court's central justification for adopting this approach was its belief that limiting a defendant's liability to its market share will result, over the run of cases, in liability on the part of a defendant roughly equal to the injuries the defendant actually caused (*id.,* 26 Cal.3d at 612, 163 Cal.Rptr. 132, 607 P.2d 924).

In the recent case of Brown v. Superior Ct., 44 Cal.3d 1049, 245 Cal.Rptr. 412, 751 P.2d 470, the California Supreme Court resolved some apparent ambiguity in Sindell v. Abbott Labs., and held that a manufacturer's liability is several only, and, in cases in which all manufacturers in the market are not joined for any reason, liability will still be limited to market share, resulting in a less than 100% recovery for a plaintiff. Finally, it is noteworthy that determining market shares under *Sindell v. Abbott Labs.* proved difficult and engendered years of litigation. After attempts at using smaller geographical units, it was eventually determined that the national market provided the most feasible and fair solution, and this national market information was compiled (*see,* In re Complex DES Litig., No. 830/109, Cal. Super. Ct.).

Four years after *Sindell v. Abbott Labs.*, the Wisconsin Supreme Court followed with Collins v. Lilly & Co., 116 Wis.2d 166, 342 N.W.2d 37. Deciding the identification issue without the benefit of the extensive California litigation over market shares, the Wisconsin court held that it was prevented from following *Sindell* due to "the practical difficulty of defining and proving market share" (*id.,* at 189, 342 N.W.2d, at 48). Instead of focusing on tying liability closely to the odds of actual causation, as the *Sindell* court attempted, the *Collins* court took a broader perspective, and held that each defendant is liable in proportion to the amount of risk it created that the plaintiff would be injured by DES. Under the *Collins* structure, the "risk" each defendant is liable for is a question of fact in each case, with market shares being relevant to this determination (*id.,* at 191, 200, 342 N.W.2d 37). Defendants are allowed, however, to exculpate themselves by showing that their product could not have caused the injury to the particular plaintiff (*id.*, at 198, 342 N.W.2d 37).

The Washington Supreme Court, writing soon after Collins v. Lilly & Co., took yet another approach (*see, Martin v. Abbott Labs.*, 102 Wash.2d 581, 689 P.2d 368). The *Martin* court first rejected the *Sindell* market share theory due to the belief (which later proved to be erroneous in *Brown v. Superior Ct.*) that California's approach distorted liability by inflating market shares to ensure plaintiffs of full recovery. * * * The *Martin* court instead adopted what it termed "market share alternative liability," justified, it concluded, because "[e]ach defendant contributed to the risk of injury to the public, and, consequently, the risk of injury to individual plaintiffs" * * *.

Under the Washington scheme, defendants are first allowed to exculpate themselves by proving by the preponderance of the evidence that they were not the manufacturer of the DES that injured plaintiff. Unexculpated defendants are presumed to have equal market shares, totaling 100%. Each defendant then has the opportunity to rebut this presumption by showing that its actual market share was less than presumed. If any defendants succeed in rebutting this presumption, the liability shares of the remaining defendants who could not prove their actual market share are inflated, so that the plaintiff received a 100% recovery * * *.[1] The market shares of defendants is a question of fact in each case, and the relevant market can be a particular pharmacy, or county, or State, or even the country, depending upon the circumstances the case presents (George v. Parke–Davis, 107 Wash.2d 584, 733 P.2d 507).

Turning to the structure to be adopted in New York, we heed both the lessons learned through experience in other jurisdictions and the realities of the mass litigation of DES claims in this State. Balancing these considerations, we are led to the conclusion that a market share theory, based upon a national market, provides the best solution. As California discovered, the reliable determination of any market smaller than the national one likely is not practicable. Moreover, even if it were possible, of the hundreds of cases in the New York courts, without a doubt there are many in which the DES that allegedly caused injury was ingested in another State. Among the thorny issues this could present,

---

1. The actual operation of this theory proved more mathematically complex when the court was presented with the question of what to do about unavailable defendants. Recognizing that the possibility of abuse existed when defendants implead unavailable defendants, who would then be assumed to have had an equal share of the market, the court placed the burden upon appearing defendants to prove the market share of the absent ones (George v. Parke–Davis, 107 Wash.2d 584, 733 P.2d 507). If this can be proved, the plaintiff simply cannot recover the amount attributable to the absent defendant, and thus recovery in the case is less than 100%. If the market share of the absent defendant cannot be shown, the remaining defendants who cannot prove their market shares have their shares inflated to provide plaintiff with full recovery. Finally, if all appearing defendants can prove their market shares, their shares are never inflated, regardless of whether the market share of a nonappearing defendant can be proved or not; thus, in this situation, the plaintiff again will not recover her full damages (*id.*).

perhaps the most daunting is the spectre that the particular case could require the establishment of a separate market share matrix. We feel that this is an unfair, and perhaps impossible burden to routinely place upon the litigants in individual cases.

Nor do we believe that the Wisconsin approach of assessing the "risk" each defendant caused a particular plaintiff, to be litigated anew as a question of fact in each case, is the best solution for this State. Applied on a limited scale this theory may be feasible, and certainly is the most refined approach by allowing a more thorough consideration of how each defendant's actions threatened the plaintiff. We are wary, however, of setting loose, for application in the hundreds of cases pending in this State, a theory which requires the fact finder's individualized and open-ended assessment of the relative liabilities of scores of defendants in every case. Instead, it is our perception that the injustices arising from delayed recoveries and inconsistent results which this theory may produce in this State outweigh arguments calling for its adoption.

Consequently, for essentially practical reasons, we adopt a market share theory using a national market. We are aware that the adoption of a national market will likely result in a disproportion between the liability of individual manufacturers and the actual injuries each manufacturer caused in this State. Thus our market share theory cannot be founded upon the belief that, over the run of cases, liability will approximate causation in this State (*see, Sindell v. Abbott Labs.*, 26 Cal.3d at 612). Nor does the use of a national market provide a reasonable link between liability and the risk created by a defendant to a particular plaintiff (*see, Collins v. Lilly & Co.; Martin v. Abbott Labs.*). Instead, we choose to apportion liability so as to correspond to the over-all culpability of each defendant, measured by the amount of risk of injury each defendant created to the public-at-large. Use of a national market is a fair method, we believe, of apportioning defendants' liabilities according to their total culpability in marketing DES for use during pregnancy. Under the circumstances, this is an equitable way to provide plaintiffs with the relief they deserve, while also rationally distributing the responsibility for plaintiffs' injuries among defendants.

To be sure, a defendant cannot be held liable if it did not participate in the marketing of DES for pregnancy use; if a DES producer satisfies its burden of proof of showing that it was not a member of the market of DES sold for pregnancy use, disallowing exculpation would be unfair and unjust. Nevertheless, because liability here is based on the over-all risk produced, and not causation in a single case, there should be no exculpation of a defendant who, although a member of the market producing DES for pregnancy use, appears not to have caused a particular plaintiff's injury. It is merely a windfall for a producer to escape liability solely because it manufactured a more identifiable pill, or sold only to certain drugstores. These fortuities in no way diminish the culpability of a defendant for marketing the product, which is the basis of liability here.[2]

Finally, we hold that the liability of DES producers is several only, and should not be inflated when all participants in the market are not before the court in a particular case. We understand that, as a practical matter, this will prevent some plaintiffs from recovering 100% of their damages. However, we eschewed exculpation to prevent the fortuitous avoidance of liability, and thus, equitably, we decline to unleash the same forces to increase a defendant's liability beyond its fair share of responsibility.[3]

Accordingly, in each case the order of the Appellate Division should be affirmed, with costs, and the certified question answered in the affirmative.

MOLLEN, JUDGE (concurring * * *).

The issue presented to the court in this appeal is to determine whether the revival statute for DES claims is constitutional and has properly "opened the window" to enable injured parties to recover for their injuries caused by DES and, if so, how to best enable such plaintiffs to overcome the practical impossibility of bearing their normal burden of proof of demonstrating that the defendants caused their injuries. The majority has selected one approach to meet this issue. However, I am

---

2. Various defendants argue here that although they produced DES, it was not sold for pregnancy use. If a defendant was not a member of the national market of DES marketed for pregnancy, it is not culpable, and should not be liable. Consequently, if a particular defendant sold DES in a form unsuitable for use during pregnancy, or if a defendant establishes that its product was not marketed for pregnancy use, there should be no liability. From the record before the court here, however, the facts are not developed well enough to establish that any defendants were not in the national market of DES sold for pregnancy use. Thus summary judgment cannot at this time be granted on this issue as to any defendants.

3. The dissenter misapprehends the basis for liability here. We have not by the backdoor adopted a theory of concerted action. We avoided extending this theory, because its concomitant requirement of joint and several liability expands the burden on small manufacturers beyond a rational or fair limit. This result is reached by the dissent, not by the majority, so that criticism on this front is misplaced. We are confronted here with an unprecedented identification problem, and have provided a solution that rationally apportions liability. We have heeded the practical lessons learned by other jurisdictions, resulting in our adoption of a national market theory with full knowledge that it concedes the lack of a logical link between liability and causation in a single case. The dissent ignores these lessons, and, endeavoring to articulate a theory it perceives to be closer to traditional law, sets out a construct in which liability is based upon chance, not upon the fair assessment of the acts of defendants. Under the dissent's theory, a manufacturer with a large market share may avoid liability in many cases just because it manufactured a memorably shaped pill. Conversely, a small manufacturer can be held jointly liable for the full amount of every DES injury in this State simply because the shape of its product was not remarkable, even though the odds, realistically, are exceedingly long that the small manufacturer caused the injury in any one particular case. Therefore, although the dissent's theory based upon a "shifting the burden of proof" and joint and several liability is facially reminiscent of prior law, in the case of DES it is nothing more than advocating that bare fortuity be the test for liability. When faced with the novel identification problem posed by DES cases, it is preferable to adopt a new theory that apportions fault rationally, rather than to contort extant doctrines beyond the point at which they provide a sound premise for determining liability.

compelled to concur in part and dissent in part because I am convinced that another more appropriate method of approaching this issue is fairer and more just and equitable to the plaintiffs and to those defendants who could not have caused the plaintiff's injuries, and which is consistent with established principles of tort law. * * * I am * * * in complete agreement with the majority's view that the market share theory of liability, based upon a national market, is an appropriate means by which to accord DES plaintiffs an opportunity to seek recovery for their injuries. However, I respectfully disagree with the majority's conclusion that there should be no exculpation of those defendants who produced and marketed DES for pregnancy purposes, but who can prove, by a preponderance of the evidence, that they did not produce or market the particular pill ingested by the plaintiff's mother. Moreover, in order to ensure that these plaintiffs receive full recovery of their damages, as they are properly entitled to by any fair standard, I would retain the principle of imposing joint and several liability upon those defendants which cannot exculpate themselves.

The emergence of the market share concept of liability in the field of products liability reflects a recognition by several jurisdictions throughout the United States that due to the incidence of mass production and marketing of various drugs and fungible goods, consumers are many times harmed by a product which is not easily traceable to a specific manufacturer, particularly in those situations where the harm occurred many years prior to the discovery of the injuries and the cause thereof. Such is the situation in the DES cases now before us. Under traditional common-law tort principles, a plaintiff is required to establish the existence of a causal relationship between the act or omission of the defendant or defendants and the injury sustained (*see,* Morrissey v. Conservative Gas Corp., 1 N.Y.2d 741, 152 N.Y.S.2d 289, 135 N.E.2d 45; Prosser and Keeton, TORTS § 41, at 263 [5th ed.]). However, given the reality of the situation in DES cases, including the lengthy passage of time, the generic form of most DES pills and the unavailability of pharmaceutical and physician records, it is, as a practical matter, impossible for most DES plaintiffs to bear the burden of proof of establishing the traditional tort element of causation.

Moreover, as noted by the majority, the tort doctrines of alternative liability and concerted action, both of which provide for recovery in situations where a plaintiff, through no fault of his or her own, cannot identify the actual wrongdoer, do not provide appropriate relief to these DES plaintiffs. Unlike the scenario present in the DES cases, the principle of alternative liability presupposes that the number of possible wrongdoers are few in number, that one of the joined defendants had to have actually caused the plaintiff's injury and that the defendants are in a much better position than the plaintiff to identify the actual wrongdoer and, therefore, the burden is shifted to the defendants to prove who was the actual wrongdoer and who among them are to be exculpated (*see,* *Summers v. Tice,* 33 Cal.2d 80; RESTATEMENT [SECOND] OF TORTS § 433B[3]). However, in view of the difference in the factual circumstances, the theory of alternative liability does not provide a workable solution for DES plaintiffs.

* * *

Clearly, the development and underlying purpose of the various concepts of liability in DES cases has been to provide a means whereby the plaintiffs, who cannot identify the actual manufacturer of the pill ingested by their mother, are alleviated of the traditional burden of proof of causation and to shift that burden to the defendants. The various theories of collective liability which have been adopted in the several jurisdictions in an effort to provide plaintiffs with a means to recovery for their injuries, were not intended to, and did not, provide DES plaintiffs with an unprecedented strict liability cause of action. However, the majority herein, by precluding exculpation of those defendants in DES cases who produced DES for pregnancy purposes but who can establish, by a preponderance of the evidence, that they did not and could not have produced or marketed the pill which caused the plaintiff's injuries, has created such a radical concept and purports to limit it to DES claims. In the majority's view, the defendant's liability in DES cases is premised upon the over-all risk of injury which they created to the public-at-large in producing and marketing DES for pregnancy purpose and, therefore, exculpation of those defendants who can establish that the plaintiff's mother did not ingest their pill, would be inconsistent with the over-all risk theory of liability. By taking this view, however, the majority, while stating that it is adopting a market share theory of liability, is, in essence, despite its disclaimer of doing so, adopting a concerted action theory of liability, but has eliminated therefrom the requirement that the plaintiffs establish that the defendants tacitly agreed to produce and market DES for pregnancy use without proper testing and without adequate warnings of the potential dangers involved. Such a result, represents a radical departure from fundamental tenets of tort law and is unnecessarily unfair and inequitable to the defendants who have proven, or can prove, that they did not produce the pill which caused the injury. Moreover, this result is directly contrary to the majority's own statement that it is rejecting the "conscious parallelism" theory utilized in *Bichler v. Lilly & Co.*, (79 A.D.2d 317), because, as stated by the majority herein, "[p]arallel behavior, the major justification for visiting liability caused by the product of one manufacturer upon the head of another under this analysis, is a common occurrence in industry generally. We believe, therefore, that inferring agreement from the fact of parallel activity alone improperly expands the concept of concerted action beyond a rational or fair limit; among other things, it potentially renders small manufacturers, in the case of DES and in countless other industries, jointly liable for all damages stemming from the defective products of an entire industry." * * *

I fully concur with the above-stated position of the majority and thus, I cannot agree that the imposition of liability on drug companies, in this case DES manufacturers, solely upon their contribution, in some measure, to the risk of injury by producing and marketing a defective drug, without any consideration given to whether the defendant drug companies actually caused the plaintiff's injuries, is appropriate or warranted. Rather, I would adopt a market share theory of liability, based upon a national market, which would provide for the shifting of the burden of proof on the issue of causation to the defendants and would impose liability upon all of the defendants who produced and marketed DES for pregnancy purposes, except those who were able to prove that their product could not have caused the injury. Under this approach, DES plaintiffs, who are unable to identify the actual manufacturer of the pill ingested by their mother, would only be required to establish, (1) that the plaintiff's mother ingested DES during pregnancy; (2) that the plaintiff's injuries were caused by DES; and (3) that the defendant or defendants produced and marketed DES for pregnancy purposes. Thereafter, the burden of proof would shift to the defendants to exculpate themselves by establishing, by a preponderance of the evidence, that the plaintiff's mother could not have ingested their particular pill. Of those defendants who are unable to exculpate themselves from liability, their respective share of the plaintiff's damages would be measured by their share of the national market of DES produced and marketed for pregnancy purposes during the period in question.

I would further note that while, on the one hand, the majority would not permit defendants who produced DES for pregnancy purposes to exculpate themselves, the majority at the same time deprives the plaintiffs of the opportunity to recover fully for their injuries by limiting the defendants' liability for the plaintiff's damages to several liability. In my view, the liability for the plaintiff's damages of those defendants who are unable to exculpate themselves should be joint and several thereby ensuring that the plaintiffs will receive full recovery of their damages. In addition to being fair to the DES plaintiffs, the imposition of joint and several liability is consistent with that portion of the revival statute which specifically exempted DES claims from those provisions which provide, with certain exceptions, for several liability of joint tort-feasors (*see,* L.1986, ch. 682, § 12; CPLR 1600 *et seq.*). Moreover, in order to ease the financial burden on the specific defendants named in the lawsuit, the defendants would have the option of seeking contribution from their fellow defendants for damages in excess of each defendant's particular market share, and a defendant should be permitted leave to implead those DES manufacturers who the plaintiff has not joined, in order to ensure, where possible, full contribution (*see, e.g.,* Dole v. Dow Chem. Co., 30 N.Y.2d 143, 331 N.Y.S.2d 382, 282 N.E.2d 288). Admittedly, adherence to joint and several liability could result in a disproportion between a defendant's potential liability for the damages suffered by the plaintiff and defendant's actual national market share; however, the opportunity to present exculpatory evidence reduces the risk of imposing liability on innocent defendants.

The application of the aforesaid principles, although somewhat innovative and a modification of traditional tort law, (i.e., the burden of proof is on the plaintiff to prove proximate causation) would, in view of the exigent circumstances, be in furtherance of a valid public policy of imposing the burden of bearing the cost of severe injuries upon those who are responsible for placing into the stream of commerce the causative instrumentality of such injuries. Adherence to this principle would not be too dissimilar from the accepted doctrine of *res ipsa loquitur* which provides, in essence, that where an instrumentality which caused the plaintiff's injuries was in the exclusive control of the defendant and the accident which occurred is one which would not ordinarily happen without negligence, these facts are sufficient to justify an inference of negligence and to shift the burden upon the defendant of coming forward with an explanation (*see, e.g.,* Galbraith v. Busch, 267 N.Y. 230, 234, 196 N.E. 36; Richardson, EVIDENCE § 93, at 68 [Prince 10th ed.]). Thus, this approach, unlike that taken by the majority, does not represent an unnecessary and radical departure from basic principles of tort law. By characterizing this approach as "nothing more than advocating that bare fortuity be the test for liability" * * * the majority fails to perceive that this is no more and no less than a basic principle of tort law; i.e., a plaintiff may not recover for his or her injuries from a defendant who could not have caused those injuries. When the majority eliminates this fundamental causative factor as a basis for recovery, it effectively indulges in the act of judicial legislating. I would further note that if the Legislature had intended to adopt this radical approach which is at total variance with traditional tort law, it could readily have done so when it enacted the revival statute for, among others, DES plaintiffs. Its refusal to do so can certainly not be deemed to be an invitation to this court to assume the legislative role.

SANTIAGO v. SHERWIN–WILLIAMS COMPANY

United States District Court, District of Massachusetts, 1992.
782 F.Supp. 186.

MEMORANDUM

TAURO, CHIEF JUDGE.

Plaintiff Monica Santiago brought this action against several defendants [2] that manufactured lead pigment contained in lead-based paint, charging that their negligence caused her to become lead poisoned. Although the defendants used pigment themselves in their own paint, the gravamen of Santiago's complaint against them relates to their role as manufacturer of lead pigment and bulk supplier to other paint producers. The defendants were all members of defendant Lead Industries Association ("LIA"), a trade association.

---

2. Defendants include Sherwin–Williams Company, NL Industries, Inc., Eagle–Picher Industries, Inc., Atlantic Richfield Corp. (successor to International Smelting & Refining Company), and SCM Corporation (successor to Glidden Company). On January 7, 1991, defendant Eagle–Picher filed for bankruptcy in Ohio, thus automatically staying this action against it. See 11 U.S.C. § 362

Santiago was born on November 9, 1972. From her birth until 1978, she and her family lived in an apartment at 20 Liston Street in Dorchester, Massachusetts. She alleges that, during those years, she ingested lead from paint on the walls of the family's apartment. The walls contained multiple layers of paint, the first of which had been applied around the time the apartment house was built in 1917. In November 1973, Santiago was first diagnosed as having lead poisoning. She was hospitalized in July 1976, and underwent chelation therapy to remove lead from her body.

Santiago alleges that defendants, or their predecessors in interest, marketed all or virtually all of the lead used in lead-based paints sold in the United States between 1917 and 1972. Specifically, the complaint charges defendants with negligent product design, negligent failure to warn, breach of warranty, and concert of action. She maintains that defendants, by and through defendant LIA, "mislead retailers, users, applicators, and parents of young children ... with respect to the unreasonable risks and hazards posed to young children by the lead produced and marketed by them and by the paint containing such lead." * * * She seeks $2.5 million in compensatory and punitive damages.

Presently at issue is the applicability of market share liability as a theory of recovery for Santiago, given the uncontradicted material facts involved in this case. Defendants move for partial summary judgment on the ground that she cannot identify which of them allegedly caused her harm. They contend that, in the absence of a market share liability theory, identification is essential to plaintiff's case. They further argue that market share liability is not the law in Massachusetts, and that the Supreme Judicial Court would not adopt market share in the context of the circumstances involved here. Santiago, in her motion for partial summary judgment, argues to the contrary.

I.

Market Share Generally

[Extensive description and discussion of *Summers v. Tice* and *Sindell*, omitted—ed.]

Market share theory, therefore, permits a plaintiff to bypass the traditional threshold requirement of identifying the defendant that caused the alleged harm. * * * In general,[4] a plaintiff "need only allege inability to identify the actual manufacturer, and join as defendants those manufacturers that compose a 'substantial share' of the market."

---

4. There are several variations of market share theory. For example, *Sindell* requires the plaintiff to join a substantial share of the manufacturers that produced the defective product. 163 Cal.Rptr. at 145, * * *. By contrast, under Martin v. Abbott Laboratories, 102 Wash.2d 581, 689 P.2d 368, 382 (1984), a plaintiff need only sue one manufacturer of the defective product. That defendant can produce evidence of its market share, and then be liable only to that degree. In other words, if this defendant shows that it occupied only 20% of the market, it will be liable for 20% of the judgment. 689 P.2d at 382. Under *Sindell*, the named defendants, constituting a substantial share of the manufacturers that produced the drug, will be liable for 100% of the judgment, even if, together, they actually had less than 100% of the market.

Hannon v. Waterman S.S. Corp., 567 F.Supp. 90, 91 n.1 (E.D.La.1983)(quoting Note, *"Market Share Liability for Defective Products: An Ill–Advised Remedy for the Problem of Identification,"* 76 Nw.U.L.Rev. 300, 301 (1981)). Once a plaintiff establishes negligence, the burden of exculpation shifts to the defendants. * * * For those defendants ultimately found liable, the court will apportion damages based on each defendant's share of the product market. * * * Under market share theory, therefore, "a particular defendant's potential liability is proportional to the probability that it caused plaintiff's injury." * * * *See also McCormack*, 617 F.Supp. at 1526 ("Theoretically, then, the extent of a defendant's liability approximates the amount of harm such defendant has caused in the market.").

The courts that have accepted market share liability have generally done so in the context of DES cases. But other courts have rejected it in both DES and non-DES situations.

The application of market share liability to childhood lead poisoning is a matter of first impression.

* * *

[Discussion of market share theory in Massachusetts omitted—*ed*.]

III.

Applicability of Market Share to Santiago's Claim

Massachusetts' courts would accept the market share theory here if the defendants would be "held liable only for the harm that they have caused." *Payton* [*v. Abbott Laboratories,* 386 Mass. 540,], 437 N.E.2d at 188. Defendants argue that, because of the nature of lead poisoning, and the variety of its possible causes, such certainty is impossible to achieve. To support this contention, defendants point out that in the DES cases, there is a unique, so-called "signature" injury, from a product manufactured, marketed and controlled by identifiable parties. Defendants maintain that no such certainty is present here, and that a jury, therefore, would have to resort to speculation and guesswork in assigning liability. Each of these factors merits discussion.

A. *Absence of a Unique Injury*

In DES cases, the market share theory succeeded in separating wrongdoers from innocent actors, because DES plaintiffs suffered from a signature DES injury—a rare form of cancer, adenocarcinoma, that was directly attributable to exposure to DES. *See* Nancy Lee Firak, *The Developing Policy Characteristics of Cause-in-Fact: Alternative Forms of Liability, Epidemiological Proof and Trans–Scientific Issues,* 63 Temp. L.Rev. 311, 334 (1990)("In the DES cases there is no doubt that DES, and not a background risk, caused plaintiff's injury."). In contrast, defendants here assert that hereditary, social and environmental factors, or lead in other products, could have caused, or at least contributed to, Santiago's injuries. In other words, defendants argue that Santiago does not suffer from a signature lead paint injury.

Santiago claims that lead poisoning retarded her "educational, social, vocational and intellectual development." * * * Plaintiff's injury is manifested by "difficulties in spelling/language arts, in organization, in requiring extra time and effort to check her work, and with frustration in learning to type." * * * Defendants counter that none of the deficits associated with Santiago "can ever be attributed solely or primarily to lead," * * * and that such "injuries" have been "strongly associated in the vast literature on childhood development with a large variety of factors including heredity, child-rearing techniques, mental and physical health of the parents, and other factors in the social and educational setting in which children develop." * * * Santiago's own expert estimates that some of the deficits that she exhibits are attributable to factors other than lead poisoning. * * *

Moreover, even if all of Santiago's injuries could be attributed to lead poisoning, she cannot prove that defendants' lead pigment was the cause of her lead poisoning. Defendants have shown that lead is widespread in many different forms, * * *, and that more than 90 percent of lead used in this country during the relevant period was contained in products other than paint. * * * They further show that the air and water in and around Santiago's home during the relevant period may have contained lead that contributed to her blood levels. * * * In addition, the City of Boston identified Santiago's neighborhood in Dorchester as a "hot spot" in soil lead contamination requiring attention by the Environmental Protection Agency. * * * Defendants' expert asserts, as well, that vehicular traffic is a major source of elevated soil lead levels. * * *

* * *

The public policy reasons favoring the use of market share do not control where there is a possibility that the defendants did not cause the harm in question. In deciding not to apply market share liability in an asbestos injury case, the court in Case v. Fibreboard Corp., 743 P.2d 1062 (Okl.1987), stated that [b]ecause market share liability theory is a theory which eliminates proof of causation of injury for public policy reasons, it must also be clearly founded in facts which support the link between the injury suffered and the risk to which plaintiff was exposed. In the DES arena this cause and effect was clear cut. In the application to asbestos related injuries there are more complications. * * * [S]ee also Starling, 533 F.Supp. at 191 (refusing to apply market share in an asbestos case because "[t]he injuries caused by asbestos exposure are not restricted to asbestos products—other products, such as cigarettes, may have caused or contributed to the injury").

Defendants have produced evidence to show that factors other than lead pigment in paint were adequate producing causes of Santiago's injuries. The jury in this case, therefore, could only speculate as to the degree to which, if at all, the defendants' conduct caused her harm. * * *

B. Defendants' Market Share

Market share liability holds defendants responsible only to the extent that their product has contributed to the risk of injury to the public. *See McCormack*, 617 F.Supp. at 1525. Presumably, defendants can calculate this risk by determining the percentage of the market that their product occupied during the relevant period. If factors significantly skewing this calculation exist, then Massachusetts would not apply market share, because of the danger that defendants could be held liable for harm "exceeding their responsibility." * * *

Here, defendants argue that two factors make it impossible for them to determine the contribution each defendant made to the risk of harm. For one, they contend that the period in which plaintiff seeks to hold defendants liable spans fifty-four years, during which time the defendants moved in and out of the market. Second, defendants point out that Santiago seeks to hold them liable as bulk suppliers of lead pigment, not as paint manufacturers. As such, defendants argue that they are even further removed from any injury to Santiago because they did not package or market the allegedly offending paint. The court considers these arguments *seriatim*.

1. Scope of the Market

In *Payton*, the SJC indicated that, in order to hold defendants liable, each had to have been "actively in the DES market during all or a substantial part of the relevant period of time in which the mothers of the plaintiffs ingested DES." * * * There, the market was limited to the year in which the named plaintiff's mother ingested DES. Here, the market spans five decades. Santiago contends that the house was first painted around 1917, and that the walls inside the house contain five layers of paint, with the last layer having been applied between 1955 and 1969.

Defendants show that, by 1954, three of the five defendants had ceased producing white lead pigments. * * * In addition, defendant Glidden did not begin producing white lead pigment until 1924, and it stopped in the late 1950's. * * * Defendant Sherwin–Williams has shown, moreover, that by the mid–1930's its lead pigment was used primarily for commercial and industrial applications. * * * Finally, defendants contend that, given the fifty-four year window here, there is insufficient data to establish to what degree each defendant's product was used in lead-based paint.[13]

Courts adjudicating asbestos cases have refused to apply market share, because of the difficulty of defining a market over a period of years. In *In re Related Asbestos Cases*, the court stated that "a factor contributing to the difficulty in calculating market shares is the fact that

---

13. Plaintiff relies heavily on data compiled by the U.S. government for a Federal Trade Commission proceeding reviewing the five defendant manufacturers' monopolistic behavior in the sale of white lead carbonate. This information, however, covers only four years—from 1938 to 1941—out of the fifty-four for which plaintiff seeks to hold defendants liable.

some plaintiffs were exposed to asbestos over a period of many years, during which time some defendants began or discontinued making asbestos products." * * *

Similarly, in *Starling,* an asbestos case, the court refused to apply market share because of the difficulty in calculating the risk associated with the defendants' product.

This court concludes that there is insufficient evidence that would warrant a jury in finding that all the defendants, or any of them, actively participated in the lead pigment market for lead based paint during the fifty-four year period involved here.

2. *Defendants as Bulk Supplier*

Of particular significance as well is the fact that defendants here supplied lead pigment in bulk to paint manufacturers. They are not being sued as manufacturers or marketers of the allegedly offending paint. They, therefore, could not control all of the risks that their products may have presented to the public.

Santiago acknowledges that the paint manufacturers, not these defendants, were the ones that decided what amount of lead pigment to use, and whether to use any lead pigment at all. * * * Santiago further admits that the paint manufacturers knew the hazards associated with lead paint, * * * and that they controlled the packaging of the paint and the warnings placed thereon.

No court has applied market share theory to a defendant that supplies an ingredient for a product packaged and sold by others. *See e.g.,* Tidler v. Eli Lilly & Co., 851 F.2d 418, 425 (D.C.Cir.1988); George v. Parke–Davis, 107 Wash.2d 584, 733 P.2d 507, 515 (1987); Lyons v. Premo Pharmaceutical Labs, Inc., 170 N.J.Super. 183, 406 A.2d 185, 191–92, *cert. denied,* 82 N.J. 267, 412 A.2d 774 (1979). The facts of this case do not warrant a different result.

CONCLUSION

For all the reasons discussed above, this court determines that it would be inappropriate to permit Santiago to proceed under a market share theory of liability. Defendants' Motion for Summary Judgment to preclude Santiago from utilizing market share liability theory is ALLOWED. Santiago's Motion to the contrary is, therefore, DENIED.

Notes and Questions

1. As the cases demonstrate, courts have struggled to define and apply an appropriate theory of joint liability in mass tort cases involving indeterminate defendants. The cases also demonstrate the difficulties of articulating such theory in the context of equally vexing problems of causation, explored in section E, *infra.* And, similar to the way in which mass tort litigation has stretched the boundaries of procedural rules and doctrine, mass tort litigation also has inspired the expansion of substantive tort doctrine, especially as it relates to liability theory.

Sindell is the landmark case where the California Supreme Court led the way in developing a joint liability theory in the presence of indeterminate defendant responsibility. As the case excerpts indicate, subsequent state and federal courts have taken various approaches to joint liability theory derived from *Sindell,* variously expanding, limiting, qualifying, or rejecting *Sindell's* market-share liability theory. It is worth noting that unlike problems relating to procedural doctrine—where the federal courts have taken the lead in interpreting existing rules to apply to mass tort cases—the state courts have been the primary expositors of new substantive tort theories for mass tort cases. Under *Erie* doctrine (including *Klaxon v. Stentor*), federal courts in their diversity jurisdiction have followed the substantive law requirements of the jurisdictions in which they sit. Because different states have taken different approaches to joint liability in mass tort litigation, what are the applicable law consequences for diversity mass torts with national reach? These problems of applicable law in mass tort are discussed in Part Four, *infra.*

2. An interesting precursor of *Sindell,* and Judge Jack Weinstein's first experience with an early proto-type mass tort litigation, was the 1972 case of Hall v. E.I. Du Pont De Nemours & Co., Inc. and Chance v. E.I. Du Pont De Nemours & Co., Inc., 345 F.Supp. 353 (E.D.N.Y.1972)(discussed and rejected in *Sindell*). In *Hall,* the children of three families in different states were injured by blasting caps manufactured by two identifiable companies; because the manufacturers were clearly identifiable by products labels, Judge Weinstein held that no theory of joint liability applied and he severed and transferred these cases back to the district court from which they had been transferred for consolidation. In the *Chance* group of cases, however, thirteen children had been injured in twelve unrelated accidents across ten states, and the plaintiffs could not identify the manufacturer of the caps that had caused the injury. The complaint named six corporate defendants and their trade association, the Institute of Makers of Explosives. After considering various theories of joint liability and aspects of substantive tort law, including joint control of risk, enterprise liability, causation and burdens of proof, Judge Weinstein permitted joinder of the plaintiffs' claims under Federal Rule of Procedure 20(a). Not only is the *Hall* case a seminal opinion grappling with joint liability issues in the context of indeterminate defendants, but it also is useful in apprehending the close connection between substantive tort theory and the application of procedural joinder rules.

3. The mass tort cases through *Sindell* suggest at least four possible theories of joint liability. The RESTATEMENT (SECOND) OF TORTS supplies two of these theories: alternative liability, illustrated by *Summers v. Tice* and embodied in Restatement § 433B, and concert of action, *see* RESTATEMENT (SECOND) OF TORTS § 876, which looks to commission of a tortious act pursuant to a common design with another, or giving assistance to another's tortious conduct. The third possible theory is enterprise liability, which Judge Weinstein endorsed in *Hall,* but the California court rejected in *Sindell.* According to the court's opinion in *Sindell,* what factual predicates must be present for a court to apply an enterprise theory of liability in the mass tort context? Is the *Sindell's* court's reading of the requirements of enterprise liability so narrow that it has limited use for conferring joint

liability in most mass tort contexts? Does the subsequent *In re Asbestos Related Cases* decision suggest that where enterprise liability may not be an available theory, a concert-of-action theory may be instead? The fourth theory, of course, is market share liability, first articulated at length in *Sindell*. What effect, if any, does the existence of varying state substantive liability theories have on the mass tort settlement process? *See* Jean Macchiaroli Eggen, *Understanding State Contribution Laws and Their Effect on the Settlement of Mass Tort Actions,* 73 Texas L. Rev. ___ (1995).

4. For commentary discussing the problem of apportioning liability in DES litigation, in the aftermath of *Sindell, see* Thomas F. Campion, *DES and Litigation: The First Ten Years,* 2 Rev.Litig. 171 (1982); Margaret A. Ciemiega, Comment, *DES: Alternative Theories of Liability,* 59 U.Det. J.Urb.L. 387 (1982); Thomas J. Currie, Note, *Risk Contribution: An Undesirable New Method for Apportioning Damages in DES Cases,* 10 J.Corp.L. 743 (1985); Andrew R. Klein, *Beyond DES: Rejecting the Application of Market Share Liability in Blood Products Litigation,* 68 Tul.L.Rev. 883 (1994); O. Lee Reed & Art Davidson, Comment, *The DES Cases and Liability Without Causation,* 19 Am.Bus.L.J. 511 (1982); David M. Shultz, *Market Share Liability in DES Cases: The UnWarranted Erosion of Causation in Fact,* 40 DePaul L.Rev. 771 (1991); Naomi Sheiner, Comment, *DES and a Proposed Theory of Enterprise Liability,* 46 Ford.L.Rev. 963 (1078); Peter N. Sheridan, Sindell *and Its Sequelae—or—From a Defendant's Perspective, How to Manage Multiple Party Litigation Under Nontraditional Theories of Litigation,* 17 Forum 1116 (1982).

5. As the case excerpts suggest, the *Sindell* decision generally has provided the analytical basis for most subsequent mass tort cases involving joint liability issues. What questions did *Sindell* leave unanswered, and to what extent is *Sindell* only applicable to certain types of mass tort cases? Although the federal court in the Northern District of California determined in the *Asbestos Related Cases,* that *Sindell*-style market-share liability was not available in that asbestos litigation, a federal district court in the Eastern District of Texas held that Texas courts could adopt and apply a *Sindell* theory of market-share liability to asbestos manufacturers. *See* Hardy v. Johns–Manville Sales Corp., 509 F.Supp. 1353 (E.D.Tex.1981), *reversed on other grounds,* 681 F.2d 334 (5th Cir.1982). Can these two decisions be reconciled? *See also* Brown v. Superior Court (Abbott Laboratories), 44 Cal.3d 1049, 245 Cal.Rptr. 412, 751 P.2d 470 (1988), in which the California Supreme Court endorsed a theory of several, rather than joint liability, wherein "each defendant's liability for the judgment would be confined to the percentage of its share of the market." To what extent does this decision reflect either a refinement, retreat, or expansion of *Sindell*?

6. How have other states adopted or modified the *Sindell* decision? To what extent has joint liability theory become intertwined with burdens of production and proof? The *Hymowitz* decision supplies a good summary of the developing *Sindell* doctrine in Wisconsin and Washington states. In New York, the Court of Appeals first confronted a DES joint liability issue in Bichler v. Eli Lilly and Co., 55 N.Y.2d 571, 450 N.Y.S.2d 776, 436 N.E.2d 182 (1982)(discussed in *Hymowitz*). On appeal that court upheld a jury finding that the DES defendants were jointly liable on a concert-of-action theory, but the decision was of limited import because the defendants had not

objected to the jury instruction on the concert-of-action theory. It was not until 1989 that the Court of Appeals directly addressed the apportionment of liability problem in *Hymowitz*. Although the *Hymowitz* court adopted a *Sindell-Brown* approach, in what significant way did it depart from these decisions? California law provides for exculpation of manufacturers that can prove its product did not injure a plaintiff; what approach has New York taken, and why? To what extent is the *Hymowitz* rule a modification of conventional tort principles beyond the California cases? How does *Hymowitz* address the problem of defining and determining what constitutes "market share"?

7. Judge Weinstein's decision in *Hall* and *Chance* demonstrated the close link between substantive liability theory and procedural joinder rules. Recall that in the *In re DES Cases, supra* at Part Two, Section D.1, Judge Jack Weinstein similarly linked the personal jurisdiction inquiry over multistate defendants to a reading of New York state substantive tort liability theory as articulated in *Hymowitz*. Thus, Judge Weinstein interpreted *Hymowitz* to conclude that:

> In short, without imposing collective responsibility on each manufacturer for the acts of others * * *, the Court of Appeals effectively converted the geographically dispersed companies that manufactured DES into a unitary, national industry for purposes of allocating the cost of DES-related injuries. By recognizing that the particular corner of the market within which a given defendant happened to operate is, for the purposes of apportioning liability for injuries caused by a nationally marketed generic good, entirely fortuitous and arbitrary, the Court of Appeals struck upon "an equitable way to provide plaintiffs with the relief they deserve, while also rationally distributing the responsibility for plaintiffs' injuries among defendants."

In re DES Cases, 789 F.Supp. 552, 564 (E.D.N.Y.1992). To what extent, then, has expansive substantive tort law also become the handmaiden of expansive jurisdictional principles?

8. Although New York's *Hymowitz* decision represents possibly one of the most expansive applications of the *Sindell-Brown* approach to apportioning liability in mass tort litigation, there are indications that the New York courts are in the process of limiting that decision. *See e.g.,* Besser v. E.R. Squibb & Sons, 146 A.D.2d 107, 539 N.Y.S.2d 734 (1st Dep't 1989), *affirmed* 75 N.Y.2d 847, 552 N.Y.S.2d 923, 552 N.E.2d 171 (1990)(*Hymowitz* rule available only to claimants with substantial connection to New York; New York borrowing statute requires application of shorter foreign statutes of limitations to claims arising outside of New York); Enright v. Eli Lilly and Co., 77 N.Y.2d 377, 568 N.Y.S.2d 550, 570 N.E.2d 198, *cert. denied* 502 U.S. 868, 112 S.Ct. 197, 116 L.Ed.2d 157 (1991)(barring liability to third generation DES plaintiffs). *See* Marisa L. Mascaro, *Preconception Tort Liability: Recognizing a Strict Liability Cause of Action for DES Grandchildren,* 17 Am.J.L. & Med. 435 (1991); John B. Maynard, *Third-Generation–DES Claims,* 27 New Eng.L.Rev. 241 (1992); Christopher J. McGuire, Note, *Market-Share Liability After* Hymowitz *and* Conley: *Exploring the Limits of Judicial Power,* 24 Mich.J.L.Reform 759 (1991).

9. Are DES plaintiffs entitled to a jury trial on the issue of market share liability? In the wake of *Hymowitz,* the Supreme Court in Erie County issued an order severing the market share issue from every DES case pending in New York and consolidating those actions so that the market share issue could be resolved in a single proceeding. The defendants then urged that the market share liability issue was a separable, collateral issue to be determined by a judge. In In the Matter of DES Market Share Litigation, 79 N.Y.2d 299, 582 N.Y.S.2d377, 591 N.E.2d 226 (Ct.App.1992), Judge Wachtler, speaking for the New York Court of Appeals, rejected this contention:

> In the case now before us, the DES plaintiffs have the right to a jury trial on the merits of their personal injury claims because these causes of action are for money damages and would have been tried by a jury at common law. The question that remains is whether the severance and consolidation of the market share inquiry in one court converts an examination of the defendants' relative culpability into a wholly separate equitable proceeding to which no right to a jury trial attaches.

> The defendants argue that in adopting a market share theory in *Hymowitz,* this Court created a new equitable remedy, unknown in the common law, that absolved DES plaintiffs from identifying the particular product that caused their injury and that apportioned liability in accordance with over-all culpability. In support of their argument, the defendants point to our use of the word "equitable" to describe our decision to use a market share theory in DES cases (Hymowitz v. Lilly & Co., 73 N.Y.2d at 508, 541 N.Y.S.2d 941, 539 N.E.2d 1069, * * * ["(w)e turn then to the question of how to fairly and equitably apportion the loss occasioned by DES" * * *], at 512, 541 N.Y.S.2d 941, 539 N.E.2d 1069, * * * ["this is an equitable way to provide plaintiffs with the relief they deserve, while also rationally distributing the responsibility for plaintiffs' injuries among defendants" * * *]). They argue that this use of the word "equitable" signalled that litigation of the market share issue was akin to a traditional action in equity, and that consequently no right to a jury trial attached as a constitutional matter.

> When we used the word "equitable" in *Hymowitz,* we were not categorizing the market share theory; rather, we were indicating the extent to which our decision was compelled by simple fairness. We adopted a market share theory because, as we noted at the time, "the ever-evolving dictates of justice and fairness, which are the heart of our common-law system, required * * * formation of a remedy for injuries caused by DES" * * *

> * * *

> *Hymowitz* simply relaxed the DES plaintiffs' burden of proof on that portion of the causation requirement which would have obligated the plaintiffs to establish the identity of the manufacturer of the drug their mothers ingested. It did not create a new equitable cause of action, as defendants contend.

* * *

Thus, because we agree with the Appellate Division that market share is an issue in the plaintiffs' cause of action for money damages and not a separate cause of action, plaintiffs are entitled to a jury trial by virtue of article I, § 2 of the New York Constitution and CPLR 4101. Although the Trial Judge had the power to sever and consolidate the market share issue for the sake of judicial economy, he did not have the added power to defeat the plaintiffs' right to a jury trial.

Because of our holding that adoption of the market share theory did not create a new equitable remedy or cause of action, but instead modified an existing common-law remedy, we need not consider defendants' arguments that the market share theory is analogous to a long account, a bill of peace or equitable contribution. We would simply note that we do not accept the defendants' argument that the sheer complexity of the market share proceeding converts it into an equitable cause of action as a matter of law. This conclusion would have enormous ramifications in the area of complex litigation and is completely unwarranted under the facts of this case. Market share is a discrete legal issue that is an integral part of the plaintiffs' cause of action in tort for money damages. Since the issue is so clearly legal in nature, we decline to hold that the complexity of its resolution alone magically transforms it into an equitable matter that can defeat the plaintiffs' constitutional right to a trial by jury.

10. For general commentary on the problems of apportioning liability in mass and toxic tort litigation, *see generally* American Bar Association, *Towards a Jurisprudence of Injury: The Continuing Creation of a System of Substantive Justice in American Tort Law: Report to the American Bar Association, Special Committee on the Torts Liability System* (1984); American Law Institute, *Reporter's Study,* ENTERPRISE RESPONSIBILITY FOR PERSONAL INJURY (1991)(volumes I & II); Annot., *Defective Product–Enterprise Liability,* 22 A.L.R. 4th 183 (1986); Wendell B. Alcorn, Jr., *Liability Theories for Toxic Torts,* Nat. Resources & Env't, Spring 1988, at 3; Robert A.B. Bush, *Between Two Worlds: The Shift From Individual to Group Responsibility,* 33 U.C.L.A.L.Rev. 1473 (1986); James G. Middlebrooks, Note, *Industry-Wide Liability and Market–Share Allocation of Damages,* 15 Ga.L.Rev. 423 (1981); Diane K. Wohlfarth, Comment, *Joint Tortfeasors in Toxic Substance Litigation: Paying Your Fair Share,* 29 Duq.L.Rev. 325 (1991); Richard W. Wright, *Allocating Liability Among Multiple Responsible Causes: A Principled Defense of Joint and Several Liability for Actual Harm and Risk Exposure,* 21 U.C. Davis L. Rev. 1141 (1988).

2. ENVIRONMENTAL TORTS

AMERICAN LAW INSTITUTE, REPORTER'S STUDY, ENTERPRISE RESPONSIBILITY FOR INJURY (1991)

Vol. I, pp. 311–317; 332–333.

TORT AND ENVIRONMENTAL LAW

In the early 1960's both the general public and legislators became aware of the subtle dangers posed by environmental toxins. Rachel

Carson's pathbreaking book, SILENT SPRING, documented the dangers of pesticides. Concerns about the spread of hard-to-detect toxic fumes, gases, and water-soluble materials—the same issues that spurred on the reformation in trespass and nuisance law—provided increasing pressure to control pollution. These concerns coincided with and supported increasing awareness of the destruction of the physical beauty of the country. Thus began the modern environmental movement, based on concern for health as well as for preservation of wild places. Given the peculiarity interstate aspect of the problem of dispersion of many pollutants which showed no respect for state lines, as well as the need to protect unique sites and ecosystems, many thought a major federal role was necessary.

The federal initiative took two forms. One was an effort to ensure that agencies of the federal government would give suitable consideration to environmental issues. The other was the promulgation of specific standards to control the pollution of major media, especially water and the atmosphere. Most of the standards were intended to reduce the general burden of the widespread pollutants such as sulfur dioxide, particulates, and organic wastes which deplete the oxygen and receiving waters, not to address specific personal injuries. Concerns about more localized "toxic" pollutants that pose targeted risks to human health developed more slowly.

For example, in 1970 Congress embraced a "technology forcing" approach to six conventional air pollutants, as codified in Section 109(a)(1) of the Clean Water Act. Large-scale epidemiological studies in the fifties and sixties had suggested that the six "conventional" air pollutants could be hazardous to health, particularly as causes of respiratory disease and perhaps of lung cancer. Their effect, however, was diffused throughout the environment and did not lead to attributable fractions of disease in specific individuals. The best evidence concerning health hazards was based instead on comparisons of disease rates in different metropolitan areas. So the impetus underlying the initial effort to clean the air was concern over a generally unhealthy environment rather than over specific hazardous or toxic substances. It was assumed that cleaning the air would improve the nation's health, but there was no assurance that this would remove a particular form of disease hazard.

Concern about specific toxic substances in air pollution, especially carcinogens, developed slowly in the seventies. Section 112 of the Clean Air Act has long required the regulation of hazardous air pollutants. Hazardous air pollutants are those for which no ambient air quality standards are applicable, but which, in the judgment of the administrator, may increase general mortality or result in serious irreversible or chronic illness. Although the 1977 amendments to the Clean Air Act were meant to spur agency action regarding toxics, only in the mid-eighties did the Environmental Protection Agency begin to speed promulgation of regulations regarding Section 112 pollutants.

The recent history of water pollution control also reflects a dual focus, not only on general "cleanup" and protection of natural beauty, but also on limiting individuals' exposure to hazardous substances. The Federal Water Pollution Control Act (FWPCA) was perhaps even less "toxics"-oriented than was the Clean Air Act in the early 1970's. Its underlying purpose was to define uniform effluent standards for various industries. Agency inaction regarding toxics in water eventually led to litigation and to development of a compromise between the EPA and environmental advocates, a compromise that resulted in a comprehensive program for regulation of toxic pollutants under the Clean Water Act. Recently the EPA has undertaken systematic investigation of whether these legal controls have been effective in removing toxic wastes from surface water.

The rather slow progress of the federal government's effort to control toxic water and air pollution was already apparent as the Love Canal disaster emerged in the late seventies and early eighties. Efforts to control air and surface water pollution ignored and in some respects encouraged the dumping of harmful residuals in the ground. The sense that dumping of industrial chemicals, many with toxic properties, might be widespread had given new impetus to the existing Resource Conservation and Recovery Act (RCA), enacted in 1976, and led to passage in 1980 of the Comprehensive Environmental Response, Compensation, and Liability Act (CERCLA). CERCLA created the so-called Superfund, financed by taxes on petroleum and chemical products as well as by other legislative appropriations; a structure for financing the cleanup of hazardous waste sites; and legal authority for the federal government to recover the cost of cleanup from the private parties responsible. The liability of these parties is strict, joint and several, and based on attenuated proof of causation, and they have extremely limited defenses available to them. In particular, CERCLA required EPA to compile a National Priority List of hazardous waste sites, as well as a National Contingency Plan specifying the timetable for cleanup of these waste sites.

The courts have generally been willing to enforce the broad liability measures of CERCLA, but the cleanup task has nonetheless proceeded at a snail's pace. More sites continue to be identified. CERCLA imposes retroactive strict liability on those who contribute to the toxic stream. The threat of such liability has basically eliminated any interest on the part of the insurance industry in writing coverage for environmental liability. But this effect of CERCLA must be considered separately from its role in addressing the health hazards of waste sites. In the latter capacity CERCLA has much less impact during its first decade than its proponents hoped it would.

In short, the main story of environmental law in the 1970's and 1980's was the rather slow, though in certain fields steady, pace at which the Environmental Protection Agency and other federal agencies moved to address the hazards of toxics.

* * *

Injuries from environmental toxins will no doubt continue to be a problem in the future. If the past provides a lesson, it is that regulatory agencies will move only slowly to curb exposure to such toxins. Tort litigation therefore could play an important role in both deterrence and compensation of such injuries. Unfortunately, even when they are based on good scientific evidence, environmental tort claims are difficult to win. On the other hand, given the complicated scientific issues involved, the possibility that plaintiffs employing fringe scientists may obtain compensation for groundless claims cannot be dismissed either.

Fortunately, methods are available for improving the reliability and predictability of environmental tort litigation. Each method relies in one way or another on further evolution of the growing synthesis between environmental regulation and tort litigation. First, plaintiffs must have available better information regarding both exposure and the potential toxicities of hazardous substances. If utilized properly, the ATSDR model * and the citizen suit provisions and right-to-know aspects of various federal and state law can provide just that sort of information. These statutory innovations would decrease barriers to litigation by decreasing the cost of the scientific evaluations necessary to bring such suits and to establish their merit.

Second, if citizen suit provisions and administrative agency assistance in the development of scientific data do lower the threshold for environmental injury litigation, the need to help courts in judging causal evidence will become even more acute than it is today. As we suggest in * * * [ ] the companion volume, judges could be assisted greatly by court-appointed experts or science panel determinations of major scientific issues. Moreover, the federal judiciary as a whole could develop policies for controlling the use of fringe sciences such as clinical ecology. These procedural devices would help to make the results of environmental litigation more accurate and predictable.

Finally, compensation for environmental injury requires overt recognition of the role of epidemiology in proof of causation, and thus the relationship of statistical attribution of disease and proportionate compensation for injury. While epidemiological proof now plays a major role in environmental regulation, environmental toxins rarely cause attributable fractions of disease that are greater than 50 percent. The simple more-probable-than-not standard will inevitably preclude most claims. If we are to take even a modest step toward closing the gap between significant environmental injuries and successful environmental litigation, we will have to entertain seriously the idea of a proportionate causation standard for such cases. * * *

* * *

---

* Agency for Toxic Substances and Disease Registry, created as part of the Superfund Amendments and Reauthorization Act of 1986 (SARA), 42 U.S.C. §§ 9601–9675. This agency was entrusted with the task of performing health assessments on every waste disposal site on the National Priority List. 42 U.S.C. § 9604(c).

UNITED STATES CODE ANNOTATED
TITLE 42. THE PUBLIC HEALTH AND WELFARE
CHAPTER 103—COMPREHENSIVE ENVIRONMENTAL RESPONSE, COMPENSATION, AND LIABILITY
SUBCHAPTER I—HAZARDOUS SUBSTANCES RELEASES, LIABILITY, COMPENSATION

§ 9607. Liability

(a) Covered persons; scope; recoverable costs and damages; interest rate; "comparable maturity" date

Notwithstanding any other provision or rule of law, and subject only to the defenses set forth in subsection (b) of this section—

(1) the owner and operator of a vessel or a facility,

(2) any person who at the time of disposal of any hazardous substance owned or operated any facility at which such hazardous substances were disposed of,

(3) any person who by contract, agreement, or otherwise arranged for disposal or treatment, or arranged with a transporter for transport for disposal or treatment, of hazardous substances owned or possessed by such person, by any other party or entity, at any facility or incineration vessel owned or operated by another party or entity and containing such hazardous substances, and

(4) any person who accepts or accepted any hazardous substances for transport to disposal or treatment facilities, incineration vessels or sites selected by such person, from which there is a release, or a threatened release which causes the incurrence of response costs, of a hazardous substance, shall be liable for—

(A) all costs of removal or remedial action incurred by the United States Government or a State or an Indian tribe not inconsistent with the national contingency plan;

(B) any other necessary costs of response incurred by any other person consistent with the national contingency plan;

(C) damages for injury to, destruction of, or loss of natural resources, including the reasonable costs of assessing such injury, destruction, or loss resulting from such a release; and

(D) the costs of any health assessment or health effects study carried out under section 9604(i) of this title.

The amounts recoverable in an action under this section shall include interest on the amounts recoverable under subparagraphs (A) through (D). Such interest shall accrue from the later of (i) the date payment of a specified amount is demanded in writing, or (ii) the date of the expenditure concerned. The rate of interest on the outstanding unpaid balance of the amounts recoverable under this section shall be the same rate as is specified for interest on investments of the Hazardous Substance Superfund established under subchapter A of chapter 98 of Title 26. For purposes of applying such amendments to interest under this subsection, the term "comparable maturity" shall be determined with reference to the date on which interest accruing under this subsection commences.

(b) Defenses

There shall be no liability under subsection (a) of this section for a person otherwise liable who can establish by a preponderance of the evidence that the release or threat of release of a hazardous substance and the damages resulting therefrom were caused solely by—

(1) an act of God;

(2) an act of war;

(3) an act or omission of a third party other than an employee or agent of the defendant, or than one whose act or omission occurs in connection with a contractual relationship, existing directly or indirectly, with the defendant (except where the sole contractual arrangement arises from a published tariff and acceptance for carriage by a common carrier by rail), if the defendant establishes by a preponderance of the evidence that (a) he exercised due care with respect to the hazardous substance concerned, taking into consideration the characteristics of such hazardous substance, in light of all relevant facts and circumstances, and (b) he took precautions against foreseeable acts or omissions of any such third party and the consequences that could foreseeably result from such acts or omissions; or

(4) any combination of the foregoing paragraphs.

* * *

§ 9613. Civil Proceedings

* * *

(f) Contribution

(1) Contribution

Any person may seek contribution from any other person who is liable or potentially liable under section 9607(a) of this title, during or following any civil action under section 9606 of this title or under section 9607(a) of this title. Such claims shall be brought in accordance with this section and the Federal Rules of Civil Procedure, and shall be governed by Federal law. In resolving contribution claims, the court may allocate response costs among liable parties using such equitable factors as the court determines are appropriate. Nothing in this subsection shall diminish the right of any person to bring an action for contribution in the absence of a civil action under section 9606 or section 9607 of this title.

(2) Settlement

A person who has resolved its liability to the United States or a State in an administrative or judicially approved settlement shall not be liable for claims for contribution regarding matters addressed in the settlement. Such settlement does not discharge any of the other potentially liable persons unless its terms so provide, but it reduces the potential liability of the others by the amount of the settlement.

(3) Persons not party to settlement

(A) If the United States or a State has obtained less than complete relief from a person who has resolved its liability to the United States or the State in an administrative or judicially approved settlement, the United States or the State may bring an action against any person who has not so resolved its liability.

(B) A person who has resolved its liability to the United States or a State for some or all of a response action or for some or all of the costs of such action in an administrative or judicially approved settlement may seek contribution from any person who is not party to a settlement referred to in paragraph (2).

(C) In any action under this paragraph, the rights of any person who has resolved its liability to the United States or a State shall be subordinate to the rights of the United States or the State. Any contribution action brought under this paragraph shall be governed by Federal law.

UNITED STATES v. MONSANTO COMPANY

United States Court of Appeals, Fourth Circuit, 1988.
858 F.2d 160.

Before WIDENER, SPROUSE and ERVIN, CIRCUIT JUDGES.

SPROUSE, CIRCUIT JUDGE:

Oscar Seidenberg and Harvey Hutchinson (the site-owners) and Allied Corporation, Monsanto Company, and EM Industries, Inc. (the generator defendants), appeal from the district court's entry of summary judgment holding them liable to the United States and the State of South Carolina (the governments) under section 107(a) of the Comprehensive Environmental Response, Compensation, and Liability Act of 1980 (CERCLA). 42 U.S.C.A. § 9607(a) (West Supp. 1987). The court determined that the defendants were liable jointly and severally for $1,813,624 in response costs accrued from the partial removal of hazardous waste from a disposal facility located near Columbia, South Carolina. The court declined, however, to assess prejudgment interest against the defendants. We affirm the district court's liability holdings, but we vacate and remand for reconsideration its denial of prejudgment interest.

I.

In 1972, Seidenberg and Hutchinson leased a four-acre tract of land they owned to the Columbia Organic Chemical Company (COCC), a

South Carolina chemical manufacturing corporation. The property, located along Bluff Road near Columbia, South Carolina, consisted of a small warehouse and surrounding areas. The lease was verbal, on a month-to-month basis, and according to the site-owners' deposition testimony, was executed for the sole purpose of allowing COCC to store raw materials and finished products in the warehouse. Seidenberg and Hutchinson received monthly lease payments of $200, which increased to $350 by 1980.

In the mid–1970s, COCC expanded its business to include the brokering and recycling of chemical waste generated by third parties. It used the Bluff Road site as a waste storage and disposal facility for its new operations. In 1976, COCC's principals incorporated South Carolina Recycling and Disposal Inc. (SCRDI), for the purpose of assuming COCC's waste-handling business, and the site-owners began accepting lease payments from SCRDI.

SCRDI contracted with numerous off-site waste producers for the transport, recycling, and disposal of chemical and other waste. Among these producers were agencies of the federal government and South Carolina, and various private entities including the three generator defendants in this litigation. Although SCRDI operated other disposal sites, it deposited much of the waste it received at the Bluff Road facility. The waste stored at Bluff Road contained many chemical substances that federal law defines as "hazardous."

Between 1976 and 1980, SCRDI haphazardly deposited more than 7,000 fifty-five gallon drums of chemical waste on the four-acre Bluff Road site. It placed waste laden drums and containers wherever there was space, often without pallets to protect them from the damp ground. It stacked drums on top of one another without regard to the chemical compatibility of their contents. It maintained no documented safety procedures and kept no inventory of the stored chemicals. Over time many of the drums rusted, rotted, and otherwise deteriorated. Hazardous substances leaked from the decaying drums and oozed into the ground. The substances commingled with incompatible chemicals that had escaped from other containers, generating noxious fumes, fires, and explosions.

On October 26, 1977, a toxic cloud formed when chemicals leaking from rusted drums reacted with rainwater. Twelve responding firemen were hospitalized. Again, on July 24, 1979, an explosion and fire resulted when chemicals stored in glass jars leaked onto drums containing incompatible substances. SCRDI'S site manager could not identify the substances that caused the explosion, making the fire difficult to extinguish.

In 1980, the Environmental Protection Agency (EPA) inspected the Bluff Road site. Its investigation revealed that the facility was filled well beyond its capacity with chemical waste. The number of drums and the reckless manner in which they were stacked precluded access to various areas in the site. Many of the drums observed were unlabeled, or their labels had become unreadable from exposure, rendering it impossible to identify their contents. The EPA concluded that the site posed "a major fire hazard."

Later that year, the United States filed suit under section 7003 of the Resource Conservation and Recovery Act, 42 U.S.C. § 6973, against SCRDI, COCC, and Oscar Seidenberg. The complaint was filed before the December 11, 1980, effective date of CERCLA, and it sought only injunctive relief. Thereafter, the State of South Carolina intervened as a plaintiff in the pending action.

In the course of discovery, the governments identified a number of waste generators, including the generator defendants in this appeal, that had contracted with SCRDI for waste disposal. The governments notified the generators that they were potentially responsible for the costs of cleanup at Bluff Road under section 107(a) of the newly-enacted CERCLA. As a result of these contacts, the governments executed individual settlement agreements with twelve of the identified off-site producers. The generator defendants, however, declined to settle.

Using funds received from the settlements, the governments contracted with Triangle Resource Industries (TRI) to conduct a partial surface cleanup at the site. The contract required RAD Services, Inc., a subsidiary of TRI, to remove 75% of the drums found there and to keep a log of the removed drums. RAD completed its partial cleanup operation in October 1982. The log it prepared documented that it had removed containers and drums bearing the labels or markings of each of the three generator defendants.

The EPA reinspected the site after the first phase of the cleanup had been completed. The inspection revealed that closed drums and containers labeled with the insignia of each of the three generator defendants remained at the site. The EPA also collected samples of surface water, soil, and sediment from the site. Laboratory tests of the samples disclosed that several hazardous substances [4] contained in the waste the generator defendants had shipped to the site remained present at the site.[5]

Thereafter, South Carolina completed the remaining 25% of the surface cleanup. It used federal funds from the Hazardous Substances Response Trust Fund (Superfund), 42 U.S.C. § 9631, as well as state money from the South Carolina Hazardous Waste Contingency Fund,

---

4. The term "hazardous substance" is defined in section 101(14) of CERCLA, 42 U.S.C.A. § 9601(14) (West Supp.1987). The definition incorporates by reference the substances listed as hazardous or toxic under the Clean Water Act, 33 U.S.C.A. §§ 1317(a), 1321(b)(2)(a) (West 1986), the Clean Air Act, 42 U.S.C. § 7412(b), the Resource Conservation and Recovery Act of 1976, 42 U.S.C.A. § 6921 (West 1983 & Supp. 1987), and the Toxic Substances Control Act, 15 U.S.C. § 2606. Section 102(a) of CERCLA also authorizes EPA to list ad-

ditional substances that "may present substantial danger to the public health or welfare or the environment." 42 U.S.C.A. § 9602(a) (West Supp. 1987).

5. It is undisputed that hazardous substances of the sort contained in each of the generator defendants' waste materials were found at the site. These substances included 1,1,1-Trichloroethane, acetone, phenol, cresol (methyl phenol), chlorophenol, and 2,4-dichlorophenol.

S.C. Code Ann. 44–56–160, and in-kind contribution of other state funds to match the federal contribution.

In 1982, the governments filed an amended complaint, adding the three generator defendants and site-owner Harvey Hutchinson, and including claims under section 107(a) of CERCLA against all of the nonsettling defendants. The governments alleged that the generator defendants and site-owners were jointly and severally liable under section 107(a) for the costs expended completing the surface cleanup at Bluff Road.

In response, the site-owners contended that they were innocent absentee landlords unaware of and unconnected to the waste disposal activities that took place on their land. They maintained that their lease with COCC did not allow COCC (or SCRDI) to store chemical waste on the premises, but they admitted that they became aware of waste storage in 1977 and accepted lease payments until 1980.

The generator defendants likewise denied liability for the governments' response costs.[6] Among other defenses, they claimed that none of their specific waste materials contributed to the hazardous conditions at Bluff Road, and that retroactive imposition of CERCLA liability on them was unconstitutional. They also asserted that they could establish an affirmative defense to CERCLA liability under section 107(b)(3), 42 U.S.C. § 9607(b)(3), by showing that the harm at the site was caused solely through the conduct of unrelated third parties. All parties thereafter moved for summary judgment.

After an evidentiary hearing, the district court granted the governments' summary judgment motion on CERCLA liability. The court found that all of the defendants were responsible parties under section 107(a), and that none of them had presented sufficient evidence to support an affirmative defense under section 107(b).[7] The court further concluded that the environmental harm at Bluff Road was "indivisible," and it held all of the defendants jointly and severally liable for the governments' response costs. United States v. South Carolina Recycling & Disposal, Inc., 653 F.Supp. 984 (D.S.C.1984)(SCRDI).

As to the site-owners' liability, the court found it sufficient that they owned the Bluff Road site at the time hazardous substances were deposited there. Id. at 993 (interpreting 42 U.S.C.A. § 9607(a)(2) (West Supp. 1987)). It rejected their contentions that Congress did not intend to subject "innocent" landowners to CERCLA liability. The court

---

6. Section 101(25) of CERCLA provides that " 'respond' or 'response' means remove, removal, remedy, and remedial action, all such terms (including the terms 'removal' and 'remedial action') include enforcement activities related thereto." 42 U.S.C.A. § 9601(25) (West Supp. 1987). The terms "remove" and "removal," and "remedy" and "remedial action" are in turn defined at sections 101(23) and 101(24), 42 U.S.C.A. §§ 9601(23), (24) (West Supp. 1987).

7. In its initial summary judgment order, the court refused to hold COCC liable for response costs. After subsequent proceedings, however, the court found that COCC was engaged in a joint venture with SCRDI and therefore shared its liability for the governments' costs. COCC has not appealed from that ruling.

similarly found summary judgment appropriate against the generator defendants because it was undisputed that (1) they shipped hazardous substances to the Bluff Road facility; (2) hazardous substances "like" those present in the generator defendants' waste were found at the facility; and (3) there had been a release of hazardous substances at the site. SCRDI, 653 F.Supp. at 991–93 (interpreting 42 U.S.C.A. § 9607(a)(3) (West Supp. 1987)). In this context, the court rejected the generator defendants' arguments that the governments had to prove that their specific waste contributed to the harm at the site, and it found their constitutional contentions to be "without force." SCRDI, 653 F.Supp. at 992–93, 995–98. Finally, since none of the defendants challenged the governments' itemized accounting of response costs, the court ordered them to pay the full $1,813,624 that had been requested. * * * It refused, however, to add prejudgment interest to the amount owed. * * * This appeal followed.

II.

The site-owners and the generator defendants first contest the imposition of CERCLA liability vel non, and they challenge the propriety of summary judgment in light of the evidence presented to the trial court. The site-owners also reassert the "innocent landowner" defense that the district court rejected, and claim that the court erroneously precluded them from presenting evidence of a valid affirmative defense under section 107(b)(3), 42 U.S.C. § 9607(b)(3). The generator defendants likewise repeat their arguments based on the governments' failure to establish a nexus between their specific waste and the harm at the site. They also claim that the trial court ignored material factual issues relevant to affirmative defenses to liability. We address these contentions sequentially, but pause briefly to review the structure of CERCLA's liability scheme.

In CERCLA, Congress established "an array of mechanisms to combat the increasingly serious problem of hazardous substance releases." Dedham Water Co. v. Cumberland Farms Dairy, Inc., 805 F.2d 1074, 1078 (1st Cir.1986).[8] Section 107(a) of the statute sets forth the principal mechanism for recovery of costs expended in the cleanup of waste disposal facilities. At the time the district court entered judgment, section 107(a) provided in pertinent part:

> (a) Covered persons; scope Notwithstanding any other provision or rule of law, and subject only to the defenses set forth in subsection (b) of this section—

. . . . .

---

8. As one district court has stated, the statute provides the federal government with "the tools necessary for a prompt and effective response to problems of national magnitude resulting from hazardous waste disposal," and it evinces congressional intent "that those responsible for problems caused by the disposal of chemical poisons bear the costs and responsibility for remedying the harmful conditions they created." United States v. Reilly Tar & Chemical Corp., 546 F.Supp. 1100, 1112 (D.Minn. 1982).

(2) any person who at the time of disposal of any hazardous substance owned or operated any facility at which such hazardous substances were disposed of, [and]

(3) any person who by contract, agreement, or otherwise arranged for disposal or treatment, or arranged with a transporter for transport for disposal or treatment, of hazardous substances owned or possessed by such person, by any other party or entity, at any facility owned or operated by another party or entity and containing such hazardous substances, and

(4) ... from which there is a release, or a threatened release which causes the incurrence of response costs, of a hazardous substance, shall be liable for—(A) all costs of removal or remedial action incurred by the United States Government or a State not inconsistent with the national contingency plan. 42 U.S.C.A. § 9607(a) (West Supp. 1987).

In our view, the plain language of section 107(a) clearly defines the scope of intended liability under the statute and the elements of proof necessary to establish it. We agree with the overwhelming body of precedent that has interpreted section 107(a) as establishing a strict liability scheme.[11] Further, in light of the evidence presented here, we are persuaded that the district court correctly held that the governments satisfied all the elements of section 107(a) liability as to both the site-owners and the generator defendants.

A. Site–Owners' Liability

In light of the strict liability imposed by section 107(a), we cannot agree with the site-owners contention that they are not within the class of owners Congress intended to hold liable. The traditional elements of tort culpability on which the site-owners rely simply are absent from the statute. The plain language of section 107(a)(2) extends liability to owners of waste facilities regardless of their degree of participation in the subsequent disposal of hazardous waste.

Under section 107(a)(2), any person who owned a facility at a time when hazardous substances were deposited there may be held liable for all costs of removal or remedial action if a release or threatened release of a hazardous substance occurs. The site-owners do not dispute their ownership of the Bluff Road facility, or the fact that releases occurred there during their period of ownership. Under these circumstances, all

11. *See, e.g.,* Levin Metals Corp. v. Parr–Richmond Terminal Co., 799 F.2d 1312, 1316 (9th Cir.1986); New York v. Shore Realty Corp., 759 F.2d 1032, 1042 (2d Cir.1985); Violet v. Picillo, 648 F.Supp. 1283, 1290 (D.R.I.1986)(and cases cited therein); *see also* United States v. Northeastern Pharmaceutical & Chemical Co., 810 F.2d 726, 732 n.3 (8th Cir.1986), *cert. denied,* 484 U.S 848, 108 S.Ct. 146, 98 L.Ed.2d 102 (1987)(*dictum*). In addition to the unanimous judicial viewpoint that Congress intended CERCLA liability to be strict, we observe that CERCLA section 101(32), 42 U.S.C.A. § 9601(32) (West Supp. 1987), provides that the standard of liability applicable to CERCLA actions shall be that which governs actions under section 311 of the Clean Water Act, 33 U.S.C. § 1321. In Steuart Transportation Co. v. Allied Towing Corp., 596 F.2d 609, 613 (4th Cir.1979), we held that the standard of liability under section 311 is strict liability.

the prerequisites to section 107(a) liability have been satisfied.[13] *See* Shore Realty, 759 F.2d at 1043–44 (site-owner held liable under CERC-LA section 107(a)(1) even though he did not contribute to the presence or cause the release of hazardous substances at the facility).[14]

The site-owners nonetheless contend that the district court's grant of summary judgment improperly denied them the opportunity to present an affirmative defense under section 107(b)(3). Section 107(b)(3) sets forth a limited affirmative defense based on the complete absence of causation. *See* Shore Realty, 759 F.2d at 1044. It requires proof that the release or threatened release of hazardous substances and resulting damages were caused solely by "a third party other than ... one whose act or omission occurs in connection with a contractual relationship, existing directly or indirectly, with the defendant...." 42 U.S.C. § 9607(b)(3). A second element of the defense requires proof that the defendant "took precautions against foreseeable acts or omissions of any such third party and the consequences that could foreseeably result from such acts or omissions." * * * We agree with the district court that under no view of the evidence could the site-owners satisfy either of these proof requirements.

First, the site-owners could not establish the absence of a direct or indirect contractual relationship necessary to maintain the affirmative defense. They concede they entered into a lease agreement with COCC. They accepted rent from COCC, and after SCRDI was incorporated, they accepted rent from SCRDI. *See* United States v. Northernaire Plating Co., 670 F.Supp. 742, 747–48 (W.D. Mich.1987)(owner who leased facility to disposing party could not assert affirmative defense). Second, the site-owners presented no evidence that they took precautionary action

---

13. The site-owners' relative degree of fault would, of course, be relevant in any subsequent action for contribution brought pursuant to 42 U.S.C.A. § 9613(f)(West Supp. 1987). Congress, in the Superfund Amendments and Reauthorization Act of 1986, Pub.L. 99–499, § 113, 100 Stat. 1613, 1647 (1986) [hereafter SARA], established a right of contribution in favor of defendants sued under CERCLA section 107(a). Section 113(f)(1) provides:

> Any person may seek contribution from any other person who is liable or potentially liable under section 9607(a) of this title, during or following any civil action under section 9606 of this title or under section 9607(a) of this title. Such claims shall be brought in accordance with this section and the Federal Rules of Civil Procedure, and shall be governed by Federal law. In resolving contribution claims, the court may allocate response costs among liable parties using such equitable factors as the court determines are appropriate. Nothing in this subsection shall diminish the right of any per-

son to bring an action for contribution in the absence of a civil action under section 9606 or section 9607 of this title. 42 U.S.C.A. § 9613(f) (West Supp. 1987).

The legislative history of this amendment suggests that in arriving at an equitable allocation of costs, a court may consider, among other things, the degree of involvement by parties in the generation, transportation, treatment, storage, or disposal of hazardous substances. H.R. Rep. No. 253(III), 99th Cong., 1st Sess. 19 (1985), reprinted in 1986 U.S. Code Cong. & Admin. News 2835, 3038, 3042.

14. Congress, in section 101(35) of SARA, acknowledged that landowners may affirmatively avoid liability if they can prove they did not know and had no reason to know that hazardous substances were disposed of on their land at the time they acquired title or possession. 42 U.S.C.A. § 9601(35) (West Supp. 1987). This explicitly drafted exception further signals Congress' intent to impose liability on landowners who cannot satisfy its express requirements.

against the foreseeable conduct of COCC or SCRDI. They argued to the trial court that, although they were aware COCC was a chemical manufacturing company, they were completely ignorant of all waste disposal activities at Bluff Road before 1977. They maintained that they never inspected the site prior to that time. In our view, the statute does not sanction such willful or negligent blindness on the part of absentee owners. The district court committed no error in entering summary judgment against the site-owners.

B. Generator Defendants' Liability

The generator defendants first contend that the district court misinterpreted section 107(a)(3) because it failed to read into the statute a requirement that the governments prove a nexus between the waste they sent to the site and the resulting environmental harm. They maintain that the statutory phrase "containing such hazardous substances" requires proof that the specific substances they generated and sent to the site were present at the facility at the time of release. The district court held, however, that the statute was satisfied by proof that hazardous substances "like" those contained in the generator defendants' waste were found at the site. * * * We agree with the district court's interpretation.

Reduced of surplus language, sections 107(a)(3) and (4) impose liability on off-site waste generators who: "arranged for disposal ... of hazardous substances ... at any facility ... containing such hazardous substances ... from which there is a release ... of a hazardous substance." 42 U.S.C.A. §§ 9607(a)(3), (4) (West Supp. 1987). * * * In our view, the plain meaning of the adjective "such" in the phrase "containing such hazardous substances" is "[a]like, similar, of the like kind." BLACK'S LAW DICTIONARY 1284 (5th ed.1979). As used in the statute, the phrase "such hazardous substances" denotes hazardous substances alike, similar, or of a like kind to those that were present in a generator defendant's waste or that could have been produced by the mixture of the defendant's waste with other waste present at the site. It does not mean that the plaintiff must trace the ownership of each generic chemical compound found at a site. Absent proof that a generator defendant's specific waste remained at a facility at the time of release, a showing of chemical similarity between hazardous substances is sufficient.[15]

The overall structure of CERCLA'S liability provisions also militates against the generator defendants' "proof of ownership" argument. In *Shore Realty,* the Second Circuit held with respect to site-owners that requiring proof of ownership at any time later than the time of disposal would go far toward rendering the section 107(b) defenses superfluous.

15. CERCLA plaintiffs need not perform exhaustive chemical analyses of hazardous substances found at a disposal site. * * * They must, however, present evidence that a generator defendant's waste was shipped to a site and that hazardous substances similar to those contained in the defendant's waste remained present at the time of release. The defendant, of course, may in turn present evidence of an affirmative defense to liability.

Shore Realty, 759 F.2d at 1044. We agree with the court's reading of the statute and conclude that its reasoning applies equally to the generator defendants' contentions. As the statute provides—"[n]otwithstanding any other provision or rule of law"—liability under section 107(a) is "subject only to the defenses set forth" in section 107(b). 42 U.S.C.A. § 9607(a)(West Supp. 1987). Each of the three defenses [16] established in section 107(b) "carves out from liability an exception based on causation." *Shore Realty,* 759 F.2d at 1044. Congress has, therefore, allocated the burden of disproving causation to the defendant who profited from the generation and inexpensive disposal of hazardous waste. We decline to interpret the statute in a way that would neutralize the force of Congress' intent.[17]

Finally, the purpose underlying CERCLA's liability provisions counsels against the generator defendants' argument. Throughout the statute's legislative history, there appears the recurring theme of facilitating prompt action to remedy the environmental blight of unscrupulous waste disposal. In deleting causation language from section 107(a), we assume as have many other courts, that Congress knew of the synergistic and migratory capacities of leaking chemical waste, and the technological infeasibility of tracing improperly disposed waste to its source.[19] In view of this, we will not frustrate the statute's salutary goals by engrafting a "proof of ownership" requirement, which in practice, would be as onerous as the language Congress saw fit to delete. *See* United States v. Wade, 577 F.Supp. 1326, 1332 (E.D.Pa.1983)("To require a plaintiff under CERCLA to 'fingerprint' wastes is to eviscerate the statute.").

The generator defendants next argue that the trial court ignored evidence that established genuine factual issues as to the existence of an affirmative defense to liability. They maintain that summary judgment was inappropriate because they presented some evidence that all of their waste had been removed from Bluff Road prior to cleanup. We agree

16. In addition to the limited third-party defense discussed above, sections 107(b)(1) and (2) respectively allow defendants to avoid liability by proving that the release and resulting damages were "caused solely" by an act of God or an act of war. 42 U.S.C. § 9607(b)(1), (2).

17. In fact, Congress specifically declined to include a similar nexus requirement in CERCLA. As the Second Circuit in *Shore Realty* observed, an early House version of what ultimately became section 107(a) limited liability to "any person who caused or contributed to the release or threatened release." 759 F.2d at 1044, quoting H.R. Rep. 7020, 96th Cong., 2d Sess. § 3071(a)(1980), reprinted in 2 *A Legislative History of the Comprehensive Environmental Response, Compensation and Liability Act of 1980* at 438. As ultimately enacted after House and Senate compromise, however, CERCLA "imposed liability on classes of persons without reference to whether they caused or contributed to the release or threat of release." *Shore Realty,* 759 F.2d at 1044. The legislature thus eliminated the element of causation from the plaintiff's liability case. *Id.; see also* United States v. Bliss, 667 F.Supp. 1298, 1309 (E.D.Mo.1987)("traditional tort notions, such as proximate cause, do not apply"); Violet v. Picillo, 648 F.Supp. 1283, 1290–93 (D.R.I.1986)(minimal causal nexus); United States v. Conservation Chemical Co., 619 F.Supp. 162, 190 (W.D.Mo. 1985); United States v. Wade, 577 F.Supp. 1326, 1331–34 (E.D.Pa.1983).

19. In advancing their arduous proof requirements, the generator defendants make little mention of the fact that leaking chemicals may combine to form new compounds or escape into the atmosphere before proper response action can be taken.

with the trial court, however, that the materials on which the generator defendants rely were insufficient to create a genuine issue of material fact.

The generator defendants offered only conclusory allegations, principally based "on information and belief," that their waste, originally deposited at Bluff Road, was at some time prior to 1979 transported from that facility to other sites operated by SCRDI. To withstand summary judgment under section 107(b)(3), however, the generator defendants had to produce specific evidence creating a genuine issue that all of their waste was removed from the site prior to the release of hazardous substances there. *See* 42 U.S.C. § 9607(b)(3). In light of the uncontroverted proof that containers bearing each of the defendants' markings remained present at the site at the time of cleanup and the fact that hazardous substances chemically similar to those contained in the generators' waste were found, the generator defendants' affidavits and deposition testimony simply failed to establish complete removal as a genuine issue. *See* Celotex v. Catrett, 477 U.S. 317, 106 S.Ct. 2548, 91 L.Ed.2d 265 (1986)(summary judgment appropriately granted against nonmoving party who failed to produce evidence supporting an element essential to its case on which it bore burden of proof at trial).

III.

The appellants next challenge the district court's imposition of joint and several liability for the governments' response costs.[22] The court concluded that joint and several liability was appropriate because the environmental harm at Bluff Road was "indivisible" and the appellants had "failed to meet their burden of proving otherwise." *SCRDI*, 653 F.Supp. at 994. We agree with its conclusion.

While CERCLA does not mandate the imposition of joint and several liability, it permits it in cases of indivisible harm. *See* Shore Realty, 759 F.2d at 1042 n.13; United States v. Chem-Dyne, 572 F.Supp. 802, 810–11 (S.D.Ohio 1983).[23] In each case, the court must consider traditional and evolving principles of federal common law, which Congress has left to the courts to supply interstitially.

---

22. The site-owners limit their joint and several liability argument to the contention that it is inequitable under the circumstances of this case, i.e., their limited degree of participation in waste disposal activities at Bluff Road. As we have stated, however, such equitable factors are relevant in subsequent actions for contribution. They are not pertinent to the question of joint and several liability, which focuses principally on the divisibility among responsible parties of the harm to the environment.

23. As many courts have noted, a proposed requirement that joint and several liability be imposed in all CERCLA cases was deleted from the final version of the bill. *See, e.g.*, Chem-Dyne, 572 F.Supp. at 806. "The deletion," however, "was not intended as a rejection of joint and several liability," but rather "to have the scope of liability determined under common law principles." *Id.* at 808. We adopt the *Chem-Dyne* court's thorough discussion of CERCLA's legislative history with respect to joint and several liability. We note that the approach taken in *Chem-Dyne* was subsequently confirmed as correct by Congress in its consideration of SARA's contribution provisions. See H.R. Rep. No. 253(I), 99th Cong.2d Sess., 79–80 (1985), *reprinted in* 1986 U.S.Code Cong. & Admin. News at 2835, 2861–62.

Under common law rules, when two or more persons act independently to cause a single harm for which there is a reasonable basis of apportionment according to the contribution of each, each is held liable only for the portion of harm that he causes. Edmonds v. Compagnie Generale Transatlantique, 443 U.S. 256, 260 n. 8, 99 S.Ct. 2753, 2756 n. 8, 61 L.Ed.2d 521 (1979). When such persons cause a single and indivisible harm, however, they are held liable jointly and severally for the entire harm. *Id.* (citing RESTATEMENT (SECOND) OF TORTS § 433A (1965)). We think these principles, as reflected in the RESTATEMENT (SECOND) OF TORTS, represent the correct and uniform federal rules applicable to CERCLA cases.

Section 433A of the RESTATEMENT provides: "(1) Damages for harm are to be apportioned among two or more causes where (a) there are distinct harms, or (b) there is a reasonable basis for determining the contribution of each cause to a single harm. (2) Damages for any other harm cannot be apportioned among two or more causes." RESTATEMENT (SECOND) OF TORTS § 433A (1965).

Placing their argument into the RESTATEMENT framework, the generator defendants concede that the environmental damage at Bluff Road constituted a "single harm," but contend that there was a reasonable basis for apportioning the harm. They observe that each of the off-site generators with whom SCRDI contracted sent a potentially identifiable volume of waste to the Bluff Road site, and they maintain that liability should have been apportioned according to the volume they deposited as compared to the total volume disposed of there by all parties. In light of the conditions at Bluff Road, we cannot accept this method as a basis for apportionment.

The generator defendants bore the burden of establishing a reasonable basis for apportioning liability among responsible parties. Chem-Dyne, 572 F.Supp. at 810; RESTATEMENT (SECOND) OF TORTS § 433B (1965). To meet this burden, the generator defendants had to establish that the environmental harm at Bluff Road was divisible among responsible parties. They presented no evidence, however, showing a relationship between waste volume, the release of hazardous substances, and the harm at the site.[25] Further, in light of the commingling of hazardous substances, the district court could not have reasonably apportioned liability without some evidence disclosing the individual and interactive qualities of the substances deposited there. Common sense counsels that a million gallons of certain substances could be mixed together

---

25. At minimum, such evidence was crucial to demonstrate that a volumetric apportionment scheme was reasonable. The governments presented considerable evidence identifying numerous hazardous substances found at Bluff Road. An EPA investigator reported, for example, that in the first cleanup phase RAD Services encountered substances "in every hazard class, including explosives such as crystal-lized dynamite and nitroglycerine. Numerous examples were found of oxidizers, flammable and nonflammable liquids, poisons, corrosives, containerized gases, and even a small amount of radioactive material." Under these circumstances, volumetric apportionment based on the overall quantity of waste, as opposed to the quantity and quality of hazardous substances contained in the waste would have made little sense.

without significant consequences, whereas a few pints of others improperly mixed could result in disastrous consequences.[26]   Under other circumstances proportionate volumes of hazardous substances may well be probative of contributory harm.[27]   In this case, however, volume could not establish the effective contribution of each waste generator to the harm at the Bluff Road site.

Although we find no error in the trial court's imposition of joint and several liability, we share the appellants' concern that they not be ultimately responsible for reimbursing more than their just portion of the governments' response costs.[28]   In its refusal to apportion liability, the district court likewise recognized the validity of their demand that they not be required to shoulder a disproportionate amount of the costs. It ruled, however, that making the governments whole for response costs was the primary consideration and that cost allocation was a matter "more appropriately considered in an action for contribution between responsible parties after plaintiff has been made whole." *SCRDI,* 653 F.Supp. at 995 & n.8.   Had we sat in place of the district court, we would have ruled as it did on the apportionment issue, but may well have retained the action to dispose of the contribution questions. *See* 42 U.S.C.A. § 9613(f) (West Supp. 1987).   That procedural course, however, was committed to the trial court's discretion and we find no abuse of it. As we have stated, the defendants still have the right to sue responsible parties for contribution, and in that action they may assert both legal and equitable theories of cost allocation.

VI.

In view of the above, the judgment of the district court as to the CERCLA liability of the site-owners and generator defendants is affirmed.   The case is remanded, however, for reconsideration of the question of prejudgment interest.

Affirmed in part, vacated in part, and remanded.

---

26. We agree with the district court that evidence disclosing the relative toxicity, migratory potential, and synergistic capacity of the hazardous substances at the site would be relevant to establishing divisibility of harm.

27. Volumetric contributions provide a reasonable basis for apportioning liability only if it can be reasonably assumed, or it has been demonstrated, that independent factors had no substantial effect on the harm to the environment. *Cf.* RESTATEMENT (SECOND) OF TORTS § 433A comment d, illustrations 4, 5 (1965).

28. The final judgment holds the defendants liable for slightly less than half of the total costs incurred in the cleanup, while it appears that the generator defendants collectively produced approximately 22% of the waste that SCRDI handled.   Other evidence indicates that agencies of the federal government produced more waste than did generator defendant Monsanto, and suggests that the amounts contributed by the settling parties do not bear a strictly proportionate relationship to the total costs of cleaning the facility.   We note, however, that a substantial portion of the final judgment is attributable to litigation costs.   We also observe that the EPA has contributed upwards of $50,000 to the Bluff Road cleanup, and that any further claims against the EPA and other responsible government instrumentalities may be resolved in a contribution action pursuant to CERCLA section 113(f).

UNITED STATES v. ASARCO, INC.

United States District Court, District of Colorado, 1993.
814 F.Supp. 951.

MEMORANDUM OPINION AND ORDER

CARRIGAN, DISTRICT JUDGE.

The United States filed its complaint in this consolidated action on August 6, 1986, seeking to recover its response costs incurred and to be incurred in responding to releases or threatened releases of hazardous substances at the California Gulch Superfund Site under section 107 of CERCLA, 42 U.S.C. § 9607, and to obtain injunctive relief to abate the release or threatened release of hazardous substances under section 106 of CERCLA, 42 U.S.C. § 9606. The United States asserted claims against twelve defendants, including ASARCO, Inc. (ASARCO), Res–ASARCO Joint Venture (Res–ASARCO) and Hecla Mining Company (Hecla), as current or past owners or operators of the site. ASARCO and Res–ASARCO asserted cross-claims against the other defendants, including Hecla.

On April 9, 1992, the United States lodged with the court a proposed partial consent decree to resolve its claims against Hecla. Public notice was published in the Federal Register on April 20, 1992. A thirty day public comment period was provided, which expired on May 20, 1992. Resurrection Mining Company, ASARCO and Res–ASARCO submitted comments on the proposed Hecla decree. Thereafter, the United States filed a motion to enter the proposed partial consent decree. ASARCO and Res–ASARCO responded by opposing that motion. The United States and Hecla also filed a motion to add a substitute addendum to the partial consent decree defining the term "Malta Gulch Tailings." On August 12, 1992, oral argument was heard on whether the proposed partial consent decree should be entered. On January 6, 1993, the partial consent decree and addendum were entered by this court. This order sets forth my reasoning for entering the partial consent decree.

The California Gulch Superfund Site encompasses the Leadville, Colorado mining district where extensive mining, milling, and smelting of gold, silver, zinc and lead ores occurred for more than a century. The environmental legacy of these activities includes acid mine drainage from point sources; numerous tailings, slag and waste rock dumps; demolition debris from smelters and other ore processing facilities; and contaminated surface alluvial channels, sediments and soil. This litigation, spawned by these mining activities, began in December 1983.

* * *

II. HECLA DECREE.

The Hecla decree constituted a cash settlement of the United States' claims against Hecla under section 107(a) of CERCLA, 42 U.S.C. § 9607(a), for all matters at the California Gulch Site, except Hecla's obligations and liability for: (1) investigation and clean-up of the Malta Gulch tailings and areas contaminated by those tailings, and (2) natural resource damages.

Congress intended the judiciary to take a "broad view of proposed settlements, leaving highly technical issues and relatively petty inequities to the discourse between parties." *Cannons*, 899 F.2d at 85–86. Applying that standard, I conclude that only one specific challenge to the Hecla partial consent decree merits in-depth discussion—whether the contribution protection provision of the partial consent decree, § VII.A, bars ASARCO and Res–ASARCO's cross-claims against Hecla. Apart from that challenge, I conclude, based on the content of the partial consent decree, the comments and responses, the motion and response, and the statements of counsel at the hearing, that the remainder of the Hecla decree is legal, fair, reasonable and consistent with the purposes that CERCLA is intended to serve.

Section VII.A of the proposed partial consent decree provides, in pertinent part that: "With regard to claims for contribution against Hecla brought by any third parties pursuant to sections 107(a) and 113(f)(1) of CERCLA ..., the parties herein agree and the Court hereby finds and concludes that Section 113(f)(2) of CERCLA ... shall govern." [2]

ASARCO and Res–ASARCO argue that: (1) their cross-claims against Hecla are independent cost recovery claims under § 107, and therefore are not subject to the contribution protection granted in § VII.A of the partial consent decree; and (2) an "inherent authority" settlement does not allow for contribution protection.

A. Whether ASARCO and Res–ASARCO's Claims Are for Contribution.

ASARCO and Res–ASARCO seek clarification of the breadth of the protection granted by § VII.A. They argue that the government has no authority to provide protection to Hecla from ASARCO and Res–ASARCO's independent cross-claims for costs they have incurred in performing remedial actions, including the Yak Tunnel surge pond and water treatment plant, because their cross-claims are not contribution claims. ASARCO and Res–ASARCO assert that the: "government wholly fails to honor the distinction between cost recovery claims and contribution claims.... Whereas the former are independent claims a party brings to recover its own costs, a contribution claim instead is derivative; thus a party would bring a cost recovery action to recoup its own costs, but would bring a contribution claim to pass off a portion of liability imposed on it for someone else's costs." * * *

The government responds that ASARCO and Res–ASARCO misconstrue CERCLA. It contends that ASARCO's and Res–ASARCO's cross-claims against Hecla under § 107 are indeed for contribution.

---

2. Section 113(f)(2) of CERCLA, 42 U.S.C. § 9613(f)(2), provides, in pertinent part, that: "A person who has resolved its liability to the United States ... in a judicially approved settlement shall not be liable for claims for contribution regarding matters addressed in the settlement. Such settlement does not discharge any of the other potentially liable persons unless its terms so provide, but it reduces the potential liability of others by the amount of the settlement."

Courts that have considered the issue are split on whether one jointly liable party can assert an independent cost recovery claim against another jointly liable party and thereby negate the latter party's contribution protection. *Compare* United States v. Hardage, 733 F.Supp. 1424 (W.D.Okla.1989)(reporter's transcript)(recognizing a "marked distinction" between a contribution claim and a response cost claim); with Transtech Industries, Inc. v. A & Z Septic Clean, 798 F.Supp. 1079 (D.N.J.1992)(claim against one liable party by another liable party who incurred response costs is a claim for contribution) and Dravo Corp. v. Zuber, 804 F.Supp. 1182, 1187 (D.Neb.1992)(response cost claim indistinguishable from claim for contribution).[3]

"Contribution is a statutory or common law right available to those who have paid more than their equitable share of a common liability." County Line Investment Co. v. Tinney, 933 F.2d 1508, 1515 (10th Cir.1991). Contribution is available because of CERCLA's "imposition of joint and several liability, regardless of fault, on persons deemed responsible under CERCLA section 107 for the release or threatened release of hazardous substances from a facility." * * * Congress amended CERCLA by adding section 113(f) which expressly recognizes a right of contribution. * * * Section 113(f), however, does not create the right of contribution—rather the source of a contribution claim is section 107(a). * * * Under CERCLA's scheme, section 107 governs liability, while section 113(f) creates a mechanism for apportioning that liability among responsible parties. * * *

I conclude that where parties are jointly and severally liable under CERCLA, response costs can only be shifted by one party to another party by way of contribution. Where a liable party has incurred response costs for which it is jointly liable, and then attempts to exercise its statutory right to recover another party's share of that common liability, the claim is one for contribution. *See County Line*, 933 F.2d at 1515–16; *Transtech Industries*, at 1086; *Dravo Corp.*, 804 F.Supp. at 1187. Absent a provision to the contrary in CERCLA, the fact that ASARCO and Res–ASARCO have incurred response costs does not alter the substance of their claims so as to enable them to void the contribution protection provided to Hecla by CERCLA § 113(f)(2).[4]

This interpretation is consistent with Congress' intent that Superfund sites be cleaned up expeditiously and fairly. Section 113(f)(2) has

---

3. A number of courts have held that when one liable party sues another to recover an equitable share of its response costs under CERCLA, the action is one for contribution. See In re Dant & Russell, Inc., 951 F.2d 246, 248–49 (9th Cir.1991); Amoco Oil Co. v. Borden, Inc., 889 F.2d 664, 672 (5th Cir.1989); and Smith Land & Improvement Corp. v. Celotex Corp., 851 F.2d 86, 88–89 (3d Cir.1988), *cert. denied,* 488 U.S. 1029, 109 S.Ct. 837, 102 L.Ed.2d 969 (1989). As ASARCO and Res–ASARCO point out, these cases are of limited persua-sive value because the courts did not consider whether there is a distinction, in this setting, between contribution claims and cost recovery claims.

4. On the other hand, if two parties are not jointly and severally liable because the harm is divisible, one party could assert an independent cost recovery claim against the other because there is no common liability and therefore no right of contribution. *See County Line*, 933 F.2d at 1515 n.11, 1516.

been aptly described as creating a carrot and stick. "The carrot the EPA can offer potential settlors is that they need no longer fear that a later contribution action by a non-settlor will compel them to pay still more money to extinguish their liability.... As for the stick, if the settlor pays less than its proportionate share of liability, the nonsettlors, being jointly and severally liable, must make good the difference." In re Acushnet River & New Bedford Harbor, 712 F.Supp. 1019, 1027 (D.Mass.1989). The possibility of disproportionate liability created by CERCLA "promotes early settlements, and deters litigation for litigation's sake, and is an integral part of the statutory plan." *Cannons*, 899 F.2d at 92. The wisdom of Congress in providing this incentive to settle is illustrated by the instant case, now in its tenth year of costly and time consuming litigation.

The interpretation suggested by ASARCO and Res–ASARCO would severely undermine the effectiveness of § 113(f)(2). As a result, there would be far less incentive for Hecla and other defendants to expediently settle the claims against them. In the real world created by CERCLA, litigation expenses have consumed inordinately large sums that could far better have been applied to cleanup. Obviously each day of delay adds to the "transaction" costs of litigation.

Unless a party in Hecla's situation can receive reasonable assurance that its settlement payment will buy a peace with finality, it may see little advantage in early settlement. Absent the contribution claim protection provided by Congress, one recalcitrant party might be able to hinder and delay indefinitely the settlement efforts of other parties. While the contribution protection rule may sometimes result in disproportionate liability, the possibility of such results is speculative, whereas the manifold advantages of early, final, individual settlements are highly probable.

* * *

Notes and Questions

1. The subject of environmental law as it relates to pollution, injuries, and remedies is outside the scope of this casebook and is dealt with extensively in other law school courses. However, environmental litigation deriving from exposure to toxic substances obviously is related to, and can be manifested as, mass tort litigation—asbestos litigation is the most prominent example. To what extent are environmental injuries overlapping or co-extensive with mass tort litigation? To what extent do environmental injury cases share attributes with other mass tort litigation? As described in the ALI *Reporter's Study*, ENTERPRISE RESPONSIBILITY FOR PERSONAL INJURY (1991):

> * * * However, the waves of asbestos litigation were soon joined by other mass tort actions involving a variety of other products. These suits were supported by reasonably firm causal attributions, in the sense that it was possible to prove that the victim had been exposed to some documented quantity of a disease-producing product.

But the end of the seventies witnessed the appearance of tort litigation based on "environmental injury"—injury caused by exposure to something in the outside environment, as opposed to exposure to a consumer product or to a substance in a confined workplace. Beginning with litigation over the Love Canal dumpsite, individuals who had been personally injured by exposures to water or air-borne hazardous substances sought relief through tort litigation for environmental injuries, in addition to compensation for property damages.

These tort claims for environmental injuries are representative of what RAND researchers have labelled Tier III tort litigation—that is, mass tort claims from latent injuries. In these cases the causal connection between the injury and the substance is typically uncertain because the toxic material is dispersed by its contact with water, air, or soil. In addition, the substances involved are typically solvents or heavy metals that cause subtle neurological or metabolic injuries, or carcinogens that have long latency periods. As a result, the difficulty of proving causation in toxic tort litigation and the unpredictability of outcome that attends such difficulty are greatly exacerbated in environmental injury tort claims.

Id., Vol. I at 301–02.

2.   Environmental law is governed by a intricate web of federal statutory provisions. Among these statutes are the Clean Air Act, 42 U.S.C.A. §§ 7401–7642 (1967); the National Environmental Policy Act of 1969 (NEPA), 42 U.S.C.A. § 4332 *et seq.* (1969)(requiring federal agencies to conduct environmental impact studies of the consequences of federal regulation); the Resource Conservation and Recovery Act (RCRA), 42 U.S.C.A. §§ 6901–6991 (1976); the Federal Water Pollution Control Act (Clean Water Act), 33 U.S.C.A. §§ 1251–1387 (1977); the Federal Insecticide, Fungicide, and Rodenticide Act (FIFRA), 7 U.S.C.A. §§ 136 *et seq.* (1982); the Comprehensive Environmental Response, Compensation and Liability Act of 1980 (CERCLA), 42 U.S.C.A. §§ 9601–9675 (1980); and the Toxic Substances Control Act, 15 U.S.C.A. §§ 2607 *et seq.* (1982).

3.   To what extent does CERCLA and creation and administration of the Superfund provide a possible federal statutory model for handling mass torts other than those arising from environmental pollution or contamination? Do the CERCLA provisions adequately resolve liability and causation problems so evident in non-environmental products liability mass torts? As the ALI *Reporter's Study* indicates, the Superfund is financed by taxes on petroleum and chemical products, supplemented by other legislative appropriations. Would it be possible to create similar industry-financed superfunds in products cases and to provide for an administrative distribution scheme in products mass tort litigation? *ASARCO* illustrates the government's use of the consent decree as a settlement mechanism under CERCLA provisions. To what extent is the federal court's review of the consent decree and settlement different than or similar to a federal court's scrutiny of a mass tort settlement class? Does this CERCLA consent decree/settlement resolve the environmental injury any more effectively than other mass tort settlements? Does it more effectively resolve transaction cost and delay problems? *See* J.B. Ruhl, *Toxic Tort Remedies: The Case Against the*

"Superduper Fund" and Other Reform Proposals, 38 Baylor L. Rev. 597 (1986).

4. The 1991 ALI's *Reporter's Study,* ENTERPRISE LIABILITY FOR PERSONAL RESPONSIBILITY at 319–20 suggested that courts have neither been overwhelmed with environmental injury lawsuits, nor overcompensating victims of such injuries. The *Study* indicated that a review of environmental injury litigation from 1983 through 1986 demonstrated total awards significantly less than the monumental settlements achieved in prominent mass torts such as the Agent Orange litigation. *See, e.g.,* In re Love Canal Actions, 145 Misc.2d 1076, 547 N.Y.S.2d 174 (1989)(award of $20 million to over 100 plaintiffs claiming personal injury and property damage); Ayers v. Jackson Township, 106 N.J. 557, 525 A.2d 287 (1987)(compensation for loss of potable water for twenty months and medical monitoring, but no personal injury awards); In re Three Mile Island Litigation, 557 F.Supp. 96 (M.D.Pa.1982)(initial settlement of $24 million for economic and property damage; second settlement of $15 million for medical injuries; $5 million for medical monitoring). In attempting to explain this phenomenon, the Reporters conclude: "Recall that even conservative estimates indicate that there are over 10,000 environmental carcinogen deaths each year; so it is evident that environmental injury victims have enjoyed very little tort success. * * * Why are there so few of these claims? The answer is that environmental injury tort cases are difficult to win." *See id.* at 320–21. *But see* Nick Madigan, *Largest-Ever Toxic Waste Suit Opens in California,* N.Y. Times, Feb. 5, 1993 at B16.

5. Apart from groundwater and toxic air pollution, another category of environmental injury cases have involved persons injured by exposure to radiation in nuclear fallout resulting from atomic weapon testing. In 1985 Congress enacted legislation designating the United States government as the sole defendant in any litigation arising from atomic testing. *See* Pub. L. No. 98–525, § 1331, 98 Stat. 2492, 42 U.S.C.A. § 2212 (Supp. III 1985)(the so-called "Warner amendment"). Plaintiffs who have pursued relief have generally been unsuccessful as the federal courts have rejected claims against the United States under the discretionary function exception to the Federal Torts Claim Act. *See* Allen v. United States, 816 F.2d 1417 (10th Cir.1987)(government not liable because Atomic Energy Commission made policy decisions protected by FTCA discretionary function exception); In re Consolidated United States Atmospheric Testing Litig., 616 F.Supp. 759 (C.D.Cal.1985), *affirmed* 820 F.2d 982 (9th Cir.1987)(discretionary function exception barred claims by 43 individuals exposed to nuclear fallout in Japan, the Pacific, and Nevada). *See generally* ALI *Reporter's Study,* ENTERPRISE RESPONSIBILITY FOR PERSONAL INJURY (1991) at 323–27; *see also,* Note, *Constitutional Fallout From the Warner Amendment: Annihilating the Rights of Atomic Weapons Testing Victims,* 62 N.Y.U.L.Rev. 1331 (1987). The federal government has attempted to provide for the contingency of massive nuclear disaster litigation; *see* Presidential Commission on Catastrophic Nuclear Accidents, *Report to the Congress* (1990).

6. There is a fairly extensive literature relating to environmental injury litigation. *See generally,* Gail Bingham, RESOLVING ENVIRONMENTAL DISPUTES. A DECADE OF EXPERIENCE (1986); P. Brown and E. Mikkelsen, NO SAFE PLACE: TOXIC WASTE, LEUKEMIA, AND COMMUNITY ACTION (1990); Allan R.

Talbot, SETTLING THINGS, SIX CASE STUDIES IN ENVIRONMENTAL MEDIATION (1983); Austin, *The Rise of Citizens Suit Enforcement of Environmental Law: Reconciling Private and Public Attorneys General,* 81 Nw.U.L.Rev. 220 (1987); Roy A. Cohen & Jodi F. Minich, *Expert Testimony and the Presentation of Scientific Evidence in Toxic Tort and Environmental Hazardous Substance Litigation,* 21 Seton Hall L. Rev. 1009 (1991); Peter J. Kalis, et al., *The Choice-of-Law Dispute in Comprehensive Environmental Coverage Litigation: Has Help Arrived From the American Law Institute's Complex Litigation Project?,* 54 La. L. Rev. 925 (1994); Sanford E. Gaines, Foreword, *Rethinking Tort and Environmental Liability Laws: Needs and Objectives of the Late 20th Century and Beyond,* 24 Hous.L.Rev. 1 (1987); Leslie S. Gara, *Medical Surveillance Damages: Using Common Sense and the Common Law to Mitigate Dangers Posed by Environmental Hazards,* 12 Harv.Envt.L.Rev. 265 (1988); Peter Huber, *Environmental Hazards and Liability Law, in* LIABILITY: PERSPECTIVES AND POLICY (R. Litan and C. Winston eds.1988); Francis E. McGovern, *The Alabama DDT Settlement Fund,* 53 Law & Contemp.Probs. 61 (Autumn 1990); Mintz, *Agencies, Congress and Regulatory Enforcement: A Review of EPA's Hazardous Waste Enforcement Effort, 1970–1987,* 18 Envtl.L. 683 (1988); Robert L. Rabin, *Environmental Liability and the Tort System,* 24 Hous.L.Rev. 27 (1987); Palma J. Strand, Note, *The Inapplicability of Traditional Tort Analysis to Environmental Risks: The Example of Toxic Waste Pollution Victim Compensation,* 35 Stan.L.Rev. 575 (1983); Jeffrey Trauberman, *Statutory Reform of Toxic Torts: Relieving Legal, Scientific, and Economic Burdens on the Chemical Victims,* 7 Harv. Envtl.L.Rev. 177 (1983); Developments in the Law, *Toxic Waste Litigation,* 99 Harv.L.Rev. 1458 (1986).

D. STRICT LIABILITY
BESHADA v. JOHNS–MANVILLE PRODS. CORP.

Supreme Court of New Jersey, 1982.
90 N.J. 191, 447 A.2d 539.

PASHMAN, J.

The sole question here is whether defendants in a product liability case based on strict liability for failure to warn may raise a "state of the art" defense. Defendants assert that the danger of which they failed to warn was undiscovered at the time the product was marketed and that it was undiscoverable given the state of scientific knowledge at that time. The case comes to us on appeal from the trial court's denial of plaintiffs' motion to strike the state-of-the-art defense. For the reasons stated below, we reverse the trial court judgment and strike the defense.

I

These six consolidated cases are personal injury and wrongful death actions brought against manufacturers and distributors of asbestos products. Plaintiffs are workers, or survivors of deceased workers, who claim to have been exposed to asbestos for varying periods of time. They allege that as a result of that exposure they contracted asbestosis (a non-malignant scarring of the lungs), mesothelioma (a rare cancer of the lining of the chest, the pleura, or the lining of the abdomen, the peritoneum) and other asbestos-related illnesses. * * * Plaintiffs have raised a variety of legal theories to support their claims for damages. The important claim, for purposes of this appeal, is strict liability for failure to warn. Prior to the 1960's, defendants' products allegedly contained no warning of their hazardous nature. Defendants respond by asserting the state-of-the-art defense. They allege that no one knew or could have known that asbestos was dangerous when it was marketed.

There is substantial factual dispute about what defendants knew and when they knew it. A trial judge in the Eastern District of Texas, the forum for numerous asbestos-related cases, has concluded that "[k]nowledge of the danger can be attributed to the industry as early as the mid–1930's. . . ." Hardy v. Johns–Manville Sales Corp., 509 F.Supp. 1353, 1355 (E.D.Tex.1981). * * * Defendants respond, however, that it was not until the 1960's that the medical profession in the United States recognized that a potential health hazard arose from the use of insulation products containing asbestos. Before that time, according to defendants, the danger from asbestos was believed limited to workers in asbestos textile mills, who were exposed to much higher concentrations of asbestos dust than were the workers at other sites, such as shipyards. Defendants claim that it was not discovered until recently that the much smaller concentrations those workers faced were also hazardous.

We need not resolve the factual issues raised. For purposes of plaintiffs' motion to strike the defense, we assume the defendants' version of the facts. The issue is whether the medical community's presumed unawareness of the dangers of asbestos is a defense to plaintiffs' claims.

* * *

III

Our inquiry starts with the principles laid down in *Freund v. Cellofilm Properties, Inc., Suter v. San Angelo Foundry & Machine Company*, and Cepeda v. Cumberland Engineering Company, Inc., 76 N.J. 152, 386 A.2d 816 (1978). In *Suter,* we summarized the principle of strict liability as follows: "If at the time the seller distributes a product, it is not reasonably fit, suitable and safe for its intended or reasonably foreseeable purposes so that users or others who may be expected to come in contact with the product are injured as a result thereof, then the seller shall be responsible for the ensuing damages." * * * The determination of whether a product is "reasonably fit, suitable and safe" depends on a comparison of its risks and its utility (risk-utility equation). Central to this theory is the risk-utility equation for determining liability. The theory is that only safe products should be marketed—a safe product being one whose utility outweighs its inherent risk, provided that risk has been reduced to the greatest extent possible consistent with the product's continued utility. * * *

In *Cepeda,* we explained that in the context of design defect liability, strict liability is identical to liability for negligence, with one important caveat: "The only qualification is as to the requisite of foreseeability by the manufacturer of the dangerous propensity of the chattel manifested at the trial—this being imputed to the manufacturer." * * * In so holding, we adopted the explication of strict liability offered by Dean Wade: "The time has now come to be forthright in using a tort way of thinking and tort terminology [in cases of strict liability in tort]. There are several ways of doing it, and it is not difficult. The simplest and easiest way, it would seem, is to assume that the defendant knew of the dangerous condition of the product and ask whether he was then negligent in putting it on the market or supplying it to someone else. In other words, the scienter is supplied as a matter of law, and there is no need for the plaintiff to prove its existence as a matter of fact. Once given this notice of the dangerous condition of the chattel, the question then becomes whether the defendant was negligent to people who might be harmed by that condition if they came into contact with it or were in the vicinity of it. Another way of saying this is to ask whether the magnitude of the risk created by the dangerous condition of the product was outweighed by the social utility attained by putting it out in this fashion." [Wade, *"On the Nature of Strict Tort Liability for Products,"* 44 Miss. L.J. 825, 834–35 (1973), quoted in *Cepeda,* 76 N.J. at 172, 386 A.2d 816.] Stated differently, negligence is conduct-oriented, asking whether defendant's actions were reasonable; strict liability is product-oriented, asking whether the product was reasonably safe for its foreseeable purposes * * *.[3]

"Warning" cases constitute one category of strict liability cases. Their relation to the strict liability principles set forth above can best be analyzed by focusing on the definition of safe products found in footnote 1 of *Freund.* * * * For purposes of analysis, we can distinguish two tests for determining whether a product is safe: (1) does its utility outweigh its risk? and (2) if so, has that risk been reduced to the greatest extent possible consistent with the product's utility? * * * The first question looks to the product as it was in fact marketed. If that product caused more harm than good, it was not reasonably fit for its intended purposes. We can therefore impose strict liability for the injuries it caused without having to determine whether it could have been rendered safer. The second aspect of strict liability, however, requires that the risk from the product be reduced to the greatest extent possible without hindering its utility. Whether or not the product passes the initial risk-utility test, it is not reasonably safe if the same

---

3. The imputation of knowledge is, of course, a legal fiction. It is another way of saying that for purposes of strict liability the defendant's knowledge of the danger is irrelevant. *See* Freund v. Cellofilm Properties, Inc., 87 N.J. at 239, 432 A.2d 925, quoting Keeton, *"Products Liability—Inadequacy of Information,"* 48 Tex.L.Rev. 398, 407–08 (1970). The imputation of knowledge does not represent any presumption that defendants knew or even that they could have known of the product's dangers.

product could have been made or marketed more safely.[4]

Warning cases are of this second type.[5] When plaintiffs urge that a product is hazardous because it lacks a warning, they typically look to the second test, saying in effect that regardless of the overall cost-benefit calculation the product is unsafe because a warning could make it safer at virtually no added cost and without limiting its utility. *Freund* recognized this, noting that in cases alleging "an inadequate warning as to safe use, the utility of the product, as counter-balanced against the risks of its use, is rarely at issue." * * *

Freund is our leading case on strict liability for failure to warn. In *Freund,* Justice Handler applied the principles set forth above, initially laid down in *Suter* and *Cepeda,* to warning cases. The issue there was whether there is any difference between negligence and strict liability in warning cases. We stated unequivocally that there is. That difference is the same difference that we noted in *Suter* and *Cepeda* concerning other design defect cases: when a plaintiff sues under strict liability, there is no need to prove that the manufacturer knew or should have known of any dangerous propensities of its product—such knowledge is imputed to the manufacturer. * * * Thus, we held in *Freund* that it was reversible error for the trial judge to instruct the jury only with a negligence charge.

With these basic principles of design defect strict liability in New Jersey as our framework for analysis, we turn now to a discussion of the state-of-the-art defense.

IV

As it relates to warning cases, the state-of-the-art defense asserts that distributors of products can be held liable only for injuries resulting from dangers that were scientifically discoverable at the time the product was distributed. Defendants argue that the question of whether the product can be made safer must be limited to consideration of the available technology at the time the product was distributed. Liability would be absolute, defendants argue, if it could be imposed on the basis of a subsequently discovered means to make the product safer since technology will always be developing new ways to make products safer. Such a rule, they assert, would make manufacturers liable whenever

4. This dichotomy is created only for purposes of analysis, because it will help explain the role of state-of-the-art in strict liability cases. In actuality, the only test for product safety is whether the benefit outweighs the risk. However, in calculating the benefit from any product, one must consider alternate products that can yield the same benefit at lower risk. Wade, 44 Miss.L.J. at 837–38.

5. This two-part distinction can best be clarified by looking at how it would apply to automobiles without seatbelts. Because of the great utility of cars, few would dispute that even without seatbelts, a car's utility to society outweighs its risks. Thus, cars would be considered safe under the first aspect of the test. However, since seatbelts make cars safer without hindering utility, cars without seatbelts are deemed unsafe by virtue of the second part of the *Freund* test. Warnings are like seatbelts: regardless of the utility and risk of a product without warnings, a warning can generally be added without diminishing utility. *Freund v. Cellofilm Properties, Inc.,* 87 N.J. at 238–39, n.1, 432 A.2d 925.

their products cause harm, whether or not they are reasonably fit for their foreseeable purposes.

Defendants conceptualize the scientific unknowability of the dangerous propensities of a product as a technological barrier to making the product safer by providing warnings. Thus, a warning was not "possible" within the meaning of the *Freund* requirement that risk be reduced "to the greatest extent possible."

In urging this position, defendants must somehow distinguish the *Freund* holding that knowledge of the dangers of the product is imputed to defendants as a matter of law. A state-of-the-art defense would contravene that by requiring plaintiffs to prove at least that knowledge of the dangers was scientifically available at the time of manufacture.

Defendants argue that *Freund* did not specify precisely what knowledge is imputed to defendants. They construe *Freund* to impute only that degree of knowledge of the product's dangerousness that existed at the time of manufacture or distribution.

While we agree that *Freund* did not explicitly address this question, the principles laid down in Freund and our prior cases contradict defendants' position. Essentially, state-of-the-art is a negligence defense. It seeks to explain why defendants are not culpable for failing to provide a warning. They assert, in effect, that because they could not have known the product was dangerous, they acted reasonably in marketing it without a warning. But in strict liability cases, culpability is irrelevant. The product was unsafe. That it was unsafe because of the state of technology does not change the fact that it was unsafe. Strict liability focuses on the product, not the fault of the manufacturer. "If the conduct is unreasonably dangerous, then there should be strict liability without reference to what excuse defendant might give for being unaware of the danger." Keeton, 48 Tex.L.Rev. at 408.

When the defendants argue that it is unreasonable to impose a duty on them to warn of the unknowable, they misconstrue both the purpose and effect of strict liability. By imposing strict liability, we are not requiring defendants to have done something that is impossible. In this sense, the phrase "duty to warn" is misleading. It implies negligence concepts with their attendant focus on the reasonableness of defendant's behavior. However, a major concern of strict liability—ignored by defendants—is the conclusion that if a product was in fact defective, the distributor of the product should compensate its victims for the misfortune that it inflicted on them.

If we accepted defendants' argument, we would create a distinction among fact situations that defies common sense. Under the defendants' reading of *Freund*, defendant would be liable for failure to warn if the danger was knowable even if defendants were not negligent in failing to discover it. Defendants would suffer no liability, however, if the danger was undiscoverable. But, as Dean Keeton explains, if a defendant is to be held liable for a risk that is discoverable by some genius but beyond the defendant's capacity to do so, why should he not also be liable for a risk that was just as great but was not discoverable by anyone? [Keeton, 48 Tex.L.Rev. at 409].

* * *

The most important inquiry, however, is whether imposition of liability for failure to warn of dangers which were undiscoverable at the time of manufacture will advance the goals and policies sought to be achieved by our strict liability rules. We believe that it will.

Risk Spreading. One of the most important arguments generally advanced for imposing strict liability is that the manufacturers and distributors of defective products can best allocate the costs of the injuries resulting from it. The premise is that the price of a product should reflect all of its costs, including the cost of injuries caused by the product. This can best be accomplished by imposing liability on the manufacturer and distributors. Those persons can insure against liability and incorporate the cost of the insurance in the price of the product. In this way, the costs of the product will be borne by those who profit from it: the manufacturers and distributors who profit from its sale and the buyers who profit from its use. "It should be a cost of doing business that in the course of doing that business an unreasonable risk was created." Keeton, 48 Tex.L.Rev. at 408. *See* Prosser, THE LAW OF TORTS, § 75, p. 495 (4th Ed.1971).

Defendants argue that this policy is not forwarded by imposition of liability for unknowable hazards. Since such hazards by definition are not predicted, the price of the hazardous product will not be adjusted to reflect the costs of the injuries it will produce. Rather, defendants state, the cost "will be borne by the public at large and reflected in a general, across the board increase in premiums to compensate for unanticipated risks." There is some truth in this assertion, but it is not a bad result.

First, the same argument can be made as to hazards which are deemed scientifically knowable but of which the manufacturers are unaware. Yet it is well established under our tort law that strict liability is imposed even for defects which were unknown to the manufacturer. It is precisely the imputation of knowledge to the defendant that distinguishes strict liability from negligence. * * * Defendants advance no argument as to why risk spreading works better for unknown risks than for unknowable risks.

Second, spreading the costs of injuries among all those who produce, distribute and purchase manufactured products is far preferable to imposing it on the innocent victims who suffer illnesses and disability from defective products. This basic normative premise is at the center of our strict liability rules. It is unchanged by the state of scientific knowledge at the time of manufacture.

Finally, contrary to defendants' assertion, this rule will not cause the price and production level of manufactured products to diverge from the so-called economically efficient level. Rather, the rule will force the price of any particular product to reflect the cost of insuring against the possibility that the product will turn out to be defective.

Accident Avoidance. In *Suter,* we stated: "Strict liability in a sense is but an attempt to minimize the costs of accidents and to consider who should bear those costs." *See* the discussion in Calabresi & Hirschoff, *"Toward a Test for Strict Liability in Torts,"* 81 Yale L.J. 1055 (1972), in which the authors suggest that the strict liability issue is to decide which party is the "cheapest cost avoider" or who is in the best position to make the cost-benefit analysis between accident costs and accident avoidance costs and to act on that decision once it is made. * * * Using this approach, it is obvious that the manufacturer rather than the factory employee is "in the better position both to judge whether avoidance costs would exceed foreseeable accident costs and to act on that judgment." * * * Defendants urge that this argument has no force as to hazards which by definition were undiscoverable. Defendants have treated the level of technological knowledge at a given time as an independent variable not affected by defendants' conduct. But this view ignores the important role of industry in product safety research. The "state-of-the-art" at a given time is partly determined by how much industry invests in safety research. By imposing on manufacturers the costs of failure to discover hazards, we create an incentive for them to invest more actively in safety research.

Fact Finding Process. The analysis thus far has assumed that it is possible to define what constitutes "undiscoverable" knowledge and that it will be reasonably possible to determine what knowledge was technologically discoverable at a given time. In fact, both assumptions are highly questionable. The vast confusion that is virtually certain to arise from any attempt to deal in a trial setting with the concept of scientific knowability constitutes a strong reason for avoiding the concept altogether by striking the state-of-the-art defense.

Scientific knowability, as we understand it, refers not to what in fact was known at the time, but to what could have been known at the time. In other words, even if no scientist had actually formed the belief that asbestos was dangerous, the hazards would be deemed "knowable" if a scientist could have formed that belief by applying research or performing tests that were available at the time. Proof of what could have been known will inevitably be complicated, costly, confusing and time-consuming. Each side will have to produce experts in the history of science and technology to speculate as to what knowledge was feasible in a given year. We doubt that juries will be capable of even understanding the concept of scientific knowability, much less be able to resolve such a complex issue. Moreover, we should resist legal rules that will so greatly add to the costs both sides incur in trying a case.

The concept of knowability is complicated further by the fact, noted above, that the level of investment in safety research by manufacturers is one determinant of the state-of-the-art at any given time. Fairness suggests that manufacturers not be excused from liability because their prior inadequate investment in safety rendered the hazards of their product unknowable. Thus, a judgment will have to be made as to whether defendants' investment in safety research in the years preceding distribution of the product was adequate. If not, the experts in the history of technology will have to testify as to what would have been knowable at the time of distribution if manufacturers had spent the proper amount on safety in prior years. To state the issue is to fully understand the great difficulties it would engender in a courtroom.

In addition, discussion of state-of-the-art could easily confuse juries into believing that blameworthiness is at issue. Juries might mistakenly translate the confused concept of state-of-the-art into the simple question of whether it was defendants' fault that they did not know of the hazards of asbestos. But that would be negligence, not strict liability.

For precisely this reason, Professor Keeton has urged that negligence concepts be carefully avoided in strict liability cases. My principal thesis is and has been that theories of negligence should be avoided altogether in the products liability area in order to simplify the law, and that if the sale of a product is made under circumstances that would subject someone to an unreasonable risk in fact, liability for harm resulting from those risks should follow. * * * This Court has expressed the same concern in Freund, reversing the trial court's jury charge because the "terminology employed by the trial judge was riddled with references to negligence, knowledge and reasonable care on the part of a manufacturer." * * * "[W]e must be concerned with the effect of the trial judge's articulation upon the jury's deliberative processes." * * *

V

For the reasons expressed above, we conclude that plaintiffs' position is consistent with our holding in *Freund* and prior cases and will achieve the various policies underlying strict liability. The burden of illness from dangerous products such as asbestos should be placed upon those who profit from its production and, more generally, upon society at large, which reaps the benefits of the various products our economy manufactures. That burden should not be imposed exclusively on the innocent victim. Although victims must in any case suffer the pain involved, they should be spared the burdensome financial consequences of unfit products. At the same time, we believe this position will serve the salutary goals of increasing product safety research and simplifying tort trials.

Defendants have argued that it is unreasonable to impose a duty on them to warn of the unknowable. Failure to warn of a risk which one could not have known existed is not unreasonable conduct. But this argument is based on negligence principles. We are not saying what defendants should have done. That is negligence. We are saying that defendants' products were not reasonably safe because they did not have a warning. Without a warning, users of the product were unaware of its hazards and could not protect themselves from injury. We impose strict liability because it is unfair for the distributors of a defective product not to compensate its victims. As between those innocent victims and the distributors, it is the distributors—and the public which consumes their products—which should bear the unforeseen costs of the product.

The judgment of the trial court is reversed; the plaintiff's motion to strike the state-of-the-art defense is granted.

Notes and Questions

1. In *Beshada,* the New Jersey Supreme Court reviews basic principles of a cause of action based in strict liability (as opposed to negligence) and the consequences of each for available defenses. In the early 1960s the American Law Institute's Section 402A of the RESTATEMENT (SECOND) OF TORTS articulated the modern concept of strict liability, which courts subsequently generally applied to actions based on manufacturing defects. Through the 1970s, courts expanded strict liability theory to also reach claims of defectively designed products, including both warning defects as well as failure to inform consumers of the risk level of product use. Further, a product could fail the design defect test either by failing to meet consumer expectations, or a "risk-utility" standard. The modern development of the strict products liability cause of action has been summarized:

> The phrase "strict liability" has two meanings in product litigation. The first refers to the rejection of the traditional norms of sales law: liability is strict in this sense when exculpatory clauses are banned and warranty prerequisites to liability are repealed. This conception of strict liability applies to actions brought in consequence of any defect type; the firm is held liable independently of any contract between the parties. The second meaning of strict liability refers to judicial regulation of manufacturer behavior. Liability is strict in this sense when the manufacturer must compensate victims even though the manufacturer took all cost-justified steps to produce a safe product. This alternative conception of strict liability applies only to actions brought in consequences of manufacturing defects: here the manufacturer is liable regardless of its behavior. In contrast, at least in the way that it operates, product liability is not strict in this second sense for design and warning defects. * * * [T]he concept of "defect" utilized in product design or warning litigation incorporates the key elements of standard negligence law by asking whether, given the state of the art at the time, the manufacturer's design or warning created an unreasonable risk of consumer injury.

American Law Institute, *Reporter's Study,* ENTERPRISE RESPONSIBILITY FOR PERSONAL INJURY at 39 (1991); *see also id.* at 33–82 (discussing issues relating to development of strict products liability law).

What theory of strict product liability law does the New Jersey Supreme Court endorse in *Beshada?* Is this a legitimate interpretation and extension of strict products liability? Is the *Beshada* ruling limited to the asbestos context, or does it have implications for other products liability or mass torts? *See e.g.,* Alison Joy Arnold, Comment, *Developing, Testing, and Marketing An AIDS Vaccine: Legal Concerns for Manufacturers,* 139 U.Pa. L.Rev. 1077 (1991); Richard C. Ausness, *Unavoidably Unsafe Products and*

Strict Products Liability: What Liability Rule Should Be Applied to the Sellers of Pharmaceuticals?, 78 Ky.L.J. 705 (1989–90); Richard L. Cupp, Jr., *Sharing Accountability for Breast Implants: Strict Products Liability and Medical Professionals Engaged in Hybrid Sales/Service Cosmetic Products Transactions*, 21 Fla.St.U.L.Rev. 873 (1994).

2. The subsequent history of *Beshada* as a precedent for supplying a strict products liability theory leaves these questions in considerably clouded. In 1984 the New Jersey court again considered the failure to warn issue in Feldman v. Lederle Laboratories, 97 N.J. 429, 452, 479 A.2d 374, 386 (1984). The court reversed its former position and said, "[g]enerally the state-of-the-art * * * and available knowledge are relevant factors" and "generally conduct should be measured by knowledge at the time the manufacturer distributed the product." 479 A.2d at 386. *Feldman* acknowledged *Beshada* only by saying, "we do not overrule *Beshada*," but proceeded to "restrict [it] to the circumstances giving rise to its holding." *Id.* 479 A.2d at 388. The opinion further noted "in passing, that, although not argued and determined in *Beshada*, there were or may have been data and other information generally available, aside from scientific knowledge, that arguably could have alerted the manufacturer at an early stage in the distribution of its product to the dangers associated with its use." *Id.* In addition, the *Feldman* court concluded that *Beshada* would not demand a contrary conclusion in "the typical design defect or warning case." *Id.* 479 A.2d at 387. The court also refused to agree that *Beshada* held "generally or in all cases * * * that in a warning context knowledge of the unknowable is irrelevant in determining the applicability of strict liability." *Id.* See generally David R. Gross, Practising Law Institute, *The State of the Art Is Alive and Well in New Jersey (* Beshada *Is No More)*(1984).

Whatever qualifications are embodied in *Feldman,* the New Jersey Supreme Court revisited the *Beshada* holding again in Fischer v. Johns–Manville Corp., 103 N.J. 643, 512 A.2d 466 (1986), and seemed to validate its earlier holding in the asbestos context. *Fischer* determined that one manufacturer did know the hazards of asbestos by the 1930s and that other manufacturers could have gained similar knowledge through articles published at that time in scientific journals. *Feldman* had earlier held that "a reasonably prudent manufacturer will be deemed to know of reliable information generally available or reasonably obtainable in the industry." 479 A.2d at 387.

3. Deans Page and Wade, favorably cited in *Beshada,* subsequently criticized the decision. Dean Wade remarked that "[t]he Pennsylvania and New Jersey courts appear to be straining too hard in their efforts to develop a different standard of product actionability for strict liability actions.... [B]ecause of the way in which insurance premiums are set ... these tests may render a disservice to both product suppliers and consumers throughout the country." Wade, *On Effect in Product Liability of Knowledge Unavailable Prior to Marketing,* 58 N.Y.U.L.Rev. 734, 744 (1983). Dean Page described the policy reasons articulated in *Beshada* as "weak justification[s] for a narrower rule of strict liability." Joseph A. Page, *Generic Product Risks: The Case Against Comment K and for Strict Tort Liability,* 58 N.Y.U.L.Rev. 853, 879 (1983).

4. Academic criticism of *Beshada* has been harsh. *See generally The Passage of Time: The Implications for Product Liability,* 58 N.Y.U.L.Rev. 733 (1983). One commentator termed the decision "unjustifiable on grounds of logic and public policy." Schwartz, *The Post–Sale Duty to Warn: Two Unfortunate Forks in the Road to a Reasonable Doctrine,* 58 N.Y.U.L.Rev. 892, 902 (1983). Another said, "[b]y and large I regard the decision as indefensible.... If our only goal is compensation, we should not handle products liability cases through the tort system." Richard A. Epstein, *Commentary,* 58 N.Y.U.L.Rev. 930, 933 (1983). *See also* Andrew T. Berry, Beshada v. Johns–Manville Products Corp.: *Revolution—Or Aberration—In Products Liability Law,* 52 Ford.L.Rev. 786 (1984); Christopher M. Placitella and Alan M. Darnell, Beshada v. Johns–Manville Products Corp.: *Evolution or Revolution in Strict Products Liability?,* 51 Fordham L.Rev. 801 (1983); Ellen Wertheimer, *Unknowable Dangers and the Death of Strict Products Liability: The Empire Strikes Back,* 60 U.Cinn.L.Rev. 1183 (1992).

5. The duty to warn as it relates to product labeling has played a major role in some incipient mass torts, especially litigation relating to cigarette smoking. The ability of plaintiffs to pursue claims in state court based on failure to warn theories effectively has been frustrated by federal preemption doctrine; the Supreme Court has held that federal regulatory statutes preempt state tort liability under "duty to warn" theories for manufacturer conduct that complies with federal regulations. *See* Cipollone v. Liggett Group, Inc., ___ U.S. ___, 112 S.Ct. 2608, 120 L.Ed.2d 407 (1992)(but not preempting state claims based on other tort theories); *see also* Kotler v. American Tobacco Co., 685 F.Supp. 15 (D.Mass.1988). *See generally,* Richard C. Ausness, *Cigarette Company Liability: Preemption, Public Policy, and Alternative Compensation Systems,* 39 Syracuse L.Rev. 897 (1988); C.F. Fenswick, Recent Development, *Cipollone v. Liggett Group, Inc.: Supreme Court Takes Middle Ground in Cigarette Litigation,* 67 Tul.L.Rev. 787 (1993); James C. Thronton, Comment, *Cigarette Manufacturers for Lung Cancer: An Analysis of the Federal Cigarette Labeling and Advertising Act and Preemption of Strict Liability in Tort Against Cigarette Manufacturers,* 76 Ky.L.J. 569 (1987–88). *Cf.* Andrew Ready & Robert Carter, *Tobacco Litigation: Looking for Cover,* Legal Times of Wash., March 6, 1995 at S37; Richard K. Shuter, *Recent Decision, Apportionment of Damages—Third Circuit Predicts Pennsylvania Courts Would Not Allow Jury to Apportion Liability in a Cigarette Smoking, Asbestos Exposure Case,* 66 Temp. L. Rev. 223 (1993).

6. The American Law Institute is in the process of drafting a RESTATEMENT (THIRD) OF TORTS, a project which may significantly modify and erode the doctrine of strict products liability as it has developed in the common law subsequent to the RESTATEMENT (SECOND)'s promulgation of Section 402A. For discussions of proposed revisions, *see generally* Symposium: *The Revision of Section 402A of the Restatement (Second) of Torts: Occasion for Reform of Products Liability Law?,* 10 Touro L.Rev. 1 (1993)(collected articles); James A. Henderson, Jr. & Aaron D. Twerski, *A Proposed Revision of Section 402A of the Restatement (Second) of Torts,* 77 Corn.L.Rev. 1512 (1992); James A. Henderson, Jr. & Aaron D. Twerski, *Closing the American Products Liability Frontier: The Rejection of Liability Without Defect,* 66 N.Y.U.L.Rev. 1263 (1991); Michael A. Pittenger, *Reformulating the Strict*

Liability Failure to Warn, 49 Wash. & Lee L.Rev. 1509 (1992); William Powers, Jr., *A Modest Proposal to Abandon Strict Products Liability,* 1991 U.Ill.L.Rev. 639 (1991). *See also* Nina S. Appel, *Liability in Mass Immunization Programs,* 1980 B.Y.U. L. Rev. 69 (1980).

E.   GENERAL AND SPECIFIC CAUSATION
IN RE AGENT ORANGE PROD. LIAB. LITIG.

United States Court of Appeals, Second Circuit, 1987.
818 F.2d 145.

Review "Agent Orange" decisions, supra, for summary of facts and proceedings.

Before VAN GRAAFEILAND, WINTER, and MINER, CIRCUIT JUDGES.

WINTER, CIRCUIT JUDGE:

* * *

The present litigation justifies the prevalent skepticism over the usefulness of class actions in so-called mass tort cases and, in particular, claims for injuries resulting from toxic exposure. First, the benefits of a class action have been greatly exaggerated by its proponents in the present matter. For example, much ink has been spilled in this case over the distinction between generic causation—whether Agent Orange is harmful at all, regardless of the degree or nature of exposure, and what ailments it may cause—and individual causation—whether a particular veteran suffers from a particular ailment as a result of exposure to Agent Orange. It has been claimed that the former is an issue that might appropriately be tried in a class action, notwithstanding that individual causation must be tried separately for each plaintiff if the plaintiff class prevails.

We do not agree. The generic causation issue has three possible outcomes: 1) exposure to Agent Orange always causes harm; 2) exposure to Agent Orange never causes harm; and 3) exposure to Agent Orange may or may not cause harm depending on the kind of exposure and perhaps on other factors. It is indisputable that exposure to Agent Orange does not automatically cause harm. The so-called Ranch Hand Study of Air Force personnel who handled and sprayed the herbicide proved that much beyond a shadow of a doubt in finding no statistically significant differences between their subsequent health histories and those of similar personnel who had not been in contact with Agent Orange. Further, defendants have conceded that some kinds of exposure to Agent Orange may cause harm. They stated at both the argument of the mandamus petition and the argument of the appeal that Agent Orange, like anything else, including water and peanuts, may be harmful. The epidemiological studies on which defendants rely so heavily prove no more than that Vietnam veterans do not exhibit statistically significant differences in various symptoms when compared with other groups. They in no way exclude the possibility of injury, and tend at best to prove only that, if Agent Orange did cause harm, it was in isolated instances or in cases of unusual exposure.

The relevant question, therefore, is not whether Agent Orange has the capacity to cause harm, the generic causation issue, but whether it did cause harm and to whom. That determination is highly individualistic, and depends upon the characteristics of individual plaintiffs (e.g. state of health, lifestyle) and the nature of their exposure to Agent Orange. Although generic causation and individual circumstances concerning each plaintiff and his or her exposure to Agent Orange thus appear to be inextricably intertwined, the class action would have allowed generic causation to be determined without regard to those characteristics and the individual's exposure.

GLEN O. ROBINSON, MULTIPLE CAUSATION IN TORT LAW: REFLECTIONS ON THE DES CASES

68 Va.L.Rev. 713, 736–749, 768–769 (1982).

* * *

IV. LIABILITY OBJECTIVES AND THE ROLE OF CAUSATION

If "compensation" has little to say about the shape of liability rules, neither does "fairness." Few if any would quarrel with the proposition that liability rules should be "fair." The difficulty arises when one tries to use "fairness" to define concrete requirements of a liability rule. According to Epstein, causation is the key to a liability system based on fairness; in his jurisprudence, causation is not merely a necessary, but a sufficient, condition of liability. At least since the nineteenth century, however, there has not been much support for the notion that fairness supports causation as a sufficient condition of liability.

There may be more support for the proposition that fairness dictates specific causation as a necessary condition of liability. In fact, it appears that just such a notion created the major problem in the DES cases: there was no proof of a causal link between the actions of any one DES manufacturer and the plaintiff's injuries. But does fairness require such a link? In the criminal context, it is considered fair to impose liability for some crimes—for instance, reckless driving or attempted crimes—even though no specific harm results. Similarly, fairness in the civil context seems to require only that a defendant's liability be related to his conduct, and that liability, where imposed, be roughly proportional to the seriousness of the risks that he has created. Despite Cardozo's insistence that liability not be imposed for "negligence in the air," considerations of fairness do not forbid it. From the standpoint of fairness, the critical point is the creation of a risk that society deems to be unreasonable, not whether anyone was injured by it.

On this premise, imposition of liability in the DES cases is fair. By assumption, each defendant made a "defective" product that created an unreasonable risk of the harm the plaintiff suffered. "Fault" can be imputed to a defendant's conduct from the fact that it made a product that created such a risk. Whether the defendant's actions caused injury in the particular case does not alter the character of its conduct, which was as final as the defendant could make it. Furthermore, in *Sindell,* the court imposed liability on the defendants according to their market shares, thereby allocating the loss in proportion to the degree of risk created.

The argument from a deterrence perspective yields a similar conclusion. To deter only unnecessarily risky behavior, the law must require a causal link between the defendant's behavior and the risk that it seeks to deter. It is not necessary, however, that there be a link between the defendant's risky conduct and a particular victim's injury. Normally, of course, deterring the risk will deter the harm; nevertheless, legal rules that are forced on only the latter may not deter the former effectively.

The DES cases illustrate this point. To insist that a particular injury be linked to a particular manufacturer's product is to invite underdeterrence of the risk in every case where there is no proof of specific causation. There is no question of causal responsibility for the risk. Although there may be some evidentiary problems in establishing that DES was the cause of the plaintiff's cancer, that has not been a critical issue in the litigation to date, and for the present this article assumes that this relationship is clear and unequivocal. The question is, why insist on anything more?

One answer might be that imposing liability regardless of causation would destroy a manufacturer's incentives to take special precautions in the manufacture or marketing of its product, because it still could be held liable regardless of such individual measures. The argument fails on two counts, however.

First, it proceeds on the erroneous premise that a manufacturer would be held liable regardless of its individual actions and its individual care. That would be the case only if such actions did nothing to differentiate the manufacturer's product from those of others in the industry in such a manner as to reduce the risk of harm from its product and either to preclude its being found negligent or, if liability is strict, to reduce its share of the damages. No such product differentiation appears in the DES cases; each case involved products that were identical in all respects relevant to the risk of cancer. * * * For now it is enough simply to stress that *Sindell* and the other cases imposing liability did so on the premise that the defendants were distinguished only by the respective magnitudes of their contributions to the risk, as measured by their respective output of DES.

Second, the argument that liability in these cases would reduce incentives for individual care by tortfeasors ignores the fact that, under the conventional rule requiring proof of a causal link between a tortfeasor and the victim, there also is no incentive for individual care. Under the conventional rule, each manufacturer of a product can insulate itself from liability by following the practices of others, thereby making it difficult to distinguish its product as the cause of an injury. In effect, it is a case of safety in numbers and safety in conformity.

If the foregoing is persuasive as a rationale for the "alternative liability" rule for multiple tortfeasors, it remains to be considered whether and how the burden of liability should be shared. As noted earlier, the DES cases have divided on the question. One approach follows the conventional *Summers v. Tice* approach of joint and several liability, which holds each defendant liable for the entire amount of the plaintiff's damage. The second approach is that of *Sindell,* which makes each defendant liable only for the proportion of the plaintiff's damage corresponding to its market share of the product.

If the defendants under the first rule are able to demand contribution from other negligent manufacturers, then the results in the two cases will not be radically different. Liability will be shared under either approach. Because rules allowing contribution among joint tortfeasors are increasingly common, liability will be shared in most cases. Nevertheless, because the arguments in favor of loss apportionment are not accepted universally, and because those arguments underlie much of what follows, it may be appropriate to consider the arguments for apportionment.

On fairness principles, the argument for apportionment is a judgment that all tortfeasors should bear their "fair share" of the accident costs they created. Without contribution, the rule of joint and several liability may lead to unfair results insofar as it permits plaintiffs to discriminate among tortfeasors—requiring some to pay all, or a disproportionate amount, of the accident costs while allowing others to escape their proper share of the costs. A similar sentiment underlies the trend toward comparative negligence: the traditional contributory negligence rule arguably is unfair insofar as it requires the plaintiff to bear the entire cost even when both he and the defendant were "at fault." The concern of fairness is bolstered by the argument that efficiency requires apportionment among joint tortfeasors (and between plaintiffs and defendants) in order to prevent underdeterrence of those who escape their share of costs and overdeterrence of those who bear more than their share.

Landes and Posner have suggested counterarguments to this reasoning. They posit two types of cases: one in which the optimal level of care is achieved by having all tortfeasors take joint care; the other—so-called "alternative care"—in which it is most efficient for a single tortfeasor to take care.

In the joint care case, they argue that contribution is not necessary for deterrence, because what is critical to the incentive is not the burden of liability *ex post*, but the expected liability *ex ante*. Because no manufacturer could be assured that it would not be the one held liable, even with joint and several liability, all would have an incentive to take the care necessary to avoid being found negligent. Even if one tortfeasor were likely to be singled out, the other tortfeasors would recognize the targeted tortfeasor's increased incentive to avoid being found negligent, thus restoring their own risk of liability and incentive to take care. In such a case, because a rule of contribution is unnecessary to develop proper economic incentives, it is said to be inefficient to the extent of the administrative costs it entails.

In the alternative care case, the argument presumes that a single tortfeasor is the cheapest cost avoider, and that he alone should take the necessary care to avoid the accident. A rule that requires the cost of care to be shared creates incentives for joint care by other tortfeasors, which is, by assumption, inefficient.

As far as efficiency criteria are concerned, the logic of the Landes and Posner theory is appealing, though it rests on assumptions that can be challenged. In the alternative care case, it assumes each tortfeasor can reliably and efficiently calculate not only what conduct is efficient for itself but what conduct is efficient for every other tortfeasor that might contribute to the risk. This is a plausible assumption only where the costs of information are small relative to the costs of risk avoidance. An illustrative case might be one in which the nature of the care required is similar among the different tortfeasors—involving, say, a common industry, manufacturing, or marketing practice. Where this condition holds, however, one also might suppose that the entire allocation problem would be resolved by an arrangement among the tortfeasors to have the cheapest cost avoider accept full responsibility for risk avoidance.

Nevertheless, the case for apportionment on efficiency grounds alone is hard to make for cases in which efficient risk avoidance requires action by a single party. It remains to be considered, of course, whether that condition characterizes most multiple-activity cases. Implicit in my argument for apportionment is a hunch that the alternative care model does not hold widely in these cases.

In the joint care situation, the logic of the Landes and Posner argument assumes that certain classes of defendants—the large manufacturers in the DES situation—will not be routinely singled out for liability and found negligent. Although in theory the smaller manufacturers may be expected to be deterred by the knowledge that the larger manufacturers may take the care required to avoid liability, in fact the smaller manufacturers likely will know what care the larger manufacturers are taking and will insulate themselves simply by following suit. The question then becomes whether it is more efficient to deter only the larger manufacturers but to make the deterrence as heavy as the injury it caused, or to deter all of the manufacturers by imposing a somewhat smaller burden on each of them. The answer to that question is not clear, but seen in this light the efficiency argument hardly seems to outweigh the fairness concern, which supports forcing all of the tortfeasors to share the loss.

Although Landes and Posner purport at one point to deal with the question of fairness, their treatment of it is subordinated to efficiency considerations. They appear simply to assume that the demands of fairness parallel the needs of efficiency in regard to *ex ante* equality among tortfeasors. Given the vagaries of fairness it would be convenient to suppose that they may. It is not clear, however, that common notions of fairness are satisfied by an *ex post* allocation of liability that is disproportionate to respective fault or responsibility, merely because the expected burden of the loss, *ex ante*, is allocated equitably. In other words, the fact that the allocation of the risk is actuarially "fair" does not necessarily imply that it is ethically "fair."

Of course, many present contribution rules also deviate from the concept of *ex post* fairness to the extent that they require equal sharing of liability regardless of relative fault or causal contribution. It appears, however, to be precisely in recognition of this point that comparative negligence apportionment is made on the basis of relative fault and/or causal contribution, and the contribution rules are being modified to conform to this model. The *Sindell* approach to contribution—apportionment according to relative causation—follows the trend of recent decisions accepting causation as at least a partial basis for apportionment in comparative negligence and contribution cases.

The court in *Sindell* did not have to address a situation where the defendants had created risks of different magnitudes. Its market share apportionment rule, therefore, does not properly apportion liability among tortfeasors who create different risks that combine to produce an injury. Nevertheless, the *Sindell* court's apportionment scheme is noteworthy on two counts. First, it is an important step toward recognizing that both fairness and efficiency are well served by allocating loss according to the risk created by each tortfeasor. Second, it recognizes the logical implications of the alternative liability theory of *Summers v. Tice* and in effect imposes liability on a manufacturer for creating a risk, despite the absence of a specific causal link between that risk and a plaintiff's injury. Both of these developments point toward a rule that imposes liability for the creation of a risk and apportions liability according to the magnitude of that risk. * * *

* * *

VI. CONCLUSION

These far-reaching speculations on causation and loss apportionment appear to have carried us far beyond the problem that introduced them—shifting the burden of proof on causal responsibility. To those who think that *Sindell* is an unprecedented departure from settled principles of tort law, this attempt to derive from *Sindell* a principle of causal apportionment for all multiple-causation cases must seem doubly radical.

In fact, the departure from traditional doctrine is not so large as may appear, as I have tried to emphasize throughout. *Sindell* itself is essentially an application of *Summers v. Tice*, modified to include a rule of contribution. To be sure, the application of *Summers* to an entire industry, as distinguished from two hunters, stretches that precedent, at least as it has been construed heretofore. Yet it does no violence to the underlying principle of *Summers,* rationalized either in terms of shifting the burden of proof on causation or in terms of a substantive liability rule. Indeed, this application of *Summers* is conservative insofar as it incorporates a rule of contribution limiting each tortfeasor's liability commensurate with its particular contribution to the aggregate risk created by the product. There is, of course, no novelty in contribution, or in causation-based apportionment, which *Sindell's* market-share rule essentially represents. The fact that there is uncertainty and debate over the proper bases of apportionment should not be allowed to obscure the fact that causal contribution is now widely accepted as a proper element of loss apportionment. In this regard, the *Sindell* court unwittingly ignored its prior decisions on contribution, but followed the main current of judicial trends in other states.

If *Sindell* is not radically out of line with conventional tort doctrine, neither are the extended applications I have suggested—at least not as a matter of principle. To begin with, it was argued that apportionment need not, and should not, be conditioned on joinder of all or most tortfeasors. Contrary to the *Sindell* opinion, there is no reason to insist that a substantial share of the causal agents be before the court. Such joinder in no way affects the strength of the presumed causal responsibility in respect to any tortfeasor, and each tortfeasor should be liable only for its individual contribution to the risk. This result is more favorable to defendants than the conventional joint tortfeasor case, where the law does not require joinder and it is a defendant's burden to implead or institute a separate suit for contribution. The *Sindell* situation differs from this general case only with regard to the degree of certainty as to individual causal contributions; joinder is irrelevant to the resolution of this issue.

In this suggested application of *Sindell* lies the germ of another: fixing liability according to a party's causal contribution to risk, considering all causal contributions whether innocent or wrongful. This suggestion essentially builds on present contribution rules to the extent that they apportion liability on the basis of causation. It goes beyond existing law in two respects: it eliminates any threshold of "substantiality" as a prerequisite to liability, and it includes in its apportionment causal factors that are not subject to liability—innocent and unknown causes. Under this scheme, the present distinction between environmental conditions and causal factors would continue to be drawn, on a case-by-case basis.

These proposed extensions of the loss-apportionment rule give new importance to an old problem, that of defining causation. For purposes of causal apportionment, this article adopted a probabilistic conception. * * * The conception is not without its difficulties, both practical and conceptual. As a vehicle for allocating relative shares, however, it seems workable. The important point, not to be overlooked in the search for conceptions of causation, is the need for a practical conception of responsibility that allows us to assign liability in a fair and reasonably efficient manner.

RICHARD DELGADO, BEYOND SINDELL: RELAX-ATION OF CAUSE–IN–FACT RULES FOR IN-DETERMINATE PLAINTIFFS

70 Calif.L.Rev. 881, 892–908 (1982).

* * *

A. *Compensation*

A central purpose of tort law is to compensate victims. Extending *Sindell-Summers* doctrine to indeterminate plaintiffs would promote this goal, although in a somewhat uneven or inexact manner. If all members of the plaintiff class are permitted to recover fully, many will receive possibly substantial awards even though the defendant did not injure them. One solution is to provide only proportional recovery, in which each member of the plaintiff class is compensated in proportion to the damages sustained by the class as a whole. This method of distributing damages undercompensates some victims while overcompensating others, a result some class members will see as unfair. The only plausible alternative, however, is that provided under present rules—no recovery at all.

Relaxation of the burden of proof with respect to causation would be more attractive to plaintiffs, of course. A similar modification has occurred in selected areas, such as Title VII litigation. But the hope for such an extension to environmental suits seems unrealistic. Suits for damages in both paradigms, though meritorious, are not supported by the powerful historical and ideological policies against racial discrimination. Moreover, they would be resisted by defendants on the ground that they would impose "crushing liability" far beyond the damage actually caused by their actions.

The modification proposed permits recovery corresponding to the damage actually done, and thereby achieves a form of rough-hewn justice. All the persons who suffered injury after exposure to the agent recover something, though less than what they would recover by establishing that causation was probable. No one recovers who does not suffer an injury of the kind caused by defendant's conduct, and who was not placed at risk by the defendant's acts. The extension thus promotes the goal of compensating victims, although the promotion is less than perfect.

B. *Loss Spreading, Deterrence, and Economic Efficiency*

From the viewpoint of the plaintiff who seeks complete compensation, the proposed scheme of proportional recovery operates imperfectly. From the defendant's perspective, however, the fit of certain policies is perfect. Loss spreading is advanced without the inexactness found in connection with compensation. The plaintiff class passes the exact amount of accident costs on to the defendant, who can then pass this amount on to the public through additional charges or insurance. At the same time, the increased costs deter the defendant from engaging in the liability generating practice. The in terrorem effect is tailored to the deed; there is neither over-nor under-deterrence. Unlike its effect on compensation, the extension of the *Sindell-Summers* rule strongly promotes the tort goals of loss spreading and deterrence.

For the same reasons, the extension of *Sindell-Summers* reasoning to the case of indeterminate plaintiffs advances the goal of economic efficiency. Tortfeasors will face potential liability corresponding to the damages they cause the public. Where injuries are avoidable at lower cost by taking safety precautions, tortfeasors will have an incentive to do so. A new rule permitting liability in the two paradigms thus encourages businesses and individuals to act to maximize economic wealth and social welfare.

C. *Knowledge and Justice*

The extension of *Sindell* and *Summers* to cases of indeterminate plaintiffs should also have a beneficial knowledge generating effect. At present, inability to trace causation aids defendants, who consequently lack incentive to carry out research into injury causation. Imposing liability on defendants encourages them to investigate the manner in which their actions endanger others so that they may escape liability by showing that they are not to blame. It is possible to argue that plaintiffs have an equal stake in avoiding injury and that the cost of developing knowledge about mechanical or biological causation should be placed on them. Ordinarily, however, the defendant-disseminator will have greater access to the information and technology necessary to develop this knowledge, and will be in a position to do so more cheaply than members of the public. The burden is thus appropriately placed on him or her.

Once it is seen that extension of *Sindell's* cause-in-fact treatment to indeterminate plaintiffs serves goals of compensation, deterrence, economic efficiency, and knowledge generation, the conclusion seems inescapable that such an extension is morally just. Existing causation rules allow a blameworthy party to escape liability. The proposed modification imposes liability and compensates victims in proportion to the likelihood that they were, individually, injured by the defendant. Faced with a choice between manifest injustice and inexact justice, the law should prefer the latter.

III

THEORIES AND MECHANISMS OF RELIEF

If tort policies and parallel reasoning support extension of the *Sindell-Summers* result to situations in which uncertainty lies in the plaintiff class, how might such a reform be effected? Two approaches seem possible. In the first, existing tort mechanisms are manipulated to accomplish the desired result. In the second, a new mechanism is created. Although both approaches have merit, this Article urges courts to adopt a new mechanism.

A. Modification or Extension of Existing Mechanisms

Courts may accommodate suits brought by plaintiffs in indeterminate classes by modifying or extending existing mechanisms. They could, for example, find that exposure to certain forms of risk is a harm in itself, thus avoiding causal problems entirely. Thus, when the plaintiff knows of the exposure and suffers fear and anxiety, recovery could be permitted for negligent or intentional infliction of emotional distress. Second, courts could shift the burden of proof to the defendant once risk-creation plus harm is shown, as was done in a leading English case. More drastically, they could "estop" the defendant from denying causation once his or her negligent conduct and materialization of the harm are shown.

Courts could also lower the burden of proof where the defendant's action appears especially reprehensible, so as to allow plaintiffs to recover by showing that causation is possible, or conceivable, rather than probable. They could hold plaintiffs "vicariously compensable," by analogy to the concepts of transferred intent or vicarious liability, thereby permitting recovery on a showing that causation exists with respect to some member of the plaintiff class. If through jury nullification, a jury finds the defendant liable in one of our paradigm cases and awards punitive damages, the court might condition the award on plaintiff's willingness to share it with other similarly situated victims, or might use it to benefit the injured class.

Finally, all or most of the claims of the indeterminately bounded class might be assigned to a given individual or proxy, who would sue for the known number of claims in return for a promise to distribute any recovery. Subrogation could create the same result. Consider, for example, a large health insurance carrier forced to pay the medical expenses of all 190 victims in our first paradigm. The carrier can argue that it is entitled to sue and to be compensated for the 90 additional cases, even without specific identification of the victims.

All these approaches are promising, and could be adapted by a court to provide a method of recovery for indeterminate plaintiffs. Some have the drawback that they stretch existing doctrine to a possibly undesirable extent. Others permit overcompensation and "crushing liability" against the defendant which exceeds the amount of damages actually caused.

B. The Proposed Solution

The best solution would combine the elements of the second and final approaches described above. When a defendant has caused a known number of injuries to a class, as in one of the paradigm situations, the burden of proof should be reversed, and the defendant should be required to prove noncausation with respect to each injury. The "prima facie case" that plaintiff must satisfy to obtain the described relaxation of causal rules consists of the following elements: (i) that plaintiffs have suffered an injury; (ii) that the injury be one that could have resulted from either natural or human causes, acting separately and without synergy; (iii) that the injuries be causally indeterminate—that is, not identifiable as humanly or naturally caused; (iv) that the defendant is the only possible human cause; and (v) that the population injured, mode of risk, and other variables be uniform and stable enough to permit calculation of the increased number of victims. Once the plaintiff has established the prima facie case, the burden of proof shifts to the defendant to prove noncausation with respect to each injury. If he or she fails to do so, liability will be imposed for the number of unproved victims. The defendant will be able to shoulder this burden of proof in one of two ways. First, he or she can show the plaintiff's calculation of the number of humanly caused cases is exaggerated. This would reduce his or her liability in proportion to the reduction in number of victims. Second, he or she can show that there is another human defendant who has injured some of the victims.

In return for relaxation of the causation requirement, a plaintiff will be required to share any recovery with the other members of the class. The named plaintiff would thus prosecute a representative suit, and would be bound by the rules normally applied in such cases, including a fiduciary relationship to the class members. The plaintiff class, if successful, would recover an amount corresponding to its combined losses attributed to defendant's actions. This amount would be allocated among the members pro rata, after subtracting litigation costs. Even if damages vary greatly from one class member to another, or cannot be known precisely, established methods exist for ensuring just compensation to each class member.

From the defendant's perspective, the result corresponds exactly to the harm created and cannot reasonably be viewed as unfair. From the perspective of the plaintiff, the scheme compensates all who suffer the injury and who were within the zone of risk. Society as a whole benefits because of the deterrent effect of the tort sanction, and because defendants are no longer permitted to expose others to injury with impunity merely because causation is difficult or impossible to trace. Tortfeasors, particularly corporate ones, will have an incentive to carry out research that will permit them to carry the burden of disproof on the issue of causation, thus avoiding liability. Once the specific mechanism of causation is known, it may be possible to reduce the risk or even eliminate it entirely.

OBJECTIONS TO THE PROPOSED SOLUTION

The conclusion that there ought to be compensation for indeterminate plaintiffs and the method by which it is reached are mirror images to those in *Sindell*. In both cases, modification of causation rules avoids technological impossibility of proof, while the practical difficulties of calculating liability or distributing relief are circumvented by proration. Similar policy grounds support both extensions.

Because the two reforms stand on similar footings, this section omits any discussion of criticisms that can be levelled at both *Sindell* and the proposed companion remedy. For example, no attention is given to the objections that both "open the floodgates" of liability, violate due process, or unduly burden entrepreneurial activity. Nor is there discussion of the objection that both problems are best left to an administrative remedy or a scheme of social insurance. These aspects of *Sindell* have already spurred a lively body of commentary; some of them were discussed in the opinion itself. *Sindell* seems likely to survive them.
* * *

A number of objections do affect the argument for modified causation rules for plaintiffs uniquely, however, or at any rate more forcefully than when applied to *Sindell* alone, and therefore merit separate consideration. These objections include: (i) that the remedy imposes liability on defendants who are non-negligent vis-a-vis plaintiffs, i.e., because of risk-creation simpliciter; (ii) that the remedy contravenes doctrine and policy forbidding liability based on probabilistic evidence; (iii) that the fact situations * * * that call for application of a reverse-*Sindell* rule are unlikely to be found in the real world; and (iv) that *Sindell* and our remedy could be combined, resulting in liability of multiple defendants toward multiple plaintiffs, and virtually endless liability.

A. Compensation for Plaintiffs Not Demonstrably Injured by Defendant's Actions

It is a basic principle of tort law that the plaintiff must show that the defendant injured him or her. The Anglo–American system does not award damages simply because a defendant has done something reprehensible, created a risk, or behaved irresponsibly. It could be argued that an award of damages to indeterminate plaintiffs would violate this principle by compensating individuals who cannot show that they have been injured by the defendant, or, indeed, by any human being at all. In *Sindell,* the court permitted the plaintiff to recover against drug manufacturers, many of whom did not injure her, because of overriding policy grounds favoring recovery.

But overlooking causal indeterminacy for plaintiffs may seem a more radical departure than permitting recovery for known plaintiffs against indeterminate defendants, because an indeterminate plaintiff may well have no reason to deserve recompense. Sindell deserved compensation; her problem was that she did not know who had injured her, and thus did not know from whom she was entitled to recover. This may appear a less serious problem than that confronting indeterminate plaintiffs, who cannot prove that they belong in court—that they have a cause of action at all.

A number of responses seem possible. First, the defendants in each of our paradigms unquestionably injured members of the plaintiff class; plaintiffs cannot use the proposed remedy unless they first establish this. Defendants are thus not penalized for risk creation alone, as they have demonstrably injured a number of victims. Further, the plaintiffs' inability to trace causation and thus identify which of their number were injured by the defendant is a result of defendant's action, rather than any failure on the part of plaintiffs to investigate and develop their case. Every plaintiff will be highly motivated to trace causation and thus recover a full, rather than a partial, share of the damages. Reverse-*Sindell* suits will be filed only when a conventional suit is not feasible.

Finally, the proposed remedy gives only partial relief to members of the indeterminate plaintiff class. The amount of each plaintiff's recovery is measured by the proportion of culpably injured to nonculpably injured members of the class. If a class contains only a small proportion of culpably injured victims, each member will recover only a small amount. If the class contains a high proportion, each member will receive an award approximating his or her actual damages. Any unfairness or "windfall" effect is mitigated by this *pro rata* scheme of distributing damages. Classes that contain a high proportion of "deserving" plaintiffs will be in a position to provide each member with nearly full compensation. Classes composed of a high proportion of "undeserving" plaintiffs will recover only a small amount.

B. *Probabilistic Evidence*

A second objection to a reverse-*Sindell* rule is that it awards damages on the basis of probabilistic evidence. Of course, only one of the paradigms under consideration presupposes the use of probabilistic evidence. In the second paradigm, the plaintiff proves causation mechanically; probability theory plays no part.

The first paradigm does entail the use of statistical evidence, but only to establish the number of culpably injured members of the plaintiff class. The comparison of before and after frequencies that the model entails thus presents few of the dangers that courts fear in connection with probabilistic evidence and that have on occasion led them to exclude it. Probabilities are not used to single out the defendant nor to establish a causal link between conduct of a certain type and a particular injury. There is little risk that judge and jury will be paralyzed by obscure arguments or calculations. Unlike identification cases, there is little danger that the jury will apply a probability coefficient to the wrong population or variable, or that plaintiffs will deliberately use statistics to conceal a weak case. The danger of dependent variables masquerading as independent is minimal. Thus, the arguments against the use of probability evidence do not apply to the paradigms under discussion.

C. *A Model Without Application?*

A further objection that might be made to new causation rules for indeterminate plaintiffs is that there would be few, if any, applications for them. If so, their proposal would be little more than an exercise in symmetrical reasoning. * * * When an injury is mechanically caused, it will often be possible for the plaintiff to eliminate natural causation and make a case for human liability. Mechanical forces generally operate quickly and without a latency period or complex physiological mediating mechanisms to obscure cause and effect. In these cases, we properly expect the plaintiff to make his or her case under conventional rules. Indeed, most plaintiffs will prefer to do so in order to obtain full, rather than proportional, relief.

Some * * * cases do seem likely to arise; witness the recent "Medfly" spraying cases. Moreover, even if [these] cases arise only rarely their infrequency is not a good reason for courts to refuse them careful consideration when appropriate examples come before them. *Summers v. Tice,* the defendant-side analog * * *, was "unusual" case when it was decided, as was *Sindell.* This was no reason for denying the *Summers* and *Sindell* plaintiffs relief.

[Other type] cases are likely to arise somewhat more often. The principal difficulties will arise from the requirements that there be only one possible human cause, and that the population, mode of risk, and other variables be stable enough to permit a statistical calculation of the increased number of injuries above a background level. Such a suit will be impossible if, for example, the population is shifting or highly mobile, or if the background rate of the disease or injury varies greatly. A Paradigm I suit will also be barred if there is not one but a multitude of potential human defendants, as might be the case in a region that contains several polluters.

The requirements * * * would be most easily satisfied in connection with immobile or "captive" populations, such as members of a work-force, inmates of a mental or penal institution, students at a school, or residents of small, isolated communities. Uniformity of exposure could be met if it appeared that each individual suffered a common risk, for example from airborne distribution of a harmful substance in a confined area or contamination of food or water supply. The requirement of a single human defendant not only preserves doctrinal symmetry but also guards against inordinate expansion of the lawsuit and the spectre of undeserving plaintiffs recovering from defendants who were not personally responsible for their injuries. These requirements would thus tend to assure that [these] suits would be manageable both in number and in size.

Sindell, however, permitted a suit against a class of multiple defendants. This raises a final objection—that extending tort compensation to indeterminate plaintiffs would inexorably combine with existing theory to permit causes of action against indeterminate defendants. The ultimate result might be open-ended liability, with damages exceeding anything the legal system has hitherto known.

D. Combining Both Theories: Indeterminate Plaintiffs Versus Indeterminate Defendants

If causation rules are relaxed for indeterminate plaintiffs, the sobering possibility exists that ingenious counsel will combine both the *Sindell* doctrine and its inverse in a suit by a class of indeterminate plaintiffs against a class of indeterminate defendants. Imagine, for example, several manufacturers which, acting independently, market an identical substance known to cause a certain type of injury. The injury also occurs naturally, so that its occurrence does not in itself implicate any of the manufacturers. A substantial rise in the incidence of the injury immediately follows. Investigation eliminates other possible causes of the increase.

Neither the *Sindell* nor the reverse-*Sindell* doctrine will apply. But there seems to exist no theoretical reason not to permit a plaintiff to unite both principles and thus launch a massive lawsuit presenting complex problems of proof and requiring a large investment of judicial resources. The distribution of any damage award would be an accountant's nightmare, requiring proration with respect to both the defendant and plaintiff classes. Because of the high costs and special dangers of such suits, courts may well refuse to hear them at least until there has been an adequate period of experimentation with both types of *Sindell* causation rules.

Conclusion

The development of special cause-in-fact rules to aid plaintiffs confronted with indeterminacy in the defendant class suggests that a similar modification might occur when indeterminacy lies in the plaintiff class. Although current law does not permit recovery when the defendant is identifiable but the specific plaintiffs are not, many of the same considerations that supported recovery in *Summers v. Tice* and in *Sindell v. Abbott Laboratories* support it here. Permitting indeterminate plaintiffs to sue for their injuries promotes tort goals of compensation, deterrence, efficiency, knowledge generation, and justice. Distribution of damages can be accomplished by a variety of allocation schemes, employing a form of proportional recovery. This extension is maintainable in the face of objections that it would compensate persons who do not deserve it, would award damages based on probabilistic evidence, and would be available either too rarely or too often. It would eliminate an existing asymmetry in causal doctrine, and would advance the policy objectives of the substantive areas in which it is likely to be applied.

Modified tort rules for indeterminate plaintiffs are thus a logical and desirable next step in the development of tort doctrine.

Notes and Questions

1. As the Second Circuit decision in the *Agent Orange* appeal suggests, federal courts, at least, continue to be concerned about the legal requirements of actual causation-in-fact. Did the *Sindell* decision relating to the problem of apportioning liability among indeterminate defendants open the door for relaxation of tort causation requirements? Both Professors Robinson and Delgado seized upon the *Sindell* decision to argue in favor of such relaxed causation rules. To what extent do Robinson and Delgado agree about the relationship of causation rules and the purposes of the tort system? Does Professor Delgado's arguments favoring a "reverse-*Sindell*" rule for indeterminate plaintiffs, make sense? Is there a symmetry in tort law between the problem of indeterminate defendants and indeterminate defendants?

2. *See generally* James A. Henderson, Jr., Fred Bertram & Michael J. Toke, *Optimal Issue Separation in Modern Products Liability Litigation,* 73 Texas L. Rev. 1653 (1995).

F.   SCIENTIFIC PROOF

1.   PROBLEMS OF SCIENTIFIC UNCERTAINTY

AMERICAN LAW INSTITUTE, REPORTER'S STUDY, ENTERPRISE RESPONSIBILITY FOR PERSONAL INJURY (1991)

Vol. II at 321–328.

* * *

II.   The Nature of Scientific Uncertainty

Much of the confusion about causation in hazardous substance litigation is a result of uncertainty in the toxicological evidence that produces the basis for inferring causation in those cases. Some background on toxicological uncertainty is essential for analyzing alternative methods of presenting scientific evidence.

A.   *Forms of Evidence*

Toxicology is the science of poisons and their effects. The toxicology of environmental and occupational toxins as well as toxic consumer products relies on four types of scientific evidence: (1) cluster analysis, (2) short-term molecular assays, (3) animal bioassays, and (4) epidemiological studies.

1.   *Cluster Analysis*

Cluster analysis was the first important type of toxicological information and is perhaps the easiest for the lay person to understand. Cluster analysis involves review of "clusters" of cases of rare diseases and a search for a common exposure as a potential cause. For example, in the late 1960's clusters of rare hepatic angiosarcomas were observed in tire manufacturing plants. These were eventually traced to worker exposure to high levels of vinyl chloride. Cluster analyses usually result in the identification of a "signature" disease, a disease rarely found outside the particular type of exposed population. In this type of study, then, an "effect" has been observed and the search is for a potential "cause."

But signature diseases are not the rule in toxicology. Much more frequently hazardous substances cause diseases that also occur sporadically without this exposure. In most cases the fraction of the overall incidence of a disease that can be attributed to the hazardous substance is small. In addition, any people who are exposed to one hazardous substance are also exposed to others. This phenomenon makes the causation issue more difficult than the simple cluster analysis and signature disease concepts.

2. Short–Term Molecular Assays

The second type of toxicological evidence is the short-term screening assay. Scientists doing short-term screening assays take advantage of the similarities between the metabolic processes of humans and other forms of life to develop experiments that are relatively inexpensive and quick to complete. For instance, the general toxicity and potential carcinogenicity of substances can be evaluated by analyzing their tendency to cause mutations in bacteria. Short-term assays generally rely on the assumption that carcinogens interact with human genetic material to cause cancer and other diseases.

3. Animal Bioassays

More expensive and difficult to complete are animal bioassays. In an animal bioassay experiment scientists give several hundred mammals prescribed doses of a particular toxic substance and then identify causes of death in the animal cohort. Calculation of proper doses and careful monitoring of animal populations are critical to the process. Even more difficult is the mathematical modeling of the data generated by such studies, data that is used to determine safe doses.

4. Epidemiological Cohort Studies

The fourth kind of toxicological evidence is epidemiological. Epidemiology is the application of statistical techniques to the study of disease in groups of individuals. Epidemiologists do not conduct experiments because they have no control over factors that produce effects in their study populations. Rather, the epidemiologist looks for statistical correlations between exposures and disease outcomes. In epidemiological "cohort" studies a potential "cause" (such as cigarette smoking) has been observed and there is a search for "effect." Of course, epidemiology does not make direct observations of causation; rather, the epidemiologist can determine only how frequently a certain exposure would be associated with a particular effect as a matter of chance.

B. FORMS OF UNCERTAINTY

Given the nature of toxicological evidence, it is clear that any attribution of toxic causation may be attended by one or more of several kinds of uncertainty. Four different types of uncertainty are encountered in hazardous causation.

1. Trans–scientific Uncertainty

The first is trans-scientific uncertainty. Trans-scientific issues are those which can be cast in scientific terms but which are not amenable to scientific proof. For instance, we accept that animal carcinogens are human carcinogens as a matter of policy, yet for most animals carcinogens this proposition cannot be proven, given our present understanding of carcinogenesis. Trans-scientific propositions are policy decisions that inform discussion of hazardous substance toxicology.

2. Confidence Interval Uncertainty

The second kind of uncertainty that bests toxicological causal propositions is confidence interval uncertainty. The technical definition of a confidence interval is the range within which a study parameter lies 95 percent of the time. This definition derives from the fact that statisticians tend to use p-values of .05 as the standard for statistical significance.

A little background helps to clarify these technical terms. After collecting and analyzing epidemiological data, the epidemiologist usually can calculate a relative risk ration for the development of a disease. For example, a scientist studying lung cancer may find that workers exposed to a certain substance in the workplace for over five years have a relative risk of developing lung cancer that is twice the risk of similar workers who are not so exposed.

With the same data used to calculate the risk ration, the scientist can also calculate a p-value, which is the frequency with which a given exposure would be associated with a disease process solely as a matter of chance. The threshold of statistical significance is customarily set at the p-value of .05. For example, a study may show that a certain substance doubles the lung cancer risk. The study is statistically significant, however, only if the p-value generated by the study is less than .05, meaning that the association would be observed as a matter of chance only 5 in 100 times.

Confidence intervals can be calculated using the same statistical information. If many subjects are used in the study and the exposure data are very precise, the confidence intervals will tend to be quite narrow. But if there are few subjects in the study, perhaps because it is difficult to obtain exact exposure data on a large number, the confidence intervals may be quite wide. When a causal attribution in the form of a risk ratio is based on wide confidence intervals, the statistical uncertainty associated with the attribution is greater.

3. Individual Attribution Uncertainty

A third kind of uncertainty occurs when individual causal attribution is based on statistical evidence. Because statistical analysis deals with groups of subjects, any generalizations arising out of such analysis are about the effects on groups, not individuals. For example, a group of asbestos workers has an increased statistical risk of developing lung cancer. If there is an excess of lung cancer in the group, any given individual in the group might have contracted his lung cancer either from exposure to the asbestos or from another cause. Individual attribution is indeterminate in this context. Statistics can tell us only about increased risk, not about individual causation.

However, statistics can be used to infer causal attribution based on degrees of risk. The so-called attributable fraction is the portion of contracting a disease that can be attributed to a particular exposure. For instance, in an asbestos worker who smoked and later developed lung cancer, we can calculate attributable fractions for the smoking exposure and the asbestos exposure. These attributable fractions are based on studies of large groups of asbestos workers, some of whom smoked. The risk ratios calculated in these studies are then used to estimate the attributable fractions.

4. Multiple Causation Uncertainty

The fourth kind of uncertainty, "multiple causation uncertainty," attends discussion of any scientific field. Science-laden disputes bring judges and juries face to face with the fact that a single disability has many potential causes. Although the same dilemma may also arise in traditional tort litigation, mass tort litigation, with its complex technical vocabulary, generally exacerbates the problem.

In a sense individual attribution uncertainty is a subset of multiple causation uncertainty. Whenever a certain kind of illness has multiple potential causes it is difficult to attribute one single cause to a single individual. For example, hypertension, diabetes, smoking, and hyperlipidemia are all considered risk factors for development of heart disease. If an individual suffers from heart disease and also smokes and has hypertension, he has several potential causes of his heart disease. Consequently, it is difficult to attribute the heart disease to either smoking or hypertension.

The critical difference between multiple causation and individual attribution uncertainty is that the latter arises when findings of causation are based on inferences that derive from data gathered on groups. Multiple causation problems imply that there is a causal chain explanation for the causal relationship. On the other hand, individual attribution problems arise only when epidemiological studies suggest there are multiple causes. In cases of individual attribution uncertainty, causal chain explanations have receded into the background, and epidemiological and statistical evidence have come to the forefront.

JOSEPH SANDERS, THE BENDECTIN LITIGATION: A CASE STUDY IN THE LIFE CYCLE OF MASS TORTS

43 Hastings L.J. 301, 321, 331–347 (1992).

IV. The Science

Science is discussed first because it was, in a sense, a leading indicator of what was to happen in the *Bendectin* trials. To know the science was, to some extent, to be able to predict what would come. On the other hand, the law, especially as reflected in appellate opinions, was a lagging indicator—a reflection of what already had occurred.

A. Background

Bendectin was already in the marketplace when Merrell experienced problems with Thalidomide and later with MER/29. In part because Bendectin was comprised of existing drugs, the compound had not undergone substantial testing when introduced. At that time, FDA standards did not require testing for teratogenicity, and Merrell did not test Bendectin for teratogenicity until after the Thalidomide disaster in 1961. Indeed, the Thalidomide disaster acted as an important catalyst for reformation of the Food and Drug Act.

In the aftermath of that disaster, Merrell began investigating the safety of Bendectin. As is typical, early research involved *in vitro* and *in vivo* studies. Later, when questions arose regarding Bendectin's safety, new *in vivo* studies were undertaken, and researchers conducted a series of epidemiological studies assessing Bendectin's effect on human fetuses. Because the relative probative value of various types of data became a determining factor in the *Bendectin* cases, the next sections provide an overview of each type of research: *in vitro*, *in vivo*, and epidemiological. * * *

* * *

The history of the *Bendectin* litigation has been marked by questions concerning the relative probative value of each type of evidence and the causal inferences that can be drawn from statistical correlations.

B.   The Bendectin Studies

* * * The purpose here is not to determine whether Bendectin is a teratogen; rather, it is to examine the flow of science over the life cycle of the *Bendectin* litigation. In mass tort cases, the importance of the science cannot be overemphasized. Without *in vitro*, *in vivo* and epidemiological findings, and experts prepared to present them, the plaintiff has no case. In order to understand the litigation, something first must be known about the science.

Further, there are two other issues suggested by the idea of a congregation of cases. First, the science, like the law, of a case congregation develops and matures; the science also experiences a life cycle. We should expect that the science will be relatively poorly developed in the early stages of litigation, but that over time the mobilization efforts of the parties will produce a richer body of scientific evidence.

This leads to the second point: We should anticipate that the science itself is influenced by the legal process. As the congregation of cases grows and matures, it creates its own gravity field, attracting and distorting the science that comes near it. In turn the science affects the law. Ultimately, science and law interact in complex ways to produce unique patterns of development in various case congregations. In the following three sections, I show how the science developed in the *Bendectin* cases.

(1) In Vitro Studies

While probably all *Bendectin* cases have contained some testimony on *in vitro* research, the number of studies on point is limited. In a recent letter published in the Journal of the American Medical Association, Dr. Stuart Newman cites six *in vitro* studies that examine Bendectin or its antihistamine component, two of which were published in 1989. Compared to *in vivo* or epidemiological research, *in vitro* studies are the least accessible to the lay person. Summarizing the findings is difficult. One study that is damaging with respect to Bendectin's safety is by Budroe, Shaddock, and Casciano, who conclude that Doxylamine may be a weak DNA-damaging agent. Hassell and Horigan report that Bendectin inhibits limb bud mesenchyme cell differentiation. Dr. Newman interprets the other studies as indicating doxylamine also curtails the formation of embryonic cartilage. The authors of these studies, however, apparently do not conclude that their research indicates that Bendectin or doxylamine is teratogenic. Cumulatively, the evidence suggests that Bendectin's antihistamine component may have some adverse effects on embryonic cell development, but there is relatively little research, and the findings are not clear cut.

This circumstance is not surprising since the purpose of most of these studies is not to prove or disprove that Bendectin causes specific types of developmental defects in animals or children. Instead, most appear to have a different purpose: to study a group of known teratogens alongside a group of known nonteratogens and determine whether the procedure used in the study is in fact able to differentiate the two groups of drugs. If a procedure is able to distinguish known teratogens from known nonteratogens then it will be a better predictor as to whether a new compound will in fact be teratogenic in humans. To return to the distinction developed earlier between studies used to regulate risk versus studies used to prove causation in a tort case, the primary goal of most of these *in vitro* studies appears to have been the development of techniques that will be most helpful in regulating risk.

Perhaps this is why, in comparison to the *in vivo* and epidemiological research discussed below, relatively little Bendectin-specific *in vitro* research has occurred. As a consequence, the *in vitro* data is second best evidence when used in the courtroom to demonstrate that Bendectin is a teratogen.

(2) In Vivo Studies

In the aftermath of the Thalidomide disaster, the first *in vivo* tests of Bendectin were conducted by Merrell employees in 1963, using rabbits and rats. The principal investigator, Dr. Robert Staples, concluded that the study did not reveal teratogenicity. However, he noted some malformations in rabbits given the highest doses, and therefore recommended further research be conducted at higher dose rates. In 1966 and 1967 further tests were done on the individual components of Bendectin by two other Merrell employees, Drs. James Newberne and John Gibson. These results were published in 1968. Since that time there have been surprisingly few published *in vivo* studies designed to explore the teratogenic effect of Bendectin or its constituent ingredients. * * *

[Concerning] the development of the literature, [t]he first thing to note is the erratic nature of the research-bursts of activity separated by several years during which no research occurred. In fact, the pattern reflects the regulatory purpose of most *in vivo* studies and, later, the demands of the *Bendectin* litigation. The early 1967 research represents Merrell's response to Thalidomide. It was followed by a long period of quiet. The mid–1970s work reflects the impact of the epidemiological effectiveness study that found two ingredient Bendectin to be as effective as the three ingredient version. Subsequently, Merrell conducted *in vivo* studies to test the safety of the new formulation on animals. The final and largest wave of studies, from the early 1980s to date, reflects the need for new evidence regarding the drug's safety, driven largely by the interest in and demand for information resulting from the *Bendectin* litigation.

* * *

One would expect that as the *Bendectin* litigation matured, so too should the quality of the *in vivo* evidence have improved, allowing the parties and the courts to reach a consensus regarding the drug's teratogenicity. And there is some evidence that the quality of the research did improve over time. Early studies rarely utilized any statistical analysis of experimental results, while later ones employed some rather sophisticated analytic tools. Additionally, the sample sizes of the studies have grown, and dose rates have been increased. Both of these methodological changes increase a study's ability to detect minor defects. On the other hand, the limited number of *in vivo* studies, which employed a variety of test animals and tested a variety of component drugs, makes it difficult to draw any conclusions as to whether Bendectin has a specific teratogenic effect on humans.

How to account for the relatively limited number of *in vivo* studies, as well as their relatively late appearance? The small number of studies cannot be explained by a direct depletion effect. While Bendectin is no longer available as a prescription drug, it remains available for laboratory studies. Indeed, the most recent research occurred subsequent to Merrell's withdrawal of Bendectin from the market. Nevertheless, the volume of published work is thin. Why?

In part, the answer is found in the relationship of this research to all Bendectin research and to the ongoing litigation surrounding the product. While *in vivo* studies in general are cheaper to conduct than epidemiological studies, with respect to a particular drug the relative advantage is lessened. Large scale epidemiological studies can be used to investigate a wide variety of drugs simultaneously. Most of the epidemiological research on Bendectin, for instance, uses data sets collected for more general purposes. Animal studies, by contrast, must focus on the drug in question. Consequently, there has been less interest in mobilizing the resources necessary to conduct Bendectin-specific *in vivo* experiments.

This has proven especially true since Bendectin was removed from the market. Further study of the drug is of limited interest to people who are not in some way involved with Bendectin as a legal, as well as scientific, issue. In other words, Merrell's decision to remove Bendectin from the market did lessen demand for animal research. This fact is reflected in the sponsorship of the published studies that do exist. * * * The first (Gibson) was sponsored and conducted by Merrell. The second (Khera) was done to explore the teratogenicity of pyridoxine; it did not directly involve Bendectin. The third (McBride) was independent. Hendrickx's work began independently, but the research reported in the second 1985 article was funded by Merrell. Tyl's study, the largest and most sophisticated *in vivo* study to date, was undertaken by the National Toxicology Program at the specific request of the FDA's Bureau of Drugs. Given the fact that Merrell was, by far, more interested in such research than any other entity, its decision to drop Bendectin naturally led to a decrease in animal studies of the drug's teratogenicity.

If those not involved in the litigation had little interest in new research, neither did the parties themselves have strong incentives to conduct new studies. Once litigation began, Merrell's incentive to continue its own research was substantially diminished. New studies done by Merrell scientists in Merrell laboratories were, from the company's point of view, a lose-lose proposition. If they showed an effect, the studies would be used against the company in subsequent litigation. If they failed to show an effect, their persuasiveness would be seriously limited by the fact that Merrell had conducted them. Any slight technical flaw in the design or execution of the experiment would be exploited by plaintiffs to undermine Merrell's findings. A similar analysis would apply to research funded by Merrell, especially if it was conducted by someone who had previously testified on the firm's behalf.

In this respect it is interesting to note that while the Hendrickx study, which was funded by Merrell, did involve some risk of an adverse finding, from the firm's perspective it had the benefit that it was conducted by a non-Merrell employee who had previously concluded Bendectin causes heart defects in monkeys. Merrell thus could hope to make effective use of a negative finding in court. Even so, the researchers used a double-blind design so as to minimize the potential that the study might appear biased. Even this strategy, however, did not shield Merrell from the suggestion that because they funded the study its results were suspect.

It is not only the existence of litigation that alters the incentives to conduct *in vivo* research; so too does the existence of a large body of epidemiological data diminish the market for animal research. Inevitably, the direct evidence on human effects provided by the epidemiological evidence diminishes the demand for *in vivo* studies insofar as they are designed to answer the question of whether a drug causes harm to humans. Although there is considerable disagreement about the proper role of *in vivo* studies in answering that question, many would agree they are less probative than epidemiological evidence. As the following discussion shows, the *Bendectin* litigation and epidemiology eventually interacted in a way that seriously undermined the worth of animal studies. Increasingly, courts simply refused to rely on or even to admit *in vivo* evidence. Considering the declining demand for *in vivo* research, it is not surprising that the supply has been limited.

(3) Epidemiological Studies

The epidemiological evidence stands at the center of the *Bendectin* cases. As noted earlier, a number of judges and scientists have argued that a coherent body of epidemiological evidence trumps other information.

a. Background

I have found and examined thirty-nine published epidemiological studies that discuss Bendectin. * * *

What do these studies show concerning the teratogenic effects of Bendectin? Needless to say, much of the litigation in this and other drug cases centers on varying interpretations of the epidemiological findings. However, as with the *in vivo* studies, two summary facts are worth reporting: (1) the authors' conclusions about the drug; and (2) whether the study contains any objective indication that Bendectin has adverse effects.

In no study did the authors clearly conclude that Bendectin does have teratogenic effects. In six studies, the authors report at least one significant correlation between Bendectin and some adverse effect and conclude that while their findings alone are insufficient to support an attribution of causation, one may exist. In the remaining thirty-three studies, the authors either draw no conclusion or conclude that there is no statistical relationship.

Apart from the author's own conclusions, a second measure of Bendectin's effect is the odds ratio or the relative risk reported in the study. For each study, I have attempted to extract the "most important" odds ratio or relative risk. Either by using the statistic reported or by calculating an odds ratio based on the raw data published, it was possible to extract one or both measures in twenty-six of the thirty-nine studies. In general, odds ratios and relative risks are not strictly comparable-either with each other or across studies. But one crude type of comparison that can be made is whether the statistic is greater or less than 1. An odds ratio or relative risk greater than one indicates that children whose mothers took Bendectin are more likely to have suffered a defect than those whose mothers did not. An odds ratio or relative risk of less than one indicates the opposite. If Bendectin truly has no effect, given a large number of equally valid studies, half should produce statistics greater than one and half should result in measures of less than one. With regard to the twenty-six studies for which I was able to extract a value, in thirteen the most important measure is greater than one and in twelve it is less than one. One study reports a relative risk of exactly one.

b. The Evolution of Bendectin's Epidemiological Research

While the aggregate findings of the studies are critical to the ultimate disposition of the *Bendectin Cases* as a group, the key point for this analysis is that the studies, like the case law, evolved over time. In the early years, the epidemiological research tended to parallel the *in vivo* research. A number of investigations were conducted in the early 1960s, partly in response to the Thalidomide disaster. Then the epidemiological research virtually ceased for a number of years. In the late 1970s, a number of new studies were published, although it is important to note that most of them did not target Bendectin specifically. Rather, they reported the results of broad epidemiological studies of drugs taken during pregnancy, including Bendectin and its constituent ingredients.

A turning point in the epidemiological research occurred in 1979 with the publication of the first article suggesting an association of Bendectin with birth defects. The study was important for several reasons: It was published in one of the leading American journals on epidemiology; the analysis was relatively sophisticated; and the senior author, Kenneth Rothman, was a professor in the Department of Epidemiology in the Harvard School of Public Health. With the publication of the Rothman study, Bendectin, like Thalidomide and MER/29 before it, became epidemiologically suspect.

To demonstrate the importance of the Rothman study, I have coded the thirty-nine studies as either pre-or post–1979 * * * prior to 1979 most of the studies focused on teratogenicity in general, not Bendectin in particular. The Rothman finding, plus the emerging litigation concerning Bendectin, generated study after study of this particular drug. With this increased focus came an increase in the sophistication and the power of the studies.

c. *The Increase in Statistical Sophistication and Power*

* * * [S]tudies rarely reported more than a basic Chi-square statistic prior to 1980, but uniformly began to report more after that date. Most importantly, they began to report confidence intervals for estimates and started to control for other factors through the use of multiple regression techniques, most frequently logistic regression.

As time passed, the power of individual studies also increased. The power of a study is its ability to detect a difference of some given magnitude. Epidemiological studies, like all statistical analyses, are vulnerable to two types of errors.

* * *

In sum, from the mid–1970s to the mid–1980s the quantity and quality of the epidemiological evidence on Bendectin improved dramatically. The research focused on the drug and used increasingly sophisticated methods to control for confounding factors. Specifically, it used a combination of increased sample size, a shift to case-control studies, and a focus on particular types of defects to greatly increase the power of the research. During this period, the probability of making either * * * errors was significantly reduced.

d. The End of Research

Suddenly, in 1985 with nearly three dozen studies in print, epidemiological research on Bendectin came to a virtual halt. As noted earlier, *in vivo* research experienced a similar, contemporaneous decline. Figure 1 shows the number of *in vivo* and epidemiological studies published each year from the early 1960s to the present.

Figure 1
Published Bendectin Epidemiological
and *In vivo* Studies, by Year

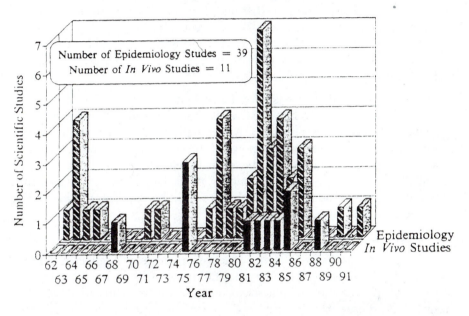

The figure illustrates two phenomena. First, and most important, it clearly shows that the science was driven by the law. The study of Bendectin became a hot topic and substantial resources were mobilized to study it. This mobilization can be understood at several levels. Because Bendectin was a hot topic, articles on the subject were relatively likely to find their way into print. Careerist concerns may have caused academics to select topics that would lead to publication in prestigious journals. Moreover, the federal government, through the FDA, encouraged research by offering grants to fund the study of Bendectin's effects. Finally, the Bendectin litigation itself generated research, as parties encouraged and even funded work on Bendectin. Legal needs gave shape and direction to the epidemiological study of teratogenic effects. The volume and sophistication of studies focusing specifically on Bendectin was, in large part, the result of the litigation.

Second, Figure 1 demonstrates the relatively sudden cessation of studies in the mid–1980s. Galanter's hypotheses about holistic effects can be extended to explain the decline of scientific investigations as well as case congregations. Because Bendectin was removed from the market in 1983, and because its sales had plummeted in the preceding year or two, there eventually were no new data bases to exploit. By withdrawing the product from the market Merrell created an epidemiological depletion effect as well as the intended case depletion effect.

It would be a mistake, however, to attribute the decline of Bendectin studies entirely to depletion effects. Two other factors were also at work. The scientific community seems to have reached something close to a consensus concerning the drug. While no study can remove all residual uncertainty regarding Bendectin's safety, if the drug is a teratogen, it is à relatively mild one (having effects too subtle to be measured reliably with existing techniques). As a result, many felt that Bendectin had been overstudied. There arose the desire to ration Bendectin studies and save limited resources to study other drugs. As Lewis Holmes notes in an influential essay:

> While we can always wish for more and better studies, two issues must be borne in mind. First, well-designed and extensive epidemiologic studies are expensive. Where will the funds to support these studies come from in this period of limited funding? Second, in view of the extensive data cited above on Bendectin and the limited data available on many other commonly used drugs one can argue that well-designed studies of other drugs would be of greater value to the public at this time.

(4) The Life Cycle of the Bendectin Science

The preceding analysis of the research regarding Bendectin demonstrates that the science has followed a life cycle of its own. There was a substantial mobilization of resources devoted to the study of Bendectin, much of it apparently in response to the litigation and concomitant political pressure. The quantity and quality of epidemiological research increased dramatically in the 1980s, to the point where people like Holmes concluded that we knew more about the teratogenic potential of this drug than nearly any other. The extent of the epidemiological literature stands in contrast to the paucity of *in vivo* studies. In part, this may be understood as a consequence of the fact that there were few if any basic science questions to be answered through the study of Bendectin, and as a legal resource the *in vivo* studies were of increasingly little value in the face of a mounting body of epidemiological evidence. In a sense, epidemiology drove out animal studies.

Finally, in the mid–1980s came the end of new epidemiological studies as well. The combination of depletion effects and an emerging scientific consensus that if Bendectin has any teratogenic effects they are virtually undetectable by existing methods together led to the cessation of research. The leading indicator, published scientific articles, had stabilized at an essentially pro-defendant conclusion. But while the science was winding down, the law was just getting into full swing. * * *

Notes and Questions

1. Issues relating to scientific proof obviously are entailed in traditional tort litigation, but as Professor Sanders suggests, these problems are exacerbated in complex mass tort litigation. Professor Sander's in-depth study of the *Bendectin* litigation explores another dimension of the science debate: namely, the relationship of the development of scientific knowledge to the development of legal causes of action. This is an especially significant point for mass tort litigation—to what extent does the development of scientific knowledge precede or follow the development of a mass tort litigation? What is the relationship of the development of scientific knowledge and the formation of a mass tort class of claimants, and how might the state of scientific information effect settlement negotiations? The relationship of scientific knowledge to the development of a nascent mass tort played a controversial role in the *Silicone Breast Implant* litigation, where it has been suggested that the law was in advance of the scientific knowledge of silicone as an injury-producing agent. After the silicone breast implant class settlement was achieved, industry-sponsored studies were published questioning the validity of silicone as a disease-causing agent. Should the settlement have been approved in the presence of such evidence?

2. There is a considerable literature discussing the problems of science in the law. *See generally,* Peter Huber, GALILEO'S REVENGE: JUNK SCIENCE IN THE COURTROOM (1991); Kenneth S. Abraham & Richard A. Merrill, *Scientific Uncertainty in the Courts*, Issues Sci. & Tech., Winter 1986, at 93; David M. Benjamin, *Elements of Causation in Toxic Tort Litigation*, 14 J. Legal Med. 153 (1993); Bert Black, *A Unified Theory of Scientific Evidence*, 56 Ford. L.Rev. 595 (1988); Bert Black & David E. Lilienfeld, *Epidemiological Proof in Toxic Tort Litigation*, 52 Ford.L.Rev. 732 (1984); Gerald W. Boston, *A Mass–Exposure Model of Toxic Causation: The Content of Scientific Proof and the Regulatory Experience*, 18 Colum.J.Envtl.L. 181 (1993); Troyen A. Brennan, *Causal Chains and Statistical Links: The Role of Scientific Uncertainty in Hazardous–Substance Litigation*, 73 Cornell L.Rev. 469 (1988); Michael Dore, *A Proposed Standard for Evaluating the Use of Epidemiological Evidence in Toxic Tort and Other Personal Injury Cases*, 28 How.L.J. 667 (1985); Steve Gold, *Causation in Toxic Torts: Burdens of Proof, Standards of Persuasion, and Statistical Evidence*, 96 Yale L.J. 376 (1986); Thomas W. Henderson, *Toxic Tort Litigation: Medical and Scientific Principles in Causation*, 132 Am.J. Epidemiology S69 (1990); Constantine Kokkoris, Comment, Deluca v. Merrell Dow Pharmaceuticals, Inc.: *Statistical Significance and the Novel Scientific Technique*, 58 Brook. L. Rev. 219 (1992); Joseph Sanders, *From Science to Evidence: The Testimony on Causation in the Bendectin Cases*, 46 Stan. L. Rev. 1 (1993); Melissa M. Thompson, Comment, *Causal Inference in Epidemiology: Implications for Toxic Tort Litigation*, 71 N.C.L.Rev. 247 (1992); Jack B. Weinstein, *Litigation and Statistics*, 3 Sta. Sci. 286 (1988); Richard W. Wright, *Causation, Responsibility, Risk, Probability, Naked Statistics, and Proof: Pruning the Bramble Bush by Clarifying Concepts*, 73 Iowa L.Rev. 1001 (1988); Special Committee on Science and the Law, American Bar Association, *An Analysis of Proposed Changes in Substantive and Procedural Law in Response to Perceived Difficulties in Establishing Whether or Not Causation Exists in Mass Toxic Tort Litigation*, 41 Record Ass'n Bar City New York 905 (1986); Symposium,

Legal and Scientific Perspectives on Causation in Mass Tort Litigation, 1
Cts. Health, Sci. & L. 287 (1991); *Toxic Torts: Science, Evidence, Causation,*
61 Def. Couns. J. 19 (1994).

2. ALTERNATIVES FOR PRESENTATION OF SCIENTIFIC EVIDENCE TO COURTS

TROYEN A. BRENNAN, HELPING COURTS WITH TOXIC TORTS: SOME PROPOSALS REGARDING ALTERNATIVE METHODS FOR PRESENTING AND ASSESSING SCIENTIFIC EVIDENCE IN COMMON LAW COURTS

51 U.Pitt.L.Rev. 1, 4–18 (1989).

* * *

I. ALTERNATIVES TO TRADITIONAL LITIGATION

As even the briefest review of depositions or testimony will indicate,
the litigation of toxic tort cases proceeds within an adversarial atmosphere. The parties are often hostile, a hostility that extends even to
the opposing scientific experts. Polarization of views occurs as financial
incentives push the experts to extreme positions, especially regarding the
critical causation question. This adversarial science, and the "hired
gun" witnesses it appears to engender, are what seems to trouble
members of the judiciary, as well as some expert witnesses. Judges fear
that juries can be misled by highly paid experts who will find at least
some support in the voluminous scientific literature for any position,
even when that position is repudiated by the majority of scientists.

In addition to the hired gun phenomenon, there is concern that
judges and juries often do not understand the scientific information
presented by experts, even when the experts are impartial and knowledgeable. As I have argued elsewhere, statistical and epidemiological
evidence is especially troubling for common law courts, largely because
of the difference between statistical and legal notions of causation.
Thus triers of fact can be misled by expert witnesses even when those
witnesses present impartial, rational testimony. Courts' problems with
scientific data on causation have created an interest in alternative means
for presenting such data.

* * *

A. Modification of Existing Rules and Procedures

One way to ensure better and more understandable scientific evidence on causal issues is to allow the judge to become an active
participant in the presentation of the case. While the paradigm of
judging in the American common law has emphasized a passive role for
the judge, this conception of judging is not universal. Indeed, in the
past few years, judges on the federal bench have become more creative in
their approaches to complicated evidence. The challenge of complex,

multi-party litigation has led experts in procedure to push the judges, especially the federal judiciary, toward innovation.

Procedural rules offer some promise for helping judges assume the initiative and develop reliable expert testimony on hazardous substance cases. For example, motions can be used to determine the kind of evidence that will be admitted at trial. Joint pretrial meetings can help educate a judge before the trial begins on the shape of the parties' cases. The judge can use summary judgment to police the causal evidence.

Perhaps most promising, Special Masters appointed under Federal Rule of Civil Procedure 53 can be used to coordinate evidence available on causal issues. For example, Special Masters have assisted courts with asbestos litigation, hazardous waste site litigation, and Dalkon Shield litigation. In each of these cases, however, the Special Master was not involved in providing the court with a determination regarding the causal relationship; rather, the Special Master tended to develop methods for processing claims and dealing with issues other than causation.

Since the major problem which courts have with causal issues is the evidence presented by the parties, innovations in evidentiary rules might provide greater promise. To understand the manner in which judges might control evidence, a brief historical digression, and review of the *Frye* rule, is helpful. As set forth in *Frye v. United States,* the *Frye* rule required that an expert testify that the theory or process on which he relied was generally accepted by the relevant scientific peer group. This rule thus created a special, and arguably higher, threshold for scientific evidence than for other sorts of evidence introduced at trial. It no doubt gave judges great control over scientific evidence. By 1970, the overwhelming number of American jurisdictions accepted some form of the *Frye* rule.

In the 1970s, as more innovative scientific evidence was being presented to courts, the federal government adopted new Federal Rules of Evidence. The new rules gave judges generally more discretion, but also effectively removed the high threshold of the *Frye* rule. Indeed, several federal courts held that Rule 702, which states that expert testimony can be admitted if it "will assist the trier of fact to understand the evidence or determine a fact in issue", overturns the *Frye* rule. Paradoxically, then, the grant of greater discretion to trial judges appears to have removed some of their power to exclude scientific evidence.

There are, however, numerous ways in which the discretionary nature of the Federal Rules of Evidence can be used to a judge's advantage, if the judge wishes to exercise some control over the scientific evidence. Rule 703 allows experts to rely on hearsay if that data is sufficiently trustworthy. Rule 803(8)(C) allows admission of epidemiological studies as evidence. Exceptions to the hearsay rule for learned treatises and other reports under Rule 803 also allow the judge greater discretion in educating the jury. In addition, judges also retain their traditional authority to exclude evidence when the prejudice the evidence might create outweighs its probative value.

The greatest potential in the Federal Rules of Evidence for judges to control scientific testimony is presented by Rule 706. Rule 706 provides that a judge can appoint an expert witness in addition to those of the parties. This witness can be deposed by the litigants, and the fact that he is court-appointed can be shielded from the jury. Nonetheless, judges have not often exercised this prerogative, probably because of fear of appearing partial or of unfairly influencing the jury.

A court-appointed expert changes the entire dynamic of a hazardous substance case. Without the court-appointed expert, the experts for the opposing sides have every incentive to take as radical a position as possible. For instance, a plaintiff's expert might testify that one molecule of a substance is enough to cause a variety of illnesses, while the defendant's expert would posit that the substance is essentially harmless. The adversarial nature of the proceeding creates a perception that moderation of expert opinion will sway the jury in favor of the other party.

The court-appointed expert changes this dynamic. If the court-appointed expert outlined a position which was intermediate within the spectrum of views that exist on a particular causal relationship, and the jury knew this, the parties' experts would have great incentive to demonstrate how their views relate to those of the court-appointed expert. The incentive to maintain a radical position is essentially eliminated. The judge thus forces the parties to moderate, and to address the conventional testimony of the court's expert.

So, why are there not more court-appointed experts? Possibly because judges do not know where to find such experts. Usually appointed for reasons other than their strong technical backgrounds, judges are not equipped to anticipate the nature of scientific testimony and react to it by identifying a suitable, objective expert. A judge who wants to appoint an expert has neither a ready source of experts, nor a set of criteria which indicate the kind of expert best suited for the particular case. The fear of unfairly influencing the jury is magnified once the other side demonstrates that the court's expert is inappropriate for the particular causal issue, or nothing more than an industry hack or a plaintiff's hired gun. Thus before Federal Rule 706 can become quite useful for judges trying hazardous substance cases, the problem of selection of experts must be solved.

The beauty of Rule 706 is that it does not require judges themselves to make decisions regarding difficult scientific issues. Some fears regarding the use of court-appointed experts center on the power it gives the court over the proceeding. This power pales in comparison with the power judges could wield using summary judgment and interpretations of Rule 702. Indeed there are signs that the federal judiciary may prove more willing, likely too willing, to use summary judgment and evidentiary thresholds as a method for keeping plaintiffs out of court when the judges themselves do not find evidence probative. It seems to me much more reasonable to maintain an impartial role for judges regarding determinations of scientific merit, yet allow them to call their own witnesses when necessary.

In summary, there are a number of options using existing rules of civil procedure and evidence for judges to control expert testimony. The most promising of these, the use of court-appointed experts, requires that judges have some technical sophistication, an understanding of the kind of expert that is needed, and a source of such experts. Moreover, concerns about impartiality must be overcome. In addition, court-appointed experts might not be appropriate for all types of hazardous substance litigation. Before making assessments about appropriateness, however, it is necessary to define other alternatives to traditional litigation.

B. Science Panels

The science panel, as I use the term in this essay, is a panel of scientists, possibly aided by lawyers and concerned citizens, who adjudicate a specific question regarding a technical dispute and formulate a consensus opinion. As a reform measure for hazardous substance litigation, the science panel would provide a consensus opinion on a given causal dispute for the court. There are many problems with this approach. Again, a historical digression can help clarify these problems; particularly useful is a review of the debate over the intellectual forbearer of the science panel, the science court.

In the late 1970s, questions about the courts' handling of scientific issues largely centered on the manner in which federal appellate courts decided technical disputes arising out of regulatory agencies' actions. The intellectual leadership of the Court of Appeals for the District of Columbia Circuit was especially important. While judges debated the relative merits of a "hard" versus a "soft" look at regulations that relied heavily on the agency's technical expertise, some scientists and industry representatives fretted that ignorant decisions by courts might inhibit the development of new technology. In response to this, they proposed the science court.

The most thoroughgoing of the science court proposals was championed by Dr. Arthur Kantrowitz. As early as 1967, Kantrowitz argued that scientific advisory functions should be institutionalized to increase the "presumptive validity of the scientific input." Central to Kantrowitz's proposal was a separation of the scientific from the moral or political issues presented by a controversy, adjudication of the scientific issues before a panel, with presentation made in an adversarial fashion, and publication of any decisions. Kantrowitz's leadership eventually gave rise to the report by the Task Force of the Presidential Advisory Group on Anticipated Advances in Science and Technology. This report advocated the concept of resolution of scientific disputes through an adversarial proceeding before a panel of scientists.

Clearly, the science court was intended to respond to the inability of courts to address the complicated scientific issues arising out of disputes between industry and regulatory agencies. The paradigmatic cases were the Department of Transportation's concern about the environmental impact of SST flights and the Food and Drug Administration's regulation of the use of saccharin as a food additive. Since these kind of problems had already led to costly disputes, the added cost of the science court was thought to be minimal. Thus, the original Science Court proposals were intended to address "big picture" technical concerns, in turn aiding the regulatory agencies and federal appeals courts.

This sort of model would seem unsuitable for the many thousands of individual hazardous substance cases, each of which raises particular causal issues. While the expense of a science court might be justified if the court's function was to replace much of the work regulatory agencies were doing in the development of scientific bases for regulations, this is certainly not true with regard to toxic tort litigation. No science court could possibly do all the work involved in preparing the particular scientific case for each litigant in thousand of cases.

There are other problems with science courts. First, many observers have pointed out that scientific issues are not readily separated from political issues. For instance, consider the example of the regulation of benzene in the workplace. In the late 1970s, the Occupational Safety and Health Administration ("OSHA") attempted to lower the standard for benzene from ten parts per million to one part per million. The basis of OSHA's regulatory decision was its Generic Carcinogen Policy ("GCP"). The GCP, thought OSHA, would justify stringent regulation of benzene even though the differential effects of one versus ten parts per million were not available. This led to expensive litigation, finally resulting in the Supreme Court's rejection of the standard in 1980. The Court based its definition on OSHA's enabling legislation, and the role that legislation created for the use of cost-benefit analysis.

Since the agency's decision to regulate was based largely on trans-scientific issues, namely policies concerning scientific issues, and the court's rejection based on interpretation of the statute, it is difficult to understand the role a strictly technical science court might have played in this extremely important dispute. The science and policy issues were inextricably linked in this case. Turning such decisions over to scientists would be inappropriate.

A second major problem with the science court is the use of adversarial methods. Since many legal scholars have expressed concern with the manner in which factual issues are treated in courtrooms, it seems odd to subject science to an adversary process. Certainly consensus development models make more sense for reaching a considered opinion among scientists.

The third major problem with science courts concerns the role which their decisions might play in the courtroom. Would opposing parties be able to discover the records upon which the court relied and depose the members of the court? What form would the science court's opinion take? Would the science court's opinion decide the case, or act as a rebuttable presumption, or be merely advisory? These difficult questions have not been addressed by science court proponents.

Finally there are the practical issues. Who pays for the cost of the science court? Who recruits its members, and are they paid? Is the science court to do original research or not? Faced with these questions, the science court notion faded quickly in the early 1980s.

The death of the science court concept did not eliminate all interest in science panels. Throughout the 1980s, various science panel hybrids have found niches in regulatory agencies. For example, the Environmental Protection Agency ("EPA") has an independent peer review body entitled the Scientific Advisory Board ("SAB") which reviews critical scientific issues for the agency. The SAB has three duties: 1) to provide scientific advice requested by EPA or the Congressional committees overseeing EPA; 2) to complete annual reviews of the EPA's Office of Research and Development; and 3) to comment on selected regulations.

SAB has an executive committee and several subcommittees. Most members are academics or are recruited from industry and public interest groups. There are published requests for nominations of qualified individuals, and industry public interest groups frequently nominate people. The members spend only 30 days per year working on EPA matters and none receives more than $270 per day in compensation. While one might not agree with its opinions, the SAB has played a major role in at least two scientific controversies. The SAB experience suggests at least that experts are available to serve on science panels, and that these panels can reach a consensus.

Another science panel hybrid, one that is more exciting as a model for a science panel that could be useful to courts faced with a difficult causal issue, is the Agency for Toxic Substances and Disease Registry ("ATSDR"). This agency was created as part of the original Comprehensive Environmental Response Compensation and Liability Act ("CERCLA") in 1980. In late 1986, heavily influenced by the litigation about ground water pollution in Woburn, Massachusetts, Congress passed sweeping changes in CERCLA. These amendments, entitled the Super Fund Amendments and Reauthorization Act ("SARA"), provided ATSDR with much broader duties. Specifically, SARA required ATSDR to prepare toxicological profiles of at least 100 substances, to perform health assessments at all existing National Priority List hazardous waste sites, and to complete epidemiological studies at particular sites if the agency deems it appropriate. The evidence gathered in such health assessments can be used by litigants bringing toxic tort suits.

Soon after passage of SARA, ATSDR began the process of naming priority substances and evaluating their toxicity. The methodology for production of the toxicological profiles was published in the Federal Register in April of 1987. In essence, the Agency is to review all available toxicological and human data, and to produce a document which summarizes this data in nontechnical terms. Scientific peer review of all profiles is built into the system, as is opportunity for public comment. Thus, the ATSDR acts as a science panel with regard to the toxicity of certain common substances.

In the last year, ATSDR has begun to produce the profiles themselves, drafts of which have been circulated to industry and public interest groups. In addition, health assessments of 220 NPL sites have been completed. Disease registries have been completed at several sites, allowing long term surveillance of exposed individuals. Finally the agency made 27 site visits as part of the emergency response program. The agency is unaware of any situations in which agency information has been used in hazardous substance litigation case, but fully expects this to happen in the future. As such, ATSDR will soon begin to play a role as a science panel which provides information for toxic tort litigants. Courts' reactions to such information is difficult to predict.

Another science panel which deserves mention is the Industrial Disease Standard Panel of the Province of Ontario ("Panel"). In 1984, Ontario amended its workers' compensation statute to create an Industrial Disease Standards Panel. The mandate for the Panel is to investigate potential industrial diseases, make findings about the causal connection between disease and exposure, specify criteria for evaluation of claims, and advise compensation boards about eligibility rules. The impetus for the panel was the recognition by Weiler and others that the understanding of industrial diseases, and the resources devoted to compensation for them, were inadequate.

The Panel is made up of nine members appointed by the Ontario Executive. They are to represent the public, the scientific community, and technical and professional persons. The Panel is empowered to appoint specialist panels which conduct work in epidemiology, toxicology and clinical medicine. The Workers' Compensation Board refers issues of concern to the Panel, and the Panel then develops its consensus opinion. After consideration, a final report is issued on the subject, and the information regarding causal connection and eligibility criteria is utilized by the compensation boards.

The Panel has completed reviews concerning the relation of gold mining to stomach and lung cancer, and concerning the carcinogenic potential of PCB's. In these reports, the Panel wrestled with questions regarding the kind of evidence upon which it should rely, and the difficulty of developing eligibility criteria. After referral in each case to a scientific committee, the Panel did manage to develop findings regarding causation and eligibility which are straightforward and readily employed by local boards. The budget for the year in which these two criteria were developed was $526,000.

In summary, the examples of the Ontario Industrial Disease Standards Panel, the Agency for Toxic Substances and Disease Registry and the Scientific Advisory Panel of the Environmental Protection Agency all suggest that the science panel approach is a reasonable way to consider issues of causation and compensation for hazardous substance induced injury. At the very least they show that experts are available to serve, that scientific issues can be delegated to experts in a manner that is not undemocratic and elitist, that an adversarial approach to such problems is not required, and that experts are available to serve on such panels.

The experience of these panels raises many questions concerning the role of science panels in hazardous substance litigation. First, it is unclear how a science panel might be integrated with expanded use of court-appointed experts. Second, the evidentiary role which findings by science panels might play in common law courts is an open question. Third, the efficiency of science panels must be evaluated; one cannot expect a science panel to address all of the causal issues raised by the thousands of hazardous substances which might become the subject of litigation in the next few years.

Notes and Questions

1. In addition to his suggestions relating to expansive application of federal evidence rules, use of special masters and science panels, Professor Brennan concludes his article with a proposal for a "Federal Toxic Substance Board" to monitor ongoing hazardous substance litigation in federal courts and to provide education to federal judges regarding toxicology. He also suggests that such a board could develop policy positions, maintain an expert witness list, and develop science panels for federal courts. *See id.* at 62–71. For a similar list of suggestion for assisting courts and judges in handling scientific issues in litigation, *see also* American Law Institute, *Reporter's Study*, ENTERPRISE RESPONSIBILITY FOR PERSONAL INJURY (1991), Vol. II at 332–351 (alternatives for presentation of scientific evidence to the courts).

2. For other possible suggestions for improving the use of science in the courts, *see generally,* David M. Bernstein, *Out of the Fryeing Pan and Into the Fire: The Expert Witness Problem in Toxic Tort Litigation,* 10 Rev.Litig. 117 (1990); Bert Black, *Evolving Legal Standards for the Admissibility of Scientific Evidence,* 239 Science 1508 (1988); Roy A. Cohen & Jodi F. Mindnich, *Expert Testimony and the Presentation of Scientific Evidence in Toxic Tort and Environmental Hazardous Substance Litigation,* 21 Seton Hall L.Rev. 1009 (1991); Margaret G. Farrell, *Coping With Scientific Evidence: The Use of Special Masters,* 43 Emory L.J. 927 (1994); Michael D. Green, *Expert Witnesses and Sufficiency of Evidence in Toxic Substances Litigation: The Legacy of Agent Orange and Bendectin Litigation,* 86 Nw. U.L.Rev. 643 (1992); Laurel J. Harbour, *Increasing Judicial Scrutiny of Expert Testimony in Toxic Tort Cases,* 30 Washburn L.J. 428 (1991); William V. Nordenberg & Mark A. Nordenberg, *Specially Qualified Juries and Expert Non Jury Tribunals: Alternatives for Coping with the Complexities of Modern Civil Litigation,* 67 Va.L.Rev. 887 (1981); Sheldon L. Trubach, *Informed Judicial Decisionmaking: A Suggestion for a Judicial Office for Understanding Science and Technology,* 10 Colum.J.Envtl.L.255 (1985); Jack B. Weinstein, *Improving Expert Testimony,* 20 Rich.L.Rev. 473 (1986).

3. SCIENTIFIC PROOF: EXPERT WITNESS TESTIMONY

DAUBERT v. MERRELL DOW PHARMACEUTICALS, INC.

Supreme Court of the United States, 1993.
___ U.S. ___, 113 S.Ct. 2786, 125 L.Ed.2d 469.

BLACKMUN, J., delivered the opinion for a unanimous Court with respect to Parts I and II–A, and the opinion of the Court with respect to Parts II–B, II–C, III, and IV, in which WHITE, O'CONNOR, SCALIA, KENNEDY, SOUTER, AND THOMAS, JJ., joined. REHNQUIST, C.J., filed an opinion concurring in part and dissenting in part, in which STEVENS, J., joined.

JUSTICE BLACKMUN delivered the opinion of the Court.

In this case we are called upon to determine the standard for admitting expert scientific testimony in a federal trial.

I

Petitioners Jason Daubert and Eric Schuller are minor children born with serious birth defects. They and their parents sued respondent in California state court, alleging that the birth defects had been caused by the mothers' ingestion of Bendectin, a prescription anti-nausea drug marketed by respondent. Respondent removed the suits to federal court on diversity grounds.

After extensive discovery, respondent moved for summary judgment, contending that Bendectin does not cause birth defects in humans and that petitioners would be unable to come forward with any admissible evidence that it does. In support of its motion, respondent submitted an affidavit of Steven H. Lamm, physician and epidemiologist, who is a well-credentialed expert on the risks from exposure to various chemical substances.[1] Doctor Lamm stated that he had reviewed all the literature on Bendectin and human birth defects—more than 30 published studies involving over 130,000 patients. No study had found Bendectin to be a human teratogen (i.e., a substance capable of causing malformations in fetuses). On the basis of this review, Doctor Lamm concluded that maternal use of Bendectin during the first trimester of pregnancy has not been shown to be a risk factor for human birth defects.

Petitioners did not (and do not) contest this characterization of the published record regarding Bendectin. Instead, they responded to respondent's motion with the testimony of eight experts of their own, each of whom also possessed impressive credentials.[2] These experts had

---

1. Doctor Lamm received his master's and doctor of medicine degrees from the University of Southern California. He has served as a consultant in birth-defect epidemiology for the National Center for Health Statistics and has published numerous articles on the magnitude of risk from exposure to various chemical and biological substances.

2. For example, Shanna Helen Swan, who received a master's degree in biostatics from Columbia University and a doctorate in statistics from the University of California at Berkeley, is chief of the section of the California Department of Health and Services that determines causes of birth defects, and has served as a consultant to the World Health Organization, the Food and

concluded that Bendectin can cause birth defects. Their conclusions were based upon *"in vitro"* (test tube) and *"in vivo"* (live) animal studies that found a link between Bendectin and malformations; pharmacological studies of the chemical structure of Bendectin that purported to show similarities between the structure of the drug and that of other substances known to cause birth defects; and the "reanalysis" of previously published epidemiological (human statistical) studies.

The District Court granted respondent's motion for summary judgment. The court stated that scientific evidence is admissible only if the principle upon which it is based is " 'sufficiently established to have general acceptance in the field to which it belongs.' " 727 F.Supp. 570, 572 (S.D.Cal.1989), quoting United States v. Kilgus, 571 F.2d 508, 510 (9th Cir.1978). The court concluded that petitioners' evidence did not meet this standard. Given the vast body of epidemiological data concerning Bendectin, the court held, expert opinion which is not based on epidemiological evidence is not admissible to establish causation. * * * Thus, the animal-cell studies, live-animal studies, and chemical-structure analyses on which petitioners had relied could not raise by themselves a reasonably disputable jury issue regarding causation. * * * Petitioners' epidemiological analyses, based as they were on recalculations of data in previously published studies that had found no causal link between the drug and birth defects, were ruled to be inadmissible because they had not been published or subjected to peer review. * * *

The United States Court of Appeals for the Ninth Circuit affirmed. 951 F.2d 1128 (1991). Citing Frye v. United States, 54 App. D.C. 46, 47, 293 F. 1013, 1014 (1923), the court stated that expert opinion based on a scientific technique is inadmissible unless the technique is "generally accepted" as reliable in the relevant scientific community. * * * The court declared that expert opinion based on a methodology that diverges "significantly from the procedures accepted by recognized authorities in the field * * * cannot be shown to be 'generally accepted as a reliable technique.' " * * *

The court emphasized that other Courts of Appeals considering the risks of Bendectin had refused to admit reanalyses of epidemiological studies that had been neither published nor subjected to peer review. * * * Those courts had found unpublished reanalyses "particularly problematic in light of the massive weight of the original published studies supporting [respondent's] position, all of which had undergone full scrutiny from the scientific community." * * * Contending that reanalysis is generally accepted by the scientific community only when it is subjected to verification and scrutiny by others in the field, the Court of Appeals rejected petitioners' reanalyses as "unpublished, not subjected to the normal peer review process and generated solely for use in

Drug Administration, and the National Institutes of Health. * * * Stewart A. Newman, who received his master's and a doctorate in chemistry from Columbia University and the University of Chicago, respectively, is a professor at New York Medical College and has spent over a decade studying the effect of chemicals on limb development. * * * The credentials of the others are similarly impressive. * * *

litigation." * * * The court concluded that petitioners' evidence provided an insufficient foundation to allow admission of expert testimony that Bendectin caused their injuries and, accordingly, that petitioners could not satisfy their burden of proving causation at trial.

We granted certiorari, * * *, in light of sharp divisions among the courts regarding the proper standard for the admission of expert testimony. *Compare, e.g.,* United States v. Shorter, 257 U.S.App.D.C. 358, 363–364, 809 F.2d 54, 59–60 (applying the "general acceptance" standard), *cert. denied,* 484 U.S. 817, 108 S.Ct. 71, 98 L.Ed.2d 35 (1987), with DeLuca v. Merrell Dow Pharmaceuticals, Inc., 911 F.2d 941, 955 (3d Cir.1990)(rejecting the "general acceptance" standard).

II

A

In the 70 years since its formulation in the *Frye* case, the "general acceptance" test has been the dominant standard for determining the admissibility of novel scientific evidence at trial. *See* E. Green & C. Nesson, PROBLEMS, CASES, AND MATERIALS ON EVIDENCE 649 (1983). Although under increasing attack of late, the rule continues to be followed by a majority of courts, including the Ninth Circuit.[3]

The *Frye* test has its origin in a short and citation-free 1923 decision concerning the admissibility of evidence derived from a systolic blood pressure deception test, a crude precursor to the polygraph machine. In what has become a famous (perhaps infamous) passage, the then Court of Appeals for the District of Columbia described the device and its operation and declared: "Just when a scientific principle or discovery crosses the line between the experimental and demonstrable stages is difficult to define. Somewhere in this twilight zone the evidential force of the principle must be recognized, and while courts will go a long way in admitting expert testimony deduced from a well-recognized scientific principle or discovery, the thing from which the deduction is made must be sufficiently established to have gained general acceptance in the particular field in which it belongs." * * * Because the deception test had "not yet gained such standing and scientific recognition among physiological and psychological authorities as would justify the courts in admitting expert testimony deduced from the discovery, development, and experiments thus far made," evidence of its results was ruled inadmissible. * * *

The merits of the *Frye* test have been much debated, and scholarship on its proper scope and application is legion.[4] Petitioners' primary

---

3. For a catalogue of the many cases on either side of this controversy, *see* P. Gianelli & E. Imwinkelried, SCIENTIFIC EVIDENCE § 1–5, pp. 10–14 (1986 & Supp.1991).

4. *See, e.g.,* Green, *Expert Witnesses and Sufficiency of Evidence in Toxic Substances Litigation: The Legacy of Agent Orange and Bendectin Litigation,* 86 Nw.U.L.Rev. 643 (1992)(hereinafter Green); Becker & Orenstein, *The Federal Rules of Evidence After Sixteen Years—the Effect of "Plain Meaning" Jurisprudence, the Need for an Advisory Committee on the Rules of Evidence, and Suggestions for Selective Revision of the Rules,* 60 Geo. Wash. L.Rev. 857, 876–885 (1992); Hanson, *"James Alphonso*

attack, however, is not on the content but on the continuing authority of the rule. They contend that the *Frye* test was superseded by the adoption of the Federal Rules of Evidence.[5] We agree.

We interpret the legislatively-enacted Federal Rules of Evidence as we would any statute. Beech Aircraft Corp. v. Rainey, 488 U.S. 153, 163, 109 S.Ct. 439, 446, 102 L.Ed.2d 445 (1988). Rule 402 provides the baseline: "All relevant evidence is admissible, except as otherwise provided by the Constitution of the United States, by Act of Congress, by these rules, or by other rules prescribed by the Supreme Court pursuant to statutory authority. Evidence which is not relevant is not admissible." "Relevant evidence" is defined as that which has "any tendency to make the existence of any fact that is of consequence to the determination of the action more probable or less probable than it would be without the evidence." Rule 401. The Rule's basic standard of relevance thus is a liberal one.

Frye, of course, predated the Rules by half a century. In United States v. Abel, 469 U.S. 45, 105 S.Ct. 465, 83 L.Ed.2d 450 (1984), we considered the pertinence of background common law in interpreting the Rules of Evidence. We noted that the Rules occupy the field, * * *, but, quoting Professor Cleary, the Reporter, explained that the common law nevertheless could serve as an aid to their application: "In principle, under the Federal Rules no common law of evidence remains. 'All relevant evidence is admissible, except as otherwise provided....'" In reality, of course, the body of common law knowledge continues to exist, though in the somewhat altered form of a source of guidance in the exercise of delegated powers." * * * We found the common-law precept at issue in the *Abel* case entirely consistent with Rule 402's general requirement of admissibility, and considered it unlikely that the drafters had intended to change the rule. * * * In Bourjaily v. United States, 483 U.S. 171, 107 S.Ct. 2775, 97 L.Ed.2d 144 (1987), on the other hand,

---

Frye is Sixty–Five Years Old; Should He Retire?," 16 W.St.U.L.Rev. 357 (1989); Black, *A Unified Theory of Scientific Evidence,* 56 Ford.L.Rev. 595 (1988); Imwinkelried, *The "Bases" of Expert Testimony: The Syllogistic Structure of Scientific Testimony,* 67 N.C.L.Rev. 1 (1988); *Proposals for a Model Rule on the Admissibility of Scientific Evidence,* 26 Jurimetrics J. 235 (1986); Gianelli, T*he Admissibility of Novel Scientific Evidence:* Frye v. United States, *A Half–Century Later,* 80 Colum.L.Rev. 1197 (1980); *The Supreme Court, 1986 Term,* 101 Harv.L.Rev. 7, 119, 125–127 (1987). Indeed, the debates over *Frye* are such a well-established part of the academic landscape that a distinct term—*"Frye*-ologist"—has been advanced to describe those who take part. *See* Behringer, *Introduction, Proposals for a Model Rule on the Admissibility of Scientific Evidence,* 26 Jurimetrics J., at 239, *quoting* Lacey, *Scientific Evidence,* 24 Jurimetrics J. 254, 264 (1984).

5. Like the question of *Frye* 's merit, the dispute over its survival has divided courts and commentators. *Compare, e.g.,* United States v. Williams, 583 F.2d 1194 (2d Cir. 1978), *cert. denied,* 439 U.S. 1117, 99 S.Ct. 1025, 59 L.Ed.2d 77 (1979)(*Frye* is superseded by the Rules of Evidence), *with* Christophersen v. Allied–Signal Corp., 939 F.2d 1106, 1111, 1115–1116 (5th Cir.1991)(*en banc*)(*Frye* and the Rules coexist), *cert. denied,*503 U.S. 912, 112 S.Ct. 1280, 117 L.Ed.2d 506 (1992), 3 J. Weinstein & M. Berger, WEINSTEIN'S EVIDENCE ¶ 702[03], pp. 702–36 to 702–37 (1988)(hereinafter Weinstein & Berger)(*Frye* is dead), and M. Graham, HANDBOOK OF FEDERAL EVIDENCE § 703.2 (2d ed.1991)(*Frye* lives). *See generally* P. Gianelli & E. Imwinkelried, SCIENTIFIC EVIDENCE § 1–5, pp. 28–29 (1986 & Supp.1991)(citing authorities).

the Court was unable to find a particular common-law doctrine in the Rules, and so held it superseded.

Here there is a specific Rule that speaks to the contested issue. Rule 702, governing expert testimony, provides: "If scientific, technical, or other specialized knowledge will assist the trier of fact to understand the evidence or to determine a fact in issue, a witness qualified as an expert by knowledge, skill, experience, training, or education, may testify thereto in the form of an opinion or otherwise." Nothing in the text of this Rule establishes "general acceptance" as an absolute prerequisite to admissibility. Nor does respondent present any clear indication that Rule 702 or the Rules as a whole were intended to incorporate a "general acceptance" standard. The drafting history makes no mention of *Frye,* and a rigid "general acceptance" requirement would be at odds with the "liberal thrust" of the Federal Rules and their "general approach of relaxing the traditional barriers to 'opinion' testimony." *Beech Aircraft Corp. v. Rainey*, 488 U.S. at 169 (*citing* Rules 701 to 705). *See also* Weinstein, *Rule 702 of the Federal Rules of Evidence is Sound; It Should Not Be Amended,* 138 F.R.D. 631, 631 (1991)("The Rules were designed to depend primarily upon lawyer-adversaries and sensible triers of fact to evaluate conflicts"). Given the Rules' permissive backdrop and their inclusion of a specific rule on expert testimony that does not mention "general acceptance," the assertion that the Rules somehow assimilated *Frye* is unconvincing. *Frye* made "general acceptance" the exclusive test for admitting expert scientific testimony. That austere standard, absent from and incompatible with the Federal Rules of Evidence, should not be applied in federal trials.

B

That the *Frye* test was displaced by the Rules of Evidence does not mean, however, that the Rules themselves place no limits on the admissibility of purportedly scientific evidence.[7] Nor is the trial judge disabled from screening such evidence. To the contrary, under the Rules the trial judge must ensure that any and all scientific testimony or evidence admitted is not only relevant, but reliable.

The primary locus of this obligation is Rule 702, which clearly contemplates some degree of regulation of the subjects and theories about which an expert may testify. "If scientific, technical, or other specialized knowledge will assist the trier of fact to understand the evidence or to determine a fact in issue" an expert "may testify thereto." The subject of an expert's testimony must be "scientific ... knowledge." The adjective "scientific" implies a grounding in the methods and procedures of science. Similarly, the word "knowledge" connotes more than subjective belief or unsupported speculation. The term "applies to any body of known facts or to any body of ideas inferred from such facts or accepted as truths on good grounds." Webster's

---

7. The Chief Justice "do[es] not doubt that Rule 702 confides to the judge some gatekeeping responsibility," * * *, but would neither say how it does so, nor explain what that role.

THIRD NEW INTERNATIONAL DICTIONARY 1252 (1986). Of course, it would be unreasonable to conclude that the subject of scientific testimony must be "known" to a certainty; arguably, there are no certainties in science. *See, e.g.,* Brief for Nicolaas Bloembergen *et al.* as Amici Curiae 9 ("Indeed, scientists do not assert that they know what is immutably 'true'—they are committed to searching for new, temporary theories to explain, as best they can, phenomena"); Brief for American Association for the Advancement of Science and the National Academy of Sciences as Amici Curiae 7–8 ("Science is not an encyclopedic body of knowledge about the universe. Instead, it represents a process for proposing and refining theoretical explanations about the world that are subject to further testing and refinement."). * * * But, in order to qualify as "scientific knowledge," an inference or assertion must be derived by the scientific method. Proposed testimony must be supported by appropriate validation—i.e., "good grounds," based on what is known. In short, the requirement that an expert's testimony pertain to "scientific knowledge" establishes a standard of evidentiary reliability.[9]

Rule 702 further requires that the evidence or testimony "assist the trier of fact to understand the evidence or to determine a fact in issue." This condition goes primarily to relevance. "Expert testimony which does not relate to any issue in the case is not relevant and, ergo, non-helpful." 3 Weinstein & Berger ¶ 702[02], p. 702–18. *See also* United States v. Downing, 753 F.2d 1224, 1242 (3d Cir.1985)("An additional consideration under Rule 702—and another aspect of relevancy—is whether expert testimony proffered in the case is sufficiently tied to the facts of the case that it will aid the jury in resolving a factual dispute"). The consideration has been aptly described by Judge Becker as one of "fit." * * * "Fit" is not always obvious, and scientific validity for one purpose is not necessarily scientific validity for other, unrelated purposes. *See* Starrs, Frye v. United States *Restructured and Revitalized: A Proposal to Amend Federal Evidence Rule 702,* and 26 Jurimetrics J. 249, 258 (1986). The study of the phases of the moon, for example, may provide valid scientific "knowledge" about whether a certain night was dark, and if darkness is a fact in issue, the knowledge will assist the trier of fact. However (absent creditable grounds supporting such a link),

---

9. We note that scientists typically distinguish between "validity" (does the principle support what it purports to show?) and "reliability" (does application of the principle produce consistent results?). *See* Black, *A Unified Theory of Scientific Evidence,* 56 Ford.L.Rev. 595, 599 (1988). Although "the difference between accuracy, validity, and reliability may be such that each is distinct from the other by no more than a hen's kick," Starrs, Frye v. United States *Restructured and Revitalized: A Proposal to Amend Federal Evidence Rule 702,* 26 Jurimetrics J. 249, 256 (1986), our reference here is to evidentiary reliability—that is, trustworthiness. *Cf., e.g.,* Advisory Committee's Notes on Fed.R.Evid. 602 (" '[T]he rule requiring that a witness who testifies to a fact which can be perceived by the senses must have had an opportunity to observe, and must have actually observed the fact' is a 'most pervasive manifestation' of the common law insistence upon 'the most reliable sources of information.' " (citation omitted)); Advisory Committee's Notes on Art. VIII of the Rules of Evidence (hearsay exceptions will be recognized only "under circumstances supposed to furnish guarantees of trustworthiness"). In a case involving scientific evidence, evidentiary reliability will be based upon scientific validity.

evidence that the moon was full on a certain night will not assist the trier of fact in determining whether an individual was unusually likely to have behaved irrationally on that night. Rule 702's "helpfulness" standard requires a valid scientific connection to the pertinent inquiry as a precondition to admissibility.

That these requirements are embodied in Rule 702 is not surprising. Unlike an ordinary witness, see Rule 701, an expert is permitted wide latitude to offer opinions, including those that are not based on first-hand knowledge or observation. See Rules 702 and 703. Presumably, this relaxation of the usual requirement of first-hand knowledge—a rule which represents "a 'most pervasive manifestation' of the common law insistence upon 'the most reliable sources of information,' " Advisory Committee's Notes on Fed.R.Evid. 602 * * *—is premised on an assumption that the expert's opinion will have a reliable basis in the knowledge and experience of his discipline.

C

Faced with a proffer of expert scientific testimony, then, the trial judge must determine at the outset, pursuant to Rule 104(a),[10] whether the expert is proposing to testify to (1) scientific knowledge that (2) will assist the trier of fact to understand or determine a fact in issue.[11] This entails a preliminary assessment of whether the reasoning or methodology underlying the testimony is scientifically valid and of whether that reasoning or methodology properly can be applied to the facts in issue. We are confident that federal judges possess the capacity to undertake this review. Many factors will bear on the inquiry, and we do not presume to set out a definitive checklist or test. But some general observations are appropriate.

Ordinarily, a key question to be answered in determining whether a theory or technique is scientific knowledge that will assist the trier of fact will be whether it can be (and has been) tested. "Scientific methodology today is based on generating hypotheses and testing them to see if they can be falsified; indeed, this methodology is what distinguishes science from other fields of human inquiry." Green, at 645. *See also* C. Hempel, PHILOSOPHY OF NATURAL SCIENCE 49 (1966)("[T]he statements constituting a scientific explanation must be capable of empirical test"); K. Popper, CONJECTURES AND REFUTATIONS: THE GROWTH

10. Rule 104(a) provides: "Preliminary questions concerning the qualification of a person to be a witness, the existence of a privilege, or the admissibility of evidence shall be determined by the court, subject to the provisions of subdivision (b) [pertaining to conditional admissions]. In making its determination it is not bound by the rules of evidence except those with respect to privileges." These matters should be established by a preponderance of proof. * * *

11. Although the *Frye* decision itself focused exclusively on "novel" scientific techniques, we do not read the requirements of Rule 702 to apply specially or exclusively to unconventional evidence. Of course, well-established propositions are less likely to be challenged than those that are novel, and they are more handily defended. Indeed, theories that are so firmly established as to have attained the status of scientific law, such as the laws of thermodynamics, properly are subject to judicial notice under Fed.R.Evid. 201

OF SCIENTIFIC KNOWLEDGE 37 (5th ed.1989)("[T]he criterion of the scientific status of a theory is its falsifiability, or refutability, or testability").

Another pertinent consideration is whether the theory or technique has been subjected to peer review and publication. Publication (which is but one element of peer review) is not a *sine qua non* of admissibility; it does not necessarily correlate with reliability, *see* S. Jasanoff, THE FIFTH BRANCH: SCIENCE ADVISORS AS POLICYMAKERS 61–76 (1990), and in some instances well-grounded but innovative theories will not have been published, *see* Horrobin, *The Philosophical Basis of Peer Review and the Suppression of Innovation,* 263 J.Am.Med.Assn. 1438 (1990). Some propositions, moreover, are too particular, too new, or of too limited interest to be published. But submission to the scrutiny of the scientific community is a component of "good science," in part because it increases the likelihood that substantive flaws in methodology will be detected. *See* J. Ziman, RELIABLE KNOWLEDGE: AN EXPLORATION OF THE GROUNDS FOR BELIEF IN SCIENCE 130–133 (1978); Relman and Angell, *How Good Is Peer Review?,* 321 New Eng.J.Med. 827 (1989). The fact of publication (or lack thereof) in a peer-reviewed journal thus will be a relevant, though not dispositive, consideration in assessing the scientific validity of a particular technique or methodology on which an opinion is premised.

Additionally, in the case of a particular scientific technique, the court ordinarily should consider the known or potential rate of error, *see, e.g.,* United States v. Smith, 869 F.2d 348, 353–354 (7th Cir.1989)(surveying studies of the error rate of spectrographic voice identification technique), and the existence and maintenance of standards controlling the technique's operation. See United States v. Williams, 583 F.2d 1194, 1198 (2d Cir.1978)(noting professional organization's standard governing spectrographic analysis), *cert. denied,* 439 U.S. 1117, 99 S.Ct. 1025, 59 L.Ed.2d 77 (1979).

Finally, "general acceptance" can yet have a bearing on the inquiry. A "reliability assessment does not require, although it does permit, explicit identification of a relevant scientific community and an express determination of a particular degree of acceptance within that community." United States v. Downing, 753 F.2d, at 1238. *See also* 3 Weinstein & Berger ¶ 702[03], pp. 702–41 to 702–42. Widespread acceptance can be an important factor in ruling particular evidence admissible, and "a known technique that has been able to attract only minimal support within the community," *Downing, supra,* at 1238, may properly be viewed with skepticism.

The inquiry envisioned by Rule 702 is, we emphasize, a flexible one.[12] Its overarching subject is the scientific validity—and thus the

---

12. A number of authorities have presented variations on the reliability approach, each with its own slightly different set of factors. *See, e.g., Downing,* 753 F.2d at 1238–1239 (on which our discussion draws in part); 3 Weinstein & Berger ¶ 702[03], pp. 702–41 to 702–42 (on which the *Downing* court in turn partially relied); McCormick, *Scientific Evidence: Defining a New Approach to Admissibility,* 67 Iowa L.Rev. 879, 911–912 (1982); and *Symposium on Science and the Rules of Evidence,* 99 F.R.D. 187, 231 (1983)(statement by Margaret Berger). To the extent that they

evidentiary relevance and reliability—of the principles that underlie a proposed submission. The focus, of course, must be solely on principles and methodology, not on the conclusions that they generate.

Throughout, a judge assessing a proffer of expert scientific testimony under Rule 702 should also be mindful of other applicable rules. Rule 703 provides that expert opinions based on otherwise inadmissible hearsay are to be admitted only if the facts or data are "of a type reasonably relied upon by experts in the particular field in forming opinions or inferences upon the subject." Rule 706 allows the court at its discretion to procure the assistance of an expert of its own choosing. Finally, Rule 403 permits the exclusion of relevant evidence "if its probative value is substantially outweighed by the danger of unfair prejudice, confusion of the issues, or misleading the jury...." Judge Weinstein has explained: "Expert evidence can be both powerful and quite misleading because of the difficulty in evaluating it. Because of this risk, the judge in weighing possible prejudice against probative force under Rule 403 of the present rules exercises more control over experts than over lay witnesses." Weinstein, 138 F.R.D., at 632.

* * *

IV

To summarize: "general acceptance" is not a necessary precondition to the admissibility of scientific evidence under the Federal Rules of Evidence, but the Rules of Evidence—especially Rule 702—do assign to the trial judge the task of ensuring that an expert's testimony both rests on a reliable foundation and is relevant to the task at hand. Pertinent evidence based on scientifically valid principles will satisfy those demands.

The inquiries of the District Court and the Court of Appeals focused almost exclusively on "general acceptance," as gauged by publication and the decisions of other courts. Accordingly, the judgment of the Court of Appeals is vacated and the case is remanded for further proceedings consistent with this opinion.

It is so ordered.

CHIEF JUSTICE REHNQUIST, with whom JUSTICE STEVENS joins, concurring in part and dissenting in part.

The petition for certiorari in this case presents two questions: first, whether the rule of *Frye* v. United States, * * *, remains good law after the enactment of the Federal Rules of Evidence; and second, if *Frye* remains valid, whether it requires expert scientific testimony to have been subjected to a peer-review process in order to be admissible. The Court concludes, correctly in my view, that the *Frye* rule did not survive the enactment of the Federal Rules of Evidence, and I therefore join

focus on the reliability of evidence as ensured by the scientific validity of its underlying principles, all these versions may well have merit, although we express no opinion regarding any of their particular details.

Parts I and II–A of its opinion. The second question presented in the petition for certiorari necessarily is mooted by this holding, but the Court nonetheless proceeds to construe Rules 702 and 703 very much in the abstract, and then offers some "general observations." * * *

"General observations" by this Court customarily carry great weight with lower federal courts, but the ones offered here suffer from the flaw common to most such observations—they are not applied to deciding whether or not particular testimony was or was not admissible, and therefore they tend to be not only general, but vague and abstract. This is particularly unfortunate in a case such as this, where the ultimate legal question depends on an appreciation of one or more bodies of knowledge not judicially noticeable, and subject to different interpretations in the briefs of the parties and their *amici*. Twenty-two amicus briefs have been filed in the case, and indeed the Court's opinion contains no less than 37 citations to amicus briefs and other secondary sources.

The various briefs filed in this case are markedly different from typical briefs, in that large parts of them do not deal with decided cases or statutory language—the sort of material we customarily interpret. Instead, they deal with definitions of scientific knowledge, scientific method, scientific validity, and peer review—in short, matters far afield from the expertise of judges. This is not to say that such materials are not useful or even necessary in deciding how Rule 703 should be applied; but it is to say that the unusual subject matter should cause us to proceed with great caution in deciding more than we have to, because our reach can so easily exceed our grasp.

But even if it were desirable to make "general observations" not necessary to decide the questions presented, I cannot subscribe to some of the observations made by the Court. In Part II–B, the Court concludes that reliability and relevancy are the touchstones of the admissibility of expert testimony. * * * Federal Rule of Evidence 402 provides, as the Court points out, that "[e]vidence which is not relevant is not admissible." But there is no similar reference in the Rule to "reliability." The Court constructs its argument by parsing the language "[i]f scientific, technical, or other specialized knowledge will assist the trier of fact to understand the evidence or to determine a fact in issue ... an expert ... may testify thereto...." Fed.R.Evid. 702. It stresses that the subject of the expert's testimony must be "scientific ... knowledge," and points out that "scientific" "implies a grounding in the methods and procedures of science," and that the word "knowledge" "connotes more than subjective belief or unsupported speculation." * * * From this it concludes that "scientific knowledge" must be "derived by the scientific method." * * * Proposed testimony, we are told, must be supported by "appropriate validation." * * * Indeed, in footnote 9, the Court decides that "[i]n a case involving scientific evidence, evidentiary reliability will be based upon scientific validity." * * *

Questions arise simply from reading this part of the Court's opinion, and countless more questions will surely arise when hundreds of district judges try to apply its teaching to particular offers of expert testimony. Does all of this dicta apply to an expert seeking to testify on the basis of "technical or other specialized knowledge"—the other types of expert knowledge to which Rule 702 applies—or are the "general observations" limited only to "scientific knowledge"? What is the difference between scientific knowledge and technical knowledge; does Rule 702 actually contemplate that the phrase "scientific, technical, or other specialized knowledge" be broken down into numerous subspecies of expertise, or did its authors simply pick general descriptive language covering the sort of expert testimony which courts have customarily received? The Court speaks of its confidence that federal judges can make a "preliminary assessment of whether the reasoning or methodology underlying the testimony is scientifically valid and of whether that reasoning or methodology properly can be applied to the facts in issue." * * * The Court then states that a "key question" to be answered in deciding whether something is "scientific knowledge" "will be whether it can be (and has been) tested." * * * Following this sentence are three quotations from treatises, which speak not only of empirical testing, but one of which states that "the criterion of the scientific status of a theory is its falsifiability, or refutability, or testability[.]" * * *

I defer to no one in my confidence in federal judges; but I am at a loss to know what is meant when it is said that the scientific status of a theory depends on its "falsifiability," and I suspect some of them will be, too.

I do not doubt that Rule 702 confides to the judge some gatekeeping responsibility in deciding questions of the admissibility of proffered expert testimony. But I do not think it imposes on them either the obligation or the authority to become amateur scientists in order to perform that role. I think the Court would be far better advised in this case to decide only the questions presented, and to leave the further development of this important area of the law to future cases.

Notes and Questions

1. To what extent did the Court in *Daubert* "bury" the *Frye* rule? What now is the test or standard for scientific expert-witness testimony in federal court? How are federal judges to function in their gatekeeper role? Has *Daubert* eliminated problems relating to scientific expert witness testimony, or created newer, even more complicated ones? *See generally* Stanley Pierce, et al., *Expert Testimony in Technically Complex Litigation*, 40 Def. L.J. 697 (1991). Is Justice Rehnquist correct in his insight that the Court would have been better off by not describing the judicial gatekeeper role?

2. Federal courts are just beginning to grapple with the meaning and significance of *Daubert* for scientific expert witness testimony in both traditional and mass tort litigation. *See Standards and Procedures for Determining the Admissibility of Expert Evidence After* Daubert, 157 F.R.D. 571 (1994). The commentary generated by the *Daubert* decision has been

massive; for a partial selection of the literature, *see generally*, Margaret A. Berger, *Procedural Paradigms for Applying the* Daubert *Test,* 78 Minn. L.Rev. 1345 (1994); Bert Black, *et al., Science and the Law in the Wake of* Daubert: *A New Search for Scientific Knowledge,* 72 Tex.L.Rev. 715 (1994); Robert G. Blomquist, *The Dangers of "General Observations" on Expert Scientific Testimony: A Comment on* Daubert v. Merrell Dow Pharmaceuticals, Inc., 82 Ky.L.J. 703 (1993–94); Joe S. Cecil and Thomas E. Willging, *Accepting* Daubert*'s Invitation: Defining a Role for Court–Appointed Experts in Assessing Scientific Validity,* 43 Emory L.J. 995 (1994); Rochelle C. Dreyfuss, *Is Science a Special Case? The Admissibility of Scientific Evidence After Daubert v. Merrell Dow,* 73 Texas L. Rev. 1779 (1995); Michael H. Gottesman, *Admissibility of Expert Testimony After* Daubert: *The "Prestige" Factor,* 43 Emory L.J. 867 (1994); Thomas W. Henderson, Daubert *Unlikely to Change Court's Treatment of Expert Evidence,* 8 Toxics L. Rep. (BNA) 33 (Summer/Fall 1993); Jean Macchiaroli, *Causation and Scientific Evidence After* Daubert, 55 U.Pitt.L.Rev. 889 (1994); Paul S. Milich, *Controversial Science in the Courtroom:* Daubert *and the Law's Hubris,* 43 Emory L.J. 913 (1994); Nancy A. Miller, Daubert *and Junk Science: Have Admissibility Standards Changed?,* 61 Def.Couns.J. 501 (1994); Susan R. Poulter, Daubert *and Scientific Evidence: Assessing Evidentiary Reliability in Toxic Tort Litigation,* 1993 Utah L. Rev. 1307 (1993); Joseph Sanders, *Validity, Admissibility, and Mass Torts After* Daubert, 78 Minn.L.Rev. 1387 (1994); Andrew E. Taslitz, Daubert *'s Guide to the Federal Rules of Evidence: A Not–So–Plain Meaning Jurisprudence,* 32 Harv.J.Legis. 3 (1995).

Chapter VI

MASS TORTS AND AFFIRMATIVE DEFENSES

A. STATUTE OF LIMITATIONS PROBLEMS

BESSER v. E.R. SQUIBB & SONS

New York Supreme Court, 1989.
146 A.D.2d 107, 539 N.Y.S.2d 734, *affirmed* 75 N.Y.2d
847, 552 N.Y.S.2d 923, 552 N.E.2d 171 (1990).

Before KUPFERMAN, J.P., and SULLIVAN, ASCH and WALLACH, JJ.

SULLIVAN, JUSTICE.

This appeal from the dismissal of a complaint on the ground that the action, commenced pursuant to the "revival statute", was barred by the "borrowing statute" involves the interplay between the latter (CPLR 202)[1] and the 1986 statute which revived causes of action arising out of exposure to diethylstilbestrol (DES) and other toxic substances, even if such causes had been previously dismissed as time-barred.[2] Since her action is time-barred if the borrowing statute controls, plaintiff argues that, inasmuch as the revival statute begins with the words "[n]otwithstanding any other provision of law," the borrowing statute is to be disregarded in revival statute actions. The motion court rejected this argument and granted defendants' motion for summary judgment.

Plaintiff's construction of the revival statute does not comport with the Legislature's intent to provide to New York residents only—not the entire world—a one-year window period in which to sue for claims otherwise barred by law. Plaintiff was a resident of Pennsylvania at the time her cause of action accrued, a resident of New Jersey at the time her injury manifested itself, and a resident of Virginia at the time she first commenced a lawsuit for *in utero* exposure to DES. Despite the

---

1. CPLR 202 provides: An action based upon a cause of action accruing without the state cannot be commenced after the expiration of the time limited by the laws of either the state or the place without the state where the cause of action accrued, except that where the cause of action ac- crued in favor of a resident of the state the time limited by the laws of the state shall apply.

2. In Hymowitz v. Eli Lilly & Co., 139 A.D.2d 437, 526 N.Y.S.2d 922, this court upheld the revival statute in the face of a constitutional challenge. * * *

absence of any nexus to New York, she contends that this action, and many others which similarly have no connection to the state, can be maintained in this jurisdiction. We believe that such a result is contrary to logic and foreclosed by the legislative history and policy underlying the revival statute. Accordingly, we affirm.

Plaintiff, who was born in Philadelphia, was allegedly exposed, *in utero*, to DES during her gestation. Thus, any such exposure occurred wholly in Pennsylvania. In September 1975, while she was a resident of New Jersey and attending college in Massachusetts, plaintiff became ill and was diagnosed as having clear cell adenocarcinoma of the cervix, a condition allegedly caused by the exposure to DES. She thereafter underwent treatment in New Jersey and Pennsylvania. After graduating from college in 1977, plaintiff returned to her home in New Jersey. Since that time, she has resided in Illinois, Virginia and Massachusetts, but now apparently resides in New York.

On December 29, 1980, plaintiff commenced an action solely against E.R. Squibb & Sons, Inc. to recover for her alleged exposure to DES. At the time, she was a resident of Virginia, and had never lived in New York. That action was dismissed on July 27, 1982 because the court found that under the then applicable three-year statute of limitations, plaintiff's cause of action accrued at the time of her "last exposure" to DES, and that, even allowing for a toll of the limitation period until she reached majority, she had commenced her action more than three years after she attained her majority on September 1, 1974.

In 1986, as part of a tort reform package, the Legislature enacted the Toxic Tort Revival Statute (L.1986, ch. 682, § 4), which provides:

> Notwithstanding any other provision of law, * * * every action for personal injury, injury to property or death caused by the latent effects of exposure to diethylstilbestrol, tungsten-carbide, asbestos, chlordane or polyvinyl-chloride upon or within the body or upon or within property which is barred as of the effective date of this act or which was dismissed prior to the effective date of this act solely because the applicable period of limitations has or had expired is hereby revived and an action thereon may be commenced provided such action is commenced within one year from the effective date of this act. * * *

Although the 1986 legislation made significant changes in the rules governing the conduct of personal injury suits, its focus was on the elimination of New York's "last exposure" rule and the adoption of a "discovery" statute of limitations. (L.1986, ch. 682 § 2, adding CPLR 214–c). The new statute of limitations provides that a personal injury claim arising out of the "latent effects of exposure to any substance or combination of substances" accrues on the earlier of "the date of discovery of the injury by the plaintiff or from the date when through the exercise of reasonable diligence the injury should have been discovered...." (CPLR 214–c.) Henceforth, an injured party is permitted to assert a cause of action within three years from the date of discovery of the injury, regardless of the time of exposure. In addition, in an effort to eliminate the unfairness of the state's last exposure rule, the revival statute provided a one-year window period to sue for persons who were or would have been barred by operation of the preexisting last exposure rule.

Commenced on August 6, 1986, this action was also brought initially only against Squibb. In addition to a general denial, Squibb's answer asserted as affirmative defenses the bar of the applicable statute of limitations and the unconstitutionality of the revival statute. When plaintiff moved to dismiss these affirmative defenses, Squibb cross-moved for summary judgment on the ground, inter alia, that the action was barred by the statute of limitations. While the motion was pending, plaintiff commenced similar actions against The Upjohn Company and Eli Lilly & Company.

Squibb argued, and plaintiff did not contest, that where a cause of action accrues outside New York in favor of a nonresident, the borrowing statute requires that the foreign statute of limitations apply if it is shorter than the applicable New York limitation period * * *; that plaintiff's injuries accrued in 1955 in Pennsylvania;[3] and that, as a result, she must satisfy the Pennsylvania limitation rule, which, as long as the revival statute is upheld as constitutional, is shorter than the New York period. In response, plaintiff's sole contention was, as it is on appeal, that since the revival statute commences with the words "[n]otwithstanding any other provision of law . . . ," the borrowing statute was intended to be excluded from any application to revived claims.

Finding that exposure to the drug occurred in Pennsylvania, while discovery of the illness took place in New Jersey, the court held that either the Pennsylvania or New Jersey law would apply by virtue of the borrowing statute. Applying that statute, the court ruled that the claim was untimely under the statute of limitations of either state, and dismissed the complaint. The court rejected the argument that the initial words to the revival statute excluded the application of the borrowing statute, citing In re "Agent Orange" Product Liability Litigation, 597 F.Supp. 740, *affd.*, 2nd Cir., 818 F.2d 145. At the court's direction, the parties stipulated that the separate actions be consolidated and that Squibb's cross-motion be deemed to have been made by Upjohn and Lilly as well. This appeal followed.

Plaintiff contends that "the borrowing statute is simply . . . to be disregarded" because the revival statute bestows its benefits "[n]otwithstanding any other provision of law. . . ." Plaintiff further argues that because the revival statute's plain language conveys a definite meaning there is "no occasion for resorting to rules of statutory construction." Strict construction, however, should not be used to reach unintended

3. For the purposes of the borrowing statute, a cause of action sounding in negligence or strict product's liability accrues where the injury occurs. * * * In cases involving exposure to a chemical substance, the Court of Appeals has consistently held that "injury", if any, occurs at the time, and thus the place of exposure. * * *

results. "The rules of strict construction do not command such inflexibility; they do not constrain a court to defeat the evident intention of the lawmaker...." * * *

In determining a statute's meaning, the court's function is not to adhere slavishly to the statute's literal language, but, rather, to ascertain the legislature's intent. As the court stated in Matter of River Brand Rice Mills, Inc. v. Latrobe Brewing Co., 305 N.Y. 36, 110 N.E.2d 545: "The intent of the Legislature in enacting legislation is the primary object to be found. Whenever such intention is apparent it must be followed in construing the statute." * * * "[A] thing which is within the letter of the statute is not within the statute unless it be within the intention of the lawmakers, but a case within the intention of a statute is within the statute, though an exact literal construction would exclude it. It is a familiar legal maxim that 'he who considers merely the letter of an instrument goes but skin deep into its meaning,' and all statutes are to be construed according to their meaning, not according to the letter." * * * ["It is a fundamental principle of statutory interpretation that a court should attempt to effectuate the intent of the Legislature...."]; * * *. ["[A] primary command to the judiciary in the interpretation of statutes is to ascertain and effectuate the purpose of the Legislature"].

This principle is so well-established that even where, as here, the statute "may appear literally 'unambiguous' on [its] face, the absence of ambiguity facially is never conclusive." * * * Indeed, "[s]ound principles of statutory interpretation generally require examination of a statute's legislative history and context to determine its meaning and scope." * * * Thus, "[i]nquiry into the meaning of statutes is never foreclosed at the threshold...." * * *

As noted previously, the 1986 tort reform legislation was principally intended to remedy the unfair consequences suffered by injured persons under the last exposure rule. The legislation furthered that purpose by providing a one-year window period for those New Yorkers whose claims were previously barred by the operation of that rule. As the memorandum prepared by its Senate sponsor noted, "This bill will provide relief to injured New Yorkers whose claims would otherwise be dismissed for untimeliness simply because they were unaware of the latent injuries until after the limitation period had expired." In contrast, the borrowing statute was primarily intended to prevent forum shopping by nonresident plaintiffs, as well as to afford resident defendants the benefit of the shortest limitation period. * * * These policy concerns are achieved through a choice of law mechanism. Where a cause of action accrues outside New York in favor of a nonresident, the foreign statute of limitations is "borrowed."

Thus, the revival statute is concerned solely with the harshness of a time-bar that focused on a victim's exposure to a toxic substance, witting or otherwise, as a cause of action's accrual date, not the policies served by the borrowing statute. In enacting the revival statute, therefore, the

Legislature's remedial purpose was merely to remove the obstacle of the last exposure rule, not to repeal the salutary purposes underlying the borrowing statute. It is a long standing rule of statutory construction that a law will not be interpreted so as to modify pre-existing law by implication. "[I]n the absence of a manifestation of intent to change a long-established practice, ordinarily no design to do so will be attributed to legislative action...." * * * Thus, in the absence of some manifestation of intention by the Legislature to limit the borrowing statute, the revival statute should not be interpreted to override its provisions.

Rather, the two statutes should be construed, if possible, to accommodate the policies underlying each. "It is a familiar and salutary canon of construction that courts, in construing apparently conflicting statutory provisions, must try to harmonize them...." (* * * In this connection, it should also be noted that statutes which revive causes of action previously time-barred must be narrowly construed.) * * * "Revival is an extreme exercise of legislative power. * * * Uncertainties are resolved against consequences so drastic." * * *

As already noted, the primary impetus behind enactment of the revival statute was to relieve the harsh results of New York's exposure-based statute of limitations, which, due to the latent effects of exposure to some toxic substances, might have expired before the injured party even knew of his injuries. Such a result is, of course, avoided in those states where the statute of limitations begins to run from the date of discovery. Thus, the New York Legislature would not have an interest in reviving the claims of nonresident plaintiffs who were adequately protected under their own states' statutes of limitations. Only New York residents whose causes of action accrued here were in need of relief from the consequences of the exposure-based statute of limitations. It should be noted that both Pennsylvania, the state where plaintiff was exposed to DES, and New Jersey, where her injuries were manifested and diagnosed, have statutes of limitations which begin to run upon discovery of the injury. Thus, plaintiff, unlike those New Yorkers for whom the revival statute was intended, had a viable cause of action in, at least, either Pennsylvania or New Jersey at the time of the diagnosis of her injury, had she chosen to pursue it.

The policy underlying the revival statute can be harmonized with the policies of the borrowing statute. As already noted, the borrowing statute was primarily enacted to prohibit nonresident plaintiffs from forum shopping and to afford New York defendants the benefit of the shortest possible statute of limitations. By construing the revival statute so that revived claims are subject to the borrowing statute, the policies of each statute are afforded due regard. New York residents formerly subject to the harsh exposure-based statute of limitations will have access to the New York courts, while nonresident plaintiffs will be barred from forum shopping; moreover, New York defendants will be afforded the benefit of the shortest possible statute of limitations for claims accruing outside the state.

Thus, when read consistently with the statute's underlying purpose, the introductory phrase of the revival statute can only mean that the CPLR's three-year limitations period on personal injury actions shall not apply to claims brought within the revival period. Accordingly, the phrase "[n]otwithstanding any other provision of law" is intended to obviate the proscriptions of CPLR 214, which, if applied, would result in the dismissal of any causes of action brought more than three years after the discovery of the injury. This was the interpretation reached in *In re "Agent Orange" Product Liability Litigation*, * * * where the court interpreted a nearly identical statute which provided that the claims of Vietnam War veterans arising out of exposure to Agent Orange would be governed by a discovery rule "[n]otwithstanding any provision of law to the contrary...." [4] Recognizing that many of those asserting claims would be residents of different states and, hence, that the borrowing statute would present an impediment, the court asserted:

While the introductory clause of the statute, CPLR 214–b, states: "Notwithstanding any provision of law to the contrary," the reference appears to have been intended to avoid application of CPLR 214, the three-year statute for personal injury cases, to New York veterans. It does not suggest that CPLR 202 is inapplicable. (Id. at 803–804.) Similarly, Judge McLaughlin in his Practice Commentaries to the CPLR noted that "a nonresident plaintiff would be permitted to rely upon the [*Agent Orange* Revival Statute], although such a plaintiff would also have to deal with the additional hurdle of CPLR 202, the borrowing statute." (McKinney's CONSOL. LAWS, BOOK 7B § 214–b [1981 Supp. Practice Commentary].)

The *Agent Orange* and Practice Commentary interpretation clearly governs the identical issue presented here.[5] Indeed, were CPLR 202 not to apply to actions commenced pursuant to the revival statute, claims caused by the effects of any of the enumerated five substances for injuries which accrued in any other state and which are time-barred under that state's law could be imported to New York. Nothing in the

---

4. The statute involved, CPLR 214–b, provides: Notwithstanding any provision of law to the contrary, an action to recover damages for personal injury caused by contact with or exposure to phenoxy herbicides while serving as a member of the armed forces of the United States in Indo–China from January first, nineteen hundred sixty-two through May seventh, nineteen hundred seventy-five, may be commenced within two years from the date of the discovery of such injury, or within two years from the date when through the exercise of reasonable diligence the cause of such injury should have been discovered, whichever is later. (L.1981, ch. 266, § 3, amended L.1982, ch. 153, § 1.) In addition, a special "Preservation of Rights and Remedies" section expressly revived any action which was or would be barred prior to June 16, 1985

because the statute of limitations had run. (L.1981, ch. 226, § 4, amended L.1982, ch. 153, § 2; L.1983, ch. 358, § 1; L.1985, ch. 498, § 1.)

5. Plaintiff's claim that the revival statute's reference to the General Municipal Law or the Education Law, but not to CPLR 214, evinces an intent that "any other provision of law" was to be disregarded is also unavailing. The cited provisions involve conditions precedent to the commencement of an action and are in the nature of statutes of limitations. Accordingly, their inclusion is consistent with the Legislature's intention to eliminate all vestiges of the last exposure rule judicially grafted onto CPLR 214, and should not be read as a purposeful omission of the borrowing statute, a statute of a wholly different nature.

revival statute or its legislative history suggests that the statute was intended to create a national safe harbor for second chance litigation by otherwise time-barred claimants. Furthermore, this is precisely the kind of forum-shopping evil which the borrowing statute was designed to avoid.

Moreover, the failure to apply the borrowing statute herein would divest defendants of those vested rights created by the laws of sister states where the action would otherwise be barred. The Legislature could hardly have contemplated, much less intended, such a result. The bill specifically sought to "provide relief to injured New Yorkers...."

Finally, we note that the dissent premises its entire argument on plaintiff's claim that she is now a New York resident, a circumstance which is irrelevant, since plaintiff can avoid the operation of CPLR 202 only if she was a New York resident at the time her cause of action accrued. * * * Moreover, such statutory distinction in treatment has been constitutionally upheld. * * *

All concur except Asch, J., who dissents in an Opinion.

Asch, Justice (dissenting):

This is a products liability action in which plaintiff-appellant Karen Sue Besser seeks damages for personal injuries against three defendant pharmaceutical companies. The claim results from the ingestion by plaintiff's mother, during pregnancy, of defendants' drug, diethylstilbestrol ("DES"). The appeal presents to this court, for the first time, a novel issue pertaining to the recent Toxic Tort Revival Statute (L.1986, ch. 682, § 4) passed by the Legislature of New York to afford a remedy to victims of five separate toxic substances, when claims, in many instances, were time-barred even before some of those injured were even aware of their existence.

We are asked to decide whether the plaintiff, a New York resident at the time her action was commenced, is barred under the New York "borrowing statute" (CPLR 202) from taking advantage of the benefits conferred by the revival statute.

Plaintiff appeals from an order of the Supreme Court, New York County, which granted defendant Squibb's cross motion for summary judgment, in which the other defendants had joined. The basis of this order was that the "borrowing statute" (CPLR 202) invoked a statute of limitations which barred the action. The same order also denied plaintiff's motion to dismiss two of defendant Squibb's affirmative defenses.

Plaintiff's mother, while she was pregnant with plaintiff some 33 years ago, ingested DES, produced and marketed by defendants. She had no way of knowing that the consequences of such use might be catastrophic to her daughter, as yet unborn. Plaintiff was born in Pennsylvania, where she had been conceived and exposed to the DES, in 1955. She became ill with cervical cancer in 1975, some 20 years later, in New Jersey, where she underwent surgery. A prior action she commenced on December 29, 1980, in New York, was dismissed as untimely. Thereafter, plaintiff brought the present action on August 6, 1986, as a resident of New York. While the record does not indicate when this residency began, the defendants cannot persuasively establish that plaintiff was only a resident of convenience for purposes of this action.

CPLR 202, New York's borrowing statute, is a protective device for New York defendants to be raised so as to bar suits brought by foreign plaintiffs. In effect, CPLR 202 provides that with respect to a cause of action accruing outside of the state, commenced by a non-resident, a New York defendant will be able to invoke whichever statute of limitations has already expired, the foreign jurisdiction's or New York's. However, section 202 preserves for the resident plaintiff the benefit, or the detriment, of New York's statute of limitations.

In this case, it is undisputed that the action would be time-barred in both New Jersey and Pennsylvania (two years from date of injury). And, ordinarily, under CPLR 202, plaintiff's action would be time-barred for all purposes if plaintiff was a non-resident. Fortunately, for her, she is protected by her procedural status as a resident of New York.

In 1986, the Legislature passed the so-called revival statute (L.1986, ch. 682, § 4). It revived for one year certain causes of action which had been time-barred under New York Law. It is not disputed that this action would be deemed timely commenced, then, if plaintiff could take advantage of the revival statute. Chapter 682 of the 1986 New York Laws * * *.

Both the defendants and the plaintiff engage in substantial argument whether the revival statute addresses only New York claims barred by the New York statute of limitations, or whether it can revive an action time-barred not by New York's statute of limitations, but by that of foreign jurisdictions, pursuant to CPLR 202.

As noted, the revival statute commences with the qualifying language that it will apply "[n]otwithstanding any other provision of law", and it then enumerates certain such other limiting provisions of law. Plaintiff contends that this statutory language is to be taken at face value and serves to nullify the application of section 202 and any other statute of limitations. Defendants urge that such a literal interpretation misreads the legislative intent of the statute, which was to be narrowly construed; it was never intended to apply to non-resident causes of action, into which category they include the instant case.

The case law on this specific point is virtually a blank slate and, so, general principles of statutory construction will control.

Judge Breitel has stated with respect to statutory interpretation that "purpose cannot be a warrant to go beyond the language used. The language is a limitation on construction even as the purpose may be a liberalizing factor" * * * McKinney's CONSOLIDATED LAWS OF N.Y., BOOK 1, Statutes § 111 states, in pertinent part, that "the intent of the Legislature is the primary object.... While such intention is first to be sought from a literal reading of the text itself ... giving such language its natural and obvious meaning ... the literal meaning of words are not to be adhered to ... to defeat the general purpose and manifest policy intended to be promoted." * * * Further, "statutes are not to be read with literalness that destroys meaning, intention, purpose or beneficial end for which the statute has been designed." This permissiveness of departure from literal language, however, appears to address the situation where, in light of the statute's explicit intent, the words, ill-chosen, make no sense in terms of application. * * *

The purpose to be examined would be that of the revival statute, not the purpose of section 202. The objective of the revival statute appears to be to afford relief in tort to hapless victims of a tragedy which they had no part in making. To construe the statute in the way urged by the defendants would be to subvert its beneficial purposes, giving recognition to the increasing mobility of Americans, the complexity of determining pernicious consequences of modern "wonder drugs", and the long-term consequences of the ingestion of medical drugs, the lethal consequences of which may not become apparent for a generation or more. Both the literal language "notwithstanding any other provision of law" as well as the "equity of the statute" * * * support plaintiff's position. To deny the plaintiff the right to seek legal redress in this case, because her mother lived in New Jersey at the time she took DES, would be the equivalent of the long-time rejected punishment of attainder and corruption of the blood by which the acts of the mother (which in this case were innocent) are used to penalize the daughter.

However, all the speculation as to whether plaintiff is to be afforded the beneficial effect of the revival statute is predicated on an erroneous premise. What is significant is that plaintiff commenced an earlier action in 1980, in New York, and after the enactment of the revival statute. The extensive discussion as to where the cause of action arose, or whether the revival statute protects a non-resident, is irrelevant. Although plaintiff was not a resident when the DES was ingested (since she was not yet born) nor when injury manifested itself, she commenced a prior action in New York on December 29, 1980, which, significantly, was then dismissed by application of New York's statute of limitations. Consequently, when, on August 6, 1986, she brought a new action under the revival statute, she was then an "injured New Yorker" whose day in court in New York initially had been precluded for untimeliness and whose situation is expressly covered by the language of the statute: "[E]very action ... which was dismissed ... solely because the applicable period of limitations ... had expired is hereby revived and an action thereon may be commenced within one year...." The statutory language simply revives such claims which had been brought in New York courts and which had been dismissed in New York by operation of the statute of limitations; it does not appear to exclude those causes of action for toxic torts which had accrued in other forums. Hence, plaintiff herein should be accommodated by the statute, and deemed a

New York resident, notwithstanding the lack of language which is explicit on this point.

The practice commentary to section 202 (McLaughlin, J. 1985: C202:2) relied upon by defendants actually supports the above conclusion. Citing Antone v. General Motors Corp., 64 N.Y.2d 20, 29, 484 N.Y.S.2d 514, 473 N.E.2d 742, Judge McLaughlin notes that plaintiff's domicile may not be relevant, although plaintiff's residence in New York, even if it is not the domicile, would be the focus. The *Antone* case departs from the instant case in that it involved a car accident in Pennsylvania which necessarily was contemporaneous with the accrual of the cause of action. The whole nature of toxic torts, however, which the revival statute addressed, makes accrual of the cause of action a much more elastic concept. Defendant Upjohn even seems to concede that plaintiff "now apparently resides in New York." Accordingly, the conclusion is warranted that the legislative purpose of the revival statute was to include the instant plaintiff within the class of persons to be accommodated by that statute. Defendants' conclusion that the legislative purpose was only to protect plaintiffs who were residents when the cause of action accrued or, in the alternative, that the Legislature intended that section 202 act as a limiting device upon a party such as plaintiff, would not seem warranted. While not every literal nuance of a statute need be "slavishly" adhered to (Statutes, *supra,* § 111), the clear meaning of the introductory phrase "[n]otwithstanding any other provisions of law" seems not only clear on its face, but is not inconsistent with the body of the statute nor with the above legislative memoranda.

Hence, if plaintiff has been a resident, and it appears that such is the case * * * insofar as she has "a significant connection ... living there for some length of time during the course of a year" ..., the "hurdle" of section 202 never arises and plaintiff is entitled to invoke the revival statute. If plaintiff's residency is questionable (and one wishes that the record was clearer), then the facial reading of the revival statute would appear to nullify the limitation otherwise imposed by section 202. By limiting this introductory language only to section 214, the Statute of Limitations, and not extending it so as to nullify section 202, the borrowing statute, the court below appears to have read in a statutory purpose which is not supported either by expressed language or by legislative memoranda.

Finally, while forum shopping is not to be encouraged, the public policy impact of reading the subject statutory language literally will be limited. The plaintiff may well be the only person in her category who brought an earlier action in New York, dismissed because of the Statute of Limitations, and who now proceeds under the revival statute. The revival statute opened only a one-year window period which has since closed, thereby limiting the class of plaintiffs which may take advantage of such an interpretation. That defendant Upjohn refers to two other such cases by the same trial court ought not be viewed as undermining such a conclusion.

Defendants argue that the Legislature did not intend to revive the claims of those plaintiffs whose causes of action accrued in states other than New York. Nothing persuasive has been cited, however, in the legislative history of the bill in support of this proposition. In fact, the best evidence to the contrary is the language of the statute itself that its provisions were to apply "[n]otwithstanding any other provision of law."

If the Legislature intended that the borrowing statute should be applicable, why did it not say "[n]otwithstanding any other provision of law except section 202 of the Civil Practice Law and Rules" instead of setting forth a blanket exclusion of any other provision of law? Certainly the Legislature was aware of the existence of the borrowing statute, and if it had so chosen, it could have made it clear that it was still to be applicable to revived claims. Defendants are, in effect, arguing that the Legislature should have barred claims accruing in other states, a judgment which is not for our courts to make, but for the Legislature.

It is unnecessary for this court to dwell on the meaning of the language of the revival statute ("[n]otwithstanding any other provision of law") which may or may not exclude the application of section 202 of the CPLR with respect to non-residents. Plaintiff in this case was a New York resident. It should be noted that at the time that plaintiff commenced her action against Squibb, she was a New York resident, having personally verified a complaint which set forth that "[p]laintiff is a resident of the City of New York, Borough of Manhattan." Thus, at the time that she commenced the action, she was indeed an "injured New Yorker." In fact, when her prior action was dismissed, it had been on the basis of the application of New York's statute of limitations. It was precisely for the purpose of affording relief to injured victims of toxic substances, like this plaintiff, that the Legislature enacted the revival statute. Thus, Senator Ronald B. Stafford, in a legislative memorandum dealing with the Toxic Torts/Discovery Statute of Limitations, noted, *inter alia:* "This bill will provide relief to injured New Yorkers whose claims would otherwise be dismissed for untimeliness simply because they were unaware of the latent injuries until after the limitation period had expired" * * *

In this connection, defendants contend that our courts have narrowly construed the borrowing statute to apply only to those who were New York residents at the time the cause of action accrued. * * * Thus, according to defendants' interpretation, a New York resident living here for the last 10 or 15 years could easily have been barred from bringing an action under the revival statute by application of the borrowing statute, assuming she was conceived and born in another state where her mother ingested the toxic material. Another resident for 10 or 15 years, whose mother lived in New York at the time of conception up to birth, would not be so barred. Such a narrow interpretation in this case would be a violation of the equal protection and due process clauses of the U.S. Constitution, 14th Amendment, and the N.Y. Constitution, article I, §§ 6 and 11. It would be a violation because it would create an arbitrary class of victims of toxic substances who were residents of New

York when their actions were commenced, but because their mothers fortuitously were exposed to the substances many years earlier in another state, before these plaintiffs were ever born, were exempted from revival by such a happenstance. Such a result would turn a statute which is not unconstitutional on its face into a statute which is unconstitutional as applied to certain persons or under certain circumstances. * * *

* * *

Notes and Questions

1. Although traditional tort litigation often involves statute of limitations problems, mass tort litigation has engendered interesting limitations issues because of the long latency of many mass tort injuries, plus the multi-forum nature of aggregated mass tort claims. The American Law Institute, *Reporter's Study,* ENTERPRISE RESPONSIBILITY FOR PERSONAL INJURY (1991) described mass tort statute of limitations problems:

> One potentially serious obstacle to effective litigation of environmental injuries is the statute of limitations. These statutes establish a time limit after the action has "accrued," perhaps two or three years, for filing a tort claim. Accrual is conventionally understood to have occurred once the defendant has acted wrongfully and thereby caused injury to the victim. That interpretation occasions no particular difficulties when the harm done is immediately visible, as it generally is following a motor vehicle accident or a plane crash, for instance. However, the diseases that follow toxic exposures—most notably, though by no means solely, cancers—typically have latency periods of decades between original exposure and ultimate manifestation of the disease; yet it is the manifestation that typically alerts the victims to the need to seek redress for the harm done. Without some qualifications to this legislative policy, then, the vast majority of environmental injury claims could never be filed, let alone succeed on their merits.

> Fortunately, the courts have responded to this problem, heavily influenced by a 1949 U.S. Supreme Court ruling that under the Federal Employers' Liability Act the limitations period did not begin to run until the individual employee had discovered the silicosis inflicted by long-term exposure to silica dust on the job.[16] By now approximately forty states have explicitly adopted some form of this "discovery" rule. The discovery principle, which also figures prominently in medical malpractice litigation, needs to be carefully and generously interpreted in order to ameliorate the effect of standard limitations periods on environmental exposure cases. A person who lives near a hazardous waste site may learn that he has developed leukemia, for example, but it may not be until some time later that he connects his disease to exposure to the waste in question. Perhaps the victim did not know of the presence of the waste site in the area, or the scientific community itself may as yet be unaware of the connection between the disease and the type of exposure. The courts have developed a variety of doctrinal formulas

16. *See* Urie v. Thompson, 337 U.S. 163 (1949).

that give plaintiffs some latitude in discerning the causal connection between their current illness and the defendant's prior activity. However, even forty years after the emergence of the discovery principle, the statute of limitations appears to be the most successful defense regularly asserted in asbestos litigation.

A vigorous scholarly debate has been going on for the last several years about the pros and cons of statutory limitations periods, particularly in the toxic tort area. Some scholars advocate the enactment of ten-or-twenty year statutes of repose, which would remove from enterprises any specter of liability for a multiplicity of subsequently discovered tort suits involving cases that may turn on lost or state evidence of initial exposures. Others have argued, persuasively, in our opinion, that the substantive goals of tort law in the environmental area are better served by avoiding rigid statutes of repose and by a relaxed interpretation of when "discovery" will trigger the running of limitation periods.

Id., Vol. II at 362-64.

2. The *Besser* decision illustrates another dimension of the statute of limitations problem in mass tort litigation: the application of another state's limitations period through a borrowing statute. Does the *Besser* court do an adequate job of reconciling New York state's revival statute with its borrowing statute? Is the court correct to be concerned about the problem of plaintiff forum-shopping? *See* Walker, *Forum Shopping for Stale Claims: Statutes of Limitations and Conflict of Laws,* 23 Akron L.Rev. 19 (1989). Is this inquiry completely fact-bound? Approximately two-thirds of the states have borrowing statutes that direct dismissal of a plaintiff's claim if that claim would be barred by the limitations period of the state where the action "arose," "accrued," or "originated." *See generally* American Law Institute, COMPLEX LITIGATION: STATUTORY RECOMMENDATIONS AND ANALYSIS at 390. Some courts have had difficulties under their borrowing statutes in determining where an action accrued for limitations purposes. *See, e.g.,* Renfroe v. Eli Lilly & Co., 686 F.2d 642 (8th Cir.1982)(DES claims originated "where plaintiffs first developed cancer capable of ascertainment.").

3. The American Law Institute, in COMPLEX LITIGATION: STATUTORY RECOMMENDATIONS AND ANALYSIS (1994), has recommended the following provision to resolve interstate conflicts among statutes of limitation in mass torts consolidated and transferred under its recommended procedures:

§ 6.04   Statutes of Limitation

In actions consolidated * * * or removed * * * and based on state law, the transferee court shall apply the limitations law of the state whose law is chosen to govern the claims * * *, except that any claim that was timely where filed but is not under the law chosen pursuant to this section will be deemed timely by the transferee court and remanded to the transferor court.

Comment:

a. *Rationale.* This section proposes a choice of law rule tying the limitations law to the law chosen to control liability. * * * [T]he transferee court will select the law governing liability under principles reflecting policies germane to the types of claims presented, as well as to the objectives of efficiency, economy, and fairness fostered by this complex litigation scheme. Thus, linking the choice of law decision for the limitations period to that for the liability determination establishes a coherent legal framework under which consolidated cases can be decided. Further, reference to a single state's law to control all limitations questions in a complex case offers the possibility of achieving the consistent treatment of similar claims arising from the same events or course of conduct, as well as promoting judicial economy by avoiding the need to decide multiple individual limitations issues.

American Law Institute, COMPLEX LITIGATION: STATUTORY RECOMMENDATIONS AND ANALYSIS (1994) at 383.

4. The variation among state statutes of limitation create "horizontal" conflicts of law in the interstate judicial system as well as for federal courts handling aggregate diversity mass tort cases. However, the 1986 Superfund Amendments and Reauthorization Act (SARA) to CERCLA provide a possible model for federalization of statute of limitations period for environmental toxic torts. *See* 42 U.S.C.A. § 9658. These provisions impose a federal minimum period on state personal injury or property damage for claims arising from exposure to hazardous materials, which period does not begin to run until the plaintiff knows or should have known that the injury or property damage was caused by the hazardous substance. The federal SARA limitations rules have not been applied to asbestos litigation. *See, e.g.,* Covalt v. Carey Canada, Inc., 860 F.2d 1434 (7th Cir.1988)(SARA provision did not apply against asbestos manufacturer because interior of workplace not an "environment" for CERCLA purposes); Knox v. A.C. & S., Inc., 690 F.Supp. 752 (S.D.Ind.1988). *See also* American Law Institute, *Reporter's Study,* ENTERPRISE RESPONSIBILITY FOR PERSONAL INJURY (1991), Vol. II at 364 (endorsing the SARA limitations provisions as a commendable model for state common and statutory law).

5. For general commentary on statute of limitations problems as they relate to mass or toxic tort litigation, *see generally,* Kim M. Covell, Note, Wilson v. Johns–Manville Sales Corp. *and Statutes of Limitations in Latent Injury Litigation: An Equitable Expansion of the Discovery Rule,* 32 Cath. U.L.Rev. 471 (1983); Richard Epstein, *The Temporal Dimension in Tort Law,* 53 U.Chi.L.Rev. 1175 (1986); Susan D. Glimcher, *Statutes of Limitations and the Discovery Rule in Latent Injury Claims: An Exception or the Law,* 43 U.Pitt.L.Rev. 501 (1982); Michael D. Green, *The Paradox of Statute of Limitations in Toxic Substance Litigation,* 76 Cal.L.Rev. 1965 (1988); Francis H. Hare Jr. & James L. Gilbert, *Discovery in Products Liability Cases: The Plaintiff's Plea for Judicial Understanding,* 12 Am.J. Trial Advoc. 413 (1989); Francis F.E. McGovern, *The Status of Statutes of Limitations and Statutes of Repose in Products Liability Actions: Present and Future,* 16 Forum 416 (1989); Francis McGovern, *The Variety, Policy, and Constitutionality of Product Liability Statutes of Repose,* 30 Am.U.L.Rev. 571 (1980); William J. Warfel, *Tolling of Statutes of Limitation in Long–Tail Product Liability Litigation: The Transformation of the Tort System into a Compensation System,* 13 Prod.Liab. 205 (1991); Note, *Fairness and Constitutionality of Statutes of Limitation for Toxic Tort Suits,* 96 Harv.L.Rev. 1683 (1983).

B. STATE OF THE ART DEFENSE
JOHNSON v. RAYBESTOS–MANHATTAN

United States Court of Appeals, Ninth Circuit, 1987.
829 F.2d 907.

Before FERGUSON, CANBY and HALL, CIRCUIT JUDGES.

PER CURIAM:

This appeal raises a controlling question of Hawaii State tort law which we certified to the Supreme Court of Hawaii and which that court has now decided. *See* Johnson v. Raybestos–Manhattan, Inc., 69 Haw. 287, 740 P.2d 548 (1987). Because the decision of the Supreme Court of Hawaii conflicts with the ruling of the district court in this case, we reverse and remand.

I

Plaintiff-appellant Anita Johnson appeals from the decision of the district court denying her motion in limine and permitting the introduction of state of the art evidence as a defense to her tort claim of strict liability. Plaintiff initiated this negligence and strict liability action for the death of her husband, Ray Johnson. Ray Johnson was exposed to asbestos products during his work at Pearl Harbor Naval Shipyard from 1941 to 1944. He was later diagnosed as having asbestosis and lung cancer. Defendant Raybestos–Manhattan (Raybestos) is an asbestos textile manufacturer which the jury found had provided some of the asbestos products to which Ray Johnson was exposed.

Plaintiff's complaint, filed August 22, 1980, alleged that Raybestos was negligent and strictly liable for failing to warn Ray Johnson of the dangers of asbestos products. Plaintiff's motion *in limine* sought to exclude all state of the art evidence. The district court denied plaintiff's motion, holding that previous Hawaii decisions stating that strict liability would not be interpreted as absolute liability demonstrated that the courts of Hawaii would not exclude all state of the art evidence in strict liability cases.

Trial proceeded on negligence and strict liability theories with state of the art evidence presented by both parties. Under the strict liability theory, the jury was instructed that a product is defective if it contains substances that are dangerous to the user and does not contain directions or warnings regarding "dangers in its use [that] were known, or by the use of reasonabl[y] developed human foresight, could have been known." The jury returned a verdict for defendant on both theories. On appeal, the plaintiffs challenge the introduction of state of the art evidence on the strict liability theory.

II

We certified the following issue to the Supreme Court of Hawaii: "In a strict products liability case for injuries caused by an inherently unsafe product, is the manufacturer conclusively presumed to know the dangers inherent in his product, or is state of the art evidence admissible to establish whether the manufacturer knew or through the exercise of reasonable human foresight should have known of the danger?" *See* Johnson, ___ Haw. at ___, 740 P.2d at 549 (footnote omitted). On July 22, 1987, the Supreme Court of Hawaii decided the certified issue.

The Supreme Court of Hawaii held "that in a strict products liability action, state-of-the-art evidence is not admissible for the purpose of establishing whether the seller knew or reasonably should have known of the dangerousness of his or her product." *Id.* at ___, 740 P.2d at 549. The court explained that in a strict products liability case in Hawaii "the issue of whether the defendant knew or reasonably should have known of the dangers inherent in his or her product is irrelevant to the issue of liability." *Id.* at ___, 740 P.2d at 549 (citation omitted). This is the case because "strict products liability does not require a showing that the defendant was negligent." *Id.* at ___, 740 P.2d at 549. Rather, in Hawaii courts, the plaintiff need only show that the manufacturer is "engaged in the business of selling the product, that the product contains a defect dangerous to the user or customer, and that the defect is the cause of the injury." *Id.* at ___, 740 P.2d at 549. * * *

III

The district court incorrectly determined that Hawaii courts would admit state of the art evidence in connection with Johnson's strict products liability claim, and it incorrectly instructed the jury with respect to Johnson's strict liability claim. We therefore reverse the district court's judgment and remand for a new trial on the strict products liability count of Johnson's complaint in accordance with the rules expressed in the opinion of the Supreme Court of Hawaii. * * *

Reversed and Remanded.

Review Beshada v. Johns–Manville, *supra, and accompanying Notes describing the subsequent New Jersey decisions in* Feldman *and* Fischer.

IN RE ASBESTOS LITIGATION

United States Court of Appeals, Third Circuit, 1987.
829 F.2d 1233.

Before WEIS, BECKER and HUNTER, CIRCUIT JUDGES.

OPINION OF THE COURT

WEIS, CIRCUIT JUDGE.

The district court has certified to us the question whether decisions of the New Jersey Supreme Court violate the Equal Protection Clause in abolishing the state-of-the-art defense in asbestos personal injury cases. We determine that a common law precedent announced by a state's highest court is "law" within the meaning of the Equal Protection Clause. Using the rational basis standard, we conclude that the state court rulings survive the constitutional challenge.

The district court of New Jersey consolidated all of its pending asbestos cases for argument and disposition of the defendants' attack on the state supreme court's bar against "state-of-the-art" evidence in those personal injury cases. Sitting *[e]n banc,* the district court rejected the defendants' contention that they were denied equal protection and certified the question to us under 28 U.S.C. § 1292(b). We accepted the interlocutory appeal.

[Discussion of history of asbestos litigation, New Jersey's adoption of strict product liability, the *Beshada-Feldman–Fischer* case line, omitted; *see Beshada, supra—ed.*]

* * *

The present appeal arises out of this unsettled background. In various personal injury cases brought in the district court, defendant asbestos manufacturers attempted to introduce evidence on the state-of-the-art defense. They alleged that *Beshada's* preclusion of that defense had the effect of treating them discriminatorily and less favorably than all other manufacturers. * * *

A majority of the district judges decided that the defendants' request should be denied. In their view, legitimate concerns of case management, economics, as well as social welfare policy affecting exposed plaintiffs justified preclusion of the state-of-the-art defense. * * * Noting that strict liability in workmen's compensation had withstood similar equal protection attacks, * * * as, and finding a rational relationship between the *Beshada* ruling and its goals, the judges rejected the constitutional challenge.

A minority of the judges dissented on the grounds that the state supreme court had neither clearly articulated its rationale for eliminating the defense nor substantiated its expectations that the anticipated benefits would result.[2]

On appeal to this court, defendants contend that the New Jersey Supreme Court's decisions unconstitutionally discriminate among categories of civil litigants because no rational basis for the classification can be posited. Defendants also maintain that by failing to give adequate reason for its action, the state court violated the Due Process Clause of the Fourteenth Amendment.

Plaintiffs assert that the rational basis test is the appropriate standard for reviewing this equal protection challenge and that the wisdom of the state common law rule is not at issue.

First, we observe the somewhat unusual posture in which this case reaches us. The attack on the ruling, or more accurately the series of rulings, of the state supreme court did not come to the district court as a direct appeal.

---

2. *See* In re Asbestos Litigation, 628 F.Supp. 774 (D.N.J.1986)(*en banc*), Judge Bissell wrote the opinion for the majority of eight judges and Chief Judge Fisher wrote for the six dissenting judges.

A United States District Court may not entertain an appeal from judgments of the highest court of a state. Only the United States Supreme Court may exercise such review, and then only in cases within its jurisdiction. * * * The parties to the cases at hand constitute different groups than those in the challenged state court litigation, and hence neither res judicata nor law of the case principles apply. Defendants here have no avenue to attack the precedential effect of the New Jersey judgment governing their case except through objections to rulings in these cases filed in federal court.

The question presented to the district court, and now to us, is a variation on the theme of Erie R. Co. v. Tompkins, 304 U.S. 64, 58 S.Ct. 817, 82 L.Ed. 1188 (1938), that is, whether the New Jersey decisions are binding even if their tenor is not in harmony with the federal constitution.

* * *

The threshold issue, thus, is whether *Erie* controls in circumstances where state law violates the federal constitution. Because the United States District Courts have the primary obligation to interpret and apply federal law, undoubtedly they can, and must, abjure *Erie* if its application would conflict with the United States Constitution.

This case presents several other curious features. Defendants do not contest being included within the scope of the *Beshada* doctrine along with other manufacturers. Rather, they complain that they were not excluded from it as were the other manufacturers in *Feldman.* Essentially, they do not argue that the strict liability holding of *Beshada* is constitutionally defective, whatever its other failings may be, but that asbestos manufacturers have been singled out for discriminatory treatment compared to other producers. Phrased differently, they protest the failure of the New Jersey Supreme Court to reverse *Beshada* in its entirety, rather than only partially.

In addition, unlike the usual equal protection case that challenges a legislative enactment, this attack is directed at the common law as announced by a state's highest court. [Lengthy discussion of *Erie* doctrine omitted.—*ed.*]

* * *

Whatever may have been the reaction of the courts in earlier times, we are persuaded that the district court properly considered the common law of New Jersey to be within the scope of the Equal Protection Clause.

II

Because equal protection claims may be reviewed under a number of standards which differ in intensity, we find it necessary to select the proper test for use in this case. As a general rule, classifications that neither regulate suspect classes nor burden fundamental rights must be sustained if they are rationally related to a legitimate governmental interest. * * *

The matter at issue here, the right of a manufacturer to invoke the state-of-the-art defense, is not fundamental under the Constitution nor is it a suspect classification. The Supreme Court has observed that "despite the fact that 'otherwise settled expectations' may be upset," a state may modify or abolish a cause of action at common law. Duke Power Co. v. Carolina Envtl. Study Group, 438 U.S. 59, 88 n.32, 98 S.Ct. 2620, 2638 n. 32, 57 L.Ed.2d 595 (1978), * * *.

* * *

Other legislative alterations in the tort field have also withstood constitutional challenge. Of particular interest are the drastic changes in the traditional negligence standard for liability. The no-fault workmen's compensation program is one illustration of such treatment. * * * Legislation that treats medical malpractice suits differently than other negligence claims provides another example. * * *

In short, the nature of the right to assert a particular defense in a tort action is not among those characterized as "fundamental." It is not included in the field of human rights that touches on personal liberty, an area of special concern to the courts. Nothing inherent in the right to a tort defense lends itself to demand more scrupulous review than the other social and economic matters traditionally examined under the rational relationship test. See G.D. Searle & Co. v. Cohn, 455 U.S. 404, 102 S.Ct. 1137, 71 L.Ed.2d 250 (1982). * * *

It is by now well established that in confronting a problem in the area of economic and social welfare, a state does not violate the Equal Protection Clause merely because the classifications drawn by its laws are imperfect. "If the classification has some 'reasonable basis,' it does not offend the Constitution simply because the classification 'is not made with mathematical nicety or because in practice it results in some inequality.'" Dandridge v. Williams, 397 U.S. 471, 485, 90 S.Ct. 1153, 1161, 25 L.Ed.2d 491 (1970). * * *

Having determined that the nature of the right asserted here does not place it in a category requiring heightened scrutiny, we must now consider whether the judicial rather than legislative origin of the alleged infringement mandates a more searching review. As noted earlier, classifications subject to the Equal Protection Clause generally originate in the legislature. In the case before us, the dissenting district judges observed that where judicial action creates the classification, the "efficacy of the checks and balances inherent in 'the democratic process' is substantially reduced." * * * For that reason, they concluded that a more critical equal protection test should be applied here.

The presumption of validity attaching to state legislation is based to some extent on the proposition that improvident decisions will be rectified eventually by the democratic process. Vance v. Bradley, 440 U.S. 93, 97, 99 S.Ct. 939, 942, 59 L.Ed.2d 171 (1979). However, we are not persuaded that this consideration carries any particular weight in the present circumstances.

The common law ruling by the New Jersey Supreme Court is susceptible to prompt and uncomplicated reversal by the state legislature if it deems fit. That procedure is not in the least more complex than if the precedent promulgated by the state supreme court had been enacted as a statute by the legislature. It is important to remember that speedy statutory revision remains available to correct any imprudent state court common law precedent. In fact, a bill intended to overrule *Beshada* was introduced in the New Jersey legislature. This bill never emerged from the Committee on Judiciary to which it was referred, consequently aborting the legislative effort to restore the state-of-the-art defense in products liability litigation to pre-*Beshada* status. § 1465, 201st N.J. Leg., 1st Sess. (1984).

The democratic process is as readily accessible to overrule a common law precedent created by the state's highest court as it is to repeal a statutory enactment. We recognize that in a democracy the legislature may be the more appropriate branch to draw classifications based on public policy. As a popularly elected body, the legislature is in a position to tap the thinking of its constituency and has the resources to secure data generally not available to the courts.

Nevertheless, particularly in the tort field, the common law tradition remains strong. States exercise considerable latitude to accomplish fundamental shifts in policy by judicial action as well as by legislation. For example, the abolition of contributory negligence as a complete defense and the substitution of comparative negligence has been effected in some states by the courts, * * *, while in other jurisdictions by the legislature * * *.

We are not convinced that either the nature of the subject matter or the procedure utilized in arriving at the challenged ruling constitutes sufficient grounds for requiring a stricter standard of review for common law decisions subjected to equal protection attacks.

One other element present here—case management—tips the scale in favor of the state court ruling. The *Beshada* court gave prime consideration to this concern, a subject in which the expertise of a court substantially outweighs that of a legislature and deserves due deference.

Taking the significant elements entering into the state court's ruling and balancing them against the valid competency concerns of court and legislature, we discern no measurable imbalance that weakens the presumption of regularity attaching to the state's choice of alternatives. Considering the social, economic, and administrative nature of the issues before the state court, we cannot say that its action in deciding the state-of-the-art defense question warrants strict scrutiny. We therefore conclude that the rational basis test is applicable to the classification drawn by the *Beshada* and *Feldman* courts.

III

We now turn to a closer examination of the challenged state decisions. [Summary and review of *Beshada, Feldman,* and *Fischer* omitted.—*ed.*]. * * *

These imprecise statements and the unequivocal ruling in *Middlesex Asbestos Litigation* that *Beshada* applies to pending asbestos cases leads us to the following assessment: (1) in New Jersey, *Beshada* does apply to asbestos cases but not to all products liability cases; and (2) *Feldman* does not govern asbestos cases, but does not necessarily apply to all other products liability cases.

New Jersey, therefore, does treat asbestos cases differently than other products liability cases. However, we do not know if this disparate treatment applies exclusively to asbestos cases. In addition to the expressed justifications of risk-spreading, accident avoidance, and simplification of the fact-finding process, *Feldman* provides yet another underlying reason for precluding the state-of-the-art defense in the asbestos setting. The opinion suggests that these manufacturers knew the dangers of asbestos and, consequently, the state-of-the-art defense could not be sustained.

* * *

We do not overlook the fact that exposure to asbestos may vary in degree depending on whether an individual works in a plant that manufactures asbestos products or simply drives an automobile equipped with asbestos brake linings. Nevertheless, *Beshada*'s broad language, when applied to the concrete facts of asbestos litigation and read together with *Fischer,* is not completely divorced from reality, despite its abstract appearance of assessing culpability for failure to know and warn of the unknowable.

In the case at hand, the dissenting district judges have mounted powerful arguments to sustain the equal protection challenge. Ultimately these arguments are grounded in the wisdom and correctness of *Beshada* and its progeny, an appraisal not within the function of the federal courts when called upon to assess equal protection attacks on state law. This restraint is especially appropriate when the reviewing court employs the rational basis standard, a test that does not permit federal courts to strike down classifications because they are unwise or inartfully drawn. * * *

Moreover, we must not overlook the importance of allocating the burden of proof. In equal protection cases, those who challenge state law must convince the court that the factual assumptions on which the classification is apparently based could not reasonably be conceived as true by the governmental decision maker. * * * We cannot say that the asbestos manufacturers have met that burden.

Nor may we ignore the federalism concerns that color this controversy. These considerations are invoked by long-standing acceptance of the notion that tort law, much like the law of domestic relations, belongs almost exclusively to the states. Although that principle alone would not require a federal court to stay its hand when a violation of equal protection occurs, we must recognize that the states possess a high degree of competence as well as a traditional claim of independence in this field.

From that perspective, too, it is unrealistic to ignore the fact that the doctrine of strict products liability advocated by the RESTATEMENT (SECOND) OF TORTS § 402A and adopted by New Jersey is in itself a classification that imposes discriminatory liability on a particular group of defendants. At the turn of the century, the common law held manufacturers and defendant-distributors of defective products liable in most instances only if proved negligent. State court decisions, however, developed tort law to wipe out the reasonable conduct defense and to establish liability without fault not only for manufacturers of defective products, but also for the utterly fault-free retailer. Nevertheless, no equal protection challenge has successfully undermined that doctrine.

In refining and narrowing the § 402A theory, *Beshada* eliminates one more defense to the liability of asbestos defendants. Because the court's reasoning may be applicable to other defendants in similar circumstances, the justification advanced both directly and indirectly by the New Jersey court may be regarded as weak and ill-advised. We cannot, however, conclude that the state court's position is irrational. The concepts of risk-spreading and compensation for victims by manufacturers of unreasonably dangerous products are cornerstones of § 402A, and they may be consistently applied to asbestos as well as to other products.

Although not in itself a determinative factor in the elimination of a substantive defense, the desirability of simplifying the fact-finding process and thus making it easier for victims to recover has been recognized by the law. Workmen's compensation programs and no-fault auto insurance plans share that common goal. Under workmen's compensation laws, both the employer and the employee yield common law rights in exchange for a plan of prompt, fixed payments controlled by an administrative agency. Nevertheless, the Supreme Court made it clear in *Duke Power* that the lack of a *quid pro quo* is not a prerequisite to approval of modification of traditional common law tort doctrine. * * *

Administrative convenience standing alone is not an adequate ground for the elimination of a substantive defense. * * * However, we cannot help but be conscious of the extraordinary size of the asbestos personal injury litigation. As we commented in *In Re School District Asbestos Litigation,* this unprecedented phenomenon in American tort law requires states be given some leeway in devising their own solutions.

In reaching its decision, the *Beshada* court considered the possibility that a jury might become confused by the testimony of experts who would "speculate as to what knowledge was feasible in a given year." Consequently, the court opined that it should "resist legal rules that will so greatly add to the costs both sides incur in trying a case."

It might be questioned whether the defendants themselves worried about the potential cost of producing evidence necessary to reduce or eliminate their liability and whether they, in fact, welcomed the court's concern about their litigation expenses. Moreover, *Beshada*'s interest in simplifying the trial of asbestos cases was substantially undercut by *Fischer,* where the state supreme court permitted personal injury plaintiffs to receive punitive damages on proof that the defendants had failed to comply with the state-of-the-art. Notwithstanding the distinction between what was known and what was knowable, for all practical purposes what *Beshada* precluded from coming in the front door, *Fischer* allows in the back door. Thus, the goal of simplifying asbestos litigation is eroded by the New Jersey decision to award punitive damages in these cases.

Although we find the *Fischer* case troubling, we once again acknowledge our limited function in reviewing cases of this type. We cannot overlook the fact that those plaintiffs who wish to avoid the cost of proving the foundation for an uncertain award of punitive damages still may take advantage of the simplified compensation claim Beshada makes available. While the use of that alternative may be conspicuous by its rarity, we have no empirical data that suggests it will never be employed.

IV

We further conclude that the due process challenge raised on appeal is not sustainable. Appellants have not been deprived of their due process right to be heard; they have only been denied one available defense. Because other defenses remain in their arsenal, they have not lost their ability to defend against the claims brought by asbestos victims. Nor can the contention that the New Jersey court's reasoning is unarticulated and irrational stand in light of the steady evolution over the last twenty years of the doctrine of strict products liability in that state's law. As our discussion of equal protection indicated, there are legitimate state interests here that have a reasonable basis, enabling the New Jersey law to survive scrutiny under the Due Process Clause.

V

In summary, we conclude that common law decisions of state supreme courts are subject to equal protection scrutiny under the same rational basis standard applicable to legislative enactments. Decisions of the state supreme court that fall within the economic and social fields are to be evaluated under the rational relationship test. We further decide that the policies of risk-spreading, compensation for victims, and simplification of trials in the highly unusual circumstances of asbestos claims furnish an adequate, albeit minimal, basis for eliminating the state-of-the-art defense in these cases and preclude a successful equal protection challenge to the New Jersey Supreme Court decision abolishing that defense.

The district court has presented to us the question whether, in strict liability failure to warn cases in New Jersey, the judicially imposed denial of the state-of-the-art defense to manufacturers of asbestos-containing products constitutes a violation of the Equal Protection Clause of the Fourteenth Amendment.

We answer in the negative.

BECKER, CIRCUIT JUDGE, concurring.

I join in Parts I, II and IV of Judge Weis's opinion and concur wholly in the result. I also join in portions of Part III, in which Judge Weis explains why he finds a rational basis for New Jersey's distinguishing asbestos cases from prescription drug cases in terms of the state-of-the-art defense. However, I do not believe that Judge Weis has identified with sufficient precision the New Jersey Supreme Court's reasons for making the distinction under review, a distinction I believe to be supported by a valid government objective and rational within our equal protection jurisprudence. Specifically, I believe that, on the basis of adjudicative facts determined in cases that had the full panoply of procedural protections, the New Jersey Supreme Court has determined a legislative fact—that the hazards of asbestos exposure were knowable to the industry at all relevant times. The subject of legislative factfinding is rarely discussed in the jurisprudence, and I write separately to explain why I think it validates the New Jersey Supreme Court's distinction.

* * * I believe that we need not find constitutional infirmity even if we assume for the sake of argument appellants' worst case scenario, *i.e.,* that New Jersey singles out the asbestos industry.

I

As I read the New Jersey Supreme Court's cases, the court does not deny asbestos defendants the state-of-the-art defense on theoretical grounds. Instead, I believe that the New Jersey court, *via* the *Beshada–Feldman–Fischer* trilogy, has determined a legislative fact—that, at all relevant times, asbestosis harms were knowable to the industry. That being the case, the New Jersey Supreme Court has reasonably decided to preclude endless relitigation of what was "knowable" to the asbestos industry.

* * *

The determination of knowability implicates the standard to which the state is willing to hold a manufacturer of a product: not only must a manufacturer stay abreast of what has already been discovered about his product, but he must also diligently pursue information about its possible dangers before he introduces it for distribution throughout the marketplace. * * * As such, under the aegis of "constructive knowledge," the New Jersey Supreme Court has made a policy judgment concerning the diligence with which the manufacturers should have undertaken additional investigation. * * * Thus, regardless of whether a given manufacturer is found to have actually known of the harms, the New Jersey Supreme Court could find that the industry was chargeable with the knowledge that was attainable had the manufacturers undertaken the task of discovery. As Judge Weis indicates, the court in *Feldman* made clear that "a reasonably prudent manufacturer will be deemed to know of reliable information generally available or reasonably obtainable in the industry." * * * Such a determination cannot be made without reference to facts concerning the availability of information to the asbestos industry as a whole. However, once this factual assessment had been made, the court was also justified in precluding the relitigation of the factual basis of the state-of-the-art defense.

II

Judge Hunter in dissent argues that, because the use of legislative facts concerning the knowability of asbestos harms does not satisfy the requirements of the collateral estoppel doctrine, it violates due process. I disagree. The above discussion demonstrates that, in choosing to allow the state-of-the-art defense for other industries, the New Jersey Supreme Court did not have to turn a blind eye to its belief that the harms of asbestos were knowable to the asbestos industry as a whole. Common law courts could not fashion rules grounded in reality if they were obliged to proceed without aid of legislative facts. As is evident from other cases that have found legislative facts, legislative fact-finding by such a court need not conform to the requirements of collateral estoppel to pass due process muster. I therefore do not believe that the New Jersey Supreme Court can be held to have acted unconstitutionally in finding the legislative facts it did when fashioning the law at issue in this case.

* * *

III

I have not joined the balance of Part III of Judge Weis' opinion because I do not find a rational basis for New Jersey's distinction in any of the other justifications he advances. I briefly note my differences with the remainder of Judge Weis' Part III.

For the most part, the other rationales advanced by Judge Weis do not explain the New Jersey Supreme Court's distinction; rather, they imply that, because of the New Jersey Supreme Court's conceded hegemony over the development of that state's tort law, we must defer to whatever distinction the court draws. For example, he appears to regard the differentiation in and of itself as a matter of state policy in a matter of state expertise, which is said to deserve our deference. * * * Additionally, Judge Weis draws attention to "the federalism concerns that color this controversy"—concerns, I must note, that are ever present in Fourteenth Amendment challenges. * * *

To determine the issue on the basis of such deference, however, assumes the answer to the equal protection inquiry. If we were to defer to the extent suggested by Judge Weis in all equal protection cases, no differentiation could be found irrational. Moreover, this extra dose of deference is duplicative. As Judge Weis so artfully demonstrates in Part II of his opinion, deference to legislative and state decisionmakers is part of the rationale behind the rational relation standard itself. To add greater deference would totally eviscerate that standard. This is clearly not the intended result of rational relation scrutiny. * * * Rather, the rational relation standard requires at least one justification for the challenged differentiation. It may be that the justification is to be judged by the lax standard enunciated in Vance v. Bradley, 440 U.S. 93, 99 S.Ct. 939, 59 L.Ed.2d 171 (1979)(reviewing court must be convinced "that the legislative facts on which the classification is apparently based could not reasonably be conceived to be true by the governmental decisionmakers"), but one such justification must nonetheless exist.

Additionally, although Judge Weis does not rely on administrative convenience simpliciter, he justifies the differentiation at least partially on that basis. I agree with Judge Weis to the extent that he holds that administrative convenience may play a role in prompting differentiation when an independent reason also supports it. As I have explained supra, I find that the New Jersey Supreme Court has reached the conclusion that that the state-of-the-art defense should not be available to the asbestos manufacturers because the harms of asbestos were knowable to the industry. Administrative convenience is thus a justification for the differentiation because state courts are not proscribed by the Equal Protection Clause from refusing to hear a defense that, as a matter of law, is doomed to fail. However, beyond such considerations, administrative convenience fails as a justification.

IV

While states must be allowed to make their own policy judgments in matters such as tort law, they cannot use that discretion to arbitrarily discriminate against a class of litigants. Where a factual basis supports a differentiation, however, both the policy decision and the underlying factual determination deserves our deference. In an equal protection case, those challenging the state law "must convince the court that the legislative facts on which the classification is apparently based could not reasonably be conceived to be true by the governmental decisionmaker." * * * Because the court has found that at least one asbestos manufacturer had actual knowledge of the harms of asbestos at all relevant times, I do not believe that its determination of knowability "could not reasonably be conceived to be true by the governmental decisionmaker." I therefore concur in this aspect of Part III of Judge Weis's opinion.

JAMES HUNTER, III, CIRCUIT JUDGE, dissenting:

PRELIMINARY STATEMENT

In these diversity cases, we look to the law of New Jersey. New Jersey has embraced the full panoply of products liability law. * * * The "state-of-the-art" defense is normally available to defendants in products liability actions. This defense precludes liability where the manufacturer can prove that it did its work properly and produced the product in accordance with the practices and procedures appropriate to the product's known dangers. Today this court has ruled that the manufacturers of one product may not use the state-of-the-art defense. That product is asbestos. The court has said to asbestos manufacturers: there are too many asbestos cases, these cases have clogged up the court calendars, schedules and statistics; the proof of "state-of-the-art" is too time-consuming and concerned with too many variables; and, in any event, we do not think you could prove the defense even if we gave you the chance. Thus, one narrow class of defendants is deprived of a potentially exculpatory defense in the interest of expediency and calendar control. The manufacturers of all other products—including Agent Orange, the Dalkon Shield and DES—may use the defense, even if they are also clogging up the court calendar and causing statistical chaos. Only the asbestos industry is treated differently. This is just plain wrong and I dissent.

I

It is beyond dispute that a classification that neither discriminates against a suspect class nor impinges upon a fundamental right does not violate the Equal Protection Clause if it is rationally related to a legitimate governmental purpose. *See* United States Railroad Retirement Bd. v. Fritz, 449 U.S. 166, 175, 101 S.Ct. 453, 459, 66 L.Ed.2d 368 (1980). While it is beyond our authority to strike down laws simply because we conclude that they are unwise or inartfully drawn, *id.*, neither are we required to give our stamp of approval to classifications that are arbitrary or wholly insubstantial. * * * Whether or not the lawmakers' "governmental purpose" under review must be clearly articulated by the lawmakers in order to be deemed legitimate cannot be definitively answered by reference to Supreme Court precedent. * * * However, our own precedents teach us that "[s]o long as we are careful not to attribute to the legislature purposes which it cannot reasonably be understood to have entertained, we find that in examining the challenged provisions we may consider purposes advanced by counsel ... or suggested initially by ourselves." * * * Our job then, is to determine whether the common law doctrine challenged in this case is in furtherance of a legitimate state purpose put forward by the New Jersey Supreme Court, the appellees, the United States District Court for the District of New Jersey, or ourselves, and whether the common law rule fits closely enough with any of those purposes that it can be said to be rationally related to them. I conclude that New Jersey's common law rule creates a classification that is not rationally related to a legitimate governmental purpose, and therefore deprives asbestos manufacturers of the equal protection of the laws in violation of the Constitution of the United States. * * *

* * *

III

By "restrict[ing] *Beshada* to the circumstances giving rise to its holding," the New Jersey Supreme Court created the classification challenged here. My review of the *Beshada-Feldman* line of cases leads me to conclude that the challenged classification represents nothing more than an unprincipled, expedient, and ineffective response to widespread criticism of the *Beshada* doctrine combined with an unwillingness to give up the application of *Beshada* to asbestos manufacturers. If so, the *Beshada-Feldman* classification is undeniably arbitrary. Worse yet, I fear that the New Jersey Supreme Court's sole purpose may have been to inflict a special punishment on asbestos manufacturers. The Constitution does not permit the New Jersey courts to level either an arbitrary or a punitive sanction against asbestos manufacturers (or the manufacturer of any other product, for that matter). Proper analysis of this classification under the rational basis test should disclose to us whether the classification is impermissibly arbitrary or punitive. I will address each of the justifications for the common law rule advanced by Judge Weis and Judge Becker: the asbestos manufacturers' knowledge of the dangers of asbestos; case-management; and jury confusion. * * *

A

Judge Weis and Judge Becker agree that the principal "legitimate state purpose" underlying the *Beshada-Feldman* doctrine is "the New Jersey Supreme Court['s reasonable decision] to preclude [the] endless relitigation of what was 'knowable' to the asbestos industry." * * * I have trouble accepting this aim as a "legitimate state purpose" under the Equal Protection Clause, because I believe it violates the Due Process Clause of the Fourteenth Amendment. *See* U.S. Const. amend. XIV, Sec. 1 cl. 3.

This so-called legitimate state purpose can best be described as a *de facto* exercise of collateral estoppel without benefit of the procedural niceties. On the basis of the New Jersey Supreme Court's declaratory *dicta* in *Feldman* that asbestos manufacturers did indeed possess culpable knowledge at all relevant times, those manufacturers must be collaterally estopped from litigating the question of their knowledge ever again. Judge Weis feels that this "legitimate state purpose" is a creature somehow related to collateral estoppel, as his discussion of a series of fifth circuit opinions dealing with the procedural complexity of collateral estoppel in massive asbestos litigation demonstrates. * * * [I]t is clear that Judge Weis has concluded that, since plaintiffs have experienced difficulties in prevailing on their collateral estoppel motions heretofore, * * *, the courts may constitutionally grant all plaintiffs the benefit of collateral estoppel through application of their own wisdom rather than the traditional channels of legal process. * * * The grant of a collateral estoppel motion where these conditions are not met violates a party's right to due process. *See* Blonder–Tongue Laboratories, Inc. v. University of Illinois Found., 402 U.S. 313, 329, 91 S.Ct. 1434, 1443, 28 L.Ed.2d 788 (1971). *A fortiori,* Judge Weis' *sua sponte* grant of collateral estoppel to all future asbestos plaintiffs violates the Due Process Clause and thus cannot provide a legitimate state purpose under the rationality test. Indeed, "to use collateral estoppel in this context would be to 'elevate judicial expedience over considerations of justice and fair play.'"

* * *

B

Judge Becker attempts to circumvent the collateral estoppel problem by characterizing the New Jersey Supreme Court's conclusion in Feldman "that the hazards of asbestos exposure were knowable to the industry at all relevant times," Becker at 1245, as a "legislative fact" of which the court may freely take judicial notice. I believe that Judge Becker's argument fails because it relies on a misapprehension of the nature of the legislative facts that may be judicially noticed under the common law of evidence. There are two kinds of fact of which courts may take judicial notice: "adjudicative" and "legislative." "Adjudicative facts are simply the facts of the particular case." Fed.R.Evid. 201 advisory committee's note. " 'Adjudicative facts,' ... are the ultimate facts in the case, plus those evidential facts that are sufficiently central to the controversy that they should be left to the jury unless clearly indisputable." 21 C. Wright & K. Graham, FEDERAL PRACTICE AND PROCEDURE § 5103, at 478 (1977). "Legislative facts, on the other hand, are those which have relevance to legal reasoning and the lawmaking process, whether in the formulation of a legal principle or ruling by a judge or court or in the enactment of a legislative body." Fed.R.Evid. 201 advisory committee's note.

My understanding of what constitutes a "legislative fact" seems to be at odds with Judge Becker's. In my view, legislative facts are those social, economic and philosophical facts upon which we rely to fashion just, appropriate and suitable rules of law. We derive these legislative facts from a common-sense assessment of how modern-day Americans live and view their world. Legislative facts are broad conceptions or beliefs about the interaction of law and society that inform judicial policy-making. As such, these legislative facts may be truisms, or may be wholly incapable of proof or disproof. The United States Supreme Court regularly takes judicial notice of legislative facts to resolve cases involving major policy determinations in the areas of constitutional law and criminal procedure. * * *

I realize, of course, that not all judicially noticed legislative facts involve the kinds of fundamental and glamorous policy questions central to the cases cited in the previous paragraph. Indeed, the observations made through the medium of judicial notice are just as likely to be obvious and mundane. * * * Furthermore, courts may take judicial notice of legislative facts for reasons totally unrelated to the development of policy. For example, courts regularly take judicial notice of legislative facts in order to determine whether or not particular activities come within specified statutory prohibitions. * * * However, I have never heard of any case in which the resolution of an ultimate fact—e.g., the innocence or culpability of a products liability defendant—was reached through the judicial notice of legislative facts.

The asbestos manufacturers' actual or constructive knowledge of the potential harms of asbestos does not bear any resemblance to the legislative facts judicially noticed in the cases cited above or in any other case I have found. The knowledge question does not rest upon a generalized assumption or conclusion about the state of things in order to come to a rational policy decision; rather, it demands the resolution of a hard, cold, specific factual dispute that is central to the products liability litigation between the injured plaintiffs and defendant asbestos manufacturers before the court in each case. The question posed involves a determination of who knew what, when they knew it, and when they should have known it. To my way of thinking, this has every indicia of an adjudicative fact. When a court * * * finds facts concerning the immediate parties—who did what, where, when, how, and with what motive or intent—the court * * * is performing an adjudicative function, and the facts are conveniently called adjudicative facts. * * * Stated in other terms, the adjudicative facts are those to which the law is applied in the process of adjudication. They are the facts that normally go to the jury in a jury case. They relate to the parties, their activities, their properties, their businesses. * * *

* * *

A court may only take judicial notice of an adjudicative fact where that fact is "generally known within the territorial jurisdiction of the trial court [; and] * * * capable of accurate and ready determination by resort to sources whose accuracy cannot reasonably be questioned." Fed.R.Evid. 201. Even assuming that some potential hazards of asbestos were known in the 1930's, it is by no means "generally known" or indisputable that the various specific uses of asbestos (*e.g.,* the use of asbestos to insulate automobile brake linings) were all known to be hazardous to workers or consumers as far back as the 1930's. The fifth circuit and the Southern District of Ohio were not even willing to take judicial notice of the fact that asbestos necessarily causes the various diseases with which it has been associated. According to the fifth circuit in *Hardy II,* "[t]he proposition that asbestos causes cancer, because it is inextricably linked to a host of disputed issues— . . . [including whether or not] this manufacturer [was] reasonably unaware of the asbestos hazards in 1964—is not at present so self-evident a proposition as to be subject to judicial notice." *Hardy II,* 681 F.2d at 347–48. Similarly, the issue of knowledge or knowability is "not at present so self-evident a proposition to be subject to judicial notice." Therefore, the issue of knowledge or knowability cannot properly be judicially noticed as an adjudicative fact under Fed.R.Evid. 201.

Fed.R.Evid. 201 also provides that "[a] party is entitled upon timely request to an opportunity to be heard as to the propriety of taking judicial notice and the tenor of the matter noticed." The parties in this case were not given such an opportunity. Judge Becker argues that "the affected industry [i.e., asbestos manufacturers] had relevant opportunities to respond to the New Jersey Supreme Court's determination of the pertinent legislative facts." * * * The significant opportunities cited by Judge Becker include the industry's participation in two fifth circuit cases, *Hardy* and *Borel,* and in two cases decided by the New Jersey Supreme Court after the Beshada–Feldman classification had been developed, *Fischer* and *In re Asbestos Litigation Venued in Middlesex County,* 99 N.J. 201, 491 A.2d 700 (1984). Judge Becker's conclusion is unprecedented. I have never heard of any case that has permitted a party's "opportunity to be heard" to be satisfied in subsequent litigation before the same court, or—even more incredibly—in prior litigation before an unrelated tribunal. * * * I find the New Jersey Supreme Court's failure to give the asbestos manufacturers an opportunity to be heard as to the propriety of taking judicial notice understandable, in light of the fact that they probably did not realize they were taking judicial notice (of either a legislative or an adjudicative fact) until so informed by Judge Becker.

In sum, Judge Becker has grasped the notion of legislative facts—a notion that this court has viewed with the greatest of skepticism, City of New Brunswick, 686 F.2d at 131—in an attempt to fix the broken shell of the *Beshada* decision and to patch-over New Jersey's violation of the Equal Protection and Due Process clauses. "All the King's horses...."

C

Judge Weis observes that although "[a]dministrative convenience standing alone is not an adequate ground for the elimination of a substantive defense * * * [the court] cannot help but be conscious of the extraordinary size of the asbestos personal injury litigation." While Judge Weis has rejected explicit reliance on the case management rationale as an independent justification for the *Beshada-Feldman* classification, he continues to believe that it buttresses the other justifications he has put forward. Because I find none of the other arguments advanced by Judge Weis or Judge Becker persuasive, I will examine the administrative convenience argument separately to determine whether it provides any support for the challenged classification. I find that it does not. The simple fact that elimination of a defense for one group saves time is not enough to justify discriminating between that group and another that is similarly situated. The case management rationale simply cannot provide a legitimate basis for depriving this one class of manufacturers of an exculpatory defense, particularly in light of the massive expenditure of court time and judicial energy required by DES, Dalkon Shield, *Agent Orange* and miscellaneous pharmaceutical and environmental disaster litigation. I do not mean to imply that the Fourteenth Amendment bars any effort to address a perceived crisis in a particular kind of litigation; legislatures all over the country have demonstrated that such crises can be dealt with constitutionally by developing means that are rationally related to the aim of averting them.

* * *

D

The final "legitimate state purpose" advanced by Judge Weis is the reduction of jury confusion through the complete elimination of the state-of-the-art defense in asbestos cases. The *Beshada* court had observed that "vast confusion ... is virtually certain to arise from any attempt to deal in a trial setting with the concept of scientific knowability," *Beshada,* 90 N.J. at 207, 447 A.2d at 548, and that "discussion of state-of-the-art could easily confuse juries into believing that blameworthiness is at issue." *Id.* This confusion does not stem from the nature of asbestos litigation, however, but from the interplay of the strict liability failure-to-warn action with the state-of-the-art defense. *See Beshada,* 90 N.J. at 204, 447 A.2d at 546. The likelihood of jury confusion provides a justification for one of two paths not taken by the New Jersey Supreme Court: (a) the elimination of a strict liability cause of action requiring the defendant to warn of the unknown and unknowable through the reversal of *Freund* and *Beshada;* or (b) the continued unavailability of the state-of-the-art defense to any defendant in a strict liability failure-to-warn action. The New Jersey Supreme Court balked and refused to make this difficult choice. The jury confusion rationale is, in my opinion, totally undermined by the New Jersey Supreme Court's recent decision in Fischer v. Johns–Manville Corp., 103 N.J. 643, 512 A.2d 466 (1986), holding that punitive damages were available to plaintiffs against asbestos defendants in strict liability failure-to-warn cases. The evidence introduced to determine a punitive damages award is the very same evidence—the state of scientific knowledge at the time of manufacture—that is relied upon in a state-of-the-art defense. Thus, if jury confusion is to be minimized by the exclusion of such evidence, the *Fischer* rule is sure to restore that confusion by the introduction of such evidence. I think the *Fischer* holding is fatal to the jury confusion rationale.

CONCLUSION

My position by no means constitutes the establishment of tort law for New Jersey. It simply means that since New Jersey common law is subject to the operation of the Equal Protection Clause, that clause quite plainly works to bar New Jersey from depriving asbestos manufacturers alone of the state-of-the-art defense, a defense that is available to all other manufacturers in products liability cases. The Supreme Court of New Jersey simply cannot establish a law that violates the Federal Constitution. And this court cannot look the other way and ignore its duty to defend that Constitution.

My answer to the question presented is that the judicially imposed denial of the state-of-the-art defense to manufacturers of asbestos-containing products does constitute a violation of the Equal Protection Clause of the Constitution.

Notes and Questions

1. As the cases suggest, applying the state-of-the art defense in federal diversity mass torts is a matter of *Erie* doctrine, and this defense may or may not be available in federal court from depending on how a particular jurisdiction construes its tort law. As Judge Weis indicates in his opinion, the defendants' objections in the New Jersey asbestos cases raises an interesting *Erie* problem: appeal from a state's judiciary's expansion of common law doctrine (in this instance, rejection of the state-of-the-art defense). Obviously, the *Erie* problem becomes more complicated when a consolidated mass tort involves claimants and defendants from different jurisdictions where the defense is both recognized and rejected. Does this

potential raise an equal protection problem similar to the one complained about by the asbestos defendants? Or is this simply a consequence and price of federalism?

2. The *Beshada* decision cited Hardy v. Johns–Manville Sales Corp., 509 F.Supp. 1353 (E.D.Tex.1981)(excerpted in Part II, Section F on preclusion doctrine, *supra*), one of a series of cases within the Fifth Circuit reflecting varying judicial responses to the state-of-the-art defense in asbestos litigation. *See, e.g.,* Hardy v. Johns–Manville Sales Corp. (*Hardy II*) 681 F.2d 334 (5th Cir.1982); Migues v. Fibreboard Corp., 662 F.2d 1182 (5th Cir.1981); Borel v. Fibreboard Paper Products Corp., 493 F.2d 1076 (5th Cir.1973); Hardy v. Johns–Manville Sales Corp. (*Hardy I*), 509 F.Supp. 1353 (E.D.Tex.1981); Flatt v. Johns Manville Sales Corp., 488 F.Supp. 836 (E.D.Tex.1980); Mooney v. Fibreboard Corp., 485 F.Supp. 242 (E.D.Tex. 1980). *See also* Spartanburg County School Dist. Seven v. National Gypsum Co., 805 F.2d 1148 (4th Cir.1986); Reed v. Tiffin Motor Homes, Inc., 697 F.2d 1192 (4th Cir.1982).

3. Although Judge Weis recognized that the Fifth Circuit repudiated Judge Parker's use of collateral estoppel doctrine to foreclose relitigation of the to state-of-the-art defense, Judge Weis nonetheless seems to suggest that these decisions somehow justify the Third Circuit's affirming the *Beshada/Fischer* decisions, which reject the defense altogether. After reviewing the Fifth Circuit precedents, Judge Weis concludes: "We do not overlook the fact that exposure to asbestos may vary in degree depending on whether an individual works in a plant that manufactures asbestos products or simply drives an automobile equipped with asbestos brake linings. Nevertheless, *Beshada*'s broad language, when applied to the concrete facts of asbestos litigation and read together with *Fischer,* is not completely divorced from reality, despite its abstract appearance of assessing culpability for failure to know and warn of the unknowable."

Isn't Judge Hunter correct in attacking Judge Weis's rationale based on the collateral estoppel precedents? Does Judge Weis's conclusion make sense, at all? Do these precedents in any way support the Third Circuit's affirmance of the New Jersey decisions? Has Judge Weis in his *In re Asbestos Litigation* opinion accomplished what Judge Parker failed to accomplish in the Fifth Circuit? Similarly, is Judge Becker's concurring opinion, arguing at length the distinction between legislative and adjudicative facts, a backdoor method of approving judicial notice that also was attempted by Judge Parker in his asbestos cases, but again rejected by the Fifth Circuit?

4. Typical of many mass tort cases, Judge Weis rests his conclusions concerning the constitutionality of New Jersey's common law rejection of asbestos state-of-the-art defense on additional rationales relating to administrative convenience and judicial efficiency. As Judge Hunter suggests, don't these compelling rationales similarly apply to other mass torts, in addition to asbestos litigation? Judge Hunter argues that not only does *Beshada/Fischer* discriminate as to other tort defendants, but those rulings do not apply even to other mass tort litigations, such as DES or *Agent Orange.* Is Judge Hunter correct? Could the *Beshada/Fischer* ruling conceivably apply to other mature mass tort litigation, depending on the development of historical knowledge relevant to the product design and manufacture?

5. *See generally* Rexford M. Reynolds & Michele Sunahara, Note, Johnson v. Raybestos–Manhattan, Inc.: *The Death of the State of the Art Evidence in Strict Products*, 11 U. Haw. L. Rev. 175 (1989); William J. Warfel, *State-of-the-Art Evidence in Long–Tail Product Liability Litigation: The Transformation of the Tort System into a Compensation System*, 13 J. prod. Liab. 183 (1991).

C. REGULATORY COMPLIANCE DEFENSES

1. THE GOVERNMENT CONTRACTOR DEFENSE

IN RE "AGENT ORANGE" PRODUCT LIABILITY LITIGATION MDL NO. 381

United States Court of Appeals, Second Circuit, 1987.
818 F.2d 187.

Before VAN GRAAFEILAND, WINTER, and MINER, CIRCUIT JUDGES.

WINTER, CIRCUIT JUDGE:

This opinion addresses the disposition of 287 appeals in cases brought by plaintiffs who chose to opt out of the *Agent Orange* class action. These cases remained in the Eastern District of New York after the class settlement as a result of the multidistrict referral. Chief Judge Weinstein granted summary judgment against each of the optout plaintiffs, most of whom now appeal. To avoid repetition, this opinion assumes familiarity with the discussion of the fairness of the settlement in the first of this series of opinions, 818 F.2d 145, and with Chief Judge Weinstein's opinions reported at: 597 F.Supp. 740, 775–99, 819–50 (E.D.N.Y.1984)("Settlement Opinion"); 611 F.Supp. 1223 (E.D.N.Y. 1985)("Opt–Out Opinion"); and 611 F.Supp.1267 (E.D.N.Y.1985)("Lilley Opinion").

After they had settled with the class, the defendant chemical companies moved for summary judgment against the opt-out plaintiffs. Chief Judge Weinstein granted the motion on the alternative dispositive grounds that no opt-out plaintiff could prove that a particular ailment was caused by Agent Orange,* * * that no plaintiff could prove which defendant had manufactured the Agent Orange that allegedly caused his or her injury * * *, and that all the claims were barred by the military contractor defense. * * * We do not address either of these grounds for the grant of summary judgment because we affirm on the military contractor defense.

* * *

The district court granted summary judgment on military contractor grounds because it found no genuine factual dispute as to whether the government possessed as much information as the chemical companies about possible hazards of Agent Orange at pertinent times. * * * This information concerned an association between dioxin exposure and cases of chloracne and liver damage. We agree with the district court that the information possessed by the government at pertinent times was as great as, or greater than, that possessed by the chemical companies. We add a further reason for affirming the grant of summary judgment based on the military contractor defense. Even today, the weight of present scientific evidence does not establish that Agent Orange injured personnel in Vietnam, even with regard to chloracne and liver damage. The chemical companies therefore could not have breached a duty to inform the government of hazards years earlier.

Our consideration of the military contractor defense has been greatly impaired by the inexplicable and unjustifiable failure of the opt-outs' counsel to brief the issue even though it was a dispositive ground for the grant of summary judgment. On appeal, their brief offers only the conclusory statement that "[t]he district court clearly committed error in holding that the government contract defense presented no genuine issues of material fact." We are then referred to 569 pages of deposition excerpts and documents, which are said to "raise clear questions of material fact." No explanation is given of the relevance of these materials, however, and we are left in ignorance of appellants' view of the legal contours of the defense. Appellees, having no discussion to which they might respond, also do not address the issue.

We believe that federal law shields a contractor from liability for injuries caused by products ordered by the government for a distinctly military use, so long as it informs the government of known hazards or the information possessed by the government regarding those hazards is equal to that possessed by the contractor. The military contractor defense has been the subject of several recent judicial decisions, *see* Boyle v. United Technologies Corp., 792 F.2d 413, 414–15 (4th Cir.1986), *cert. granted,* 479 U.S. 1029, 107 S.Ct. 872, 93 L.Ed.2d 827 (1987), Tozer v. LTV Corp., 792 F.2d 403 (4th Cir.1986), *petition for cert. filed,* 55 U.S.L.W. 3337 (U.S. Oct. 23, 1986)(No. 86–674); Shaw v. Grumman Aerospace Corp., 778 F.2d 736 (11th Cir.1985), *petition for cert. filed,* 54 U.S.L.W. 3632 (U.S. Mar.17, 1986)(No. 85–1529); Bynum v. FMC Corp., 770 F.2d 556 (5th Cir.1985); Tillett v. J.I. Case Co., 756 F.2d 591, 596– 600 (7th Cir.1985); Koutsoubos v. Boeing Vertol, 755 F.2d 352 (3d Cir.), *cert. denied,* 474 U.S. 821, 106 S.Ct. 72, 88 L.Ed.2d 59 (1985); McKay v. Rockwell Int'l Corp., 704 F.2d 444 (9th Cir.1983), *cert. denied,* 464 U.S.1043, 104 S.Ct. 711, 79 L.Ed.2d 175 (1984), and has figured prominently in the instant litigation, *see* In re Diamond Shamrock Chemicals Co., 725 F.2d 858, 861 (2d Cir.), *cert. denied,* 465 U.S.1067, 104 S.Ct. 1417, 79 L.Ed.2d 743 (1984); In re "Agent Orange" Product Liability Litigation, 597 F.Supp. at 847–50; 580 F.Supp. 690, 701–05 (E.D.N.Y. 1984); 565 F.Supp.1263 (E.D.N.Y.1983); 534 F.Supp.1046, 1053–58 (E.D.N.Y.1982); 506 F.Supp. 762, 792–96 (E.D.N.Y.1980). Our rationale for the defense is similar to that recently expressed by the Court of Appeals for the Fourth Circuit: Traditionally, the government contractor defense shielded a contractor from liability when acting under the direction and authority of the United States. Yearsley v. W.A. Ross Constr. Co., 309 U.S. 18, 20 (1940). In its original form, the defense covered only construction projects, McKay v. Rockwell Int'l Corp., 704 F.2d 444, 448 (9th Cir.1983), *cert. denied,* 464 U.S. 1043, 104 S.Ct. 711, 79 L.Ed.2d 175 (1984). Its application to military contractors, however, serves more than the historic purpose of not imposing liability on a contractor who has followed specifications required or approved by the United States government. It advances the separation of powers and safeguards the process of military procurement. * * *

* * *

Subjecting military contractors to full tort liability would inject the judicial branch into political and military decisions that are beyond its constitutional authority and institutional competence. *See* Gilligan v. Morgan, 413 U.S. 1, 10, 93 S.Ct. 2440, 2446, 37 L.Ed.2d 407 (1973)("The complex, subtle, and professional decisions as to the composition, training, equipping, and control of a military force are essentially professional military judgments, subject *always* to civilian control of the Legislative and Executive Branches.")(emphasis in original). The allocation of such decisions to other branches of government recognizes that military service, in peace as well as in war, is inherently more dangerous than civilian life. Civilian judges and juries are not competent to weigh the cost of injuries caused by a product against the cost of avoidance in lost military efficiency. Such judgments involve the nation's geopolitical goals and choices among particular tactics, the need for particular technologies resulting therefrom, and the likely tactics, intentions, and risk-averseness of potential enemies. Moreover, military goods may utilize advanced technology that has not been fully tested. *See McKay,* 704 F.2d at 449–50 ("in setting specifications for military equipment, the United States is required by the exigencies of our defense effort to push technology towards its limits and thereby to incur risks beyond those that would be acceptable for ordinary consumer goods"). Whereas judges and juries may demand extensive safety testing for goods marketed in the civilian sector, such testing could impose costs and delays inconsistent with military imperatives.

The procurement process would also be severely impaired if military contractors were exposed to liability for injuries arising from the military's use of their products. Military contractors produce goods for the government according to specifications provided by the government and for uses determined by the government. As long as the government is aware of known hazards, the decision to take the risk is made by the government, and it would be destructive of the procurement process and thereby detrimental to national security itself to hold manufacturers liable for injuries caused by the military's use of their products. Costs of procurement would escalate if contractors were exposed to liability. Contractors would find insurance difficult or impossible to procure, and bankruptcies might occur among companies supplying products essential to national security. Firms would take steps to avoid entering into government contracts, including resort to litigation. The effect on procurement would be particularly acute where claims of toxic exposure might be made and the number of potential claimants would be impossible to determine.

We also note that, absent the shield of the military contractor defense, the legal exposure of the contractor would be much greater than the exposure of a manufacturer that sells to a private corporation that uses its product. In the latter case, the user corporation will also be a defendant and bear some or all of the exposure. Under Feres v. United States, 340 U.S. 135, 71 S.Ct. 153, 95 L.Ed. 152 (1950), and Stencel Aero Engineering Corp. v. United States, 431 U.S. 666, 97 S.Ct. 2054, 52 L.Ed.2d 665 (1977), however, the government cannot be sued and need not even cooperate with the contractor in defending personal injury litigation. Obtaining discovery from the government as a non-party might be difficult or even barred by a claim of national security privilege. The military contractor thus faces the great exposure of being the sole "deep pocket" available. In the instant matter, for example, the United States has avoided all claims against it and has refused to participate in settlement negotiations. Moreover, while the Veterans' Administration ("VA") and the Congress have declined to recognize any ailments other than chloracne and porphyria cutanea tarda ("PCT"), a rare liver disorder, as related to Agent Orange exposure, *see infra,* the chemical companies found it prudent to pay $180 million notwithstanding the weakness of the plaintiffs' case.

At various stages in this litigation, Judge Pratt and Chief Judge Weinstein articulated somewhat different standards to govern the military contractor defense. Judge Pratt stated that each defendant would be required to prove the following elements:

1. That the government established the specifications for "Agent Orange";

2. That the "Agent Orange" manufactured by the defendant met the government's specifications in all material respects; and

3. That the government knew as much as or more than the defendant about the hazards to people that accompanied use of "Agent Orange."

In re "Agent Orange" Product Liability Litigation, 534 F.Supp. at 1055. In elaborating on the third element, Judge Pratt stated that a defendant could not employ the defense if it "was aware of hazards that might reasonably have affected the government's decision about the use of 'Agent Orange,'" * * *, but failed to disclose them to the government. * * *

After discovery and various motions, Judge Pratt concluded that disputes of material fact were involved in determining the third element—the relative knowledge possessed by the government and the chemical companies. * * * However, he concluded that all defendants were entitled to summary judgment with respect to the first two elements—that the government established the specifications for Agent

Orange and that the Agent Orange manufactured by the defendants met these specifications in all material respects. * * *

In approving the settlement, Chief Judge Weinstein addressed the military contractor defense as a potential bar to recovery by the plaintiffs. * * * While adopting the first two elements of the defense as defined by Judge Pratt, he modified the third element as follows:

> A plaintiff would be required to prove, along with the other elements of his cause of action, that the hazards to him that accompanied use of Agent Orange were, or reasonably should have been known, to the defendant. The burden would then shift to each individual defendant to prove (1) that the government knew as much as or more than that defendant knew or reasonably should have known about the dangers of Agent Orange or (2), even if the government had had as much knowledge as that defendant should have had, it would have ordered production of Agent Orange in any event and would not have taken steps to reduce or eliminate the hazard.

* * * "In practical terms," Chief Judge Weinstein explained, this standard means "that a defendant would not be liable despite the fact that it negligently produced a defective product if it could show either that the government knew of the defect or that it would not have acted any differently even if it had known." * * *

We need not define the precise contours of the defense because we believe that under any formulation, and regardless of which party bears the burden of proof, the defendants here were entitled to summary judgment.

Agent Orange was a product whose use required a balancing of the risk to friendly personnel against potential military advantage. That balancing was the exclusive responsibility of military professionals and their civilian superiors. The responsibility of the chemical companies was solely to advise the government of hazards known to them of which the government was unaware so that the balancing of risk against advantage was informed.

Given the purpose of the duty to inform, a hazard that triggers this duty must meet a two-pronged test. First, the existence of the hazard must be based on a substantial body of scientific evidence. A court addressing a motion for summary judgment based on the military contractor defense must thus look to the weight of scientific evidence in determining the existence of a hazard triggering the duty to inform. The hazard cannot be established by mere speculation or idiosyncratic opinion, even if that opinion is held by one who qualifies as an expert under Fed.R.Evid. 702. A military contractor is no more obligated to inform the government of speculative risks than it is entitled to claim speculative benefits. Second, the nature of the danger to friendly personnel created by the hazard must be serious enough to call for a weighing of the risk against the expected military benefits. Otherwise, the hazard would not be substantial enough to influence the military decision to use the product. Neither prong of the test is satisfied in the case of *Agent Orange*.

The use of Agent Orange in Vietnam was believed necessary to deny enemy forces the benefits of jungle concealment along transportation and power lines and near friendly base areas. Its success as a herbicide saved many, perhaps thousands of, lives. At the time of its use, both the government and the chemical companies possessed information indicating that dioxin posed some danger to humans. Indeed, there is evidence that the chemical companies feared that the presence of dioxin in Agent Orange might lead the government to restrict the sale of pesticides and herbicides in the civilian market. *See* P. Schuck, AGENT ORANGE ON TRIAL 85–86 (1986). However, the knowledge of the government and the chemical companies related to chloracne and certain forms of liver damage, ailments now known to be very rare among Vietnam veterans, and not to the numerous other ailments alleged in the instant litigation. Moreover, for the reasons stated in Chief Judge Weinstein's opinions, * * * we agree that the critical mass of information about dioxin possessed by the government during the period of Agent Orange's use in Vietnam was as great as or greater than that possessed by the chemical companies. Nevertheless, the government continued to order and use Agent Orange. The second prong of the test is therefore not met.

Because of the paucity of scientific evidence that Agent Orange was in fact hazardous, the first prong also is not met. This is not a case in which a hazard is known to have existed in hindsight and the issue is whether the defendant had sufficient knowledge at an earlier time to trigger an obligation to inform. Rather, this is a case in which subsequent study indicates the absence of any substantial hazard and therefore negates any claim that the chemical companies breached a prior duty to inform.

When Agent Orange was being used in Vietnam, there was some evidence, possessed as we have said by both the government and the chemical companies, relating chloracne and liver damage to exposure to dioxin. Of course, the fact that dioxin may injure does not prove the same of Agent Orange, which contained only trace elements of dioxin. The precise hazard of the herbicide, if any, was thus a matter of speculation at the time of its use. Now, some 15 to 25 years after military personnel were exposed to Agent Orange, we have considerably more information about the effects of Agent Orange. As noted in our opinion upholding the settlement, * * *, and explained in greater detail in the district court's opinions approving the settlement, * * *, and granting summary judgment against the opt-outs,* * *, epidemiological studies of those very personnel and their families fail to show that Agent Orange was hazardous, even with regard to chloracne and liver damage. While the decisions to use Agent Orange were being made, the most relevant question was not, "What will dioxin do to animals?" or even, "What will dioxin do to humans exposed to it in industrial accidents?" The most relevant question was, "What will Agent Orange do to friendly personnel exposed to it?" The epidemiological studies ask the latter question in hindsight and answer, "Nothing harmful so far as can be told." The fact that the epidemiological studies do not exclude the possibility of harm in isolated or unusual cases or in future cases is of no moment because it does not constitute evidence material to the military decisions in question. Hardly any product of military usefulness is known to be absolutely risk free. Consequently, the existence of a hazard of which the government should have been informed remains unproven to this date, long after the relevant events. Indeed, although chloracne is a leading indicator of exposure to dioxin, it is very rare among Vietnam veterans. Accordingly, there never was information about material hazards that should have been imparted by the chemical companies to the government.

The military decision to use Agent Orange was, therefore, not ill-informed, much less ill-informed as a result of any action by the chemical companies. This conclusion is underscored by the actions of the VA and the Congress in addressing claims by veterans asserting injury by Agent Orange. The VA has recognized only chloracne and PCT as ailments related to Agent Orange. By May 1984, it had granted only 13 chloracne and two PCT claims. It later concluded that none of the 13 chloracne claims actually involved chloracne. * * * In adopting the Veterans' Dioxin and Radiation Exposure Compensation Standards Act, Pub. L. No. 98–542, 98 Stat. 2725 (1984), Congress declined to compensate veterans claiming exposure to Agent Orange for ailments other than chloracne and PCT. It thus rejected earlier versions of the Act that would have compensated such veterans for other medical conditions, including soft tissue sarcomas and birth defects. * * *

The VA and the Congress thus continue to act on the factual conclusion that Agent Orange was hazardous, if at all, only with regard to chloracne and PCT. We believe these actions further demonstrate that the military decision to use Agent Orange was fully informed. To hold the chemical companies liable in such circumstances would be unjust to them and would create a devastating precedent so far as military procurement is concerned.

Affirmed.

2. THE DISCRETIONARY FUNCTION EXEMPTION

IN RE "AGENT ORANGE" PRODUCT LIABILITY LITIGATION

United States Court of Appeals, Second Circuit, 1987.
818 F.2d 210.

Before VAN GRAAFEILAND, WINTER and MINER, CIRCUIT JUDGES.

VAN GRAAFEILAND, CIRCUIT JUDGE:

The above captioned appeals raise a number of issues distinct from that of causal relation, the dominant issue in most Agent Orange cases, and will be disposed of largely on the basis of those unrelated issues.

The appeals are from a dismissal pursuant to Fed.R.Civ.P. 37(b)(2) and from summary judgments, granted by Chief Judge Weinstein of the United States District Court for the Eastern District of New York in opinions reported at 611 F.Supp. 1290 and 611 F.Supp. 1285. The Rule 37(b)(2) dismissal was against Dr. Gerald Hogan, a resident of Nevada. The summary judgments dismissed the complaints of three residents of Hawaii, James K. Oshita and Masao Takatsuki, who sue for personal injuries, and Clara Fraticelli, who sues for the wrongful death of her husband, William. Our discussion of the background and procedural history of this litigation appears in Judge Winter's lead opinion, 818 F.2d 145. * * *

* * *

THE HAWAIIAN APPEALS

In 1967, while James Oshita, Masao Takatsuki and William J. Fraticelli were working for the University of Hawaii at its College of Tropical Agriculture and Human Resources, they allegedly sustained injuries caused by exposure to Agent Orange which was being tested in the fields by University employees. All three filed Worker's Compensation claims, Oshita and Fraticelli in 1979 and Takatsuki in 1981, and all were awarded benefits. Fraticelli died in April 1981. On January 12, 1981, Oshita and Takatsuki presented administrative claims to the United States pursuant to 28 U.S.C. § 2401(b), no such claim has been filed by Fraticelli's widow, Clara. On January 11, 1982, Oshita, Takatsuki and Clara Fraticelli, on behalf of herself and her husband's estate, commenced this suit in the United States District Court for the District of Hawaii seeking relief not only for themselves but also for a proposed class consisting of everyone on the Island of Kauai who had been exposed to Agent Orange. In addition to the several chemical companies which allegedly manufactured the injurious herbicide, the complaint named as defendants ten Regents or former Regents of the University of Hawaii, together with the United States and its Department of Defense. Over the objection of the plaintiffs, the case was transferred to the Eastern District of New York by the Judicial Panel on Multidistrict Litigation.

* * *

A well-recognized exception to the Government's waiver of immunity for tort liability is the "discretionary function" exception found in 28 U.S.C. § 2680(a). The governmental acts of which the Hawaiian plaintiffs complain fall within this exception. It cannot be seriously contended that the decision to use Agent Orange as a defoliant was anything but a discretionary act. In pursuance of this decision, the Government entered into a contract with the University of Hawaii to perform field tests with the herbicide. Plaintiffs, who claim to have been injured during the course of those field tests, cannot remove them from the category of discretionary functions by vague and irrelevant allegations of negligent labeling, shipping, handling, etc. *See* Dalehite v. United States, 346 U.S. 15, 73 S.Ct. 956, 97 L.Ed. 1427 (1953); First National

Bank in Albuquerque v. United States, 552 F.2d 370, 374–77 (10th Cir.), *cert. denied,* 434 U.S. 835, 98 S.Ct. 122, 54 L.Ed.2d 96 (1977).

The Supreme Court's holding in *Dalehite* is summarized well in United States v. S.A. Empresa De Viacao Aerea Rio Grandense (*Varig Airlines*), 467 U.S. 797, 810–11, 104 S.Ct. 2755, 2762–63, 81 L.Ed.2d 660 (1984), where Chief Justice Burger, writing for the Court, said:

> *Dalehite* involved vast claims for damages against the United States arising out of a disastrous explosion of ammonium nitrate fertilizer, which had been produced and distributed under the direction of the United States for export to devastated areas occupied by the Allied Armed Forces after World War II. Numerous acts of the Government were charged as negligent: the cabinet-level decision to institute the fertilizer export program, the failure to experiment with the fertilizer to determine the possibility of explosion, the drafting of the basic plan of manufacture, and the failure properly to police the storage and loading of the fertilizer. The Court concluded that these allegedly negligent acts were governmental duties protected by the discretionary function exception and held the action barred by § 2680(a).

In *Varig,* the Court held that the failure of Federal Aviation Administration employees to check certain potentially dangerous items in certifying the safety of an airplane was the exercise of a discretionary function for which the Government was not liable. 467 U.S. at 820, 104 S.Ct. at 2767.

These two decisions teach us that, where, as here, the Government is performing a discretionary function, the fact that discretion is exercised in a negligent manner does not make the discretionary function exception inapplicable. *See also* Cisco v. United States, 768 F.2d 788, 789 (7th Cir.1985); Begay v. United States, 768 F.2d 1059, 1062–66 (9th Cir.1985); General Public Utilities Corp. v. United States, 745 F.2d 239, 243, 245 (3d Cir.1984), *cert. denied,* 469 U.S. 1228, 105 S.Ct. 1227, 84 L.Ed.2d 365 (1985); Green v. United States, 629 F.2d 581, 585–86 (9th Cir.1980).

* * * The summary judgment in favor of appellees and against appellants, Oshita and Takatsuki, is affirmed. The chemical companies moved for summary judgment against Mrs. Fraticelli on the ground that her claim was barred by the military contractor defense. The district court did not rule upon this claim, and we address it only in general terms. Mr. Fraticelli was a civilian. Nevertheless, his exposure to Agent Orange occurred after the United States government had purchased the herbicide and while the government was testing it for military use. We believe, therefore, that the military contractor defense, as discussed in Judge Winter's opinion affirming summary judgment against the opt-out plaintiffs, 818 F.2d 187, applies to Mrs. Fraticelli's claim. We vacate the dismissal of her claim and remand to the district court for a determination on the motion for summary judgment. The summary judgment dismissing Fraticelli's cause of action against the

United States is vacated and this cause of action is remanded to the district court with instructions to dismiss for lack of jurisdiction. * * *

Notes and Questions

1. The *Agent Orange* decisions illustrate dimensions of the problem of the "regulatory compliance defense." In general, when federal actors have been involved as defendants, they have been successful in invoking the regulatory compliance defense. As described by the American Law Institute, *Reporter's Study,* ENTERPRISE RESPONSIBILITY FOR PERSONAL INJURY (1991):

> The most striking application of regulatory compliance concepts has been in defense of the federal government. Government policy decisions that cause injury, such as the decision to approve a pharmaceutical drug for public use, are protected from liability by the "discretionary function" exemption of the Federal Torts Claim Act. The military cannot be sued in tort by armed service personnel who sustain injuries "incident to service." At the crossroads of these two doctrines is the rule that government contractors who supply the military with products that meet precise specifications determined by the military, and who disclose all foreseeable product risks to the military, are shielded from liability for injuries associated with the products. These three doctrines found joint operation in *In re "Agent Orange" Product Liability Litigation*, in which the court dismissed claims of civilians against the military and the Agent Orange manufacturers, and claims of service personnel against the military and the manufacturers, under each relevant rule. The net result is that fewer federal tortfeasors are liable in tort for the exercise of policy judgment or military authority, and contractors who comply with contract specifications based on such judgment or authority are similarly shielded.

Id., Vol. II at 93–94.

2. At the time of the Second Circuit appeals in the *Agent Orange* litigation, the Supreme Court had granted *certiorari,* but had not yet decided, the appeal in *Boyle* (decided in 1988). *Boyle* is the reigning precedent outlining the contours of the government contractor defense. *See* Boyle v. United Technologies, 487 U.S. 500, 108 S.Ct. 2510, 101 L.Ed.2d 442 (1988). *See also* Feres v. United States, 340 U.S. 135, 71 S.Ct. 153, 95 L.Ed. 152 (1950)(government immunity from military personnel suits). For discussions of the *Boyle* decision, *see generally,* Colin P. Cahoon, Boyle *Under Siege,* 59 J. Air L. & Comm. 815 (1994); Michael D. Green and Richard A. Matasar, *The Supreme Court and the Products Liability Crisis: Lessons From* Boyle*'s Government Contractor Defense,* 63 S.Cal.L.Rev. 637 (1990); Joanne Marie Lyons, Note, Boyle v. United Technologies Corp.: *New Ground for the Government Contractor Defense,* 67 N.C.L.Rev. 1172 (1989). For commentary on the so-called *Feres* doctrine, *see generally* John Astley, Note, United States v. Johnson: Feres *Doctrine Gets New Life and Continues to Grow,* 38 Am.U.L.Rev. 185 (1988); Robert Cooley, Note, *Method to This Madness: Acknowledging the Legitimate Rationale Behind the* Feres *Doctrine,* 68 B.U.L.Rev. 981 (1988); Carole A. Loftin, Note, *Expansion of the Government Contractor Defense: Applying* Boyle *to Vaccine Manufacturers,* 70 Tex. L. Rev. 1261 (1992); J. Thomas Morina, Note, *Denial of Atomic*

Veterans' Tort Claims: The Enduring Fallout from Feres v. United States, 24 Wm. & Mary L. Rev. 259 (1983); Anne R. Riley, Note, United States v. Johnson: *Expansion of the* Feres *Doctrine to Include Servicemembers' FTCA Suits Against Civilian Government Employees,* 42 Vand.L Rev. 233 (1989); David E. Seidelson, *The* Feres *Exception to the Federal Torts Claim Act: New Insight Into An Old Problem,* 11 Hofstra L.Rev. 629 (1983).

3.   The government contractor defense and the FTCA's discretionary function exception have limited application to mass torts generally, insofar as they apply only when named defendants are federal actors. With regard to non-federal actors, federal courts have taken a mixed approach to permitting a regulatory compliance defense. In some jurisdictions a regulatory compliance defense may be available where defendants have complied with federal regulatory requirements and courts apply preemption doctrine to supercede state tort liability. *See* American Law Institute, *Reporter's Study,* ENTERPRISE RESPONSIBILITY FOR PERSONAL INJURY (1991), Vol. II at 92–93 (compiling cases relating to automobile passive restraint design, tampon product labeling approved by the Federal Drug Administration, and cigarette labeling). On the other hand, the general trend has been to deny preemptive effect to federal regulatory schemes unless the applicable law explicitly manifests a Congressional intention to pre-empt state law. *See id.* at 94 n.27, collecting cases.

4.   *See generally* Susan L. Barna, *Abandoning Ship: Government Liability for Shipyard Asbestos Exposures,* 67 N.Y.U. L. Rev. 1034 (1992); James H. Hanes, *Agent Orange—Liability of Federal Contractors,* 13 U. Tol. L. Rev. 1271 (1982); Lora Tredway, Comment, *When a Veteran "Wants" Uncle Sam: Theories of Recovery for Service Members Exposed to Hazardous Substances,* 31 Am. U. L. Rev. 1095 (1982).

Chapter VII

DAMAGES

A. AGGREGATE COMPENSATORY DAMAGES
ORDER, CIMINO v. RAYMARK INDUSTRIES

Review Order in Cimino v. Raymark Industries, *Chapter II, Sections A.5 and Chapter IV, Section D, supra.*

IN RE FIBREBOARD CORP.
United States Court of Appeals, Fifth Circuit, 1990.
893 F.2d 706.

Review Fifth Circuit decision in *In re Fibreboard*, Chapter II, Section A.5, *supra.*

KENNETH S. ABRAHAM & GLEN O. ROBINSON, AGGREGATIVE VALUATION OF MASS TORT CLAIMS
53 Law & Contemp.Probs. 137 (1990) at 139–146, 149–152.

* * *

II
From Necessity to Virtue

Until quite recently, the attention given to innovative techniques for handling mass claims in the judicial system has been focused on procedural mechanisms for centralizing jurisdiction over the claims. Consolidation of claims in class actions is one vehicle for such centralizing; consolidation of cases for pretrial processes and facilitating settlements is another. Both types of consolidation are important means of achieving efficiencies in the adjudication of mass claims. The mere consolidation of claims or cases, however, is only partially responsive to the problems presented by cases like the *Agent Orange*, *Dalkon Shield*, and asbestos actions. The central problem in all of these cases does not lie only in the resolution of the front-end questions of liability and general causation that consolidation is designed primarily to facilitate. Rather, the sticking point in these cases often lies in the back-end allocation of awards to individual claimants once liability and general causation have been established. Consolidation of claims by itself does little to solve this problem. Further innovation is plainly needed.

Until now, the focus of most of the innovation has been on managerial techniques for processing, evaluating, and settling claims, and on the use of alternative dispute resolution ("ADR") procedures for claims that do not settle. These techniques are fairly conventional and largely unexceptionable. All are limited, however, by the boundaries set by the parties themselves; none attempts to modify the basic process by which disputed claims ultimately are adjudicated. The architects of these techniques appear to have assumed that the conventional common law trial procedures for adjudicating disputes cannot be effectively changed in ways that would materially improve the disposition of individual claims when managerial or consensual techniques fail. If this is the assumption, it should not go unchallenged.

Some of the settlement techniques also offer hope for important reforms in the conduct of formal claims adjudication. Especially noteworthy is the use of statistical claims profiles in evaluating individual claims, a technique explored (in practice and in scholarship) by Francis McGovern and outlined by Kenneth Feinberg in his discussion of the Dalkon Shield Option 3 plan. Essentially the strategy is to promote settlement of claims by presenting information to the parties on the valuation of similar claims in prior settlements and/or adjudications. Such a profile provides an indication of the amounts paid, in judgment or settlement, to different categories of claimants. These categories are defined as functions of certain variables that affect liability and the severity and duration of a claimant's injury or illness. Of course, statistical valuation here is at least implicitly, if not explicitly, a function of both probability and payout. More precisely, it is the set of probabilities of different payouts ranging from zero (no liability or no injury) to some upper limit (liability and positive damages up to an amount where the probability of award approaches zero).

This settlement strategy assumes that rational parties are kept from reaching settlement primarily by their different valuations of a claim, and that these different valuations in turn reflect different predictions of the probability and size of an award if the case is adjudicated. The trick, then, is to reduce these disparate valuations, which can be done by presenting profiles of awards in similar cases to both sides. This can be viewed as an attempt to construct a "market value" for the claims. Since the sale of tort claims to third persons is prohibited virtually everywhere, the development of an objective market valuation for such claims is precluded. Absent a true claims market, statistical claims profiles constitute an alternative source of objective valuation.

Of course, the effectiveness of this "surrogate market valuation" is dependent on the parties having a genuine interest in settling the claim on the basis of market value. Where this is the case, the convergence of the parties' respective valuations is expected to produce settlement;

parties will settle when the difference in their valuations is smaller than the expected cost of litigation. It is obvious, however, that whether parties litigate or settle is determined not merely by their respective valuation of the claim and the cost of the two options. Strategic considerations, including idiosyncratic preferences not measured by ordinary information about the market value of a claim, often play a large role in whether parties settle or litigate. It is notoriously true that defendants who face large exposure to multiple claims may adopt a strategy of litigating claims regardless of their individual value to discourage future claims or to encourage more favorable settlements. It is equally notorious that plaintiffs—more precisely, plaintiffs acting through their attorneys—may hold out against settlement at fair value, choosing instead to play a lottery with litigation. In effect this choice reflects a preference, usually the attorney's preference, for risk: the small probability of a large payoff is preferred to the claim's expected value. Notice that if such strategic objectives defeat settlement efforts, they are just as likely to frustrate attempts to implement ADR inasmuch as ADR depends on consent.

* * *

A. Claim Profiles as Evidence

An important first step in promoting settlement would be to permit the claim profiles used in settling claims to be employed in formal adjudication as well. The most modest use would be to permit a profile to be introduced as statistical evidence that the trier of fact—a jury in virtually all of these cases—could consider in evaluating the claim. These profiles would likely be constructed, under the auspices of the courts, by statisticians and other technically qualified experts under the direction of special masters. The profiles would be defined only by "legally relevant" factors: the characteristics of claims or claimants that the finder of fact in any individual trial may consider in making determinations of liability, causation, and damages. For example, in cases in which the asserted basis of liability is the failure to warn of an unavoidably dangerous quality in a product, profiles might take into account variations in different claimants' independent knowledge of the dangerous properties of the product in question if data showed that such differences in information were correlated with variations in earlier awards and settlements. Similarly, in a toxic exposure case, such data might show that awards and settlements varied with the type of disease the plaintiff had contracted and with the probability that contracting different diseases was a result of exposure to a substance produced by the defendant. In such cases, it would be permissible to define profiles by reference to differences in the variation in the severity of the diseases as well as the causal probabilities of contracting these different diseases.

In contrast, it would be impermissible to define the profiles by reference to legally irrelevant factors such as the race, gender, or religion of the claimant, even if data revealed that differences among claimants in these respects actually had affected recoveries in earlier awards and settlements in the same litigation. Although any such differences would be captured by the data aggregated in a given profile, the profile would tend to average the differences, evenly distributing the effect of a legally irrelevant factor among all persons whose claims fit the profile. For example, black and white claimants falling within a particular profile would be entitled to the same award, notwithstanding that, other things being equal, blacks had recovered less (or more) than whites in the cases upon which the profile had been based. By using only legally relevant factors to define the profiles, the risk that legally irrelevant factors had affected the earlier awards and settlements would be distributed equally among all claimants within a particular profile.

Although employing claim profiles formulated in this manner may seem unconventional, the use of statistical evidence has become routine in modern tort cases on questions of liability, causal responsibility, and damages. For instance, epidemiological studies have been the acknowledged basis for establishing general causation in a number of toxic exposure cases. Such evidence is not only relevant but necessary in certain cases. Moreover, even in ordinary tort cases involving permanent injury, the calculation of future damages is heavily dependent on general statistics concerning, for example, life expectancy, economic earnings, and medical costs. In making each calculation, the trier of fact necessarily draws inferences from general statistical evidence on the value of a particular claim. Under our proposal, the trier of fact would draw the same kind of inference from the statistical evidence summarized in a claim profile. Of course, there are differences between the statistical evidence used in conventional tort cases and mass tort claim profile data. The most obvious difference is that the profiles do not represent any objective reality; rather, they are a collection of opinions (those of juries or settling parties in prior cases) as to the value of a particular type of claim, and, legally, they are hearsay opinions that are generally inadmissible into evidence.

We can quickly push aside the hearsay objection. The profiles are hearsay, of course, since they are comprised of what out-of-court declarants (juries or settling parties in other cases) have (implicitly) asserted to be the value of a particular type of claim. All statistical evidence generally is hearsay, however, insofar as it depends on the credibility of persons who put together the underlying observations contained in the statistics. Despite its status as hearsay, statistical evidence is routinely used either directly or as a basis for expert testimony.

The more substantial objection to the introduction of the model profiles is relevance. The argument against admission is that the opinions of prior juries or settling parties as to the value of certain types of claims have no relevance to the particular claim before the court. In part this argument rehashes an old debate about the extent to which disputed issues in a particular case can be resolved by reference to general probabilities (reflected in statistics or simply in intuited generalities, such as in the case of *res ipsa loquitur*) or can be decided only on "particularistic evidence." More than enough has been written on this subject. It is enough for us to record summarily our view that the objections to probabilistic proof rest on an exaggerated distinction between general probability and "particularistic" evidence. In all but the simplest case, determinations about particular facts depend on inferences drawn from generalized knowledge and hence on general probability. In fact, it is difficult to imagine how a mass tort case would be adjudicated without probabilistic inferences drawn from general data.

To be sure, not all data are equally useful, not all probabilities equally strong, and not all permissible inferences equally relevant. Even acknowledging the general use of statistics and probabilistic proof to determine such questions as general causation (for example, asbestos causes mesothelioma), some will no doubt object that the disposition of similar tort claims by prior juries or parties is simply irrelevant to the disposition of any other claim. However, legal relevance is not a free-standing proposition of pure logic; it is always tied to an accepted convention or rule about what the basis for a legal claim should be. The relevance objection to the admissibility of claim profile data rests on the assumption that every claim is unique and that its value therefore must be determined without reference to the value of any other claim, no matter how similar.

Although this is a fairly conventional assumption about the way common law adjudications are supposed to work, it is not a sacred principle of the tort system or of the common law that every claim be completely independent of the results of other claims. Over a century ago, Oliver Wendell Holmes argued that courts should be permitted to crystallize, into more or less fixed rules of law, the accumulated findings of juries on certain commonly occurring issues. His notion has never taken hold in ordinary common law adjudication, in part because of the perceived variousness of common law claims and because of general concerns about invading the province of juries. Neither of these concerns seems very compelling in the context of mass claims adjudication. That we permit collective determinations of common legal and factual issues in class actions and in consolidated cases indicates that there is nothing sacrosanct about individualized adjudication. In the mass tort context, individual determinations are usually unavailable for plaintiffs; settlement therefore is a practical necessity. Being relegated to settlement, these plaintiffs are also relegated to some form of aggregative claims valuation. The same conditions that preclude trial of most such claims also preclude individualized negotiation. The use of claim profiles would extend recognition of this imperative to formal adjudication.

Admittedly, transplanting statistical valuation from settlement to adjudication presents a conceptual problem not confronted in voluntary settlement. As statistical artifacts, the valuations aggregate determinations of liability, causation, and injury that are formally separate in adjudication. In ordinary adjudication, juries are not asked to determine the "value" of a claim on the basis of the claim's distinct elements; rather, they are asked first to determine whether the facts support liability, causal relationship, and injury, and, if so, then to proceed to value the injury. Profile valuations conflate these two types of determinations into a single question of valuation. This aggregation is not unfamiliar to juries, however, as they often informally mix these issues, for instance, by making adjustments in awards based on degrees of certainty about liability or causation. Moreover, it should be emphasized that we are dealing with the "back-end" of the mass tort case. The general questions of liability, or fault, and generic causation have already been determined for the general class of cases. While issues may remain concerning an individual plaintiff's own fault or contribution to her injury, the predominating factor in "back-end" controversies is the existence and amount of injury conventional valuation question.

A more serious difficulty is that developing reliable claim profiles could entail methodological difficulties that can be finessed in consensual settlement, where parties can make their own discount for any methodological infirmities they detect. One concern is that the profiles might be skewed by earlier parties' strategic choices in settling or litigating claims. Though this possibility cannot be overlooked, it is not a substantial obstacle to the use of claim profiles. Any strategic moves of one party can be checked by countermoves of the other. As repeat players, defendants would naturally have the greatest incentive (and ability) to engage in such moves. Sometimes, however, plaintiffs' lawyers are also repeat players because they represent thousands of claimants; then they too would have the incentive (and ability) to manipulate settlement or litigation of some claims for the benefit of others. Moreover, attempts to manipulate the database of the claim profiles are unlikely to be worth the effort unless the party can be assured of having a significant effect on the ultimate shape of the profiles. If the database is large, this would be difficult to accomplish. Recalling our market analogy earlier, one can think of the task as being roughly comparable to the conditions for setting prices in the market: a buyer/seller must have monopoly power or be a member of an effective and durable cartel in the "market" of relevant claims, or attempts to manipulate the market will fail.

Strategic concerns aside, skeptics will undoubtedly be able to identify other problems in constructing reliably representative claims data. For instance, mixing settlements and adjudicated awards in the data base might present a problem to the extent they contain different valuation biases. We cannot pursue these methodological problems further here. It is enough to note that questions of methodology would be the subject of a judicial hearing. We do not propose to allow every plaintiff to challenge the general features of the profiles; this would defeat the purpose of the exercise by threatening to transform every claim adjudication into a trial of statistical methods if not a game of jury confusion. Instead, courts should hold a separate hearing on all of the profiles in order to yield a definitive determination of the validity of methodology and general relevance to the classes of claims to which they will be applied. There is precedent for such a separate hearing on legal and general factual issues in mass tort cases.

* * *

C. Fixed Awards

As long as settlement profiles are used only as evidence, or even as a rebuttable presumption of the value of plaintiffs' claims, our proposal may be seen as making only a modest change in the existing structure of mass tort claims administration. Under our proposal, the parties would be free to settle or not, and juries would have the same power as in conventional cases to make the award they considered correct. However, because profiles would be admitted into evidence and, under our stronger proposal, be rebuttably presumed a correct reflection of the value of the plaintiff's claim, the parties would be encouraged to reach a settlement governed by the relevant profile. Indeed, creating this incentive is an important purpose of the proposal, which is designed to promote voluntary settlement of individual mass tort claims.

Nevertheless, it would be disingenuous for us to claim that our proposal is merely a strategy for encouraging settlement. Although it undoubtedly will do just that, it would do so by altering both parties' substantive rights to the extent that the value of the asserted claim becomes more or less fixed by the profiles of other claims. The change in the parties' formal rights at trial also limits their freedom to reject settlement. Having come this far from traditional common law processes, it is natural to ask whether even more far-reaching modification of the rules governing liability and damages in mass tort cases would be appropriate. For instance, if our aim of limiting jury discretion in making awards is sensible, why not further limit jury discretion? Our concern about the possible ineffectiveness of a rebuttable presumption could easily be solved by making claim profiles dispositive of individual claims. The rebuttable presumption then becomes a fixed schedule of damages—in effect an irrebuttable or conclusive presumption about the value of the plaintiff's claim. Under this further limitation, the jury's only job would be to determine which profile best represents a particular claim. Of course, such a complete collectivization of claims adjudication would radically change the common law system and would probably require legislative authorization. As this is written, a federal trial court in Texas (Judge Parker) has implemented such a collective scheme for a class of some 2300 parties, based on a trial of selected claims that represented the different disease categories into which the class had been divided. This is a bold, as well as unique, experiment. However, the odds are against it being sustained on appeal or emulated by other courts.

Perhaps the most striking feature of a fixed valuation schedule of the sort we propose would be the difference in treatment between the early and later claims associated with the same mass tort. Of necessity the early claims would have to be resolved by current procedures, because there would be no previously resolved claims from which a set of claim categories could be constructed. Once a sufficient number of claims had been tried or settled, however, categories could be constructed and a fixed valuation schedule could be employed. Early claimants would be subject to the full panoply of conventional tort rights and constraints; decisions concerning liability, causation, and damages would be individualized. By contrast, later claimants' tort rights would be determined by the resolution of the earlier claims. Similarly, the rights and liabilities of the defendant (or defendants) would be conventionally "open" at the outset but subject to "closure" after a base of early claims had been categorized.

How can this difference in treatment be justified? The only apparent justification is an entirely practical and obvious one: in the absence of large numbers of resolved claims, there is insufficient data to support the creation of a fixed valuation schedule through the categorization of claimants and claims. Under this view, there can be no presumption, either rebuttable or conclusive, that the value of one claim is equal to the value of others in its category unless there are large numbers of resolved claims to which the claim can be compared.

It might follow that there can be no departure from individualized adjudication through the use of aggregative or fixed valuation as long as the size and components of any given tort claim are dependent on characteristics unique either to that claimant or to the members of a group of similar claimants. However, if fixed valuations are acceptable when they are based on the resolution of an earlier set of similar claims, then the principle underlying individualized adjudication in any tort claim is called into question. Were it not for the absence of a set of previously resolved claims from which to create a fixed valuation schedule, it might make sense to subject the early claims to a fixed schedule of values as well. It may well be, then, that tort liability is imposed on an individual basis and damages are assessed individually simply because we have no other satisfactory way of doing so. Under this view, individual adjudication of liability and damages becomes merely an unavoidable inconvenience rather then a principled requirement of the system.

Once the notion that individualized adjudication is required as a matter of principle has been called into question, the special treatment that mass tort claims has received also becomes problematic. The major argument for special treatment is entirely practical: restricting claimants' access to court, either through consensual or coercive methods, is expedient in mass tort cases because the judicial system would be overwhelmed if it were forced to treat mass tort claims like conventional, individual claims. It does not follow, however, that conventional claims should be privileged at the expense of mass claims. It is expedient to treat an avalanche of mass tort claims in a special manner because the judicial system does not anticipate them; when these claims are initiated, they seem special. But the processing burden these claims place on the courts is not unique; the claims are simply the latest to be filed. The burdens on the judicial system might be removed just as easily by subjecting all conventional claims to special procedures as a matter of course and permitting mass tort claimants unfettered access to individualized adjudication. No principle would preclude such a reversal of priorities. Only the difficulties of categorizing claims and applying fixed

valuations in conventional cases and anticipating mass tort case loads
would stand in the way.

In short, for those who have surrendered the idea that principle
requires individualized adjudication of either conventional or mass tort
claims, adopting something like a conclusive presumption that like
claims have equal value would simply be a problem of legal engineering.
The main obstacle would be finding a model to use in awarding nonindi-
vidualized damages; that problem could be solved, however. For example, out-of-pocket losses usually can be proved easily and paid periodically to avoid most factual disputes. Assessing these losses would be
"individualized," but nevertheless simple and uncontroversial. For obvious reasons, fixing pain and suffering damages would be a bit trickier.
Assuming one were committed to compensating claimants for pain and
suffering, however, it should be possible to construct some kind of
valuation schedule indexed to the type of injury or to medical costs. In
theory, the liability determination itself would have to be adjudicated
individually in conventional tort cases. Once uncertainty about the
magnitude of a claimant's damages were removed, however, in practice
there probably would be very few trials. At this point, consideration of
the use of a conclusive presumption about a claimant's damages would
merge with many of the proposals for general tort reform that have
surfaced in recent years.

What would remain of the traditional cause of action in tort if this
approach were adopted? The very notion of a tort action would simply
be a name given to the process of paying compensation according to a
schedule that bears only an attenuated relationship to the characteristics
of particular claims. Although this compensation might be paid in a
setting that was labelled "tort," in fact most of the characteristics that
would identify that setting as "tort" would have disappeared. The
question would then become whether these claims should disappear from
courts of law as well.

Notes and Questions

1. In a portion of their article omitted from this excerpt, Professors
Abraham and Robinson also suggest that in mass tort cases the jury ought to
give "rebuttably presumptive weight" to the claimant statistical profiles:

> If the profiles were considered simply as evidence, juries, in their (more
> or less) unfettered discretion, would be free to give the profiles such
> force as they considered appropriate. Leaving the jury wholly free to
> act on its discretion, however, would be somewhat at odds with our basic
> premise that unconstrained jury determinations produce excessive varia-
> tion in claim valuations. In optimistic moments, we think that allowing
> juries to consider claim profiles might make juries more skeptical about
> apparently idiosyncratic claims. We cannot be confident, however, that
> self-enforced jury restraint would prevail? It may be useful, therefore,
> to consider giving the profiles special legal authority by making them
> presumptive of the value of each claim within the class to which the
> profile applies.

Abraham & Robinson, *Aggregative Valuation of Mass Tort Claims,* 53 Law & Contemp. Prob. at 146 (1990). To what extent do the Abraham/Robinson proposals meet the concerns about aggregate damages articulated by the Fifth Circuit in *In re Fibreboard*? The authors subsequent admit that "the proposal that claim profiles carry a presumption is awkward." *Id.* at 148. How so? What role would or should a jury have in the damages portion of an aggregated mass tort case? Will their proposals led to a more efficient, streamlined damage allocation? Do the Abraham/Robinson proposals impinge on Seventh Amendment guarantees? If a presumption were to apply as to statistical profiles, why have a jury at all for the damages portion of the case?

2. An non-adjudicative method of allocating aggregative damages is through the auspices of a "claims resolution facility." *See* Chapter XII, *infra* on Administrative Models and Claims Facilities. The concept of a mass tort claim facility for administration distribution of compensation was pioneered in asbestos litigation. From a law-and-economics perspective, Professor Ian Ayres has examined the problem of damage awards allocated by claims resolution facilities. He believes that such claims resolution facilities can provide an effective alternative to individualized litigation, provided that such claim facilities can devise compensation categories that are "cheap to prove, but still costly to fake." Ian Ayres, *Optimal Pooling in Claims Resolution Facilities,* 53 Law & Contemp. Prob. 159, 173 (1990). Professor Ayres endorses compensation grids, but recognizes the gaming aspects that are involved in claimant selection. In endorsing pooling of claims, Professor Ayres explains:

> Because the deterrent effect of tort law turns primarily on a defendant's total liability, aggregate caps on damages shift the focus away from inducing efficient precaution to a concern with the cost of implementation. The most efficient way to distribute damage awards is to minimize the transaction costs in compensating victims. A large component of the transaction costs in compensating mass tort victims concerns the cost of individualized proof of damage and causation. Categorical compensation systems of claims facilities have the potential to increase dramatically the percentage of the defendant's aggregate damages that is actually paid to mass tort victims.

> Categorical compensation of mass tort victims is likely to be Kaldor–Hicks efficient [3] relative to traditional individualized litigation, because such a distribution system will increase the average compensation for victims. It may be difficult, however, to construct categorical compensation packages that are also Pareto-efficient relative to litigation.[4] The pooling of dissimilar victims into dissimilar categories often results in some claimants receiving less damages from a claims facility than from

3. A policy is Kaldor–Hicks efficient if the "winners" could potentially compensate the "losers" so that no one in society suffers a welfare loss. Categorical compensation, which increases the average level of compensation, is likely to be Kaldor–Hicks efficient because those victims who receive less from a claims facility than from litiga-

tion could potentially be compensated by those who made more. Richard Posner, ECONOMIC ANALYSIS OF LAW 12–14 (Little Brown, 3d ed.1986).

4. The standard of Pareto efficiency would require that claimants receive [more] from a claims facility than from litigation.

litigation. This will be especially true if categorical compensation systems induce claimants to file frivolous actions that dilute the average compensation in the pool.

The adverse selection of frivolous claimants represents an important transaction cost of claims facilities that non-frivolous claimants must bear. The adverse selection costs, in a sense, substitute for the litigation costs of individualized proof of causation and damage. Claims facilities are most likely to be Pareto-efficient when the adverse selection costs of claims facilities are less than the litigation costs of proof.

When categorical compensation is not Pareto-efficient, undercompensated claimants will attempt to separate from the pool through litigation. For this reason, claims facilities may face significant "participation constraints" in channeling claimants to lower-cost categorical pools. In some situations, forced pooling, which denies plaintiffs the option of individualized litigation, may be welfare enhancing.

Id. at 160.

B. PUNITIVE DAMAGES
IN RE RELATED ASBESTOS CASES

United States District Court, Northern District of California, 1982.
543 F.Supp. 1152.

* * *

On Motion for Punitive Damages

Defendants' motion on the issue of punitive damages came before this court for hearing on March 23, 1982. The court having reviewed the memoranda submitted in support of and in opposition to this motion, and having heard argument of counsel, rules as follows.

Defendants object to plaintiffs' requests for punitive damages on several grounds.

... First, they argue that plaintiffs' allegations are insufficient to support their claims for punitive damages. In California, punitive damages are governed by California Civil Code Section 3294, which states that punitive damages may be recovered "where the defendant has been guilty of oppression, fraud, or malice." CCP § 3294 (a). Under federal pleading standards, plaintiffs have made allegations of malice sufficient to state a claim for punitive damages. Fed.R.Civ.P. 8(a)(2); Conley v. Gibson, 355 U.S. 41, 47, 78 S.Ct. 99, 102, 2 L.Ed.2d 80 (1957).

Second, defendants argue that even if plaintiffs have properly pleaded malice, plaintiffs will be unable to prove malice, so that the claims for punitive damages should be stricken at the outset. Defendants contend in this regard that only the deliberate falsification of information concerning a product qualifies as malice within the meaning of CCP § 3294. For this proposition, defendants cite Toole v. Richardson–Merrell, Inc., 251 Cal.App.2d 689, 60 Cal.Rptr. 398 (1967), in which it was held that such deliberate falsification constituted a showing of malice sufficient to justify an award of punitive damages. However, the *Toole* case did not define deliberate falsification as the only form of malice sufficient to justify an award of punitive damages. The question whether punitive damages should be awarded is within the discretion of the jury, Davis v. Hearst, 160 Cal. 143, 116 P. 530 (1911), provided that the jury is properly instructed that malice can consist of the intent to vex, injure, or annoy, or to act with conscious disregard for the plaintiffs' rights or safety. Taylor v. Superior Court of Los Angeles County, 24 Cal.3d 890, 895, 157 Cal.Rptr. 693, 598 P.2d 854 (1979). Thus, the jury is empowered to decide that conduct other than deliberate falsification justifies an award of punitive damages. *See, e.g.,* Grimshaw v. Ford Motor Co., 119 Cal.App.3d 757, 174 Cal.Rptr. 348 (1981). We cannot say at the present time that the plaintiffs will be unable to prove malice sufficient to support an award of punitive damages.

However, in order to avoid undue prejudice to defendants in the event that the plaintiffs are unable to prove malice, we will follow the model suggested by California Civil Code Section 3295 (a), and will require each plaintiff to produce evidence of a *prima facie* case of liability for punitive damages prior to allowing the introduction of any evidence of the defendants' profits or financial condition.

The defendants further contend that the purpose of punitive damages, which is to deter further wrongful acts, Evans v. Gibson, 220 Cal. 476, 490, 31 P.2d 389 (1934), would not be served in the present context, where the defendants are already sufficiently deterred from further misconduct by their exposure to cumulative, potentially crippling damages in the nationwide asbestos litigation. This issue is not appropriate for pretrial resolution. It is possible that the plaintiffs will be unable to establish a *prima facie* case of liability for punitive damages as to some or all of the defendants. Such an eventuality would render moot the punitive damages issue as to those defendants. If any plaintiff does establish a *prima facie* case as to some or all defendants, it will be appropriate at that time to consider whether the purpose of deterrence will be served by the imposition of punitive damages upon particular defendants.

Finally, defendants raise various constitutional challenges to the awarding of punitive damages. These issues, too, are unsuitable for pretrial resolution. As noted above, at the present stage of litigation, it is not clear that the awarding of punitive damages is factually applicable to the cases before us. Thus, it would be inappropriate to reach the constitutionality of the awarding of punitive damages at the present time.

Accordingly, the defendants' motion that the claims for punitive damages should be stricken on the grounds that imposition of punitive damages here will not serve the purpose of deterrence, and that the imposition of punitive damages would be unconstitutional, is denied without prejudice.

This order will apply to all related asbestos cases in the Northern District of California, where counsel have had notice and an opportunity to participate in the hearings on these issues, subject to new developments in the law, or to factual inapplicability of our rulings to specific asbestos cases.

So ordered.

IN RE NORTHERN DISTRICT OF CALIFORNIA, DALKON SHIELD IUD PRODUCTS LIABILITY LITIGATION

United States Court of Appeals, Ninth Circuit, 1982.
693 F.2d 847.

Review the Ninth Circuit's rejection of a punitive damages class action certification at Chapter II, Section A.2, supra.

IN RE FEDERAL SKYWALK CASES

United States Court of Appeals, Eighth Circuit, 1982.
680 F.2d 1175.

Review the Eighth Circuit's decision repudiating the district court order enjoining class members from settling their punitive damage claims at Chapter II, Section A.3 (class punitive damages action does not satisfy limited fund requirements).

IN RE "AGENT ORANGE" PRODUCT LIABILITY LITIGATION.

MDL No. 381.
United States District Court, Eastern District of New York, 1984.
580 F.Supp. 690.

PRETRIAL ORDER NO. 92
PRELIMINARY MEMORANDUM ON CONFLICTS OF LAW

WEINSTEIN, CHIEF JUDGE:

A considerable number of Vietnam war veterans resident in all or almost all states, Puerto Rico and the District of Columbia and a number of foreign countries, and members of their families, claim to have suffered injury as a result of the veterans' exposure to herbicides in Vietnam. Defendants produced those herbicides. Individual claims, originally filed in all parts of the country, were transferred for pretrial purposes to this court. Subject to some powers to opt out, common issues presented by plaintiffs' claims will now be tried together since a class has been certified pursuant to Rule 23.

* * *

3. *Punitive Damages*

The third issue of substantive law whose policies must be analyzed for choice-of-law purposes is punitive damages. The states of the veterans' domicile do not have an interest in whether or not punitive damages are imposed on the defendants. The legitimate interests of those states are limited to assuring that the plaintiffs are adequately compensated for their injuries and that the proceeds of any award are distributed to the appropriate beneficiaries. *See, e.g.,* In re Air Crash Disaster Near Chicago, Ill. on May 25, 1979, 644 F.2d 594, 612–613 (7th Cir.1981); Roginsky v. Richardson–Merrell, Inc., 378 F.2d 832 (2d Cir.1967); Hurtado v. Superior Court, 11 Cal.3d 574, 584, 114 Cal.Rptr. 106, 112, 522 P.2d 666, 672 (1974). The only jurisdictions concerned with punitive damages are those, including the federal government, with whom the defendants have contacts significant for choice of law purposes. Those contacts include defendants' place of incorporation, principal place of business, location of the plants that manufactured Agent Orange, and the site of any action taken in furtherance of what plaintiffs refer to as "the conspiracy of silence."

The purposes underlying the allowance of punitive damages are punishment of the defendant and deterrence of future wrongdoing. The purpose underlying the disallowance is protection of defendants from excessive financial liability. *See, e.g.,* Chicago Air Crash Disaster, 644 F.2d at 613; Forty–Eight Insulations, Inc. v. Johns–Manville Products, 472 F.Supp. 385 (N.D.Ill.1979); Pancotto v. Sociedade de Safaris de Mocambique, S.A.R.I., 422 F.Supp. 405 (N.D.Ill.1976).

Courts disagree as to whether, as between the place of misconduct and the primary place of business, the former or the latter has the greater interest in awarding punitive damages. *Compare* Jackson v. K.L.M., 459 F.Supp. 953 (S.D.N.Y.1978) [*with*] Chicago Air Crash Disaster, 614 F.2d at 614–15. It is not necessary to decide that question for purposes of this litigation. The same reasons that justified the application of a single federal law or national consensus law to the government contract defense and to the standard of liability in this product liability case apply to the question of punitive damages. There is no rational method by which a state court could choose the law of any one state to govern the issue. The allegedly wrongful activity has contacts significant for choice of law purposes with at least twelve different jurisdictions. The Agent Orange was manufactured in many states by companies having their principal places of business in many other states, and the meetings and conferences which furthered the alleged "conspiracy of silence" took place in a variety of states.

On the other hand, there is an overriding federal interest in the award of punitive damages. The federal government is interested in the defense contractors' continued willingness and ability to supply material vitally needed for the national defense. The government also has an interest in assuring that defective war material does not injure American soldiers. How the balance should be struck in this case need not be decided now. It is enough to recognize that the federal government's interest parallels its interest in the defendants as war contractors, outlined above, and is demonstrably greater and more specific than the interest of any individual state.

* * *

IN RE SCHOOL ASBESTOS LITIGATION

United States Court of Appeals, Third Circuit, 1986.
789 F.2d 996.

Review Third Circuit's decisions rejecting punitive damages class certification under Rule 23(b)(1)(B) as under-inclusive "limited generosity" class; see Chapter II, Section A.4, supra.

Notes and Questions

1.   Similar to statute-of-limitations and other defenses, the availability and scope of punitive damage claims in mass tort cases are governed by state substantive standards, and in federal diversity cases, through application of state law under *Erie* doctrine.   Among the fifty states, punitive damage issues have become the focus of much litigation and heated public policy debate.   The punitive damage debate centers on two different concerns. The first cluster of problems relate to the availability and standards for award of punitive damages under state law.   Some states do not permit the award of punitive damages at all (Louisiana, Massachusetts, Michigan, Nebraska, New Hampshire, and Washington);   while others restrict punitive damages by statute or common law rules.   In addition, states define differently the standards of conduct that may give rise to punitive damages, the standard of proof required, as well as the method of calculation to award such damages.   *See generally* Mark A. Peterson, *et al.*, PUNITIVE DAMAGES: EMPIRICAL FINDINGS (Santa Monica: The Institute for Civil Justice, Rand 1987).

In the 1990s the Supreme Court has attempted to delimit the constitutional due process parameters for state jury awards of punitive damages;   in each instance a losing defendant challenged a state jury's award of punitive damages under the Eighth Amendment "excessive fines" clause of the constitution, as well as a denial of procedural due process (under the Fifth or Fourteenth Amendments).   *See* Honda Motor Co., Ltd. v. Oberg, ___ U.S. ___, 114 S.Ct. 2331, 129 L.Ed.2d 336 (1994)(Oregon's denial of judicial review of punitive damage award violated due process); TXO Production Corp. v. Alliance Resources Corp., ___ U.S. ___, 113 S.Ct. 2711, 125 L.Ed.2d 366 (1993);   and Pacific Mutual Life Insurance Co. v. Haslip, 499 U.S. 1, 111 S.Ct. 1032, 113 L.Ed.2d 1 (1991).   *See generally* John C. Jeffries, A *Comment on the Constitutionality of Punitive Damages,* 72 Va.L.Rev. 139 (1986);   and Andrew M. Kenefick, *The Constitutionality of Punitive Damages Under the Excessive Fines Clause of the Eighth Amendment,* 85 Mich.L.Rev. 1699 (1987);   Wheeler, *The Constitutional Case for Reforming Punitive Damages,* 69 Va.L.Rev.139 (1986).

Defendants in federal mass tort cases have asserted due process challenges to punitive damage claims.   In addition to the cases excerpted above, *see also* In re "Agent Orange" Prod. Liab. Litig., 100 F.R.D. 718 (E.D.N.Y. 1983), *mandamus denied,* 725 F.2d 858 (2d Cir.), *cert. denied* 465 U.S. 1067,

104 S.Ct. 1417, 79 L.Ed.2d 743 (1984); *but cf.* Leonen v. Johns–Manville Corp., 717 F.Supp. 272 (D.N.J.1989)(allowing punitive damages despite defendant's exposure to multiple punitive damage awards).

2. The second concern relating to punitive damages, which has great relevance for many products mass tort cases, centers on the problem of multiple, repetitive punitive damage awards against the same defendant for the same conduct. The American Law Institute's *Reporter's Study,* ENTERPRISE RESPONSIBILITY FOR PERSONAL INJURY (1991), describes the multiple punitive damage problem:

> Problems arise especially in the context of product litigation alleging defective designs or warnings. * * * If a defectively designed product is unduly hazardous, it may injure hundreds or even thousands of purchasers and users. If liability for punitive damages can be established for any of the resulting tort claims, then such an award should be available for all the claims arising out of the single corporate misdeed. Yet the consequence is that beyond compensatory damages it must pay for the actual losses of its victims, the firm will be penalized again and again for a single wrongful judgment or action, a sanction that is antithetical to the protection against double jeopardy that characterizes overtly penal regimes. In addition, substantial payments for the earlier punitive damage awards may strip the firm of its insurance coverage and assets, thus endangering the ability of later claimants to realize their fundamental tort right to compensatory redress.

* * *

> As an illustration, the A.H. Robins Co. manufactured and sold the Dalkon Shield from June 1970 to June 1974, producing total revenue of about $11 million and profits of about $500,000. By 1985 Robins had paid $530 million to settle 9000 claims and had another 5000 claims pending. By this time the propriety of punitive damages had been established, with some $25 million paid or awarded in a dozen so cases. Faced with escalating liability, the firm filed for Chapter 11 protection.

Id., Vol. II at 260–61 n.50.

3. Georgia and Missouri have made legislative attempts to deal with the multiple punitive damage award problem. *See* Ga. Code Ann. 51–12–5.1 (e)(1) (1990)(allowing only single punitive damage award, to first claimant, for all claims arising out of same conduct); *but see* McBride v. General Motors Corp., 737 F.Supp. 1563 (M.D.Ga.1990)(declaring punitive damage limitation unconstitutional); Mo. Stat. Ann. § 510.263 (4) (Vernon 1952 & Supp.1990)(allowing defendant to credit prior punitive damage award in subsequent litigation arising from same conduct). The Supreme Court has granted certiorari in BMW of North America v. Gore, 646 So.2d 619 (S.Ct.Ala.1993), *cert. granted,* ___ U.S. ___, 115 S.Ct. 932, 130 L.Ed.2d 879 (1995) and will address this issue in this case during the 1995–96 Supreme Court Term.

4. The problem of multiple punitive damage awards in mass tort cases has the additional consequence of depleting the available pool of assets for subsequent future claimants (seeking both compensatory and punitive damages). If this is true, doesn't this situation counsel a class approach to punitive damage awards in mass tort litigation? The American Bar Associa-

tion, in light of the experience of the Dalkon Shield and other mass tort cases, recommended enactment of a federal class action procedure for punitive damage claims. Under the ABA recommendations, a nationwide punitive damages class action could be triggered upon the request of a defendant potentially subject to multiple punitive damage claims for the same conduct. A judicial panel would be required to make a finding that there was a "reasonable possibility" that inadequate compensatory damages would be available if multiple punitive damages were awarded in individual cases. After such a finding and class certification, state and federal punitive damages cases would be consolidated in a binding federal punitive damages class. A federal common law of punitive damages would govern, there would be one mass trial of punitive damages claims, and punitive damages would be distributed *per capita* to class members with a residual amount withheld to compensate future punitive damage claimants. *See* American Bar Association, Section of Litigation, *Report of the Special Committee of Punitive Damages, Punitive Damages: A Constructive Examination* 71–85 (1986). *See also* American College of Trial Lawyers, *Report on Punitive Damages of the Committee on Special Problems in the Administration of Justice* (1989)(similarly recommending federal multi-district or national class action approach to punitive damage awards using either a federal-choice-of-law standard or federal tort standard to determine punitive damages in a mass trial).

To what extent do these proposals address the problems generated by the reluctance and resistance of the federal courts to certify punitive damage class actions, as illustrated by the case excerpts? Doesn't the Rule 23(b)(1)(B) class seem especially tailored for certifying a punitive damages class? Do the Ninth and Third Circuit decisions denying such certification make sense? To what extent do the ABA and ACTL proposals endorse Judge Weinstein's approach to the punitive damage issue in the *Agent Orange* litigation? *See generally* C. Delos Putz, Jr., *et al., Punitive Damage Claims of Class Members Who Opt Out: Should They Survive?,* 16 U.S.F.L.Rev. 1 (1981); Note, *Class Actions for Punitive Damages,* 81 Mich. L.Rev. 1787 (1983).

5. Obviously, multiparty, multistate mass torts give rise to complicated choice-of-law issues relating to applicable punitive damage law. This problem exists for state-based mass torts, where the forum court has to determine which state's punitive damages law will apply (a horizontal choice-of-law issue; *see* Part Four, Chapter VIII, Section B, *infra,* for a discussion of horizontal choice-of-law problems in state mass tort litigation). The applicable punitive damage issue also exists in federal, consolidated diversity mass tort cases (vertical choice-of-law issues). In order to deal with the punitive damages applicable-law problem, the American Law Institute proposed the following set of standards to guide a federal courts determination of applicable punitive damages rules in consolidated mass tort litigation:

§ 6.06 Punitive Damages

(a) In actions consolidated under § 3.01 or removed under § 5.01 in which punitive damages are sought and in which the parties assert the application of laws that are in material conflict, the transferee court shall choose the law governing the award of punitive damages by applying the criteria set forth in the following subsections with the objective of applying a single state's law to all punitive damage claims asserted against a defendant.

(b) In determining the governing law under subsection (a), the court shall consider the following factors for purposes of identifying each state having a policy on punitive damages that would be furthered by the application of its laws:

(1) the place or places of injury;

(2) the place or places of the conduct causing the injury;

(3) the primary places of business or habitual residences of the defendants.

(c) If, in analyzing the factors set forth in subsection (b), the court finds that only one state has a policy that would be furthered by the application of its law, that state's law shall govern. If more than one state has a policy that would be furthered by the application of its punitive damages law, those damages may be awarded if the laws of the states where any two of the factors listed in subsection (b) are located authorize their recovery and the court finds that the possible imposition of punitive damages reasonably was foreseeable to the defendants. If multiple places of injury are involved and they differ as to the availability of punitive damages, the law of the state where the conduct causing the injury occurred governs. When conduct occurred in more than one state, the court will choose the law of the conduct state that has the most significant relationship to the occurrence.

(d) If the court determines that punitive damages are authorized under subsection (c), but the state law identified in subsection (b) differ with respect to the standard of conduct giving rise to the availability of punitive damages, the standard of proof required, the method of calculation, limitations on the amount of punitive damages, or other matters, the order of preference for the governing law on these issues, among the states authorizing punitive damages, is the place of conduct, the primary place of business or the habitual residence of the defendant, and the place of injury.

American Law Institute, COMPLEX LITIGATION PROJECT, *Proposed Final Draft* (1993) at 499–01. Is the ALI's proposed set of choice-of-law principles relating to punitive damages superior to those of the ABA, ACTL, or Judge Weinstein in the *Agent Orange* litigation? What possible problems do the ALI provisions entail? In partial justification for their punitive damage proposals, the Reporters indicate:

* * * [A]n important objective of the rules set out in this section is to allow a single legal standard to control the punitive damage claims asserted against each defendant. Reference to a single punitive damages standard should help increase predictability with regard to these awards, as well as avoid inconsistent treatment of similarly harmed victims. Under the current regime, some plaintiffs receive a windfall and others receive nothing. The application of a single state's law also will foster the consolidation of punitive damages claims, facilitating the imposition of only one punitive damages award to be made against each

defendant, and thereby lessening the potential for a series of awards whose cumulative effect may be disproportionate. Without significant changes in the preclusion rules, however, the consolidation of punitive damages claims does not itself guarantee the avoidance of multiple recoveries. If some claims remain lodged in the state court, for example, additional punitive damage awards might be made.

Id. at 504. Do you agree with the Reporter's optimistic hope that their punitive damage rules will foster mass tort consolidations?

6. For commentary on the problems of punitive damages in the mass tort context, *see generally* Howard T. Edelman, *Punitive Damages Crash in the Second Circuit:* In Re Air Disaster at Lockerbie, Scotland on December 21, 1998, 58 Brook.L.Rev. 497 (1992); Kevin M. Forde, *Punitive Damages in Mass Tort Cases: Recovery on Behalf of a Class,* 15 Loy.U.Chi.L.J. 397 (1984); Donna Fowler, Note, *After the Hyatt Tragedy—Rethinking Punitive Damages in Mass Disaster Litigation,* 23 Washburn L.J. 64 (1983); J.K. Ivery, *Punitive Damages in Mass Product Liability Cases: Hope for Reform?,* 6 Rev.Litig. 69 (1987); Joseph A. Mahoney, *Note, Senate Bill 640: Proposed Federal Product Liability Reform and Its Potential Effect on Pharmaceutical Cases and Punitive Damages Claims,* 36 St. Louis U.L.J. 475 (1991); David G. Owen, *Problems in Assessing Punitive Damages Against Manufacturers of Defective Products,* 49 U.Chi.L.Rev. 1 (1982); Mark D. Peters, Comment, *Punitive Damages, The Common Question Class Action, and the Concept of Overkill,* 13 Pac.L.J. 1273 (1982); Richard A. Selzer, *Punitive Damages in Mass Tort Litigation: Addressing the Problem of Fairness, Efficiency and Control,* 52 Fordham L.Rev. 37 (1983); Tobin L. Briggs, Comment, *The "Limited Generosity" Class Action and a Uniform Choice of Law Rule: An Approach to Fair and Effective Mass–Tort Punitive Damage Adjudication in the Federal Courts,* 38 Emory L.J. 457 (1989).

7. For generalized commentary on the problem of punitive damages, *see generally* Frank J. Barrett & James E. Merriman, *Legislative Remedies for Punitive Damages,* 28 Fed.Ins.Couns.Q. 339 (1978); Griffin B. Bell & Parry E. Pearce, *Punitive Damages and the Tort System,* 22 U.Rich.L.Rev. 1 (1987); Jason S. Johnston, *Punitive Liability: A New Paradigm of Efficiency in Tort Law,* 87 Colum.L.Rev. 1385 (1987); James B. Sales & Kenneth B. Cole., Jr., *Punitive Damages: A Relic That Has Outlived Its Origins,* 37 Vand.L.Rev. 1117 (1984).

Part Four

MASS TORT LITIGATION AND CHOICE OF LAW

Chapter VIII

THE APPLICABLE LAW PROBLEM

A. THE AIRPLANE CRASH CASES
IN RE PARIS AIR CRASH OF MARCH 3, 1974
United States District Court, Central District of California, 1975.
399 F.Supp. 732.

MEMORANDUM OF OPINION IN RE CHOICE OF LAW ON DAMAGES

PEIRSON M. HALL, SENIOR DISTRICT JUDGE.

* * *

On March 3, 1974, shortly after takeoff from Paris, France, a Douglas DC–10 passenger airplane owned and operated by Turkish Air Lines crashed in France, destroying the plane and killing all human occupants (346) aboard, 13 of whom were crew. The number of dependents and claims are unknown, but unofficial estimates have placed that number at about 1,000.

There are 203 suits involving 337 decedents arising from that crash pending in this court. One hundred ninety-one were initially filed here and transferred to the undersigned judge * * * Ten were transferred here from other districts under 28 U.S.C. § 1407 by the Judicial Panel on Multidistrict Litigation and given MDL Docket No. 172.

* * *

That case and all the other cases have been separated on the issue of liability from damages and consolidated with the lead cases and with each other for discovery and related matters.

* * *

Although some counsel have urged the Court to defer to an indefinite date a decision on the question of the law applicable to damages, it seems that advance resolution of that issue is necessary in evaluating the claims for purposes of settlement.

Various arguments have been advanced as to which law should be applied on damages. These include: (1) California, (2) domicile of decedents, (3) domicile of claimants, (4) France, (5) Japan, and (6) California plus French "moral" damages.

We come now to the merits of the questions raised by the motions for determination of the choice of law applicable to damages in this case, with its own unusual set of facts.

The law on "choice of law" in the various states and in the federal courts is a veritable jungle, which, if the law can be found out, leads not to a "rule of action" but a reign of chaos dominated in each case by the judge's "informed guess" as to what some other state than the one in which he sits would hold its law to be. In Wilbur v. Mullaney, 496 F.2d 1303 (1st Cir.1974), the Circuit Court and District Court agreed on the interpretation of state law, but the State Court not only disagreed with both of them but also with "the propriety of [their] effort to interpret it." 496 F.2d at 1305. Most of the cases are involved with such a "guess" as to the law of one other state or perhaps as many as three. Here, if the rule laid down in some cases (not California) were followed, this Court would have to "guess" what the courts in 24 foreign and 12 domestic jurisdictions would hold on the facts in this case, including their "choice-of-law" rules, and who knows what laws of what country or state that would lead to.

Nevertheless, it is my task to discover, if possible, the way damages should be assessed in this case.

The Court is not unmindful of the June 26, 1975, opinion of the Ninth Circuit in Forsyth v. Cessna Aircraft Co., 520 F.2d 608, which discussed "the *judicial nightmare* known as Conflicts of Laws." [emphasis supplied.] Suit was for damage to a plane on the grounds of products liability, rather than for wrongful death or personal injuries. The plane was manufactured and sold in Kansas; the plaintiff's residence and the place of the crash were both Washington; and the suit was filed in Oregon.

The District Court held that: The product was defectively designed; under the Oregon conflict-of-laws rule the law of Kansas applied; and Kansas having no product liability law, the action was barred by the Kansas statute of limitations. The Appellate Court reversed the District Court, holding that the Kansas statute of limitations did not bar the action, and directed the District Court to enter appropriate findings on strict liability and, if found, assess the damages. Nothing was said about the choice of law on damages in any of the three separate opinions written by each judge. This suggests the conclusion that the choice of law on liability should also be the choice of law on damages. It is interesting to note in the *Forsyth* case (Oregon) that reference is made to the place of the accident, while California law adopts the place of the wrong.

The three opinions in *Forsyth* omit discussion on some points which are important in this litigation. There is no mention made of (1) the alternative purpose of strict liability, *viz.*, deterrence; (2) the distinction which should be made between the place of the wrong and that of the accident—if the wrong is in defective design or manufacture, it occurred *at the time and in the place of design and manufacture;* the place where it came to fruition is purely fortuitous; (3) the rights of the manufacturer. In short, the discussions in *Forsyth* assume that the place of the accident governs compensation to all injured within the borders of that state. Under that analysis, the Court would apply French law to determine the damages by the designers and manufacturers in the Paris crash, certainly an undesirable result which could not have been so intended under the California decisions.

In the *Forsyth* case the Court cited with approval a Kansas case which, in turn, cited with approval the following from Richards v. United States, 369 U.S. 1, 11–12, 82 S.Ct. 585, 592, 7 L.Ed.2d 492 (1962): "The general conflict-of-laws rule, followed by a vast majority of the States, is to apply the law of the place of the injury to the substantive rights of the parties." *Richards* did not follow that reasoning in holding that Oklahoma, the place of the alleged negligence, applied the law of the place of death (or accident causing the death) under Oklahoma's conflict-of-laws rules, thus leading to the decision that under Oklahoma law, the law of Missouri (the place of the accident) controlled over Oklahoma's more liberal law.

Upon recourse to the *Richards* case, we find the above-quoted statement was an historical recital of conflict-of-law rules. It was immediately followed by the statement * * *:

"Recently there has been a tendency on the part of some States to depart from the general conflicts rule in order to take into account the *interests of the State* having *significant contact* with the parties to the litigation. We can see no compelling reason to saddle the Act [Tort Claims] with an interpretation that would prevent the federal courts from implementing this policy in choice-of-law rules where the State in which the negligence occurred has adopted it." [emphasis supplied.]

Using the reasoning for that decision (*Richards*), California has seen fit to adopt a well-defined policy of "governmental interest" in its choice-of-law rule set forth in several California cases, but best expressed in Hurtado v. Superior Court, 11 Cal.3d 574, 114 Cal.Rptr. 106, 522 P.2d 666 (1974).

California's choice-of-law rule on damages is not statutory, but has been developed by case law. Under it, in an ordinary case, if diversity of citizenship were the only basis of jurisdiction, this Court would be required to follow the law of the domicile [7] at the time of the crash * * * of each of the plaintiff litigants in the United States and the domiciles of the thousand or so foreign claimants, which are presently unknown to

---

7. The distinction between "citizenship" and "domicile," or "residence" does not appear to be taken note of in the nine representative and leading California cases. In fact, many lawyers file complaints alleging only diversity of "residence" or "domicile"; and the complaints, unless amended, must be dismissed. But inasmuch as the California cases use "domicile," this Memorandum will use "domicile," instead of "citizenship," in speaking of California's conflict-of-laws rule.

this Court, although the decedents are reported to have been nationals of 24 countries. In spot-checking some of the cases, it was noted that the "domicile" of some of the claimants of the same decedent at the time of the crash was in different states or countries than the decedent or each other, which means, if the California rule were to be applied, the heirs or dependents of one decedent would have as many as two or more states or countries apply their individual and different damage rules to the heirs of the same decedent.

Taking one of the cases at random * * *, the heirs are alleged, at the time of the crash, to be citizens and domiciliaries distributed among four countries, *viz.*, France, United Kingdom, Morocco, and Israel. This is not the only case with such a divergence, which produces an unanswerable enigma. If the law of damages of each country controlled, i.e., if in one country (or state) beneficiaries are limited to linear descendants, in another they may be lateral descendants, and in another they may be dependents regardless of blood affinity, and if one country (or state) limited damages, another imposed a penal fine regardless of damages (Colorado), and another permitted punitive damages, the result would be chaotic, and against the faintest instinct for justice by unequal results to those standing in the same relationship to each other and to the decedent.

* * *

So far as the Court can find out from all sources available to it without violating the prohibition of the appellate court, the decedents were from 24 countries, and at least 12 states of the United States were represented among the suits filed—a total of 36 jurisdictions. According to information furnished voluntarily by THY, the human occupants of the plane came from the following countries: Argentina, Australia, Belgium, Brazil, Canada, Cyprus, Denmark, England (United Kingdom), France, India, Northern Ireland (United Kingdom), Republic of Ireland, Italy, Japan, Morocco, New Zealand, North Korea, Pakistan, Senegal, South Viet Nam, Switzerland, Turkey, United States, and West Germany. (Claimants are from all of these countries plus Israel and Sweden.) So far, it presently appears to the Court that claimants are from the states of California, Indiana, Kansas, Maryland, New Jersey, New York, Pennsylvania, South Carolina, Texas, Utah, Virginia, and Washington. How many countries or states are actually involved as to either claimants or decedents neither the Court nor his staff has had time to tabulate, and accurate and complete information has not been supplied to the Court by the parties.

The Court decided from the bench in the early stages of the proceedings, without written opinion, that the law of California and the United States statutes and regulations applicable to these cases would govern the matter of product liability and negligence as well as all other grounds for liability, and that a decision on the choice of law on damages would be deferred to a later date. * * *

The complexity of the problem of the choice of law applicable to damages is further illustrated by some facets of the distinctions in the conflicts rules of the 12 states listed above: Five of them use the "significant contacts" (state-with-substantial-ties-to-a-transaction) approach, sometimes interchangeably with "governmental-interest" or "public-interest" approach; six apply the "place-of-the-wrong," i.e., accident, approach; and California specifically uses the "governmental-interest" approach, and such governmental interest exists when the act or omission which ultimately caused the accident occurred in California.

The measure of damages recoverable also varies: One state limits the amount to $50,000; another, to $75,000; four allow full recovery with varying limitations; one has full recovery plus pain and suffering and mental anguish; and five use "compensatory" and, in some instances, "pecuniary."

No standard or rules for choice of law on damages (where there may be a conflict) of any of the foreign nations involved has been cited to the Court by the parties, and none has been found on independent research, although the parties have set forth the elements of the measure of damages in death cases in some, but by no means all, of the countries involved.

The objective of the governmental-interest approach is "to determine the law that most appropriately applies to the issue involved." Reich v. Purcell, *supra,* at 554, 63 Cal.Rptr. at 34, 432 P.2d at 730. The search must consider the interests of the litigants and involved states.
* * *

Applying this to our case, California has no interest in the distribution of proceeds to foreign beneficiaries, but is interested mainly in (1) deterring conduct of its defendants, (2) avoiding the imposition of excessive financial burdens of its resident defendants, and, I now add, (3) providing a uniform rule of liability and damages so that those who come under the ambit of California's strict product liability law and market their product outside of California and/or in foreign countries may know what risks they are subject to when they make and sell their products. Under the holdings of *Reich* and *Hurtado,* California courts would not apply foreign standards which limit recovery, and would hold that the foreign jurisdiction has no interest in so holding because the latter has no California resident defendant to protect.

When a foreign jurisdiction would allow greater recovery than California, a more liberal standard should NOT be adopted. Gordon v. Eastern Air Lines, 391 F.Supp. 31 (S.D.N.Y.1975). The case arose in the Florida Everglades crash case. After the defendant eliminated liability in Florida in the multi-district litigation proceedings, the case was returned for damage trial to New York, which was plaintiff's residence and the place where the case was originally brought. The case analyzed various jurisdictions to see which had the strongest interest in the outcome, much the same as what California terms the "governmental-interest" approach, and applied New York's measure of damages instead of the Florida law, which permits higher measures of damages. Since conduct was not involved, the place of defendant's business (Florida) was insignificant, and the fact that it was also the crash site was fortuitous. It was argued that Florida also had an interest in promoting tourism, which might be furthered by inducing carriers to exercise greater care through awards of greater damages. This was answered by saying that due care was not in issue since liability was eliminated and that Florida has no interest in how much a New York jury gives a New York resident in a New York court. The Court found New York public policy to be to protect its own residents against unfair foreign laws, but not to enhance recovery by application of more liberal foreign rules. To allow this would induce forum shopping.

Applying the same principles, the California courts would protect resident defendants and would not allow enhanced recovery to plaintiffs because of the fortuitous place of the crash or residence of the litigants. A *fortiori* California would not allow nonresidents a greater recovery than the law of this forum allows its own resident plaintiffs.

* * *

There is no question that three of the four defendants have actual contacts with California, and they will be affected by the outcome of this MDL litigation. The acts and omissions alleged occurred here, and plaintiffs have chosen to bring their suits in this forum. It is, therefore, fitting that the latter be bound by a measure of damages designed to deter misconduct, yet to protect resident defendants against excessive claims.

Counsel for some Japanese claimants, as do counsel for a large block of other claimants, argue that inasmuch as both Japan and France have a broader base for calculating damages, which should result in higher verdicts, the Court should apply Japanese law to the Japanese claimants and French law to all others, including Americans. If that argument were adopted, then it seems to the Court that it would violate the defendants' rights in that it would deny to the defendants the equal protection of the laws guaranteed by the Fourteenth Amendment to the U.S. Constitution. *Kasel, supra,* 24 Cal.App.3d at 741, 101 Cal.Rptr. 314, specifically refuses to adopt a rule that the law most favorable to a plaintiff, whether he be a resident or a nonresident, a citizen or an alien, be applied. Moreover, the Japanese and other foreign plaintiffs voluntarily filed here, and "[he] who takes the benefit must bear the burden" (Cal.C.C. § 3521) is as much a part of the California law as its judge-created conflict-of-laws rule.

It has been argued that the California policy of deterrence will not be impaired by applying foreign law, but that begs the question. Generally a forum applies its own law, and it is incumbent on a litigant who wishes to apply the law of a foreign state to demonstrate that the latter rule of decision "will further the interest of the foreign state and therefore that it is an appropriate one for the forum to apply to the case before it." *Hurtado, supra,* at 581, 114 Cal.Rptr. at 110. That has not been shown here.

Early in these proceedings defendants urged the application of English law of damages (considerably lower than California's) because plaintiffs should not be entitled to recover more than they could recover under the law of their residence. The same argument was rejected in *Hurtado,* at page 586, 114 Cal.Rptr. at page 114, saying:

> Limitations of damages express no such state interest. A policy of limiting recovery in wrongful death actions "does not reflect a preference that widows and orphans should be denied full recovery."

As for those countries or states where recovery would be less than by applying California law, surely they have no interest in limiting recovery of their resident plaintiffs as against a nonresident of their country or state which is a defendant here. Surely the interest of those states would be satisfied so long as there is full recovery for "such damages as may be just," as California allows. Where there is no showing that a foreign interest is greater, or where the interests are equal, California will apply its own law. *See* Bernhard v. Harrah's Club, 42 Cal.App.3d 1024, 1032, 117 Cal.Rptr. 351 (1974).

The Court in this case must consider more than the California governmental interest. It must include the United States interest in this multi-nation situation, as was recently pointed out in Challoner v. Day and Zimmermann, Inc., 512 F.2d 77, 82 (5th Cir.1975).

* * *

It would be as improper to apply forum law merely because it allows a higher return as it would be improper to apply foreign law merely because it allows a lower return; and the converse is true.

Mention has been made of the argument that applying California law on damages would put the California designers and manufacturers at a competitive disadvantage, although it is not clear just how or why this would result from applying the California law on damages. On the contrary, the state of residence of designers and manufacturers has a most significant interest in applying its measure of damages to a product distributed throughout the world for the sake of uniformity of decisions involving such designers and manufacturers, to give only one reason.

Moreover, it must not be forgotten, inasmuch as the United States has preempted the field of regulating aviation * * * to the extent that *no plane manufactured anywhere in the United States can fly without a United States certificate of airworthiness,* that the United States Government has as much, or greater, interest in the products which it certifies as airworthy as any state or any nation in order to insure the integrity of its products in this very competitive world market and also to insure that anyone coming within the ambit of strict products liability shall know that its liability for a defect shall be uniform, no matter where or how the defect is discovered, through accident or otherwise.

As a corollary to the aforementioned integrity of the product put in commerce, the United States has a great concern with its designers and manufacturers of such product. Anyone injured throughout the world should be assured that he can obtain recourse under the law of the state of design and/or manufacture. There is no indication that the designers or manufacturers would be amenable to process or otherwise liable to suit in any other nation of the world. On June 17, 1974, in arguing a motion to dismiss on the ground of forum non conveniens, counsel for McDonnell Douglas suggested that if the Court granted its motion in connection with a suit brought on behalf of an English decedent, McDonnell Douglas would agree to a condition that it consent to jurisdiction in England, without assurance that England would accept this attempt to confer jurisdiction. McDonnell Douglas refused to agree that it was or would be amenable to suit in every foreign country and state of the United States potentially involved. Clearly it is not compatible with American principles of justice and fairness that liability and damages should be determined in accordance with the whim or volition of a defendant designer or manufacturer.

* * *

The Court can take judicial notice that:

The DC–10 plane was designed, constructed, manufactured, and tested in California; it is known throughout the world; it is in direct domestic, foreign, and international competition with wide-bodied jets manufactured abroad as well as with other American-made jets; McDonnell Douglas advertises that the DC–10 is sold to and used by 34 carriers, 25 of which are foreign; according to FAA statistics, there were 110 DC–10's in service throughout the world on March 4, 1974; the airlines using the DC–10 fly into 83 countries or protectorates; 113 foreign cities are serviced by regularly scheduled flights of the DC–10.

The number of million or billion passenger miles flown annually by the DC–10's domestically and internationally is not available, but every mile is a danger to the passenger if he is flying in a plane whose design and construction cannot withstand the decompression explosion caused by a sudden opening into its pressurized baggage compartment. * * *

Clearly the United States and the State of California both have governmental interests in applying the law of California, a state of the United States, in the measure of damages for each claimant, which interests are significantly greater than the interest of the countries or states of which either the decedents or claimants are citizens.

The United States having no general statute promulgating the measure of damages in a death case, the Court, under the Rules of Decision Act (28 U.S.C. § 1652), must, and will, apply the California measure of damages, which is "such damages ... as ... may be just."

In addition to the above, the elements of the measure of damages of the states of the United States whose citizens have sued here are not of enough difference to apply any other law than California's. In doing so, in view of the federal interest, this Court will adopt the liberalization over California's interpretations of the phrase "pecuniary loss" as laid down by the Supreme Court in Sea–Land Services v. Gaudet, 414 U.S. 573, 94 S.Ct. 806, 39 L.Ed.2d 9 (1974).

* * *

ANDREAS F. LOWENFELD, MASS TORTS AND THE CONFLICT OF LAWS: THE AIRLINE DISASTER

1989 U.Ill.L.Rev. 157–163 (1989).

I. INTRODUCTION

Of all the mass torts we have come to know, airplane crashes have been around the longest and have remained among the most puzzling from the conflict-of-laws perspective. With employment-related injuries such as asbestosis, following the law of the place of employment makes sense; with product-related injuries, courts may need to choose between the law of the place of manufacture and the place of consumption. Normal expectations would link the law governing a fire or other disaster in a hotel to the hotel's location. Airplanes, however, have no fixed location, and no given link seems superior to any other. Moreover, in the past fifteen years most litigation resulting from airplane disasters has involved at least two major defendants, the airline operator and the manufacturer, and often a third, the federal government as operator of air traffic control. To complicate the choice of law decision further, add the odd combination of multistate litigation under federal auspices but applying state law, plus the *Erie*,[2] *Klaxon*,[3] *Van Dusen*[4] trilogy as it works out in airline accident litigation, and further, the numerous issues of substantive law that different states resolve differently. If airplane accidents a quarter century ago contributed strongly to the unshackling of conflict of laws from the bonds of Holmes and Beale—* * *—the airplane cases in the 1970s and 1980s seem to have made a parody not only of the conflict of laws but of the law of torts in general.

Conflict of laws has become a game—or rather an element in a game—quite skillfully played by certain masters who have realized that neither resourceful discovery nor seduction of a jury is the whole story of an airplane accident case. I fly a good deal, and my wife has instructions that if I go down, she is to get in touch with a particular New York attorney who is skilled in discovery, working juries, and conflict of laws. That is because in such an event, I would hope that my widow and children would receive the most money possible, without any concern about what such a result would do to airline fares, litigation costs, insurance rates, or justice. While I am alive and privileged to look at the

2. Erie R. Co. v. Tompkins, 304 U.S. 64 (1938).

3. Klaxon Co. v. Stentor Elec. Mfg. Co., 313 U.S. 487 (1941).

4. Van Dusen v. Barrack, 376 U.S. 612 (1964).

issue from the vantage point of a professor who has taught torts, civil procedure, aviation law, international law, and conflict of laws, I hope I can address the subject somewhat more dispassionately.

II. THE ISSUES

For me, airplane disasters raise many of the questions of the purpose of law generally—of deterrence and retribution, of allocation of risk, of equality of treatment, of expectation and reliance, of compensation and grief, and of the meaning, or at least the valuation, of a life. I suspect that no two persons, and certainly no two legislators, share my views on these questions precisely. Indeed, I am not sure that my own views on these questions are the same today as they were two decades ago, when for a time I had some impact (for good or ill) on the rules for compensating victims of airplane disasters in international air transportation.

. . . At the end of the day, however, conflict of laws is supposed to teach how to decide specific cases. What law, to take a familiar case, should govern the consequences of a crash in Illinois of a plane bound from Chicago to Los Angeles? [16] Should the victims all be treated alike for this purpose, or should distinctions be drawn according to where the passengers began their journey, where they planned to end their journey, or where they were domiciled? Does it matter where the airline had its corporate headquarters, or its maintenance base? Does it matter where the airplane was put together, or where the manufacturer had its headquarters? Does it matter where a given action was initiated, and for what purpose it was transferred? Are the answers the same for all the issues that may arise—strict liability vs. negligence; punitive damages vs. compensatory damages only; compensation for pain and suffering, or for grief or for economic loss only? And so on. * * *

III. THE *CHICAGO DC–10* CASE

All these issues were raised in the *Chicago DC–10* case, which involved the crash with complete loss of life of an American Airlines plane bound from Chicago to Los Angeles; many of these issues are raised in almost every airline disaster litigation. I mention the *Chicago DC–10* case in particular because the court there made an extraordinary effort to cope with the 118 actions filed on behalf of 271 persons aboard the plane plus two persons on the ground. The decedents were residents of ten states of the United States, plus Puerto Rico, Japan, the Netherlands, and Saudi Arabia. Apparently the accident occurred because one of the giant jet engines came loose and fell to the ground just as the plane was taking off from O'Hare Airport in Chicago, causing the aircraft to flip over, crash, and burn. All the plaintiffs sought punitive damages both from the plane's manufacturer, McDonnell–Douglas, and from the carrier, American Airlines.

16. In re Air Crash Disaster Near Chicago, Ill. on May 25, 1979, 500 F.Supp. 1044 (N.D.Ill.1980), *rev'd in part, aff'd in part,* 644 F.2d 594 (7th Cir.), *cert. denied,* 454 U.S. 878 (1981).

The district court determined (1) that the choice-of-law rule in each case depended on the state where the action had been brought, and (2) that by one theory or another the courts of each of those states would look to the law of the principal place of business of the respective defendant. This conclusion led the court to disallow the claim for punitive damages against the airline, because its principal place of business (as the court found) was New York, which at the time did not permit punitive damages in wrongful death cases. The manufacturer, however, had its principal place of business in Missouri, and that state did not prohibit punitive damages; accordingly, the district court declined to grant McDonnell–Douglas's motion to strike the claims for punitive damages.

One might object right here: if the plane was designed or manufactured with egregious disregard of the duty of care, that conduct must have taken place in California, at the former Douglas Aircraft facility in Long Beach where the plane was principally designed and assembled, and not in Missouri at corporate headquarters. As for American Airlines, if it was egregiously at fault in maintaining the aircraft, that conduct probably took place at its maintenance base in Oklahoma, and not where the board of directors met in New York. Moreover, if the disaster resulted from failures by both the manufacturer and the carrier, a decision that would effectively place all the excess liability—*i.e.*, all the damages greater than an amount found to equal the loss—on one of the two parties without determination of their relative responsibility seems unfair, without, I think, any redeeming attraction. But we must not spend too long on the decision of the district court, because the Court of Appeals for the Seventh Circuit, in effect, started over.

First, the court of appeals asked whether it had real or merely apparent conflicts before it. It examined not only the six states already mentioned—three principal places of business (because American Airlines was moving), a place of manufacture, a maintenance base, and the place of accident—but also Hawaii, because one plaintiff had brought suit in that state and its courts might apply Hawaii law as the law of the forum or of the decedent's domicile. As one might expect in this time of transition, the law on punitive damages in wrongful death actions in all of these states was not perfectly clear. Missouri's law was ambiguous, California's law was uncertain, and Hawaii's law was unknown. Eventually, the Seventh Circuit concluded that punitive damages were permitted in Missouri, Texas, and Oklahoma, but not in Illinois, New York, California, and Hawaii. All that proved, however, was that there was a real, not just an apparent conflict-of-laws problem.

Next, the court had to play the *Van Dusen v. Barrack* game, looking for the choice-of-law rules for each of the six states where actions arising out of the crash had been brought. The court understood that this search was not a general one, but a search with regard to each state's interest in punitive damages. *Depecage,* in other words.

The court's research was nothing if not thorough: For actions begun in Illinois, the court concluded that RESTATEMENT (SECOND) OF CONFLICT OF LAWS was applicable, which the court read as pointing to the place of injury, unless another state had a more significant relationship to the occurrence or the parties. How can one tell whether "unless clause" applies? The diligent court went through the general criteria of section 6 of the RESTATEMENT, and then through the more specific criteria of section 145—*i.e.,* "contacts." This led the court to examine (i) the place of injury; (ii) the place of misconduct; (iii) the domicile, residence, nationality, place of incorporation, and place of business; and (iv) the place where the relationship between the parties was centered. First, this inquiry was aimed at McDonnell–Douglas. As to the relationship of plaintiffs with McDonnell–Douglas, the court was temporarily lucky. It did not have to decide for the Illinois plaintiffs between Illinois law (the place of departure) and California law (the place of destination), because neither law permitted punitive damages in death cases. As to domicile, the court imported the interest connection: does the state of the defendant's domicile have an interest in punishing resident defendants? The court went back and forth, but came down eventually for deterrence and corporate accountability: it held that Missouri, the state with punitive damages (according to the court) and the place of McDonnell–Douglas's corporate headquarters had an interest as great as that of California, where the aircraft was assembled.

Remember, the federal appeals court performed this exercise to determine how Illinois state courts would view the problem. The court concluded that as between California and Missouri, the balance on the scales was even. As to Illinois itself, the place of injury was fortuitous. But the court, sitting in Chicago, took judicial notice "that the DC–10 crash sent shock waves throughout the metropolitan Chicago area. Illinois special emergency disaster units responded to the crash. The state certainly incurred significant expense in attempted rescue operations, clean-up operations . . ." and so on. "As the home of O'Hare International Airport, one of the world's busiest airports, Illinois certainly has strong interests in encouraging air transportation corporations to do business in the state." Where did all this probing lead (apart from a fluid drive shift from contacts to interests)? The court concluded:

> Although either California or Missouri, taken separately, would have a greater interest than Illinois, the fact that the laws of these states are in absolute conflict indicates that neither state has an interest greater than the other's. Thus, in terms of a principled basis upon which a choice can be made, neither state has a "more significant interest" than Illinois. Since neither California nor Missouri can be chosen on a principled basis, the application of the "most significant relationship" test leads to the use of Illinois law.

I do not stop to cavil at the apparent interchangeability in Judge Sprecher's opinion between "most significant interest" and "most significant relationship." More ominous is that by now twenty-two pages in the Federal Reporter have been filled, covering only the claims against one of the two defendants, and only by those plaintiffs who sued in Illinois. The opinion has another defendant to go for the Illinois plaintiffs, and actions from five other forums brought by persons with fifteen or so other domiciles to take through both defendants. I do not pause to paraphrase the remaining seventeen pages of the court's opinion, except to report that eventually both California's "comparative impairment" approach and New York's "functional equivalent of the RESTATEMENT (SECOND) test" (as the court put it) led to Illinois as the tie breaker; those initial forums, such as Michigan and Puerto Rico, that would apply lex loci also pointed to Illinois. Thus in the end, no one was entitled to punitive damages.

IV. THE BURDENS OF *KLAXON* AND *VAN DUSEN*

Could we do better? I wish I could be sure. I cannot detect any reversible error in the decision of the court of appeals in the Chicago DC–10 case. It is only fair, moreover, to mention that Judge Sprecher expressed his own frustration at the end of his opinion and pleaded for a uniform federal law applicable to airline torts. * * *

* * *

Notes and Questions

1. As Professor Lowenfeld suggests in his article, an earlier generation of airplane crash accidents led the way in modernizing modern conflicts-of-law thinking. *See e.g.* Gore v. Northeast Airlines, Inc., 373 F.2d 717 (2d Cir.1967); Long v. Pan Am. World Airways, Inc., 16 N.Y.2d 337, 213 N.E.2d 796, 266 N.Y.S.2d 513 (1965); Griffith v. United Air Lines, Inc., 416 Pa. 1, 203 A.2d 796 (1964); Pearson v. Northeast Airlines, Inc., 309 F.2d 553 (2d Cir.1962)(*en banc*), *cert. denied,* 372 U.S. 912, 83 S.Ct. 726, 9 L.Ed.2d 720 (1963); Kilberg v. Northeast Airlines, Inc., 9 N.Y.2d 34, 172 N.E.2d 526, 211 N.Y.S.2d 133 (1961). But as he also suggests, the modern air crash disaster cases have evolved into almost a parody of conflicts-of-law problems that arise in multiparty, multiforum disaster litigation. To what extent, if any, do the airplane disaster cases provide a reasonable model for state and federal courts to determine applicable law in contemporary products-liability mass tort litigation? Keep in mind that airplane crashes are the paradigmatic "single-site" mass accident case. To what extent do the choice-of-law principles developed in this context provide a reasonable basis for thinking about multiforum contemporary mass tort litigation? *See generally* Thomas M. Reavley and Jerome W. Wesevich, *An Old Rule for New Reasons: Place of Injury as a Federal Solution to Choice of Law in Single–Accident Mass–Tort Cases,* 71 Tex. L.Rev. 1 (1992).

2. At a minimum, the airplane crash cases are instructive for illustrating generic choice-of-law issues that arise in multiple victim disaster cases. First, the determination of applicable law depends on whether a case is filed in state or federal court. Both the Paris and Chicago air crash disasters were filed in federal court and therefor subject to *Erie* rules to determine applicable law. *See* notes 3–4, *infra.* If, instead, these cases had been filed in state court, then the state court judge would have referred to California or Illinois choice-of-law principles to determine which possible state or foreign

law applied to issues in the case. This is known as a "horizontal" choice of law determination, and as the excerpts above suggest, state approaches to determining applicable law are quite varied. *See* discussion of possible state choice-of-law regimes, *infra* at Section B.

Second, the air crash disaster cases also illustrate that courts must make independent choice-of-law determinations for each issue in the case: in tortious actions, that will mean an independent applicable law determination for liability, limitations, damages, etc. *See e.g.,* In Re Air Crash Disaster at Sioux City Iowa, 734 F.Supp. 1425 (N.D.Ill.1990)(punitive damages issue not governed by plaintiff's domicile); In Re Air Crash Disaster at Stapleton Int'l Airport, Denver Colorado on November 15, 1987, 720 F.Supp. 1505 (D.Colo.1989)(negligence issues governed by Colorado law but compensatory damages resolved with reference to law of each plaintiff's domicile); *cf.* In Re Air Crash Disaster Near New Orleans, Louisiana on July 9, 1982, 789 F.2d 1092 (5th Cir.1986), *rehearing en banc* 821 F.2d 1147 (5th Cir.1987), *vacated on other grounds sub nom.* Pan American World Airways, Inc. v. Lopez, 490 U.S. 1032, 109 S.Ct. 1928, 104 L.Ed.2d 400 (1989)(compensable losses determined by same law governing liability).

3. For air crash disaster and other mass tort litigation filed in federal court, the federal judge must apply state law under *Erie* principles if the applicable law is substantive. In 1941, the Supreme Court in Klaxon Co. v. Stentor Elec. Mfg. Co., 313 U.S. 487, 61 S.Ct. 1020, 85 L.Ed. 1477 (1941), determined that state choice-of-law principles are substantive for *Erie* purposes. The Supreme Court subsequently announced that in cases transferred within the federal system under 28 U.S.C.A. § 1404(a)—whether the transfer is initiated either by the defendant or the plaintiff—the federal judge is to apply the law of the transferee court. *See* Van Dusen v. Barrack, 376 U.S. 612, 619, 84 S.Ct. 805, 810, 11 L.Ed.2d 945 (1964); Ferens v. John Deere, 494 U.S. 516, 110 S.Ct. 1274, 108 L.Ed.2d 443 (1990). This "trilogy" (now four) of *Erie* cases (*Erie–Klaxon–Van Dusen–Ferens*) supplies the analytical framework for federal judges in attempting to determine applicable law in federally transferred and consolidated litigation; it also supplies the analytical framework in MDL cases transferred and consolidated under 28 U.S.C.A. § 1407. Why does Professor Lowenfeld somewhat cynically call this process as the *"Van Dusen* game"? Although Professor Lowenfeld believes Judge Sprecher did a commendable job of ascertaining the applicable law relating to the punitive damages issue in the Chicago air crash disaster, he clearly also believes that this choice-of-law process leaves much to be desired. Why?

4. Federal courts, applying *Erie-Klaxon–Van Dusen* principles, have adopted various state choice-of-law approaches to resolving applicable law issues in air crash disaster litigation. *See e.g.,* Lewis–DeBoer v. Mooney Aircraft Corp., 728 F.Supp. 642 (D.Colo.1990)(applying RESTATEMENT SECOND, CONFLICTS OF LAWS principles); In Re Air Crash Disaster Near New Orleans, 789 F.2d 1092 (5th Cir.1986)(interest analysis); In Re Air Crash Disaster at Stapleton Int'l Airport, Denver, Colorado on November 15, 1987, 720 F.Supp. 1505 (D.Colo.1989)(subclassing parties and claims as governed by different applicable law).

5. In the remainder of his article, Professor Lowenfeld questions whether the *Klaxon* rule makes any sense in limiting the ability of federal judge to make independent choice-of-law decisions in federal multiparty, multiforum diversity cases, suggesting that *Klaxon* either ought to be judicially limited or legislatively overruled:

> Would such an act be constitutional? Could Congress provide, for example, that in state-created actions involving a given number of plaintiffs and an air carrier or aircraft manufacturer as defendant, a federal court could make its own choice-of-law decisions, without reference to the choice-of-law doctrine of any state? I believe the answer is yes, though there are not many examples of state-created actions partly governed by federal law. * * * It seems to me as a constitutional matter that if a claim arising out of a state-created right can be made into a federal matter by virtue of federal legislation focusing on a particular class of defendants, the same could be said about a case being heard in federal court by virtue of legislation concerning the removal, transfer, and consolidation of a particular class of actions. Thus we need not, I think, ask whether *Klaxon* could or should be legislatively reversed to conclude that Congress could carve out aviation accidents— or all mass torts—from the burdens that have overwhelmed the federal courts in *Chicago DC–10* and in so many other cases.

Lowenfeld, *Mass Torts and the Conflict of Laws: The Airline Disaster,* 1989 U.Ill.L.Rev. at 164. Whether *Klaxon* is constitutionally compelled or should be overruled legislatively is the central issue that has informed most of the applicable-law debate for modern mass tort litigation. *See* Chapter X, *infra.*

6. *See generally* John B. Austin, *A General Framework for Analyzing Choice-of-Law Problems in Air Crash Litigation,* 58 J. Air L. & Com. 909 (1993); James A.R. Nafzinger, *Choice of Law in Air Disaster Cases: Complex Litigation Rules and the Common Law,* 54 La.L.Rev. 1001 (1994); Prewitt, *Federal Common Law of Aviation and the* Erie *Doctrine,* 40 J. Air L. & Com. 653 (1974); Williard Reese, *The Law Governing Airplane Accidents,* 39 Wash. & Lee L. Rev. 303 (1982).

B. CHOICE OF LAW IN STATE–BASED MASS TORTS

GIOVANETTI v. JOHNS–MANVILLE CORP.

Supreme Court of Pennsylvania, 1988.
372 Pa.Super. 431, 539 A.2d 871.

JUDGES: CIRILLO, PRESIDENT JUDGE, and McEWEN and MONTEMURO, JJ.

Opinion by: CIRILLO

This is an appeal from the Court of Common Pleas of Philadelphia County in which a jury relieved various corporations of liability to Louis Giovanetti for injuries allegedly resulting from his exposure to asbestos. We affirm.

Louis Giovanetti, a New Jersey resident, initiated this action in the Philadelphia Court of Common Pleas to recover for injuries allegedly sustained as a result of exposure to asbestos. The exposure allegedly occurred during his employment as a tinsmith and a welder in both New Jersey and Pennsylvania over the course of nearly thirty years. Giovanetti named various manufacturers and distributors of the asbestos products as defendants. The trial was conducted in reverse bifurcated form, with the questions of damages and causation being determined before liability.

On the second day of trial, the defendants indicated for the first time that they were seeking the application of New Jersey law to the facts of the case. The court complied, and the jury was told to disregard any of counsel's opening arguments that were based on the application of Pennsylvania law. The jury determined that Giovanetti suffered no compensable injury as a result of his exposure to asbestos, thereby obviating the need to proceed to the second phase of the trial. Giovanetti filed for post-trial relief, which was denied. This appeal followed.

Giovanetti contends that he should be granted a new trial for the following reasons: (1) the inherently prejudicial effect of the court's application of New Jersey law at the appellee's behest when both parties had completed a portion of the trial with the tacit understanding that Pennsylvania law would apply; * * * [Other grounds for appeal omitted.—*ed.*]

Giovanetti first contends that he was prejudiced by the application of New Jersey law to the facts of his case. Although he does not suggest that the choice of New Jersey law was invalid, he maintains that Pennsylvania law should have been chosen in light of the tacit agreement among the parties that Pennsylvania law would apply. This agreement, according to Giovanetti, was evidenced by the fact that before the conflict of law issue was raised, twenty-three of the twenty-nine points for binding instruction submitted to the court by the appellees referred to Pennsylvania cases, and none referred to New Jersey law. Additionally, counsel for both parties based their opening statements on Pennsylvania law and Giovanetti had already presented his first witness, whose testimony was based on Pennsylvania law.

When faced with choice of law questions, Pennsylvania courts have abandoned the rule of *lex loci delicti* in favor of a less restrictive approach combining the methodologies of a "government interest analysis" and the "significant relationship" approach of the Restatement (Second) of Conflicts § 145 (1971). *See also* Griffith v. United Air Lines, Inc., 416 Pa. 1, 203 A.2d 796 (1964). The paramount consideration under this analysis is:

> the extent to which one state rather than another has demonstrated, by reason of its policies and their connection and relevance to the matter in dispute, a priority of interest in the application of its rule of law.

McSwain v. McSwain, 420 Pa. 86, 94, 215 A.2d 677, 682 (1966). Furthermore, in reviewing the relative interests of each jurisdiction in a cause of action, Pennsylvania courts will weigh their respective contacts qualitatively, rather than quantitatively. *See* Cipolla v. Shaposka, 439 Pa. 563, 267 A.2d 854 (1970).

In weighing the relative interests of Pennsylvania and New Jersey in this particular litigation, we conclude that New Jersey law is more appropriately applied. Because six of the appellee corporations are Pennsylvania-based, Pennsylvania can certainly be viewed as possessing a legitimate interest in ensuring that Pennsylvania companies do not manufacture or distribute hazardous products which cause injury. That interest, however, is clearly eclipsed by the numerous contacts between New Jersey and the present cause of action. Giovanetti, a resident of New Jersey, spent twenty-seven of his working years in New Jersey, as opposed to only two years working in Pennsylvania. Any relationship he had with the manufacturers and distributors of the asbestos products was centered in New Jersey. Considering the fact that asbestos-related disease is proportionally related to the extent and duration of exposure, it is not unreasonable to assume that any injury he may have suffered as a result of exposure to asbestos occurred primarily in New Jersey. Furthermore, all of the appellees were doing business in New Jersey at the time of his alleged exposure. New Jersey, then, has a compelling interest in seeing that its citizens are compensated for injuries which occurred within its borders, allegedly as a result of the appellees' business there.

In light of the quality and number of contacts between New Jersey and Giovanetti's exposure to asbestos, it is clear that the trial court properly applied New Jersey law. In so holding, we reject Giovanetti's initial contention that either New Jersey or Pennsylvania law could have been applied under a *Griffith* analysis. Giovanetti further argues, however, that his case was prejudiced by the timing of the appellees' request. Specifically, he suggests that the defense's belated request that New Jersey law be applied confused the jury, hampered him in the presentation of his case, and prejudiced his right to recover.

Regardless of the theorized effect of the appellees' mid-trial request that New Jersey law should apply, Giovanetti's claim must fail for the simple reason that the application of New Jersey law to the facts of the case put him in no worse a position than he would have been in had Pennsylvania law been applied. In fact, an analysis of the respective laws of the two states reveals that Giovanetti actually benefits from the application of New Jersey law.

The primary difference between the laws of Pennsylvania and New Jersey with respect to the litigation of asbestos-related suits is fundamental. Pennsylvania treats all injuries arising from the same tortious conduct of a defendant as one cause of action subject to the standard limitations period. *See* Cathcart v. Keene Industrial Insulation, 324 Pa.Super. 123, 471 A.2d 493 (1984). Because of the constraints such an approach imposes on a plaintiff's ability to obtain compensation for foreseeable, but distant injuries arising from the same tortious conduct, Pennsylvania courts allow an injured plaintiff to produce expert testimony as to the possible future effects of that conduct. *See* Schwegel v. Goldberg, 209 Pa.Super. 280, 228 A.2d 405 (1967). Thus, if Pennsylvania law is applied, Giovanetti would be able to recover for any injuries he could presently prove as well as for the increased risk of cancer. On the other hand, New Jersey recognizes cancer as an injury separate and distinct from asbestosis and considers the cause of action for such an injury to accrue only when the individual has discovered, or should have discovered, that he has cancer. *See, e.g.,* Herber v. Johns–Manville Corp., 785 F.2d 79 (3d Cir.1986).

Thus, the application of New Jersey law can be viewed as actually benefiting Giovanetti rather than hindering his cause of action. Because the jury determined that he suffered no compensable present injury as a result of his exposure to asbestos, it is unlikely that they would have awarded him damages based on an increased risk of cancer under Pennsylvania law. This is especially true when Giovanetti himself testified that he was advised that the risk of cancer was "damn near none." Should that risk ever become realized, Giovanetti would be free to pursue a future action in his home state and would not be barred by either a statute of limitations period or res judicata, because New Jersey recognizes asbestosis and asbestos-related cancer as two distinct actions.

With respect to the "timing" issue, we find no merit in Giovanetti's claim that, in requesting that New Jersey law be applied, the appellees violated a tacit agreement that Pennsylvania law would apply. This agreement, as envisioned by Giovanetti, was based primarily on the defense's submission of points for binding instructions which cited Pennsylvania cases almost exclusively. Although the numerous and substantial contacts between New Jersey and the present litigation would lead us to believe that both parties should have recognized the possible application of New Jersey law to the case, we recognize that points for instruction are often submitted to the court in a prefabricated or "canned" form. Thus, although defense counsel committed some degree of error in submitting instructions based on Pennsylvania law, we are not prepared to find that they did so with the intent to mislead Giovanetti.

Furthermore, as a result of the jury's finding that Giovanetti suffered no compensable present injury as a result of his asbestos exposure, it was unlikely that he could have proven a compensable risk of future injury under Pennsylvania law. Therefore, we fail to see how he was prejudiced by the adoption of New Jersey law after he had elicited testimony as to that risk, especially when New Jersey law permits a later suit if that risk becomes realized. As to Giovanetti's claim that the mid-trial shift in law unduly confused the jury, we are satisfied that the trial judge's exhaustive instructions that they should disregard only those arguments made pursuant to Pennsylvania law were sufficiently clear to safeguard against any possible prejudice. In light of the foregoing, we reject Giovanetti's claim that the application of New Jersey law was prejudicial to his cause of action.

* * *

Order affirmed.

BAROLDY v. ORTHO PHARMACEUTICAL CORP.

Arizona Court of Appeals, 1988.
157 Ariz. 574, 760 P.2d 574.

JUDGES: CORCORAN, PRESIDING JUDGE. JACOBSON and BROOKS, JJ., concur.

Opinion by: CORCORAN

Defendant-appellant Ortho Pharmaceutical Corporation (Ortho) appeals from the judgment entered in favor of appellees Roberta Baroldy and Lee Baroldy (plaintiffs) after a jury awarded them $1,500,000 in this products liability suit.

Ortho is incorporated in Delaware with headquarters in New Jersey. It does business in all 50 states. Ortho contends on appeal that the trial court erred in applying Arizona law rather than North Carolina law, and then applied that law erroneously in its evidentiary rulings, resulting in prejudice to Ortho that requires a new trial. Ortho does not claim that Arizona courts do not have jurisdiction or provide a proper venue.

Because we find no reversible error, we affirm the judgment.

1. FACTUAL BACKGROUND

Approximately 6 weeks after the birth of her first child in April 1982, Roberta Baroldy's obstetrician prescribed an Ortho All–Flex diaphragm. Ortho has manufactured and sold many millions of diaphragms for more than 40 years. Roberta began using the diaphragm in early July 1982, and experienced discomfort. She returned to her obstetrician on July 8, 1982, to check the fit of the diaphragm, and was assured it fit well. During the next three days, she inserted and removed the diaphragm repeatedly, wearing it for extended periods. On July 11, 1982, Roberta awoke with a high fever and a flushed appearance. Her husband, Lee, took her to the emergency room of the local hospital, where she was told she had the flu. Roberta returned home, where her symptoms worsened. She returned to the emergency room late that afternoon, and was admitted for treatment. Her hospital record indicates that a culture taken from her diaphragm tested positive for *Staphylococcus aureus* (*S. aureus*), a common symptom of toxic shock syndrome (TSS). *See generally* Chesney, Bergdoll, Davis & Vergeront, THE DISEASE SPECTRUM, EPIDEMIOLOGY, AND ETIOLOGY OF TOXIC-SHOCK SYNDROME, 38 Ann. Rev. Microbiol. 315 (1984). The admitting physician recorded in Roberta's medical record that his initial evaluation was "Toxic shock state secondary to retained vaginal diaphragm." Roberta was hospitalized for 41 days with TSS, at times comatose and near death.

Ortho does not dispute on appeal that Roberta had TSS, although that issue was litigated at trial. Plaintiffs' medical witnesses testified at trial that Roberta will continue to have physical problems the rest of her life as a result of the disease.

At the time Roberta's diaphragm was prescribed, the Patient Information Booklet (PIB) accompanying the device contained the following statements:

> You need not feel any urgency about removing the diaphragm. It is safe to let it remain in position for 24 hours. Should you forget to remove it for some hours, or should removal be inconvenient at any particular time, that is no cause for concern. Just bear in mind that if you desire to have intercourse again, you must first apply more spermicidal jelly or cream.

Prior to and during Roberta's hospitalization, plaintiffs were living in North Carolina, where Lee was temporarily stationed in the United States Army. After Roberta's release from the hospital, plaintiffs returned to Arizona, where they had lived prior to Lee's enlistment. In October 1983, plaintiffs filed this products liability suit against Ortho in Arizona, claiming first, that the diaphragm was defective under 2 RE-STATEMENT (SECOND) OF TORTS § 402A (1965)(§ 402A) because Ortho's PIB failed to warn diaphragm users of the danger of TSS, and second, that the product was defective under § 402B because the PIB contained false or misleading statements. Plaintiffs also asserted claims of negligence and breach of warranty, which were later withdrawn.

After a lengthy trial, the court entered judgment for the plaintiffs on the jury's verdict. The jury awarded plaintiffs compensatory damages in the amount of $1,500,000. Although the issue of punitive damages was submitted to the jury, none were awarded. Ortho has timely appealed from this judgment, but Ortho does not claim that the judgment is excessive.

2. CHOICE OF LAW

Ortho first argues that the trial court erred in applying the products liability law of Arizona rather than the negligence law of North Carolina. Arizona has adopted §§ 402A and 402B, but North Carolina has not. *Compare* Salt River Project Agric. Improvement & Power Dist. v. Westinghouse Elec. Corp., 143 Ariz. 368, 694 P.2d 198 (1984) *with* Smith v. Fiber Controls Corp., 300 N.C. 669, 268 S.E.2d 504 (1980). North Carolina thus does not recognize the doctrine of strict products liability. Byrd Motor Lines, Inc. v. Dunlop Tire and Rubber Corp., 63 N.C.App. 292, 304 S.E.2d 773 (1983). Ortho contends that 1 RESTATEMENT (SECOND) OF CONFLICTS § 146 (1971)(§ 146) [1] creates a presumption that the law of the state where the injury occurred—here, North Carolina—governs the choice of law issue. Ortho also contends that, under the

---

1. Section 146 provides as follows:

Personal Injuries

In an action for a personal injury, the local law of the state where the injury occurred determines the rights and liabilities of the parties, unless with respect to the particular issue, some other state has a more significant relationship under the principles stated in § 6 to the occurrence and the parties, in which event the local law of the other state will be applied.

general principles of § 145,[2] North Carolina law should apply because North Carolina has more contacts with the parties and the occurrence than does Arizona.

The parties argued this issue at trial after plaintiffs sought partial summary judgment on the choice of law question. The trial court found that "Arizona law clearly applies and controls this case, rather than the law of either North Carolina or New Jersey," after concluding that "the most significant relationship to the occurrence and the parties exists in this jurisdiction and Arizona has the greater interest in the determination of this matter."

Because choice of law is a question of law, our review of this issue is *de novo*. *See, e.g.*, Bryant v. Silverman, 146 Ariz. 41, 703 P.2d 1190 (1985); Ambrose v. Illinois–California Express, Inc., 151 Ariz. 527, 729 P.2d 331 (App.1986). Our analysis has three parts. First, we must consider the general principles of § 145 to determine the number of contacts and the weight of each state's contacts with the parties and the occurrence. Second, those contacts must be taken into account in applying the principles of 1 RESTATEMENT (SECOND) OF CONFLICTS § 6[3] to determine which state has the most significant to the occurrence and the parties. Third, the specific principles of § 146 must be applied. *See generally* Bates v. Superior Court, 156 Ariz. 46, 749 P.2d 1367 (1988); Bryant v. Silverman; Ambrose v. Illinois–California Express, Inc.; Kimble & Lesher, PRODUCTS LIABILITY §§ 331–36 (1979).

A. *Section 145.* Beginning with § 145, we find that Arizona has the most significant contacts with the parties and occurrence. First,

---

2. Section 145 provides as follows:

The General Principle

(1) The rights and liabilities of the parties with respect to an issue in tort are determined by the local law of the state which, with respect to that issue, has the most significant relationship to the occurrence and the parties under the principles stated in § 6.

(2) Contacts to be taken into account in applying the principles of § 6 to determine the law applicable to an issue include:

   (a) the place where the injury occurred,

   (b) the place where the conduct causing the injury occurred,

   (c) the domicile, residence, nationality, place of incorporation and place of business of the parties, and

   (d) the place where the relationship, if any, between the parties is centered. These contacts are to be evaluated according to the relative importance with respect to the particular issue.

3. Section 6 provides as follows:

Choice-of-Law Principles

(1) A court, subject to constitutional restrictions, will follow a statutory directive of its own state on choice of law.

(2) When there is no directive, the factors relevant to the choice of the applicable rule of law include

   (a) the needs of the interstate and international systems,

   (b) the relevant policies of the forum,

   (c) the relevant policies of other interested states and the relative interests of those states in the determination of the particular issue,

   (d) the protection of justified expectations,

   (e) the basic policies underlying the particular field of law,

   (f) certainty, predictability and uniformity of results, and

   (g) ease in the determination and application of the law to be applied.

although the "place of injury" was North Carolina, that location was a mere happenstance because Roberta was in North Carolina because of temporary military assignment over which her husband had no control, and because the same injury could have happened to her regardless of where she lived. *Cf.* Hitchcock v. United States, 665 F.2d 354 (D.C.Cir. 1981)(place of injury was fortuitous when plaintiff was injured while temporarily assigned to a location in connection with government service). Additionally, here plaintiffs demonstrated damages for both future medical expenses and loss of future income, indicating that the injuries are likely to continue in Arizona, where plaintiffs are domiciled. *Cf.* Moore v. Montes, 22 Ariz.App. 562, 566, 529 P.2d 716, 720 (1974)(Arizona has an interest in insuring that its injured residents do not become wards of the state as a result of long-term injuries that require medical treatment).

Second, although the place where the conduct causing the injury occurred is unclear, it is unlikely that the conduct occurred either in Arizona or North Carolina. *Cf.* Ambrose, 151 Ariz. at 530, 729 P.2d at 334. In a failure to warn case, the "place of conduct" is where the tortious decision is made. *See* § 146, comment d; Danner v. Staggs, 680 F.2d 427, 430 (5th Cir.1982)(place of misconduct in a negligence action is where the negligent decision is made). Thus, plaintiffs' incidental conduct is not relevant to the choice of law issue. *Hitchcock,* 665 F.2d at 359–61. Here, Ortho's corporate decision about what to include in its PIB most likely occurred at its principal place of business in New Jersey.[4] *See* Bates, 156 Ariz. at 49–50, 749 P.2d at 1370–71. The parties have agreed that the products liability laws of Arizona and New Jersey are virtually identical for purposes of this analysis; New Jersey law thus presents no "conflict" to resolve. Comment i to § 145 indicates that, when the law of two states does not conflict, the contacts from those two states should be considered as if they were from the state involved in the choice of law question. *See also* Myers v. Cessna Aircraft Corp., 275 Or. 501, 513, 553 P.2d 355, 367 (1976). Thus, for purposes of our § 145 analysis, the place where the conduct occurred—New Jersey—can be considered an Arizona contact.

Third, the domicile, residence, and principal place of business of the parties again indicate an Arizona contact. Ortho does not dispute that plaintiffs have always been Arizona domiciliaries. Although plaintiffs were residing in North Carolina at the time of the injury, we have already dismissed that temporary circumstance as fortuitous. Ortho has its principal place of business in New Jersey. Comment e to § 145 indicates that the corporate place of business is a more important contact than the place of incorporation. Again, grouping New Jersey contacts with Arizona contacts because the laws of those states do not conflict, the "domicile" factor weighs heavily in favor of Arizona. In § 145 analyses, the domicile of the plaintiff often carries the greatest

---

4. Neither party argued in the trial court that Delaware law should apply to this matter. The parties further agreed that, although New Jersey has an interest in regulating Ortho's conduct, New Jersey law would not apply.

weight. *See, e.g., Bates; Bryant; Ambrose.* This is because "the state where the injury occurs does not have a strong interest in compensation if the injured plaintiff is a nonresident. * * * Compensation of an injured plaintiff is primarily a concern of the state in which plaintiff is domiciled." *Bryant,* 146 Ariz. at 45, 703 P.2d at 1194. In this case, the fact that plaintiffs are Arizona domiciliaries is the most significant factor.

Fourth, the place where the relationship between the parties was centered was undisputedly North Carolina. This factor, however, carries little weight in our analysis because of the fortuitous location of the injury. Plaintiffs could have duplicated their relationship with Ortho anywhere.

Section 145 thus indicates that Arizona is the state with the most qualitative contacts between the parties and the occurrence.

B. *Section 6.* We next turn to the choice-influencing factors of § 6 relevant to choosing the applicable rule of law.

First, the parties agree that the needs of the interstate system will not be impaired by the application of Arizona law. Second, the relevant policies of the forum indicate that Arizona has the more significant interest. Arizona has adopted §§ 402A and 402B to protect its citizens from defective products by compensating resident tort victims and preventing future misconduct. *See, e.g.,* Salt River Project Agric. Improvement & Power Dist., 143 Ariz. at 375, 694 P.2d at 205. North Carolina courts, on the other hand, have declined to adopt §§ 402A and 402B out of deference to the legislature as a policymaker. *Smith v. Fiber Controls Corp.* Furthermore, even if North Carolina declined to adopt strict products liability because of a policy aimed at protecting its resident defendants from liability, Ortho would be outside of that protected class as a foreign corporation. *See* Turcotte v. Ford Motor Co., 494 F.2d 173 (1st Cir.1974). In this case, Arizona's policy concerns clearly supersede any competing North Carolina policy. *Cf.* Trahan v. E.R. Squibb & Sons, Inc., 567 F.Supp. 505 (M.D.Tenn.1983)(applying Tennessee products liability law rather than North Carolina negligence law).

Similarly, a consideration of the relevant policies of New Jersey and the basic policies underlying its tort law reinforces Arizona's significant interest. Because New Jersey has virtually the same relevant law, its policies are not disrupted by holding its resident corporation Ortho liable under Arizona law. Application of Arizona law also promotes the basic policies underlying all tort law: to compensate victims and to deter future misconduct. *See* Gordon v. Kramer, 124 Ariz. 442, 604 P.2d 1153 (App.1979).

The § 6 considerations of "protection of justified expectations" and "certainty, predictability, and uniformity of result" are largely irrelevant in this analysis for several reasons. First, because Ortho does business in all 50 states, it can expect to be subject to liability in those states that have adopted strict products liability. Second, Ortho has not indicated that it altered its business activity in North Carolina in reliance on that law. *See Trahan,* 567 F.Supp. at 510 ("[A] large national corporation doing business in all states does not make its marketing decisions on the basis of whether a state has or has not adopted § 402A"). Third, because an outbreak of TSS cases in diaphragm users is hardly a planned occurrence, predictability and uniformity are not important considerations. See *Gordon.*

Finally, we find that an Arizona jury could apply either Arizona products liability law or North Carolina negligence law with equal ease.

Our § 6 analysis compels the conclusion that Arizona is the state with the most significant interest.

C. *Section 146.* Applying § 145 and § 6 principles to the specific rule in § 146, we hold that Arizona's significant relationship to the occurrence and the parties justifies the application of Arizona law as the exception to the rule that the local law of the state where the injury occurs generally applies.

We thus conclude that the trial court properly applied Arizona law in this case.

Notes and Questions

1. The *Giovanetti* and *Baroldy* cases illustrate how state courts resolve applicable law issues in products liability litigation where arguably more than one state's law might supply the relevant liability, limitations, and damages standards. Because state law differs in significant respects, litigants often challenge court determination of applicable law. The *Giovanetti* and *Baroldy* cases involve simple two-party tort litigation; but the plaintiffs' underlying claims (asbestos injury and toxic shock syndrome) represent proto-typical nascent mass torts. As such, the cases are useful for thinking about the dimensions of choice-of-law problems in mature mass tort that aggregate hundreds (if not thousands) of claimants residing in multiple states. In this respect, mature mass torts involve the same choice-of-law problems entailed in the airplane crash cases, *supra,* and courts must conduct a choice-of-law analysis that replicates the analyses in the *Giovanetti* and *Baroldy* excerpts. To what extent, however, are traditional conflicts rules useful for solving choice-of-law problems in dispersed mass torts?

2. Both the *Giovanetti* and *Baroldy* courts utilize a RESTATEMENT (SEC-OND) OF CONFLICTS OF LAW approach to deciding the applicable law issue. Although most states have adopted the RESTATEMENT (SECOND) as their choice-of-law regime, this is not the only analytical choice-of-law scheme that states utilize. The *Giovanetti* decision suggests two other possible approaches: (1) the *lex loci delicti* or "place of injury" approach embodied in the RESTATE-MENT (FIRST), and (2) governmental interest analysis. The central concept of the RESTATEMENT (SECOND) is that of identifying the state with the "most significant relationship" to the issue (embodied in Section 145), relying on a multi-factor test to determine which state has that "most significant relationship" (set forth in Section 6, choice-of-law principles). As the Paris Air Crash Disaster case, *supra,* indicates, California has developed a "comparative impairment" approach to determining applicable law. In addition, some states have adopted an analytical approach suggested by Professor Leflar in

his writings on conflicts, which relies on a set of "choice-influencing factors" to decide applicable law. For a very thorough and excellent description of the possible choice-of-law regimes, *see* Judge Weinstein's discussion in In re "Agent Orange" Prods. Liab. Litig., 580 F.Supp. 690 (E.D.N.Y.1984)

3. With regard to the array of possible state choice of law schemes, the American Law Institute's COMPLEX LITIGATION PROJECT has noted:

> State approaches to choice of law are quite varied in their methodology. *See* E. Scoles & P. Hay, *Conflicts of Laws* 11–44 (2d ed.1992); Kay, *Theory into Practice; Choice of Law in the Courts*, 34 Mercer L.Rev. 521 (1983); Smith, *Choice of Law in the United States*, 38 Hast.L.J. 1041 (1987). Because choice of law standards are in a state of flux, it often is difficult to ascertain the applicable choice of law rule in a particular state with any assurance or accuracy, making the federal court's task of applying state choice of law rules very problematic. Certification has not provided an answer to those problems and, most likely, will not. *See* Corr & Robbins, *Interjurisdictional Certification and Choice of Law*, 41 Vand.L.Rev. 411 (1988).

American Law Institute, COMPLEX LITIGATION PROJECT, *Proposed Final Draft* (1993) at 380.

4. In *Giovanetti*, the Pennsylvania court applied New Jersey law and concluded, over Mr. Giovanetti's protest on appeal, that New Jersey law coincidentally benefited Mr. Giovanetti more so than Pennsylvania law. In contrast, the Arizona court—also conducting an analysis under the RESTATE-MENT (SECOND)—suggested that Arizona, rather than North Carolina, had the most significant relationship to issues raised in Roberta Baroldy's claims. Are both analyses convincing? The *Baroldy* decision is more consistent with most state choice-of-law determinations, where state courts frequently conclude that forum law is most appropriately applied in preference to any other state's law.

C. CHOICE OF LAW IN FEDERAL DIVERSITY MASS TORTS

1. THE PROBLEM OF DETERMINING WHICH STATE'S LAW APPLIES

IN RE UNION CARBIDE CORP. GAS PLANT DISASTER

United States District Court, Southern District of New York, 1986.
634 F.Supp. 842, *affirmed* 809 F.2d 195 (2d Cir.1987).

Review the In Re Union Carbide Corp. Gas Plant Disaster decision at Part Two, Chapter II.E.2 (forum non conveniens), supra.

* * *

C. THE APPLICABLE LAW

Gilbert and *Piper* explicitly acknowledge that the need of an American court to apply foreign law is an appropriate concern on a *forum non conveniens* motion, and can in fact point toward dismissal. *Gilbert* at 509; *Piper* at 260. Especially when, as here, all other factors favor dismissal, the need to apply foreign law is a significant consideration on this type of motion. *Piper* at 260, n.29. A federal court is bound to apply the choice of law rules of the state in which an action was originally brought; even upon transfer to a different district, "the transferee district court must be obligated to apply the state law that would have been applied if there had been no change of venue." Van Dusen v. Barrack, 376 U.S. 612, 639, 84 S.Ct. 805, 821, 11 L.Ed.2d 945 (1964). Thus, this Court, sitting over a multidistrict litigation, must apply the various choice of law rules of the states in which the actions now consolidated before it were brought.[26] Rather than undertake the task of evaluating the choice of law rules of each state separately, the Court will treat the choice of law doctrine *in toto*. The "governmental interest" analysis, employed by many jurisdictions, requires a court to look to the question of which state has the most compelling interest in the outcome of the case. India's interest in the outcome of the litigation exceeds America's, *see supra*.... The *lex loci delicti* analysis used in other jurisdictions indicates that the law of the state where the tort occurred should be applied. The place in which the tort occurred was, to a very great extent, India. Other states apply the "most significant relationship" test, or "weight of contacts" test, which evaluate in which state most of the events constituting the tort occurred. The contacts with India with respect to all phases of plant construction, operation, malfunction and subsequent injuries are greater in number than those with the United States. Thus, under any one of these three doctrines, it is likely that Indian law will emerge as the operative law. An Indian court, therefore, would be better able to apply the controlling law than would this United States Court, or a jury working with it. This public interest factor also weighs in favor of dismissal on the grounds of *forum non conveniens*.

IN RE RICHARDSON–MERRELL, INC.

United States District Court, Southern District of Ohio, 1984.
545 F.Supp. 1130, *affirmed sub. nom.*
Dowling v. Richardson–Merrell, Inc. 727 F.2d 608 (6th Cir.1984).

CARL B. RUBIN, CHIEF JUDGE.

This matter is before the Court on defendant Merrell–Dow Pharmaceuticals, Inc's., (hereinafter Merrell–Dow) renewed Motions to Dismiss the above-captioned complaints based on the doctrine of forum non conveniens. Plaintiffs filed a memorandum contra the original Motions.

I. INTRODUCTION

Plaintiffs in the cases addressed herein are all residents of the United Kingdom. These suits were originally filed in the Southern

---

26. Upon a cursory review of the individual complaints comprising this action, the Court notes that suits were brought in California, Connecticut, the District of Columbia, Florida, Illinois, Louisiana, Maryland, New Jersey, New York, Pennsylvania, Tennessee, Texas and West Virginia, at a minimum.

District of New York against Richardson–Merrell, Inc., the predecessor of defendant Merrell–Dow, based on diversity of citizenship. In their complaints, plaintiffs alleged that they were injured as a result of their mothers' ingestion of the drug Debendox during pregnancy, and that defendant is liable to them based on its conduct in the development, marketing, testing, and promotion of Debendox as well as the related drug Bendectin. Debendox is manufactured and distributed in the United Kingdom by Richardson–Merrell Ltd., a wholly-owned British subsidiary of the defendant. Richardson–Merrell Ltd. was not named as a defendant in these actions.

The motions at issue herein were originally filed in the Southern District of New York. After oral argument on the motion, but prior to the Court's ruling, plaintiffs moved to voluntarily dismiss these actions pursuant to Rule 41(a)(2), or, in the alternative, to transfer these actions to the Southern District of Ohio. In his Memorandum and Order of February 1, 1982, as modified by a subsequent Memorandum and Order of February 25, 1982, Judge Brieant ordered that these cases be transferred to this Court pursuant to 28 U.S.C. § 1404(a). Defendant has since renewed its pending motion to dismiss these cases based on the doctrine of *forum non conveniens*.

An initial question raised by defendant's motion is whether federal or state law controls the application of the doctrine of *forum non conveniens* in these cases. This issue once again eludes decision, however, because New York courts appear to follow the same standards set forth in the federal cases. Gulf Oil Corp. v. Gilbert, 330 U.S. 501, 509 (1947); Fosen v. United Technologies Corp., 484 F.Supp. 490, 503 n.8 (S.D.N.Y.1980), *aff'd* 633 F.2d 203 (2d Cir.1980). We note, however, that given the discretionary nature of the *forum non conveniens* inquiry and the factors established by the Supreme Court to guide such a determination, it would appear anomalous for the Court to apply anything but federal principles. In any event, this Court will consider the defendant's Motions to Dismiss under the standards recently set forth in Piper v. Reyno, 454 U.S. 235, 102 S.Ct. 252, 70 L.Ed.2d 419 (1981), as well as prior federal cases.

* * *

The more impressive arguments in favor of dismissal of these cases address the "public interest" factors which are involved in the *forum non conveniens* inquiry. Defendant argues that to allow these foreign plaintiffs access to American courts on the bare nexus that a product was developed and tested in this country, when it was manufactured and sold abroad by a foreign corporation, would flood this country with cases in which its own interest is minimal and the United Kingdom's great. We find this argument highly persuasive from both a practical and theoretical viewpoint.

One of the public interest factors which the Court may consider in a *forum non conveniens* inquiry is whether it will be necessary to apply foreign law. Because this case was transferred to this Court pursuant to

28 U.S.C. § 1404(a), we must apply the same substantive law and choice of law rules which would have governed the transferor court. Van Dusen v. Barrack, 376 U.S. 612, 84 S.Ct. 805, 11 L.Ed.2d 945 (1964); Martin v. Stokes, 623 F.2d 469, 473 (6th Cir.1980). New York choice of law rules must therefore apply in these cases. Defendant contends that there is "no question" that New York courts would apply British law and plaintiffs have made no specific assertion to the contrary.

In Babcock v. Jackson, 12 N.Y.2d 473, 191 N.E.2d 279, 240 N.Y.S.2d 743 (1963), the New York Court of Appeals held that controlling effect should be given to "the law of the jurisdiction which, because of its relationship or contact with the occurrence or the parties, has the greatest concern with the specific issue raised in the litigation." *Id.* at 481, 191 N.E.2d at 283, 240 N.Y.S.2d at 749; Loebig v. Larucci, 572 F.2d 81, 84 (2d Cir.1978), Danser v. Firestone Tire and Rubber Co., 86 F.R.D. 120 (S.D.N.Y.1980). When the interests of New York and the United Kingdom in this litigation are compared, the United Kingdom has the unquestionably greater interest. This action involves the safety of drugs manufactured in the United Kingdom and sold to its citizens pursuant to licenses issued by that government. The interest of the United Kingdom is overwhelmingly apparent. New York, and Ohio for that matter, have a minimal interest in the safety of products which are manufactured, regulated and sold abroad by foreign entities, even though development or testing occurred in this country.[6] At this juncture, then, it appears virtually certain that the substantive tort law of the United Kingdom will govern these actions. This Court's unfamiliarity with the foreign law which will govern these actions supports dismissal on the basis of *forum non conveniens*. Piper Aircraft Co. v. Reyno; Calavo Growers of California v. Belgium, 632 F.2d 963, 967 (2d Cir.1980), *cert. denied,* 449 U.S. 1084, 101 S.Ct. 871, 66 L.Ed.2d 809 (1981).

Consistent with the New York choice of law inquiry, we find that from a theoretical or policy perspective, the United Kingdom is the more appropriate forum for trial of the issues raised herein. As the Court in *Harrison* stated:

> Questions as to the safety of drugs marketed in a foreign country are properly the concern of that country; the courts of the United States are ill-equipped to set a standard of product safety for drugs sold in other countries. The issues raised here concern the knowledge, if any, of an allegedly unreasonable risk, and the sufficiency of the warning of that risk to users of the product. Both the British and the American governments have established require-

6. In *Reyno,* which involved an American manufacturer, the Supreme Court noted:

Respondent argues that American citizens have an interest in insuring that American manufacturers are deterred from producing defective products, and that additional deterrents might be obtained if Piper and Hartzell were tried in the United States where they could be sued on the basis of both negligence and strict liability. However, the incremental deterrents that would be gained if this trial were held in an American court is likely to be insignificant.

___ U.S. ___, 102 S.Ct. at 268.

ments as to the standards of safety for drugs and the adequacy of any warnings to be given in connection with its use. Each government must weigh the merits of permitting the drug's use and the necessity of requiring a warning. Each makes its own determination as to the standards of degree of safety and duty of care. This balancing of the overall benefits to be derived from a product's use with the risk of harm associated with that use is peculiarly suited to a forum of the country in which the product is to be used. 510 F.Supp. at 4.

* * *

This Court is aware that Judge Battisti of the Northern District of Ohio has recently denied a Motion to Dismiss based on similar grounds in five Bendectin cases pending before that Court. Lake v. Richardson–Merrell, Inc., 538 F.Supp. 262 (1982). We note, however, some distinguishing aspects of that decision. In two of the cases considered by Judge Battisti, the Canadian plaintiff had the equivalent of no remedy at all under the law of Quebec because its rules of prescription had extinguished their right of action. The Court, relying on *Piper,* therefore found that dismissal based on *forum non conveniens* was totally inappropriate in those cases. Judge Battisti also found that under Ohio choice of law rules, the substantive tort law of Ohio would govern the actions considered therein. Finally, we note that the determination to dismiss on the basis of *forum non conveniens* is fundamentally a matter of the trial court's discretion. Paper Operations Consultants Intern., Ltd. v. S.S. Hong Kong Amber, 513 F.2d 667 (9th Cir.1975).

* * *

Notes and Questions

1. Compared to the *Paris Air Crash Disaster* case, the Southern District of New York's discussion of the applicable law issue in the Bhopal litigation is cursory, at best. To what extent was this skimpy analysis driven by the fact that the court had already concluded, after lengthy analysis, that a *forum non conveniens* dismissal was appropriate in the Bhopal litigation? Why does the court even address the choice-of-law issue?

2. Federal diversity suits relating to the Bhopal disaster were originally filed in federal district courts in California, Connecticut, the District of Columbia, Florida, Illinois, Louisiana, Maryland, New Jersey, New York, Pennsylvania, Tennessee, Texas, and West Virginia. These states variously had adopted different choice-of-law approaches: *lex loci delecti,* governmental interest analysis, and the RESTATEMENT (SECOND) "most significant relationship" standards. Was the federal district court in the Southern District of New York, where the cases were transferred, correct in concluding that under any of these choice-of-law schemes the state courts would apply Indian law?

3. In *Piper Aircraft v. Reyno,* discussed in Judge Rubins' *Richardson-Merrell* opinion, the Supreme Court seemed to suggest that the possibility of different applicable law in alternative forums was not a consideration that

should weigh in a court's evaluation of a *forum non conveniens* dismissal. Yet Judge Rubin analyzes possible applicable law as a dimension of *Piper's* "public interest" factor. Does Judge Rubin violate the spirit of *Piper Aircraft* in his assessment of the applicable law question in the *Richardson–Merrell* bendectin litigation? Has Judge Rubin done an adequate job of distinguishing his bendectin cases involving foreign plaintiffs from Judge Battisti's refusal to dismiss such cases?

2. RESTATEMENT (SECOND) APPROACHES

BAROLDY v. ORTHO PHARMACEUTICAL, CORP.

Arizona Court of Appeals, 1988.
157 Ariz. 574, 760 P.2d 574.

Review Baroldy v. Ortho Pharmaceuticals, supra.

IN RE BENDECTIN LITIGATION

United States Court of Appeals, Sixth Circuit, 1988.
857 F.2d 290, *cert. denied* 488 U.S. 1006, 109 S.Ct. 788, 102 L.Ed.2d 779 (1989).

ENGEL, CHIEF JUDGE.

* * *

III.   GOVERNING LAW OF PROXIMATE CAUSATION
IN CONFLICT OF LAWS CONTEXT

Before determining whether proximate causation should properly be considered a separate issue for purposes of Rule 42(b), it is necessary first to determine under which jurisdiction's law of proximate causation we are operating. At trial, Judge Rubin applied the substantive law of Ohio to any case brought in Ohio, citing *Erie,* 304 U.S. 64, and required all plaintiffs who transferred their cases to the Southern District of Ohio under MDL 486 and 28 U.S.C. § 1404 also to consent to have the liability issues tried in accordance with the substantive law of Ohio. Since the question of proximate causation was tried under the law of Ohio for all cases, and since the judge determined that the law of Ohio considered causation a separate issue from fraud, he prohibited the plaintiffs from introducing evidence that defendant had committed fraud in its submission to the FDA of test results regarding the safety of Bendectin. Because he found that fraud, even if proved, had no relation to the causation question under Ohio law, he concluded that the trifurcated case could proceed on the separate issue of causation.

While we are in agreement with the result reached by Judge Rubin, our course of reaching that decision differs from his in one important respect which requires closer analysis. On appeal, those plaintiffs not represented by Plaintiffs' Lead Counsel Committee argue that Judge Rubin could not assign to them the burden of proof on the proximate causation question because the law of their home states would place this burden on the defendant. They argue that had the law of Ohio not been applied, and had there not been trifurcation, they could have proved a rebuttable presumption of negligence because of the defendant's violation of the FDCA, and the proof of that statutory violation would shift to the defendant the burden of proof regarding causation. They also argue that, as under Ohio law, the law of their home states would shift the burden of proof because of defendant's fraud. The alleged fraud they assert consisted of defendant's failure to report to the FDA the results of animal and human studies concerning Bendectin's propensity to cause birth defects. Even if Ohio law did not recognize this doctrine, it is argued by the Wood plaintiffs that the district judge was obligated to apply the law of Texas because Ohio's choice of law rules dictate that Texas law governs their claims, notwithstanding that the *Wood* plaintiffs originally filed their case in Ohio federal court. Since the law of Texas does not consider causation and liability to be separate issues in this type of case, they argue that the district court abused its discretion in trifurcating the claims brought by these Texas plaintiffs. They ask us to allow them to opt out of the common issues trial, presumably permitting them to have their case transferred to Texas and tried under the law of Texas, with the burden of proof upon the defendant.

The *Davis* plaintiffs, who filed originally in other states and then transferred their cases to the multidistrict litigation in the Southern District of Ohio, raise a slightly different argument. Rather than merely arguing, as do the *Wood* plaintiffs, that the district court could not force them to have their cases tried by the law of any state other than that which the conflicts rules of Ohio dictate, they assert that the district judge could not require that they submit to the law of any state other than that where the complaint was originally filed. The *Davis* plaintiffs claim that the law of Arizona should govern their case, and that since the district judge applied Ohio law, their case should be returned to Arizona to be tried under the law of Arizona, with the burden of proof upon the defendant in at most a bifurcated trial.

In response, defendant contends that the plaintiffs never argued at trial that they could not prove that Bendectin caused birth defects because the defendant concealed evidence of teratogenicity. Rather, defendant asserts that plaintiffs' argument was that the evidence was sufficient to prove that the drug caused all varieties of birth defects. Likewise, at trial the plaintiffs' own proposed instructions placed the burden of proof on themselves, contrary to lead counsel's assertion on appeal. Further, the plaintiffs themselves urged the district judge to apply the law of Ohio to this case, and never argued that any other law should apply. Those plaintiffs who transferred into the common issues trial had the unfettered discretion to accept the Ohio forum and the district court's previously announced decision to apply Ohio law, or to return their cases to the district in which they were originally filed.

We agree with Judge Rubin's conclusion that under Fed.R.Civ.P. 51 any objections that the instructions on causation were not couched in terms of Arizona or Texas law were waived when not made before the jury retired. Even if such a claim were construed as plain error, we observe that there was no showing that the law of these states differed in any material respect from that of Ohio. Out of caution, however, we inspect this issue more closely.

The Supreme Court has long held that a federal district court exercising diversity jurisdiction must apply the same conflict of laws rules that the state court would apply.

> The conflict of laws rules to be applied by the federal court in [a state] must conform to those prevailing in [that] state['s] courts. Otherwise, the accident of diversity of citizenship would constantly disturb equal administration of justice in coordinate state and federal courts sitting side by side.... Any other ruling would do violence to the principle of uniformity within a state, upon which the *Tompkins* decision is based.

Klaxon Co. v. Stentor Electric Manufacturing Co., 313 U.S. 487, 496, 61 S.Ct. 1020, 1021–22, 85 L.Ed. 1477 (1941)(citations omitted). "The conflict-of-laws rules to be applied by a federal court in Texas must conform to those prevailing in the Texas state courts. A federal court in a diversity case is not free to engraft onto those state rules exceptions or modifications which may commend themselves to the federal court, but which have not commended themselves to the State in which the federal court sits." Day & Zimmermann, Inc. v. Challoner, 423 U.S. 3, 4, 96 S.Ct. 167, 168, 46 L.Ed.2d 3 (1975)(per curiam).

Applying *Klaxon* here, it is apparent that it is Ohio's conflict of laws rules that must normally determine which substantive state law should govern the rights of the parties. Although determining what law should apply is not altogether without doubt, the Ohio Supreme Court appears to have clarified the issue substantially in this past decade. In the most recent of a series of cases, Morgan v. Biro Mfg. Co., 15 Ohio St. 3d 339, 474 N.E.2d 286 (1984)(per curiam), the Ohio Supreme Court reaffirmed its intention to abandon a strict adherence to the traditional rule of *lex loci delicti* in favor of a more flexible rule based on which state has "a more significant relationship to the lawsuit," *id.* at 289, in light of the factors set forth in section 145 of 1 RESTATEMENT (SECOND) OF CONFLICT OF LAWS § 145 (1971). *Morgan* involved a product liability action against the manufacturer of a meat grinder. There the court concluded that even though the product was manufactured in Ohio and the defendant manufacturer was incorporated in Ohio, Kentucky had the most significant relationship to the parties since that is the state where the injury occurred, the plaintiff resided, and the workers' compensation benefits were determined, and Kentucky was the state responsible for inspection of the condition and safety of the product for use in that state. As a basis for its holding, the court quoted both section 145 and section 6, as incorporated in section 145, of the RESTATEMENT OF CONFLICTS. It is thus apparent that the Supreme Court of Ohio recognizes the limitations of the *lex loci delicti* rule that are imposed by the broader considerations of sections 145 and 6 of the RESTATEMENT, since it quotes both of these sections in full. Morgan, 474 N.E.2d at 289 n.56.

Applying here the flexible approach adopted in recent Ohio case law and codified in sections 145 and 6 requires an inquiry into which state possesses the most significant relationship. If this question cannot be determined, the law of the place of the injury controls. *Id.* at 289; 1 RESTATEMENT (SECOND) OF CONFLICT OF LAWS § 146 (1971).

Throughout this litigation there has been some discussion of the law of states in which non-Ohio plaintiffs are domiciled. We, however, see the law of the state of manufacture of the product as being more significant in this type of case than that of the state where an individual plaintiff happens to live. Merrell Dow manufactured and distributed a uniform drug internationally. The company issued a uniform set of warnings and instructions for use. The regulations governing the labeling, research, and distribution of the drug were governed either by Ohio law or by the federal Food, Drug and Cosmetic Act. Standards against which defendant's wrongful or negligent conduct may be measured are also set by Ohio and federal law.

In contrast, plaintiffs seem to allege either that their domicile states have a more substantial interest in the outcome of this litigation or that no state has a particularly substantial interest, and thus the law of the state of the place of injury should prevail. Both of these arguments fail, however. Domicile states do have a strong interest in the protection and well-being of their citizens, and the RESTATEMENT plainly regards domicile as one consideration in determining the existence of a substantial state interest. *See id.* § 145. Those plaintiffs who seek to apply the law of their state of domicile may also do so on the assumption that this is where the injury occurred. Such an assumption, however, is not at all clear, for the state of domicile at the time of suit may bear little or no relation to where a mother may have taken a morning sickness drug years before. A plaintiff presently residing in Arizona, for example, might nonetheless be found to have taken Bendectin while traveling in many different states. In short, it is difficult if not impossible to perceive any meaningful relationship to the subject matter of the lawsuit for the law of the state of domicile at the time of the suit, or the state in which the drug may have been prescribed, dispensed, ingested, or the state in which the child may have been conceived, or born. This is far different from the circumstances which led the Ohio Supreme Court to apply Kentucky law in *Morgan.* The application of the same principles which led the court to Kentucky law in *Morgan* points unmistakably to Ohio law here. The State of Ohio is responsible for regulating local aspects of the marketing, manufacture, distribution, and labeling of the drug, and thus the relationship between the parties is essentially centered in Ohio, where the tortious conduct and the safety of the product are regulated. The fact that federal regulation through the FDCA impacts pervasively upon the development and approval of the drug in question tends further to minimize the significance of the law of other states and to focus emphasis upon the state of manufacture as the state in which application of the federal standards and oversight is most likely to occur.

The choice of Ohio law is even more persuasive when we apply, as we must under *Morgan,* the factors set forth in section 6 of the Restatement: "The needs of the interstate and international systems"; "the protection of justified expectations"; "the basic policies underlying the particular field of law"; "certainty, predictability and uniformity of result"; and "ease in the determination and application of law to be applied" provide, in our judgment, a persuasive basis for holding that the more significant relationships were those of the place of manufacture. We therefore conclude that under Ohio conflicts law as applied to the circumstances of these cases, the substantive law of Ohio was properly applied to those parties over whom the district court had jurisdiction.

One final choice of law problem, however, remains. When a defendant transfers a case to another district under 28 U.S.C. § 1404, the *Erie* doctrine requires that the court apply the choice of law rules of the transferor state. Van Dusen v. Barrack, 376 U.S. 612, 637–39, 84 S.Ct. 805, 819–21, 11 L.Ed.2d 945 (1964). The holding of *Van Dusen* is that when a plaintiff files suit in a federal court with proper venue, and the defendant transfers it to a new federal court for convenience, the transferor state's law (including its conflicts law) applies. The Supreme Court noted that section 1404(a) was not designed to defeat the plaintiff's right to obtain the state law advantages that might accrue from the exercise of the venue privilege. *Id.* at 635, 84 S.Ct. at 818-19. "A change of venue under § 1404(a) generally should be, with respect to state law, but a change in courtrooms." *Id.* at 639, 84 S.Ct. at 820-21 (footnote omitted). The Court expressly reserved the question whether section 1404(a) would require the application of the law of the transferor state when the plaintiff, rather than the defendant, seeks transfer under that statute. That is the situation here for the plaintiffs who voluntarily transferred their cases to the Southern District of Ohio after they had been originally filed in federal courts in other states.

"Although much can be said for applying the law of the transferee state when it is plaintiff who has moved, the cases increasingly seem to be applying the law of the transferor court regardless of which party moved for transfer if that court was proper in terms of venue and personal jurisdiction." 15 C. Wright, A. Miller & E. Cooper, *Federal Practice & Procedure* § 3846 at 367 (footnotes omitted). We have adopted the majority position on this issue.

Once a plaintiff has exercised his choice of forum by selecting a permissible forum, the state law of that forum should govern the action, regardless of the wisdom of the plaintiff's selection. Thus, no matter who seeks to transfer the action to a more convenient forum under § 1404(a), the state law of the forum in which the action was originally commenced remains controlling. In this manner, the outcome in the transferee district court will be the same as the outcome would have been in the state courts of the state where the action was originally brought.

> Accordingly, we conclude that the choice of law is dependent upon the nature of the transfer. If an action is transferred under § 1404(a), the state law of the transferor court should be applied.

Martin v. Stokes, 623 F.2d 469, 473 (6th Cir.1980). No true conflict exists, however, where another state's choice of law rules would have applied the substantive law of Ohio to this case.

Rather than attempting to analyze the conflict of laws rules of every state in the union, we will assume that the only state laws that could apply to any individual suit would be that of the state where the injury occurred or the plaintiff was domiciled, or that of Ohio, as those would be the only places with interests sufficient to have their law govern under prevailing conflict of laws theory. In short, the district court would not have committed error if the pertinent state choice of law rules commanded that the substantive law of Ohio apply. Likewise, if the laws of any other state were the same as Ohio's on the issue of proximate causation in this case, any error on the conflict question would be harmless, for it could not have adversely affected the court's decision of the plaintiffs' rights. Instead of analyzing each state's law, then, we consider whether the district court properly concluded that the plaintiffs must prove proximate causation in these cases under Ohio law, and then determine whether any case that the plaintiffs have cited to us, or any other source of law in other jurisdictions, holds that on the facts alleged here, proximate causation was not a separate issue. * * *

* * *

Notes and Questions

1. Does the RESTATEMENT (SECOND) OF THE CONFLICTS OF LAWS provide a reasonable methodology for determining applicable law in mass tort cases? What does due process require in determining applicable law? *See* Joyce R. Berman, Note, *Choice of Law and the Supreme Court:* Phillips Petroleum Co. v. Shutts, 19 Conn. L. Rev. 171 (1986). If the RESTATEMENT (SECOND) does provide an adequate analytical approach, why should reformers be concerned with the applicable law problem in aggregate mass tort cases? *See, e.g,.* Digges & Wharton, *Choice of Law in Products Liability Actions: Order for the Practitioner in a Reign of Chaos,* 33 Def.L.J. 467 (1984)(approving of the RESTATEMENT (SECOND) methodology as applied to products liability actions); Linda S. Mullenix, *Beyond Consolidation: Post–Aggregative Procedure in Asbestos Mass Tort Litigation,* 32 Wm. & Mary L.Rev. 475 (1991) (describing how Judge James McGirr Kelly decided applicable law on an issue-by-issue basis in the *School Asbestos Litigation*). Do mass tort cases give rise to more complex choice-of-law problems that are not reasonably solved by recourse to the RESTATEMENT (SECOND)?

2. The American Law Institute basically has expanded on the RESTATEMENT (SECOND) methodology in its proposals for determining choice-of-law in mass tort litigation. Similar to the RESTATEMENT, the ALI COMPLEX LITIGATION: STATUTORY RECOMMENDATIONS AND ANALYSIS (1994) suggests a choice-of-law approach that focuses on issues rather than claims in a litigation. *See*

Chapter X, B, *infra.; see also* American Law Institute, COMPLEX LITIGATION: STATUTORY RECOMMENDATIONS AND ANALYSIS at 315 (1994).

3. Compare the various analyses and holdings in *Baroldy, Richardson–Merrell,* and *In re Bendectin Litigation.* In each case, what factor provides the "most significant contact" under the RESTATEMENT (SECOND) methodology for the purpose of determining which state's law applies? Are the courts' conclusions consistent on the facts? Is there any reason for preferring to choose applicable law based on the plaintiff's or defendant's domicile, corporate residence, the place of injury, the place of manufacture, or any other affiliating facts? Do the RESTATEMENT (SECOND) criteria make sense for dispersed mass torts? *See generally* Louise Weinberg, *The Place of Trial and the Law Applied: Overhauling Constitutional Theory,* 59 Colo.L.Rev. 67 (1988).

4. For commentary relating to choice-of-law issues in mass tort litigation generally, with reference to various choice-of-law regimes, *see* Barbara A. Atwood, *The Choice of Law Dilemma in Mass Tort Litigation, Kicking Around* Erie, Klaxon, *and* Van Dusen, 19 Conn.L.Rev. 9 (1986); Friedrich K. Jeunger, *Mass Disasters and the Conflicts of Laws,* 1989 U.Ill.L.Rev. 105 (1989); William D. Torchiana, *Choice of Law and the Multistate Class: From Interests in Matters Distant,* 134 U.Pa.L.Rev. 913 (1986); Russell J. Weintraub, *Methods for Resolving Conflicts-of-Laws Problems in Mass Tort Litigation,* 1989 U.Ill.L.Rev. 129 (1989).

Chapter IX

MASS TORTS AND FEDERAL COMMON LAW

A. THE POSSIBILITY OF FEDERAL COMMON LAW

IN RE "AGENT ORANGE" PRODUCT LIABILITY LITIGATION

United States District Court, Eastern District of New York, 1984.
580 F.Supp. 690.

PRETRIAL ORDER NO. 92

PRELIMINARY MEMORANDUM ON CONFLICTS OF LAW

WEINSTEIN, CHIEF JUDGE:

A considerable number of Vietnam war veterans resident in all or almost all states, Puerto Rico and the District of Columbia and a number of foreign countries, and members of their families, claim to have suffered injury as a result of the veterans' exposure to herbicides in Vietnam. Defendants produced those herbicides. Individual claims, originally filed in all parts of the country, were transferred for pretrial purposes to this court. Subject to some powers to opt out, common issues presented by plaintiffs' claims will now be tried together since a class has been certified pursuant to Rule 23. *See* In re "Agent Orange" Product Liability Litigation, P.T.O. 72, 100 F.R.D. 718 (E.D.N.Y.1983). *Petit. for Writ of Mandamus denied,* 725 F.2d 858 (2d Cir.), *cert. denied, sub nom.* Diamond Shamrock Chemicals Co. v. Ryan, 465 U.S. 1067, 104 S.Ct. 1417 (1984).

Plaintiffs have failed to state a cause of action under federal common law for jurisdictional purposes. In re "Agent Orange" Product Liability Litigation, 635 F.2d 987 (2d Cir.1980), *cert. denied sub nom.* Chapman v. Dow, 454 U.S. 1128, 102 S.Ct. 980, 71 L.Ed.2d 116 (1981). Accordingly, the litigation is grounded upon diversity jurisdiction raising the issue of what substantive law should apply.

As required by Klaxon Co. v. Stentor Elec. Mfg. Co., 313 U.S. 487, 61 S.Ct. 1020, 85 L.Ed. 1477 (1941), this court has examined the conflict of law rules of the states in which the transferor courts sit. Van Dusen

894

v. Barrack, 376 U.S. 612, 84 S.Ct. 805, 11 L.Ed.2d 945 (1964). For the reasons set forth below, it is concluded that under the special circumstances of this litigation, all the transferor states would look to the same substantive law for the rule of decision on the critical substantive issues.

I. INTRODUCTION

Plaintiffs originally sought to base jurisdiction on federal common law relying on federal question jurisdiction. 28 U.S.C.§ 1331. This court sustained their contention. In re "Agent Orange" Product Liability Litigation, 506 F.Supp. 737 (E.D.N.Y.1979). The Second Circuit reversed, concluding, for the purpose of denying federal question jurisdiction, that "there is [no] identifiable federal policy at stake in this litigation that warrants the creation of federal common law rules." 635 F.2d 987, 993, *cert. denied sub nom.* Chapman v. Dow, 454 U.S. 1128, 102 S.Ct. 980, 71 L.Ed.2d 116 (1981). The court held that if the action was to continue in the federal courts, jurisdiction must be based on diversity of citizenship. 28 U.S.C.§ 1332.

In applying state law, following what is assumed to be the mandate of *Klaxon,* the choice of law methodology used by the states in which transferor courts sit has been examined to predict what law each state would apply.

We recognize that *Klaxon* has been widely criticized and that learned scholars have suggested on the basis of policy and possible constitutional grounds that a federal conflicts of law rule should be applied in diversity cases such as the one before us. *See, e.g.,* R. Bridwell & R. Whitten, *The Constitution and the Common Law* 135 (1977); R.C. Cramton, D.P. Currie & H.H. Kay, CONFLICT OF LAWS, 927–932 (3d ed.1981); Hart & Wechsler's *The Federal Courts and the Federal System,* 713–717 (2d ed. by P.M. Bator, P.V. Mishkin, D.L. Shapiro & H. Wechsler, 1973); W.L.M. Reese & M. Rosenberg, *Conflict of Laws,* 692, 694–695 (7th ed.1978); E.F. Scoles & P. Hay, *Conflict of Laws* 112 (1982); C. Wright, *Law of Federal Courts,* 366–370 (4th ed.1983); Hill, *The* Erie *Doctrine and the Constitution,* 53 Nw.U.L.Rev. 427, 444–45 (1958); Korn, *The Choice of Law Revolution: A Critique,* 83 Colum.L.Rev. 772, 971 (1983); Trautman, *The Relation Between American Choice of Law and Federal Common Law,* 41 Law & Contemp.Prob. 105, 120 (Spring 1977). The Supreme Court has, however, "made it clear that the *Klaxon* rule is not to yield to the more modern thinking of conflicts-of-laws scholars." C. Wright, *id.* at 368. *See, e.g.,* Day and Zimmermann, Inc. v. Challoner, 423 U.S. 3, 96 S.Ct. 167, 46 L.Ed.2d 3 (1975).

Much of the law of conflicts is in a state of flux, development and refinement. Any dogmatism as to the result were the issue to be certified to the highest court of each jurisdiction involved is unwarranted. *See, e.g.,* the most current authoritative and comprehensive review of choice of law problems, Korn, *The Choice-of-Law Revolution: A Critique,* 83 Colum.L.Rev. 772, 956 (1983), and the shorter but trenchant Juenger, *Conflict of Laws: A Critique of Interest Analysis,* 32 Am.

J.Comp.L. 1 (1984). Nevertheless, given the special facts of this litigation, under any approach utilized today, so far as can reasonably be predicted, the result would be the same: each state would probably apply the same law, that is to say either federal or national common law.

Before starting the analysis, it is well to keep in mind the admonition of Chief Judge Fuld whose "impact upon choice of law has been greater than that of any living judge and probably greater than that of any judge during the present century." Reese, *Chief Judge Fuld and Choice of Law,* 71 Colum.L.Rev. 548 (1971). Justice, fairness and "the best practical result" * * * may best be achieved by giving controlling effect to the law of the jurisdiction which, because of its relationship or contact with the occurrence or the parties has the greatest concern with the specific issue raised in the litigation. Babcock v. Jackson, 12 N.Y.2d 473, 481, 240 N.Y.S.2d 743, 749, 191 N.E.2d 279, 283 (1963). Hope of obtaining a universally accepted result is tempered by Professor von Mehren's reminder that one who expects to achieve results in multistate cases that are as satisfying in terms of standards of justice and of party acceptability as those reached in purely domestic cases is doomed to disappointment. von Mehren, *Choice of Law and the Problem of Justice,* 41 Law & Contemp.Probs. 27, 42 (1977).

In view of a growing consensus about what the law governing manufacturer's liability is—a problem to be dealt with in a subsequent opinion—there is a convergence between the result required in the instant case under the separate state conflicts of law rules and the separate state substantive tort rules. Thus, the obviously sensible result of treating members of this nation's armed forces and their families in essentially the same way for any injuries suffered in a national war fought on foreign soil would, it is now provisionally found, be reached by each of the states.

The issue is particularly difficult to deal with because of a number of definitional and conceptual issues that tend to make some problems appear more murky than they are. While we disclaim any capacity to clarify the law of conflicts, it does seem helpful for purposes of this opinion to restate some definitions and distinctions.

Essentially, there are five different conflicts of laws methodologies widely used in this country. These may be summarized as (1) traditional or RESTATEMENT (FIRST) based upon Professor Beale's work, (2) RESTATEMENT (SECOND) being in large part a pragmatic and conservative revision by Professor Reese of Professor Currie's interest analysis school, (3) governmental interest, (4) Leflar, and (5) forum. There is a sixth proposed approach that has some of the aura of Leflar, but which we treat separately as the von Mehren approach. Some states use a combination or variation of these techniques. See, e.g., for various other characterizations of state approaches: R.C. Cramton, D.P. Currie & H.H. Kay, CONFLICTS OF LAWS, 326 ff. (3d ed.1981); W.L.M. Reese & M. Rosenberg, CONFLICTS OF LAWS, 478 ff. (7th ed.1978); Korn, *The Choice-of-Law Revolution: A Critique,* 83 Colum.L.Rev. 779–780, 819–820

(1983)(stressing New York cases); Rosenberg, *The Comeback of Choice-of-Law Rules,* 81 Colum.L.Rev. 946 (1981)(stressing California cases). For purposes of this opinion, we have eschewed specific discussion of the effects of modern doctrine leading to renvoi (*see, e.g.,* W.L.M. Reese & M. Rosenberg, CONFLICTS OF LAWS 550 (7th ed.1978)("Renvoi Returns")), or the increased likelihood of depecage, applying the law of different jurisdictions to different aspects of the case (R.J. Weintraub, COMMENTARY ON THE CONFLICT OF LAWS 72 (2d ed.1980)), though, as will be seen, both doctrines are implicated in the present case. Finally, it is unnecessary to consider whether any state's conflict of law rule would deprive a litigant of due process, equal protection, or other constitutional right since each of the states whose conflict rule might apply has sufficient nexus with the matter through residence or the like. *See, e.g.,* R.C. Cramton, D.P. Currie & H.H. Kay, CONFLICT OF LAWS, 499–508 (3d ed.1981); Hart & Wechsler's THE FEDERAL COURTS AND THE FEDERAL SYSTEM, 717–718 (2d ed. by P.M. Bator, D.L. Shapiro, P.J. Mishkin & H. Wechsler, 1973). *Cf.* Allstate Insurance Co. v. Hague, 449 U.S. 302, 101 S.Ct. 633, 66 L.Ed.2d 521 (1981), discussed in Currie, *The Supreme Court and Federal Jurisdiction: 1975 Term,* 1976 Sup.Ct.Rev. 183, 217 (questioning constitutionality), and Korn, *The Choice-of-Law Revolution: A Critique,* 83 Colum.L.Rev. 772, 792–799 (1983).

A. *Federal Law—for jurisdictional purposes; for substantive purposes; for evidentiary and procedural purposes; and as a model for the states to incorporate in their own law.* As already suggested, the Court of Appeals has decided that there is no federal substantive law directly controlling in this case upon which federal question jurisdiction of federal district courts may be based under 28 U.S.C. § 1331. Thus, this is not a civil action "arising under the ... laws ... of the United States." *Id.* Federal substantive law—that is, the law of the United States Congress, Executive and courts—does not, according to the Second Circuit, apply by direct authority and compulsion of the federal government and the Supremacy clause of the Constitution. For procedural purposes, however, the federal rules of procedure and evidence apply. Federal Rules of Evidence, Rules 101; Federal Rules of Civil Procedure, Rule 1. This means, for example, that in this case, based upon the predicate of diversity of citizenship jurisdiction, the Federal Rules of Civil Procedure governing class actions control. *See* In re "Agent Orange" Product Liability Litigation, P.T.O. 72, 100 F.R.D. 718 (E.D.N.Y.1983). * * *

Even though federal substantive law does not control by its own force, states will often look to non-controlling federal decisions, statutes, executive orders and administrative decisions in deciding what state policy and substantive law ought to be. "The overarching presence of federal law has moved state judges to view federal law ... as a source of inspiration for the development of a state jurisprudence." The Supreme Court, 1982 Term, 97 Harv.L.Rev. 70, 224 (1983) * * *. Often, then, federal substantive law becomes state substantive law, not because the federal government has willed it so, but because the state has deemed it should be so through its governing institutions including the state's courts.

B. *State Law.* By "state law" we mean the substantive law, as far as it can be predicted to be, devised and enforced by the state within the limits of its constitutional powers. Since this is a diversity jurisdiction case, pursuant to 28 U.S.C. § 1332, this court, as to those claims originally filed in this court, sits much as a state trial court would in New York, applying New York substantive law except when, under the New York law of conflicts, a New York court would look to substantive law other than New York's in deciding what substantive law would apply. Cases commenced in other districts are treated as if they are pending in those other districts whether transferred to this court for pretrial purposes under the multi-district litigation statute, 28 U.S.C. § 1407, or transferred for trial for the convenience of witnesses, 28 U.S.C. § 1404. *See* Van Dusen v. Barrack, 376 U.S. 612, 84 S.Ct. 805, 11 L.Ed.2d 945 (1964); W.L.M. Reese & M. Rosenberg, *Conflict of Laws,* 194–96 (7th ed.1978); R.J. Weintraub, *Commentary on the Conflict of Laws,* 584–87 (2d ed.1980); Note, *Choice of Law in the Federal Court after Transfer of Venue,* 63 Cornell L.Rev. 149 (1977).

Certifying this as a class action with residents of different states as plaintiffs does not, we assume for present purposes, by analogy to *Van Dusen v. Barrack,* reduce all disputes within the litigation to one subject to the substantive and conflicts of laws rules of New York. This is arguably clear where the suits were begun in other states and transferred to this court under section 1404 or 1407 of Title 28. It also may be assumed to be the case as to those plaintiffs who never brought suit, but became parties as a result of certification pursuant to Rule 23 of the Federal Rules of Civil Procedure. Where relevant state substantive and conflicts rules are not uniform, certification does not, we will assume, provide uniformity. *Cf.* Snyder v. Harris, 394 U.S. 332, 334, 89 S.Ct. 1053, 1055, 22 L.Ed.2d 319 (1969); Klaxon Co. v. Stentor Elec. Mfg. Co., 313 U.S. 487, 496, 61 S.Ct. 1020, 1023, 85 L.Ed. 1477; Erie R. Co. v. Tompkins, 304 U.S. 64, 58 S.Ct. 817, 82 L.Ed. 1188 (1938); In re No. Dist. of Cal. "Dalkon Shield" IUD Product Liability Litigation, 693 F.2d 847, 850 (9th Cir.1982), *cert. denied sub nom.* A.H. Robins v. Abed, 459 U.S. 1171, 103 S.Ct. 817, 74 L.Ed.2d 1015 (1983).

This assumption is made despite the contrary argument—with great appeal for reasons beyond the scope of this opinion—that these class members are subject to New York conflicts law since they constructively sued in the New York case by analogy to Fed.R.Civ.P. Rule 24 (intervention) or Rule 42 (consolidation). Although we do not find it necessary to adopt this argument, it is clear that class action certification provides no added support for applying conflicts of law rules to require differing substantive law. *Cf.* Young v. That Was The Week That Was, 312 F.Supp. 1337 (N.D.Ohio 1969), *aff'd,* 423 F.2d 265 (6th Cir.1970)(class action certification, particularly where the law respecting conflicts was not clear, warranted using the law of one state even though members of the class came from many states whose law would apply under traditional conflicts rules).

C. *National-Consensus Law.* While those close to the American law scene tend to emphasize the diversity of substantive law among the states and between the states and the federal government, to outside observers much of the differences must appear as significant as that among the Lilliputians to Swift's hero. Faced with a unique problem, American lawmakers and judges tend to react in much the same way, arriving at much the same result.

There are, of course, centrifugal forces in the law leading to different substantive and procedural results even in a single nation like the United States. With thousands of municipalities, 50 states, the District of Columbia and the Federal jurisdiction having many law-creating legislative bodies, executive departments, administrative bodies, and courts, this is to be expected. Yet, powerful centripetal tendencies often encourage the formulation of national consensus law. First, is the essential homogeneity of our unified technological-social structure increasingly tied together by national transportation, communication and educational-cultural networks. Second, is an Anglo–American legal system with common roots and a strongly integrated law school educational system relying upon national scholars, treatises and cases. National casebooks and fungibility of teaching materials, for example, create a strong unifying influence making it possible for lawyers to be trained in one section of the country and to transfer to other areas for practice. It allows development of a national bar examination and a national bar even though lawyers are licensed in different states. The result is that law-making and law-applying authorities tend to utilize national standards and approaches.

Institutions such as the American Law Institute with its Restatements, the National Commissioners on Uniform State Laws with many widely-adopted uniform statutes and the National Municipal League with its uniform charters aid these unifying national tendencies. So, too, do many quasi-public bodies setting manufacturing and safety standards. The pressure, for example, for a uniform manufacturers liability substantive law is well known, having even led the Department of Commerce to draft federal legislation on the subject.

When presented with a new problem, we tend to proceed by analogy and by precedent. Analogies available are much the same for all courts. Even though one state is not bound by the precedents of another, when a new problem arises courts tend to follow the decisions of courts of other American jurisdictions since the reasoning and pool of factual and legal data will tend to be the same.

The concept of a national law already exists in federal common law since federal law, by definition, is created to deal with problems that are national in scope. In determining the content of that federal law courts have long looked to state law sources, the Restatement of Law of the American Law Institute and other "non-federal" sources. *See, e.g.,*

Miree v. DeKalb County, 433 U.S. 25, 30, 97 S.Ct. 2490, 2494, 53 L.Ed.2d 557 (1977); Clearfield Trust Co. v. United States, 318 U.S. 363, 367, 63 S.Ct. 573, 575, 87 L.Ed. 838 (1943); Owens v. Haas, 601 F.2d 1242, 1250 (2d Cir.), *cert. denied*, 444 U.S. 980, 100 S.Ct. 483, 62 L.Ed.2d 407 (1979); Southern Pacific Transportation Co. v. United States, 462 F.Supp.1193 (E.D.Cal.1978); Weinberger v. New York Stock Exchange, 335 F.Supp. 139, 143 (S.D.N.Y.1971).

* * *

FRIEDRICH K. JUENGER, MASS DISASTERS AND THE CONFLICT OF LAWS

1989 U.Ill.L.Rev. 105, 109–110 (1989).

* * *

In consequence of *Erie, Klaxon,* and *Van Dusen,* identical facts may have to be tried under fifty or more different laws. Such fragmentation can cause striking disparities in the recovery for the death or injury of victims of the same accident, and the plaintiffs' fates may depend less on the justice of their causes than on their selection of an initial forum. Commenting on *Van Dusen,* which only involved two groups of plaintiffs, a noted French comparatist called their disparate treatment "scandalous." Where, as in *Agent Orange,* the victims come from all parts of the United States and from several foreign countries, the lack of a uniform law increases the likelihood of discrimination among different classes of victims.

Accordingly, something is to be said in favor of a federal common law of conflicts for mass disaster cases. As the *Preliminary Study* [of the ALI COMPLEX LITIGATION PROJECT] notes, there is general agreement on the proposition that *Klaxon* is not constitutionally mandated and that Congress has the power to enact conflicts statutes. The full faith and credit clause as well as other constitutional provisions would support such an enactment. Even in the absence of congressional action, the Supreme Court, in light of the staggering burden that the lack of uniformity imposes on the federal judiciary in complex litigation, might conceivably overrule *Klaxon,* at least to the extent of allowing federal courts to create conflicts rules for mass disasters.

The real problem, however, is whether the rules that Congress or the federal courts might devise can adequately resolve the choice-of-law issues posed by truly multistate cases. Ideally, all litigation prompted by a mass tort would be governed by the same rules of decision. Choice-of-law approaches that subject the victims' claims to different substantive laws are not merely unfair: by necessitating separate trials they further complicate complex litigation. How, then, do the various conflicts approaches proffered for application to mass disasters meet the twin goals of fairness and efficiency?

B. FEDERAL COMMON LAW REJECTED

IN RE "AGENT ORANGE" PRODUCT LIABILITY LITIGATION

United States Court of Appeals, Second Circuit, 1980.
635 F.2d 987, *cert. denied* 454 U.S. 1128, 102 S.Ct. 980, 71 L.Ed.2d 116 (1981).

Before FEINBERG, CHIEF JUDGE, and VAN GRAAFEILAND and KEARSE, CIRCUIT JUDGES.

KEARSE, CIRCUIT JUDGE:

This appeal presents the question whether claims asserted by veterans of the United States armed forces against companies which supplied the United States government with chemicals that are alleged to have been contaminated and to have injured the veterans and their families, are governed by federal common law. Defendants-appellants Diamond Shamrock Corporation, Monsanto Company, Thompson–Hayward Chemical Company, Hercules Incorporated and the Dow Chemical Company were the manufacturers of various herbicides including "Agent Orange" (hereinafter collectively referred to as "Agent Orange") for use by the military as defoliants in the Vietnam War. The plaintiffs, veterans of that war and their families, allege that they have sustained various physical injuries by reason of the veterans' exposure to Agent Orange. Plaintiffs seek redress of those injuries under federal common law, and have invoked the "federal question" jurisdiction of the district court. 28 U.S.C. § 1331(a)(1976). Defendants contest the existence of a federal common law cause of action, and moved below to dismiss for lack of subject matter jurisdiction. The United States District Court for the Eastern District of New York, George C. Pratt, Judge, denied their motion. * * *

We agree with defendants that there is no federal common law right of action under the circumstances of this litigation. Accordingly, we reverse.

* * *

B. THE DECISION OF THE DISTRICT COURT

Plaintiffs argue that federal common law should be applied to their claims principally because of the unique federal nature of the relationship between the soldier and his government, relying chiefly on United States v. Standard Oil Co., 332 U.S. 301, 305, 67 S.Ct. 1604, 1606 , 91 L.Ed. 2067(1947)("Perhaps no relation between the Government and a citizen is more distinctively federal in character than that between it and members of its armed forces."). They contend that this interest brings the case within the doctrine of Clearfield Trust Co. v. United States, 318 U.S. 363, 366, 63 S.Ct. 573, 574, 87 L.Ed. 838 (1943), which held that, in order to ensure uniformity and certainty, "[t\]he rights and duties of the United States on commercial paper which it issues are governed by federal rather than local law." Plaintiffs argue that the government similarly has an interest in having all of its veterans compensated by government contractors who manufactured or marketed Agent Orange, and that application of the respective state laws would impede recovery on a uniform basis.

The district court rejected the contention that *Clearfield Trust* stated the controlling principle, recognizing that the United States, a party to *Clearfield Trust*, is not party to the plaintiffs' claims here. Rather, the court recognized that since the present action involves only private parties, the federal common law issue is controlled by the principles set forth in Miree v. DeKalb County, 433 U.S. 25, 97 S.Ct. 2490, 53 L.Ed.2d 557 (1977), and Wallis v. Pan American Petroleum Corp., 384 U.S. 63, 86 S.Ct. 1301, 16 L.Ed.2d 369 (1966). After reviewing the latter decisions, the district court applied a three-factor test to determine whether federal common law governs plaintiffs' claims:

> (1) the existence of a substantial federal interest in the outcome of a litigation;

> (2) the effect on this federal interest should state law be applied; and

> (3) the effect on state interests should state law be displaced by federal common law.

* * *

II

Both plaintiffs and defendants accept the three-part test that the district court applied to the federal common law issue, and for purposes of discussion we accept that framework. But, focusing our consideration chiefly on the first factor of the test, i.e., "the existence of a substantial federal interest in the outcome of the litigation," we disagree with the district court's analysis and conclude that the court gave insufficient weight to the Supreme Court's repeated admonition that

> [i]n deciding whether rules of federal common law should be fashioned, normally the guiding principle is that a *significant conflict between some federal policy or interest and the use of state law in the premises must first be specifically shown* ....

Wallis v. Pan American Petroleum Corp., *supra,* 384 U.S. at 68, 86 S.Ct. at 1304, *quoted with emphasis* in Miree v. DeKalb County, *supra,* 433 U.S. at 31, 97 S.Ct. at 2494. Principally we reject the district court's conclusion that there is an identifiable federal policy at stake in this litigation that warrants the creation of federal common law rules.[11]

In considering plaintiffs' contentions, it is essential to delineate precisely the relation of the United States to the claims here at issue. These claims are brought by former servicemen and their families

11. Since we conclude that there is not now an identifiable federal policy, we need not reach the second and third factors of the test and speculate as to how state law, if it were already developed, would affect the federal policy if it were identifiable-or vice versa.

against private manufacturers; they are not asserted by or against the United States, and they do not directly implicate the rights and duties of the United States. They are thus unlike the claims in *United States v. Standard Oil Co., supra,* in which the government brought suit to recover for its payments to a soldier injured as a result of the defendant's negligence, and *Clearfield Trust Co. v. United States, supra,* in which the government brought suit to enforce its rights in commercial paper issued by it. In each of those cases the government was a party seeking to enforce its own asserted rights, and analysis reveals two federal concerns which are inherent in such cases. First, the government has an interest in having uniform rules govern its rights and obligations. Second, the government has a substantive interest in the contents of those uniform rules. The first interest prizes uniformity for its own sake and is content-neutral; it does not dictate the substance of the federal common law rule to be applied. Thus, in *United States v. Standard Oil Co., supra,* the Court applied federal common law, recognizing the government's interest in uniformity, but refused to impose the liability argued for by the United States as the substance of that law.

The present litigation is fundamentally different from *Standard Oil* and *Clearfield Trust* with respect to both uniformity interest and substantive interest in the content of the rules to be applied. Since this litigation is between private parties and no substantial rights or duties of the government hinge on its outcome, there is no federal interest in uniformity for its own sake.[12] *See e. g., Miree v. DeKalb County, supra,* 433 U.S. at 28, 97 S.Ct. at 2493. The fact that application of state law may produce a variety of results is of no moment. It is in the nature of a federal system that different states will apply different rules of law, based on their individual perceptions of what is in the best interests of their citizens. That alone is not grounds in private litigation for judicially creating an overriding federal law. Indeed, even where a federal statutory program governs the rights of private litigants and Congress has left gaps to be filled by the courts, uniformity is not prized for its own sake. For example, in Auto Workers v. Hoosier Corp., 383 U.S. 696, 701–05, 86 S.Ct. 1107, 1110–1113, 16 L.Ed.2d 192 (1966), the Court dealt with a suit under § 301 of the National Labor Relations Act, 29 U.S.C. § 185 (1976), to which federal common law applied. Yet in determining the timeliness of such suits, the Court ruled that the appropriate state statutes of limitations should apply, and refused to impose a uniform federal period of limitations:

> [T]imeliness ... is clearly a federal question, for in § 301 suits the applicable law is "federal law, which the courts must fashion from the policy of our national labor laws." Textile Workers v. Lincoln Mills, 353 U.S. 448, 456, 77 S.Ct. 912, 917, 1 L.Ed.2d 972.

---

12. *Compare* Bank of America Nat'l Trust & Sav. Ass'n v. Parnell, 352 U.S. 29, 32–34, 77 S.Ct. 119, 120–121, 1 L.Ed.2d 93 (1956), private litigation involving the issues of whether certain government bonds were "overdue" and whether the defendant had taken title to the bonds in good faith. The Court observed that the question of when a government bond is overdue is a matter of federal law, but held that questions as to a party's good faith are left to local law.

We are urged instead (of referring to state laws,) to devise a uniform time limitation to close the statutory gap left by Congress. But the teaching of our cases does not require so bald a form of judicial innovation. 383 U.S. at 701, 86 S.Ct. at 1110. Thus, the prospect of uniformity is insufficient reason to invoke federal common law in private litigation; and if federal common law were invoked, it would not ensure uniformity since frequently that law takes its substance from local law.

The second fundamental difference between the present litigation and the *Clearfield Trust* type of case is that in the latter, the government's substantive interest in the litigation is essentially monothetic, in that it is concerned only with preserving the federal fisc, whereas here the government has two interests; and here the two interests have been placed in sharp contrast with one another. Thus, the government has an interest in the welfare of its veterans; they have given of themselves in the most fundamental way possible in the national interest. But the government also has an interest in the suppliers of its materiel; imposition, for example, of strict liability as contended for by plaintiffs would affect the government's ability to procure materiel without the exaction of significantly higher prices, or the attachment of onerous conditions, or the demand of indemnification or the like. As plaintiffs' counsel has observed, "this litigation will have a direct and lasting impact on the relationship between the federal government and war contractors ... and between the federal government and veterans." * * * It is obvious that the government is interested. But unlike a simple uniformity interest, neither the government's interest in its veterans nor its interest in its suppliers is content-neutral. Each interest will be furthered only if the federal rule of law to be applied favors that particular group.

The extent to which either group *should* be favored, and its welfare deemed "paramount" (*see* dissent of Chief Judge Feinberg), is preeminently a policy determination of the sort reserved in the first instance for Congress. The welfare of veterans and that of military suppliers are clearly federal concerns which Congress should appropriately consider in setting policy for the governance of the nation, and it is properly left to Congress in the first instance to strike the balance between the conflicting interests of the veterans and the contractors, and thereby identify federal policy. Although Congress has turned its attention to the Agent Orange problem, it has not determined what the federal policy is with respect to the reconciliation of these two competing interests. Thus, this case is unlike Owens v. Haas, 601 F.2d 1242 (2d Cir.), *cert. denied,* 444 U.S. 980, 100 S.Ct. 483, 62 L.Ed.2d 407 (1979), or Ivy Broadcasting Co. v. American Tel. & Tel. Co., 391 F.2d 486 (2d Cir.1968), in which the court was asked to supplement with federal common law a federal statutory program which itself embodied Congressional policy determinations.[14] In *Owens,* as Chief Judge Feinberg observes, * * *, the Court

---

14. Plaintiffs contend that FIFRA * * * evinces a federal interest in regulation of   herbicides sufficient to call into play the federal common law. But as this court has "discerned a 'federal regulatory scheme' " for the protection of prisoners. It is one thing to discern a federal regulatory scheme from the statutes Congress has enacted, as in *Owens*; it is another to devise such a scheme in the face of inaction by Congress. The dissent finds it anomalous that federal common law may apply to prisoners but not to veterans. We suggest that the anomaly lies not with the court in declining to devise a scheme, but with Congress which has made specific provision for protection of the government's prisoners but not for its soldiers.

We conclude that in the present case, while the federal government has obvious interests in the welfare of the parties to the litigation, its interest in the *outcome* of the litigation, i.e., in how the parties' welfare should be balanced, is as yet undetermined. The teaching of *Wallis* and *Miree* is that before federal common law rules should be fashioned, the use of state law must pose a threat to an "identifiable" federal policy. *Wallis v. Pan American Petroleum Corp.*, 384 U.S. at 68; *Miree v. DeKalb County*, 433 U.S. at 31–33. In the present litigation the federal policy is not yet identifiable. We conclude, therefore, that the district court erred in ruling that plaintiffs' claims were governed by federal common law. The order denying defendants' motion to dismiss for lack of subject matter jurisdiction is accordingly

Reversed.

FEINBERG, CHIEF JUDGE (dissenting):

This case presents us with a unique set of facts, parties, and pleadings. Many aspects of plaintiffs' case are troublesome, because plaintiffs seek unusual relief, both procedural and substantive, as to which I express no view. But the issue now before us is far narrower, and raises more familiar considerations. That issue is whether a federal district court has federal question jurisdiction over the action, see 28 U.S.C. § 1331(a), because the action arises under federal common law. I agree with District Judge Pratt that this case should be tried in federal court under rules of federal common law. I therefore dissent from the opinion of the majority.

That the present case is *sui generis*, and national in its proportions, is evident from the complaint itself. * * * The plaintiffs in these cases complain of injuries sustained as the result of service in our nation's military, in a national endeavor in a foreign land. To the non-legal mind, it would be an odd proposition indeed that this litigation, so patently of national scope and concern, should not be tried in federal court.

As for the legal mind, all involved in this case—the parties, Judge Pratt, and the panel on appeal—appear to agree that federal question

noted, FIFRA was not intended to preempt state law even with respect to those matters it specifically regulates. Chemical Specialties Mfrs. Ass'n v. Lowery, 452 F.2d 431 (2d Cir.1971). It is certainly an insufficient basis for a displacement of the entire body of state product liability law.

jurisdiction depends upon whether a federal common law rule of product liability should be applied.

* * *

Looking, as the *Owens* court did, to *Miree* and *Wallis*, the first question we must answer is whether the federal government has a "substantial interest" in the outcome of this litigation. It is plain that this question must be answered affirmatively. As the Supreme Court observed in United States v. Standard Oil Company, 332 U.S. 301, 67 S.Ct. 1604, 91 L.Ed. 2067 (1947),

> Perhaps no relation between the Government and a citizen is more distinctively federal in character than that between it and members of its armed forces. To whatever extent state law may apply to govern the relations between soldiers or others in the armed forces and persons outside them or non-federal governmental agencies, the scope, nature, legal incidents and consequences of the relation between persons in service and the government are fundamentally derived from federal sources and governed by federal authority.... So also we think are interferences with that relationship such as the facts of this case involve. For, as the Federal Government has the exclusive power to establish and define the relationship by virtue of its military and other powers, equally clearly it has power in execution of the same functions to protect the relation once formed from harms inflicted by others.

* * * This obviously federal relationship does not depend primarily upon any particular statute, but rather inheres in the federal government's exclusive capacity to wage war. * * *

The majority concludes that on the facts of this case "there is no federal interest in uniformity for its own sake," and that there is no federal "substantive interest in the content of the rules to be applied." I disagree on both counts. As to uniformity of treatment, this court noted in *Owens* that "[b]ecause there is a federal regulatory scheme, there is a federal interest in assuring uniform treatment of federal prisoners." * * * It is anomalous for this court to hold, on the one hand, that the federal government has an interest in "uniform treatment" of its *prisoners* sufficient to warrant the use of a federal rule of recovery, and, on the other hand, that the federal government has no such interest in "uniform treatment" of its *soldiers*. The majority suggests that the anomaly here lies "with Congress, which has made specific provisions for the protection of the government's prisoners but not for its soldiers." But a review of the statutory and regulatory provisions ..., as well as myriad, detailed Army Regulations, demonstrates beyond doubt that Congress has made specific provisions for the protection of its soldiers, both directly and by delegation.

The majority also concludes that because the government has arguably conflicting substantive interests in the outcome of the litigation, "the federal policy is not yet identifiable." The allegedly conflicting federal interests are in the welfare of veterans and in the welfare of suppliers of war materiel. But that the plaintiff veterans and the defendant contractors have opposing interests in this litigation hardly means that the paramount federal interest is somehow divided or self-contradictory. The United States has a clear interest in the protection of its soldiers from harm caused by defective war materiel. What other interests does the United States arguably have that might conflict with this clear interest? One such interest might be in seeing that defendants, as suppliers of war materiel, are treated fairly. But that interest cannot be said to conflict with the government's interest in the safety of its soldiers. Another such interest might be in preventing defendants from being driven to bankruptcy by large damage awards to *Agent Orange* plaintiffs, who have already made claims assertedly greater than defendants' combined liquid assets. This, I take it, is what the majority means by its reference to the federal interest in the "welfare" of defendants. But this interest lies in the future, and in the realm of speculation. There will be time enough to deal with the potential impact of defendants' financial liability if and when they incur any, if it is truly in the interest of the United States to do so. By contrast, plaintiffs' injuries-assuming for the moment that plaintiffs have a viable cause of action-lie in large part in the present, and in the realm of the concrete. The conclusion seems inescapable to me that the United States' interest in the "welfare" of defendants cannot approach, either in magnitude or in quality, its interest in the welfare of the *Agent Orange* plaintiffs. In short, in the case before us the paramount interests of the United States are in the welfare of its veterans and in their fair and uniform treatment.

Having discerned a significant federal interest, we are next required to determine whether or not a "significant conflict" exists between that interest and the application of state law. This factor is not reached by the majority. But that such a conflict does exist in the present case can hardly be disputed. Given the "distinctively federal" character of the relationship between the federal government and its soldiers, there is an inherent federal interest in the uniform definition of the aspects of that relationship involved in this case. As noted earlier, this inherent interest in uniformity was observed by this court in *Owens*, * * *. The application of state law to the present case would severely frustrate this federal interest: If state law is applied in the present litigation, and assuming again that the allegations in the complaint are true, then veterans may well be subjected to sharply differing rules of law in the pursuit of their remedies. For example, the law of the various states is in flux, diverging widely in the definition of what constitutes a "defective" product-especially with respect to defectively designed products—and in the availability of defenses based on the "state of the art" and technological feasibility. * * * As a result, if the laws of 30 or 40 state jurisdictions are separately applied, veterans' recoveries for Agent Orange injuries will vary widely—despite the fact that these soldiers fought shoulder to shoulder, without regard to state citizenship, in a national endeavor abroad. In sum, the federal interest here in uniformity would be defeated by the application of discrete and differing state laws. It is thus not necessary to reach the question whether the other federal interest present in this case—in seeing that soldiers are not harmed by defective war materiel—would be frustrated by the application of state law. Because the federal interest in uniformity would be defeated by such an application, I conclude that the first two requirements of *Miree* and *Wallis,* as interpreted by this court in *Owens,* are satisfied, as Judge Pratt concluded.

The third and last factor involves the extent to which state interests would be affected, if state law were to be "displaced" by federal common law in the present case. This factor is also not reached by the majority. I agree with Judge Pratt's conclusion that the claims made by plaintiffs in this unique and unprecedented litigation do not fall within the developed area of state tort law. As noted above, the states' product liability law is in flux; with respect to a case as novel as the one before us, a consistent and established body of state law is even less discernible. Accordingly, I think that Judge Pratt was correct in holding that the application of federal common law to the case before us would not "displace" state law, because there is no substantial body of state law on this point to be displaced. I thus conclude that all three factors, accepted by the majority as the proper analytical framework, point to the use of a federal common law rule in the present case, giving rise to federal question jurisdiction.

Because I conclude that the district court does have jurisdiction over the case before us, I dissent from the opinion of the majority.

IN RE DIAMOND SHAMROCK CHEMS. CO.

United States Court of Appeals, Second Circuit, 1984.
725 F.2d 858, *cert. denied* 465 U.S. 1067, 104 S.Ct. 1417, 79 L.Ed.2d 743 (1984).

WINTER, CIRCUIT JUDGE:

This multi-district litigation in the Eastern District of New York involves several hundred actions brought by veterans of the armed forces of the United States, Australia and New Zealand who served in Vietnam at some time during the period 1961 to 1972 and by their spouses, parents and children. Jurisdiction is based upon diversity of citizenship. In re "Agent Orange" Product Liability Litigation, 635 F.2d 987 (2d Cir.1980), *cert. denied,* 454 U.S. 1128 (1981). * * * On December 16, 1983, Chief Judge Weinstein certified two classes, one pursuant to Fed.R.Civ.P. 23(b)(3) and the other pursuant to Rule 23(b)(1)(B). In re "Agent Orange" Product Liability Litigation, 100 F.R.D. 718 (E.D.N.Y. 1983). Familiarity with his Memorandum and Order is assumed. This petition for a writ of mandamus ensued. We deny the petition.

* * *

Chief Judge Weinstein also found that the divergence among states as to choice of law and product liability rules is insignificant and that "a consensus among the states * * * provides, in effect, a national substantive rule governing the main issues in this case." It is, of course, the law of this case that plaintiffs' claims arise under state law, *In re* "Agent Orange" Product Liability Litigation, 635 F.2d 987 (2d Cir.1980), *cert. denied,* 454 U.S. 1128, 102 S.Ct. 980, 71 L.Ed.2d 116 (1981), and it is possible that the law of every state and Australia and New Zealand, including choice of law rules, will at some point come into play. While we will not disclaim considerable skepticism as to the existence of a "national substantive rule," we note Chief Judge Weinstein's declared intention to create subclasses as dictated by variations in state law. Given the unique aspects of this case arguably creating a need for a single dispositive trial on the common issues described above, we cannot say that the use of subclasses corresponding to variations in state law is a palpable error remediable by mandamus.

Chief Judge Weinstein also certified a mandatory class under Rule 23(b)(1)(B). Relying upon findings of a Special Master, he found that the defendants' assets are at this time sufficient to meet a judgment for compensatory damages. He reasoned, however, that because punitive damages are designed solely to punish rather than to compensate, courts adjudicating later individual claims would admit evidence as to the payment of punitive damages in prior cases. Since this might induce juries to reduce punitive awards to later claimants, he found that an "adjudication with respect to individual members of the class ... would as a practical matter be dispositive of the interests of the other members not parties to the adjudication." He then certified a class under Rule 23(b)(1)(B) for the award of punitive damages. Given the large number of potential claimants, estimated by the Special Master to be over 40,000 and given the fact that punitive damages ought in theory to be distributed among the individual plaintiffs on a basis other than date of trial, the argument against his ruling does not justify issuance of a writ of mandamus.[4]

JACKSON v. JOHNS–MANVILLE SALES CORP.

United States Court of Appeals, Fifth Circuit, 1985.
750 F.2d 1314.

Before CLARK, CHIEF JUDGE, GEE, RUBIN, GARZA, REAVLEY, POLITZ, RANDALL, TATE, JOHNSON, GARWOOD, JOLLY, HIGGINBOTHAM, DAVIS and HILL, CIRCUIT JUDGES.

RANDALL, CIRCUIT JUDGE:

In this Mississippi diversity case, plaintiff James L. Jackson, a former shipyard worker, seeks recovery of actual and punitive damages against defendants Johns–Manville Sales Corporation, Raybestos–Manhattan, Inc., and H.K. Porter Company, manufacturers of asbestos

4. Subclasses may also be necessary here because of variations in state law governing the award of punitive damages.

products, for injuries allegedly caused by the defendants' failure to warn of the dangers associated with exposure to their asbestos products. Following extensive discovery and a lengthy jury trial, the district court entered judgment in favor of Jackson and against all defendants except H.K. Porter Company for $391,500 in compensatory damages and $625,-000 in combined punitive damages. On appeal, a panel of this court affirmed in part, reversed in part, and remanded the case for a new trial. Jackson v. Johns–Manville Sales Corp., 727 F.2d 506 (5th Cir.1984). We granted *en banc* rehearing, 727 F.2d at 533, and now decide to certify to the Mississippi Supreme Court three significant questions of Mississippi law.

* * *

II

* * *

B. SUBSTANTIVE LAW—PUNITIVE DAMAGES, MENTAL ANGUISH AND PROBABLE FUTURE CONSEQUENCES.

In the original appeal of this case, Johns–Manville and Raybestos–Manhattan argued that punitive damages should not be recoverable as a matter of law in the context of asbestos litigation because of certain public policy considerations described below. The defendants also insisted that the district court erroneously allowed the jury to award compensatory damages for mental anguish allegedly associated with Jackson's increased risk of contracting cancer. Finally, before the *en banc* court the defendants argued that the district court was also erroneous in allowing the jury to award compensatory damages for cancer as a probable future consequence of Jackson's present condition. Because a plaintiff under Mississippi law can usually recover both types of compensatory damages if they are sufficiently tied to the defendants' wrong, *see* Entex, Inc. v. Rasberry, 355 So.2d 1102, 1103 (Miss.1978)("where . . . future consequences from an injury will ensue, recovery therefor may be had, but such future consequences must be established in terms of reasonable probabilities"); Sears, Roebuck & Co. v. Devers, 405 So.2d 898, 901 (Miss.1981)(damages for mental anguish are recoverable when they are the natural and proximate result of a wrong), whether these damages are available in the instant case may depend on the nature of the actionable injury. If the actionable injury here was the exposure to asbestos, as Jackson insists, he may be entitled to recover damages for those future consequences, such as the manifestation of cancer, that could be established in terms of reasonable probabilities and for the mental suffering that is the direct consequence of the increased risk of cancer caused by the asbestos exposure. If, on the other hand, exposure to asbestos is regarded as too abstract an invasion, either as a general rule or in the context of latent disease, mass tort litigation, and instead Jackson's asbestosis itself is considered to be the only actionable harm, Jackson may have no right to recover these damages since asbestosis alone does not result in an increased risk of cancer. In voting to rehear the case en banc, this court requested the parties additionally to consider in their briefings whether this case was an appropriate one for the fashioning and imposition of federal common law.[14] Upon careful review of the excellent briefs submitted and the applicable caselaw, we now conclude that Mississippi law governs the resolution of the punitive damages, cancer as a probable future consequence, and mental anguish issues. Moreover, because Mississippi courts have yet to give a definite answer to the questions these issues pose, we have determined to certify all three issues to the Mississippi Supreme Court.

1.   The Unique Nature of Asbestos Litigation.

In advocating the application of federal common law, both the defendants and the dissent distinguish the instant case from routine personal injury actions on the ground that asbestos-related injuries have become a national problem of immense proportions. Studies cited in the panel opinion indicate that in the last forty years over 21 million Americans have been significantly exposed to asbestos. These studies further estimate that at least 200,000 people will die from asbestos-related cancer alone by the end of the century. As a result of the widespread exposure to asbestos, over 20,000 personal injury lawsuits have already been filed, seeking billions of dollars in damages. Johns–Manville reports that it alone is named as a defendant in over 14,000 suits, almost 10,000 of which seek substantial punitive damages in addition to compensatory relief.

It is feared that, unless present plaintiffs are soon limited in the damages they can collect, early recoveries will create a substantial possibility that the responsible corporate entities will be unable to satisfy the compensatory awards of future claimants. Defendants, the dissent, and a number of commentators urge that, specifically, assessments of punitive damages not only threaten to destroy the viability of enterprises through which loss distribution can be accomplished, but also are incapable of fulfilling their dual functions of punishment and deterrence in the face of the asbestos industry's virtual limitless liability. Similarly, awards for mental and prospective damages related to possible future manifestations of a disease, theoretically recoverable when exposure is considered as the actionable injury, require asbestos companies to expend their resources at a more accelerated pace to the detriment of future plaintiffs. To the defendants and the dissent, these problems and the need for national solutions form an ample basis for the formulation of federal common law.

2.   The Question of Federal Common Law.

Any discussion of federal common law must begin with Erie R. Co. v. Tompkins, 304 U.S. 64, 58 S.Ct. 817, 82 L.Ed. 1188 (1938). In *Erie*, the

---

14. Our request read in pertinent part as follows: Please refer to the discussion in Part VI of the panel opinion, * * * (727 F.2d 526–530). Supplement or include in your briefing in this case a discussion of what consideration *Erie R. Co. v. Tompkins*, 304 U.S. 64, 58 S.Ct. 817, 82 L.Ed. 1188, *Clearfield Trust Co. v. United States*, 318 U.S. 363, 63 S.Ct. 573, 87 L.Ed. 838, and subsequent interpretative decisions would permit this court to give to the impact of punitive damage awards on future federal court litigants notwithstanding Mississippi rules of substantive law.

Supreme Court established that federal courts do not have the general law-making powers commonly exercised by state courts. The *Erie* Court held that federal courts, as courts of limited jurisdiction, are empowered to make only those laws authorized by the Constitution or by enactments of Congress. 304 U.S. at 78. Nevertheless, since *Erie,* the Supreme Court has recognized "a responsibility in the absence of legislation, to fashion federal common law in cases raising issues of uniquely federal concern." Northwest Airlines, Inc. v. Transport Workers Union of America, 451 U.S. 77, 95, 101 S.Ct. 1571, 67 L.Ed.2d 750 (1981). These instances, however, are "few and restricted." Wheeldin v. Wheeler, 373 U.S. 647, 651, 83 S.Ct. 1441, 1444, 10 L.Ed.2d 605 (1963). With respect to the kinds of cases that do raise issues of "uniquely federal concern," the Supreme Court has most recently stated:

> [A]bsent some congressional authorization to formulate substantive rules of decision, federal common law exists only in such narrow areas as those concerned with the rights and obligations of the United States, interstate and international disputes implicating the conflicting rights of States or our relations with foreign nations, and admiralty cases. In these instances, our federal system does not permit the controversy to be resolved under state law, either because the authority and duties of the United States as sovereign are intimately involved or because the interstate or international nature of the controversy makes it inappropriate for state law to control.

Texas Industries, Inc. v. Radcliff Materials, Inc., 451 U.S. 630, 641, 101 S.Ct. 2061, 2067, 68 L.Ed.2d 500 (1981).

Johns–Manville and Raybestos–Manhattan, while conceding that Congress has yet to take any action to remedy the problems of asbestos exposure, present what can be taken as two arguments for the proposition that these problems involve uniquely federal concerns justifying the displacement of state law. First, the defendants, echoed by the dissent, argue that the potential conflict among plaintiffs for the limited resources of the asbestos companies is analogous to the interstate conflicts over water rights and pollution that have been held to involve uniquely federal interests. According to the defendants, just as one state cannot divert the waters of a river flowing partially within its borders without regard for those downstream, one group of states should not be able by allowing the recovery of noncompensatory damages to divert and deplete scarce corporate resources at the expense of injured plaintiffs in other states.

We find this argument, although superficially plausible, to be ultimately unpersuasive. Defendants in drawing their analogy necessarily rely on such cases as Hinderlider v. La Plata River & Cherry Creek Ditch Co., 304 U.S. 92, 58 S.Ct. 803, 82 L.Ed. 1202 (1938), and Illinois v. City of Milwaukee, 406 U.S. 91, 92 S.Ct. 1385, 31 L.Ed.2d 712 (1972). *Hinderlider* concerned the allocation of water rights between Colorado and New Mexico in regard to the La Plata River, which flowed from Colorado to New Mexico and was used beneficially by both states. The

Supreme Court, in requiring the river to be equally apportioned, held that "whether the water of an interstate stream must be apportioned between the two States is a question of 'federal common law' upon which neither the statutes nor the decisions of either State can be conclusive." 304 U.S. at 110. Similarly, in *Illinois v. City of Milwaukee*, the Supreme Court, faced with a dispute over water pollution in Lake Michigan, a body of water bounded by four states, found that the conflict was fundamentally interstate in nature and thus touched basic interests in federalism. The Court held that, in such a situation, federal common law applied. 406 U.S. at 105 & n. 6, 92 S.Ct. at 1393 & n. 6.

In both cases, the essential conflict was between states as quasi-sovereign bodies over shared resources. Under such circumstances, a single state's statutes or decisions could not be considered conclusive. In the realm of asbestos litigation, on the other hand, any conflict between plaintiffs, even assuming one to exist, may transcend state lines but does not involve the rights and duties of states as discrete political entities. A conflict over the resources of the asbestos industry would be not merely between plaintiffs in different states but between plaintiffs in the same state and between past, present, and future plaintiffs. Clearly, if federal courts are to remain courts of limited powers as required under *Erie,* a dispute over a common fund or scarce resources cannot become "interstate," in the sense of requiring the application of federal common law, merely because the conflict is not confined within the boundaries of a single state.

Second, the defendants argue that there is a uniquely federal interest in assuring compensation to injured persons and in maintaining government asbestos suppliers. Both interests, the defendants insist, would be substantially served by the creation of federal rules restricting the types of damages recoverable in asbestos suits. We think the defendants in making this argument misconceive the nature of the uniquely federal interest requirement. "Uniquely federal interests" are not merely national interests, and the existence of national interests, no matter their significance, cannot by themselves give federal courts the authority to supersede state policy. Indeed, as the Supreme Court recently stated, "[t]he enactment of a federal rule in an area of national concern, and the decision whether to displace state law in doing so, is generally made not by the federal judiciary, purposefully insulated from democratic pressures, but by the people through their elected representatives in Congress." City of Milwaukee v. Illinois, 451 U.S. 304, 312–13, 101 S.Ct. 1784, 1789–90, 68 L.Ed.2d 114 (1981)(*Milwaukee II*). It is well-established instead that to be "uniquely federal" and thus a sufficient predicate for the imposition of a federal substantive rule, an interest must relate to an articulated congressional policy or directly implicate the authority and duties of the United States as sovereign. *See, e.g., Texas Industries, supra,* at 641, 101 S.Ct. at 2067 (authority and duties of United States must be "intimately involved"); *Northwest Airlines, supra,* at 95, 101 S.Ct. at 1582 (uniquely federal concern is "the definition of rights and duties of the United States"); United States v.

Kimbell Foods, Inc., 440 U.S. 715, 726, 99 S.Ct. 1448, 1457, 59 L.Ed.2d 711 (1979)(federal law governs rights of United States arising under nationwide federal program); Clearfield Trust Co. v. United States, 318 U.S. 363, 366, 63 S.Ct. 573, 574, 87 L.Ed. 838 (1943)(federal common law governs rights and duties of United States on commercial paper which it issues).

Although individual members and committees of Congress have expressed concern with the problem of asbestos litigation, Congress itself has yet to make policy on this issue. Moreover, defendants have been unable to point to any substantial right or duty of the federal government that would be directly affected by the outcome of this litigation. Any effect state law recoveries would eventually have on the government's ability to obtain needed materials is far too indirect to justify the imposition of federal common law. *See, e.g.,* In re "Agent Orange" Product Liability Litigation, 635 F.2d 987, 993 (2d Cir.1980)(no federal policy at stake in action by war veterans against manufacturers of defoliants used in Vietnam War that is sufficient to warrant creation of federal common law), *cert. denied,* 454 U.S. 1128, 102 S.Ct. 980, 71 L.Ed.2d 116 (1981); *cf.* Miree v. DeKalb County, 433 U.S. 25, 29–32, 97 S.Ct. 2490, 2493–97, 53 L.Ed.2d 557 (1977)(federal interest in air travel insufficient basis for creation of federal law in action between private parties that will have no direct effect on United States or its treasury); Bank of America National Trust & Savings Ass'n v. Parnell, 352 U.S. 29, 33–34, 77 S.Ct. 119, 121, 1 L.Ed.2d 93 (1956)(interest of government too speculative and remote in action between private parties that does not touch rights and duties of the United States). Similarly, ensuring the availability of compensation for injured plaintiffs is predominately a matter of state concern and, in the absence of congressional enactments, state law, both as to the extent of compensation available and punitive damages, must apply. As recently as last term, the Supreme Court reaffirmed this basic principle of American federalism when it stated in a related context: "Punitive damages have long been a part of traditional principles of state law. As noted above, Congress assumed that traditional principles of state tort law would apply with full force unless they were expressly supplanted." Silkwood v. Kerr–McGee Corp., 464 U.S. 238, 104 S.Ct. 615, 625, 78 L.Ed.2d 443 (1984).

A related interest that has been suggested to justify the exercise of federal judicial power in this case is the federal court's own interest in "doing justice." It could be argued that federal courts have an institutional interest in maintaining a federal judicial system that is fundamentally "just." While we are sympathetic to such an argument, it is clear that such an abstract, all-encompassing interest cannot form a sufficient basis upon which to rest the displacement of state law. First, we find implicit in *Erie* the idea that in diversity actions federal court concerns in a just judicial system cannot be used as a reason for supplanting substantive state policies. Second, certainly as a practical matter, the effect of resting assertions of federal judicial power on so vague an interest as "justice" would be to eviscerate *Erie* completely and thus ignore its constitutional underpinnings. Third, the Supreme Court itself has already rejected a similar interest in Guaranty Trust Co. v. York, 326 U.S. 99, 65 S.Ct. 1464, 89 L.Ed. 2079 (1945). In that diversity case, the plaintiff argued, *inter alia*, that the federal court's equitable powers and discretion constituted an exception to *Erie* and that, therefore, the federal court was not bound by the state statute of limitations. The Supreme Court, in rejecting the plaintiff's claim, stated:

> But since a federal court adjudicating a state-created right solely because of the diversity of citizenship of the parties is for that purpose, in effect, only another court of the State, it cannot afford recovery if the right to recover is made unavailable by the State nor can it substantially affect the enforcement of the right as given by the State.

Id. at 108–09. A federal court's interest in "doing equity" is closely related to its interest in "doing justice." It is doubtful that the Supreme Court in *Guaranty Trust* would have been any more willing to displace state law if the plaintiff additionally had successfully shown that the applicable state statute of limitations was "unjust." Obviously, if justice could be used as a justification for the naked exercise of federal judicial power, the Supreme Court's oft-repeated assertion that the instances in which federal common law governs are "few and restricted" would no longer be true. *Cf. Texas Industries, Inc.*, at 640 (denying rights of contribution against antitrust co-conspirators).

Finally, we note the impracticalities of fashioning a federal common law in the context of asbestos litigation. First, any decision by this court to displace state law would be effective only within our geographical jurisdiction. While it is of course possible that other circuits would in time follow our lead, at least one circuit has already expressly refused to apply federal common law in these circumstances. *See Moran, supra,* at 817 ("relief sought ... may be more properly granted by the state or federal legislature than by this Court"). Unless and until the Supreme Court imposes a similar federal common law on the country as a whole, any federal substantive rules fashioned by us would only exacerbate the alleged inequities among claimants, with punitive and certain types of compensatory damages being available outside the circuit but not within. Such a result, in turn, would encourage a massive effort at forum shopping to bring suits outside this circuit.

Second, we are unable to discern any governing principle of easy application for the imposition of federal common law in the asbestos context. Although the amount of recovery available to plaintiffs depends in large part on the availability of punitive damages and the scope of the actionable injury, many other aspects of the litigation similarly play a significant role in determining the size of potential awards. The applicable limitations period for the bringing of an action, for example, has a direct impact on aggregate recovery and thus the availability of funds for future claimants. The simple fact is that, once the need to limit plaintiffs' recoveries is used to justify the creation of federal substantive rules precluding the recovery of punitive damages and narrowing the scope of the actionable injury, there would be no principled means of restricting the application of federal common law to other matters, either in the context of asbestos litigation or in relation to similar legal problems. As a consequence, federal courts would become increasingly responsible for establishing a general federal tort law in a manner we think is inconsistent with the teachings of *Erie* and the logic behind our federal system. *Cf.* Parratt v. Taylor, 451 U.S. 527, 544, 101 S.Ct. 1908, 1917, 68 L.Ed.2d 420 (1981)(due process clause not intended to be "a font of tort law to be superimposed upon whatever systems may already be administered by the States")(*quoting* Paul v. Davis, 424 U.S. 693, 701, 96 S.Ct. 1155, 1160, 47 L.Ed.2d 405 (1976)).

Third, displacement of state law in asbestos cases would require federal courts to reexamine the major issues and principles involved in asbestos litigation, most of which are presently settled under state tort law. As a result, the progress of currently pending asbestos cases through the federal court system would come to a virtual standstill. The need to ensure quick resolution of the claims militates strongly against taking such action.

In sum, we find that this case is not an appropriate one for the creation of a federal common law because of the absence of a uniquely federal interest and the practical problems that would attend the displacement of state law. Although federal common law may at times be a "necessary expedient," *Milwaukee II,* at 314, 101 S.Ct. at 1791 (*quoting* Committee for Consideration of Jones Falls Sewage System v. Train, 539 F.2d 1006, 1008 (4th Cir.1976)(*en banc*)), under our federal system Congress is generally the body responsible for balancing competing interests and setting national policy. There is no doubt that a desperate need exists for federal legislation in the field of asbestos litigation. Congress' silence on the matter, however, hardly authorizes the federal judiciary to assume for itself the responsibility for formulating what essentially are legislative solutions. Displacement of state law is primarily a decision for Congress, and Congress has yet to act. *See Miree,* at 32, 97 S.Ct. at 2495.[18]

* * *

CLARK, CHIEF JUDGE, with whom GEE, GARZA, POLITZ AND E. GRADY JOLLY, CIRCUIT JUDGES, join, dissenting.

The nub of the disagreement with the majority opinion lies in its essential premise that justice is too abstract, too all-encompassing a

18. Because we find that the imposition of federal common law is clearly not appropriate in this context, we have determined not to certify the question to the United States Supreme Court pursuant to 28 U.S.C. § 1254(3), as suggested by the dissent. *See* Wisniewski v. United States, 353 U.S. 901, 902, 77 S.Ct. 633, 634, 1 L.Ed.2d 658 (1957)(per curiam)(certification only proper in rare instance when advisable in the proper administration and expedition of judicial business); United States v. Perrin, 131 U.S. 55, 58, 9 S.Ct. 681, 682, 33 L.Ed. 88 (1889)(question certified must pose "a real question of a difficult point of law"). *See generally* 17 C. Wright, A. Miller & E. Cooper, *Federal Practice and Procedure* § 4038.

concept to serve as a basis for supplanting state substantive law in diversity cases. Therefore, the aim of this dissent will be to develop the values that support the premise that existing precedent creates a duty to ask the Supreme Court of the United States to instruct us on whether federal common law should be applied in this litigation.

The majority labels this a "Mississippi diversity case." While this is literally accurate, it is misleading. *Jackson* is a seminal case that will control the rights of untold thousands of litigants in this court. The panel opinion cannot form a proper premise for dissent, for, like the majority, it too gave less than adequate consideration to the impact of the unprecedented volume of the asbestos litigation in the federal court system. The number of the claims is already legion and increasing at a geometric rate. Compensation for these actions, most of which are founded on the concept of liability without fault, must be paid by a finite and indeed limited group of business entities and insurers. These facts prevent consideration of James Leroy Jackson's case in isolation. They also preclude our dealing with Jackson and his cohorts as a group of litigants whose cases should be governed by Mississippi law under ordinary diversity principles. The only just resolution this court can achieve here is to certify to the United States Supreme Court under 28 U.S.C. § 1254(3) the question of whether federal common law must be developed to govern this uniquely interdependent mass of tort litigation.

I

In the fifteen years since the filing of the first suits, the field of asbestos litigation has exploded. We are confronted with an already astronomical and still growing number of plaintiffs seeking individual recoveries against a finite pool of assets belonging to a relatively small group of defendants. Because the insidious diseases giving rise to these claims have latency periods ranging up to forty years, the injuries of many plaintiffs will not become manifest for years to come. There is a real and present danger that the available assets will be exhausted before those later victims can seek the compensation to which they are entitled. This threat is exacerbated by inconsistent state policies pertaining to many elements of litigation. The clearest sources of this danger are the two major concepts at issue here: the availability of punitive damages and the propriety of restricting the accrual of each of the many distinct diseases that can result from asbestos exposure to the actual date of manifestation. In this unique context, the continued case-by-case implementation of these policies on an inconsistent basis will permit initial plaintiffs, through disproportionate awards, to consume the only assets available to compensate later-filing but equally deserving plaintiffs.

Each of the many states touched by this litigation has a strong interest in ensuring that its citizens receive full compensation, regardless of when their individual claims accrue. Uncompensated victims could directly or indirectly burden the state itself. However, no state can control the tort law of another. A state seeking to protect its own citizens can only shape its law to maximize the recovery of its own early plaintiffs, so that at least those individuals will not be impeded in the legal scramble for a share of insufficient assets.

We do not deal here with a question of limited scope and impact such as the application of a state statute of limitations governing breach of trust actions as did *Guaranty Trust* on which the majority relies. As Justice Frankfurter pointed out, even before *Erie* such statutes generally governed diversity suits. Rather, we confront a sequence of massive tort claims that has unparalleled geographic and financial dimensions. We confront cases where the application of divergent governing principles can destroy the rights of similarly situated claimants. We confront no less than a challenge to our purpose as courts.

II

Just as the rote application of inconsistent state laws cannot resolve this problem, so too, any action by this inferior appellate court alone would be ineffective. Our creation of a federal common law to govern asbestos actions within the Fifth Circuit would only eliminate inequities among federal claimants in the area we serve. Courts outside our jurisdiction could continue to apply disparate policies. The question of resolving a proper federal common law rule must be certified to the Supreme Court of the United States—the only judicial forum capable of providing the right answer.

III

Modern strict liability and, indeed, almost all tort principles are products of state law. Since *Erie Railroad v. Tompkins* state law principles have governed diversity trials. This dissent invokes no departure from that well established rule. However, there is equally authentic authority that federal forums must impose an overarching rule to accomplish justice in litigation where the application of inconsistent rules generated by states with conflicting interests can consume the purpose of the state law itself.[5] Even in diversity cases we do not become courts of the states. That is why, with fidelity to the decision of the Supreme Court to apply state substantive law in diversity cases, it is necessary to remember that we always retain the duty to perform our tasks under our system of federalism.

The instances where the formulation of federal common law is justified are "few and restricted."[6] Federal common law only governs situations where "our federal system does not permit the controversy to

---

5. On the day Justice Brandeis wrote in *Erie Railroad Co. v. Tompkins*, "There is no federal *general* common law," 58 S.Ct. 817, 822 (1938)(emphasis added), in Hinderlider v. La Plata River and Cherry Creek Ditch Co., 304 U.S. 92, 58 S.Ct. 803, 811, 82 L.Ed. 1202 (1938), another case between private parties, he also wrote: "whether the waters of an interstate stream must be apportioned between the two states is a question of 'federal common law' upon which neither the statutes nor the decisions of either state can be conclusive."

6. Wheeldin v. Wheeler, 373 U.S. 647, 83 S.Ct. 1441, 10 L.Ed.2d 605 (1963).

be resolved under state law, either because the authority and duties of the United States as sovereign are intimately involved or because the interstate or international nature of the controversy makes it inappropriate for state law to control." [7]   Here the competing state interests presented by the nationwide flood of asbestos litigation place this case well within the second category as the interstate nature of the controversy makes the application of state law inappropriate.

IV

The majority concludes that federal common law is available to resolve an interstate conflict only if the essential conflict is between the states as "discrete political entities." I respectfully disagree. This conclusion ignores Justice Burger's statement that the application of federal common law is not precluded in all matters involving only private citizens.[8]   It is inconsistent with Hinderlider v. La Plata River and Cherry Creek Ditch Co., 304 U.S. 92, 58 S.Ct. 803, 82 L.Ed. 1202 (1938), the companion case to *Erie* in which Justice Brandeis announced the continuing vitality of federal common law under the proper circumstances.[9]   *Hinderlider* itself was an action to enforce private rights of a Colorado corporation.

The basis for *Hinderlider* was an earlier water apportionment case, Kansas v. Colorado, 206 U.S. 46, 27 S.Ct. 655, 51 L.Ed. 956 (1906). In *Kansas*, the Court ruled that an interstate dispute over the water in a nonnavigable stream was necessarily subject to federal common law because there was no viable means of resolving the conflict under state law. Therefore, the Court was obliged to formulate a body of federal common law to "settle that dispute in such a way as will recognize the equal rights of both and at the same time establish justice between them." *Id.* at 667.

Although both *Hinderlider* and *Kansas* specifically addressed the apportionment of water, their underlying rationale governs the equitable division of any scarce resource between citizens of different states where conflicting state interests make the use of either state's law inappropriate. The asbestos cases present this precise quandary. The finite pool of assets available to satisfy an infinite number of claimants is an identical value to the limited water available to serve many riparian owners.

An equitable resolution of this nationwide competition for scarce assets is surely as important to the basic interests of federalism as the equities invoked to justify the formulation of a common law of nuisance to resolve the dispute between the several bordering states over the

---

7. Texas Industries, Inc. v. Radcliff Materials, 451 U.S. 630, 101 S.Ct. 2061, 68 L.Ed.2d 500 (1981).

8. Miree v. DeKalb County, 433 U.S. 25, 97 S.Ct. 2490, 53 L.Ed.2d 557 (1977)(Burger, C.J., concurring).

9. *See* Banco Nacional de Cuba v. Sab-

pollution of Lake Michigan.[10]

V

Although certainly not presuming to tell the Supreme Court what course of action to take, it is appropriate, in seeking instructions, to say what divides us. We are not just divided on whether to reach for a single judicial resolution through Supreme Court certification, but also on whether that resolution should be left to state law. Our uncertainty is demonstrated by the conflict between the reasoning of the panel and the en banc majority on the substantive issues posed.

In capsule, the panel found punitive damages inappropriate in a mass tort context. Repeated awards of "smart money" for the same conduct do nothing to deter socially undesirable behavior. The enormous liability imposed by the compensatory awards in these cases has already achieved such deterrence. Aside from the inequity resulting from the fact that some states do not permit such awards, they carry the seeds to ultimately defeat the basic purpose of product liability law—to ensure that the manufacturers of a dangerous product, not the injured consumers, bear the costs of the injury. If punitive awards to early-filing plaintiffs exhaust the assets, late-comers or their state health and welfare programs must bear the costs of the injury. These are values that no single-case application of any state's law can be expected to consider.

The panel opinion also explains that separate accrual dates for a cause of action for each of the diseases which may result from asbestos exposure is vital to ensuring a rational and equitable distribution of available assets. In some cases asbestos exposure does lead to cancer. Present experience indicates, however, that the majority of individuals exposed do not develop the disease. If a plaintiff who does not have asbestos-related cancer is allowed to recover for cancer damage because he finds a medical witness who will opine that there is a reasonable probability that he may later develop the disease, that individual's damage award will be a windfall if the disease never materializes. That windfall may leave later plaintiffs unable to secure compensation for diseases actually suffered. Without uniform rules to govern this accrual procedure courts cannot ensure that such assets as are available will be distributed to claimants in proportion to injuries suffered. Such claims must mature only as each disease is diagnosed so that each plaintiff may bring separate claims based on facts, not speculation, and receive proper compensation. Only a single source of authority can avoid the destruction of the rights of valid claimants by the application of inconsistent rules generated by forums with inconsistent and competing interests.

VI

The majority says, and we agree, that legislation would be the preferred solution to the dilemma of providing an adequate scheme for

---

batino, 376 U.S. 398, 84 S.Ct. 923, 11 L.Ed.2d 804 (1964).

10. Illinois v. City of Milwaukee, 406 U.S. 91, 92 S.Ct. 1385, 31 L.Ed.2d 712 (1972).

the proper distribution of compensation. But Congress has failed to enact any of the asbestos compensation bills proposed to date. Courts enjoy no comparable ability to refuse to decide cases brought before them. We must decide Jackson's claims. But it is not just Jackson's rights which are at stake. Literally, the rights of tens of thousands of claimants in cases presently being litigated depend on what we do. Untold thousands more who have not yet manifested the symptoms of the insidious diseases that can result from asbestos fibre inhalation also depend upon our decision. We cannot wait to see if the impasse in Congress ultimately will be broken by lawmaking.

The Supreme Court, as the only institution other than Congress capable of imposing the uniformity necessary to resolve this problem in a just manner, should be afforded the chance to deal with the singular problem presented by these cases. That Court has the power to formulate federal common law which will ensure equitable compensation for all claimants. Its ability to address the controlling issues with a single voice is not only necessary for just resolution of pending litigation; it is even more important to expeditious and equitable settlement of claims. A uniform set of rules would not only protect the rights of individual claimants and the effective functioning of the judicial system, but would also aid the efforts of the asbestos companies and their insurers to develop an effective procedure for resolving these disputes on a rational basis without resorting to the courts. The potential for disparate outcomes in the different states could encourage many plaintiffs to remain in the courts rather than resorting to a unified nationwide facility for resolving these disputes.

Making judicial rules will not preclude legislative resolution. If Congress does decide to act in this area, federal common law declared by the courts would be preempted. However, the possibility of a future legislative solution does not justify a refusal by this court to deal properly with the cases now before us.

Rather than infringing the prerogatives of Congress, immediate unified judicial action would enhance the ability of Congress to address a recognized problem. All the asbestos compensation legislation proposed is premised on the assumption that asbestos manufacturers will provide most, if not all, of the necessary funding. This option will be foreclosed if these assets are exhausted prematurely by excessive awards to current plaintiffs. Moreover, the interests of individual states in protecting their claimants with later maturing disease will be facilitated and any unseemly conflict between state law rules will be eliminated.

VII

Jackson's legal rights have been a long time maturing. However, the overriding importance of their proper development makes the minor delay in certifying these issues to the single forum that possesses the power to provide an effective remedy relatively insignificant. A Supreme Court decision not to answer the questions certified, or an answer that a federal common law rule should not be applied can be quickly given. Because of the importance of an affirmative substantive response to the myriad asbestos cases confronting the federal courts, any delay resulting from a certification procedure that would deal with the merits certainly would be worth the wait. The decision not to ask is an opportunity irretrievably lost.

* * *

C. THE CASE FOR FEDERAL COMMON LAW IN MASS TORTS

GEORGENE M. VAIRO, MULTI-TORT CASES: CAUSE FOR MORE DARKNESS ON THE SUBJECT, OR A NEW ROLE FOR FEDERAL COMMON LAW?

54 Fordham L.Rev. 167, 200–224 (1985).

* * *

III. AN ANALYTIC FRAMEWORK FOR APPLYING FEDERAL
COMMON LAW IN MULTI-TORT CASES

A. A Choice of Law Approach to the Problem

One should separate the following issues: what jurisdiction provides or creates the cause of action and right to sue; what jurisdiction provides or fashions the standards of conduct; and what jurisdiction determines the available remedies. Indeed, *Guaranty Trust Co. v. York* clearly distinguishes between the right to sue and the remedy. *Clearfield Trust* shows that the jurisdiction providing the right to sue may be different from the one providing the applicable legal standards.

It is axiomatic that in multi-tort cases the laws of the fifty states create the cause of action on which the plaintiffs sue. A much more significant and thorny question remains, however. How should a federal court decide whether to apply state or federal law to each of the issues raised in a multi-tort case?

. . . in multi-tort cases, questions such as burden of proof, defenses, remedies and statutes of limitations are neither strictly substantive nor procedural. . . . [I]t is easy, but unwise, to fall into the quagmire of determining whether an issue is substantive or procedural in the multi-tort context. Thus, rather than characterizing the issue presented as substantive or procedural, the federal courts must be allowed to consider whether to develop and apply federal common law to these issues regardless of their labels in a choice of law analysis because a multi-tort case should be viewed as a hybrid.

A plaintiff's cause of action or right to sue for negligence, strict liability or breach of warranty may arise under state law. Yet, the federal courts are not without power to provide a remedy that may differ from one rendered by a state court. The myriad federal statutes regulating various hazardous products and substances together with the implied authority to create rules to "do justice" when cases are consolidated pursuant to section 1407, provide authority for a federal court to create a federal rule when competing state interests and identifiable federal interests are presented. If a federal court decides that uniquely federal interests are presented, and substantive state policies clash or are unclear, implied congressional authority for common law lawmaking exists, and the state policies must yield.

B. Procedural Enhancement: The Role of Federal Procedure in Justifying Application of Federal Common Law

In the context of multi-tort cases, the commerce clause, the federal regulatory statutes, and the equal protection clause provide the basis for Congress and the federal courts to find sufficient federal interests to support application of federal law. Section 1407, a procedural rule, exists to assist federal courts in expediting the fair adjudication of mass tort claims by providing for a transfer of related cases to one federal district court for pretrial purposes. The express command of Congress when it enacted section 1407 was that the statute be used to assure "the just and efficient conduct" of multidistrict proceedings.

The Court in *Hanna v. Plumer* stated that Congress' power to enact procedural rules supports an implied power in the courts to regulate in the murky area that is found in the midst of the substantive/procedural continuum. As discussed * * *, the issues in multi-tort cases lie in this range. Accordingly, the congressional mandate in enacting section 1407 can be satisfied only if federal courts can freely examine the federal policies underlying the relevant regulatory schemes to determine whether federal common law should be applied. By doing this, courts will ensure equal administration of the law with respect to the parties in mass tort litigation, and will also ensure that any federal policy embodied in the statute is not undermined.

Thus, while most courts have accepted without question the rule that requires that the transferee court apply the law the transferor court would have applied, it is not unlikely that Congress intended the transferee court to consider applying a uniform rule to expedite the disposition of the consolidated lawsuits.

A uniform federal rule should be considered by a court when federal regulatory schemes relate to the product that caused the harm. Indeed, if federal interests predominate and a federal rule is not adopted, enforcing divergent state standards of liability may undermine the salutary purposes of the federal acts. Moreover, a federal rule may be needed to vindicate the anti-bias purpose of diversity jurisdiction and to prevent the equivalent of the equal protection problems raised in *Erie*. Thus, in a case involving a product that has injured plaintiffs throughout the United States, section 1407 transfer, together with interstate harm and a federal regulatory scheme, provides the basis for applying a federal common law rule.

Federal interests, as evidenced in regulatory statutes, are enhanced when procedural devices such as section 1407 are used. Until this device is used, the case has not become a truly multi-tort litigation; rather, the case arguably retains its character as essentially a single plaintiff, single defendant lawsuit. Using section 1407 provides the court with the opportunity to engage in the kind of federal-state balancing urged in *Byrd v. Blue Ridge Rural Electric Cooperative,* and the power to regulate in the murky area discussed in *Hanna.* As a result, a court might apply a federal rule to certain issues in a case. Whether one characterizes the rules thus created as substantive or procedural is irrelevant. The point is that *Erie* does not require application of state law when conflicting state interests are present and sufficient federal interests are implicated.

C. Implying a Federal Rule of Decision

In two recent cases, the Second and Fifth Circuits refused to apply federal common law in mass toxic tort cases. In *Jackson v. Johns–Manville Sales Corp.,* the Fifth Circuit declined to adopt a federal rule on the issue of punitive damages in an asbestos case. In *In re Agent Orange Product Liability Litigation,* the Second Circuit held that the product liability action brought by United States veterans against several chemical companies that produced herbicides containing Agent Orange was not the kind of case properly "governed by federal common law." These cases will now be examined to demonstrate law a federal court should determine, as a choice of law question, whether to exercise its power to apply a federal or state rule in mass toxic tort cases.

1. In Re Agent Orange Product Liability Litigation

Agent Orange, described by some as *sui generis,* is in fact the archetypal mass toxic tort case. Indeed, although the plaintiffs' claims were unique because they related to the veterans' exposure to Agent Orange while serving in Vietnam, the case clearly had "national dimensions." Lawsuits were filed in twenty-five federal district courts, with 2,400,000 potential plaintiffs, against five of the largest chemical companies in the United States. All the federal actions, many of which were class actions, were eventually consolidated in the Eastern District of New York.

In *Agent Orange,* the court was presented with a motion to dismiss for lack of subject matter jurisdiction. Thus, the question facing the Second Circuit was whether the case arose under federal common law, thereby establishing federal question jurisdiction.

The problem *Agent Orange* presents ... is that both the majority and dissent viewed the question of whether to apply federal common law as an all or nothing proposition. The majority concluded that the case did not arise under federal common law because there was no "identifiable federal policy at stake in this litigation that warrants the creation of federal common law rules." The court distinguished the private lawsuit before it from cases such as *Clearfield Trust Co. v. United States* and *United States v. Standard Oil Co.* because the case did not "directly implicate the rights and duties of the United States." The majority believed that uniformity is not a federal interest in a private lawsuit not involving substantial rights or duties of the federal government. In addition, the majority noted that even if a federal statute creates private rights, Congress has occasionally allowed federal courts to borrow state law to fill in the gaps.

The Second Circuit indicated that it would take an extremely narrow view of the use of federal common law. The majority could not decide whether the government's interest in the welfare of its veterans outweighed its interest in protecting its relations with government contractors. It concluded that the issue of which group should be favored is the kind of policy matter that should be left to Congress. Because Congress had failed to enact a statute to deal with the issues raised in the *Agent Orange* case, the court declined to devise judicially such a scheme. Thus, it appears that federal common law may not be applied unless the government's interest is essentially monolithic.

The majority's approach confuses the need to find some federal interest to justify applying federal common law with the need to find some federal interest to determine the content of the common law rule. This Article maintains that a federal court is free to consider whether to develop a common law rule in appropriate cases. The federal interest need not dictate the content of the rule; determining the rule's substance is the role of the federal courts. As the *Agent Orange* majority necessarily conceded, a court is not always going to create a rule promoting a substantive federal interest.

For example, in *United States v. Standard Oil Co.* the question was whether the United States could seek indemnification for its expenses from a private party due to injuries suffered by a United States serviceman. The Court decided that the question was one of federal common law because of the government's interest in a uniform rule. However, the Court declined to adopt the rule of liability urged by the government, believing that it was a matter better decided by Congress. The federal interest in a case not involving the government as a party might not be readily apparent, and therefore the need for uniformity might be less apparent. However, as even the *Agent Orange* Second Circuit majority conceded, federal interests do exist in mass toxic tort cases.

The distinction between finding a federal interest sufficient to justify applying federal common law in a choice of law context and finding enough of an interest sufficient to support federal question jurisdiction is critical. In many federal common law cases, the question is whether the case "arises under" federal common law so that federal question subject matter jurisdiction exists. Federal question jurisdiction is limited. Thus, when a court needs to decide whether federal common law exists in order to determine whether there is federal question subject matter jurisdiction, the plaintiff should be required to demonstrate a significant and identifiable federal interest.

However, when the issue before the court is not subject matter jurisdiction, but rather choice of law, the degree of federal interest required need not be as high because the federal court already has jurisdiction over the matter. The federal interest must still outweigh any applicable state interest but need not meet the threshold required for a federal question. Once the case rises to the level of a multi-tort, the court has the power to imply a federal rule of decision based on the policies and interests Congress intended to serve when it enacted the various statutes regulating toxic materials.

While concluding that the federal interests presented in *Agent Orange* were insufficient to support federal question jurisdiction, the Second Circuit nevertheless noted—perhaps anticipating the choice of law problems that would be presented if the case reemerged—that the use of state law could threaten an " 'identifiable' federal policy." To support its position, the court cited two Supreme Court private party federal common law cases. Significantly, the question in those cases was not whether federal question subject matter jurisdiction existed, but rather whether a federal common law rule should be created. The majority concluded, however, that, as in those cases, the federal policy in *Agent Orange* was "not yet identifiable."

It is submitted here, however, that the federal interests were sufficiently identifiable for choice of law purposes because section 1407 was used to transfer the *Agent Orange* cases to the Eastern District of New York. The district court, when presented with the case after the plaintiffs filed an amended complaint alleging diversity, had the power to apply federal common law.

In making its choice of law decision, the district court appeared to believe it was constrained by the *Erie Railroad v. Tompkins, Van Dusen v. Barrack, Klaxon Co. v. Stentor Electric Manufacturing Co.* trilogy, which requires a transferee court to apply the substantive and choice of law rules that the transferor court would have applied. Moreover, the court believed that it was bound by the Second Circuit's statement that the case was not governed by federal common law. Despite these limitations, the court held that something called "national consensus law"—which can only be a euphemism for federal common law—would apply to particular issues in the case. The following analysis will demonstrate that the court's instincts served it correctly. * * *

The first step in the analysis is to determine whether the various competing interested states' policies cancel each other out such that a federal rule should be considered. Because the plaintiffs and defendants are citizens of so many different jurisdictions, no one state's interest can be said clearly to predominate. Next, the court should ask whether Congress intended that a uniform rule be applied in the case. There are at least two indications of congressional intent in the *Agent Orange* litigation. First, the statute cited by plaintiffs as well as other statutes regulating products similar to *Agent Orange* that may have been relied on by plaintiffs in other cases, suggests that Congress intended that such products be held to a uniform minimum accepted level of safety. Second, Congress' enactment of section 1407 provides the basis for allowing a federal court to engage in a choice of law analysis in complex lawsuits such as *Agent Orange*.

Section 1407 helps explain why in the private party cases cited by the Second Circuit, which involved neither a 1407 transfer nor interstate harm of the kind presented in multi-tort litigation, the federal interests were too remote or speculative to support applying federal common law. For example, in the first case cited by the *Agent Orange* majority, *Miree v. DeKalb County,* the plaintiffs were representatives of passengers killed in a plane crash. They sued the county that operated the airports, and claimed to be third party beneficiaries of a contract between the county and the Federal Aviation Administration. The contract provided that the county would restrict the use of the land surrounding the airport. The question before the Court was whether Georgia law or federal law applied to the issue of whether third party beneficiary claims were barred by the county's governmental immunity.

Although holding that state law applied, the Court made clear that even in private party cases there may be enough federal interests to consider applying federal common law:

> [I]n deciding whether rules of federal common law should be fashioned, normally the guiding principle is that a significant conflict between some federal policy or interest and the use of state law in the premises must first be specifically shown. It is by no means enough that, as we may assume, Congress could under the constitution readily enact a complete code of law governing transactions.... Whether latent federal power should be exercised to displace state law is primarily a decision for Congress.

In *Miree,* the Court concluded that any federal interest in the outcome of the question was "far too speculative, far too remote a possibility to justify the application of federal law to transactions essentially of a local concern." In *Agent Orange,* there is much more than a "transaction essentially of a local concern." No mere localized tort, such as an aircrash case, is presented. Moreover, the use of section 1407 enhances the interests presented by the relevant federal regulatory statutes and justifies concluding that the supremacy of federal interests should prevail over the inchoate state interests that might otherwise be relevant. Finally, the salutory policy of section 1407, as well as that of any applicable federal regulatory statutes, may be undermined if federal common law is ignored as a possible rule of law in a multi-tort case. Thus, in the final analysis, the question is whether applying state law would conflict with either the remedial purposes of the federal regulatory scheme or the federal interest in providing fair administration of justice in multi-tort cases. If the answer is yes, then the court should be free to imply a federal rule of decision.

2. *Jackson v. Johns–Manville Sales Corp.*

In *Jackson v. Johns–Manville Sales Corp.,* the Fifth Circuit, sitting *en banc,* ruled that a federal rule on punitive damages should not displace a state rule providing for such damages in a single-plaintiff asbestos case. Nine judges were in the majority; five dissented. Like the majority in the *Agent Orange* case, the majority in *Jackson* acknowledged the "massive,"—in other words, national—nature of the asbestos litigation confronting the federal courts. According to the court, however, that alone was not a basis for creating a federal rule. The court also rejected the interstate nature of the conflict as a rationale even though it has been applied in cases such as *Hinderlider v. La Plata River & Cherry Creek Ditch Co.* and *Illinois v. City of Milwaukee.* The *Jackson* court did so because it concluded that the conflicts in those cases were between discrete political entities. Second, according to the court, federal common law could not be fashioned because there was no "uniquely federal interest" evidenced by "an articulated congressional policy."

Implicit in the majority's reasoning is that a uniquely federal interest can be evidenced only by a statute created by Congress providing an injured plaintiff with the right to sue. This ignores the possibility that Congress has made policy on the substance in issue in other federal statutes, as it did on the water pollution issue in the City of Milwaukee litigations and as it has in the area of toxic substances. From such statutes, a court may infer or imply an appropriate legal rule to be applied in a case involving the product. Moreover, it is Congress' provision of a useful procedural too—section 1407—for achieving a just result that triggers the opportunity for the court to create a federal rule in multi-tort cases.

Jackson, then, should serve as an invitation to the Multidistrict Litigation Panel to use section 1407 to solve the conflicts of law problems presented in mass toxic tort litigations. "Doing justice" may be an inadequate criterion for permitting a federal court to engage in lawmaking in the single tort case, as the Fifth Circuit found. But, 20,000 cases similar to *Jackson* were in the court system. The pervasiveness of the problem shows the need for the federal courts to "do justice." Had the 20,000 cases been consolidated by the Multidistrict Litigation Panel, the Fifth Circuit majority could not have ignored the express command of Congress when it enacted section 1407 to use the statute to assure "the just and efficient" conduct of multidistrict proceedings.

Finally, when this inquiry is undertaken pursuant to section 1407 consolidation, the last problem raised by the *Jackson* court—application of federal common law would open the way for each district to formulate a new rule of law—disappears. Because the Multidistrict Litigation Panel transfers the cases, and future "tag along" cases the insidious forum shopping problem and "equal protection" concerns of the *Erie* and *Hanna* Courts also disappears. Under this Article's analysis, the decision of the district court handling the proceedings after a section 1407 transfer would provide the only federal rule. Thus the need for uniformity is protected. There would not be ninety-one or twelve other federal rules competing with the fifty state rules. Admittedly, the task of determining the content of the federal rule may not be easy, but the common law as expressed by the courts has always been the primary source of tort rules.

Should the courts go too far, by either misreading the policy underlying a federal statute, or by excessively encroaching on viable state
interests, Congress can enact an explicit statute more clearly defining
the legislative scheme, as it did in the City of Milwaukee. Once
Congress enacted a comprehensive scheme, the federal common law
rules that the Supreme Court had formulated to give the Court jurisdiction and to provide a cause of action had to yield. It is not enough to say
that Congress alone is responsible for balancing competing interests.
Indeed, in *Byrd v. Blue Ridge Electric Cooperative,* and in *Illinois v. City
of Milwaukee,* the Court recognized that this was a function of the
federal courts as well. Therefore, until Congress enacts a comprehensive federal products liability and toxic tort compensation act, the federal
courts should accept their responsibility and exercise their implicit
authority to create federal rules of decision in multi-tort cases.

* * *

CONCLUSION

The presence of relevant federal regulatory statutes, in addition to
the national scope of the harm and the availability of a section 1407
transfer, compels a federal court to engage in a choice of law analysis
that considers the propriety of creating a federal rule in multi-tort cases.
The court should first determine whether the policies of any of the
interested states essentially cancel each other out. If so, it should next
explore whether applying a federal rule offends a particular state's
interest or undermines the twin purposes of *Erie.* Finally, a court
should analyze whether federal interests evoked by federal statutes
outweigh state interests. If they do, the court should create and apply a
federal rule on the issue.

This Article's proposal to allow federal courts to consider whether a
federal rule should be applied to particular issues when a multi-tort case
has been transferred pursuant to section 1407 will not unduly interfere
with the development of state law. Indeed, it is not proposed that
federal common law must apply in state court actions. Rather the
Article suggests a choice of law analysis that would permit only the
federal courts hearing a case after a section 1407 transfer to consider the
distinctly national aspects of the case.

We need not fear forum shopping or the kind of unequal administration of law discussed in *Erie Railroad v. Tompkins* that provided the
basis for *Klaxon Co. v. Stentor Electric Manufacturing Co.* and *Van
Dusen v. Barracks* because the Multidistrict Litigation Panel, not the
parties, chooses the federal court to which the case would be transferred,
and because multi-tort cases are not simple two party actions. The
courts should engage in a choice of law analysis that requires them to
measure competing state interests, as well as federal interests evidenced
by statutes and the need to treat litigants fairly, to determine whether
state law or a federal rule should be applied. This kind of analysis is
always necessary to resolve choice of law questions and is no more
burdensome in this context than in any other. Finally, although adopt-

ing this approach may lead some litigants to choose a federal forum, the more insidious form of state-to-state forum shopping will probably be eliminated in most cases. The federal courts will thus be in the best position to provide a fair resolution of the myriad problems raised in mass toxic tort litigation.

Notes and Questions

1. When may a federal court apply "federal common law"? Is it possible to apply federal common law in a diversity case? Did Judges Pratt and Weinstein do a capable job of attempting to bring the *Agent Orange* litigation within existing Supreme Court precedent on federal common law? Both the Second and Fifth Circuits repudiated the efforts of district judges to apply federal common law in the asbestos and *Agent Orange* contexts. Do the dissenters make sensible objections based on the scope of the litigation crisis, coupled with legislative inaction? *See* Lindsey How–Downing, *The Agent Orange Litigation: Should Federal Common Law Have Applied?*, 10 Ecology L.Q. 611 (1983); Jeffrey D. Steinhardt, Note, *Agent Orange and National Consensus Law: Trespass on* Erie *or Free Ride for Federal Common Law?*, 19 U.C. Davis L. Rev. 201 (1985).

2. Doesn't authorization of federal common law make sense as an applicable law regime for multi-party, multiforum mass torts? Wouldn't such authorization solve the complicated problems evident under interest analysis or RESTATEMENT (SECOND) approaches to determining choice-of-law in mass tort cases? The American Law Institute's COMPLEX LITIGATION: STATUTORY RECOMMENDATIONS AND ANALYSIS eschewed adopting a federal common law approach to its choice-of-law provisions, concluding:

> * * * Resort to federal common law as a means of resolving choice of law questions in complex litigation would facilitate the consolidated handling of these cases. It would free the transferee courts from the complicated inquiry now required, * * * and would avoid the difficulties of trying to achieve political consensus on the details of the choice of law regime.

> Nonetheless, the federal common law approach has several distinct disadvantages. Not only will uncertainty and a lack of uniformity continue, at least until the courts determine what the standards should be, but also there is no assurance that a single federal standard ever will evolve. Rather, just as the states have had difficulty in reaching agreement in various substantive contexts as to what choice of law standard seems most appropriate, it is likely that variations will develop among the federal circuits. If the transferee court alternatively were directed to evaluate the policies fostered by the application of a given state's law and to determine which states might assert a legitimate governmental interest in the controversy in light of those policies (that is, to engage in a form of governmental interest analysis), similar problems are likely to arise because of the intrinsic indeterminacy of that form of analysis. To expect the Supreme Court to review two or three cases a year to resolve choice of law differences between the circuits and provide some certainty seems totally unrealistic. * * *

American Law Institute, COMPLEX LITIGATION: STATUTORY RECOMMENDATIONS AND ANALYSIS at 314 (1994).   Are the ALI's concerns about the discovery and application of federal common law in the mass tort context well-placed? How would Judges Pratt and Weinstein respond?

3.   Although the possibility of creating and applying federal common law in consolidated mass torts has been repudiated by the federal appellate courts, it has received some favorable notice by some academic commentators.   In addition to Professor Juenger's and Vairo's articles, excerpted *supra, see* Linda S. Mullenix, *Class Resolution of the Mass–Tort Case: A Proposed Federal Procedure Act,* 64 Tex.L.Rev. 1039 (1986)(endorsing authorization of federal common law under proposed statute); Linda S. Mullenix, *Federalizing Choice of Law For Mass–Tort Litigation,* 70 Tex.L.Rev. 1623 (1992); Steven L. Schultz, *Mass Torts: In Re Joint Eastern & Southern Asbestos Litigation: Bankrupt and Backlogged—A Proposal For the Use of Federal Common Law in Mass Tort Class Actions,* 58 Brook.L.Rev. 553 (1992); *see generally,* Donald Trautman, *The Relation Between American Choice of Law and Federal Common Law,* 41 Law & Contemp.Prob. 105 (1977); Louise Weinberg, *Federal Common Law,* 83 Nw.U.L.Rev. 805 (1989).

Chapter X

MASS TORTS AND FEDERALIZED CHOICE OF LAW

A. STATUTORY CHOICE OF LAW
103RD CONGRESS; 1ST SESSION IN THE HOUSE OF REPRESENTATIVES AS INTRODUCED IN THE HOUSE 1993 H.R. 1100; 103 H.R. 1100

A BILL

To amend title 28, United States Code, to provide for Federal jurisdiction of certain multiparty, multiforum civil actions.

SPONSOR(S): MR. HUGHES (for himself and MR. MOORHEAD) introduced the following bill; which was referred to the Committee on the Judiciary.

Be it enacted by the Senate and House of Representatives of the United States of America in Congress assembled,

* * *

Section 1. Short Title. This Act may be cited as the "Multiparty, Multiforum Jurisdiction Act of 1993"

* * *

Sec. 6. Choice of Law.

(a) Determination by the Court.—Chapter 111 of title 28, United States Code, is amended by adding at the end the following new section:

1659. Choice of law in multiparty, multiforum actions

"(a) In an action which is or could have been brought, in whole or in part, under section 1368 of this title, the district court in which the action is brought or to which it is removed shall determine the source of the applicable substantive law, except that if an action is transferred to another district court, the transferee court shall determine the source of the applicable substantive law. In making this determination, a district court shall not be bound by the choice of law rules of any State, and the factors that the court may consider in choosing the applicable law include—

"(1) the place of the injury;

"(2) the place of the conduct causing the injury;

"(3) the principal places of business or domiciles of the parties;

"(4) the danger of creating unnecessary incentives for forum shopping; and

"(5) whether the choice of law would be reasonably foreseeable to the parties.

The factors set forth in paragraphs (1) through (5) shall be evaluated according to their relative importance with respect to the particular action. If good cause is shown in exceptional cases, including constitutional reasons, the court may allow the law of more than one State to be applied with respect to a party, claim, or other element of an action.

"(b) The district court making the determination under subsection (a) shall enter an order designating the single jurisdiction whose substantive law is to be applied in all other actions under section 1368 arising from the same accident as that giving rise to the action in which the determination is made. The substantive law of the designated jurisdiction shall be applied to the parties and claims in all such actions before the court, and to all other elements of each action, except where Federal law applies or the order specifically provides for the application of the law of another jurisdiction with respect to a party, claim, or other element of an action.

"(c) In an action remanded to another district court or a State court under section 1407(i)(1) or 1441(e)(2) of this title, the district court's choice of law under subsection (b) shall continue to apply.".

* * *

Notes and Questions

1. The Multiparty, Multiforum Jurisdiction Act of 1993 is the latest version of federal legislation that has been successively introduced in Congress since 1988. *See* Part II, Chapter II.D.3, *supra* (discussing the jurisdiction proposals of both the American Law Institute's COMPLEX LITIGATION project and the Multiparty, Multiforum Jurisdiction Act). Recall that the bill's choice-of-law provision is part of a statutory amendment of the multidistrict litigation statute, designed to provide for minimal diversity jurisdiction for single site, single-event tortious occurrences. As of 1995, no version of the Multiparty, Multiforum Jurisdiction Act has been passed by both houses of Congress. In addition, no new version of the Multiparty, Multiforum Jurisdiction Act has been introduced during the 104th Congress. It remains to be seen whether this reformist Congress will turn its attentions to legislatively solving mass tort litigation problems, after addressing problems relating to traditional products liability litigation.

2. What is the general choice-of-law approach of the 1993 version of the Multiparty, Multiforum Jurisdiction Act? Why have the drafters of this legislation selected those particular five affiliating contacts as the locus of the choice-of-law determination? Do these factors make sense? How are they related, in any way, to the analytical elements required for a choice-of-law determination under the RESTATEMENT (SECOND) OF CONFLICT OF LAWS (1971)? Are the section 6 factors neutral in impact? Does the section 6 analysis result in the application of one state's law, and will the factors enumerated in the statute result in a principled selection of that state's law? What problems might you anticipate in applying section 6 to determine applicable law? Will section 6 assist a federal judge in determining applicable law in a dispersed mass tort?

3. Earlier versions of section 6 the Multiparty, Multiforum Jurisdiction Act enumerated longer lists of factors to be considered by a transferee court in determining applicable law in mass tort cases. In combination with the American Law Institute proposals, *see infra,* academic commentators have widely criticized these earlier Congressional choice-of-law proposals. *See generally* Friedrich K. Jeunger, *Mass Disasters and the Conflict of Laws,* 1989 U.Ill.L.Rev. 105 (1989); Andreas F. Lowenfeld, *Mass Torts and the Conflicts of Laws: The Airline Disaster,* 1989 U.Ill.L.Rev. 157 (1989); Robert A. Sedler, *Interest Analysis, State Sovereignty, and Federally–Mandated Choice of Law in Mass Tort Cases: Another Assault on State Sovereignty,* 54 La.L.Rev. 1085 (1994); Robert A. Sedler & Aaron D. Twerski, *State Choice of Law in Mass Tort Cases: A Response to "A View From the Legislature,"* 73 Marq. L.Rev. 625 (1990); Russell J. Weintraub, *Methods For Resolving Conflict-of-Laws Problems in Mass Tort Litigation,* 1989 U.Ill.L.Rev. 129 (1989).

4. For commentary dealing with the problems of legislatively providing for federal statutory choice-of-law principles, *see generally* Paul S. Bird, *Mass Tort Litigation: A Statutory Solution to the Choice of Law Impasse,* 96 Yale L.J. 1077 (1987); Symposium, *Conflict of Laws and Complex Litigation Issues in Mass Tort Litigation,* 1989 U.Ill.L.Rev. 35 (1989).

B. THE AMERICAN LAW INSTITUTE CHOICE OF LAW PRINCIPLES

1. CHOICE OF LAW PRINCIPLES IN STATE–CREATED ACTIONS

AMERICAN LAW INSTITUTE, COMPLEX LITIGATION: STATUTORY RECOM- MENDATIONS AND ANALYSIS

at 321–325; 330–331 (1994).

§ 6.01. Mass Torts

(a) Except as provided in § 6.04 through § 6.06, in actions consolidated under § 3.01 or removed under § 5.01 in which parties assert the application of laws that are in material conflict, the transferee court shall choose the law governing the rights, liabilities, and defenses of the parties with respect to a tort claim by applying the criteria set forth in the following subsections with the objective of applying, to the extent feasible, a single state's law to all similar tort claims being asserted against a defendant.

(b) In determining the governing law under subsection (a), the court shall consider the following factors for purposes of identifying each state having a policy that would be furthered by the applications of its laws:

(1) the place or places of injury;

(2) the place or places of the conduct causing the injury; and

(3) the primary places of business or habitual residences of the plaintiffs and defendants.

(c) If, in analyzing the factors set forth in subsection (b), the court finds that only one state has a policy that would be furthered by the application of its law, that state's law shall govern. If more than one state has a policy that would be furthered by the application of its law, the court shall choose the applicable law from among the laws of the interested states under the following rules:

(1) If the place of injury and the place of conduct causing the injury are in the same state, that state's laws governs.

(2) If subsection (c)(1) does not apply, but all of the plaintiffs habitually reside or have their primary places of business in the same state, that state's law governs the claims with respect to that defendant, Plaintiffs shall be considered as sharing a common habitual residence or primary place of business if they are located in states whose laws are not in material conflict.

(3) If neither subsection (c)(1) or (c)(2) applies, but all of the plaintiffs habitually reside or have their primary places of business in the same state, and that state also is the place of injury, then that state's law governs. Plaintiffs shall be considered as sharing a common habitual residence or primary place of business if they are located in states whose laws are not in material conflict.

(4) In all other cases, the law of the state where the conduct causing the injury occurred governs. When conduct occurred in more than one state, the court shall choose the law of the conduct state that has the most significant relationship to the occurrence.

(d) When necessary to avoid unfair surprise or arbitrary result, the transferee court may choose the applicable law on the basis of additional factors that reflect the regulatory policies and legitimate interests of a particular state not otherwise identified under subsection (b), or it may depart from the order of preferences for selecting the governing law prescribed by subsection (c).

(e) If the court determines that the application of a single state's law to all elements of the claims of a single state's law to all elements of the claims pending against a defendant would be inappropriate, it may divide the actions into subgroups of claims, issues, or parties to foster consolidated treatment under § 3.01, and allow more than one state's law to be applied. The court also may determine that only certain claims or issues involving one or more of the parties should be governed by the law chosen by the application of the rules in subsection (c), and that other claims or parties should be remanded to the transferor courts for individual treatment under the laws normally applicable in those courts. In either instance, the court may exercise its authority under § 3.06(c) to sever, transfer, or remand issues or claims for treatment consistent with its determination.

Comment:

a. *Rationale.* Section 6.01(a) authorizes the transferee court to apply the rules contained in the subsequent subsections to determine what law or laws will govern in mass tort claims in complex litigation when the parties assert that more than one state's law should apply and that the laws are in material conflict. Subsection (a) also acknowledges that the objective underlying the rules is to allow a single state's tort law to apply to all similar claims asserted against each defendant, to the extent it is feasible to do so. In this way, the application of § 6.01 fosters the consolidated treatment of the mass tort claims under this proposal.

Subsections (b) and (c) are the heart of the mass choice of law scheme. Section 6.01(b) sets out the factors identifying states that may have interests in the litigation and thus whose laws arguably may apply. The places listed generally represent those states having significant contacts with the parties or events in light of the policies underlying tort law. Each of the contacts identified must be evaluated in light of its relative importance to the types of policies that the state where that contact is located has chosen to follow in developing its tort law. Thus, the factors identified in subsection (b) assume significance only in relation to that state's regulatory objectives. This approach reflects modern choice of law analysis and is consistent with the RESTATEMENT, SECOND, OF CONFLICT OF LAWS (1971) [hereinafter, RESTATEMENT, SECOND]. * * * If the location of the factors suggests that only one state has a policy that would be furthered by the application of its law to the claims against a particular defendant, then, as provided in subsection (c), that state's law will govern. However, identification of states having significant contacts often may suggest more than one state whose law may be applied, particularly in the context of complex multiparty litigation. Thus, the rules set out in subsection (c) are included to provide guidance as to how the transferee court should choose among the competing interests of those states having policies that would be furthered by the application of their laws in order to identify a single state's law to govern the consolidated tort claims.

As is discussed later in this Comment, the preference rules set out in subsection (c) reflect, in large measure, the conclusion that most of the tort rules that will be at issue are directed toward conduct regulation rather than at loss allocation, and thus that certain contacts or factors have more significance than others given that objective. Although the general assumption seems appropriate, some issues involved in tort cases clearly may be decided differently by the states because of differences in their views on how to allocate losses, rather than how to regulate conduct. The most obvious of these may involve decisions regarding what types of damages are available for certain losses. * * *

Thus, the last two subsections in § 6.01 are included to provide the court with the necessary authority to avoid unfair surprise or arbitrary results * * *, and to subdivided the cases into issues when it would be appropriate to do so. * * * This power to subdivide the cases is important because not only does it ensure that the special policies surrounding particular issues will be evaluated to determine whether the application of the laws designated in § 6.01(c) truly would foster the policy objectives, but it also allows the court to recognize the actions or claims to adjust for the application of more than one state's law if doing so fosters the fairness to the litigants and the consolidated treatment of the cases, or portions thereof. In this way, the transferee court can determine whether and how the cases can be treated efficiently and economically.

The identification of contacts in subsection (b) relevant to determining whether a particular state or states have a policy that would be furthered by the application of its laws parallels the inquiry made in single-claim cases under § 145 of the Restatement, Second, which seeks to identify the state or states having a significant relationship with the issues before the court. In addition, the objective of identifying those states for purposes of determining which have policies that would be advanced by applying their laws to the particular claim involved is consistent with the broader guidelines of § 6 of the RESTATEMENT, SECOND.

However, introduction of four preference rules in subsection (c) departs from that general approach by providing clear choices rather than relying on the general balancing of competing interests on a case-by-case basis. *See generally* RESTATEMENT, SECOND § 6. The inclusion of more precise rules responds to the special problems and circumstances of complex litigation. The federal transferee court sits as a truly disinterested tribunal, with the task of resolving possible conflicts among the laws of interested states. Consequently, it seems both desirable and necessary to provide some specific guidance as to how to accommodate the competing interests of multiple states in having their particular laws govern.

* * *

The rules just described are designed to apply in litigation arising out of a single tortious event, as well as dispersed or latent tort litigation. * * * The use of a single set of choice of law rules for all consolidated tort cases offers the advantage of avoiding confusion or arguments about whether a particular set of claims should be viewed as part of a single event or whether, because they are products liability claims, involve a dispersed tort situation. Nonetheless, the need to formulate rules premised on factors or contacts general enough to be relevant in either situation necessitates eliminating certain formulations that might be viewed as more refined and clearer. For example, a choice of law rule for single event torts could refer to the injury state (because in that setting there would be only one state and it could be identified easily), unless the place of injury was fortuitous, as in most aircrashes. In that event, an alternative reference could be made to the place of defendant's conduct. A choice of law rule for products liability cases could be modeled much like the one set out in this section, except that rather than focusing on the place of the defendant's conduct as provided in subsection (b)(2), reference could be made to the place where the product was first acquired through commercial channels, or the place of injury if the product were distributed there regularly.

The application of the rules set out in this section should not produce results different from those obtained under these more precise approaches. As explored in the following * * * comments * * *, the principles set out in this section are fully consistent with those approaches, but § 6.01 represents a preference for more flexible treatment. The objectives are (1) to provide some certainty to the choice of law process in mass tort cases, (2) to prescribe rules that are reasonably easy to administer, and yet (3) to leave "some play in the joints so that the rule does not compel a bad result in an unusual or unforeseen circumstance." Weintraub, *Methods for Resolving Conflict-of-Laws Problems in Mass Tort Litigation,* 1989 U.Ill.L.Rev. 129, 145.

2. GOVERNING LAW IN ACTIONS BASED ON FEDERAL LAW

AMERICAN LAW INSTITUTE, COMPLEX LITIGA-TION: COMPLEX LITIGATION: STATUTORY RECOMMENDATIONS AND ANALYSIS
at 430—432 (1994).

§ 6.08 Intercircuit Conflicts

In actions consolidated under § 3.01 or removed under § 5.01, the transferee court shall not be bound by the federal law as interpreted in the circuits in which the actions were filed, but may determine for itself the federal law to be applied to the federal claims and defenses in the litigation

Comment:

a. *Rationale.* When claims are consolidated under § 3.01 and transferred from federal courts sitting in different circuits, a governing law problem will arise if there is a conflict between the circuits on the interpretation of the relevant federal laws. This situation is likely to be a common one because of the limited number of cases the Supreme Court can take to resolve intercircuit conflicts. The problem is magnified in the complex litigation context because the class of cases eligible for consolidation and transfer by definition are dispersed in multiple fora and thus likely to be lodged in several circuits. Further, * * *, courts currently are not agreed as to whether, under the general transfer statute, 28 U.S.C. § 1404(a), the transferee court is obliged to apply the federal law interpretation of the circuit from which the claims were transferred or may follow the view prevailing in its own circuit. This means that applying existing standards for resolving intercircuit conflicts to cases transferred under § 3.01 would not result in consistency, thereby undermining the objectives of encouraging the uniform and predictable [   ] treatment of complex cases.

This section provides that the transferee court may decide for itself the interpretation of federal law applicable to the federal claims and defenses in litigation transferred and consolidated [under provisions of the PROJECT]. reference to the law of the transferee circuit is an easy rule to administer and permits a single version of the federal law to apply to all the consolidated claims, thereby offering the potential for uniform treatment of similar claims.

* * *

Reference to the law of the circuit in which a defendant is located also does not foster the objectives of efficiency and consistency as well as allowing the transferee court to apply its own circuit's understanding of the federal law. In many federal law cases, the United States may be a party, raising problems of defining where the defendant resides. Even if a private defendant is involved, identifying a defendant's principal place of business may necessitate a detailed factual inquiry. Finally, in federal litigation involving multiple defendants, use of the defendant's location could result in more than one governing version of the federal law being applied to the case. For these reasons, allowing the transferee circuit's law to control is the preferred solution for handling intercircuit conflicts in the complex litigation setting.

* * *

Notes and Questions

1. Section 6.01 of the ALI's COMPLEX LITIGATION: STATUTORY RECOMMENDATIONS AND ANALYSIS supplies the general analytical framework for choice-of-law determinations in mass tort cases transferred, removed, and consolidated under other provisions of the Project. Section 6.01 is itself supplemented with a series of further provisions governing choice-of-law considerations for particular issues. *See e.g*, § 6.02 (contractual choice-of-law); § 6.03 (mass contracts, law governing in absence of effective party choice); § 6.04 (statute of limitations); § 6.05 (monetary relief); and § 6.06 (punitive damages). Section 6.07 provides guidance relating to procedural aspects of determining applicable law. Each of these particular sections adheres to the basic analytical concept embodied in Section 6.01: that for each issue involved in

a mass tort case, the judge will determine a single state's law as applicable to that issue, based on recourse to alternative preference rules, if necessary. For insight into the Reporter's approach to constructing a set of choice-of-law rules for complex litigation, *see* Mary K. Kane, *Drafting Choice of Law Rules for Complex Litigation: Some Preliminary Thoughts,* 10 Rev.Litig. 309 (1991).

2.   Does the ALI's choice-of-law provisions provide a sensible, workable solution for multiparty, multiforum mass tort cases? Are the rules clear, coherent, and easy to apply? Will these choice-of-law principles serve the goals of justice and efficiency? In what ways do the ALI proposals depart from the RESTATEMENT (SECOND) OF CONFLICT OF LAWS requirements in §§ 6 and 145? Should they be preferred to the principles set forth in section 6 of the Multiparty, Multiforum Jurisdiction Act? Review the airplane crash and products liability cases, *supra.* How would the applicable law have been determined under the ALI proposals? Would the outcome have been different with regard to the forum's choice-of-law? In applying one forum's law to a multiparty, multiforum litigation, do the ALI provisions satisfy due process considerations? Does this approach impinge on state sovereignty concerns, as Professors Sedler and Twerski have argued? *See generally* Joyce R. Berman, Note, *Choice of Law and the Supreme Court:* Phillips Petroleum Co. v. Shutts, 19 Conn.L.Rev. 171 (1986).

3.   The ALI's choice-of-law proposals, similar to those of Congress in the Multiparty, Multiforum Jurisdiction Act, have been subjected to thorough-going criticism, much of its negative. *See generally* Friedrich K. Juenger, *The Complex Litigation Project's Tort Choice-of-Law Rules,* 54 La.L.Rev. 907 (1994); John P. Kozyris, *The Conflicts Provisions of the ALI's Complex Litigation Project: A Glass Half Full?,* 54 La.L.Rev. 953 (1994); Robert A. Sedler, *The Complex Litigation Project's Proposal for a Federally–Mandated Choice of Law in Mass Tort Cases: Another Assault on State Sovereignty,* 54 La.L.Rev. 1085 (1994); David E. Seidelson, *Section 6.01 of the ALI's Complex Litigation Project: Function Follows Form,* 54 La.L.Rev. 1111 (1994); Gene Shreve, *Reform Aspirations of the Complex Litigation Project,* 54 La.L.Rev. 1139 (1994); Symeon C. Symeonides, *The ALI's Complex Litigation Project: Commencing the National Debate,* 54 La.L.Rev. 843 (1994); Donald T. Trautman, *Some Thoughts on Choice of Law, Judicial Discretion, and the ALI's Complex Litigation Project,* 54 La.L.Rev. 835 (1994); Louise Weinberg, *Mass Torts and the Neutral Forum: A Critical Analysis of the ALI's Proposed Choice Rule,* 56 Alb.L.Rev. 80 (1993).

C.   CRITIQUES OF THE PROPOSALS FOR FEDERALIZATION

LINDA S. MULLENIX, FEDERALIZING CHOICE OF LAW IN MASS TORT LITIGATION

70 Tex.L.Rev 1623 (1992).

I.   INTRODUCTION

* * *

Judges, lawyers, legislators, and academicians already have written massive amounts concerning the resolution of the applicable law problem in mass-tort litigation. Indeed, it hardly seems possible that anything new can be added either to describe the problem or to resolve this debate. As is true generally in conflicts scholarship, the lists of choice-influencing factors to determine applicable law in consolidated mass-tort cases grows longer as each conflicts scholar weighs in with his or her own particular conflicts predilections. Furthermore, such is the nature of the task that even perennial optimists are skeptical whether law reformers will be able to achieve a consensus solution to this choice-of-law problem in the near future. Someone's predilections will prevail, however, and it is a fairly certain bet that the scheme for resolving choice-of-law questions in mass tort will resemble a federalized version of the RESTATEMENT (SECOND) OF CONFLICT OF LAWS.

While federal courts bumble along solving choice-of-law issues in mass-tort cases in the old-fashioned way, Congress has experienced multiple false starts in attempting to enact a multiparty, multiforum bill, and the American Bar Association's proposals for mass-tort legislation ignominiously died in the back rooms and public forums of the ABA House of Delegates. The remaining institutional law-reform group still actively grappling with the mass-tort choice-of-law problem is the American Law Institute in its COMPLEX LITIGATION PROJECT.

The COMPLEX LITIGATION PROJECT proposals relating to choice of law have come to occupy the mass-tort field almost by default. This Article therefore primarily examines these ALI proposals and critically assesses the wisdom of adopting a modified, federalized RESTATEMENT (SECOND) approach to resolving the choice-of-law problem in mass-tort litigation. The basic thesis is that in proposing to federalize various choice-of-law determinations along RESTATEMENT principles, the reformers are recycling tired conflicts principles and adapting them, Rube Goldberg fashion, to a bigger tort model. In the final analysis, using the collection of RESTATEMENT rules to determine applicable law in mass-tort litigation will not work for the truly dispersed mass-tort case. Like their colleagues in Congress, the ALI Reporters have, at best, solved the choice-of-law problem for the single-site accident, but have not really supplied a workable choice-of-law scheme for a nationwide or regional calamity.

In the larger context of remedial reform, the American Law Institute's proposals relating to choice of law are but another frustrating illustration of the basic refusal of law-reform groups to grapple with the underlying substantive law problem of mass tort. In this sense, the story of the choice-of-law proposals is also the story of the failure of law reform writ large and writ small. The Institute and other institutional players have consistently offered federal solutions for all procedural aspects of mass-tort litigation but have resolutely eschewed proposing a substantive federal tort statute that would address the underlying substantive legal issues.

Characteristically, the American Law Institute Reporters offer their proposals to federalize choice of law as a federal solution to a federal problem. This proposed federalization of conflicts law is accompanied by the full flush of constitutional rhetoric that has supported each new piece of this Project. And although every law reform group that has considered the problems of mass-tort litigation has characterized this litigation as constituting a set of legal problems of national scope, the reformers uniformly have stopped short of federalizing substantive tort law.

Thus, to date, the reformers have offered a piecemeal approach to mass-tort litigation that would federalize jurisdiction and consolidation procedure, federalize various coercive devices to collect individual cases in one forum and enjoin litigation elsewhere, and federalize applicable law.

In the larger sense, then, the ALI Complex Litigation Project as a whole reflects a failure of political will. On a smaller scale, with regard to its various proposals for procedural reform, the Project also reflects a failure of creative thinking in its general approach of harnessing existing, often problematic rules to complex mass-tort litigation. And this is nowhere more evident than in the Project's provisions for determining applicable law.

In federalizing applicable-law rules, the Institute's proposals are troubling because they subvert basic *Erie* doctrine in garden-variety diversity cases, blithely endorse vertical forum shopping, and inadequately justify a federalized regime in mass-tort cases. It is not enough to simply keep repeating that mass-tort cases are bigger and more complicated and therefore justify overriding all pre-existing rules and doctrines in the interest of sound judicial administration. While stating that the objective of the choice-of-law proposals is to curb judicial discretion, in reality the proposed multifactor approaches encourage creative judicial deductive reasoning from the judge's choice of applicable law to the factors supporting that choice. And if it is true that a purpose of multifactor choice-of-law schemes is to reduce unbridled judicial discretion, then perhaps what we ought to do, if we choose a modified Restatement route, is to take the judge out of the decisional process altogether and have applicable law determined by computer. If ever an area of law was susceptible to decision-tree analysis, then surely it would be multifactor choice-of-law rules.

Perhaps the most disturbing aspect of the ALI choice-of-law proposals is that they will not meaningfully assist in determining law in truly dispersed mass-tort litigation. For the hard cases, the reformers have proposed virtually useless rules. Although the provisions and commentary sound perfectly plausible and reasoned (albeit reflecting the proposers' own conflicts preferences), the proposed rules will not work for truly massive tort cases. Furthermore, when considering actual or hypothesized dispersed mass-tort scenarios, the Reporters' typical solution is to recommend subclassing claimants or remanding cases for a choice-of-law determination. This punting approach to the really complicated conflicts questions again reflects a failure of will and imagination.

* * *

III. Some Troubling Points About the ALI Proposal to Federalize
Choice-of-Law Determinations in Mass–Tort Litigation

A. *The ALI Proposals Do Not Really Represent a Unified, Federalized*
Choice-of-Law Scheme That Is Conceptually Simple to Understand
or Judicially Efficient to Apply

What the ALI has proposed is a series of rules for determining applicable law with regard to a discrete set of legal issues: tort, contract, limitations, and damages. What the ALI proposals do not do is supply one overarching set of guiding principles for determining applicable law, similar to the factors set out in sections 6 and 145 of the Restatement (Second) of Conflicts, or the ten factors listed in Congress's proposed Multiparty, Multiforum Jurisdiction Act of 1991.[68]

This observation about the overall structure of the ALI proposals obviously is neither a fatal criticism of the enterprise nor an endorsement of the alternatives. Indeed, it is something of a compliment to the ambitiousness of the undertaking. From this perspective, the Complex Litigation Project, in its choice-of-law chapter, has become the victim of its own sophisticated success. Once the ALI Reporters recognized that the simple, comprehensive list of choice-influencing factors in sections 6 and 145 of the Restatement or Congress's version would not supply adequate conflicts rules for the multiple issues present in mass-tort cases, they understood that each separate legal issue probably required its own separate choice-of-law rules.

Once launched on this methodology, however, there is no logical stopping point until and unless the Reporters restate the entire Restatement (Second) of Conflicts, only re-tailored for mass-tort cases. Al-

---

68. The 10 factors in the original version of the bill are:

1. The law that might have governed if the jurisdiction created by section 1368 of this title did not exist;

2. The forums in which the claims were or might have been brought;

3. The location of the accident on which the action is based and the location of related transactions among the parties;

4. The place where the parties reside or do business;

5. The desirability of applying uniform law to some or all aspects of the action;

6. Whether a change in applicable law in connection with removal or transfer of the action would cause unfairness;

7. The danger of creating unnecessary incentives for forum shopping;

8. The interest of any jurisdiction in having its law apply;

9. Any reasonable expectation of a party or parties that the law of a particular jurisdiction would apply or would not apply; and

10. Any agreement or stipulation of the parties concerning applicable law.

Multiparty, Multiforum Jurisdiction Act of 1991, supra note 15. This list, incidentally, has one less factor than the 1990 version of the choice-of-law provision. *See* Multiparty, Multiform Jurisdiction Act of 1990.
* * *

though the Reporters have flagged the most obvious substantive issues in need of modification for the mass-tort context, their selective list is necessarily incomplete and underinclusive. What the Reporters have embarked on, then, is nothing so much as a kind of RESTATEMENT (THIRD) of Conflicts for complex mass-tort litigation.

B.   The ALI Proposals Do Not Really Supply Viable
Conflicts Rules for the Dispersed Mass Tort

Section 6.01 of the COMPLEX LITIGATION PROJECT details the analytical structure that a transferee judge should use in determining applicable law for tort claims, with the goal of applying one state's law to all similar tort claims asserted against a defendant.

The structure of these provisions is relatively simple: section 6.01(b) sets forth the factors or affiliating contacts to consider when determining which states have legitimate interests in having their state tort policies govern. These criteria look to the place of injury, conduct, business, or habitual residences of the plaintiffs and defendants. Subsection (c) then instructs that if more than one state has an interest that would be furthered by application of its law, the judge should consider four tie-breaking or preference rules. In dispersed mass-tort cases such as *Agent Orange, Dalkon Shield, Bendectin-DES*, or asbestos-related injury, the choice-of-law determination will always be subject to section 6.01(c) preference rules, because the factors listed in section 6.01(b) will indicate multiple interested states.

The tie-breaking rules in section 6.01(c), however, will most likely prove unavailing to supply a single choice-of-law rule in dispersed mass-tort cases, because these cases rarely, if ever, meet the provisions' descriptive criteria. For example, subsection (c)(1) specifies that if the place of injury and conduct causing the injury are in the same state, then that state's law applies. But dispersed mass-tort cases, such as *Agent Orange, Dalkon Shield, Bendectin-DES*, and asbestos cases, will fail this test. So too with subsection (c)(2), which would apply the law of the state where all the plaintiffs habitually reside or have their principal places of business and the defendant also has its principal place of business.

Subsection (c)(3) provides the third tie-breaking rule: this provision would apply the law of the place of all the plaintiffs' habitual residences or principal places of business, if that state was also the place of injury. Again, it is highly unlikely that this provision will supply the rule of decision for the dispersed mass-tort case, because all the plaintiffs, businesses, and injuries are going to be dispersed all over the map.

The first three preference rules will perhaps deal nicely with single-site events or mass-accident (but not mass-tort) cases. For example, section 6.01(c)(1) will probably provide applicable law for local environmental pollution cases such as Love Canal. Subsection (c)(2) might assist in determining applicable law for the crash of a Southwest Airlines plane somewhere in Texas. Subsection (c)(3) might supply the applicable law for all asbestos plaintiffs residing in the Eastern District of Texas who worked at a particular Beaumont or Port Arthur refinery. The problem here is not that the ALI has failed to supply choice-of-law rules or to justify those preferences, but that the tie-breaking rules deal with easy single-site accident cases that have little relevance to major dispersed mass-tort cases.

Subsection (c)(4) of section 6.01 provides the catch-all preference rule applicable when no other tie-breaking provisions apply. Here the Reporters tell us: "In all other cases, the law of the state where the conduct causing the injury occurred governs. When more than one place of conduct is involved, the court shall choose the state that has the most significant relationship to the occurrence." There are some definitional problems with this formulation. First, what does it mean to say that judges ought to look to the place of the "conduct causing the injury"? As a conflicts term of art, it is not intuitively clear where this place is. In products liability cases, does this mean the place of product design? The place of manufacturing or marketing? The place of sale or distribution? Does the rule look to the defendant's conduct, or to the plaintiff's conduct?

Second, if there is more than one identifiable place of the "conduct causing the injury," how is the judge to assess which state has the "most significant relationship to the occurrence"? Clearly this language tracks the "most significant relationship" concept of section 145 of the RESTATEMENT (SECOND) OF CONFLICTS, but it is unclear how a judge in a dispersed mass-tort case with multiple plaintiffs and defendants in a products liability manufacturing and distribution chain is to determine which of many possible states has this relationship.

To further complicate this scheme, but to alleviate possible harsh or arbitrary results, section 6.01(d) provides an escape valve permitting a transferee judge "to take into account pertinent factors in addition to those listed in subsection (b) that indicate the regulatory policies and legitimate interests of a particular state not otherwise identified under that subsection." While it is undoubtedly useful to provide some mechanism to mitigate an arbitrary determination of applicable law, it would be interesting to speculate what a judge would have to do, analytically, to arrive at the point of invoking subsection (d) and then applying its criteria to reach a fair applicable-law determination.

Finally, subsection (d) also permits a judge to "depart from the preferences for selecting the governing law under subsection (c) in order to avoid unfair surprise or arbitrary results." Again, it is unclear what it means when a judge is permitted to "depart from the preferences." Moreover, assuming that no preference rule under subsection (c) provides a method for selecting one state's law in a dispersed mass-tort case, then application of subsection (d) seems to result in the judge exercising precisely the kind of unbridled discretion that the PROJECT attempts to limit by its detailed rules.

In fairness, the Reporters' comments recognize that the section 6.01 factors may not provide an applicable-law solution to dispersed mass-tort cases. In recognition of this special category of cases, the Reporters allow the court to divide such complicated litigation into subgroups of claims, issues, or parties, and allow more than one state's law to apply. Further, the Reporters suggest that in certain "appropriate cases," other claims and parties should "be remanded . . . for individual treatment under the laws normally applicable there." These two recommendations, then, are the PROJECT'S solution for the difficult complications of truly dispersed mass-tort cases. But the solution is essentially a nonsolution, and does little more than existing rules and procedure already allow. If this analysis of the probable utility of section 6.01 is correct, why has the ALI bothered to supply a set of slightly modified RESTATEMENT (SECOND) rules for single-site accident cases?

C.   *The ALI Proposals Will Encourage Forum–Shopping for More Favorable Law in Contravention of Erie Doctrine in the Absence of an Interstate Consolidation Mechanism for Complex Mass–Tort Litigation*

The initial grand design for the COMPLEX LITIGATION PROJECT was to provide procedural mechanisms for federal intrasystem consolidation, federal-state intersystem consolidation, and state-to-state consolidation of mass-tort cases. In the federal realm, at least, the Reporters have adapted existing multidistrict litigation procedure and proposed a Complex Litigation Panel with authority to transfer and consolidate cases within the federal system. These procedural mechanisms were relatively easy to design, building on pre-existing federal transfer and consolidation procedures.

More difficult are proposals relating to federal-to-state or state-to-state consolidation, both of which implicate Tenth Amendment concerns and require state consent and cooperation. Here the ALI proposals are offered as models or "illustrations" of the way future law reformers might "conceptualize an interstate transfer system." In other words, while the ALI may have a fair shot at implementing a federal complex-litigation scheme, it probably will do this without a concomitant parallel state consolidation reform.

If the ALI proposals for federalized complex-litigation procedure and choice of law are ever implemented in the absence of parallel state-consolidation procedures, then the ALI proposals open opportunities for forum-shopping for more favorable law—provided of course that anyone is prescient (and intelligent) enough to be able to anticipate what law is going to be applied in either state or federal court. The ALI's federalized choice-of-law scheme effectively overrides the requirements of *Klaxon, Van Dusen,* and *Ferens,* and substitutes another new, modified RESTATEMENT (SECOND)-like set of criteria for determining applicable law. Indeed, if the ALI proposals work as designed, their application ought to result in a different choice of law than would occur under existing choice-of-law schemes, because the whole point of the exercise is to tailor federalized choice of law to mass-tort cases. Or, in other words, mass-tort litigation in federal court is supposed to provide litigants with a better (or at least a different) choice of law than they would otherwise be subject to under state choice-of-law statutes.

But if it also remains possible to litigate mass-tort cases exclusively in state courts as well, then plaintiffs will have an incentive to forum-shop horizontally for a preferable state choice-of-law statute, if they can find one, or vertically if diversity jurisdiction will ensure a more favorable law determination under the federalized criteria. Defendants also will have an incentive to forum-shop vertically, through removal procedure, for federalized choice of law. On balance, defendants under the ALI proposals will have the choice-of-law advantage, a benefit that the Reporters recognize but think is a small and fair price for federalized, efficient procedure. What is disconcerting in this tacit admission, however, is that it runs counter to the Reporters' repeated insistence that any federalized choice-of-law scheme be neutral and not favor any class or type of litigant.

The proposal for a federalized choice-of-law scheme overrides *Klaxon* in saying that federal courts need not be bound by state choice-of-law statutes: state law is rendered irrelevant for the choice-of-law determination in federal mass-tort cases. Presumably, the national scope of mass-tort litigation presents a national problem requiring federalized procedural and choice-of-law rules. Although this mind-set permits overriding *Klaxon,* it ignores the fact that federal mass-tort cases are diversity-based. A federalized choice-of-law scheme, then, subverts not so much *Klaxon* as it does basic *Erie* doctrine: in providing for federal diversity jurisdiction, the object is to provide potentially state-biased litigants with another choice of forum, but not another choice of law.

The ALI proposals are likely to leave two choice-of-law systems in place: one in federal court and another in state court. Therefore, it should not be long before litigants realize the potential for applicable-law manipulation. Federalized choice-of-law standards, in the absence of federalized state choice-of-law, are a return to *Swift*-vintage forum-shopping opportunities. It should be remembered that the plaintiff in the infamous *Black & White Taxicab* case strategically reincorporated in another state to take advantage of a federal court determination of applicable law. What was good lawyering then will become good lawyering now, *Erie* notwithstanding.

D. THE ALI PROPOSALS WILL NOT REALLY CIRCUMSCRIBE THE DISCRETION OF FEDERAL JUDGES IN MAKING AN APPLICABLE-LAW DETERMINATION

One of the major ALI criticisms of the option of using federal common law is that the dubious process of finding federal common law gives the judge unbridled discretion in making this determination. In essence, the trend to curb judicial discretion is a reaction, in the choice-of-law realm, to Justice Holmes's notion that law is not some brooding omnipresence in the sky, or that we don't want our judges' heads in the clouds, at least. Thus, in general, conflicts scholars in cahoots with legislators have circumscribed judicial discretion through various formulations of multifactor choice-influencing concerns. What the entire field of conflicts seems to have done over the last century is move from a set of purportedly rigid, black-letter rules that were covertly manipulable to a modernized set of flexible principles that are overtly manipulable. But these modern multifactor approaches belie the notion that laundry lists for determining applicable law curb judicial discretion.

The ALI provisions for determining applicable law in complex cases are but a variation on this theme, with the factors retailored and rejustified for mass-tort litigation. The Reporters admit that their principles are largely modeled on and derived from the RESTATEMENT (SECOND) OF CONFLICTS. But the Reporters' notes inadvertently make an interesting point about judicial application of the RESTATEMENT (SECOND): the cited cases demonstrate the wide variation in judges' assessment of applicable law, particularly under RESTATEMENT section 145, to products liability cases. Although one virtue of adopting a RESTATEMENT (SECOND) approach is that federal judges will already be familiar with its provisions, one might question the wisdom of championing a system in which judicial discretion results in widely varying interpretations and results.

In addition, there comes a point when there are so many relevant factors that the notion of "bridled" discretion is meaningless. When everything is relevant, without any instruction as to persuasive weight, the judge must necessarily exercise unbridled discretion to choose among options.

Commendably, the ALI Reporters have attempted to tie their choice-influencing factors to the purposes underlying tort law. In the dispersed mass-tort case, however, the judge is going to be faced with a choice of up to fifty states' laws, and the ALI scheme effectively forces the judge to resort to the various mitigating provisions. In default instances, when all else fails, these sections typically instruct the judge to apply the law of the state most significantly interested or to consider the regulatory policies and legitimate interests of states not otherwise interested. This is pretty thin guidance for curbing judicial discretion. At that point, a fair-minded judge might as well put on a blindfold and throw a dart at a map of the United States.

Furthermore, limiting judicial discretion in determining applicable law is supposed to support the fairness values of consistency and predictability. But it is difficult to contemplate how the values of consistency and predictability will be achieved under this scheme given the broad range of factors and authority of judges under the ALI provisions. This observation is not so much an indictment of the current ALI proposals as it is of multifactor choice-of-law schemes generally. * * *

[*Discussion and Analysis of Other Objections to ALI Proposals, Omitted.—ed.*]

* * *

IV. POSSIBLE CHOICE-OF-LAW APPROACHES IN MASS TORT: A REPRISE

A. The Problem of Determining the Content of a Federalized Choice-of-Law Scheme

The possibility of overriding *Klaxon* in mass-tort litigation and imposing a federalized choice-of-law regime stems from the probably correct instinct that a federal judge ought to have one choice-of-law rule for such cases rather than the possibility of fifty states' choice-of-law schemes. In essence, the great appeal of a federalized choice-of-law rule is that it liberates judges from the constraints of state choice-of-law rules, and in so doing avoids favoring any one state's choice-of-law preferences over any other state's preferences.

Federalized choice-of-law reduces incentives for horizontal forum-shopping across states, but perhaps increases incentives for vertical forum-shopping from state to federal court. If this is true, then, the proposed federalized choice-of-law schemes violate *Erie* in diversity cases. Reformers cannot escape the anomaly that federalized choice-of-law schemes, in the absence of federal question jurisdiction, undermine the *Erie* stricture against forum-shopping. While federalized choice-of-law schemes may alleviate one kind of bias against out-of-state defendants, these proposed rules infuse the system with another kind of bias that favors litigants in federal court.

Of course, much depends on the content of the federalized choice-of-law scheme that is eventually enacted into law, or that becomes the authoritative rules through court recognition, as in the instance of ALI RESTATEMENT provisions. The debate over applicable law in mass tort now centers almost exclusively on defining the content of a federalized choice-of-law scheme. Here, the virtues and weaknesses of the conflicts academy are readily apparent—a conflicts scholar loves to do nothing so much as delineate a set of choice-influencing factors. The literature is now filled with these proposals, each expressing the conflicts predilections of its author. The ALI COMPLEX LITIGATION PROJECT is but one extended treatment of a possible federalized choice-of-law scheme.

B. Federalized Choice of Law in the Multiparty, Multiforum Bill: Ten Little Factors, and Then There Were None

Reviewing each scholar's list of relevant preference factors for a federalized, mass-tort choice-of-law scheme tends to induce intellectual vertigo. The apotheosis of this process was epitomized by Congress's first draft version of its Multiparty, Multiforum Jurisdiction Act of 1991, which inadvertently parodied the worst excesses of conflicts law. In this version, Congress would have had a transferee federal judge in a consolidated mass-tort case determine the source of applicable federal law according to the following factors:

> (1) the law that might have governed if the jurisdiction created ... by this title did not exist;

> (2) the forums in which the claims were or might have been brought;

(3) the location of the accident on which the action is based and the location of related transactions among the parties;

(4) the place where the parties reside or do business;

(5) the desirability of applying uniform law to some or all aspects of the action;

(6) whether a change in applicable law in connection with removal or transfer of the action would cause unfairness;

(7) the danger of creating unnecessary incentives for forum shopping;

(8) the interest of any jurisdiction in having its law applied;

(9) any reasonable expectation of a party or parties that the law of a particular jurisdiction would apply or not apply; and

(10) any agreement or stipulation of the parties concerning the applicable law.

As Professor Lowenfeld said of an earlier congressional version of this legislation, "No reasonable Restater ... could object to this list of factors." But he went on to "wonder[ ] how a transferee court would cope with all the factors listed, plus the mandate to decide all issues by the laws of a single state."

Clearly, Congress had serious second thoughts about its federalized choice-of-law rules, because it went back to the drawing board and reported new draft legislation six months later in November 1991. This version of the bill would have a transferee federal judge determine applicable law in consolidated mass-tort cases according to the following considerably pared-down list:

(1) the principal place of injury;

(2) the place of the conduct causing the injury;

(3) the principal places of business or domiciles of the parties;

(4) the danger of creating unnecessary incentives for forum shopping; and

(5) whether choice of law would be reasonably foreseeable to the parties.

Congress then instructs that "[t]he factors set forth in paragraphs (1) through (5) shall be evaluated according to their relative importance with respect to the particular actions."

Congress's revised approach is a highly distilled pastiche of conflicts concerns: territorialism, contacts, and *Erie* jurisprudence, with the policy value of foreseeability thrown in for good measure. It is a kind of essence of conflicts law. Congress's latest approach is, more important-ly, a fascinating variation on Professor Juenger's proposed rules for mass-tort cases, which would reduce the choice-of-law inquiry to what are essentially Congress's first three concerns. Professor Juenger said it first, though. Thus, Professor Juenger would resolve mass-tort choice-of-law problems as follows:

> In selecting the rule of decision applicable to any issue in a mass disaster case, the court will take into account the laws of the following jurisdictions:
>
> (a) the place of the tortfeasor's conduct;
>
> (b) the place of injury;
>
> (c) the home state of each party.

As to each issue, the court shall select from the laws of these jurisdictions the most suitable rule of decision.

Professor Juenger explains that his formulation is preferred because it "favors application of the better substantive law," rather than favoring one of the parties. This approach, he argues, "has a venerable history dating back to the Roman *ius gentium*, [e]arly English admiralty practice and Justice Story's opinion in *Swift v. Tyson....*"

The problems with Congress's original ten-factor choice-of-law scheme are evident, and Congress abandoned that idea. Congress's revised five-factor scheme reflects an interesting conflicts triage, but why these factors made the short list can only be subject to speculation and forthcoming legislative history, if the legislators choose to enlighten the citizenry concerning their own conflicts preferences. But if Congress's proposed five-factor list is an improvement over its earlier version, then why is Professor Juenger's three-factor list not an even further improvement? And if Professor Juenger is conceptually correct in suggesting that his list merely embodies the old notion of federal common law, then why not simply go all the way and authorize federal common law?

Was Judge Jack Weinstein right in *Agent Orange* after all? Professor Juenger tantalizingly hints that this might be so:

> A federal common law of the kind Story had hypothesized would of course obviate the need for this symposium [on mass disasters and the conflict of laws]. If federal judges were free to shape the law in complex cases, they could be expected to develop appropriate rules of decision as the law of admiralty demonstrates. But in matters outside the purview of federal law-making power, *Erie* has seemingly deprived the federal judiciary of the creative powers that are the normal attributes of common law judges. Yet, nothing in the Constitution precludes courts from making choice-of-law decisions in a critically evaluative fashion.

Professor Juenger's insight in locating his choice-of-law rules for mass-tort litigation in "better substantive law" resonates in federal common-law making. Perhaps what conflicts analysis in mass-tort litigation ultimately may teach is some reasonable response to the *Erie* problem of the brooding omnipresence in the sky.

* * *

Notes and Questions

1. The author summarizes the possible approaches that reformers might use in address the applicable-law determination in mass tort litigation:

> There are and always have been [three] basic methods that law reformers could use to design a set of choice-of-law rules for mass-tort cases. The first is simply to enact federal substantive tort or products liability legislation that would incorporate not only substantive legal standards, but also jurisdictional provisions, limitations requirements, and available remedies. In one fell swoop, then, Congress could, if it wanted to, "solve" the entire array of mass-tort litigation problems.

> But, as indicated above, there has not to date been a general clamor for substantive mass-tort law reform, which suggests that legislative politics are working either too well or too poorly. This is unfortunate because in the absence of serious consideration of substantive mass-tort law reform, reformers must instead cobble together all the separate pieces of mass-tort litigation: rules for aggregate consolidation, jurisdictional predicates, remedies, and choice of law, to name a few. Rather than having one politically unpleasant substantive tort statute, we now have a collection of analytically unpleasant procedural proposals. It is also interesting to note that none of the major institutional law reform organizations—the ABA, the ALI, and Congress—have ever seriously even mentioned the possibility of substantive mass-tort legislation. Only a stray academician here and there has sheepishly suggested that substantive law reform might provide a preferable solution, but this simple-minded recommendation has been given no serious consideration.

> The second possible approach for determining applicable law in mass-tort litigation would be to authorize the creation and application of federal common law. If suggestions of substantive mass-tort law are sheepishly made, then proposals for federal common law are even more perilously ventured. Few legal concepts carry such heavy intellectual baggage as does federal common law. *Clearfield Trust* and *Lincoln Mills* notwithstanding, the notion of general federal common law has never recovered from *Erie* and Justice Holmes's famous dictum about the "brooding omnipresence in the sky." In short, the legal profession has a longstanding, collective psychological block with regard to even the mention of federal common law, and its occasional messengers are typically received with polite disregard.

> Because the notion of federal common law is so widely and rotely discredited, it follows that no serious scholar (or at least no scholar who wants to be regarded as serious) will champion its case. Thus, Justice Holmes very effectively induced a longstanding chilling effect on legal discourse relating to federal common law. If this point needs any further support, consider that when Judge Jack Weinstein wanted to exercise federal lawmaking authority in the *Agent Orange* litigation, even he felt compelled to label this exercise as one of seeking "national consensus law." This disdain for federal common law has, of course, carried into mass-tort law reform. Any suggestions to adopt federal

common law for mass-tort litigation essentially have been accorded scant attention, as befits this intellectual poor relation.

The third possible approach for determining applicable law in mass-tort litigation is to enact a federalized choice-of-law scheme. Both the American Law Institute and Congress now take this approach, justifying it on various expansive justice and prudential rationales. This federalized choice-of-law option basically overrides the requirements of *Klaxon* and enables federal judges to apply new federal choice-of-law provisions without regard to possible state choice-of-law rules. In the constitutional realm, a federalized choice-of-law regime effectively means that the Commerce Clause, the Full Faith and Credit Clause, and the Judicial Power Clause trump the Tenth Amendment. The option of a federalized choice-of-law scheme is the preferred approach of conflicts scholars; they only disagree as to the content of the federalized choice-of-law criteria.

See Linda S. Mullenix, *Federalizing Choice of Law in Mass Tort Litigation,* 70 Tex.L.Rev. at 1631–37. Of the possible approaches to determining applicable law in multiparty, multiforum mass tort litigation, which proposals seem best designed to fairly and effectively resolve choice-of-law issues in these cases? *See also* Donald T. Trautman, *Toward Federalizing Choice of Law,* 70 Tex. L. Rev. 1715 (1992).

*

Part Five

MASS TORTS AND ALTERNATIVE DISPUTE RESOLUTION TECHNIQUES

Chapter XI

INNOVATIVE USE OF SPECIAL MASTERS

A. APPOINTMENT, SCOPE OF REFERENCE, AND DUTIES

IN RE JOINT EASTERN AND SOUTHERN DISTRICTS ASBESTOS LITIGATION

United States District Courts, Eastern & Southern Districts of New York, 1990.

IN RE NEW YORK CITY ASBESTOS LITIGATION

Supreme Court of the State of New York, 1990.
129 F.R.D. 434.

APPOINTMENT OF SPECIAL MASTER/REFEREE

Before WEINSTEIN, DISTRICT JUDGE, and FREEDMAN, SUPREME COURT JUSTICE.

Several hundred cases from the United States District Courts in the Southern and Eastern Districts of New York have been assigned to Judge Jack B. Weinstein. Several hundred similar state cases have been assigned to New York Supreme Court Justice Helen E. Freedman.

Plaintiffs claim injuries from exposure to asbestos at the Brooklyn Navy Yard during and after World War II. They seek hundreds of millions of dollars in compensatory damages. They also demand punitive damages of billions of dollars. Defendants deny liability.

Scores of similar cases have already been tried or settled in the Eastern and Southern Districts of New York and in the Supreme Court of the State of New York. Tens of thousands of such cases have been disposed of across the country. More than a hundred thousand are still pending.

It is simply not possible for our court system to clear this huge backlog in a way fair to both plaintiffs and defendants on a case-by-case trial basis. The taxpayers cannot afford to pay the costs of "business-as-usual" in disposing of this litigation. Creativity and cooperation are vital.

This major litigation has now matured. Little in law or fact concerning general liability remains in doubt. Only the details of individual claims vary from case to case. The attorneys representing the parties have had so much experience with worker-asbestos cases that they are in a position to agree on fair settlement values in every case.

We have now consulted with the other judges in the Southern and Eastern Districts and in the Supreme Court of the State of New York. Two extensive meetings with the attorneys for plaintiffs and defendants have been conducted with Justice Freedman and Judges Weinstein and Charles P. Sifton participating.

It is the consensus of all the judges involved that these cases can and should be settled now on terms fair to both the plaintiffs and defendants. Settlement is required to alleviate the terrible calendar congestion in the State and Federal courts of New York. There is an urgent need to clear our dockets to make room for the increases in drug cases. More criminal drug cases will be brought if promises of increased anti-drug law enforcement are met.

Accordingly, the Supreme Court of the State of New York and the United States District Courts for the Eastern and Southern Districts of New York jointly appoint Kenneth R. Feinberg, Esq., as Referee and Settlement Master. His appointment as a Referee is made pursuant to sections 4301 *et seq.* of the New York Civil Practice Law and Rules and as Master pursuant to Rule 53 of the Federal Rules of Civil Procedure. The powers of Settlement Master and Referee are for this purpose equivalent. The emergency nature of this problem requires a joint appointment and close cooperation between the State and Federal courts.

Mr. Feinberg has special expertise, competence and experience as a Settlement Master and Referee. He will assist the parties and the courts in promptly settling these cases subject to further orders of the courts. Fees will be based upon rates and procedures approved in County of Suffolk v. Long Island Lighting Co., 710 F.Supp. 1477 (E.D.N.Y.1989).

The parties are directed promptly to meet with Mr. Feinberg. They will assist him and each other in the disposition of these cases without trial. The courts reserve the power to take such further steps as may appear to be desirable.

So ordered.

IN RE NEW YORK COUNTY DES LITIGATION

Supreme Court of the State of New York, New York County, 1992.

IN RE DES CASES

United States District Court, Eastern District of New York, 1992.
142 F.R.D. 58.

APPOINTMENT OF SPECIAL MASTER/REFEREE

WEINSTEIN, DISTRICT JUDGE, and IRA GAMMERMAN, SUPREME COURT JUSTICE.

Plaintiffs claim injuries from their mothers' exposure to diethylstilbestrol (DES) from the 1940s through 1971. Defendants were manufacturers and distributors of DES. Cases pending in the state Supreme Court have been assigned to Justice Ira Gammerman. Cases pending in the federal district court have been assigned to Judge Jack B. Weinstein.

This major litigation has now matured. Little in law concerning general liability remains in doubt. *See* generally Enright v. Eli Lilly & Co., 77 N.Y.2d 377, 568 N.Y.S.2d 550, 570 N.E.2d 198 (no cause of action by third-generation DES daughters against manufacturers), *cert. denied,* 502 U.S. 868, 112 S.Ct. 197, 116 L.Ed.2d 157 (1991)....

Only the issue of relative market share, now before Justice James B. Kane (but previously litigated in California), and the details of individual claims require resolution. The attorneys representing the parties have the requisite skill and experience to negotiate a fair settlement without further trials. These cases can and should be settled now on terms fair to both the plaintiffs and defendants.

Individual trials of the hundreds of pending DES cases would require more than fifty judge-years and thousands of jurors. Delays would adversely affect plaintiffs who have not had speedy dispositions of their claims; add to the costs of defendants, both in heavy jury verdicts and unnecessary transactional costs in discovery, trials and appeals; unnecessarily burden jurors, witnesses and parties; and require large expenditures of court resources which are in short supply and are required for other purposes, including criminal trials.

Accordingly, the Supreme Court of the State of New York and the United States District Court jointly appoint Kenneth R. Feinberg, Esq., as Referee and Special Master for DES cases. His appointment as a Referee is made pursuant to sections 4301 *et seq.* of the New York Civil Practice Law and Rules and as Special Master pursuant to Rule 53 of the Federal Rules of Civil Procedure. The powers of Settlement Master and Referee are for relevant purposes equivalent. The shared problems of the two court systems and the litigants requires a joint appointment and close cooperation between the state and federal courts.

Mr. Feinberg has special expertise, competence, and experience as a Special Master and Referee. He will assist the parties and the courts in promptly settling these cases subject to further orders of the courts. Fees will be based upon rates and procedures approved in In re Joint Eastern & Southern Dists. Asbestos Litig., In re New York City Asbestos Litig., 129 F.R.D. 434, 435 (E.D.N.Y.1990).

The parties are directed to meet forthwith with Mr. Feinberg. They will assist him and each other in the prompt disposition of these cases without trial. The courts reserve the power to take such further steps as may appear to be desirable.

So ordered.

PRUDENTIAL INSURANCE COMPANY OF AMERICA v. UNITED STATES GYPSUM COMPANY

United States Court of Appeals, Third Circuit, 1993.
991 F.2d 1080.

Before: BECKER, ALITO and GARTH, CIRCUIT JUDGES.

OPINION OF THE COURT

GARTH, CIRCUIT JUDGE:

Petitioners, Prudential Insurance Company of America and PIC Realty Corporation ("Prudential"), seek the issuance of a writ of mandamus that requires the review of an order of the district court appointing Dean Henry G. Manne of the George Mason University School of Law as a special master. Because the record before us does not satisfy the exceedingly high standard that must be met before the reference of a special master can be made pursuant to Fed.R.Civ.P. 53(b), we will grant the writ.

I

The underlying dispute from which this petition arises involves several products liability actions brought by Prudential against the United States Gypsum Company, W.R. Grace and Co.-Conn., the Celotex Corporation, U.S. Mineral Products Company, Keene Corporation, Pfizer, Inc., Asbestospray Corporation, National Gypsum Company, and John Doe Companies (collectively, "the Defendants"). Prudential seeks to recoup the cost of testing, air-monitoring, removing and encapsulating asbestos-containing products allegedly installed by the Defendants in thirty-nine Prudential properties located in eighteen different states.

In early 1992, after more than four years of pre-trial activity (the original complaint was filed in October of 1987), several motions were made before the district court. By order dated February 14, 1992, the district court judge *sua sponte* appointed a special master to supervise all pre-trial matters and make recommendations as to all pre-trial motions. However, after it was brought to the attention of the district court that the individual who had been appointed was statutorily barred from serving as a special master under 28 U.S.C. § 458, the district court rescinded the appointment.

At a subsequent status conference before the magistrate judge, who had been handling discovery matters since the inception of the case, all parties agreed that the litigation did not require the services of a special master and asked that the magistrate judge inform the district court of their determination.

The district court apparently did not agree with the litigants' conclusion. Citing "the complexity of both the legal claims and the factual scenario involved in the litigation," the district court appointed Dean Manne to serve as a special master in the litigation pursuant to Fed.R.Civ.P. 53. In his order dated July 31, 1992, the district court judge defined the role of Dean Manne as follows:

> A. To confer promptly with the parties regarding the status of this matter and determine what type and nature of proceedings are necessary for the master to become knowledgeable regarding the matters at issue herein and to carry out his duties as specified below;

> B. To consider and resolve expeditiously any and all future disputes between the parties relating to discovery and other nondispositive motions made prior to the time of trial;

> C. To fully consider and prepare reports to be submitted to the Court, including an exposition of all relevant facts and conclusions of law, concerning any and all future dispositive motions made prior to the time of trial.

The order specified Dean Manne's rate of compensation and provided that one-half of the master's bill was to be paid by Prudential and the other half by the Defendants.

Prudential subsequently moved to vacate the appointment on two grounds. First, it contended that Rule 53 does not permit the appointment of a special master to hear dispositive legal motions. Second, Prudential asserted that Dean Manne's prior work in the field suggests that he is unsympathetic to litigants such as Prudential and, therefore, incapable of dealing with a party in Prudential's position in an impartial manner.

By opinion dated October 13, 1992, the district court denied Prudential's motion to vacate the reference to the special master, and Prudential subsequently moved to certify the issue for immediate interlocutory appeal pursuant to 28 U.S.C. § 1292(b) and to stay the proceedings before Dean Manne pending appeal. The district court denied the motion by opinion and order of October 21, 1992, and on November 3, 1992, Prudential filed the instant petition.

* * *

III

A

The historical role of the special master informs our decision. Special masters were first utilized as judicial assistants to the court in the early years of the English chancery practice. *See* Kaufman, *Masters in the Federal Courts: Rule 53,* 58 Colum.L.Rev. 452, 452 (1958). Although the practice was continued in the United States, id. at 453, beginning in 1912 the rules of equity restricted the use of masters to situations where an "exceptional condition" required it. Silberman, *Masters and Magistrates Part II: The American Analogue,* 50 N.Y.U.L.Rev. 1297, 1322 (1975).

In fact, much of today's Rule 53(b) is taken directly from Equity Rule 59 which was adopted by the Supreme Court in 1912 and provided:

> *Reference to Master—Exceptional, Not Usual*
>
> Save in matters of account, a reference to a master shall be the exception, not the rule, and shall be made only upon a showing that some exceptional condition requires it. . . .

Rules of Practice in Equity, 226 U.S. 666 (1912).

As stated by Professor Silberman,

> There seems to be no official comment as to why the restriction [requiring an exceptional condition] was added. However, in Los Angeles Brush Mfg. Corp. v. James, 272 U.S. 701, 47 S.Ct. 286, 71 L.Ed. 481 (1927), the Court, per Chief Justice Taft, ascribed the rule's purpose to a shielding of equity litigants from the delay and expense that often accompanied reference to a master. Id. at 707, 47 S.Ct. at 288.

Id. at 1325, n.161.[5]

It was not until the Federal Rules of Civil Procedure were adopted in December of 1937 that a clause was added to the rule that distinguished between jury trials and nonjury trials. The new language read: "in actions to be tried by a jury, a reference shall be made only when the issues are complicated." Although we have been unable to find any contemporaneous explanation as to why the Rules Committee saw fit to add the "complicated" standard to actions involving juries, statements made during a 1938 symposium on the Federal Rules suggest that the new clause was not intended to depart in any substantial way from Equity Rule 59:

> [Complicated] is a very broad word and subject to a variety of interpretations, but coupled with the first sentence, "[A] reference to a master shall be the exception and not the rule," it undoubtedly sets a limitation which the district judges will be inclined to feel is a rigorous limitation upon the exercise of their discretion in that regard. Robert G. Dodge, statement to the Institute of Federal Rules, Cleveland, Ohio, July, 1938, in American Bar Association, Rules of Civil Procedure for the District Courts of the United States,

---

5. Although in more recent times this rationale seems to have taken a back seat to the Supreme Court's concern for the "abdication of the judicial function," *La Buy,* 352 U.S. at 256, there can be little doubt that Chief Justice Taft's concerns also inform the rule's purpose.

with Notes, and Proceedings of the Institute on Federal Rules, Cleveland, Ohio, July 21–23, 1938, ed. by William W. Dawson, at 330 (1938).

B

Ordinarily, in order to determine whether a reference to a special master is permissible, it is necessary to ascertain the type of action underlying the reference. Fed.R.Civ.P. 53(b) presently provides:

> *Reference.* A reference to a master shall be the exception and not the rule. In actions to be tried by a jury, a reference shall be made only when the issues are complicated; in actions to be tried without a jury, save in matters of account and of difficult computation of damages, a reference shall be made only upon a showing that some exceptional condition requires it.

Thus, if the case is to be tried by a jury, the issues involved must be "complicated" before a special master may be appointed. If, however, there is to be a nonjury trial, an "exceptional condition" is required before a special master may be authorized. We emphasize, however, as did Mr. Dodge, who focused on the sentence preceding these directives, that in all cases a reference is to be "the exception and not the rule."

It is a matter of dispute between the parties as to whether the jury or nonjury standard applies in this case. Although Prudential's complaint in the underlying action seeks a jury trial, Prudential urges that the relevant standard to be applied at this stage of the proceeding is nevertheless the more demanding "exceptional condition" requirement. This is so because, as argued by Prudential, the determination of core issues, which must be decided prior to trial, must be tested under the nonjury standard of Rule 53, particularly since such issues are, and have always been, within the province and special competence of the appointed judiciary to decide.

Indeed, in this very case the matters consigned by the district court to the master involve proceedings having to do with motions to dismiss, motions to strike defenses, summary judgment motions and discovery. * * * All of these proceedings must be resolved prior to trial and all universally and traditionally have been decided by judges without jury involvement. Jack Walters & Sons Corp. v. Morton Bldg., Inc., 737 F.2d 698, 712 (7th Cir.1984)(reference to special master required exceptional condition since "it was not made to assist a jury and did not call for an accounting or a damage calculation.").

Nevertheless, Rule 53 enables a judge to appoint a special master to "assist the jury in those exceptional cases where the legal issues are too complicated for the jury to handle alone." Dairy Queen, Inc. v. Wood, 369 U.S. 469, 478, 82 S.Ct. 894, 900, 8 L.Ed.2d 44 (1962). The court in *Dairy Queen* cautioned, however, that "[e]ven this limited inroad upon the right to a jury should seldom be made and if at all only when unusual circumstances exist." *Id.* at n. 18, 82 S.Ct. at 900 n. 18, *quoting La Buy,* 352 U.S. at 258, 77 S.Ct. at 314.[6]

It is at least clear to us from the historical evidence that the "complicated" standard of Rule 53 was conceived to provide assistance to juries and for no other reason.[7] Significantly, in this case neither the original order of reference, nor any subsequent statements made by the district court in regard to the reference, mention any role the special master might play in assisting a potential jury. Rather, the district court, without making specific findings or giving explicit reasons as to the need for a special master in this case, stated only that Dean Manne was appointed "[b]ecause of the complexity of both the legal claims and the factual scenario involved in the litigation." District Court Opinion of October 13, 1992 at 2.

As defined by the district court's order of July 31, 1992, Dean Manne's role was to confer with the parties, resolve nondispositive motions made prior to the time of trial, resolve discovery disputes between the parties and "prepare reports to be submitted to the Court, including an exposition of all relevant facts and conclusions of law, concerning any and all future dispositive motions made prior to the time of trial." * * * These tasks are normally conducted by a district court with, perhaps, the assistance of a magistrate judge, whether or not a jury is destined to try the underlying case.[8]

Moreover, rather than utilizing the special master to perform some specialized matters of account or difficult computation of damages, see Fed.R.Civ.P. 53(b), or some other time consuming or detailed tasks that the district court judge or a magistrate judge would be less efficient in accomplishing, the district court in this case merely appears to have substituted a master for the magistrate judge, who had been managing the case for five years with the approval of all parties. * * * Indeed, the district court has neither given us specific reasons for appointing a

---

6. Ex parte Peterson, 253 U.S. 300, 40 S.Ct. 543, 64 L.Ed. 919 (1920), explained the functions that a special master could perform in assisting a jury. Because the district court's order of reference in the instant case assigned no such tasks to Dean Manne and because we have concluded that all of the functions to be performed by the master were to be conducted prior to trial and were inherently pre-trial in nature, the teaching of *Ex parte Peterson,* even if relevant today, cannot inform our decision. In particular, we call attention to the fact that *Ex parte Peterson* was decided before the enactment of the Federal Rules of Civil Procedure, the Federal Rules of Evidence and the Federal Magistrates Act, 28 U.S.C. §§ 631–639 (West Supp.1992)(originally enacted in 1968). Therefore, the decision in *Ex parte Peterson,* rendered in 1920, did not, and could not, interpret Rule 53(b) because, as we have observed, the Federal

Rules of Civil Procedure were not adopted until 1937.

7. For one of the more provocative and interesting discussions of Rule 53, see Brazil, *Authority to Refer Discovery Tasks to Special Masters: Limitations on Existing Sources and the Need for a New Federal Rule,* in W. Brazil, G. Hazard Jr. & P. Rice, Managing Complex Litigation: A Practical Guide to the Use of Special Masters 305 (1983).

8. As Prudential points out, "... by definition summary judgment motions are legal motions to be granted by the judge only when no disputed facts exist. *See* Fed. R.Civ.P. 56." * * * *See also* Stauble v. Warrob, 977 F.2d 690, 696–97 (1st Cir.1992)(holding that it is impermissible to refer liability determinations to a special master over the objections of a party where the particular determination is essentially a judicial function).

special master nor has it called our attention to any particular, unique, special or exceptional circumstances with which a magistrate judge could not deal effectively or which would require that a magistrate judge be replaced by a special master.[9]

Finally, the plain language of the rule supports Prudential's contention that the jury standard of Rule 53 is inapplicable to the instant petition. Recall that Rule 53(b) provides, *"[i]n actions to be tried by a jury* a reference shall be made only when the issues are complicated" (emphasis added). Although, admittedly, Prudential has requested a jury trial in its complaint, the action currently before us is not yet a jury trial, nor is there any assurance, or even probability, that Prudential's claims ever will be presented to a jury. Depending on the disposition of the various motions to dismiss petitioner's claims and motions for summary judgment, a jury may never be empaneled in this case. Since, as we have shown, the "complicated" standard of Rule 53(b) contemplates the use of a master only for purposes of assisting a jury, we decline to apply the jury standard in this case where the need for a jury is as yet undetermined. Thus, in light of the pre-trial role that the district court assigned to the special master, we will measure the district court's appointment of a special master by the nonjury standard of Rule 53.

C

The "exceptional condition" standard of Rule 53(b) has been addressed by a significant number of courts.[10] As noted, the seminal Supreme Court case regarding the application of the rule is La Buy v. Howes Leather Co., 352 U.S. 249, 77 S.Ct. 309, 1 L.Ed.2d 290 (1957), which involved two underlying antitrust actions affecting ninety-three plaintiffs and twelve defendants. Concerned by the complicated nature of the case, the time it would take to try and the congestion of the court calendar, the district court in La Buy referred the case to a special master, authorizing him to "take evidence and to report the same to [the] Court together with his findings of fact and conclusions of law." *Id.* at 253, 77 S.Ct. at 312.

The Supreme Court affirmed the Seventh Circuit's issuance of the mandamus writ to withdraw the reference, holding, in part, that the complexity of the legal and factual issues did not warrant the appointment of a special master: "[o]n the contrary, we believe that this is an impelling reason for trial before a regular, experienced trial judge rather than before a temporary substitute appointed on an *ad hoc* basis and

---

9. The notes to Rule 53 recognize that "... the existence of [magistrate judges] may make the appointment of outside masters unnecessary in many instances...." Fed.R.Civ.P. 53(a) Advisory Committee's note (1983 amendment).

10. Because we conclude that the nonjury standard applies in this case, we need not reach the question of how, if at all, the

Rule 53(b) jury standard differs from the nonjury standard. We note, however, that as a definitional matter, it is difficult to understand how a reference to a master may be "the exception," as required by the first sentence of Rule 53(b), and yet be made in the absence of an "exceptional condition."

ordinarily not experienced in judicial work." *Id.* at 259, 77 S.Ct. at 315. Therefore, according to *La Buy,* as the complexity of the litigation increases, so, too, does the need for the district judge's personal attention.[11] A district court has no discretion to delegate its adjudicatory responsibility in favor of a decision maker who has not been appointed by the President and confirmed by the Senate. *See La Buy,* 352 U.S. at 256, 77 S.Ct. at 313.

Given the constraints that *La Buy* places on Rule 53, we cannot say on the record before us, and on the various representations made to us on appeal based on the record, that Prudential's claims establish an exceptional case. As we have noted, the district court has not called our attention to any exceptional qualities of this case nor has it fashioned any findings of fact nor given us any compelling, specific reasons from which we could discern that this case is, indeed, exceptionally different from other cases that have presented complex legal and factual claims, but in which no special masters were sought or appointed. *See, e.g.,* In re Japanese Electronic Products, 723 F.2d 238 (3d Cir.1983), *aff'g in part and rev'g in part* 513 F.Supp. 1100 (E.D.Pa.1981), *rev'd,* 475 U.S. 574, 106 S.Ct. 1348, 89 L.Ed.2d 538 (1986), *on remand,* 807 F.2d 44 (3d Cir.1986), *cert. denied,* 481 U.S. 1029, 107 S.Ct. 1955, 95 L.Ed.2d 527 (1987)(action against 24 Japanese electronics producers alleging antitrust, tariff, and antidumping violations); *see also* In re School Asbestos Litigation, 977 F.2d 764 (3d Cir.1992)(asbestos litigation involving over 30,000 school districts' and the laws of 54 jurisdictions). Beyond the district court's generalized statement that Prudential's legal claims and the factual scenario developed are complex, it provides only the following explanation for the reference:

> [T]he volume of documents, the length of the proceedings, the number of the motions and the breadth of documents accompanying the motions, and the inherent complexity of an asbestos litigation all demonstrate that the matters encompassed in the reference in this case not only meet the "complexity" standard of the Rules but also are unique in their complexity. . . .

* * *

11. In its opinion of October 13, 1992, the district court distinguishes its reference to Dean Manne from that in *La Buy* by suggesting that while the district court in *La Buy* referred the entire action to a special master for trial on the merits, in this case only pre-trial motions were referred. Moreover, the district court stated that it planned to "review *de novo* every finding of law by the special master to ensure that the final dispositive decision-making comes from an Article III judge rather than a Special Master appointed solely to facilitate the disposition of a complex and lengthy case." * * * We are troubled by the distinction made by the district court. Even in those cases where a district court has exceeded its authority by referring an entire trial to a special master, the district court presumably has retained authority to review *de novo* all conclusions of law. Stauble v. Warrob, 977 F.2d 690, 697 (1st Cir.1992). Indeed, such conclusions must be adopted by the district court before orders pursuant to them can be issued. Additionally, depending upon how the summary judgment motions and the motions to dismiss are decided by Dean Manne, the district court's reference in this case may well encompass the entire action.

Far from justifying the appointment of a special master, however, the factors listed by the district court have been specifically rejected by the Supreme Court as justifications for referring a case to a special master. Neither the volume of work generated by a case nor the complexity of that work will suffice to meet the "exceptional condition" standard promulgated by Rule 53. *La Buy,* 352 U.S. at 259.

Additionally, *La Buy* was decided more than a decade prior to the enactment of the Federal Magistrate's Act, 28 U.S.C. §§ 631–639 (West Supp.1992)(originally enacted in 1968). Since the implementation of that Act, the analysis, reasoning and conclusions of *La Buy* are even more compelling in disfavoring the appointment of special masters. Much of the concern over docket congestion has been addressed by the appointment of magistrate judges who are expressly authorized by statute to assist the district court with pre-trial matters, including discovery and dispositive legal motions. 28 U.S.C. § 636(b)(1)(West Supp.1992); *see also* Mathews v. Weber, 423 U.S. 261, 270–72, 96 S.Ct. 549, 554–55, 46 L.Ed.2d 483 (1976)(magistrate judge assisting with pre-trial proceedings is not performing the role of a special master pursuant to Fed.R.Civ.P. 53). It stands to reason, therefore, that any contemporary examination of the "exceptional condition" standard must be made in light of the Magistrate's Act and the current availability of magistrate judges to whom Congress has specifically authorized the referral of pre-trial matters.

Accordingly, we next turn our attention to the question of whether there is some exceptional aspect of the underlying proceedings giving rise to this petition that might require the appointment of a special master in lieu of a magistrate. *See* In re Dept. of Defense, 848 F.2d 232, 240–41 (D.C.Cir.1988)(Starr, J., dissenting). Again, nothing in the record informs us that Dean Manne is more qualified to recommend how the pre-trial motions in this case should be decided than is a magistrate judge who has been involved with the Prudential claims and the defenses thereto for more than five years and who has attended approximately forty status conferences. We are not persuaded that the academic credentials of Dean Manne, as impressive as they are, can justify replacing a federally appointed magistrate judge, who, by all accounts, has an excellent working knowledge of the facts and issues in the case and who has thus far ably supervised pre-trial activities.

We are familiar with representative instances in which special masters have not been approved, as well as those cases in which they have been authorized. On the one hand, the appointment of a special master has been disapproved in the following cases: Apex Fountain Sales, Inc. v. Kleinfeld, 818 F.2d 1089, 1096–97 (3d Cir.1987)(referral to special master of contempt motion made during implementation stage of court order was inappropriate where motion presented simple question of law, and depending on disposition of legal issue, a relatively simple factual question); Bennerson v. Joseph, 583 F.2d 633 (3d Cir.1978)(reference to special master to conduct hearings in nonjury case was error where hearings assigned to master took only three days, produced 444 page transcript and concerned simple factual matters that turned on credibility); Stauble v. Warrob, 977 F.2d 690 (1st Cir.1992)(special master disapproved in nonjury case involving complex issues, voluminous record, and multiple defendants where reference authorized master to try the case); In re U.S., 816 F.2d 1083, 1088–91 (6th Cir.1987)(calendar congestion, complexity of issues, possibility of lengthy trial, extraordinary pretrial management in case with 250 parties, and public interest in quick resolution of case did not satisfy "exceptional condition" for appointment of special master to determine dispositive pre-trial legal issues); Jack Walters & Sons Corp. v. Morton Bldg., 737 F.2d 698, 712 (7th Cir.1984)(lack of time for lengthy trial, several thousand pages of materials, and large number of issues did not satisfy "exceptional condition" standard); Wilver v. Fisher, 387 F.2d 66, 69 (10th Cir.1967)(reference to special master in nonjury case was error where district court should have heard plaintiff's motion for default based on defendant's failure to answer interrogatories rather than appointing master to supervise answers to interrogatories).

On the other hand, the appointment of a special master has been approved in the following cases: Halderman v. Pennhurst State School and Hosp., 612 F.2d 84, 111–12 (3d Cir.1979)(special master appropriate to supervise reorganization of major health institution); Ruiz v. Estelle, 679 F.2d 1115, 1160–61 (5th Cir.1982)("exceptional condition" as well as court's inherent equitable power justified reference where special master appointed to supervise implementation of order at remedy stage); Gary W. v. Louisiana, 601 F.2d 240, 244–45 (5th Cir.1979)(special master appropriate to supervise multi-year implementation of court order affecting care of all mentally retarded children in Louisiana); U.S. v. Horton, 622 F.2d 144 (5th Cir.1980)(reference to special master was proper for purpose of assisting jury with complex accounting dispute); Williams v. Lane, 851 F.2d 867, 884 (7th Cir.1988)(upheld appointment of master in nonjury case to supervise enforcement of court order pertaining to prison conditions where judge's busy docket prevented him from doing so himself); Arthur Murray, Inc. v. Oliver, 364 F.2d 28 (8th Cir.1966)(reference to master for accounting analysis approved in nonjury case).

Our reading of these authorities bolsters our conclusion that here, on the instant record, the Rule 53(b) requirement of an "exceptional circumstance" is not satisfied. In short, we cannot in good conscience, and in light of the record and of those authorities that have approved or disapproved of special masters, hold this case to be more the exception than the rule.

IV

In normal course, where we have looked to a different legal standard than that applied by the district court, we have generally vacated the district court's order and remanded so that the district court might give effect to the correct standard we announced. U.S. v. Gypsum, 333 U.S.

364, 68 S.Ct. 525, 92 L.Ed. 746 (1948); Black United Fund of N.J., Inc. v. Kean, 763 F.2d 156 (3d Cir.1985).

In this case, however, we see little point in adhering to a remand procedure because we can envisage no possibility that the applicable nonjury standard of Rule 53 can be satisfied. This being so, no order of reference defining or redefining the master's role, no matter how restrictive in scope, could be framed. The instruction of *La Buy,* the availability of a competent magistrate judge familiar with the earlier proceedings, the overwhelming preference of the Supreme Court and other case authorities for legal issues to be determined by Article III judges and, in particular, the absence of any exceptional conditions revealed by the record all persuade us that in this case, at this time, it would be both error and a waste of valuable judicial resources not to direct that the order of reference be vacated.

We will therefore issue a writ of mandamus directing the district court to withdraw and vacate its reference to the special master.[13]

* * *

Notes and Questions

1. As the materials excerpted above (and that follow) demonstrate, federal courts have made extensive and innovative use of special masters in mass tort cases. When may a federal judge appoint a special master, and what functions may a special master perform? Is complexity a sufficient ground for appointing a special master to assist in a complex mass tort case? Are Judge Weinstein's appointment orders in the Brooklyn Navy Yard Asbestos and New York DES litigations consistent with the Third Circuit's mandamus decision in *Prudential Insurance Co*? Why does complexity in the first two litigations support appointment of a special master, but not so in the *Prudential* asbestos abatement litigation?

2. What functions may a special master perform? In what capacity was Kenneth Feinberg to serve in the *Brooklyn Navy Yard* Asbestos litigation and *New York DES* litigation? Was the district court in the *Prudential* litigation contemplating a different role for Dean Manne in the asbestos abatement litigation? Does the promulgation of the United States Magistrate's Act, as the Third Circuit suggests, undercut the need for special masters? What is the relationship of United States Magistrate judges to special masters in terms of the scope of their powers and authority?

3. Who determines the need for a special master and how are special masters selected? As the readings will suggest, mass tort litigation has given rise to a professional career group of special masters such as Mr. Feinberg. Is this a desirable development, or does it also entail problems? How are special masters paid for their services? For commentary discussing the historical development and current use of special masters, *see generally*

---

13. In support of its petition, Prudential also argues that the appointment of Dean Manne should be vacated because of his alleged appearance of partiality evidenced by his academic writings. * * * Because we conclude that the district court exceeded its authority in appointing a special master in the first instance, we neither consider nor address the argument concerning alleged biases of Dean Manne.

Wayne D. Brazil, SETTLING CIVIL SUITS (Chicago: American Bar Association 1985); Wayne D. Brazil, *Referring Tasks to Special Masters: Is Rule 53 a Source of Authority and Restrictions?*, 1983 Am.B.Found.Res.J. 143 (1983); Wayne D. Brazil, *Special Masters in the Pretrial Development of Big Cases: Potential and Problems*, 1982 Am.B.Found.Res.J. 287 (1982); James S. DeGraw, *Rule 53, Inherent Powers, and Institutional Reform: The Lack of Limits on Special Masters*, 66 N.Y.U.L.Rev. 880 (1991); Geoffrey C. Hazard Jr. and Paul R. Rice, *Judicial Management of the Pretrial Process in Massive Litigation: Special Masters as Case Managers*, 1982 Am.B.Found. Res.J. 375 (1982); David Rosenberg, *Comment: Of End Games and Openings in Mass Tort Cases: Lessons From a Special Master*, 69 B.U.L.Rev. 695 (1989).

4. Historically, special masters have been used for limited particular purposes, such as performing an accounting for the court, in certain kinds of litigation (most notably in patent infringement, copyright, and securities cases). In the 1960s and 1970s, the role of special masters was expanded to assist the court in various oversight functions generated by institutional reform litigation. Thus, special masters helped federal judges in designing and implementing desegregation plans, prison or mental health facility reform, or environmental cleanup plans. *See e.g.* David I. Levine, *The Authority for the Appointment of Remedial Special Masters in Federal Institutional Reform Litigation: The History Reconsidered*, 17 U.C. Davis L.Rev. 753 (1984); Timothy G. Little, *Court-Appointed Special Masters in Complex Environmental Litigation:* City of Quincy v. Metropolitan District Commission, 8 Harv.Envtl.L.Rev. 435 (1984). How has the mass tort litigation of the 1980s and 1990s expanded and redefined the role of the special master?

5. Judge Robert Parker of the Eastern District of Texas appointed Professor Francis McGovern to serve as a special master in Jenkins v. Raymark, 109 F.R.D. 269 (1985), *affirmed* 782 F.2d 468 (5th Cir.1986) to gather information relating to the composition of the asbestos-injury class members (described *infra* at section C). Subsequently, after provisional certification of the class action in *Cimino v. Raymark Industries*, Judge Parker appointed Professor Jack Ratliff of the University of Texas Law School to formulate a trial plan for *Cimino* (*see supra*). Why would a federal judge need a special master to formulate a trial plan? Both plaintiffs and defendants initially opposed appointment of Professor Ratliff as a special master for this purpose. For a discussion of this novel use of the special master's office, *see* Linda S. Mullenix, *Beyond Consolidation: Post–Aggregative Procedure in Asbestos Mass Tort Litigation*, 32 Wm. & Mary L.Rev. 475 (1991); Jack Ratliff, *Special Master's Report in* Cimino v. Raymark Industries, Inc., 10 Rev.Litig. 521 (1991).

6. In *Carlough v. Amchem Prods., Inc.*, the district court judge appointed Professor Stephen Burbank of the University of Pennsylvania Law School to serve as special master to perform an independent assessment of past and current personal injury asbestos claim values, with a view towards determining the fairness of a "futures" class action settlement. The court relied on the special master's findings in its fairness opinion. *See* Georgine v. Amchem Prods., Inc., 157 F.R.D. 246 (E.D.Pa.1994)(fairness hearing).

B. SPECIAL MASTERS IN MASS TORT: CONFLICTS AND DISQUALIFICATION

IN RE JOINT EASTERN AND SOUTHERN DISTRICTS ASBESTOS LITIGATION

United States District Courts, Eastern & Southern Districts of New York, 1990.

IN RE NEW YORK CITY ASBESTOS LITIGATION

Supreme Court of New York, 1990.
737 F.Supp. 735.

WEINSTEIN, DISTRICT JUDGE, and HELEN E. FREEDMAN, SUPREME COURT JUSTICE.

On January 30, 1990 Kenneth R. Feinberg, Esq. was appointed a federal Special Master and a state Referee by joint order of the United States District Court for the Eastern District of New York and the Supreme Court of the State of New York, respectively. See In re Joint Eastern and Southern Districts Asbestos Litigation; In re New York City Asbestos Litigation, 129 F.R.D. 434 (E.D.N.Y. & N.Y.Sup.Ct.1990). Mr. Feinberg was to act as a settlement master-referee, mediating between the parties to avoid the necessity of extended trials in cases involving asbestos exposure at the Brooklyn Navy Yard. He was directed to attempt to settle the cases in four months, by June 1, 1990.

Owens–Illinois, Inc., one of the defendants in these cases, offered no objection during discussions with the court. Nevertheless, Owens–Illinois sought on April 24, 1990 by motion returnable May 15 to disqualify Mr. Feinberg. Its ground was that some years ago he and his law firm, Kaye, Scholer, Fierman, Hays & Handler, had acted on its behalf and that of other asbestos manufacturers in connection with public education and legislative efforts aimed at promoting alternative compensation systems to mass tort litigation.

The motion must be denied because: (1) the special position of a mediator renders inappropriate disqualification under the circumstances alleged by the moving party; (2) it has already been denied in connection with consolidated asbestos litigation pending in Maryland in which Mr. Feinberg was appointed as mediator; and (3) the motion is untimely.

I. FACTS

Kenneth R. Feinberg, Esq. is a nationally recognized mediator of great skill whose services have been frequently utilized by private litigants and by courts. He has also taken a leading role in legislative, bar association and academic circles in connection with the development of important alternative dispute resolution (ADR) innovations. In addition to his duties as mediator in the Brooklyn Navy Yard cases, Mr. Feinberg was appointed to a similar position last year by the Baltimore Circuit Court for Baltimore City and charged with settling some 9000 consolidated asbestos personal injury cases in the state of Maryland.

That litigation is currently pending. Mr. Feinberg, with the consent of the Maryland, New York and federal courts, continues to act simultaneously as a settlement master in both the Maryland and New York litigations.

From 1980 to 1983 Mr. Feinberg represented a group of asbestos manufacturers known as the Asbestos Compensation Coalition. The Coalition was formed to develop or respond to federal legislative proposals and to other governmental activities relating to alternative compensation systems for asbestos claimants. During the course of his representation of the Coalition Mr. Feinberg drafted legislative proposals for alternative compensation systems and worked with congressional personnel and representatives of other companies. Owens–Illinois, the moving party in the instant case, was not a member of the Coalition, although a number of the other defendants in the instant case—none of whom have joined in the motion to disqualify—were members.

In early 1983 the Coalition disbanded and in its place a number of asbestos companies, including Owens–Illinois, formed the Committee for Equitable Compensation, an organization with purposes similar to that of the Coalition. Mr. Feinberg personally represented the Committee through the end of 1983. Neither he nor his firm represented or advised the Committee or any of its individual members in the defense or settlement of asbestos claims brought under existing laws. Mr. Feinberg worked with Congress on behalf of the Committee looking towards federal legislation establishing a no-fault administrative compensation program for asbestos claimants to which the United States Government would contribute. He and his firm also undertook public education projects on the Committee's behalf and reacted to proposals for a uniform national product liability law. Although a number of the other defendants in the instant litigation were members of the Committee, none have joined Owens–Illinois' motion to disqualify.

Although his personal involvement had ceased by early 1984, Mr. Feinberg's law firm and in particular, his colleague, Lawrence Novey, continued to represent the Committee until mid–1987.

In January 1990, some five months into Mr. Feinberg's tenure as settlement master in the Maryland asbestos litigation, Owens–Illinois moved to disqualify him in that litigation. The motion was denied by Judge Marshall A. Levin, who was supervising the Maryland asbestos litigation, in February 1990. *See* In re Asbestos Personal Injury Litigation, AMOF No. 87048500, (Balt. City Cir.Ct. Feb. 14, 1990)(Letter–Order) .... The Owens–Illinois appeal was dismissed in April 1990 by the Maryland Court of Special Appeals. See Owens–Illinois, Inc. v. Kenneth R. Feinberg, PHC No. 93 (Ct. Special App. Apr. 19, 1990) .... In April 1990, after Mr. Feinberg was moving towards a final critical phase of his mediation efforts in the *Brooklyn Navy Yard* cases, Owens–Illinois moved to disqualify him in the instant litigation. The Owens–Illinois papers are almost verbatim copies of its papers in the Maryland litigation.

II. THE IMPORTANCE OF ALTERNATIVE DISPUTE RESOLUTION ADVANCES AND PROPOSALS

Mediation in mass tort litigation such as the asbestos cases is of vital importance to the public, interested parties, the courts and the legal profession. The cost, both in specific outlays of the parties and the burdens these complex cases place on the courts by preventing or substantially delaying adjudication in criminal and other civil matters, as well as in high transactional costs that prevent claimants from obtaining reasonable awards promptly, warrants every effort to avoid expensive and unnecessary litigation. Without such mediation efforts by judges, magistrates and others our calendar system would break down. Many litigants would simply find the courthouse door closed.

The mediator—whether judge or special master—must work independently with each of the parties. It must be assumed that the relationship between the mediator and each of the parties and their counsel will be open, candid and forthcoming. *See, e.g.,* Henderson, *Settlement Masters,* in Center for Public Resources Legal Program, ADR AND THE COURTS: A MANUAL FOR JUDGES AND LAWYERS 233 (E. Fine ed.1987)(district judge's views on mediation process). The settlement master must hold *ex parte* "frank, confidential discussion[s]" with all parties so that each privately can inform the master of the strengths and weaknesses of its case and hear the master's evaluation of the case. * * * Neither the judge nor opposing counsel is privy to these individual discussions. * * * The parties engaged in a mediated settlement process recognize that they must, if the process is to work, fully disclose to the mediator their needs and tactics—not only those that have been publicly revealed, but also their private views and internal arrangements. Information revealed to the mediator should include—absent a confidential communication privilege—relationships to insurers, overall strategy, corporate politics and the like.

Much the same position is taken when the court itself acts as a mediator in the large number of cases in which a judge or a magistrate works closely with the parties to assist them in settling pending cases. It is standard practice for the presiding judge or magistrate to meet separately with each of the parties for a candid discussion of strategy and the needs of the party. Sometimes these sessions will be attended by high officials of one of the parties in addition to the attorneys. Often insurance counsel will attend so that the judge can appreciate fully the difficulties faced and positions taken by each party and make helpful suggestions.

Thus the mediator, in the form of judge, magistrate, special master, referee or other privately appointed person, must be fully apprised if he or she is to take advantage of the special circumstances of each case. The role of the mediator is often that of the honest broker who must suggest a solution giving advantage to both sides and minimizing the price that each must pay. *See generally* W. Brazil, *Effective Approaches to Settlement* (1988); D. Provine, *Settlement Strategies for Federal*

Judges (1986); R. Fisher and W. Vry, *Getting to Yes* (1981); H. Will, R. Merhige, Jr. and A. Rubin, *The Role of the Judge in the Settlement Process* (1977); F. Lacey, *The Judge's Role in the Settlement of Civil Suits* (1977); Lynch and Levine, *The Settlement of Federal District Court Cases: A Judicial Perspective,* 67 Or.L.Rev. 239 (1988); Galanter, *The Emergence of the Judge as a Mediator in Civil Cases,* 69 Judicature 256 (1986); Schuck, *The Role of Judges in Settling Complex Cases: The Agent Orange Example,* 53 U.Chi.L.Rev. 337 (1986). Examples of this technique are found in general litigation, mass torts, labor and elsewhere. *See, e.g.,* Center for Public Resources Legal Program, ADR AND THE COURTS: A MANUAL FOR JUDGES AND LAWYERS 11, 207–255 (E. Fine ed.1987); A. Talbot, SETTLING THINGS (1983)(evaluating mediation of environmental disputes); Rowe, *Study on Paths to a "Better Way": Litigation, Alternatives, and Accommodation,* 89 Duke L.J. 824 (1989). A considerable amount of teaching in the law schools is now devoted to mediation and alternative dispute resolution. *See, e.g.,* n.Rogers and C. McEwen, MEDIATION: LAW, POLICY, PRACTICE (1989)(treatise); L. Riskin and J. Westbrook, DISPUTE RESOLUTION AND LAWYERS (1987)(casebook); L. Kanowitz, CASES AND MATERIALS ON ADR (1986)(casebook); *Journal of Dispute Resolution* (published since 1984 by the University of Missouri at Columbia School of Law).

III. ETHICAL OBLIGATIONS OF MEDIATOR

A. Law

In general a special master or referee should be considered a judge for purposes of judicial ethics rules. *See* Code of Judicial Conduct For United States Judges, 69 F.R.D. 273, 286 (1975)(approved by Judicial Conference of the United States, April 1973 and amended)(Code of Judicial Conduct applicable to special masters); Standards Relating to Judicial Discipline and Disability Retirement, Rule 1.2, Comment (same). *Accord* Belfiore v. New York Times Co., 826 F.2d 177, 185 (2d Cir. 1987)(Code of Judicial Conduct For United States Judges applies to special masters), *cert. denied,* 484 U.S. 1067, 108 S.Ct. 1030, 98 L.Ed.2d 994 (1988). This conclusion is not undermined by the fact that the federal and state statutes governing the recusal of judges, justices or magistrates, *see* 28 U.S.C. § 455 and N.Y.Jud.Law § 14, do not by their terms cover special masters or referees.

The Court of Appeals for the Second Circuit appears not to have explicitly addressed the question of whether the same standard governing disqualification of a judge should apply to special masters. *See* Rios v. Enterprise Ass'n of Steamfitters Local 638, 860 F.2d 1168, 1173–74 (2d Cir.1988)(observing that federal case law is ambivalent regarding whether special masters should be held to same standards of impartiality as judges). Other federal courts have required special masters to meet the same ethical standards as judges. *See, e.g.,* Jenkins v. Sterlacci, 849 F.2d 627, 630 n.1, 631–32 (D.C.Cir.1988)("[I]nsofar as special masters perform duties functionally equivalent to those performed by a judge, they must be held to the same standards as judges for purposes of disqualification.''); United States v. Conservation Chemical Co., 106 F.R.D. 210, 234 (W.D.Mo.1985)(same). But see Morgan v. Kerrigan, 530 F.2d 401, 426 (1st Cir.)(applying lower standard of impartiality to masters than to judges), *cert. denied,* 426 U.S. 935, 96 S.Ct. 2648, 49 L.Ed.2d 386 (1976).

Section 4301 of the New York Civil Practice Law and Rules provides that a referee appointed to determine an issue or perform an act "shall have all of the powers of a court in performing a like function." Impliedly, then, the standards of judicial conduct applicable to judges also apply to a referee. *See, e.g.,* Moers v. Gilbert, 175 Misc. 733, 25 N.Y.S.2d 114, 118 (Sup.Ct.), *aff'd,* 261 A.D. 957, 27 N.Y.S.2d 425 (1st Dep't 1941)(holding that the provisions of New York judicial disqualification statute apply to court-appointed referees).

For purposes of deciding this motion we accept the movant's proposition that special masters and referees should be held to the same standards as judges. We see no need to distinguish between state or federal appointees. Both should be held to equally high standards. Both should be above suspicion. Since the use of special masters for purposes of settlement is more prevalent in the federal courts, the statutory and case precedents are primarily federal.

Under federal law, a judge may be disqualified in two situations that are relevant to the instant motion: 1) where "impartiality might reasonably be questioned," 28 U.S.C. § 455(a), and 2) where there is "a personal bias or prejudice concerning a party, or personal knowledge of disputed evidentiary facts concerning the proceeding." *Id.* § 455(b)(1). Section 455(a) "sets out an objective standard for recusal, creating the so-called 'appearance of justice' rule." DeLuca v. Long Island Lighting Co., 862 F.2d 427, 428 (2d Cir.1988)(citation omitted).

The federal test of impartiality "is what a reasonable person, knowing and understanding all the facts and circumstances, would believe." In re Drexel Burnham Lambert Inc., 861 F.2d 1307, 1309 (2d Cir.1988). As the legislative history of the 1974 amendments to section 455 emphasizes when explaining subsection (a): [d]isqualification for lack of impartiality must have a reasonable basis. Nothing in this proposed legislation should be read to warrant the transformation of a litigant's fear that a judge may decide a question against him into a "reasonable fear" that the judge will not be impartial. H.R.Rep. No. 1453, 93d Cong., 2d Sess. 4–5, *reprinted in* 1974 U.S.Code Cong. & Admin.News 6351, 6354–55.

With regard to § 455(b)(1), any "alleged bias and prejudice to be disqualifying must stem from an extrajudicial source and result in an opinion on the merits on some basis other than what the judge learned from his participation in the case." United States v. Grinnell Corp., 384 U.S. 563, 583, 86 S.Ct. 1698, 1710, 16 L.Ed.2d 778 (1966). Accord People v. Moreno, 70 N.Y.2d 403, 407, 521 N.Y.S.2d 663, 666, 516 N.E.2d 200, 202–03 (1987)(holding New York State judges to same disqualification standard)(*citing Grinnell,* 384 U.S. at 583, 86 S.Ct. at 1710).

The sole statutory authority for disqualification of a judge under New York State law is Section 14 of the Judiciary Law. That provision states that a judge may not take part in a proceeding involving either the judge or the judge's relatives up to the sixth degree of consanguinity or in a proceeding in which the judge or relatives have a direct interest in the litigation. The New York Court of Appeals has held that "absent a legal disqualification under Judiciary Law § 14, a Trial Judge is the sole arbiter of recusal." People v. Moreno, 70 N.Y.2d 403, 405, 521 N.Y.S.2d 663, 665, 516 N.E.2d 200, 201 (1987).

There are also rules governing judicial conduct which are made binding upon New York State Judges by the Rules of the Chief Administrator of the Courts. *See* 22 N.Y.C.R.R. § 100.1 *et seq.* These rules follow the language of the Code of Judicial Conduct promulgated by the American Bar Association, adopted by the New York State Bar Association and codified in Book 29 of McKinney's Consolidated Laws of New York. Under the heading "avoiding impropriety and the appearance of impropriety," Rule 100.2 of the New York Code of Rules and Regulations states that a judge should "conduct himself or herself at all times in a manner that promotes public confidence in the integrity and impartiality of the Judiciary."

In defining avoidance of the appearance of impropriety, Rule 100.3 states a judge should disqualify himself or herself "in a proceeding in which his or her impartiality might reasonably be questioned" including situations in which "the judge served as a lawyer in the matter in controversy...." The determination of impropriety in any given situation, however, remains within the discretion of the judge. *See* People v. Moreno, 70 N.Y.2d 403, 407, 521 N.Y.S.2d 663, 666, 516 N.E.2d 200, 202–03 (1987)(absent statutory disqualification, standard of review is abuse of discretion); Johnson v. Hornblass, 93 A.D.2d 732, 461 N.Y.S.2d 277, 279 (1st Dep't 1983).

Owens–Illinois raises an additional issue concerning the appointment of a referee under New York law, claiming that consent of the parties is a prerequisite. While consent is necessary for a referee appointed to hear and determine a controversy pursuant to CPLR § 4317(a), it is not necessary for an appointment under CPLR § 4311 or CPLR § 4320(a). The order appointing Mr. Feinberg in no way authorizes him to hear and determine controversies. Rather his position is to "assist the parties and the courts in promptly settling these cases subject to the further order of the courts." In re Joint Eastern and Southern Districts Asbestos Litigation; In re New York City Asbestos Litigation, 129 F.R.D. 434, 435 (E.D.N.Y. & N.Y.Sup.Ct.1990).

This is the same role that Mr. Feinberg has played in Maryland. If the settlement process is not successful, all parties retain the right to a jury trial. Therefore, the limitations imposed by CPLR § 4317 are irrelevant.

The issue of whether a judge should be disqualified requires careful examination of the particular setting of the dispute to determine whether the charge could reasonably be construed as bringing into question the trier's impartiality. *See* In re Drexel Burnham Lambert Inc., 861 F.2d 1307, 1309 (2d Cir.1988).

Examination of the context is particularly important in the case of mediators, where the courts have recognized that it is inevitable that special masters—like court-appointed experts, but unlike judges—will often be chosen from the ranks of practicing attorneys who themselves have prior expertise in the subject matter and prior association with experts in the field. *See* Rios v. Enterprise Ass'n of Steamfitters Local 638, 860 F.2d 1168, 1174–75 (2d Cir.1988). Cf. Scott v. Spanjer Bros., Inc., 298 F.2d 928, 931–32 (2d Cir.1962)(finding that medical expert appointed by court to assist court and jury need not be disqualified because he allegedly had a great deal of experience as "plaintiff's doctor"). In light of this inevitability, the Court of Appeals for the Second Circuit has found as a "general 'rule that disqualification [of a special master] is a matter for the exercise of discretion by the district judge, unless actual bias has been demonstrated.'" Rios v. Enterprise Ass'n of Steamfitters Local 638, 860 F.2d 1168, 1174 (2d Cir.1988). *Cf.* Lipton v. Lipton, 128 Misc.2d 528, 489 N.Y.S.2d 994, 1000 (Sup.Ct. 1985)("[A] referee should be removed only for good and substantial reasons.")

As an officer of the court the special master remains bound to respect the confidentiality of and refrain from using to Owens–Illinois' disadvantage any information imparted to him under seal of confidentiality by that company in the course of his legislative or mediation efforts. *Cf.* Code of Professional Responsibility, N.Y.Jud.Law App., EC 4–5.

B. *Facts and Conclusion*

The gravamen of Owens–Illinois' complaint is that Mr. Feinberg, in the context of a prior attorney-client relationship during the early and mid–1980's, became privy to "highly sensitive" and candid internal information and that, as a result, his impartiality in the current case might reasonably be questioned. Mr. Feinberg must now possess, in less dated but presumably equally forthcoming form, confidential information of a similar nature as a result of his current mediation efforts in Maryland and New York. As already noted *supra* in Part I, Mr. Feinberg obtained the earlier information for purposes of general legislative representation, distinct from the representation or advising of Owens–Illinois in its defense of asbestos personal injury litigation. In his present role as a neutral mediator charged with assisting the parties in achieving a settlement and with pursuing the goals of the alternative dispute resolution process outlined by the courts, he is not an advocate for either Owens–Illinois, or for any other party whose interests may be inimical to those of Owens–Illinois.

Owens–Illinois has failed to make any showing that as a result of any alleged conflict of interest, it has or will be adversely affected. See McLaughlin v. Union Oil Co. of California, 869 F.2d 1039, 1047 (7th

Cir.1989)("Bias ... requires evidence that the [judicial] officer had it 'in' for the party for reasons unrelated to the officer's view of the law, erroneous as that view might be."). Under these circumstances it can not be said that it has demonstrated by any possible standard that Mr. Feinberg is biased against Owens–Illinois. *See, e.g.,* Rios v. Enterprise Ass'n of Steamfitters Local 638, 860 F.2d 1168, 1174 (2d Cir.1988)(citation omitted). Here, as already pointed out by the Maryland court, it is clear from the record that no reasonable lawyer or member of the public who understood the nature of the mediator's role or the facts relied upon by the moving party could possibly question the impartiality of Mr. Feinberg.

IV.   Res Judicata and Collateral Estoppel

A.   Facts

The same issue of disqualification has already been fully adjudicated between the same parties in the Maryland asbestos litigation. *See* In re Asbestos Personal Injury Litigation, AMOF No. 87048500, (Balt. City Cir.Ct. Feb. 14, 1990)(Letter–Order denying Owens–Illinois' Motion to Disqualify Special Master Kenneth R. Feinberg, Esq.), app. dismissed sub nom., Owens–Illinois, Inc. v. Kenneth R. Feinberg, PHC No. 93 (Ct.Special App. Apr. 19, 1990).

During the course of the Maryland litigation Owens–Illinois raised objections to Mr. Feinberg's appointment as settlement master based on his prior representation of the Committee for Equitable Compensation on two occasions. Both times the objections were rejected. The first occurred in early September 1989 shortly after the presiding judge announced his intention to appoint Mr. Feinberg. At that time Owens–Illinois, together with at least one plaintiff firm, objected informally by letter and in a conference with the Judge. After "considering carefully" the claim, Judge Levin held that even if, as Owens–Illinois claimed, the information, strategies and positions explained to Mr. Feinberg and his law firm colleagues and the knowledge they gained while representing the Committee were relevant to Owens–Illinois' current position in the Maryland asbestos personal injury litigation, "that furnishes no basis for disqualifying Mr. Feinberg from acting as a Special Master for this court." Letter from Judge Levin to Messrs. B. Ford Davis and Harry S. Johnson (Sept. 19, 1989)(overruling Owens–Illinois' objections).

Judge Levin went on to observe that as a settlement master, Mr. Feinberg will not act or be in the position of hearing daily two sides of continuing controversies and then impartially deciding in favor of one side or the other. He will not act in a judicial role. Rather, he will be charged with devising and creating an ADR system within 90 days (plus a reasonable implementation time). The resultant procedures and techniques will be designed to dispose of the Baltimore City cases on a fair and efficient basis. This court feels that the vast majority of the cases can be disposed of in this manner. Any cases that cannot be so resolved will be disposed by either some consensual ADR method or ultimately by trial. Indeed, I feel that we shall know very soon whether such ADR system can work in Baltimore City, (and possibly in the rest of the State, for that matter). I feel confident that it will work. Therefore, I do not feel that [Owens–Illinois'] objection is well-founded. It is further significant to this court that even though there are many other members of [the Committee for Equitable Compensation] who are presently defendants in asbestos personal injury cases in Baltimore City, none save [Owens–Illinois] has objected even though the interest and objectives of such [Committee for Equitable Compensation] members is analytically the same as [Owens–Illinois']. While this court is aware that there are many other qualified persons who could act as impartial mediators, the appointment of a Special Master is not a mediation-specific appointment. It is rather an ADR-specific appointment. In this latter connection, Mr. Feinberg comes very well equipped * * *. He has already spent an enormous amount of time with counsel for plaintiffs and counsel for defendants and has specific plans for further activity. He works well with the court system. *Id.*

In a December 1989 conference with all the Maryland parties Mr. Feinberg himself raised the fact that there had been an objection lodged against him. Neither Owens–Illinois nor any other party responded. On January 12, 1990, however, Owens–Illinois made a formal motion to disqualify Mr. Feinberg. The matter was subsequently briefed by both Owens–Illinois and Mr. Feinberg. On February 14, 1990 Judge Levin determined that the motion must be denied for two reasons: 1) on the basis of laches or, alternatively, 2) because the relief sought was both unnecessary and unwarranted since Owens–Illinois could adequately protect itself by simply withdrawing from the ADR process at any time. In re Asbestos Personal Injury Litigation, AMOF No. 87048500, (Balt. City Cir.Ct. Feb. 14, 1990)(Letter–Order). Judge Levin wrote:

> To ... derail an ADR process that has been in operation for more than five months seems to be pure overkill. Moreover, the fact that [Owens–Illinois] is the only member of [the Committee for Equitable Compensation] to object serves to fortify this Court's conclusion that disqualification would not be appropriate. * * *

Id. Owens–Illinois' subsequent appeal to the Maryland Court of Special Appeals—which was opposed by several other asbestos manufacturers who had been Committee members and who are also defendants in the instant litigation—was dismissed, apparently on the ground of lack of finality. Owens–Illinois, Inc. v. Kenneth R. Feinberg, PHC No. 93 (Md.Ct. Special App. Apr. 5, 1990). *See also* Memorandum [of other defendants] in Support of Defendants' Motion to Dismiss, In re Owens–Illinois, Inc.'s Motion to Disqualify Special Master Kenneth R. Feinberg for Alleged Conflict of Interest, PHC No. 93 (Md.Ct.Special App. Apr. 5, 1990)("The ADR procedure is clearly voluntary, and nothing that the Special Master does is binding upon any of its participants. Owens–Illinois, Inc. is therefore free to participate or not in the ADR process as it chooses, and to accept or reject what the Special Master proposes. Thus, the Order neither determines nor concludes Owens–Illinois, Inc.'s rights in any sense.").

B.   Law

A state or federal judgment regarding a motion for disqualification of a judge must be accorded res judicata effect. *See, e.g.,* Tonti v. Petropoulous, 656 F.2d 212, 216–17 (6th Cir.1981)(affirming district court ruling that doctrine of res judicata barred plaintiff's claim that he was denied a fair trial because of bias and prejudice of presiding probate judge where same claim had been fully and fairly litigated in and decided by state appellate courts); Patterson v. Aiken, 628 F.Supp. 1068, 1076 (N.D.Ga.1985)(claim that certain federal district judges were biased is barred by principles of res judicata and collateral estoppel because it was argument that could have been or was raised in prior lawsuits), *aff'd mem.,* 784 F.2d 403 (11th Cir.1986); Collins v. Collins, 597 F.Supp. 33, 36 n.3 (N.D.Ga.1984)("The fact that a court of competent jurisdiction has adjudicated the issue of whether [the judge] should have been recused from further involvement in the [lawsuit] would preclude relitigation of that issue in this court under the doctrine of res judicata."). *Cf.* Margoles v. Johns, 798 F.2d. 1069, 1072 n.4 (7th Cir.1986)(citation omitted)(noting that failure to raise question of judge's impartiality in any post-judgment or appeal proceeding creates substantial questions of waiver and res judicata), *cert. denied,* 482 U.S. 905, 107 S.Ct. 2482, 96 L.Ed.2d 374 (1987).

C.   Conclusion

Mr. Feinberg's role as settlement master and referee in the instant litigation has been essentially identical to that which he pioneered in the consolidated Maryland cases. The New York courts appointed Mr. Feinberg in part on the basis of his Maryland experience and with the understanding that he would attempt to reproduce that methodology, if possible, in settling the Brooklyn Navy Yard litigation. Nor did this intention come as a surprise to the parties. At a mid-January conference with the parties, which was attended by Owens–Illinois, these courts explicitly discussed their desire to appoint a "Ken Feinberg-type . . . settling master [to do] what he's doing in Maryland." At a subsequent conference in mid-February the courts again informed the parties, including counsel for Owens–Illinois, that "[t]he Maryland approach seems . . . desirable." On neither occasion did Owens–Illinois raise any objection.

The only discernible difference in the Maryland and New York litigations is one of re-labelling the same argument rather than of raising a new and distinct theory. Whereas the Owens–Illinois Maryland motion relied solely on a claimed breach of attorney-client privilege, in the instant litigation it has added to the privilege argument a federal appearance-of-impropriety charge. This "new" argument is based on the applicability to special masters of the Code of Judicial Conduct for United States Judges. 69 F.R.D. 273 (1975).

* * *

V. Laches and Waiver

A. *Law*

Laches will rarely be applied in cases of claimed lack of impartiality. The reason is almost jurisdictional. It flows not only from the natural desire of the courts to both be and appear impartial so that their judgments will be accepted by the parties and the public at large, but also from the fact that there is no applicable statute of limitations. Thus, even after a case has been fully decided, should information come to the attention of a litigant suggesting partiality, the matter can be raised anew. *See, e.g.,* Liljeberg v. Health Services Acquisition Corp., 486 U.S. 847, 108 S.Ct. 2194, 100 L.Ed.2d 855 (1988)(citation omitted)(in appropriate cases a judgment may be set aside under Fed.R.Civ.P. 60(b)(6) when a judge fails to recuse himself in violation of 28 U.S.C. § 455(a)); Noli v. Commissioner of Internal Revenue, 860 F.2d 1521, 1527 (9th Cir.1988)(citation omitted)(failure to move for recusal at trial level does not absolutely preclude raising on appeal issue of recusal under 28 U.S.C. § 455).

Nonetheless, where the alleged conflict of interest is known to a party at the outset of the proceeding, the party must make a motion for disqualification in a timely manner. *See* Hardy v. United States, 878 F.2d 94, 97 & n.4 (2d Cir.1989)(§ 455(a) recusal claim, whether made in collateral attack or on direct appeal, must be asserted by a timely motion); In re Int'l Business Machines Corp., 618 F.2d 923, 932 (2d Cir.1980)(finding timeliness requirement under 28 U.S.C. § 455 even in absence of explicit statutory provision).

Courts that have insisted upon holding special masters and referees to the high standards applicable to judges in matters affecting disqualification have acknowledged that parties objecting on the basis of an appearance of partiality must take action to eliminate the perceived conflict-of-interest in a timely fashion or risk being barred from the attempt. *See, e.g.,* Jenkins v. Sterlacci, 849 F.2d 627, 633 (D.C.Cir. 1988). *See also* National Auto Brokers v. General Motors Corp., 572 F.2d 953, 958–59 (2d Cir.1978)(affirming denial of motion to disqualify judge in large part because the motion was not made at threshold of litigation, but in untimely fashion after five weeks of trial and months after facts had become known to counsel and because the alleged conflict had been public knowledge for years), *cert. denied,* 439 U.S. 1072, 99 S.Ct. 844, 59 L.Ed.2d 38 (1979).

* * *

B. *Facts and Conclusion*

The facts in the case at bar provide even stronger support for a finding that Owens–Illinois has effectively waived objection to any appearance of partiality than did the circumstances in *Jenkins.* There can be no doubt that Owens–Illinois possessed not merely constructive, but actual knowledge of the special master's alleged conflict of interest.

The existence of the alleged conflict of interest was known to Owens–Illinois, as well as to the other defendants who had been members of the Asbestos Compensation Coalition or Committee for Equitable Compensation, from the outset of Mr. Feinberg's appointment. Prior to his appointment by Judge Levin Mr. Feinberg had disclosed to the Baltimore court and the parties the details of his earlier representation of both the Coalition and the Committee. *See* Code of Judicial Conduct, *supra,* Canon 3.D (one disqualified by reason of appearance only may, instead of withdrawing, disclose on the record the basis of disqualification which parties and lawyers may waive); 28 U.S.C. § 455(e) (same). Owens–Illinois first raised reservations in September 1989 regarding Mr. Feinberg's ability to serve as an impartial special master in settling thousands of asbestos claims the company was defending in the Maryland litigation. Nevertheless, Owens–Illinois waited nearly five and one-half months, until January 1990, before moving to disqualify Mr. Feinberg.

Owens–Illinois' conduct in the instant litigation is reminiscent of its conduct in Maryland. When the courts and the special master-referee met with liaison counsel for the parties in the instant litigation on February 13, 1990 they set a rigid schedule as follows: (1) one month, from March 1–April 1, 1990 for collecting data on the Brooklyn Navy Shipyard cases; (2) one month, from April 1–May 1 to agree on a settlement methodology; (3) one month, from May 1 to June 1 to actually settle all or appreciably all of the cases and, failing that; (4) appropriate action by the courts for prompt disposition. Owens–Illinois has waited until Mr. Feinberg's term as special master-referee in the *Brooklyn Navy Yard* cases is close to complete before taking any action. This delay, coupled with the lack of specificity concerning the purported prejudice, suggests that the partiality claimed is more a figment of imagination and an attempt to delay settlement than a matter of real concern.

VI. ACTUAL PREJUDICE

There remains only the argument that Mr. Feinberg's participation will or has actually prejudiced Owens–Illinois. But, as noted *supra* in Part III, no evidence has been presented of that eventuality that could be credited by a reasonable observer with knowledge of these proceedings. Owens–Illinois acknowledged at oral argument the complete absence of any actual prejudice.

Mediation and settlement negotiations are now moving toward the critical stage. Delays should not be encouraged. The mediator has already expended an enormous amount of effort meeting individually with the parties and in meetings with various groups in assembling information, in conducting research, in consulting with the courts involved, and in making numerous suggestions. See Rios v. Enterprise Ass'n of Steamfitters Local 638, 860 F.2d 1168, 1175 (2d Cir.1988)(upholding district court's refusal to disqualify special master in part because he had been serving in that capacity for a number of years before any suggestion of recusal was made and had already acquired a considerable body of experience in the proceedings in question); National Auto Brokers v. General Motors Corp., 572 F.2d 953, 958–59 (2d Cir.1978)(affirming denial of motion to disqualify where judge had, in course of presiding over case, acquired valuable background of experience), *cert. denied,* 439 U.S. 1072, 99 S.Ct. 844, 59 L.Ed.2d 38 (1979).

With less than two weeks before a final report is due, to replace the mediator at this stage would be to largely negate the enormous amount of effort by all those involved to date. Moreover, it would impinge on the court's calendar in connection with hundreds of cases. If settlement is not consummated, the courts will move towards trial early in September and a huge expenditure of effort in connection with discovery, preparation and research by the courts will be required. In addition, scores of other cases will have to be moved from the trial docket. This will affect the work of many other lawyers and judges.

In this case it cannot be doubted that whatever knowledge of the moving party's internal procedure was acquired by Mr. Feinberg some years ago is by now stale and outmoded. It has been replaced by more current knowledge required in the course of mediation efforts in the Maryland and New York cases.

VII. CONCLUSION

The motion has no merit. The court does not, however, find that it was made in bad faith. It is the obligation of the parties to bring to the court's attention anything that may lead to the questioning of its reputation for impartiality and fairness. Owens–Illinois did not act improperly in making the motion. In the Maryland litigation the court noted that the moving party agreed that if its motion were denied, it would proceed with the alternative dispute resolution mediation efforts without holding back in any way. It is assumed that this is the position of the moving party in the New York Litigation.

The motion was denied from the bench in view of the necessity of speed in the mediation efforts. This opinion is being issued now to explain the reasons for that oral decision from the bench.

So ordered.

* * *

Notes and Questions

1. As the readings suggest, mass tort litigation has given rise to a small group of professional mass-tort special masters who have served in this capacity in multiple mass tort cases in several jurisdictions. Special masters most often are lawyers, many with previous careers in private practice. What is the potential for ethical problems in this setting? What professional responsibility rules govern mass tort special masters? Does it make a difference what tasks have been delegated to the special master? If the special master is serving as a mediator or settlement negotiator, what ethical rules apply? Should special masters be subject to attorney professional

responsibility rules relating to conflicts-of-interest and confidentiality strictures? Does it make sense to analogize a special masters' ethical duties to those of judges? Does the nature of mass tort litigation compel a relaxation of professional responsibility duties of special masters? For a discussion of ethical issues arising out of use of special masters, *see* Jack B. Weinstein, *Ethical Dilemmas in Mass Tort Litigation*, 88 Nw.U.L.Rev. 469 (1994). What ethical standards apply in federal court litigation? *See generally* Linda S. Mullenix, *Federal Multiforum Practice: Ethics and* Erie, 9 Geo. J. Legal Ethics ___ (1995).

2. Similar to ethical problems in the use of special masters, litigants in mass tort litigation also have sought to disqualify federal judges who serve in a dual capacity as trial and settlement judge. Should a federal judge who negotiates a mass tort settlement be permitted to then sit as the trial judge evaluating the settlement? *See* Bilello v. Abbott Laboratories, 825 F.Supp. 475 (E.D.N.Y.1993)(defendants in DES products liability actions moved to disqualify trial judge; conferences that trial judge conducted in his role as settlement judge did not require disqualification).

C. CASE STUDIES AND CRITIQUES

FRANCIS E. McGOVERN, TOWARD A FUNCTIONAL APPROACH FOR MANAGING COMPLEX LITIGATION

53 U.Chi.L.Rev. 440–441; 478–491 (1986).

I. INTRODUCTION

The managerial horse is out of the judicial barn. Federal Judicial Center and National Judicial College programs, the Federal Rules of Civil Procedure, and the *Manual for Complex Litigation Second* illustrate the significant commitment made by academics and leaders of the judiciary in encouraging judges to become more active litigation managers.

* * *

IV. MASS TORTS: CAN WE PRIORITIZE THE QUEUE?
A. *Problem*

* * *

In some jurisdictions the resolution of asbestos disease cases correlates with normal disposition rates. In other jurisdictions there is substantial stagnation. The variance can largely be explained by the rate and number of filings, the number of competing cases, the attention given by the judiciary, the behavioral patterns of the local bar, and the incentives of parties and attorneys. In jurisdictions where dockets have become overloaded, the resources of courts, attorneys, and parties are simply inadequate to cope. Typically an extremely small number of firms represents massive numbers of plaintiffs; it would not be unusual for a single lawyer with four associates to represent over a thousand clients. Defense teams are typically of similar size. The defendants' resources—in both defending suits and paying judgments—are often strained. These problems become particularly acute in the absence of cooperation among the lawyers. After August of 1982 the absence of the Manville attorneys, who had been the natural leaders of the defense effort, sometimes left an organizational vacuum which has exacerbated this situation.

Regardless of the local situation, approximately 98 percent of the asbestos disease cases that were resolved were settled; only 2 percent of the cases concluded with a jury verdict. Most settlements, however, occurred on the eve of trial. The major bottleneck was the scarcity of trial dates; judicial trial time became the scarcest resource in the dispute resolution process.

In 1983 there were almost 80 asbestos cases pending in the Northern District of Ohio. Some of them had been on file for over three years and had been assigned to nine different judges. Two trials had been held in federal court, one in state court, and 64 cases had been settled. Judge Thomas D. Lambros decided that the resolution rate of the asbestos disease cases had been sufficiently desultory and was so delaying the progress of unrelated cases that a new methodology was needed to handle them. He consolidated all the asbestos cases in his court and appointed two special masters to develop an Ohio Asbestos Litigation Case Management Plan (OAL Plan) for resolving all pending cases within a two-year period.

B. *Diagnosis*

The high settlement rates in asbestos disease cases can be explained in part by the medical consensus that asbestos does cause certain diseases—asbestosis, mesothelioma, and certain other cancers. The genuine issues in these lawsuits typically concern whether this plaintiff was exposed to asbestos, whether the asbestos was manufactured by these defendants, whether it was manufactured at a time when defendants did not fulfill their legal obligations to users of their products, and whether this plaintiff's injuries were asbestos-related. For individuals who had a disease caused by asbestos and who had experienced massive exposure to asbestos when the producers had a legal duty to reduce the risk of exposure to asbestos but did not, the only argument was over the amount of money that should be paid.

Ironically, the success of the obviously-injured plaintiffs created much of the asbestos litigation problem. Virtually anyone who had ever worked with asbestos had an incentive to bring suit. The commons became standing room only. Our traditional litigation mechanism, which values minimizing false-positive damage awards—awarding no compensation to undeserving plaintiffs—mandated first-come, first-served individual trials. As a result, a lengthy queue of litigants developed. Defendants and even some plaintiffs' attorneys had little incentive to expedite the decisionmaking process—the plaintiffs themselves bore the brunt of the slowdown.

Because of the extensive history of asbestos litigation, however, there was some theoretical support for an ADR methodology to prioritize the cases in the queue that Judge Lambros regarded as unacceptably long. [S]ome mechanism could identify the probable true positive and true negative plaintiffs early and inexpensively, then plaintiffs who had greater chances of succeeding might be placed at the head of the queue. Defendants appeared willing to settle in clear cases, but desired more scrutiny for the less obviously meritorious suits. If greater judicial resources were allocated to the more serious cases, they should settle quickly; then public acceptance should develop for the remaining cases to compete with other lawsuits for judicial attention. This was precisely what the Speedy Trial Act did by expediting the resolution of criminal cases.

This theory views litigation as an information system generating massive amounts of data, from which one can isolate the variables critical to jury awards and settlements. It then might be possible to list the outcome-determinative factors, weigh their relative importance, and create a model to predict the value of pending cases. Prioritizing can then be performed on a reasoned basis.

The arguably idiosyncratic nature of litigation outcomes might limit the predictive power of the information generated. In the mass tort context, however, it has been suggested that a marketplace of multiple trials, over time, results in a rough equilibrium of case values. This cyclical theory of mass torts holds that a defined pattern in these cases will culminate in trials and settlements having approximately equivalent outcomes. In the early stages of the cycle, defendants tend to win more cases than plaintiffs because of strategic and informational superiority. If the litigation has any merit, however, plaintiffs will eventually develop successful information and strategies and win an extremely high percentage of the cases tried. Next, the plaintiffs will bring cases for trial that stretch the envelope of viable plaintiffs too far, and defendants will create more effective counterstrategies, resulting in a reduced percentage of plaintiff victories. Eventually, after full aggregation and dissemination of information, crystallization of the law, and thorough development of strategies, there will be a rough equilibrium of trial results. Remaining variations will then be due to jury demographics, attorney caliber, and random events during trials. Although perhaps it is counterintuitive, settlements will also reflect this equilibrium: the average settlement amount will be virtually identical to the average jury verdict. The variance, however, will be substantially different. Settlements for similarly situated plaintiffs will be extremely similar; verdicts will vary in accordance with idiosyncrasies of the trial process.

If this cyclical theory of mass torts were remotely correct, it would be feasible to extrapolate from the information generated in the equilibrium state to predict the values of pending cases. If the parties could use these predictions to evaluate their cases prior to expending the substantial transaction costs associated with discovery and trial, both sides would have an incentive to settle. Under classic negotiation theory, most personal injury suits are viewed as zero-sum games or distributive bargains. Each additional dollar received by a plaintiff comes directly from a defendant's pocket. In contrast, furnishing both sides with case value predictions should permit them to bargain integratively. When the difference between defendant's offer and plaintiff's demand is less than the projected transaction costs for traditional trial, each side would benefit by settling anywhere between that offer and demand.

The key problem with this scenario relates to the fundamental goal of expediting payments to plaintiffs through private settlements. Defendants, eager to retain their limited resources by slowing the velocity of cash outflow, might still resist early settlements, particularly if they perceived that several jurisdictions would adopt similar procedures. Plaintiffs' attorneys might prefer traditional procedures because they tend to satisfice [sic] under the traditional system and would find the lack of public knowledge of jury verdicts detrimental to their efforts to seek recompense for as yet unidentified plaintiffs. Other incentives, such as limiting fees for plaintiffs' attorneys and structuring settlements over time, might be necessary to encourage defendants further. Given the small number of plaintiffs' attorneys and a recognition that their contingent fees involved little contingency, mass settlements might still be palatable even with these limitations. The fundamental problem here was to determine how far the court could and should go in creating artificial incentives that arguably would rob a party of its rights to due process by effectively coercing settlements.

C. Prescription

In accordance with the appointment by Judge Lambros, the special masters designed a case management plan that alters the traditional procedural model by adding both cooperative and inquisitorial components. Not all parties had complete data concerning past trials and settlements. Typically, a plaintiff achieved settlement by negotiating with individual defendants, who seemed less concerned with how much they paid in absolute dollars than with how much they paid relative to other defendants. As a result, some defendants preferred to keep their settlement amounts secret. Plaintiffs, not reluctant to play defendants off against each other, were the only ones to know the total settlement value of most cases. The masters arranged to gather that information and compile it in a form that each party could use.

The parties were interviewed in great detail concerning the objective and subjective factors by which they evaluated cases. Then discovery was scheduled so that the minimum information essential for an acceptable case evaluation would be gathered first. Next, a pretrial conference allowed the parties to explore settlement possibilities prior to expending substantial funds to obtain data that would be more valuable for trial. To assist this process, we examined the kinds of evidence typically gathered for various purposes, and attempted to ensure that the marginal cost of obtaining information for settlement did not exceed its marginal value. One by-product of applying this theory was to defer the most expensive discovery until after the initial settlement conference, thereby increasing the chances for integrative bargaining. Finally, the masters felt that communication breakdowns among the parties warranted the use of mediation. We recommended that Judge Lambros, who has a national reputation as an effective settlement facilitator, fulfill that role.

This prescription relied upon procedures that were generally acceptable to the parties as long as they felt they had the ultimate option of seeking a jury determination. We deferred recommending more draconian proposals that would intensify the pressures for settlement. The OAL Plan did, however, list a number of alterations that might be considered if the process did not function satisfactorily. Despite the mildness and acceptability of its innovations, the OAL Plan was criticized for valuing expedition over accuracy.

1. *Parties.* Given the large number of plaintiffs and the limited time Judge Lambros had allocated, it was necessary to consolidate cases for disposition. The cases were organized into separate clusters of five cases each. The key issue was how to constitute each cluster. Should we select cases by the traditional first-come, first-served method, or group similar cases to facilitate presenting evidence at trial, or combine cases representing each of the plaintiff categories? Differences-oriented negotiation theory suggested that settlements would be easier to achieve by creating bargaining groups including both weaker and stronger cases from each side's perspective. We decided, therefore, to select a representative case from each disease category. To streamline the process further, the clusters were organized into two separate tracks that would proceed concurrently through the litigation schedule. Thus, ten cases would be available for treatment at each stage of discovery, settlement negotiation, and trial.

While increasing the number of plaintiffs, the OAL Plan suggested reducing the number of defense counsel as much as possible. Since the local bar had de facto leaders, it was not necessary to appoint lead counsel. The negotiations among producers of asbestos and their insurers subsequently improved on this approach by hiring single counsel to represent multiple defendants.

These so-called Wellington negotiations also solved another problem encountered under the OAL Plan. Settlement and judgment dollars were generally paid by producers, multiple insurers, excess carriers, and reinsurers. Early in the asbestos litigation producers and insurers heatedly debated which parties bore the risk for asbestos-related injuries. Some focused on the time a plaintiff was exposed to asbestos, while others emphasized the time the disease manifested itself. Circuit courts of appeals have sharply differed on this issue, but it had become moot in the Sixth Circuit prior to the creation of the OAL Plan. The Wellington negotiations created a common mechanism for producers and insurers to pay settlements.

Another equally serious insurance problem remained. The majority of general comprehensive insurance policies provided a defined sum of money to indemnify the insured producers for settlement and judgment costs, and an undefined sum to pay defense costs associated with protecting the insured in the litigation. This type of contractual relationship created a moral hazard. The producers had already paid premiums entitling them to a virtually infinite amount of defense costs associated with indemnity payments up to the limits of the primary policy. Therefore, their incentives were to force the insurers to spend those dollars in order to protect the finite amount of indemnity dollars purchased. Many primary insurers, on the other hand, recognized that they would eventually have to tender all of the indemnity dollars contracted for. Their incentives were to reduce the transaction costs associated with compensating plaintiffs for their injuries because once indemnity dollars were exhausted, they would no longer be obliged to pay defense costs. These disparate incentives created disparate defense strategies. To assist the parties in resolving their conflict, Judge Lambros brought insurance company representatives into the negotiation process. The Wellington agreement eventually accomplished the same goal by creating a defined method for its members to pay both defense and indemnity costs.

Besides altering the configuration of existing parties, the OAL Plan expected the special masters and their assistants to act as neutral third parties, gathering and organizing information not otherwise available. The judge would also mediate between the parties, to seek areas for cooperation.

2. *Issues.* The OAL Plan neither expanded nor contracted issues. However, it divided issues into two categories and reconstituted the agenda for considering each category. In the first category were issues related to case evaluation. One of the masters concentrated on insuring that the minimal amount of discovery necessary for a threshold case evaluation was gathered first, including the total values of earlier similar cases. If the parties did not settle, then extensive discovery would be undertaken for trial.

The second category covered issues related to apportioning damages among defendants. The parties received information concerning the historic shares paid by each defendant in past trials and settlements. The Wellington negotiations obviated the need to develop these issues fully by undertaking separate negotiations to allocate responsibility among defendants using a system similar, but national in scope, to that proposed in the OAL Plan.

3. *Information.* In addition to the normal kinds of evidence generated in litigation, the OAL Plan provided two types of information concerning case values: historic trial and settlement values, and summary jury trial values. Neutral third parties gathered data on over 300 variables for each completely resolved case. Data collection was performed by trained individuals completing a data collection protocol, and

the data was entered into a computer for subsequent analysis. In conjunction with policy analysts, we created a decision support system to facilitate the parties' use of the collected data through computer-assisted negotiation.

First, a case-matching program listed the data from a pending case, located the three cases that it most resembled, and indicated which characteristics did and did not match. Second, the parties could use a decision tree analysis to evaluate cases by folding back sequential estimates of outcomes on preliminary issues and ultimately reaching a single case value. Third, a mathematical model using standard statistical analysis was designed to incorporate the relative importance of the critical variables during a final case evaluation. Finally, an expert system was created to mimic the decisionmaking process of attorneys who evaluate cases.

The case-matching program became the only operational form of assistance for the parties. Once the computer had produced the matching cases and their values, a hearing was held to discuss the pending cases. The parties could briefly state their analysis of each case, the matching cases were reviewed, and we estimated a settlement range from all this information. The settlement ranges generally varied between 10 and 20 percent, which was usually less than the transaction costs associated with trial. If both parties commenced negotiations within the suggested range, the chances of a settlement increased greatly.

D. Results

All 112 cases settled within 27 months of the implementation of the OAL Plan. All of the eventual settlements were within the special masters' range of predicted values.

1. *Economy.* At first glance, the OAL Plan appears enormously successful, but substantial problems cropped up in its implementation which deserve closer scrutiny. The cost for special masters, experts, computer runs, and other expenses of designing and implementing the OAL Plan during the three-year period was over $250,000, although a major grant from the National Institute for Dispute Resolution softened the impact on the parties. The court's and parties' time expenditures were also substantial. Multiple separate negotiations took place, some persisting over extended periods of time. Forty-three OAL Plan orders have been promulgated by the court.

Although some savings were produced because no trials had to be held, everyone's opportunity costs were nevertheless substantial. A pending evaluation of the OAL Plan will attempt to make simplifying assumptions and suggest how the cost in time and money compares to more traditional litigation. In all probability, any economic justification for the OAL Plan would have to be made in terms of a capital investment. In other words, funds were invested to produce an asset which is not exhausted by a single use. This approach could be justified in part by the adoption of OAL Plan components in other jurisdictions, such as the Eastern District of Texas and the District of Massachusetts, and by the Wellington Plan. However, the individual plaintiffs, who absorbed some of the costs of the OAL Plan, would find the capitalization argument less persuasive.

A reduction in error costs may be the strongest argument for the OAL Plan. Virtually all plaintiffs who received settlements had long histories of asbestos exposure and had received a medical diagnosis of some asbestos-related disease. There were no false negatives in the OAL Plan—anyone who met the exposure and injury criteria received some compensation. There may have been a small number of false positives, but the rigorous entry criteria minimized them.

2. *Fairness.* An evaluation for fairness also gives mixed reviews. The plaintiffs and their attorneys generally seemed pleased that the cases were being resolved speedily, without full trials and expensive discovery. Defendants and their attorneys seemed less satisfied. They found the original OAL Plan overly complex, the constant revisions disconcerting, and the court's interventionist posture constraining on their ability to represent their clients as they saw fit. Defendants did not feel that the settlements were excessive, but that they had insufficient opportunity to prepare complete defenses. They believe that as product liability law has been applied to asbestos cases, plaintiffs have the advantage and defendants must engage in extensive discovery to prove that a person does not deserve compensation. Plaintiffs' attorneys have typically responded to these arguments by noting a propensity for defense counsel to churn cases and for defendants to hold on to their assets as long as possible. The ongoing evaluation should give a clearer picture of the reality behind these sentiments.

3. *Other Values.* Plaintiffs and their attorneys also appeared to appreciate being able to participate in the evaluation conferences and did not view the decision support system as impinging on their individual sense of worth. Defendants and their attorneys, on the other hand, preferred the more traditional methodology for resolving cases and felt that the court had partially usurped their usual case management prerogatives. As a result, they reacted negatively to losing control of the litigation.

A final, compelling argument in favor of the OAL Plan is its consistency with the underlying values of product liability law. Most states, including Ohio, have adopted strict liability in tort, thereby making it easier for plaintiffs to recover. Society, through its expression of tort law, has decided to accept a greater frequency of personal injury awards in order to heighten the incentives to manufacturers to produce safer products. Much of the defendants' criticism concerning the value of expediting the litigation process can be viewed as a basic disagreement with the policies underlying strict tort liability.

Judge Lambros had decided in 1982 that traditional litigation was biased toward inefficient dispute resolution, and had asked the special masters to design a management plan that would reduce that inefficiency while maintaining other due process values. Far more sophisticated analysis will be necessary to determine the relative merits of the OAL Plan and the traditional litigation model. In this instance the ex ante analysis of the OAL Plan may appear more favorable than an ex post one.

FRANCIS F.E. McGOVERN, RESOLVING MATURE MASS TORT LITIGATION

69 B.U.L.Rev. 659, 663–667; 669–688 (1989).

* * *

I. ASBESTOS LITIGATION: HAS JUDGE ROY BEAN RETURNED?

* * *

[Description of Judge Parker's certification of the *Jenkins v. Raymark* class action, and procedures, omitted—*ed.*]

3. *Information*

Aside from the usual decisions common to any asbestos trial concerning liability and state-of-the-art, Judge Parker would also have asked the jury to determine a multiple of compensatory damages to be awarded to an entire class of plaintiffs. Normally, either jurors would receive individualized evidence for each plaintiff or the plaintiffs would be so similar that the evidence presented for each would be virtually identical. In most personal injury cases, however, the mechanics of causation and the extent of damages tend to vary considerably from plaintiff to plaintiff.

Judge Parker decided to appoint a special master, the author of this Article, to gather relevant information concerning each member of the class. By this process, the jury could benefit from both an individualized and a collective view of class members (1) for analyzing the proportionality of any award of punitive damages; and (2) for appreciating the typicality of the named representative class plaintiffs. The special master decided that the most effective approach would be to seek the cooperation of the parties and view the entire project as a joint venture. Rather than making this solely a court process, the parties' participation would both reduce cost and add to the legitimacy of the project.

The special master commenced negotiations with the parties to devise a data collection protocol. Experts hired by the special master began the process by composing a proposed list of critical asbestos disease case variables. Once the parties agreed on the appropriate information to be collected, negotiations began on a format for collecting that information. The court's experts then designed a data collection instrument. Eventually everyone agreed on two virtually identical protocols—one to be completed by the plaintiffs and one by the defendants—containing 109 questions requesting 512 separate pieces of data. Paralegals and attorneys for the parties, under the supervision of carefully screened public health professionals selected by the special master, completed their respective protocols. In addition, a team of neutral professionals spot-checked a percentage of the protocols to insure accuracy.

Once the data had been collected, it was entered into a central computer. A total of approximately 2.3 million items of information were gathered. The special master, in conjunction with neutral programmers, prepared a system of programming logic that organized the data into an aggregate compilation of information. Background information consisted of the class members' average age, sex, vital status, income, and alleged disease, as well as a distribution of these characteristics among the class plaintiffs. Asbestos disease data included dates of first exposure to asbestos, total years of exposure to asbestos, level of exposure to asbestos, employment, smoking history, knowledge of asbestos danger, use of protective devices, applicable statutes of limitations, and exposure to other substances. Finally, medical data concerning clinical symptoms, pulmonary function tests, radiographic findings, blood gas studies, pathology/biopsy results, type, cause, and origin of cancer, other diseases, and medical expenses was also compiled. The special master and experts prepared a computer program that would display this information for each individual plaintiff. The special master also prepared a slide series that displayed the characteristics of the class members. In addition, he made a video tape of the proposed presentation for the jury.

Judge Parker contemplated two separate presentations to the jury by the special master. First, the special master would present introductory evidence concerning the general characteristics of the plaintiffs, accompanied by a preview of their more detailed asbestos exposure and medical history. Second, following testimony by plaintiffs and defendants concerning liability and general causation, the special master would offer further evidence on exposure and medical data. Once the parties saw the programming logic, data, slides, and video tape, they agreed to present the information to the jury with the special master available to answer questions. The data collection process was begun on December 23 and ended with the presentation at trial on March 12—a period of less than three months.

D. Results

Jenkins v. Raymark was tried for twenty days. The trial commenced with the special master's presentation of the vital statistics of the class members and with a preview of data to be presented after the jury had heard evidence concerning exposure and medical aspects of asbestos related diseases. The plaintiffs called thirteen witnesses, but before the defendants presented their case, the parties settled for a total of $137 million—$107 million in new money to be paid over three years and $30 million from earlier partial settlements. The settlement allocated a separate amount of money to each plaintiffs' attorney and provided that the attorney, subject to review by the court, would allocate the money among his clients. The judge examined the award to each class member, reviewed the awards in light of composite and individual data, and then made several changes. The average value of the class action cases was twenty-five percent lower than the mean of prior settlement values.

The court also reduced the attorneys' fees by limiting the normal thirty to forty percent contingent fee contracts to no more than twenty percent. Lead counsel for the plaintiffs received one percent of the settlement for his role in the trial.

1. Economy

The cost to the judicial system for the class action approach in both time and money was substantially less than what an equivalent number of individual trials would have generated, even taking into account the supplemental judicial resources devoted to appeals, pre-trial matters, and settlement negotiations. The cost to the parties, however, was greater than a trial with a smaller number of plaintiffs. In addition, the parties bore the expenses of the lead trial counsel and the special master. Yet if costs were pro-rated over the entire class, the per-plaintiff transaction costs were substantially less than for a similarly situated group of individual plaintiffs.

Though opportunity costs were negligible, potential error costs remained considerable. The defendants vigorously argued that a jury was incapable of making error-free decisions when confronted with such a staggering amount of complex information; the decision-making process was simply unworkable. Jurors would average, anchor, or utilize emotional techniques to help them cope with an otherwise unintelligible mass of data. The plaintiffs, however, contended that asking the jury to look at the big picture—all relevant asbestos products over a large period of time in the context of determining who knew what and when—would improve overall accuracy and consistency.

The special master's presentation concerning the members of the class alleviated some of these concerns, particularly in regard to punitive damages. Rather than answering questions concerning individual plaintiffs, the jury could focus on the group as a whole. They could be wrong in any specific instance but, as long as their aggregate analysis was correct, their overall error rate would be low. The data was also effective in the attorneys' and judge's allocation of monies among the plaintiffs.

2. Fairness

The defendants protested that the entire process failed on grounds of predictability, rationality, and equality of opportunity and strategy. A number of plaintiffs' attorneys agreed but, since they decided to opt out of the class, their arguments went unheard.

Notwithstanding the guidelines in the Federal Rules of Civil Procedure, Rule 23 had never before been used in the context of a mass tort trial prior to *Jenkins*. The defendants viewed the class action as leading inexorably to an unfavorable financial result. Instead of resolving the

753 cases individually over a several-year period, the claims would all be paid at once. Many of them would be paid long before resolution of similarly situated claims in other jurisdictions.

If these cases had proceeded to trial, a jury might have denied liability or punitive damages, but the consensus among attorneys for both sides was that a $300 million punitive damage award was probable. The defendants felt that they simply could not take that risk, even with prospects for a favorable appeal. A single $300 million award would also have severely damaged the Asbestos Claims Facility.

The plaintiffs' attorneys representing the class reacted differently. They felt certain that the East Texas courts would not devote a disproportionate amount of trial time to asbestos cases. They feared they would face tremendous delays like those burdening the dockets in Philadelphia or Boston. This overwhelming delay shifts bargaining power from plaintiffs to defendants; defendants have practically unilateral power to settle prior to trial. When plaintiffs' attorneys realize that they will not get full trial value for many years, they discount their cases to present value, and settlement becomes more appealing. The net effect of such tremendous court delay may be a more rapid resolution of cases, but at a substantially lower value.

Faced with this alternative, the weaknesses the plaintiffs' attorneys saw in the class action approach seemed almost trivial. They did, however, dislike the single roll-of-the-dice verdict, judicial control over attorney's fees, and the elimination of liability and punitive damages from individual trials. They worried that, if the cases did not settle, subsequent trials on individual causation and damages would result in lower verdicts; the "heat" generated by the defendants' documents, testimony, and trial strategy would no longer be available to stimulate a large jury award.

* * *

The special master's report in *Jenkins* was opposed by defendants because it seemed to advocate the use of the class action device. Both plaintiffs and defendants were skeptical of the report's value and cost effectiveness. Once completed, however, the data presented by the special master seemed to support each side's interests sufficiently to warrant its use. In general, the report suggested that the parties had little factual disagreement. The data revealed that plaintiffs and defendants had similar information on the fundamental characteristics of the plaintiffs' cases—items such as age, family history, income, asbestos exposure, and smoking history. They differed, however, on the legal and factual implications of this shared information.

Significant variances also existed in the parties' medical data. For example, the defendants' medical experts had generally found that many plaintiffs suffered only from pleural plaques or thickening of pulmonary membranes through their analysis of radiographic evidence. Plaintiffs' doctors, however, often found interstitial fibrosis, a much more serious and advanced condition, from similar evidence.

On balance, the data revealed that the members of the class were very similar in their work and personal histories. The report provided, however, sufficient strengths and weaknesses to afford each side ample opportunity for argument. In particular, the defendants relished the opportunity to portray plaintiffs presented to the jury as representative of the class, as not "representative" at all.

Once the case was settled, the data provided an opportunity to evaluate any perceived unfairness of a group settlement. Because extensive information concerning individual plaintiffs already existed, the court could review each plaintiff's case and insure that the allocation of awards was equitable. In addition, the court could determine the adequacy of the overall settlement amount.

3. Other Values

Plaintiffs' attorneys were interested in resolving their cases at full value and remained confident that the class action would result in either a favorable verdict or settlement. They were willing, therefore, to sacrifice a degree of individual autonomy, dignity, participation, and control in order to facilitate the mass resolution of their cases. Moreover, the relatively small number of plaintiffs' attorneys involved in the class action preserved a respectable level of individual control. In fact, the settlement allocated separate lump sums of money to each attorney for their respective clients.

Plaintiffs' attorneys who opted out of the class expressed more strenuous objections. They felt that control over their clients' fate as well as trial participation would have been seriously diluted by lead plaintiffs' counsel. They also perceived the risks associated with the class action somewhat differently. Although East Texas might be an acceptable forum for plaintiffs, results from other parts of the country indicated that a class action vehicle might prove less favorable.

A vigorous debate arose over whether the class action approach was consistent with the policies underlying the substantive tort law. The defendants contended that an award of punitive damages could not be determined without reference to each plaintiff and each plaintiff's compensatory damages. The United States Court of Appeals for the Fifth Circuit held that the purpose of punitive damages under Texas law was "to create deterrence and to protect the public's interest." Because the jury would be asked to focus on the defendant's conduct, a concurrent decision on punitive damages and compensatory damages was not required. It was necessary, however, for the court to insure a reasonable proportionality between compensatory and punitive awards. Arguably, the jury's award would be a more precise deterrent because it would be founded on a broader based information matrix than would normally be available in single plaintiff trials.

II. DALKON SHIELD: ARE MASS TORT BANKRUPTCIES BANKRUPT?

A. *Problem*

On August 21, 1985, the A.H. Robins Company filed for bankruptcy. Prior to filing, Robins had been sued by approximately 16,000 plaintiffs because of alleged defects in its Dalkon Shield intrauterine device. Almost 9,500 cases had been settled for approximately $530 million; sixty cases had been tried to a jury verdict with the plaintiffs winning thirty-three and Robins winning twenty-seven; and 7,000 lawsuits were still pending in August of 1985. Among the jury awards were two large judgments for punitive damages—one for $7.6 million and one for $6.2 million.

After filing under Chapter 11, Robins attempted to establish a bar date for plaintiffs to file new claims. At a minimum, Robins wanted all claimants who had filed lawsuits or whose causes of action had accrued prior to the bar date to file a claim in the bankruptcy court or forfeit their claims. Robins also wanted a bar date for all unaccrued causes of action against the debtor—all persons in the future who might eventually have actions for personal injuries associated with the use of the Dalkon Shield. In addition, Robins desired to establish a close-ended fund to compensate those claimants who had not been barred. All liabilities from Dalkon Shield related claims would rest with a trust fund while the company could proceed unencumbered in its normal business operations. Bankruptcy would thus create "global peace" except for actions against the trust fund.

When the case was filed in Richmond, Virginia, where the headquarters of Robins was located, it was automatically referred to U.S. Bankruptcy Judge Blackwell N. Shelley. Upon motion by Robins, U.S. District Judge Robert R. Merhige, Jr., entered an order retaining the non-core portions of the proceedings. On November 21, 1985, Judge Merhige approved Robins's motion to establish a bar date and its proposal to spend $4.5 million advertising to all present and future claimants that they must file a claim in the bankruptcy court by April 30, 1986. By March of 1986, it became obvious that the bar date had created a new problem for the debtor: instead of an anticipated 30,000–50,000 claims, the advertising campaign was generating filings at a rate that would eventually total 300,000 claims from over one hundred countries.

In an effort to obtain more information concerning the claims, the court sent a two-page questionnaire to each claimant requesting certain basic information: name, address, nature of injury, and details of Dalkon Shield use. The parties had estimated that up to one-third of the claims were duplicates, made in error, or involved no injuries. The court questionnaire was designed to give Robins an opportunity to object to any claim that was facially invalid and eliminate the claims of those who failed to return the questionnaire. Even with that fallout, approximately 200,000 claimants remained, about 193,000 of whom had never entered the tort system during the fifteen years of Dalkon Shield litigation.

B. Diagnosis

Chapter 11 of the Bankruptcy Code is premised upon negotiated solutions. Typically, the parties are united by a common interest in maximizing returns from a fixed asset base that diminishes over time. Each party owns a common resource and, since neither party can act unilaterally, the parties must agree on how to share that resource. In the *Robins* case, however, the natural bargaining strengths of the parties were somewhat different. A management that highly valued the integrity of the company owned forty percent of the debtor. This management continued to run the company without significant interruption; profits and salaries increased, and prospects for future earnings were not significantly diminished even during bankruptcy.

Management seemed convinced that it would retain its statutory exclusive period for filing a plan of reorganization even though it was under judicial pressure to file quickly. In particular, management was convinced that the total value of all Dalkon Shield related claims, except for punitive damages, would be a manageable amount. If it were possible to eliminate the threat of punitive damages, the company itself could provide more than sufficient funds for relief—a fund of $800 million could be created by using company assets as collateral. Yet Robins insisted upon a close-ended fund—a single lump payment or a payment of a single amount over time—without any further recourse to the company. It was concerned that the extreme rancor pervading the Dalkon Shield litigation would follow *Robins* if it remained liable for an unlimited amount of damages.

The claimants' committee was unsympathetic to management's concerns. The Bankruptcy Code provided that claimants must be paid in full before any money can be allocated to equity. At historic settlement rates, the claimants' committee argued that billions of dollars in claims might arise against a company that had a much smaller estimated value. The committee argued for sale of the company, or at least an open-ended fund to pay all Dalkon Shield claims. Any remainder would go to equity. Further, the committee argued that the claimants should not bear the risk of an inadequate fund once the shareholders had received payment for their stock in the company. In addition, the claimants' committee could, under the Bankruptcy Code, move for the appointment of a trustee or for the termination of the debtor's exclusive period for filing a reorganization plan.

No one was optimistic about the chances for an early settlement. If the debtor attempted a reorganization plan without the participation of the claimants' committee and failed to garner the requisite number of claimant votes, practical termination of the exclusive period could result, and creditors could proceed with virtually any plan they desired. On the other hand, if the debtor succeeded on a claimant vote, the claimants' committee would have functionally diluted their role in the development of a reorganization plan.

There were two ways to view the negotiations: the parties could either look to the total value of the company and divide the pie or they could decide the total value of the claims and set aside a payment fund. Although uncertainty in settlement negotiations can encourage parties to reach an agreement, the uncertainty here merely crippled negotiations. A multi-billion dollar difference between management's estimates and the plaintiffs' alleged total value of the Dalkon Shield claims, coupled with over a one billion dollar difference in estimates of the total value of the company, prevented negotiations from progressing past the preliminary stages.

Ill will among the parties also inhibited settlement negotiations. Not only had Dalkon Shield litigation created animosities in its fifteen year history, but a cultural chasm separated bankruptcy lawyers from tort lawyers. In addition, Robins had fired its initial bankruptcy lawyers, the judge had fired the claimants' committee, and the plaintiffs' lawyers had attempted to disqualify the judge. It was clear that a negotiated solution would be difficult to reach.

C. Prescription

Judge Merhige took a two-pronged approach. In August, 1986, he appointed an examiner, former U.S. Bankruptcy Judge Ralph R. Mabey, to facilitate negotiations by increasing the total value of the company. In March, 1986, Judge Merhige named a court appointed expert, the author of this Article, to devise a system for estimating the total value of the Dalkon Shield related claims. If the examiner could reduce uncertainty concerning Robins's value by increasing its total worth in the marketplace, and the court appointed expert could accurately estimate the range of value of the claims, a consensual plan might prove more accessible. The theory was to create an artificial negotiation deadline that would act as a surrogate for the normally successful negotiation incentive of a trial date.

The negotiations sponsored by the examiner partially succeeded in February of 1987. A potential purchaser offered to establish a $1.75 billion cash fund for the claimants, pay $100 million to trade creditors, and $550 million in stock for equity. This offer was accepted by the claimants' committee after they had negotiated the fund up from $1.5 billion to $1.75 billion. Negotiations with Robins, however, stalled and the purchaser withdrew.

The debtor then developed a reorganization plan that offered trade creditors $100 million and claimants a $1.75 billion letter of credit to be paid over time. The claimants opposed the plan because the payment would not be in cash and because the company retained a reversionary interest in the fund. Yet another suitor offered to purchase the company with a $1.75 billion fund for claimants to be paid over time, $100 million for trade creditors, and approximately $720 million for equity holders. The claimants also opposed this plan because they contended it was inferior to the proposal made in February, 1987.

On July 27, 1987, Judge Merhige scheduled a hearing to estimate the total value of the Dalkon Shield related claims in accordance with Section 502 (c) of the Bankruptcy Code. His goal remained encouraging a consensual plan that would expedite Dalkon Shield claims resolution as well as "global peace" for the debtor.

1. Parties

There were six major players: the company, the trade creditors, the equity committee, claimants, future claimants, and the company's insurer. The Robins family members acted through counsel for the debtor and had their own separate bankruptcy counsel. The equity committee represented the non-Robins family shareholders; their goal was to maximize stock value. The trade creditors were primarily interested in swift claims resolution. The sooner they received their funds, the more they would have in their pockets.

The situation concerning the claimants and future claimants was more complex. For instance, the U.S. Trustee originally appointed a claimants' committee of thirty-eight plaintiffs' attorneys with Dalkon Shield experience. Radical differences in tactics and strategy among the tort lawyers and between the tort and bankruptcy lawyers sometimes became so acute that communications ground to a standstill. Eventually, Judge Merhige disbanded the committee and replaced it with one that consisted of three claimants and one attorney. The legal representative for the future claimants worked closely with the claimants' committee, but his interests diverged when the rights of present and future claimants conflicted.

Another interested party was Aetna Life and Casualty Company, Robins's insurer. Although the insurer-insured relationship between Robins and Aetna had been terminated in 1977, Aetna remained a major trade creditor because of Dalkon Shield related damage awards and settlement funds it had advanced to Robins. In addition, Aetna had been sued as a joint tortfeasor with Robins for failing to remedy the problems associated with the use of the Dalkon Shield. Judge Merhige consolidated all of those cases in his court.

2. Issues

The first issue confronting the court concerned its powers under Section 502 (c) of the Bankruptcy Code. It is not uncommon for courts to estimate the value of claims for voting purposes. Nor is it unusual for them to estimate a single claim to provide full information for a disclosure statement. Here, Robins was asking the court to estimate the total value of 200,000 still viable individual claims that had been filed, plus an unknown number of future claims, and to use that estimated number to set a cap on the total award Robins would owe all Dalkon Shield claimants.

In theory, the estimation hearing was intended to provide sufficient information to the parties so that they could negotiate a consensual plan. In fact, the impending release of raw and unanalyzed data for the estimation necessitated a substantial negotiation effort. If negotiations proved unsuccessful, the court could rule, at least for purposes of a disclosure statement, on the total value of the claims. If the parties still could not reach a settlement, the court could then limit Robins's Dalkon Shield liability to that value.

The court faced two issues in its estimation process: (1) what was the appropriate amount of money for the fund? and (2) how would it be distributed? A 502 (c) estimation had never been conducted in a mass tort action, so little precedent existed in law or in practice. The method of distributing the fund proved just as important as the amount placed in it; until the parties had a good perspective on the general rules for payment, an estimated value of the claims would remain impossible. Judge Merhige asked his court-appointed expert, with the concurrence of the examiner, to serve as a mediator with the parties in devising a claims resolution facility and if necessary, to make recommendations to the court when there were differences among the parties.

This claims resolution facility, eventually included in Robins's proposed disclosure statement, offered four options for claimants: (1) a relatively small flat payment upon an affirmation of Dalkon Shield use and injury; (2) a schedule of benefits for specific injuries for claimants who could provide documentary evidence of use and injury; (3) a deferral option for those who later decided to make a claim; and (4) a procedure to proceed through a series of offers and demands culminating in settlement, binding arbitration, or trial. With the exception of the elimination of punitive damages, the applicable law and venue was as if the cases had never been in bankruptcy.

The theory behind the claims resolution facility was that there was no single "best" remedy for all the claimants. For those who had minor damages or who were unable to prove a Dalkon Shield related injury, the flat payment of option one was optimal. Plaintiffs who had substantial proof of injuries could elect the scheduled payment in option two, rather than the more intense process required by option three. Those who felt they deserved higher awards and individualized treatment could choose the more traditional litigation process in the final option. The more compensation sought by a claimant, the more information the fund required.

These options recognized that claimants are in the best position to make these individual process selections. At the same time, the fund would not expend precious resources conducting a full and complete investigation in every case, regardless of its worth. The design of the facility resembled a manufacturer's attempt to capture consumer surplus through price discrimination. The fund was "selling" its "product"— the resolution of Dalkon Shield cases—by having "purchasers" self-select the optimal combination of price and transaction costs.

3. Information

To resolve the specifics of the 200,000 pending claims, the court-appointed expert decided to utilize an analytic approach he had developed in the Ohio Asbestos Litigation with Professor Eric D. Green. Approximately 9,500 previous cases provided data on key variables essential to the outcomes and values of Dalkon Shield claims. The 200,000 pending cases also afforded information concerning these same variables. Using historical experience, one could extrapolate the total value of the pending claims based upon previous case values.

The first issue arose over data collection. Due to the controversial nature of the estimation process, and because the court had not yet mandated a Section 502 (c) estimation, each party had its own experts to assemble data. The entire process would thus be consensual—experts from all parties would collaborate with court-appointed neutrals and subcontractors to develop a common data base. If all parties agreed on the data base, then each side could use its own methodology to analyze the data and make its own estimation.

The next concern was whether the parties, now accustomed to acrimonious discourse, could possibly agree on each step in the claims estimation process. Following a long series of negotiations, the experts agreed on virtually every aspect of the data collection. During the estimation hearing, not a single complaint was raised regarding the data base; during the entire process only three issues were raised before Judge Merhige.

The experts agreed upon two data collection instruments—one for previously resolved cases and one for pending claims. The previously resolved case questionnaire consisted of 150 questions culled from the range of relevant variables. The statisticians decided that the questionnaire would be used for a random sample of 1,600 of the 9,500 cases and a stratified sample of the 100 highest and 100 lowest cases. Neutrals hired specifically for this purpose gathered complaints, interrogatories, depositions, and medical records from the files of Robins, its attorneys, its insurance carrier, and plaintiffs' attorneys. Once the files were re-created, neutral medical personnel completed the questionnaire and translated the information into an international language for the coding of diseases, treatments, and tests—a format known as the ICD–9. Neutral computer personnel then entered the information onto computer tapes to facilitate analysis.

The experts realized that the task of reaching a consensus on a corresponding questionnaire for the pending cases would be far more difficult. Preliminary data showed that fewer than one-fourth of the claimants were represented by attorneys, so the form had to be comprehensible to all potential lay plaintiffs. On the other hand, a significant amount of information was required to verify the details of each claim. The experts, therefore, decided to send a fifty-page claim form to 6,000 claimants. Following drafting and approval, the claim form was pretested on claimants from a variety of socio-economic groups to determine if they could understand the questions and respond completely and accurately.

The final design of the claim form accomplished two goals: it gathered information on certain specifics of a claimant's personal history, and it identified the essential facts of a claimant's OB/GYN medical history so that medical records could then be obtained. The claim form consisted of eleven sections: background information; use of Dalkon Shield; medical history; pregnancies; contraception; medical problems, illnesses, or injury claims from the Dalkon Shield; other medical information; claims of future medical problems; financial losses; certification; and optional additional comments. Partially because it was product of intense negotiations the form contained imperfections. For example, Robins favored open-ended questions concerning a claimants' allegations of harm, since choosing from a list of potential harms might prompt erroneous responses. On the other hand, the claimants' committee favored a checklist that claimants could readily mark. The compromise claim form contained a checklist in the section on medical history, and two sections later, open-ended questions regarding medical problems, illnesses, or injury claims from the Dalkon Shield.

Once a claimant completed and returned the claim form, she would be responsible for obtaining medical records verifying her Dalkon Shield use and describing any related injuries. Once received, neutrals hired by the court gathered all other relevant medical records. In addition, the parties established a toll-free telephone line to assist the sampled claimants. Because of concerns over interviewer bias, all responses made by the 800 number operators were limited to scripts approved by all the parties.

As the claim form and requested medical records were returned, neutrals logged them on a sophisticated data tracking system and entered the data directly into computers using programs specifically designed for that purpose. As in previously resolved cases, the medical records were coded into ICD–9 and entered onto computer tape.

The parties received the final tapes in July, 1987. Over 75 million pieces of information had been collected; the entire process had taken fourteen months. The materials prepared for the parties had two components, a tape of the raw data organized to facilitate analysis and a hard copy which translated the raw data from the master tape into a printout of a case summary for each sampled claimant. The printout organized the case summaries to approximate traditional Dalkon Shield case summaries. Thus, the parties had two formats for analyzing data— the tape, for computer manipulation of the information as a whole, and case summaries that could be reviewed individually by attorneys, physicians, nurses, or paralegals.

D. *Results*

Judge Merhige conducted as estimation hearing from November 5 through November 11, 1987. Fifteen witnesses testified; 212 exhibits were offered into evidence. Testimony concerning the total value of pending claims from the five experts who participated in the consensual data collection process varied from $1.0 billion to $7.3 billion, with the second highest estimate at $2.5 billion. They used at least three distinct analytic techniques—regression analysis, decision tree analysis, and an expert system.

Although the absolute estimates diverged substantially, all the experts agreed on the role of the data base with the discrepancies in their testimony attributable to disagreements on five basic assumptions: (1) the effect of statutes of limitations; (2) the level of proof required to demonstrate Dalkon Shield use and injury; (3) the effect of alternative causes of injury; (4) the value of the previously resolved cases; and (5) the number of claimants who would pursue the various claims resolution facility options.

Of these five assumptions, the experts disagreed the most on the size of the claimant pool. Experts for Robins, for example, assumed that a relatively small number of claimants would qualify to receive historic settlement values. Robins's expert based his assumption on the number of claimants who returned a completed claim form, and sent in medical records that confirmed Dalkon Shield use and injuries, and demonstrated in the file a lack of obvious alternative causes for alleged Dalkon Shield related injuries. On the other hand, the expert for Aetna assumed a much larger number of eligible claimants. She focused on the total number of claimants who sent some portion of the claim form, alleged Dalkon Shield use and injury, and presented at least some, if not complete, medical records. The expert for the claimants took a different, and more expansive, approach. He assumed that all claimants would be eligible unless their claims form or medical records showed an absence of Dalkon Shield related injuries.

The basic differences among the parties became more acute as the hearing proceeded. At one point, Judge Merhige requested that certain assumptions be changed and estimates recalculated. By the conclusion of the hearing, however, it was reasonably clear that the remaining issues were well within the expertise of the court. Notwithstanding these efforts, subsequent settlement negotiations failed to resolve the differences between the parties. Therefore, on December 11, 1987, Judge Merhige announced that he would rule on the total value of the Dalkon Shield related claims. His ruling set the estimated value of the claims at $2.475 billion, to be paid over a reasonable length of time.

Within two weeks of the announcement, two additional parties offered to purchase the company. Robins decided to sell after it became evident that its stand-alone purchase plan could not be self-financed. The company proposed a sale of fifty-eight percent of the stock for $600 million, with a $2.475 billion letter of credit to be paid over five years, and $100 million to trade creditors. The claimants' and equity committees, on the other hand, preferred a sale involving 100 percent of the stock for $700 million, a $2.34 billion cash payment at consummation for claimants, $100 million to trade creditors, and a settlement of the plaintiffs' independent tort action against Aetna.

After extensive negotiations, the parties accepted the latter offer in March of 1988. The final plan also included provisions that relaxed the bar date originally requested by Robins. Future claimants could receive compensation, but only if their medical problems were manifested after the bar date, or they lacked knowledge of the bar date. Under the amended bar date, late filing claimants would be subordinated to timely claimants but would be compensated if sufficient funds still remained.

1. Economy

When completed, the estimation process represented the largest and most expensive social science survey ever conducted under the auspices of a court. The data collection process itself cost approximately $5 million. The study cost represented 0.2% of the $2.475 billion in dispute and 0.7% of the change in the value of the claimants' fund. The parties also incurred expenses in both monitoring the process and in presenting evidence at the estimation hearing. Total expenses for the data collection process could probably have been reduced by half, however, if the court-appointed experts, rather than all the parties, had conducted the process.

The cost of the study can be justified on two grounds independent of the estimation: (1) for the benefit of the trustees of the claims resolution facility in designing their processes; and (2) for scientists studying the medical phenomena associated with IUD use. In addition, in any future litigation, a substantial cost reduction can be realized by using the process as a model.

Despite these benefits, the opportunity costs associated with the estimation process may have been significant. For example, it could be argued that, absent the estimation process, the case might have settled much earlier and at lower cost. Had the parties known that no additional information concerning the value of the pending claims would be forthcoming, they might have become reconciled to a high level of uncertainty, and thus resolved the case earlier. Most of the parties believed that they required some sort of estimation based upon gross data; it did not seem feasible to have extensive formal discovery in 200,000 cases before the resolution of the bankruptcy. Moreover, while the estimation might have been much less sophisticated and expensive or relied on more hypothesis than data, successful case resolution required a greater degree of certainty.

The most troublesome costs of the estimation process related to potential errors. Only time will determine the accuracy of the process, although estimates can often become self-fulfilling prophecies. Given the painstaking and costly checks made on the underlying data, the experts all agreed on the level of accuracy of the data base. Yet, a comparison to the information gathered following exhaustive discovery under the Federal Rules of Civil Procedure in a typical Dalkon Shield case would necessarily render the study second best. In addition, the nature of the evidence—purely statistical—may have its own problems. There is a bona fide doubt by some decision-makers of making a ruling based on anything other than detailed and individualized facts. That is one reason why the parties received both raw data tapes and individualized case summaries.

2. *Fairness*

The fairness criteria constitute both the greatest strengths and weaknesses of the process. On one hand, genuine equal opportunity and strategy existed among the parties. On the other hand, the exigencies of the project did not permit a high level of predictability concerning the rules of the study. In addition, continuous doubt remained whether the court would allow the project to be completed and, if so, how it would be used by the court. Nevertheless, the transparent nature of the process, as well as the continuous interaction among the parties, helped allay these fears. The court-appointed expert worked carefully with the parties during each step of the process, thereby insuring that each decision received a full opportunity for input from all sides.

Views of the rationality of the study varied but the close agreement among the experts suggests that the data base was reliable. Therefore, despite the lack of an official ruling or opinion, the fact that the parties all agreed to the final estimate suggests their approval of both its rationality and its fairness.

3. *Other Values*

The reaction to other, less tangible, values varied among the attorneys and their clients. The attorneys, for example, generally noted a strong sense of participation, full information, and significant control in the process. The attorneys did not consider values such as dignity.and autonomy as important.

The claimants' level of participation was extraordinary. Of a potential 300,000 claimants, sixty-six percent returned the court's two-page questionnaire. In addition, sixty-six percent of the 6,000 survey claimants indicated a desire to pursue their claims by returning at least one document. Sixty-five percent of the sampled survey claimants from the group of 200,000 viable claims returned the fifty-page claim form. Indeed, claimants seemed to relish the opportunity to tell their own stories without the indignities often suffered in the formal litigation discovery process. Minimal assistance from the toll-free telephone number for legal and medical advice as well as by the inability to locate the appropriate medical records, however, generally frustrated them.

A desire to protect the privacy value of each claimants' file resulted in high levels of confidentiality. The court neutrals went so far as to enclose all communications with claimants in envelopes to prevent even casual revelations to third parties. In addition, the parties limited the public exposure of the data base only to the estimation hearing.

The degree to which the process furthered the underlying values of the substantive tort and bankruptcy law is not as clear. If $2.475 billion is the "true value" of the eventually liquidated claims, then the results would be superb. If not, at least one of the parties will have been shortchanged. Yet, the lack of viable alternatives and the parties acceptance of the estimate offered by the court indicates that these values were served.

WAYNE D. BRAZIL, SPECIAL MASTERS IN COMPLEX CASES; EXTENDING THE JUDICIARY OR RESHAPING ADJUDICATION?

53 U.Chi.L.Rev. 394, 394–406; 412–414; 417–423 (1986).

In recent years, courts have used special masters to help manage complex civil cases. But this use has raised serious questions of efficacy and ethics. This paper first identifies the needs and ambitions that inspire courts to appoint masters, in order to demonstrate why recourse to this tool can be so rich in potential yet so controversial. Then, in describing some recent roles masters have played, it assays their potential contributions as well as the risks attending their use. It concludes that as masters are used more ambitiously, the potential benefits and risks increase. Masters can bring significant new skills and flexibility to bear on cases whose complexity threatens to overwhelm our traditional system. However, a correlative danger exists that using masters will fundamentally alter that system in ways we find troubling: by making adjudication too informal, by removing it from public scrutiny and challenge, and by encouraging judges to rely on masters to a degree incompatible with appropriate exercise of the judicial function.

I. Background

A. Needs That Inspire the Use of Masters

Courts appoint special masters as a means of addressing three overlapping categories of problems: judicial limitations, shortcomings of the traditional adjudicatory system, and shortcomings of parties and counsel. Judicial limitations include time constraints; lack of expertise in esoteric or technologically sophisticated areas; lack of skill in certain roles, such as the facilitation of settlement negotiations; and limitations that stem from the proprieties of judicial conduct, at least for the judge who will try the case.

The shortcomings of the traditional adjudicatory process are more subtle. First, our adversarial and dialectical pretrial process institutionalizes and legitimates both distrust and the pursuit of selfish ends. Friction is the norm in this process; yet friction saps energy and consumes resources. Second, adjudication is hampered by formalism. Pleading can be ritualistic and uncommunicative. Discovery, which was designed to compensate for pleading limitations, has become similarly stultified. Preoccupation with form and fear of loss often displace substantive communication, common sense, and good faith.

Users of the system (clients and counsel) also behave inappropriately. Parties sometimes commence litigation unwisely—where there is no hope of victory, where victory would not provide an effective remedy, or for ulterior purposes—either as a weapon to extend economic combat beyond the marketplace, or to demonstrate power or tenacity. Parties often experience considerable difficulty communicating, and may act more out of misunderstanding than by clear calculation. Relations between parties are also complicated by pervasive distrust. Although distrust can help parties to protect themselves, it also clouds their judgment and inspires overkill tactics or opaque responses to pleading and discovery. Even if individual instances of tactical excess are negligible, they can provoke cycles of retaliations. Occasionally hostility or bad faith so pollutes a case that movement toward disposition becomes virtually impossible.

B.   Uses of Masters

Courts appoint special masters in an effort to circumvent these obstacles to adjudication. But the precise roles that masters play are changing. The oldest and least controversial uses of special masters developed in response to limitations on judges' time and are wholly ministerial in character. Examples include accountings and calculations of damages using court-approved formulae.

In these roles the work of masters is not controversial because it involves no significant exercise of judgment or discretion, no legal analysis, and no determinations of policy.

A more recent ministerial use of special masters is in the administration and distribution of large funds generated by settlements or judgments in civil class actions or in criminal cases involving large-scale fraudulent schemes. The court may determine in advance how money will be invested and how potential claimants will prove their membership in the class and their proportionate share of the fund. Such detailed judicial guidance, coupled with a requirement that the master submit thorough reports to both court and counsel, prevents the master from usurping judicial functions.

These uses of special masters conserve substantial judicial resources for the tasks of judging. However, masters cannot make major contributions to the larger objectives of expediting and rationalizing the resolution of complex disputes if their powers are so limited. This fact undoubtedly underlies the trend toward expanding masters' responsibilities. It also helps explain why even masters with clearly limited mandates seem pressured or tempted to gravitate into larger spheres. With broader duties, masters might contribute more, but they also may invade the proper preserve of the judiciary, change the character of adjudication, or interject themselves into sensitive aspects of attorney-client relations.

Recent and proposed uses of special masters that are more ambitious and controversial involve tasks that require the skills and responsibilities of judging or interventionist behavior that is generally regarded as improper for a judge. Today these categories have begun to blur because of major changes in the courts' functions, at least in the federal system. Judges are under considerable pressure to participate actively in case development. The Federal Rules of Civil Procedure invite judges to look behind the pleadings, to narrow the issues, and to improve communication between litigants. The rules also encourage judges to help parties acquire and share information, contain their costs, explore settlement, and experiment with unusual mechanisms to resolve their differences.

These changes in the judicial role have two implications for the use of masters. First, the assignment of some case management and settlement duties to masters becomes less controversial because broader precedent exists for a neutral person to assume this role. The second and rather ironic point is that these changes intensify pressure on courts to appoint masters (or magistrates) to perform certain interventionist functions. Greater judicial involvement in case development raises ethical concerns insofar as the judge may become biased by contact with the parties prior to trial and the judge's power may intimidate counsel (even unintentionally) during the formative stage of litigation, which could distort case development. By harping on these ethical concerns, critics may pressure judges to delegate the more intrusive or sensitive tasks to masters or magistrates.

Not surprisingly, courts have used masters most ambitiously in the most complex, resource-threatening cases. Three types of cases are prototypical: mass torts (such as actions involving asbestos, *Agent Orange*, or DDT), massive commercial litigation, and public law cases requiring courts to fashion and implement equitable decrees that cover complex institutional relationships and extend over considerable periods of time. The discussion below focuses primarily on the first two categories, in part because much literature already exists regarding masters and public institutional reform.

* * *

II. CASE MANAGEMENT AND EVALUATION

* * *

A. *The Ohio Asbestos Litigation*

In the Ohio asbestos litigation (OAL) Judge Thomas D. Lambros appointed law professors Eric Green and Francis McGovern to develop a case management plan for each category of asbestos case (for example, insulation cases, suits by plant workers, suits by brake repairers). The goals were to streamline pleading and discovery practice and to set time schedules for completion of all major aspects of case preparation. Working closely with counsel and drawing on materials generated by national organizations or in other asbestos litigation, the masters developed two sets of standardized documents: questionnaires for plaintiffs to provide information about their claims, and discovery forms for interrogatories, document production requests, and witness disclosures. Parties who desired information not accessible through the standardized procedures, or relief from some element of the program, could petition a single designated magistrate for assistance.

Because no systematic empirical evaluation of the costs and benefits of this program has been completed, we cannot yet assess its value. The establishment of presumptive time frames for completing each pretrial stage, based on substantial inputs from affected parties, probably sped up case development and undercut excuses offered by dilatory lawyers. And hammering out the discovery questions probably helped educate counsel about the dynamic between facts and law.

On the other hand, negotiating the development and acceptance of standardized discovery forms was costly. A lengthy set of interrogatories (containing hundreds of questions, counting subparts) emerged as the approved form. This invites speculation that the masters felt constrained to include something for everyone in order to gain support for the concept itself. Having supervised discovery and hosted settlement conferences in asbestos cases in California, I question the need for all the data requested by the forms. Counsel with asbestos litigation experience seem able to value individual claims, at least for serious settlement negotiations, with only modest amounts of information about the plaintiff. This observation is somewhat unfair because the case development plan had two purposes—to equip parties for settlement negotiations and to prepare for trial. Since only a few cases are tried, however, the procedures may have over-rationalized the pretrial process. If the information necessary for settlement is much less elaborate than that necessary for trial, the Ohio asbestos plan might have overburdened the parties in an effort to achieve a quite secondary goal.

Judge Lambros and masters Green and McGovern were well aware that rational, expedited settlement was a paramount goal of their overall strategy. Toward that end, the Judge ordered the masters to undertake an even more ambitious task: to develop a quantified system for appraising individual asbestos claims and apportioning financial responsibility among defendants. The objective was to develop computer-based models or formulae for different kinds of claims, so that the computer could digest a case's data and decide the otherwise thorny questions about which parties owed what to whom.

The masters originally contemplated drawing extensively on many different kinds of data, particularly from asbestos litigation in Cleveland and elsewhere, then integrating that data with two "dynamic" decision models from academic literature. The goal of the first stage was to ascertain the settlement values of terminated cases and to isolate and ascribe relative weight to each operative factor in those valuations. Working with experienced local counsel, the masters developed a list of some 300 variables that could affect the valuation of individual asbestos cases. The second stage would refine the historical analysis by imposing an overlay of dynamic decision theory.

The objective of this plan is unimpeachable, yet in conceptual reach it far exceeds our current abilities to grasp. It seems fair to ask whether a mechanism of such sophistication is necessary, and whether sufficient dividends could result to justify the massive investment of effort that it would entail. To be effective, the formulae must be credible to affected parties. Credibility would require, at a minimum, substantial efforts to educate lawyers and clients about how the formulae were developed. The formulae probably reflect compromises or choices between debatable positions, and each such compromise or choice could be used by a skeptical lawyer or client to justify rejecting the whole concept. Moreover, persuading lawyers and clients to accept elaborate academic decision models might pose an even larger obstacle to "selling" this kind of procedure. Many attorneys and clients would sense artificiality in this heavily conceptual undertaking and would therefore distrust it.

A thorough evaluation is impossible, since the masters were unable to produce the comprehensive set of formulae originally envisioned. Still, the masters have developed quantified portraits of numerous terminated asbestos cases from the Cleveland area, and have used this data base to propose outer limits for settlement negotiations. To achieve this end, they gather as much information about the pending case as is feasible and feed that data into their computer. The computer locates the three most similar cases in its historical file, then lists the characteristics of those three cases and the amounts of the settlements or judgments therein. These figures shape the ensuing negotiations. Professor McGovern reports that because all parties "had the computerized value ranges, the lawyers could not be too far apart and still be realistic and credible. We ended up having demands and offers within a range of about 20 percent of the values we thought the cases would be worth."

But is even this scaled-down plan worth all the effort? If we focus only on asbestos litigation in Ohio, the answer is probably no. I have seen experienced counsel produce reasonable valuations of asbestos cases with relatively few elements of information. And networks of lawyers share information about values of roughly comparable cases. As Professor McGovern has pointed out, however, the work done in Ohio might be valuable if the recently established national claims handling facility will be processing significant numbers of claims. The computer programs, lists of variables, and valuation data generated in Ohio could prove very useful in setting guidelines to guard against arbitrary or inconsistent recommendations by adjusters, and in bolstering claimant confidence in the fairness of settlement offers.

We know too little at this juncture to fairly assess the worth of the masters' approach. Yet the experience in Ohio compels us to recognize a potential problem: where a court tentatively concludes that masters are needed because a case cannot adequately be handled through established procedures, masters may feel pressured to design wholly new systems or experiment with elaborately innovative dispute resolution techniques that are expensive to generate and to "sell" to the affected community. They may overlook available resources and downplay the utility of adapting or refining established ways of solving problems. Given these pressures, judges who appoint masters might consider advising them to try first to build on traditional or accepted methods. Getting large groups of people to adopt new ways of doing things carries a cost (in resistance and education) that should be considered at the outset and avoided if possible.

* * *

B. Agent Orange in New York

Separating the trial judge from a master who is facilitating settlement has one obvious drawback: it may reduce the master's leverage with and ability to persuade the parties. This consideration apparently affected how Judge Jack B. Weinstein structured his relationship with the settlement masters in the *Agent Orange* litigation. Judge Weinstein's first task for special master Ken Feinberg was to write a detailed memorandum outlining the issues presented by the case and suggesting principles on which to allocate damages among the defendants. Feinberg's ability to persuade parties to consider his settlement recommendations depended in part on whether he could convince them of his sophisticated understanding of relevant law. His effectiveness also depended somewhat on parties' perceptions about how much influence his views had on the judge, or at least on the likelihood that the judge would similarly resolve important issues.

This connection between settlement master and judge may have been uniquely necessary in *Agent Orange* because of the great uncertainty in the law. Since so much was left to the almost unfettered judgment of the court, the parties might well have ignored the master's opinions unless they were tied to the judge. The situation in *Agent Orange* was loaded with socio-political sensitivities, and desperately in need of a solution perhaps not achievable through more cautiously crafted procedures. On balance, it was arguably worth risking so much communication between settlement facilitator and trial judge.

However, separation generally seems much wiser. It would be unseemly if the settlement master were ostensibly only an instrument for the judge to exercise power over the litigants; judicial coercion of settlement is no less attractive when indirect. Moreover, substantial communication between a settlement master and the judge could damage the negotiation process. Parties might become more reluctant to speak candidly to the master and the master might be so identified with the judge that parties resume the posturing and other strategic behavior we hoped to avoid by using masters. Off-the-record communication between master and judge also risks creating the impression that the master is unduly influencing the court. Parties could justifiably object that such *ex parte* communication deprives litigants of an opportunity to challenge the information and ideas that might influence the court's subsequent decisions.

Concern about a judge's indirect (or direct) participation in settlement negotiations could be especially acute in class actions. As Vincent

Nathan has pointed out, the public might well doubt that a judge who participated in settlement negotiations can later make an independent determination that a proposed class settlement is reasonable and fair to all members.

* * *

V.   Some Cautions

As has been shown, special masters are making innovative contributions to our system of dispute resolution and helping the courts successfully process the most unwieldy, potentially interminable cases.   The achievements of special masters in the areas of case management, settlement facilitation, and ongoing decree implementation give us cause for celebration.   Yet this success is at best partial: new dangers lurk just below the surface as we move out of the mainstream.   This final section discusses some of the problems we must confront and solve if we are to continue delegating ambitious tasks to special masters.

A.   Masters' Discretion and Judicial Responsibility

Two competing schools of thought exist about how courts should supervise masters.   According to one school, the best orders of reference are phrased only in generalities.   This frees the master, who will get to know the case much more intimately than will the judge, to tailor procedures to evolving needs, to act quickly and informally, and to acquire the influence (or power) over litigants and counsel necessary to serve effectively and minimize appeals of his rulings.   Advocates of this approach tend to trust masters' discretion, to be skeptical of judges' capacity to predict how best to employ masters, and to disparage procedural formalism.   They fear that the cost and time savings of using a special master will be dissipated if the judge invades the master's sphere or forces the master to make lengthy reports or to obtain judicial approval for most acts.

The other school of thought emphasizes the court's need to maintain tight control over both the master and the case.   Orders of reference should describe the master's duties and powers as specifically as possible.   Courts also should require the master to file frequent and formal reports, and should prohibit him from any *ex parte* communication with either the court or any litigant.   Adherents to this school believe that insulating the assigned judge from case development, as was done in the Michigan fishing rights litigation, can have serious negative consequences.   The judge may learn too little about the relevant facts, law, or the lawyers' behavior to rule properly on appeals from the master's decisions.   If his knowledge remains superficial, the judge is more likely to defer to the master and thus be unable to verify the correctness and wisdom of the master's actions.   A master operating in such an environment acquires a great deal of power that is susceptible to abuse.   Parties who perceive few restraints on the master's power may be intimidated or frustrated into abandoning significant rights.

The judge who stands aloof from case development may be unable to control litigants and their lawyers, whereas a judge familiar with the case can by his presence encourage parties to act responsibly and civilly and avoid contentious behavior. In contrast, if the parties observe the judge's detachment they may succumb to temptations to posture for undeserved advantages. If the special master is weak, the parties may try to manipulate him. Thus the remote judge poses three threats to case development: the judge will be unable to discharge his judicial function, the master will abuse his power, and litigants will skew the process through undisciplined behavior.

When a special master conducts substantial out-of-court investigation,* * *, new problems arise. The master is functioning like a court-appointed expert (or a continental judge), but without the procedural safeguards that check the reliability of an expert's reasoning and conclusions. As the *Manual for Complex Litigation, Second,* points out, court-appointed experts, unlike masters, may be targeted for pretrial discovery, may be deposed, and usually testify at trial, where they are subject to full cross-examination. Moreover, the appointed expert's work enjoys no presumption of correctness, whereas in matters tried to the bench a special master's findings of fact, unless clearly erroneous, must be accepted by the court. In addition, a court-appointed expert has less power than a master to frame issues and to control their exploration. Because the court receives less from an appointed expert, it is less likely to rely as heavily on or defer completely to her as it might to a master having both a broader mandate and legal training.

The procedural differences between using masters and using court-appointed experts might make judges hesitate to use masters to ameliorate the court's lack of expertise in an esoteric subject area. For example, special masters in high-tech intellectual property cases are often lawyers with specialized engineering backgrounds. Their dual expertise in substantive law and science can create a real risk of judicial abdication of the ultimate responsibility to decide legal issues. Use of a court-appointed expert, in contrast, poses less of a threat to the court's independence of mind, since the expert's views are testable through cross-examination and must compete openly, on even terms, with the views of the parties' experts.

Thus, when a special master is employed to investigate a complex situation and propose solutions, or to lend the court expertise in some sophisticated technological or other esoteric subject, serious dangers may face our dispute resolution system. Because parties often lack an opportunity to challenge the master's findings, and generalist judges may be tempted to rely too heavily on the master's expertise, the resulting decision may be less well reasoned and less acceptable to affected parties than if a court-appointed expert had been utilized instead. The rules applying to experts incorporate mechanisms to test publicly the appointee's work and to guard against the problems that can arise when the court's agent is not limited, in forming his opinions, to information on the record. This issue is especially sensitive in public law cases, where a master can affect important policies or social institutions. These cases demonstrate an acute need to maximize public confidence in the openness and fairness of the decision process.

B. Informality

Special masters are touted for their ability to proceed much more informally than a judge in managing case development, fostering settlement, and implementing equitable decrees. Informality has much to commend it: it can refresh relations, open communications, reduce self-protective actions, cut costs, and generally infuse litigation with common sense. It can eliminate the delay and expense associated with full briefing, staged argumentation, and written opinions. I have found, in my work as a magistrate, that informal conferences often suffice to resolve emerging discovery disputes or to plan for sharing information and for advancing the pretrial process.

Informality, however, may also impose costs and create problems. For example, one informal procedure masters use is the quick-fix discovery ruling, often given over the telephone after a brief argument by counsel. Prompt rulings can save parties considerable expense and expedite the pretrial process. But the depth of consideration, by both counsel and the neutral, is necessarily limited. I have been forced to acknowledge that fact by parties urging reconsideration of my tentative discovery rulings. In some instances, my initial instinct was misplaced, the situation was more complex than I appreciated, and after more careful consideration I have reversed my original decision. These sobering experiences have not led me to conclude that most discovery disputes require formal briefing and argument. But I have become more sensitive to the dangers inherent in speedy and wholly oral procedures.

Informality may create a related danger of imprecision. If the neutral renders fuzzy decisions, or imposes poorly-specified obligations, he sets the stage for breaches, disputes, and disillusion. He also creates opportunities for lazy or unscrupulous counsel to take advantage of others. Without a precise foundation, it is virtually impossible to impose sanctions or otherwise control the litigants. These unfortunate consequences of imprecision can be especially troublesome and costly in complex cases, where duties are less self-evident and where the ripple effects of poor communication on one matter can extend to many others.

Conducting business off the record is a potentially more troublesome informality. Arguably, communicating without the costs, inhibition, and posturing that accompany recorded proceedings is a virtue of using special masters, especially in the pretrial period. A master working away from public scrutiny may more easily convince the parties to talk candidly about their objectives and concerns and be more flexible in eschewing impractical but technically defensible positions to pursue commonsense solutions. Communicating *ex parte* can arguably increase these benefits of proceeding off the record. A master may discern the parties' real agendas and induce cooperative attitudes through sympathy, frankness, or pressure.

Private proceedings may well offer significant advantages in some pretrial situations, most obviously in settlement conferences. Yet we may exaggerate how much counsel's behavior changes simply because no transcript is being made. Also, we may not fully appreciate the risks entailed in proceeding in this manner. In my experience the absence of recording often affects the tone or style of conversation, but not its substance or purpose. Counsel remain quite self-conscious; they continue to posture, albeit more gently and subtly, for the neutral's sympathy. Litigators seldom forget that a key objective is to shape the neutral's perceptions to serve their client's interests. Thus, lawyers are not suddenly transformed from self-protective partisans into trusting nonpartisans, interested only in justice, responsibility, and cost-effective information sharing: they remain lawyers. This counsels some caution in going off the record, for litigators may become even more manipulative, less forthright, and less thoughtful than if they knew the neutral could reproduce their words later and hold them strictly accountable.

The absence of a record can create similarly perverse incentives for the neutral. A retired judge who recently served as a master handling discovery in a complex case told me that he acted very differently when a record was being made. Off the record he felt freer to cajole or pressure counsel. He also may have felt less constrained in arriving at and articulating his decisions. Yet this master, as a former judge, had been schooled for years in the virtues of thoughtfulness and restraint. Other special masters might be even more likely to slide into unbecoming, unwise, or unfair behavior.

The absence of a record can both exaggerate a master's sense of power (by removing the constraint of appellate review) and increase temptations to abuse it. The most likely abuse is not born of malice or bias, but of sloppiness or sloth. Thus risks arise that the master's reasoning will be faulty and that the parties will disparage his rulings because of failure to understand the reasoning underlying them. In our system, power is illegitimate unless we expose the basis upon which it is exercised. This observation should make us cautious about proceeding off the record or *ex parte*. The distrust that such communications can engender could negate all the benefits that informality is intended to achieve.

C. *Masters in Political Roles*

Masters' apparent successes as quasi-judicial politicians raise many perplexing questions about masters' roles in these cases. Given that judges issue orders affecting complex institutional relationships and having significant political and economic implications, should we consider expanding or changing the processes by which courts reach their decisions? These decisions may impinge on all of society, but who should be allowed to participate in the decisionmaking processes? Should courts be explicitly permitted to take into account political considerations, for example, in selecting feasible remedies? Should courts attempt to influence public opinion in order to facilitate implementation of legal rulings? Should the judiciary's capacity to perform administrative functions be expanded so that it could implement its own orders or step in to fill legally mandated but unmet administrative needs? Changes along these lines might rob the judiciary of the appearance of neutrality and objectivity arguably essential to perceptions of its legitimacy and authority.

Some commentators argue that the risk of polluting the judiciary with politics is greater than the potential benefits of more politically sophisticated judicial behavior. If that is true, should courts tolerate quasi-political behavior by special masters that would be unacceptable or unwise in judges? We must recognize that judges may employ the less visible and less accountable master to play roles or pursue ends deemed improper for the courts. Such use of masters might jeopardize public confidence in the integrity of the judiciary itself.

D. Neutrality

One difficult issue regarding a master's proper role arises frequently in nearly every context. What should or may a master do when he perceives a legal theory, or a line of reasoning, or a source of evidence, that would substantially improve one party's position but to which that party seems oblivious? Does a master have a right or a duty to share his perception? More generally, should the master help a clearly weaker party against a stronger opponent, or prevent a party from accepting an unfairly low settlement? These questions go to the heart of the adversary system. The answers for masters may be the same as for judges—but the answers for judges are less than self-evident.

CONCLUSION

None of this should be read as an argument against using masters or as a blanket condemnation of more flexible, less structured procedures. The ponderousness and cost of our inherited procedures create a pressing need to develop more efficient means to achieve justice. But we must take care that new methods include adequate safeguards against subtle corruptions of neutrals and misbehavior by litigants. In the past we have relied on the public visibility of our procedures and on precision in our pronouncements to assure the accountability essential to all actors in the litigation drama. We should hesitate to abandon these features of the system until we have developed similarly effective sources of restraint and intellectual discipline.

We must also keep in mind that the special master is not a procedural panacea. The problems that embarrass and encumber our system have roots too deep in our institutions and in human nature to admit of complete solution. Appointing special masters will not convert litigants and lawyers into saints. We can reasonably hope only for modest gains. Carefully used, masters will help the courts sustain the tension that prevents the dispute process from unravelling altogether.

Notes and Questions

1. In addition to his work in the Ohio and East Texas asbestos litigation and Dalkon Shield litigation, Professor McGovern has served as a court-appointed special masters in numerous other complex and mass tort litigations, including a Great Lakes fishing rights dispute, *see* United States v. Michigan, 471 F.Supp. 192 (W.D.Mich.1979), *remanded* 623 F.2d 448 (6th Cir.1980), *as modified* 653 F.2d 277, *cert. denied* 454 U.S. 1124, 102 S.Ct. 971, 71 L.Ed.2d 110 (1981); and an Alabama public utilities ratemaking controversy. These and other mass tort cases are described in his articles, *supra; see also* Francis E. McGovern, *The Alabama DDT Settlement Fund,* 53 Law & Contemp.Probs. 61 (1990); Francis E. McGovern, *Management of Multiparty Toxic Tort Litigation: Case Law and Trends Affecting Case Management,* 19 Forum 1 (1983); Francis E. McGovern, *Toxic Substances Litigation in the Fourth Circuit,* 16 U.Rich.L.Rev. 247 (1982); *On Settling Toxic Tort Cases—The Role of Special Masters: An Interview With Francis McGovern,* ALTERNATIVES TO THE HIGH COST OF LITIGATION, Center for Public Resources (Sept. 1984).

2. Professor McGovern has capably documented the role of special masters in mass tort litigation; has he effectively argued the case for their utility, fairness, and efficiency? To what extent is Magistrate Judge Brazil's rejoinder a cautionary note? Has the use of special masters in mass tort cases led to informational overkill, adding further layers of needless complexity? Has the courts' use of masters impermissibly expanded judicial authority to non-judicial court surrogates? Are litigants correctly concerned, not only about losing control of their litigation, but about judicial power being exerted by a non-judicial appointee?

Chapter XII

ADMINISTRATIVE MODELS, ADR, AND CLAIMS FACILITIES

A. ASBESTOS LITIGATION

1. ASBESTOS CLAIMS RESOLUTION FACILITIES

LAWRENCE FITZPATRICK, THE CENTER FOR CLAIMS RESOLUTION

53 Law & Contemp. Probs. 13 (1990).

* * *

I

INTRODUCTION

The Center for Claims Resolution, Inc. ("the Center") was formed on October 6, 1988 to handle asbestos-related personal injury claims filed against its members. The members of the Center are all former members of the Asbestos Claims Facility, which was officially dissolved on October 3, 1988 after three years of operation. The Center strives to deal with the asbestos personal injury problem in a rational, responsible, and cost-effective manner.

* * *

II

FORMATION AND DISSOLUTION OF THE ASBESTOS CLAIMS FACILITY

On June 19, 1985, thirty-two producers of asbestos or asbestos containing products ("producers") and sixteen insurers ("insurers") signed an agreement concerning mass resolution of asbestos-related claims. This Agreement is known as the Wellington Agreement because of the role played by Harry Wellington, then-Dean of the Yale University Law School, as a facilitator in the negotiations between the producers and the insurers. The Wellington Agreement resolved dozens of actual and potential lawsuits between the producers and their insurers over insurance coverage for asbestos losses. The agreement also established a nonprofit organization, the Asbestos Claims Facility ("the Facility"), to administer and arrange for the evaluation, settlement, payment, or defense of all asbestos-related personal injury claims against subscribing producers and insurers.

The Facility began handling claims for its members in September 1985. During the initial stages of operation, it operated through employees borrowed from its members. The Facility began hiring permanent staff during the spring of 1986 and was fully staffed and operational by August 1986.

Despite serious structural problems, the Facility achieved several significant accomplishments in its three years of existence. First, it dramatically increased the number of asbestos claims resolved. As best can be determined from historical records, Facility members resolved approximately 6,000 claims in the ten-plus years of asbestos litigation that preceded the creation of the Facility. In its three years of operation, the Facility disposed of more than 18,500 asbestos claims. While some criticized the Facility for not settling claims fast enough and far enough in advance of trial, the Facility clearly increased the disposition rate of asbestos claims by a substantial margin.

The Facility also implemented programs to deal with asbestos claimants who show signs of exposure to asbestos, but who do not show signs of impairment as a result of that exposure. Prior to the inception of the Facility, such claimants often were forced to file lawsuits to avoid being barred by statutes of limitations, and they ultimately ended their lawsuits by compromising their claims for relatively nominal amounts. Claimants who subsequently developed serious asbestos-related illness often found themselves precluded from additional compensation because of their prior settlements. The Facility instituted "Green Card" and "Pleural Registry" programs for such claimants. Under these programs, the Facility waived the limitation periods and placed the claims on inactive status. If a claimant subsequently became impaired from asbestos exposure, the claimant could seek full compensation for the injury. In its three years of existence, the Facility recorded over 5,500 such dispositions. During the first half of 1988, the number of such cases placed on inactive status exceeded the number of cash settlements.

The Facility also reduced the transactional costs associated with the processing of asbestos claims. Before the Facility was created, approximately 1,100 law firms represented asbestos defendants nationwide. Upon inception, the Facility reduced this number to sixty-three and later reduced the number to fifty-five. While quantifying the exact amount of savings attributable to the Facility is difficult because the volume of the asbestos problem significantly increased after the Facility was created, the Facility clearly saved its members substantial sums in defense costs by limiting the number of law firms in the overall defense effort. The Wellington Agreement prohibited cross-claims and third-party complaints among Facility members, thus saving additional transaction costs.

Finally, from the perspective of its members, the Facility materially improved the trial results in those cases that were tried to a verdict. Before the Facility was created, the defendants prevailed in approximately 28 percent of the cases that went to verdict. In the remaining cases, the plaintiffs' average award was approximately $600,000. With the creation of the Facility and centralization of the defense of its members in one law firm per jurisdiction, the Facility defendants prevailed in approximately 65 percent of the cases that proceeded to verdict, and the average adverse verdict was approximately $330,000.

Since its inception, however, the Facility was plagued by three serious structural problems that eventually led to its dissolution. The first problem involved the predetermined shares of each settlement to be paid by the producers. The Center calculated the shares based on the producers' experience in the tort system before the creation of the Facility. At the time the shares were originally calculated, the only kinds of asbestos claims were essentially shipyard claims and claims brought by insulators who worked with asbestos-containing products. After the formation of the Facility, the number of new asbestos claims dramatically increased and the occupational mix of the new claims significantly shifted. While claims continued to be received from shipyard workers and insulators, there was also an influx of new claims from other occupations, such as tire workers, rubber workers, and steel workers. Some producers claimed it was unfair to apply their shares, which were derived primarily from shipyard and insulator experience, to these new kinds of claims. While the sharing formula under the Wellington Agreement did have a provision for share adjustment, it contained a relatively inflexible cap, providing that no producer's share could change by more than 15 percent because of any one prospective adjustment. In the opinion of at least some producers, the Wellington Agreement's sharing formula was too inflexible to account for the changing mix of the new claims.

The second structural problem related to governance. The Facility was established basically as a one-company-one-vote organization. Some members thought this allowed members with small shares to combine and out-vote members with larger shares of some key governance questions.

The third structural problem was philosophical. Facility members came to the Facility with widely divergent claims-handling philosophies and vast differences in available assets to deal with their shares of settlements. Some members favored an aggressive claims philosophy and increased disposition rates. Other members favored a more conservative claims handling approach and disfavored settlements beyond those mandated by the tort system trial calendar. Similarly, some members favored litigating asbestos claims perceived to be meritless, and other members opposed litigating the claims in most circumstances. Rather than improving over time, these philosophical splits were exacerbated by the increasing volume of new asbestos claims and the multiplication of the number of asbestos claims set for trial.

On July 31, 1987, prompted at least in part by these structural problems, Owens Corning Fiberglas Corporation ("OCF") became the first member to withdraw from the Facility. OCF complied with the terms of the Wellington Agreement, under which a producer could withdraw its designation of the Facility as its claims-handling agent only with respect to the claims filed sixty days after notice of withdrawal was given.

During August and September 1987, several other major Facility producers expressed dissatisfaction with their liability shares and demanded share relief from other producers. During these two months, the producers held various meetings and made several proposals on share reallocation. On October 7, 1987, however, the producers informed the Facility's board of directors of their inability to agree to a reallocation and that, as a result, seven major producers wished to withdraw from Facility membership.

From October 1987 through February 1988, the Facility membership divided into three groups: the insurers, seven dissatisfied producers, and thirty producers who opted to remain with the Facility. Numerous meetings during each of these months among and between the three groups concerned potential negotiated withdrawals from the Facility by dissatisfied producers and a reconstituted Facility for the remaining producers.

On February 26, 1988, Eagle–Picher Industries, Inc., one of the dissatisfied producers, filed a complaint against the Facility in the United States District Court for the Southern District of Ohio, seeking termination of the agency relationship between the Facility and Eagle–Picher, and alleging breach of contract, mutual mistake, breach of fiduciary duty, combination and restraint of trade, and antitrust law violations.

During March and April 1988, Carey Canada, Inc., Celotex Corporation, Fibreboard Corporation, Owens–Illinois, Inc., and Pittsburgh Corning Corporation prospectively withdrew from the Facility. OCF also announced that it no longer believed the Facility was the most effective means of resolving meritorious asbestos-related claims and that it wished to withdraw its pending claims from the Facility.

In response, the Facility's board of directors appointed a special nine-person committee to evaluate the situation and to consider the ramifications of dissolution or reorganization of the Facility. For a variety of reasons, including the members' inability to agree on how to reallocate the shares of withdrawing members such as Eagle–Picher, and increasing nonpayment of Facility bills by some Facility members, the Facility was drawn inexorably toward dissolution.

On June 15, 1988, a substantial majority of Facility members agreed to dissolve the Facility effective October 3, 1988. In the interim, the Facility members pledged to use their best efforts to establish a new claims-handling organization for those members that desired one. On September 1, 1988, Facility members voted to dissolve the Facility, and, on October 3, 1988, members filed a certificate of dissolution with the Delaware Secretary of State.

III

FORMATION OF THE CENTER FOR CLAIMS RESOLUTION

Contemporaneously with the dissolution of the Facility, twenty-one companies announced the creation of the Center for Claims Resolution. While the twenty-one founders of the new claims-handling organization are all former members of the Facility, the Center is neither a continuation of nor successor to the Facility. It is independently funded and operated. Unlike the Facility, insurance companies are not members of the Center. However, virtually all insurers that were formerly members of the Facility and whose policyholders joined the Center have signed an agreement to support the Center's operational costs.

In an effort to eliminate the major structural problems that had plagued the Facility, the Center differs from the Facility in several respects. First, the Center has a much more flexible sharing formula for liability payments and expenses, which determines producer shares across four different time periods and a dozen occupational categories. In certain new categories of cases in which the data are insufficient to establish a rational sharing formula, the formula provides for per capita sharing among the members until a reasonable permanent sharing formula can be derived. The new sharing formula removes the Wellington Agreement's 15 percent cap on prospective adjustment. The Center will maintain detailed data concerning pending claims and will generate reports necessary for monitoring of the new sharing formula. The new sharing formula promises to result in a formula that more accurately reflects the changing nature of asbestos claims; its safeguards and procedures also should provide additional fairness and flexibility.

Second, in response to the governance problem, the Center weights members' votes according to each members' share of liability and expenses. Unlike the Facility, the Center thus strikes a balance between the right of each member to have a vote and the substantial disparity in the financial participation of its members.

Finally, all members of the Center have agreed to a claims-handling philosophy providing for the early resolution of meritorious asbestos claims. According to this philosophy, the Center will attempt to settle all meritorious claims on the Trial List significantly before the scheduled trial date. A substantial portion of the Center's estimated annual indemnity payments also will be used to resolve non-Trial List asbestos claims that further the goals of the Center and reduce the backlog of asbestos claims pending against its members.

IV

OBJECTIVES OF THE CENTER

The Center is focusing on the following goals and objectives for the asbestos claims of its members: (1) early resolution of meritorious asbestos claims; (2) resistance and, if necessary, litigation of nonmeritorious asbestos claims; (3) establishment and maintenance of credibility with the judiciary, claimants, members of the plaintiffs' bar, and the public; (4) development of appropriate short-term and long-term strategic plans to fulfill the mission of the Center while maintaining the flexibility to respond to changing circumstances; (5) reduction of allocated legal expenses through internalization of functions currently performed by outside counsel, while maintaining quality representation; (6) reduction of unallocated operating expenses through increased efficiency and productivity within the Center; and (7) attraction, development, and retention of high quality professional and support staff.

To achieve these goals and objectives, the Center will take various actions. As mentioned above, the Center will dispose of all appropriate asbestos claims on the Trial List in a timely and cost-effective manner, and of non-Trial List asbestos claims that further the goals of the Center and reduce the backlog of asbestos claims pending against its members. The Center also will resolve asbestos claims at a level that accurately reflects the exposures of the Center's members, and will continue and expand non-cash disposition programs, such as Pleural Registries and Green Cards. The filing of nonmeritorious asbestos claims will be resisted, and more creative and innovative methods to dispose of asbestos claims will be developed. Finally, to meet its goals and objectives, the Center will develop training programs for Claims Division personnel.

The Center also will dramatically reduce its aggregate defense expenses by (1) internalizing numerous claims-handling functions, currently performed by outside counsel, that can be more efficiently and cost-effectively performed by the Center's staff; (2) achieving the early disposition of all meritorious claims on the Trial List; and (3) participating initially in counsel-sharing arrangements with various non-members.

To deal effectively with the asbestos problem over time, the Center also will devote resources to achieving long-term goals. Among the long-term goals to be addressed by the Center are:

1. Processing of claims, not lawsuits. The Center will institute programs to resolve asbestos claims that have not yet been filed as lawsuits. The Center's staff will receive claims directly from claimants, and will conduct an investigation and secure an appropriate independent medical examination whenever necessary. At the close of the investigation, an evaluation and negotiation period will commence. The claim will be settled for a fair value or denied as nonmeritorious. Alternative dispute resolution mechanisms will be utilized for those claims with a genuine dispute as to value.

2. Independent medical examinations. The Center will consider the development of a network of independent physicians to perform medical examinations of claimants. These physicians would examine the patient, provide evaluations based on a standard protocol, and submit reports in a predetermined format. Members of the network would not be used as trial experts, thereby enhancing their credibility with, and acceptability to, the plaintiffs' bar. The Center has received a prelimi-

nary study of the feasibility of establishing such a network of examining physicians with various specialties.

3. New uses of Green Cards. The Center will attempt to expand the Green Card deferral programs that were successfully used by the Facility. For example, the Center may offer a Green Card with a promise to investigate and to attempt to negotiate a resolution of a claim within a specified period upon manifestation of an asbestos-related disease.

4. Encouragement of limited releases. With the expansion of the Green Card program, the Center will consider encouraging the use of limited releases. For example, in cases not involving malignancies, the claimant would be offered a limited release and would be encouraged to settle for a reduced dollar amount. Should a malignancy subsequently develop, the claimant would then be allowed to present another claim.

5. Improved relationships with unions. With the other long-term programs proposed by the Center, including the program of independent examinations, the Center will develop an effective program for dealing with the unions representing potential claimants. Such a program would explain the Center's various programs and detail its claims-handling philosophy.

6. Branch legal offices in target regions. On an as-needed basis, the Center will consider establishing small branch legal offices in target regions to handle routine litigation functions. The development of these branch offices would greatly reduce allocated defense expenses in high-volume areas, while not sacrificing quality legal representation.

7. Improved communication with the judiciary, press, and plaintiffs' bar. The Center will develop a program of affirmative, rather than reactive or defensive, public relations. In so doing, it is contemplated that the Center will initiate periodic meetings with judges and with plaintiffs' counsel to solicit their input about its programs.

8. Cancer insurance or life insurance programs. The Center will consider the implementation of a program that would provide life insurance as a means of disposing of claims. Such insurance could be triggered to pay proceeds upon confirmation or diagnosis of a malignancy. The Center would need to find an insurance company willing to provide a product resembling group-life insurance. In exchange for the policy, the Center would pay a premium for each nonmalignancy case that is settled.

V

ADMINISTRATION AND FUNDING OF THE CENTER

The Center's headquarters and its national claims office are located in Princeton, New Jersey. The Center's annual operating budget during its first year of existence was approximately $15.0 million. The operating budget is expected to increase substantially in subsequent years as the Center expands its staff and continues to internalize functions. Supporting insurers pay for approximately 70 percent of the operating expenses of the Center. The producer members pay the remaining 30 percent under a tiered agreement, with larger producers paying a larger share.

The Center currently employs approximately sixty professionals in its operations (claims and legal) branch and an additional sixty persons in its administrative (for example, financial and data processing) branch. The number of employees in the operational branch is expected to expand substantially over the near term and should reach approximately 100 by the end of 1989.

The Center pays its indemnity and defense commitments by billing the insurers for their shares of each Center commitment. Generally speaking, the insurance coverage provisions of the Wellington Agreement were carried over intact into the agreement establishing the Center. Accordingly, all producer members of the Center can call upon any insurance policy in effect from the date of first exposure until the date of manifestation to pay on a particular claim.

To facilitate prompt payment of Center indemnity and defense commitments, Center insurers have agreed to thirty days' advance billing of indemnity and defense costs. The Center estimates its settlements and defense costs for each upcoming month and bills its supporting insurers. The insurers pay the Center based upon the estimates, and the Center in turn compensates both claimants and defense counsel. As settlements are consummated and per claim data becomes available, the estimated bills are retroactively adjusted to conform to the Center's actual experience. This procedure should enable the Center to avoid the chronic late payments experienced by the Facility.

The Center has no particular problems with matters related to funding such as timing and contingencies. Funding is available on a current basis for all Center commitments; this situation is not expected to change during the existence of the Center.

VI

Center Claims Processing

The Center does not settle asbestos claims pursuant to a predetermined schedule of benefits. The Center staff analyzes each asbestos claim individually and makes what it considers to be a fair offer on behalf of its members. In analyzing asbestos claims, the Center staff considers several factors, including the severity of the disease, the degree to which Center members contributed to the disease process relative to contributions by nonmembers, and legal trends in the jurisdiction where the claim has been filed.

The Center's analysis of each claim on an individual basis does not preclude it from settling asbestos claims in blocks or groups. The vast majority of the claims settled to date have been disposed of in group fashion after the Center staff reviewed each claim individually. Given the scope of the asbestos problem, the Center sees no practical alternative to this approach.

Although the Center readily accepts claims filed by unrepresented claimants, more than 99 percent of the claims currently being handled by the Center involve claimants represented by counsel. Since the Center membership nearly always represents only a relatively small percentage of the total causation in any given claim, and since the claimant probably will have to proceed in the tort system against recalcitrant, nonmembers who refuse to settle, the Center does not anticipate this situation changing in the foreseeable future.

The Center staff typically negotiates settlements directly with counsel for the claimants. In a few jurisdictions, however, outside attorneys negotiate for the Center. The relationship between the Center staff and the asbestos plaintiffs' bar can be fairly characterized as "friendly adversaries." Compared to history and to the current positions of most non-Center producers, the Center staff has engaged in unprecedented dialogue with the attorneys representing asbestos claimants.

During the first four months of its existence, the Center made several positive strides. First, it disposed of more than 12,300 claims. By way of comparison, as noted above, there were approximately 6,000 total dispositions in the ten-plus years of asbestos litigation before the Facility was created, and the Facility disposed of approximately 18,500 claims in its three years of existence.

Second, the Center has resolved the 12,300 claims at average values that compare very favorably with the historical shares of its members in settlements, both before and during the existence of the Facility.

Third, the Center has decreased the backlog of asbestos claims pending against its members. Approximately 61,000 claims were pending against Center members when the Center commenced operation in October 1988. By January 31, 1989, the Center had reduced that number to 57,000, despite an increase in new filings during the period. Of the 57,000 pending claims, approximately 8,000 (14 percent) were from nontraditional occupations, which the Center did not intend to settle in the same manner as traditional claims. Furthermore, approximately 36,000 of the pending claims (63 percent) represented claims filed from 1987 through 1989. Thus, the Center made substantial progress in settling the older, more meritorious claims against its members.

Fourth, the Center has managed to limit the number and amount of adverse trial verdicts against its members. As best the Center can determine, there have been adverse verdicts against non-Center producers in excess of $240 million since the breakup of the Facility. The Center, in contrast, has been forced to go to verdict only a handful of times during the last four months and has generally prevailed at trial or received relatively small adverse verdicts.

Fifth, the Center also has limited its members' defense costs. Most producers who chose not to join the Center have at least informally admitted that their defense costs have roughly doubled since the demise of the Facility. The Center has held defense costs constant for its members and is implementing plans to reduce defense costs substantially in the future.

Finally, the Center has avoided the recent judicial trend to certify class actions or mass consolidations. Although several judges have recently certified such actions, none has yet been certified against any Center members.

The Center's claims-handling performance thus far has been very encouraging. While it is impossible to predict too much based upon only four months' history, Center members seem quite satisfied with the Center's performance.

VII

Conclusion

The greatest strengths of the Center for Claims Resolution are its professional, competent staff and a membership that is willing and able to allow that staff to explore proactive, creative approaches to the asbestos personal injury problem. Unlike the Asbestos Claims Facility, for which there was no precedent, the Center was designed with the benefit of prior experience. As a result, the Center expands upon the Facility's significant strengths and positive innovations, but avoids the Facility's most serious problems. With its clearer mission and organizational structure, smaller and more unified membership, and more flexible and refined sharing formula, the Center offers its members the best, and perhaps final, opportunity for private industry to address the asbestos problem in a collective fashion.

Appendix

A May 1991 Update

The Center for Claims Resolution has now been in existence for approximately three years. Its headquarters and national claims office are still located in Princeton, New Jersey. The Center has also established a West Coast claims office in San Ramon, California, and a Texas claims office in Richardson, Texas.

The Center has now disposed of more than 46,000 asbestos claims against its members, prevailing in more than half of the cases that have gone to verdict. The average adverse verdict against Center members have been relatively small.

The Center's annual operating budget is now approximately $17.5 million and is not expected to change substantially in the short term. Unlike the Center's first year of operation, supporting insurers now pay virtually all of the operating expenses of the Center, with such payments coming out of the insurance coverage of the producer members. Insurers continue to pay advance bills for indemnity and defense costs. The Center has accordingly managed to avoid the chronic late payments experienced by the Facility.

The Center currently employs 113 professionals in its operations (claims and legal) branch and an additional 70 persons in its administrative branch. Staff counsel and claims people do work formerly done by outside counsel. For example, they receive complaints and open the initial files, prepare case releases, conduct discovery, and direct nearly all settlement negotiations. The role and number of Center employees is expected to remain constant over the near term.

During its second year of operation, the Center adopted an administrative claims program for the processing of claims directly without the necessity of litigation. Response for the program has been mixed. While the program has been responsible for the disposal of more than 1,000 claims, the vast majority of claims currently being handled by the Center involve claimants represented by counsel who have filed lawsuits. As the Center members nearly always represent only a small percentage of the total causation in any given claim, and since the claimants probably have to proceed in the tort system against other defendants and in various bankruptcy courts against insolvent companies, the Center does not anticipate any change in this situation.

The Center has implemented several measures to control the transactional cost associated with the processing of asbestos claims. While the Center and other asbestos defendants consider information about defense cost to be confidential, the available evidence indicates that the Center spends far less for defense of all its members than most major asbestos defendants spend defending a single company. The Center and its members continue to be deeply committed to a philosophy of handling asbestos claims in a manner that minimizes the cost of processing meritorious claims.

In summary, the Center for Claims Resolution has expanded upon the Asbestos Claims Facility's significant strengths and positive innovations and has avoided the Facility's most serious problems. As noted in the main text, the Center offers its members, the judiciary, and the plaintiffs' bar the only opportunity for a private industry to address the asbestos problem in a collective fashion. To date, the Center appears to be accomplishing its goals and objectives in a manner that can sustain its membership and keep it a viable organization.

Notes and Questions

1. The immediate administrative precursors of the Center for Claims Resolution (CCR) were the Wellington and Asbestos Claims Facility, mentioned in Mr. Fitzpatrick's article. For a discussion of the Wellington and Asbestos Claims Facility, see Leland G. Smith, Comment, *Asbestos Claims Facility—An Alternative to Litigation*, 24 Duq.L.Rev. 833 (1986); Harry H. Wellington, *Asbestos: The Private Management of a Public Problem*, 33 Cleve.St.L.Rev. 375 (1985); Harry H. Wellington, *Toxic Torts: Managing the Asbestos Problem*, Yale L.Rep., Spring 1985, at 20. What lessons may be learned from these successive attempts to handle personal injury claims through administrative auspices as an alternative to the tort litigation system? What benefits are achieved through use of claims facilities, and what are the drawbacks? Who is most likely to favor this administrative

approach? In what sense do claims facilities provide fair and adequate justice for claimants?

2. Administrative resolution of asbestos personal injury claims continues to provoke heated controversy. For proposals and commentary on administrative alternatives for handling asbestos claims, *see generally* Lester Brickman, *The Asbestos Claims Management Act of 1991: A Proposal to the United States Congress,* 13 Cardozo L.Rev. 1891 (1992); Lester Brickman, *The Asbestos Litigation Crisis: Is There a Need For An Administrative Alternative?,* 13 Cardozo L.Rev. 1819 (1992); Deborah R. Hensler, *Fashioning a National Resolution of Asbestos Personal Injury Litigation: A Response to Professor Brickman,* 13 Cardozo L.Rev. 1967 (1992); Ronald L. Motley & Susan Nial, *A Critical Analysis of the Brickman Administrative Proposal: Who Declared War on Asbestos Victims' Rights?,* 13 Cardozo L.Rev. 1919 (1992); and Howard D. Samuel, *Comment on the Asbestos Claims Management Act of 1991,* 13 Cardozo L.Rev. 1991 (1992); Colloquy, *An Administrative Alternative to Tort Litigation to Resolve Asbestos Claims,* 13 Cardozo L.Rev. 1817 (1992).

3. For discussions of the merits and problems of claims resolution facilities generally, *see* Florence B. Thomas & Judith Gurney, *The Computerization of Mass Tort Settlement Facilities,* 53 Law & Contemp.Probs. 189 (1990); Deborah R. Hensler, *Assessing Claims Resolution Facilities: What We Need to Know,* 53 Law & Contemp.Probs. 175 (1990); Mark A. Peterson, *Giving Away Money: Comparative Comments on Claims Resolution Facilities,* 53 Law & Contemp.Probs. 113 (1990). *See also* Ian Ayres, *Optimal Pooling in Claims Facilities,* 52 Law & Contemp.Probs. 159 (1990), Chapter VII. A, *supra.*

2. THE JENKINS II ALTERNATIVE DISPUTE RESOLUTION AGREEMENT

ALTERNATE DISPUTE RESOLUTION AGREEMENT

United States District Court, Eastern District of Texas, 1986.
September 5, 1986.

The Alternate Dispute Resolution Agreement is applicable to all asbestos personal injury cases filed by Walter Umphrey and Marlin Thompson in the United States District Court for the Eastern District of Texas from January 1, 1985 through April 1, 1986. If any party wishes to terminate or modify the Alternate Dispute Resolution provisions, a motion must be made to the District Court and a hearing held upon the intention of any party to discontinue the Alternate Dispute Resolution.

I. Monitor. The Court shall designate a special Monitor to oversee the ADR procedure. The plaintiffs' attorneys shall certify to the Monitor those cases on the individual plaintiff attorney's case list which are in compliance with paragraphs I.a through g of the standing order for asbestos cases in the Eastern District of Texas dated July 7, 1982.

II. Negotiation Eligibility. The Monitor shall provide to Wellington attorneys a list of fifty (50) Walter Umphrey and ten (10) Marlin

Thompson cases per month eligible for the negotiation process. The list of cases eligible for negotiation shall be compiled by the Monitor after reviewing plaintiffs' attorney certification. Wellington shall have sixty (60) days from the date determined by the Monitor for each case that such case is eligible for negotiation to review said case in preparation for the negotiation. At the time of certification, plaintiffs' attorneys shall provide Wellington attorneys all information deemed appropriate for proper evaluation of the case including not only the plaintiff's examining physician's narrative report, but also pulmonary function studies and the underlying data in connection therewith, the x-rays, the results of any other tests ordered by such examining physician, and authorizations for the medical records from other physicians and hospitals at which plaintiff has been treated including company medical files where applicable. Copies of medical records will be furnished to plaintiff's attorney within thirty (30) days. Additionally, if Wellington attorneys deem it necessary, the plaintiff shall be made available for a thirty (30) minute personal videotaped interview. During the sixty (60) days following the cases being provided by the Monitor as eligible for the negotiation, the defendants may have the plaintiff examined by a physician of their choice at the defendant's expense with a travel allowance to plaintiff. The results of any such examination shall be provided to the plaintiff's attorney.

III. Negotiation Period. The negotiation period shall be forty (40) days. During such negotiation period, plaintiff's attorneys shall personally confer with a designated attorney or representative of Wellington. Plaintiff's attorney and Wellington attorney, or its designated representative, shall during such period of time negotiate in good faith and make a bona fide effort to resolve each case by negotiation. At the conclusion of the negotiation period, plaintiff's attorneys shall notify the Monitor in writing for each particular case whether the case has been settled by negotiation. Upon receipt of such written notice for cases not settled by negotiation, the Monitor shall prepare a list of cases which shall be submitted to arbitration for resolution by Arbitrators.

IV. Arbitration Period. The arbitration period shall be ninety (90) days from the date certified by the Monitor that a particular case is eligible for submission to the Arbitrator.

V. Arbitrator Selection. The defendants and the plaintiffs shall each select one person as an arbitrator selector. The two selectors designated will then meet independent of the attorneys who chose them, and they will agree on the individual number of and the Arbitrators who will ultimately decide the cases in the arbitration phase. The parties shall jointly negotiate with the individuals selected regarding agreement to serve and compensation for their services. In the event an agreement is not reached regarding compensation, the parties shall notify the court of an early date and the court shall enter an appropriate order.

VI. Cases Subject to Stay Orders. In any case that the medical evidence of a particular plaintiff demonstrates that the plaintiff is not suffering at the time of evaluation from the disease of asbestosis or cancer, such as plaintiffs with only pleural plaques for pleural thickening without restrictive impairment by pulmonary function studies, the Monitor shall place such cases on the Court's administrative docket and stay these cases for a period of two years. At any time during the two year period of time, plaintiff's attorney may, with proper medical justification, move the Monitor to remove such case from the administrative stay; at which time the case would immediately be placed on the active ADR docket. If there is no evidence of asbestosis or other asbestos-related disease at the end of the two year stay, plaintiff shall have the option of either dismissing the suit, receiving a green card from Wellington which will toll limitations, or requesting that the case be placed on the Court's active docket where it will proceed through negotiation and arbitration and ultimately, to trial if so requested.

VII. Cases Submitted to the Arbitrator. Within the ninety (90) day time period for determination of cases submitted to the Arbitrator, the parties shall by agreement and in cooperation with the Arbitrator schedule presentation of cases. In the event an agreement is not possible, the Monitor shall be promptly notified and the Monitor shall provide the parties with such schedule. The cases will be submitted to the various arbitrators on a rotating basis. The Arbitrator shall conduct a hearing and receive evidence in each case. The matters presented to the Arbitrator are not controlled by the Federal Rules of Evidence and may be presented in summary or affidavit form, or by deposition or live witness, but shall include evidence as to product exposure, whether the plaintiff suffers from an asbestos-related injury or disease and any damages to which the plaintiff may be entitled. The parties may by agreement modify the method of presentation or establish an agreed procedure concerning the trial or presentation to the Arbitrator. However, any such agreement shall be first submitted to the Court for approval.

To assist the Arbitrators in making consistent determinations, there will be seven categories of evaluation on which the arbitrator would decide the award amount of damages, if any. The cases to be considered by the arbitrator would be all those cases not placed on the pleural inactive docket by the Monitor. The seven potential findings by the Arbitrator are as follows:

(1) No asbestos-related disease and therefore no recovery by the plaintiff;

(2) Pleural changes with restrictive impairment;

(3) Pulmonary asbestosis;

(4) Asbestos-related cancer cases;

(5) Confirmed Mesothelioma;

(6) That it is a pleural case with no restrictive impairment and recommending that it be placed on the pleural inactive docket.

(7) That a particular case does not fit in any of the enumerated categories and making an appropriate determination or award.

In determining the appropriate award in each category, the Arbitrator should consider such factors as age of the plaintiff, degree of asbestos related disability, extent and type of exposure to asbestos, smoking history, significant non-asbestos health problems relating to any disability, lost wages, dependents, medical records and other reports, increased risk of cancer, progression of asbestos-related injury, and pain and suffering. The plaintiffs shall file with the Arbitrator the amounts and parties of any prior settlement in a particular case and shall furnish a copy of such information to the defendants prior to any hearing before the Arbitrator. Defendants shall receive a credit for all amounts paid by such settlements and the defendants shall subtract the total amount of prior settlements from the Arbitrator's award, if any. The arbitrator shall also make percentage findings relating to participating, non-settling manufacturers and suppliers in the arbitration and to non-participating, non-settling defendants. To determine the effect of the percentage findings on the final award, the parties shall apply the doctrine of *Duncan v. Cessna*. The Arbitrator shall have thirty (30) days from the date of hearing to render a decision based upon a review of the evidence.

Upon receipt of the decision of the Arbitrator, the parties shall have twenty (20) days to notify the Monitor whether they accept or reject the award of the Arbitrator. In the event the award is accepted, the parties shall provide the Court with an appropriate order the case shall be dismissed. In the event the award is not accepted, the Monitor shall assign the case to the docket of the individual judge to whom the case would originally have been assigned to take its place on the trial docket. If the case is to be tried, the plaintiffs waive any claim for punitive damages and the defendants waive state-of-the-art defense. The matters to be tried would include product exposure by the plaintiffs, whether the plaintiff suffer an asbestos-related injury or disease, and actual damages, if any. The procedure to be followed would be similar to that in Hardy v. Johns–Manville, 681 F.2d 334 (5th Cir.1982). The jury, however, will make the appropriate percentage findings as set out in the decisions of Duncan v. Cessna, 665 S.W.2d 414 (Tex.1984) and *Moore v. Johns–Manville Sales Corporation*, as those cases apply the law of the State of Texas.

Should any cases not be settled after proceeding through the arbitration stage, then each party shall be authorized to conduct all discovery allowed by the applicable Federal and State Rules of Civil Procedure except that there shall be no discovery related to punitive damages or state-of-the-art. No evidence shall be admitted regarding the amount of any award by the Arbitrator or that an appeal was taken therefrom.

VIII. Cases which are disposed of by settlement or through an arbitrator's award shall be paid by defendants within thirty (30) days after settlement agreement is negotiated or, where not appealed, within 30 days after receipt of arbitrator's decision.

IX. Order of Presentation. The parties shall prepare and present cases through each phase of the Alternate Dispute Resolution Procedure in the chronological order of their filing. Exceptions will be allowed by the Monitor where in the judgment of the Monitor sufficient evidence of hardship exists.

SIGNED and AGREED to on this the day of September, 1986.

Attorney for Asbestos Claims Facility

Notes and Questions

1. Judge Parker envisioned that the *Jenkins II* Alternative Dispute Resolution Agreement would dispose of all after-occurring asbestos cases that were not captured by the *Jenkins I* class action settlement. The *Jenkins II* ADR mechanism experienced limited success:

> Although *Jenkins I* settled 755 cases, approximately 1,000 cases still remained on the Eastern District of Texas docket, and plaintiffs were filing approximately 150 to 200 new cases each month. In June 1986, Judge Parker issued a preliminary ADR order and, after the defendants' objections and appeals to modify that order, the attorneys signed an ADR agreement in September 1986. This agreement set up an ADR mechanism for handling all asbestos cases filed in that district from January 1, 1985, until April 1, 1986. The agreement included cases filed after the *Jenkins I* class certification. In the fall of 1986, Judge Parker created a new class, called *Jenkins II,* for all Beaumont Division cases filed from January 1, 1985, through March 31, 1986, and issued an order staying all asbestos cases pending in the district. He viewed the ADR process as administratively efficient and beneficial to the defendants because it reduced their exposure to future damages and their transaction costs.

> The *Jenkins II* ADR agreement detailed a three-stage process for handling newly filed claims in the district. In the first stage, plaintiffs' attorneys certified to an ADR monitor the asbestos cases eligible for ADR treatment, the monitor referred sixty cases a month to the defendants for an eligibility agreement, and the defendants had sixty days to consent. If eligibility was agreed upon, the parties had forty days to negotiate a settlement in the second stage of the process. If settlement did not occur, the parties had ninety days for arbitration in the third stage. If arbitration did not result in settlement, the plaintiff had the option of filing suit in district court, except that the ADR agreement permitted no discovery relating to punitive damages or the state-of-the-art defense.

> The *Jenkins II* ADR process began in late 1986 and functioned until early 1988. Magistrate Judges McKee and Hines served as ADR monitors, and Magistrate Judge Hines set up an elaborate calendaring system that clustered asbestos filings into ADR groups. The original *Cimino* complaint was filed on May 12, 1986, and ultimately received a monitor's certification of eligibility as part of an ADR group. However, *Cimino* never advanced beyond the first stage of the ADR process because, by late 1988, Judge Parker and Magistrate Judge Hines agreed

that the ADR process was failing and that something needed to be done to handle the ever growing number of new asbestos filings in the district. Although Judge Parker successfully settled some 600 additional cases by the time *Cimino* was certified for ADR eligibility in 1988, over 2,300 asbestos cases remained on the Eastern District of Texas docket. Convinced that the *Jenkins II* ADR was not working and that newly filed claims were swamping the court, Judge Parker initiated the *Cimino* class certification by requesting plaintiff's counsel to file for class certification.

See Linda S. Mullenix, *Beyond Consolidation: Post–Aggregative Procedure in Asbestos Mass Tort Litigation*, 32 Wm. & Mary L.Rev. 475, 490–91 (1991). What, if anything, does the perceived failure of the *Jenkins II* ADR program teach about the possible use of ADR auspices to resolve thousands of mass tort claimants in a non-adjudicative setting?

2. Subsequent asbestos settlement classes such as *Georgine* and *Ahearn* have incorporated, as part of the settlement agreement, recourse to various successive ADR auspices if claimants decline to accept the court's proffered settlement value. Does the *Jenkins II* ADR experience offer any forecast concerning the utility of these ADR provisions in the asbestos settlement classes?

3. At least one commentator has suggested use of alternative dispute resolution techniques to resolve mass tort litigation. *See generally,* Jeffrey S. Brenner, Note, *Alternatives to Litigation: Toxic Torts and Alternative Dispute Resolution—A Proposed Solution to the Mass Tort Case,* 20 Rutgers L.J 779 (1989). For commentary relating to the use of alternative dispute resolution in complex litigation generally, *see* Allan R. Talbot, SETTLING THINGS, SIX CASE STUDIES IN ENVIRONMENTAL MEDIATION (1983); Robert H. Gorske, *An Arbitrator Looks at Expediting the Large, Complex Case,* 5 Ohio St.J.Disp.Res. 381 (1990); Lucy v. Katz, *The L'Ambiance Plaza Mediation: A Case Study in the Judicial Settlement of Mass Torts,* 5 Ohio St.J.Disp.Res. 277 (1990); Timothy Kratz, *Alternative Dispute Resolution in Complex Litigation,* 57 UMKCL.Rev. 839 (1989); David T. Peterson & Thomas P. Redick, *Innovations and Considerations in Settling Toxic Tort Litigation,* 3 Nat. Resources J. 9 (1988); Annual Judicial Conference—Second Circuit, *Innovative Techniques for Resolving Complex Litigation,* 115 F.R.D. 374 (1987). *See also* Dwight Golan, Making *Alternative Dispute Resolution Mandatory: The Constitutional Issues,* 68 Or.L.Rev. 487 (1989).

B. AGENT ORANGE
HARVEY P. BERMAN, THE AGENT ORANGE VETERAN PAYMENT PROGRAM
53 Law & Contemp.Probs. 49 (1990).

I
INTRODUCTION

On May 7, 1984, a settlement was reached in a class action brought by Vietnam veterans and members of their families against seven chemical companies for injuries (including disability and death of veterans and birth defects in children of veterans) alleged to have been caused by the veterans' exposure to Agent Orange and other phenoxy herbicides in Vietnam. Soon after settlement, Aetna learned of the opportunity to participate in a program to pay the settled claims. Before participating in such a program, however, Aetna had to conduct a cost-benefit analysis of its participation. From a positive standpoint, the payment program presented an opportunity for Aetna to do what it does best—process and pay claims—in a new context. Successful administration of such a program could result in new business opportunities in similar mass tort settlement situations. On the other hand, the *Agent Orange* litigation had aroused strong emotions in the veteran community. There was a danger that association with such a project, particularly in connection with the denial of claims, could create adverse publicity and alienate a significant segment of the insurance-buying public. Moreover, as an insurer, Aetna was concerned about participation in an arrangement where private corporations had assumed the burden for injuries resulting from a governmental function. Finally, Aetna was concerned that operating under the control of the court would reduce the degree of flexibility needed to administer successfully a program different from that of the usual benefit arrangements. Meetings and discussions with various veterans' groups (including Aetna-employed Vietnam veterans) and with the office of the special master of the payment program convinced us, however, that not only was Aetna able to do the job, but that such involvement could lend credibility to the project. With the court providing general guidelines and eligibility criteria, Aetna's job as claims administrator of the Agent Orange Veteran Payment Program was seen as primarily one of filling in the eligibility details and developing the necessary processes.

II

THE LITIGATION

Following settlement of the class action, Judge Jack Weinstein of the United States District Court for the Eastern District of New York appointed Kenneth R. Feinberg as special master to develop a plan for distribution of the settlement funds—expected to be almost $200 million after attorneys' fees and expenses.

Judge Weinstein accepted the special master's distribution plan with some modifications on May 28, 1985. As modified, the plan provided for a payment program to distribute approximately $150 million (subsequently grown to approximately $170 million) in cash payments to eligible veterans and families of deceased veterans, and a nonprofit foundation initially funded at $45 million to provide services to exposed veterans and their families, particularly veterans' children with birth defects. Actual distribution could not begin until all appeals were decided. The program was designed to have a ten year life, expiring in 1994, with provision for investment of unpaid funds during that period. A key element of the cash payment plan, extraordinary for a mass tort case, was the provision of awards for nontraumatic total disability or death of a veteran exposed to Agent Orange, without a showing of a causal relationship between the exposure and the health problem.

More than 200 companies—including insurers, third-party administrators, and data processing companies—expressed interest in bidding on the contract to administer the cash payment plan. On June 24, 1986, Special Master Kenneth Feinberg awarded Aetna the contract, subject to the approval of Judge Weinstein and the development of a mutually acceptable agreement. Separate contracts were awarded for the investment function.

* * *

On April 21, 1987, in nine separate opinions, the Second Circuit affirmed all of the district court judgments, with some modifications. The court did strike down the nonprofit foundation, however, indicating that the district court should consider selected projects under the control of the court to assist veterans. The payment program was not affected.

III

THE FACILITY

The facility through which the settlement was implemented is the *Agent Orange* Fund ("Fund"), an unincorporated, tax-exempt, charitable organization. Established by court order, the legal basis for the Fund lay in the discretion granted to it by the settlement agreement, the authority provided by Rule 23 of the Federal Rules of Civil Procedure, and the court's inherent equity power. The Fund includes the monies to be distributed by the payment program, those to be paid for other social services, and those to be paid to trusts in Australia and New Zealand for the benefit of veterans in those countries. The maintenance and administration of these monies is subject to the continuous jurisdiction of the court.

The Fund is managed by court-appointed officers, who are authorized to contract with various organizations for the distribution of funds to veterans and social service programs. Upon the resolution of all appeals, that portion of the settlement funds designated for the payment program was transferred from escrow to the Fund. Now being managed by investment managers, the Fund will make initial payments to each veteran or survivor once initial eligibility is certified, and yearly disability payments for each year the veteran's eligibility continues during the life of the program. If investment earnings are higher than expected, or claims are lower than expected, amounts payable in subsequent years may be increased, both for deaths and newly-arising disabilities, and for existing disabilities. No assets of the Fund may revert to the chemical company defendants or be used for non-charitable purposes.

Officers of the Fund, which is headquartered in Brooklyn, New York, consist of a president (Special Master Feinberg) and a vice president (who is the Special Master for Investment Policy). A program manager for the payment program has been designated, and an advisory board has been created to advise the court and the Fund on the implementation of the payment program.

Unless the court determines otherwise, the Fund will be dissolved by court order in 2009 at the termination of the settlement agreement, or when all funds have been distributed, whichever is earlier. Ten million dollars of the settlement funds will be held by the court until dissolution to indemnify the defendants against state court judgments.

Compensation of the claims administrator by the Fund is based upon agreed-upon hourly or daily rates for work performed in designated labor categories, and the cost of certain other services and facilities provided. Compensation of the investment managers is based upon agreed-upon percentages of Fund assets under management.

IV

THE CLAIMS ADMINISTRATION AGREEMENT

The Claims Administration Agreement governs the relationship between the Fund and Aetna and, among other things, describes the duties and responsibilities of the claims administrator. The duties of the claims administrator include document development, maintenance of veteran mailing lists and of the claim-file database, veteran information services, liaison with other consultants, claim processing (including application of eligibility criteria and adherence to performance standards), banking services, reports, quality control and audit of claims administration services, testing and staff training, and actuarial services involving analysis of claims experience. The agreement also specifies such terms as the location of operations, limits on subcontracting, prevention of conflicts of interest, changes in functions and responsibilities, and the degree of care expected of the claims administrator.

The role of the special master and the legal relationships between the special master, the court and the claims administrator also are set forth in the agreement. The special master administers the Fund "under the supervision and direction of the [c]ourt and with the advice and assistance of the [a]dvisory [b]oard." The special master, the advisory board, other representatives of the Fund, and the court are responsible for all general communication with the public. With certain limited exceptions, the claims administrator is prohibited from communicating directly with members of the public about the Fund. Finally, the special master, as well as the other representatives of the Fund, is not personally liable for any of his official actions or for any breach of the Claims Administration Agreement itself. The claims administrator may look only to the "Fund (or its successor organization) and its assets . . . for payment under [the Claims Administration] Agreement or for relief in case of breach of [the] Agreement."

Besides defining the basis for compensation (including adjustments) and the terms of payment, the agreement also provides for handling compensation if the agreement is terminated. The agreement also mandates the maintenance of minimum levels of liability and other insurance (including bonding) by the claims administrator and indemnifies both the Fund and the claims administrator against loss resulting from a breach of duty by the other party.

Under the agreement, disputes between the parties are to be submitted to binding arbitration if they cannot be resolved by negotiation. All proceedings related to the agreement are subject to the jurisdiction of the United States District Court for the Eastern District of New York, and the agreement is governed by the laws of New York. The special master may bypass negotiation and arbitration, however, and apply directly to the court for specific performance or for any other equitable relief necessary to protect the interests of the class members.

V

The Payment Program

As indicated above, the payment program is unique in that the eligibility process does not involve establishment of the normal tort elements: causation, fault, and proof of damages. Rather, the process is designed to provide as much relief as possible to those individuals most in need of assistance who can satisfy certain threshold criteria. Thus the victims avoid the need to establish a violation of a duty owed to them and a causal link to their injuries; in return, they give up the right to collect in proportion to their specific losses. This situation is analogous to that under a first-party insurance policy that offers scheduled benefits for certain types of losses such as loss of a limb or accidental death.

Eligibility for payments requires a showing that (1) the veteran was exposed to Agent Orange in or near Vietnam at any time from 1961 through 1971, (2) the veteran, or the veteran's child, suffers from a long-term total disability or has died, and (3) the death or disability arose principally from causes other than trauma, accident, or self-inflicted injury.

A. *Exposure*

The Fund has contracted with exposure consultants to develop a methodology for evaluating exposure to Agent Orange as a part of the claim process. A questionnaire was designed to elicit information about the dates and locations of the veteran's service in Vietnam and whether the veteran had duties involving the handling or application of Agent Orange. After the questionnaires are completed, the consultants analyze the data under a computerized process that also considers authenticated sources of information about military unit locations in Vietnam and records of herbicide dissemination. Finally, exposure is determined by certain criteria, such as actual handling or application of Agent Orange, or presence in a sprayed area within temporal and geographic limits established by the court. Under this methodology, there are no degrees of exposure—the veteran either has been exposed or has not. After analysis of the initial batch of processed claims, the minimum exposure threshold may be adjusted to maintain claim incidence expectations.

B. Total Disability and Death

Disability will be determined in accordance with the definition in the Social Security Act, and veterans who are receiving Social Security disability benefits will be presumed to be disabled for purposes of the payment program. For veterans who are not receiving Social Security benefits, the claims administrator will apply the Social Security definition with its own claim settlement practices, giving the benefit of the doubt to the claimant in questionable situations. Disability will be deemed to commence on the date of onset determined by the Social Security Administration, if such a finding has been made. Otherwise, disability is presumed to have commenced on the later of the first day of the program (January 1, 1985) or the date of filing a claim. The veteran may overcome this presumption, however, with a showing of "evidence clearly demonstrating the date of onset." Disability will be deemed to terminate when the veteran dies or recovers from the disability.

Under the original distribution plan, surviving spouses or dependent children of a deceased veteran who met the general eligibility criteria described above are eligible for one-time survivor payments. Spouses must have been lawfully married to the veteran at the time of his death. Surviving children (including stepchildren, adopted children, and foster children living in the veteran's home) under age nineteen or full-time students at the time of the veteran's death are eligible, but only if there is no surviving spouse. All eligible surviving children will share the payment equally. In November, 1989, the court expanded the definition of eligible survivors to include, in order, the veteran's parents, adult children, and siblings if there is no spouse or child meeting the original definition.

C. Excluded Causes

Deaths or disabilities predominantly caused by traumatic, accidental, or self-inflicted injury are not eligible for payment. Thus, excluded injuries would include war wounds, auto accidents, falls, suicides or attempted suicides, intentional drug overdoses, and gunshot wounds. These types of claims are most probably unrelated to Agent Orange exposure and are relatively easy to define and administer.

D. The Claim Process

To be considered timely, claims for disabilities or death originally had to be filed by January 1, 1989. However, the court has now removed all timely filing requirements. The current application for payment is a comprehensive yet easily readable form with complete instructions for furnishing all necessary medical, exposure, and other information. The form also contains a program description and is available in Spanish. The process is designed to obviate the need for counsel to assist the claimant. Based upon data collected on potential claimants, 295,000 preliminary letters were mailed to veterans with information about the program. The claims administrator has received

115,000 requests for claim kits, that is, applications for payments, and 48,000 completed claims, both of which are consistent with expectations.

The claims administrator acknowledges completed applications, reviews them for completeness, and requests additional information as necessary. The claims administrator then determines whether the claimant meets the eligibility criteria described above, and notifies the claimant of denial or approval of the application. The claims administrator also provides a toll-free number for questions about the program or particular claims.

Claims denied by the claims administrator must contain the reason for denial and are subject to appeal to a special master for appeals appointed by the court. Use of counsel by the claimant at this point would not be unexpected, based upon experience with other insurance arrangements, although such use has not proven to be common.

E.   *The Payment Process*

The claims administrator paid the first death claims in February of 1989 and the first disability claims in March of 1989. Initial payments have been made on a weekly basis after approval by the program manager. Before such dates, a statement is sent to the investment managers specifying the total amount to be paid. The claims administrator pays claims by drafts drawn on a payment bank. Upon presentment, the payment bank will inspect and accept the drafts and advise a depository bank to make sufficient funds available to the payment bank to cover the drafts.

F.   *Payment Amounts*

Payment levels will depend on the total number of disabled or deceased veterans for whom claims are submitted, and the number of claimants meeting exposure and other eligibility requirements. The estimated maximum award for disability was originally estimated to be about $12,800 over the life of the program, which, as noted above, is expected to terminate December 31, 1994. Disability awards will be payable in annual installments, and individual awards will vary according to the age of the veteran and the duration of the disability. Lower payments are made to older veterans and for shorter disabilities. No credit is given for any year of disability after a veteran's sixtieth birthday. In December of 1989, the court ordered one-time, "bonus" payments to be made to all veterans receiving disability benefits under the program before November 15, 1989.

Death benefits are paid in a lump sum, with the maximum benefit originally estimated at approximately $3400. Survivors of veterans who died before the program commenced receive the maximum benefit; awards for other survivors are based on the number of years remaining in the program at the time of the veteran's death. No payment is made for death occurring after the age of sixty.

Payments after the first year of the program are adjusted upward or downward based upon claim incidence in the first year, changes in projected investment earnings, and other relevant factors. Such adjustments will be made periodically throughout the life of the program. The objective of such adjustments, of course, is to provide for the maximum payout possible while maintaining funds to support payments over the life of the program. The claims administrator will provide the actuarial services necessary for such adjustments under the Claims Administration Agreement.

VI

ASSESSMENT OF THE PAYMENT PROGRAM

A. *Strengths and Assets*

There are several strengths and assets of the payment program that should enable it to achieve its objectives cost-effectively. Probably the most important is the structure of the settlement plan itself, which avoids the need to relitigate the liability and damage issues in each claim. Eligibility for awards will be determined, to the maximum extent possible, by reference to objective criteria with minimal exercise of judgment. The effect of this structure is to maximize benefits and minimize expenses.

As indicated above, determining eligibility by a process that primarily uses objective factors has enabled the claims administrator to reduce the cost of the claim process by taking maximum advantage of sophisticated computer systems. These systems also should contribute to more effective reporting and analysis of the claim experience, which supports necessary adjustments in the program and otherwise facilitates the court's and the special master's oversight functions.

Another strength is the communication system that is an integral part of the program. The preliminary letters to veterans were the first step in that process, providing a clear written description of the program and the claim process. The claim kits provide additional information. Through the toll-free telephone system, the claims administrator can answer questions and provide information about the claim process, the settlement, and counseling resources available to the veterans. More than 395,000 calls have been handled through this system, and the special needs of particular groups, including Spanish-speaking and institutionalized veterans, have been taken into account.

B. *Weaknesses and Problems*

One problem that arose after the project was well underway was the disruption caused by the Second Circuit's stay of implementation of the plan in August 1986. Obviously, this was something over which neither Aetna nor the district court had any control. At that point, Aetna had expended significant amounts of money and time to hire and train personnel and purchase equipment, and had reserved space within Aetna facilities to operate the project. During the almost two-year hiatus between the entry of the stay and the Supreme Court's denial of certiorari, it was impossible to retain all of these resources, and it was necessary to start over in some respects in June of 1988. By working as a consultant for the Fund during a portion of the hiatus, however, Aetna was able to continue development of some of the basic tools needed to process claims so that a minimum of additional time was lost from the original implementation schedule.

One operational weakness, at least from the claims administrator's standpoint, is that all of the functions and resources necessary to implement the payment program are not concentrated in one entity. Among other things, development of the exposure criteria and management of general information concerning the program are not within the control of the claims administrator, even though such functions may directly impact on the quality of its work. While this has not been an overwhelming problem, it has led to some disruptions in work schedules. For example, publication of news articles regarding the payment program has triggered more calls to the claims administrator than it was equipped to handle, thus putting a strain on the communication system. Similarly, reliance on the exposure consultants to finalize the recommended criteria caused some delay in the implementation of the claim process.

While it might be inappropriate to characterize it as a weakness, a program such as the *Agent Orange* payment program that is under the control and supervision of a court may at times experience a conflict between the legal, result-oriented operations and concerns of the court, and the business, process-oriented operations and concerns of a claims administrator. In other words, the court may be accustomed to taking months to consider a decision and then issuing an order with the expectation that it will be immediately followed. A business organization, despite (and sometimes because of) its computer resources and structure, cannot always react immediately to a change in the operation of the program, at least not without substantial disruption. This type of conflict can be minimized, however, if both the court and the contractors with whom it deals are cognizant of, and consider the effect of their actions on, the needs and functions of the others.

C. Changes and Recommendations

In planning for future claims resolution facilities of this type, the *Agent Orange* Veteran Payment Program can well be looked upon as a valuable learning experience. The lessons learned suggest that future controlling organizations should take certain steps to ensure their success. The controlling organization should determine eligibility for payment on objective factors to the maximum extent possible to avoid litigation of the issues of causation and damages, and to take advantage of the cost savings associated with computerized claim systems. The organization also should concentrate control of the claim process, and the external factors directly affecting that process, in the claims administrator to the maximum extent possible, subject to appropriate oversight by the court. If that cannot be done, the controlling organization should take steps to integrate the operation of all functions to achieve synergy and avoid disruption in the operation of one function by another.

Finally, the organization should structure the claim process to avoid a "crush" of claims at the beginning of the program to spread the claim processing burden over a reasonable period.

With regard to the unavoidable period of uncertainty between the date the trial court approves the distribution plan and the date all appeals are exhausted, the organization selected as claims administrator should focus its energies on perfecting the payment system, anticipating different levels of demand from those originally projected, and, in general, working out the "bugs" in the program. Resources needed for implementation should be planned so they can be called upon quickly when needed without incurring expense to retain them prematurely.

VII

CONCLUSION

There were some operational problems in the first year of the *Agent Orange* Veteran Payment Program that led to slower distribution of fund assets than expected. These problems have been overcome, however, and, as of August 31, 1990, the program had distributed $68.1 million in cash payments to over 21,000 individual Vietnam veterans and survivors of deceased veterans. The claims administrator continues to receive approximately 200 new applications per week; it is expected that the claim process will operate smoothly and efficiently throughout the remainder of the program.

Notes and Questions

1. Challenges to the *Agent Orange* settlement and Veterans' Payment Program continued into the mid–1990s. The Second Circuit has continued to uphold the *Agent Orange* settlement and to enjoin newly filed, independent actions brought in state court around the country. The Second Circuit also has upheld the *Agent Orange* agreement against attacks based on lack of personal and subject matter jurisdiction, unfairness of the settlement, and judicial bias. *See* In re "Agent Orange" Prod. Liab. Litig., Ivy v. Diamond Shamrock Chemicals, 996 F.2d 1425 (2d Cir.1993)(upholding *Agent Orange I* settlement agreement against various challenges).

2. For commentary concerning the *Agent Orange* settlement terms and administration of the Veterans Payment Fund, *see generally,* Robert H. Sand, *How Much Is Enough? Observations in Light of the* Agent Orange *Settlement,* 9 Harv.Envtl.L.Rev. 283 (1985).

Chapter XIII

BANKRUPTCY AND TRUST FUNDS

A. THE MANVILLE TRUST FUND

NOTE, THE MANVILLE BANKRUPTCY: TREATING MASS TORT CLAIMS IN CHAPTER 11 PROCEEDINGS

96 Harv. L.Rev. 1121 (1983).

The reorganization petition filed in federal bankruptcy court by the Manville Corporation on August 26, 1982, placed a major challenge before the new federal bankruptcy system, which the Supreme Court had recently shaken with its decision in *Northern Pipeline Construction Co. v. Marathon Pipe Line Co.* Whereas Congress had foreseen the issues raised by the *Northern Pipeline* case when it passed the Bankruptcy Reform Act of 1978 (BRA), it did not anticipate that a healthy and solvent corporation might seek refuge from potentially massive but speculative tort liability in the BRA's chapter 11 reorganization provisions. Although Manville and UNR Industries are the first such apparently healthy corporations to file chapter 11 petitions in the face of massive tort claims, manufacturers in a variety of industries that face similar liability could follow suit.

The *Manville* filing presents a stark contrast to the traditional reorganization case, in which the debtor knows the identities of its creditors and the amount of its debts. In such cases, the debtor seeks the aid of the court only in restructuring its finances and satisfying its existing creditors to the greatest extent possible. The most extraordinary aspects of the *Manville* case are that the majority of Manville's creditors are unknown and that the majority of the debts on which Manville bases its claims of prospective insolvency are contingent and unliquidated. Manville thus appears to be attempting to use the bankruptcy power largely as a tool to limit the aggregate size of its current and future liabilities. If successful, Manville's strategy will have a profound effect on all asbestos-related tort litigation; Manville is the nation's largest asbestos manufacturer and the "deepest pocket" among the codefendants in the many asbestos-related suits.

I. APPLYING THE DOCTRINE OF DISMISSAL OF BAD FAITH
REORGANIZATION PETITIONS TO *MANVILLE*

The Bankruptcy Reform Act of 1978 reaffirms bankruptcy courts'
broad equitable and statutory powers to deal flexibly with unorthodox
bankruptcy petitions by means ranging from dismissal to extraordinary
relief. The new Bankruptcy Code has been interpreted to confer the
traditional equitable power to dismiss petitions filed in bad faith, even
though the Code does not explicitly impose a good faith requirement.
The "bad faith" doctrine that was developed at common law has been
held to be incorporated into the Bankruptcy Code through section
1112(b), which permits bankruptcy courts to dismiss a petition "for
cause," whether or not such cause is among the nine explicitly enumerated in section 1112(b).

Typically, reorganization cases dismissed for bad faith have been of
four types: those in which there is no reasonable chance of successful
rehabilitation, those that attempt to work a fraud on the court, those
filed to settle internal disputes of a business entity, and those in which
the conduct of the debtor clearly indicates that its sole intent is to hinder
or delay its creditors. Manville's filing does not necessarily fit within
any of these categories. First, the strength of Manville's on-going
operations leaves no doubt that a successful reorganization is feasible.
Second, although some asbestos claimants have alleged that Manville has
attempted to defraud the court by placing assets in newly created
subsidiaries beyond the court's reach, those allegations remain unprov-
en; in any event, proof of such a segregation of assets would more likely
result in the bankruptcy judge's taking control of the segregated assets
than in the dismissal of the entire case. Third, Manville's filing is
clearly motivated by external problems with creditors rather than by
internal squabbles. Finally, although the tort claimants argue that
hindrance and delay are indeed Manville's primary motives, courts have
generally been reluctant to find such a motive except in the most
extreme cases, those in which it appears that delay is the sole reason for
the filing.

These four categories are illustrative rather than exclusive; that
Manville may not fit neatly within any of them does not mean that its
petition may not be dismissed. The underlying inquiry, as in all
instances of alleged bad faith reorganization petitions, is whether the
debtor "seeks to abuse the bankruptcy law by employing it for a purpose
for which it was not intended to be used." The Bankruptcy Code,
however, does not lend itself easily to such an inquiry; it embodies many
varied purposes—protecting jobs, ensuring a fresh start for debtors,
ensuring equitable treatment for creditors—designed to benefit debtors
and creditors alike.

Manville can argue that filing a chapter 11 petition at such an early
date is entirely consistent with the basic policy of the Bankruptcy Code
that encourages debtors to file petitions before their financial position
deteriorates to the point at which rehabilitation is no longer feasible,

even if that point would be reached before actual insolvency. Not only may creditors file involuntary petitions when debtors have waited too long without filing voluntary petitions, but moreover both section 1112(b) of the Code and the case law warn debtors that a petition will be dismissed when there is little or no likelihood of successful rehabilitation.

Nonetheless, the absence of a requirement of insolvency as a prerequisite for filing a chapter 11 petition should not be interpreted to mean that financial condition is not a relevant consideration when evaluating the good faith of such a petition. Moving along a continuum from balance sheet and equitable insolvency toward perfect financial health, one eventually reaches a point of relative financial soundness at which application of the bankruptcy laws could not have been contemplated by Congress. Unfortunately, Congress has never identified the point at which the invocation of the bankruptcy power ceases to be legitimate. Such line-drawing was left to the courts, to be accomplished by applying equitable principles and the policies of the Code to individual cases. In general, the inquiry should focus on whether the debtor is more likely than not to reach either balance sheet or equitable insolvency in the foreseeable future.

In the *Manville* case, the court's inquiry should involve a careful scrutiny of the company's present financial condition, projected earnings, and projected asbestos-related liability. The asbestos claimants should be given an opportunity to challenge the findings of the medical study of projected asbestosis occurrence that Manville commissioned as well as Manville's assessment of its financial condition. If the creditors succeed in showing that Manville is more likely than not to remain solvent for the foreseeable future, the reorganization petition should be dismissed as an attempted misuse of the bankruptcy power. If, however, the creditors are unable to show that Manville's projections of future financial ruin are inaccurate, immediate filing would appear necessary to further two basic policies of the Bankruptcy Code—the protection of future claimants and the protection of jobs. Dismissal of Manville's chapter 11 petition and a return to the status quo would deplete the company's assets and thus prejudice future asbestos claimants unable to execute their judgments fully. Further, to meet its future liabilities, Manville might be forced to liquidate in full or in part and thereby to eliminate a large number of jobs.

* * *

III. Conclusion

The new Bankruptcy Code gives bankruptcy courts broad discretion to dismiss reorganization petitions filed in bad faith. When a solvent and healthy corporation files a reorganization petition based on massive but speculative tort liability, the court should inquire, on motion of a party in interest, into the financial condition of the company and the validity of its projections of liability. If creditors are able to show that the debtor's projections are inaccurate and that the debtor corporation does not face insolvency in the foreseeable future, the court should dismiss the petition under section 1112(b) of the Bankruptcy Code.

If the creditors fail to discredit the corporation's projections and it appears that the purposes of the Code would be served by the filing, the bankruptcy court should entertain the petition. Nevertheless, the court should not undertake the estimation of each creditor's individual claim. Rather, to promote judicial economy, comity, and fairness to the plaintiffs, and in order not to interfere with the plaintiffs' right to trial by jury under state law, the bankruptcy court should limit itself to estimating the corporation's total liability, placing a ceiling on that liability, and establishing a compensation fund for the plaintiffs. The plaintiffs should be allowed to pursue their claims in the state and federal courts in which the claims were originally filed and then to return to the bankruptcy court to execute their judgments on a pro rata basis against the compensation fund.

Notes and Questions

1. The Manville Corporation filed its federal bankruptcy petition in August 1982, largely in light of the specter of its potential corporate liability for thousands of asbestos personal injury and property damage claims. To what extent, if any, was Manville's decision to pursue bankruptcy relief prompted by Manville's understanding of the judicial system's approach to mass tort cases in the late 1970s and early 1980s? Was Manville's decision to seek bankruptcy reorganization a strategic reaction to the federal courts reluctance to grant class action certification of asbestos mass torts?

2. Under what circumstances may a corporation or business entity file for Chapter 11 bankruptcy reorganization? What is the jurisdiction of federal bankruptcy court and the powers of bankruptcy judges in comparison to regular federal district courts? What relationship does Rule 23 class action procedure have to actions in bankruptcy? How are claims filed, recognized, and prioritized in Chapter 11 proceedings? What due process protections, if any, do bankruptcy proceedings provide bankruptcy creditors? How do these protections compare to class action claimants?

3. The author of the Harvard Law Review note recognized that the *Manville* bankruptcy signalled the possibility that other corporate mass tort defendants would pursue Chapter 11 bankruptcy as an alternative means of resolving massive potential liability from thousands of actual and future claimants. Do bankruptcy proceedings provide superior methods of aggregating claims in one proceeding? *See generally* Darlene Echols, *Note, Bankruptcy, Hazardous Waste and Mass Tort: A Top Priority Review,* 23 Hous.L.Rev. 1243 (1986); Margaret I. Lyle, *Note, Mass Tort Claims and the Corporate Tortfeasor: Bankruptcy Reorganization and the Legislative Compensation Versus the Common–Law Tort System,* 61 Tex.L.Rev. 1297 (1983); Christopher M.E. Painter, *Note, Tort Creditor Priority in the Second Credit System—Asbestos Times, The Worst of Times,* 36 Stan.L.Rev. 1045 (1984); Mark J. Roe, *Bankruptcy and Mass Tort,* 84 Colum.L.Rev. 846 (1984); Alan Schwartz, *Products Liability, Corporate Structure and Bankruptcy: Toxic Substances and Remote Risk Relationship,* 14 J. Legal Stud. 689 (1985); Kaighn Smith Jr., Note, *Beyond the Equity Power of Bankruptcy Courts:*

Toxic Tort Liabilities in Chapter 11 Cases, 39 Me.L.Rev. 391 (1986); Alan Schwartz, *Products Liability, Corporate Structure and Bankruptcy: Toxic Substances and Remote Risk Relationship,* 14 J. Legal Stud. 689 (1985).

4. As we have seen, a central problem in the resolution of latent-injury mass torts has been the problem of providing for future claimants. How do the bankruptcy laws treat future claimants? Does the bankruptcy system provide a better method for handling such claims? *See generally* Gregory A. Bibler, *The Status of Unaccrued Tort Claims in Chapter 11 Bankruptcy Proceedings,* 61 Am.Bank.L.J. 145 (1987); Anne Hardiman, *Recent Developments, Toxic Torts and Chapter 11 Reorganization: The Problem of Future Claims,* 38 Vand.L.Rev. 1369 (1985); Harvey J. Kesner, *Future Asbestos Related Litigants as Holders of Statutory Claims Under Chapter 11 of the Bankruptcy Code and Their Place in the Johns–Manville Reorganization,* 62 Am. Bank. L.J. 69 (1988); and Ralph R. Mabey and Jamie Andra Gavrin, *Constitutional Limitations on the Discharge of Future Claims in Bankruptcy,* 44 S.C.L.Rev. 745 (1993).

1. THE MANVILLE PERSONAL INJURY SETTLEMENT TRUST

MARIANNA S. SMITH, RESOLVING ASBESTOS CLAIMS: THE MANVILLE PERSONAL INJURY TRUST

53 Law & Contemp.Probs. 27 (1990).

I

INTRODUCTION

There was no precedent for the Manville Personal Injury Settlement Trust ("Trust"). A grantor trust, its genesis, birth, and evolution were influenced by—and its operation is still influenced by—many groups with differing agendas: the Manville Corporation, multiple federal and state courts, legal experts, investment bankers, victims' groups, plaintiffs' attorneys, Trust staff, and other trusts. The development and evolution of the Trust were further affected by a myriad of state and federal laws on, *inter alia*, trusts, securities regulation, contracts, fiduciary responsibility, bankruptcy, and civil procedure.

These often conflicting constituencies and laws were forced into a compromise "peace" during the upheaval of the Johns–Manville Corporation chapter 11 bankruptcy filing.

The Trust, an independent organization, was created by the bankruptcy court to distribute funds as equitably as possible while balancing the rights of current claimants against those of future, unknown claimants. It was established as a negotiation-based settlement organization, designating its claimants as beneficiaries. (Co-defendants are also named beneficiaries.) Plan provisions made it clear that claimants did not need to litigate or threaten to litigate in order to negotiate a fair settlement. The Trust was committed to settling as many claims as quickly and fairly as possible in the order specified in the Plan. Although the Trust never wavered from this commitment, it quickly became clear that the full Plan would be impossible to implement.

During 1990–91, the Trust participated in a process initiated by the United States District Courts for the Eastern and Southern Districts of New York in an attempt to find a workable solution to the mismatch of available funds and volume of incoming claims. To preserve remaining Trust assets, the courts, under Judge Jack B. Weinstein, ordered the Trust to renegotiate its financial relationship with Manville Corporation and to revamp its claims handling procedures. At the heart of these efforts to restructure the liabilities and assets of the Trust is broad-based attempt to have a limited-fund class action certified as a means to revise the rules governing the order and method of claims evaluation and payment.

At the time of this writing, the Trust's operations are governed by a stipulation of settlement filed on November 19, 1990, and concurrent court orders staying Trust payments and settlements. The Plan's claims resolution procedures are soon to be replaced. Fairness hearings also are currently underway to determine whether all interested parties have been fairly represented and whether the Trust's claimants should be declared a class. As a final (nonappealable) court order redefining the Trust's mandates and procedures is not expected for some time, it is premature to discuss these procedures here. Rather, this article covers the genesis of the Trust, the process that formed it, and the Trust's unique attributes, strengths, and weaknesses. It concludes with a discussion of the lessons learned that can inform the design, implementation, and operation of future claims resolution facilities.

II

THE MANVILLE BANKRUPTCY

Between 1858 and the late 1970s, Johns–Manville Corporation produced more than 600 different asbestos products for a wide variety of industrial and construction needs. By the mid–1960s, when an epidemiological study documented the health dangers of asbestos exposure, Manville owned and operated several asbestos mines, and had thirty manufacturing plants in the United States and at least a controlling interest in eight overseas plants.

Manville made and sold asbestos products in three different forms: solid, as in exterior and interior insulation; soft or pliable, as in felt blankets, packing, and other material used to insulate boilers, steam engines, pipe joints, and air compressors; and granular or loose, as in a wide range of asbestos cements. These products were used in markets described by economists as "industrial" rather than "consumer," that is, Manville sold the products, primarily through distributors, to industries that used the products to make goods for later sale in the consumer market. Thus, the individuals most likely to be exposed to asbestos fibers through the handling of Manville's asbestos products were skilled, semi-skilled, and unskilled workers in a number of different industries and trades, including shipping, construction, insulation, utilities, oil and chemical refining, and manufacturing and maintenance of automobile parts, railroad cars, aerospace, and electrical equipment. During the 1960s, workers in these industries and trades began filing lawsuits against asbestos manufacturers, including Manville, alleging personal injury from asbestos exposure. By 1982, the lawsuits against Manville alone numbered more than 16,500, with more than 400 new cases filed each month. Projections at that time for the total number of Manville personal injury claimants ranged from 50,000 to 200,000. This unexpected deluge of claims overwhelmed court dockets and confronted Manville with a then-estimated liability for personal injury claims in excess of $2 billion through the year 2001.

In August 1982, Manville filed a petition for reorganization and protection under chapter 11 of the Bankruptcy Code, which automatically suspended all personal injury lawsuits and allowed Manville to reorganize, thus preserving its financial viability to compensate asbestos claimants.

III

Establishment of the Trust

The 1988 Plan of Reorganization represented four years of negotiation between the bankruptcy court, Manville, and the court-appointed representatives for existing asbestos claimants, future, unknown claimants, and co-defendants. To finalize the agreement, the negotiators, assisted by legions of attorneys and financial advisors, were required to compromise on a wide range of extremely complicated financial and claims handling issues. Without the benefit of experts on management and claims settlement, the negotiators wrestled with various procedural questions, such as how quickly, in what priority, and through what approaches claims would be processed, evaluated, and settled.

Two goals were fundamental to the Plan's ultimate success: first, that the principles and strategies guiding the Trust's settlement of claims be fair to the parties, and, second, that the agreed-upon plan of reorganization be realistic and achievable. Only the first of these goals was met.

A. Impact of a Trust Structure

The Manville Trust is a grantor trust. During the design period, it was thought that tax benefits from a trust structure would be very beneficial to the grantor, Manville. The Internal Revenue Service subsequently carved out a special rule—the "Manville Rule"—to address the Trust's unique tax status. Since such a rule could have been attached to any organizational structure, such as non-profit, foundation, or charitable foundation, it was unnecessary to impose the significant encumbrances associated with a trust structure.

Probably the most unique characteristic of a trust is the strict accountability, and thus the liability, of the trustees. Whereas corporate directors are subject to a business rule of "reasonable business judgment," trustees are held to the "highest standards of care" in preserving and enhancing the trust estate and are subject to personal liability in the event they do not meet those standards. On paper, the trustees' unique accountability has merit. In the context of the lack of trust between those representing the injured claimants and Manville, the "higher standard of care" seemed a politic choice at the time. In practice, however, it creates financial and legal difficulties. For example, because of this unflinching accountability, the Trust must purchase separate liability insurance for its directors and officers (as trustees) at an annual premium cost of over $2 million. In the absence of such insurance, trustees would be personally liable and unlikely to volunteer to take that risk. The Trust also must self-insure by segregating $30 million of its assets as additional insurance protection. To reduce this financial sting, the Plan limits trustee accountability by specifying that trustees may be successfully sued only for gross negligence or willful misconduct. In practice, however, this limitation offers little comfort to anyone asked to serve as a trustee and thus put his or her personal fortune at risk.

The complexities associated with the trust structure are further complicated in the Manville Trust situation by the continuing jurisdiction of the bankruptcy court. The Trust, in effect, owns Manville. While there is adequate precedent on post-reorganization bankruptcy proceedings, there is little or no legal guidance for a trust that owns a post-reorganization company. Thus, the legal, procedural, and liability ramifications of every issue must be minutely examined and researched.

B.   The Operation of the Trust

Although not confirmed until October 1988, the Trust began operation in January 1987, following the bankruptcy court's appointment of trustees. During the first seven months of 1987, several consulting organizations assisted the trustees in handling a range of complex issues and developing a strategy for responding to the impending deluge of claims. In October 1987, the trustees hired this author as executive director of the Trust, and shortly thereafter established the Trust's offices in Washington, D.C. Within six months, the Trust had hired and trained nearly ninety-five employees and was prepared to settle claims.

In May 1988, the Trust began to negotiate settlements of the cases filed against Manville before August 1982, all of which had been stayed by the bankruptcy proceeding. Of the approximately 16,500 pre-bankruptcy claims submitted to the Trust, more than 15,500 were settled for a total of approximately $640 million. Upon consummation of the plan on November 28, 1988, the Trust was able to begin paying these pre-bankruptcy claims, subject to certain conditions, including the receipt of an individual proof of claim form and a signed release from each claimant. By mid–1989, an additional 48,500 post-bankruptcy claim forms were received, for a total of 65,000 claims filed with the Trust. By the end of August 1989, the total had risen to more than 97,000, and by January 1991 more than 170,000 claimants were seeking compensation from the Trust.

C. The Protection of Multiple Interests and Beneficiaries

The Trust has three principal groups of beneficiaries: present claimants, future claimants, and co-defendants. As fiduciaries, the trustees, who are responsible for supervising and administering the claims resolution facility, must treat the groups equally, showing no favoritism toward any one group despite the inherent conflicts. Such conflicts exist because, for example, claimants may be both Trust beneficiaries and litigants, and co-defendants are beneficiaries of the Trust as well as litigants of the Trust and of the claimants.

The Trust's directives to "enhance and preserve the Trust estate" in order to "deliver fair, adequate and equitable compensation to [claimants], whether known or unknown," and to give "Full" compensation to all claimants give rise to additional conflicts. With insufficient assets to pay even the current, known claimants in full, the conflict is obvious.

D. Long–Term Funding Versus Immediate Liabilities

The Trust is funded for twenty-seven years through a complicated array of financial instruments that form the unique financial relationship between the Trust and Manville. The Trust is Manville's principal stockholder, holding 24 million shares (50 percent) of common stock and 7.2 million shares of Manville series A convertible preferred stock, which is convertible into 72 million shares of common stock. After conversion, the Trust would own 80 percent of Manville's common stock. As holder of two bonds with an aggregate face value of more than $1.8 billion, the Trust is also Manville's largest creditor. The total assets with which the Trust was funded have a face value well in excess of $3 billion. Beginning in 1992 and continuing as long as the Trust needs additional funds, the Trust also will receive up to 20 percent of Manville's profits under a profit-sharing agreement.

As part of the 1990 court-ordered restructuring, Manville and the Trust entered into agreements to enhance the Trust's available cash to pay claims. The Trust's funding mechanisms, both before and after more recent modifications, provide limited funds during early years with restrictions on the sale of assets, and insufficient funds in the aggregate to pay all claimants.

As noted above, the bankruptcy reorganization plan states that all claimants will receive payment from the Trust of 100 hundred percent of full value. When the value of present claims exceeded the value of available assets, it became clear the Trust could not meet that mandate. Even the attempt to do so would mean selling the Trust's asset, Manville stock, and would violate another requirement of the Plan: to preserve assets to pay future, as-yet-unfiled claims. Despite this requirement, the Plan provided no mechanism to hold back money for such a purpose.

E. The Evaluation of Claims

The Trust may compensate claimants only for injuries caused by exposure to Manville asbestos. Thus, the Plan mandates that each claim be evaluated on its own merits considering the nature and severity of the injury, as well as factors such as the extent of exposure to Manville products, exposure to other manufacturers' products, jurisdictional values, and the claimant's age, wage loss, and medical costs. So that the less costly, less risky settlement process provided by the Trust would be more attractive to claimants, the evaluation process was designed to consider the same factors that would be considered if settlement, award, and verdict values were derived through litigation.

Since many of the claims resolution procedures set forth in the Plan are expected to change dramatically under the class action settlement, it is inappropriate in this article to discuss the old structure and premature to discuss the new. Therefore, the remaining paragraphs in this section will discuss some of the more unusual legal and operational aspects of the Trust, independent of the procedures that are likely to change.

F. Payments to Pre–bankruptcy Claimants

The bind in which the Trust found itself when it came time to pay the pre-bankruptcy claims illustrates the conflicts discussed in the previous section. The controversy did not surface, however, until early 1990 when the Trust announced an extended payment plan on current and future settlements, under which settlements were to be paid 40 percent at settlement and 60 percent over five years.

Despite extensive efforts to call the attention of the courts and the plaintiff bar to the critical shortfall of Trust assets available to pay claims, only the step away from 100 percent claims payments finally brought wide awareness of the problem. That awareness manifested itself, however, not by addressing the cash shortfall issue directly. Instead the discussion revolved around the amounts of the pre-bankruptcy settlements. In addition, the Trust was criticized for its decision to pay 100 percent on all pre-bankruptcy claims, even though the bankruptcy plan specified such and the decision was endorsed at the time by the parties to the bankruptcy. Many appeared to feel that the Trust had paid out too much, too soon, to the earliest claimants.

In its first year alone, the Trust disbursed over $600 million to pre-bankruptcy claimants. While a large sum by anyone's measure, in perspective this amount is considerably less than it seems. Many of the 16,500 claimants were high-value, acute injury cases; some were "Manville-only" cases (for example, Manville plant workers), for which the Trust assumed full, rather than the usual partial, liability. Also driving up claim value was the long wait the pre-bankruptcy claimants had endured, a wait ranging from six to twelve years depending on their states' docket backlog.

Despite annual medical cost increases of 11.5 percent after 1982, the Trust kept its average settlement value at $41,150. Thus, the initial $600 million represents less than 15,000 of the earliest, sickest claimants. At the time of Manville's 1982 bankruptcy filing, Trust planners estimated they would have to pay some 50,000 claimants $40,000 each. A broader study conducted some years later estimated a greater number of claims at a lower cost per claim. As the Trust settles the "newer" claims, the lower estimate may yet be proven accurate.

G. Litigation—Not Settlement—Driven

Although heavy litigation against the Trust was not contemplated by the crafters of the reorganization plan, it was unavoidable, operationally unmanageable, and ultimately contributed substantially to the Trust's already troubled financial situation. As evidenced by one of the articulated purposes of the Trust, the crafters of the Plan genuinely wanted the Trust to be a negotiation-based settlement organization. They wanted claimants to explore all avenues of negotiation and alternative dispute resolution before turning to litigation as a last resort. To meet this objective, the Plan established a "formula" for ordering the payment of claims, allowing the Trust to take cases docketed and scheduled for trial out of queue and settle them. This appeared to be a reasonable approach. However, two factors led to the Trust's inundation with active litigation. The first factor was purely operational: the Plan permitted claimants to sue the Trust 120 days after filing their claims with the Trust. Because the Trust had received such an enormous volume of claims and was unable to make offers on all of them within 120 days, claimants had the right to sue and did so to improve their position in the queue.

The second factor influencing the volume of litigation was an acceleration in the volume of cases tried in the courts compared to the relative handful of asbestos cases that came to trial in the mid–1980s. By 1990 four significant class actions and tens of thousands of individual cases demanded judicial attention. As noted above, this deluge had not been anticipated, and the Plan did not allow modification of the Trust's operations to accommodate the problem.

H. Settlement Transaction Costs

The excessive unplanned litigation also had a significant financial impact on the Trust. Prior to July 1989, before the trial docket began to drive the Trust's business conduct, the cost of settling claims, or transaction cost (measured as operating costs, including start-up costs as a percentage of settlement values), was 6.1 percent of total costs. When litigation costs are excluded, this percentage drops only slightly to 5 percent. Even with the heavy impact of the trial docket, from inception of the Trust to the end of 1990, the Trust kept overall transaction costs to 10.4 percent. Transaction costs excluding litigation defense costs were kept to 5.5 percent of settlements. Had the Trust been able to avoid the cost of litigation defense, it would have offered a low-cost alternative to traditional settlement techniques.

IV

LESSONS FOR FUTURE SETTLEMENT ORGANIZATIONS

As the Trust awaits final direction from the courts on how to proceed, it is a good time to reflect on how lessons learned by the Trust might serve to guide crafters of future claims resolution facilities.

A. *Build In Flexibility.* In crafting any plan, it is essential to articulate the plan's objectives and devise the procedures to implement the objectives. However, enough flexibility must exist during implementation to revise or replace operational approaches when they fail to promote their intended goals.

B. *Authorize the Balance of Assets and Liabilities.* When the ultimate liability of a mass tort is unknown, as will often be the case with toxic torts, and when lengthy disease latencies preclude the imposition of a cut-off date to limit the number of potential claims, the plan must authorize the balance of assets and liabilities in the most equitable and fair fashion. One viable solution to the Trust's difficulty would have been to offer partial payments, known as a pro-rata distribution. That proposal, now under consideration in the class action settlement, would distribute a share of the available cash to each settled claim based upon its proportionate value of total liability.

C. *Protect Constitutional Rights.* While no legal document may limit or deny constitutionally guaranteed protections (such as the right to trial), careful thought must be given to building incentives that promote the behavior patterns required for ultimate success of the settlement program. In particular, attention should focus on building disincentives for claimant alternatives such as litigation that will dissipate assets. The Trust is a prime example of a case where the right to trial became a driver rather than a fallback for claimants when all settlement approaches failed.

D. *Simplify the Legal Structure.* It is critical to minimize the bodies of law with which a new organization is burdened. The Manville Trust is subject to the law of all fifty states, as well as bankruptcy law, tort law and traditions, corporate and business law, rules of the Securities and Exchange Commission, and complex federal legislation. Unless a compelling reason to do so exists, placing the law of trusts in this mix is unnecessarily burdensome.

E. *Consider Management Input During the Design Stage.* When lawyers and judges without extensive business experience create procedural and operational documents, they must involve specialists, such as operations planners, management consultants, and organization designers, who know how to make organizations function in the real world. Experienced operations experts need to advise on the practicality of the organization design, and on its goals and flexibility. Reaching consensus through compromise can reap great initial benefits from a settlement perspective, but may lead to later failure in its practical implementation phase.

V

CONCLUSION

Solutions to the Trust's dilemma are no more easily found now than they were in 1982. The same opposing forces are struggling over the same issues that were raised ten years ago. However, experience has shown at least two features of claims resolution facilities that do not work:

    1. Allowing easy and immediate access to the tort system forces the Trust into a "courthouse steps settlement" posture, which is expensive, wastes assets, skews claims values artificially high, and neglects many needy beneficiaries.

    2. Inconsistent and sometimes conflicting goals, written to achieve settlement through compromise, create confusion, delay, and additional litigation, slowing down or even halting operations.

There has been tremendous pressure from the media, the courts, and the Trust beneficiaries to provide an "answer" to the asbestos liability problem. Unfortunately, there is no quick, simple, or easy answer. To oversimplify these complex problems only will exacerbate them in the long run. Consideration of some of the painful lessons learned over the past three years of Trust operation will be critical to the success of future efforts.

    Review **In Re Keene Corp.,** *Chapter II, Part A.5, supra;* **In re Joint Eastern and Southern District Asbestos Litigation,** *Chapter III, Part A.2, supra*.

IN RE JOINT EASTERN AND SOUTHERN DISTRICT ASBESTOS LITIGATION
IN RE JOHNS–MANVILLE CORPORATION, DEBTOR

United States Court of Appeals, Second Circuit, 1992.
982 F.2d 721, 23 Bankr.Ct.Dec. 1237, Bankr.L.Rep. ¶ 75,047.

Before: FEINBERG, NEWMAN, and WINTER, CIRCUIT JUDGES.

JON O. NEWMAN, CIRCUIT JUDGE:

This appeal challenges significant rulings made jointly by a district judge and a bankruptcy judge in an effort to restructure the mechanism for distributing compensation to thousands of persons claiming asbestos-related injuries from products manufactured by the Johns–Manville Corporation. The rulings are presented for review on appeal from a judgment jointly entered on August 21, 1991, by the District Courts of the Eastern and Southern Districts of New York and the Bankruptcy Court of the Southern District of New York (Jack B. Weinstein, District Judge, and Burton R. Lifland, Chief Bankruptcy Judge) approving the settlement of a class action.

Some indication of the scope of the rulings is revealed by the fact that the principal opinion explaining them consumes 525 typescript pages—201 printed pages of the Bankruptcy Reporter, supplemented by 68 pages of appendices. *See* In re Joint Eastern & Southern District Asbestos Litigation ("*Asbestos Litigation II*"), 129 B.R. 710 (E. & S.D.N.Y., Bankr.S.D.N.Y.1991). The dimensions of the controversy are indicated by the polar characterizations of the contending sides on this appeal. For the principal appellants, the proceedings giving rise to the challenged rulings are "unique in jurisprudential history, if not bizarre," * * * "frightening," * * *, and "grossly" beyond "the bounds of judicial power," * * *. The appellees consider the rulings to be simply the valid settlement of a class action within the jurisdiction of the District Court, accomplished to enhance the fairness of the ultimate distribution of compensation to asbestos victims.

We conclude that the judgment approving the settlement must be vacated because, to the extent that the judgment rests on diversity jurisdiction, the use of a mandatory non-opt-out class action without proper subclasses violates the requirements of Rule 23 of the Federal Rules of Civil Procedure, and, to the extent that the judgment rests on bankruptcy jurisdiction, it represents an impermissible modification of a confirmed and substantially consummated plan of reorganization in violation of section 1127(b) of the Bankruptcy Code.

BACKGROUND

A. *The Manville Reorganization.* The current controversy arises in the aftermath of the confirmation of a plan of reorganization of the Johns–Manville Corporation ("the Debtor") the world's largest manufacturer of asbestos. Facing claims from current and future victims of asbestos-related deaths and injuries estimated to total $2 billion, the Debtor filed a voluntary petition in bankruptcy under Chapter 11 on August 26, 1982. The reorganization proceeding involved both "present claimants," i.e., persons who, prior to the petition date, had been exposed to Manville asbestos and had developed an asbestos-related disease, and "future claimants," i.e., persons who had been exposed to Manville asbestos prior to the petition date but had not shown any signs of disease at that time. The Bankruptcy Court appointed a legal guardian to represent the interests of the future claimants.

After four years of negotiation, a Second Amended Plan of Reorganization ("the Plan") was presented to the Bankruptcy Court, *see* Manville Corp. v. Equity Security Holders Committee (In re Johns–Manville Corp.), 66 B.R. 517, 518–33 (Bankr.S.D.N.Y.1986), and confirmed in 1986, In re Johns–Manville Corp., 68 B.R. 618 (Bankr.S.D.N.Y.1986). The cornerstone of the Plan was the Manville Personal Injury Settlement Trust ("the Trust" or "the PI Trust"), a mechanism designed to satisfy the claims of all asbestos health claimants, both present and future. The Trust was to be funded from several sources: the proceeds of the Debtor's settlements with its insurers; certain cash, receivables, and stock of the reorganized Manville Corporation ("Manville"); long term notes; and the right to receive up to 20 percent of Manville's yearly profits for as long as it might take to satisfy all asbestos disease claims.

As a condition precedent to confirmation of the Plan, the Bankruptcy Court issued an injunction channeling to the Trust all asbestos-related personal injury claims against the Debtor ("the Injunction"). The Injunction specifies that asbestos health claimants may proceed only against the Trust to satisfy their claims against the Debtor and may not sue Manville, its related operating entities, or its insurers. The Injunction applies to all health claimants, both present and future, regardless of whether they technically have dischargeable "claims" under the Code. Those with present claims unquestionably have dischargeable "claims" within the meaning of 11 U.S.C. § 101(4)(1988) and hold what the Plan categorizes as "AH Claims"; holders of AH Claims are Class–4 unsecured creditors under the Plan. If future claimants are ultimately determined to hold "claims" within the meaning of section 101(4), they too will be Class–4 unsecured creditors. If it is determined that they do not hold "claims," they will then fall within a category denominated by the Plan as "Other Asbestos Obligations." Whether or not the future claimants have creditor status under the Plan, they are nevertheless treated identically to the present claimants, at least to the extent of being obliged to look to the Trust as the sole source of compensation. All health claimants are required to attempt settlement with the Trust. If a settlement cannot be reached, the claimant may elect mediation, binding arbitration, or traditional tort litigation in state or federal court, including trial by jury. The claimant may collect from the Trust the full amount of whatever compensatory damages are awarded. The only restriction on recovery is that punitive damages are prohibited.

* * * The Trust Agreement contains Annex B, establishing Claims Resolution Procedures. A significant provision of Annex B, pertinent to one of the major issues raised on this appeal, specifies that claims will be processed "in order of initial filing, whether in a court or with the MSV [the Manville Settlement Vehicle, the mechanism established to attempt settlement of individual claims], whichever is earlier, on a first-in-first-out basis except that claims which have been settled with all defendants except defendants which are petitioners in these bankruptcy proceedings may be negotiated separately on a first-in-first-out basis with representatives of the MSV." * * *

Challenges to the confirmation of the Plan were rejected by this Court, at least those challenges that the appellants had standing to bring. *See* Kane v. Johns–Manville Corp., 843 F.2d 636 (2d Cir.1988).

Pursuant to the Plan, the Trust received $909 million in cash, two bonds with an aggregate value of $1.8 billion, 24 million shares of Manville common stock, and 7.2 million shares of Manville convertible preferred stock, aggregating 80 percent of the stock of the reorganized Manville. *See* In re Joint Eastern & Southern District Asbestos Litigation ("Asbestos Litigation I"), 120 B.R. 648, 652 (E. & S.D.N.Y., Bankr. S.D.N.Y.1990). Despite this funding, it soon became apparent that the liquidation of the claims of thousands of asbestos victims was substantially depleting the Trust's cash. By March 30, 1990, the Trust had received more than 150,000 claims, 50 percent above the highest number estimated when the Plan was approved. * * * The Trust settled 22,386 of those claims at an average liquidated value of $42,000. * * * By the spring of 1990, "the Trust was effectively out of money to pay its current and short term obligations." * * *

B. *The Evolution of the Trust Restructuring.* Inevitably, the financial plight of the Trust came to the attention of trial judges in the Eastern and Southern Districts of New York, who were struggling to cope with the mounting flood of asbestos cases. On June 1, 1990, Judge Weinstein of the Eastern District and Justice Freedman of the New York Supreme Court, who had been jointly endeavoring to settle a number of federal and state court asbestos cases pertaining to the Brooklyn Navy Yard, issued a joint order *sua sponte.*[1] The order did not require anything, but contained several suggestions. One paragraph noted both the financial plight of the Trust and a suggestion that Manville should advance between 200 and 300 million dollars to the Trust. Another paragraph noted a need to restrict payments and urged that the Plan should be amended to permit inquiry into attorney's fees and that the Trust should consider amending its "Payment Program" to provide for installment payments and to reject the FIFO order of payments, with payments scheduled instead based on fixed criteria such as disease, age, and availability of funds.

On July 9, 1991, Judge Weinstein issued a further order, *sua sponte.* This Order contained several provisions. First, under the heading "Directions to Leon Silverman, Advisor to Bankruptcy Judge," it pointed out the need to restructure the Trust and noted that Judge Lifland had given Silverman until August 6 "to arrange the restructuring outlined." Second, explicitly exercising authority as a district judge of the Southern District pursuant to an assignment by the Chief Judge of the Circuit, dated January 23, 1990, Judge Weinstein issued a partial stay of payments by the Trust, staying until August 6, 1990, payments of judgments, settlements, and legal fees. Third, the Order stated that the circumstances "appear to warrant a non-opt-out class under Rule 23(b)(1)(B)," which would "provide substantial benefit to those injured, the economy and the courts." Judge Weinstein stated that he would not "today mandate such a step," but urged all those involved to make recommendations for "a Rule 23(b)(1)(B) global settlement" and warned, "Failure to do so will leave this Court no alternative but to consider other available options."

On July 20, 1990, Judge Weinstein was granted supervisory responsibility over the Plan, pursuant to a designation by the Circuit Chief Judge and an assignment order by the Chief Judge of the Southern District. *See Asbestos Litigation II*, 129 B.R. at 762. In effect, what had occurred was a partial removal of the Chapter 11 proceeding from the Bankruptcy Court to the District Court under 28 U.S.C. § 157(d)(1988)(district court may, on its own motion, withdraw, in whole or in part, any proceeding referred under section 157 to bankruptcy judge).

---

1. The caption of this Order indicates that it was entered with respect to In re New York City Asbestos Litigation, a group of cases pending in the New York Supreme Court (in all counties within New York City), and In re Joint Eastern and Southern District Asbestos Litigation, a group of cases pending in the District Courts of the Eastern and Southern Districts of New York.

On September 18, 1990, Judge Weinstein appointed Marvin E. Frankel, Esq., as a special master to hold hearings and to report on two questions: (1) whether the financial assets of the Trust were so limited as to create a substantial risk that payments for present and future claimants would be in jeopardy, and (2) whether there was a substantial probability that payment of damage awards would exhaust the Trust's available and projected assets. * * * This appointment was made in response to a motion by the Trust for a determination that its assets constituted a limited fund within the meaning of Rule 23(b)(1)(B). * * * The Special Master's report, submitted November 3, 1990, concluded that the Trust was "deeply insolvent." * * * The Special Master estimated that the Trust's assets had a value between $2.1 and $2.7 billion, that current and future claims were estimated at $6.5 billion, and that the Trust currently lacked the cash to pay the then liquidated total of $448.5 million in claims. * * *

There then ensued a negotiation among lawyers representing present claimants, future claimants, the Trust, asbestos manufacturers who were co-defendants of the Trust in pending lawsuits, and Manville. The negotiations resulted in a proposal, agreed to by lawyers representing many of the interested parties but not all of the claimants, for paying present and future claimants. The proposal called for a revised Trust Distribution Process, which we outline below. With the proposed revision widely though not universally agreed to, the restructuring was accomplished by means of the filing and rapid settlement of a class action.

C. *The Class Action.* On Nov. 19, 1990, five plaintiffs with claims against the Trust for death or injury caused by exposure to asbestos filed a class action complaint on behalf of all beneficiaries of the Trust against the trustees of the Trust and simultaneously filed a proposed Stipulation of Settlement of the class action. The judgment approving the settlement is the subject of the pending appeal. The complaint, styled *Findley [et al.] v. Blinken [et al.]* was captioned as filed both in *In re Joint Eastern and Southern District Asbestos Litigation*, pending in the Eastern and Southern Districts, and in *In re Johns–Manville Corp.*, the Chapter 11 proceeding pending in the Bankruptcy Court of the Southern District. The complaint was filed on behalf of the named plaintiffs and "all others similarly situated as Beneficiaries of the Trust.... Each Class member has or will have a claim either for death or personal injury caused by exposure to asbestos, or a claim for warranty, guarantee, indemnification or contribution arising from an obligation of the Trust for the payment of a Trust death or personal injury claim." * * *

The complaint invoked both diversity jurisdiction and bankruptcy jurisdiction. Diversity jurisdiction was based on allegations that diversity of citizenship existed between the named plaintiffs, on the one hand, and the defendant Trustees, on the other, and the matter in controversy exceeded $50,000. *See* 28 U.S.C. § 1332 (1988 & Supp. II 1990). Bankruptcy jurisdiction was based on the allegation that the action was "related" to the Manville reorganization proceeding, over which the Court had retained jurisdiction. * * *

The complaint alleged a single count "Seeking to Establish An Equitable Distribution of the Trust Res." * * * It alleged that the Trust is required to pay all claims in full shortly after claims are liquidated, that the assets of the Trust are insufficient to permit such payment without jeopardizing the payment of the claims of other beneficiaries, that "[e]quitable principles of trust law and other applicable law require that the Court determine an equitable allocation of the Trust res among its Beneficiaries and a restructuring of the Trust's procedures for payment to its Beneficiaries," * * *," that 70,000 actions are currently pending against the Trust, * * *, and that continued prosecution of these actions will defeat the purposes of the Trust by depleting the Trust *res*," * * *. As relief, the complaint sought a judgment determining an equitable allocation of the Trust res among all beneficiaries, determining the "relative rights and priorities" of all beneficiaries, determining an equitable, efficient, and inexpensive method for fixing the amount each beneficiary is entitled to receive and for distribution of Trust assets, and "enjoining permanently all pending and future proceedings by Beneficiaries against the Trust in all state and federal courts except in accordance with the procedures determined hereby." * * *

On the day the complaint was filed, District Judge Weinstein and Bankruptcy Judge Lifland (hereafter "the Trial Courts") jointly entered orders to show cause why orders should not be entered (a) conditionally certifying the class, (b) appointing a legal representative for beneficiaries of the Trust who have not yet asserted asbestos claims, and (c) staying all proceedings against the Trust pending determination of the class action. A hearing was scheduled for November 23, four days after the complaint was filed (and the day after Thanksgiving). On November 23, after hearing oral argument, the Trial Courts entered orders (1) conditionally certifying the class and appointing representative counsel, * * *, (2) setting fairness hearings in four cities and approving a form of notice, * * *, (3) staying payments by the Trust, * * *, (4) staying proceedings against the Trust, * * *, (5) making exceptions to the order staying proceedings, * * *, and (6) appointing counsel as representatives for defendants, other than the Trust, in pending asbestos litigation, * * *.

Copies of the foregoing orders were mailed to counsel for each known claimant and each co-defendant and to approximately 1,500 *pro se* claimants. * * * Copies were also distributed to all courts in which the Trust was a party to litigation, and to various other interested persons. * * * Notice of the proposed settlement was published in 11 major newspapers. * * * Hearings on the fairness of the proposed settlement were conducted in four cities. The hearings, conducted over eight days, received evidence from proponents of the settlement and objectors. Thirty-seven witnesses and attorneys were heard.

On February 13, 1991, the Trial Courts issued an Order and Partial Judgment, certifying a mandatory non-opt-out class under Rule

23(b)(1)(B). * * * At that time a motion by a member of the class to opt out was denied.

On June 27, 1991, the Trial Courts filed an Amended Memorandum, Order, and Final Judgment, * * *, after affording the parties an opportunity to comment on an earlier version, * * *. The judgment (1) approves the settlement, (2) makes permanent the prior stay of proceedings against the Trust, and (3) reaffirms the prior injunction, issued in the Chapter 11 proceeding, restricting suits against the Manville Corporation. * * *

D. *The Settlement.* The settlement, set out in *Asbestos Litigation I,* * * *, contains numerous provisions. First, it specifies that it is binding on the class that consists of all beneficiaries of the Trust who now have or in the future may have (a) any unliquidated claims for death or injury resulting from exposure to Manville asbestos, (b) any warranty, guarantee, indemnification, or contribution claims against the Trust arising from exposure to asbestos by any class member, and (c) settlements or judgments arising from any of the foregoing claims. * * * Trust beneficiaries include those with death or personal injury claims arising from exposure to Manville asbestos prior to the confirmation date. * * *

Second, and a source of major dispute on this appeal, the Settlement establishes a Trust Distribution Process ("TDP"), and specifies that Trust payments will be made only in compliance with the TDP. * * * The objective of the TDP is stated to be "to treat all claimants alike by paying all claimants an equal percentage of their claims' values over time." * * * The TDP divides all asbestos disease claims into two levels. The most seriously injured claimants are placed in Level One; these include all claims for asbestos-related cancers, all claims "of a sufficient severity to justify treatment with cancer cases," and claims for death substantially caused by asbestos-related disease. * * * All other health claimants are placed in Level Two.

* * *

The TDP also makes a distinction in the method of adjudication of health claims in an effort to divert claims out of the tort system (i.e., jury trial). The TDP establishes two payment pools. Claimants who accept liquidated values offered by the Trust or determined in binding or non-binding arbitration will be paid from Pool A. Claimants who opt for jury trials will be paid their judgment from Pool A only to the extent of the upper limit of the disease category established by the Trust or by non-binding arbitration, or such higher amount as may have been offered by the Trust or awarded through arbitration; the excess amount of any judgment will be collectable only from Pool B. * * * Payments can be made from Pool B in any one year only after all Pool A claims available for payment in that year have been fully paid, * * * an outcome that the appellants contend is impossible.

Third, to facilitate the restructuring of the Trust, the Settlement includes a Master Agreement between the Trust and Manville, requiring Manville to supply additional financing beyond the 20 percent profit-sharing called for by the Plan. Manville is to pay the Trust $280 million during the first four years and become obligated to pay a special dividend, depending on profitability, that will provide the Trust with sums up to an additional $240 million through the seventh year. * * * Refinancing of the Trust's bonds will also occur.

Fourth, the Settlement includes a provision limiting the fees of lawyers for health claimants to the lesser of their contracted fee or 25 percent of any recovery. * * *

Fifth, Section H of the Settlement includes a complicated provision purporting to reduce the Trust's litigating expenses by preventing all Trust beneficiaries from litigating their claims in state or federal courts. * * * Section H provides for an injunction ordering all Trust beneficiaries, including health claimants and asbestos manufacturers who are co-defendants of the Debtor in pending state and federal asbestos lawsuits, to dismiss, without prejudice, all pending cases, to be barred from filing future cases against Manville or the Trust, and to pursue their claims against the Trust only to the extent permitted by the Settlement. Section H also provides that in any litigation between beneficiaries of the Trust (health claimants and co-defendant manufacturers) all beneficiaries are enjoined from asserting or introducing evidence that the Trust is a joint and/or several tortfeasor, that the Trust is responsible for any injury, or that the Trust would have been responsible for any injury if it had been made a party. In the view of the co-defendant manufacturers, these prohibitions ban the introduction of Manville-related causation evidence at trial, establish national rules of joint and several liability and pro tanto (i.e., dollar for dollar) setoff for the Manville liability share, and ban impleader of the Trust. Such provisions, the co-defendants contend, trench on state law provisions and shift hundreds of millions of dollars of Manville asbestos liability from the Trust to the co-defendants.

In approving the Settlement, the Trial Courts recognized that Section H "presents substantial risk of altering constitutional and state law rights of certain parties if read *literally* and expansively." * * * The Trial Courts suggested that they might be entitled to impose a uniform national rule governing the contribution and related rights of co-defendants "[d]rawing on the courts' continuing bankruptcy jurisdiction." * * * However, they refrained from attempting to invoke bankruptcy court jurisdiction to impose uniform tort rules, noting that the matter before them was "a class action, based primarily on diversity jurisdiction, rather than a pure bankruptcy proceeding." * * * Instead, the Trial Courts sought to relax the rigor of Section H by "interpret[ing]" it, * * *, stating that "[m]uch of section H is precatory," * * *.

The "interpretation" permits the states "to exercise their evidence and substantive law policies to regulate the relationship between plaintiffs and codefendants so long as the method of recovery from the Trust is not affected and the Trust is not required to participate in any way in any litigation." * * * More specifically, states are authorized to "apply state policy and law to control set-off and contribution in contravention of the terms of section H," * * *, and state and federal courts are authorized to "admit or exclude evidence in contravention of the terms of section H," * * *. The standard of Section H is not abandoned, however; rather, it is to govern state and federal court litigation "except where it violates either a fundamental public policy of New York or any other state." * * *

* * *

DISCUSSION

The pending appeal presents a broad array of challenges to the Settlement brought primarily by two groups of appellants—health claimants who objected to the Settlement and co-defendant manufacturers of asbestos. The objecting health claimants contend essentially (1) that the Trial Courts acted beyond judicial authority in developing and engineering the adoption of a legislative solution to the financial difficulties of the Trust, (2) that the Trial Courts exceeded their subject matter jurisdiction, (3) that the Trial Courts lacked personal jurisdiction over absent asbestos disease claimants, (4) that the Settlement violates the Bankruptcy Code in that it modifies a confirmed and substantially consummated plan of reorganization in violation of 11 U.S.C. § 1127(b)(1988), (5) that, even if the Trial Courts have authority to reopen the reorganization and modify the Plan, the Settlement violates specific limitations of the Code, notably the requirement that members of each class receive the "same treatment," *id.* § 1123(a)(4), (6) that the Settlement denies health claimants their rights to procedural due process and violates the requirements of Fed.R.Civ.P. 23 because of defects in the class notice, lack of an adequate opportunity to be heard, lack of appropriate subclasses, and lack of an opportunity to opt out of the class, (7) that the Settlement is unfair, (8) that the orders respecting state court actions violate the Anti–Injunction Act, 28 U.S.C. § 2283 (1988), and exceed the Trial Courts' authority under the All–Writs Act, 28 U.S.C. § 1651 (1988), and (9) that the Trial Courts erred in denying one law firm's fee application. The co-defendant manufacturers advance essentially two contentions. First, they urge that the class definition improperly groups them with the health claimants in disregard of a fundamental adversity of interests between the two groups. Second, they urge that Section H of the Settlement unlawfully impairs their state law rights and that the Trial Courts' opinion confirming the Settlement is fatally imprecise to the extent that it endeavors to lessen the rigor of Section H through "interpretation."

I. JUDICIAL AUTHORITY

Though the jurisdictional challenges are substantial and merit careful attention, we first consider the even more basic contention that the entire course of events that culminated in the Settlement of the class action represent action beyond the scope of legitimate judicial authority. Specifically, the objecting health claimants contend that Judge Weinstein acted in a legislative capacity in initiating the restructuring of the Trust and shaping the contours of the Settlement.

Judge Weinstein was duly designated to act as a district judge of the Southern District by designation of the Chief Judge of this Circuit on January 23, 1990. In that capacity and in his normal capacity as a district judge of the Eastern District, he was exercising entirely legitimate authority in supervising the trial preparation of the group of asbestos cases collectively identified as *In re Joint Eastern and Southern District Asbestos Litigation.* As a district judge with responsibilities for cases seeking recovery from the Manville Trust, he was surely entitled to be concerned with the ability of that Trust to fulfill its expectations. And, having become aware of the developing economic plight of the Trust, he was entitled to act within the framework of the Judicial Branch to initiate remedial steps.

At that point, however, Judge Weinstein had no bankruptcy court authority, and the Trust was an integral component of a then pending bankruptcy reorganization. We believe the more prudent course would have been to alert the Bankruptcy Judge then supervising the Manville reorganization as to the adverse effects the Trust's financial condition was having upon the resolution of pending asbestos cases and also to alert the Chief Judge of the Circuit and the Chief Judge of the Southern District so that those officials could consider the exercise of their authority to effect any necessary special designations. Instead, Judge Weinstein issued *sua sponte* the orders of June 1, 1990, and July 9, 1990, 1990 WL 115761. We think these actions were ill-advised, as they concerned a reorganization proceeding over which Judge Weinstein then had no judicial authority.

On July 20, 1990, 1990 WL 115785, however, Judge Weinstein's authority to take judicial action with respect to the Manville reorganization was fully supplied by a grant of supervisory responsibility over the Plan, pursuant to a designation by the Circuit Chief Judge and an assignment order by the Chief Judge of the Southern District. *See Asbestos Litigation II*, 129 B.R. at 762. Whether or not his actions from that point on were in any respect erroneous, they were fully within his judicial authority. We reject the contention that Judge Weinstein assumed a legislative role in proposing steps to restructure the Trust and working rather forcefully with the parties to accomplish the restructuring. A judge with responsibilities for a lawsuit is not a bystander. Nor is the judge relegated to the role of umpire, awaiting the submission of precisely framed disputes by the parties. Especially in the course of a complex and continuing proceeding such as a bankruptcy reorganization, a judge has an entirely legitimate *judicial* role in suggesting constructive solutions and assisting the parties in achieving them.

Of course, there are limits to the exercise of that role. There is a line to be observed between suggesting the resolution of a dispute and insisting upon it. And all who have exercised judicial authority are aware that, unless a judge acts with caution and sensitivity, there is a risk that what the judge tenders as a suggestion will be perceived as a command. In this proceeding, we are satisfied that, once duly authorized to act with respect to the Manville reorganization, Judge Weinstein did not exceed judicial authority. And whatever infirmity may have attended the issuance of the orders of June 1 and July 9, issued before the July 20 designations, provides no basis for complaint. To a large extent, those orders were advisory only. To whatever extent the July 9 order went beyond advice, it was effectively ratified and validated by the grant of authority conveyed on July 20.

II. The Hybrid Nature of the Lawsuit

The Trial Courts purported to be exercising both bankruptcy court jurisdiction under 28 U.S.C. § 1334 and diversity jurisdiction under 28 U.S.C. § 1332. *Asbestos Litigation II*, 129 B.R. at 795. Their elaborate opinion does not relate specific rulings to one or the other source of jurisdiction. They observe only that the matter before them is "based primarily on diversity jurisdiction, rather than a pure bankruptcy proceeding." * * * Before reviewing the challenges to the exercise of either basis of jurisdiction, we pause to dispel some confusion, reflected in some of the parties' arguments, as to the respective spheres of authority of a diversity court and a bankruptcy court in this unusual hybrid action.

Though the appellants challenge the exercise of both diversity and bankruptcy jurisdiction, they appear, at times, to argue that only bankruptcy jurisdiction is available to deal in any way with the Manville Trust because it is an integral component of a confirmed plan of reorganization. If that is their contention, it is not correct. The Bankruptcy Court in the Chapter 11 proceeding had authority to make changes in the state law rights of creditors and to replace those rights with a new set of state law rights. Just as a reorganized corporation is subject to state law, so also is a trust that emerges from a plan of reorganization. Of course, state law might not, *as a substantive matter*, be able to alter any of the state law rights enjoyed by those dealing with the reorganized corporation, or in this case, with the Trust, either because state law does not authorize the requested relief or because its attempt to do so encounters constitutional obstacles. Some changes in rights, notably the rights of creditors, can be involuntarily altered only in the exercise of bankruptcy authority. But if a lawsuit is filed asserting a valid state law cause of action against an entity that has emerged from a reorganization plan, that suit may be settled, and any state law rights may be voluntarily modified so long as the settlement is within the subject matter jurisdiction of the court approving it and the settlement is accomplished in observance of all applicable procedural requirements. That is what the appellees contend has occurred in this case—the filing of a state law cause of action to restructure the Trust in a diversity court with subject matter jurisdiction and the settlement of that suit in observance of the procedural requirements of Rule 23. We therefore turn first to the objections to the exercise of the Trial Courts' diversity jurisdiction and then proceed, in the event deficiencies are encountered, to consider whether the changes wrought by the Settlement may be accomplished in the exercise of bankruptcy jurisdiction[.] * * *

III.   EXCLUSIVE EXERCISE OF DIVERSITY JURISDICTION

[Discussion of the court's diversity jurisdiction omitted—*ed.*].

* * *

C.   Rule 23 Requirements—The (b)(1)(B) Non-opt-out Class

Normally, we would first consider the appellants' challenges to the specific criteria of Rule 23(a), especially the requirements of typicality and adequacy of representation, and then proceed to consideration of the relevant category of Rule 23(b), in this case, the appropriateness of a mandatory non-opt-out class under Rule 23(b)(1)(B). In this case, however, for reasons to be discussed, we take up these contentions in the reverse order.

The Trial Courts certified a class under Rule 23(b)(1)(B), * * *. In their view, this case presented the sort of "limited fund" for which the Advisory Committee's note to the 1966 amendment of Rule 23 makes a (b)(1)(B) class "plainly" available—"when claims are made by numerous persons against a fund insufficient to satisfy all claims." Fed.R.Civ.P. 23 advisory committee's note to 1966 amendment; *see Asbestos Litigation II*, 129 B.R. at 825.

The Trial Courts concluded that the insolvency of the Manville Trust rendered it a "limited fund." Plainly, insolvency does not present the classic instance of a "limited fund," such as would be involved if a group of claimants asserted claims of an aggregate amount that would deplete a fixed sum of money. Whether, and for what purposes, (b)(1)(B) may be used with respect to an insolvent entity are perplexing issues that we would have expected to have received more extended consideration than is apparent in the cases thus far decided.

With respect to aggregate claims in excess of a fixed sum of money, a (b)(1)(B) class action is appropriate to avoid an unfair preference for the early claimants at the expense of later claimants. With respect to an insolvent entity, however, bankruptcy law is normally the source of protection to assure a fair and orderly distribution of assets insufficient to meet claims. Insolvency exerts powerful pressures upon contending creditors to compromise their positions so that a fair distribution of assets is achieved—through a reorganization that contemplates the continuation of the debtor where feasible, and otherwise through liquidation. To lessen the risk that these pressures will lead to unfair compromises, bankruptcy law provides numerous safeguards not contained in class action procedures. For example, for a plan of reorganization to be approved, the plan must be put to a vote of all members of impaired classes of creditors, 11 U.S.C. § 1126, the vote is taken only after a solicitation based on a detailed description of the plan, *id.* § 1125, the plan can be "crammed down" over the objection of a dissenting class of creditors only if strict fairness standards are met, *id.* § 1129(b)(1), and the plan may not be imposed against the wishes of an impaired class that would fare better under liquidation, *id.* § 1129(a)(7).

By contrast, Rule 23 is less elaborate in its protections, for example, permitting named representatives of a class, or subclass, to consent to a settlement that binds all the members of the class, or subclass, without a vote of the class or subclass members. And there is no option for those who would fare better under liquidation than under settlement of the class action followed by reorganization to insist on liquidation.

These differences raise a substantial question whether a class action may be used to adjust claims against an insolvent entity that is eligible for bankruptcy protection. And, even if, in the context of insolvency, a "limited fund" class action may be used for its traditional purpose of effecting a pro rata reduction of all claims, *see* Dickinson v. Burnham, 197 F.2d 973 (2d Cir.1952), *cert. denied,* 344 U.S. 875, 73 S.Ct. 169, 97 L.Ed. 678 (1952), an even more substantial question is raised as to whether a class action may be used against an insolvent entity to adjust the claims of creditors *vis-a-vis* each other, without observing the protections that would be available under bankruptcy law.

Thus far, with one notable exception to be discussed below, courts have moved sparingly in approving class action settlements that adjust creditors' claims vis-a-vis each other against insolvent entities through the use of a mandatory non-opt-out (b)(1)(B) class. In upholding the use of a (b)(1)(B) "limited fund" class, the Trial Courts relied on two class action rulings of the Eastern District (both rendered by Judge Weinstein), which were affirmed by this Court. *See* County of Suffolk v. Long Island Lighting Co., 710 F.Supp. 1407 (E.D.N.Y.1989), *aff'd,* 907 F.2d 1295 (2d Cir.1990); In re Agent Orange Product Liability Litigation, 100 F.R.D. 718 (E.D.N.Y.1983), *aff'd,* 818 F.2d 145 (2d Cir.1987), *cert. denied,* 484 U.S. 1004, 108 S.Ct. 695, 98 L.Ed.2d 648 (1988). Our affirmance of those rulings does not support the (b)(1)(B) non-opt-out class certified in this case. In *Suffolk County,* we faced no issue of the propriety of a (b)(1)(B) class. The class action issue was whether the District Judge had exceeded his discretion in allowing one member of the class to opt out. We ruled he had not. * * * In *Agent Orange,* we upheld the certification of a (b)(3) class because of the centrality of one major issue—the military contractor defense, and we found it unnecessary to consider the propriety of a (b)(1)(B) class. * * *

An earlier decision of this Court in the *Agent Orange* litigation is arguably more pertinent. In In re Diamond Shamrock Chemicals Co., 725 F.2d 858 (2d Cir.1984), we declined to issue mandamus to vacate Judge Weinstein's certification of a (b)(1)(B) class limited to the issue of punitive damages. The denial of mandamus does not imply approval, but, in any event, we note that the (b)(1)(B) punitive damages class was not certified to permit the involuntary adjustment of the rights of competing creditors with claims against an insolvent entity. *Diamond*

Shamrock presented a situation much closer to the traditional concept of a limited fund than occurs whenever an entity becomes insolvent. Though the potential amount of aggregate punitive damages had not yet been determined, that amount was finite and was not claimed to have rendered the defendant insolvent. The (b)(1)(B) class was thought appropriate because the recoveries of early successful claimants for punitive damages would quickly reach a total sufficient to assure deterrence, thereby precluding later claimants as a matter of law.

> Given the large number of potential claimants . . . and given the fact that punitive damages ought in theory to be distributed on a basis other than the date of trial, the argument against [the class action] ruling does not justify mandamus. . . . There was no prospect of the involuntary revision of the rights of competing creditors in contemplation of insolvency. No bankruptcy protections were circumvented.

We also take note of the following dictum in Green v. Occidental Petroleum Corp., 541 F.2d 1335 (9th Cir.1976):

> It is conceivable of course, that the claims of named plaintiffs would be so large that if the action were to proceed as an individual action the decision "would as a practical matter be dispositive of the interests of the other members not parties to the adjudications or substantially impair or impede their ability to protect their interests." Fed.R.Civ.P. 23(b)(1)(B). This would be the case where the claims of all plaintiffs exceeded the assets of the defendant and hence to allow any group of individuals to be fully compensated would impair the rights of those not in court.

Id. at 1340 n.9. That dictum implied the possible availability of a (b)(1)(B) class action in the context of an insolvent entity, but had no occasion to go further and reckon with the prospect of using such a device to achieve the involuntary adjustment of rights of competing creditors with claims against such an entity. We note that when the Ninth Circuit next considered the *Occidental Petroleum* dictum, it rejected the certification of a (b)(1)(B) class, even for purposes of punitive damage claims. *See* In re Northern District of California, Dalkon Shield IUD Products Liability Litigation, 693 F.2d 847, 851 (9th Cir.1982).

One district court decision has certified a (b)(1)(B) class because of the likelihood that the aggregate total of claims would render the defendant insolvent. *See* Coburn v. 4–R Corp., 77 F.R.D. 43 (E.D.Ky. 1977). That decision, however, had no occasion to reckon with the objection that the class action device might be used to circumvent bankruptcy procedures. Nor did it involve an involuntary modification of creditors' rights vis-a-vis each other, such as abrogation of the clear order-of-filing priority of rights enjoyed by the objecting health claimants in the pending litigation.

If the cases discussed to this point exhausted our jurisprudence, we would seriously doubt whether a mandatory non-opt-out (b)(1)(B) class action may be used to readjust the rights of creditors vis-a-vis each other against an insolvent entity. Though we recognize that the Bankruptcy Rules make Rule 23 of the Civil Rules applicable to adversary proceedings, *see* Fed.R.Bankr. 7023, we would be wary of any class action settlement that accomplished more than a liquidation and pro rata reduction of the claims of a group of creditors and risked circumvention of Bankruptcy Code protections. *See* In re Shulman Transport Enterprises, Inc., 21 B.R. 548, 551 (Bankr.S.D.N.Y.1982)("[A] bankruptcy court must consider the fact that in most instances class action principles are antithetical to those in bankruptcy."), *aff'd*, 33 B.R. 383 (S.D.N.Y.1983), *aff'd*, 744 F.2d 293 (2d Cir.1984). However, respect for the binding force of precedent within this Circuit obliges us to take careful note of the recent decision in In re Drexel Burnham Lambert Group, Inc., 960 F.2d 285 (2d Cir.), *cert. filed*, 61 U.S.L.W. 3151 (Aug. 13, 1992), which approved a more adventuresome use of a class action settlement to make a non-uniform adjustment of creditors' rights against an insolvent entity.

Drexel involved claims by purchasers of securities sold by the ill-fated firm of Drexel Burnham Lambert. A forerunner of the case was a suit filed by the Securities and Exchange Commission against Drexel seeking, among other things, disgorgement of profits it had made, allegedly on unlawful transactions. The SEC's suit was settled by Drexel's payment of $200 million into a fund for defrauded purchasers, with the fund to be augmented by an additional payment of $150 million. Before the second payment was made, Drexel filed for reorganization under Chapter 11.

Judge Pollack, before whom were pending suits by many of the defrauded purchasers, then supervised the filing and settlement of a class action, which is highly pertinent to the issues we face in the pending appeal. After the claims of the defrauded purchasers were withdrawn from bankruptcy jurisdiction pursuant to 28 U.S.C. § 157(d) on the ground that they involved issues arising under the securities laws, an elaborate settlement of the claims was reached through the formation of a class action. The principal elements were the division of the purchaser claimants into two subclasses and the specification of the payment rights of each subclass. Subclass A, which held claims with a face amount of $20 billion, was to receive 75 percent of the $350 million fund, plus 75 percent of stated percentages of the liquidation value of various Drexel assets. In addition Subclass A was to pool with Drexel the proceeds from the suits each had against officers and directors of Drexel. Subclass B, which held claims with a face amount of $3.6 billion, was to receive 25 percent of the $350 million fund plus 25 percent of the stated percentages of the funds resulting from liquidation of Drexel assets, but had no participation in the pooling arrangement with respect to suits against Drexel officers and directors.

The judgment approving the settlement was affirmed by this Court, over the objection of some members of Subclass B. * * * A major contention of some of the appellants was that the use of a mandatory non-opt-out (b)(1)(B) class constituted an impermissible circumvention of bankruptcy law protections. * * * Though the opinion contains no explicit consideration of this contention, the Court's affirmance, in the face of a detailed presentation of the argument, must be regarded as a holding that, at least in the circumstances of the *Drexel* case, a mandatory non-opt-out (b)(1)(B) class action may be used to accomplish some readjustment of creditors' rights against an insolvent entity, without observing the protections of bankruptcy law.

Especially pertinent to the pending appeal is the designation of subclasses in *Drexel* for settlement purposes. Recognizing that Subclasses A and B were being treated differently, the District Court accepted the settlement only after receiving the consent of representatives of each of the subclasses, who were adjudged to fairly and adequately represent the interests of all of the members of their respective subclasses.

Drexel acknowledges that class actions are not normally to be used in the context of bankruptcy. 960 F.2d at 292. Two circumstances not present in the pending case may have influenced the decision to approve the class action settlement. First, the case involved, at least in part, a traditional limited fund, since the claimants were asserting claims against the $200 million paid by Drexel to the fund assembled by the SEC and to the additional $150 million to be paid to that fund. Second, the settlement was regarded by this Court as a necessary prerequisite to a successful reorganization plan. *Drexel*, 960 F.2d at 293. By contrast, the pending case involves a "limited fund" only in the sense that, like any insolvent entity, the assets of the Manville Trust, including its income stream, are insufficient to pay present and future claims. And the class action here is not a prerequisite to a reorganization, but a change in rights already established in a confirmed and substantially consummated plan of reorganization. Indeed, it is arguable that the Settlement in the pending case, by abandoning the order-of-payment priority, accomplishes a more substantial adjustment of creditors' rights than occurred in *Drexel*, where creditors with only an expectation of recovery in effect had those expectations valued by being relegated to specified percentages of different asset pools for their recoveries. These differences make us somewhat skeptical of permitting the use of a mandatory non-opt-out class in this case. But, though the question is close, we are not persuaded that the need to insist on bankruptcy law protections is greater in this case than it was in *Drexel*, and the reasonableness of using a (b)(1)(B) non-opt-out class is at least as compelling in this case as in *Drexel*.

We are therefore willing to permit the use of such a class action in the pending case, so long as there exists, as occurred in *Drexel*, appropriate designation of subclasses to provide assurance that the consent of groups of claimants who are being treated differently by the settlement is being given by those who fairly and adequately represent only the members of each group. The inevitable tension between the limited protections of Rule 23 and the more complete protections of the Bankruptcy Code is strained by any use of a mandatory non-opt-out class to settle claims against an insolvent entity that is subject to bankruptcy jurisdiction. But that tension reaches the breaking point when, instead of the traditional limited fund settlement that achieves a pro rata reduction of the claims of all members of the plaintiff class, the rights of the plaintiff class are revised *vis-a-vis* each other and consent to the resulting settlement is given by representatives who purport to represent the undifferentiated class of plaintiffs as a whole, rather than the interests of each of the subclasses whose rights are being altered. We therefore proceed to an examination of the appellants' contentions regarding the lack of subclasses, mindful that these contentions require careful scrutiny in the unusual context where settlement of a class action is used to readjust creditors' claims against an insolvent entity, without observance of the protections that would otherwise be available under the Bankruptcy Code.

* * *

IV. EXERCISE OF BANKRUPTCY JURISDICTION

Though the Trial Courts relied primarily on the exercise of diversity jurisdiction and the application of Rule 23(b)(1)(B) as authority to approve the Settlement restructuring the Trust, they also invoked their bankruptcy jurisdiction to some unspecified extent. We therefore proceed to inquire whether approval of the Settlement is valid in the exercise of the Trial Courts' bankruptcy jurisdiction. The objecting health claimants contend that the modification of their rights as Class–4 creditors is not authorized by the Plan or its attached documents and, in any event, violates section 1127 of the Code. We consider first the amending authority within the Plan.

A. *Amending Authority Within the Plan*

The modification of the rights of the Class–4 claimants is accomplished under the Settlement by an amendment of the document entitled "Claims Resolution Procedures," which is Annex B to the Trust Agreement. * * *

Section 11.6 of the Plan, concerning amendment of Plan-related documents, provides:

> Amendments. The authority of the Company, the Trustees, the PD Trustees and holders of Claims to agree to modifications, supplements or amendments of or to the agreements and instruments attached as Exhibits hereto or as Annexes to any such Exhibit shall be as provided in such agreements and instruments.

The Trial Courts, after citing this authority, invoked the amending authority of the Trust Agreement. Section 6.03(a) of the Trust Agreement provides:

> Amendments. (a) The Company ... and the Trustees ... may, after consultation with Selected Counsel for the Beneficiaries, modify, supplement or amend this Trust Agreement [with exceptions not relevant to this dispute] in any respect. . . .

The Trial Courts apparently reasoned that the explicit authority to amend the Trust Agreement carried over to the six annexes attached to the Trust Agreement, including Annex B, with which we are concerned. We cannot agree.

Though we might have expected the drafters to provide that the authority to amend the Trust Agreement carries over to all of the documents appended to it, they chose a different approach. The Plan expressly provides that the authority to amend *"agreements* and instruments *attached* as Exhibits hereto or *as Annexes* to any such Exhibit *shall be as provided in such agreements* and instruments." Plan § 11.6 (emphasis added). Annex B contains no amending authority whatsoever. This omission is striking when Annex B is compared to other Plan-related documents.

* * *

The care with which the drafters granted and withheld amending authority in the various documents attached to the Plan persuades us to read section 11.6 of the Plan to mean, as it appears to say, that amending authority with respect to a particular Plan-related document must be found in the document itself. An exception to this approach is apparently available for the PD Claims Resolution Facility, since amending authority is contained in the definition of the term "PD Claims Resolution Facility," and this authority is thereby arguably incorporated by reference into Annex B to the PD Trust Agreement, the annex establishing the PD Claims Resolution Facility. No comparable authority is contained in Annex B to the PI Trust Agreement, or elsewhere in the Plan or in any Plan-related document.

Apparently, the asbestos health claimants not only negotiated the FIFO principle into the terms of Annex B of the PI Trust Agreement but were also able to prevent the granting of any authority for abandonment or alteration of this principle, save only for section 10.1(H) of the Plan, which authorizes the Court to retain jurisdiction "[t]o modify any provision of the Plan to the full extent permitted by the Code."

We conclude that the restructuring of the Trust was not permitted pursuant to any of the specific amending powers reserved to the various parties identified in the Plan and the Plan-related documents. We therefore consider whether the changes were authorized by the more general reserved power of the Bankruptcy Court to modify the Plan "to the full extent permitted by the Code." Plan § 10.1(H).

B.　*Conflict With the Code*

The extent to which a bankruptcy court may make changes in a confirmed reorganization plan is largely uncharted terrain. *See* David A. Lander & David A. Warfield, *A Review and Analysis of Selected Post–Confirmation Activities in Chapter 11 Reorganizations,* 62 Am.Bankr.L.J. 203 (1988). Appellants contend that the restructuring violates the Code in two respects. First, they contend, it violates the fundamental bar of section 1127(b), which prohibits modifications of a confirmed and substantially consummated plan of reorganization. Second, they contend, it violates section 1123(a)(4), which requires that a plan "provide the same treatment for each claim or interest of a particular class."

1. *Section 1127(b).* The Trial Courts sought to avoid the bar of section 1127(b) by maintaining that the restructuring of the Trust was not a "modification." We cannot agree. Even if the concept of "modification" implies some distinction between significant changes of substance, which are prohibited, and minor changes of procedure, which might be allowed, the alterations accomplished by the Settlement are both substantive and significant. Health claimants who formerly stood on an equal footing, entitled to payment in the order their claims were filed, and with jury trial rights unimpaired, emerged divided into two groups, with differing rights as to maximum amounts recoverable and as to timing and rate of payments. The FIFO ordering of payments was scrapped. For all claimants, the opportunity to have a jury determine the amount of their damages was drastically curtailed by the disincentive created by the payment of jury verdicts in excess of offers or arbitration awards only out of a secondary pool of money, unlikely to have sufficient resources to meet its obligations.

The Trial Courts additionally sought to avoid the restrictions of section 1127(b) by contending that the settlement effects no change in the Plan, but only in Plan-related documents. As the Trial Courts' Opinion states, "We have found no case that has applied section 1127(b) to bar variations in a plan-related document." * * * That argument will not suffice. It could be said with equal conviction that no case has ever approved variations in a plan-related document, without regard to section 1127(b), where the effect is to alter substantial rights of creditors. The question remains whether a change that would contravene section 1127(b) if made in the provisions of a plan can be accomplished by modifying the provisions of a plan-related document. The answer must be no. The rights of creditors, bargained for during the negotiations that preceded the presentation and confirmation of the Plan cannot depend on whether those rights were spelled out in a document labeled "plan" or in an attached document labeled "exhibit" or "annex." What controls is the substance of the change, not the title of the document that is changed. In this case, the Plan requires payment of the full amount of all allowed Class–4 claims. The change effectively alters that payment right.

* * *

2. *Section 1123(a)(4).* Since the purported exercise of bankruptcy jurisdiction violates the bar of section 1127(b), we need not decide whether the Settlement also violates section 1123(a)(4) by failing to accord the "same treatment" to the health claimant members of Class–4. We have summarized the extensive changes that the Settlement makes in the rights of the Class–4 claimants in pointing out why those changes qualify as "modifications" for purposes of section 1127(b).

* * * Whether the Settlement permissibly classifies according to seriousness of injury or impermissibly denies health claimant creditors the "same treatment" need not be resolved, since any effort to use bankruptcy authority to accomplish the objectives of the Settlement would in any event require a second reorganization.

* * *

CONCLUSION

With considerable regret, we hold that the Settlement must be set aside, and we vacate the judgment of the Trial Courts. Our regret arises from two sources: both the extraordinary efforts that have been made by all concerned with this litigation—judges, lawyers, and court-appointed experts—in crafting an ingenious set of arrangements to resolve an extremely difficult set of problems, and the obvious benefits that the result of their combined labors would have brought to most of those with interests in this litigation. But we cannot uphold as "sensible" or "useful" or "fair" or even "achieving the most good for the most people" an impairment of rights accomplished in violation of applicable legal rules.

We need not consider at this time whether any of the changes in claim adjudication and payment can yet be made by the settlement of a proper class action or by procedures other than the settlement of a class action, such as a Chapter 11 proceeding for the Trust itself (if it qualifies as a business trust, *see* 11 U.S.C. § 101(8)(A)(v)), a "reopen[ing of] all aspects of the Plan" * * *, a consensual modification of the Plan, or, more likely, a second Chapter 11 proceeding for the debtor, *see* In re Jartran, Inc., 71 B.R. 938 (Bankr.N.D.Ill.1987). Unattractive as the prospect of pursuing other devices may be, we cannot permit the virtues of the present technique to supplant the legal requirements of Rule 23 and the Bankruptcy Code. Those requirements may not be cast aside no matter how beneficial the outcome may seem to the majority of those affected by the class action settlement. A reorganization is assuredly governed by equitable considerations, but that guiding principle is not a license to courts to invent remedies that overstep statutory limitations nor to approve arrangements that some parties to a reorganization proceeding find preferable to the arrangements incorporated in a confirmed and consummated plan. "[W]hatever equitable powers remain in the bankruptcy courts must and can only be exercised within the confines of the Bankruptcy Code." Norwest Bank Worthington v. Ahlers, 485 U.S. 197, 206, 108 S.Ct. 963, 969, 99 L.Ed.2d 169 (1988).

Accordingly, we vacate the judgment of the District Courts and the Bankruptcy Court and remand for further proceedings not inconsistent with this opinion. The petition for mandamus is denied.

FEINBERG, CIRCUIT JUDGE, concurring in part and dissenting in part:

Judge Newman's opinion for the majority in this important case is characteristically thoughtful and comprehensive. I concur in much of it. I cannot agree, however, with the majority's holding that the Trial

Courts' approval of the treatment of the health claimants in the restructured Manville Personal Injury Settlement Trust (the Trust) was improper under both Rule 23 of the Federal Rules of Civil Procedure and the bankruptcy laws. As discussed below, I believe that the Trial Courts' ruling violated neither Rule 23 nor the bankruptcy laws.

* * *

II

It is against this background that the rulings of the majority from which I dissent must be considered. I believe that those rulings are the product of three misconceptions. The first is that the use of Rule 23 to change the rights of creditors of an insolvent entity should be accepted only grudgingly, if at all. Prior authority in this court does not require such reluctance. *See, e.g.,* In re Drexel Burnham Lambert Group, Inc., 960 F.2d 285 (2d Cir.), *cert. filed,* 61 U.S.L.W. 3151 (Aug. 13, 1992); In re Diamond Shamrock Chemicals, Co., 725 F.2d 858 (2d Cir.1984). *Cf.* In re American Reserve Corp., 840 F.2d 487, 488–93 (7th Cir.1988); Green v. Occidental, 541 F.2d 1335, 1340 n.9 (9th Cir.1976). It is true that we stated in *Drexel* that "a mandatory class action will not be appropriate in most bankruptcy cases." 960 F.2d at 292. But we nevertheless approved the use of Rule 23 in a bankruptcy context because of the exigencies noted there. The same justification applies here.

Moreover, there is at least doubt as to whether the bankruptcy laws alone can effectively deal with the problem of future claimants in the context of mass torts whose damage may not surface for many years. *See* Kane, 843 F.2d at 639; In re Joint Eastern & Southern Districts Asbestos Litigation, 129 B.R. at 839; In re Johns–Manville Corp., 68 B.R. at 628. *See also* NEWBERG ON CLASS ACTIONS §§ 20.28, 20.31 (Cum. Supp., pt. one. Mar. 1992). The usefulness of Rule 23 in this situation is thus apparent, particularly when the future asbestos-diseased claimants were "the *raison d'etre*" of the reorganization, and these claimants as a group stand to suffer the most if the Settlement fails. Certainly, as the majority recognizes, the Bankruptcy Rules themselves "make Rule 23 of the Civil Rules applicable to adversary proceedings." At the very least, the use of Rule 23 in this context should not be scrutinized with undue wariness.

Second, in its discussion of the use of Rule 23, the majority appears to focus on the plaintiff beneficiaries' class action against the Trust as though that action stood by itself, apart from the history set forth above. But that is not the case. The Trust is not simply any insolvent entity. Nor, as the majority notes, is the Trust "an ordinary private understanding of a settlor to carry out private preferences." It is a payment mechanism created by a plan of reorganization. The efforts of the Trial Courts to restructure the Plan's payment mechanism are not an attempt to subvert the bankruptcy laws; they are an attempt to carry out the purposes of a trust that itself was the product of a reorganization under those laws. Moreover, the restructuring of the Trust is entirely proper since the purpose of creating the Trust was to carry out the provision of the Plan that called for payment of health claims in full. It may be that unforeseen events have made that purpose difficult, and perhaps impossible, to achieve. We should nevertheless be slow to set aside the efforts of all those involved to achieve it, including those of the experienced trial judges who have lived with these massive proceedings on a daily basis.

Third, the majority appears to attribute unwarranted substantive importance to the Trust's FIFO procedure for the processing of beneficiaries' health claims. In 1988, this court wrote: "Not all present asbestos claims must be paid immediately upon confirmation [of the Plan], and many will not be liquidated and presented for payment even within the first five years. More likely, payment of present health claims will be spread out over roughly a ten-year period." *Kane*, 843 F.2d at 650. With the benefit of hindsight, we now know that this assumption as to when present health claimants would be paid was too optimistic; as it turned out, the Trust was "deeply insolvent," in the words of the special master, only two years later. If you assumed, as this court did as late as 1988, that all present health claimants would be paid in full within ten years, then a FIFO preference simply meant you could get your money sooner. While this was not insignificant, it did not mean the difference between getting 100% compensation and zero. FIFO "rights" became that valuable only when people realized that the money would run out, not before. From this perspective, it is easy to see why the FIFO procedure had to be discarded: The most basic assumption upon which it rested, namely, full payment of all present health claimants over a period of years, had proved to be wrong.

The most that can reasonably be said for FIFO is that it seemed like an efficient procedure when the Trust Agreement, which makes frequent reference to the necessity for "efficient" resolution of claims, was drafted. But what had seemed like an efficient procedure proved to be otherwise. FIFO simply did not work. In re Joint Eastern & Southern Districts Asbestos Litigation, 129 B.R. at 759. In fact, FIFO and related procedures may have been the single most important factor leading to the insolvency of the Trust. To explain this requires considering the FIFO procedures in detail. Annex B provided that all claims be processed, from filing of claim forms to issuance of check, within 120 days of filing. * * * If the Trust did not process a claim within 120 days, a claimant had a right to go to trial and thereby jump the FIFO queue. * * * "Therefore, even claimants with late filing dates were able to receive early processing and payment by going to trial." Mark A. Peterson, *Giving Away Money,* 53 L. & Contemp. Probs. 113, 119 (Autumn 1990). Many claims took more than 120 days to process; consequently, many claimants were permitted to sue the Trust. *See* Marianna S. Smith, *Resolving Asbestos Claims: The Manville Personal Injury Trust,* 53 L. & Contemp. Probs. 27, 34 (Autumn 1990). This defeated one of the express purposes of the Trust.

As evidenced by one of the articulated purposes of the Trust, the crafters of the Plan genuinely wanted the Trust to be a negotiation-based settlement organization. They wanted claimants to explore all avenues of negotiation and alternative dispute resolution before turning to litigation as a last resort. To meet this objective, the Plan established a "formula" for ordering the payment of claims, allowing the Trust to take cases docketed and scheduled for trial out of queue and settle them. This appeared to be a reasonable approach. However, two factors led to the Trust's inundation with active litigation. The first factor was purely operational: the Plan permitted claimants to sue the Trust 120 days after filing their claims with the Trust. Because the Trust had received such an enormous volume of claims and was unable to make offers on all of them within 120 days, claimants had the right to sue and did so to improve their position in the queue.

The second factor influencing the volume of litigation was an acceleration in the volume of cases tried in the courts compared to the relative handful of asbestos cases that came to trial in the mid–1980's.

* * * The costs of defending the "inundation" of litigation ate up the Trust's funds faster than anybody expected and made the compensation process unworkable. Peterson, *Giving Money Away,* 53 L. & Contemp. Probs. at 119–20.

Once the inadequacy of the Trust's assets became apparent, the need to adjust the payment mechanism became paramount. The Trial Courts were faced with the prospect that many health claimants would get little or no compensation while others would receive 100%. But under the Plan, *all* present health claimants were to be paid in full. *Kane,* 843 F.2d at 649. Unlike FIFO, which was merely one procedural aspect of the payment mechanism, the right of all present health claimants to the full value of their claims was a substantive right they received under the Plan. Moreover, if *present* health claimants were in danger of not getting their due under the Plan, a fortiori, the goal of meeting future asbestos-related liability was not likely to be met.[5]

* * *

III

This analysis leads me to conclude that the Trial Courts' approval of the treatment of the health claimants, present and future, in the restructured Trust was not improper under Rule 23 or the bankruptcy laws. Based upon its misconceptions, the majority subjects the Settlement to "careful scrutiny" and concludes that under Rule 23 the health claimants should have been subdivided into four subclasses in order to

---

5. Abandoning FIFO was only one of the ways the Settlement sought to reduce transactional costs and enhance the fairness of distribution. Another change approved by the Settlement was a cap on attorneys' fees payable in connection with liquidated claims, limiting them to the fee provided in the contract between claimant and counsel or 25%, whichever is less. The fee provision in the Settlement "compels all to share in the necessary adjustments to account for the Trust's limited resources." In re Joint Eastern & Southern Districts Asbestos Litigation, 129 B.R. at 869.

modify the Trust, and that the representatives of Level One and Level Two health claimants could not validly settle the class action on behalf of the health claimants. Respectfully, I disagree.

I have already discussed why I believe that FIFO rights did not require subdividing the health claimants into subclasses. Nor was such action required by the change in payment procedures to allow the most seriously ill health claimants (Level One) to obtain 45% payment on their claims before the remaining health claimants (Level Two) get 45%, with both sharing pro rata thereafter. This not only made compassionate good sense but also represented a good-faith effort to realize the Plan's stated objective to pay all liquidated health claims in full, or, short of that, to pay equal percentages of all claims over time in accordance with the purposes for which the Trust was created. It is true that Level Two claimants have to wait longer and have a greater risk of non-payment in full. But all health claimants—even those who were present claimants when the Plan was confirmed—were faced with the same rapidly deteriorating financial situation, which the Settlement halted. The majority notes that the Trial Courts estimated that the Manville stock would have to reach a price of $24 to $25 per share before the Trust could raise enough money to pay Level Two claimants the same 45 percent share of awards paid to Level One claimants, and that in the period prior to the Settlement, Manville shares traded at only between $4 and $5 per share. It seems equally worth noting that Manville shares are now selling at approximately $9 a share with a 52–week high of $10⅞.

On this record, and free of any undue wariness about the use of Rule 23 in this situation, I do not discern the extensive "adversity" in the group of health claimants that the majority does, or the inadequacy of representation. The Trial Courts found that the claims of the representatives were typical of those of remaining class members:

> [T]he representative cases embody a cross-section of the claims filed against the Manville Trust nationwide. Their cases arise out of the same underlying course of conduct and are based on the same legal theories as those of the class generally.... The class members and their representatives possess an identity of interest and appear to lack any critical inimical interests for purposes of Rule 23 certification.

In re Joint Eastern & Southern Districts Asbestos Litigation, 129 B.R. at 820. In addition, the Trial Courts found that

> [t]he class representatives include persons who would qualify as Level Two Claimants under the Settlement, and each of the class counsel has clients who suffer from injuries which similarly fall within the definition of a Level–Two asbestos-related disease * * *. These claimants' interests have been vigorously prosecuted throughout the negotiation process and resulted in the Settlement before the courts.

* * * With regard to the health claimants, I see no persuasive basis for reversing the Trial Courts on these issues, * * *. With respect to the health claimants, the Settlement carried out the intentions of the Plan and the Trust, and the class representatives accepted it. We should abide by that.

Finally, the majority states that there is a "substantial" question whether the "alteration of beneficiaries' rights" under the Trust "had a sufficiently plausible basis" in New York trust law "to make the Settlement a reasonable compromise of the lawsuit." The majority finds it unnecessary to answer that question because it concludes that "[a]t a minimum," the Settlement required "the separately obtained consents of representatives who fairly and adequately speak for each of the significant subclasses," which the majority had already ruled had not been obtained. As to the adequacy of representation of the health claimants, I disagree for reasons already given. Moreover, if it were crucial to determine whether New York law allowed the restructuring of the Trust, the sensible course would be to certify that issue to the New York Court of Appeals. That tribunal can speak more appropriately (and more authoritatively) than we on whether the restructuring permissibly serves the interests of the beneficiaries, so many of whom are undoubtedly New York residents.

Accordingly, I concur in part and dissent in part, as set forth above.

Notes and Questions

1. Marianna Smith was the executive Director of the Manville Trust. At the time she wrote her article for the symposium issue of *Law and Contemporary Problems* on claims facilities, the Manville Trust was experiencing serious difficulties and beginning to unravel. To what extent did Ms. Smith recognize the problems in the Manville Trust? What optimistic forecast did she have for the Trust? Do the lessons she outlines at the end of her article make sense in light of subsequent developments relating to the Manville Trust?

2. In 1992, exactly ten years after the Manville Corporation had first filed for bankruptcy, the Second Circuit overruled Judge Weinstein's and Judge Lifland's approval of a class action/bankruptcy settlement with Manville. As a district court judge assigned a docket of asbestos cases, what authority did Judge Weinstein have for intervening in the Manville Trust bankruptcy and reorganization plan? Is the Second Circuit convincing in finding an authority for the judge's actions? Didn't Judge Weinstein's actions, as the appellants contended, border on a legislative solution to the Manville Trust problems? Recall that in summer 1990 a group of federal district judges, also faced with the asbestos litigation crisis, attempted to certify a nationwide class of asbestos cases that was overturned by the Sixth Circuit in *In re Allied Signal; see In re Allied Signal*, Chapter II.A, section 5, *supra*. To what extent are Judge Weinstein's actions with regard to the Manville Trust a part of this history? Does an announced litigation crisis justify the judges' intervention in an ongoing bankruptcy reorganization plan?

3. Does the Second Circuit's decision in the *Joint Eastern & Southern Dist. Asbestos Litigation* appeal preclude recourse to a Rule 23(b)(1)(B) class certification to settle creditors' claims against a mass tort bankruptcy debtor? Can a district court and/or bankruptcy court jointly utilize the courts' authority to use class action procedures to globally settle claims in a bankruptcy proceeding? Do the bankruptcy provisions permit or preclude use of such devices? Remember that both bankruptcy proceedings and class action procedure derive from equity. Shouldn't the equity basis of both permit greater leeway to the courts and judges in fashioning solutions to mass tort litigation? To what extent does Judge Feinberg's dissent make the argument for a more expansive use of class action procedure in a bankruptcy setting?

4. What were Judges Weinstein and Lifland trying to accomplish by their orders in restructuring the Manville Trust? In addition to invalidating the Rule 23(b)(1)(B) class, the Second Circuit also finds that the judges' approval of the settlement constituted an impermissible modification of a consummated reorganization plan under section 1127(b) of the Bankruptcy Code. Keep this ruling in mind as you read the Second Circuit's decision relating to the Manville Property Damage Settlement Trust, *infra*. To what extent does the Second Circuit's decision rely on interpretation and application of state law? Is Judge Feinberg correct that, at a minimum, this issue ought to have been certified to the New York court for a ruling on applicable law?

5. For a discussion of restructuring bankruptcy plans in the mass tort context, *see generally* Stacy L. Rahl, Note, *Modification of a Chapter 11 Plan in the Mass Tort Context,* 92 Colum.L.Rev. 192 (1992).

2. THE MANVILLE PROPERTY DAMAGE SETTLEMENT TRUST

IN RE JOHNS–MANVILLE CORPORATION

United States Court of Appeals, Second Circuit, 1990.
920 F.2d 121.

MAHONEY, CIRCUIT JUDGE:

The State Government Creditors' Committee for Property Damage Claims (the "State Committee") appeals from an order and judgment of the United States District Court for the Southern District of New York, Leonard B. Sand, Judge, entered March 16, 1990. The district court's order and judgment affirmed an order of the United States Bankruptcy Court for the Southern District of New York, Burton R. Lifland, Chief Judge, dated February 26, 1990 that authorized the temporary suspension of the operations of a claims resolution facility (the "PD Facility") established to resolve asbestos-related property damage claims against Johns–Manville Corporation and certain of its subsidiaries (collectively "Manville") pursuant to the Manville Property Damage Settlement Trust (the "PD Trust").

Manville's Second Amended and Restated Plan of Reorganization (the "Plan") established two trusts; the PD Trust at issue in this appeal, the affairs of which are conducted by three trustees (the "PD Trustees"), and a separate trust for the benefit of asbestos-related personal injury claimants against Manville (the "PI Trust"). The PD Trustees moved before the bankruptcy court to suspend the operations of the PD Facility as of October 31, 1992, at which date the PD Trust would not, for the indefinite future, have funds to pay claims. The trustees sought thereby to free an estimated $35.25 million in projected administrative expenses of the PD Facility and use that money instead to pay claims established against the PD Trust. The bankruptcy court granted the application, and the district court affirmed the ruling of the bankruptcy court.

The State Committee contends on appeal that these rulings authorized a modification of the Plan that violates 11 U.S.C. § 1127(b)(1988), and that in any event they were an abuse of discretion because holders of claims not perfected prior to the October 31, 1992 suspension of the PD Facility would be irreparably harmed by that suspension with regard to the ultimate establishment and payment of their claims. Appellees defend the rulings on the merits; the PD Trustees additionally contend that this appeal should be dismissed for lack of jurisdiction because it was taken from an interlocutory, rather than final, order.

We conclude that we have appellate jurisdiction, and affirm the district court's order and judgment affirming the bankruptcy court's order authorizing suspension of the operations of the PD Facility.

Background

This appeal arises out of reorganization proceedings under chapter 11 of title 11 of the United States Code initiated by Manville's filing of a petition for reorganization on August 26, 1982.[1] The Plan, which was intended to amend, modify, and supersede earlier proposed reorganization plans, was proposed, confirmed by the bankruptcy court, and consummated during these proceedings.

The PD Trust was established for the benefit of schools, colleges, hospitals, governmental bodies, and other persons and entities (the "Claimants") seeking recovery in the Manville bankruptcy for property damage due to asbestos and asbestos-containing products manufactured and/or sold by Manville, and is governed by New York law. According to the Claims Resolution Guidelines (the "PD Guidelines") that were annexed to the agreement establishing the PD Trust, the PD Facility "provide[s] the exclusive method for the disposition and payment of [p]roperty [c]laims [ ] against the PD Trust as provided in the Plan." The PD Guidelines govern "[d]eterminations as to the allowance and payment of [property] claims ... [and] ... are designed to provide a no-fault, non-litigated, low transaction cost method of effectuating the consensual settlement of [p]roperty [c]laims asserted against [Man-

---

1. As to the history of these proceedings, *see* Kane v. Johns–Manville, 843 F.2d 636, 639–41 (2d Cir.1988); In re Johns–Manville Corp., 824 F.2d 176, 178–79 (2d Cir.1987); In re Johns–Manville Corp., 36 B.R. 727 (Bankr.S.D.N.Y.), *appeal denied*, 39 B.R. 234 (S.D.N.Y.1984).

ville]." Supplementary "Allowance Procedure and Distribution Guidelines" (the "Allowance Guidelines") address the sequence for allowance and payment of approved claims.

The PD Trust received substantial cash and insurance settlement proceeds in its early years of operation, but will not receive significant additional funds until the PI Trust no longer requires funds from Manville to pay personal injury claimants. Thereafter, the PD Trust will be entitled to receive from Manville twenty percent of its annual profit, assuming that Manville is still in business and profitable.

Pursuant to the PD Guidelines, the PD Facility receives and reviews documentation of asbestos property damage claims, determines the allowed amounts of claims, and makes distributions thereon from assets of the PD Trust. The Allowance Guidelines dictate timetables for the review and periodic payment of claims. Claims are reviewed and allowed in "cycles" determined by their filing dates. The first cycle encompassed six months from the activation of the PD facility; subsequent cycles cover twelve months. No payment on a claim filed in a given cycle may be made until all claims filed in that cycle have been allowed or disallowed. At the close of each cycle, the funds remaining in the PD Trust after the creation of a specified reserve are paid to holders of allowed claims. The unpaid balances due such holders, together with newly filed claims, become part of the claims payable in subsequent cycles. The first cycle ended on October 31, 1989, and payments to the first cycle Claimants were scheduled to be completed by March, 1990.

The Plan was confirmed on December 22, 1986. Subsequently, but prior to the Plan's consummation, the PD Trustees, anticipating a possible "drought" period during which the PD Trust would incur administrative expenses but would lack the wherewithal to pay claims, sought and obtained from the bankruptcy court an order, entered October 28, 1988, which provided in pertinent part: "[A]t any time after the expiration of the time for the filing of claims in the first allowance cycle and prior to the payment of any claim filed in the first allowance cycle, the PD Trustees are authorized to apply to this Court, upon adequate notice to all interested parties, for relief necessary to permit the PD Trust to fulfill its purposes under the Plan, including application * * * (2) for approval of a plan providing for the modification or suspension of operations of the PD Claims Resolution Facility during cycles in which the PD Trust is not expected to have sufficient income to make payments on claims while maintaining all authorized reserves, and * * * after hearing on 30 days' notice to [interested parties] the Court may grant an adequately documented application for such relief."

In accordance with the quoted order, the PD Trustees applied to the bankruptcy court on January 18, 1990 for a suspension of the operations of the PD Facility upon completion of the fourth allowance cycle on October 31, 1992. The supporting affidavit of Kurt H. Schaffir, executive director of the PD Trust, stated that after October 1992 the PD Trust could expect no significant income until the PI Trust no longer required Manville funds to pay claims, and that the chief financial officer of the PI Trust had advised Schaffir that the PI Trust would require Manville funds "well beyond the year 2024." Further, Schaffir opined that the PD Trust would have to set aside an operating reserve of $35.25 million to cover operating expenses of the PD Trust and Facility through 2024, which reserve would accordingly have to be withheld from the payment of first-cycle claims scheduled for March 1990, absent relief from the anticipated thirty-year operating expenses.

The State Committee and the Hospitals, Colleges, and Universities Property Damage Group (the "Hospitals Group," which is not a party to this appeal) objected to the application, contending that the temporary suspension would "irreparably harm holders of unfiled Property Claims." Noting that the PD Facility had theretofore routinely required that Claimants provide additional information after submitting claims, the State Committee and Hospitals Group concluded: "Under the Guidelines, a Property Claim for which the claimant cannot provide additional documentation deemed by the Facility to be necessary will automatically be disallowed. The result of a thirty-year suspension of claims processing will inevitably be the disallowance of meritorious claims that would have been allowed had they been addressed promptly after they were submitted."

The Creditors' Committee for Asbestos Related Property Damage School Claimants ("Schools Committee") and Big City Property Damage Creditors Committee ("Big City Committee"), which together make up the large majority of claimants, did not join in this opposition. Although they "share[d] the very serious and real concerns of the States and the Hospitals," they concluded in their response to the application for suspension: "We agree with the PD Trustees' assertion that the interests of the property damage claimants ("PD Claimants") will be better served by the distribution of $35 million to PD Claimants who file claims in the first four cycles than by the reserve and possible use of those funds to maintain a claims-review bureaucracy when there is no money for payment of claims and payment at anytime [sic] after the first four cycles is somewhat speculative." The Schools Committee and Big City Committee expressly reserved, however, the right to object to the PD Trustees' detailed plan for suspension of the PD Facility when thereafter submitted.

In response to the objections and concerns raised by the various creditors' committees, the PD Trustees adopted "the claimants' suggestion that a supplemental instruction package be prepared to help claimants avoid errors which have been encountered frequently to date", and further proposed that "the functions of receiving and date-stamping claims should continue even while processing is suspended" in order to relieve claimants from the burden of storing records.

After a hearing on the application on February 20, 1990, the bankruptcy court entered an order granting the application, as modified. The order directed "that the PD Trustees shall plan operations of the

[PD Facility] in the expectation that the Facility will suspend operations after the end of the fourth allowance cycle," and further provided:

> [T]he PD Trustees shall prior to the commencement of the fourth allowance cycle submit for approval of the Court ... a detailed plan of how the PD Trust shall operate during the period of suspension of the Facility[,] ... [which plan] shall provide, among other matters, for receiving and date-stamping the receipt of claims during the period of suspension, and for dissemination to claimants of a detailed manual designed to assist claimants in filing complete and accurate claims, including information on how to avoid most frequently encountered deficiencies in claims filed prior thereto.

The State Committee appealed to the district court pursuant to 28 U.S.C. § 158(a)(1988) and sought a stay of the bankruptcy court order pending appeal, attempting thereby to preclude any first-cycle distribution without the prior establishment of a $35.25 million reserve for future operating expenses, which would in turn prevent distribution of that sum to the first-cycle Claimants. The district court did not rule on the motion for a stay, but instead accelerated the hearing on the merits of the appeal. At the conclusion of the hearing, the court delivered an opinion affirming the order of the bankruptcy court.

The district court characterized the bankruptcy order as approving a "lowering of the voltage in the processing of claims" by the PD Facility. The court rejected the State Committee's contention that the bankruptcy court order constituted an impermissible modification of the Plan within the meaning of 11 U.S.C. § 1127 (1988), concluding instead that it was "entirely consistent with and pursuant to the provisions of the reorganization plan."

Accordingly, by order and judgment entered March 16, 1990, the district court: (1) affirmed the bankruptcy court order; but (2) stayed that order and the district court's affirmance thereof "on an interim basis through and until 6:00 pm on March 19, 1990;" and (3) further ordered "that the Trustees of the [PD] Trust shall not make any distribution of funds to First–Cycle Claimants until after the expiration of the interim stay."

The State Committee thereupon appealed to this court pursuant to 28 U.S.C. § 158(d)(1988), and moved for a stay of (1) the order permitting suspension of the operation of the PD Facility and (2) the distribution of $35.25 million. An interim order of this court entered March 15, 1990 preserved the status quo until the State Committee's motion could be heard by a panel of this court. By order entered March 20, 1990, the motion was granted "only until argument of the appeal," which was expedited. An order entered March 28, 1990 further provided that: "the Trustees are required, until oral argument of this appeal is held before this Court, to hold in reserve, from the cash and liquid assets otherwise included in the computation of amounts available for payment on the first-cycle payment date, the amount of $35.25 million in addition to reserves the Trustees are otherwise required to maintain." * * *

DISCUSSION

[Court's discussion of interlocutory appeal jurisdiction under 28 U.S.C. § 158 (1988) omitted; jurisdiction upheld—*ed.*] * * *

B. The Merits.

Turning to the merits, the State Committee makes two arguments: first, that suspension of the operations of the PD Facility was impermissible as a matter of law; and second, that in any event, the bankruptcy court's approval of the suspension was an abuse of discretion.

The State Committee argues that the proposed suspension of the PD Facility impermissibly modifies a substantially consummated plan in violation of 11 U.S.C. § 1127(b)(1988), which provides in relevant part: "The proponent of a plan or the reorganized debtor may modify such plan at any time after confirmation of such plan and before substantial consummation of such plan...." This provision is interpreted to prohibit modification of a reorganization plan that has been substantially consummated. *See, e.g.,* In re Olsen, 861 F.2d 188, 190 (8th Cir.1988).[4]

The PD Trustees do not contest the State Committee's position that the Plan, whose consummation date was November 28, 1988, has been substantially consummated. In any event, we need not address the question of consummation, because we agree with the district court that "the proposed lowering of the voltage in the processing of claims is not a Modification pursuant to the provisions of the above-cited bankruptcy statute."

Section 1127 does not define the term "modification," nor does the definitional section (§ 1101) of chapter eleven. Accordingly, we turn to the Plan for guidance. The Plan includes "Modification" among the phrases defined in its glossary, which states: "Modification has the meaning assigned to it in Section 6.03 of the PD Trust Agreement." Section 6.03 does not expressly define the term; rather this section describes the method by which Manville and the PD Trustees "may modify, supplement, or amend this PD Trust Agreement." The PD Guidelines and Allocation Guidelines may not be modified under this section, which specifies that "[t]he Company shall have the exclusive right to propose a Modification."

In contrast, the Plan contemplates that the PD Trustees, acting alone, may make other needed adjustments. The definition of the PD Facility, included in the Plan's glossary, provides in pertinent part:

> [T]he PD Trustees, by a majority vote after consultation with the Company, representative counsel for the PD Beneficiaries selected by the PD Trustees and any other interested parties whom the PD Trustees desire to consult, may amend, delete or add to any of the

---

4. "Substantial consumption" is defined in 11 U.S.C. § 1101(2)(1988) to mean: (A) transfer of all or substantially all of the property proposed by the plan to be transferred; (B) assumption by the debtor or by the successor to the debtor under the plan of the business or of the management of all or substantially all of the property dealt with by the plan; and (C) commencement of distribution under the plan.

procedural provisions with respect to the operation of the PD Claims Resolution Facility except for Modifications, provided that no such amendment, deletion or addition may affect any of the substantive provisions set forth in [the PD Guidelines].

* * * Further, the PD Guidelines state that "[t]he [PD] Facility may establish procedures designed to reduce administrative costs, which do not prejudice Claimants' substantive rights." Thus, the Plan expressly grants the PD Trustees discretion to suspend operation of the PD Facility, provided that such suspension constitutes a procedural, rather than substantive, change.

The State Committee insists that the suspension constitutes a substantive amendment to the Guidelines. Applying an "outcome-determinative test," the State Committee argues that in view of the thirty-year time lapse, the proposed suspension "would effectively destroy claimants' abilities to secure allowance of their claims."

In our view, the suspension is more properly deemed, as suggested by the district court, to be "a variation ... with respect to the timing and intensity of claim processing." The substantive rights of the Claimants remain unchanged, and we see no basis for the State Committee's prediction that the suspension will result in the wholesale frustration of legitimate claims. Rather, we agree with the district court's assessment: "It is clear that when the plan was adopted the parties were embarking into unknown territory and that the operation of the Manville claims facility might require adjustments and changes as additional knowledge and experience were gained. Thus, we find that the [bankruptcy court's] order is entirely consistent with and pursuant to the provisions of the reorganization plan and that there was no error of law by the bankruptcy court in approval of the order."

Finally, the Plan provides ample authority for the bankruptcy court's action. Under section 10.1(G) of the Plan, the bankruptcy court retains jurisdiction for a number of purposes, including "[t]o enforce and administer the provisions of the Plan, and, to the extent expressly provided therein, the Exhibits thereto and the Annexes to the Exhibits." The PD Guidelines are set forth in Annex B to the PD Trust Agreement, which is Exhibit D to the Plan. The Allowance Guidelines constitute Exhibit A to Annex B. The October 28, 1988 order gave the Trustees specific authority to return to the bankruptcy court to apply for relief necessary to permit the PD Trust to fulfill its purposes under the Plan, including application * * * for approval of a plan providing for the modification or suspension of operations of the PD Claims Resolution Facility during cycles in which the PD Trust is not expected to have sufficient income to make payments on claims while maintaining all authorized reserves. That order, taken in conjunction with section 10.1(G) of the Plan, clearly contemplates the action taken by the PD Trustees in returning to the bankruptcy court for approval of the proposed suspension.

Having concluded that there was no legal impediment to the suspension of operations of the PD Facility, we turn to the question whether the bankruptcy court's ruling that the suspension would be in the best interest of the Claimants was an abuse of the court's discretion. At the hearings on the suspension application, the bankruptcy court stated:

I do find [the PD Trustees'] suggestion, as modified today and on this record, as accommodating the essentials of the objections which have already been filed and adopting the suggestions in that regard, leaving open the detailing of the final plan. And under all of those circumstances I think the application, to the extent it recognizes that a suspension or a lowering of the voltage of the operation or the dynamics of the operation, substantially is in the best interests of all the beneficiaries. And to that extent I will grant the application. . . .

As noted by the district court in reviewing the bankruptcy court's decision, the bankruptcy court balanced "the interests of the State Committee in having reduced to a liquidated amount at the earliest possible date claims by members of this committee ... against the interest of those in the first cycle who would be the recipients of an immediate distribution of funds." The bankruptcy court carefully scrutinized the proposed suspension, and mandated measures to safeguard the rights of the Claimants. In our view, far from constituting an abuse of discretion, the outcome was a practical and economically sensible balancing of the interests of all parties involved.

CONCLUSION

We affirm the order and judgment of the district court affirming the order of the bankruptcy court authorizing suspension of the operations of the PD Facility. The order of this court entered May 7, 1990, continuing the stay imposed by the court's previous orders entered March 20 and 28, 1990 pending the decision of this appeal, is vacated.

Notes and Questions

1. In its decision relating to the Manville Personal Injury Trust, the Second Circuit held that Judge Weinstein and Lifland's restructuring of the trust constituted an impermissible modification of a Chapter 11 bankruptcy reorganization plan. *See supra.* Yet the Second Circuit also held that the suspension of the Manville Property Damage Claims Facility did not constitute an impermissible modification under the same bankruptcy provision, section 1127(b). Are these decisions reconcilable? What is the consequence of the Second Circuit's decision with regard to the property damage claimants? What relationship do the property damage claimants against Manville have in relation to the personal injury claimants?

2. In describing the creation and operation of the Manville Property Damage Trust Fund, Professor Robert B. McKay noted:

The central feature of the bankruptcy plan established two trusts, one for health claims—the Manville Personal Injury Settlement Trust—and one for property damage claims—the Manville Property Damage

Settlement Trust. It is important to note the structural similarities of the two trusts and their interrelatedness. Both trusts use claims facilities designed to settle the numerous claims against Manville through the use of specified alternative dispute resolution mechanisms. The funding of the two trusts gives rise to their interrelatedness. The PI Trust is generally accorded priority of funding. According to estimates at the time of filing the reorganization plan, the PI trust will receive about $2.5 billion over a twenty-six-year period. The PD Trust, Inc. in contrast, will receive in the foreseeable future only a fraction of that amount, which can provide payment of at best a fraction of allowable claims.

* * *

A. The PD Claims Resolution Facility

The Plan provides for the creation of the PD Claims Resolution Facility for the determination any payment of property damage claims that meet the guidelines established by the Plan. The guidelines contemplate a no-fault, no-product-identification reimbursement for specified expenses made by eligible claimants because of asbestos-containing materials located in buildings. Punitive damages are not recoverable. * * *

* * *

C. Claims and Claimants

Unlike the PI Trust guidelines, which provide relief for future claimants—individuals who have been exposed to asbestos but who had not filed a claim by the date of the bankruptcy order or even by the date of consummation—the PD Trust guidelines bar all property damage claims by claimants who had not filed with the bankruptcy court by a specified date in 1984. Accordingly, when the PD Trust commenced in late 1986, a finite list of potential claimants existed. * * *

* * *

III

Conclusion

It is too early to draw conclusions about the ultimate success of the PD Trust. Nevertheless, this much can be said: the bankruptcy plan attained its principal goals of (1) assuring payment to personal injury claimants, present and future, that might otherwise have been denied, as well as at least partial compensation to property damage claimants, and (2) avoiding the almost certain destruction of a viable company. Manville has emerged from its asbestos ashes into the economic sunlight of profitability.

* * *

Robert B. McKay, *Asbestos Property Damage Settlement in a Bankruptcy Setting,* 53 Law & Contemp. Probs. 37, 39, 43–44 (1990). See Professor McKay's article for a more detailed description of the terms of the Manville

Property Settlement Trust. In theory, at least, did the Manville Property Damage Trust provide a satisfactory set of provisions for resolving the asbestos property damage claims? Because of the interrelatedness of the two trusts, were property damage claimants doomed in their prospects for recovery of claims? Could the bankruptcy reorganization plan have been structured differently to avoid this seemingly inevitable consequence?

3. Professor McKay's discussion of the Manville Trust funds ends on the cheery note that the bankruptcy approach to settlement of mass tort claims enables viable companies to continue in business while providing compensatory relief to injured claimants. Is the bankruptcy approach the fairest resolution of mass tort injury? *See generally* Thomas A. Smith, *A Capital Markets Approach to Mass Tort Bankruptcy,* 104 Yale L.J. 367 (1994).

B.   THE DALKON SHIELD TRUST FUND

Review Morton Mintz, AT ANY COST: CORPORATE GREED, WOMEN, AND THE DALKON SHIELD, Chapter I.A, *supra;* In re Northern Dist. of Cal. "Dalkon Shield" IUD Prods. Liab. Litig., Chapters II.A, II.B, and VII.B, *supra;* In re A.H. Robins, Chapter II.A, section 6, and II.B, section 2, *supra;* Richard B. Sobol, BENDING THE LAW: THE STORY OF THE DALKON SHIELD, Chapter IV. G, *supra;* Grady v. A.H. Robins, Chapter V.A, section 2, *supra;* and Francis F.E. McGovern, *Resolving Mature Mass Tort Litigation,* Chapter XI.C, *supra.*

IN RE A.H. ROBINS (DALKON SHIELD LITIGATION)

United States Court of Appeals, Fourth Circuit, 1989.
880 F.2d 694.

Before RUSSELL, WIDENER, and CHAPMAN, CIRCUIT JUDGES.

WIDENER, CIRCUIT JUDGE:

On July 26, 1988, the bankruptcy court and the district court jointly confirmed the "Sixth Amended and Restated Plan of Reorganization" (the Plan) submitted by A.H. Robins Company, Inc. (Robins). In Re A.H. Robins Co. Inc., 88 B.R. 742 (E.D.Va.1988). Rosemary Menard–Sanford and certain other personal injury claimants, who voted against the Plan, appeal. They challenge the district court's approval of the disclosure statement, the district court's use of a one claimant one vote voting procedure, the district court's feasibility finding, and a certain injunction found in the Plan. We affirm.

On August 21, 1985, Robins filed a petition for reorganization relief under Chapter 11 of the Bankruptcy Code. For an explanation of the details surrounding Robins' bankruptcy and some of the resulting litigation, see the district court's opinion in In Re A.H. Robins Co., Inc., 88 B.R. 742 (E.D.Va.1988), and our other published opinions regarding this bankruptcy.[1]

On April 1, 1988, the district court approved the "Sixth Amended and Restated Disclosure Statement." The appellants argue that the disclosure statement does not contain adequate information. 11 U.S.C. § 1125(b) requires that before solicitation of approval or disagreement of a plan of reorganization the disclosure statement must contain "adequate information" and be approved by the court. 11 U.S.C. § 1125(a)(1) defines "adequate information" as "information of a kind, and in sufficient detail, as far as is reasonably practicable in light of the nature and history of the debtor and the condition of the debtor's books and records, that would enable a hypothetical reasonable investor typical of holders of claims or interests of the relevant class to make an informed judgment about the plan." The determination of whether the disclosure statement has adequate information is made on a case by case basis and is largely within the discretion of the bankruptcy court. In the Matter of Texas Extrusion Corp., 844 F.2d 1142, 1157 (5th Cir.1988), *cert. denied*, 488 U.S. 926, 109 S.Ct. 311, 102 L.Ed.2d 330 (1988). The challenged disclosure statement began its 261 pages of information with a thorough summary of the complex plan in terms that almost anyone could understand. It explained, among much more, the amount to be put into trust and made available for the payment of claims, the various estimates of how much money was required, a warning that the funds furnished to pay the estimates might not be enough to pay all claims in full, the sources of funding, an explanation of the various funding provisions which depended on the outcome of various appeals, how claims would be handled, the four options for processing claims and the background of the case. The disclosure statement continued with a discussion of the Robins company, the Dalkon Shield, various litigation regarding the Dalkon Shield, the reorganization, the proposed merger with American Home Products Corporation (AHP), the historical stock values of both AHP and Robins, and federal income tax consequences. The final part of the disclosure statement contains actual copies of the Plan, the Claimants Trust Agreement, the Other Claimants Trust Agreement, the Claims Resolution Facility, the Merger Agreement, Aetna's

---

1. In Re A.H. Robins Co. Inc., 880 F.2d 769 (4th Cir.1989); In Re A.H. Robins Co. Inc., 88–1755(L) 880 F.2d 709 (Breland settlement)(heard Dec. 6, 1988)(4th Cir.1989); In Re A.H. Robins Co. Inc., 862 F.2d 1092 (4th Cir.1988); In Re A.H. Robins Co. Inc., 846 F.2d 267 (4th Cir.1988); Maressa v. A.H. Robins Co. Inc., 839 F.2d 220 (4th Cir.1988), *cert. denied*, 488 U.S. 826, 109 S.Ct. 76, 102 L.Ed.2d 53 (1988); Grady v. A.H. Robins Co. Inc., 839 F.2d 198 (4th Cir.1988), *cert dismissed*, 487 U.S.1260, 109 S.Ct. 201, 101 L.Ed.2d 972 (1988); Official Committee of Equity Security Holders v. Mabey, 832 F.2d 299 (4th Cir.1987), *cert. denied*, __ U.S.__, 485 U.S. 962, 108 S.Ct. 1228, 99 L.Ed.2d 428 (1988); Beard v. A.H. Robins Co. Inc., 828 F.2d 1029 (4th Cir. 1987); In Re A.H. Robins Co. Inc., 828 F.2d 1023 (4th Cir.1987), *cert. denied*, 485 U.S. 969, 108 S.Ct. 1246, 99 L.Ed.2d 444 (1988); Committee of Dalkon Shield Claimants v. A.H. Robins Co. Inc., 828 F.2d 239 (4th Cir.1987); Van Arsdale v. Clemo, 825 F.2d 794 (4th Cir.1987); Vancouver Women's Health Soc. v. A.H. Robins Co. Inc., 820 F.2d 1359 (4th Cir.1987); In Re Beard, 811 F.2d 818 (4th Cir.1987); and A.H. Robins Co. Inc. v. Piccinin, 788 F.2d 994 (4th Cir. 1986), *cert. denied*, 479 U.S. 876, 107 S.Ct. 251, 93 L.Ed.2d 177 (1986).

additional insurance policy, AHP's Annual Report, the Liquidation Analysis and biographies of the proposed Trustees.

The appellants contend that the disclosure statement is misleading because it contains a statement that in order to approve the Plan the district court must make a finding that the Plan contains enough money to satisfy all claims in full. They point out that in reality there may not be enough money to cover all claims. The disclosure statement, however, makes that clear to the claimants. It states that "if the Court's estimate turns out to be too low, Robins will not have to make any more money available to pay claims. In addition, the Plan would generally take away your right to recover for Dalkon Shield injuries against any other parties." The disclosure statement later repeats that thought in explicit terms: "[e]stimation is not an exact science. The money available to pay Dalkon Shield claims may prove to be more or less than the actual value of such claims. If the estimation decision underestimated the value of the claims, there may not be enough money for the Claimants Trust to pay all claims in full." Thus, we think appellants' contention is without merit.

The appellants' principal challenge to the disclosure statement, however, is that it is inadequate because it does not contain ranges of recovery for claimants with specified injuries. The disclosure statement notes that "[t]here is no certain way to predict the amount that you could receive under option 3. Each claim is different. Factors that affect the value of a claim include the nature of the injury, the medical evidence available to prove the injury, the medical evidence to prove Dalkon Shield use, the presence of other causes of your injury, how long ago you were injured, and what steps you took to enforce your legal rights after your injury became apparent." There is no requirement in case law or statute that a disclosure statement estimate the value of specific unliquidated tort claims. In fact, with so many various unliquidated personal injury claims which vary so much in the extent and nature of injury, medical evidence and causation factors, any specific estimates may well have been more confusing than helpful and certainly would be more calculated to mislead. Given the quantity and quality of the information in the disclosure statement we can not say that the district court abused its discretion in finding that it contained "adequate information."

The appellants next challenge the legality of the voting procedure used to confirm the Plan. The difficulty surrounding the voting procedure resulted from the 195,000 unliquidated claims for personal injuries (Dalkon Shield Claims). The controlling legal provisions for the reorganization include 11 U.S.C. § 1126(a) which provides that a "holder of a claim or interest allowed under section 502 of this title" is entitled to vote on the acceptance of a plan. 11 U.S.C.§ 502(a) provides that a claim filed "is deemed allowed unless a party in interest" objects. Robins objected to all the Dalkon Shield Claims. B.R. 3018(a) provides that "[n]otwithstanding objection to a claim or interest, the court after notice and hearing may temporarily allow the claim or interest in an amount which the court deems proper for the purpose of accepting or rejecting a plan." The district court, after notice and a hearing, ordered that, for purposes of voting, each Dalkon Shield Claim was estimated and allowed to be equal. It found, fully supported by the record, that any attempt to evaluate each of the 195,000 individual claims for voting purposes would cause intolerable delay. The challenge to the voting procedure relies on 11 U.S.C. § 1126(c) which requires that for a plan to be approved by a class the creditors "that hold at least two-thirds in amount and more than one-half in number" accept the plan. The argument is that § 1126(c) requires use of a weighted voting method which estimates the value of the claims and gives larger claims more votes.

We do not decide whether the district court's voting procedure violated § 1126(c) because, in view of the outcome of the vote, the challenged procedure was at most harmless error. 139,605 claimants voted. Of that 131,761 (94.38%) voted in favor of the Plan. In Kane v. Johns–Manville Corp., 843 F.2d 636, 641–647 (2d Cir.1988),[2] the district court, faced with 52,440 unliquidated personal injury claims, assigned each claim the value of one dollar for voting purposes. 95.8% of those claims voted to approve the plan. The Second Circuit in reviewing the decision did not decide whether the equal voting plan was error and decided instead that the alleged irregularities were at most harmless error. Given that 94.38% of the Dalkon Shield Claimants voted for the Plan, we hold that, at most, harmless error was committed.[3]

Appellants' next point on appeal is that the district court erred in finding that the Plan complied with 11 U.S.C. § 1129(a)(7)(A)(ii) which requires that an impaired class of claims such as the Dalkon Shield claimants must "receive ... under the Plan ... property of a value ... that is not less than the amount that ... [they would] receive ... if the debtor were liquidated under Chapter 7" and § 1129(a)(11) which requires that confirmation is not likely to be followed by liquidation or the need for further reorganization. This latter is called the feasibility requirement.

2. We have previously noted the "striking similarity both factually and on the legal issues" of the *Robins* and *Johns-Manville* cases. A.H. Robins Co. Inc. v. Piccinin, 788 F.2d 994, 1007 (4th Cir.1986), *cert. denied*, 479 U.S. 876, 107 S.Ct. 251, 93 L.Ed.2d 177 (1986).

3. We are not persuaded by the argument that the 5.62% NO votes were from the claimants with the largest claims, that being necessary of course to make up more than one-third of the claims in amount. The argument goes that such claimants have the most to gain from a rejection of the Plan, but that proposition, we think, is not only supported by no evidence, it is not supported by logic, and is no more likely than the fact that the largest claimants have the most to lose by a rejection of the

Plan. Indeed, it would seem that the latter is the more likely if one must choose between the two. Appellants take no exception to the findings of the district court that the liquidation value of the company is considerably less than its value in reorganization, and the part allocated to the claims of the Dalkon Shield claimants is considerably less, $2.5+ billion under the Plan as opposed to $1.6+ in liquidation. So, with a rejection of the Plan which resulted in liquidation, the largest claimants would be the biggest losers. We remain convinced, in view of the 94.38% affirmative vote, that had a weighted voting system been practicable and utilized, the required two-thirds in amount would have approved the Plan. It follows that the error, if any, is harmless.

Both such complaints are based on the "same source: the failure of the district court to break out the components of the $2.475 billion figure." The argument is that since the figure was not broken down, if it turned out to be too low, then the Plan would not be feasible because it could not pay all the claimants in full, which, as the appellants note, is an assumption of the Plan and the disclosure statement. The appellants thus complain about the same fact again, except in slightly different context. In all events, we think there is no merit to the claim, but that the care the district court took in arriving at its estimate deserves mention.

The challenged findings are based on an estimation process that the district court undertook as a result of our decision in A.H. Robins Co., Inc. v. Piccinin, 788 F.2d 994, 1013 (4th Cir.1986), *cert. denied* 479 U.S. 876, 107 S.Ct. 251, 93 L.Ed.2d 177 (1986). In *Piccinin,* we stated that due to the large number of unliquidated claims that if each claim was tried the process itself "would likely consume all the assets of the debtor." * * * We suggested that the bankruptcy court "arrive at a fair estimation of the value of all the claims." * * * To assist in the estimation process, the district court appointed Professor Francis E. McGovern, who was familiar with such matters, as the court's expert to develop a data base regarding Dalkon Shield Claims. The Dalkon Shield Claimant's Committee, the Unsecured Creditor's Committee, the Future Claimant's Representative, the Equity Security Holder's Committee, Robins and Aetna all had experts to assist Professor McGovern. The data base included the results of a two page "Dalkon Shield Questionnaire and Claim Form" from more than 195,000 claimants. It also contained roughly 6,000 responses to a fifty page, "McGovern Survey Questionnaire" and medical records from a random sample of 7,500 claimants. The data collection process lasted more than a year and a half. Each of the experts hired by the various parties used the basic data in various ways to arrive at an estimation.

The district court conducted an estimation hearing from November 5, 1987 to November 11, 1987. At the hearing the parties' various experts testified. The district court considered that the testimony of the various experts estimated the claims as follows: Robins'—.8 to 1.3 billion, Equity Security Holders'—1.03 billion, Unsecured Creditors'—1.54 billion, Aetna's'—2.2 to 2.5 billion, and the Dalkon Shield Claimants'—4.2 to 7 billion. The district court decided that the proper estimate was 2.475 billion.[4]

At this point it is well to relate somewhat more fully the procedure used in arriving at the estimate found by the district court. As the district court noted, the testimony as to the estimated recovery value of the Dalkon Shield claims ranged from 600 million to 7 billion dollars.

---

4. We note that the district court's figure was within the range of the second highest estimation—that of Dr. Francine F. Rabinovitz, the expert for Aetna. The district court repeatedly rejected the credibility of the expert for the Dalkon Shield Claimants, the only expert with a higher estimation than Dr. Rabinovitz.

The testimony with respect to the 7 billion dollar figure, however, was not credited by the court.

Professor McGovern was assisted by the experts mentioned representing each of the interests involved in this case, and the procedural steps which were taken were all done by consensus among the experts representing all of the interests, so that the conclusions which the various experts drew from the evidence or the findings of the court from the evidence were the only things left open to exception.

As has been previously mentioned from time to time in the reports of these cases, the district court entered a bar date on claims and prescribed a very informal method of advising the court that a claim was being filed. The bar date of course limited the potential claimants. From these potential claimants, there were eliminated, by standard statistical and analytical methods, about one-third of the initial claims which had been filed. A detailed analysis of those claims not eliminated was performed by sending the detailed questionnaire previously mentioned to a randomly selected sample of several thousand of the claims remaining. The questionnaire asked for information, which, in the most general sense, was received back, concerning the insertion of the Dalkon Shield in the claimant and the nature of the claimant's injuries, including verification by way of medical records where possible.

A detailed analysis of all of the responses was then performed by the expert witnesses who testified in the case. A good example of competent testimony was that of Dr. Francine F. Rabinovitz, who testified on behalf of Aetna. We illustrate with her testimony because her conclusions more nearly match the conclusions of the district court than any other single witness offered. She took the returned questionnaires as a representative sample and weeded out those, for example, with no medical proof of use of the Dalkon Shield. As a further example, she classified the claims into those with and without complications and the nature of the injuries claimed. She took a further random sample of the claims as she had divided them up and got three Aetna claims adjusters who had been experienced in the actual adjustment of Dalkon Shield claims and instructed those adjusters to set a value on a sample of the claims she referred to them, considering that there was liability, so the only thing the adjusters had to consider in setting a value on a claim was the nature of the injury and of course the proof required and the attendant expenses. The adjusters were instructed not to place a low estimate on the claims. Dr. Rabinovitz, by using this method, drew the conclusion that the compensation necessary, assuming that documentation that use of the Dalkon Shield were a prerequisite, would be in excess of 1.9 billion dollars, and, assuming that documentation would not be a prerequisite, a sum in excess of 2.4 billion dollars. To these sums, she would have added modest payments to all active claimants, whatever the merit of such claims, and 50 million dollars as a reserve against future injuries, which made her figures for documented injuries at slightly more than 2.0 billion dollars and for undocumented injuries slightly more than 2.5 billion dollars. Dr. Rabinovitz further concluded that she thought there might be a considerable reduction from disallowance of claims and that she would reasonably anticipate the total indemnity of the obligation to be 2.2 to 2.3 billion dollars. That some reduction is not unreasonable is illustrated by a remark we have come across in the record that one claimant apparently said she took two Dalkon Shields a day.

From our brief recital of a small part of the evidence before the district court, we see that its finding of 2.475 billion dollars as the estimate to include all Dalkon Shield claims is not clearly erroneous under Rule 8013. Indeed, we think the district court would have been quite justified in accepting Dr. Rabinovitz' testimony, so appellants may not complain about the district court's arrival at a somewhat higher figure.

Finally, the appellants challenge as without the power of the bankruptcy court the portion of the Plan which requires the injunction of suits that have connection to the Dalkon Shield, against certain entities other than Robins. Robins argues that the injunction is a proper exercise of the district court's power to channel claims to a specific res or alternately that the injunction is proper because 94.38% of the claimants voted for the Plan and thereby consented to the injunction. We affirm, but our reasoning differs somewhat from that of Robins, although its position, of course, should enter into consideration. The suits in question which some of the appellants wish to bring are against Robins' directors, Robins' and Aetna's attorneys, and Aetna, seeking to hold them as joint tortfeasors with Robins for Dalkon Shield injuries.

We begin our discussion by considering the impact of our decision in In re A.H. Robins Company Inc., 88–1755(L)(*Breland* settlement), decided this date, on this challenge to the Plan's injunction. In *Breland,* we affirmed the district court's certification of a mandatory non-opt-out class for members of class A and a class which allows an opt-out for compensatory damages for members of class B. Class A is defined as those Dalkon Shield claimants who met the filing deadlines of the district court and therefore have a non-subordinated claim against the trust fund set up for the claimants in the Robins' reorganization. Class B is defined as those Dalkon Shield claimants who did not meet the filing deadline or like procedural requirements and are therefore not eligible for a non-subordinated recovery from the trust fund for reasons not related to the abstract merits of the claims. The *Breland* settlement, however, provided all class B claimants with a second chance to pursue their Dalkon Shield claims by staying in the class and applying to the Claims Resolution Facility. For class B members the merits of their Dalkon Shield claims would be determined in the same method as is in place to determine class A members' claims except they would have no right to a jury trial. Their claims would be paid by the two Outlier policies issued by Aetna which provide for $100,000,000 to pay such claims. No party challenges the adequacy of the Outlier policies to pay the class B claims. We therefore are entitled to and do assume that the claims of all class B claimants who wish to have the merits and amount of their claims ascertained by the Claims Resolution Facility will be fully satisfied. However, the *Breland* settlement, in conjunction with the Plan, did not force the class B claimants who chose to opt-out to stay within the settlement. They could elect to forgo the benefits of the settlement and retain their right to sue Aetna and to sue medical providers for malpractice.[7] In *Breland,* we also approved the class action settlement, which expressly bars the members of class A and the members of class B who did not opt-out from further prosecuting their Dalkon Shield claims other than pursuant to the terms of the settlement. Given this bar from pursuing compensation for their Dalkon Shield injuries, other than pursuant to the order, the injunction complained of has no real effect on the rights of members of class A and the members of class B who have not exercised their right to opt-out.

The Plan's injunction, therefore, only has real impact upon members of Class B who have elected to opt-out of the *Breland* settlement. The injunction under sections 1.85 and 8.04 of the Plan prevents these claimants from suing all third parties other than "insurer[s]" (which includes Aetna) and claims based exclusively on medical malpractice. The class B members who have elected to opt-out, it is remembered, claim to have causes of action as joint tortfeasors with Robins against Robins' directors, Aetna, and law firms who represented both Robins and Aetna. A suit against any of the parties mentioned by the class B opt-out members would affect the bankruptcy reorganization in one way or another such as by way of indemnity or contribution. See A.H. Robins Co. Inc. v. Piccinin, 788 F.2d 994 (4th Cir.1986), *cert. denied,* 479 U.S. 876, 107 S.Ct. 251, 93 L.Ed.2d 177 (1986). And, in all events, provision for payment in full of all class B claimants has been made.

Bankruptcy courts are courts of equity. *See* NLRB v. Bildisco & Bildisco, 465 U.S. 513, 527, 104 S.Ct. 1188, 1196, 79 L.Ed.2d 482 (1984). 11 U.S.C.§ 105(a) gives a bankruptcy court the power to issue "any order, process or judgment that is necessary or appropriate to carry out the provisions of this title," and confers equitable powers upon the bankruptcy courts. In Matter of Old Orchard Inv. Co., 31 B.R. 599 (W.D.Mich.1983). Given the impact of the proposed suits on the bankruptcy reorganization and the fact that the class B members who chose to opt-out could have had their claims fully satisfied by staying within the settlement, the bankruptcy court's equitable powers support the questioned injunction. We think the ancient but very much alive doctrine of marshalling of assets is analogous here. A creditor has no right to choose which of two funds will pay his claim. The bankruptcy court has the power to order a creditor who has two funds to satisfy his debt to resort to the fund that will not defeat other creditors. * * * Here, the carefully designed reorganization of Robins, in conjunction with the settlement in *Breland,* provided for satisfaction of the class B claimants. However, some chose to opt-out of the settlement in order to

---

7. There are approximately 111,000 class B claims, and only 2,960 exercised their right to opt-out.

pursue recovery for their injuries from Aetna or from medical providers for malpractice. It is essential to the reorganization that these opt-out plaintiffs either resort to the source of funds provided for them in the Plan and *Breland* settlement or not be permitted to interfere with the reorganization and thus with all the other creditors. Since they have chosen opt-out rather than payment in full, they may have no complaint about a restriction placed on their ability to sue others. Permitting a suit by them in violation of the Plan is a defeat of the Plan and a resulting defeat of the other creditors. "Particularly since the insurance settlement/injunction arrangement was essential in this case to a workable reorganization, it falls within the bankruptcy court's equitable powers 'which traditionally have been invoked to the end that * * * substance will not give way to form, that technical considerations will not prevent substantial justice.'" MacArthur Co. v. Johns–Manville Corp., 837 F.2d 89, 94 (2d Cir.1988), *cert. denied,* 488 U.S. 868, 109 S.Ct. 176, 102 L.Ed.2d 145 (1988), *quoting* In re U.N.R. Industries, Inc., 725 F.2d 1111, 1119 (7th Cir.1984).

* * *

The orders of the district court appealed from are accordingly. Affirmed.

IN RE A.H. ROBINS (DALKON SHIELD LITIGATION)

United States Court of Appeals, Fourth Circuit, 1989.
880 F.2d 779.

Before RUSSELL, WIDENER, and CHAPMAN, CIRCUIT JUDGES.

CHAPMAN, CIRCUIT JUDGE:

The appellants, Barbara Blum, Ann Samani and Gene Locks were named as three of the five trustees under the Dalkon Shield Claimants' Trust ("Trust") which was created as a part of the Plan of Reorganization ("Plan") of A.H. Robins ("Robins") under Chapter 11 of the Bankruptcy Code. The Plan also created a Claims Resolution Facility ("CRF") to handle the settlement of claims against Robins resulting from its manufacture and sale of the Dalkon Shield. After hearing twenty hours of testimony in support and opposition of a motion by certain beneficiaries to remove all five trustees, the district court removed the three appellants. We find that the district court's findings of fact are not clearly erroneous, and that these findings, under Virginia law, support the conclusion to remove the three appellants.

I

On August 21, 1985, A.H. Robins, Inc. filed its petition for reorganization pursuant to 11 U.S.C. §§ 101 *et seq.* Robins sought relief under the Bankruptcy Code because of its cash flow problems resulting from the cost of defending, litigating and paying thousands of claims brought against it by persons claiming damage from use of the Dalkon Shield.

During the bankruptcy, notice was given to claimants throughout the world that they must file claims in the bankruptcy proceeding, or their claims against Robins resulting from its manufacture and distribution of the Dalkon Shield would be barred. As a result, several hundred thousand claims were filed. In order to keep records of these claims, the district court, which had retained jurisdiction over a number of questions and issues in the bankruptcy, created a record keeping and computer center under the management of the Clerk of the Bankruptcy Court for the Eastern District of Virginia. This facility employed approximately 20 people, and it became the repository of the information relating to claimants. It was an indispensable storehouse of information necessary to the eventual resolution of all claims.

After months of negotiations, a Sixth Amended and Restated Plan of Reorganization of A.H. Robins, Inc. was agreed upon and was submitted to all claimants and approved by an overwhelming majority of claimants in both number and amount. This plan called for the merger of Robins into a subsidiary of American Home Products, and the creation of a Claims Resolution Facility, a Claimants' Trust and the Other Claimants' Trust for the purpose of resolving and satisfying all claims brought against Robins as a result of the Dalkon Shield. All claims arising from the Dalkon Shield would be made against the Trusts and none of them would follow Robins after the merger.

The Plan provided for the appointment of five trustees and Barbara B. Blum, Kenneth R. Feinberg, Gene Locks, Stephen A. Saltzburg and Ann Samani were appointed and duly qualified. The Trust is to be funded in the amount of $2.3 billion. This amount will not be paid into the Trust until the Plan has been confirmed by the court and all appeals challenging the Plan have been exhausted.

In March 1988, each of the five trustees were informed that they would be selected. The selection of trustees was made by the court upon recommendation of the Claimants' Committee. On April 11, 1988 the court entered an order appointing the five trustees and on May 5, 1988 the court met with the trustees and tried to impress upon them the tremendous responsibility of handling such a large number of claims and such an enormous trust fund. He advised that he wanted them to "hit the ground running." The court was anxious to promptly pay the liquidated claims of persons who had obtained judgments against Robins prior to the bankruptcy and to pay settlements that had been agreed upon prior to the bankruptcy. Interest on these claims was running as of January 1, 1988.

On July 25, 1988, the day that the confirmation order was entered approving the plan of reorganization, the district judge and the bankruptcy judge met with the five trustees and reiterated the necessity for handling the claims expeditiously. The trustees were also advised that this was a public trust, one of the largest ever created in the United States, and that the court had a role to play to be sure that valid claims were promptly paid.

Under § 3.03(c) of the Trust, it is provided:

A trustee may be removed from office by the Court upon its own motion, the motion of any Trustee, or the motion of at least 100 Beneficiaries represented by at least five independent and unaffiliated attorneys and a determination by the court that such removal is appropriate upon good cause shown.

On September 24, 1988 a motion was made to remove the trustees for the Dalkon Shield Claimants' Trust and the Dalkon Shield Claims Resolution Facility. This motion was filed by five unaffiliated independent attorneys representing more than 1,800 Dalkon Shield personal injury claimants. Thereafter, an additional 1,101 Dalkon Shield personal injury claimants intervened in support of the motion, and at the trial more than 300 additional claimants, through their attorneys, were permitted to participate in the removal proceeding. The petition for removal of the trustees alleged in part that the trustees "are guilty of malfeasance, or at least misfeasance in the performance of their duties as set forth in the Claimants' Trust Agreement." In particular the moving parties are informed and believe that these acts consist of the following: (1) The trustees have negligently failed to act prudently and expeditiously in setting up the Claims Resolution Facility. (2) The trustees sought the employment of a managing consultant firm to advise them as to the deployment of the Claims Resolution Facility, which is a task they should be able to handle themselves without such assistance, if they have the requisite ability and background to justify their appointment as trustees. Such a request, in the opinion of the moving parties, underscores the trustees' apparent lack of ability and skill required to administer this trust fund. (3) The trustees are opposed to having their activities supervised by this court for the protection of the Dalkon Shield claimants. (4) The trustees voted to appoint Murray Drabkin, and his law firm as legal representative of the Dalkon Shield Trust Fund. The moving parties are informed and believe that some or all of the trustees have had long and close relationships with Mr. Drabkin, that such prior relationships improperly influenced the trustees to consent to Mr. Drabkin's appointment as attorney for the trust fund that Mr. Drabkin and his firm have an inherent conflict of interest which precludes their legal representation of the fund, and that this act demonstrates that the trustees are not acting prudently in the best and sole interests of the Dalkon Shield claimants, and (5) Other acts of misfeasance and improprieties which have been disclosed by Mr. Mabey's investigation and report to this court.

A trial on the issue of whether the trustees should be removed was commenced on October 31, 1988 and twenty hours of testimony was taken. On November 28, 1988, the district court filed its Order and Memorandum removing appellants Blum, Locks and Samani as trustees, and retaining trustees Feinberg and Saltzburg. The district court set forth findings of fact in its memorandum, but did not number them. We have supplied numbers for easier reference.

1.   Notwithstanding the Trust Agreement's mandate, emphasized by the Court, to effect a speedy resolution of Dalkon Shield Claims, the Trustees failed to act effectively toward the creation of an operational claims resolution process.   This failure to act was a direct result, at least in part, of conflict between the Trustees and a perceived but misguided one-sided conflict with the Court on the part of three Trustees.

2.   The Court in its findings and conclusions does not treat Locks' and Samani's challenge to the Court's authority as the basis for the removal of any of the Trustees, it is the derelictions following that challenge which requires the Court to act.   The open defiance of these Trustees, however, cannot be overlooked.   The facts are that the excessive time expended by the dissidents in arguing and discussing ways to challenge the Court's continuing supervisory role has resulted in costly delay in effecting the Trust's purposes.

3.   Mr. Locks' unwillingness to consider Mr. Sheppard's employment by the Trust was based upon Locks' belief that to do so would be to submit to the Court.

4.   At least in part as a result of Mr. Locks' belief, the Trustees failed to select a manager, or indeed any employee, of the claims record center in a timely manner.   This failure resulted in the Court's being required for a short period to assume responsibility as hereinafter described for the operation of the center.

5.   Several weeks prior to the entry of the Confirmation Order the Court, in an effort to encourage and prepare the Trustees to act expeditiously pursuant to the Trust's mandate, dispatched the Clerk of the Bankruptcy Court to meet with the Trustees.   At that meeting, held in Washington, D.C. on July 9, 1988, the Clerk endeavored to impress the Trustees with the fact that upon confirmation, Robins would no longer fund the existing claims facility, and that absent affirmative action taken by the Trustees the facility would close its doors.   Despite the Clerk's as well as the Court's advice, as shown by the evidence, no effective effort was made by the Trustees and, as of the date of transition the Trust was completely unprepared to operate the facility.

6.   Except for the Court's intervention in directing the Clerk to utilize court personnel to maintain the facility to give the Trustees further opportunity to retain employees and secure appropriate banking facilities, it would have closed.   Such a consequence would have been an extreme disservice to the approximately 200,000 remaining claimants who had voted overwhelmingly in favor of the Plan of Reorganization and who were looking to a fulfillment of that Plan by the actions of the Trustees.

7.   The Trustees' failure to prepare for acceptance of control over the Claims Facility, despite their knowledge of the possible effects of such failure, was attributable in part to Locks' refusal to acknowledge the Plan's provision transferring control to the Trustees and to Locks' belief that Robins would continue to maintain the Facility after confirmation.   Locks took this position on control over the Facility despite

Robins' prompt payment of $200,000 to the Trust for the purposes of maintaining the Facility on an interim basis.

8.   Though the Trustees have selected a records facility director, a custodial bank, and interim counsel, they failed, as of the date of this hearing, to reach final agreement on any issue of importance.

9.   The Court finds that the Trustees had initially agreed that law firms that had been heavily involved in the bankruptcy case and in the formulation of the Plan of Reorganization should not represent the Trust.   In spite of this initial decision, the law firm of Cadwalader, Wickersham & Taft ("Cadwalader"), which represented the Claimants' Committee, was among those considered, and was ultimately employed. This decision was reached with full knowledge that the firm was still counsel for Claimants' Committee and in the face of Judge Shelley's expressed view that the firm was disqualified by reason of a conflict of interest.

10.   The vote to retain the Cadwalader firm was three to two, with Saltzburg and Feinberg voting against the retention.   Both Saltzburg and Feinberg argued against employment of Cadwalader, with Saltzburg and Feinberg voting against employment of Cadwalader, with Saltzburg emphasizing that "the price which would have to be paid in terms of an inevitable battle over whether there was a conflict, and the wisdom of that choice, would be so high that it would be inconceivable that [the Trust] would want to pay it."

11.   Mr. Locks, in his testimony at the hearing in this matter, admitted that he felt the retention of the Cadwalader firm would lead to further controversy as predicted by Mssrs. Saltzburg and Feinberg. Controversy of this nature is hardly a recommended ingredient leading to the early success of a public trust whose entire mission is to endeavor to fully and fairly satisfy its contemplated beneficiaries.

12.   The delay engendered by the controversy over the selection of counsel and the ultimate retention of Cadwalader, however, cannot be laid solely at the feet of Mr. Locks.   Mrs. Blum and Mrs. Samani were fully aware of the concerns and predictions of the minority Trustees, and participated actively in the choice of Cadwalader.

13.   Cadwalader was the archetypical example of a firm which ought not to have been retained.

14.   Although Locks now admits it was a mistake to hire the Claimants' Committee counsel to represent the Trust, he, like Mrs. Blum and Ms. Samani, has declined all offers from Mssrs. Feinberg and Saltzburg to join in their minority suggestion that the Trustees vote to dismiss Cadwalader as Trust counsel.

15.   It is clear from the evidence, that the issue [the discharge of the Cadwalader firm] was raised on three separate occasions by Saltzburg, the last time following Judge Bryan's ruling which found the existence of an impermissible conflict of interest in Cadwalader's representation of the Trust.

16. As Saltzburg testified, this group of Trustees has been the most divisive he has worked with. He further stated that prior to September, six months after agreeing to hit the ground running for the benefit of the Trust, less time was spent on affirmative Trust business than was spent on discussion and actions pertaining to the retention of the Cadwalader firm.

17. It is clear from the record that consideration of Option 1 as hereinafter discussed was subordinated to the Trustees' preoccupation with Blum, Locks and Samani's insistence that the Trust retain the Cadwalader firm. The Trust accomplished very little since April.

18. As of October 31, 1988, more than six months after their appointment, no such claim form [Option 1] had been developed by the Trustees, nor had any payment amounts been established for the categories of claimants. Further, as of the date of this opinion, the Court is unaware of any final determinations concerning forms or amounts.

19. The Court relied in part upon the expert testimony of Francine Rabinowitz in estimating the value of the claims. The Trustees were free to seek advice as to the value of claims and were encouraged by the Court to consider meeting Ms. Rabinowitz promptly after their appointment. The Trustees did not meet with her until immediately prior to this hearing. Thus four months were allowed to go by before consultation with her, or so far as the Court knows, any of the other estimation experts, occurred.

20. The Plan called for prompt payment by the Trust of all holders of Dalkon Shield liquidated claims of personal injury claimants with interest from January 1, 1988. In spite of Section 4.03 of the Plan which provides "Dalkon Shield liquidated claims will be paid by the Trust as soon as practicable," the evidence before the Court is that it was September 8, 1988 before any effort to even ascertain who held liquidated claims commenced. As of the date of the hearing on the instant motion, which was more than three months subsequent to confirmation and almost six months after the Trustees agreed, at the Court's request, to prepare to act promptly in the likely event the Plan would be approved by a majority of claimants and confirmed by the Court, certain of the aforementioned liquidated claims had still not been paid.

21. Although Mr. Locks testified to having spent a great deal of time on Trust business throughout the late spring, summer and early fall of 1988, he was not until the day of the instant hearing even aware of crucial provisions of the pertinent documents. Locks stated he did not know that Section 4.07(c) of the Trust Agreement provides that in the event the Order of Confirmation is reversed on appeal funds already paid into the Trust can no longer be used to compensate Dalkon Shield claims.

22. The dilatory conduct of the Trustees may result in the nonpayment of monies which claimants would have otherwise received had Option 1 been expeditiously effected. The Trustees' failure to act may

require thousands of claimants to wait for compensation while the debtor goes "back to the drawing board" for plan formulation.

23. The Court finds it inconceivable that the Trustees of a $2.3 billion Trust would so ignore their responsibility to further the Trust's purposes. One may fairly conclude that the interests of the prospective beneficiaries was of secondary importance to these Trustees. The evidence before the Court shows the same three Trustees [Blum, Locks and Samani] have vocally or by their actions engaged in effort to thwart the law of the case and expended time, effort and Trust funds for that purpose to the ultimate delay and detriment to the Trust beneficiaries.

24. It simply is not in the best interest of this public Trust and its putative beneficiaries to permit a continuation in office of certain of these Trustees. Too much time and money has been wasted on matters unrelated to the principal purposes of the Trust. It is apparent from the evidence that the Trustees were divided to a point where they were not making decisions or progress.

25. In response to the instant motion, however, the Trustees contend that any further divisiveness among themselves has been eradicated. The Court believes that the appearance of an abatement of tensions is temporary and is the result of the motion which precipitated this hearing. The Court further believes that a lasting reduction of antagonisms among the Trustees can only be brought about through the removal of the obstructive Trustees.

26. Payment of the $2.3 billion to the Trust may not occur during the pendency of any appeal. If these funds were in the hands of the Trustees they would be drawing interest at the rate of $600,000 per day. The three Trustees, Blum, Locks and Samani supported the appeal of the Confirmation Order which exhibits disloyalty to the Trust and a lack of appreciation for the effect any further delay may have upon the beneficiaries.

27. Mrs. Samani's membership on the Claimants' Committee, which continued even after their appeal was noted, represented a breach of her obligation to the Trust.

28. All of the Trustees except Saltzburg have been paid the sum of $17,500 for six months salary between April and September 30, 1988, plus a total in excess of $111,000 for attendance at the meetings ($1,000 per meeting), as well as approximately $36,000 in expenses, as of the date of the filing of the instant motion. For this expenditure of Trust funds all that has been fully accomplished is the retention of counsel which has been disqualified, the interim retention of replacement counsel, the retention of a Claims Facility director and one other person under contract, and the selection of a bank.

The district court found: that the legal issue presented is not to be resolved by bankruptcy law, but by application of the laws of Virginia, as required by § 6.07 of the Claimants' Trust Agreement; that the Trust is a public or court created Trust and is different from a private or testamentary trust; that under Virginia law the ordinary powers of the court of equity include the removal of trustees, and that good cause for removal is shown when such removal is in the best interest of the Trust.

The district court concluded: "In the court's view it is unnecessary to make a formal ruling that the good cause standard in the trust instrument governs the instant removal action instead of the best interests standard of Virginia law. The difference the court perceives between the cause standard and the best interests standard is one of direction. Under the good cause standard the court's evaluation is primarily a retrospective view of actions taken, or not taken, by the challenged trustees. Conversely, in applying the best interest standard, the court determines whether removal will enhance the future performance of the Trust. In any event, whether looking to the past or to the future, the court finds that it must remove trustees Barbara Blum, Gene Locks, and Ann Samani. Based on the evidence adduced at the hearing in this matter, the court finds that as a result of the debilitating disagreements which have been endemic among the Trustees, and of the concomitant inaction and delay, good cause for their removal exists. The court further finds that if no change in the composition of the trustees is effected the Trust's future holds only the prospect of further discord and delay, and that the best interests of both the Trust and its beneficiaries will be served by the removal of the above-named trustees."

The removed trustees appealed. Petitions to file amici curiae briefs were received from Ralph R. Mabey, as examiner, the Official Committee of Equity Security Holders, and trustees Feinberg and Saltzburg. These Petitions were granted and all of the amici briefs urge affirmance of the district court order removing the appellants.

II

Appellants contend that good cause for their removal has not been shown; that the court's interpretation of good cause is inconsistent with the laws of Virginia and the terms of the Plan and the Trust; that the district court's findings of fact are clearly erroneous; and that the personal involvement of the district court undermined its objectivity.

The present dispute is not between the removed trustees and the district court, although the appellants would like to present the controversy in that light. The court did not act sua sponte in bringing on the motion to remove the trustees. The motion was made under the third option in Section 3.03(c) of the Trust, a motion to remove filed on behalf of at least 100 beneficiaries represented by at least five independent and unaffiliated attorneys. The present motion was brought on behalf of more than 1800 beneficiaries and by the time of the trial, the number of beneficiaries exceeded 3,200, because of the large number of beneficiaries who intervened in support of the motion to remove.

The appellants attempt to present this case as a clash of personalities between the appellants and the district court and that this conflict is at the heart of the problems that have beset the Trust from its inception. We find this unpersuasive. The appellants have spent so much time, money and energy trying to assert their independence from the district court, that they have neglected their primary duty of administering the trust so as to promptly pay the Dalkon Shield claimants. Such is manifest from the record, which is ample to support the findings of fact made by the district court. Since the district court's account of the evidence is plausible in light of the record viewed in its entirety, it may not be changed on appeal. * * *

III

The Trust Agreement at § 3.03(c) provides for the removal of a trustee, and § 6.07 requires that the interpretation and validity of the Trust Agreement be governed by the laws of Virginia.

Appellants contend that the trustees may only be removed for "good cause" and that under Virginia law "good cause" requires a showing of fraud or gross negligence. The Petition to Remove does not allege fraud or dishonesty, and no attempt was made at the hearing to prove this type of misconduct. The Petition charges the trustees with negligence in the discharge or in the failure to discharge their duties, but the district court did not make a finding of negligence or gross negligence to support its order of removal. The district judge concluded that under Virginia law "good cause" requires an examination of the Trustees' prior acts or failures to act and also requires a consideration of what is in the best interest of the Trust and whether removal of challenged Trustees will enhance the further performance of the Trust.

Virginia Code § 26–3 (1985) provides that the court "under whose order ... such fiduciary derives his authority ... whenever from any cause it appears proper, [may] revoke and annul the powers of any such fiduciary." This section requires reasonable notice to the fiduciary, which was provided in the present case. The Trustees of the Dalkon Shield Claimants' Trust were appointed to their fiduciary positions by the district court and the clear language of the statute does not set a standard of fraud or gross negligence for removal, as argued by appellants, but simply says "from any cause it appears proper." The Virginia courts have held that this language vests the appointing court with very large discretion in regard to the removal of a fiduciary. * * *

Virginia courts have not clearly defined "any cause" but have held that courts should consider "What is best for the trust estate?" *Willson v. Kable*, 177 Va. 668, 15 S.E.2d 56 (1941). *Willson* turns to Restatement on Trusts and Bogert, *Trusts and Trustees* to support its rule. Generally, the removal of a trustee is within the reasonable discretion of the court. More is required to remove a trustee appointed by the creator of the trust than is required to remove one appointed by the court. In all cases the real guide is whether or not it is best for the trust estate that the trustee be removed. Friction between the trustee and the beneficiary is not in itself sufficient ground for removal. Some beneficial end must be achieved by the removal or it will not be justified. Restatement, *Trust*, § 107; Bogert, *Trusts and Trustees,* vol. 3, § 527. *Willson*, 177 Va. at 671, 15 S.E.2d at 59.

The district court has abundantly set forth its findings of fact supporting its conclusion that it is in the best interest of the Dalkon Shield Claimants' Trust that the three named trustees be removed. The interests of the beneficiaries of the Trust require that the Trustees act promptly in establishing procedures for the expeditious payment of just claims. The delays occasioned by the three trustees have increased administrative costs, have delayed the full funding of the Trust, which when fully funded will produce approximately $600,000 per day in interest income, and have endangered the very life of the Plan by delays that could extend consummation past July 24, 1989, and allow American Home Products to revoke its offer of merger. Such revocation would eliminate the $2.3 billion contribution to the Trust.[2] They have delayed the adoption of Option 1 and payment to those claimants, who would accept payment thereunder, and they have also delayed paying Dalkon Shield liquidated claims "as promptly as practicable" as required by § 4.03 of the Plan.

Disharmony, animosity and friction among the Trustees will also support a removal under Virginia law. In Sterling v. Blackwelder, 383 F.2d 282, 286 (4th Cir.1967) we stated:

> The main thrust of the attack in the district court was to rescind or otherwise invalidate the trust. Thus, the district court was not called upon to carefully consider, in the interest of proper administration, the possibility of substituting a trustee who might be able to overcome the obvious animosity between the parties and facilitate harmonious cooperation. Although we will not, on this record, ourselves order the removal of Leroy Blackwelder as the active trustee, we think that the district court, on remand, might properly consider whether such a course would be in the best interest of the trust estate and the various parties. *See* Va. Code §§ 26–48,–52; 1 *Scott, Trusts* § 107 (2d ed. 1956).

It is clear from the record and the district court's findings that there was division and disharmony among the Trustees. The district court found that harmony and cooperation among the Trustees could best be restored by removing Trustees Blum, Lock and Samani. On the showing made at the hearing, we find this is a proper use of the considerable discretion allowed the appointing judge under Virginia law.

The law of Virginia is quite clear that the court appointing the Trustees has great discretion in determining proper cause for their removal. In Reynolds v. Zink, 68 Va. (27 Grat.) 29 (1876), the court stated: The statute, Code of 1860, ch. 132, § 11, has wisely deposited with "the court, under the order of which any (such) fiduciary derives

---

2. Mr. Locks testified that he was not aware of this provision of the merger agreement. He was also unaware that under § 4.07(c) of the Trust Agreement if the Order of Confirmation were reversed on appeal, the $100,000,000 already paid into the Trust could no longer be used to compensate claimants. Mr. Locks testified that he was an experienced attorney in mass tort litigation, but months after he became a trustee of one of the largest trusts ever created, he was unfamiliar with critical provisions of the documents making up the Plan of Reorganization.

his authority," the right and duty to revoke and annul his powers "whenever from any cause it appears proper." There must, of necessity, be vested in that court a very large discretion; and while it is a legal discretion, to be exercised in a proper case, an appellate court ought not to interfere, except in a case where manifest injustice has been done, or where it is plain that a proper case has not been made for the exercise of the powers which the legislature has specially conferred upon that court, from which the fiduciary derives his authority. This is still the law of Virginia and the above quote in its entirety, is found in Clark v. Grasty, 210 Va. at 36, 168 S.E.2d at 271.

It is obvious from the record that a real bone of contention among the Trustees is the appointment of an attorney or a firm of attorneys to represent the Trustees and handle the many legal questions that will arise in the administration of the Dalkon Shield Claimants' Trust. Mr. Lock, Ms. Blum and Ms. Samani have refused to acknowledge that Mr. Drabkin and his firm, Cadwalader, Wickersham and Taft may have a conflict of interest because the firm has been and still is counsel to the Dalkon Shield Claimants' Committee. The remaining Trustees and the disqualification order of Chief Judge Albert Bryan, Jr. have found such a conflict, but this has not diminished the loyalty of the three Trustees to Mr. Drabkin. This is a throw-back to the former bankruptcy scenario when the lawyer for the largest number of creditors elected the Trustee, and the Trustee then employed the lawyer to represent him. Such activity is no longer acceptable. The first loyalty of the Trustees must be to the Trust and to the prompt and efficient exercise of their duties thereunder.

The district court has been handling the Dalkon Shield litigation since it began and has retained jurisdiction of the present bankruptcy proceedings. It has devoted a large part of its time to the handling of these matters and it is better positioned than we are to understand the conflicts among the Trustees, the delays that have been occasioned in the carrying out of the Plan of Reorganization and what is in the best interest of the Trust. Its findings of fact are not clearly erroneous and its conclusion that removal of the three Trustees will be in the best interest of the Trust is acceptable under the law of Virginia and the provisions of the Trust.

Affirmed.

GEORGENE VAIRO, THE DALKON SHIELD CLAIMANTS TRUST: PARADIGM LOST (OR FOUND)?

61 Fordham L.Rev. 617, 651–660 (1992).

* * *

IV. THE DALKON SHIELD CLAIMANTS TRUST: A PRELIMINARY APPRAISAL

A set of recent articles in the *Duke Journal of Law and Contemporary Problems* describe the various claims resolution facilities that recently have been established to deal with mass tort claims. Nearly all of the articles focus to some extent on the Dalkon Shield Claimants Trust, and many are critical or inaccurate.

Typical criticisms are reported by Professor Francis McGovern. He wrote of the "high level of dissatisfaction over claims processing." Curiously, the source of this statement was a *Wall Street Journal* article which described two claimants' dissatisfaction with how their claims were evaluated. McGovern wrote:

> [T]his title reflects the sentiments of at least some of the participants in the claims resolution process and suggests a high level of dissatisfaction over claims processing. Commonly discussed general complaints include a lack of willingness to compromise, a failure to reveal information concerning the trust's evaluation of claims, an insensitivity to the behavioral needs of claimants, and an overemphasis on administrative convenience.

There are several problems with this statement. First, "commonly discussed general complaints" by whom? Nowhere is it disclosed that many of the chief critics of the Trust are plaintiffs' lawyers who have not been able to influence the Trust to the degree that they had hoped. Because the Trust is an independent body, it has not accepted wholesale the suggestions of the plaintiff's bar.

Other accusations are equally problematic. While it is true that the Trust will not provide claimants, or their lawyers, with a roadmap as to how claims are evaluated, the Trustees have made numerous statements about the process. For example, the Trust has informed claimants as to what elements are considered and what elements are not considered. Also, possible statute of limitations defenses are not considered during the claims resolution process, while alternative causation problems are very important.

The statements reflect a bad game of semantics. "Administrative convenience" is set forth as the justification for the Trust's unpopular policies. In fact, the Trust's purpose is to operate as leanly as possible to protect the Trust's fund for distribution to claimants.

Similarly, it is difficult to understand what "insensitivity to the behavioral needs of claimants" means. Each claimant is provided a Personal Contact at the Trust who is well-trained to answer the claimant's questions about the claims resolution process. The Trust also has provided training to each Personal Contact to insure that they can treat claimants with dignity and empathy. In addition, any claimant who rejects her initial offer from the Trust is entitled to a face-to-face meeting with Trust representatives to discuss her claim in detail, and tell her story. As Karen Hicks pointed out in her dissertation, many Dalkon Shield claimants were just as concerned about achieving justice on a personal level as with being appropriately compensated.

Much of the criticism being leveled against the Trust appears to be designed to embarrass the Trust into more fully cooperating with those who have much to gain: the lawyers and other professionals who personally benefit if business is done in the usual adversarial fashion.

Certainly, claimants in current and future mass torts would be better served by a reasoned and balanced evaluation of the Trust's performance to assess what lessons have been learned and to determine whether the Trust can serve as a paradigm. This part of this Essay attempts to provide some balance, and thus the framework for further analysis, by providing a quantitative picture of the Trust's performance to date, a comparison of the Trust's performance with the Manville Trust's performance, and a further response to some of the criticisms of the Trust.

A.   *The Trust's Performance*

The following data suggests that the Trust's philosophy is working well. About 350,000 timely and late claims have been filed. Over 106,000 of these claims were disallowed by the court in 1987 before the bankruptcy plan was approved. Roughly 60,000 Late Claims have been filed and will be reviewed for possible payment if there is any money remaining after paying the nearly 200,000 timely claims.

Since the Trust began resolving claims, it has settled over 145,000 claims at a total administrative cost of under $400 per claim. Over $410,800,000 has been paid to represented claimants. Thus, assuming a one-third contingency fee rate, represented claimants have received about $278,890,000. Unrepresented claimants have received approximately $226,100,000. In addition, claimants are currently considering Option 3 offers totalling almost $43,000,000 in the aggregate.

At first glance, the average payment to unrepresented claimants may appear far less than that for represented claimants. In fact, that is true, because 116,349 unrepresented claimants have been paid, while only 25,571 represented claimants have been paid. The average payment to unrepresented claimants must be evaluated in light of the fact that a far higher number of unrepresented claimants chose the $725 Option 1 payment. When payments under Option 3 are examined, however, unrepresented claimants are actually netting higher average amounts than the average amounts netted by represented claimants.

Moreover, the processing of claims has moved efficiently, allowing injured persons to be compensated without undue delay. The Trust is paying about $1,000,000 in claims per day, and sometimes as much as $10,000,000 per week, and will make offers on all remaining timely claims in approximately two years.

Further, the Trust's offers of compensation appear to be perceived as fair and just, given the acceptance rate of Option 3 offers. The acceptance rate on the Trust's Option 3 offers is over 82%. Taking into account those claimants who rejected their Option 3 offer but who accepted the ADR option, the acceptance rate is approximately 85%. Moreover, most of the rejections (approximately 60%) are by claimants who receive offers of less than $6,000. Additionally, 37% of those claimants who initially reject the Trust's Option 3 offer change their decision and accept the Trust's offer after the settlement conference, at which the Trust's offer is explained. Because of the high acceptance rate, the Trust has been able to keep administrative and legal costs very low.

B. Comparison With the Manville Trust

The Trust recognizes that many Dalkon Shield claimants suffered their injuries as long as twenty years ago and regrets any further delays in payment. Since the Trust was fully funded in December 1989, however, it appears that it has been able to settle more claims faster than any other compensation system devised in the mass tort context even though Option 3 payments can be quite large and are based upon complex medical evidence.

By comparison, the Manville Trust has made offers to claimants over a longer period of time. The Manville Trust has reviewed approximately 28,000 claims out of 192,000 active claims in a five and one-half year period. The Dalkon Shield Claimants Trust, on the other hand, has processed almost 150,000 claims in four years. Many of these claims, about 115,000, were Option 1 claims. In the two and a half years that it has been processing the higher valued claims, the Trust has paid about 16,000 Option 2 claims, which require an examination of medical records and a claim form. As of the end of October 1992, it also had made approximately 17,500 Option 3 offers, which require examination of voluminous medical records and a detailed claim form.

Moreover, the Manville Trust is now paying less than twenty-five cents on the dollar due to a lack of funds. In contrast, the Trust is paying 100 cents on the dollar to all claimants who accept their Option 3 offers. Another area of comparison is administrative costs. As of June 1991, Manville's transaction costs, including legal fees, were twenty-five times higher than those of the Dalkon Shield Claimants Trust. Manville's administrative cost per claim was $4,900, while the Dalkon Shield Claimants Trust's cost per claim was under $400. Although the Dalkon Shield Claimants Trust's cost per claim is likely to rise as it enters the litigation phase, the acceptance rate of its offers and its emphasis on cost effectiveness should result in significantly lower transaction costs than those of the Manville Trust.

C. Criticisms of the Trust

Curiously lacking in the criticisms of the Trust is any suggestion of a motive for the Trustees to act against the interests of the claimants. The fund belongs to the claimants, not the Trustees. The Trustees have only one motive: to see the fund distributed as fairly and efficiently as possible.

One article criticizing the Trust makes erroneous and misleading statements about the Trust's holdback policy. The article states that if a claimant refuses the Trust's offer and wins a larger recovery at trial or arbitration, the Trust will pay only $10,000 at the time of judgment and hold back the rest. This statement is inaccurate. The Trust will pay either $10,000 or the Option 3 offer amount, whichever is higher. Thus, if the Trust offered a woman $125,000, and she obtained a jury verdict of $350,000, she would be paid $125,000 at the time of the judgment, and the balance when the Trust is assured that there will be enough money to pay all claimants their settlement amounts.

The negative impression created by this inaccuracy is compounded by the article's misleading impression as to why the Trust has decided to implement the "holdback" provision of the bankruptcy plan establishing the Trust. The author states that the purpose is simply to "preserve assets." In fact, the purpose of the "holdback" is to ensure that all claimants receive a fair proportion of the $2.3 billion settlement fund. Indeed, it would be a gross violation of the Trust's fiduciary duty to the entire claimant population to risk bankrupting the fund by paying large sums to those at the head of the line when that might mean there is no money for those at the end of the line.

The article also ignores another fundamental point. Every single penny of the Trust fund, except those needed for administrative expenses, will be distributed to claimants. Any money left over after all settlement judgments and late claimants are paid, will be distributed to all claimants on a pro rata basis. By making fair offers to claimants and by creating the incentive to settle now by paying claimants the full amount of the offer, the Trust saves huge amounts in transaction costs by avoiding additional attorneys fees and other defense costs. If all or most claimants accepted their settlement offers, there would be substantially more money to be distributed on a pro rata basis.

Finally, if the Trust is prohibited from implementing the "holdback" in the manner in which it has decided is in the best interests of the claimant population as a whole, it will be forced to hold back some amount of its Option 3 settlement offers. Why should claimants who want to settle, some of whom have been waiting since the early 1970s, have to wait another minute to receive their entire settlement because of a relatively small number of claimants who wish to litigate their claims? Why should the majority who want to settle get only 12%, 25%, or 50%, or some other portion now, to preserve assets for the minority who want to litigate?

Indeed, the Trust's policies are designed to achieve a resolution of all claims in the shortest possible period of time. If more claimants were to elect trial or arbitration, rather than to settle at Option 3, the Trust would be in business for a far longer time. Thus, the Trust's policies which provide incentives to settle, rather than to litigate, should result in the Trust going out of business sooner rather than later.

The question, once again, is one of control: who should make the ultimate decisions concerning the distribution of the fund? It seems perfectly obvious that those who are in business to give all the money away are in the best position to make decisions to protect the interests of the whole. They certainly are in a better position to make these sorts of decisions than those who want to maximize individual recoveries and who have a financial stake in those recoveries.

CONCLUSION

The Dalkon Shield Claimants Trust was established to compensate women and their families who were injured by the Dalkon Shield. Several factors should be considered when analyzing the performance of the Trust. First, the Trust made serious and exhaustive attempts to insure a high degree of claimant satisfaction with its claims resolution process.

Second, the Trust has operated on a lean administrative budget, holding total administrative costs to under $400 per claim. Moreover, in the typical tort case, the defendant's costs consume about 35% of the litigation expense and recovery pie. After plaintiffs' attorneys take approximately 35%, plaintiffs are left with roughly 30%. In contrast, a Dalkon Shield claimant can expect to receive about 65% of the amount offered if she is represented by a lawyer, or 100% less approximately $400 if she represents herself.

The fact that women were the primary victims in the Dalkon Shield case motivated many of the Trustees' decisions. These decisions and the success of the CRF have serious implications for resolving claims of women and other traditionally less powerful persons, or for any victims of a mass tort. When disaster strikes along the lines of the Dalkon Shield, asbestos, etc., there will eventually be millions or billions of dollars at stake. The question should be how to distribute the most money to the victims in such a way that the victims feel that justice has been served. Only Tom Tyler's article in the Duke Symposium focused on this matter of deep concern to the Trustees. It was always the Trustees' view that claimants were concerned not simply with money, but also with dignity and justice.

The Trust believes, as does the law and economics scholarship, that the claimants are in the best position to make their own choices concerning settlement options if they receive accurate information about the process and if no special expertise is required to complete the process. To further maximize each claimant's position, the Trust relies on the submissions of each claimant and then subjects each claimant's materials to the same claims evaluation process. This creates an efficient system that protects the good of the whole, arguably a goal in accordance with feminist philosophy.

The operation of the Trust can further bridge the gap between the law and economics school and feminist jurisprudence. Both law and economics and feminist jurisprudentialists should agree that the Trust serves as an example of the need to create new ways of looking at legal problems to ensure their just resolution. There is a need to re-examine notions of individual prerogatives, sometimes forsaking them for more collective, and efficient, resolution.

Reliance on a law and economics perspective may seem "sterile," however, or lacking in feminist values of care. For instance, Professor Bender suggests that

> [I]n the Dalkon Shield cases, corporate defendants might be ordered by law to fulfill their care-giving responsibilities by finding openings in infertility clinics for victims, arranging their appointments and transportation for the necessary visits, organizing necessary clinics if what already exists is inadequate, locating competent marriage and psychological counseling, developing private adoption alternatives for those women who want children but cannot conceive, and the like.

These suggestions are valuable. In addition, however, there are other ways to demonstrate this care-giving ethic through a claims evaluation process. By ensuring such qualities as timely and fair processing of claims, effective communication lines between the Trust and the claimants, staff members willing to assist claimants, and settlement conferences whereby the Trust explains to a claimant, face-to-face, the strengths and weaknesses of her claim, the Trust is, in fact, able to act in a caring, responsive manner while still preserving efficiency in claims resolution and administrative operation.

In sum, the Trust encountered resistance to its policies because the system devised to implement the Plan differs significantly from the traditional adversarial model. Those who historically have had much to gain in mass tort cases—namely, lawyers and other professionals—would lose much of their power if the Dalkon Shield Claimants Trust succeeds in its goal of distributing the settlement fund as fairly and efficiently as possible.

It is indeed likely that, without court involvement in future cases, the claims resolution paradigm the Trustees hoped to create may well be lost. It is unlikely that those who have much to lose would agree to another Plan, like the Dalkon Shield Claimants Trust Plan, which provides the tools with which independent trustees can seek to protect the interests of a whole class of claimants.

This Essay raises numerous questions and presents the factual and conceptual materials that provide the basis for beginning a reasoned and academic discussion of all the issues presented by the Dalkon Shield case, as well as other mass torts. Further articles by this author, and hopefully by her colleagues, will explore fully the Dalkon Shield Claimants Trust experience from the three jurisprudential perspectives discussed earlier in this Essay—professional ethics, feminist jurisprudence, and law and economics. Perhaps then we will know whether the Dalkon Shield Claimants Trust represents a paradigm lost or found.

Notes and Questions

1. The Dalkon Shield Claimants Trust was established as part of the Plan of Reorganization of the A.H. Robins Company. *See* Sixth Amended and Restated Disclosure Statement Pursuant to Section 1125 of the Bankruptcy Code (Bankr.E.D.Va. Mar. 28, 1988)(No. 85–01307–R), *confirmed* In re A.H. Robins Co., 88 B.R. 742 (E.D.Va.1988), *affirmed* 880 F.2d 694 (4th Cir.), *cert. denied sub nom.* Menard–Sanford v. A.H. Robins Co., 493 U.S. 959, 110 S.Ct. 376, 107 L.Ed.2d 362 (1989).

The creation and administration of the Dalkon Shield Trust Fund has led to extended litigation over various aspects of the Trust's administration, and continues to do so. A history of the Dalkon Shield and the Chapter 11 litigation may be found in In re A.H. Robins Co., 880 F.2d 709, 711–22 (4th Cir.), *cert. denied sub nom.* Anderson v. Aetna Casualty & Surety Co., 493 U.S. 959, 110 S.Ct. 377, 107 L.Ed.2d 362 (1989). Other details regarding the A.H. Robins bankruptcy case are explained in In re A.H. Robins Co., 88 B.R. 742 (E.D.Va.1988) [the so-called *Breland* settlement], *affirmed* 880 F.2d 694 (4th Cir.), *cert. denied sub nom.* Menard–Sanford v. A.H. Robins Co., Inc., 493 U.S. 959, 110 S.Ct. 376, 107 L.Ed.2d 362 (1989). *See also* Tetuan v. A.H. Robins Co., 241 Kan. 441, 738 P.2d 1210, 1218–24 (Kan.1987)(affirming $1.75 million compensatory and $7.5 million punitive jury award).

2. The central appellate decision approving the Dalkon Shield settlement is A.H. Robins Co. v. Piccinin, 788 F.2d 994, 996 (4th Cir.), *cert. denied* 479 U.S. 876, 107 S.Ct. 251, 93 L.Ed.2d 177 (1986). For a discussion of this decision *see* David Walsh, Fourth Circuit Review, *Robins v. Piccinin: The Fourth Circuit's Response to Bankruptcy and Mass Tort,* 44 Wash & Lee L.Rev. 537 (1987). In *Piccinin,* the Fourth Circuit in upholding the Dalkon Shield bankruptcy trust agreement relied heavily on the Second Circuit's approval of the Manville Trust bankruptcy reorganization. To what extent do these two bankruptcy reorganizations resemble each other? In what regard were they different?

3. Professor Vairo's article recounts a lengthy description of the creation and operation of the Dalkon Shield Trust Fund, extending beyond the removal of the controversial trustees. As Professor Vairo notes, the Dalkon Shield Trust Fund has been the object of a tremendous outpouring of academic commentary, most of it critical. Is Professor Vairo's defense of the Dalkon Shield Trust credible? Does she adequately counter the charges of the Trust's critics? Do either the Manville Trust or Dalkon Shield Trust provide a satisfactory model for aggregating, valuing, and compensating mass tort claimants? Do either provide a preferred resolution to mass tort outside the adjudicative system?

4. There have been at least five book-length treatments of the Dalkon Shield litigation. *See* Ronald J. Bacigal, THE LIMITS OF LITIGATION: THE DALKON SHIELD CONTROVERSY (1990); Sheldon D. Engelmayer & Robert Wagman, LORD'S JUSTICE: ONE JUDGE'S BATTLE TO EXPOSE THE DEADLY DALKON SHIELD (1985); Karen M. Hicks, SURVIVING THE DALKON SHIELD IUD: WOMEN V. THE PHARMACEUTICAL INDUSTRY (1994); Morton Mintz, AT ANY COST: CORPORATE GREED, WOMEN, AND THE DALKON SHIELD (1985); Susan Perry & Jim Dawson, NIGHTMARE: WOMEN AND THE DALKON SHIELD (1985).

5. For academic commentary relating to the Dalkon Shield litigation, *see generally* Kenneth R. Feinberg, *The Dalkon Shield Claimants Trust,* 53 Law & Contemp. Probs. 79 (1990); Herbert M. Kritzer, *Public Notification Campaigns in Mass Litigation: The Dalkon Shield Case,* 13 Just.Sys.J. 220 (1988); Peggy McCollum, Note, *Dalkon Shield Claims Resolution Facility: A Contraceptive for Corporate Irresponsibility,* 7 Ohio St.J.Disp.Resol. 351 (1992); Joseph A. Page, *Asbestos and Dalkon Shield: Corporate America on Trial,* 85 Mich. L.Rev. 1324 (1987); Jason A. Rosenthal, Note, *Courts of Inequity: The Bankruptcy Laws' Failure to Adequately Protect the Dalkon Shield Victims,* 45 Fla.L.Rev. 223 (1993); Leslie E. Tick, *Beyond Dalkon Shield: Proving Causation Against I.U.D. Manufacturers for PID–Related Injury,* 13 Golden Gate I.L.Rev. 639 (1983); John M. Van Dyke, *The Dalkon Shield: A Primer in IUD Liability,* 6 West St.U.L.Rev. 1 (178); Sharon Youdelman, *Strategic Bankruptcies: Class Actions, Classification and the Dalkon Shield Cases,* 7 Cardozo L.Rev. 817 (1986).

6. In addition to the academic critical commentary, the implementation of the Dalkon Shield Fund has been the object of extensive scrutiny in the general media. *See e.g.,* Paul Blustein, *How Two Young Lawyers Got Rich by Settling IUD Liability Claims,* Wall St. J., Feb. 24, 1982, at 1; Malcolm Gladwell, *Latest Fight In a Long Case: Attorney Fees; Victims' Lawyers Getting Too Much, Critics Contend,* Wash. Post, Jan. 22, 1989, at H1; *Women Reject Settlement Offers From Stingy Dalkon Shield Trust,* Atlanta J. & Const., Nov. 14, 1991, at D4; *see also* Paul Marcotte, *$2.48 Billion Trust Fund: A.H. Robins Faces Claimants, Bankruptcy, Takeover Agreement,* A.B.A.J., Mar. 1, 1988, at 24.

7. As Professor Vairo also suggests, the Dalkon Shield litigation and other mass torts has inspired a feminist critique of the judicial system's response to mass tort litigation generally. This critique stems from the view that the primary victims of many mass torts are women (as in the DES, Dalkon Shield, and silicone breast implant litigations), and the judicial and alternative dispute resolution systems have sadly failed these claimants. *See e.g.,* Leslie Bender, *Feminist (Re)Torts: Thoughts on the Liability Crisis, Mass Torts, Power, and Responsibilities,* 1990 Duke L.J. 848 (1990); Deborah R. Hensler and Mark A. Peterson, *Understanding Mass Personal Injury Litigation: A Socio–Legal Analysis,* 59 Brook.L.Rev. 761 (1993); Joan E. Steinman, *Women, Medical Care, and Mass Tort Litigation,* 68 Chicago–Kent L.Rev. 409 (1992); and Zoe Panarites, Note, *Breast Implants: Choices Women Thought They Made,* 11 N.Y.L. Sch.J.Hum.Rts. 163 (1993). *Cf.* Tom R. Tyler, *A Psychological Perspective on the Settlement of Mass Tort Claims,* 53 Law & Contemp. Probs. 199 (Autumn 1990).

8. For further discussion of mass tort claims facilities, *see* B. Thomas Florence & Judith Gurney, *The Computerization of Mass Settlement Facilities,* 53 Law & Contemp. Probs. 189 (Autumn 1990); Symposium, *Claims Resolution Facilities and the Settlement of Mass Torts,* 53 Law & Contemp. Probs. 1 (Autumn 1990).

C. BANKRUPTCY JURISDICTION AND THIRD–PARTY SURETIES

CELOTEX CORPORATION v. EDWARDS

Supreme Court of the United States, 1995.
___ U.S. ___, 115 S.Ct. 1493, 131 L.Ed.2d 403.

CHIEF JUSTICE REHNQUIST delivered the opinion of the Court.

The United States Court of Appeals for the Fifth Circuit held that respondents should be allowed to execute against petitioner's surety on a supersedeas bond posted by petitioner where the judgment which occasioned the bond had become final. It so held even though the United States Bankruptcy Court for the Middle District of Florida previously had issued an injunction prohibiting respondents from executing on the bond without the Bankruptcy Court's permission. We hold that respondents were obligated to obey the injunction issued by the Bankruptcy Court.

I

In 1987 respondents Bennie and Joann Edwards filed suit in the United States District Court for the Northern District of Texas against petitioner Celotex (and others) alleging asbestos-related injuries. In April 1989 the District Court entered a $281,025.80 judgment in favor of respondents and against Celotex. To stay execution of the judgment pending appeal, Celotex posted a supersedeas bond in the amount of $294,987.88, with Northbrook Property and Casualty Insurance Company serving as surety on the bond. As collateral for the bond, Celotex allowed Northbrook to retain money owed to Celotex under a settlement agreement resolving insurance coverage disputes between Northbrook and Celotex.

The United States Court of Appeals for the Fifth Circuit affirmed, issuing its mandate on October 12, 1990, and thus rendering "final" respondents' judgment against Celotex. Edwards (*Edwards I*) v. Armstrong World Industries, Inc., 911 F.2d 1151 (1990). That same day, Celotex filed a voluntary petition for relief under Chapter 11 of the Bankruptcy Code in the United States Bankruptcy Court for the Middle District of Florida.[1] The filing of the petition automatically stayed both the continuation of "proceeding[s] against" Celotex and the commencement of "any act to obtain possession of property" of Celotex.[2] 11 U.S.C. §§ 362(a)(1) and (3).

On October 17, 1990, the Bankruptcy Court exercised its equitable powers under 11 U.S.C. § 105(a) and issued an injunction (the "Section

---

1. For purposes of this case, we assume respondents' judgment became final before Celotex filed its petition in bankruptcy.

2. As of the filing date, more than 141,000 asbestos-related bodily injury lawsuits were pending against Celotex, and over 100 asbestos-related bodily injury cases were in some stage of appeal, with judgments totaling nearly $70 million being stayed by supersedeas bonds that Celotex had posted.

105 Injunction'') to augment the protection afforded Celotex by the automatic stay. In pertinent part, the Section 105 Injunction stayed all proceedings involving Celotex "regardless of . . . whether the matter is on appeal and a supersedeas bond has been posted by [Celotex]." * * * [3] Respondents, whose bonded judgment against Celotex had already been affirmed on appeal, filed a motion pursuant to Federal Rule of Civil Procedure 65.1 in the District Court seeking permission to execute against Northbrook on the supersedeas bond. Both Celotex and Northbrook opposed this motion, asserting that all proceedings to enforce the bonds had been enjoined by the Bankruptcy Court's Section 105 Injunction. Celotex brought to the District Court's attention the fact that, since respondents had filed their Rule 65.1 motion, the Bankruptcy Court had reaffirmed the Section 105 Injunction and made clear that the injunction prohibited judgment creditors like respondents from proceeding against sureties without the Bankruptcy Court's permission: "Where at the time of filing the petition, the appellate process between Debtor and the judgment creditor had been concluded, the judgment creditor is precluded from proceeding against any supersedeas bond posted by Debtor without first seeking to vacate the Section 105 stay entered by this Court." In re Celotex (*Celotex I*), 128 B.R. 478, 485 (Bkrtcy.Ct. MD Fla.1991). Despite the Bankruptcy Court's reaffirmation and clarification of the Section 105 Injunction, the District Court allowed respondents to execute on the bond against Northbrook.[4]

3. The Bankruptcy Court noted that, upon request of a party in interest and following 30 days written notice and a hearing, it would "consider granting relief from the restraints imposed" by the Section 105 Injunction. * * * Several of Celotex' bonded judgment creditors whose cases were still on appeal filed motions requesting that the Bankruptcy Court lift the Section 105 Injunction (1) to enable their pending appellate actions to proceed and (2) to permit them to execute upon the bonds once the appellate process concluded in their favor. The Bankruptcy Court granted the first request but denied the second. In re Celotex (*Celotex I*), 128 B.R. 478, 484 (Bkrtcy.Ct. MD Fla.1991).

4. Two days after the District Court entered its order, the Bankruptcy Court ruled on motions to lift the Section 105 Injunction that had been filed by several bonded judgment creditors who, like respondents, had prevailed against Celotex on appeal. The Bankruptcy Court again reaffirmed the Section 105 Injunction and it again explained that the injunction prohibited judgment creditors like respondents from executing on the supersedeas bonds against third parties without its permission. In re Celotex (*Celotex II*), 140 B.R. 912, 914 (Bkrtcy.Ct. MD Fla.1992). It refused to lift the Section 105 Injunction at that time, finding that Celotex would suffer irrepara-

ble harm. It reasoned that if the judgment creditors were allowed to execute against the sureties on the supersedeas bonds, the sureties would in turn seek to lift the Section 105 Injunction to reach Celotex' collateral under the settlement agreements, possibly destroying any chance of a successful reorganization plan. * * * To protect the bonded judgment creditors, the Bankruptcy Court ordered that: (1) the sureties involved, including Northbrook, establish escrow accounts sufficient to insure full payment of the bonds; (2) Celotex create an interest-bearing reserve account or increase the face amount of any supersedeas bond to cover the full amount of judgment through confirmation; and (3) Celotex provide in any plan that the bonded claimants' claims be paid in full unless otherwise determined by the court or agreed by the claimant. *Id.* at 917. The Bankruptcy Court also directed Celotex to file "any preference action or any fraudulent transfer action or any other action to avoid or subordinate any judgment creditor's claim against any judgment creditor or against any surety on any supersedeas bond within 60 days of the entry" of its order. * * * Accordingly, Celotex filed an adversary proceeding against respondents, 227 other similarly situated bonded judgment creditors in over 100 cases, and the sureties on the supersedeas bonds, in-

Celotex appealed, and the Fifth Circuit affirmed. Edwards (*Edwards II*) v. Armstrong World Industries, Inc., 6 F.3d 312 (1993). It first held that, because the appellate process for which the supersedeas bond was posted had been completed, Celotex no longer had a property interest in the bond and the automatic stay provisions of 11 U.S.C. § 362 therefore did not prevent respondents from executing against Northbrook. *Edwards II, supra,* at 315–317. The Court then acknowledged that "[t]he jurisdiction of bankruptcy courts has been extended to include stays on proceedings involving third parties under the auspices of 28 U.S.C. § 1334(b)," 6 F.3d, at 318, and that the Bankruptcy Court itself had ruled that the Section 105 Injunction enjoined respondents' proceeding against Northbrook to execute on the supersedeas bond. *Ibid.* The Fifth Circuit nevertheless disagreed with the merits of the Bankruptcy Court's Section 105 Injunction, holding that "the integrity of the estate is not implicated in the present case because the debtor has no present or future interest in this supersedeas bond." *Id.* at 320. The Court reasoned that the Section 105 Injunction was "manifestly unfair" and an "unjust result" because the supersedeas bond was posted "to cover precisely the type of eventuality which occurred in this case, insolvency of the judgment debtor." *Id,* at 319. In concluding that the Section 105 Injunction was improper, the Fifth Circuit expressly disagreed with the reasoning and result of Willis v. Celotex Corp., 978 F.2d 146 (4th Cir.1992), *cert. denied,* 507 U.S. ___, 113 S.Ct. 1846, 123 L.Ed.2d 470 (1993), where the Court of Appeals for the Fourth Circuit, examining the same Section 105 Injunction, held that the Bankruptcy Court had the power under 11 U.S.C. § 105(a) to stay proceedings against sureties on the supersedeas bonds. 6 F.3d at 320.

Celotex filed a petition for rehearing, arguing that the Fifth Circuit's decision allowed a collateral attack on an order of the Bankruptcy Court sitting under the jurisdiction of the Court of Appeals for the Eleventh Circuit. The Fifth Circuit denied the petition, stating in part that "we have not held that the bankruptcy court in Florida was necessarily wrong; we have only concluded that the district court, over which we do have appellate jurisdiction, was right." *Id.* at 321. Because of the conflict between the Fifth Circuit's decision in this case and the Fourth Circuit's decision in *Willis,* we granted certiorari. 511 U.S. ___, 114 S.Ct. 2099, 128 L.Ed.2d 661. We now reverse.

II

Respondents acknowledge that the Bankruptcy Court's Section 105 Injunction prohibited them from attempting to execute against Northbrook on the supersedeas bond posted by Celotex. * * * In GTE

cluding Northbrook. * * * In that proceeding, Celotex asserts that the bonded judgment creditors should not be able to execute on their bonds because, by virtue of the collateralization of the bonds, the bonded judgment creditors are beneficiaries of Celotex asset transfers that are voidable as preferences and fraudulent transfers. * * * Celotex also contends that the punitive damages portions of the judgments can be voided or subordinated on other bankruptcy law grounds. * * * This adversary proceeding is currently pending in the Bankruptcy Court.

Sylvania, Inc. v. Consumers Union of United States, Inc., 445 U.S. 375, 386, 100 S.Ct. 1194, 1201, 63 L.Ed.2d 467 (1980), we reaffirmed the well established rule that "persons subject to an injunctive order issued by a court with jurisdiction are expected to obey that decree until it is modified or reversed, even if they have proper grounds to object to the order." In *GTE Sylvania*, we went on to say: "There is no doubt that the Federal District Court in Delaware had jurisdiction to issue the temporary restraining orders and preliminary and permanent injunctions. Nor were those equitable decrees challenged as only a frivolous pretense to validity, although of course there is disagreement over whether the District Court erred in issuing the permanent injunction. Under these circumstances, the CPSC was required to obey the injunctions out of respect for judicial process." *Id.* at 386–387 (internal quotation marks, citations, and footnote omitted). This rule was applied in the bankruptcy context more than 60 years ago in Oriel v. Russell, 278 U.S. 358, 49 S.Ct. 173, 73 L.Ed. 419 (1929), where the Court held that turnover orders issued under the old bankruptcy regime could not be collaterally attacked in a later contempt proceeding. Respondents acknowledge the validity of the rule but contend that it has no application here. They argue that the Bankruptcy Court lacked jurisdiction to issue the Section 105 Injunction, though much of their argument goes to the correctness of the Bankruptcy Court's decision to issue the injunction rather than to its jurisdiction to do so.

The jurisdiction of the bankruptcy courts, like that of other federal courts, is grounded in and limited by statute. Title 28 U.S.C. § 1334(b) provides that "the district courts shall have original but not exclusive jurisdiction of all civil proceedings arising under title 11, or arising in or related to cases under title 11." 28 U.S.C.§ 1334(b). The district courts may, in turn, refer "any or all proceedings arising under title 11 or arising in or related to a case under title 11 . . . to the bankruptcy judges for the district." 28 U.S.C. § 157(a). Here, the Bankruptcy Court's jurisdiction to enjoin respondents' proceeding against Northbrook must be based on the "arising under," "arising in," or "related to" language of §§ 1334(b) and 157(a).

Respondents argue that the Bankruptcy Court had jurisdiction to issue the Section 105 Injunction only if their proceeding to execute on the bond was "related to" the Celotex bankruptcy. Petitioner argues the Bankruptcy Court indeed had such "related to" jurisdiction. Congress did not delineate the scope of "related to" [5] jurisdiction, but its choice of words suggests a grant of some breadth. The jurisdictional grant in § 1334(b) was a distinct departure from the jurisdiction con-

---

5. Proceedings "related to" the bankruptcy include (1) causes of action owned by the debtor which become property of the estate pursuant to 11 U.S.C.§ 541, and (2) suits between third parties which have an effect on the bankruptcy estate. *See* 1 COLLIER ON BANKRUPTCY ¶ 3.01[1][c][iv], p. 3–28 (15th ed.1994). The first type of "related to" proceeding involves a claim like the state law breach of contract action at issue in Northern Pipeline Constr. Co. v. Marathon Pipe Line Co., 458 U.S. 50, 102 S.Ct. 2858, 73 L.Ed.2d 598 (1982). The instant case involves the second type of "related to" proceeding.

ferred under previous acts, which had been limited to either possession of property by the debtor or consent as a basis for jurisdiction. *See* S. Rep. No. 95–989, pp. 153–154 (1978). We agree with the views expressed by the Court of Appeals for the Third Circuit in Pacor, Inc. v. Higgins, 743 F.2d 984 (1984), that "Congress intended to grant comprehensive jurisdiction to the bankruptcy courts so that they might deal efficiently and expeditiously with all matters connected with the bankruptcy estate," *id.* at 994; *see also* H. Rep. No. 95–595, pp. 43–48 (1977), and that the "related to" language of § 1334(b) must be read to give district courts (and bankruptcy courts under § 157(a)) jurisdiction over more than simply proceedings involving the property of the debtor or the estate. We also agree with that Court's observation that a bankruptcy court's "related to" jurisdiction cannot be limitless. *See* Pacor, *supra,* at 994; *cf.* Board of Governors v. MCorp Financial, 502 U.S. 32, 40, 112 S.Ct. 459, 464, 116 L.Ed.2d 358 (1991)(stating that Congress has vested "limited authority" in bankruptcy courts).[6]

We believe that the issue of whether respondents are entitled to immediate execution on the bond against Northbrook is at least a question "related to" Celotex' bankruptcy.[7] Admittedly, a proceeding by

6. In attempting to strike an appropriate balance, the Third Circuit in Pacor, Inc. v. Higgins, 743 F.2d 984 (1984), devised the following test for determining the existence of "related to" jurisdiction: "The usual articulation of the test for determining whether a civil proceeding is related to bankruptcy is whether the outcome of that proceeding could conceivably have any effect on the estate being administered in bankruptcy. . . . Thus, the proceeding need not necessarily be against the debtor or against the debtor's property. An action is related to bankruptcy if the outcome could alter the debtor's rights, liabilities, options, or freedom of action (either positively or negatively) and which in any way impacts upon the handling and administration of the bankrupt estate." *Id.* at 994. The First, Fourth, Fifth, Sixth, Eighth, Ninth, Tenth and Eleventh Circuits have adopted the *Pacor* test with little or no variation. *See* In re G.S.F. Corp., 938 F.2d 1467, 1475 (1st Cir.1991); A.H. Robins Co. v. Piccinin, 788 F.2d 994, 1002, n. 11(4th Cir.), *cert. denied,* 479 U.S. 876, 107 S.Ct. 251, 93 L.Ed.2d 177 (1986); In re Wood, 825 F.2d 90, 93 (5th Cir.1987); Robinson v. Michigan Consol. Gas Co., 918 F.2d 579, 583–584 (6th Cir.1990); In re Dogpatch U.S.A., Inc., 810 F.2d 782, 786 (8th Cir.1987); In re Fietz, 852 F.2d 455, 457 (9th Cir.1988); In re Gardner, 913 F.2d 1515, 1518 (10th Cir. 1990); In re Lemco Gypsum, Inc., 910 F.2d 784, 788, and n. 19 (11th Cir.1990). The Second and Seventh Circuits, on the other hand, seem to have adopted a slightly different test. *See* In re Turner, 724 F.2d 338,

341 (2d Cir.1983); In re Xonics, Inc., 813 F.2d 127, 131 (7th Cir.1987); Home Ins. Co. v. Cooper & Cooper, Ltd., 889 F.2d 746, 749 (7th Cir.1989). But whatever test is used, these cases make clear that bankruptcy courts have no jurisdiction over proceedings that have no effect on the debtor.

7. The dissent agrees that respondents' proceeding to execute on the supersedeas bond is "related to" Celotex' bankruptcy, * * *, but noting that "only the district court has the power [under 28 U.S.C. § 157(c)(1)]to enter 'any final order or judgment' " in related "non-core proceedings," *post,* at 9, the dissent concludes that the Bankruptcy Court here did not possess sufficient "related to" jurisdiction to issue the Section 105 Injunction. * * * The Section 105 Injunction, however, is only an interlocutory stay which respondents have yet to challenge. See *infra,* at 13. Thus, the Bankruptcy Court did not lack jurisdiction under § 157(c)(1) to issue the Section 105 Injunction because that injunction was not a "final order or judgment." In any event, respondents have waived any claim that the granting of the Section 105 Injunction was a "non-core" proceeding under § 157(c)(1). Respondents base their arguments solely on 28 U.S.C. § 1334, and concede in their brief that the "bankruptcy court had subject matter jurisdiction to issue orders affecting the bond, then, only if the proceedings on the bond were 'related' to the Celotex bankruptcy itself within the meaning of § 1334(b)." * * * We conclude, and the dissent agrees, that those proceed-

respondents against Northbrook on the supersedeas bond does not directly involve Celotex, except to satisfy the judgment against it secured by the bond. But to induce Northbrook to serve as surety on the bond, Celotex agreed to allow Northbrook to retain the proceeds of a settlement resolving insurance coverage disputes between Northbrook and Celotex. The Bankruptcy Court found that allowing respondents—and 227 other bonded judgment creditors—to execute immediately on the bonds would have a direct and substantial adverse effect on Celotex' ability to undergo a successful reorganization. It stated: "[I]f the Section 105 stay were lifted to enable the judgment creditors to reach the sureties, the sureties in turn would seek to lift the Section 105 stay to reach Debtor's collateral, with corresponding actions by Debtor to preserve its rights under the settlement agreements. Such a scenario could completely destroy any chance of resolving the prolonged insurance coverage disputes currently being adjudicated in this Court. The settlement of the insurance coverage disputes with all of Debtor's insurers may well be the linchpin of Debtor's formulation of a feasible plan. Absent the confirmation of a feasible plan, Debtor may be liquidated or cease to exist after a carrion feast by the victors in a race to the courthouse." In re Celotex (*Celotex II*), 140 B.R. 912, 915 (M.D.Fla. 1992).

In light of these findings by the Bankruptcy Court, it is relevant to note that we are dealing here with a reorganization under Chapter 11, rather than a liquidation under Chapter 7. The jurisdiction of bankruptcy courts may extend more broadly in the former case than in the latter. *Cf.* Continental Illinois Nat. Bank & Trust Co. v. Chicago, R.I. & P.R. Co., 294 U.S. 648, 676, 55 S.Ct. 595, 606, 79 L.Ed. 1110 (1935). And we think our holding—that respondents' immediate execution on the supersedeas bond is at least "related to" the Celotex bankruptcy—is in accord with representative recent decisions of the Courts of Appeals. *See* American Hardwoods, Inc. v. Deutsche Credit Corp., 885 F.2d 621, 623 (9th Cir.1989)(finding "related to" jurisdiction where enforcement of state court judgment by creditor against debtor's guarantors would affect administration of debtor's reorganization plan); *cf.* MacArthur Co. v. Johns–Manville Corp., 837 F.2d 89, 93(2d Cir.)(noting that a bankruptcy court's injunctive powers under § 105(a) allow it to enjoin suits that "might impede the reorganization process"), *cert. denied,* 488 U.S. 868, 109 S.Ct. 176, 102 L.Ed.2d 145 (1988); In re A.H. Robins Co., 828 F.2d 1023, 1024–1026 (4th Cir.1987)(affirming bankruptcy court's § 105(a) injunction barring products liability plaintiffs from bringing actions against debtor's insurers because such actions would interfere with debtor's reorganization), *cert. denied sub nom.,* 485 U.S. 969, 108 S.Ct. 1246, 99 L.Ed.2d 444 (1988).[8]

ings are so related. * * * We thus need not (and do not) reach the question whether the granting of the Section 105 Injunction was a "core" proceeding.

8. We recognize the theoretical possibility of distinguishing between the proceeding to execute on the bond in the Fifth Circuit and the § 105 stay proceeding in the Bankruptcy Court in the Eleventh Circuit. One

Respondents, relying on our decision in Board of Governors v. MCorp Financial, 502 U.S. 32, 112 S.Ct. 459, 116 L.Ed.2d 358 (1991), contend that § 1334(b)'s statutory grant of jurisdiction must be reconciled and harmonized with Federal Rule of Civil Procedure 65.1, which provides an expedited procedure for executing on supersedeas bonds. In *MCorp,* we held that the grant of jurisdiction in § 1334(b) to district courts sitting in bankruptcy did not authorize an injunction against a regulatory proceeding, but there we relied on "the specific preclusive language" of 12 U.S.C. § 1818(i)(1) which stated that "no court shall have jurisdiction to affect by injunction or otherwise the issuance or enforcement of any [Board] notice or order." *MCorp, supra,* at 39, 42, 112 S.Ct. at 463, 465. There is no analogous statutory prohibition against enjoining the maintenance of a proceeding under Rule 65.1. That Rule provides: "Whenever these rules ... require or permit the giving of security by a party, and security is given in the form of a bond or stipulation or other undertaking with one or more sureties, each surety submits to the jurisdiction of the court and irrevocably appoints the clerk of the court as the surety's agent upon whom any papers affecting the surety's liability on the bond or undertaking may be served. The surety's liability may be enforced on motion without the necessity of an independent action.... " Fed.R.Civ.P. 65.1. This rule outlines a streamlined procedure for executing on bonds. It assures judgment creditors like respondents that they do not have to bring a separate action against sureties, and instead allows them to collect on the supersedeas bond by merely filing a motion. Just because the rule provides a simplified procedure for collecting on a bond, however, does not mean that such a procedure, like the more complicated procedure of a fullfledged law suit, cannot be stayed by a lawfully entered injunction.

Much of our discussion dealing with the jurisdiction of the Bankruptcy Court under the "related to" language of §§ 1334(b) and 157(a) is likewise applicable in determining whether or not the Bankruptcy Court's Section 105 Injunction has "only a frivolous pretense to validity." *GTE Sylvania,* 445 U.S. at 386 (internal quotation marks and citation omitted). The Fourth Circuit has upheld the merits of the Bankruptcy Court's Section 105 Injunction, *see Willis,* 978 F.2d, at 149–150, and even the Fifth Circuit in this case did not find "that the bankruptcy court in Florida was necessarily wrong." *See Edwards II,* 6 F.3d, at 321. But we need not, and do not, address whether the Bankruptcy Court acted properly in issuing the Section 105 Injunction.[9]

might argue, technically, that though the proceeding to execute on the bond is "related to" the title 11 case, the stay proceeding "arises under" title 11, or "arises in" the title 11 case. *See* In re Monroe Well Serv., Inc., 67 B.R. 746, 753 (Bkrtcy.Ct. ED Pa.1986). We need not and do not decide this question here.

9. The dissent contends that Celotex' attempts to set aside the supersedeas bond

are "patently meritless" because none of Celotex' claims can impair Northbrook's obligation to respondents. * * * That premise, however, is not so clear as to give the Section 105 Injunction "only a frivolous pretense to validity." There is authority suggesting that, in certain circumstances, transfers from the debtor to another for the benefit of a third party may be recovered from that third party. *See* In re Air Condi-

We have made clear that " '[i]t is for the court of first instance to determine the question of the validity of the law, and until its decision is reversed for error by orderly review, either by itself or by a higher court, its orders based on its decision are to be respected.' " Walker v. Birmingham, 388 U.S. 307, 314, 87 S.Ct. 1824, 1828, 18 L.Ed.2d 1210 (1967)(quoting Howat v. Kansas, 258 U.S. 181, 189–190, 42 S.Ct. 277, 281, 66 L.Ed. 550 (1922)). If respondents believed the Section 105 Injunction was improper, they should have challenged it in the Bankruptcy Court, like other similarly situated bonded judgment creditors have done. *See Celotex II*, 140 B.R. at 912. If dissatisfied with the Bankruptcy Court's ultimate decision, respondents can appeal "to the district court for the judicial district in which the bankruptcy judge is serving," see 28 U.S.C. § 158(a), and then to the Court of Appeals for the Eleventh Circuit. *See* § 158(d). Respondents chose not to pursue this course of action, but instead to collaterally attack the Bankruptcy Court's Section 105 Injunction in the Federal Courts in Texas. This they cannot be permitted to do without seriously undercutting the orderly process of the law.

The judgment of the Court of Appeals, accordingly, is reversed.

It is so ordered.

[Dissenting opinion by Justices Stevens and Ginsburg, omitted—*ed.*]

Notes and Questions

1. What is the implication of the *Celotex* decision for mass tort judgment creditors against companies that have sought bankruptcy protection? One commentator has suggested:

> The Supreme Court made it tougher for people to collect money they have won in lawsuits against companies that later seek bankruptcy-law protection from creditors.

> The high court ruled 7–2 yesterday that bankruptcy judges have authority to block a victorious plaintiff, at least for a while, from getting money from a defendant's insurance company.

> The decision could bolster former makers of asbestos products and other companies that have used the bankruptcy process to delay payment of large numbers of damage awards. It was a defeat for individuals and other creditors who won suits against such firms before the companies sought bankruptcy-law protection.

* * *

Jeffrey White, who filed a "friend of the court brief" in the case for the Association of Trial Lawyers of America, warned that the ruling could allow companies to "hide under the bankruptcy law tent from

tioning, Inc. of Stuart, 845 F.2d 293, 296–299 (11th Cir.), *cert. denied*, 488 U.S. 993, 109 S.Ct. 557, 102 L.Ed.2d 584 (1988); In re Compton Corp., 831 F.2d 586, 595 (1987), *modified on other grounds*, 835 F.2d 584 (5th Cir.1988). Although we offer no opinion on the merits of that authority or on whether it fits the facts here, it supports our conclusion that the stay was not frivolous.

plaintiffs who have won damages." He added that "for people suffering asbestos-related illnesses, justice delayed is justice denied."

Robert Millner, a bankruptcy lawyer representing Celotex in the Edwards case, Northbrook Property & Casualty Insurance Co., countered that the ruling was good news for all parties with an interest in a company's reorganizing and paying off its debt. "This is the first expression by the Supreme Court recognizing bankruptcy-court power to issue third-party injunctions" that temporarily shield insurers or others involved in a bankruptcy proceeding, he said. "Protection of insurers is often paramount in return for the insurers' contribution" to the larger reorganization plan, he added.

Paul M. Barrett, *Justices Make It Harder to Collect Awards,* Wall St. J., April 20, 1995, at B6.

Chapter XIV

COOPERATIVE FEDERALISM

A. INTERSYSTEM COOPERATION

Review William W. Schwarzer, Nancy E. Weiss, and Alan Hirsch, *Judicial Federalism in Action: Coordination of Litigation in State and Federal Courts,* Chapter IV.B, section 4, *supra.*

B. INTERSTATE COOPERATION

Review materials at Chapter III, Mass Torts and Federalism, *supra.*

1. STATE TRANSFER OF LITIGATION

EDWARD H. COOPER, INTERSTATE CONSOLIDATION: A COMPARISON OF THE ALI PROJECT WITH THE UNIFORM TRANSFER OF LITIGATION ACT

54 La.L.Rev. 897 (1994).

I. INTRODUCTION

The Uniform Transfer of Litigation Act (UTLA) was undertaken for purposes simpler than the mass consolidation of multiparty, multiforum litigation. It seeks to create an effective tool that can be used to reduce some of the artificial barriers that tradition has erected around the sovereign separateness of the many different court systems in this country. The fact of separate sovereignty must be recognized, however, and to this end consent of both transferring and receiving courts is required. Within the consent requirement, transfer from the court system of one sovereign to the court system of another can improve on present practices in many settings. A court that lacks subject matter or personal jurisdiction can transfer rather than dismiss. An inconvenient court can transfer to a convenient court rather than invoke forum non conveniens or perhaps struggle on with the litigation. Should complementing federal legislation be enacted, transfer can work better than dismissal when supplemental jurisdiction is declined, or when a state

1126

court concludes that a dispute lies in exclusive federal jurisdiction. Of course an effective structure must address the incidental questions that arise when one sovereign's court system transfers jurisdiction, in whole or in part, to another sovereign's court system. Good answers to these questions are important. Clear answers are even more important. The answers given by the UTLA will be described below.

These simpler purposes, however, did not obscure the opportunities for effecting consolidation of related litigation brought in different court systems. The structural problems are the same, and the effective answers are the same in dealing with many ordinary situations. A contract dispute between a Michigan seller and an Ohio buyer, for example, could give rise to closely related actions in Michigan and Ohio courts. Transfer for consolidation may serve the interests of both court systems and at least one of the parties. Beyond these ordinary situations, transfer also may provide an effective answer for more complex situations involving large numbers of related lawsuits. These situations too were considered. The succinct statement of reasons for transfer in Section 104, indeed, includes "the public interest in securing a single litigation and disposition of related matters." The comment states that this factor "establishes a starting point for consolidation in state court systems of multiparty, multiforum disputes."

The American Law Institute *Complex Litigation Project* was well under way when the National Conference of Commissioners on Uniform State Laws Committee began drafting work on the UTLA. The ALI Project had identified the problems that must be surmounted in consolidating large numbers of dispersed lawsuits and had outlined tentative answers. The UTLA Committee deliberately chose to put aside the complex problems that arise in designing a system that asks states to consent in advance to a system that, without specific later consent, can wrest litigation from the courts of an unwilling state and thrust it into the courts of another unwilling state. Any system that has this capacity must be built with great care and no small measure of prophetic vision. The ALI model, sketched in Section 4.02 and fleshed out in the Reporter's Study, seeks to address the central concerns. An Interstate Complex Litigation Panel (ICLP) would be established, composed of one judge from each participating state. The ICLP would have power to direct transfer and consolidation of state court actions without consent of the transferring or receiving courts. Standards for transfer and consolidation are set. Procedures are developed for making transfer and consolidation decisions, for review of those decisions, and for review of some decisions by the transferee court. The managerial powers of the transferee court are defined. Personal jurisdiction and choice-of-law problems are addressed.

The UTLA model is much simpler than the complex ALI model. It also may seem less threatening. Transfer requires consent of both transferring and receiving courts. No state need, against its will, send its litigants elsewhere. Nor must any state, against its will, assume the burden of litigation brought elsewhere. Each state is assured that the transfer determination is made by courts intimately familiar with all of the details of each individual case and with the procedural and systemic advantages of litigation in each system.

The UTLA model, albeit more modest, is intended to serve the same purposes as the ALI model in dealing with multiple parallel actions. It would be difficult to quarrel with the general standard set out in Section 1(a)(2) of the Reporter's Study, authorizing transfer and consolidation to promote "the just, efficient, and fair conduct of the actions" when consolidation "is superior to their separate adjudication." Although there is no central authority that can give guidance, significant consolidation remains possible. Often there will be a natural focus for potential consolidation. Common disasters provide the most obvious examples: an airplane crashes, a hotel burns, a structure collapses. Usually there is a defined geographic location for the event, and usually much of the related litigation will be filed in the local courts. There is an obvious receiving court for litigation filed in other states. The receiving court, moreover, may be willing to undertake the burden of added cases—particularly if consolidation does not entail responsibility for trying individual causation and damage issues—because the added burden is not great, and consolidation helps the court to achieve a single, consistent resolution of common issues under a single choice of law. Significant measures of consolidation may be accomplished under this model, and the experience may support creation of more ambitious programs in the future.

The common disaster example illustrates a deeper problem. Common disaster litigation arising from a single discrete event may represent the outer limits of consolidated adjudication through adversary procedure. Even with hundreds of plaintiffs and several defendants and insurers, several characteristics make effective disposition possible. There is a well-defined occurrence. Most of those injured, if not quite all, can be identified. Resolution of common liability issues often can pave the way for manageable disposition of individual issues, ordinarily by settlement. The challenges presented by widespread injuries dispersed in time and place are much more daunting. Asbestos litigation is simply the most aggravated and familiar example of many product and process liability problems. Most of these problems are not fit for disposition under current substantive doctrines of tort, contract, or property law. Even if these doctrines were intrinsically satisfactory, adversary judicial procedure is not. It has proved difficult to develop plausible means to resolve common liability issues promptly and effectively against defendants. It will prove far more difficult to develop plausible means of resolution in favor of defendants. Beyond that point, we have found no means of achieving any measure of rationally comparable treatment of individual issues. Our model insists on individual assessments of exposure, causation, and damages. Common disposition, whether the labels are those of class actions or consolidation of nominally individual actions, cannot provide individual control of common liability determinations and cannot provide individual consideration and disposition of individual issues. Individual claimants are participants—often quite remote participants—in the processing, not the adjudication, of their disputes. The ALI model is one for the relatively short-term future, and perforce assumes the continuation of present procedures. The present procedural capacities of any court system, state or federal, provide a weak and sinking foundation for the imposing structure needed to effect massive consolidation.

One fundamental contrast between the ALI project and the UTLA model, then, is that the UTLA does not make any wholesale assumptions about the adequacy of adversary judicial procedure to resolve truly massive consolidated litigation. Consolidation will occur only when both the several transferring courts and the receiving court make independent judgments that the resulting package is within the institutional and procedural capacities of the receiving court.

II. Choice of Merits Law

The ALI Project proposes a sophisticated and elegant set of choice-of-law rules for consolidated proceedings. Such rules, generalized to other settings, may provide the way out of the contemporary choice-of-law morass. * * * Such rules also will stimulate vigorous debate and disagreement, as well demonstrated by these articles. The UTLA deliberately refrained from answering these questions. This reticence was due in part to the different setting. The UTLA addresses the full range of noncriminal litigation. A choice-of-law code for the UTLA would have to reach many more questions than are addressed by the ALI Project. Another reason for reticence may be that it will prove easier to reach agreement on relatively fixed rules for the truly mammoth consolidations addressed by the ALI proposal. It is difficult to avoid deep dissatisfaction with the present system. Hundreds or thousands of people may be injured in the same way by a common course of conduct followed by a single defendant or group of defendants. Their claims may be determined by bodies of law that frequently vary in subtle but important detail and that at times vary in more fundamental ways. It is difficult to understand why some should be well compensated, others less well compensated, and still others denied any compensation. The sheer absurdity of the situation may force grudging surrender to rules that dim this sorry spectacle. There is less obvious pressure to regularize choice-of-law practice in smaller-scale disputes. Desirable transfers might often be thwarted if transfer required both transferring and receiving courts to surrender to a dictated choice of law.

Rather than a set of rules, choice-of-law concerns are addressed by the UTLA in an open-ended way. The approach is largely controlled by a central feature of the UTLA structure. Transfer carries control of the litigation to the receiving court. Divided authority is obviously unworkable. There must not be any opportunity for the parties to play one court off against the other, nor any fear that a transfer may come undone if the transferring court is displeased with the receiving court's actions. The transferring court cannot even impose binding conditions on the receiving court. Instead, Section 105 allows it to state "terms" of transfer; Section 208 permits the receiving court to depart from these terms for good cause.

Beyond the problem of divided control lies the prospect that proceedings in the receiving court may develop new information that affects any earlier disposition that might have been made by the transferring court. The affiliating circumstances that inform a choice of law may not be fully developed at the time of transfer.

Within this structure, choice-of-law considerations can be addressed in several ways. The first occasion will be the motion to transfer. The transferring court should consider the likely choice of law in determining whether to transfer. A conclusion that forum law should apply is likely to defeat transfer entirely, or to limit transfer to defined purposes such as consolidated discovery. A conclusion that a particular law should be applied, whether that of the transferring court or some other jurisdiction, can be expressed as a term of transfer. The receiving court likewise should consider the likely choice of law. Choice of its own law would provide a strong reason for accepting transfer. If a particular choice is stated as a term of transfer, the receiving court should accept transfer only if that term is likely to prove acceptable. Once transfer is accepted, however, the receiving court must be free to reconsider the choice of law as the case develops. An eventual determination that the case should be controlled by the law of the transferring court may justify transfer back under Section 217, but the disruption of repeated transfers weighs against transfer back unless the content of the controlling law is significantly uncertain.

III. Personal Jurisdiction

Recognition of personal jurisdiction is tightly bound up with the choice-of-law process. An exercise of jurisdiction inevitably imposes the court itself as forum, a choice that may be more important than any other. The forum administers whatever choice-of-law rules may be followed, whether imposed from outside as suggested by Section 9 of the ALI Reporter's Study or followed in the free will of the forum. Once the law is chosen, it is interpreted and applied by the forum.

The UTLA and the *Complex Litigation Project* reflect substantially similar views of the impact of interstate transfer and consolidation on personal jurisdiction. Consolidation of related actions in a single court may justify assertion of personal jurisdiction over an action and over parties that could not be reached if the forum sought to reach that action as a detached unit. This conclusion is influenced by the prospect that consolidation often will reduce the burdens borne by individual parties. It is more heavily influenced, however, by the public advantages that flow from consolidation. Consistent outcomes are perhaps more important in this regard than the savings of judicial resources.

The means used by the UTLA to implement this expansive view of jurisdiction is the open-ended long-arm provision of Section 203. If the transferring court has subject matter and personal jurisdiction, it can transfer to a court that could not independently command personal jurisdiction under its ordinary domestic rules. No attempt is made to enact a phrase that might capture the constitutional constraints that will limit this jurisdiction.

Application of Section 203 can be illustrated by a simple illustration, elaborated from the notes to Section 8, comment f of the ALI Reporter's Study. A Rhode Island plaintiff is injured in a Rhode Island accident involving an automobile she purchased from a Rhode Island dealer and had serviced by a Rhode Island mechanic. She brings suit in Rhode Island against the manufacturer, the dealer, and the mechanic. Consolidated litigation involving the same model automobile is pending in one of two state courts Massachusetts court sitting in Boston or a California court sitting in San Francisco. Transfer of the entire Rhode Island litigation to Massachusetts may be appropriate. Transfer of the claim against the manufacturer to California may impose untoward burdens on the plaintiff even apart from assimilation of her personal claim into the mass proceeding. Transfer of the claim against the dealer, whose only connection with California may be selling automobiles made by a manufacturer who also sells automobiles to dealers in California, may be even more obviously untoward. Transfer of the claim against the mechanic may be beyond reasonable contemplation.

The UTLA addresses the risks of improvident transfer by the structure of the transfer process. Transfer requires an order of the transferring court, which can undertake a case-specific inquiry into the burdens imposed by transfer. The transferring court also can make an informed appraisal of the costs of continuing with the action and an intelligent guess as to the benefits of transfer and consolidation. It is required by Section 104 to consider the interest of each plaintiff in selecting the forum. A decision to transfer part or all of an action provides an impressive assurance of probable fairness. Transfer also requires an order of the receiving court, which reconsiders the same factors as the transferring court from the vantage of its own familiarity with the proceedings, whether the receiving court is at the threshold of possible consolidation or already has consolidated a number of other cases. This double scrutiny should support jurisdiction in many circumstances that would not support a unilateral assertion of jurisdiction by a single court acting in stand-alone litigation. It also may provide greater assurances of fairness than the decisions of a centralized panel, such as the Interstate Complex Litigation Panel (ICLP) envisioned by the Reporter's Study.

The UTLA reaches an additional circumstance that occasionally may prove useful in dealing with large-scale consolidation. Section 103 permits a court that lacks personal jurisdiction to transfer to a court that has personal jurisdiction. Ordinarily this provision will be invoked in ordinary litigation, both when the plaintiff has overreached as to all defendants and when it is desirable to split the action by transferring rather than dismissing as to some defendants. The same need may arise, however, if a court holding consolidated proceedings concludes that it lacks personal jurisdiction as to some claims involving some parties.

IV. Limitations

The only explicit choice-of-law provision in the UTLA is found in the limitations provisions of Section 209. Section 209 prohibits the receiving court from dismissing "because of a statute of limitations a claim that would not be dismissed on that ground by the transferring court." This provision does not carry with the case all of the limitations doctrines of the transferring court. A court that would apply its own shorter limitations period as a matter of "procedure," for example, can transfer to a court that would apply a longer period. Because under Section 210 transfer takes the filing date in the transferring court to the receiving court, the result may be that transfer preserves a claim that would be barred as untimely if a new action must be filed in the receiving court.

The ALI Project sets out a somewhat similar limitations rule in Section 6.04. Section 6.04 invokes the limitations law of the state whose law is chosen to govern mass tort or mass contract claims. But it adds an exception that if that law would bar a claim that was timely where filed, the claim will be remanded to the transferor court. Apparently, remand is designed to discourage forum shopping by denying the benefits of consolidation to plaintiffs who delay filing beyond the period allowed by the law chosen to govern the claim.

It is a fair question whether either provision is quite right. For present purposes, the important question is whether plaintiffs should continue to enjoy the power that comes from the willingness of many courts to treat limitations as a procedural matter, automatically referred to the law of the forum. Under the UTLA, a court that has been chosen only for its longer limitations period may feel bound to apply its own period only because it feels caught in this traditional rule. It might prefer to transfer to a more convenient court for an independent determination of the limitations law that should govern the claim. That option is foreclosed by Section 209. If transfer is otherwise desirable, however, at least it remains possible to conduct the litigation in the court best situated to overcome the problems arising from delayed filing. Under the ALI approach, the case must be shuttled back to a court that may have no interest in the dispute beyond the power of general personal jurisdiction and the laxity of traditional limitations choice rules.

* * *

VII. Conclusion

This brief comparison is designed to demonstrate the difficulty of the task undertaken by the ALI model. The UTLA system is not simple. Many of the potential difficulties of transfer are reduced, however, by the basic structure. Much can be accomplished by requiring the conjoint consent of transferring and receiving courts and by requiring that controlling authority be surrendered to the receiving court.

The UTLA model does not provide a means for effecting consolidation as complete as can be accomplished by the ALI model. Potential transferring courts often will deny transfer. Transfer to several different receiving courts may be more likely than with the ALI model. Choice-of-law determinations are left to the unguided judgment of the receiving court, which may find it difficult to rise beyond the severe limits of all present choice-of-law models to respond to the just needs for coherent and consistent adjustment of interests affected by a common course of events.

The urge to press beyond the limits of the UTLA model, however, may properly be tempered by contemplating the difficulties that arise from any model that seeks to compel more thorough-going consolidation. Any system that asks both sending and receiving states to surrender the transfer decision to an interstate tribunal must provide persuasive answers to many troubling questions. The most troubling question is whether any court anywhere, state or federal, has the capacity to administer mammoth consolidated proceedings. The ambitious ALI model does not attempt to offer any new answers to this question. Perhaps the next most troubling question is whether an interstate consolidation tribunal can be expected to focus as clearly as need be on the specific fairness concerns that attend transfer as to each party to each related action. Transfer determinations by each court entertaining a related action inevitably will lead to fewer transfers and less consolidation; it is far from clear whether that is a bad thing. Among the other troubling questions, the difficulties of defining appeal jurisdiction stand out. Massive consolidation of common liability questions often would not be possible without subsequent dispersion of individual questions of causation and damages. There is no good answer to the ensuing questions of appeal jurisdiction. If the ALI study has proposed the least bad answer, it remains fair to weigh the ensuing costs in the cumulating balance of difficulties entailed by a centralized system for coercive consolidation.

These doubts do not amount to a demonstration that the ALI model is ill-advised. It provides a comprehensive study of the problems that must be encountered in any system for widespread consolidation of related litigation pending in different state court systems. The answers proposed often are ingenious. Some variations of many of these answers may be essential components of any workable system. Only a centralized tribunal, for example, can ensure widespread consolidation, and only a centralized tribunal can develop a sustained tradition and common-law rules. For the present, however, it may be wiser to work for general adoption of the UTLA and development of the experience it can provide with intersystem transfer. There still is something to be said for sturdy simplicity in the face of ingenious complexity.

2. STATES AS PREFERRED FORUMS FOR RESOLVING MASS TORT

MARK C. WEBER, COMPLEX LITIGATION AND THE STATE COURTS: CONSTITUTIONAL AND PRACTICAL ADVANTAGES OF THE STATE FORUM OVER THE FEDERAL FORUM IN MASS TORT CASES

21 Hastings Const.L.Q. 215–220; 253–274 (1994).

There is a paradox in current proposals for law reform in the field of complex litigation. Numerous authorities have proposed the transfer of mass tort cases, such as those that concern mass disasters and widely distributed product injuries, from dispersed state and federal trial courts to consolidated proceedings in the federal district courts. These authorities include the American Law Institute, the American Bar Association, the House Judiciary Committee, the Federal Courts Study Committee, and leading academics. The paradox is that the federal courts are poorly suited to handle those cases for a number of readily apparent reasons.

First, though federal district courts are required under the *Erie* doctrine to apply state law to these cases, they are unable to contribute to its sensible development and application in the mass tort area. Any attempt to anticipate changes in state law would be unlikely to make a positive contribution to legal development because of the political and popular isolation that marks the institutional perspective of the federal judiciary. The alternative of ignoring the *Erie* doctrine and creating a federal common law of mass tort would violate federalism principles. The policy and constitutional underpinnings of *Erie,* as well as the majoritarian character of elected state courts, support the maintenance of the *Erie* doctrine in the field of mass torts. Indeed, most of the major proposals suggest retaining it.

Second, the federal courts should not allocate their scarce resources of time and effort to mass tort cases, which must be controlled by state law. The federal courts' expertise lies in interpreting federal statutory and constitutional provisions. Just as their political isolation makes federal courts unsuited for developing state tort law, it makes them the best protectors of individual rights; they should spend their time on civil rights and other federal law cases.

Several proponents of change recognize these problems in their proposals for federal consolidation of mass tort actions. They view them as the price to pay for the important judicial economy advantage of consolidation. But there is an unexamined premise to this reasoning: that consolidation must take place in a federal, as opposed to a state, forum.

State courts are now highly desirable forums to consolidate tort cases from other states. Barriers to aggregation of cases in state courts have fallen; the larger states and many smaller ones have made changes in rules and practice to handle cases of extreme complexity in an efficient manner.

A number of doctrinal developments have facilitated these changes. State court territorial jurisdiction has broadened. The doctrine of forum non conveniens has been all but eliminated in Texas and some other states. Restrictive venue rules have disappeared. Specific procedures exist to identify and expedite cases that are likely to become complex.

Efforts have already begun to promote transfer and consolidation in state courts. In 1991, the Commissioners of Uniform State Laws promulgated a uniform act on interstate consolidation; at least one state has already adopted it. The American Law Institute's proposal for transfer and consolidation of cases in federal courts includes a proposal for interstate consolidation of cases in state courts, and thus provides an additional model for future developments. So do existing interstate cooperation statutes, such as the Parental Kidnapping Prevention Act. Finally, consolidating mass tort cases in state courts may be the path of least political resistance in efforts to achieve the efficiencies of combined treatment of common issues.

Nevertheless, some doctrinal problems will hamper any form of state court consolidation of cases whose complexity comes from interstate injuries or disasters. Some limits still exist on territorial jurisdiction and venue. No consistent system exists among states to defer to other states' assertions of jurisdiction, by application of abatement or abstention. Existing full faith and credit doctrine makes the first final decision the binding one, and so creates incentives for races to the courthouse between potential litigants. Litigants may be skeptical about the impartiality and skill of the judiciary in many states. Each of these problems has its own solutions, however, and all of them combined are not as difficult as the problems with federal transfer and consolidation.

Enhanced consolidation of mass tort cases in state courts could take one of two forms. In the first form, each state would act independently to strengthen its ability to handle complex tort litigation, increasing its willingness to take jurisdiction of cases filed within its borders and consolidating them into single proceedings. At the same time, courts could use door-closing doctrines to discourage the filing of cases that would detract from the efficiency advantages of larger, ongoing suits in other states. The second form would be the creation of an interstate compact and a uniform law in each participating state to permit the voluntary or compulsory transfer of cases filed in one state to magnet forums handling the consolidated proceedings in another state. Each of the two approaches has merits and demerits. However, either would be superior to the federal alternative.

* * *

The state forum is the undiscussed and undeveloped alternative to federal consolidation of mass torts. Its potential for achieving efficiency gains, while not disrupting important political and judicial structures, make the state forum superior for mass tort consolidation.

* * *

II. STATE COURT CONSOLIDATION: ADVANTAGES AND OPPORTUNITIES

Aggregating cases from courts now in various states into a single state court forum carries the judicial economy and consistency advantages of federal consolidation. These advantages flow from consolidation itself. Consolidation in a state forum, however, may confer additional advantages from new doctrinal developments and recently improved procedures for handling complex cases in several states. Moreover, improvements in state judicial systems that would facilitate just adjudication of complex cases may be easier to obtain than expansions of federal jurisdiction.

A. The Advantage of Transfer and Consolidation

The flaws in the idea of consolidation in a federal forum should not obscure the real benefits of consolidating individual cases into larger proceedings. The primary benefit is efficiency. Multiple cases to resolve the same factual and legal issues entail multiple costs to litigants, attorneys, witnesses, and courts. The advantage of consolidation is a familiar one, and was a primary impetus behind the liberal joinder and class action provisions of the original Federal Rules of Civil Procedure, as well as the still more liberal 1966 revisions. The objective was to make single proceedings out of multiple lawsuits. Besides eliminating duplication, consolidation can also enhance efficiency by allowing greater opportunity for the use of sampling techniques.

A secondary advantage of aggregation is a greater likelihood of consistent results in factually similar cases. The same factfinder is more likely to be consistent with itself than multiple factfinders would be with each other. Uniformity of result in mass tort cases is a major selling point for proponents of a federal common law of products liability. Nevertheless, consistency may be real or false. Differences in law that affect liability or damages for various plaintiffs should yield different, not similar, results in their cases. Consolidation of cases in the appropriate state forums promotes uniformity of result when the facts and the applicable law are the same, while permitting the difference in result that different state law causes. The disuniform results will enable states' voters and politicians to make more informed choices whether and how to modify their tort law.

Even efficiency should not be pursued too far. Individual fairness and participation interests may work in the opposite direction, as do some diseconomies of scale. Depending on the situation, consolidation into several proceedings, rather than a single one, may best meet the combined goals of efficiency, appropriate consistency, fairness, and participation. Nevertheless, the haphazard consolidation now available under the federal class action rule, the federal transfer statutes, and abstention and preclusion doctrines diminish fairness and participation without obtaining the full advantages of consolidation. The federal class action rule is drafted to exclude ordinary tort cases. Even if it were revised, changes in jurisdiction statutes would be needed to make it a true consolidation vehicle. These changes, as noted above, would be unwise. Section 1404 of Title 28 merely permits suits to be transferred to places they could have been brought in the first place, which may not be a single forum. Section 1407, in practice, is more flexible, but, once again, federal consolidation is full of difficulties. Preclusion was once thought to hold great promise as a means of promoting efficiency, but the reluctance of courts to apply preclusion in tort cases has limited its value. A federal court may abstain in favor of parallel activity in other federal courts or in the state courts, but this voluntary action does not guarantee the accumulation of those suits that ought to be heard together in the forum where they most logically would be heard. Enhanced state court consolidation would be preferable.

B. Capabilities of State Forums

State forums will frequently be those in which mass tort cases most logically would be heard. Nevertheless some question remains whether state courts are capable of hearing them and rendering fair decisions. A range of recent developments that have improved state courts' capacity to resolve mass tort cases suggests that they are.

Many state courts have adopted case management procedures, some of which compare favorably with federal court procedures for handling complex cases. One example is New Jersey, where a report from the mid–1980s told that magistrates supervised discovery and judges handled trials in complex asbestos cases under a rigid schedule of plans and reporting. At the same time, the federal court in New Jersey, faced with reluctance by judges to accept transferred cases and to supervise discovery aggressively, was "at a standstill in dispositions." Joinder has been liberalized in many states to facilitate consolidation. State class action rules are in place and may be more amenable to mass tort claims than the federal class action rule. States have successfully used bifurcation of issues and trial of representative cases to dispose of complex tort litigation. States have also established deferral registries for claims that are not yet ripe. Although deferral enhances both justice and efficiency, federal courts may lack the authority to take this step.

State courts have acquired extensive experience in complex injury and environmental suits. What is thought to be the most complex civil toxic-waste lawsuit ever heard in an American court is currently pending before a state judge in California. A Maryland Circuit Court heard the largest civil asbestos trial in the country, with 8,555 cases consolidated into it, in 1992. An action with more than 700 consolidated asbestos cases recently proceeded to partial settlement and partial adjudication in New York.

Procedural uniformity may be an advantage of federal consolidation over consolidation in the state courts, but that argument cannot be pressed too far. Not only is there a trend towards uniformity in state practice rules, but there are significant disuniformities in federal practice. Part of the disuniformity stems from the federal courts' practice tending to resemble local state court practice. A more potent centrifugal force in federal practice is the recent proliferation of local practice rules. Most recently, the Civil Justice Reform Act has spawned advisory groups to propose civil justice expense and delay reduction plans, which may turn the proliferation of variant local rules into an explosion. Of course, differences between state and federal practice that stem from state initiatives to facilitate handling mass tort cases are hardly an advantage of federal consolidation.

C. Political Considerations

The various calls for expanded federal court jurisdiction over consolidated mass tort cases all would require Congressional action. Congress, however, will not necessarily be persuaded by the same policy concerns that may move academics and judges. Perhaps the role of legal commentators is not to predict the likelihood of political success for their proposals, but anyone advocating a reform must make a rough prediction of what is likely to succeed politically if only to determine where to expend scholarly resources.

Recent experience suggests that political resources would be better spent supporting reforms aimed at enhanced state court consolidation rather than expanded federal mass tort consolidation efforts. Proposals to expand federal consolidation gain their strongest support among elite groups of lawyers and politicians, but fail when they confront more broadly representative bodies. The American Bar Association proposal sailed through committee, but could not command a majority among the House of Delegates; even a resolution to support legislation for federal consolidation of mass accidents failed to pass. House Bill 3406 succeeded in the House Judiciary Committee but failed on the Senate floor. The costs of federal consolidation proposals fall on specific groups and individuals, while judicial economy benefits the United States population as a whole. Consequently, only a strong consensus on terms of a proposal will enable it to survive the legislative process.

Important special interest groups fear federal consolidation. Consumers worry that it is the first step to a federal torts or products law that would diminish liability and curtail incentives for safety. Trial lawyers fear decreases in liability, but they are also concerned about the impact on practice, even if the underlying law were to remain unchanged. Federal courts are often thought to be the domain of large firms, rather than solo or small-firm practitioners. Many lawyers prefer the state courts, which they know intimately, rather than the sometimes forbidding federal tribunals.

Unless there is a change in underlying law, the concerns of the consumers seem groundless. The concerns of trial lawyers and small-scale practitioners are merely an expression of self-interest. The real reasons to oppose federal consolidation are the concerns about institutional competence, democracy, and allocation of resources. But the existence of widespread concern matters, even if the concerns are misplaced. If federal consolidation will not succeed, or will succeed only at a tremendous political cost, politicians will abandon it. Reformers should explore other ways to obtain the same advantages. Solving the apparent problems of state court consolidation may be the best way.

III. State Court Consolidation: Problems and Solutions

A number of existing procedural doctrines may make interstate transfer and consolidation into state forums troublesome. Nevertheless, law reform efforts, many of them already well underway, will ease nearly all of these difficulties. The problems are both doctrinal and practical.

A. Doctrinal Problems of State Court Consolidation

Some problems with interstate transfer and consolidation derive from outmoded or otherwise troublesome legal doctrines. These include territorial limits on personal jurisdiction, forum non conveniens restrictions, choice of law, possible jurisdictional conflicts among states, and potential conflict with the Constitution's interstate compacts clause and the Tenth Amendment. Although the problems are vexing, they are amenable to resolution either at the judicial or legislative level.

1. Fourteenth Amendment Due Process and Territorial Authority

If a court cannot exercise jurisdiction over anyone outside its boundaries, it will face insurmountable obstacles trying to consolidate a national products injury case; it will have difficulties even with a mass disaster case when one or more of the actors is an out-of-state entity. This problem is the main reason that reformers argue for federal, rather than state, consolidation. Nevertheless, both state law and federal constitutional law can be, and are being, modified to make territorial jurisdiction an insignificant barrier.

Although state law may limit territorial authority of state courts, the restrictions are subject to reform efforts by legislatures and by the courts themselves. A trend exists to expand the authority to the boundaries set by the Due Process Clause of the Fourteenth Amendment. Some states have done so by legislation, others by judicial interpretation of vaguely-worded long-arm statutes. Legislatures and courts who want to retain control over the development of their own tort law have a significant incentive to permit broad territorial jurisdiction in mass tort cases. Otherwise parties could be forced by jurisdictional constraints to litigate the same matter elsewhere.

Federal constitutional restrictions on state court jurisdiction are also amenable to reform. A general trend towards expansion of state court jurisdiction began almost as soon as the ink was dry on *Pennoyer v. Neff*. Through the expansion of *in rem* jurisdiction and the development of concepts of implied consent and corporate presence, courts have eroded state sovereignty-based restrictions. The interests of the states and the goal of efficient functioning of the judicial system as a whole have justified the expansion. The Supreme Court has cited judicial efficiency in upholding broad territorial jurisdiction in state court class actions. In

Phillips Petroleum Co. v. Shutts, the Court noted that plaintiffs involuntarily brought into a suit do not have as strong an objection as defendants involuntarily brought to another jurisdiction, and held that general procedural due process is the touchstone for analysis.

Furthermore, according to many authorities, the due process limits on state courts apply equally to federal courts. Federal Rule of Civil Procedure 4(f)'s limit on federal court service of process has prevented this objection from receiving full development in the courts, but a federal consolidation procedure with nationwide service of process would draw the fire. If the question comes down to one of fairness, convenience, or even reasonable expectations based on past practice, the limits on personal jurisdiction of a state or federal court should be the same for any consolidated proceeding.

Consolidation in a single state court may require other state courts to render themselves inhospitable to claimants who would rather sue there. State courts may impose restrictions on the free choice of litigants. The state creates the cause of action, and may provide that it arises only when the plaintiff observes procedures such as submitting to the jurisdiction of a different state. The Supreme Court has held that states may limit the scope of tort liability by analogous means, such as tolling rules that depend on service of process, or immunities that limit the classes of permissible defendants. Waiver of jurisdictional objections to counterclaims is another widely accepted condition of plaintiff's filing a cause of action in a state's courts. States interested in promoting a rational system of state court consolidation should require as a precondition to filing suit that the litigant has been excluded from a consolidated action in another state that plaintiff could conveniently join.

States may not subject causes of action to procedures that unfairly deny notice and hearing rights. Thus interstate transfer and consolidation procedures will still need to accommodate geographic considerations that compromise the ability to appear and prosecute one's case. The due process requirements in this context should be no different than those that would apply to federal courts consolidating complex litigation. In either case, travel costs that would defeat the right to present one's case violate due process. In either case reducing the duties of the distant plaintiff would prevent a violation of due process.

In *Burnham v. Superior Court,* the Supreme Court reaffirmed a state's power to assert personal jurisdiction over a defendant within its territory. *Burnham,* however, does not present an obstacle to state court consolidation of mass tort cases. *Burnham* may mark a return to sovereignty reasoning in cases that consider the scope of state court territorial authority. The plurality opinion stated that continuously observed traditional rules of territorial jurisdiction—which state sovereignty underlies—satisfy due process. This reasoning does not give rise to any valid objection to interstate transfer and consolidation. If the objection is based on sovereignty, the state court, as the organ of the sovereign, may waive it by agreeing to transfer the case to another forum. While the individual litigant does not have power to waive the sovereign's prerogative, the sovereign itself does. Sovereignty doctrine is often thought of as a restriction on the reach of state courts. Whatever effect *Burnham* has on sovereignty doctrine, however, the application in that case actually expanded the jurisdiction of the state court by giving broad approval to transient service of process. Indeed, the opinion declares that continually-used traditional exercises of jurisdiction satisfy due process, without saying anything about what fails to satisfy due process.

Moreover, a majority of the Court has not embraced the return to sovereignty ideas. A group of justices of equal size to that endorsing the plurality opinion in *Burnham* relied on concepts of fairness to support the assertion of state court jurisdiction in the case. Fairness concepts would make the application of territorial restrictions uniform in the state and federal courts. Those ideas would also allow for an expansion of jurisdiction to accommodate serious interests of the state and the judicial system, such as state court consolidation of mass tort cases.

An alternative possibility for achieving the same result of expanded state court territorial authority would be for Congress to authorize nationwide service of process for state courts handling mass tort cases. Congress has authorized nationwide service in some actions brought under federal jurisdiction that is concurrent with state court jurisdiction. Courts are divided whether this congressional action overrides restrictive state long-arm statutes or expands the state jurisdiction otherwise available under the minimum contacts test. Because minimum contacts applies only to defendants, and the test is flexible to accommodate interests like consolidation, minimum contacts should not create a serious difficulty.

2. Forum Non Conveniens and Venue

The state law of forum non conveniens has undergone major changes in the last generation so that it now will rarely present a serious obstacle to interstate consolidation of mass torts. The country's third-largest state has effectively abolished forum non conveniens. Other states have greatly liberalized the doctrine in recent years. State venue law may impose some restrictions, although venue laws that permit suit to be heard where any properly joined defendant is found will hardly present serious obstacles to the location of controversies with many defendants. Unlike current federal statutes, state law does not necessarily require that cases transferred in-state be tried where they could have been brought in the first instance. Of course, both forum non conveniens and venue are subject to legislative revision by the states. The legislatures might adopt broad rules only for consolidated cases without otherwise disrupting the restrictions currently in place.

3. Choice of Law

Most proposals for federal consolidation include a federal uniform choice of law standard. Actions consolidated into a single, national magnet forum all but require a single choice of law. It is hard to imagine a jury keeping straight fifty, or even a dozen, different legal rules to be applied to different plaintiffs on different issues presented at trial. No federal choice of law rule exists, however, and present doctrine under the federal consolidation statutes requires the application of the choice of law rules of the state in which the transferred action was filed, guaranteeing a multiplicity of rules in a consolidated action. Hence, the reformers propose the creation of a single rule for consolidated federal cases.

State courts, of course, have their own choice of law rules, and are quite experienced with applying them. Thus if consolidation takes place by means of state courts simply rejecting cases when the litigants can join in ongoing litigation in another state, there would be no need for a uniform choice of law rule. However, it may be that state courts could never obtain the greatest practical advantage from consolidation of similar litigation unless they accept cases transferred from other state or federal forums. Even in this instance, the states need not adopt the same choice of law rules. The application of another state's choice of law would be another factor for litigants to consider if their transfer decision is to be voluntary, and another for the judge to consider if it were compulsory. In either case, the scope of consolidation may diminish somewhat, but one should not ignore the advantage of consolidating one thousand cases into one in each of a dozen interested forum states. Moreover, manageability may be greater in a dozen consolidated cases that go along in parallel than in one giant case in a single forum. If one were willing to accept the drawbacks—largely the damage to federalism—of a uniform choice of law, Congress could create one for state courts to use when they handle transferred or otherwise consolidated mass tort cases.

State courts should have no more difficulty applying other states' law in mass tort cases than they do in other cases. But a serious problem lies in the fact that the courts of one state will need to apply, and thus necessarily to develop, foreign states' law, negating some of the will-of-the-majority and adaptation-to-local-conditions advantages of state, rather than federal, transfer and consolidation. If it is undesirable to have federal judges, even those drawn from the state, developing a state's mass tort law, it is also unwise to have judges of another state developing the law.

The short response to this objection would begin by noting the strong tendency among states using the *Restatement (Second) of Conflict of Laws* to apply their own law to issues of liability and damages in tort cases. If no mechanism exists to transfer cases from state court to state court around the country, state courts should feel free to apply their own law to the consolidated cases of all those who opted to sue within the forum. This should occur even if the choices were constrained by other states discouraging the litigants from filing in those forums.

A somewhat more elaborate response would apply if states adopted a transfer and consolidation mechanism: the mechanism they adopt should take the tendency to apply forum state law into account. More specifically, cases should be sent to a given state largely on the basis of whose law would apply to the case under the state's choice of law rules. Erroneous predictions could be remedied by remand or further transfer to a different state forum. This idea is not as far-fetched as it might seem. Courts frequently frame separate subclasses in class action litigation on the basis of the law to be applied to the subclass. Mechanism for interstate consolidation might divide a mass tort case along similar lines and transfer particular groupings of plaintiffs and defendants to different states according to the law to be applied in the cases. Uniformity of result would suffer in comparison to that found in cases consolidated into a single proceeding in a single forum, but the disuniformity may be appropriate given the identity of the various groups of parties. Even if state courts would need to develop other states' mass tort law in some instances, an elected state judge is still a better expositor of tort law than a life-tenured judge from the federal system.

4. Interstate Conflicts in the Assertion of Jurisdiction and Application of Binding Effect

There are two basic means by which enhanced consolidation of mass tort cases in state courts could be achieved. In the first, each state would act independently to improve its ability to handle complex tort litigation, increasing its willingness to take jurisdiction of cases filed within its borders and consolidating them into single proceedings in an appropriate state trial court. At the same time, the court would use door-closing doctrines to discourage the filing of cases that would detract from the efficiency advantages of ongoing mass tort suits in other states, creating incentives for the plaintiffs in the cases to join those suits. Cases that otherwise might be heard in federal court could be kept from that forum if the federal courts made sensible use of abstention doctrines.

In the second approach, the states would create an interstate compact and adopt a uniform law to permit the voluntary or compulsory transfer of cases filed in one place to magnet forums handling consolidated proceedings in the other state. This latter option could also be accomplished by Congressional action, at least if the state voluntarily opted to participate in the plan.

The first option has a significant advantage in not requiring any formal concerted action by the states, nor any intervention from Washington. States can simply work towards it on their own. Efficiency gains will be lost during the period of drift, and the efficiency gains will never by quite as great as those of a more formal system, but few expenditures, political or otherwise, would be necessary to bring the transition about. Indeed, the mere continuation of existing trends should lead to it.

The disadvantage of this approach is that some state courts might resist the trend and issue rulings asserting jurisdiction when both efficiency and fairness dictate that the court should decline to hear the case in favor of another forum. An injunction by one state of the proceedings in another state risks triggering an injunction by the second state against proceedings in the first. When parallel proceedings go ahead in two states, existing full faith and credit law holds that the first valid judgment binding the parties is the effective one. Parties vying for the advantages of different forums might thus engage in a race to, and a race through, the courthouse to gain the first valid judgment.

The widespread state adoption of some doctrinal reforms might minimize these jurisdictional conflicts, however. This independent action by states would move towards a true system of interstate consolidation of mass tort cases in the state courts. Currently, the law in many jurisdictions provides that an action will abate if there is a prior pending action between the same parties on the same cause of action. Courts could facilitate interstate consolidation by expanding this doctrine to allow abatement or dismissal of the action when a case exists elsewhere against the same defendant and plaintiff conveniently can join his or her cause of action in the proceeding. Courts could also induce interstate consolidation with the careful use of forum non conveniens doctrine. As has been discussed, this doctrine has weakened in recent years, facilitating consolidation of mass torts in state forums. A modification of the doctrine would help consolidation more than abolition would, however. The courts should consider the existence of an action the plaintiff conveniently could join when they determine whether to grant the defendant's motion for dismissal under the doctrine. The absence of actions elsewhere and the likelihood that other parties could conveniently join the action under challenge should be reasons to deny the motion to dismiss.

States could transform this tentative promotion of interstate consolidation into a real system of interstate transfer by adopting the Uniform Transfer of Litigation Act, which permits the transfer of all or part of a suit brought in one state to the courts of another state. The grounds for transfer are simply that the transfer "serve the fair, effective, and efficient administration of justice and the convenience of the parties and witnesses." As drafted, the law applies both to multiparty and simple proceedings, but a relevant factor in the transfer decision is "the public interest in securing a single litigation and disposition of related matters." The law expands the personal jurisdiction of the court receiving the litigation to incorporate the jurisdiction of the transferring court. Whether the states will voluntarily adopt this provision is unclear. Currently, only one state has adopted the law, although several more have it under consideration.

Fear that these reforms would not be widely adopted or that they would not be effective may counsel for a second form of consolidation, one that has a more formal mechanism backing it. One such mechanism would be the creation of a panel of judges from various states issuing orders about which cases should be transferred and consolidated with which other cases to what courts. An interstate compact or act of

Congress would be required for this latter initiative. It would also require an organization to administer the system once created.

An even more elaborate device would be the actual creation of a multistate court, but this has little advantage over mechanisms that simply steer the cases to state forums that can handle them. It also has some of the drawbacks of federal consolidation: judges who are not responsible to the voters of a state will be developing and applying the state's law and may need to have some universal choice of law standard for the mega-consolidations that would occur.

A third proposal, a kind of compromise between the two principal choices of relying on independent state action and creating an interstate or federal bureaucracy, might follow the model of the Parental Kidnapping Prevention Act. Section 1738A of Title 28 requires states to enforce, and not to modify, child custody determinations made by the courts of other states, when those courts have properly asserted jurisdiction under the Act. By requiring full faith and credit be given to these determinations, the Act induces parties to join in a single proceeding in a logically chosen jurisdiction. Application of this model to mass tort cases would require Congress to pass a full faith and credit provision compelling dismissal of tort cases that could be joined with actions in other states that had properly been determined to meet the statutory criteria for magnet proceedings.

Nevertheless, the model of § 1738A may not be ideal. Because it confers jurisdiction on the first state to properly assert it, § 1738A both encourages races to the courthouse and fails to guarantee that the forum obtaining jurisdiction is the optimal one to decide the action. Moreover, § 1738A has received mixed reviews about its ability to operate without a private cause of action to enforce it in federal court, which the Supreme Court found that Congress did not intend to confer. If the § 1738A model were adopted, Congress would be well advised to add an effective remedy in an impartial tribunal, and perhaps to modify the standard so that being first to assert jurisdiction does not necessarily grant control. Mediation of competing state assertions of jurisdiction under a new full faith and credit law would be a more appropriate role for the federal courts than monopolizing the development of substantive state tort law.

Each of the principal models for state court consolidation of mass torts thus has its advantages and drawbacks, as does a compromise between the two. Considerations of competence, federalism, and allocation of resources, combined with realistic observations of state courts' abilities, still dictate that any of these proposals would be superior to consolidation of mass tort cases in federal courts.

5. Federal Constitutional Objections

An agreement among states permitting interstate transfer and consolidation may face doctrinal difficulties under the interstate compact clause of the United States Constitution. Although the interstate compact clause appears to require congressional approval of all agreements between states, the Supreme Court has limited the scope of the provision to include only those arrangements that add a new political presence between the state and the federal governments or increase the states' basic sphere of authority. An interstate agreement to transfer cases, even if it entails a panel of judges from different states to preside over the transfers, does not alter federal-state power relationships in such a way as to require congressional approval under the compact clause.

Congressional action to promote transfer and consolidation in the state courts might conceivably face a Tenth Amendment objection. Nevertheless, if the congressional act merely permitted states to voluntarily participate in the system, the law would face no difficulties. Although the Supreme Court has recently held unconstitutional a federal regulatory effort that required state legislative or executive action and left no choice to the state, the Court has permitted Congress to impose significant involuntary law-enforcement obligations on the state courts under the authority of the Supremacy Clause and the Constitution's implicit understanding that state courts would be a primary means to enforce federal law.

B. Practical Problems of State Court Consolidation

Beyond doctrine, there are practical problems to a regime of transfer and consolidation in the state courts. Nevertheless, two of the most serious problems, practice rules differences and uneven judicial personnel, are amenable to solution. They do not present difficulties any worse than those faced by federal courts in consolidated proceedings.

1. Differences in Practice Rules

Although practice rules differ from state to state, the differences are not so great that they would present insurmountable obstacles to interstate consolidation. As noted above, though practice from state to state has grown more uniform in recent years, federal practice has blossomed into a multitude of different forms. The Civil Justice Reform Act will increase federal multiplicity. At the state level, there are only two basic regimes, one that is similar to the Federal Rules, and the other that has grown out of the Field Codes adopted in the mid-nineteenth century. Even between the two systems, significant aspects of practice overlap. For example, liberal discovery is a hallmark of the Federal Rules, but code states now have discovery rules that are similar to the federal ones. Pleading standards, once thought to be a major difference between practice influenced by the federal rules and code practice, now show close similarity between federal courts and the courts of many code states.

2. Corruption and Incompetence

Corruption and incompetence may continue to worry litigants subject to consolidation of their cases before a state judge. The problem is smaller than imagined, however. The tort system now relies largely on state judges; the only danger of consolidation is placing greater responsibility in the hands of a single judge. The uneven quality of some states' judicial personnel also reflects the range of jobs that state judges perform. State courts of general jurisdiction hear only eight percent of state court cases; the quality of judges in traffic, small-claims, and family courts that hear the other ninety-two percent do not affect the desirability of consolidation of mass tort claims in state courts of general jurisdiction. State supreme courts and court administrators may be expected to choose the judges receiving the consolidated cases with some care. Moreover, incompetence and corruption are hardly unknown among federal judges, and life tenure makes dishonest or bumbling federal judges extremely difficult to weed out.

An additional consideration is the strong effort by many states to train and assist their judiciaries, particularly in the handling of mass tort cases. One state has produced a judges' manual for complex litigation, with an entire chapter devoted to mass tort cases. At least twenty-four states have judicial evaluation programs in some stage of operation. The State Justice Institute, which provides financial support to projects improving the administration of justice in the states, has given priority to establishing procedures for the selection and removal of judges, and for the education and training of judges and other court personnel. From 1987 to 1992 the Institute funded 183 training projects, most at levels in excess of six figures. Because enhancing the capacity of the state courts to handle consolidated mass tort cases will benefit the federal court system by freeing the federal courts' time, it is entirely appropriate for the federal government to fund projects to improve the state judiciary's ability to handle the suits. Given the current fiscal problems of many state governments, further judicial improvement projects may well depend on increases in federal funding.

Finally, trying consolidated mass tort cases in state court systems may induce politically powerful forces such as organized trial lawyers, associations of manufacturers, and insurers to push for further improvement of the state courts. Recently, a group studying an urban juvenile court suffering from inefficient and irregular procedures suggested recruiting associates from large law firms to represent parties in proceedings there in order to increase the visibility of problems and generate political pressure for reform. If improvement is needed in the courts that receive consolidated mass tort cases, the persons with the greatest stake in improvement will be among those most able to obtain it. Assigning mass tort cases to the federal courts would diminish the quality of justice in that system, but adding the cases to the states' dockets would be likely to cause an increase in the quality of state judicial performance.

CONCLUSION

Federal jurisdiction should not be treated as the default option in the consolidation of mass tort proceedings. Efficiency gains of consolidation can be obtained without violence to federalism by use of the state courts. The values of federalism are important ones: experimentation, adaption to local conditions, and popular participation. There is no good reason to displace the elected judiciaries of the states in a role they perform well and can perform even better if doctrinal and practical reforms are made. Use of the state courts would be a better allocation of scarce adjudicatory resources, and would strengthen the states in an area in which constitutional structures give them independence. At the minimum, the alternative of state consolidation deserves the serious discussion that consolidation in the federal courts has received.

Notes and Questions

1. Is the Uniform Transfer of Litigation Act a superior statutory approach to securing interstate cooperation in mass tort litigation? Does it solve problems that are present in the ALI's proposed Model System for State-to-State Transfer and Consolidation, *supra*? For a state judge's analysis, *see* Herbert P. Wilkins, *The ALI's Complex Litigation Project: A State Judge's View,* 54 La.L.Rev. 1155 (1994).

2. As Professor Weber observes, the major proposals for resolving the problems of mass tort litigation have focused chiefly on various reforms of the federal adjudicative system. Are state courts better forums for resolving mass torts, and does the Uniform Transfer of Litigation Act or other state-based proposals offer a better approach to resolving mass tort litigation? Does the Uniform Transfer of Litigation Act, as described by Professor Cooper, solve many of the difficulties of multiparty, multiforum mass tort cases? In addition to states' adoption of the Uniform Transfer of Litigation Act as a procedural vehicle for interstate transfer and consolidation of dispersed mass tort cases, another possibility is for states to enter into interstate compacts to resolve mass torts. For a discussion of the legal basis and practical implementation of the interstate compact approach, *see* Leonard J. Feldman, *The Interstate Compact: A Cooperative Solution to Complex Litigation in State Courts,* 12 Rev.Litig. 137 (1992).

3. Has Professor Weber adequately canvassed the arguments on behalf of states as the preferred forums for resolving mass tort cases? Is his thesis—that state substantive and procedural rules have undergone major reform in recent years, making state courts the better system to resolve these cases—realistic and persuasive? For a review of Professor Weber's thesis and counter-arguments favoring federalization of mass tort law, *see* Linda S. Mullenix, *Mass Tort and the Dilemma of Federalization,* 44 DePaul L.Rev. 755 (1995).

Index

References are to Pages

†